D1238908

EVIDENCE UNDER THE RULES

EVIDENCE UNDER THE RULES
Text, Cases, and Problems

FIFTH EDITION

CHRISTOPHER B. MUELLER
Henry S. Lindsley Professor of Procedure & Advocacy
University of Colorado School of Law

LAIRD C. KIRKPATRICK
Philip H. Knight Dean and Hershner Professor of
Jurisprudence
University of Oregon School of Law

ΛSPEN
P U B L I S H E R S

76 Ninth Avenue, New York, NY 10011
http://lawschool.aspenpublishers.com

Aspen Publishers
Attn: Permissions Department
76 Ninth Avenue, 7th Floor
New York, NY 10011-5201

Printed in the United States of America

2 3 4 5 6 7 8 9 0

ISBN 0-7355-4062-4

Library of Congress Cataloging-in-Publication Data

Mueller, Christopher B.
   Evidence under the rules : text, cases, and problems / Christopher B. Mueller,
   Laird C. Kirkpatrick—5th ed.
      p. cm
   Includes bibliographical references and index.
   ISBN 0-7355-4062-4 (alk. paper)
   1. Evidence (Law)—United States—Cases.   I. Kirkpatrick, Laird C.   II. Title.

   KF8934.M84   2004
   347.73′6—dc22   2003070803

About Aspen Publishers

Aspen Publishers, headquartered in New York City, is a leading information provider for attorneys, business professionals, and law students. Written by preeminent authorities, our products consist of analytical and practical information covering both U.S. and international topics. We publish in the full range of formats, including updated manuals, books, periodicals, CDs, and online products.

Our proprietary content is complemented by 2,500 legal databases, containing over 11 million documents, available through our Loislaw division. Aspen Publishers also offers a wide range of topical legal and business databases linked to Loislaw's primary material. Our mission is to provide accurate, timely, and authoritative content in easily accessible formats, supported by unmatched customer care.

To order any Aspen Publishers title, go to *www.aspenpublishers.com* or call 1-800-638-8437.

To reinstate your manual update service, call 1-800-638-8437.

For more information on Loislaw products, go to *www.loislaw.com* or call 1-800-364-2512.

For Customer Care issues, e-mail *CustomerCare@aspenpublishers.com*; call 1-800-234-1660; or fax 1-800-901-9075.

Aspen Publishers
A Wolters Kluwer Company

To Martha, Gretchen, and David
CBM

To My Family
LCK

SUMMARY OF CONTENTS

CONTENTS

Two | RELEVANCE   51

Six | COMPETENCY OF WITNESSES   449

Eight | IMPEACHMENT OF WITNESSES   **501**

As we wrote in the Preface to earlier editions, this book takes as its focus the Federal Rules of Evidence. American evidence law underwent a sea change in 1975 when the Rules were adopted, and they are now law in 42 states (listed in footnote 2 of Chapter 1). A great body of interpretive tradition has gathered around these Rules, and today few decisions on evidence issues can be made without taking the Rules into account. Hence the Rules provide a natural core for the study of evidence. Most of the Problems set out in this book, and most of the cases, notes, and essays too, examine the Rules and how they work.

The enthusiasm of professors and students using this book has reinforced the ideas we had in mind in writing it: To study evidence law effectively, we need more than cases. We refer to the present work as a *coursebook* that combines the better features of standard materials (casebook, problems, hornbook). Here the basics are set forth in narrative form, with live issues presented in modern cases and problems that we put together, trying to be sure to include enough facts to make the evidence issue concrete and vivid. We hope these materials are largely self-contained—we think a conscientious student can grasp what is most important from this book alone, without constantly going elsewhere to fill in the gaps.

The subject of evidence law—what evidence law is *about*—is one that carries great intrinsic interest. That subject is something akin to epistemology: In an adversary system, how do we go about finding the facts? The challenge for the Rules is to regulate the process of inquiry in a setting in which lawyers, witnesses, courts, and jurors are the important players. Not surprisingly, and we hope we may be forgiven as teachers for making the following claim, we think the course in Evidence is the most absorbing course in law school.

Evidence law raises larger issues of policy, principle, and philosophy, often with constitutional dimensions. And because we have the Rules, evidence law brings narrower issues of application and construction. This book aims to raise both the larger and the narrower issues, to be philosophical and policy-oriented as well as practical and concrete.

The coming of the Rules did not, of course, put a stop to growth or change in the law of evidence. In 1997, for example, a new hearsay exception was added: Under FRE 804(b)(6), a party who has "engaged or acquiesced in wrongdoing" that makes another unavailable forfeits the right to exclude the latter's statements, and the implications of this exception are only beginning to unfold. And in the same year, FRE 407 was amended to make it applicable in product liability cases. In the year 2000, changes were made in FRE 103 (offers of proof and objections), 404 (character evidence), and 701-703 (opinion and expert testimony). Pending in 2003 were changes to FRE 608 (governing aspects of impeachment by showing bad character for truth and veracity) and FRE 804(b)(3) (the against-interest exception). In anticipation of ultimate approval of the pending language, this book notes and deals with these developments.

This edition brings other changes.

For one thing, the Supreme Court's decision in the *Crawford* case, handed down in March 2004, marks a new departure in confrontation jurisprudence. See Crawford v. Washington, 124 S.Ct. 1354 (2004). We include *Crawford* in the materials on the Confrontation Clause in Chapter 4G (page 368). Perhaps just as important, *Crawford* is likely to have considerable impact on various hearsay exceptions, at least when "testimonial" hearsay is offered against the accused. Hence forward-looking references to *Crawford*, and suggestions as to its likely impact, are included in note materials not less than a dozen times prior to the confrontation materials themselves. In some places, the likely impact of *Crawford* is clear, but in others courts must resolve the question whether *Crawford* applies at all and, if it does apply, what its effect really is. Although *Crawford* displaced prior doctrine in large part, and delivered scathing criticisms of the approach begun by the *Roberts* decision in 1980, nevertheless *Crawford* did not necessarily discard the *Roberts* approach for various forms of hearsay that might be offered against the accused that do not fit the "testimonial" category. For this reason, we retain *Roberts* in the confrontation section of this book.

In some other areas, we decided it was time for a fresh look at some old problems. Hence this edition uses the Seventh Circuit decision in *Manske* to illustrate the use of FRE 608, and we add *Kumho Tire* as a feature case in the treatment of scientific and expert testimony (it was covered in notes in earlier editions). We have also added new problems illustrating the problem of authentication of email messages (Problem 13-C, *"The Wizard" and the Incriminating Email*) and the use of computer animations (Problem 13-L, *"The Animation Will Help The Jury"*).

Other new material, apart from updated references and newer citations, include revised Notes on Conditional Relevancy in Chapter 2, a reworking of the material on Borderland of Hearsay in Chapter 3, new Notes on Required Disclosure and the Fifth Amendment in Chapter 12, and extensive revisions in the Notes on present sense impressions, the against-interest exception, the *Havens* doctrine, and scientific evidence.

We retain some cases that were new in the fourth edition: Thus we stay with the Maryland decision in the *Tuer* case to illustrate subsequent remedial measures in the setting of medical malpractice (page 433), the Iowa decision in *Weaver* to illustrate the catchall exception in the setting of evidence that helped win a new trial, and ultimately an acquittal, for a woman charged with killing a child in her care (page 348), and the *Norcon* case to illustrate the business records exception in the distinctly modern context of an internal investigation into sexual harassment on the job (page 278).

In offering what we have called a coursebook, and claiming for it a kind of completeness that cannot be found in casebooks, we don't mean at all to steer students away from other sources. Excellent studies of evidence law abound, and even students using this coursebook may find value in consulting some of these. Here are some of the books we recommend:

Michael Graham, Handbook of Federal Evidence (5th ed. 2001) (3-volume set)

Graham Lilly, Introduction to the Law of Evidence (3d ed. 1996) (very compact single-volume summary of evidence law)

McCormick on Evidence (J. Strong 5th ed. 1999) (compact single-volume source; updated revision of classic work)

Christopher Mueller and Laird Kirkpatrick, Evidence (3d ed. 2003) (compact single-volume source)

Christopher Mueller and Laird Kirkpatrick, Federal Evidence (2d ed. 1994) (5-volume set with supplementation)

Roger Park, David Leonard & Steven Goldberg, Evidence Law: A Student's Guide (1998) (compact single-volume source)

Charles Wright & Kenneth Graham, Federal Practice and Procedure, volumes 21-26A (FRE 101 through Rejected Rule 513); 27-29 (C. Wright and V. Gold) (FRE 601-706); 30 (K. Graham) (Hearsay Policy); 31 (FRE 801-1103) (M. Graham)

Among our friends whose comments have helped us in revising this book we want to acknowledge the following: David Bernstein, Chris Blair, Mark Bonner, Sherry Colb, David Crump, David DeMuro, David Dorsen, James Duane, Michael Green, Steven Heyman, Edward Kimball, Paul Janicke, John Junker, Ronald Lansing, Lash LaRue, Graham Lilly, Peter Lushing, Donna Mathew, Dayna Matthew, Pedro Malavet, Tom Mason, Kevin McMunigal, David McCord, Jean Montoya, the Honorable Gerald Rosen, David Siegel, Alex Stein, George Strickler, Eleanor Swift, Suja Thomas, the Honorable Richard Unis, Robert Weninger, Mimi Wesson, and Wayne Westling. All of these colleagues in evidence have from time to time commented on these pages and helped us to improve them, and the book is much the better for their suggestions.

The authors wish also to extend their appreciation to Dean David Getches and former Dean Hal Bruff at Colorado, and to President Dave Frohnmayer and former Dean Rennard Strickland at Oregon for their help and support in the task of writing and revising this book.

Student assistants too were essential to this project. At Colorado, we thank Christopher Estoll and Laura Sturges for work on this edition. At Oregon, we thank Melissa Aubin, and for work on prior additions, Brooke Burns, Eric Dahlin, J. Scott Denko, Richard Handley, Scott Johansen, Vera Langer, Philip Simon, and Lore Rutz.

Patient and careful secretarial work is always essential to the task of revision. At Oregon, we wish to thank Sue Wilson, Maxine Lee, Jackie Snider, and Karen Spradling. At Colorado, we wish to thank Cynthia Carter, Linda Spiegler, Diana Stahl, Kay Wilkie, and Cindy Winn.

Finally some words about our families. Spouses and children are always in the wings, and often in the thoughts of authors working on long projects. They are expected to understand when we get tired or can't quite leave the work at school, and in thousands of ways, both large and small, they support what we do. It is to our families that we dedicate this work. On Laird Kirkpatrick's side, we wish to acknowledge his wife Lind and his sons Ryan and Morgan. On Christopher Mueller's side, we wish to acknowledge his wife Martha and their children Gretchen and David. We trust that our families know how much they mean to us.

Laird C. Kirkpatrick
Eugene

Christopher B. Mueller
Boulder

March 2004

ACKNOWLEDGMENTS

We gratefully acknowledge the following sources, which granted us permission to reprint excerpts from the works listed below:

Belli, Demonstrative Evidence: Seeing Is Believing. Trial (July 1980). Copyright © 1980 by the Association of Trial Lawyers of America. Reprinted by permission.

N. DeLange, Apocrypha: Jewish Literature of the Hellenistic Age. (Viking Press 1978). Copyright © 1978 by the B'nai B'rith Commission on Adult Jewish Education. Reprinted by permission.

Falknor, The "Hear-Say" Rule as a "See-Do" Rule: Evidence of Conduct, 33 Rocky Mtn. L. Rev. 133 (1961). Copyright © 1961 by the Rocky Mountain Law Review. Reprinted by permission.

Finman, Implied Assertions as Hearsay: Some Criticisms of the Uniform Rules of Evidence, 14 Stan. L. Rev. 682 (1962). Copyright © 1962 by the Board of Trustees of Leland Stanford Junior University. Reprinted by permission.

James, Relevancy, Probability and the Law, 29 Calif. L. Rev. 689 (1941). Copyright © 1941 by the California Law Review. Reprinted by permission.

R. Keeton, Offering Documentary Evidence, in Basic Expressions for Trial Lawyers §2.25. Copyright © 1979 by Little, Brown and Company. Reprinted by permission.

C. Mueller and L. Kirkpatrick, Federal Evidence (2d ed. 1994). Copyright © 1994 by the Lawyers Co-Operative Publishing Co. Reprinted by permission.

Marcus, The Perils of Privilege: Waiver and the Litigator, 84 Mich. L. Rev. 1605 (1986). Copyright © 1986 by Richard L. Marcus. Reprinted by permission.

SPECIAL NOTICE

The problems and examples in this book are drawn, for the most part, from actual cases. But facts have been changed for predictable reasons—to add human interest, to adapt the situation to classroom use, to combine in a single example the conflicts that have arisen in several decided cases, to present particular issues or sharpen the presentation of issues, and to achieve other educational purposes. Names used in the problems and examples are inventions of the authors. None of the examples or problems should be read as referring to an actual person, and none is intended to make any comment about any person.

CBM
LCK

EVIDENCE UNDER THE RULES

One | EVIDENCE LAW AND THE SYSTEM

A. WHY RULES OF EVIDENCE?

1. Why Evidence Law at All?

Many reasons have been advanced in answer to the second question posed above, but five stand out. At the end of the course you will be better able to evaluate them, but keeping them in mind from the outset may help on your journey through the subject.

The first sounds strange in a republic that places great faith in the jury system, but mistrust of juries is the single overriding reason for the law of evidence. The hearsay doctrine exists, for example, largely because we believe that a lay jury (an amateur factfinder) cannot properly evaluate statements made outside its presence, and the rules governing character evidence assume that juries place too much weight on such proof or employ it improperly for punitive purposes.

A second reason for the law of evidence is to serve substantive policies relating to the matter being litigated. Rules that set and allocate burdens of persuasion are examples. They amount to substantive evidence law, existing in the hope and belief that they affect outcome—recovery or exoneration from liability in civil litigation and conviction or acquittal in criminal cases—in ways nearly as significant as purely substantive principles. Everyone understands that the prospect for recovery in negligence is enhanced or inhibited by adjusting substantive law to allow or preclude recovery where plaintiff is himself partly to blame. Similar results may be achieved by setting and allocating burden of persuasion: Plaintiff has a better chance if he only needs to prove his case by a "preponderance" (lowest standard of proof known to the law), as opposed to "clear and convincing" evidence; his prospects also improve if defendant bears the burden of showing plaintiff's negligence, and diminish if plaintiff must prove due care.

A third reason is to further substantive policies *unrelated* to the matter in litigation—what we may call *extrinsic* substantive policies. Typically rules in this category seek to affect behavior or quality of life outside the courtroom, and

1

privileges are the prime example. Thus the two spousal privileges (one covering marital confidences, the other regulating the use of one spouse as witness against another) aim to protect marriage, vindicating the widespread public assumption that marital privacy is protected and removing (or limiting) the specter of pitting spouse against spouse in court.

A fourth reason for the law of evidence is to ensure accurate factfinding.[1] Thus the rules governing authentication of documents and things ("laying the foundation") and the Best Evidence doctrine (which requires the content of a writing to be proved by means of the writing itself) exist largely to ensure accuracy—to force litigants and courts to be careful.

The fifth reason for evidence law is pragmatic—to control the scope and duration of trials, because they must run their course with reasonable dispatch. Achieving resolution is itself valuable, even if it is not perfect. To this end, the Rules authorize the trial judge to confine and organize the dispute. Rule 403, for example, permits the judge to exclude evidence that would be otherwise admissible, simply because it would take more time than it is worth and might confuse the jury. And Rule 611 gives the judge power to control the sequence of proof and the manner of examining witnesses.

2.   Why Rules Rather Than Common Law?

Accessibility is the main reason advanced by the framers of what has become the most influential body of American evidence law—the Federal Rules of Evidence. This code sets forth the bulk of the law of evidence in 63 short provisions, in language easily read and largely free from technicality and cross-referencing. The text of the Rules may be printed in a small book easily carried to court, quickly perused and readily understandable.

Success of the Federal Rules. It is in part because of their brevity and simplicity that the Federal Rules have become so influential. Their quality and widespread success make them a logical focal point for a course in American evidence law, and they are central to this text.

Consider just how important the Rules have become:

They apply in federal courts across the land in both criminal and civil cases, and generally they apply regardless whether federal or state law supplies the rule of decision. (In diversity cases where federal courts apply state substantive law, however, the Rules require federal courts to apply state evidence rules in limited areas—namely, presumptions, privileges, and competency of witnesses. See FRE 301, 501, and 601.)

Within the first 12 years after the Rules were adopted in the federal system, a majority of states adopted codes closely tracking the Federal Rules, and the

---

1. To some extent, this concern overlaps with the first one, for another way of expressing mistrust of juries is to say that we fear that juries will not soundly appraise certain types of evidence and will be misled to wrong conclusions. Nobody really thinks that hearsay evidence, for example, is worthless, and we all routinely rely on hearsay in daily life. Mistrust of juries results from a belief that jurors will not (and to some extent cannot) adequately evaluate hearsay, which is another way of saying that we fear they will fail to perform accurate factfinding.

number of state adoptions has reached 42.[2] Even in states that have not adopted the Rules, appellate opinions cite them and sometimes adopt their underlying principles.

It was not always so.

Pre-Rules evidence law. Until the Federal Rules appeared, evidence law was mostly a creature of common law tradition. To be sure, in most jurisdictions there were statutes addressing such matters as physician-patient privilege, admissibility of business and public records, and some aspects of impeaching witnesses. But comprehensive codes were longer in coming and slower to gain acceptance.

Numerous efforts to codify evidence law preceded the Federal Rules, of which the following four are most notable:

1. Dean Wigmore wrote an early code in 1909 when he was a young man. It was a long and cumbersome document that achieved no success in practice, except perhaps in proving that evidence law could be codified. See J. Wigmore, Code of Evidence (1909).

2. A generation later the American Law Institute proposed the Model Code of Evidence (1942). Professor Edmund Morgan drafted and later defended it, and he vigorously disagreed with Wigmore on important points. But the Model Code was both radical and technical. It would have largely discarded the hearsay doctrine, and its cross-referencing and precise terminology put it on a par with the modern Uniform Commercial Code in complexity. No jurisdiction adopted the Model Code.

3. In 1953 the original Uniform Rules of Evidence appeared, proposed by the National Commissioners on Uniform State Laws. It drew from the Model Code but was shorter, less technical in wording, simpler in design, and not so radical. The Uniform Rules were adopted (with local variation) in a handful of states. (In 1974 the Commissioners abandoned the original Rules and adopted the new Uniform Rules, which largely track the Federal Rules, and the states that adopted the original rules mostly went along.)

4. In 1965 a fourth codification appeared—the California Evidence Code, a comprehensive statutory scheme put together by a public commission and enacted by the legislature. It proved highly successful, and made important modifications in common law tradition.

The Federal Rules. The Federal Rules of Evidence are the most recent and most successful codification. They were proposed by a distinguished Advisory Committee that comprised practitioners, judges, and law professors appointed by the United States Supreme Court. The Committee was chaired by Albert Jenner (a prominent Chicago trial attorney), and the principal task of drafting

---

2. By 2003, these states had adopted codes based on the federal model: Alabama, Alaska, Arizona, Arkansas, Colorado, Connecticut, Delaware, Florida, Hawaii, Idaho, Indiana, Iowa, Kentucky, Louisiana, Maine, Maryland, Michigan, Minnesota, Mississippi, Montana, Nebraska, Nevada, New Hampshire, New Jersey, New Mexico, North Carolina, North Dakota, Ohio, Oklahoma, Oregon, Pennsylvania, Rhode Island, South Carolina, South Dakota, Tennessee, Texas, Utah, Vermont, Washington, West Virginia, Wisconsin, and Wyoming.

the Rules fell to Professor Edward Cleary (then of the University of Illinois). The Committee labored more than eight years, publishing two drafts which it distributed to bench and bar, and a would-be final version, which the Supreme Court accepted and transmitted to Congress pursuant to the Enabling Act (28 U.S.C. §2072).

By accident of history, the Rules arrived at Congress as the Watergate scandal was erupting. Amidst claims of executive privilege by President Nixon stirring impassioned resentment in Congress, the privilege provisions in the Rules attracted immediate attention. Acutely sensitive on the matter of legislative prerogative as against presidential power, members of Congress saw the Rules as an encroachment by the other branch—an infringement of legislative prerogative by the judiciary. Hence the Rules were not destined to pass quietly into law (under the Enabling Act, as it existed then, Rules proposed by the Court became law after 90 days if Congress took no action). Instead Congress held hearings, scrutinized the Rules, changed them substantially, and finally enacted the changed version in statutory form.

Most significant among congressional changes was the deletion of the privilege rules, and the adoption in their place of a single provision (Rule 501) leaving privilege to common law evolution. In 2004, some 29 years after adoption of the Rules in 1975, an Advisory Committee is working on drafting comprehensive privilege Rules, but these Rules have not yet been adopted or even submitted to the Court or to Congress for possible adoption. Also significant, when the Rules were adopted in 1975, was congressional rejection of a proposal to admit prior inconsistent statements by testifying witnesses as "substantive" (and not merely "impeaching") evidence, by defining them as "not hearsay." Congress would not go along with this proposal, even though years earlier the Supreme Court had implied that such a provision would pass constitutional muster.

There are those who believe strongly that evidence law should *not* be codified and that the Federal Rules are a mistake. Consider, for example, the viewpoint of the Supreme Judicial Court of Massachusetts, which in 1982 declined to adopt the Federal Rules in that state:

> A majority of the Justices conclude that promulgation of rules of evidence would tend to restrict the development of common law principles pertaining to the admissibility of evidence. The valid objective of uniformity of practice in Federal and State courts would not necessarily be advanced because the Proposed Rules, in their present form, depart significantly from the Federal Rules of Evidence. Additionally, in the view of some of the Justices, the Federal Rules of Evidence have not led to uniform practice in the various Federal courts and are, in some instances, less well adapted to the needs of modern trial practice than current Massachusetts law.

Announcement of the Judicial Court of Massachusetts Concerning the Proposed Massachusetts Rules of Evidence (December 30, 1982). The announcement went on, however, to suggest that the proposal being rejected has "substantial value as a comparative standard" and that parties may "cite the Proposed Rules, wherever appropriate, in briefs and memoranda"!

B.   WHAT HAPPENS AT TRIAL

In both civil and criminal cases, the trial is the culmination of preliminary work and skirmishes. The decision whether to bring a claim or prosecute charges was made long before, and evidence has been collected, witnesses located and interviewed, and negotiations aimed at settlement ("plea bargaining" in criminal cases) have been attempted and abandoned. And the court has already played a role. Pleadings, motions, and in civil cases discovery and perhaps pretrial conferences have gone forward to their conclusion.

   Comes now the main event—the trial itself.

1.   Jury Selection

In most jurisdictions a jury panel has been assembled when the lawyers enter the courtroom on the first day of trial. The jurors may be sitting in the spectator section behind the "bar" or assembled in waiting rooms or milling in the hall. One by one the clerk summons an adequate number (usually 12 in criminal cases, sometimes less; in civil cases often 12, but often as few as six) plus two alternates, and they take their seats in the jury box.

   The jurors usually introduce themselves one at a time, and the trial lawyers note their names. Particularly in large urban centers, the lawyers may already have information about each juror: Often jury selection forms are available to the lawyers, and private agencies rent "jury books" containing whatever information can be unearthed about members of the panel—age, marital status, occupation, prior jury service (with details about the nature and outcome of the case), and so forth.

   The next step is called "voir dire," in which court and counsel try to find out whether any members of the panel should not serve in the case at hand. Sometimes this process brings to light the fact that a potential juror does not meet the statutory qualifications, which typically set minimum and maximum age (often 18 to 72), require that each be a citizen, and sometimes include quaint prerequisites (not being "decrepit"). But usually these standards are implemented by the clerk in issuing the summonses and do not arise during voir dire. More people on the panel are eligible, but one or another should not serve for a reason specific to the case. If a juror is related to a party (by blood or marriage, or by business connection such as being his creditor or debtor, employer or employee), or is "prejudiced" on one or another issue or against one or another party, he should be excluded "for cause." Each party may challenge any number of people for cause, and the judge must determine any such challenge, excluding if cause is found. In addition, each party (or each "side") has a fixed number of "peremptory" challenges (often three), which entitles him to exclude potential jurors for any reason at all—and the reason need not be stated.[3]

_____

3.   In criminal cases, the government must be prepared to show that its exercise of peremptory challenge does not rest on racial considerations. See Batson v. Kentucky, 476 U.S. 79 (1986). Later the Court extended the same principle to private litigants in civil cases and defendants in criminal

In addition to specific questions aimed at uncovering "cause" to exclude potential jurors, voir dire involves talking to them in general terms about the case and asking them whether they are ready and able to serve conscientiously. In state courts, the lawyers often conduct voir dire. They prize the right to make direct contact, and use it to establish rapport. In federal court and many states, voir dire is conducted by the trial judge. She may well question the panel as a whole, rather than one by one, and counsel must be content with submitting questions to her, in hopes that she will put them to the panel.

2. *Opening Statement*

The opening statement gives each side its first opportunity to set before the jury "the story" that the ensuing proof will tell. Here the lawyer presents an overview that will help the jury understand what is to come, for the evidence will likely seem fragmented and disjointed. The courtroom is a kind of theater, the trial a kind of drama, but it is not a well-made play—few witnesses on the stand perform as well as actors on stage.

Customarily the party bearing the burden of persuasion—usually plaintiff in civil litigation and prosecutor in criminal cases—has the right to make the first opening statement, and the opponent follows. (If the court permits, the opponent may delay his opening until the other party has presented her case and rested, although this approach is seldom taken.)

In theory the opening statement is not an "argument," it simply sums up "the facts" that each party contends that her proof will later establish. But the opening statement *is* an argument of sorts, for the lawyer tries to persuade, in the sense of predisposing the jury to favor the cause of her client. She points out the direction, the themes, the meaning of it all, so testimony and other proof will come as echoes or continuities of thoughts already in the minds of the jurors, and her opening remarks begin to draw the shape of things to come. The opening statement is "the first act" in the theater of trial.

It is during opening statement that the jury learns background facts about the parties—for example, plaintiff is a laboratory technician at Carle Clinic who was driving to work when the accident occurred. Such humanizing information may not be relevant to the legal issues in the case, but may garner sympathetic reaction, so inevitably it comes out as part of the presentation and is likely to receive early mention. And it is during opening statement that the jury hears that plaintiff was injured in a car accident, that he sustained serious injuries requiring treatment and convalescence, and that defendant was speeding (or drunk or inattentive). In a phrase that counsel will likely repeat often, "the evidence will show" all these points.

3. *Presentation of Proof*

Now comes the main act—the presentation of proof, where each party seeks to build his case and tear down his opponent's. Ordinarily the party with the

---

cases. See Edmonson v. Leesville Concrete Co., Inc., 500 U.S. 614 (1991) (civil litigants); Georgia v. McCollum, 505 U.S. 42 (1992) (criminal defendants).

burden of persuasion goes first, followed by his adversary, and each may have additional turns if needed. Thus plaintiff usually begins in a civil suit, followed by defendant; the prosecutor goes first in criminal cases, followed by the accused.

During his first appearance each party presents his "case-in-chief." Now he holds center stage: He need not "speak all his lines," but he cannot hold back much of substance. He has to establish everything he must prove in order to prevail, keeping in reserve only what he will use to rebut whatever his opponent presents. When he is finished, he "rests" and yields the stage to his adversary. After both have put on their cases-in-chief, the party who opened has another chance, this time to present his "case-in-rebuttal," and then his adversary has a similar opportunity. The process may go on until each side is satisfied, or the judge decides that proof and counterproof have become repetitive or trivial. Rebuttal cases are narrower than cases-in-chief, for the only purpose is to give each side a chance to refute what the adverse party presented during his most recent appearance, and each succeeding rebuttal should be narrower (hence usually shorter) than the one before.

During his case-in-chief, then, each party seeks to establish everything he must prove to prevail, calling every witness on whom he depends, seeking to build his case by means of testimony elicited on "direct examination" (of which more later). He also introduces tangible evidence, such as the allegedly defective steering link that caused the accident, or the contract sued on, or medical records, or models and photographs of the accident scene. Such tangible things are often swept up under the general heading "demonstrative evidence," and sometimes more particular labels apply. Thus the objects actually involved in the events in litigation (the steering link) are called "real" or "original" evidence, and almost always such things are admitted, if physical limitations of the courtroom permit. Writings are called "documentary" evidence, and they are so common that special rules apply.

During the time when one party holds center stage, he is in control. He calls the witnesses and puts the initial questions, thus determines the subjects and sequence, and trial lawyers prize and jealously guard that control. But even during his case-in-chief each party must share the stage with the opposition: After direct examination of each witness is completed, the opponent gets a turn to ask questions, this time by "cross-examination" (of which more below). Thus in effect the opponent interrupts the calling party's case, though in most jurisdictions the opponent can cross-examine only on subjects opened up on direct, and may not go into other relevant matters not explored on direct. (The question whether cross should be limited by the "scope of direct" is hotly debated. See the discussion in section D of this chapter, infra.)

When cross-examination is finished, the calling party may engage in "redirect" examination, and then the adversary may again cross-examine (now "recross-examination"), and so on. Each succeeding round of questioning becomes narrower until the parties are satisfied or the judge decides that repetition has set in or that the sparring has become trivial.

To sum it up, the order of proof goes this way:

1. Plaintiff (or prosecutor) presents his case-in-chief, then rests;
2. Defendant presents his case-in-chief, then rests;

3. Plaintiff (or prosecutor) presents his case-in-rebuttal;
4. Defendant presents his case-in-rebuttal (sometimes called his "case-in-rejoinder");
5. Each side presents further cases-in-rebuttal (again sometimes called cases-in-rejoinder).

And the order of examination is as follows:

1. Direct examination by the calling party;
2. Cross-examination by the adverse party;
3. Redirect examination by the calling party;
4. Re-cross by the adverse party;
5. Further redirect and re-cross as may be necessary.

4.   Trial Motions

When the evidence on both sides is in (sometimes earlier), a party confident that a reasonable person could only find in his favor may make a motion for judgment (only the defense may do so in a criminal prosecution). Here the court has an opportunity to assess the sufficiency of the proof, and to take the case from the jury if a reasonable person could resolve the dispute only one way.

In ruling on such motions, the trial judge follows well-recognized rules of thumb (though they vary among jurisdictions). She assumes that the jury (if given the case) will believe witnesses for the party opposing the motion, which means that the judge does not determine credibility issues (or "resolves them in favor of the party opposing the motion"). In some jurisdictions the judge considers only evidence offered by the party opposing the motion, but it is usually said that she considers that evidence *and* evidence offered by the moving party that a reasonable juror could not reject. She also may take "judicial notice" of facts so well known and universally accepted as to be indisputable (it is hot in Phoenix in August). The trial judge only rejects evidence that runs contrary to the "laws of nature" or to matters that can be judicially noticed.

Typically such motions are denied; they are seldom granted for the party bearing the burden of proof in a civil case, and seldom granted in negligence cases. They are perhaps most often granted for defendants in criminal cases, and for defendants in civil contract suits. As a practical matter, they are routinely denied in jury-tried cases even where the judge is inclined to go along with the movant, if only because the outcome is better protected from reversal if the jury takes the case and comes in with a verdict for the moving party. (If the jury comes in the other way, the judge has the chance after the verdict to grant a similar motion, and if she does so and is found on appeal to have erred, the original verdict can be reinstated.) Particularly in civil cases, these motions are attended by procedural complexities that help ensure that they are rarely granted.

5. Closing Argument

When presentation of proof is finished, the time comes for lawyers and judge to have their final say. The lawyers argue and the judge instructs. In federal court and most state systems it is done in that order (hence instructions are the last thing the jury hears before it "retires"). In a number of state systems, however, the judge speaks first and the lawyers have the last word, an approach much preferred by the trial bar.

The party bearing the burden of persuasion (usually plaintiff or prosecutor) has the right to make two closing arguments, one before and one after his adversary. The notion is that he needs an extra chance to persuade, since he loses if the jury finds the evidence equally balanced. In short, the party with the burden opens first and closes first and last. His adversary goes second, in both opening and closing.

In closing argument each side gets its chance to put its "last word" to the jury. The lawyer has seen the ebb and flow of trial, and perhaps expressions of sympathy or doubt on the faces of jurors, and now he has his last chance to clear away doubts, reinforce sympathetic reactions, and explain why the jury should find for his client.

Often the trial lawyer has already written a draft of his close, and he devotes final preparation to finding the best words. He concentrates on phrasing, allusions, tone, cadence. He thinks about the relationship that has grown up between him and the jury, seeking words and expressions in keeping with the positive aspects of that relationship. And he works on continuities—ideas already set out in the opening statement and supported by testimony.

The matter of closing argument is highly personal to each attorney and dependent on the course of trial. But the attorney is not the subject of the close—the plight of the client is. Hence a good close does not overwhelm the jury with the skill or brilliance of the lawyer, but instead leaves the jury with an inexorable feeling that the client's cause is clearly the stronger, and that any lawyer worth his salt would have shown as much (just as *this* lawyer happened to do).

6. Instructions

The judge instructs the jury on the law, so it understands what it must decide in order to reach a verdict for either party. Instructions explain the applicable substantive principles, and allocate and define the burdens of proof on the various issues. Usually they also contain standard admonitions about the manner in which deliberations are to be conducted, the need to decide on the basis of the evidence, and so forth. The parties draft the instructions and submit their requests to the court (providing copies to the adverse parties) before the process of proof has been completed (in the wording of FRCP 51 and FRCrimP 30, before "the close of the evidence"), and in fact the judge often expects and gets instructions before trial even begins.

Often the judge also instructs the jury on evidentiary matters. Such instructions may take many different forms:

They may admonish the jury to exclude from consideration certain testimony that it heard or information suggested by a question during trial. Such instructions are often given when the incident occurs, and the repetition is for good measure. These are "curative" instructions whose purpose is to save the verdict and judgment to come from later reversal on account of inevitable errors as trial progresses. On some points, a "curative" instruction cannot work and may even be counterproductive—emphasizing the very point it asks the jury to forget. Hence for the most part the question whether to give such instructions is left in the first instance to the party whose case might be damaged by the incident in question.

Often instructions advise the jury to consider certain proof only on one point and not others or against one party and not others. These are "limiting" instructions, made necessary by the unavoidable fact that a great deal of evidence that is essential at trial has unwanted side effects, and the aim is to obviate or minimize these. Again such instructions are likely to be given during trial when such incidents occur, and again the party who might be hurt by the evidence in question ordinarily decides in the first instance whether he wishes the jury to be admonished in this way.

Another kind of instruction seeks to convey to juries the effect of "presumptions" and certain formal inferences. Sometimes the instruction is simple. In civil cases, for example, a presumption sometimes *requires* the jury to accept a fact as established if no counterproof has been adduced. But in criminal cases, and in civil cases where counterproof *has* been adduced, the matter of instruction is complicated. The jury is sometimes told that it may draw an inference from particular proof, although the parties may quarrel over language and may not agree that the evidence even warrants the instruction. (See Chapter 10, infra.)

Still other instructions tell the jury that it must decide certain points before it may consider certain evidence. In criminal cases, for example, a defendant who contends that a confession admitted against him was "coerced" may be entitled to have the jury consider the coercion claim before it takes the confession as proof of any element of guilt. (The accused is constitutionally entitled to have the judge resolve his claim of coercion, but if the judge decides against him and admits the confession, the accused may be entitled to a "second bite"—that is, to make the same argument to the jury, in hopes that it will come out on his side.)

7. *Deliberations*

After lawyers and judge finish talking to the jury, the curtain falls. The characters have left the stage. Their lines have been spoken, their performances watched and heard. Judge and lawyers, themselves producers and directors (and actors too) make their exits as well. Now it is the turn of the jury: The audience becomes actor.

The performance of the jury takes place behind closed doors. There it selects a leader and deliberates its verdict. The lines spoken in the jury room, and the performances of individual jurors, are hidden from view. Necessarily hidden as well are the factors that prove persuasive and the personalities that become influential, among witnesses and lawyers, and among the jurors themselves.

This secrecy is intentional. One purpose is to encourage jurors to share their views with one another, a notion reflecting our democratic ideals and faith in the value of free expression and exchange of views—the faith that underlies the First Amendment. Another purpose is to insulate verdicts, both from public scrutiny (which would lead to relentless examination and criticism in the press) and from judicial review (which could have no purpose but to provide additional ground for reversal). Paradoxically, one reason for such precautions is the widespread belief that jury deliberations may not live up to an ideal of enlightened exchange of views and sifting of evidence, and that the jury as an institution might not survive close scrutiny of its deliberative process.

In modern practice jurors usually go home at the end of each day, although they are admonished not to discuss the case among themselves or with outsiders. If the case is notorious or controversial, however, the jury may be sequestered during trial and deliberations to insulate it from outside influence and pressures.

Questions often arise during deliberations, and jurors seek clarification of testimony or instructions. Typically the leader passes a note to the bailiff to be forwarded to the judge, who summons the jury and the opposing lawyers to the courtroom, where the jury's request can be heard and considered. Often instructions are repeated, or portions of the trial transcript are read aloud by the reporter.

If deliberations bog down in disagreement, the leader may again communicate with the judge, and the question arises whether to declare a mistrial. Often the judge admonishes the jury to try again, reminding it of the time already spent and the expense of a new trial and telling each juror to reconsider her position. Commonly the admonition suggests that jurors who find themselves in the minority or alone in their view should take into account the contrary view of most of the others and carefully consider whether that view might not be right. It suggests to those in the majority that they should reconsider the objections of the others once again. Particularly in criminal cases, defendants object to this so-called "dynamite charge" as infringing the constitutional safeguard requiring proof beyond a reasonable doubt for conviction.

8. The Verdict

When the jury reaches its verdict, the actors in the drama assemble in court—judge and jury, lawyers and parties, and the court reporter. The jury leader announces the verdict or hands a written verdict to the judge or court clerk, who reads it into the record. Generally the judge asks appropriate questions to ensure that all jurors agree on the verdict as thus rendered, closing the door to any later claim that what was announced is not what was agreed to.

Usually the jury gives a "general verdict," which in civil cases states simply who wins and (if it is the plaintiff) the amount of recovery, and in criminal cases states simply that the defendant is found "guilty" or "not guilty" of the various charges. But sometimes in civil cases the jury answers special interrogatories (with or without a "bottom line" general verdict), which ensures that the jury addresses and resolves particular issues. And in criminal prosecutions where the death penalty is possible, the jury may retire a second time to deliberate and recommend punishment.

9.   *Judgment and Post-Trial Motions*

After the verdict is announced, the court enters judgment. In civil cases, generally the prevailing party prepares the judgment for the court's signature, and the clerk "enters" the judgment by notation in the docket book. Now the time for appeal begins to run, and now a judgment awarding relief becomes effective in the sense of becoming the basis for "execution" against property owned by the debtor. In criminal cases in which the jury returns a verdict of "not guilty," a judgment of acquittal is signed by the judge and entered by the clerk forthwith, and the defendant is released from custody immediately. Where the jury returns a verdict of "guilty," the judgment is signed and entered after a sentencing hearing has been held and sentence has been pronounced. In civil and criminal cases alike, entry of judgment starts the time for appeal, although the prosecutor usually has no appeal from an acquittal.

Post-trial motions present the parties with their last opportunity at the trial level to obtain the result they have sought. Routinely the losing parties in civil cases move for judgment as a matter of law (formerly called a J.N.O.V. or "judgment notwithstanding the verdict"), requesting in the alternative a new trial. In federal court and in many states such motions must be made not later than ten days after entry of judgment, a time constraint that is rigorously enforced. And routinely the defense in criminal cases moves for a judgment of acquittal, which in federal court and most states is once again subject to a rigid time limit.

Other kinds of post-trial motions may be made. Some are less sweeping, such as motions to correct "clerical" or "ministerial" mistakes in the judgment, and motions for permission to interview jurors (if the parties suspect some impropriety during deliberations). Others seek to begin the contest anew, such as motions to reopen on account of "newly discovered evidence."

10.   *Appellate Review*

Federal courts and most state judicial systems adhere to the principle of finality, under which appellate review may be had only at the end of the case, when the trial court has entered a "final judgment" that dismisses the claims or charges for jurisdictional or other "technical" reasons (thus in effect denying the relief sought) or disposes of them "on the merits" (perhaps awarding relief and perhaps not, but in any event resolving substantive issues). There are notable exceptions to this pattern: In New York, parties in civil cases may obtain "interlocutory" appellate review of a wide range of orders and rulings by trial courts. And even jurisdictions observing the finality principle permit interlocutory review of some rulings and orders.

The finality principle applies to appellate review of evidence points, with the result that usually a party aggrieved by a ruling on an evidence point must await final judgment before seeking review. (There are a few exceptions to this pattern, taken up below in section F.)

Even when judgment has been entered, a party may obtain full appellate review only if it has "preserved" its claim of error by stating its position promptly and clearly at trial (see sections C and D, infra). If these procedural steps have been taken, appellate review of evidence rulings may lead to relief (reversal and often a new trial), but only if the reviewing court concludes both that the trial court erred and that the error probably affected substantial rights of the appellant, hence that the error was "reversible" rather than merely "harmless" (see section E, infra).

C. MAKING THE RECORD

1. *What Is the Record and How Is It Made?*

Trying a case involves a performance designed to affect both a live and a remote audience. The live audience is the judge and the jury (if any), who see and hear the goings on in the theater of trial. The remote audience is the appellate tribunal, which neither sees nor hears the performance, and depends entirely on a secondhand source—the "cold" written "record." Hence trial lawyers are aware of the immediate impact of their performances (and those of the witnesses), but are also conscious of the picture that their words (and those of witnesses) will make when printed for remote scrutiny.

In the first instance it is the responsibility of the court reporter to prepare the record of trial. One might think that in the twenty-first century and the era of the computer, it would no longer be necessary for a human agent actually to hear and record a trial, and that a machine should be able to pick up the sights and sounds of a trial and produce, almost instantaneously, a readable transcript and a video with sound. That day may come, and it is already true that sometimes the proceedings are recorded electronically, and the court reporter later works from the recording to produce a record. (For reasons that might not occur to you at first, using a recording machine rather than a live court reporter has some drawbacks: A reporter will speak up if he cannot hear or spell a word, and a judge will "protect" her reporter by reminding witnesses to speak clearly and to use the microphone when necessary. Most machines don't "say something" when voices become inaudible, and the judges and lawyers are prone to forget that the machine is even there, so transcripts produced from recordings tend to be inferior to those produced by a reporter actually sitting in the courtroom.) For the most part, in any event, a court reporter is still to be found in most American trials making a record of what is said.

The reporter is a skilled public servant and officer of the court, and his task is exactly what the title implies: He puts into permanent written form, as best he can, the words actually uttered at trial. He is neither editor nor dramatist, and he tries not to add to or subtract from what is actually said. Hence in a real sense it is also the responsibility of court and counsel to prepare the record—to try hard to ensure that the words spoken at trial will make sense when written down—and making the record is, in the end, a cooperative venture requiring coordinated efforts by trial lawyer, judge, and reporter.

The "official record" of a trial actually comprises five different kinds of material:

1. The pleadings.   In civil actions these include complaint and answer, and often third-party claims, counterclaims (sometimes called cross-complaints), cross-claims, and answers to these. In criminal actions the pleadings include the indictment or complaint and the plea of the accused (usually entered orally and recorded in a verbatim transcript).

2. Filed documents.   The record includes all other papers filed in court, such as motions and accompanying briefs, documents seeking and providing discovery, jury instructions, and court orders. Many of these fade into oblivion as the action proceeds: Complaint and answer are often superseded by pretrial order; many discovery requests and responses lead nowhere and are quite rightly forgotten. But any one may be critical later on: A judgment, for example, becomes the basis for executing upon a claim successfully brought, and for enforcing the doctrines of res judicata and collateral estoppel, which block prosecution of a subsequent claim or charge and relitigation of points decided. And often the jury instructions and the findings and conclusions play a central role in later appellate review.

3. The record of proceedings.   One of the most important parts of the record is the verbatim memorial of what transpires in the courtroom when the action is tried. It captures what is said by the parties, witnesses, and court in public session. It also captures whatever spoken words are considered important by the court or any of the parties in private conferences, conducted sometimes in whispers at the bench, occasionally while the jury (and perhaps even the public) is excluded from the courtroom, and sometimes "in camera" (the office or "chambers" of the judge), at least when the court or a party requests the reporter's presence. Thus the record of proceedings puts into permanent form the testimonial evidence presented in the trial of a case, as well as questions, objections, arguments, comments, and stipulations offered by the trial lawyers during the proceedings, and orders and rulings announced orally by the trial judge.

It is important to note that inevitably much of the ebb and flow of the proceedings is of little or no subsequent importance, whatever immediate influence it might have on the live audience. For that reason, the reporter does *not* routinely prepare an actual transcript in readable typewritten form. Indeed, the record that he produces is for the most part simply stored away in the original form of stenographic notes, once comprised of fanfold pages resembling an adding machine tape and now more often comprised of computer memory produced by the reporter's use of a keyboard, but in either case the content is the reporter's personalized arrangement of symbols. For the most part, these are readable only by their maker, being so much Greek to anybody else.

It is equally important to note that any part of this portion of the record may become critical in post-trial motions seeking a new trial or other relief and on appellate review of the proceedings. Hence the reporter stands ready to prepare the transcript whenever asked to do so by one of the parties—and the party who wants a transcript must pay the reporter for this additional service, which is not financed by taxpayers through the judicial system. In "big" cases, heavily supported by one or more parties, the lawyers may request a "daily transcript," and the task of taking down the proceedings may be divided up between two or more reporters who operate in shifts, alternately spending an hour or so in court stenographically recording what goes on, and then an hour or so setting down in typewritten form the tape just completed. Through their combined efforts they produce at day's end an "instant transcript" for lawyers to review that night in preparation for the next day.

As should be obvious by now, this portion of the record is critical in preserving for review the various points of evidence raised by the parties during trial. The appellate opinions set out in this book depend heavily on this portion of the record as a primary source, even though they may not actually quote or even mention it.

4. The exhibits.   The record includes all the physical exhibits offered during trial (much is documentary, but some may be other kinds of physical objects). These are identified by one or more of the parties and lodged with the court, whether or not actually "admitted" for consideration by the trier of fact. Here the job of the reporter involves more care than technical skill, and doing it well is critical in preserving for review the contentions of the parties concerning such items of proof. Here too cooperation between reporter and trial lawyer is essential. In many modern courts, computers alleviate some of the physical clumsiness of this process, as documents can be stored in computer memory, accessed simultaneously by the lawyers and the court for viewing on individual screens, and "published" so a jury can see them (either in the form of printouts or images on a larger monitor).

5. Docket entries.   Finally, the record includes the court's own "ledger" of the proceedings—the "docket" or "docket book" kept by the clerk of court, which contains dated line items entered in chronological order from the beginning to the end of the proceedings (that is, from summons and complaint or indictment through judgment, post-trial motions, and notice of appeal). In this form the clerk simply lists each filed document and all important orders made by the judge, although the latter are generally entered in the docket book only if put in written form and filed. The docket book is a virtual "table of contents" for the proceedings, and sometimes the moment when each item is "entered" has great legal significance: For example, the time for appeal and for making some post-trial motions begins to run when the clerk "enters" the judgment in the docket book.

The record as a whole, including the five categories of material described above, is not actually assembled until and unless one or more of the parties decides to seek appellate review. Then an early task of the appellant is to "designate" the record, part of which involves directing the reporter to prepare a transcript of important parts of the proceedings.

2.   *Beware the Pitfalls—What Not to Do*

Trial lawyers, particularly beginners who suffer stage fright in their early performances, make a number of common mistakes that tend to muddy the record.

1. Echoing.   Often a nervous trial lawyer, particularly the novice, repeats the answers before putting the next question. This practice swells the record, distracts the listening audience and later the reviewing court, and conveys hesitancy and unease which tend to undermine the cause that the attorney seeks to advance. No doubt the practice gives the attorney some breathing room between questions, but the real reason is not so much the need for reflection as discomfort with the surroundings. Consider this example:

Q *(by Phillips):*   Were you present in the operating room?
A *(Mr. Irwin):*   Yes, I was.
Q: You were. And who made the incision?
A: Dr. Young made the incision, and Dr. Hansen closed and cleaned up afterwards.
Q: Dr. Young made the incision, and Dr. Hansen closed. Very good. And were any other physicians in attendance?

2. Overlapping.   The reporter's feat in taking down the spoken word verbatim is considerable, but even skill and dedication can be overwhelmed when several voices speak at once and at cross-purposes. When lawyers or judges interrupt each other or the witness, the reporter tries to continue to set down the words of whoever had the floor, but often the interrupted speaker stops or hesitates in surprise, and the reporter tries to pick up the ongoing words of the interrupter, which may be impossible if the original interrupting voice has itself been joined or interrupted by yet another. The result is an unreadable mishmash and a disgusted reporter. Consider the following:

A: Yes, Dr. Roth stepped in toward the end to examine the abdominal wall before—
Q *(Rogers):*   Nothing to do with this lawsuit, and isn't even—
Q *(Phillips):*   Interrupted by such discourtesy, which he knows, as Your Honor has again and again said you would—
A *(Mr. Irwin):*   That again—
[Whereupon a discussion was had off the record.]

3. Numbers, names, and big words.   When a witness recites a number in her testimony, her spoken word may be susceptible to many different interpretations. What does a witness mean when she says "thirty-four O seven"? She could mean 3,407, 34.07, or even 30,407. Context may make one or another interpretation by far the more probable: "Thirty-four O seven" likely means "$3,407" (rather than either of the other two possibilities) if the witness had been asked how much it cost to rebuild the engine of the car, but the context will not always make clear the intended meaning of the answer, and the trial lawyer is well advised to clarify the record on such points.

Q *(by Phillips):*   By "thirty-four O seven" do you mean three thousand four hundred seven dollars?
A *(Rogers):*   Yes, that's right.

In everyday experience, names present spelling difficulties. Witnesses named "Meyer," "Myer," "Meier," "Mayer," "Meir," or "Maier" may utter the very same sound when asked their last name. What is the reporter to do? In fact, he may interrupt the proceedings and ask for a spelling then and there, but if the pace of questioning is hectic there may be no chance, and the problem may go unnoticed until the transcript appears. Sometimes the witness spells her name on her own, recognizing the problem. A thoughtful lawyer provides a list of names to the reporter in advance, so the reporter will know the spelling already.

Difficult or uncommon words, especially technical medical terms, create difficulties for the reporter. The witness who uses them should be asked first to spell them for the reporter, then explain them to the jury:

Q (by Phillips): Doctor, what did the abdominal incision reveal?
A (Dr. Young): Acute secondary peritonitis caused by bacterial invasion from the biliary system, entering through a perforation in the viscus brought on by acute cholecystitis.
Q: Doctor, would you be kind enough to assist the reporter by spelling those technical terms? Then I'll ask you to explain your answer in lay terms, as best you can, so that the jury and I can understand you.

4. Exhibits. The problem of laying the foundation for tangible evidence is taken up in detail in Chapter 13. Suffice it to note here that in addition to laying the foundation, the trial lawyer must find an unambiguous way of referring to such evidence so his questioning is intelligible in the transcript. Instead of referring only to "that X-ray" or "the letter in your hand," the lawyer should refer to the object in question by reference to its exhibit number.

Q (by Phillips): Doctor, I hand you what we have marked as plaintiff's exhibit number 35 for identification, and ask you to identify it if you can.
A (Dr. Young): Certainly. Yes, that is the X-ray which Dr. Knight prepared at my direction, showing Carl Deaver's abdominal cavity.
Q: Thank you, sir. Your Honor, if there is no objection, we now offer in evidence plaintiff's exhibit number—let's see, it'll be number 32 in evidence, I believe.
Court: Any objection?
Ms. Dreeves: No, your honor.
Court: Very well, it is admitted.
Q (by Phillips): Thank you, Your Honor. Now Dr. Young, calling your attention again to plaintiff's exhibit number 32 in evidence, can you tell us in lay terms what it shows?

5. Pantomime, nonverbal cue, gesture, internal reference. From time to time the witnesses follow the conventions of everyday conversation, conveying information by use of nonverbal cues or words whose significance depends entirely on reference to the immediate physical surroundings. Here the meaning is likely clear to the observer at trial, but lost completely to readers of the written transcript.

For example, the witness may give his answer in pantomime: Holding arm to his side with shoulder raised, elbow out and hand turned inward, he might say, "He was carrying the book this way." Here the trial lawyer conducting the questioning would be wise to state, "Let the record show that the witness is indicating that the subject carried the book at his side in one hand at about waist level." (If the lawyer on the other side disagrees, she should say so, and either the witness must convey his meaning in words or the parties must agree as to what the witness in fact indicated.)

Or the witness may answer by nonverbal cue: A nod or shake of the head, a shrug of the shoulders. Usually such a response evokes a gentle reminder from trial judge or questioning lawyer: "Please give an audible response. The reporter can write down only what you say."

Sometimes the witness answers by gesture, indicating a direction or object or identifying a person by pointing. Again usually the lawyer fills the gap: "Let the record show that the witness pointed northward" (or "up" or "at his right knee"), or "Let the record show that the witness pointed to the defendant, Leon Hall." Once again, if opposing counsel disagrees, she should so state, and silence is likely to be taken as assent.

Sometimes the witness answers by making reference to objects in the courtroom, and again a clarifying remark by counsel helps, with an express or tacit stipulation by opposing counsel, or an additional answer by the witness:

A: The hammer I saw was about as big as her honor's gavel.
Q: Let the record show that the gavel has a handle about eight inches long and a head about an inch in diameter and about two inches long. That's about right, isn't it?
Ms. Dreeves: Yes, I think that's the burden of his testimony.
Q (Phillips): Thank you counsel—
A (Gordon): Yes, that's about what it was.
Q: Thank you.

6. *Going "off the record."*   Trial lawyers are very much in the habit of going "off the record" at difficult moments during depositions and occasionally during trial. The point is to avoid cluttering the transcript with bickering or long discussion that may end in agreement on a small point and a stipulation that can ultimately be briefly and simply stated.

But going off the record produces problems of its own.

For one thing, the need to do so may not appear until a discussion has already begun, with the result that one of the lawyers sings out "Off the record, don't take this down," and the discussion then continues. The reporter is now in a quandary: He is professionally responsible to record all that transpires; he has no wish to be entangled in disagreement between the parties or lawyers, in case one of them wants what is said to be recorded; if he stops taking notes, he may not know when to begin again. The better part of wisdom is to keep on recording until all parties agree to go "off the record," then to note in his transcript, "Whereupon a discussion was held off record."

For another thing, the lawyers themselves may forget that the reporter has stopped recording the proceedings. If an important answer or concession goes unrecorded, the lawyer who later needs the record faces acute embarrassment. Having gone off the record, lawyers must take care to signal the reporter that he is to begin again to record. Catching his eye or pointing to the stenograph may do it, but the careful lawyer might prefer to leave no doubt: "Alright, let's go back on the record now. We need to get this down."

7. *The sidebar conference.*   Frequently during trial the need arises for lawyers and court to speak on procedural or evidentiary points that might confuse the jury or convey matters that might ultimately be ruled inadmissible. See Rule 103(c). In such cases the court summons the lawyers to the bench, or one or another of them asks permission "to approach the bench." Often the judge

moves her chair to the side of the bench furthest from the jury, the better to talk with the lawyers without being heard. These "sidebar" conferences are necessarily "off the record" if the court reporter cannot hear them, though he may be invited to join (and record) the huddle.

Physical limitations of the courtroom usually make it awkward to conduct a sidebar conference that is "on the record" yet outside the hearing of jurors in the nearby box. It can be done in modified stage whispers if the reporter hears well and moves close to the participants, but lengthy conversations are best conducted in chambers or after the jury has been momentarily excused from the courtroom.

3. Taking Care—What to Do

As the foregoing discussion suggests by negative inference, two important contributions that the trial lawyer makes in preparing a useful record of the proceedings are (1) to ensure that utterances important to his cause, whether his own or those of witnesses or the judge in the case, are spoken clearly enough to be understood and put down by the reporter, and (2) to ensure that those utterances will have meaning when they appear in typewritten form in the transcript. Accomplishing just these aims requires the trial lawyer to be aware of the court reporter and his task, and to pitch his performance toward both the live and the remote audience.

The procedural requirements for preserving points for review by appropriate offer of proof and objection are described below, as are the formalities of introducing tangible evidence (whether in documentary or other form). Both require care in building the record of proceedings.

D. HOW EVIDENCE IS ADMITTED OR EXCLUDED

1. Getting Evidence In: Foundation and Offer

a. Testimonial Proof—Direct Examination

Almost always, the bulk of the trial (in terms of time spent) involves the presentation of live testimony by witnesses. Initially each party presents such testimony by "direct examination," during which she tries to do basically three things with each witness:

First, she brings out background information—name and address and other basic facts, such as occupation and perhaps age or marital status. Several things are going on here: Opening questions help put the witness at ease, and along with the ritual of the oath impress on him that now is an occasion to behave responsibly; the jury wants to know who is talking, and needs a few moments to get used to the person and voice before focusing on the issues at hand; in a trial of public record a person giving evidence should be identified rather than faceless and anonymous.

Second, each party "lays the foundation" for the testimony to follow by asking questions that show that the witness has "personal knowledge" of the matters to which he will speak, such as by placing him at the scene of the accident or the signing of a will (see Chapter 6J, infra). In the case of an expert witness, the party brings out the special skill or training that provides the basis for his testimony on unfamiliar or technical matters (see Chapter 9, infra).

Third, the lawyer asks "substantive questions" getting at the witness' knowledge of pertinent facts—the direction from which the car was coming, how fast it was going, which car had the light, and so forth.

Form of questioning. For the most part, direct examination must proceed by nonleading questions. See FRE 611(c). The point is that the questioning should not *unnecessarily* push the witness toward a particular response—it should not be too suggestive of the answers sought. In most instances, lawyer and witness have already gone over the substance of the expected testimony, and usually they reach a mutual understanding of the narrative that is to unfold before the trier of fact, so there should be no particular need to lead the witness.

There is no simple test for the "leading question," which is to be avoided during direct examination. Sometimes it is said that any question seeking a yes or no answer is leading, but that is plainly not so: Asking a witness whether he was at a certain place at a certain time calls for such a response, for example, but would not likely be considered leading. Consider this description of what makes a question leading:

> Sometimes it is simply a matter of phrasing: Even in cold print, a question which begins "Isn't it a fact that" or "Did you not" suggests a response and is leading. So is one that is phrased in the alternative to highlight the desired response in careful detail while diminishing the other choice in vagueness: "Did you understand that you were to meet him at your home at ten o'clock, or what?" But a question that frames the only likely alternatives in an evenhanded way is not leading: "Did you call him, or did he call you?" Sometimes phrasing tells little, and context is more important: In a trial for battery where defendant claims he struck no blow, the defense might ask an eyewitness "Did you see the defendant beat the victim?" and it would hardly be considered leading, but the same question would be leading if put by the prosecutor. And sometimes inflection, facial expression, voice dynamics, or gestures tell the story. It is easy enough to imagine asking the question "Did he seem really angry to you?" in a leading manner that conveys clearly that either a "yes" or a "no" answer is the one sought, but also easy to imagine the same words spoken in a neutral, nonleading way.

3 C. Mueller and L. Kirkpatrick, Federal Evidence §296 (2d ed. 1994).

The idea is that the *witness* should do the testifying during direct examination, and not the attorney. Questions pushing too hard in one direction or another are bad because they may (1) invoke in the witness a false memory of events, (2) induce him to lessen efforts to relate what he actually remembers and to acquiesce instead in the examiner's suggested version, and (3) distract him from important detail by directing his attention only to selected aspects of the story. (Important departures from this pattern are taken up in Chapter 7, infra.)

b. Testimonial Proof—Cross-Examination

With each witness, "direct examination" is followed by cross-examination by the adverse party. During plaintiff's case-in-chief, defendant has opportunities to cross-examine after plaintiff's direct is finished, and plaintiff has similar opportunities during defendant's case-in-chief. Cross-examination seeks to set limits or bring out inconsistencies in the direct testimony.

So important is this process that cross-examination has been extolled as a bulwark of our liberty, and the most powerful weapon in the arsenal of the trial lawyer: Wigmore called it "the greatest engine ever invented for the discovery of truth." 5 Wigmore on Evidence §1390 (J. Chadbourn rev. 1974).

Leading questions. Cross-examination differs markedly from the direct. Here counsel is in the limelight, and the substance of what is conveyed to the jury emerges more from questions than answers—the latter serving to confirm an idea already planted by counsel in the question. Much has been written about this process, perhaps because lawyers sometimes see this function as their highest calling and greatest challenge. The following advice to practitioners gets to the heart of the matter:

> The name of the game in cross-examination is control. However, such control should perhaps more properly be categorized as subtle control. While it is certainly in your interest to control the witness, it may not be in your interest to convey the fact of control too overtly to either the witness or the jury. Sympathies are a fickle thing and can shift rather easily without much provocation or justification. Thus, you cannot make it appear, despite what you may be attempting to accomplish with respect to a particular witness, that you are taking unfair advantage of the witness, brow-beating the witness or otherwise treating the witness with less respect than you would treat any other human being. This is made all the more difficult when you know the witness is a liar or is capable of providing you with information which is extremely helpful to your case, but won't do so without a certain amount of intimidation. . . . [B]y the same token, you cannot permit the witness to take advantage of you. While there is nothing wrong with permitting it to appear as if the witness is taking advantage of you for the purpose of setting the witness up for the big fall, you cannot permit the momentum to become such that the cross-examination and its direction [are] actually being dictated by the responses of the witness as opposed to the questions you ask.

M. Dombroff on Direct and Cross-Examination 191-192 (1985).

Apart from the personality of counsel, the main instrument of control during cross-examination is the leading question. From the standpoint of the litigant, the leading question narrows the inquiry and limits the opportunity of the witness to stray from the chosen path.

From the standpoint of the system, leading the witness on cross is acceptable because the qualities in this form of questioning that seemed bad during direct now seem beneficial. Thus during cross-examination leading questions may (1) invoke the conscience of the witness and awaken his memory sufficiently to dislodge him from his previous version of events in favor of what he himself considers a more complete or accurate version, (2) expose limits or inaccuracies in his memory, and (3) focus his attention on important details.

Scope-of-direct rule. A critical limit on cross-examination is the principle, observed in most jurisdictions, that the questioning is limited to the matters explored on direct examination. This traditional rule aims to minimize the interruption of the calling party's case caused by the opponent's cross-examination. It is fundamental to the philosophy of the adversary system that each party is responsible to make his own case, and it follows that each should have considerable latitude to arrange his own presentation, hence to control the order in which he introduces his evidence.

Critique of scope-of-direct rule. Scholars and some judges have vigorously attacked the scope-of-direct rule, mounting two main objections: First, it is said to be hard to administer and to lead to "quibbling" objections. Second, it is said to be an impediment to truth, for it may prevent the cross-examiner from exploring admittedly relevant matters within the knowledge of the witness.

1. Administration. Difficulties in administration arise from the imprecision of the principle. Consider a suit by a contractor for final payment on a home that he planned and built. Plaintiff calls an architect who inspected the house and looked at the plans, and he testifies on direct that it is "substantially complete." All would agree that defendant may cross-examine the architect on things remaining undone (painting trim, completing cabinets or fixtures, and so forth), for completeness is the very "matter" to which the architect testified on direct.

But may defendant ask about the soundness of the plan or quality of its execution—whether, for example, the foundation ought to have broader footings than the plan specifies, in light of soil conditions, or whether the contractor graded the premises to ensure proper drainage, where the contract calls for "basic grading," which was done, but perhaps not well? If the scope-of-direct rule embraces the "transaction" described by the witness, arguably the questions are proper: After all, the architect described the contractor's performance, and the cross goes to this point. But if the rule is intended to confine the cross-examiner to the very matter opened up on direct, then such questions seem improper, for they do not affect "substantial completion."

May the defendant ask the architect whether 11 months is a "reasonable time" to complete such a house? If the rule embraces every "issue" to which the direct testimony relates, then the answer would seem to be yes, for "substantial completion" and "timely performance" both relate to "breach" and the propriety of recovering damages. See Degnan, Non-Rules Evidence Law: Cross-Examination, 6 Utah L. Rev. 323, 330-331 (1959) (suggesting not fewer than six possible interpretations of the scope-of-direct limit).

2. Impediment to truth. It has long been asserted, mostly by scholars and some judges, that the scope-of-direct rule impedes the truth-finding mission by keeping the adverse party from pursuing matters relevant to the case but not raised during direct by the calling party. For reasons perhaps best put by McCormick, it is no answer to say that the adverse party may later call the same witness and put such questions:

> [I]n many instances a postponement of the questions will not be the only result of a ruling excluding a cross-question as outside the scope of the direct. Unless the question is vital and he is fairly confident of a favorable answer, the cross-examiner might be unwilling to run the risk of calling the adversary's witness at

a later stage as his own and will abandon the inquiry. Getting concessions from the opponent's witness hot on the heels of the direct while his story is fresh is worth trying for. It is a much less attractive option to call an unfriendly witness later when his first testimony is stale.

C. McCormick on Evidence §23 (J. Strong 5th ed. 1999).

Defense of the scope-of-direct rule. Despite these strong objections, most jurisdictions continue to prefer the scope-of-direct rule. One reason has proved persuasive to many observers, and two others are often advanced in support of the result thus reached:

1. The order of proof. The strongest single reason for the scope-of-direct rule is that it enables the parties to control the order in which they present their evidence. Trial lawyers carefully plan their presentation, and while they cannot put on a well-made play, in which every line is spoken in just the right place, still they take pains to present their case in coherent fashion, and they do not want their adversary to disrupt this process.

Does the scope-of-direct limit actually serve this interest? The answer seems to be yes and no, which is to say that it is an imperfect means to achieve this end.

The yes part runs this way: When the calling party introduces evidence of a single act or event in the case, limiting cross to the subject of that act or event does protect the order in which the calling party has decided to present his case. The no part is as follows: If Witness 1 testifies to the color of the light at the intersection and Witness 2 describes the speed of the vehicles, then disallowing cross-examination of the latter on the color of the light does not preserve the order of proof. *That* cat is already out of the bag, and the calling party would likely have questioned Witness 2 on the subject if he could have expected favorable answers.

2. The special case of the accused as witness. The Fifth Amendment entitles the accused not to testify for himself and bars the prosecutor from calling him as a witness. That constitutional protection reinforces, in this special context, the tradition of limiting cross-examination to the scope of the direct.

It is settled that when the accused does testify, he cannot raise the Fifth Amendment as a shield against reasonable cross-examination:

> [The accused] has the choice, after weighing the advantage of the privilege against self-incrimination against the advantage of putting forward his version of the facts and his reliability as a witness, not to testify at all. He cannot reasonably claim that the Fifth Amendment gives him not only this choice but, if he elects to testify, an immunity from cross-examination on the matters he has himself put in dispute. It would make of the Fifth Amendment not only a humane safeguard against judicially coerced self-disclosure but a positive invitation to mutilate the truth a party offers to tell.

Brown v. United States, 356 U.S. 148, 155-156 (1958).

The question then becomes, How broad is the waiver of the Fifth Amendment right? To put it another way, Does the waiver coincide with cross-examination that would be permitted by the scope-of-direct rule, or is it broader or narrower?

There is every indication that the waiver is limited to matters related to the direct testimony. See Brown v. United States, 356 U.S. 148, 154-155 (1958) (defendant "determines the areas of disclosure and therefore of inquiry" and thereby "the breadth of his waiver"); Fitzpatrick v. United States, 178 U.S. 304, 315-316 (1900) (after testifying to an alibi, defendant could be cross-examined on his whereabouts, but going "farther" would present "a clear case of the defendant being compelled to furnish original evidence against himself"); United States v. Hernandez, 646 F.2d 970, 978-979 (5th Cir.), cert. denied, 454 U.S. 1082 (1981); Tucker v. United States, 5 F.2d 818, 822 (8th Cir. 1925). See also Carlson, Cross-Examination of the Accused, 52 Cornell L.Q. 705 (1967), and Scope of Cross-Examination and the Proposed Federal Rules, 32 Fed. B.J. 244 (1973).

In one opinion, however, the Supreme Court seems to have squinted in the opposite direction. See Johnson v. United States, 318 U.S. 189, 195 (1943) (in testifying the accused waives his privilege against self-incrimination "as to *all other relevant facts*"). And in the much-publicized prosecution of kidnapped heiress Patricia Hearst for bank robbery, the reviewing court demonstrated that even a limited waiver may be construed broadly. See United States v. Hearst, 563 F.2d 1331, 1341 (9th Cir. 1977) (in support of her claim that she was coerced into participating in bank robbery, defendant described what happened during her lengthy period of captivity but omitted reference to happenings during one "lost year" in that period; on cross-examination, the prosecutor could inquire about that "interim year" even though he might uncover other criminal acts, for this line of inquiry was "more than 'reasonably related' to the subject matter" of her direct testimony), cert. denied, 435 U.S. 1000 (1978).

3. The voucher principle.   It was once said that the calling party "vouched" for his witnesses and was thus "bound" by their testimony.[4] In practice, this principle meant that a party could not impeach witnesses he called, and it reinforced the notion that the calling party should not cross-examine such witnesses by leading questions. It seemed to follow that the cross-examiner should not be permitted to explore matters that had not been "opened up" on direct, for doing so would let him (1) "make his own case" by leading questions, (2) avoid "vouching" for a witness who would become in substance "his" witness although not actually called by him, and (3) build his case by testimony of a witness for whom his opponent had vouched and whom his opponent could not impeach.

These somewhat formalistic objections have disappeared. FRE 607 does away with the voucher rule in no uncertain terms, providing that "any party" may impeach, "including the party calling the witness," and it is no longer open to doubt that a party who cannot cross-examine a witness adequately at the outset may recall her later, without fearing that he thereby "vouches" for her or becomes "bound" by her testimony, and with the right to "impeach" and put "leading questions" to her.

---

4. Here was a dog whose bark was worse than its bite. A party could always adduce evidence conflicting with what one of its witnesses said, and there were so many ways around the rule that it came to be honored more in the breach than the observance. But it was pernicious. It rested on the half-truth that a party really has a choice of what witnesses to call, and sometimes it produced gross injustice, as happened in the case of Chambers v. Mississippi, 410 U.S. 284 (1973) (see Chapter 4H, infra).

If it be argued that the freedom made possible by throwing out the voucher rule makes it *unnecessary* to permit cross-examination beyond the scope of the direct, the answer may be the one advanced by McCormick: Questioning delayed is likely to be questioning denied, for the adverse party often will not dare recall the witness later.

Striking a compromise. The framers of the Federal Rules were unable to choose between the scope-of-direct limit or wide-open cross. They seesawed back and forth. In his testimony before Congress, Albert Jenner described the debate in Committee:

> *Mr. Jenner:* The committee went up the mountain and down the mountain on the question of the scope of cross-examination. The rule in the Federal court today is and has been that the scope of cross-examination is limited to the scope of the direct examination.
>
> There are very strong views around the country that the scope of cross-examination is not limited where a party is a witness. You may ask a party any questions. He tenders the whole issue when he is on the stand.
>
> Well, the committee took many votes on this subject. It was either one way or the other by 1 vote. It was 8 to 7 one way or the other and [in] the final vote, virtually within the last few weeks of the meetings of the committee, the committee opted for the present proposed rule 611 that the scope of cross-examination be limited to the direct. [This version was originally suggested by the Committee and ultimately enacted by Congress.—EDS.]
>
> Now, there is an area in which the Congress and you may very well [differ]—it is a close question. Litigators are of the view that the scope of cross should be limited to the direct. The scholars in their great wisdom feel that it should be wide open as it is now [in subsequent Committee drafts of Rule 611, including the one finally recommended by the Committee to the Court, and thereafter endorsed by the Court and sent to Congress for approval].
>
> *Mr. Cleary:* I think we could probably aline [*sic*] the judges on our side, Mr. Chairman.
>
> *Mr. Jenner:* Align those judges who had not been litigators before they assumed the bench.
>
> *Mr. Hungate:* They will have to qualify as scholars, then won't they?
>
> *Mr. Smith:* On your final option was it still a one vote decision?
>
> *Mr. Jenner:* Yes, it was, one vote.
>
> *Judge Maris:* It was one vote in the Advisory Committee. It was by one vote in the Standing Committee. We approved the draft that the majority of that committee had presented.

Hearings on Proposed Rules of Evidence before the Special Subcommittee on Reform of Federal Criminal Laws of the House Committee on the Judiciary, 93d Cong., 1st Sess., ser. 2, at 526-527 (1973).

In all this vacillation the Committee was debating only a matter of emphasis in a very flexible provision—one that would say *either* that cross-examination "should be limited to the subject matter of the direct" but that the judge may "permit inquiry into additional matters" *or* that cross-examination may delve into "any matter relevant to any issue in the case" but that the judge might "limit cross-examination with respect to matters not testified to on direct." The former was to prevail, so usually the scope-of-direct rule applies, but the trial judge may permit broader cross. The rule in this form largely obviates the objection that it is hard to administer, since the trial judge is not likely to be reversed for choosing either alternative and there is little "percentage" trying to make an issue out of the choice she makes in any given case.

The divisions in the Committee are reflected in conflicts in state practice. Although most states adhere to the scope-of-direct rule, a substantial minority has gone the other way. By recent count, more than a dozen states have abandoned or diluted the scope-of-direct rule.[5] See Arizona Rule of Evidence 611(b) (permitting cross-examination on "any relevant matter"); Maine Rule of Evidence 611(b) (trial judge may limit cross-examination "in the interests of justice"); Boller v. Cofrances, 42 166 N.W.2d 129 (Wis. 1969) (landmark opinion adopting wide-open rule).

PROBLEM 1-A. *How Did It Happen?*

At the intersection of Folsom and Valmont two cars collide—a yellow Fiat driven by Abby Barton, in which Carl Dreeves rode as passenger, and a blue Buick driven by Eric Felsen. In a Rules jurisdiction, Barton sues Felsen for personal injuries and property damage. During her case-in-chief, Barton calls Carl Dreeves, who testifies on direct examination that "the Buick ran a red light."

On cross-examination, Felsen's counsel asks the following questions:

Q: Now Mr. Dreeves, you and Ms. Barton are seeing each other socially, isn't that right?
Q: Isn't it true, Mr. Dreeves, that at the time of the accident Ms. Barton here had turned clear around in her seat and was looking out the back window of the car?
Q: Tell me, Mr. Dreeves, you and Ms. Barton here had just finished lunch at Sebastian's where she drank three glasses of wine just before the accident, isn't that true?

To each question Barton's counsel objects, "Improper as beyond the scope of direct, your honor." How should the judge rule in each instance, and why? What arguments do you expect from Barton and Felsen?

c. Real Evidence

"Real evidence" refers to tangible things directly involved in the transactions or events in litigation—the defective steering assembly involved in the accident, the weapon used in the homicide or armed robbery, the wound or injury suffered by the claimant, the written embodiment of the terms of agreement.

Apart from writings, the law of evidence ordinarily does not *require* production of such items, and their existence and nature may be established by testimonial account. But the Best Evidence doctrine (Chapter 14) generally does require the introduction of writings (or an excuse for not producing them),

---

5. States with decisions or positive law seemingly adopting the wide-open rule include Alabama, Arizona, Georgia, Louisiana, Maine, Massachusetts, Michigan, Mississippi, Missouri, North Carolina, South Carolina, Tennessee, Texas, and Wisconsin.

and all such items are generally considered relevant. They are likely to be admitted unless practical considerations preclude receipt.

The proponent's task in getting them admitted is to lay the necessary "foundation." Even if the thing in question looks very much like what it is supposed to be, the law of evidence is a Doubting Thomas, taking the skeptical position that the thing may *not* be taken "at face value" and the trier of fact may *not* assume it is "what it seems to be." Instead, the proponent must prove this point, and the process is called "authenticating" the evidence. Few specific Rules govern this process, and the ones we have are found in Article IX (see Chapter 13). Usually authentication is taken care of by stipulation, or by testimony from a witness having firsthand knowledge:

Q (Ms. Phipps): Now, Lieutenant Goldbloom, I hand you a gun which has been marked for identification as People's Exhibit Number Seven, and ask whether you can tell us what it is. Don't worry, sir, I've checked to be sure that it is not loaded.

A (Mr. Goldbloom): Thank you, but I always like to check these things myself. (Witness pauses to examine the gun.) Yes, I can identify this weapon. It is a Smith & Wesson .38 caliber revolver.

Q: And have you seen this particular weapon before?

A: Yes.

Q: How can you tell?

A: Here on the handle, it has my identification mark on it, which means that I found it in the course of my duties and wrote it up in a report.

Q: And could you tell us how you happened to find it?

A: Certainly. It was during the investigation of the death of Irving Stiffle, and I found the gun on the floor of the bedroom about five feet from his body.

Q: Your honor, I now offer this gun into evidence—what number will it be, Mr. Glade?

Court Clerk: It would be People's Number Three in evidence.

Ms. Phipps: I offer this gun into evidence as People's Exhibit Number Three.

The Court: Any objection from the defense?

Mr. Darnell: Yes, your honor, I do object, on several grounds. In the first place, nothing Lieutenant Goldbloom has said here connects that gun in any way to the defendant, or even to the alleged homicide. Moreover, the Lieutenant's testimony fails to account for the whereabouts of that gun from the time he picked it up until now. For all we know, the Property Room has fouled up again, and that's an entirely different weapon.

The Court: Ms. Phipps, any counter?

Ms. Phipps: Yes, your honor, it should suffice that the gun was found in the same room with the victim, but in any event we will offer ballistics testimony proving that the bullet that killed the victim was fired from this gun, and testimony from Forensics that defendant's fingerprints were found on the gun. As to the objection that we have not established the chain of custody, such proof should be unnecessary when we have the Lieutenant's testimony based on his mark that this is the very weapon which he found at the scene.

The Court: I'm inclined to agree. Objection overruled. Exhibit—what number is it, now?

Court Clerk: Number Three in Evidence.

The Court: Yes, the gun is admitted as Exhibit Number Three in Evidence.

In the above exchange, notice that the authenticating witness Goldbloom recognized the gun and knew from memory that it was the weapon he found at the scene. In effect, the trial court has ruled that this information suffices to "authenticate" the weapon, even *without* "chain-of-custody" evidence establishing that the gun he found was carefully kept in a safe place under watch (or at least lock and key). Implicit here is a judgment that the proponent need not show precautions against a switch, at least when the authenticating witness says, in effect, that no switch occurred. Note too that the trial judge did not decide whether "authentication" requires proof connecting the gun to the homicide (the ballistics evidence) or to the defendant (forensics evidence), taking the prosecutor at her word that she would supply such proof later. If she does not deliver, the defense may force the issue by moving to strike the evidence.

Note too that the gun was "marked for identification" before even being mentioned. All physical objects that a party expects to offer are routinely marked in this preliminary way. This precaution helps keep track of them and enables the parties to refer to them, in a way that will later make sense in the transcript, even before they are admitted. If the trial judge *excludes* an object, still it is lodged with the clerk, and the record of the offer may become important later on. When the judge *admits* the object, it is renumbered as an exhibit in evidence, and the number finally assigned may differ from the one originally assigned for identification.

d. Demonstrative Evidence

As the name implies, demonstrative evidence is tangible proof that in some way makes graphic the point to be proved. It differs from real evidence in that it is created for illustrative purposes and for use at trial, and it played no actual role in the events or transactions which gave rise to the lawsuit. Diagrams, photographs, maps, and models are all within the present category. So are computer-aided reconstructions, which can depict in color and from multiple perspectives an automobile accident or a crime, such as a robbery or murder or assault. See generally Fred Galves, Where the Not-So-Wild Things Are: Computers in the Courtroom, The Federal Rules of Evidence, and the Need for Institutional Reform and More Judicial Acceptance, 13 Harv. J.L. & Tech 161 (2000).

Such materials are usually considered relevant and are routinely admitted. Once again there are no specific rules or principles that apply, and the task of the proponent is to show that the proffered item amounts to a fair and accurate depiction of the matter in question. The growing sophistication of computer-aided reconstructions, which have the power to convey a sense of movement, mass, and perspective that cannot easily be captured in verbal descriptions, but also have the power to distort or overwhelm, have "raised the ante" for such foundational issues. These reconstructions must usually be supported by testimony showing that the dimensions and perspectives are correctly depicted, and may require experts rather than ordinary eyewitnesses. For more routine and less dramatic forms of demonstrative evidence, usually the proponent simply calls a witness who has seen the matter and who then testifies that the exhibit fairly represents it:

Q (Ms. Phipps): Lieutenant Goldbloom, may I call your attention to the drawing on the stand over here, which has been marked for identification as People's Exhibit Number Eight. This drawing is intended to show the layout of the bedroom where the victim was found. Is that a fair and reasonably accurate diagram of the room as you remember it?

A (Lt. Goldbloom): Yes, the bed came out more or less from the center of the wall farthest from the door, there was a bureau along the wall to the left as you came in—that's supposed to be the bureau, isn't it?

Q: Perhaps you could label the various items with this marker. (Counsel hands marker to Witness.)

A: OK, here's the bed. (Witness marks drawing.)

Q: You've written the word "bed." OK, Thank you. Would you also mark where the window is? (Pause. Witness marks drawing.) You've written the word "window" with an arrow. Is that where the window is located?

A: Yes.

Ms. Phipps: Your Honor, we now offer into evidence what has been marked for identification as People's Exhibit Eight.

The Court: Mr. Darnell?

Mr. Darnell: No objection, Your Honor.

The Court: Very well, then. The diagram of the room will be received as People's Exhibit—what number are we at now?

Court Clerk: This will be People's Number Four in Evidence, Your Honor.

The Court: It is admitted as People's Exhibit Number Four.

Notice in this exchange that the drawing was taken only as illustrating the testimony of the witness, Lieutenant Goldbloom. You will see that a drawing produced to make graphic the testimony of a witness has no evidential force independent of that testimony. Sometimes jurors are instructed to this effect, and sometimes the parties even argue that material of this sort should not be taken to the jury room or even displayed to them because of the risk that the jury will *treat* it as evidence, uncritically accepting the things that it represents as having been established, when in fact they have no more support than the testimony of the witness, which the material merely illustrates. Of course the same is true of computer-aided reconstructions.

e. Writings

Writings are one kind of physical evidence that generally *must* be introduced at trial rather than proved by means of testimonial description. Often writings amount to real evidence because so many transactions generating lawsuits involve documents. But often writings provide a means to prove what someone has said about a matter in dispute: Laboratory reports and medical records, for example, are routinely admitted into evidence as proof of the matters that they relate. Again electronic technology sometimes aids courts and litigants, for written documents can be stored and organized on computers, made available to the lawyers and judges for simultaneous access on computer screens, and "published" for juries to see on larger screens, or printed out for ease in access on a selective basis.

With writings, once again the job of the proponent is to establish authenticity, and we have some specific rules on authenticating writings (Article IX, taken up in Chapter 13). Suffice it to say here that in civil suits the parties usually authenticate writings involved in the underlying transaction by means of discovery or stipulations during pretrial. Taking time at trial to authenticate such writings is a sign that there is a genuine dispute over authenticity or that trial counsel are not well prepared.

With respect to writings offered to prove what somebody has said about the matters in litigation, laying the foundation is usually a twofold task. First, the proponent establishes that the writing is what he says it is—in other words he authenticates it. Second, he shows that it falls within a hearsay exception:

Q (Irwin): Dr. Rogers, I hand you now a book and would ask you now to look at it and tell me whether you are acquainted with this work?

A (Dr. Rogers): Oh, Appleby on Thoracic Surgery, Littleton Publishing Company, Sixth Edition 1984. Yes, this is a standard work in my field.

Q: Would you be good enough to turn to page 287 and read aloud to us the paragraph which has been marked? Mr. Steed, here is a copy of the page in question.

Mr. Steed: One minute, Your Honor, please. I have not seen this before.

The Court: Yes, of course. Dr. Rogers, please wait with your response.

Mr. Steed: I'm going to have to object, Your Honor. Obviously this book is hearsay, and since the doctor here has not said that he relied on it in formulating whatever opinion he is going to offer, the passage in question is not admissible.

Mr. Irwin: Your Honor, Dr. Rogers has testified that Appleby on Thoracic Surgery is a standard work in his field, and that should suffice to satisfy Rule 803(18), which is the exception for learned treatises.

Mr. Steed: But there's been no reliance on this book, and without reliance it cannot be offered in evidence.

Mr. Irwin: Perhaps that was the common law rule, counsel, but the Federal Rules have changed that. Exception 18 doesn't say the witness has to rely on it, so long as the book is shown to be authoritative.

The Court: Mr. Steed, I think he's right. I'm going to let it in.

In this exchange, proving that the object is what the proponent claims it to be is easy. A physician acquainted with a published work can authenticate a particular bound volume as a counterpart of that published work, and ordinarily there would be no contest on this point whatsoever. In this particular exchange, laying the foundation involves mostly a demonstration that what the book contains is competent evidence.

2. *Keeping Evidence Out*

a. The Objection

Perhaps the one practice known to everybody is that lawyers object when they want to keep evidence out. You have probably concluded that there must be a reason and that failing to object must carry a cost. Right on both points. Broadly speaking, the aim of the rules surrounding this custom is to provide the parties a fair opportunity to make their case, but not an endless one. If a party aggrieved by particular evidence were permitted to await the outcome and *then* complain that it should not have been admitted, the trial process would be even more drawn out and costly. The eventual loser could hold his peace during trial, and perhaps even encourage error, then avoid the result by obtaining a reversal. Requiring objections helps limit this risk. Of course this approach carries a cost, for it means that some errors (those not objected to) go uncorrected, and the fact that we take this risk is one indication that the system tolerates imperfection.

There are two other (more particular) reasons to require objections to be raised at trial. One is that the objection helps the trial court. The law of evidence is vast and sometimes complicated, and trial judges (like other mortals) do not always have the right answer close at hand. The other is to help the offering party cure on the spot any problem in his proof. If an objection is sustained, the offering party may be able to accomplish her original aim by rephrasing the question, laying a further foundation, or asking the question of another witness.

These aims imply two further points about objections:

The objection must be timely, meaning that it must be raised at the earliest reasonable opportunity. Thus an objection to testimony by a witness should usually be stated after the proponent has put a question but before the witness answers. (If the witness "jumps the gun," perhaps with the connivance of the other lawyer, the objection can be stated after the fact, when it becomes a "motion to strike.") The obvious drawback of this "after objection" is that the jury has heard the answer, so an instruction to disregard may be ineffective, even counterproductive (emphasizing the point to be forgotten). Hence the objecting party often couples a motion to strike with a request for a mistrial, arguing that the damage cannot be undone, and therefore that the trial must begin anew before another jury. You can probably guess why this part of the motion is not likely to succeed.

And the objection should include a statement of the underlying reason ("ground"). When the context leaves room for doubt, the objection should specify what the objector seeks to exclude. In other words, the objection should be "specific" and not "general." The alliterative phrase "irrelevant, incompetent, and immaterial" is viewed as a general objection, even though a more detailed argument that evidence is "irrelevant" would be considered specific.

The specific grounds that support an objection may be, for want of better terms, either "substantive" in nature or "formal."

Substantive objections. These rest on particular exclusionary principles in the Rules of Evidence, which are examined in detail in this course. The fervent hope of the party raising such an objection is to keep the evidence out altogether. He may not entirely succeed, of course, even if his objection is sustained, as the proponent may find another way to offer substantially the same proof. Examples of substantive grounds include the hearsay and Best Evidence doctrines, the attorney-client and marital confidence privileges, and the rules governing character evidence and "subsequent remedial measures" (these last are usually framed in terms of limitations upon the general notion of relevancy). Consider the following exchange:

Q (Mr. Parsons):   Were you at the intersection of Fourth and Green in the commercial
   area in Champaign near campus on Wednesday afternoon, June 16th of this year?
A (Ms. Gordon):   Why yes, I think I was. I can't remember the date for sure, but you're
   talking about the day of the accident, aren't you?
Q: Yes, that occasion. You were present then?
A: Yes.
Q: And did you see an accident between two cars at that time?
A: Well yes, I happened to be looking at the station wagon when it collided with the
   other car.
Q: And did you have occasion to speak to Mr. Cronan shortly after that?
A (Ms. Gordon):   Yes, I did.
Q: And what was his reaction?
A: Well, he told me—
Mr. Dawson: I'm going to have to object, your honor. The jury has no way of knowing
   whether Mr. Cronan was speaking accurately or even whether he was truthful. What
   he said is inadmissible hearsay.
Mr. Parsons: Your Honor, Mr. Cronan's statement fits within the exception for excited
   utterances. That's Rule 803(2), I believe—Yes, that's it.
Mr. Dawson: He hasn't shown that that exception applies, your honor.
The Court: Well, Mr. Dawson, I'm inclined to agree. Mr. Parsons, you'd best lay the
   foundation first or call Mr. Cronan himself to the stand.

Pay attention to several things here. One is that the objection is both specific and timely. Another is that it imparts the necessary information to the judge, and yet it conveys sympathy for the jury rather than mistrust of its judgment. Because the jury hears most objections, trial lawyers need to find a way to object without seeming to obstruct, to make the necessary legal point without seeming to hide information from the jury. Finally, the objection serves one of the underlying purposes, which is to alert the proponent to a problem in his proof, so he may cure it if he can, and here perhaps he can: He may be able to call Cronan ("declarant" who made the statement), hoping he will say the same thing on the stand, or to "lay the foundation" by satisfying the excited utterance exception so that Gordon can testify to Cronan's statement.

Formal objections. These focus on the manner of questioning, and they are standard equipment for trial lawyers. Many of them are mere tactical weapons, used to obstruct, delay, or break the cadence of the opposition. But in the right circumstances they raise proper points and will be sustained. Apart from the objection to leading questions, these objections are not enshrined in particular Rules, but they speak to the broad authority of the trial judge to regulate the presentation of proof in the interest of getting at the truth while avoiding confusion and delay and preventing abuse of witnesses. See FRE 611, and see generally Roger C. Park, David P. Leonard, and Steven H. Goldberg, Evidence Law: A Student's Guide to the Law of Evidence as Applied in American Trials, Chapter 3 (1998).

Here is a list of what may be the most frequently encountered of these objections:

1. "Asked and answered."   Here the objecting lawyer accuses the questioner of drumming away too hard on the witness, putting the same question time and again in hopes of coercing the desired response. Clearly the questioner must be allowed to press the witness (particularly on cross) and need not take the first answer given, or else the witness would soon catch on that she can get out of the hot seat by simple denials or the time-honored evasion of "I don't know/remember." But when the questioner has gotten his response and has had a reasonable chance to expose falsehood or awaken the memory and conscience of the witness, then the questioning must move on to other matters, and this objection can force the point.

2. "Assumes facts not in evidence."   If the questioner imparts important information in his query, it should be supported by proof already admitted. If such support is missing, the question is objectionable as assuming too much. Thus, asking "How long did it take to drive the 20 miles from the ranch to town?" would be objectionable if nothing in the record indicated that the ranch was 20 miles from town.

3. "Argumentative."   Sometimes the questioner tries to contradict the witness or wants more to confront her with disbelief than to get a response. Questions in this vein, usually dripping with sarcasm and contempt, amount to "grandstanding," which may be permissible in closing argument but not while evidence is being presented. "What you mean when you say Martin wasn't speeding is that his car hadn't taken off like an airplane, isn't that it?" is a question that cannot be taken seriously and is objectionable as argument thinly disguised.

4. "Compound."   Sometimes a question apparently seeks more than one answer or suggests alternative responses, while being framed in a way that invites a yes or no response. The problem is that the witness may answer yes or no and her meaning will then be obscure. For example, "Did you telephone or see the decedent after that?" If the witness says yes, a strict construction of the question and response suggests that she telephoned *or* saw the decedent, but not both. But in the more relaxed everyday parlance the yes might mean that the witness *both* telephoned and saw the decedent, or perhaps simply that she saw the decedent (that being the last and perhaps more inclusive possibility). A careful witness might see the ambiguity and answer clearly ("I saw the decedent after that but did not speak to him on the phone"), but a timely objection will likely persuade the judge to tell the questioner to rephrase, so as to lessen the risk of ambiguity in the upcoming response.

5. "Leading the witness."   Here the suggestion is that counsel is telling the witness what to say, and the net impression is that the lawyer is doing the testifying, with the witness simply acceding to the will of counsel. We have already looked at the underlying problems in this technique.

6. "Misleading."   Here the question misstates the evidence. If the only proof on point suggests that the ranch is 40 miles from town, a question asking "Why did it take you an hour to drive the ten miles to town?" would be objectionable as misleading. The same is true of a question that misquotes the testimony of a previous witness.

7. "Speculation or conjecture."   This objection raises the point that witnesses are expected to say what they "know," not what they "guess" or "suppose" or "expect" is true. Like objections to hearsay, this one has substantive content. It may be impossible for the questioner to offer what he wants because lay witnesses are expected to say what they know and to be factual and specific. (Experts have more leeway and often testify to what they would expect in hypothetical circumstances, where these are supported by evidence.) Asking a lay witness, for example, "what she would have done" if she knew something then that she knows now, or what someone else "was thinking when he did that," is typically objectionable on this ground. (Categorical certainty is not required, for in court as in life it is hard to come by. Someone who saw a robbery and "thinks" X did it may testify to this effect, even if she is "not absolutely certain." We expect a reasonable belief; a "guess" is not good enough.) Sometimes the problem is less substance than form, as when the questioner cannot figure out how to get what he wants in a nonleading way. A court that does not let a lawyer ask "what you would have done" with other information would probably let him ask, "What was the most important reason you did what you did?"

8. *"Ambiguous, uncertain, and unintelligible."* Like the alliterative general objection ("incompetent, irrelevant, and immaterial"), this three-part protest is time-honored. It isn't pretty, but it does point out the flaw in questions that simply cannot be understood or whose meaning depends entirely on inflection that the record cannot capture. Sometimes the problem is that the lawyer has garbled his words and needs to start over. Sometimes the query is a close cousin to the argumentative question, where there is no serious expectation of a response. Here is an example: "In arranging the lineup, you picked seven men who weighed the same and didn't weigh the same, who were the same height but not the same height, and who looked alike but didn't look alike, didn't you?"

9. *"Nonresponsive to the question."* Lawyers who ask proper questions on specific points are entitled to answers addressing those points. Suppose counsel for plaintiff asks defendant in an accident case, "Weren't you driving faster than the posted limit?" If he replies, "Maybe so, but your client darted out in front of me and I couldn't have stopped no matter how fast I was going," the questioner can ask the court to "strike the answer as nonresponsive and instruct the witness to answer the question." (The judge will do so and, on request or maybe even without it, tell the jury to "disregard the answer.") Anyone who watches televised interviews knows questioners and respondents have agendas and work at cross-purposes—sometimes it's hard to know who's manipulating whom. In the courtroom, the judge decides such things and ordinarily gives the lawyer leeway to decide what points to make and when, and the witness has to cooperate. Clients are usually stuck with evidence their lawyers offer, so when a witness answers a question that wasn't asked, striking the answer as nonresponsive may be important. (A fair answer to an open-ended question is *not* nonresponsive. If the lawyer says, "Tell us what happened," and the witness replies, "Your client darted out in front of me," that answer *is* responsive and the lawyer is stuck with it.)

The general objection. If overruled, a general objection does not preserve for review whatever point the objector had in mind, and in this sense it gives less than maximum protection.

Yet a general objection is far from useless, and trial lawyers make such objections all the time. Sometimes the reason is that they (like the rest of us) do not always find the right words immediately—they sense that something is wrong but cannot say exactly what. Sometimes the reason is almost the converse—which is to say that *everybody* knows exactly what is wrong, and the point is too obvious for words. Here the trial lawyer may well resort to the alliterative "incompetent, irrelevant, and immaterial," or (better yet, to avoid evoking the stereotypical lawyer's image, never much liked by lay people) might simply say "I object, Your Honor; he can't do that" or "That's unfair" or words of similar effect.

If the problem is that the objecting attorney has for the moment lost his wits and cannot think of the specific ground, these words at least halt the proceedings momentarily while he gropes in his mind to formulate his point. If lawyers and judge already know what is wrong, the judge may well sustain the objection in peremptory fashion, and a general objection sustained will survive attack by the other party on appeal if there are *any grounds* upon which it may be supported.

So a general objection may be a sign of poor lawyering, but not necessarily and not always. And in the right circumstances it can aptly serve the objector's purpose.

b. The Motion in Limine

Often a party anticipates that particular evidence will be offered to which he will object. Sometimes he anticipates that an item of proof that he plans to offer will meet serious objection from the adversary. In either case, he may want to obtain a ruling in advance, and the mechanism of a "motion in limine" (literally, "at the threshold") provides the means. This procedural device is sometimes authorized by statute or rule, and it exists by common law tradition in almost all other jurisdictions (including the federal system).[6]

The attraction of this device is readily explained. It provides a chance for both parties to brief an important evidence issue and present more elaborate argument than is possible during trial. It allows the movant to isolate and emphasize a point, and in the process obtain a carefully considered ruling. It may affect trial strategy: In the common situation in which the accused seeks an order forbidding the prosecutor from questioning him on past criminal convictions, the ruling may determine whether he should testify on his own behalf. And trial judges may be more than willing to consider and rule in advance upon such matters, in hopes of making a sounder decision and avoiding delays that are awkward while trial is in process.

But motions in limine are not always satisfactory.

From the standpoint of the trial judge, the motion may seem to seek an "advisory opinion" that she is loathe to provide. It grates on her judicial temperament to be asked to decide a point not yet actually presented, and its very isolation from the trial may persuade her that she does not yet know how the issue should be resolved. In the frequent case in which the accused wants to foreclose cross-examination about his own criminal convictions, ruling correctly may involve the trial judge in considering the nature of testimony as yet unheard.

---

6. The motion to suppress evidence, which is generally authorized by specific provision in the rules of criminal procedure (see, e.g., FRCrimP 12(b)) and routinely made by the defense as a means of asserting rights based upon the Fourth and Fifth Amendments, is the best known instance of this procedure in operation.

And the trial judge may want to know more about the entire complexion of the case than she can know before trial has begun.

Motions in limine sometimes create procedural ambiguities for the parties. If the trial judge denies a motion to exclude certain evidence, must the movant object again during trial in order to protect his right to obtain later appellate review? Decisions conflict on this point, but FRE 103(a) was amended in 2000 so that it now provides that an objection need not be renewed at trial if the judge makes a "definitive ruling" on a pretrial motion. If the trial goes differently from what was anticipated at the time of the ruling, however, it seems that the judge may change the ruling. See United States v. Gaertner, 705 F.2d 210, 214-216 (7th Cir. 1983) (in drug trial, court first ruled that prosecutor could not ask defendant about prior narcotics convictions, but after he implied in his testimony that he was a person of good character, court permitted cross-examination on the prior convictions), cert. denied, 464 U.S. 1071 (1984). Thus, even a clear ruling in limine still leaves the lawyers with the problem of deciding when (and whether) events have gone sufficiently far astray to justify reconsideration.

3. The Offer of Proof

The counterpart to the objection is the offer of proof. Making an offer of proof is not nearly so ingrained in the popular image of lawyers as objecting, but it is equally important, and failing to make offers when necessary is a common and serious shortcoming. Here is the basic point: A lawyer faced with a ruling excluding evidence *must* make a formal offer of proof, if he wants to preserve the point for later appellate review, which means demonstrating to the trial court exactly what he is prepared to introduce if permitted.

Broadly speaking, offers of proof are required for the same reason as objections. The idea is to accord the offering party (the "proponent") a fair procedural opportunity to get in his proof, but not endless chances. He must be ready to present his evidence when the objection is made and must make its "substance" known to the court (see FRE 103(a)(2)). If it were otherwise, if the proponent could await the outcome and only *then* make it known that he has additional evidence and disclose the details of what he would have proved if allowed, the end result would be a costly and potentially interminable trial process. An offer of proof is also necessary in order to "preserve the record" for purposes of review. Without an offer, an appellate court normally has no way to determine whether excluded evidence might have affected the outcome.

Like the objection, the offer of proof serves a disclosive function and thus achieves two additional ends. One is to enable the objector to refine his objection if need be, and perhaps to frame it more fully. The other is to assist the trial judge to arrive at the correct ruling, since a detailed exposition of the evidence in question might lead her to change her mind and admit.

If the evidence offered is a document or other physical exhibit, it will likely have been marked for identification before trial. At the time of the offer, the proponent will hand it to the clerk ("lodge" is the usual expression), to become part of the record regardless whether it is ultimately admitted in evidence. (You already saw this ritual in the examples of the gun and drawing, offered with

Lieutenant Goldbloom's testimony.) With documentary evidence, technology can make this process simpler, since a document stored on computers can be accessed by the lawyers and the court at the same time, and "calling it up on the screen" can enable the court to consider and rule on the proffer without handing pieces of paper around. If the evidence is testimonial, usually counsel for the proponent makes his offer by means of an oral description *on the record* of the substance of the expected testimony. If the judge entertains any doubt that the witness would testify in the manner described, she may ask counsel to put him on the stand: In the words of FRE 103(b), the court may "direct the making of an offer in question and answer form." Needless to say, in all these cases the offer of proof is made (in the words of FRE 103(c)) "to the extent practicable, so as to prevent inadmissible evidence from being suggested to the jury by any means." It follows that ordinarily the jury is excused when a proffer is heard.

It should be obvious from the description of objecting that the party wishing to exclude evidence bears the initial burden of raising the objection. When the objection has been made, however, ordinarily the proponent bears the burden of showing that his evidence is admissible. In other words, in making his offer of proof he must be prepared to explain why the pertinent rule or principle supports receipt of the evidence. The necessary showing may involve simply winning an argument over the meaning and applicability of the rules, but often it involves presentation of testimony or other proof to establish facts and conditions that bring a rule of admissibility into play. The apparently successful objection voiced by Dawson in the exchange quoted above might lead to an offer of proof by Parsons:

Mr. Parsons: Your Honor, may I be heard further on this matter? I believe that I can establish that Mr. Cronan's statement fits within the excited utterance exception set out in Rule 803(2), and I would like to make an offer of proof for the record.

Mr. Dawson: Cronan's statement does not fit, and the court has quite rightly sustained my objection. If we're going to get into a legal argument on this point, may I suggest that the jury be excused while we fight it out? The jury has to leave if he's going to make an offer of proof, anyway.

The Court: Gentlemen, please approach the bench.

[Discussion is held off the record.]

The Court: Ladies and gentlemen, we have not been able to reach an understanding yet, and since the dispute concerns a rather technical question of law, I'd like to ask you to step out in the hall for about 20 minutes while we get to the bottom of this thing. The bailiff will show you out. You may want to take this opportunity to go down to the snack room in the basement for a cup of coffee or other refreshment. There are some vending machines down there, and you can take a midmorning break.

[Jury leaves the courtroom.]

The Court: Alright, gentlemen, let's get this over with. Mr. Parsons, you say I should let Ms. Gordon tell us what Mr. Cronan said shortly after the accident. You claim that his statement fits within the excited utterance exception and you want to make a record of Cronan's statement, is that right?

Mr. Parsons: Exactly, Your Honor. The exception was practically designed for this very situation, and we want to preserve a record of what he said.

The Court: Alright. Mr. Dawson, you say the statement is hearsay, and I should not let Ms. Gordon testify to what Cronan said, is that right?

Mr. Dawson: Right, Your Honor. Cronan's statement is pure hearsay, and Mr. Parsons should call him as a witness if he wants the jury to hear what he has to say.

The Court: The ball's in your court, Mr. Parsons.

Q (Parsons):   Thank you, Your Honor. Ms. Gordon, where were you when the accident occurred?

A (Gordon):   As I said before, I was on the sidewalk about 40 feet away from where the two cars collided.

Q: And where was Mr. Cronan at the time?

A: He was about ten feet away from me.

Q: And did you two know each other?

A: No, sir. But we both went into the gas station on the corner to call for help, and then we stayed around in case we were needed. And when the police came, they took statements from both of us, and it was then that I picked up his name.

Q: I see. And shortly after the collision, but before you found out his name, did Mr. Cronan say something to you about the accident?

A: Yes.

Q: How long after the accident, would you say?

A: Well, hardly any time had passed. It's a little hard to say, since I was concerned about the condition of the people in those cars, and worried that we were going to have other collisions. But to answer your question, I would say that Mr. Cronan said what he said not more than half a minute after the impact.

Q: Thank you. And Ms. Gordon, could you tell us how he sounded? Did he speak to you in—

Mr. Dawson: Just a minute, Your Honor. He's about to put words in the mouth of the witness. Let her tell us how he sounded in her own words.

The Court: Yes, I agree. Ms. Gordon, you heard the question. Tell us how Mr. Cronan sounded.

A (Gordon):   Well, he just said it. I suppose we were both a bit upset—probably more surprised than anything. You know how it is when you're walking along the street and all of a sudden out of nowhere you hear tires screech and that terrible sound of metal crashing together and you don't know for sure whether you're out of harm's way. I'd say Mr. Cronan said the first thing that came to him, and he kind of blurted it out.

Q: You said that Mr. Cronan sounded upset. Could you elaborate on that?

A: Well, I don't know what more to say. He was startled and sounded sort of aggravated.

Q: And now tell us, please, what you heard him say.

Mr. Dawson: Your Honor, you haven't ruled yet that what Mr. Cronan said is admissible. Let me just state for the record that I continue to object that his statement is hearsay.

The Court: Yes, counsel, I haven't forgotten your objection. You may answer, Ms. Gordon. What did he say?

A (Gordon):   Well, he said "I knew that guy in the stationwagon wasn't going to stop. He never did slow down." Then he added something like, "Too much of a hurry to obey the rules the rest of us live by."

Mr. Parsons: Thank you, Ms. Gordon. Your Honor, I submit that Cronan's statement is within the excited utterance exception of Rule 803(2). Ms. Gordon has said that he seemed "startled," to use her word, and subdivision (2) expressly mentions statements "relating to a startling event or condition" when such statements are made while declarant was "under the stress of excitement" brought on by that event. Well, a car accident is a startling event, and Mr. Cronan was obviously excited. His statement relates to the event. It should be received.

The Court: I take your point. Mr. Dawson, your turn.

Q (Dawson):   Ms. Gordon, the intersection of which you spoke was Fourth and Green, was it not?

A (Gordon):   Yes.

Q: And what were the traffic conditions at the time, if you remember?

A: Well, it was about three o'clock on a Wednesday afternoon, and there were quite a few cars coming down Green from both directions, and up and down Fourth too.

Q: So would you say things were pretty quiet, or on the noisy side?

A: Well, rather noisy. It is a busy street corner, and with the buses and the students and all, it's fairly noisy.

Q: So you heard the sounds of the accident against a background of pretty substantial traffic noise?

A: Yes, I would say so.

Q: Thank you, Ms. Gordon. Your Honor, this is not a case—

The Court: Excuse me just a minute. Are you both through with the witness?

Mr. Parsons: Yes, Your Honor. For the moment.

Mr. Dawson: Yes, sir.

The Court: Ms. Gordon, you may step down. Would you be good enough to wait in the hall for a few minutes? We'll tell you shortly whether we will be needing you any further.

[Witness leaves.]

The Court: OK gentlemen, where are we?

Mr. Dawson: Your Honor, may I be heard? Ms. Gordon has told us that neither she nor Mr. Cronan were afraid for their personal safety. They were far enough away from the accident to be out of danger. She has also testified, and I don't know how she could have said otherwise, that there was considerable noise in the intersection at the time. The noise of the collision was not like a sudden thunderclap. It wasn't any more than a loud sound in the general rumble of traffic, nothing you could even call unusual. The excited utterance exception contemplates a person exclaiming something "under the stress of excitement," and these people were not under stress and were certainly not excited. No more than you or I would be under similar circumstances.

Mr. Parsons: Your Honor,—

The Court: Unless you have something new to add that you haven't already said, I'd just as soon not hear anything further.

Mr. Parsons: Let me just say that the Rule does not require the declarant to be frightened for his life. It speaks of a "a startling event" and "excitement," and we have that here. Moreover, this evidence is critical to my case.

The Court: Well, it's a close question. You've made a record of what you want to get in, Mr. Parsons, so if this case goes up on appeal you can point out exactly what you wanted to prove. I still think this is just hearsay, and I'm inclined to agree with Mr. Dawson that there wasn't enough excitement here to guarantee reliability. If you want to get in Mr. Cronan's opinion, you'll have to call him. The objection is sustained. Gentlemen, unless you have any objection, I am going to excuse Ms. Gordon. Bailiff, please ask Ms. Gordon to step back in the courtroom, and I'll tell her she is excused. Then you may bring the jury back in.

If Parsons' client loses the case and takes an appeal, he now has the fullest possible on-the-record offer of proof, done in "question-and-answer form" so as to preserve the very testimony ultimately excluded and including testimony supporting the ground upon which he contends that the statement should have been admitted. If error was committed, the reviewing court should be able to see it and assess its significance. Consider for a moment how much harder those tasks would be if no offer had been made—if the record had stopped short when the objection was originally sustained.

Fortunately such an elaborate offer of proof is not always necessary. In the example above, Parsons put Gordon on the stand to get her to testify to what Cronan said about the conduct of the driver of the station wagon. Testimony as to what another person said raises hearsay issues, which cannot properly be resolved simply on the basis of Parsons' initial question to Ms. Gordon ("And what was his [Cronan's] reaction?"), so further inquiry is in order when the defense makes its objection. But if Parsons sought to elicit from Ms. Gordon *her own* account of what happened when the cars collided, the nature of her expected response would likely be apparent on the face of the question. Recall that Parsons placed her at the scene ("Were you at the intersection of Fourth and Green. . . ?" "Why yes,. . .") and established that she saw what happened ("And did you see an accident. . . ?" "Well yes, I happened to be looking at the stationwagon.. . ."). Assume the questioning then proceeded in this way:

Q (Parsons): If you can, Ms. Gordon, please tell us about how fast the station-wagon was going as it entered the intersection.

Mr. Dawson: Your Honor, please, Ms. Gordon can't give her opinion on points like that.

Mr. Parsons: Your Honor, I don't know where Mr. Dawson got that idea. Under the Rules, let's see, I think it's 701, any witness can testify to matters based on personal observation, so long as it's helpful to the jury. Certainly a person who sees a car driving along can give an estimate as to speed, and that's all I propose for Ms. Gordon to do here.

Court: No Mr. Parsons, I don't think so. She couldn't see the speedometer from outside the car and I don't think I'll allow it. Now if you want to cover any other points with her, go right ahead.

In this situation a careful attorney in Parsons' position might well request permission to approach the bench and would whisper to the court, the reporter, and to opposing counsel, "Let the record show that if permitted, Ms. Gordon would testify that she saw the station wagon driving along Fourth Street at approximately 50 mph just prior to the collision." Unless court or counsel did not believe that Ms. Gordon would testify in that vein, this representation would likely be accepted as true, satisfying the requirement of an offer of proof.

It is even probable that if Parsons made *no* further statement of the expected tenor of Gordon's testimony, the record would suffice to show the appellate court that Ms. Gordon was expected to testify that the vehicle was speeding and that the ruling disallowing such testimony would be reviewable for error. (Most courts permit an eyewitness such as Ms. Gordon to testify to the speed of an automobile, and the court probably erred in refusing to permit her to answer. See Chapter 9A, infra.)

4. *Judicial "Mini-Hearings"*

Objections and offers of proof can involve court and parties in what amounts to "mini-hearings" raising all sorts of questions. Does the hearsay doctrine permit Appleby on Thoracic Surgery to be used to prove proper surgical technique? Is a gun sufficiently connected to the crime to be admitted into evidence in a murder prosecution, on the basis of testimony by Lieutenant Goldbloom that he found it "on the floor of the bedroom about five feet from [the victim's] body"? Was Cronan excited when he spoke, since apparently the hearsay doctrine would permit this use of his out-of-court statement about the speed of a stationwagon if he was?

Obviously the judge has a role to play. But does he decide these questions himself? Or just screen them, passing them to the jury if a reasonable person could decide them either way, on the basis of the evidence or common sense and experience?

Rule 104 describes the functions of judge and jury in deciding evidence questions. Rule 104(a) says that the judge determines "preliminary questions"—witness competency, privilege, and "admissibility of evidence." Rule 104(b) says it is different when "relevancy" turns on "fulfillment of a condition of fact." Here the judge merely screens the evidence, and when different answers are possible the jury decides. That is, it decides whether the condition is satisfied ("fulfilled"), and evidence that is conditionally relevant is admitted "upon, or subject to" the introduction of sufficient other evidence to support "a finding" (by the jury) that the condition is satisfied.

Sometimes Rule 104(a) and 104(b) operate without a hitch.

Pretty clearly Rule 104(a) applies to the first and third questions noted above, for example, because both involve application of the hearsay doctrine. In Rules terms, the proposed use of the treatise and the bystander's remark about speed raise questions of "admissibility." Rule 104(a) also applies to questions of witness competency. The only common question of competency involves qualifying a witness as an expert, and the trial judge alone decides this point. And Rule 104(a) also allocates to the judge alone issues involving the application of privileges, such as attorney-client and spousal.

And there are clear applications of Rule 104(b). It governs the question raised by the gun that Lieutenant Goldbloom found next to the body. In Rules terms, the question whether the gun is sufficiently connected to the crime raises an issue of "authentication," which is treated as a matter of conditional relevancy (see the ACN to Rule 901, and Chapter 13, infra). That is, the jury decides whether such an item is what its proponent claims. The task of the judge is to ensure that there is enough evidence to enable a reasonable juror to conclude that the item is (or is not) what it is claimed to be. Only in extreme cases does the judge take over this decision. (At one extreme, he excludes for failure to authenticate where there is not enough foundational evidence to enable a reasonable person to find the item authentic, or where the counterproof is so cogent and compelling that a reasonable person could only find the item *not* authentic. At the opposite extreme, he could instruct that the item is what its proponent claims, though such an instruction is seldom given in fact, and conceivably it would be improper against the accused in a criminal case.) And Rule 104(b) applies to the question of personal knowledge of witnesses (see ACN FRE 602, and see generally Chapter 6J, infra).

As you will see in succeeding chapters, however, sometimes application of Rule 104 is more difficult. While connecting a gun to an alleged murder is a clear instance of conditional relevancy, other instances are not at all certain. And while applying the hearsay doctrine is mostly a matter for the judge under

Rule 104(a), a few hearsay issues are sometimes given to juries, such as the question whether a party "adopted" a statement made by another and the question whether a person who makes what is offered as a "dying declaration" actually knew he was dying (see Chapter 4B2 and 4D3, infra). Note too the language in Rule 104(a) that the judge is not bound by "the rules of evidence" (apart from privileges) in deciding questions of admissibility. That implies that he may consider matters that the jury cannot consider in deciding the case on the merits, and this point too creates problems in applying the admissions doctrine and the exception for excited utterances (see Chapter 4B3, 4B4, 4B5, and 4C1, infra).

E. CONSEQUENCES OF EVIDENTIAL ERROR

Few trials make it from beginning to end without error on points of evidence, and claims of evidence error are commonplace in appeals. It is doubtful that perfection in administering evidence law may be had at all, let alone at a price worth paying. There are three main causes of imperfection, and for each the system has developed an adaptive technique that helps separate errors requiring correction from those that do not.

First, some evidence rules are slippery or complex. Hence unerring application under the pressures of trial is too much to expect. Judges who make the initial decision, lawyers who guide and influence that decision by framing the issues and setting out the factual picture, commentators and authors of appellate opinions—all are mortals who make mistakes. This reason alone suggests that there can be no such thing as "automatic" reversal on account of evidence errors. The reviewing court awards relief only when errors seem to have made a real difference in result.

Second, some evidence rules are framed as vague standards, and close appellate scrutiny would make no more sense than trying to fix a computer with a wrench. Many of the more particular rules require someone—usually the judge—to resolve factual issues, and the remoteness of the reviewing court suggests that deference to the trial judge is very much in order. Moreover, freewheeling review of efforts by the trial judge to apply vague standards or find facts affecting application of specific rules would be demoralizing, and would discourage trial judges from taking care in the first instance.

Third, ours is an adversary system, which places the lion's share of responsibility for the conduct of trial in the litigants themselves (acting through their lawyers). There is good reason to hold them to the choices they (their lawyers) make at trial, and to refuse relief for errors they cause or might reasonably have been expected to prevent.

In sum, our system tolerates a less-than-perfect world. The three adaptive techniques are worth a closer look.

1. Appraising Such Error on the Merits

Assume that the reviewing court means to resolve an evidence point on the merits. One of its tasks is to identify error and instruct the trial court (and the rest of us) how to do the right thing next time. But since reversal is not to be automatic, identifying error is only the beginning. The rest of the job is to distinguish errors that matter from those that do not.

The distinction turns on two somewhat connected points. One is that the evidence error must have affected what Rule 103 calls "a substantial right," meaning essentially outcome (the verdict in jury cases, hence a judgment based thereon; the judgment alone in judge-tried cases). The other is that there must be some assurance that the error had such effect, for otherwise we are stuck at the extremes, with automatic reversal or no possibility of correction at all. In short, we need a standard of proof. The usual standard directs appellate courts to reverse a judgment only for error which "probably affected" the result, although this formula tells little and does not capture the flavor of the cases.[7]

Kinds of error. In explaining what they do, reviewing courts classify evidence errors in four categories:

One is "reversible" error, which refers to the kind of mistake that probably *did* affect the judgment. Generally the term also means that appellant took the necessary steps at trial to preserve his claim of error (usually by raising an appropriate objection or making a formal offer of proof).

Another is "harmless" error, meaning the kind of mistake that probably did *not* affect the judgment. This label expresses the reviewing court's conclusion that appellant has not shown that a ruling affected the verdict.

The third is "plain" error, meaning the kind that in the estimation of the reviewing court warrants relief on appeal even though appellant failed at trial to take the steps usually necessary to preserve its rights (objecting or making an offer of proof). It bears emphasis that the plain error doctrine provides only a slim hope for the trial lawyer whose wits and instincts failed at an important moment, and appellate opinions routinely reject claims of plain error and emphasize that the lawyer failed to object or offer proof, thus waiving the right to argue error. Generally reviewing courts insist that error is "plain" only if it is in some sense "obvious" (the judge should have known better even if the lawyer did not) and more "serious" in the sense of providing greater certainty (more even than "reversible" error imparts) that outcome was affected at trial. Sometimes courts go so far as to say that error can be viewed as plain only if the judgment below amounts to a "miscarriage of justice." See Rule 103(d).

The fourth is "constitutional" error in criminal cases, which usually means a mistake by the trial court in admitting evidence for the prosecution that should have been excluded under the Constitution. Most often invoked are

---

7. Most courts apply the standard quoted above, but the matter is not free of doubt. A famous scholar of the bench preferred a formulation requiring reversal unless the reviewing court "believes it highly probable that the error did not affect the judgment." R. Traynor, The Riddle of Harmless Error 35 (1970). And it has been argued that in criminal cases the standard applied on review should track the standard of proof observed at trial, meaning that the prosecutor should be prepared to establish beyond reasonable doubt that the error did not affect the result. See Saltzburg, The Harm of Harmless Error, 59 Va. L. Rev. 988, 991-1007 (1973). In its most thorough consideration of this subject, the Supreme Court admonished against "technicality," emphasized the importance of considering the proceedings "in their entirety," but then stated its conclusion in elusive language. Kotteakos v. United States, 328 U.S. 750, 765 (1946) (reversal proper unless reviewing court can say with "fair assurance" that error did not affect the judgment).

the search and seizure provision of the Fourth Amendment (source of the doctrine requiring exclusion of illegally seized evidence, see Mapp v. Ohio, 367 U.S. 643 (1961)), the privilege against self-incrimination set out in the Fifth Amendment (source of the doctrine requiring police to warn suspects in custody of their rights, see Miranda v. Arizona, 384 U.S. 436 (1966)), and the Confrontation Clause of the Sixth Amendment (source of the doctrine entitling the accused to cross-examine witnesses against him, see Davis v. Alaska, 415 U.S. 308 (1974)). Here is a place where it was once thought that the general rule required "automatic" reversal, without a showing that the error affected the results below. But the Supreme Court repudiated that position in Chapman v. California, 387 U.S. 18 (1967), adopting for most such cases (though perhaps not all) a more lenient standard under which the judgment may be affirmed if the prosecution shows beyond a reasonable doubt that the error was harmless. Less often, constitutional error occurs when courts exclude evidence offered by the defense, see Chambers v. Mississippi, 410 U.S. 284 (1973) (Chapter 4H).

Distinguishing "harmless" from "reversible" error. You will discover that appellate courts are likely to find that a party has lost or limited her "standing" to complain of error on review by the way she (her lawyer) conducted herself at trial. Tremendous energy goes into explaining why one or another contention cannot be fully considered on appeal. Putting this difficulty aside for a moment, the hardest task for appellate courts (and for lawyers trying to decide whether to appeal) is to distinguish between harmless and reversible error.

Viewed in isolation, many errors might have affected the outcome: Evidence admitted in error might have been the reason why the trier decided against the appellant on a critical issue; evidence excluded in error might (if only it had been admitted) have tipped the balance on an issue that the jury decided against the appellant. An impeaching attack (or cross-examination) undertaken by the appellant but erroneously cut short by the trial court might have undercut a critical witness for the adverse party if allowed to run its full course. And an improper attack (or cross-examination) undertaken by the adverse party might have destroyed a witness for appellant whom the trier would otherwise have believed. Convincing an appellate court that such errors "probably" had such effect is the second task of the appellant (the first being to persuade the reviewing court that indeed there was error below).

In this quest appellant usually must also convince the reviewing court that other circumstances disclosed by the record (and emphasized by the party who won below) do not turn what seems to be reversible error into harmless error.

Three doctrines have evolved, each describing and responding to a circumstance that turns the poignant into the bland (reversible into harmless error):

First is the "cumulative evidence" doctrine, which supports affirmance despite errors by the trial court both in admitting and in excluding. Nothing is so common as to read in appellate opinions that while the trial judge erred in *admitting* evidence offered *against* the appellant, still so much other proof was properly received on the same point that the jury would likely have found against her even if the judge had correctly excluded the evidence in question. And you will read almost as often the appellate view that while the trial judge erred in *excluding* evidence offered *by* the appellant, still so much other proof was admitted on the same point that the jury would not likely have changed its mind even if the judge had correctly admitted the evidence in question.

A point that needs to be made here—and appellate opinions sometimes overlook it—is that the "cumulative evidence" doctrine does *not* justify affirmance merely because other evidence in the case was *sufficient* to sustain the result reached below: The question in every case is whether evidence erroneously admitted *probably affected* outcome or whether evidence erroneously excluded *probably would have* affected outcome. If the answer is yes, the error calls for corrective action even though there is enough other evidence in the case to support the conclusion that the trier actually reached below.

Second is the "curative instruction" doctrine. When a trial judge commits an evidence error, he may be able to avoid reversal by means of an instruction to the jury. When the risk is great that evidence admitted on one point or against one party may be improperly considered by the jury as proof on a different point or against another party, a "limiting" instruction may be sought (see FRE 105), and such instruction is usually viewed as effective, thus disposing of any contention on appeal that the evidence was used improperly. When it becomes clear after the fact that evidence already admitted should not have come in at all, an instruction to "disregard" may be equally effective in preserving the judgment on appeal. These instructions are said to "cure" the error, rendering it harmless. Occasionally an instruction even cures an error in *excluding* evidence, as happens when a judge implies in his instructions that the issue has been (or should be) resolved in favor of the party who offered the evidence. Sometimes the verdict itself cures the error, as happens when the jury finds in favor of the appellant on the only issues affected by any error.

Third is the "overwhelming evidence" doctrine. If a reviewing court concludes that evidence properly admitted supports the judgment below overwhelmingly, generally it affirms, even in the face of errors admitting or excluding evidence that might otherwise have been considered serious. The opinions seem almost to suggest that the evidence was such as to invite a directed verdict.

2. *Appellate Deference: The Discretion of the Trial Judge*

The doctrine of judicial "discretion" has led to the practice of limiting appellate review of evidential rulings. One source of this discretion is found in evidential doctrines that are framed in loose terms. It is settled, for example, that trial judges may exclude even competent and relevant evidence if it seems likely to prejudice the jury against one of the parties or confuse it by introducing collateral issues leading far afield. See FRE 403. And it is settled that the trial judge may control the manner and sequence of presenting evidence and questioning witnesses. See FRE 611.

Doctrines such as these may be viewed in different ways. Clearly they confer great power in the trial judge to affect the presentation of evidence; they amount to a vote of confidence in her ability to fashion sensible ad hoc solutions to the inevitable problems of trial; the generality of such doctrines concedes that specific rules do not exist and suggests that such could not be framed. Lawyers are inclined to describe the decisions which these doctrines invite in terms of "balancing," by which is usually meant selecting between one course and another by considering and comparing dissimilar factors (in effect "choosing between apples and oranges").

In such cases the trial judge is likely to be upheld no matter which choice she makes. Appellate opinions refer to the "broad discretion" of the trial judge, and often they suggest that her decision is reviewable only for "abuse," which is perhaps only another way of saying that the appellate court strongly disagrees. (If the claimed error falls into a discretionary category, sometimes reversal can be had if it can be shown that the trial judge failed to exercise discretion in the mistaken belief that she was bound by a particular rule.)

There is another source of judicial discretion. It is the more particular evidential doctrines whose application turns in the first instance upon factfinding by the trial judge. Even in criminal trials and civil jury cases, where we think of the jury as the factfinder, the trial judge performs factfinding duties in administering the law of evidence. Recall the discussion between Parson and Dawson over Cronan's remark about the fellow in the stationwagon being in "too much of a hurry." There the trial judge was asked to apply Rule 803(2)— the "excited utterance" exception, which applies only where (1) there was an occasion which startled the declarant, (2) he spoke while excited, (3) his statement expressed his reaction to the occasion. It is the trial judge who must determine whether these requirements are satisfied, and her conclusions are reviewed under either a "clear error" or "abuse-of-discretion" standard. These terms seem in this context to coalesce, and they mean that the reviewing court defers to the conclusions of the trial judge, and reverses only if it strongly disagrees.

3. Procedural Pitfalls and Adversarial Gambits

Often reviewing courts do not reach the question whether error was harmless, or even whether it was committed. And often they do not reach the question whether the ruling below should be affirmed because the matter at hand is committed to the sound discretion of the trial judge and her decision was within reasonable parameters. Instead, courts often limit review or foreclose relief altogether because of the trial behavior of the appellant (acting through counsel). In hindsight, that behavior may fall somewhere on a continuum from gross blunder to understandable mistake, calculated risk, or carefully planned (but unsuccessful) strategy.

In general, three kinds of behavior generate such effects:

1. *Failing to object or offer proof.*   We have already considered the need to object and to make offers of proof. When a case goes up on appeal, a serious consequence usually flows from failing to object or offer proof: Failing to object waives the right to claim error in admitting evidence, and failing to offer proof waives the right to claim error in excluding evidence. In both cases relief is denied in the absence of "plain error," and review is limited *because* appellant failed to "preserve the point" by objecting or making an offer. Plain error is seldom found in rulings admitting evidence, and almost unheard of in rulings excluding evidence (absent a record of the unoffered proof, a reviewing court can hardly tell that it would have affected the result).

More refined consequences flow from the manner in which objection or offer of proof is made. Thus, an objection on particular grounds suffices only to preserve errors made on those very grounds: If appellant unsuccessfully objected that certain testimony violates the hearsay doctrine, he can prevail on appeal only if the testimony did offend the hearsay doctrine (as well as outcome). He might argue on appeal that the testimony also offended the rule against proving conduct by character evidence, but failing to raise this ground in his original objection waived his right to assert it on appeal. (He might still win on this ground, but only if the reviewing court concludes that failing to see and apply the character rule was plain error.)

Likewise, an unsuccessful offer of proof resting on a particular ground for admitting evidence suffices only to preserve that ground for review: If appellant invokes a particular hearsay exception in his offer, he can prevail only if the trial court erred in refusing to apply that exception (and the excluded evidence would likely have affected outcome). The fact that the evidence fits another exception avails appellant little, for failing to advance this ground in his proffer waived his right to rely on it, and once again he can argue this new exception only if the failure to see and apply it was plain error.

And there is more:

In objecting and making offers of proof, appellant may limit or lose his right to review if some significant part of the proof in question does not fit the objection or the offer. If *part* of a document is not excludable under the hearsay doctrine, an objection on that ground may be viewed as inadequate even though other parts of the document *should be excluded* for that reason. Conversely, if part of a document does not fit a particular hearsay exception, an offer of the whole document may be viewed as inadequate even though part *does* fit the exception. In short, rulings by the trial judge adverse to the party who later appeals may be sustained if that party was not sufficiently precise in specifying the evidence subject to the objection or offer.

Finally, and here we see real determination of the system to sustain the trial court if possible, appellate courts often say that where the trial judge sustains an objection or accepts an offer of proof *on the wrong ground* (a ground later shown inapplicable or erroneous), her ruling will likely be sustained on appeal if *some other ground, though unmentioned below,* supports her action. Thus if the trial judge accepts an offer of proof dependent upon a particular hearsay exception, she is likely to be sustained even though that exception is shown to be inapplicable, if the offering party can demonstrate that some other exception supports receipt of the evidence. In short, the system favors affirmance of judgments, imposing what amounts to a double standard operating in favor of the trial judge and against trial counsel.

2. Inviting error. Trial behavior of a very different sort may affect review, for counsel sometimes put questions that produce otherwise excludable answers. Assuming that the witness has fairly replied to the question asked, the questioner is said to have "invited" any error that would otherwise have arisen in admitting the answer. And a party also "invites" error by relying on (and in this sense endorsing) evidence offered by his opponent that he might otherwise have succeeded in excluding by raising appropriate objection.

3. Opening the door. Finally, trial behavior may "open the door" to evidence that would otherwise be excludable. In the typical instance, a party testifying on direct examination by his own counsel makes an ill-advised and overbroad assertion that he has a blemish-free past. Thus a criminal defendant sometimes testifies that he has "never been in trouble with the law before," and if this statement is false it "opens the door" to devastating evidence of prior arrests or convictions, which he might otherwise have kept out. And a party in a civil negligence suit sometimes testifies that he "has never had an accident before," which (if false) "opens the door" to damaging proof that indeed he has had other accidents. (See the material on impeaching witnesses in Chapter 8, infra.)

PROBLEM 1-B.   He Didn't Object!

Carl Dreeves joins with Abby Barton as the second plaintiff in the suit against Eric Felsen (Problem 1-A). The defense offers testimony by police officer Hill, based on measurements of skidmarks at the scene, that Barton's Fiat was traveling at a speed of about 50 mph just before entering the intersection. (The posted limit was 35 mph.) Counsel for Barton objects that "officer Hill is not qualified as an expert in accident reconstruction," and that "estimates of speed based on skidmarks involve sheer speculation and are not helpful to the jury."

The court overrules the objection; the jury returns a verdict for Felsen; the court enters judgment that Barton and Dreeves take nothing, and that their claims be dismissed with prejudice. Dreeves appeals, and Felsen argues that his appeal should be dismissed because of his failure to object below. Should he prevail on this argument? Why or why not?

F.   OBTAINING REVIEW OF EVIDENCE POINTS

1.   Appeal from Judgment

Evidence rulings are, for the most part, prime examples of the nonappealable interlocutory order. When such rulings are made during trial, immediate review would be impractical: The resultant interruption of trial would be an imposition upon trial courts, not to mention juries and witnesses; piecemeal review could become another weapon of delay for a party fearful of an adverse judgment; the very nature of the review would change radically if appellate courts had to evaluate evidential error without the record of a completed trial.

Hence rulings admitting or excluding evidence, rulings on examination of witnesses (whether dealing with the form or the substance of the questions), and rulings on such evidential devices as presumptions and burden of persuasion are almost always reviewed only after judgment. Generally (though not always) rulings on claims of privilege are likewise reviewed only after judgment.

2.   Interlocutory Appeal

There are two important exceptions to the pattern sketched above—two instances where interlocutory appeal is commonly permitted. One arises when a person claims a privilege and refuses to answer despite an order of the trial court directing him to do so, and the other involves pretrial orders suppressing evidence in criminal cases.

Privilege rulings. Here the cases are in disarray.

Under one approach, the threshold question is whether the person from whom information was sought has been held in contempt. If not, no review may be had. If so, some authority would permit the reviewing court to consider the merits of the privilege ruling only if the person was held in criminal contempt, and otherwise would limit review to the matter of the authority of the trial judge to impose the contempt sanction.

Under another approach, the threshold question is whether the nondisclosing person is a party to the action. If he is a party, he may be permitted to obtain review of the privilege ruling only by suffering an adverse judgment on the merits of the case, then raising the privilege issue (and all other points of error) on appeal from the judgment. If he is not a party, he may obtain review of the privilege issue without suffering a judgment of contempt, simply because the final judgment in the proceedings will never afford him a chance to obtain such review.

Not surprisingly, many modern cases present the issue of review in the context of orders of production directed to criminal defense lawyers. As you will see, a lawyer may (indeed must) invoke the attorney-client privilege on her client's behalf, and of course *the lawyer* is not herself a party to her client's case. In this circumstance, some modern federal authority applies the doctrine of Perlman v. United States, 247 U.S. 7 (1918) (party permitted to appeal, on ground of Fourth Amendment violation, from disclosure order directed to court clerk), and permits the attorney to appeal immediately from a disclosure order overruling her claim of privilege, advanced on her client's behalf. See, e.g., In re Grand Jury Proceedings (Fine), 641 F.2d 199, 201-203 (5th Cir. 1981).

Suppression motions. In criminal cases in federal court, applicable statute paves the way for government appeals "from a decision or order. . . suppressing or excluding evidence. . . not made after the defendant has been put in jeopardy and before the verdict or finding on an indictment or information" if the U.S. Attorney certifies that the appeal has not been taken "for purpose of delay and that the evidence is a substantial proof of a fact material in the proceeding" (18 U.S.C. §3731). Many states have similar statutes. For the most part, such pretrial suppression motions raise issues under the Constitution rather than the Rules of Evidence, but any pretrial defense motion to exclude evidence may generate an appeal by the prosecutor under such statutes.

Two | RELEVANCE

INTRODUCTION

"Relevance" is an everyday word describing factors that bear on the decisions we make and problems we set out to solve, and the term carries similar meaning in the law of evidence. As rational beings, we know as a matter of habit or common sense what we ought to consider in making decisions and solving problems. A picnic in the park? We think about whether we have time, whether the sun is out, what the temperature might be, whether the roads are congested or the park crowded, and so forth.

Long ago Thayer said that the very existence of a judicial system, created to resolve disputes affecting private rights of citizens and administration of regulatory and criminal laws, implies the principle that "relevant" evidence should generally be considered, and not irrelevant evidence. J. Thayer, Preliminary Treatise 264-265 (1898). This principle finds expression in FRE 402, which says that relevant evidence is generally admissible and irrelevant evidence is not.

A relational concept. By nature, relevance is relational—it carries meaning only in context. If we learn that *E* is employed as a driver by the Corporation and that this fact is "relevant," we would ask, "relevant to what?" In a suit against the Corporation for injuries allegedly caused by a truck owned by it and driven by *E*, his employment is some indication that he was acting pursuant to his duties, hence that the Corporation may be responsible under the tort doctrine of respondeat superior if *E* was negligent. But in a suit by *E* for injuries he sustained crossing a street, his employment would not likely be "relevant" to any issue at hand. *E* might argue that his employment in a responsible position shows that he is careful, hence that he was being careful when he was struck. But we would likely conclude that relevancy is marginal at best and reject his argument as unconvincing.

The context in which relevance questions arise is defined partly by applicable substantive law (like the doctrine of respondeat superior) and partly by the issues that the parties raise. In criminal cases the issues are raised by the information or indictment and the defendant's plea. In civil cases the pleadings raise the issues generally, though they are refined through discovery and motions and narrowed by pretrial conference and order.

No modern thinker considers it profitable to codify relevance in detail. Disputes leading to litigation are too varied, as are problems of proof. Not that the possibility of detailed rules governing relevance has been ignored: John Henry Wigmore, who did much for the law of evidence, tried early in life to draft such rules, and anyone who believes the task worthwhile should begin with a look at the compendious banalities that found their way into his Code of Evidence (1909). Thayer hit on a more durable truth when he said "the law furnishes no test of relevancy," but relies instead on "logic and general experience." J. Thayer, Preliminary Treatise 265 (1898).

Following Thayer, FRE 401 furnishes no test and is content to set out a general standard: Evidence is relevant if it has "any tendency" to make the existence of any consequential fact "more or less probable."

Direct and circumstantial. If the question is whether E is employed by the Corporation, nobody doubts the relevance of his own testimony to that effect, or testimony by W that she saw E loading boxes on a truck with the Corporation logo painted on the side. Both are relevant on the question of E's employment, but here a distinction is commonly drawn: The former is usually called "direct" and the latter "circumstantial" evidence.

"Direct" describes evidence that, if accepted as genuine or believed true, necessarily establishes the point for which it is offered (if E is believed, the trier must conclude that he was employed by the Corporation). "Circumstantial" means evidence that, even if fully credited, may nevertheless fail to support (let alone establish) the point in question, simply because an alternative explanation seems as probable or more so (perhaps E *was* seen loading the truck, but other facts suggest he was helping a friend employed by the Corporation).

The Federal Rules draw no distinction between direct and circumstantial evidence, and the latter is not necessarily inferior: Alternative explanations may be so much less likely than the one advanced by the proponent as to seem preposterous, and direct proof may be unavailable, either because there are no witnesses or because the issue is such that direct proof cannot be had (usually "mens rea," the mental element of a crime, is proved circumstantially). Courts recognize these realities. See Michalic v. Cleveland Tankers, 364 U.S. 325, 330 (1960) (circumstantial evidence may be "more certain, satisfying and persuasive than direct evidence"). Even criminal convictions may rest on such proof, see United States v. Young, 568 F.2d 588, 589 (8th Cir. 1978) (conviction may "rest solely on circumstantial evidence, which is intrinsically as probative as direct evidence").

Still, circumstantial evidence poses special problems. In popular imagination, the very term connotes weakness, and closing arguments often exploit that preconception. And circumstantial evidence poses the only real challenge in administering the requirement of logical relevancy and assessing the sufficiency of proof to take a case to the jury. Moreover, circumstantial evidence raises questions of coordinating the responsibilities of judge and jury.

Rationality. There are some differences between the common understanding of "relevance" and its meaning in the law of evidence. For one thing, experience seems time and again to affirm that even thoughtful decisions in life rest only in part on reason and logic, that decisionmaking is as much

experience ✓

psychological as analytical, and that <u>intuition and emotion play large roles.</u> But <u>evidence law,</u> especially its notion of relevance, <u>emphasizes reason and logic.</u> Intuition and emotion in the trier of fact are matters to be controlled and minimized, and numerous exclusionary rules serve that end, along with a tradition of discretionary power in the trial judge to exclude evidence so as to obviate or minimize extrarational forces.

Another difference is that everyday decisions generally look forward rather than backward, while courts have the task of determining matters of historical fact—what happened, why, and how. <u>So our legal concept of relevance seeks to describe clues that enable the trier of fact to understand the past, rather than to decide on a future course of action.</u> But the difference is not great, simply because the historical facts are contested by the parties and unknown to the trier.

The law of evidence serves a pragmatic profession, so it ignores the philosophical problem, which is illuminated in literature and experienced in science,[1] whether anyone can ever really know what happened. It affirms implicitly that we *can* know enough, and that relevant evidence offered in court can help the trier of fact arrive at a close enough understanding to warrant entry of a judgment which materially alters the positions and fortunes of the parties. Carl Sandburg put it this way:

> Do you solemnly swear before the everliving God that the testimony you are about to give in this cause shall be the truth, the whole truth, and nothing but the truth?
>
> No, I don't. I can tell you what I saw and what I heard and I'll swear to that by the everliving God but the more I study about it the more sure I am that nobody but the everliving God knows the whole truth and if you summoned Christ as a witness in this case what He would tell you would burn your insides with the pity and the mystery of it.

C. Sandburg, The People, Yes 193 (1936).

A. LOGICAL RELEVANCE

1. *Relevance and Materiality*

Relevance readily divides into two subparts, and common law tradition distinguished them by separate terms. Evidence was "<u>relevant</u>" if it tended to establish the point for which it was offered, and "<u>material</u>" if the point bore on issues in the case.

Assume that *X* says publicly that *J* is embezzling money from her employer and tells *J* privately that he will repeat the story to *J*'s boss unless *J* pays *X* for his silence. If *X* were the defendant in a libel suit or a prosecution for extortion,

---

1. Consider the Japanese saga of Rashomon, where witnesses to a single event see vastly different happenings, and the Heisenberg Uncertainty Principle, which holds that the process of observing subatomic particles alters their position or velocity, so that it is possible to determine one or the other but not both.

evidence that *J* altered the books of her employer and lived beyond her means would be "relevant" in tending to show that she embezzled. But the evidence would only be "material" in the libel suit, and then only if *X* raised truth as an affirmative defense. Truth would not matter in an extortion trial, where the heart of the crime is obtaining by threat something of value to which one is not entitled, and the evidence would not be "material."

No one doubts that evidence should be admitted only if it is, in the terminology of the common law, "relevant" and "material." But since both conditions must always be satisfied, insisting on two terms was a fetish, and the modern approach embraces both ideas within the single term "relevance." Under FRE 401, evidence is relevant if it tends to make more or less probable the existence of any consequential fact.

OLD CHIEF v. UNITED STATES (I)
Supreme Court of the United States
519 U.S. 172 (1997)

JUSTICE SOUTER delivered the opinion of the Court.

[Defendant Johnny Lynn Old Chief was charged with being a convicted felon in possession of a firearm. As is usual when this charge is brought, defendant allegedly committed other crimes that are more visible and likely to attract the attention of law enforcement: Old Chief was also charged with assault with a deadly weapon and using a firearm in a crime of violence. His prior felony conviction was for assault causing serious bodily injury, so the defense offered to stipulate to the conviction in hope of keeping its title and the details from the jury. In this opinion, the Supreme Court ultimately decides that the trial court should have excluded proof of the name and details of the prior conviction as too prejudicial. (See *Old Chief (II)* in section B of this chapter, infra.) Before dealing with the prejudice issue, the Court addresses the basic question whether the name of the crimes of which Old Chief had been convicted was relevant.]

In 1993, petitioner, Old Chief, was arrested after a fracas involving at least one gunshot. The ensuing federal charges included not only assault with a dangerous weapon and using a firearm in relation to a crime of violence but violation of 18 U.S.C. §922(g)(1). This statute makes it unlawful for anyone "who has been convicted in any court, of a crime punishable by imprisonment for a term exceeding one year" to "possess in or affecting commerce, any firearm. . . ." "[A] crime punishable by imprisonment for a term exceeding one year" is defined to exclude "any Federal or State offenses pertaining to antitrust violations, unfair trade practices, restraints of trade, or other similar offenses relating to the regulation of business practices" and "any State offense classified by the laws of the State as a misdemeanor and punishable by a term of imprisonment of two years or less." 18 U.S.C. §921(a)(20).

The earlier crime charged in the indictment against Old Chief was assault causing serious bodily injury. Before trial, he moved for an order requiring the government "to refrain from mentioning—by reading the Indictment, during jury selection, in opening statement, or closing argument—and to refrain from offering into evidence or soliciting any testimony from any witness regarding the prior criminal convictions of the Defendant, except to state that the Defendant has been convicted of a crime punishable by imprisonment exceeding one (1) year." He said that revealing the name and nature of his prior assault conviction would unfairly tax the jury's capacity to hold the Government to its burden of proof beyond a reasonable doubt on current charges of assault, possession, and violence with a firearm, and he offered to "solve the problem here by stipulating, agreeing and requesting the Court to instruct the jury that he has been convicted of a crime punishable by imprisonment exceeding one (1) year." He argued that the offer to stipulate to the fact of the prior conviction rendered evidence of the name and nature of the offense inadmissible under FRE 403, the danger being that unfair prejudice from that evidence would substantially outweigh its probative value. He also proposed this jury instruction:

> The phrase "crime punishable by imprisonment for a term exceeding one year" generally means a crime which is a felony. The phrase does not include any state offense classified by the laws of that state as a misdemeanor and punishable by a term of imprisonment of two years or less and certain crimes concerning the regulation of business practices. . . .

As a threshold matter, there is Old Chief's erroneous argument that the name of his prior offense as contained in the record of conviction is irrelevant to the prior-conviction element, and for that reason inadmissible under FRE 402. FRE 401 defines relevant evidence as having "any tendency to make the existence of any fact that is of consequence to the determination of the action more probable or less probable than it would be without the evidence." To be sure, the fact that Old Chief's prior conviction was for assault resulting in serious bodily injury rather than, say, for theft was not itself an ultimate fact, as if the statute had specifically required proof of injurious assault. But its demonstration was a step on one evidentiary route to the ultimate fact, since it served to place Old Chief within a particular sub-class of offenders for whom firearms possession is outlawed by §922(g)(1). A documentary record of the conviction for that named offense was thus relevant evidence in making Old Chief's §922(g)(1) status more probable than it would have been without the evidence.

Nor was its evidentiary relevance under FRE 401 affected by the availability of alternative proofs of the element to which it went, such as an admission by Old Chief that he had been convicted of a crime "punishable by imprisonment for a term exceeding one year" within the meaning of the statute. [Court quotes ACN to FRE 401, which states: "The fact to which the evidence is directed need not be in dispute. While situations will arise which call for the exclusion of evidence offered to prove a point conceded by the opponent, the ruling should be made on the basis of such considerations as waste of time and undue prejudice (see FRE 403), rather than under any general requirement that evidence is admissible only if directed to matters in dispute."]

[If relevant evidence must sometimes be excluded because of its connection to other evidence, the reason is not] that the other evidence has rendered it "irrelevant," but on its character as unfairly prejudicial, cumulative or the like, its relevance notwithstanding.[4] . . .

[T]he Government invokes the familiar, standard rule that the prosecution is entitled to prove its case by evidence of its own choice, or, more exactly, that a criminal defendant may not stipulate or admit his way out of the full evidentiary force of the case as the government chooses to present it. The authority usually cited for this rule is Parr v. United States, 255 F.2d 86 (CA5), cert. denied, 358 U.S. 824 (1958), in which the Fifth Circuit explained that the "reason for the rule is to permit a party 'to present to the jury a picture of the events relied upon. To substitute for such a picture a naked admission might have the effect to rob the evidence of much of its fair and legitimate weight.'"

This is unquestionably true as a general matter. The "fair and legitimate weight" of conventional evidence showing individual thoughts and acts amounting to a crime reflects the fact that making a case with testimony and tangible things not only satisfies the formal definition of an offense, but tells a colorful story with descriptive richness. Unlike an abstract premise, whose force depends on going precisely to a particular step in a course of reasoning, a piece of evidence may address any number of separate elements, striking hard just because it shows so much at once; the account of a shooting that establishes capacity and causation may tell just as much about the triggerman's motive and intent. Evidence thus has force beyond any linear scheme of reasoning, and as its pieces come together a narrative gains momentum, with power not only to support conclusions but to sustain the willingness of jurors to draw the inferences, whatever they may be, necessary to reach an honest verdict. This persuasive power of the concrete and particular is often essential to the capacity of jurors to satisfy the obligations that the law places on them. Jury duty is usually unsought and sometimes resisted, and it may be as difficult for one juror suddenly to face the findings that can send another human being to prison, as it is for another to hold out conscientiously for acquittal. When a juror's duty does seem hard, the evidentiary account of what a defendant has thought and done can accomplish what no set of abstract statements ever could, not just to prove a fact but to establish its human significance, and so to implicate the law's moral underpinnings and a juror's obligation to sit in judgment. Thus, the prosecution may fairly seek to place its evidence before the jurors, as much to tell a story of guiltiness as to support an inference of guilt, to convince the jurors that a guilty verdict would be morally reasonable as much as to point to the discrete elements of a defendant's legal fault.

But there is something even more to the prosecution's interest in resisting efforts to replace the evidence of its choice with admissions and stipulations, for beyond the power of conventional evidence to support allegations and give life to the moral underpinnings of law's claims, there lies the need for evidence

---

4. Viewing evidence of the name of the prior offense as relevant, there is no reason to dwell on the Government's argument that relevance is to be determined with respect to the entire item offered in evidence (here, the entire record of conviction) and not with reference to distinguishable sub-units of that object (here, the name of the offense and the sentence received). We see no impediment in general to a district court's determination, after objection, that some sections of a document are relevant within the meaning of FRE 401, and others irrelevant and inadmissible under FRE 402.

in all its particularity to satisfy the jurors' expectations about what proper proof should be. Some such demands they bring with them to the courthouse, assuming, for example, that a charge of using a firearm to commit an offense will be proven by introducing a gun in evidence. A prosecutor who fails to produce one, or some good reason for his failure, has something to be concerned about. "If [jurors'] expectations are not satisfied, triers of fact may penalize the party who disappoints them by drawing a negative inference against that party." Saltzburg, A Special Aspect of Relevance: Countering Negative Inferences Associated with the Absence of Evidence, 66 Calif. L. Rev. 1011, 1019 (1978) (footnotes omitted).[9] Expectations may also arise in jurors' minds simply from the experience of a trial itself. The use of witnesses to describe a train of events naturally related can raise the prospect of learning about every ingredient of that natural sequence the same way. If suddenly the prosecution presents some occurrence in the series differently, as by announcing a stipulation or admission, the effect may be like saying, "never mind what's behind the door," and jurors may well wonder what they are being kept from knowing. A party seemingly responsible for cloaking something has reason for apprehension, and the prosecution with its burden of proof may prudently demur at a defense request to interrupt the flow of evidence telling the story in the usual way.

In sum, the accepted rule that the prosecution is entitled to prove its case free from any defendant's option to stipulate the evidence away rests on good sense. A syllogism is not a story, and a naked proposition in a courtroom may be no match for the robust evidence that would be used to prove it. People who hear a story interrupted by gaps of abstraction may be puzzled at the missing chapters, and jurors asked to rest a momentous decision on the story's truth can feel put upon at being asked to take responsibility knowing that more could be said than they have heard. A convincing tale can be told with economy, but when economy becomes a break in the natural sequence of narrative evidence, an assurance that the missing link is really there is never more than second best.

[Court concludes, however, that the prosecutor's need for "evidentiary depth" has virtually no application "when the point at issue is a defendant's legal status, dependent on some judgment rendered wholly independently of the concrete events of later criminal behavior."]

[A dissenting opinion of JUSTICE O'CONNOR, joined by CHIEF JUSTICE REHNQUIST and JUSTICES SCALIA and THOMAS, is omitted.]

---

9. Cf. Green, "The Whole Truth?": How Rules of Evidence Make Lawyers Deceitful, 25 Loyola (LA) L. Rev. 699, 703 (1992) ("[E]videntiary rules. . . predicated in large measure on the law's distrust of juries [can] have the unintended, and perhaps ironic, result of encouraging the jury's distrust of lawyers. The rules do so by fostering the perception that lawyers are deliberately withholding evidence" (footnote omitted)). The fact that juries have expectations as to what evidence ought to be presented by a party, and may well hold the absence of that evidence against the party, is also recognized in the case law of the Fifth Amendment, which explicitly supposes that, despite the venerable history of the privilege against self-incrimination, jurors may not recall that someone accused of crime need not explain the evidence or avow innocence beyond making his plea. The assumption that jurors may have contrary expectations and be moved to draw adverse inferences against the party who disappoints them undergirds the rule that a defendant can demand an instruction forbidding the jury from drawing such an inference.

NOTES ON RELEVANCE, "FIT," AND OFFERS TO STIPULATE

1. *Old Chief* is right, isn't it, to hold that proof of a prior *felony assault conviction* is relevant when the point to be proved is a prior *felony conviction?* The statute speaks of a conviction for "a crime punishable by imprisonment exceeding one (1) year," which basically means felony. Under the statute, it doesn't matter *what kind of felony* (even though certain felonies don't count, including those for "antitrust violations, unfair trade practices, restraints of trade," and "similar offenses relating to the regulation of business practices"). Still, every conviction that *does count* will be for some particular crime, such as assault, so the basic concept of relevance cannot require a one-to-one "fit" between the proof and the element in the case to which the proof relates.

2. It is true, isn't it, that in ordinary cases the prosecution proves points of detail that aren't, strictly speaking, necessary to the case? In a murder trial, for example, the prosecution shows the circumstances surrounding the killing (the victim was killed in front of his spouse, for instance, or died of multiple stab wounds, or pleaded for his life, or was shot in the abdomen, and so forth). And in the negligence suit described in Problem 1-A (*How Did It Happen?*), proof that Abby Barton was driving a yellow Fiat and that Eric Felsen was driving a blue Buick would be relevant even if it were *not* needed as a means to connect those people to the accident, wouldn't it? Partly the reason such proof is relevant is that we want witnesses to communicate in ways that are comfortable to them and to juries, and ordinary language does not easily mesh with (or reduce to) the various categories that are important in lawsuits. Partly the reason is that even "background" evidence has some relevance under FRE 401, as the ACN recognizes (even evidence that is "essentially background in nature" is routinely admitted "as an aid to understanding"). See also United States v. Daily, 842 F.2d 1380, 1388 (2d Cir. 1988) (can show "the circumstances surrounding the events"). In this vein, courts routinely let witnesses testify to their name and address, and often occupation or business, although questioning about such things as hobbies and military service may be disallowed as getting too far afield. See, e.g., United States v. Solomon, 686 F.2d 863, 873-874 (11th Cir. 1982) (barring inquiry into family history and military service). And see generally Mueller and Kirkpatrick, Evidence §§4.2 and 6.58 (3d ed. 2003).

3. *Old Chief* is also wise, isn't it, in holding that an offer to stipulate does not make relevant evidence irrelevant? The Court rests its conclusion partly on the ACN to FRE 401. Compare Cal Evidence Code §210 (defining relevance to mean "having any tendency in reason to prove or disprove *any disputed fact* that is of consequence to the determination of the action") (emphasis added). In *Old Chief*, the Court also relies on notions of policy, stressing party autonomy in presenting evidence, jury expectations, and "descriptive richness." What does all this have to do with relevance? When you revisit this decision a few pages hence, in *Old Chief (II)*, you will see that an offer to stipulate bears on whether evidence should be excluded under FRE 403 because of the risk of "unfair prejudice."

4. The majority in *Old Chief* also says particularized evidence is important "to sustain the willingness of jurors to draw the inferences" required for a verdict, and to convince them that a guilty verdict "would be morally reason-

able." Does this point mean that the *defense* should be allowed to offer particularized proof that isn't strictly relevant to the matter of guilt or innocence, but that might bear on what is "morally reasonable"? See generally James Joseph Duane, "Screw Your Courage to the Sticking Place": The Roles of Evidence, Stipulations, and Jury Instructions in Criminal Verdicts, 49 Hastings L.J. 463, 469 (1998) (asking whether *Old Chief* majority would "embrace the logical implications of this position" by letting the defendant "call his wife and children to testify" to the ways "their lives would be devastated" by extended incarceration, or by letting defendant show a "graphic but accurate film of living conditions in the only local prison").

5. In Shannon v. United States, 512 U.S. 573 (1994), the Supreme Court held that a defendant, who had been charged with a violent crime and offered an insanity defense, was not entitled to an instruction that he would be committed involuntarily if the jury accepted the defense, to keep the jury from mistakenly believing that a finding of insanity would allow the defendant to go free. The majority in *Shannon* wrote that the jury's function is to find the facts and decide guilt or innocence, hence that information on "the consequences of a verdict" is irrelevant to this task. This decision has been broadly applied to deny defense requests that the jury be instructed on mandatory minimum sentences that would follow from a verdict of guilty. Do *Shannon* and *Old Chief,* taken together, construct a pro-prosecution bias by inviting prosecutors to prove the consequences of criminal acts without allowing defendants to offer analogous proof relating to the consequences of conviction? See James Joseph Duane, supra note 4, at 474 (arguing that *Shannon* and *Old Chief* create an inconsistency that "borders on madness," since the former says juries cannot consider evidence relevant to the moral reasonableness of a guilty verdict but the latter says juries can consider such evidence).

2. *Establishing Relevance: The Evidential Hypothesis*

Often the relevance of circumstantial evidence is obvious. Everyone may see how it bears on the case, what point it tends to prove and why the point counts. If the question is whether defendant is the one who robbed the bank, evidence that he said he intended to do so requires no explaining.

But relevance may not be so apparent, and explanation may be needed—for the judge as well as the jury. And if the adverse party raises a relevance objection, the judge may ask the proponent to justify the proffer, even if relevance seems apparent. It is one thing to see that evidence bears on a pertinent point, and something else again to understand how and to what extent. It may not support the proponent's case so strongly as first appears. Ambiguities crop up, as well as explanations that would lead a thoughtful person to another conclusion—one that may leave the positions of the parties unchanged or even assist the adverse party.

Evidential hypothesis. The proponent should be prepared to advance an "evidential hypothesis" explaining why his proof is relevant. The adverse party should be ready to destroy it, if possible, or show its limitations, or even offer a counterhypothesis that explains away the evidence or enlists it in aid of his own cause.[2] An evidential hypothesis contains one or more of what logicians call a "general premise"—a proposition of general knowledge about the ways of the world or human nature. It also contains at least one specific premise linking the proof to the general premise. Finally, it sets out the conclusion toward which the evidence points.

The evidential hypothesis sets out the steps of reasoning and inference that logicians describe as argument by "deduction" or "induction." Both forms involve appraising known or accepted data in order to reach a new understanding of matters not directly observed. Logicians define deductive argument as one in which the stated premises *necessarily* lead to a particular conclusion. In the classic example, the major (or general) premise holds that "all humans are mortal," and the minor (or particular) premise asserts that "Socrates is human." Hence necessarily the conclusion, "Socrates is mortal." The "inductive" argument is less categorical. Logicians define it as one in which the conclusion *does not* necessarily follow from the underlying premises, though they at least support the conclusion. Proving that defendant robbed a bank by evidence that he stated an intent to do so involves an inductive argument: The major premises are that "People who intend to do something likely do it" and "People who state an intent likely have it." The minor premise is "Defendant stated his intent to rob the bank"; the conclusion is that "He likely did rob the bank."

Deduction. Deductive and essentially categorical logic sometimes appears in litigation: Again consider a bank robbery trial, but this time the government offers a surveillance film. This film may be well-nigh conclusive proof that a crime was committed and that the person depicted is the perpetrator, but other evidence may only circumstantially link defendant to the crime, and there may be a question whether he is the person in the film. The government might call a photographic expert who examined the film and elicit his testimony that defendant is the person shown. The prosecutor might not set out his argument as a deductive syllogism, but if the evidential hypothesis were stated it would fit the model: The man in the film is the perpetrator; defendant is the man in the film; hence he is the perpetrator.

Induction. Not only in litigation, but in science and everyday thinking, inductive argument is far more common. In a sense it is the more potent and inventive of the two forms, for it reaches further than deduction in seeking to increase understanding. One scholar put it this way:

Valid deductive arguments are demonstrative; that is, if the premises are true, the conclusion must necessarily be true also. Because of this, the conclusion cannot embody conjectures about the empirical world that go beyond what the premises say; in this sense the conclusion of a valid deductive argument must be "contained in" its premises. However, an inductive argument. . . has a conclusion embodying empirical conjectures about the world that do go beyond what its premises say; in an inductive argument the conclusion is not wholly "contained in" the premises.

2.   The parties will not likely agree on interpreting the evidence. Their differences are aired in closing argument and ultimately resolved by the trier of fact. Such differences are said to affect "weight" of the evidence and "credibility" of witnesses, rather than "admissibility." But sometimes the proponent's hypothesis is so weak, or the adversary's so strong, that admissibility is the issue.

S. Barker, The Elements of Logic 223 (3d ed. 1980).

Consider again evidence that defendant said he intended to rob the bank. One major premise was, "People who intend to do something likely do it." Wigmore pointed out that this premise itself—and remember that it serves as a foundation of an inductive argument—rests on induction: How do we know people act as they intend? The answer is, by observing particular instances in which they do so—in other words, by drawing an inductive inference (a generalization) to the major premise, which serves then as the basis for an inductive inference to the particular point in issue (that *this* person acted on *his* intent). So Wigmore noticed that in every inductive argument it is possible to "forc[e] into prominence the implied law or generalization on which it rests more or less obscurely." But he then reached a questionable conclusion: It is "undesirable" and "useless" to do so, since forcing the premise into prominence simply requires the court "to take it up for examination," which can be undertaken only by resort to the very inductive inference for which the proponent argued in the first place. See 1 J. Wigmore, Evidence §12 (1943).

If you think something is fishy, you are not alone. Wigmore was confronting the riddle that plagues logicians, which is that inductive argument seems circular.

In a seminal article, Professor James took Wigmore on:

Wigmore does not deny that in every instance proof must be based upon a generalization connecting the evidentiary proposition with the proposition to be proved. Conceding this, he argues that the generalization may as well be tacitly understood as expressed, . . . "because the Court's attention is merely transferred from the syllogism as a whole to the validity of the inference contained in the major premise." Yet it is precisely in this transfer of attention that the value. . . lies. [Wigmore's] own examples illustrate the point. In the case of the repaired machinery we are told: "'People who make such repairs [after an accident] show a consciousness of negligence; *A* made such repairs; therefore, *A* was conscious of negligence.'" Before this. . . proof can be evaluated, ambiguity must be eliminated from the major premise. By "people" shall we understand "some people" or "all people"? If the argument is intended to read, "Some people who make such repairs show consciousness of negligence; *A* made such repairs; therefore *A* was conscious of negligence," it contains an obvious logical fallacy. If intended to read, "All people who make such repairs show consciousness of negligence; *A* made such repairs; therefore, *A* was conscious of negligence," it is logically valid. However, few could be found to accept the premise that *all* persons who repair machinery after an accident show consciousness of guilt; that is, that no single case could be found of one who, confident of his care in the past, nevertheless made repairs to guard against repetition of an unforeseeable casualty or to preserve future fools against the consequence of their future folly. Here the result of [forcing the premise into prominence] is discovery that it is invalid—at least in the terms suggested.

James, Relevancy, Probability and the Law, 29 Calif. L. Rev. 689, 696-697 (1941).

Consider evidence that defendant said he intended to rob a bank. The government advances the evidential hypothesis: People who intend to do something likely do it, and people who announce an intent likely have it. Combine the evidence with the premises, and the conclusion follows—not that defendant must have robbed the bank, but that he likely did so. How likely is hard to say. James again:

> Once one attempts to deal, in a quasi-syllogistic form, not with certainties but with probabilities, additional opportunities for fallacy are presented. Suppose that it is argued: "Most *As* are *X, B* is an *A,* therefore *B* is probably *X;* or Nine-tenths of all *As* are *X, B* is an *A,* therefore the chances are nine to one that *B* is an *X.*" Neither of these arguments is logically valid except upon the assumption that *As* may be treated as a uniform class with respect to the probability of their being *X.* This can be because there really is no way of subdividing the class, finding more *X*s in one subclass than in another, or because no subdivision can be made in terms of available data. Suppose that nine-tenths of all people in the world have dark eyes. If absolutely all one knew about *B* was that he was a person, it would be an apparent nine-to-one chance that *B* had dark eyes. But if one knew *B* to be a Swede, the percentage of dark eyes in the total population of the world would no longer be important. One would want to know about the proportion of dark-eyed Swedes, which might differ from the ratio among humans generally.

James, id. at 697.

How about the government's two premises? Do all persons having a particular intent carry it out? (Of course not, common experience cries out. Hence the conclusion is less than certain, and the argument is inductive rather than deductive.) Do most—say, seven out of ten? (Nobody knows, and we cannot be sure that the conclusion is more probable than not.) Do some—say, two out of ten? (Surely yes—often we act in accordance with earlier-formed intent—and the evidence provides some support for the conclusion.) Does it matter *what* is intended? (Just as the percentage of Swedes with dark eyes may differ—one supposes it is smaller—from the percentage of people in general with dark eyes, so the percentage of people intending to take a walk who actually do so may differ—one supposes it is higher—from the percentage of people intending to commit serious crimes who actually do so.) Does the age or circumstance of the person matter? (Surely it does: One who despairs of lawful profits and sustains himself in criminal endeavors may be more likely to carry out an intent to commit a now-familiar sort of act than, say, a hitherto law-abiding college student, who may want or need money too, but for whom the world holds promise of moderate profit from lawful pursuits.)

And what of the second premise—that persons who announce an intent likely have such intent? (Again, surely less than all who make such announcement actually harbor such intent, but at least some do. Again the nature of the announced intent may matter, and again the situation of the person in question probably matters.)

PROBLEM 2-A.   *Was He Going Too Fast?*

On an open stretch of two-lane highway in Nevada, Jay Gadsby, traveling eastbound in a red Z-Car with racing stripe, collided with Roy Reinhart, headed westbound in a pickup truck with gunrack. Both Jay and Roy were killed instantly. The road was straight, the noonday sun bright overhead, and afternoon thermal winds had not yet picked up—in short, driving conditions were optimal. Physical facts yield no clues as to the cause of the accident.

In her wrongful death action against Gadsby's estate, Roy's widow offers testimony by another eastbound driver—one Hill, who was the first to come upon the accident—that 30 miles west of the point of collision the red Z-Car had overtaken him going "at least 80 miles per hour." The defense objects, arguing that Hill's testimony is "irrelevant" when offered as proof that Jay was speeding at the time of the accident, at least in the absence of further proof that Gadsby likely continued to travel at the rate observed for the 30 miles between the sighting and the point of impact.

Is the evidence relevant on the question of Gadsby's speed at the time of impact? Should the judge admit the evidence only if the proponent offers additional proof to satisfy the condition suggested by defendant?

3. Relevance As Threshold: The Standard of Probative Worth

Rule 401 provides no particularized test of relevancy, but sets a general standard requiring a "tendency" to prove or disprove a consequential fact. So it is tempting to ask: How strong must the tendency be?

Over the years four answers have been suggested:

One is that evidence has the required tendency only if it makes the point more probably true than not. But the standard must be applied again and again during trial because evidence is offered piece by piece. Hence defining the tendency this way seems too strict: It would exclude many items of proof that, taken together, might have high probative value. In civil cases usually the party with the burden of persuasion must satisfy the trier that the facts on her side are more probably true than not, so in these cases adopting this measure as the standard would mean that evidence is *relevant* only if it is also *sufficient*.

A second answer holds that evidence is relevant only if the suggested inference is more probable than any other. Some courts have taken this view. See Standafer v. First National Bank, 52 N.W.2d 718 (Minn. 1952) (in wrongful death action arising out of accident in which decedent fell down elevator shaft, error to admit evidence that a heel was knocked from his shoe, offered as proof that he tripped on L-beam while working on top of the elevator car; it was equally probable that heel was knocked off during fall) (harmless). But setting the standard at this level would produce a sliding scale, in which evidence would be scrutinized more strictly at the beginning of trial, when little or nothing is known of the facts, than at the end, when probative worth would be more apparent in light of evidence already presented. See Trautman, Logical or Legal Relevancy—A Conflict in Theory, 5 Vand. L. Rev. 385, 390 (1952).

A third answer rejects the first two, but insists that the necessary tendency requires more than minimal probative worth, hence that there is a standard of "legal relevancy" that is more strict than logic and reason alone would indicate. Wigmore took this view, writing that legal relevance demands an incremental "plus value." Occasionally courts agree. See Frank R. Jelleff, Inc. v. Braden, 233 F.2d 671, 679 (D.C. Cir. 1956). Wigmore thought the accumulation of legal precedent would create rules that resolve relevance problems, and that resort to logic and experience on an ad hoc basis is inappropriate. See 1 J. Wigmore, Evidence §28 (1943).

The fourth answer holds that evidence is relevant if it makes the point to be proved more probable than it was without the evidence. Here is the most lenient standard of all—the one most favoring admissibility. It is the one adopted in FRE 401. The idea is captured in some downhome aphorisms: "A brick is not a wall," McCormick on Evidence §185 (E. Cleary 3d ed. 1984); "Not every witness can make a home run" (ACN to FRE 401, paraphrasing McBaine). Consider the explanation set out by Professor James, writing about evidence of intent as proof of subsequent action:

> Persons who are unwilling to agree that men's fixed designs (at least in the case of murder) are "probably" carried out—or, even conceding the fact of murder, that proof of A's fixed design to kill B establishes A, more likely than not, as B's killer—still agree that somehow this bit of evidence does have some tendency to indicate A's guilt. What form of general statement can reconcile these views? Perhaps something like this: "Men having such a fixed design are more likely to kill than are men not having such a fixed design." Those who contend that even fixed designs to kill are more often abandoned or thwarted than carried out can and doubtless will still concede that enough such designs are carried to execution so that the percentage of murderers is higher among persons entertaining such a fixed design than among the general public. Obviously this proposed generalization does not lead us from A's fixed design to kill B to the conclusion that A probably did kill B. There is nothing disturbing in this. This conclusion simply does not follow from the evidence of design. The error was in the original "direct induction." In fact, no useful conclusion about A's guilt can be drawn from design or intent alone. On the basis of an acceptable generalization we are able only to place A in a class of persons in which the incidence of murder is greater than among the general public. We cannot now say that A is probably guilty, but we can say that *the apparent probability of his guilt is now greater than before the evidence of design was received.* This is logical relevancy—the only logical relevancy we can expect in dealing with practical affairs where strict demonstration is never possible. The advantage of [forcing the general premise into prominence] is that we know to what degree of proof we have attained, and do not overstate our results.

James, Relevancy, Probability and the Law, 29 Calif. L. Rev. 689, 698-699 (1941).

In effect this fourth answer holds that the question we began with is unanswerable. Thayer was right: There is no real test; attempting to refine the idea of "tendency" is like trying to bring in a test by the back door.

4.   Relevance In Operation: Hypothesis and Standard Applied

Assessing relevance involves understanding the evidential hypothesis that leads by inductive argument to the sought-after conclusion and deciding whether the argument really does increase the likelihood of the conclusion. Consider these matters in the context of a common kind of evidence—proof of flight by the accused, offered by the prosecutor as evidence of guilt.

PROBLEM 2-B.   *Flight and Guilt*

As Joe and his assistant Andy are closing the mobile fish-and-chip stand they operate from a truck in a parking lot near a lighted baseball field, a man armed with a sawed-off shotgun robs them of the evening's proceeds.

The next day Joe and Andy examine mug books at the stationhouse and independently identify Carl as the thief. Later that day police arrest Carl at his home.

At trial, the state calls Brenda. She is Carl's girlfriend, and she answered the door at the time of the arrest. The state offers her testimony that when Carl saw the police approaching he first ran to the back door, then hid in a closet after discovering an officer standing guard in the alley. Carl objects, arguing that proof of his behavior at the time of arrest is irrelevant. In a sidebar conference, his lawyer points out that Carl's arrest was based on an outstanding default warrant, issued two years earlier on unrelated charges.

State the evidential hypothesis supporting the proffer. State a counterhypothesis favoring exclusion. How should the judge rule, and why?

NOTES ON EVIDENCE OF ATTEMPTS TO AVOID CAPTURE

1.   Evidence of efforts to avoid capture is generally admissible in criminal trials. We even have a Biblical aphorism: "The wicked flee when no man pursueth; but the righteous are bold as a lion." Proverbs 28:1. The Supreme Court has long thought such evidence is relevant, Allen v. United States, 164 U.S. 492, 499 (1896) (flight by the accused is competent evidence having a tendency to establish guilt), and it usually comes in. See United States v. Martinez, 681 F.2d 1248, 1257 (10th Cir. 1982) (few cases are found in which such evidence is excluded); State v. Payne, 280 S.E.2d 72, 80 n.2 (W. Va. 1981) (citing authority from all but three states approving such evidence).

2.   Evidence of flight does not create a "presumption of guilt" or suffice for conviction. Hickory v. United States, 160 U.S. 408, 416 (1896). And the Court has declared that the Biblical aphorism does not state "an accepted axiom of criminal law," noting that there may be reasons for flight apart from guilt:

> Innocent men sometimes hesitate to confront a jury,—not necessarily because they fear that the jury will not protect them, but because they do not wish their names to appear in connection with criminal acts, are humiliated at being obliged to incur the popular odium of an arrest and trial, or because they do not wish to be put to the annoyance or expense of defending themselves.

Alberty v. United States, 162 U.S. 499, 511 (1896). See also United States v. Stewart, 579 F.2d 356, 359 n.3 (5th Cir.) (approving instruction warning jury that flight might result from "fear of being apprehended, unwillingness to confront the police, or reluctance to confront the witness"), cert. denied, 439 U.S. 936 (1978). While flight bears generally on guilt, it clearly cannot be taken as proof of some specific elements in the alleged crime. See United States v.

Owens, 460 F.2d 467, 470 (5th Cir. 1972) (alleged interstate transportation of stolen money orders; evidence of defendant's flight in Louisiana could not be taken to establish that the money orders in question had been forged in New Jersey).

3. Such evidence can be troublesome because the very idea of flight is interpretive, amounting to a gloss or reading of human conduct. Sometimes there is no room for doubt, as happens when defendant leads arresting officers driving a clearly marked vehicle on a high-speed chase or runs when uniformed officers approach. But often the evidence is subject to doubt. It may show, for example, only that after the crime defendant could not be located in his usual haunts, see United States v. Sims, 617 F.2d 1371, 1378-1379 (9th Cir. 1980) (failure to return to "halfway house" could be viewed as flight); Commonwealth v. Toney, 433 N.E.2d 425, 431-432 (Mass. 1982) (after homicide, inability of law enforcement officers to locate defendant at her home or workplace or by contacting four sisters and one cousin amounted to evidence of flight). Or it may show only that he left the environs after the crime, see United States v. Beahm, 664 F.2d 414, 419-420 (4th Cir. 1981) (on receipt of note from FBI requesting interview three weeks after crime, defendant went from Virginia to Florida; not flight). Or it may show that he was arrested in another jurisdiction, with no indication when he left the area, see United States v. Howze, 668 F.2d 322, 324-325 (7th Cir. 1982) (charged with robbing bank in Illinois, defendant was arrested four months later in Minnesota; court should reconsider whether these facts indicate flight). Yet even in such cases, the inference of flight might be persuasive if other factors are present. See United States v. Martinez, 681 F.2d 1248, 1254-1259 (10th Cir. 1982) (attorney disappeared after television and newspaper reports said he was wanted in connection with letter bombs, abandoning family and law practice, allowing driver's license to lapse and failing to attend mother's funeral; seven years later he was arrested entering from Mexico with false name and passport; trial judge erred in excluding proof of these facts to show flight; defendant "had to know" he was wanted, and there was enough evidence that he disappeared shortly after issuance of arrest warrant).

4. Courts often suggest that relevancy depends on the reasonableness of the assumption that defendant knew he was under investigation and that this inference becomes weaker as lapsed time between the crime and alleged flight increases. See United States v. Jackson, 572 F.2d 636, 640-641 (7th Cir. 1978).

5. Important to the prosecutor is an instruction that invites the jury to consider flight as evidence of possible guilt. Kevin F. O'Malley, Jay E. Grenig, and Honorable William C. Lee, Federal Jury Practice and Instruction §14.08 (5th ed. 2000); United States v. Blue Thunder, 604 F.2d 550, 556 (8th Cir.) (approving flight instruction), cert. denied, 444 U.S. 902 (1979). If defendant's conduct cannot support an inference of flight, it may be reversible error to invite the jury to consider flight as evidence of possible guilt. See United States v. Myers, 550 F.2d 1036, 1048-1051 (5th Cir. 1977) (conviction reversed).

6. Similar kinds of proof include evidence that the accused (1) employed false identification or aliases, (2) destroyed or concealed evidence ("spoliation"), (3) fabricated evidence or suborned perjury, (4) killed, threatened, or otherwise impeded witnesses for the prosecution, (5) sought to escape detention, (6) attempted suicide, or (7) sought to bribe public officials. See generally Mueller and Kirkpatrick, Evidence §4.4 (3d ed. 2003); Hutchins and Slesinger,

Some Observations on the Law of Evidence—Consciousness of Guilt, 77 U. Pa.
L. Rev. 725 (1929).

5. *Relevance Reconsidered: The Problem of Induction*

We have looked at the difference between inductive and deductive reasoning.
Logicians who specialize in epistemology have paid close attention to induction.
They have classified it, exposed its central dilemma, refined and defended it.
The problem of induction is largely a problem of relevance, and the challenge
to logicians is the challenge of FRE 401.

Varieties of inductive reasoning. Logicians divide inductive logic into four
categories.

1. Inductive generalization. In this form, the inquirer draws an inference
from a sample of observed instances to a conclusion about further instances
not observed:

> All observed jadestones are green;
>
> Therefore the next jadestone we see will be green.

or

> Studies show that smokers suffer eventually from lung cancer much more often
> than people who do not smoke;
>
> Therefore, smokers in general are much more likely to suffer from lung cancer
> than nonsmokers.

In the first example the premise is in a sense categorical (all observed samples
are "green"), but it tacitly concedes that not all jadestones have actually been
seen, so the conclusion (although stated categorically) cannot be said to be
certain. In the second example the premise is qualified (it says "more often"
rather than "always"), and the conclusion is also qualified (it says "more
likely"), and sometimes such a qualified premise may be set out with numerical
precision using a percentage, which adds precision to the conclusion. As the
smoking example suggests, induction can involve predicting future
consequences.

2. Inductive analogy. Here the reasoning proceeds from resemblances between known instances and some aspects of the instance under study, then
suggests an inference that an unknown aspect of the latter follows a known
aspect of the former:

> Known instances *a*, *b*, and *c* have qualities (or behave in the manner of) *Q*, *R*,
> and *S*;
>
> Instance *d* (under study) resembles *a*, *b*, and *c* in that it too has qualities (or
> behaves in the manner of) *Q* and *R*;
>
> Therefore, instance *d* probably has the quality (or behaves in the manner of) *S*.

Reasoning by analogy is common, in everyday thinking and evaluating evidence at trial: You need clothes cleaned and pressed in a hurry. Three times before you chose Q-Cleaners and they promised the job done by Friday, but the clothes were not ready until Monday and were badly done. (So you wouldn't go to the same place with the same request a fourth time; you'd choose another cleaner.) On numerous prior occasions construction cranes collapsed under load, and it was discovered that the accidents resulted from the failure of clamp-like fittings that secure the support cables; when another crane with similar fittings collapses, the court rejects arguments by the maker of the clamps that they could not cause such accidents. See Jones & Laughlin Steel Corp. v. Matherne, 348 F.2d 394 (5th Cir. 1965).

   3. Inductive inference to cause.   In this form, the inductive argument proceeds upon observation of an event that seems to be the "effect" of something else, and draws an inference that a previous event or condition was the cause. Carelessly advanced, this form of argument falls into the fallacy captured in the Latin expression *post hoc ergo propter hoc* ("after this, therefore on account of this"). In litigation, reconstruction of accidents involves reasoning of this sort, as does much other proof.

   4. Inductive explanation or hypothesis.   In the three forms of argument described above, the conclusion involves a particular assertion, but inductive argument may be more in the nature of hypothesis, advanced as the best explanation of observed phenomena. Scientists and detectives reason in this way, seeking to account for or explain observed data, as do prosecutors and law enforcement officers seeking to explain how a web of circumstantial proof establishes defendant's guilt.

   The dilemma of inductive logic. For more than two centuries, philosophers have been plagued by doubt concerning induction. The Scottish philosopher David Hume voiced that doubt:

> [A]ll inferences from experience suppose, as their foundation, that the future will resemble the past, and that similar powers will be conjoined with similar sensible qualities. If there be any suspicion that the course of nature may change, and that the past may be no rule for the future, all experience becomes useless, and can give rise to no inference or conclusion. It is impossible, therefore, that any arguments from experience can prove this resemblance of the past to the future; since all these arguments are founded on the supposition of that resemblance.

D. Hume, An Enquiry Concerning Human Understanding 37-38 (33-34) (posthumous edition of 1777, reprinted 1975). Thus the problem:

> When we make an inductive statement, . . . such as "The sun always rises" or "All larks build their nests on the ground," we are stating something *more* than experience tells us. We jump to a conclusion the evidence does not strictly warrant. What experience does tell us is that *in the past* the sun has always risen and larks have built their nests on the ground. . . . But experience does not tell us that the sun will rise tomorrow, [or] that larks will build their nests on the ground next spring. . . .

J. Brennan, Handbook of Logic 185 (1957). And the twentieth-century English philosopher Bertrand Russell captured the Humean dilemma thus:

A chicken may have been fed by a certain man throughout its life, and have come to look to him confidently for food; but one day he wrings its neck instead. It would have been better for the chicken if its inductive inferences had been less crude.

B. Russell, The Art of Drawing Inferences, in The Art of Philosophizing and Other Essays 37, 48 (1968).

Why then has inductive argument survived?

Hume thought that induction is not so much a reflective process as the result of habit, for that alone "is the great guide of human life," which "renders our experience useful to us, and makes us expect, for the future, a similar train of events with those which have appeared in the past." D. Hume, id. at 44 (36). He did not mean to slight human worth or mental agility in drawing that conclusion. Russell again:

> Experience of apples causes you to expect confidently that *this* apple, which you are about to eat, will taste like an apple and not like a beefsteak. The inductive logician tries to turn this into an argument: "Since the former apples tasted like apples, so will this one." But in fact former apples are probably not in your thoughts. You have an expectation about *this* apple, which has causes in your physiology, but not grounds in your thinking. When the logician tries to find grounds, he also tries to weaken your confidence; he tells you it is only *probable* that this apple will not taste like a beefsteak. At this point you will probably say: "Away with logicians! They only try to confuse me about things that everybody knows perfectly well." But what everybody knows, or thinks he knows, are the *conclusions* of inductions, not their connection with the premises. It is the body rather than the mind that does the connecting of premises and conclusions in an induction.

B. Russell, id. at 73-74.

Defense of inductive logic. John Stuart Mill (1806-1873) defended induction, arguing that the cornerstone of inductive logic is the principle that nature is uniform. Unfortunately this conclusion too is inductive, resting on the premise that induction has proved reliable in the past and should remain so. Hence the logic is circular:

> You may say: "Well, at least you must admit that induction works." "*Has* worked, you mean," the skeptic will reply: for it is only induction itself that assures us that what has worked will work. Perhaps tomorrow stones will be nourishing and bread will be poison, the sun will be cold and the moon hot. The cause of our disbelief in such possibilities is our animal habits; but these equally might change, and we might suddenly begin to expect the opposite of everything that we expect at present.

B. Russell, id. at 74-75. But Mill's defense is not so easily dismissed:

> Mill was aware of this difficulty, and argued that the law of uniformity was excep-tional among inductive statements. He was convinced that the usual challenge. . . could not be brought against this single, all-embracing principle, unique in its comprehensive generality, verified by evidence from all possible quarters, with no known case to the contrary.

J. Brennan, id. at 187.

A more serious challenge rests on the vagueness in the idea of uniformity, because every event supporting the notion can be counted a favorable instance, and an unexplained event tempts the response that "if only we knew all the attendant circumstances, we should see that this too is an instance of Nature's uniformity." Id. Modern commentators emphasize that uniformities can be found in *any* sequence of observations, hence that the notion of general uniformity in nature is "trivial." See Skyrms, The Goodman Paradox and the New Riddle of Induction, in New Readings in Philosophical Analysis 489 (H. Feigl, W. Sellars, and K. Lehrer eds. 1972).

The dilemma cut to size. Modernists have recast the basic inquiry, concerning themselves less with justifying inductive reasoning than with finding principled distinctions between sound and unsound inductive arguments:

> That a given piece of copper conducts electricity increases the credibility of statements asserting that other pieces of copper conduct electricity, and thus confirms the hypothesis that all copper conducts electricity. But the fact that a given man now in this room is a third son does not increase the credibility of statements asserting that other men now in this room are third sons, and so does not confirm the hypothesis that all men now in this room are third sons. Yet in both cases our hypothesis is a generalization of the evidence statements. The difference is that in the former case the hypothesis is a *lawlike* statement; while in the latter case, the hypothesis is merely a contingent or accidental generality. Only a statement that is *lawlike*—regardless of its truth or falsity or its scientific importance—is capable of receiving confirmation from an instance of it; accidental statements are not. Plainly, then, we must look for a way of distinguishing *lawlike* from accidental statements.

N. Goodman, The New Riddle of Induction, in Fact, Fiction, and Forecast 73, 81 (4th ed. 1983).

So how *do* we distinguish between "lawlike" and "accidental" statements—between reliable and spurious hypotheses about the world? Try your hand at pure inductive logic in a legal context.

PROBLEM 2-C. *Too Much Wax on the Floor?*

Juliette Bryant, a 60-year-old married woman, went grocery shopping at her local Alpha Market on Tuesday, January 3. The weather was unseasonably warm and dry.

While pushing a cart down one of the aisles, Mrs. Bryant fell and sustained a fractured distal of the lower one-third of the right fibula (the small bone that goes into the ankle). Her foot and leg had to be put in a cast for six weeks, and she was hospitalized for 30 days. According to her doctor's testimony, she developed traumatic arthritis causing chronic partial disability that might be permanent.

Bryant and her husband sue Alpha Market, claiming that it failed to maintain its floor in a safe condition. At trial she shows that each Saturday night Alpha cleans the floor by scrubbing with water and detergents, followed by machine-scrubbing to remove old wax and dirt and then the application of a solution of new wax and water. The evidence indicates that the amount of water in the solution determines how much wax adheres to the floor, and that improper mixtures lead the wax to "cake" and become slick. This procedure was followed on the Saturday before the mishap, and the store was closed on the following Sunday and Monday in observance of the New Year's holiday. Mrs. Bryant was among the earliest customers on Tuesday morning.

Plaintiffs call Mr. Walters, the manager of Alpha Market, as an "adverse witness." Over Alpha's objection, plaintiffs get Walters to admit that "twice before I slipped and fell on the floor when it was overwaxed," and that he received "several other reports" of customers falling in the past year.

Should plaintiffs have been permitted to ask Walters about his prior falls? About the reports he received that others fell?

B.   PRAGMATIC RELEVANCE

1.   Prejudice and Confusion

It is said that FRE 401 giveth, but FRE 403 taketh away. The logical relevancy standard in FRE 401 is satisfied by evidence having even slight probative worth, but FRE 403 lets the judge exclude relevant evidence on account of any "danger" described there ("unfair prejudice, confusion of the issues, or misleading the jury") or any of the "considerations" also set out there ("undue delay, waste of time, or needless presentation of cumulative evidence").

FRE 403 confers broad discretion on the trial judge. Note, however, that FRE 403 is cast in language favoring admissibility. Evidence is to be excluded only if probative value is "substantially outweighed" by the various dangers and considerations listed. Apparently evidence is to be admitted if probative worth and (for instance) the danger of unfair prejudice are in equal balance. Does it make sense to set a low standard of relevance and then authorize exclusion in broad terms? Does the cast of FRE 403 mean that this power should be exercised sparingly?

STATE v. CHAPPLE
Arizona Supreme Court
660 P.2d 1208 (Ariz. 1983)

Is Dolan "Dee"?

[Alleged first-degree murder, arising out of apparent dispute over drug money. Victim Bill Varnes was found in the bedroom of a house trailer, dead of a gunshot wound in the head. At his trial, defendant Dolan Chapple claimed to have been in another state at the time. He was convicted on the basis of testimony by Malcolm Scott and Pamela Buck, who were themselves involved in the drug transaction and who did not actually see the killing. They placed one Dee at the scene of the crime, however, and Buck testified that Dee had confessed to killing Varnes. And both Scott and Buck identified defendant as Dee by picking out his picture from a photographic display.]

FELDMAN, J.

Defendant contends that the trial court erred by admitting pictures of the charred body and skull of the victim, Bill Varnes. The four pictures were admitted in conjunction with the testimony of Detective Hanratty, the investigating officer, and Dr. Thomas Jarvis, the medical examiner. In vivid color, the photographs portray Varnes' burned body, face and skull, the entry wound of the bullet, a close-up of the charred skull with a large bone flap cut away to show the red-colored, burned dura matter on the inside rim of the skull with the pink brain matter beneath and a pencil pointing to the location of the bullet embedded in the brain. The last photograph shows the brain as the bullet is being removed. On appeal, defendant contends that these pictures were gruesome and inflammatory and therefore should not have been admitted.

We have previously stated the law on this issue as follows:

> Photographs having probative value are admissible in evidence whether they are in black and white or color. *They must, of course, be relevant* to an issue in the case and may be admitted in evidence to identify the deceased, to show the location of the mortal wounds, to show how the crime was committed and to aid the jury in understanding the testimony of the witnesses. *If the photographs have any bearing upon any issue in the case, they may be received although they may also have a tendency to prejudice the jury against the person who committed the offense.* The discretion of the trial court will not be disturbed on appeal unless it has been clearly abused.

State v. Mohr, 476 P.2d 857, 858 (Ariz. 1970) (citations omitted) (emphasis supplied).

The facts of this case and the presence of the issue of inflammatory photographs in many other cases recently argued to this court lead us to reexamine the often quoted language from State v. Mohr. That language should not be interpreted to mean that any photograph which is relevant may be admitted despite its tendency to prejudice the jury. If this were the rule, any photograph of the deceased in any murder case would be admissible because the fact and cause of death are always relevant in a murder prosecution. Relevancy is not the sole test of admissibility for the trial court. Where the offered exhibit is of a nature to incite passion or inflame the jury—and the photographs in the case at bench certainly fall within that category—the court must go beyond the question of relevancy and consider whether the probative value of the exhibit outweighs the danger of prejudice created by admission of the exhibit. State v. Beers, 448 P.2d 104, 108-110 (Ariz. App. 1968). . . . We first adopted this rule in these words:

> Relevancy is thus not the sole test of the admissibility of evidence; admissibility depends, rather, on a balancing of the various effects of the admission of such evidence, considered in the light of recognized rules of law governing the administration of criminal justice.

The. . . test has since been codified in Arizona Rule 403.

Thus, the correct rule is that exhibits which may tend to inflame the jury must first be found relevant. The trial court must then consider the probative value of the exhibits and determine whether it outweighs the danger of prejudice. . . . In making this determination, the trial court must examine the purpose of the offer. In State v. Thomas, 515 P.2d 865 (Ariz. 1973), we identified the following uses for which photographs of a corpse may be admitted in a homicide prosecution: to prove the corpus delicti, to identify the victim, to show the nature and location of the fatal injury, to help determine the degree of atrociousness of the crime, to corroborate state witnesses, to illustrate or explain testimony, and to corroborate the state's theory of how and why the homicide was committed. If any of these questions is contested, either expressly or implicitly, then the trial court may find that the photographs have more than mere technical relevance; it may find that the photographs have "bearing" to prove a contested issue in the case and may, therefore, be admissible notwithstanding a tendency to create prejudice.

However, if the photographs have no tendency to prove or disprove any question which is actually contested, they have little use or purpose except to inflame and would usually not be admissible.

In this case the State had the burden of proving all the elements of first degree murder as well as responding to defendant's sole argument that he was not Dee. In meeting this burden, the State not only had to establish that the defendant was at the scene of the crime, but also that he was responsible for murder. The State argues that the photographs were relevant to these purposes for several of the reasons enumerated in Thomas, supra. We agree that the photographs were relevant to the issues raised by the state's burden of establishing a case for first degree murder. We also agree with the State's claim that the photographs are useful to prove that Dee (who told Buck that he had "shot that _____ in the head") had committed one of the killings.

While both of these arguments establish the relevancy of the photographs, under the facts of this case we find that they had little probative value. The fact that Varnes was killed, the medical cause of his death, and what was done with his body after death were not in controversy. The defense did not dispute, controvert or contradict the State's testimony from the two witnesses on this subject, Detective Hanratty and Dr. Jarvis, and even offered to stipulate to the cause of death. The facts illustrated in the photographs were simply not in dispute or at issue. As the prosecution accurately told the jury in final argument, the only issue to be tried was whether Malcolm Scott and Pamela Buck were correct in identifying the defendant as Dee.

While the exhibits did illustrate the testimony of Hanratty and Jarvis and thus helped the jury comprehend that testimony,[7] there was simply no conflict with regard to the point at which the bullet entered Varnes' skull, the depth of its penetration, the lobe of the brain in which it was lodged, the damage which it did, or over whether it or some other condition had caused death. Nor was there any value to the photographs on the theory that they were

---

7. The trial judge admitted three of the photographs over objection, informing the jurors that the photographs were "distasteful, perhaps to some even shocking. The. . . sole purpose for which you are to consider their admission into evidence, is the fact that they do show where the slug which the detective described was in the skull of one of the victims." The detective and medical examiner both testified without contradiction to the area of the brain in which the bullet was found and the cumulative effect of the photographs could serve no purpose under these facts. We do not believe that the court's statement to the jury regarding the purpose of the admission can be relied upon to negate the admittedly "shocking" effect of the photographs.

[handwritten margin note: D argues only that he wasn't "Dee"]

relevant to Buck's testimony that after the killings Dee admitted that he had shot Varnes in the head. This admission may well serve to establish that Dee was the one who killed Varnes, but defendant did not deny that Dee had killed Varnes by shooting him in the head. Defendant argued only that he was not Dee. The photographs showing the bullet hole in the skull and the bullet in the burned brain were not probative on the only issue being tried, which was whether defendant was Dee.

[handwritten margin note: narrow issue? identification]

In summary, the narrow issue on which this case turned was identification. The matters illustrated by the photographs were cumulative of uncontradicted and undisputed testimony, as well as the subject of a stipulation offered by the defendant. We find, therefore, that the photographs in question had little probative value on the issues being tried and that their admission in evidence could have almost no value or result except to inflame the minds of the jury. Under such circumstances, there was nothing for the trial court to weigh, nothing on which its discretion could be exercised, and the admission of the photographs was error.

[handwritten margin note: Holding]

In reaching this conclusion, we recognize that the state cannot be compelled to try its case in a sterile setting. Exhibits which have the tendency to cause prejudice may often be admissible despite offers to stipulate or the absence of controverting or contradicting evidence. Many times the accuracy of a witness' testimony is not conceded and can be better understood when illustrated by photographs. Testimony may be difficult to comprehend without photographs, or exhibits may corroborate or illustrate controverted testimony. In such cases, the exhibits have probative value on issues expressly or tacitly in dispute. In every case in which there is probative value to the exhibit, it is for the trial court to weigh that value against the danger of prejudice and its conclusion on this point will not be disturbed absent a clear abuse of discretion.

In this case, however, there was nothing of significance to weigh and the only possible use of the photographs would have been to inflame the minds of the jury or to impair their objectivity. Since there was so little probative value to these photographs and since their capacity to inflame is obvious, the admission was legally erroneous and an abuse of discretion. . . .

[The conviction is reversed on account of errors in admitting the photographs and excluding expert testimony offered by the defense concerning the reliability of eyewitness identification.]

OLD CHIEF v. UNITED STATES (II)
Supreme Court of the United States
519 U.S. 172 (1997)

JUSTICE SOUTER delivered the opinion of the Court.

[Recall that Johnny Lynn Old Chief was charged with being a felon in possession of a firearm. Recall too that he was also charged with assault with a dangerous weapon and use of a firearm in a crime of violence. The prior conviction involved an assault causing serious bodily injury, so the defense offered to stipulate to the conviction in hope of keeping details from the jury. Early in the opinion, the Court concludes that the *name* of the prior conviction is relevant, that the defense offer to stipulate did not make this point irrelevant, and that it is important for a variety of reasons to admit evidence rather than try cases on stipulated facts. See *Old Chief (I)* in section A of this chapter, supra. Here the Court addresses the matter of unfair prejudice under FRE 403.]

As for the analytical method to be used in FRE 403 balancing, two basic possibilities present themselves. An item of evidence might be viewed as an island, with estimates of its own probative value and unfairly prejudicial risk the sole reference points in deciding whether the danger substantially outweighs the value and whether the evidence ought to be excluded. Or the question of admissibility might be seen as inviting further comparisons to take account of the full evidentiary context of the case as the court understands it when the ruling must be made.[6] This second approach would start out like the first but be ready to go further. On objection, the court would decide whether a particular item of evidence raised a danger of unfair prejudice. If it did, the judge would go on to evaluate the degrees of probative value and unfair prejudice not only for the item in question but for any actually available substitutes as well. If an alternative were found to have substantially the same or greater probative value but a lower danger of unfair prejudice, sound judicial discretion would discount the value of the item first offered and exclude it if its discounted probative value were substantially outweighed by unfairly prejudicial risk. As we will explain later on, the judge would have to make these calculations with an appreciation of the offering party's need for evidentiary richness and narrative integrity in presenting a case, and the mere fact that two pieces of evidence might go to the same point would not, of course, necessarily mean that only one of them might come in. It would only mean that a judge applying FRE 403 could reasonably apply some discount to the probative value of an item of evidence when faced with less risky alternative proof going to the same point. Even under this second approach, as we explain below, a defendant's FRE 403 objection offering to concede a point generally cannot prevail over the Government's choice to offer evidence showing guilt and all the circumstances surrounding the offense.[7]

The first understanding of the rule is open to a very telling objection. That reading would leave the party offering evidence with the option to structure a trial in whatever way would produce the maximum unfair prejudice consistent with relevance. He could choose the available alternative carrying the greatest threat of improper influence, despite the availability of less prejudicial but equally probative evidence. The worst he would have to fear would be a ruling sustaining a FRE 403 objection, and if that occurred, he could simply fall back to offering substitute evidence. This would be a strange rule. It would be very odd for the law of evidence to recognize the danger of unfair prejudice only to confer such a degree of autonomy on the party subject to temptation, and the Rules of Evidence are not so odd.

6. It is important that a reviewing court evaluate the trial court's decision from its perspective when it had to rule and not indulge in review by hindsight. . . .

7. . . . [O]ur holding is limited to cases involving proof of felon status. On appellate review of a FRE 403 decision, a defendant must establish abuse of discretion, a standard that is not satisfied by a mere showing of some alternative means of proof that the prosecution in its broad discretion chose not to rely upon.

Rather, a reading of the companions to FRE 403, and of the commentaries that went with them to Congress, makes it clear that what counts as FRE 403 "probative value" of an item of evidence, as distinct from FRE 401 "relevance," may be calculated by comparing evidentiary alternatives. The ACN to FRE 401 explicitly say that a party's concession is pertinent to the court's discretion to exclude evidence on the point conceded. . . . As already mentioned, the Notes make it clear that such rulings should be made not on the basis of FRE 401 relevance but on "such considerations as waste of time and undue prejudice (see FRE 403). . . ." The ACN to FRE 403 then take up the point by stating that when a court considers "whether to exclude on grounds of unfair prejudice," the "availability of other means of proof may. . . be an appropriate factor.". . . Thus the notes leave no question that when FRE 403 confers discretion by providing that evidence "may" be excluded, the discretionary judgment may be informed not only by assessing an evidentiary item's twin tendencies, but by placing the result of that assessment alongside similar assessments of evidentiary alternatives.

In dealing with the specific problem raised by §922(g)(1) and its prior-conviction element, there can be no question that evidence of the name or nature of the prior offense generally carries a risk of unfair prejudice to the defendant. That risk will vary from case to case, for the reasons already given, but will be substantial whenever the official record offered by the government would be arresting enough to lure a juror into a sequence of bad character reasoning. Where a prior conviction was for a gun crime or one similar to other charges in a pending case the risk of unfair prejudice would be especially obvious, and Old Chief sensibly worried that the prejudicial effect of his prior assault conviction, significant enough with respect to the current gun charges alone, would take on added weight from the related assault charge against him.[8]

The District Court was also presented with alternative, relevant, admissible evidence of the prior conviction by Old Chief's offer to stipulate, evidence necessarily subject to the District Court's consideration on the motion to exclude the record offered by the Government. Although Old Chief's formal offer to stipulate was, strictly, to enter a formal agreement with the Government to be given to the jury, even without the Government's acceptance his proposal amounted to an offer to admit that the prior-conviction element was satisfied, and a defendant's admission is, of course, good evidence. See FRE 801(d)(2)(A).

Old Chief's proffered admission would, in fact, have been not merely relevant but seemingly conclusive evidence of the element. The statutory language in which the prior-conviction requirement is couched shows no congres-

---

8. It is true that a prior offense may be so far removed in time or nature from the current gun charge and any others brought with it that its potential to prejudice the defendant unfairly will be minimal. Some prior offenses, in fact, may even have some potential to prejudice the Government's case unfairly. Thus an extremely old conviction for a relatively minor felony that nevertheless qualifies under the statute might strike many jurors as a foolish basis for convicting an otherwise upstanding member of the community of otherwise legal gun possession. Since the Government could not, of course, compel the defendant to admit formally the existence of the prior conviction, the Government would have to bear the risk of jury nullification, a fact that might properly drive the Government's charging decision.

sional concern with the specific name or nature of the prior offense beyond what is necessary to place it within the broad category of qualifying felonies, and Old Chief clearly meant to admit that his felony did qualify, by stipulating "that the Government has proven one of the essential elements of the offense." As a consequence, although the name of the prior offense may have been technically relevant, it addressed no detail in the definition of the prior-conviction element that would not have been covered by the stipulation or admission. Logic, then, seems to side with Old Chief.

[Here Court discusses "descriptive richness," "moral underpinnings" of the law, and jury "expectations." See *Old Chief (I)* in section A of this chapter, supra.]

[Recognition that the prosecution] needs evidentiary depth to tell a continuous story has, however, virtually no application when the point at issue is a defendant's legal status, dependent on some judgment rendered wholly independently of the concrete events of later criminal behavior charged against him. As in this case, the choice of evidence for such an element is usually not between eventful narrative and abstract proposition, but between propositions of slightly varying abstraction, either a record saying that conviction for some crime occurred at a certain time or a statement admitting the same thing without naming the particular offense. The issue of substituting one statement for the other normally arises only when the record of conviction would not be admissible for any purpose beyond proving status, so that excluding it would not deprive the prosecution of evidence with multiple utility; if, indeed, there were a justification for receiving evidence of the nature of prior acts on some issue other than status (i.e., to prove "motive, opportunity, intent, preparation, plan, knowledge, identity, or absence of mistake or accident," FRE 404(b)), FRE 404(b) guarantees the opportunity to seek its admission. Nor can it be argued that the events behind the prior conviction are proper nourishment for the jurors' sense of obligation to vindicate the public interest. The issue is not whether concrete details of the prior crime should come to the jurors' attention but whether the name or general character of that crime is to be disclosed. Congress, however, has made it plain that distinctions among generic felonies do not count for this purpose; the fact of the qualifying conviction is alone what matters under the statute. . . . Finally, . . . proof of the defendant's status goes to an element entirely outside the natural sequence of what the defendant is charged with thinking and doing to commit the current offense. Proving status without telling exactly why that status was imposed leaves no gap in the story of a defendant's subsequent criminality, and its demonstration by stipulation or admission neither displaces a chapter from a continuous sequence of conventional evidence nor comes across as an officious substitution, to confuse or offend or provoke reproach.

Given these peculiarities of the element of felony-convict status and of admissions and the like when used to prove it, there is no cognizable difference between the evidentiary significance of an admission and of the legitimately probative component of the official record the prosecution would prefer to place in evidence. . . . In this case, as in any other in which the prior conviction is for an offense likely to support conviction on some improper ground, the only reasonable conclusion was that the risk of unfair prejudice did substantially

[handwritten margin note: admission was an abuse of discretion!]

outgoing the discounted probative value of the record of conviction, and it was an abuse of discretion to admit the record when an admission was available.[10] . . .

The judgment is reversed, and the case is remanded to the Ninth Circuit for further proceedings consistent with this opinion.[11]

It is so ordered.

JUSTICE O'CONNOR, with whom THE CHIEF JUSTICE, JUSTICE SCALIA, and JUSTICE THOMAS join, dissenting.

[The dissent argues that the relevant statute shows that Congress thought jurors would learn "the name and basic nature" of the prior offense. The statute uses the term "crime punishable by imprisonment for a term exceeding one year," and does not refer merely to "felons," and it does provide that certain "business crimes" and misdemeanors that happen to be punishable by imprisonment of two years or less. Hence "crime" is not an "abstract or metaphysical" concept, and the government must prove that the defendant "committed a particular crime."

More importantly, one is not found guilty of a crime or felony, but of "a specified offense." Thus the prior case found that Old Chief "did knowingly and unlawfully assault Rory Dean Fenner, said assault resulting in serious bodily injury," and the name and nature of his crime were "inseparable from the fact of his earlier conviction."

Still more troubling is the majority's argument that the general principle favoring evidentiary depth has "virtually no application" here, for a jury is "as likely to be puzzled" by a "missing chapter" relating to a prior felony conviction as it would be by a concession of any other element in the crime.]

NOTES ON PREJUDICE, GRUESOME PHOTOGRAPHS, AND PRIOR CRIMES

1.   What is "prejudice" in *Chapple*? What is it in *Old Chief*? Are defendants complaining that the evidence (photographs and prior conviction) "hurt" or "harms" their case? Doesn't all relevant evidence do that? *Chapple* and *Old Chief* agree that a stipulation offered by the defense is not enough by itself *to require*

---

10.   There may be yet another means of proof besides a formal admission on the record that, with a proper objection, will obligate a district court to exclude evidence of the name of the offense. A redacted record of conviction is the one most frequently mentioned. Any alternative will, of course, require some jury instruction to explain it (just as it will require some discretion when the indictment is read). A redacted judgment in this case, for example, would presumably have revealed to the jury that Old Chief was previously convicted in federal court and sentenced to more than a year's imprisonment, but it would not have shown whether his previous conviction was for one of the business offenses that do not count, under §921(a)(2). Hence, an instruction, with the defendant's consent, would be necessary to make clear that the redacted judgment was enough to satisfy the status element remaining in the case. The Government might indeed, propose such a redacted judgment for the trial court to weigh against a defendant's offer to admit, as indeed the government might do even if the defendant's admission had been received into evidence.

11.   In remanding, we imply no opinion on the possibility of harmless error, an issue not passed upon below.

exclusion of evidence. As you know from *Old Chief (I)*, the reason has to do with the definition of relevant evidence and with certain policies. Yet a proffered stipulation clearly means there is less need for the evidence, so the risk of prejudice (or "unfair prejudice") weighs more heavily in the balance and may require exclusion of the evidence.

2.   As noted in *Chapple*, courts often admit photographs of the victim in homicide cases. Defendants often offer to stipulate to the appearance of the scene and cause of death—points they are unlikely to contest anyway—in hope of keeping such pictures from the jury. But prosecutors have a laundry list of points on which such photographs bear: To establish cause of death, to show position of the body, to show nature and relationship of wounds, to prove viciousness of attack, and so forth. On one or more of these arguments, prosecutors regularly prevail, and some modern authority holds that the logic of *Old Chief* in requiring courts to accept defense offers to stipulate in felon-in-possession cases does *not* require courts to exclude bloody photographs in homicide trials. See Edwards v. United States, 767 A.2d 241 (D.C. Ct. App. 2001) (in trial for murder of 2-year-old placed in tub of hot water, admitting photographs of body despite defense offer to stipulate to the identity of the body and the cause of death; *Old Chief* did not require otherwise).

3.   Often the cases hold, like *Chapple*, that the mere fact that photographs are "gruesome" does not mean they should be excluded. See State v. Smith, 684 N.E.2d 668, 687-688 (Ohio 1997) (admitting "gruesome" photographs of body, crime scene, and autopsy; details included "the depressed skull fracture caused by a hammer-like object" which conflicted with defendant's testimony about what he had done). Indeed, they are sometimes admitted because they demonstrate atrocity. See State v. Green, 48 P.3d 1276, 1278 (Kan. 2002) (in trial for "incredibly violent and gruesome homicide" where death was caused by "massive blows to the head" that "did horrific damage to the face and skull" and "near decapitation resulted from multiple sawing motions from a sharp object," admitting photographs to help medical examiner describe cause of death; fact that juror fainted at the sight was irrelevant: "Gruesome crimes result in gruesome photographs"); Commonwealth v. Rogers, 222 N.E.2d 766, 772 (Mass.) ("repulsive pictures of mutilated corpse, which left no gruesome detail of this macabre event to the imagination" were relevant on question whether homicide was committed with "extreme atrocity and cruelty"), cert. denied, 389 U.S. 991 (1967); Hopkinson v. State, 632 P.2d 79, 139 (Wyo. 1981) (photographs of victim who had been "brutally tortured before his death"; manner of death was relevant to prosecutor's theory, which was that defendant, who was himself in prison at time of slaying, arranged killing for revenge: "[I]t has never been held that *probative* evidence is inadmissible solely because of repugnancy. Murder is repugnant"), cert. denied, 455 U.S. 922 (1982). Color slides are sometimes allowed, magnifying the awful image of violent death. See Goffer v. State, 430 So. 2d 896, 898-899 (Ala. Crim. App. 1983) (rejecting claim that color slides of victim in hospital should have been excluded because they "produced a magnification of the wounds and a distortion of the injuries"; the slides were "just enlargements").

4.   Sometimes courts exclude gruesome photographs under FRE 403 when probative worth is minimal and inflammatory impact is great. The chance for exclusion improves when the numbing impact of such pictures results from

changed conditions, so they are "misleading" under FRE 403 as well as prejudicial. See People v. Coleman, 451 N.E.2d 973, 977-978 (Ill. App. 1983) (reversible error to admit "color slide of the decedent's decomposing, maggot-infested, partially autopsied body"); Terry v. State, 491 S.W.2d 161, 164 (Tex. Crim. App. 1973) (reversible error to admit pictures of month-old murder victim, showing "massive mutilation" caused by autopsy and depicting "severed parts of a human body"). And see Ritchie v. State, 632 P.2d 1244, 1245-1246 (Okla. Crim. 1981) (reversible error to display enlarged photograph of three-year-old victim taken before attack, surrounded by photographs of his body afterwards and during subsequent autopsy; jury "should not have been concerned with what the child looked like prior to the offense," and "use of a billboard to display the numerous photographs could have served no other purpose than to prejudice and arouse the passions," and "the billboard became an item of evidence notwithstanding the fact that it was never introduced").

5.   The majority in *Old Chief* is right, isn't it, that the felon-in-possession charges against did not turn on the *nature* of the prior conviction? That is to say, Johnny Lynn Old Chief had been convicted of felonies that were not in the exempt category relating to "business practices," so it made no difference to the *present* charges whether he had been convicted of burglary, embezzlement, murder, or something else. It follows, doesn't it, that telling the jury the nature of the convictions served no legitimate purpose? And it's obvious, isn't it, that proving that Old Chief had been convicted of assault might incline the jury to conclude that he was up to no good when found in possession of a gun, and that he is a bad person who deserves to go to jail? As the Court notes, prior criminal acts are often relevant in a very different way: They may shed light on points such as motive (defendant had committed a robbery, so he needed to steal a car to get away) or intent (defendant had often sold cocaine, so this time when he possessed cocaine he probably intended to sell it). In such cases, *Old Chief* says, a defense offer to stipulate will not likely tip the balance as it did in this instance. Still, courts often exclude prior crimes in this setting when relevance seems attenuated and the risk of prejudice seems large. You will take up this issue in Chapter 5 of this book. At least one commentator thinks that the typical outcomes (bloody photographs are routinely admitted; prior crimes are often excluded) are backwards. See Michael Risinger, John Henry Wigmore, Johnny Lynn Old Chief, and "Legitimate Moral Force": Keeping the World Safe for Heartstrings and Gore, 49 Hastings L.J. 403, 421 (1998) (arguing that proof of "bloody photos and weeping widows" ought to be more readily excludable than prior convictions, which at least are not "wholly irrelevant by anyone's definition," but that "the opposite is in fact the case" and *Old Chief* does not change this practical reality).

6.   *Old Chief* determines an issue of federal evidence law, so its holding does not bind states. That means that states could, if they chose, continue to admit proof of the names of prior convictions in state felon-in-possession cases. Not surprisingly, however, *Old Chief* has proven influential in state courts and its reasoning has been applied in other areas. See, e.g., Carter v. State, 824 A.2d 123 (Md. 2003) (trial for possession of regulated firearm by one previously convicted of crime of violence); State v. James, 81 S.W.3d 751 (Tenn. 2002) (trial for escape by convicted felon). But see Rigby v. State, 826 S.2d 694 (Miss. 2002) (in trial on felony DUI charges, prior DUI convictions were admissible

despite defense offer to stipulate; in *Old Chief,* the nature of prior convictions did not matter; here they do); Cox v. State, 819 S.2d 705, 715 (Fla. 2002) (in penalty phase of trial for commission of crime while under sentence for previous violent felony, defendant could not exclude proof of prior conviction by offer to stipulate), cert. denied, 123 S.Ct. 8899 (2003).

7.   *Old Chief* is careful to say that its holding applies only to felon-in-possession cases. You will see that prior crimes are often proved in efforts to show particular points like "intent" or "motive" under FRE 404. *Old Chief* says that this situation is very different. We revisit this issue in Chapter 5, infra.

PROBLEM 2-D.   *The Battered Wife*

Virginia died of a stab wound in her chest, and the state has charged her ex-husband Donald with murder and, in the alternative, manslaughter. Donald has pleaded innocent to the charges, claiming that the killing was accidental.

There is no doubt of the cause of death. Virginia's body was found in the trailer where she lived with Todd and Jason (children of hers from a previous marriage), dead from massive hemorrhaging caused by a chest wound. Nor is there any doubt that Donald played a role in her death: The evidence shows that he called the sheriff's office at 2:00 A.M., saying that he had just stabbed his wife and giving the address of the trailer. (Officers who went to the scene found the children asleep.)

During the state's case-in-chief, the prosecutor proves cause of death (stab wound) and introduces a knife said to be the fatal weapon, along with lab analysis connecting the blood on the knife to Virginia, forensic testimony that a knife of that size made the wound, and evidence that Donald's latent fingerprints were found on it.

During the defense case, Donald testifies that he spent the evening at the trailer watching television with Virginia while the children slept, and that the two quarreled when she said she was going to leave him and take Todd and Jason with her. He testifies that he "asked her not to go, and told her how important her children had become to him, and that he would try to get a court order to stop her from leaving." He testifies that Virginia then attacked him with a baseball bat and admits that he picked up the knife from the countertop, but says, "She just fell into the blade, and I didn't even know she was hurt, at least not right away."

During its case-in-rebuttal, the state offers testimony by a counselor at a Shelter for Battered and Abused Women that two years earlier Virginia had sought refuge there for about 30 days, during which time she divorced Donald.

Donald objects to the testimony of the counselor at the shelter, arguing that it is irrelevant and prejudicial. Should that testimony get in? How is it relevant? How is it prejudicial?

PROBLEM 2-E.   *The Exploding Gas Tank*

Struck from behind by a vehicle exceeding the speed limit on the highway, the car in which Risner was riding as a passenger bursts into flames as a result of a ruptured fuel tank. Within 24 hours Risner dies from burns sustained in the accident, and his widow thereafter sues the automaker, alleging that negligent design of the fuel tank caused Risner's death—that if the tank had been properly designed it would not have ruptured when the car was struck from behind.

At trial, defendant automaker introduces testimony by a state trooper that the impacting vehicle was going about 68 mph at the time of impact. The automaker also introduces a certified copy of a guilty plea, entered by the driver of the impacting vehicle to charges of involuntary manslaughter arising from the accident. In the end, the jury returns a verdict for defendant.

Mrs. Risner appeals, urging that the trial court should have excluded the guilty plea under FRE 403. In response, defendant automaker argues that the plea was properly received to show the speed of the impacting vehicle and establish cause of death.

Who should prevail in these arguments and why?

2. Limited Admissibility—Confining the Impact of Proof

It is a perennial headache for judges and trial lawyers that evidence tends to prove too much.

Time and again evidence that seems perfect to prove one point also tends to prove another, on which it is incompetent. Or the other point is itself highly prejudicial. Or evidence is admissible in support of one claim but not another, or admissible against one party but not another. Rule 403 permits the trial judge to balance probative worth against risks of "unfair prejudice" or "confusion" of issues or "misleading the jury" and admit or exclude accordingly.

Rule 105 authorizes a very different approach: Admit the evidence, on the point for which or against the parties as to whom it is competent, but give "limiting instructions" to prevent misuse on other issues or as against other parties. More often than not courts admit evidence having unwanted spillover effect, and parties raising objection on this ground must content themselves with a limiting instruction. The reason is practical necessity, for little proof would be admissible if its relevance or impact in the case had to match exactly its competency. Thus a great deal of evidence is admitted for purposes of impeachment despite the fact that it cannot properly be considered as proof of any number of other points that it may seem to establish, and out-of-court statements and prior criminal acts may be proved in different contexts despite rules restricting their use.

PROBLEM 2-F.   "My Insurance Will Cover It"

While driving on the left (inside) lane of a busy four-lane street in Miami, Lina hears a sudden metallic scraping and feels her (new shiny white) Chrysler being shoved roughly leftward. Myra, who is driving in the right (outside) lane hears the same awful noise, and feels her (bright red) Porsche being nudged sharply to the right. The two regain control of their cars. Lina drops back behind Myra, and they pull over to the curb and inspect the damage.

They exchange names and addresses, and Lina says: "Whoever screws up, her insurance pays. I'm sure my insurance will cover it. They'll pay for what happened to your Porsche."

It takes more than $3,000 to fix Myra's Porsche and almost as much to repair Lina's Chrysler. Despite their promising amicable beginning, the two women do not manage to work out their differences amicably. Myra sues, and Lina counterclaims.

At trial, Myra proposes to testify to what Lina said.

Lina objects, invoking FRE 411, which says that evidence of liability insurance cannot be offered to prove that a person "acted negligently or otherwise wrongfully." But Myra insists: "What Lina said is admissible to prove she was negligent. She admitted it, for heaven's sake."

How should the court rule, and why?

NOTES ON LIMITED ADMISSIBILITY

1. You will see that what a party says is usually admissible against her, under the admissions doctrine contained in Rule 801(d)(2)(A). See Chapter 4B1, infra. Myra is right that nothing prevents use of a statement by Lina to prove she was negligent. But Lina is also right that under Rule 411 the fact of insurance cannot be used to prove negligence. See Chapter 5F, infra. The challenge is to sort out the admissible from the inadmissible aspects of the proffered evidence. There's no way, is there, that Myra could testify to part of what Lina said? Should Lina's statement be excluded altogether under Rule 403 or admitted for a limited purpose under Rule 105? Should Lina ask for a limiting instruction? What would it say?

2. As a practical matter, there is no alternative to the doctrine of limited admissibility, is there? Consider these statements in defense of the doctrine:

> To say that the jury might have been confused amounts to nothing more than an unfounded speculation that the jurors disregarded clear instructions of the court in arriving at their verdict. Our theory of trial relies upon the ability of a jury to follow instructions.

Opper v. United States, 348 U.S. 84, 95 (1954) (no "confusion" resulted here).

> Unless we proceed on the basis that the jury will follow the court's instructions where those instructions are clear and the circumstances are such that the jury can reasonably be expected to follow them, the jury system makes little sense. Based on the faith that the jury will endeavor to follow the court's instructions, our system of jury trial has produced one of the most valuable and practical mechanisms in human experience for dispensing substantial justice.

Delli Paoli v. United States, 352 U.S. 232, 242-243 (1957) (but there are "practical limitations" on doctrine of limited admissibility). The Court is right, isn't it?

3. In *Opper* and *Delli Paoli*, the Court struggled with limited admissibility in a recurrent situation—the criminal trial of several defendants, where the

prosecutor offers a statement by one that mentions others. Often such a statement is admissible against the person who made it, but *not* against others. The question was whether the Constitution could tolerate receipt of such a statement against its maker, with a limiting instruction to protect the others. Finally the Court concluded that even clear limiting instructions were not good enough, noting that the prosecutor could sever and proceed separately against the various defendants. Bruton v. United States, 391 U.S. 123 (1968) (set forth and examined in detail in Chapter 4B1, infra).

3. *Completeness—Providing Context* 403 v 106

[handwritten margin note: 403 ↓ balance d admit /exclude]

Another headache for judges and trial lawyers comes from the fact that a bit of evidence that might be competent on a point is so connected with other evidence that it would be a distortion to consider the one without the other. Sometimes the difficulty is that there is not enough competent evidence to make the point fairly. But usually the problem is that the proponent chooses to present a small piece of a larger picture and thus distorts meaning.

[handwritten margin note: 106 ↓ Rule of completeness]

Here again FRE 403 authorizes one approach (balance, and admit or exclude the whole accordingly). And at least in connection with "a writing or recorded statement," FRE 106 authorizes another: The adverse party may require introduction of "any other part" of the statement that "ought in fairness to be considered contemporaneously" with the part already offered. This "rule of completeness," as it is sometimes called, obviously could apply to statements that have not been written or recorded and to other sorts of evidence as well, and trial courts have authority enough under Rules 401 through 403 and 611 to apply the same principle to such other proof.

PROBLEM 2-G. *"Power Rollback Caused the Crash"*

While serving as a Navy flight instructor, Lieutenant Commander Erin Ranney died in a T44 training aircraft that crashed while climbing and turning hard right during "touch-and-go's" (exercises in which the plane lands, then accelerates and takes off again). Her student, Ensign Dan Knowls, also died in the crash. Jim Ranney, her surviving husband and also a Navy flight instructor, sued manufacturer Rockwood Aircraft.

Jim Ranney thinks that sudden failure of engine power at a crucial moment during take-off caused the crash. He personally investigated the plane and the scene and the available records, and wrote a detailed letter to Commander Martin concluding that "power rollback caused the crash."

At trial, Ranney presents his evidence of power rollback, mostly in the form of expert testimony developed for trial. During the defense case, Rockwood introduces official findings based on Commander Martin's investigation, that pilot error caused the crash. Those findings suggest that Knowls was in the left student seat in control of the plane, that Erin Ranney did not at first see a second craft approaching from the left because Knowls blocked her view, and that when she did see the second plane she took the controls and banked right. The findings indicate that Knowls "released the stick" to let her do what she had to do, but that he had improperly trimmed the plane (the trim tabs were set wrong). Releasing the stick brought the nose up, causing a sudden loss of airspeed leading to stall and crash.

Counsel for Rockwood calls Jim Ranney as an adverse witness, and asks about several comments in his letter. In one, he said the plane "violated pattern integrity as it turned crosswind" when his wife "reacted instinctively and abruptly by initiating a hard right turn" away from the nearby craft. In another, he said Erin Ranney was under "unnecessary pressure" and tried to "cancel the exercise because Knowls was tired and emotionally drained." Counsel for Ranney rose to examine:

Ranney Counsel: In the same letter you were just asked about, didn't you conclude that power rollback caused the crash?

Rockwood Counsel: Well, I'm going to have to object to that, your Honor. We went into the letter because he wrote it and we can do that, but he can't offer his own letter because it's hearsay. Of course he can go over the passages about how fatigued his wife was, and how she was out of the pattern, but he's getting into other subjects now. It's hearsay and beyond the direct.

Ranney Counsel: Your honor, he's trying to pick and choose. If he's going to use the letter, he can't distort it. We need to correct that.

The Court: I'm going to sustain the objection. If you want to ask your client what he learned about the crash by investigating, I'll let you get into that again, just to clear up what he thinks. But don't go into other parts of the letter.

After a jury verdict and judgment for the defense, Jim Ranney appeals, arguing that the court erred under FRE 106 in restricting redirect. What result, and why?

NOTES ON THE COMPLETENESS DOCTRINE

[handwritten annotation: → 106 Trumps hearsay to provide context]

1. FRE 106 invites the adverse party to "require" the proponent to offer another "writing" (or "other part" of a writing) *at the same time* as the writing (or part) being offered. But in the Problem counsel for Ranney acted to bring out additional parts of the Ranney letter during what amounted to "friendly cross-examination" *after* counsel for Rockwood had brought out part of the letter on direct. Indeed, counsel for Ranney might have deferred this effort until putting on his case-in-rebuttal. Although framed as what one commentator calls an "interruption rule," FRE 106 clearly authorizes adverse parties to answer an incomplete presentation later in trial, thus also serving as a "rebuttal rule." See generally Dale Nance, A Theory of Verbal Completeness, 80 Iowa L. Rev. 825, 847-849 (1995).

2. Later you will see that what Ranney wrote in his letter could be used *against him* as his *admission,* but Ranney could not normally put the letter in evidence himself, since the admissions doctrine does not authorize one to introduce his own statements. (Probably the letter does not fit the exception for public records, although Commander Martin's official findings might fit this exception.) Does this fact make a difference? Some courts take the view that FRE 106 affects only the *order* or *sequence* of proof, which would mean that

*[handwritten annotation: * admissions doctrine]*

it does not authorize a person in Ranney's position to offer his own letter later in the trial. The better view, however, is that FRE 106 can sometimes "trump" hearsay and other objections when necessary to provide context. For a good development of this view, see Dale Nance, Verbal Completeness and Exclusionary Rules Under the Federal Rules of Evidence, 75 Texas L. Rev. 51 (1996).

4.   "The Shortness of Life"   *403 ⇒ practicality*

Trial judges can exclude even probative evidence not only because of prejudice and confusion—factors likely to distort or undermine the jury's decisionmaking process—but also for more mundane reasons. FRE 403 speaks of "undue delay, waste of time, or needless presentation of cumulative evidence." Here the concern is purely practical, and this aspect of judicial power amounts to what Holmes called "a concession to the shortness of life." Reeve v. Dennett, 11 N.E. 938, 943 (Mass. 1887).

Thus courts may limit the number of witnesses called to prove any particular point. See Michelson v. United States, 335 U.S. 469, 480 (1948) (judge may control number of character witnesses called by the accused); Mills v. Nahabedian, 824 A.2d 500, 503 (R.I. 2003) (in doctor's suit alleging that odors from new carpet made her patients ill, trial judge properly limited number of witnesses that plaintiff could call to five). And judges may exclude, as cumulative, evidence that is duplicative of that already presented. See United States v. Crosby, 713 F.2d 1066, 1071-1072 (5th Cir.) (judge properly excluded journal entries and poetry offered to support defense of post-traumatic stress disorder from Vietnam experience, for these were "cumulative of other testimony"), cert. denied, 464 U.S. 1001 (1983). Judges may also insist that a trial continue once it has begun and deny requests for time to locate new witnesses or evidence.

Consider the following explanation for these powers:

> The court's time is a public commodity that should not be squandered. Witnesses and jurors have private lives, and ought not to be asked to give more of their time than is necessary to resolve disputes. A tireless or resourceful litigant should not have unlimited freedom to wear down his opponent by repetitious proof or unnecessary waiting. In short, FRE 403 is evidence law's answer to the adage, "Enough is enough."

1 C. Mueller and L. Kirkpatrick, Federal Evidence §96 (2d ed. 1994).

5.   The Functions of Judge and Jury

Recall that the trial judge alone determines questions of "admissibility" under Rule 104(a) (Chapter 1D4, supra). When it comes to relevancy, he is not always the sole decisionmaker. Sometimes he shares responsibility with the jury, and it is fair to say that roles of judge and jury in these cases are commingled, even confused.

Simple relevance. The judge alone decides whether a particular point, which a proffered item of evidence concededly tends to establish or refute, is "consequential" within the meaning of FRE 401. Only a judge is qualified to decide this point, for it turns on substantive and procedural rules, which establish and limit the issues. See Prather v. Prather, 650 F.2d 88, 90 (5th Cir. 1981) (in suit on oral contract, court erred in admitting statements by plaintiff describing his understanding of the terms, instructing jury to determine whether his belief was relevant; whether state of mind is a relevant issue "is for the court to determine," and if it had performed this duty it would have concluded that declarant's state of mind was "not a relevant issue").

Also the judge decides whether proffered evidence really has a tendency in reason to prove the point for which it is offered. This question is sometimes described as one of "simple" (as opposed to "conditional") relevance. But it is up to the jury to "weigh" the evidence, as Rule 104(e) implicitly recognizes. "Simple relevance" (or "admissibility") is often clearly distinguishable from "weight," but these matters occupy a continuum and merge in an indistinct haze in the middle. Telling simple relevancy from weight is like distinguishing between cases that go to the jury because reasonable minds could assess the evidence differently and cases that require a directed verdict because only one outcome is reasonable.

Conditional relevance. Rule 104(b) provides that when relevance turns on "the fulfillment of a condition of fact," the judge performs only a screening function: When different answers are reasonable, the jury decides. That is, the jury decides whether the condition is satisfied. Conditionally relevant evidence is admitted "upon, or subject to" introduction of enough other evidence to support the appropriate jury "finding."

There are a few well-understood instances of "conditional relevance" in operation. As you have seen (Chapter 1D4, supra), questions of authenticity (like connecting the gun found by Lieutenant Goldbloom to the crime) fall into this category, as does the question whether a witness has personal knowledge. The ACN to FRE 104 advances two other examples, said to be in this category: "[W]hen a spoken statement is relied upon to prove notice to X, it is without probative value unless X heard it"; when a letter apparently from Y is offered as his admission, "it has no probative value unless Y wrote or authorized it." In the first case, relevance of the statement turns on satisfying the condition of proving that X heard it. In the second, relevance of the letter turns on satisfying the condition of proving that Y wrote it.

Yet distinguishing "conditional relevancy" under FRE 104(b) from "simple" relevancy and other questions of "admissibility" under FRE 104(a) can be surprisingly difficult. Try your hand at the following problem.

PROBLEM 2-H.   The Bicycle Brake

Seven-year-old Raysha borrows her older brother's 24-inch bicycle and rides down the steep hill in front of her home. She brakes to keep the speed down, but at a curve in the road the brakes fail. The bicycle hits the curb, throwing Raysha over the handlebars into a tree, fracturing her skull. Three years later, her parents sue the manufacturer and the retailer, claiming that the brake was defectively designed because of the use of a plastic cap. The cap fit onto a short metal tube in the wheel hub that permitted the mechanism to be oiled, and plaintiffs assert that the metal threads on the tube destroyed those in the cap, resulting in its loss, then loss of oil, introducing dust and dirt in the mechanism, ultimately causing brake failure. At trial Raysha's brother testifies that the cap was missing at the time of the accident.

Plaintiffs then offer testimony by Mundel, a consulting engineer who examined the bicycle two years after the accident, to the effect that the brake did not work properly.

Defendants object, claiming that plaintiffs failed to lay the necessary "foundation" by establishing that the bicycle was in substantially the same condition when examined by Mundel as it was on the day of the accident. To overcome this objection, plaintiffs call Carter, a mechanical engineer who experimented with the bicycle a few weeks after the accident. He attached to the pedal a piece of steel about as heavy as Raysha and rode down the hill about 40 times, to simulate what would happen if she applied the brake. (Carter could not support plaintiff's case, for he experienced no "total loss" of braking power.) Raysha's father testifies that at all other times since the accident the bicycle was not used, but was kept in storage in the basement. The defense continues to object, arguing now that Carter's experiments altered the condition of the brake.

The trial court excludes Mundel's testimony, finding that plaintiffs failed to establish that the bicycle was in the same condition when Mundel inspected it as it was at the time of the accident. The court directs a verdict for defendants.

Raysha's parents appeal. Does Mundel's testimony raise a problem of simple relevancy within FRE 104(a) or one of "conditional relevancy" within FRE 104(b)? Whichever it is, did the trial judge err in excluding it?

NOTES ON CONDITIONAL RELEVANCY

1.   Can testimony by Mundel be relevant if the condition of the bicycle was substantially changed when he inspected it, because of passage of time or Carter's experiments? If Mundel thinks he has something useful to say about the bicycle, don't we have an issue of "admissibility" of expert testimony?

2. Lawsuits tend to spill beyond neat boundaries, and one side often charges that the other behaved in ways suggesting that its case is weak or false. When such attacks are mounted in sloppy or cavalier fashion, the trial judge can block the effort: Sometimes there is no evidence on which a jury could base a finding of the necessary condition under Rule 104(b). Sometimes the judge decides the point as a matter of admissibility under Rule 104(a), and the decision is that the proof is inadmissible. Consider these examples:

(a) In a trial for manslaughter committed during an aborted drug transaction, defendant objected to evidence that he threatened his girlfriend from jail. The theory was that he was trying to force her to marry him in the belief that being married would keep her from testifying. The reviewing court found that a necessary condition was not satisfied: While attempts to suppress testimony suggest consciousness of guilt, the state "failed to make the threats relevant" because it did not actually show that defendant had that purpose. See Standifer v. Commonwealth, 2003 WL 21254858 (Ky. 2003) (reversing on other grounds).

(b) In a suit against owners of a mobile home park, defendants showed that they received threatening phonecalls from plaintiff's ex-boyfriend expressing "in aggressive and profane terms" an intent to harm one of the defendants "for harassing and inflicting distress on plaintiff." Exclusion was proper, however, because a court can require a "foundational showing" that the ex-boyfriend was acting "as an agent for plaintiff," and defendants "never attempted to show agency," offering only the content of the tape and plaintiff's testimony that she "talked to the ex-boyfriend because he is her child's father." This proof did not show that plaintiff "knew of the threats or authorized them." See Sweet v. Roy, 801 A.2d 694, 705 (Vt. 2002).

(c) In a trial for sexually assaulting four-year-old MM, defendant sought to cross-examine her about charges that one Ashley had molested her before, arguing that these charges were false and that they bore on MM's credibility. The intermediate appellate court thought the jury should decide whether the previous charges were false under Rule 104(b), but the state supreme court concluded that "the trial judge should make a preliminary determination based on a preponderance of the evidence that the statements are false." Here he could reasonably decide that defendant had not proved the falsity of the prior charges. State v. West, 24 P.3d 648, 652-655 (Hi. 2001) (conviction reinstated).

3. The government condemns the Cook farm in Kentucky to make way for the Taylorsville Reservoir. The Cooks reject as inadequate the $90,000 offered by the government, arguing that this valuation rests on farm use, and that the property can be subdivided into recreational parcels and sold for $225,000. They introduce testimony by a planning coordinator that the county is feeling population pressures, as children return to rural homes and urbanites seek recreational property. They also offer testimony by a real estate broker, estimating value for recreational use. Should he be allowed to testify? See United States v. 478.34 Acres of Land, 578 F.2d 156 (6th Cir. 1978) (error to exclude broker's testimony, for FRE 104(b) requires jury to decide whether potential for recreational use is shown).

4. Recall Problem 2-A (Was He Going Too Fast?). Should the trial court, before admitting Hill's testimony as to speed of Gadsby's vehicle 30 miles before the accident, require proof that driving conditions were the same between the place where Hill saw Gadsby and the place of the accident? Does that problem too present an issue of "conditional relevance"?

5. Consider examples of conditional relevancy (like those given by the Advisory Committee), in which both of two seemingly independent facts must be established before a critical conclusion is possible—notification by spoken word, for example, in which speaking and hearing are necessary to the conclusion. Are you satisfied that evidence of one without the other is "irrelevant" under FRE 104? See Ball, The Myth of Conditional Relevancy, 14 Ga. L. Rev. 435 (1980) (arguing that unless the trier has determined that one of two necessary facts does not exist, evidence tending to prove either one is relevant, and that FRE 104(b) should be repealed).

6. The concept of conditional relevance connects with a larger phenomenon that modern commentators call the problem of "conjunction." The fortunes of a litigant may depend on acceptance of testimony by two witnesses and thus on the "conjunction" of what they say. Here the relevance of what each says might be said to be conditional on what the other says. Consider an

example drawn from the Advisory Committee's Note: X sues Y on a debt, and X's case depends on proving that Y admitted the debt by letter. The Note describes this situation as one of conditional relevance, and the judge will likely admit testimony by X that he received the letter, as well as testimony by some third person Z that Y wrote or authorized it.

If the proof shows a 60 percent likelihood that X received such a letter and a 60 percent likelihood that Y authorized it, should the jury find for X? The "product rule" describes the "conjoint" probability that two independent events occur: If there is a 50 percent likelihood of getting a head or a tail on a single flip of a coin, the product rule tells us that there is a 25 percent likelihood of getting a head (or a tail) on both of two flips (50 percent $\times$ 50 percent). In the suit of X against Y, applying this rule suggests that the evidence favoring X reaches only a likelihood of 36 percent. See generally Nesson, The Evidence or the Event? On Judicial Proof and the Acceptability of Verdicts, 98 Harv. L. Rev. 1357, 1388 (1985) (in this situation a jury "will not consider and accept each of the witness's accounts separately"; it will not "ignore questionable aspects of one witness's testimony when considering the other's," but will "consider the conjunction of the two accounts" in deciding the issue).

C. THE RELEVANCE OF PROBABILISTIC ANALYSIS

The task of the trier of fact is usually to determine whether plaintiff in a civil suit has proved his case by a preponderance of the evidence, which is usually defined in terms of establishing that the necessary facts are more probably true than not. The task in a criminal prosecution is to determine whether the prosecutor has proved guilt beyond a reasonable doubt, which also suggests probability but at a much higher level.

Seldom does the degree of probability suggested by evidence lend itself readily to mathematical expression or attain numeric precision. But probabilistic evidence is sometimes offered, and in certain kinds of cases (such as discrimination suits and litigation over paternity) mathematical proof has become common.

| PEOPLE v. COLLINS
| California Supreme Court
| 438 P.2d 33 (Cal. 1968)

SULLIVAN, J.

We deal here with the novel question whether evidence of mathematical probability has been properly introduced and used by the prosecution in a criminal case. While we discern no inherent incompatibility between the disciplines of law and mathematics and intend no general disapproval or disparagement of the latter as an auxiliary in the fact-finding processes of the former, we cannot uphold the technique employed in the instant case. As we explain in detail infra, the testimony as to mathematical probability infected the case with fatal error and distorted the jury's traditional role of determining guilt or innocence according to long-settled rules. Mathematics, a veritable sorcerer in our computerized society, while assisting the trier of fact in the search for truth, must not cast a spell over him. We conclude that on the record before us defendant should not have had his guilt determined by the odds and that he is entitled to a new trial. We reverse the judgment.

A jury found defendant Malcolm Ricardo Collins and his wife defendant Janet Louise Collins guilty of second degree robbery. Malcolm appeals from the judgment of conviction. Janet has not appealed.

On June 18, 1964, about 11:30 A.M. Mrs. Juanita Brooks, who had been shopping, was walking home along an alley in the San Pedro area of the City of Los Angeles. She was pulling behind her a wicker basket carryall containing groceries and had her purse on top of the packages. She was using a cane. As she stooped down to pick up an empty carton, she was suddenly pushed to the ground by a person whom she neither saw nor heard approach. She was stunned by the fall and felt some pain. She managed to look up and saw a young woman running from the scene. According to Mrs. Brooks the latter appeared to weigh about 145 pounds, was wearing "something dark," and had hair "between a dark blond and a light blond," but lighter than the color of defendant Janet Collins' hair as it appeared at trial. Immediately after the incident, Mrs. Brooks discovered that her purse, containing between $35 and $40, was missing.

About the same time as the robbery, John Bass, who lived on the street at the end of the alley, was in front of his house watering his lawn. His attention was attracted by "a lot of crying and screaming" coming from the alley. As he looked in that direction, he saw a woman run out of the alley and enter a yellow automobile parked across the street from him. He was unable to give the make of the car. The car started off immediately and pulled wide around another parked vehicle so that in the narrow street it passed within six feet of Bass. The latter then saw that it was being driven by a male Negro, wearing a mustache and beard. At the trial Bass identified defendant as the driver of the yellow automobile. However, an attempt was made to impeach his identification by his admission that at the preliminary hearing he testified to an uncertain identification at the police lineup shortly after the attack on Mrs. Brooks, when defendant was beardless.

In his testimony Bass described the woman who ran from the alley as a Caucasian, slightly over five feet tall, of ordinary build, with her hair in a dark blond ponytail, and wearing dark clothing. He further testified that her ponytail was "just like" one which Janet had in a police photograph taken on June 22, 1964.

On the day of the robbery, Janet was employed as a housemaid in San Pedro. Her employer testified that she had arrived for work at 8:50 A.M. and that defendant had picked her up in a light yellow car[2] about 11:30 A.M. On that day, according to the witness, Janet was wearing her hair in a blonde

---

2. Other witnesses variously described the car as yellow, as yellow with an off-white top, and yellow with an egg-shell white top. The car was also described as being medium to large in size. Defendant drove a car at or near the times in question which was a Lincoln with a yellow body and a white top.

ponytail but lighter in color than it appeared at trial.[3] There was evidence from which it could be inferred that defendants had ample time to drive from Janet's place of employment and participate in the robbery. Defendants testified, however, that they went directly from her employer's house to the home of friends, where they remained for several hours.

In the morning of June 22, Los Angeles Police Officer Kinsey, who was investigating the robbery, went to defendants' home. He saw a yellow Lincoln automobile with an off-white top in front of the house. He talked with defendants. Janet, whose hair appeared to be a dark blonde, was wearing it in a ponytail. Malcolm did not have a beard. The officer explained to them that he was investigating a robbery specifying the time and place; that the victim had been knocked down and her purse snatched; and that the person responsible was a female Caucasian with blonde hair in a ponytail who had left the scene in a yellow car driven by a male Negro. He requested that defendants accompany him to the police station at San Pedro and they did so. There, in response to police inquiries as to defendants' activities at the time of the robbery, Janet stated, according to Officer Kinsey, that her husband had picked her up at her place of employment at 1 P.M. and that they had then visited at the home of friends in Los Angeles. Malcolm confirmed this. Defendants were detained for an hour or two, were photographed but not booked, and were eventually released and driven home by the police.

Late in the afternoon of the same day, Officer Kinsey, while driving home from work in his own car, saw defendants riding in their yellow Lincoln. Although the transcript fails to disclose what prompted such action Kinsey proceeded to place them under surveillance and eventually followed them home. He called for assistance and arranged to meet other police officers in the vicinity of defendants' home. Kinsey took a position in the rear of the premises. The other officers, who were in uniform and had arrived in a marked police car, approached defendants' front door. As they did so, Kinsey saw defendant Malcolm Collins run out the back door toward a rear fence and disappear behind a tree. Meanwhile the other officers emerged with Janet Collins whom they had placed under arrest. A search was made for Malcolm who was found in a closet of a neighboring home and also arrested. Defendants were again taken to the police station, were kept in custody for 48 hours, and were again released without any charges being made against them.

Officer Kinsey interrogated defendants separately on June 23 while they were in custody and testified to their statements. . . . According to the officer, Malcolm stated that he sometimes wore a beard but that he did not wear a beard on June 18 (the day of the robbery), having shaved it off on June 2, 1964.[5] He also explained two receipts for traffic fines totaling $35 paid on June 19, which receipts had been found on his person, by saying that he used funds

---

3. There are inferences which may be drawn from the evidence that Janet attempted to alter the appearance of her hair after June 18. Janet denies that she cut, colored or bleached her hair at any time after June 18, and a number of witnesses supported her testimony.

5. Evidence as to defendant's beard and mustache is conflicting. Defense witnesses appeared to support defendant's claims that he had shaved his beard on June 2. There was testimony that on June 19 when defendant appeared in court to pay fines on another matter he was bearded. By June 22 the beard had been removed.

won in a gambling game at a labor hall. Janet, on the other hand, said that the $35 used to pay the fines had come from her earnings.[6]

On July 9, 1964, defendants were again arrested and were booked for the first time. While they were in custody and awaiting the preliminary hearing, Janet requested to talk with Officer Kinsey. There followed a lengthy conversation during the first part of which Malcolm was not present. During this time Janet expressed concern about defendant and inquired as to what the outcome would be if it appeared that she committed the crime and Malcolm knew nothing about it. In general she indicated a wish that defendant be released from any charges because of his prior criminal record and that if someone must be held responsible, she alone would bear the guilt. The officer told her that no assurances could be given, that if she wanted to admit responsibility disposition of the matter would be in the hands of the court and that if she committed the crime and defendant knew nothing about it the only way she could help him would be by telling the truth. Defendant was then brought into the room and participated in the rest of the conversation. The officer asked to hear defendant's version of the matter, saying that he believed defendant was at the scene. However, neither Janet nor defendant confessed or expressly made damaging admissions although constantly urged by the investigating officer to make truthful statements. On several occasions defendant denied that he knew what had gone on in the alley. On the other hand, the whole tone of the conversation evidenced a strong consciousness of guilt on the part of both defendants who appeared to be seeking the most advantageous way out. . . . [S]ome parts of the foregoing conversation were testified to by Officer Kinsey and in addition a tape recording of the entire conversation was introduced in evidence and played to the jury.

At the seven-day trial the prosecution experienced some difficulty in establishing the identities of the perpetrators of the crime. The victim could not identify Janet and had never seen defendant. The identification by the witness Bass, who observed the girl run out of the alley and get into the automobile, was incomplete as to Janet and may have been weakened as to defendant. There was also evidence, introduced by the defense, that Janet had worn light-colored clothing on the day in question, but both the victim and Bass testified that the girl they observed had worn dark clothing.

In an apparent attempt to bolster the identifications, the prosecutor called an instructor of mathematics at a state college. Through this witness he sought to establish that, assuming the robbery was committed by a Caucasian woman with a blond ponytail who left the scene accompanied by a Negro with a beard and mustache, there was an overwhelming probability that the crime was committed by any couple answering such distinctive characteristics. The witness testified, in substance, to the "product rule," which states that the probability of the joint occurrence of a number of *mutually independent* events

---

6.   The source of the $35, being essentially the same amount as the $35 to $40 reported by the victim as having been in her purse when taken from her the day before the fines were paid, was a significant factor in the prosecution's case. Other evidence disclosed that defendant and Janet were married on June 2, 1964, at which time they had only $12, a portion of which was spent on a trip to Tiajuana. Since the marriage defendant had not worked, and Janet's earnings were not more than $12 a week, if that much.

is equal to the product of the individual probabilities that each of the events will occur.[8] *Without presenting any statistical evidence whatsoever in support of the probabilities for the factors selected,* the prosecutor then proceeded to have the witness *assume* probability factors for the various characteristics which he deemed to be shared by the guilty couple and all other couples answering to such distinctive characteristics.[10]

Applying the product rule to his own factors the prosecutor arrived at a probability that there was but one chance in 12 million that any couple possessed the distinctive characteristic of the defendants. Accordingly, under this theory, it was to be inferred that there could be but one chance in 12 million that defendants were innocent and that another equally distinctive couple actually committed the robbery. Expanding on what he had thus purported to suggest as a hypothesis, the prosecutor offered the completely unfounded and improper testimonial assertion that, in his opinion, the factors he had assigned were "conservative estimates" and that, in reality "the chances of anyone else besides these defendants being there, . . . having every similarity, . . . is somewhat like one in a billion."

Objections were timely made to the mathematician's testimony on the grounds that it was immaterial, that it invaded the province of the jury, and that it was based on unfounded assumptions. The objections were "temporarily overruled" and the evidence admitted subject to a motion to strike. When that motion was made at the conclusion of the direct examination, the court denied it, stating that the testimony had been received only for the "purpose of illustrating the mathematical probabilities of various matters, the possibilities for them occurring or re-occurring."

Both defendants took the stand in their own behalf. They denied any

---

8.   In the example employed for illustrative purposes at the trial, the probability of rolling one die and coming up with a "2" is 1/6, that is, any one of the six faces of a die has one chance in six of landing face up on any particular roll. The probability of rolling two "2's" in succession is 1/6 × 1/6, or 1/36, that is, on only one occasion out of 36 double rolls (or the roll of two dice), will the selected number land face up on each roll or die.

10.   Although the prosecutor insisted that the factors he used were only for illustrative purposes—to demonstrate how the probability of the occurrence of mutually independent factors affected the probability that they would occur together—he nevertheless attempted to use factors which he personally related to the distinctive characteristics of defendants. In his argument to the jury he invited the jurors to apply their own factors, and asked defense counsel to suggest what the latter would deem as reasonable. The prosecutor himself proposed the individual probabilities set out in the table below. Although the transcript of the examination of the mathematics instructor and the information volunteered by the prosecutor at that time create some uncertainty as to precisely which of the characteristics the prosecutor assigned to the individual probabilities, he restated in his argument to the jury that they should be as follows:

Characteristic	Individual probability
A. Partly yellow automobile	1/10
B. Man with mustache	1/4
C. Girl with ponytail	1/10
D. Girl with blond hair	1/3
E. Negro man with beard	1/10
F. Interracial couple in car	1/1000

In his brief on appeal defendant agrees that the foregoing appeared on a table presented in the trial court.

knowledge of or participation in the crime and stated that after Malcolm called for Janet at her employer's house they went directly to a friend's house in Los Angeles where they remained for some time. According to this testimony defendants were not near the scene of the robbery when it occurred. Defendant's friends testified to a visit by them "in the middle of June" although she could not recall the precise date. Janet further testified that certain inducements were held out to her during the July 9 interrogation on condition that she confess her participation.

Defendant makes two basic contentions before us: First, that the admission in evidence of the statements made by defendants while in custody on June 23 and July 9, 1964, constitutes reversible error. . . and second, that the introduction of evidence pertaining to the mathematical theory of probability and the use of the same by the prosecution during the trial was error prejudicial to defendant. We consider the latter claim first.

As we shall explain, the prosecution's introduction and use of mathematical probability statistics injected two fundamental prejudicial errors into the case: (1) The testimony itself lacked an adequate foundation both in evidence and in statistical theory; and (2) the testimony and the manner in which the prosecution used it distracted the jury from its proper and requisite function of weighing the evidence on the issue of guilt, encouraged the jurors to rely upon an engaging but logically irrelevant expert demonstration, foreclosed the possibility of an effective defense by an attorney apparently unschooled in mathematical refinements, and placed the jurors and defense counsel at a disadvantage in sifting relevant fact from inapplicable theory.

We initially consider the defects in the testimony itself. As we have indicated, the specific technique presented through the mathematician's testimony and advanced by the prosecutor to measure the probabilities in question suffered from two basic and pervasive defects—an inadequate evidentiary foundation and an inadequate proof of statistical independence. First, as to the foundation requirement, we find the record devoid of any evidence relating to any of the six individual probability factors used by the prosecutor and ascribed by him to the six characteristics as we have set them out in footnote 10, ante. To put it another way, the prosecution produced no evidence whatsoever showing, or from which it could be in any way inferred, that only one out of every ten cars which might have been at the scene of the robbery was partly yellow, that only one out of every four men who might have been there wore a mustache, that only one out of every ten girls who might have been there wore a ponytail, or that any of the other individual probability factors listed were even roughly accurate.[12]

The bare, inescapable fact is that the prosecution made no attempt to offer any such evidence. Instead, through leading questions having perfuncto-

---

12. We seriously doubt that such evidence could ever be compiled since no statistician could possibly determine after the fact which cars, or which individuals, "might" have been present at the scene of the robbery; certainly there is no reason to suppose that the human and automotive populations of San Pedro, California, include all potential culprits—or, conversely, that all members of these populations are proper candidates for inclusion. Thus the sample from which the relevant probabilities would have to be derived is itself undeterminable. (See generally Yamane, Statistics, An Introductory Analysis (1964), ch. I.)

rily elicited from the witness the response that the latter could not assign a probability factor for the characteristics involved,[13] the prosecutor himself suggested what the various probabilities should be and these became the basis of the witness' testimony (see fn. 10, ante). It is a curious circumstance of this adventure in proof that the prosecutor not only made his own assertions of these factors in the hope that they were "conservative" but also in later argument to the jury invited the jurors to substitute their "estimates" should they wish to do so. We can hardly conceive of a more fatal gap in the prosecution's scheme of proof. A foundation for the admissibility of the witness' testimony was never even attempted to be laid, let alone established. His testimony was neither made to rest on his own testimonial knowledge nor presented by proper hypothetical questions based upon valid data in the record. . . .

But, as we have indicated, there was another glaring defect in the prosecution's technique, namely an inadequate proof of the statistical independence of the six factors. No proof was presented that the characteristics selected were mutually independent, even though the witness himself acknowledged that such condition was essential to the proper application of the "product rule" or "multiplication rule." To the extent that the traits or characteristics were not mutually independent (e.g., Negroes with beards and men with mustaches obviously represent overlapping categories[15]), the "product rule" would inevitably yield a wholly erroneous and exaggerated result even if all of the individual components had been determined with precision.

In the instant case, therefore, because of the aforementioned two defects—the inadequate evidentiary foundation and the inadequate proof of statistical independence—the technique employed by the prosecutor could only lead to wild conjecture without demonstrated relevancy to the issues presented. It acquired no redeeming quality from the prosecutor's statement that it was being used only "for illustrative purposes" since, as we shall point out, the prosecutor's subsequent utilization of the mathematical testimony was not confined within such limits.

We now turn to the second fundamental error caused by the probability testimony. Quite apart from our foregoing objections to the specific technique employed by the prosecution to estimate the probability in question, we think that the entire enterprise upon which the prosecution embarked, and which

---

13. The prosecutor asked the mathematics instructor:

Now, let me see if you can be of some help to us with some independent factors, and you have some paper you may use. Your specialty does not equip you, I suppose, to give us some probability of such things as a yellow car as contrasted with any other kind of car, does it?. . . I appreciate the fact that you can't assign a probability for a car being yellow as contrasted to some other car, can you?

A. No, I couldn't.

15. Assuming arguendo that factors B and E (see fn. 10, ante) were correctly estimated, nevertheless it is still arguable that most Negro men with beards also have mustaches (exhibit 3 herein, for instance, shows defendant with both a mustache and a beard, indeed in a hirsute continuum); if so, there is no basis for multiplying 1/4 by 1/10 to estimate the proportion of Negroes who wear beards and mustaches. Again, the prosecution's technique could never be meaningfully applied, since its accurate use would call for information as to the degree of interdependence among the six individual factors. Such information cannot be compiled, however, since the relevant samples necessarily remain unknown. (See fn. 10, ante.)

was directed to the objective of measuring the likelihood of a random couple possessing the characteristics allegedly distinguishing the robbers, was gravely misguided. At best, it might yield an estimate as to how infrequently bearded Negroes drive yellow cars in the company of blonde females with ponytails.

The prosecution's approach, however, could furnish the jury with absolutely no guidance on the crucial issue: *Of the admittedly few such couples, which one, if any, was guilty of committing this robbery?* Probability theory necessarily remains silent on that question, since no mathematical equation can prove beyond a reasonable doubt (1) that the guilty couple in fact possessed the characteristics described by the People's witnesses, or even (2) that only one couple possessing those distinctive characteristics could be found in the entire Los Angeles area.

As to the first inherent failing we observe that the prosecution's theory of probability rested on the assumption that the witnesses called by the People had conclusively established that the guilty couple possessed the precise characteristics relied upon by the prosecution. But no mathematical formula could ever establish beyond a reasonable doubt that the prosecution's witnesses correctly observed and accurately described the distinctive features which were employed to link defendants to the crime. Conceivably, for example, the guilty couple might have included a light-skinned Negress with bleached hair rather than a Caucasian blonde; or the driver of the car might have been wearing a false beard as a disguise; or the prosecution's witnesses might simply have been unreliable.[16]

The foregoing risks of error permeate the prosecution's circumstantial case. Traditionally, the jury weighs such risks in evaluating the credibility and probative value of trial testimony, but the likelihood of human error or of falsification obviously cannot be quantified; that likelihood must therefore be excluded from any effort to assign a *number* to the probability of guilt or innocence. Confronted with an equation which purports to yield a numerical index of probable guilt, few juries could resist the temptation to accord disproportionate weight to that index; only an exceptional juror, and indeed only a defense attorney schooled in mathematics, could successfully keep in mind the fact that the probability computed by the prosecution can represent, at best, the likelihood that a random couple would share the characteristics testified to by the People's witnesses—*not necessarily the characteristics of the actually guilty couple.*

As to the second inherent failing in the prosecution's approach, even assuming that the first failing could be discounted, the most a mathematical computation could ever yield would be a measure of the probability that a random couple would possess the distinctive features in question. In the present case, for example, the prosecution attempted to compute the probability that a random couple would include a bearded Negro, a blonde girl with a ponytail, and a partly yellow car; the prosecution urged that this probability was no more

16. In the instant case, for instance, the victim could not state whether the girl had a ponytail, although the victim observed the girl as she ran away. The witness Bass, on the other hand, was sure that the girl whom he saw had a ponytail. The demonstration engaged in by the prosecutor also leaves no room for the possibility, although perhaps a small one, that the girl whom the victim and the witness observed was [not], in fact, the same girl.

than one in 12 million. Even accepting this conclusion as arithmetically accurate, however, one still could not conclude that the Collinses were probably the guilty couple. On the contrary, as we explain in the Appendix, the prosecution's figures actually imply a likelihood of over 40 percent that the Collinses could be "duplicated" by at least *one other couple who might equally have committed the San Pedro robbery.* Urging that the Collinses be convicted on the basis of evidence which logically establishes no more than this seems as indefensible as arguing for the conviction of X on the ground that a witness saw either X or X's twin commit the crime.

Again, few defense attorneys, and certainly few jurors, could be expected to comprehend this basic flaw in the prosecution's analysis. Conceivably even the prosecutor erroneously believed that his equation established a high probability that no other bearded Negro in the Los Angeles area drove a yellow car accompanied by a ponytailed blonde. In any event, although his technique could demonstrate no such thing, he solemnly told the jury that he had supplied mathematical proof of guilt.

Sensing the novelty of that notion, the prosecutor told the jurors that the traditional idea of proof beyond a reasonable doubt represented "the most hackneyed, stereotyped, trite, misunderstood concept in criminal law." He sought to reconcile the jury to the risk that, under his "new math" approach to criminal jurisprudence, "on some rare occasion. . . an innocent person may be convicted." "Without taking that risk," the prosecution continued, "life would be intolerable. . . because. . . there would be immunity for the Collinses, for people who chose not to be employed to go down and push old ladies down and take their money and be immune because how could we ever be sure they are the ones who did it?"

In essence this argument of the prosecutor was calculated to persuade the jury to convict defendants whether or not they were convinced of their guilt to a moral certainty and beyond a reasonable doubt. Undoubtedly the jurors were unduly impressed by the mystique of the mathematical demonstration but were unable to assess its relevancy or value. Although we make no appraisal of the proper applications of mathematical techniques in the proof of facts, we have strong feelings that such applications, particularly in a criminal case, must be critically examined in view of the substantial unfairness to a defendant which may result from ill conceived techniques with which the trier of fact is not technically equipped to cope. We feel that the technique employed in the case before us falls into the latter category.

We conclude that the court erred in admitting over defendant's objection the evidence pertaining to the mathematical theory of probability and in denying defendant's motion to strike such evidence. The case was apparently a close one. The jury began its deliberations at 2:46 P.M. on November 24, 1964, and retired for the night at 7:46 P.M.; the parties stipulated that a juror could be excused for illness and that a verdict could be reached by the remaining 11 jurors; the jury resumed deliberations the next morning at 8:40 A.M. and returned verdicts at 11:58 A.M. after five ballots had been taken. In the light of the closeness of the case, which as we have said was a circumstantial one, there is a reasonable likelihood that the result would have been more favorable to defendant if the prosecution had not urged the jury to render a probabilistic verdict. In any event, we think that under the circumstances the "trial by mathematics" so distorted the role of the jury and so disadvantaged counsel for the defense, as to constitute in itself a miscarriage of justice. After an examination of the entire cause, including the evidence, we are of the opinion that it is reasonably probable that a result more favorable to defendant would have been reached in the absence of the above error. The judgment against defendant must therefore be reversed.

In view of the foregoing conclusion, we deem it unnecessary to consider whether the admission of defendants' extrajudicial statements constitutes error. . . .

The judgment is reversed.

APPENDIX

If "Pr" represents the probability that a certain distinctive combination of characteristics, hereinafter designated "C," will occur jointly in a random couple, then the probability that C will *not* occur in a random couple is $(1 - Pr)$. Applying the product rule (see fn. 8, ante), the probability that C will occur in *none* of N couples chosen at random is $(1 - Pr)^N$, so that the probability of C occurring in *at least one* of N random couples is $[1 - (1 - Pr)^N]$.

Given a particular couple selected from a random set of N, the probability of C occurring in that couple (i.e., Pr), multiplied by the probability of C occurring in none of the remaining $N - 1$ couples (i.e., $(1 - Pr)^{N-1}$), yields the probability that C will occur in the selected couple and in no other. Thus the probability of C occurring in any particular couple, and in that couple alone, is $[(Pr) \times (1 - Pr)^{N-1}]$. Since this is true for each of the N couples, the probability that C will occur in precisely *one* of the N couples, without regard to which one, is $[(Pr) \times (1 - Pr)^{N-1}]$ added N times, because the probability of the occurrence of one of several *mutually exclusive* events is equal to the *sum* of the individual probabilities. Thus the probability of C occurring in *exactly one* of N random couples (*any* one, but *only* one) is $[(N) \times (Pr) (1 - Pr)^{N-1}]$.

By subtracting the probability that C will occur in *exactly one* couple from the probability that C will occur in *at least one* couple, one obtains the probability that C will occur in *more than one* couple: $[1 - (1 - Pr)^N] - [(N) \times (Pr) \times (1 - Pr)^{N-1}]$. Dividing this difference by the probability that C will occur in at least one couple (i.e., dividing the difference by $[1 - (1 - Pr)^N]$) then yields *the probability that* C *will occur more than once in a group of* N *couples in which* C *occurs at least once.*

Turning to the case in which C represents the characteristics which distinguish a bearded Negro accompanied by a ponytailed blonde in a yellow car, the prosecution sought to establish that the probability of C occurring in a random couple was $1/12,000,000$—i.e., that $Pr = 1/12,000,000$. Treating this conclusion as accurate, it follows that, in a population of N random couples, the probability of C occurring *exactly once* is $[(N) \times (1/12,000,000) \times (1 - 1/12,000,000)^{N-1}]$. Subtracting this product from $(1 - [1 - 1/12,000,000]^N)$, the probability of C occurring in *at least one couple*, and dividing the resulting difference by $[1 - (1 - 1/12,000,000)^N]$, the probability that C will occur in at least one couple, yields the probability that C will occur more than once in a group of N random couples of which at least one couple (namely, the one seen by the witnesses) possesses characteristics C. In other words, the probability of *another* such couple in a population of N is the quotient A/B, where A designates the numerator $[1 - (1 - 1/12,000,000)^N] - [(N) \times 1/12,000,000) \times (1 - 1/12,000,000)^{N-1}]$, and B designates the denominator $[1 - (1 - 1/12,000,000)^N]$.

N, which represents the total number of all couples who might conceivably have been at the scene of the San Pedro robbery, is not determinable, a fact which suggests yet another basic difficulty with the use of probability theory in establishing identity. One of the imponderables in determining N may well be the number of N-type couples in which a single person may participate. Such considerations make it evident that N, in the area adjoining the robbery, is in excess of several million; as N assumes values of such magnitude, the quotient A/B computed as above, representing the probability of a second couple as distinctive as the one described by the prosecution's witnesses, soon exceeds $4/10$. Indeed, as N approaches 12 million, this probability quotient rises to approximately 41 percent. We note parenthetically that if $1/N = Pr$, then as N increases indefinitely, the quotient in question approaches a limit of $(e - 2)/(e - 1)$, where "e" represents the transcendental number (approximately 2.71828) familiar in mathematics and physics.

Hence, even if we should accept the prosecution's figures without question, we would derive a probability of over 40 percent that the couple observed by the witnesses could be "duplicated" by at least one other equally distinctive interracial couple in the area, including a Negro with a beard and mustache, driving a partly yellow car in the company of a blonde with a ponytail. Thus the prosecution's computations, far from establishing beyond a reasonable doubt that the Collinses were the couple described by the prosecution's witnesses, imply a very substantial likelihood that the area contained more than one such couple, and that a couple other than the Collinses was the one observed at the scene of the robbery.

TRAYNOR, C.J., and PETERS, TOBRINER, MOSK, and BURKE, J.J., concur.

MCCOMB, J.

I dissent. I would affirm the judgment in its entirety.

| NOTES ON *COLLINS*

1.   The Court in *Collins* makes important technical criticisms of the prosecutor's mathematical theory and its application. The court also raises policy-based objections that seem to apply even if these technical problems could be overcome. What are these objections?

2.   For a moment, forget the policy-based objections. Assume the identical case of *Collins-2* arises, but now the prosecutor has proof of the relative frequency of the qualities of the guilty couple and shows they are independent. He makes the same statistical argument. In *Collins*, doesn't the court tell us that the argument would still be mathematically misconceived? Why is that so? In thinking about this question, consider a parlor trick. The wizard puts three complete decks of cards in a hopper and mixes them. Blindfolded, he draws a card,

which turns out to be the Queen of Hearts. He replaces it and mixes the cards again, and (blindfolded) draws a second card. Lo, it too is the Queen of Hearts. His patter runs as follows:

> The 156 cards in the hopper make three complete decks, so the proportion of hearts and queens is the same that we find in a single deck. The probability of drawing a heart is one in four because a quarter of the cards in each deck are hearts. And the probability of drawing a queen is one in 13 because each suit has 13 cards, only one of which is a queen.
>
> Knowing we drew a heart tells us nothing about the likelihood that we drew a queen. The reason is that even among hearts we still have only one chance in 13 of getting the queen. And conversely, knowing we drew a queen tells us nothing about the likelihood that we drew a heart. The reason is that even among queens we have only one chance in four of getting a heart. In short, being a heart and being a queen are independent qualities.
>
> So what's the probability that we will draw a Queen of Hearts? Easy: It may be calculated by the product rule, and it comes to 1/52, which is 1/4 times 1/13.
>
> Now, you just saw me draw the Queen of Hearts twice in a row. That astonishing feat was not accidental, and only the wizard can do it. There's only one chance in 52 of drawing such a card, so there's only one chance in 52 that the Queen of Hearts I picked on the second draw is a *different card* from the one I picked on the first draw. Imagine getting the same card twice. Try it if you think it's easy.

Isn't this patter similar to the prosecutor's argument in *Collins?* Admittedly it was a coincidence (perhaps magic) that the wizard drew a Queen of Hearts twice in a row. But the likelihood that he drew a different Queen of Hearts the second time is 2/3, isn't it? (Given three decks and replacement of the first draw, there were three Queens of Hearts in the hopper each time.) So when he said the likelihood is only 1/52 that the second card was different, he was exaggerating, if not just plain wrong.

When the wizard got 1/52 with the product rule, what does it describe? Doesn't it describe the same kind of thing that 1/12,000,000 describes in *Collins?* And just as 1/52 in the parlor trick does *not* accurately describe the likelihood that the wizard drew a different card the second time, so 1/12,000,000 in *Collins* does not accurately describe the likelihood that defendants are different from the culprits.

3.   The Appendix in *Collins* addresses the problem of distribution. Even if a particular outcome is likely to occur half the time (or half the people are likely to have brown eyes), it does not follow that this predicted frequency will be seen in a particular series of events or a particular sample. There may be a probability that half the coin tosses produce heads, but in any series of ten tosses we might get heads four times or even ten times, or not at all. Similarly in *Collins,* if the estimates are taken as describing the frequency of the observed characteristics in the known universe, they do not necessarily describe the frequency of those characteristics in Los Angeles. In one population of 12 million couples, we might find two or three matching the description of the culprits; in another, we might find none. The Appendix calculates the likelihood of finding more than one such "magic couple," given that we know one exists in a population of 12 million couples. If the calculations are right in *Collins,*

how do they affect the prosecutor's argument? If we had evidence of the frequency of the important characteristics *in Los Angeles itself*, would the Appendix still make an important point?

4.   You might think nobody would be foolish enough to make the mistake that the prosecutor made in *Collins*, but even now such mistakes are sometimes made. See, e.g., Wilson v. State, 803 A.2d 1034, 1047 (Ct. App. Md. 2002) (reversing conviction of father for murder of infant son where prosecutor argued, on basis of statistical evidence of rarity of SIDS deaths, that the chance was only "1 in 10 million that the man sitting here is innocent"). In two settings, the product rule has smoother sailing. One involves the use of DNA evidence, where prosecutors routinely show that the genetic profile of the defendant, as measured by analyzing samples of blood or other fluid or tissue taken from him, matches the genetic profile of the apparent culprit, as measured by analyzing samples found at the crime scene. Here prosecutors routinely offer proof of the probability that these characteristics would be found in the population as a whole. See, e.g., State v. Belken, 633 N.W.2d 786, 790, 799-801 (Iowa 2001) (in trial for kidnapping and sexual abuse, admitting evidence that defendant's DNA matched that found at crime scene, and that there was "a random match probability of 1 in 431 billion"). As in the *Collins* case, such probabilities describe scarcity, and do *not* describe the probability that defendant is guilty, or even the probability that he left the sample found at the crime scene. The other setting in which statistical evidence is routinely accepted is paternity cases, where a "match" between the profile of the paternal gene in the child and the genes of the defendant generates a similar statistic: "Only one in ten million men chosen at random would have this genetic profile." In this setting, courts *also* admit expert testimony describing the "probability of paternity," in which essentially an expert testifies as follows: "Based on these probabilities, we can say that there is a 97 percent probability that defendant is the father." See, e.g., Child Support Enforcement Agency v. Doe, 51 P.3d 366 (Hawai'i 2002) (99.96 percent probability of paternity). We revisit these issues in Chapter 9D, infra.

5.   On the problem of *Collins;* see McCord, A Primer for the Nonmathematically Inclined on Mathematical Evidence in Criminal Cases: *People v. Collins and Beyond*, 47 Wash. & Lee L. Rev. 741 (1990).

PROBLEM 2-I.   *The Exploding Tire*

Herb Lewis installs tires and batteries for the Auto Service Center operated by Nationwide Mercantile. One day he begins to mount four snow tires on a car. He finishes three and places the fourth on the wheel rim. Inflating it, he watches the bead rise along the inner edges of the rim, waiting for the "pop" when it would jump and firmly seat itself in the lip of the rim. This time the bead strikes the lip and the tire explodes, sending Herb to the emergency room with serious injuries. Len Small, manager of the Service Center, gathered up the burst tire and sent it to be tested by Failsafe Automotive Laboratory.

Herb sues Grather Tire Company, alleging that it made the tire and it was defective. During his case-in-chief, Herb seeks to establish (1) through testimony by Len Small that Grather made the exploding tire, and (2) through testimony by Michael Treaver (who tested the tire Failsafe got from Small) that the tire was defective. Unfortunately, Small did not note the markings on the tire, and Treaver failed to record them in his report, so nobody knows who made the exploding tire.

Herb seeks to elicit from Small that Grather made 80 percent of the tires at the Service Center, and that four other manufacturers account for the remaining 20 percent in about equal proportion. Grather objects, arguing that the court should not permit "gambling odds" testimony and that "mere numbers" cannot support a verdict.

Should Small and Treaver be allowed to testify? If there is no other proof that Grather made the tire that injured Herb, should such testimony suffice to take the issue to the jury?

NOTES ON PROBABILISTIC PROOF IN CIVIL CASES

1. In civil litigation ordinarily the burden of persuasion is framed in terms of a "preponderance" of the evidence. When it comes time to instruct the jury, the most natural explanation involves saying that the party bearing the burden must establish that the matters in question are "more likely so than not so." See generally Kevin F. O'Malley, Jay E. Grenig & Hon. William C. Lee, Federal Jury Practice and Instructions §104.01 (5th ed. 2000) (preponderance instruction using that phrase). Of course "more likely so than not so" stops short of quantifying the necessary probability. Arguably it means the evidence "preponderates" even if it *just barely* favors the party bearing the burden—a layperson might express that notion as a 51 percent likelihood (or "odds" of 51:49). If this likelihood satisfies the preponderance standard, should a plaintiff like Herb Lewis be permitted to take his case to the jury? If the answer is yes, are we on a slippery slope that leads to the conclusion that plaintiff should also get his case to the jury on proof that defendant made 51 out of 100 tires in the shop?

2. Recall the famous case of the two careless hunters who both negligently fired guns. Sympathizing with the plaintiff because he could not show which one fired the shot that hurt him, the California court put the burden on each defendant to prove he did not cause the injury. See Summers v. Tice, 199 P.2d 1 (Cal. 1948). Recall too that the idea behind *Summers* came to life in theories of market-share liability and enterprise liability in cases like Sindell v. Abbott Laboratories, 607 P.2d 924 (Cal.) (market share; antimiscarriage drug DES), cert. denied, 449 U.S. 912 (1980), and Hall v. E.I. Du Pont De Nemours & Co., 345 F. Supp. 353 (E.D.N.Y. 1972) (enterprise; blasting caps). Under *Sindell's* market-share liability theory, a plaintiff who sues makers of identical products may get a judgment against them all, with each to pay the percentage corresponding to its market share. Later the California court cleared up an ambiguity in *Sindell* by holding that recovery is limited to the proportion of total damages corresponding to the combined market share of the defendants sued. Brown v. Superior Court, 751 P.2d 923 (Cal. 1988). Under *Hall's* enterprise liability theory, a plaintiff who sues all or most makers of essentially identical dangerous products may hold each liable on a theory of joint liability, and may win a judgment for the full amount of damages. Are there good reasons to adopt

substantive theories of market-share or enterprise liability in cases like *Sindell* and *Hall* (with the result that plaintiffs can recover) but not in cases like The Exploding Tire? That question seems more substantive than evidential, doesn't it? If The Exploding Tire *is* different from cases like *Sindell* and *Hall,* does it make sense to adhere to an evidential standard that rejects "naked numerical proof"?

3. Consider the following arguments against allowing the party bearing the burden of persuasion to prevail on the basis of "numbers alone." Doing so would be bad because it would

(a) Lead to the unjust result that each of 100 similar plaintiffs win, even though the evidence means that defendant should be liable to only 80;

(b) Permit recovery on proof inherently inferior to particularized evidence, which at least tends "directly" to establish critical points;

(c) Misinterpret reality, because particularized proof usually exists and failing to offer it suggests not so much that it isn't there, but that it is unfavorable to the party relying on numerical probabilities;

(d) Create an undesirable counterincentive, discouraging active pursuit of particularized proof;

(e) Either (1) leave nothing for the jury to decide in the exercise of reason, so that it would have to be directed to find in accordance with the numbers (thus significantly and undesirably reducing its role), or (2) render the jury's work transparent, thus subjecting particular juries and the institution of jury trial to criticism, since observers will see that juries decide cases "by" or "against" the "odds";

(f) Undesirably quantify the margin for error tolerated in the system, revealing that a civil claimant may recover nothing even when the probability is as high as .49 that he should have won;

(g) Lessen public respect for and acceptance of courts by showing that they "gamble" on serious matters.

Do any of these arguments justify excluding probabilistic evidence or establishing a rule that such proof does not suffice to establish a point? See generally Nesson, The Evidence or the Event? On Judicial Proof and the Acceptability of Verdicts, 98 Harv. L. Rev. 1357, 1389 (1985); Tribe, Trial by Mathematics: Precision and Ritual in the Legal Process, 84 Harv. L. Rev. 489 (1970); L. Cohen, The Probable and the Provable (1977); Kaye, The Paradox of the Gatecrasher and Other Stories, 1979 Ariz. St. L.J. 101.

4. Consider the problem of "conjunction." Lewis must prove (a) that Grather made the tire and (b) that it was defective. He can prevail only by establishing the conjunction of both elements. Assume this time that the proof is *not* "nakedly" quantified, but the evidence suggests that each element is "probably" established: Small remembers that the exploded tire was made by Grather, but his credibility is impaired by cross-examination; Treaver gives a hedged opinion that the tire was defective. If we were to quantify the evidence ourselves, we might conclude there is an 80 percent likelihood that Grather made the tire Small sent to Failsafe and a 60 percent likelihood that it was

defective. A jury might do the same thing, assigning rough numeric values to the proof. Who should win, Lewis or Grather? If, as seems true here, the two probabilities are independent, doesn't the product rule tell us the "conjoint" likelihood of the two facts crucial to Lewis is only 48 percent? One astute commentator argues that juries do not "assess the conjunction of the elements of a case," and instead (quite properly) determine each element separately. Trials, it is argued, generate a kind of history:

> Any narrative history recounts the occurrence of many events. If we asked what the conjunctive probability of the narrative's independent elements is and dismissed the narrative when this probability was low, then we would have no history. We would constantly face a paradox. We could accept the truth of each event comprising the narrative but could not accept the narrative itself. We could believe every element that the historian recounted, but we could not believe the history as a whole.

Nesson, The Evidence or the Event? On Judicial Proof and the Acceptability of Verdicts, 98 Harv. L. Rev. 1357, 1389 (1985). Some have criticized the Nesson view. See Allen, Rationality, Mythology, and the "Acceptability of Verdicts" Thesis, 66 B.U. L. Rev. 541 (1986); Cohen, The Costs of Acceptability: Blue Buses, Agent Orange, and Aversion to Statistical Evidence, 66 B.U. L. Rev. 563 (1986).

5.   Recall that the problem of conjunction also affects different items of proof directed at single elements in a case (item 5 in Notes on Conditional Relevancy, supra). Why should the factfinder "conjoin" separate items of proof relating to a single element in a case (thus diminishing aggregate likelihood) but *not* the proofs of separate elements?

Three | HEARSAY

A. WHAT IS HEARSAY?

1. Underlying Theory: Risks and Safeguards

A simple definition. To put it about as simply as it can be put, hearsay is an out- *one*
of-court statement offered to prove the matter asserted—or as lawyers usually *liner*
say, "offered to prove the truth of the matter asserted." ✗

Assume that plaintiff Abby wants to prove that the blue car ran a red light, and that she calls Faraway to testify that he heard (but did not see) the accident and heard Bystander (who did see the accident) say shortly thereafter, "the blue car ran a red light." Here Bystander's statement is being offered (through Faraway's testimony) to prove what it asserts—that the blue car ran a red light—and it is hearsay.

The result would be the same if the party calls Faraway in order to lay the foundation for a letter he received from Bystander, in which Bystander wrote that "the blue car ran the red light." When the letter is offered in evidence, it too amounts to an out-of-court statement of Bystander. It too is offered to prove what it asserts, and it too is hearsay. (Nor would things be different if Faraway testified to what he read in the letter from Bystander, for again Bystander's out-of-court statement is offered to prove what it asserts. As you will see, there is an additional barrier to Faraway's testimonial account of what was in the letter, for the Best Evidence doctrine would require the party seeking to show what the letter says to offer the letter itself, or an excuse for not producing it. See Chapter 14.)

Assume now that Bystander is called as a witness, and that a party to the suit seeks to establish that the blue car ran a red light. If Bystander were asked on the witness stand whether the blue car had the light in its favor, he might well answer by testifying, "no, the blue car ran the red light." Now there would be no hearsay objection, for Bystander is saying in court what he knows and remembers.[1]

---

1. The hearsay objection might reappear, however, if for some reason Bystander answered the question by testifying, "I told Faraway that the blue car ran the red light." The problem is that once again Bystander's out-of-court statement is being offered in proof of what it asserts,

The simple one-liner suggested above gets to the heart of the matter, and everyone would agree that Faraway's testimonial account of Bystander's statement in the example is hearsay. If you look for a moment at FRE 801(a) through (c), you will see that our one-liner agrees substantially with the more elaborate formal definition adopted by the Federal Rules. But the hearsay doctrine draws a line through a vast domain of human expression, and charts a course across a boundless sea of evidential uses of human behavior, so we must take the one-liner for what it is and not expect too much. It is "right," but like the definition of justice offered by Glaucon in the early going of Plato's Republic ("giving every man his due") it leaves much unsaid and is capable of mischief. (We will look further at the definition contained in FRE 801 in section C, infra, and we will explore continuing challenges in applying the doctrine in marginal cases in section D, infra.)

Note that our focus for now is on recognizing hearsay, not on deciding whether it is admissible. Much that is hearsay is still admissible, and much that is not hearsay is not admissible anyway. Yet it is necessary to be able to recognize hearsay because of the general principle, central to Anglo-American evidence law, that hearsay evidence is inadmissible unless it falls within one of many exceptions. Rule 802 states that general principle and hints at the exceptions. But for the time being our *only* concern is to get straight what hearsay is.

Reasons to exclude hearsay. Why do we so often exclude hearsay? Three reasons are usually given:

First and most important is the absence of cross-examination. Out-of-court statements are not subject to this truth-testing technique, at least when uttered, and in our example Bystander was not cross-examinable when he spoke. (Never mind for the moment the question whether *deferred* cross-examination might be just as good—in other words, whether it would do to admit his statement in evidence if Bystander takes the stand and testifies at some point during the trial, and is then subject to cross-examination concerning his prior statement.) It is true that when Faraway testifies to what Bystander said, *Faraway* is subject to cross-examination, which is to say that *his in-court testimonial account* of what Bystander said can be probed by cross-questioning, and this fact is valuable in itself. (Can you see why?) But it is Bystander on whom we rely when we take his statement as evidence of what happened at the intersection.

Second is the absence of demeanor evidence. The out-of-court declarant (Bystander in our example) is not under the gaze of the trier of fact, at least at the time he speaks, so the trier lacks those impressions and clues which voice, inflection, expression, and appearance convey. (Again, put aside for the moment the question whether *deferred* demeanor evidence might be an adequate substitute, if Bystander testifies during the proceedings, so that his demeanor may be observed by the trier of fact when he is asked about his earlier statement.) Again it is true that Faraway's demeanor is observable by the trier and that this fact is helpful (why?). But again we are relying on Bystander when we come to consider his statement as evidence.

---

even though *now* that statement is proved by Bystander's own testimony. Therefore, under our one-line definition Bystander's answer is hearsay. (The cure for the problem is to direct Bystander "to tell us what happened, and not what you told someone else," a directive that might make little sense to him but that he will likely understand well enough to comply with.)

Third is absence of the oath. Usually the out-of-court declarant was not under oath at the time he spoke (as of course Bystander was not, in our example), so the trier of fact has no indication that he felt any sense of moral or legal obligation to speak the truth.[2] (Once again let us put off the question whether a *deferred* oath might suffice—whether it would be good enough to call Bystander as a witness and question him under oath at trial about his prior statement.) Of course Faraway is under oath, which helps to some extent in our example (why?), but still it is Bystander on whom we rely when we consider his statement.

These three reasons for the hearsay doctrine express a clear preference for live testimony over out-of-court statements. They also describe three major safeguards in the trial process: Testifying witnesses all swear (or affirm) under penalty of perjury that they will tell the truth, their demeanor is on display for the trier of fact to observe, *and* they are subject to immediate cross-examination. Why should these safeguards matter? Remember that the hearsay issue disappears from our example when Bystander takes the stand and testifies that "the blue car ran a red light." A testimonial account is obviously subject to the same human frailties as a substantially identical out-of-court statement. So why prefer the testimonial account?

The hearsay risks. The answer usually given is fourfold, which is to say that there are four "hearsay risks" associated with out-of-court statements that are substantially reduced (though certainly not removed entirely) by the safeguards of the trial process:

First is the risk of misperception. Maybe the car Bystander saw was not blue but silver; maybe what he thought to be a red light was glare from the sun; maybe the light changed after the blue car entered the intersection. The risk is not only a function of sensory capacity (such as acuity of vision) but of physical circumstance (such as distance and alignment of the sun) and of mental capacity and psychological condition. Even a well-situated witness with excellent vision can misinterpret or misunderstand what he sees, for lack of mental sharpness or because he is thinking of something else or is amused or expectant or angry or worried—in short, distracted or preoccupied.

Second is the risk of faulty memory. It is true that if Bystander related what he saw only moments after the event, his observation is not likely to suffer in accuracy on account of failed or faulty memory. Indeed, memory problems would likely increase with the time lapse between his original observation and his court appearance. But even a statement that follows close on the heels of an observed event might be affected by something like a memory problem: If Bystander glanced at the traffic light moments before the incident, then directed his attention elsewhere, and only *then* saw the blue car enter the intersection, his subsequent remark might reflect a conflation of his memories of the earlier condition of the light and later path of the car. As to this risk, cross-examination may be very useful in establishing, eliminating, or reducing uncertainties.

---

2. Of course he would have been sworn if his statement was in the form of an affidavit, executed with the cooperation of a notary public. But affidavits as such do not fit within any hearsay exception. To be sure, they have limited evidential use in connection with motions for summary judgment and applications for warrants. And it is true that various kinds of certificates, which are like affidavits in being sworn out-of-court statements, have important evidential use in authenticating other documents. See FRE 902(1) through (3) and (8). But the hearsay doctrine makes affidavits generally inadmissible as proof of what they assert.

Third is the risk of misstatement, perhaps most often called the risk of "ambiguity" or "faulty narration." In saying that the car "ran the red light," perhaps Bystander meant to say that the light changed to red before the car made it across the intersection; he said "blue" but might have meant to describe the car as "silver"; maybe what he really wanted to say was that the blue car "did *not* run a red light." As to this risk, the trial safeguards seem truly useful: Cross-examination can get at the limits and intended meaning of what Bystander has to say; the oath or affirmation should bring home to him the need to speak with care; his demeanor adds dimension to the ways he affirms or qualifies his story of what happened.

Fourth is the risk of distortion (whether conscious or unconscious) and outright deliberate lying or deception, or (to put it in the customary and more gentle way) the risk of insincerity or lack of candor. Bystander may have shaded the truth in saying that the blue car ran the red light, while knowing that the light changed to red only after the blue car entered the intersection. Perhaps he did so because he knew and liked the other driver or felt animus toward the driver of the blue car, and the distortion may have been subconscious rather than calculated. Or he may have known full well that the driver of the blue car had the light in his favor and Bystander fully intended to fool the trier of fact. As to distortion, it is thought that trial safeguards really do help, and we at least *hope* that they do when the witness intentionally tries to deceive. Surely there is reason to think that the oath and the whole environment of the courtroom quell at least casual impulses to deceive, that the visible demeanor of the witness provides clues when the witness tries to mislead, and that cross-examination works well to bring to light subconscious distortion and sometimes succeeds in exposing lies.

2. Out-of-Court Statement Offered for Its Truth

Often the hearsay doctrine is simple in application, as illustrated by the statements of Bystander in Abby's suit. But people do not always express themselves so directly. Consider now a series of statements, all describing the same incident.

PROBLEM 3-A.   Three See a Robbery

Higgins is charged with the armed robbery of BankSouth. As part of its case-in-chief, the state calls to the stand one Lissner, who entered BankSouth shortly after the fact and conversed with three people who apparently saw what happened. The prosecutor proposes to have Lissner describe these conversations, and specifically to testify

1. That Plaintalk said, with reference to the robbery and to defendant, "Higgins is the one who did it";
2. That Sirchev said, again with reference to the robbery and to defendant, "That fellow Higgins went out of here carrying money bags";
3. That Oblique said, once again with reference to the robbery of BankSouth and to defendant, "they ought to put Higgins in jail for this, and throw away the key."

[handwritten: automatically assumes what they said is true → put in context]

The defense objects that the statements by Plaintalk, Sirchev, and Oblique are inadmissible hearsay. Without worrying for the moment whether the statements are admissible, are they hearsay? Why or why not?

B. A CLOSER LOOK AT THE DOCTRINE

1. *What Is a Statement?*

a. Assertive Conduct   *[handwritten: verbal + nonverbal cues]*

The examples considered so far have obvious hearsay implications because they involve the use of language to express ideas. The very term "hearsay" describes what one person hears another say, and suggests a concern with human verbal expression. But the hearsay doctrine rests upon the four risks of misperception, faulty memory, ambiguity, and insincerity, and these risks appear not only with verbal expression but with nonverbal conduct where the actor has assertive intent.

Hence any reasonable definition of hearsay must embrace assertive conduct when offered to prove the point asserted. There has never been much doubt on this score, and obviously Rule 801(a) embraces such conduct, since its definition of statement includes "nonverbal conduct of a person, if it is intended by the person as an assertion." Perhaps the most common instance of such conduct involves use of one of the standard nonverbal cues—nodding or shaking the head or shrugging the shoulders in answer to a question, pointing as a means of identifying or selecting. Evidence of such behavior, offered to prove the idea which the actor sought to convey is clearly hearsay. See United States v. Caro, 569 F.2d 411, 416 n.9 (5th Cir. 1978) (where co-offender "pointed out" his "source" to law enforcement officers, apparently indicating a dwelling, his act was "assertive conduct" that, "like an oral declaration," was "subject to the hearsay rule"); United States v. Ross, 321 F.2d 61, 69 (2d Cir.), cert. denied, 375 U.S. 894 (1963) (testimony that *S* pointed to a list when asked what numbers were used by the salesmen "was not outside the hearsay rule merely because [he] used no words," for "the pointing was as much a communication as a statement. . . would have been").

Nor would it matter if the conduct were a coded signal. Evidence that one lantern had been lit in the belfry of Old North Church would be hearsay if offered in court to prove that the British had moved out from Boston toward Concord and that they were coming by land rather than sea. The evidence would tend to prove the point only if the lantern were interpreted as a signal from the minuteman immortalized in Longfellow's poem[3] and taken as proof of the very point which the appearance of one lantern in that spot was intended to communicate.

In such obvious cases the hearsay issue is readily seen and easily resolved. But read on.

---

3. See H.W. Longfellow, The Landlord's Tale: Paul Revere's Ride, from Tales of a Wayside Inn, pt. I, st. 2 (1864-1873):

> One if by land, and two if by sea,
> And I on the opposite shore will be
> Ready to ride and spread the alarm
> Through every Middlesex village and farm.

b. Nonassertive Conduct

Perhaps surprisingly, even evidence of nonassertive human conduct implicates most of the hearsay risks—at least sometimes. How to treat evidence of such conduct in such situations has posed an enormous challenge to the hearsay doctrine, in both theory and application.

PROBLEM 3-B. *Kenworth and Maserati*

A huge Kenworth truck pulls up to an intersection regulated by traffic lights and stops in its righthand lane. An open Maserati sports car pulls up beside the truck in the left lane and stops, and Phillip behind the wheel guns his engine loudly. The traffic light across the street is not working, and Phillip cannot see the light nearest him, above and to his right, nor can he see cross-traffic coming from his right, for the bulk of the Kenworth obstructs his vision.

The Kenworth begins to pull forward, and the Maserati shoots into the intersection, where it is broadsided by a blue car crossing from its right and driven by Hillary. A lawsuit follows, for personal injuries and property damage, with Phillip and Hillary each claiming the other was at fault.

As proof that he had the light in his favor, Phillip offers to testify that the truck pulled forward across the pedestrian lane into the intersection before he (Phillip) stepped on the accelerator. Hillary objects, her lawyer arguing that evidence of the behavior of the truckdriver at the intersection is hearsay, when offered to prove that the light had turned green for Phillip. The trial judge is astonished: "Hearsay? What in the world are you thinking of, counsel, there isn't an assertion in sight here. Overruled."

You are Hillary's lawyer. Advance her argument that evidence of the movement of the Kenworth is hearsay, when offered for the stated purpose. For the moment, do not try to apply Rule 801. Just explain to the judge exactly what logical steps are required to proceed from the movement of the truck to the conclusion that the light was green for Phillip, and why those steps involve precisely the same risks which cause us to exclude out-of-court statements of the ordinary sort, when offered to prove what they assert. If you can't do it, read the next case and then try it.

WRIGHT v. DOE d. TATHAM
Court of Exchequer Chamber
7 Ad. & E. 313, 112 Eng. Rep. 488 (1837)

[Sandford Tatham, cousin and sole heir at law to the decedent John Marsden, brought suit to set aside his will, which was allegedly procured by fraud. By that will Marsden left valuable real property to his steward George Wright, who was named as defendant.

John Marsden, who by the standards of the time lived to the rather old age of 68, was apparently an unprepossessing fellow. By one view, advanced vigorously on behalf of Sandford Tatham, Marsden was "weak in understanding" and "ignorant of the commonest natural occurrences," hence prone "to ask childish questions on the most familiar subjects relating to his own property" and apparently "incapable of conducting business." He also displayed "imbecility in his amusements" and was "subject to irrational fears, insomuch that he sought the protection of other persons when passing by a pig or a turkey-cock." And in these unfortunate circumstances the steward George Wright "exercised an absolute control" over Marsden, treating him "with great harshness and disrespect" and even resorting to "personal violence" against him. Evidence was offered to the effect that

> Marsden was treated as a child by his own menial servants; that, in his youth, he was called, in the village where he lived, "Silly Jack," and "Silly Marsden," and was never talked to "as a man that was capable of anything, but as a child"; that a witness had seen boys shouting after him, "There goes crazy Marsden," and throwing dirt at him, and had persuaded a person passing by to see him home; and that once, when Marsden passed the evening at a gentleman's house, in company with Mr. Ellershaw. . . the elder persons of the family sat down to whist, and, Ellershaw mentioning that Marsden was unable to play, some children were sent for, and he was put to play with them at loo, at a side table, a man-servant superintending the game.

By another view (argued on behalf of the steward Wright), John Marsden "was a man of very retentive memory." While "not of strong mind or natural talent equal to the generality of men," still it was said that he had "such understanding and judgment as to be competent to conduct all the ordinary transactions of life." And in the estimate of one acquaintance, Marsden was "competent to manage his affairs with the assistance of agents and professional men, and to make such a will and codicil as these in question." 2 Russ. & M. 1, 20, 39 Eng. Rep. 295, 302 (reporting earlier proceedings in the same case).

Part of the proof adduced by George Wright was in the form of three letters written to Marsden before his death, all by persons who had themselves died before trial. One letter was personal in nature, but two others dealt with matters of business. One of the latter sort came from the Vicar of Lancaster, Oliver Marton, and it read as follows:

> Dear Sir.—I beg that you will Order your Attorney to Wait on Mr. Atkinson, or Mr. Watkinson, & propose some Terms of Agreement between You and the Parish or Township or disagreeable things must unavoidably happen. I recommend that a Case should be settled by Your and their Attorneys, and laid before Council to whose Opinion both Sides should submit otherwise it will be attended with much Trouble and Expence to both Parties.—I am, Sr. with compliments to Mrs. Coockson, Your Humble Servant, &c.
>
>   OLIVER MARTON
>
> May ye 20th 1786.
> I beg the favour of an Answer to this.
> John Marsden, Esq. Wennington.

When the case came to be heard in Exchequer Chamber, a majority of justices thought that the letters should not have been received. Baron Parke wrote what has come to be a famous opinion, set forth in part below.]

PARKE B. . . .

Each of the three letters, no doubt, indicates that in the opinion of the writer the testator was a rational person. He is spoken of in respectful terms in all. . . . Mr. Marton addresses him as competent to do business to the limited extent to which his letter calls upon him to act; and there is no question but that, if any of one of those writers had been living, his evidence, founded on personal observation, that the testator possessed the qualities which justified the opinion expressed or implied in his letters, would be admissible on this issue. But the point to be determined is, whether these letters are admissible as proof that he did possess these qualities?

I am of the opinion that, according to the established principles of the law of evidence, the letters are all inadmissible for such a purpose. . . .

That the three letters were each of them written. . . and sent. . . no doubt are facts. . . proved on oath; and the letters are without doubt admissible on an issue in which the fact of sending such letters. . . is relevant to the matter in dispute; as, for instance, on a feigned issue to try the question whether such letters were sent to the testator's house. . . .

But the question is, whether the contents of these letters are evidence of the fact to be proved upon this issue,—that is, the actual existence of the qualities which the testator is, in those letters, by implication, stated to possess: and those letters may be considered in this respect to be on the same footing as if they had contained a direct and positive statement that he was competent. For this purpose they are mere hearsay evidence, statements of the writers, not on oath, of the truth of the matter in question, with this addition, that they have acted upon the statements on the faith of their being true, by their sending the letters to the testator. That the so acting cannot give a sufficient sanction for the truth of the statement is perfectly plain; for it is clear that, if the same statements had been made by parol or in writing to a third person, that would have been insufficient; and this is conceded by the learned counsel for [Wright]. Yet in both cases there has been an acting on the belief of the truth, by making the statement, or writing and sending a letter to a third person; and what difference can it possibly make that this is an acting of the same nature by writing and sending the letter to the testator? It is admitted, and most properly, that you have no right to use in evidence the fact of writing and sending a letter to a third person containing a statement of competence, on the ground that it affords an inference that such an act would not have been done unless the statement was true, or believed to be true, although such an inference no doubt would be raised in the conduct of the ordinary affairs of life, if the statement were made by a man of veracity. But it cannot be raised in a judicial inquiry; and, if such an argument were admissible, it would lead to the indiscriminate admission of hearsay evidence of all manner of facts.

Further, it is clear that an acting to a much greater extent and degree upon such statements to a third person would not make the statements admissible. For example, if a wager to a large amount had been made as to the matter in issue by two third persons, the payment of that wager, however large the sum, would not be admissible to prove the truth of the matter in issue. You would not have had any right to present it to the jury as raising an inference of the truth of the fact, on the ground that otherwise the bet would not have been paid. It is, after all, nothing but the mere statement of that fact, with strong evidence of the belief of it by the party making it. Could it make any difference that the wager was between the third person and one of the parties to the suit? Certainly not. The payment by other underwriters on the same policy to the plaintiff could not be given in evidence to prove that the subject insured had been lost. Yet there is an act done, a payment strongly attesting the truth of the statement, which it implies, that there had been a loss. To illustrate this point still further, let us suppose a third person had betted a wager with Mr. Marsden that he could not solve some mathematical problem, the solution of which required a high degree of capacity; would payment of that wager to Mr. Marsden's banker be admissible evidence that he possessed that capacity? The answer is certain; it would not. It would be evidence of the fact of competence given by a third party not upon oath.

Let us suppose the parties who wrote these letters to have stated the matter therein contained, that is, their knowledge of his personal qualities and capacity for business, on oath before a magistrate, or in some judicial proceeding to which the plaintiff and defendant were not parties. No one could contend that such statement would be admissible on this issue; and yet there would have been an act done on the faith of the statement being true, and a very solemn one, which would raise in the ordinary conduct of affairs a strong belief in the truth of the statement, if the writers were faith-worthy. The acting in this case is of much less importance, and certainly is not equal to the sanction of an extra-judicial oath.

Many other instances of a similar nature, by way of illustration, were suggested by the learned counsel for [Tatham] which, on the most cursory consideration, any one would at once declare to be inadmissible in evidence. Others were supposed on the part of [Wright] which, at first sight, have the appearance of being mere facts, and therefore admissible, though on further consideration they are open to precisely the same objection. Of the first description are the supposed cases of a letter by a third person to anyone demanding a debt, which may be said to be a treatment of him as a debtor, being offered as proof that the debt was really due; a note, congratulating him on his high state of bodily vigour, being proposed as evidence of his being in good health; both of which are manifestly at first sight objectionable. To the latter class belong the supposed conduct of a family or relations of a testator, taking the same precautions in his absence as if he were a lunatic; his election, in his absence, to some high and responsible office; the conduct of a physician who permitted a will to be executed by a sick testator; the conduct of a deceased captain on a question of seaworthiness, who, after examining every part of the vessel, embarked in it with his family; all these, when deliberately considered, are, with reference to the matter in issue in each case, mere instances of hearsay evidence, mere statements, not on oath, but implied in or vouched by the actual conduct of persons by whose acts the litigant parties are not to be bound.

The conclusion at which I have arrived is, that proof of a particular fact, which is not of itself a matter in issue, but which is relevant only as implying a statement or opinion of a third person on the matter in issue, is inadmissible in all cases where such a statement or opinion not on oath would be of itself inadmissible; and therefore, in this case the letters which are offered only to prove the competence of the testator, that is the truth of the implied statements therein contained, were properly rejected, as the mere statement or opinion of the writer would certainly have been inadmissible.

NOTES ON NONASSERTIVE CONDUCT AS HEARSAY

1.   Baron Parke says the letters "imply[ ] a statement or opinion" of their authors and were offered to prove "the truth of the implied statements." Obviously Parke did not mean "imply" in the usual strong sense of "intentionally suggesting." Nobody thinks the Vicar's purpose was to express or communicate that "Marsden is a man of sound mind." If his letter "implies" this point, it does so in the weak sense of the term: It "indicates," because of what it says and what it tries to do, that its author must think one can do business with Marsden. That makes the Vicar's letter different from Oblique's statement in Problem 3-A ("they ought to put Higgins in jail for this"), doesn't it? Apparently Oblique intentionally expressed and communicated that Higgins was guilty, thus "implied" it in the strong sense. For Parke, an "implied statement" embraces everything one might infer about (and from) the thoughts of a person by reading what he writes or listening to what he says, whether he intended to convey it or not.

2.   From this broad view of "imply," Parke takes a broad view of hearsay, doesn't he? Under his view, the behavior of the rascals in taunting "crazy Marsden" and throwing dirt at him could be hearsay too, couldn't it? Wouldn't the same be true of the way Ellershaw and his friends treated Marsden in arranging separate entertainment while the other adults played whist? (The Oxford English Dictionary describes "loo" as "a round card-game" played with three- or five-card hands, in which one "who fails to take a trick or breaks any of the laws of the game is 'looed', i.e., required to pay a certain sum, or 'loo', to the pool.") Apparently George Wright raised no objection to this proof.

3.   Ironically, Ellershaw wrote one of the letters Wright offered. Wright's lawyers argued in Exchequer Chamber that the letter was just as proper as proof that Marsden was called "Silly Marsden" and "pelted by boys." If the opposition could prove Marsden had been "treated as a child" by Ellershaw and others, Wright's lawyers argued, then Wright should be able to get in a letter from Ellershaw in which Marsden was "differently treated." 7 Ad. & E. at 322, 112 English Reports at 492. They had a point, didn't they? For further details about Tatham's successful battle to win the Marsden estate, see Maguire, The Hearsay System: Around and Through the Thicket, 14 Vand. L. Rev. 741, 749-760 (1961).

4.   Is it an answer to the position of Wright that the authors of the letters might have thought someone in the Marsden household would intercept them and take care of things? Several Judges made this point. See the opinion of Lord Denman:

> The respectful phrases may be ironical, or employed for the very purpose of circumventing the party addressed, on the presumption of his imbecility. This might be apparent from the language itself to those who knew the habits of the writer. It is no answer to say that such remarks are rather on the effect than the

admissibility of the evidence, and fit for the consideration of the jury. We do not think it worth while to observe here that those who produce the letters may be much more reasonably expected to explain them by circumstances, than those against whom they are produced; this may be an observation on their effect, while what has been said appears to us to prove that it must be a matter of complete uncertainty whether these letters, written by strangers to the suit, do or do not express their genuine sentiments.

7 Ad. & E. at 326, 112 Eng. Rep. at 494.

5. Baron Parke's opinion is famous for its specific holding, which is pretty broad—the letters are hearsay because they imply a statement that Marsden is sound. But Parke is even more famous for his broad account of what hearsay is, which may not be necessary to the outcome but is clearly part of the underlying logic. He speaks of the ship captain embarking with his family after inspecting the vessel, as proof the vessel is sound. That too implies a statement, in Parke's view, doesn't it? Under this view, could a person accused of crime try to prove his innocence by evidence that another was observed running from the scene of the deed, or would that too be hearsay? Could a claimant seeking workers' compensation try to prove that she suffered certain injuries by introducing evidence that she was treated for such injuries? Could the prosecutor prove an alleged robbery victim was afraid by evidence that he was shaking and trembling during the crime?

6. Under Parke's view, Phillip (Problem 3-B) couldn't prove the light was green by testifying that the truck started forward into the intersection, could he? Can you describe the two-step inference that supports the conclusion, based on movement of the truck, that the light was green? If the truckdriver had yelled to Phillip, "Hey fella, the light's green," wouldn't that be hearsay if offered in court to prove the point? Using this statement to prove the light was green involves a similar two-step inference, doesn't it? Could Parke have concluded the letters to Marsden were hearsay without such a broad view of hearsay? Can you think of a narrower account that would distinguish between the letters and the truck? Lewis Carroll (actually it was Humpty Dumpty) reminds us a word can mean "just what I choose it to mean—neither more nor less" (the question being "which is to be master—that's all"), so try to make a principled argument, without resorting to quibbling distinctions, that the letters to Marsden are hearsay but the movement of the truck is not.

7. The view of Baron Parke has generated tensions that continue to this day. Consider the following statement in support of generous application of the hearsay doctrine, as Parke preferred:

[I]n many cases [the question] whether the conduct was or was not intended as an assertion will be unclear. One inference will be no more plausible than the other. For example, suppose that a confession, taken from D while he was sick in a hospital, is offered in evidence, and, in order to show that D was physically and mentally competent to make a rational statement, the prosecution offers to prove that the interrogation was conducted pursuant to permission granted by D's doctor. The purpose of this proof, of course, is to indicate that the doctor believed that D was in condition to be questioned. The problem is whether the doctor, in consenting to the interrogation, intended to communicate his belief about D's condition. How can the court know what the doctor's intent was? Or consider this set of facts: *D*, who was being prosecuted for theft of his grandmother's cow, contended that he had been given permission to make the sale; to show that permission had not been given, the prosecution wanted to prove that when the grandmother heard about the sale, she went to the purchaser and demanded not the purchase price but the return of the cow. Did she intend to assert that she had not agreed to the sale? Again, how is the court to know?

In situations like those above and innumerable others that could be mentioned, the courts will be free to decide either (a) that the actor did intend to assert the proposition his conduct is offered to prove, and thus that the offered evidence is hearsay, or (b) that the actor had no such intent, and thus that the evidence is not hearsay. The facts do not compel either decision. Consequently such cases cannot be intelligently decided by approaching the intent issue as if it could be resolved as a question of fact. Faced with equally tenable factual inferences, the judge must decide the intent question by examining the consequences of his decision. . . . But when, as in the examples above, intent cannot be determined through a factual analysis, the problem becomes one of judgment: The court must determine whether the evidence should be considered hearsay and resolve the question of intent accordingly.

Finman, Implied Assertions as Hearsay: Some Criticisms of the Uniform Rules of Evidence, 14 Stan. L. Rev. 682, 696-697, 707 (1962) (concluding that "implied assertions should be classified as hearsay").

8. Now consider a much narrower view of what hearsay means, ably defended by Professor Falknor in the following passage:

[I]t is clear that evidence of conduct must be taken as freed from at least one of the hearsay dangers, i.e., mendacity. A man does not lie to himself. Put otherwise, if in doing what he does a man has no intention of asserting the existence or non-existence of a fact, it would appear that the trustworthiness of evidence of this conduct is the same whether he is an egregious liar or a paragon of veracity. Accordingly, the lack of opportunity for cross-examination in relation to his veracity or lack of it, would seem to be of no substantial importance. Accordingly, the usual judicial disposition to equate the "implied" to the "express" assertion is very questionable. . . .

[I]t has sometimes been suggested, that the admissibility of evidence of non-assertive conduct should depend on a preliminary finding by the judge that the conduct was of a sort "as to give reasonable assurance of trustworthiness," that is to say, that it was of substantial importance to the actor in his own affairs. But for application in the "heat and hurry" of the trial, such a solution leaves a good deal to be desired. As Thayer observed, "we should have a system of evidence, simple, aiming straight at the substance of justice, not nice or refined in its details, not too rigid, easily grasped and easily applied."

The "simple, easily grasped and easily applied" rule, "not nice or refined in its details," would seem to be one which would eliminate completely the hearsay stigma from evidence of non-assertive conduct. Because such conduct is evidently more dependable than an assertion, there is rational basis for the differentiation. And there is a cogent practical argument for such a rule in the circumstance that experience has shown that very often, probably more often than not, and understandably, the hearsay objection to evidence of non-assertive conduct is overlooked in practice with the result that the present doctrine operates very unevenly.

Falknor, The "Hear-Say" Rule as a "See-Do" Rule: Evidence of Conduct, 33 Rocky Mtn. L. Rev. 133, 136-137 (1961).

CAIN v. GEORGE
United States Court of Appeals for the Fifth Circuit
411 F.2d 572 (1969)

PER CURIAM.

This is a diversity of citizenship case brought by the parents under the wrongful death statute of Texas for the death of their son who died of carbon monoxide poisoning while a guest in appellees' motel. A chair next to the heater had burned and was smoldering at the time of the arrival of the fire department. Plaintiffs alleged that the gas heater in the motel room was defective because it had been improperly installed, was improperly vented and had never been inspected or cleaned since the time of installation.

A jury verdict in the form of answers to special interrogatories found that the death of [the son] was not proximately caused by the negligence of the defendants, that the death. . . was not proximately caused by his own negligence, and that [the son's] death was due to an unavoidable accident. Thereupon, the District Court entered a final judgment for the defendants and dismissed the action on its merits. . . .

Appellants contend that the trial court erred in allowing in evidence the testimony of the motel owners concerning the number of guests who had occupied the room where the deceased was found dead and who had made no complaints. This testimony was relevant on the issue, however, that carbon monoxide came from the smoldering chair and clothing and not from the gas heater. Such testimony merely related the knowledge of the motel owners as to whether anyone was ever harmed by the heater. It was not hearsay as it derived its value solely from the credit to be given to the witnesses themselves and it was not dependent upon the veracity or competency of other persons. This testimony of Mr. and Mrs. George was clearly the best available evidence to support their position that carbon monoxide did not come from the heater. We think it was admissible to show how the heater had acted in the past. . . .

[Judgment affirmed.]

NOTES ON EVIDENCE OF NONCOMPLAINT

1. The court in *Cain* says that testimony as to noncomplaint depends solely on "the credit to be given to the witnesses" who testify *and* that such evidence tended "to show how the heater had acted in the past." Can the court be right on *both* points?

2. Can *Cain* be reconciled with *Wright*? Does *Cain* tend to prove Falknor's argument (Note 8 after *Wright*) that courts overlook hearsay issues when the proof does not include verbal expressions?

3. Evidence of noncomplaint, sometimes called "negative hearsay" or

"the sounds of silence" as a student note aptly puts it (see Note, 84 Dickinson L. Rev. 605 (1980)), is usually admitted over a hearsay objection. See also Lindheimer v. United Fruit Co., 418 F.2d 606, 607-608 (2d Cir. 1969) (evidence that during shipboard meeting of safety committee nobody reported an accident was properly admitted "as some proof that no accident did in fact occur," where testimony indicated that "it was the duty of those present to discuss accidents occurring on the voyage"; court concludes: "The fact of nonreporting is an act, not a hearsay statement."). Would Baron Parke have seen such evidence as hearsay?

4. Is it the same thing if, in order to prove that no accident occurred, a witness testifies that he inquired of a person likely to know and was told that no accident had occurred? See United States v. DeLoach, 654 F.2d 763, 770-771 (D.C. Cir. 1980) (apparently hearsay), cert. denied, 450 U.S. 933 (1981).

c. Indirect Hearsay

Consider the following testimony in light of what you understand so far:

Q: Please state your name for the record.
A: My name is Edith Harris.
Q: And where were you born, please?
A: In Bangor, Maine.
Q: And your parents were Algernon Harris and Anne Harris?
A: That's right.
Q: And your mother's given name was Anne Davies, was it not?
A: Correct.
Q: Your parents immigrated from Yorkshire, England, to this country in 1979, is that correct?
A: Yes, sir.
Q: And the date of your birth?
A: November 14, 1983.

You can see at a glance that Edith Harris cannot have firsthand knowledge of any of the facts set out in her answers, and it would appear that every one of them was in substance (though not in form) a repetition of something that was common knowledge in her house and that her parents might have told her in so many words. By that quite reasonable view, they are hearsay pure and simple.

Yet common sense cries out that on the subjects to which Harris testified, such answers should be wholly unobjectionable. There would be something terribly wrong with a system that refused to accept the word of a witness on such fundamental facts as her name, parentage, and place and date of birth.

In the usual case in which such information is developed simply as background, such answers are routinely accepted without a second thought, even though lawyers and judges know that the hearsay doctrine is very much implicated. Everyone understands that matters of this sort should be provable in exactly this way—regardless of "technical" hearsay problems. It might be different if the place of birth or the date of the arrival of the parents were central points of hotly contested fact—if, for example, such data affected citizenship rights or entitlement to benefits. Yet even in such cases judges would likely accept the testimony of the witness, though it might carry little weight if the other side had substantial counterproof in the nature of official records or other persuasive evidence.[4]

Here a short digression is in order. Technically, "hearsay" is not quite the right objection to the answers given by Edith Harris, for she never refers to statements by others. The principle that would support an objection, if the system were administered in a wooden and unyielding way, would be that Edith lacks "personal knowledge." Rule 602 instructs that every witness must be shown to have "personal knowledge of the matter" to which she is to testify, which ordinarily means knowledge gleaned directly from the senses. Clearly Edith Harris lacks personal knowledge of the facts to which she testified. But a judge would likely give equally short shrift to a personal knowledge objection in this context. Just as the hearsay doctrine seems almost "too technical" if it could block such testimony, so too the personal knowledge requirement would seem rather to obstruct than to promote justice if it could prevent a witness from testifying to her own personal and familial background. (In the case of a witness who testifies to an out-of-court statement admissible under one of the exceptions to the hearsay doctrine, the personal knowledge requirement is satisfied if the witness heard the oral utterance or read the written word, although in the latter case the Best Evidence doctrine poses an additional problem. The personal knowledge requirement is considered in Chapter 6J, infra.)

In short, the system tolerates testimony of the sort shown above even though the witness lacks personal knowledge and is, in substance, testifying to hearsay.

It is, of course, another matter altogether if a party seeks to rely on indirect hearsay to prove contested and substantial points in his case. Consider the following somewhat appalling example of an attempt to get in hearsay evidence indirectly.

UNITED STATES v. CHECK — *dirty cop*
United States Court of Appeals for the Second Circuit
582 F.2d 668 (1978)

[Sandy Check, a patrolman in the New York City Police Department, was convicted of possessing cocaine with intent to distribute and related offenses. The key witness against him was Stephen Spinelli, a detective in the force who had been assigned to investigate allegations against Check. Spinelli operated

---

4.   It is worth noting that there *are* hearsay exceptions that would likely enable the proponent of Edith's answers to vault over any hearsay objection. FRE 803(19) embraces "[r]eputation" among family members concerning such facts of "personal or family history" as "birth, adoption, marriage, divorce, death," and FRE 804(b)(4) embraces any "statement" by an unavailable declarant describing such personal matters. One or both of these exceptions would likely enable Edith to testify very much as she did, even if she was summarizing common knowledge in her household or stating knowledge she gleaned from particular conversations with her parents.

undercover and worked through an informant named William Joseph Cali to
get close to Check. Spinelli assumed the role of a prospective purchaser of
narcotics in his investigation of Check.]

WATERMAN, J. . . .

Spinelli testified that, as anticipated, Cali arranged for a meeting with
Check which was to take place on August 8, 1974 at Dave's Corner Restaurant,
located at the corner of Canal Street and Broadway in lower Manhattan. Shortly
after Spinelli and Cali had entered the restaurant Check appeared outside the
front window of the building and motioned to have Cali meet with him outside.
This Cali did and, after a conversation with Check, Cali rejoined Spinelli who
was still seated in the restaurant. Cali refused to testify at the trial. So, in view
of the potential hearsay problems connected with any attempt to elicit the
content of Spinelli's conversations with him, and after an objection on hearsay
grounds had already been voiced, the prosecutor employed a method of questioning which he argued circumvented any hearsay problems. The prosecutor,
after establishing that Check and Cali had conversed and that Cali had thereafter
returned to speak to Spinelli, inquired of Spinelli (as he would ultimately
inquire of him at least twelve additional times): "Without telling us what Mr.
Cali said to you, what did you say to him?" In response, Spinelli told the
prosecutor, and also, of course, the jury, what he had purportedly said to Cali:

> I—after we had the conversation, I instructed William Cali that by no means
> did I intend to front any sum of money to Sandy Check, I didn't particularly care
> for the fact that—initially he was supposed to come with an ounce of cocaine,
> and the taste which he had, which I was supposed to get prior to making the
> ounce buy of cocaine, was at his house, and due to the fact that it wasn't of good
> quality, I wasn't particularly concerned, as good faith wasn't being shown to me,
> especially for the fact I also told William Cali I had no intention of giving Sandy
> Check $300 which William Cali owed to him from a previous narcotics deal. . . .

The scene of the negotiations now shifted. After instructing Cali to continue
his discussions with Check, Spinelli left the restaurant, passed Check in the
street and proceeded to a nearby topless bar. Cali arrived at the bar ten minutes
later and there Spinelli and Cali had another conversation. At trial, the government asked of the undercover agent: "Without telling us what Mr. Cali said to
you, what did you say to him during that conversation?" In accordance with
the limitations of the question, Spinelli faithfully responded:

> I told William Cali that I was willing to wait until the following day to get the
> ounce of cocaine, that I could understand that there was problems with Sandy
> Check's supplier, and that I would definitely have the money with me, and as
> arrangements, I would drop Cali off to meet Sandy Check and wait for him a few
> blocks away from the location.

The indirect dealing through Cali abruptly came to an end when Check,
responding to Spinelli's gesture of disgust at the unproductive course the
negotiations had followed, motioned for Spinelli to cross the street and meet
with him personally. . . .

Turning to the merits, we agree with Check that for much of his testimony

Spinelli was serving as a transparent conduit for the introduction of inadmissible hearsay information obviously supplied by and emanating from the informant Cali. Indeed, it would be virtually impossible to draw any other conclusion. . . . Moreover, the hearsay introduced through Spinelli was not only damaging in character but extensive in scope. Thus, the jury learned from Spinelli's "I told William Cali" responses that:

1. Check wanted Spinelli to front the money not only for the narcotics he wished to purchase from Check but also to cover $300 which William Cali owed Check from a previous narcotics deal
2. Check kept narcotics at his house
3. Check was supposed to arrive at the meeting of August 8, 1974 with an ounce of cocaine and a taste of it, but, inasmuch as the cocaine was not of good quality, Check did not bring the drugs with him. . .
7. After seeing Spinelli in the street, after he departed Dave's Corner Restaurant, Check felt more comfortable about dealing with him and would go ahead and try to arrange for a sale of an ounce of cocaine to Spinelli
8. Check would produce the ounce of cocaine that same afternoon of August 8, 1974. . .

Despite its unwillingness to exclude all of Spinelli's testimony which conveyed the foregoing hearsay information, the district court did exclude or strike some of it. . . . The judge . . . expressed her misgivings about Spinelli's entire testimony by remarking that Spinelli "doesn't seem to be [testifying to just his part of the conversation]. He seems to be weaving the two together. We can't distinguish which is which." In fact some of Spinelli's "paraphrasing" was so blatant and obvious that at one point even the prosecutor felt compelled to admit that "[t]he obvious inference to be drawn [from Spinelli's testimony regarding Check's being with his runner Duky] is that he [Spinelli] knew it because Cali identified the person."

There is, furthermore, no doubt that the out-of-court statements uttered by Cali, audaciously introduced through the artifice of having Spinelli supposedly restrict his testimony to his half of his conversations with Cali, were being offered to prove the truth of the matters asserted in them. This conclusion follows inescapably from the fact that. . . the government constantly took the position at trial that the challenged portions of Spinelli's testimony avoided the proscription against the use of hearsay not because they were not being offered for the truth of the matters asserted but rather because they were Spinelli's *own* out-of-court statements and he was testifying in court and could be cross-examined. In other words, the government was apparently arguing that the out-of-court statements were admissible because they were somehow excluded from the definition of hearsay or qualified for some supposed exception to the hearsay rule. . . . A concession that *Cali's* statements would have been hearsay [as the government agreed] is an admission that the purpose for which the statements were being offered at trial (irrespective of whether they were to be regarded as Spinelli's or Cali's) was to prove the truth of the matters asserted therein. We thus conclude that, in substance, significant portions of Spinelli's testimony regarding his conversations with Cali were indeed hearsay, for that testimony was a transparent attempt to incorporate into the officer's testimony information supplied by the informant who did not testify at trial. Such a device is improper and cannot miraculously transform inadmissible hearsay into admissible evidence. The district judge. . . . should have granted Check's motion to strike all of Spinelli's testimony narrating his conversations with Cali. . . .

Judgment of conviction reversed and case remanded for a new trial on all counts of the indictment.

NOTES ON INDIRECT HEARSAY

1. Judge Waterman's care in *Check* is surely commendable, is it not? If the government could so easily avoid the hearsay doctrine with respect to proof central to its case, the doctrine would not be worth much, would it?

2. Reviewing courts may be more relaxed in less egregious situations. See United States v. Obi, 239 F.3d 662, 668 (4th Cir. 2001) (admitting testimony by detective that he began investigating defendant because informant cooperating on another matter introduced him to underworld figure *S*, who said he "knew some dude named Obi," and rejecting claim that this testimony improperly connected defendant with underworld). In *Obi*, isn't it clear that what *S* said was hearsay if offered to connect *S* with the defendant? You will see in Chapter 5 that character evidence, including proof of prior acts, is often excludable. Why do courts sometimes admit such testimony?

3. Even in situations like *Obi*, courts sometimes show great sensitivity to the risks. See State v. Litzau, 650 N.W.2d 177, 182 (Minn. 2002) (reversing drug conviction, largely because police were allowed to testify that they acted against defendant on the basis of reliable tips); Commonwealth v. Farris, 380 A.2d 486 (Pa. Super. 1977) (error to let prosecutor elicit from detective that when he arrived at robbery scene, the first thing he did was "interrogate Gary Moore," who "made a statement," as a result of which "I arrested Emmanual Farris") (testimony violated hearsay rule).

d. Machines and Animals Speak   801 (b)

Hearsay risks sometimes appear in cases where machines or animals seem to be the source of the factual data reported in court. Consider the following exchange:

Q: When did you check the price?
A: It was 11:34 A.M.
Q: How do you happen to know that so exactly?
A: I thought it might come up, so I glanced at my watch. It's a quartz digital, and very accurate.
Q: And what was the price?
A: $47.50 for May futures.
Q: What is your source for that?

A: We have Futures Instaquote at our office, and it's just a matter of typing in the question, and then we get a screen read almost instantly.

Arguably this testimony as to time and price is hearsay, isn't it? If *a person* had told our witness the time and price, then clearly the latter's testimony would be subject to either a personal knowledge or a hearsay objection. (FRE 801(b) supposes that *only* "a person" makes a "statement," doesn't it? Why?) Most courts would reject any "hearsay" objection to testimony as to what time it was based on a clock but would view the "screen read" as hearsay, when offered to prove price. Why?

And what of animal statements? Suppose that police discover a house burglary in progress and on entering they discover clear evidence of a theft just completed and a dog. Advised by the owners that the dog does not belong to them, the police surmise that the burglar left it while making his escape. They take the dog to the station, where he is surly to all comers. But a day later when they arrest the suspected burglar and bring him to the station the dog leaps up in obvious doggish enthusiasm—head up, ears relaxed, much licking, prancing, and tail wagging and happy squeals. If ever a dog said, "I know you / I love you," this dog has said it. In the later prosecution of the suspect, the prosecutor offers a testimonial account of the discovery of the dog, his behavior at the station, and his reaction on seeing the suspect, arguing that it all amounts to circumstantial evidence that the suspect is the culprit. Hearsay? Surely not. Why? (Don't make the mistake of arguing that animals never lie or err, for it is becoming clear that sometimes they do.)

As a practical matter, the question of "animal hearsay" arises most often in connection with proof of canine tracking and identification, and such evidence is usually held admissible. See United States v. McNiece, 558 F. Supp. 612 (E.D.N.Y. 1983) (approving videotape and testimonial description of behavior of dog who, after exposure to defendant's sock and an array of tools, exhibited an "alert" reaction on coming to boltcutters found at robbery scene, leading witness to conclude that defendant had been in contact with boltcutters); Annot., 13 A.L.R.3d 1221. Sometimes proof of other kinds of animal behavior is admitted. See State v. Grimsley, 30 P.2d 85 (Mont. 1934) (in trial for theft of two calves, approving testimony by complaining witness that his cows seemed to be looking for their calves, which bore on proposed test to see whether cows would claim calves as their own).

But occasionally courts balk. See State v. Storm, 238 P.2d 1161, 1176 (Mont. 1951) ("Dogs and other dumb animals do not qualify as witnesses in the courts of this state. They know not the nature of an oath. They may not be sworn. They cannot be cross-examined. They testify only through professed interpreters whose translations and conclusions are always hearsay."(!)) (murder conviction reversed for error in admitting bloodhound tracking evidence).

2.   When Is a Statement Not Hearsay?

Under FRE 801 a statement is hearsay when "offered to prove the truth of the matter asserted." The negative inference invited by this definition is that a statement is *not* hearsay when offered for any *other* purpose. What other purposes

[handwritten margin note: Clocks are dependent on people setting them correctly, battery / electricity / failure, going out ↓ computer more reliable]

[margin note: nonhearsay uses]

can there be? There are many nonhearsay uses, but usually a statement offered for purposes other than proving what it asserts falls into one of the following six categories: (1) impeachment, (2) verbal acts (or parts of acts), (3) effect on listener or reader, (4) verbal objects, (5) circumstantial evidence of state of mind, and (6) circumstantial evidence of memory or belief. These categories are not listed in the Rules, but are well accepted by courts throughout the country as nonhearsay uses.

Unfortunately the verbal act category is much overused and is sometimes an unthinking label for a statement offered for any nonhearsay purpose. The last two categories (circumstantial evidence of state of mind, and circumstantial evidence of memory or belief) are troublesome. The next seven Problems illustrate these six nonhearsay uses in the order set out above. Even with this much guidance, and suggestions in the Notes following the Problems, you should understand in advance that these nonhearsay uses are surprisingly challenging and that thorough understanding requires considerable thought.

[margin note: NON Prior unconsist. Statement]

PROBLEM 3-C.   "The Blue Car Ran a Red Light"

[margin note: H/S use Impeachment]

Abby sues Burton for property damages and personal injuries arising out of an intersection collision. (Abby had been driving a maroon stationwagon, and Burton had been driving a blue sedan.) In order to establish that Burton's blue sedan ran the light, Abby's counsel calls Bystander and establishes through preliminary questions that he saw the accident.

Then the critical question: "Which car had the light in its favor?" Bystander's response: "The light was green for the stationwagon. The blue car ran a red light."

On cross-examination, Burton asks Bystander about a conversation he had with insurance adjuster Charles three days after the accident. Over Abby's hearsay objection, Burton wants to ask Bystander whether he said to Charles, "The blue car had the green light in its favor." Burton replies to the objection, "Your honor, we seek only to impeach the witness, not to offer the statement for its truth."

How should the court rule on the hearsay objection, and why?

NOTES ON IMPEACHMENT BY PRIOR STATEMENTS

1. What is important about Bystander's prior statement, from the standpoint of Burton? If, in arguing for Burton, you said Bystander's prior statement shows the light was green for his blue sedan, wouldn't you have "made the other side's day" because the statement would be hearsay?

2. If you said, in arguing for Burton, that the important thing about Bystander's prior statement is that it shows he *once thought* the light was green for Burton's car, many would say you're home free. But think some more: Even if the statement doesn't expressly say "I think" Burton had a green light, isn't that idea implicit in the actual words Bystander used? Doesn't every statement of fact say the speaker thinks what he says is so? If so, and if that's what it's offered to prove, it's hearsay, isn't it?

3. Despite these difficulties, courts universally take the view that prior inconsistent statements are not hearsay when offered to impeach. Can you think of a better reason that supports this universal practice? If you were arguing for exclusion, could you get any help from FRE 403?

PROBLEM 3-D. *"Any Way You Like"*

The state seeks an injunction to close down the Gentleman's Massage Parlor, upon ground that its owner Ratliff operates it for purposes of soliciting prostitution. As part of its proof, the government calls undercover agent Wallis to testify that while posing as a patron there he was served by a masseuse named Debra who, in the middle of giving him a rubdown, asked him "whether I was interested in a good time." Wallis testifies further that he replied "that depends on when and where and how much" and that the masseuse replied, "the cost depends on what you want, but I'm real versatile like, and you can have it any way you like, honey."

Ratliff objects that Wallis's testimony about what he and Debra said to one another is hearsay. Is it?

PROBLEM 3-E.   *Whose Corn?*

John Lord leased part of his farm to Cartwright for payment in kind, in the amount of 40 percent of the corn Cartwright could grow. Cartwright borrowed money from First State Bank, giving the bank a security interest in part of his crop and ultimately defaulting on the loan. The bank repossessed a double crib of corn from the farm and sold it to Prager.

Now Lord sues Prager and the bank for conversion, claiming that the corn that the bank repossessed and sold was his share of Cartwright's crop. As proof, Lord offers his own testimony that he and Cartwright had gone to the field, where Cartwright "pointed out the corn in the double crib and said, 'Mr. Lord, this double crib of corn is your share for this year, and it belongs to you, sir.'" The bank and Prager object that Lord's description of what Cartwright said and did was hearsay.

As proof that the corn in the double crib was indeed the corn covered by its security interest, the bank offers testimony by its loan officer that "when we came out to see about selling the corn, Cartwright told us that the corn in the double crib was his." Lord objects that the loan officer's description of what Cartwright said and did was hearsay.

Assume that if the bank got the wrong corn, both Prager and the bank are liable to Lord for conversion.

What result on these hearsay objections, and why?

NOTES ON VERBAL ACTS

1. Does the fact that Debra and Wallis did not agree on a price make their words not hearsay? Is agreement necessary, given that her statements are

offered only to prove solicitation? To make the argument that her statements are not hearsay, is it necessary to argue that the content is not important, or only that the evidence is not being offered to prove what she asserted? Could Debra be guilty of solicitation even if she never intended to engage in whatever acts she describes?

2.   Recall your course in Criminal Law. Can you think of other crimes that are committed by words alone? By words connected with acts? To what extent, if at all, does the definition of the crime require that the speaker intend to act in accordance with what he says?

3.   Does Cartwright's statement to Lord have some operative effect? What, if anything, does it do? Does Cartwright's statement to the bank do the same thing? Think about your first year courses in Torts, Property, and Contracts. Can you come up with other examples of civil transactions in which words have operative effects and could qualify as nonhearsay verbal acts?

PROBLEM 3-F.   "I'm from the Gas Company"

While working on the job at the Crane Wrecking Company, Jack Alford thought he smelled the odor of natural gas coming from the direction of a nearby pipeline running above ground. Although Alford had not yet decided to call the gas company, a man appeared on the scene shortly thereafter: "I'm Joe Forrest from Interstate Gas," he said, "Could you show me where the pipeline is, so I can check it out? We've had reports of a leak in this area."

Alford took Forrest around to the back of the building and was pointing out the pipeline when Forrest started to light up a cigarette. The burning match ignited the escaping gas, and in the explosion Alford was seriously hurt.

Alford sues Interstate Gas on a negligence theory, and Interstate raises contributory negligence as a defense, arguing that Alford should not have gone so close to what he knew or suspected to be a gas leak. At trial, Alford offers to testify to what Forrest told him just before the explosion, as proof that Forrest was an agent of Interstate Gas and that Alford's behavior was reasonable. Interstate Gas raises a hearsay objection. When offered for either or both of these purposes, is Forrest's statement hearsay?

NOTES ON PROVING EFFECT ON HEARER OR READER

1.   Suppose a drug company defended a product liability suit by claiming the label gave proper warning against the use to which the plaintiff put the pills. Is the label hearsay? Suppose the question is whether a broker knew facts about a house she was selling, and the other side seeks to prove the point by offering a document from her file. Hearsay? In the gas leak problem, the words were spoken rather than written. For purposes of proving notice, that doesn't matter, does it?

2.   If the purpose is to prove Forrest was actually an agent for Interstate Gas, the hearsay objection becomes clearer, doesn't it? Why? If the plaintiff argued that what Forrest said proved agency because Interstate Gas *knew* he

was going around saying such things and did nothing to stop him or alert the public, could this argument support the proffered evidence as nonhearsay proof of what the law would call "ostensible" authority? In order to support this theory, the plaintiff would need lots of other proof that Interstate Gas was remiss in letting such behavior go unchecked, wouldn't it?

PROBLEM 3-G.   Eagle's Rest Bar & Grill

Whitney Seaver, Greg Flawn, and Stacey Nichols are charged in United States District Court for the Southern District of Wisconsin with conspiring to distribute cocaine, and related substantive offenses. The case depends partly on showing that the three used a rundown house at 611 Elm Street in Alton, Wisconsin, as a warehouse and occasional living quarters, and that they sold the cocaine at a night spot called Eagle's Rest Bar & Grill in the nearby resort community of Pine Meadows.

As is usual in such matters, the evidence was largely circumstantial. Scattered in the array of background evidence offered by the prosecutor were the following bits and pieces: Proof that Whitney Seaver once attended the University of Illinois in Urbana-Champaign, where he (along with many of his fraternity brothers) was an ardent supporter of his school's football and basketball teams, known in the Big Ten as the "Fighting Illini"; proof that he was known among his friends by the nickname "Witter"; proof that Greg Flawn resided in Alton at 611 Elm Street.

The prosecutor had a hard time connecting Seaver with the alleged drug venture, but she offered the following items of evidence on this point:

1. As proof that Seaver had been to the Eagle's Rest Bar & Grill, a book of matches found in his possession bearing the legend "Eagle's Rest Bar & Grill, Pine Meadows";
2. As proof that Seaver spent time at the house in Alton, a mug found there bearing the likeness of an Indian Warrior and a legend proclaiming "Chief Illiniwek" and "The Fighting Illini" and, below these, the word "Witter";
3. As proof that Seaver knew Stacey Nichols, (a) testimony by a barmaid at the Eagle's Rest Bar & Grill that she saw Nichols in the bar on numerous occasions with a man whose name she did not know and that she accurately pointed the couple out to undercover officer Isom, along with (b) Isom's testimony that the man the barmaid pointed out with Nichols was Whitney Seaver.

To each of these items of evidence, Whitney Seaver has raised a hearsay objection. Are any or all of these items hearsay? Why or why not?

NOTES ON VERBAL OBJECTS

1.   Sherlock Holmes could sometimes figure out where a person had been in London by looking at the mud on his boots. Can a verbal legend on a

matchbook serve a similar identifying function? Unlike mud, a verbal legend is also a human expression or communication, isn't it? It *says* something because some human made the appropriate arrangements, and there's a "declarant" somewhere, isn't there? What does the legend say? In order to use mud to show where a person had been, you'd have to know where mud of that sort was found. To do something like that here, you'd have to prove where matchbooks of that sort are found. How would you do that while avoiding the hearsay problem?

2. The images and legends on the mug distinguish it from other mugs, don't they? But the words assert something, don't they? What? To escape a hearsay objection to the word "Witter," would you need testimony that Whitney Seaver owned a mug with that legend written on it?

3. What was the barmaid apparently saying when she pointed out Seaver to Isom in the bar? How was the barmaid using that statement when she testified?

PROBLEM 3-H. *Anna Sofer's Will*

Anna Sofer died from injuries she suffered when run over by a bus, and her surviving husband Ira has brought a wrongful death action against the Municipal Transit Authority, operator of the bus.

Under applicable state law, the wrongful death claim belongs to Ira as Anna's next of kin and is brought in his name. Where liability is established, the law entitles the claimant to recover for loss of companionship and expected income. Anna was a dentist with significant income.

In an attempt to show that in fact Ira would have had no reasonable expectation of future financial benefit if Anna survived, and to suggest that the quality of companionship between the two was not what might have been expected between husband and wife, the Transit Authority offers into evidence a passage from Anna's will. Anna had executed the will, with the assistance of legal counsel, only a few weeks before her death. In it she had written

> Whereas I have been a faithful and loving wife to Ira, while he has reciprocated my tender feelings with utter cruelty, disrespect, and indifference, and whereas I have foolishly spent my best years trying hard to make him happy and to provide a comfortable home for us while he took me for granted and wasted the resources gathered by what was supposed to be our joint endeavor upon selfish and trivial pursuits every chance he got, now therefore I limit my bequest to Ira to $1, which is more than he deserves.

Ira objects that Anna's will is hearsay, when offered for the stated purpose. Is it? Why or why not?

PROBLEM 3-I. *"A Papier-Mâché Man"*

Zinder is prosecuted for alleged sexual assault upon eight-year-old Sharon, which allegedly occurred eight months previously. There is abundant clinical evidence of such assault, and the defense stipulates that Sharon was indeed the victim of an attack of this nature. The critical question is whether Zinder committed the offense.

On this point, the prosecutor offers two proofs. One takes the form of an account by Officer Stalwart of the description which Sharon gave of the room to which she said she was taken by the man who assaulted her:

"Memory

Hearsay
↓
given to officer out of court

> She said the room contained what she called an "old fashioned iron bed" with "a curlicue design in the metal." She said that there were windows to the outside on two walls and a door to a closet which also had a window to the outside. She said that near the bed there was, to use her own words, "a green rocking chair and a little table with a lamp on it," and in the corner there was what she called "a papier-mâché man sitting on a wooden chair, and the man was painted red and green and blue and had a book on his lap, with his legs crossed, wearing a hat," and she said the man looked "really gay and funny, and kind of short, like a leprechaun."

details distinguish room

The other proof takes the form of a testimonial account by Officer Yeoman, who made the arrest, describing the room in which Zinder resides. Yeoman's account is independent of that given by Stalwart. That is, Yeoman was not in the courtroom while Stalwart testified; he had not talked to Sharon about the room; he described what he saw with his own eyes.

These proofs seem persuasive evidence that Zinder was the culprit because the descriptions given by Sharon and Yeoman are alike in all essential details, including especially the description of the papier-mâché man.

Zinder has strenuously objected to Officer Stalwart's testimony, arguing at length that "Sharon's description is hearsay, for it is offered as proof of the room in which the assault occurred, and necessarily that requires that the jury believe in the truth of her words and believe that she really thinks that the room looks as she described it."

But the court rules, "Her description is not hearsay. It is offered to prove that she knows what the room looks like. I'm going to let it in."

not that D assaulted V ?

Has the court erred? Why or why not? What additional proof might the prosecutor offer in aid of the claim that Sharon's description of the room should be viewed as nonhearsay?

NOTES ON CIRCUMSTANTIAL EVIDENCE OF STATE OF MIND AND OF MEMORY

1. As the introductory comment says, these categories are conceptually troublesome. Note that FRE 803(3) creates a hearsay exception for a statement describing state of mind, which means that such a statement can be admitted even if it *is* hearsay. But statements admitted under the state-of-mind exception cannot be used to prove a "fact remembered or believed."

2. In *Anna Sofer's Will,* Anna's statement is not offered to prove what Ira *did,* is it? But it is being offered to prove what Anna *thought,* isn't it? Does it prove what she thought only because she *asserts* that she has these particular thoughts? Does the (prospective) publication of her statement in a will make a difference? Courts would not apply the "verbal act" doctrine here because

the point is not to prove or give effect to a will, but to show something about the relationship of Anna and Ira. Still, the fact that Anna makes the statement in a will probably counts for something.

3. In *Papier-Mâché Man*, what Sharon said is being offered to prove her memory, hence where she has been. Her statement is *much more* persuasive on these points because it describes a unique or highly unusual room, isn't it? If you had to argue "she was there because she *asserts that* she saw all those things," her statement would be hearsay. Can you argue for nonhearsay treatment in some other way?

4. Hal is tried for stealing cash from the safe of his employer Fran. She testifies that she set the combination as 687176218, that she kept it secret, and that Hal was the only employee to whom she told the number. Hal claims Jason, another employee, committed the theft, and that he must have found the secret location where the combination was recorded. After Fran testifies, Hal calls Ike, who was sequestered and did not hear her testify or learn what she said. If allowed, Ike would testify that before the theft Jason said he "knew the combination, and wrote these numbers on a slip, which he gave to me." The digits on this slip match the combination. Hearsay, if offered to prove Jason knew the combination and might be the thief?

3. What About Prior Statements by Testifying Witnesses?

Proper handling of prior statements by testifying witnesses has troubled courts and commentators for many years. It was once clear that such statements did not get special treatment and were hearsay when offered to prove what they assert, just like any other out-of-court statement.

But scholars came increasingly to the conclusion that at least *some* prior statements by persons who testify at trial under oath, with demeanor visible to the trier of fact, and (most important) subject to cross-examination, should not be excludable as hearsay. And the kind of prior statement that attracted most attention was the prior *inconsistent* statement of the witness.[5] The drafters of the Federal Rules were persuaded, and they tried from the beginning to remove the bar of the hearsay rule from any prior inconsistent statement by a witness who testifies at trial and is "subject to cross-examination concerning the statement." See Preliminary Draft of March 1969, Proposed Federal Rules of Evidence, Rule 8-01(c)(2)(iv), 46 F.R.D. 161, 331 (1969).

For the most part, however, lawyers and judges would have none of this

---

5. There are several reasons to be most interested in this sort of prior statement. For one thing, a prior inconsistent statement imparts something not found in the live testimony of the witness, so if such a statement can overcome a hearsay objection it becomes in effect "new" and "further" evidence. For another, inconsistent statements have long been admissible for impeachment, meaning that the adverse party could use them for the limited purpose of trying to destroy credibility. You already encountered this principle in operation in Problem 3-C ("The Blue Car Ran a Red Light"), supra. So trial lawyers routinely gather out-of-court statements from persons expected to testify, and routinely bring them out at trial, either by cross-examining the witness or by calling other witnesses to testify to such prior inconsistencies. In sum, prior inconsistent statements are capable of proving points the witness does not support in his testimony, and the temptation to use them in this way is ever present.

revisionism. And Congress, many of whose members are lawyers by training and inclination, refused to go along with the drafters on this matter. (Ultimately, as you can see from looking at the language of Rule 801(d)(1)(A), the drafters succeeded in their quest only in part. Congress removed the hearsay bar only from prior inconsistent statements that were themselves "given under oath subject to the penalty of perjury at a trial, hearing, or other proceeding, or in a deposition.")

Lest you think the matter is settled, you should note that many states adopting rules based on the federal model have gone their own various ways, some agreeing with the federal drafters, others agreeing with Congress, and still others compromising between orthodoxy and reform in a variety of different ways.[6]

Scholarly arguments that stress the adequacy of trial safeguards in helping the jury evaluate such statements have provided force behind the move to discard the orthodox view. Wigmore had once defended that view, but he changed his mind on "[f]urther reflection" and announced in the 1923 edition of his treatise:

> [T]he theory of the Hearsay rule is that an extrajudicial statement is rejected because it was made out of Court by an absent person not subject to cross-examination. . . . Here, however, by hypothesis, the witness is present and subject to cross-examination. There is ample opportunity to test him as to the basis for his former statement. The whole purpose of the Hearsay rule has been already satisfied. Hence there is nothing to prevent the tribunal from giving such testimonial credit to the extrajudicial statement as it may seem to deserve.

2 J. Wigmore, Evidence §1018 (1923). Other scholars came to similar conclusions, including Professors Morgan and McCormick. See Morgan, Hearsay Dangers and the Application of the Hearsay Concept, 62 Harv. L. Rev. 177, 193 (1948); McCormick on Evidence §251 (E. Cleary ed. 1984). And the Supreme Court gave a boost to the revisionist cause when it found that the Confrontation Clause does not bar the use against the accused of prior inconsistent statements as proof of what they assert, at least in some circumstances. The case was California v. Green, 399 U.S. 149, 158-159 (1970) (described in Chapter 4G,

---

6.   Among states adopting or enacting evidence codes based on the federal model, twenty-two agree with the congressional approach (with occasional variation in detail). They are Alabama, Florida, Hawaii, Idaho, Indiana, Iowa, Louisiana, Maine, Maryland (also covering statements written and signed by the witness and those contemporaneously recorded), Minnesota, Mississippi, Nebraska, New Hampshire, Ohio, Oklahoma, Oregon, Pennsylvania, South Dakota, Texas, Vermont, Washington, and West Virginia. Thirteen other states agree with the drafters in lifting the hearsay bar from all prior inconsistent statements (with occasional variation in detail): They are Alaska, Arizona, Colorado, Delaware, Kentucky, Montana, New Jersey, New Mexico, Nevada, Rhode Island, South Carolina, Utah, and Wisconsin. It is perhaps noteworthy that California, with its own unique Code, also takes this approach. See Cal. Evid. Code §1235. One state (Connecticut) admits prior inconsistent statements as substantive evidence if written and signed by the witness, and if he had personal knowledge. Three more states (Arkansas, North Dakota, and Wyoming) agree with the drafters in civil cases and with Congress in criminal cases. And three other states go about as far as one can in the opposite direction: Michigan, North Carolina, and Tennessee make no provision for prior inconsistent statements in the hearsay section of their counterparts to the Federal Rules.

infra). In that case, the Court cited the protections afforded at trial by the oath, cross-examination, and demeanor evidence, and then announced: "[I]f the declarant is present and testifying at trial, the out-of-court statement for all practical purposes regains most of the lost protections."

But for the most part lawyers and judges argue that the safeguarding effects of oath, cross-examination, and demeanor evidence do not readily transfer from the live testimonial account of the witness to his remote statements. Senator Ervin of North Carolina, once a trial lawyer himself, minced no words in attacking the attempt in proposed Rule 801(d)(1)(A) to accord nonhearsay treatment to all prior inconsistent statements by witnesses who are subject to cross-examination concerning them. In the same breath he disparaged the Supreme Court's logic in *Green:*

> You have to find beyond a reasonable doubt in a criminal case that this man told the truth when he was not sworn but told a lie when he was under oath. I just think that is an affront to the sixth amendment, the *Green* case to the contrary notwithstanding. To allow a man to be convicted upon an extra-judicial statement of a third person when you have to find that, at the trial, the third person either had no memory or was a liar is too dangerous; it is particularly dangerous in crimes that are serious. I think it denies a fair trial.
>
> I admit the Supreme Court of the United States disagrees with me on that, but I think I am right and they are wrong.

Hearings on H.R. 5463 before the Senate Committee on the Judiciary, 93d Cong., 2d Sess., at 51 (1974).

We revisit this issue in connection with impeachment of witnesses in Chapter 8, *infra*.

C. HEARSAY UNDER RULE 801

1. *Definitional Approaches*

You have considered the coverage and limits of hearsay doctrine, various nonhearsay uses of out-of-court statements, and nonassertive conduct. Now we need to look more closely at FRE 801.

Bird's eye view. Putting aside nonassertive conduct, and deferring matters of fine detail, we can see four different approaches to the problem of defining hearsay:

1. *Tradition.* At common law, hearsay was any out-of-court statement offered to prove what it asserts. This definition tracks the one-liner we started with and is conservative in the sense of being traditional and broad (excluding lots of evidence). This definition is the most common one, and it closely matches FRE 801(a)-(c).

2. *Hearsay as uncross-examinable statement.* One reformist approach defines hearsay as an uncross-examinable statement offered to prove what it asserts. This definition, which rests on the idea that the main reason

to exclude hearsay is the absence of cross, would admit statements by people who later testify, submitting to "deferred" cross (with deferred oath and demeanor too).

3. *Hearsay as a rule of preference.* Another reformist approach defines hearsay as a <u>statement by a person who is absent but available to the proponent,</u> when offered to prove what it asserts. Like the second approach, this one would admit statements by testifying witnesses. But this approach would go further, paving the way for statements by anyone who is unavailable at the time of trial.[7] This approach would make hearsay into a rule of preference: <u>Live testimony is preferred over out-of-court statements, but the latter may supplement live testimony or be substituted for live testimony</u> if it cannot be had.

4. *Hearsay as a cautionary principle.* Yet another reformist approach defines hearsay in the usual way (out-of-court statement offered to prove what it asserts), but would admit hearsay shown to be reliable under the circumstances. Under this approach, judges would scrutinize out-of-court statements but admit them whenever they seem reliable, in anticipation that often they will qualify. The framers of the Federal Rules originally wanted to go in this direction, proposing broad language admitting statements whenever "circumstances" offered "assurances of accuracy," taking into account the alternatives of calling the speaker to testify or making do without his evidence if he was unavailable.

Approach of FRE 801. Looking only to <u>FRE 801(a)-(c), we see a clear adoption of the traditional approach</u>. This basic definition embraces the three statements we encountered in Problem 3-A (Three See a Robbery), all of which are hearsay under FRE 801 if offered to prove that Higgins robbed the bank.

Looking at the <u>whole of FRE 801</u>, we find that the <u>traditional approach is augmented by elements borrowed from the second approach described above</u>, and we find a <u>new complication</u>. Consistent with the second approach, FRE 801(d)(1) says *some* out-of-court statements by testifying witnesses that *would be* hearsay if we looked only to FRE 801(a)-(c) are "not hearsay" after all: If the declarant testifies and submits to cross-examination on any statement that fits FRE 801(d)(1)(A), (B), or (C), then that statement is "not hearsay."

The complication is that this modification is done by a bit of statutory magic: Out of the "hat" of the basic definition, the drafters pull the "rabbit"

---

7. Of course "unavailable" admits of degrees: A dead declarant is absolutely unavailable, but other situations generate argument. Is a witness unavailable when beyond reach of a subpoena? (One would think so, but usually it is possible for the proponent to get the deposition testimony of such persons by going where they are. Should we require her to do so and to offer the deposition in preference to other out-of-court declarations?) How about a witness who evades the process-server? (One would think she too is unavailable, but how hard must the proponent try? Does he have to hire a search agency to find the declarant?) How about a person who comes to court but refuses to answer questions, in contempt of the tribunal or under a claim of privilege? Perhaps hardest of all, what about a witness who testifies but cannot remember? (If his prior positive statement gets in, doesn't he have an incentive to "forget" in order to avoid the unpleasantness of cross-examination?) Even when the hearsay doctrine is not viewed simply as a rule of preference, certain "restricted" exceptions have long been recognized where the declarant is unavailable. The Rules continue this tradition. See FRE 804.

of "not hearsay" since the defining language transforms what would be hearsay into "not hearsay." This same statutory magic is also visible in FRE 801(d)(2), which codifies the admissions doctrine. The various statements described in all five clauses of that provision (A through E) are "not hearsay" only because FRE 801(d)(2) defines them in that way. This extension of the statutory magic is not so odd, however, because it connects with common law tradition, where admissions were sometimes seen as nonhearsay and sometimes as hearsay but within an exception that made them admissible.

2. Nonhearsay Uses and Nonassertive Conduct Revisited

Recall for a moment the nonhearsay uses and nonassertive conduct we already considered. How does Rule 801 affect these matters?

Nonhearsay uses. It is clear that the uses for out-of-court statements that we explored in Problems 3-C through 3-F ("The Blue Car Ran a Red Light," "Any Way You Like," Whose Corn?, and "I'm from the Gas Company") lie outside the realm of hearsay under FRE 801. That is to say, these uses lie beyond reach of the defining language contained in FRE 801(a)-(c).

Again we encounter semantic confusion traceable to the statutory magic described above. These nonhearsay uses have nothing to do with the "not hearsay" category set up by FRE 801(d)(1). We must distinguish between statements that are nonhearsay because they are used in a way that puts them beyond the reach of the hearsay definition in FRE 801(a)-(c) and statements that are "not hearsay" because they fit the special categories in FRE 801(d). We are stuck with language that makes it awkward to talk about these matters.

This book uses nonhearsay or not hearsay (without quotemarks) for statements that are not hearsay because they are used for something other than proving "the truth of the matter asserted" under FRE 801(a)-(c), and "nonhearsay" and "not hearsay" (with quotemarks) for statements that fall within FRE 801(d).

Nonassertive conduct. Statutory prose and legislative history make it about as clear as it can be made that FRE 801 rejects the broad position of Baron Parke in *Wright:* Under FRE 801, nonassertive conduct offered for the familiar two-step inference—to prove the actor's belief in a fact, hence the fact itself—is not hearsay. The wording supports this conclusion because FRE 801(a)(2) defines "nonverbal conduct of a person" as hearsay *only* "if it is intended by him as an assertion." And the Advisory Committee's Note contrasts "nonverbal" conduct which is "the equivalent of words, assertive in nature" against "[o]ther nonverbal conduct," saying of the latter:

> Admittedly evidence of this character is untested with respect to the perception, memory, and narration (or their equivalents) of the actor, but the Advisory Committee is of the view that these dangers are minimal in the absence of an intent to assert and do not justify the loss of the evidence on hearsay grounds. No class of evidence is free of the possibility of fabrication, but the likelihood is less with nonverbal than with assertive verbal conduct. The situations giving rise to the nonverbal conduct are such as virtually to eliminate questions of sincerity.

Motivation, the nature of the conduct, and the presence or absence of reliance will bear heavily upon the weight to be given the evidence.

In short, if the trial judge thinks the driver of the Kenworth intended no assertion (Problem 3-B), then evidence of his behavior in pulling forward into the intersection is not hearsay under Rule 801 when offered to prove the light changed to green. If the truckdriver had simply *said* the light turned green, his statement *would* be hearsay if offered to prove that point. And both his conduct and his statement support the two-step inference—both suggest what he thought, which in turn suggests the external fact. His conduct is nonhearsay (if nonassertive), but his statement is hearsay.

evidence of behavior vs. a statement

In passing, we should note here that nonassertive conduct includes the visible psychological, physical, and emotional reaction of a person, which may of course suggest something about what happened (the two-step inference is involved once again). Consider a case in which Gwinn was charged with kidnapping and sexually assaulting a woman. On first seeing his likeness in a mugbook at the police station, the woman screamed and started crying. Her emotional reaction amounts to nonassertive conduct and was viewed as nonhearsay. People v. Gwinn, 314 N.W.2d 562, 572 (Mich. App. 1981) (crying was not a "statement" under MRE 801 because "not intended as an assertion"). Similarly the reaction of a teller, who became pale and was shaking during a robbery, is nonassertive conduct when offered to prove the robbers intimidated bank personnel, and not hearsay. See Cole v. United States, 327 F.2d 360 (9th Cir. 1964).

The ACN to FRE 801 also states that "nonassertive verbal conduct" is excluded from the definition of hearsay. You might say "there's no such thing as nonassertive verbal conduct, because words are *always* assertive," and for the most part that's true. But it is at least possible that the framers had in mind involuntary verbal behavior like screaming "ouch" when struck unexpectedly, which seems reflexive more than reflective and is closer in nature to the kind of emotional reactions described above than to most verbal behavior.

D. HEARSAY AND NONHEARSAY—BORDERLAND OF THE DOCTRINE

1. Statements with Performative Aspects

ACN to FRE 801

While FRE 801 resolves much with certainty, some situations were problematic before the Rule was adopted and are problematic still.

The hard cases involve what might best be called "indirect uses" of statements. We are *not* talking about statements like those by Plaintalk, Sirchev, and Oblique that we saw in Problem 3-A (Three See a Robbery). In the indirect-use cases, the purpose is *not* to prove what the speaker said by the ordinary meaning of his words ("Higgins is the one who did it"), *nor* to use his words this way and then draw further inferences ("Higgins went out of here carrying money bags"), *nor* to prove what the speaker *meant* to say, even though the words make the point indirectly ("they ought to put Higgins in jail for this").

In the indirect-use cases, the purpose is to use words to get at something else. In these cases, we are after something that seems to be *on the speaker's mind but is not asserted* in the statement. Recall the words of Anna Sofer in Problem 3-H ("my husband treats me with 'cruelty' and fritters away our savings 'upon selfish and trivial pursuits'") and Sharon in Problem 3-I ("there was 'a papier mâché man'"). In each case the statement suggests something else about the speaker's thoughts (Anna would not have supported her husband; Sharon must have been in that room), and it was this "something else" that the statements were offered to prove. The same is true of the Vicar's statements in Wright v. Tatham (business talk suggested Marsden could conduct business).[8] These are examples of statements whose importance lies in what they suggest about what the declarant must think, without actually saying it.

Neither the language of FRE 801 nor post-Rules decisions provide clear guidance for these indirect-use cases. In fairness, we should add that something in the nature of hearsay and human verbal expression makes such cases problematic. There is room to doubt that any brief statutory phrase can provide much guidance.

We should now look again at the ACN to FRE 801. Right after the passage about "nonverbal conduct," the Note adds:

> [V]erbal conduct which is assertive but offered as a basis for inferring something other than the matter asserted [is] also excluded from the definition of hearsay by the language of subdivision (c).

What does this comment mean? By one reading, nobody could take issue with it, for it expresses the truism that a statement offered for a nonhearsay purpose is not hearsay. The statements in the other problems you considered in the section on nonhearsay uses—Problems 3-C through 3-F dealing with the red light, the massage parlor, the corn crib, and the gas company—all involve "assertive verbal conduct" offered "as a basis for inferring something other than the matter asserted."

How much further does this comment reach? Obviously it does not embrace what Oblique said in Problem 3-A ("they ought to put Higgins in jail for this"). Extended that far, the Note would reduce the hearsay doctrine to a foolish rule where formalism reigns supreme. Hearsay would only reach statements that say literally what they are offered to prove, and the doctrine would only occasionally achieve its purposes.

The statements by Anna Sofer and Sharon probably qualify as assertive verbal conduct offered as "a basis for inferring something other than the matter

---

8. We know what FRE 801 does to the broad holding in *Wright* (hearsay embraces all conduct, offered in support of the two-step inference to prove the actor's belief in a fact, hence the fact), but it is less clear what FRE 801 does to its narrow holding (the letters were hearsay when offered to prove the sanity of Marsden). The vicar issued an invitation for Marsden's lawyer to meet with the vicar's lawyer, and if Marsden took him up on the invitation (telling his lawyer to meet the vicar's lawyer), the vicar could not gracefully refuse to go forward with the meeting. In this sense the vicar's words have important performative qualities that might justify nonhearsay treatment. But arguably the letter is hearsay because it is so completely verbal and its verbal meaning seems so important. In effect, the vicar says, "I want to do business with you." If the letter is taken as proof of that desire (hence as circumstantial evidence that Marsden must be a person of sound mind), it is hearsay, much like the statement by Sirchev (Higgins was "carrying money bags").

asserted." But if they escape the hearsay definition in FRE 801, is it because they are offered to prove an unspoken thought? Or is it because the words have performative aspects (Anna makes a public display of distaste for her husband, and Sharon displays knowledge she could not have without the underlying experience)? If some performative aspect is necessary, does it seem to be required by the Rule as illuminated by the Note?

The same passage in the Note would also exclude "nonassertive verbal conduct" from the definition of hearsay. As noted before, this comment probably reaches involuntary verbal behavior, like screaming "ouch" when struck suddenly. But does it reach further? Does "nonassertive verbal conduct" mean ordinary words that have a performative aspect and that are conduct in the sense that they *do something* independent of what they assert?

UNITED STATES v. SINGER
United States Court of Appeals for the Eighth Circuit
687 F.2d 1135, modified, 710 F.2d 431 (1983)

[Joseph Sazenski, Arturo Izquierdo, and others were prosecuted for drug offenses, arising out of an operation allegedly involving shipments of marijuana from Miami, Florida, to Minnetonka, Minnesota. Sazenski maintained a residence at 600 Wilshire in Minnetonka. Apparently Izquierdo used the alias of Carlos Almaden.]

HENLEY, J. . . .

The district court admitted into evidence an envelope addressed to Sazenski and "Carlos Almaden," 600 Wilshire, containing notice to terminate their tenancy. It was introduced to show that "Carlos Almaden" lived with Sazenski. We reject Sazenski's contention that this letter was hearsay.

FRE 801(c) states: "'Hearsay' is a statement, other than one made by the declarant while testifying at the trial or hearing, offered in evidence to prove the truth of the matter asserted." The Advisory Committee for the proposed Rules of Evidence noted that "[t]he effect of the definition of 'statement' is to exclude from the operation of the hearsay rule all evidence of conduct, verbal or nonverbal, not intended as an assertion. . . . [Some] nonverbal conduct. . . may be offered as evidence that the person acted as he did because of his belief in the existence of the condition sought to be proved, from which belief the existence of the condition may be inferred." This observation is consistent with the purpose of the hearsay rule—the exclusion of declarations whose veracity cannot be tested by cross-examination. There is some guarantee that an inference drawn from out-of-court behavior is trustworthy, because people base their actions on the correctness of their belief. If this letter were submitted to *assert* the implied truth of its *written contents*—that Carlos Almaden lived at 600 Wilshire—it would be hearsay and inadmissible. It is, however, admissible nonhearsay because its purpose is to imply from the landlord's *behavior*—his mailing a letter to Carlos Almaden, 600 Wilshire—that "Almaden" lived there. In addition, it is important that the letter was found in the residence at 600 Wilshire. . . .

[handwritten margin note: Landlord's Behavior is the Key]

From what has been said, it follows that the judgments of the district court should be, and they are, affirmed.

It is so ordered.

[The opinion of Arnold, Circuit Judge, concurring in part and dissenting in part, is omitted. On rehearing, the Eighth Circuit reversed the convictions, but the en banc opinion expressly "adopted and reaffirmed" much of the panel's original opinion, including the portion set out above.]

NOTES ON STATEMENTS WITH PERFORMATIVE ASPECTS

1. Forget about Sazenski, who is not important. The letter to Carlos Almaden *says* he lives (takes mail) at that address, doesn't it? The larger purpose of the owner in writing the address block on the envelope was probably something else (he wanted the carrier to deliver the letter to the right place and wanted Almaden to get it), but his words still intentionally express the point that Almaden lives (takes mail) at that place, don't they? Yet the letter isn't *just* an assertion, is it? It begins to throw the fellow out (commences eviction). Shouldn't that make a difference? In calling the letter nonhearsay, the court stresses the act of mailing. If the owner hadn't mailed the letter, he would not have taken the legal step of giving notice. But mailing wouldn't make any difference for purposes of hearsay analysis if the owner had written a letter to a friend and mentioned that he rented the place at 600 Wilshire to Almaden. Mailing is important because throwing out a tenant requires not just "talk" but "action." Mailing the notice is action. The court in *Singer* is right, then, in finding the notice to be nonhearsay evidence, isn't it?

2. Suppose an FBI agent asked the owner where Carlos Almaden lived and he replied "600 Wilshire." That would be hearsay if offered to prove where Almaden lived, wouldn't it? Suppose an undercover agent testified that he gave the owner a package for Almaden, then secretly followed him, and saw the owner deliver it to 600 Wilshire. Such testimony would *not* be subject to a hearsay objection, would it? Which of these examples more closely resembles the actual facts of *Singer,* the first or the second?

3. When law enforcement agents bust illegal bookmaking or drug operations, they routinely take incoming phonecalls. In the former situation, a voice at the distant end tries to place a bet. In the latter, the voice tries to line up a drug purchase. If the officer who takes the calls testifies to the substance of what the callers say, as proof that people normally on the premises take bets or sell drugs, is it hearsay? Most American courts say no. See Headley v. Tilghman, 53 F.3d 472 (2d Cir. 1995) (incoming calls could be characterized as "mixed acts and assertions" admissable because of their "performance aspects"); United States v. Long, 905 F.2d 1572, 1579-1580 (D.C. Cir.) (admitting incoming drug calls as nonhearsay proof of trafficking), cert. denied, 498 U.S. 948 (1990). Do such calls have important performative aspects? If there are *many* such calls, is the case for treating them as nonhearsay stronger? See generally Symposium: The Reach and Reason of the Hearsay Rule: How Should (or Would) the Supreme Court Decide *Kearley?* 16 Miss. Col. L. Rev. 1 (1995)

(collecting essays on an English case holding that an incoming drug call is hearsay).

NOTES ON STATEMENTS THAT ARE NOT DECLARATIVE SENTENCES

1.   In everyday usage, "assertion" connotes a strong claim that something is so, and that is part and parcel of the hearsay doctrine, both under the Rules and in common law tradition. "There is a red barn" asserts that there is a barn and it is red. But in everyday usage, other kinds of statements, like commands or imperatives ("Look at the red barn") and questions ("Is that barn red?") would not be described as assertions because they do not (at least in a formal or grammatical sense) make strong claims: The speaker's purpose does not seem to include establishing the various facts to which he refers. Still, even questions and commands usually *express* or *communicate* various factual points, don't they? In applying the doctrine, it would be wrong, wouldn't it, to construe "assertion" in the everyday sense, and wiser to construe "assertion" to mean "express" or "communicate"? If the command "Look at the red barn" were offered to prove there is a barn or that it is red, it should be viewed as an assertion of these points (ordinarily hearsay), shouldn't it? And shouldn't the same apply to the question "Is that barn red?" if it were offered to prove there is a barn? One might suppose this question would have little probative force on the question of the barn's *color*, but it is easy enough to imagine statements framed as naked questions that *do* have probative force on the very point asked. Recall Julius Caesar's last words in the Shakespeare play: "Et tu, Brutae" sounds a lot like a question. Still, you would call it hearsay, wouldn't you, if it were offered to prove that Brutus was among the assailants? See Callen, Hearsay and Informal Reasoning, 47 Vand. L. Rev. 43, 89 (1994) (commenting that "Could it be a little more quiet in here?" may convey "the speaker's opinion that the stereo is too loud, rather than a question about applied acoustics").

2.   Unfortunately courts sometimes seize on the idea that "assertion" means only simple declarative sentences, and not questions or commands, in applying hearsay doctrine. See United States v. Oguns, 921 F.2d 442, 448-449 (2d Cir. 1990) (in a drug case, an incoming telephone query whether the "apples" had arrived was not hearsay because an inquiry is not an assertion); United States v. Lewis, 902 F.2d 1176, 1179 (5th Cir. 1990) (in similar situation, court rejects defense argument that "assertions implicit in the questions" made them hearsay, concluding that "assertion" in FRE 801 carries "the connotation of a positive declaration," so questions are not hearsay because "they do not, and were not intended to, assert anything"). Do you suppose the courts that decided *Oguns* and *Lewis* would hold that Caesar's last words (as Shakespeare envisioned them) didn't assert anything? Can you believe incoming drug queries don't assert anything? It is one thing to stress performative aspects in dealing with hearsay claims in cases like *Singer* and the drug prosecutions, but quite another to say questions and commands can't be assertions, isn't it?

3.   On trial for kidnapping, defendant Danny Weeks hears the complaining witnesses testify that during their ordeal they heard their abductors refer

to each other as "Jimmy" and "Gato." As proof that Weeks is "Gato," the government offers testimony by a warden that Weeks goes by that nickname and that guards and prisoners "use" it in reference to Weeks. Should such testimony be viewed as hearsay? See United States v. Weeks, 919 F.2d 248, 251-252 (5th Cir. 1990) (objecting party must prove declarant intended to make an assertion, and defense did not carry the burden; jury could infer that warden had knowledge of the nickname acquired "by hearing other people" use it "in a nonassertive manner"). Can you believe people talking *to* or *about* Weeks in ordinary conversation would use his nickname "in a nonassertive manner"? What exactly would that mean? That the speaker didn't utter a declarative sentence ("your name is Gato" or "his name is Gato")? Can *that* be the test of what an assertion is? If a guard or a prisoner said, with obvious reference to Weeks, that "Gato seems to be edgy of late," doesn't that line *assert* that Weeks is Gato? If a prisoner in the mess hall approaches Weeks and says "Hey, Gato, trade you a roll for a milk," doesn't that line assert that Weeks is Gato? Is there a performative aspect to calling a person by name to his face that justifies nonhearsay treatment?

PROBLEM 3-J.   *"My Husband Is in Denver"*

In FBI interviews, eyewitnesses identify Greg Hensen as one of the men who robbed Girard Bank & Trust in Boston on April 10th. On April 11th, FBI agents get an arrest warrant and go to Greg's house, where they encounter his wife Barbara. "My husband is in Denver," she tells them, "because his mother just died, and he flew out to her funeral on the 9th. He's coming back day after tomorrow." On checking airline passenger and reservation lists, the FBI learn that there is no record of a Greg Hensen flying either into or out of Boston in the previous seven days, nor any reservation in his name on any incoming flights to Boston in the next three days.

On April 12, agents question another suspect, who tells them that "Greg is hiding out at his brother's in Quincy." On the basis of that tip, the agents promptly get a warrant authorizing them to search for Greg in his brother's apartment, and there they find him.

At Greg's trial in federal court for armed bank robbery, the government offers testimony by the agents describing their encounter with Barbara, quoting what she told them of her husband's whereabouts. Counsel for Greg objects: "Barbara Hensen is not on trial here, her husband is. What she said or thought is hearsay, and irrelevant besides." Is Barbara's statement relevant? Is it hearsay?

NOTES ON LYING AND HEARSAY

1. In Greg Hensen's trial, arguing for the state that the hearsay doctrine doesn't apply to Barbara Hensen's statement is duck soup, isn't it? "We're not offering it for its truth, your Honor, so it can't be hearsay." When you prevail on that point and the statement gets in, you will come in time to closing arguments. What will you say to the jury about Barbara's false statement? Won't

you naturally stress "what she was trying to do" when she talked to police? What *was* she trying to do? Does your argument in effect stress the performative aspect of her statement?

2.   Most courts that consider lying have said it is not hearsay, and they sometimes accept the duck soup argument. In a complicated conspiracy prosecution for casting false ballots in a federal election, for example, the Supreme Court rejected a hearsay objection to evidence that conspirators perjured themselves in local proceedings inquiring into election fraud. The perjury took the form of false statements about who came to the polls, and the Court concluded that these lies were not hearsay. They were not offered to prove "the truth of anything asserted," said the Court, but to show "they were false." Nor did the rationale of the hearsay doctrine come into play, said the Court, since defendants "had no interest in cross-examining" their lying cohorts inasmuch as the government did not contend that what they said was true. Anderson v. United States, 417 U.S. 211, 219-222 (1974) (perjured statements "helped prove the underlying motive of the conspiracy" by showing that false votes in the federal contest "were not an end in themselves," but part of an effort to control local results). Do you agree that defendants had no interest in cross-examining the conspirators who committed perjury in the local proceedings? Obviously perjured statements are "verbal acts" that can send the speaker to jail. Is that point critical in *Anderson?* If you were the prosecutor, how would you use the perjured testimony in closing argument to the jury? Wouldn't your argument sound very much like the one you would make in the Greg Hensen case?

3.   In Problem 3-J, Barbara committed a criminal offense if she deliberately lied to the FBI about where her husband was, didn't she? See 18 U.S.C. §1001 (one who "knowingly and willfully falsifies, conceals or covers up" a material fact or "makes any false, fictitious or fraudulent statements" on matters within the jurisdiction of the government is guilty of a felony). The reason for construing such statements as criminal misdeeds is that they can have adverse operative impact: They can lead police in the wrong direction, cause them to overlook or miss other more fruitful avenues of investigation, and produce other negative consequences. Treating such statements as crimes recognizes their performative aspect, doesn't it? Even if Barbara did not commit a crime, doesn't the impeding effect of deceiving investigative officers justify treating her statement as an act?

4.   Where the defendant himself lies to police, it doesn't much matter whether we treat what he said as hearsay or as nonhearsay. The reason is that what a party to a suit says may always be admitted against him, at least so far as the hearsay doctrine is concerned (they may be excludable for other reasons, such as constitutional violations). In the parlance of the Rules, a statement by a party, if offered for the truth of the matter asserted, is the "admission" of the party when offered against him. See FRE 801(d)(2)(A) (taken up in Chapter 4B, infra). But this rationale does not usually reach statements offered against a defendant but made by someone else after the crime was committed, as in *Anderson* and Problem 3-J. Here it makes a big difference whether the statement is viewed as hearsay or nonhearsay, and often courts follow the lead of *Anderson* and admit. See, e.g., State v. Reyes, 52 P.3d 948, 958 (N.M. 2002) (admitting against one defendant false exculpatory statements, all telling the same story, separately given by himself and three co-offenders; statements by the other three were nonhearsay because offered as proof that they were false, indicating

consciousness of guilt). <u>Sometimes, however, false statements showing a guilty</u> <u>mind on the part of one person</u> carry little or no weight when offered against <u>another person.</u> See United States v. Pedroza, 750 F.2d 187, 203-204 (2d Cir. 1984) (in trial of *P* and *H* and others for kidnapping an 11-year-old boy, testimony by arresting agent that *H* falsely said she was the boy's mother was not hearsay, and showed "consciousness of guilt," but *H* lived with a third man who "masterminded the affair" and was "his principal aide," while *P* and other codefendants were only "hired hands," so on retrial it might not be proper to attribute *H's* state of mind to "the hired hands"). Quite apart from the question whether lying should be treated as nonhearsay because of its performative quality, there is the issue whether that behavior can be properly appraised without putting the actor on the stand and grilling her by close questioning. Do you think it would be wiser to extend the hearsay doctrine so it reaches such behavior (and perhaps *all* behavior offered in support of the two-step inference from actor's belief to the point believed) or to analyze such evidence in terms of probative worth versus risk of confusing the issues?

PROBLEM 3-K.   *King Air YC-437-CP*

Bruno and others are <u>charged with theft of an airplane and with importa-</u> <u>tion and possession of marijuana.</u> The evidence indicates that the plane in question, a King Air bearing identification Number YC-437-CP, was stolen in Florida and flown to an airstrip on Bruno's rural Arkansas property. There federal agents <u>attached a transponder enabling them to track the plane</u> when Mason and Pell flew it first to Acapulco (where it was seen picking up marijuana) and then to Mississippi (where the cargo was unloaded). Arrests were made and charges brought against Bruno and three others. Pell was not charged, for he bargained a plea and testified for the government.

At his trial, <u>Bruno contends</u> that his involvement in the unsavory theft and drug scheme was <u>completely innocent.</u> He testifies that the King Air made an emergency landing at his airstrip, where he let it stay until it could be repaired, that mechanics came thereafter and fixed a ruptured oil line that forced the landing, and that the plane "was mysteriously flown away about a week later." He denies that he accepted money from his codefendants in exchange for letting the plane stay, and insists he knows nothing about the theft or use of the plane to import marijuana.

Bruno also calls Kay Dixon as a witness and offers her testimony that "Bruno told me in front of six other people that he was storing a King Air at his airstrip." <u>He argues that the fact that he said in public that he was storing</u> <u>the plane supports his claim of innocence, since "a man with guilty knowledge</u> <u>is not likely to advertise his possession of stolen property."</u> The prosecutor raises a hearsay objection. What result, and why?

NOTES ON THE SIGNIFICANCE OF DISCLOSURE

1. Should we say Bruno's statement is not hearsay because it was a naked factual assertion ("I'm storing a King Air"), rather than a forthright revelation

of knowledge ("I know about yonder King Air")? That would be going much too far, wouldn't it? It would mean that the statement "The light was red" is not hearsay when offered to prove the speaker *thinks* the light was red, and what the speaker *thinks* is not *itself* hearsay if offered to prove that what he thinks is so. That would mean the end of hearsay, wouldn't it?

2. What makes Bruno's statement relevant is not that it proves what he knows, is it? If you get Bruno's statement admitted, what would you tell the jury it means? It is relevant to the defense because of *what it does* and not because it tends to prove what Bruno says is true. What *did* the statement do, from Bruno's perspective?

2. Using Statements to Prove Matters Assumed

UNITED STATES v. PACELLI
United States Court of Appeals for the Second Circuit
491 F.2d 1108, cert. denied, 419 U.S. 826 (1974)

[Vincent Pacelli, Jr., was charged with alleged conspiracy to interfere with the constitutional rights of others. The charges arose out of the brutal stabbing of Patsy Parks, whose body was doused with gasoline and set afire in a desolate area of Long Island. On the day before her death, federal agents had tried to serve a subpoena on her. She had previously testified before a grand jury investigating drug dealing, where she gave evidence about a box apparently containing money that was delivered to Pacelli. The grand jury had indicted Pacelli and others. In the present prosecution, the government alleged that Pacelli killed Parks to keep her from testifying.]

MANSFIELD, CIRCUIT J. . . .

Appellant next urges that it was prejudicial error on the part of the trial court to have permitted Lipsky, over defense objections, to testify as to the conduct and statements of appellant's wife, Beverly, of his uncle, Frank Bassi, and of his friends Perez and Bracer on February 10, 1972, at the Bassis' apartment. We agree. Since the conspiracy to violate Parks' civil rights had terminated with her death, this proof was not admissible as declarations of a co-conspirator made in the course of a conspiracy or as evidence of acts designed to show illegal activity on the part of the conspirators themselves. The purpose of the evidence was to get before the jury the fact that various persons other than Lipsky, who had been closely associated with Pacelli, believed Pacelli to be guilty of having murdered Parks. Indeed the government frankly conceded this in its brief:

> The fact that Pacelli's wife summoned Lipsky to the Bassis' apartment is proof that she knew of his involvement with Pacelli in the murder. The fact that Pacelli's wife, uncle, and close friends were discussing at that meeting that the murder had been bungled by leaving the body where it could easily be found—rather than that Pacelli had been remanded for something he had not done—is strongly indicative that they knew that Pacelli caused Patsy Parks's death. . . . [T]he jury

was entitled to conclude, from the close relationship to Pacelli of the persons at the February 10th meeting, that the source of their knowledge was Pacelli himself, since he was the only person besides Lipsky present at the commission of the crime.

The additional fact that at this meeting Pacelli's wife told Lipsky to get instructions from Bracer, who, with Perez, then told Lipsky he should go to Florida and offered him the money to do so, was clearly evidence that they knew that Lipsky had seen Pacelli kill Parks.

Since the extra-judicial statements clearly implied knowledge and belief on the part of third person declarants not available for cross-examination as to the source of their knowledge regarding the ultimate fact in issue, i.e., whether Pacelli killed Parks, Lipsky's testimony as to them was excludable hearsay evidence.

. . . The admission of testimony as to the third party's declarations in the present case violated the central purpose of the hearsay rule, which is to give litigants "an opportunity to cross-examine the persons on whom the fact finder is asked to rely." Finman, Implied Assertions as Hearsay: Some Criticisms of the Uniform Rules of Evidence, 14 Stan. L. Rev. 682, 684 (1962). We cannot agree that the only source of the extra-judicial declarations and conduct could have been Pacelli himself. Cross-examination of the declarants, had they been produced as witnesses, might have established that the information came from Lipsky himself, from third persons, or from news media, especially since appellant had on the same day been jailed as a result of the discovery of Parks' body.

We consider it irrelevant. . . that the extra-judicial statements and conduct admitted in this case may not have been intended by those involved to communicate their belief that Pacelli murdered Parks. The government concedes that if Lipsky had testified that the various declarants (Beverly Jalaba, the Bassis, Perez and Bracer) had told him at the February 10th meeting that Pacelli had admitted to them his participation in the killing of Parks, the testimony would have been inadmissible hearsay. While the danger of insincerity may be reduced where implied rather than express assertions of the third parties are involved, there is the added danger of misinterpretation of the declarant's belief. Moreover, the declarant's opportunity and capacity for accurate perception or his sources of information remain of crucial importance. Here, for instance, there is no suggestion that the declarants actually observed Pacelli commit the crimes with which he was charged. Thus their extra-judicial implied assertions have even less indicia of reliability than the implied assertion involved in Krulewitch [v. United States, 336 U.S. 440 (1949)], which was held inadmissible. Pacelli was entitled to cross-examine the third party declarants in order to test the validity of the inference—which the government sought to have the jury draw— that he had told the declarants he had killed Parks. . . .

The judgment of conviction is reversed and the case is remanded for a new trial.

MOORE, J., dissenting. . . .

Turning now to the "hearsay" constituting, according to the majority, reversible error, of what does this hearsay, so damaging as to require reversal, consist? On February 10th at the apartment of Frank Bassi (Pacelli's uncle) were gathered, Bassi, Pacelli's wife, Beverly, Beverly's sister, Barbara, Pacelli's sister, Loretta, three friends, Al Bracer, Abby Perez and Barbara Jalaba, and a man named Bayron. By this time via the public press, Parks' murder and the burning of the body had been revealed to the public at large. Frank Bassi commented about the bungling technique used in trying to dispose of the body. Lipsky was induced to go away for a while and given $1,000 by Perez for that purpose. From this the majority conclude that these "extra-judicial statements clearly implied knowledge and belief on the part of third person declarants not available for cross-examination as to the source of their knowledge regarding the ultimate fact in issue, i.e., whether Pacelli killed Parks." However, there was no declaration that Pacelli had told them that he had killed Parks and none expressed an opinion to this effect so that any such "hearsay" problem is not before us. Thus, Lipsky's statements of the February 10th apartment conversation added so little—and this only by way of inference—to his actual eye-witness testimony as to the events on February 4th that it does not, in my opinion, fall within the category of reversible error. . . .

NOTES ON USING STATEMENTS TO PROVE UNSPOKEN THOUGHTS

1. *Pacelli* is a pre-Rules decision, but it is not clear that applying FRE 801 would change anything. Where is the hearsay statement that led to reversal? Isn't Judge Moore right in saying there was "no declaration that Pacelli had told them" he killed Parks, and nobody "expressed an opinion" to this effect? Consider these possible interpretations of what happened in *Pacelli:*

(a) Those at the meeting thought Pacelli had done the deed, and their conversations about sending Lipski into hiding expressed that belief. Hence their words are hearsay, like the words of Oblique in Problem 3-A ("They ought to put Higgins in jail for this").

(b) Those at the meeting didn't know what happened, but spoke and acted on the basis of rumors circulating among them, perhaps traceable ultimately to statements by Lipski or Pacelli. Hence an account of the behavior of those attending the meeting conveyed "indirect hearsay," like that condemned by Judge Waterman in *Check* (Chapter 3B1c, supra).

(c) Those at the meeting *behaved* as though Pacelli did the deed—as though that were commonly understood. What they did was to send Lipsky into hiding to protect Pacelli. This behavior amounts to a performative aspect of the statements made and decisions taken, justifying nonhearsay treatment, similar to the eviction notice in *Singer* or the lies to police in Problem 3-J ("My Husband is in Denver").

(d) What is so persuasive about the meeting is what did *not* happen and what was *not* said. If those at the meeting thought Pacelli was innocent and did not murder Patsy Parks, one would have expected protests at the conduct of the federal agents and prosecutors in arresting and charging Pacelli. Hence what happened at the meeting resembles *Cain* (Chapter 3B1b, supra), where the absence of complaint was not hearsay when offered to prove the heater worked.

When conduct involving words (coming together in a meeting and speaking about a problem) has both hearsay and nonhearsay aspects, as these interpretations suggest, what should we do? Admit as nonhearsay, as the dissent argued, or exclude as hearsay as the majority held?

2. Consider a case in which Parran and Reynolds were charged with conspiracy to defraud the government by cashing unemployment compensation checks belonging to others. Federal agents had been tipped by a photography studio, where the clerk reported that two men were trying to get photo IDs but did not know what names and numbers they wanted to use(!). Watched by the agents, the two emerged from the studio, conversed briefly, and then Reynolds entered a bank, which refused to cash the check that he proffered because he had no account. Agents arrested Reynolds. When Parran approached, Reynolds told him "I didn't tell them anything about you." The government proved this statement in the joint trial of the two. When Parran appealed, the government argued that what Reynolds said was not offered against Parran "for the truth of the matter asserted" because Reynolds had said nothing about Parran's guilt or involvement. Consider these possible interpretations:

(a) Although his words do not say "we both know you're in this with me up to your eyeballs," that is the apparent message that Reynolds was conveying. Hence his words were hearsay like the words of Oblique in Problem 3-A ("They ought to put Higgins in jail for this").

(b) The fact that Reynolds chose, or felt the need, to say such a thing to Parran amounts to a gesture of solidarity, which makes it more likely that Parran was involved because no such gesture would be needed among friends if Parran were innocent. As such, the gesture has a performative aspect similar to evicting a tenant (as in *Singer*) or lying to police as in Problem 3-J ("My Husband Is in Denver") that justifies nonhearsay treatment.

(c) Reynolds did not assert anything about Parran, but merely stated a fact that is true or false (he said he had not told the agents about Parran; either he did or he didn't). We infer, from the fact that Reynolds chose to say these words, that he knew Parran was involved, and the government is right—the words are not hearsay because they assume this point but do not assert it.

Which would you choose? Would you admit or exclude? In the case itself, the reviewing court concluded that what Reynolds said was hearsay, and reversed the conviction of Parran: "[S]tatements containing express assertions may also contain implied assertions qualifying as hearsay and susceptible to hearsay objections," and the probative value of what Reynolds said "depends on the truth of an assumed fact [that] it implies," making it inadmissible hearsay. United States v. Reynolds, 715 F.2d 99, 103 (3d Cir. 1983).

3. The decisions in both *Pacelli* and *Reynolds* cite the *Krulewitch* case, where the Supreme Court concluded that a statement was hearsay when offered to prove something that the speaker was assuming. In *Krulewitch*, Kay and a woman companion were charged with interstate transportation of another woman from New York City to Miami for immoral purposes. After the three were arrested, Kay's companion spoke with the transported woman. At Kay's trial, the latter summed up the conversation this way:

> She asked me, she says, "You didn't talk yet?" And I says, "No." And she says, "Well, don't," she says, "until we get you a lawyer." And then she says, "Be very

careful what you say." And I can't put it in exact words. But she said, "It would be better for us two girls to take the blame than Kay (the defendant) because he couldn't stand it, he couldn't stand to take it."

See Krulewitch v. United States, 336 U.S. 440, 441-443 (1949) (reversing Kay's conviction for admitting "the hearsay declaration attributed" to his companion, since it "plainly implied [Kay] was guilty of the crime for which he was on trial"). See also Dutton v. Evans, 400 U.S. 74 (1970) (treating as hearsay a co-offender's jailhouse comment that "we wouldn't be in this now" if it hadn't been for defendant since it "implicitly identified" defendant as the murderer, but rejecting a constitutional challenge).

4.   Suppose Nora sues Vince, claiming he is the father of Nora's infant son Christopher. Nora offers to testify that Vince's parents came to the hospital for the delivery and that Vince's "brothers and sisters and other kindred visited [the hospital] and exhibited affection" toward little Christopher after he was born. Admit in support of the claim that Vince is the father, or exclude? Is it hearsay? See Thornton v. Shows, 537 So.2d 1363, 1366 (Miss. 1989) (affection of Vince's family for Christopher was "not more than a nonverbal assertion showing the family's belief in the paternity of the child," and it was tantamount to hearsay) (error, but harmless, to admit). Do you think Vince's family intended to assert that Vince was the father? If not, should the behavior of the family members be excluded because they could not know who the father was? Or should we view their behavior as implicitly conveying an admission by Vince that he was the father?

5.   It has been suggested that a statement asserting X must be treated as hearsay when offered to prove Y, if Y "must be being asserted" to make the statement right in asserting X. See S. Saltzburg and M. Martin, Federal Rules of Evidence Manual 133 (5th ed. 1990) (noting as well that if a statement asserting X *may be true* when Y, the fact to be proved, is not true, the statement may still be hearsay if the speaker "intended to assert" Y). That suggests, doesn't it, that "the barn is red" must be hearsay if offered to prove the barn exists (X means barn is red; Y means barn exists). Surely that's the right outcome. But the test doesn't help with what Reynolds said, does it? What he said could be right (X means Reynolds did not tell the agents about Parran) whether Parran was in it with him or not (Y means Parry being in it with him).

6.   Do the difficulties presented by these cases suggest that FRE 801 should be amended? Professors Graham and Wellborn think so. Graham would amend the hearsay definition to embrace a statement where its "relevance depends" on "truth of the matter asserted" or "declarant's belief in the truth or falsity of the matter asserted." See M. Graham, "Stickperson Hearsay": A Simplified Approach to Understanding the Rule Against Hearsay, 1982 U. Ill. L. Rev. 887, 921. Apparently Wellborn would go a step further, defining hearsay as "assertions" and "verbal expressions" offered to prove any matter "explicitly asserted" or "implied" when probative value "flows from declarant's belief as to the matter." Wellborn, The Definition of Hearsay in the Federal Rules of Evidence, 61 Tex. L. Rev. 49, 92 n.191 (1982) (this definition found its way into Texas Rule 801). Under either of these revisions, the eviction notice in *Singer* and the lies in Problem 3-B would be hearsay, wouldn't they? The incoming bet-placing and drug-ordering calls would be hearsay too, wouldn't they? And how

about Anna Sofer's statement in Problem 3-H (my husband treated me with "cruelty" and frittered away our savings "upon selfish and trivial pursuits") and Sharon's statement in Problem 3-I (describing the "papier mâché man")? Wouldn't these proposals throw out the baby with the bathwater? Don't they make the mistake of overlooking the performative quality of statements by expanding their assertive dimension to the exclusion of everything else?

7. Problems such as these are inevitable in a doctrine that tries to regulate the evidential use of human statements, aren't they? Especially since modern hearsay requires us to distinguish between *saying* and *doing*. Just as *doing something* may have an assertive quality (nodding the head, pointing), so *saying something* may have a performative quality (evicting someone). There will always be cases with a foot in both camps. See generally Mueller, Post-Modern Hearsay Reform: The Importance of Complexity, 76 Minn. L. Rev. 367, 412-423 (1992) (developing this argument); Park, "I didn't tell them anything about you": Implied Assertions as Hearsay Under the Federal Rules of Evidence, 74 Minn. L. Rev. 783 (1990) (analyzing *Reynolds* and other cases and concluding that FRE 801 should *not* be amended); Millich, Re-Examining Hearsay Under the Federal Rules: Some Method for the Madness, 39 Kan. L. Rev. 1 (1990) (proposing a test for statements offered to prove matters assumed).

E. HEARSAY—TEST YOUR UNDERSTANDING

You have made your way through some of the most difficult principles of the law of evidence. Test and refine your understanding by considering another case and taking a short quiz.

BETTS v. BETTS
Washington Court of Appeals 473 P.2d 403 (Wash. App. 1970)

[Michael Betts sued his former wife Rita in Washington and obtained a judgment awarding him custody of their daughter, five-year-old Tracey Lynn. Michael and Rita had divorced in California, and she had moved to Washington with Tracey Lynn and Tracey Lynn's brother James, the second child of the marriage.

While in Washington, Rita and the children began living with Raymond Caporale. A week later James (then two years old) died from internal injuries and multiple bruises on the head and body. Tracey Lynn was placed in protective custody and Caporale was charged with second-degree murder in the death of James, but he was acquitted with a finding that the evidence was insufficient.

In the meantime, Michael Betts moved to Washington and remarried, and Rita married Caporale and moved to California. Tracey Lynn remained in a foster home in Washington.

On appeal, Rita urges that the trial court erred in admitting certain testimony by Tracey Lynn's foster mother.]

Armstrong, C.J. . . .

The foster mother saw an item in the paper relative to the remarriage of the child's mother and with reference to it, testified as follows:

A. So I told her that her mama and Mr. Ray Caporale had got married, and she started crying. She said,—she ran and put her arms around me and her head in my lap and started crying real bad and hard and said, "He killed my brother and he'll kill my mommie too,"—and she doesn't seem to ever get that out of her mind.

Q. Does she say this often?

A. Yes, she tells all her friends—explains why she is with us, and she goes into this tale, and I don't seem to be able to get her not to tell her problems to outsiders.

Q. Did she ever make statements about this prior to the incident you have just mentioned, which apparently occurred after the trial?

A. Yes, yes, she started telling about [how] her little brother was in heaven and how he had gotten there and she always blamed him for it.

Q. By "him," who do you mean?

A. Mr. Caporale.

Q. Has anyone in your presence tried to pull this information out of this child?

A. No, because I didn't want to worry her. When she talks, we let her talk; but we don't try to change her mind, one way or the other, because we aren't there to do that—just give her a home.

The foster mother further stated, "She always mentioned, 'He's mean.' That is the word she uses—'He's mean.'"

We hold that use of this testimony does not violate the hearsay evidence rule.

The hearsay evidence rule prohibits the use of testimony in court, of a statement made by another person out of court, which is being offered to show the truth of the matter asserted therein. Such evidence derives its value, not solely from the credibility of the in-court witness himself, but also in part, from the veracity and competence of the person who made the out-of-court statement.

The statements of the child were not admitted to prove the truth of the assertions she made, but merely to indirectly and inferentially show the mental state of the child at the time of the child custody proceedings.

In finding of fact 18, the trial court stated in part: "The fact that said statements had been made would tend to create a strained relationship between said Tracey Lynn Betts and her step-father, Raymond Don Caporale, and her mother, should she be awarded to the mother.". . .

It should be pointed out that there is a distinction between nonhearsay statements which circumstantially indicate a present state of mind *regardless of their truth,* and hearsay statements which indicate a state of mind *because of their truth.* The state of mind must be relevant in either instance. The distinction is based upon the question of whether the statement shows the mental state *regardless of the truth of the statement.* The distinction is usually disregarded in the cases because the statement will usually be admissible either under the exception to the hearsay rule or under the theory that it is not hearsay. In this case the distinction is important because if the statement is admitted as an exception to the hearsay rule, certain reliability requirements must be met.

An obvious example of an out-of-court non-hearsay statement which circumstantially indicates a state of mind regardless of the truth of the statement would be "I am Napoleon Bonaparte." This would be relevant in a sanity hearing.

The statements in question in this case are clearly nonhearsay statements which circumstantially indicate a state of mind regardless of their truth. Since they were relevant, they are admissible.

The mother further contends, however, that the out-of-court statements would not be admissible because the child was not competent to testify in court. At the time of the hearing she was 5 years old.

We need not decide whether hearsay statements introduced under an exception to the hearsay rule must be made by someone who is competent to testify as a witness. We note, however, that res gestae utterances of a child who would probably not have been competent as a witness were held admissible in [two earlier cases]. It was suggested in an article [by a Washington judge] that the better rule would be that with the exception of res gestae utterances, all hearsay statements introduced under any exception to the rule should be made by someone competent as a witness at the time the statement was made.

However, we are not considering the testimony of the 5-year-old child as an exception to the hearsay rule, but as a nonhearsay statement which circumstantially indicates the state of the child's mind regardless of the truth of the statement. Under such circumstances, the statement would be admissible even though the child may not have been competent to serve as a witness in the case. . . .

We conclude that the rule, that out-of-court nonhearsay statements may be admitted which circumstantially indicate a state of mind regardless of the truth of the statement, is especially applicable in child custody proceedings. The mental state of the child is an important element in determining what is best for the child's welfare. The trial court should consider the truth of the child's assertion only if such statements meet the reliability test required of the "present state of mind" exception to the hearsay rule. . . .

The judgment is affirmed.

PEARSON and PETRIE, JJ., concur.

NOTES ON STATEMENTS AS CIRCUMSTANTIAL EVIDENCE OF STATE OF MIND

1.   What did the prosecutor seek to prove with Tracey Lynn's statements in *Betts?* Whether Tracey Lynn wanted to live with Rita and Raymond, or whether they would provide a suitable environment for Tracey Lynn? Should it matter?

2.   Should Tracey Lynn's statement be treated the same way as the statement by Anna Sofer (Problem 3-H)?

3.   The court says that Tracey Lynn's statement indicates her state of mind without regard to its truth. In what sense is that surely true? In what sense is that surely false? The court also says that the statement "I am Napoleon" would be nonhearsay circumstantial evidence if offered to prove state of mind. Is that the proper outcome under FRE 801?

4.   The foster mother testified that Tracey Lynn "ran and put her arms around me and her head in my lap and started crying real bad" on learning

that her mother Rita had married Ray. Should proof of this behavior be viewed as hearsay? If not, is it easier to accept Tracey Lynn's contemporaneous statements as not hearsay?

5.   If the court had decided that Tracey Lynn's statements were hearsay, two obvious hearsay exceptions might apply—the one for "excited utterances" now contained in FRE 803(2) and the one for statements describing the declarant's state of mind now contained in FRE 803(3). But the court entertains doubt as to Tracey Lynn's competency as a witness and thinks the hearsay exceptions might be unavailable. It also implies that "reliability" might be an issue in applying those exceptions, but not in accepting her statements as nonhearsay. Do these positions make sense?

6.   Do cases like *Betts* prove the wisdom in proposals to redefine hearsay to embrace every use of a statement to prove "declarant's belief in the truth or falsity of the matter asserted" or "declarant's belief as to the matter" asserted? (The first phrase quotes Professor Graham's proposal, the second Professor Wellborn's. See item 6 in Notes on Using Statements to Prove Unspoken Thoughts, supra.) Professor Graham thinks that the statement "I am Napoleon" would not be viewed as hearsay under FRE 801 when offered to prove mental incapacity, and further, that his proposal would make it hearsay, apparently because it is offered to prove "declarant's belief as to the matter" asserted. Do you agree that this new definition would make the statement "I am Napoleon" hearsay if offered to prove mental incapacity? Of course the statement must be understood as saying "I think I am Napoleon," must it not? Even reading it this way, doesn't it tend to prove the speaker is a little bit crazy *regardless* whether or not he believes what he says? If he believes it, something is wrong; the same is true if he doesn't believe it. If it bears on the question of capacity despite what he thinks, it isn't hearsay even under Professor Graham's proposed redefinition, is it?

HEARSAY QUIZ

In each example, the only question is whether the evidence offered is or is not hearsay. Assume that Rule 801(a) through (c) provides the applicable standard. You should consider the evidence to be hearsay if it fits within those definitional provisions and not hearsay if it does not. As you have seen, some statements that qualify as hearsay under those provisions are defined to be "not hearsay" by Rule 801(d). That has no bearing on these questions. In other words, answer the questions as if FRE 801(d) did not exist. Remember that the issue is hearsay versus not hearsay, not admissibility versus excludability. You will discover when you take up the exceptions that many statements that are hearsay are also admissible, so do not let your instinct that something is admissible lead you to conclude that it must not be hearsay!

1.   As proof that *B* lacked testamentary capacity in April, evidence that several times in March he told friends that he was Woody Allen.
2.   As proof that *C* assumed the risk of accident on account of faulty brakes in riding in *D*'s car, *D*'s testimony that "I told *C* before he got in that something was wrong with my brakes."

3. In E's personal injury suit, as proof that F was an agent of defendant All-Cure Drugstore, E's testimony that F said, "I'm awfully sorry, I was running an errand for my employer All-Cure Drugstore."

4. As proof that G stole a car, evidence that police stopped him and that his girlfriend H falsely stated at that time, "This car belongs to my brother."

5. As proof that H was frightened when J brandished a plastic pistol and demanded cash, evidence that H began sweating and shaking.

6. As proof that the time was about midnight when K entered the building, testimony by L that she saw K come in and mentioned it to M ten minutes later, coupled with M's testimony that it was "just past midnight when L told me that she saw K enter."

7. As proof that N committed the robbery with which he is charged, testimony from bystander O that "I picked N out of the lineup as the one who did it."

8. As proof that P was unusually accomplished in French, evidence that in her first year of college she was accepted into a fourth-year course.

9. As proof that defendant Q participated in a criminal venture under duress, evidence that coparticipant R told him, "We will kill you if you don't help us."

10. As proof that S favored increasing the penalties for drunk driving, evidence that she joined an organization entitled Mothers Against Drunk Driving, coupled with proof that the principal aim of that organization is to increase such penalties.

11. As proof that defendant T owned a .32 caliber pistol, testimony by a police officer that when he asked T's father U whether T owned such a pistol, U went to a drawer in the house where he and T lived, pulled out a .32 caliber pistol, and handed it to the officer.

12. As proof that officer V acted in good faith in arresting W, offered by V in defending against the claim brought by W for violation of his rights, evidence that the prosecuting attorney told V "you have probable cause to arrest W."

13. As proof that St. John's beat Georgetown in basketball, evidence that Z, who had bet on Georgetown, paid off his debt.

14. As proof that X had committed a prior bank robbery, evidence that she was prosecuted for that crime and that a jury had found her guilty.

15. As proof that Y went to New Orleans on Tuesday, evidence that on Monday he said, "Tomorrow I'm going to New Orleans."

16. As proof that his brakes were bad, evidence that Z said, "I think I ought to reline my brakes before anybody drives the car."

17. As proof that B was selling pornographic literature, evidence that he received a letter from C enclosing a check and saying in substance "please send me that dirty book."

18. As proof of the manner in which X was injured in the workplace, evidence of a videotape in which X reenacts the events that led to her injury, offered in proof by X.

19. As proof that E did not have permission to drive the car to Sacramento, evidence that owner F had told E "not to drive it out of San Francisco."

20.   As proof that tenant *G* terminated his month-to-month tenancy effective November 1, evidence that *G* sent owner *H* a letter in September that stated: "October will be my last month as tenant. I am vacating by November 1."

21.   As proof that the stairs in Bloomingdeal's Department store were adequately lighted, testimony by the floor manager that in six years several customers had complained that they were a long hard climb but no one had mentioned any lighting problem.

22.   As proof that *J* had been in the law library before, evidence that on entering the library she said to the attendant, "May I please have the key to the locked cage in the basement, so I can look at Starkie on Evidence?" coupled with proof that in fact that book is shelved in a locked cage at that location.

23.   As proof that the hit-and-run driver drove a Porsche, testimony that the logo on the rear of the vehicle in question read "Porsche."

24.   On the question whether tenant *L* had paid his rent for the month of April, testimony that in handing landlord *M* a check in the appropriate amount *L* said to *M*, "This is for the April rent."

25.   On the issue set out in question 24, testimony that on day after giving the check to *M, L* was heard to say, "I paid my rent for April."

26.   As proof that the train had come from the west, testimony by eyewitness *N* that she pointed in the direction of the train when she heard it coming, coupled with testimony by a police officer present at the scene that the direction in which *N* pointed was west.

27.   As proof that HiTechCorp was a bad credit risk, evidence that Din & Broodstreet gives HiTechCorp a poor credit rating.

28.   As proof that BankWest acted reasonably in refusing to refinance HiTechCorp's debt, evidence that Din & Broodstreet gives HiTechCorp a poor credit rating.

29.   As proof that *R* was seriously ill, evidence that he was being kept in the intensive-care unit of the hospital.

30.   As proof that *S* is an honest man, evidence that he handed the store clerk a $10 bill for a $7 purchase and, on receiving a $10 bill and three ones from the clerk in change, *S* returned the $10 bill and said, "I think you've made a mistake here."

31.   As proof that *V* is a violent man, testimony that he is reputed in his community to be such.

Four | HEARSAY EXCEPTIONS

Much that is hearsay is admissible. A series of standard exceptions paves the way for statements offered to prove what they assert, although exclusion may still be required on other grounds, such as simple relevancy or "unfair prejudice." Many exceptions rest on notions of necessity and trustworthiness, although some are outgrowths of the adversary system and the mechanics of trial.

The Rules set out the exceptions in four main groups.

(1) The first group contains three exceptions, and these apply to certain prior statements by testifying witnesses. Rule 801(d)(1) defines these exceptions, and remember that statutory magic *makes* these statements "not hearsay" even though they fit the basic hearsay definition set out in Rule 801(a) through (c). In substance, these are hearsay exceptions.

[*handwritten: 801 d 1*]

(2) The second group contains five exceptions—really five variations on a single theme or idea—that together make up the "admissions doctrine." These five exceptions are set out in Rule 801(d)(2). The same statutory magic is at work here, for these too are defined as "not hearsay" even though they fit the basic definition. Once again, the result is the creation of hearsay exceptions.

[*handwritten: 801 d 2*]

(3) The third, and by far the largest group, is comprised of the 24 "unrestricted" exceptions listed in Rule 803. Statements that fit these exceptions may be offered to prove what they assert regardless whether the declarant testifies, and regardless whether or not he could be produced at trial to give testimony.

[*handwritten: 803*]

(4) The fourth and final group is comprised of five more exceptions set out in FRE 804(b), but these may be invoked only if the declarant is "unavailable as a witness" under FRE 804(a).

[*handwritten: 804*]

Of the 37 hearsay exceptions formally recognized by the Rules, about half are in everyday use, and the others appear only rarely. This chapter takes up the most important exceptions. We also examine associated constitutional doctrines that limit the use of hearsay *against* the accused in criminal cases, or obligate the prosecutor to produce available declarants rather than resort to hearsay, or require courts to admit certain hearsay offered *by* the accused.

A. EXCEPTIONS—DECLARANT TESTIFYING

FRE 801(d)(1) defines as "not hearsay" three different kinds of prior statements by testifying witnesses. Statements in the first two exceptions—certain prior inconsistencies and certain prior consistencies—would likely be admissible for limited purposes anyway. With respect to prior inconsistencies, recall Problem 3-C ("The Blue Car Ran a Red Light") in which a prior inconsistent statement was offered to impeach. This subject is examined in more detail in Chapter 8B1. With respect to prior consistent statements, you will see below that these are sometimes admissible to bolster the present testimony of the declarant/witness, and you will take up more generally the subject of rehabilitating a witness in Chapter 8C. For the moment, the basic point is that the effect of FRE 801(d)(1)(A) and (B) is not so much to let in what would surely be kept out otherwise, but to permit fuller use of such statements.

The third exception—prior statements of identification, offered under FRE 801(d)(1)(C)—is not connected with impeachment or rehabilitation. It paves the way for some statements that might not get in at all otherwise. It applies primarily in criminal cases and expresses the view that identifying statements made out of court are more to be trusted than in-court identifications.

1. Prior Inconsistent Statements 801 (d)(1)(A)

You have already seen the scholarly debate on the question whether prior statements by testifying witnesses ought to be included in the definition of hearsay. In large measure, the reluctance to admit prior statements by testifying witnesses expresses a strong preference for live testimony, along with related fears that freely admitting such statements will add to pressures to obtain such statements and encourage reliance on them at trial, and that "deferred" cross-examination is inferior to contemporaneous cross-examination.

Rule 801(d)(1)(A) amounts to a compromise. A prior statement by a witness is "not hearsay" if three conditions are met: First, the witness must now be cross-examinable "concerning the prior statement." Second, the statement must be "inconsistent" with his present testimony. Third, it must have been made under oath in a "prior proceeding" or "deposition."

For the most part, these requirements are clear in operation. But the forgetful witness (or one who *claims* to have forgotten) brings problems in applying both the first and second requirements. And where the witness denies even having made a prior statement or claims it was a lie, special problems arise in applying the cross-examinability requirement. There is even some difficulty in deciding the appropriate reach of the term "prior proceeding."

STATE v. SMITH
Washington Supreme Court
651 P.2d 207 (Wash. 1982)

DIMMICK, J.

Assault victim, Rachael Conlin, wrote out a statement on a form supplied by a detective of the Pasco Police Department, which contained *Miranda* warnings, in which she named Nova Smith (defendant) as her assailant. She signed under oath with penalty of perjury before a notary. At Smith's trial a month later, she named another man as her attacker. The trial court allowed her prior inconsistent statement to be used as substantive evidence, ruling it was not hearsay under Rule of Evidence 801(d)(1)(i). The jury found Smith guilty of assault in the second degree.

Thereafter, the judge granted a new trial, reasoning that ER 801(d)(1)(i) did not authorize the statement's admissibility as it was not given in a "proceeding." The State appealed and we accepted certification from the Court of Appeals. . . .

form supplied by PD & signed before a notary

I

At approximately 6:30 A.M. on July 10, 1980, Rachael Conlin was cruelly and severely assaulted in a room at the Double D Motel, Pasco, Washington, which she kept for work-related activities. She was struck in the face, beaten with a wire coat hanger, a belt, and a pipe, kicked several times and pulled back into the room by her hair on her attempt to escape. She received a cracked nose, bruises, black eyes, and required several stitches on her face. At 8 A.M. a police officer was called to the hospital and Conlin stated defendant had assaulted her, she was afraid, and did not know what to do. She was advised that nothing could be done unless she was willing to testify in court. About noon the officer recontacted Conlin and asked her if she wanted to give a statement concerning the incident. She came to the police station and talked with a detective indicating she was willing to press charges and testify in court. She understood that by giving a voluntary sworn statement criminal action against defendant was likely. She thereupon wrote, in her own words, a statement describing the details of the assault and identified the defendant as her assailant. She signed each page and the detective signed as a witness on pages 2, 3, and 4 of the statement. The detective then took her before a notary and read her the affidavit portion and oath. She reread the affidavit and oath and signed the affidavit. The notary subscribed the jurat and seal to Conlin's statement.

That same day Conlin, chased by defendant, ran into her manager's apartment screaming for help. Police were called when defendant, by force, took Conlin's car keys and departed.

At trial Ms. Conlin testified to the same facts regarding her assault as her original statement indicated, except for the startling deviation that her assailant was a Mr. Gomez, and that defendant had come to her aid. She freely admitted giving the sworn, voluntary statement to the detective and telling the officer at the hospital that defendant had assaulted her. She testified that she was upset with defendant over a fight the night before and blamed him for her having to stay in the motel room overnight with Gomez rather than in her apartment where defendant also lived. She further testified that she had lived with defendant both before and after the assault, and that she had left $150 for him at the jail for cigarettes, although she denied he was her pimp.

The prosecuting attorney was surprised at trial by Conlin's change in the identification of her assailant and introduced the written statement at issue for impeachment purposes. The State then moved to have it admitted as substantive evidence also, as it was apparently the only evidence that identified defendant as the perpetrator of the assault.

As previously noted, the trial judge ruled that the statement was admissible but then reconsidered and granted a new trial declaring ER 801(d)(1)(i) did not apply.

II. . .

Issue: interpret "other proceeding"

We are here concerned with the interpretation of the words "other proceeding" as used in [Washington Evidence Rule 801(d)(1)(i)]. Washington's rule is taken verbatim from FRE 801(d)(1)(A). Accordingly, it is proper to look at the federal rule's history and purposes in interpreting its provisions. In fact, the comment to the Washington rule ER 801 provides that the rule "conforms state law to federal practice."

The rule as adopted by the United States Supreme Court and passed by the Senate adopted the minority position allowing all prior inconsistent statements to be used as substantive evidence. The House Subcommittee disagreed with this unrestricted version and sought to limit the Rule by requiring that the statement be made under oath, subject to penalty for perjury, and given at a "trial, hearing, deposition, or before a grand jury." These requirements were to assure reliability. The House Committee on the Judiciary added that the original statement must have been subject to cross-examination and deleted the reference to grand jury proceedings. The Advisory Committee objected, asserting that an in-court cross-examination was adequate to discern the truthfulness of the prior statement. The committee finally reached a compromise resulting in the rule in question. One report in the House noted that the rule adopted covers statements before a grand jury. However, the term "other proceeding" was not discussed.

It is well accepted that "other proceeding" includes grand jury proceedings. The Ninth Circuit extended this interpretation and upon reviewing the rule's legislative history it determined that a taperecorded statement made under oath and taken in an immigration investigation was admissible. United States v. Castro-Ayon, 537 F.2d 1055 (9th Cir.), cert. denied, 429 U.S. 983 (1976). The court determined that the Legislature intended the term "other proceeding" to be open-ended and not restricted to grand jury proceedings. The court also compared grand jury proceedings to immigration proceedings and found enough similarities between the two to admit the statements. The court specifically added: "We do not hold, as the question is not before us, that every sworn statement given during a police-station interrogation would be admissible."

Holding

We likewise decline to answer the issue broadly. We do not interpret the rule to always exclude[1] or always admit[2] such affidavits. The purposes of the rule and

---

1. Some federal courts would apparently exclude all affidavits made to investigating officials as substantive evidence under FRE 801(d)(1)(A). Those courts, however, have not dealt with facts identical to the ones before us. E.g., United States v. Livingston, 661 F.2d 239 (D.C. Cir. 1981) (A postal inspector asked the witness questions, took notes, typed a statement based on the witness' responses and asked her to sign it. At trial the witness gave inconsistent testimony and either did not recall making the statements to the inspector or denied them.); United States v. Ragghianti, 560 F.2d 1376 (9th Cir. 1977) (The government's witness changed her story on the stand and did not recall making the prior inconsistent statement. The circumstances surrounding the prior inconsistent statement were not set forth except that it was given to an FBI agent, the investigating officer.).

2. At least one other state court which has adopted FRE 801(d)(1)(A) would admit an affidavit signed by a witness any time it is taken under oath before an official who is authorized to hear evidence and administer oaths. Slavens v. State, 614 S.W.2d 529 (Ark. App. 1981). Appellant

the facts of each case must be analyzed. In determining whether evidence should be admitted, reliability is the key. In many cases, the inconsistent statement is more likely to be true than the testimony at trial as it was made nearer in time to the matter to which it relates and is less likely to be influenced by factors such as fear or forgetfulness. One commentator has addressed the question of admissibility as follows:

> Inquiry into what other statements are encompassed by the Rule should be informed by the two purposes Congress had in mind in narrowing the provision originally proposed by the Court. The first was to remove doubt as to the making of the prior statement. . . . The second purpose was to provide at least the minimal guarantees of truthfulness which an oath and the circumstance of a formalized proceeding tend to assure. Clearly, however, the prior statement need not have been subject to cross-examination at the time made, for Congress was satisfied to rely upon delayed cross-examination of the declarant at trial to expose error or falsehood in the statement.

(Footnotes omitted.) D. Louisell & C. Mueller, [Federal Evidence] §419, at 169-71 [now 4 C. Mueller & L. Kirkpatrick, Federal Evidence §403 (2d ed. 1994)].

Here, there was no question that the statement was made since Ms. Conlin testified to that fact. Minimal guaranties of truthfulness were met since the statement was attested to before a notary, under oath and subject to penalty for perjury. Additionally, the witness wrote the statement in her own words. The jury, seeing Rachael Conlin on the stand, under oath, and hearing her explanation of the inconsistent statement while subject to cross-examination, was in a position to determine which statement was true.

III

Another factor to be considered is the original purpose of the sworn statement. It was taken as standard procedure in one of the four legally permissible methods for determining the existence of probable cause, thus allowing charges to be filed against defendant. The four methods are:

> (1) filing of an information by the prosecutor in superior court (see Const. art. 1, §25, and RCW 10.37.026); (2) grand jury indictment (see RCW 10.[27]); (3) inquest proceedings (see RCW 36.24); and (4) filing of a criminal complaint before a magistrate (see RCW 10.16).

State v. Jefferson, 485 P.2d 77 (Wash. 1971).

The first method, the one used here, is usually the result of police investigations into alleged criminal activity, and the taking of statements from witnesses and the presentment of them to the prosecuting attorney. The prosecuting attorney then exercises discretion in finding probable cause and files an infor-

---

relies heavily upon State v. Maestas, 584 P.2d 182 (N.M. Ct. App. 1978). The New Mexico court would seemingly always admit prior inconsistent statements such as the one made in the instant case. New Mexico, however, has adopted a different rule of evidence from Washington's which allows all prior inconsistent statements to be admitted as substantive evidence regardless of whether they were taken in a proceeding or under oath.

mation. "Other proceeding" under the rule would clearly cover the other three methods of finding probable cause listed above. That is, if the witness gave a statement, necessarily under oath to a grand jury, in an inquest proceeding or to a magistrate, that statement would be admissible as substantive evidence. Since the purpose of the statements in the first method is the same as the other three methods, that is determining probable cause, it should also be covered by the rule in an appropriate case such as we have before us.

To sum up, each case depends on its facts with reliability the key. Here, the complaining witness-victim voluntarily wrote the statement herself, swore to it under oath with penalty of perjury before a notary, admitted at trial she had made the statement and gave an inconsistent statement at trial where she was subject to cross examination. ER 801(d)(1)(i) is satisfied under the totality of these circumstances.

We therefore remand to the trial court with instructions to reinstate the verdict of the jury and sentence defendant thereon.

NOTES ON PRIOR PROCEEDINGS

1. Can the term "proceeding" really embrace a stationhouse interview producing an affidavit? Apart from the semantic difficulty in interpreting the language in that manner, are there differences between an affidavit and a sworn statement given in what we would normally call a "proceeding" which suggest that they should be treated differently?

2. Most federal cases exclude stationhouse declarations, as *Smith* itself recognizes. In *Livingston* (cited in *Smith* in footnote 1), the questioning that produced the affidavit proceeded in the home of the witness. See also United States v. Williams, 272 F.3d 845, 869 (7th Cir. 2001) (excluding affidavit by government witness because there was no indication that it was given in a proceeding). Would the Washington court that decided *Smith* admit the statement by Conlin if she had prepared it at home?

3. If the term "proceeding" does not embrace a stationhouse interview, is that because the word means only "judicial" proceedings? What about an agency hearing? In a prosecution for allegedly transporting illegal aliens (and related offenses), three aliens called by the government gave testimony favorable to the defense, but each admitted having made a prior statement to Agent Pearce on arrest. Those statements were made at a Border Patrol Station after Pearce had read their *Miranda* warnings and placed them under oath. Then he questioned them and recorded the interrogation. The trial court admitted the prior statements, and the reviewing court approved:

> [T]he immigration proceeding before Agent Pearce bears many similarities to a grand-jury proceeding: Both are investigatory, ex parte, inquisitive, sworn, basically prosecutorial, held before an officer other than the arresting officer, recorded, and held in circumstances of some legal formality. Indeed, this immigration proceeding provides more legal right for the witness than does a grand jury: the right to remain totally silent, the right to counsel, and the right to have the interrogator inform the witnesses of those rights.

United States v. Castro-Ayon, 537 F.2d 1055, 1056-1057 (9th Cir.), cert. denied, 429 U.S. 983 (1976). But see United States v. Day, 789 F.2d 1221, 1221-1223 (6th Cir. 1986) (recorded statement given under oath to IRS agent does not fit FRE 801(d)(1)(A); court refuses to follow *Castro-Ayon*). If *Castro-Ayon* is correct that an inquiry in the Border Patrol Station qualifies as a "proceeding," does it follow that *Smith* was rightly decided?

4. If a witness testifies both at a preliminary hearing and at trial, giving a different version of the facts on the latter occasion, it is clear that what he said at the preliminary hearing may be offered at trial (at least if he is cross-examinable on the latter occasion). In short, a preliminary hearing clearly is a "proceeding" under FRE 801(d)(1)(A). This exception often helps the prosecutor deal with a "turncoat" witness. It helps the accused less often because he typically does not call witnesses during a preliminary hearing. On that earlier occasion, both the defense and the prosecutor are represented by counsel (unless the accused chooses to represent himself), so both had a *prior* opportunity to cross-examine the witness at the preliminary hearing itself. But FRE 801(d)(1)(A) reaches further still, as the court points out in *Smith*: The term "proceeding" embraces a grand jury inquest, so the provision enables either party to offer at trial the prior grand jury testimony of a witness (again assuming inconsistency and cross-examinability *at trial*). The big difference between the preliminary hearing and the grand jury inquest is that in the latter instance the defense will not have had any *previous* chance to cross-examine the witness because grand juries operate ex parte (attended only by prosecutor, witness, court reporter, and grand jurors). Does the fact that FRE 801(d)(1)(A) reaches grand jury testimony prove that the principal safeguard is cross-examinability at trial? Does it prove that *Smith* was right to interpret "proceeding" to embrace the stationhouse interview?

PROBLEM 4-A. *"I Got Amnesia"*

In June 2003, Paul Barlow is tried on charges of racketeering and disrupting interstate commerce, arising out of the armed robbery of Halshire Foods on March 29, 2002.

At a grand jury proceeding in June 2002, Peter Breen testified that he, along with Paul Barlow and a man named Zigler, "cased" Halshire Foods several times in the days prior to the robbery. On the night in question, Breen climbed a telephone pole and broke into the store through an upstairs window. He then let Barlow and Zigler in the back door. While Zigler guarded the janitor in the office, Breen and Barlow wheeled in portable acetylene tanks and a blowtorch and "blew the safe." Barlow, Breen, and Zigler then fled with the proceeds.

The government calls Breen as its star witness at trial, but he suddenly proves unhelpful. First he claims his privilege against self-incrimination. The court immunizes him from any future use of his testimony and directs him to answer the prosecutor's questions. Then he says he can't remember what happened on March 29, 2002, because he "got under the influence of Valium in May 2002 while living at the Metropolitan Correctional Center, and that made me forget." He adds that "events in the early summer of 2002 upset me a lot because federal agents and others threatened me so I got amnesia about what happened before then, except that I remember going in the Witness Protection Program." Finally, Breen says he cannot remember making any statements to the grand jury about the robbery.

The prosecutor argues that Breen's lack of memory is "feigned," hence that his position at trial is "inconsistent with his detailed grand jury testimony in June 2002." Invoking FRE 801(d)(1)(A), she offers a transcript of that testimony. Counsel for Barlow vigorously objects:

> Your honor, Breen's grand jury transcript is absolutely inadmissible. First, under 801(d)(1)(A), the earlier statement has to be "inconsistent" with the trial testimony, and it isn't. All Breen has said here today is that he can't remember. Second, Breen has to be "subject to cross-examination" on his prior statement, but he isn't. How can I question him on his allegations about the robbery in March of a year ago when he says he doesn't remember blowing the safe at Halshire Foods? How can I question him about what he told the grand jury last April when he can't even remember testifying? Sure, he'll sit there and let me ask questions, but that can't be all that "subject to cross-examination" means. If I can't get anything out of him, how am I supposed to test his statement?

The prosecutor replies in this vein:

> Your honor, Mr. Breen is a classic turncoat witness. In June 2002 he testified to the grand jury about the Halshire Foods robbery on March 29th, but now he's got cold feet. Selective memory loss, actually. He remembers going into the Protection Program, which was in May of 2002, and the defendant can ask him about that and going to the grand jury, and anything he wants about credibility.

The trial court admits the grand jury testimony. On cross-examination, Breen still claims he cannot remember the robbery, but counsel for Barlow gets him to admit "I've been a burglar most of my life" until deciding "to lay low for a while helping the government, as long as they'll keep me in the Program and pay me a living wage." Breen admits he's been in trouble with petty crimes while in the Program, and "got more than $40,000 from the government over the last year or so, you know, for helping 'em out."

Barlow is convicted, and he appeals. Did the court properly admit Breen's prior grand jury testimony under FRE 801(d)(1)(A)? What are the best arguments for the defense and the government?

NOTES ON SUBSTANTIVE USE OF INCONSISTENT STATEMENTS: MEMORY LOSS AND CROSS-EXAMINABILITY

1. Is David Breen's grand jury testimony describing the robbery inconsistent with his testimony at trial that he doesn't remember the events of that day? Consider the approach endorsed by the Seventh Circuit:

> As long as people s peak in nonmathematical languages, such as English . . . it will be difficult to determine precisely whether two statements are inconsistent. But we do not read the word "inconsistent" in FRE 801(d)(1)(A) to include only

statements diametrically opposed or logically incompatible. Inconsistency may be "found in evasive answers, silence, or changes in positions." In addition, a purported change in memory can produce "inconsistent answers." Particularly in a case of manifest reluctance to testify, "if a witness has testified to [certain] facts before a grand jury and forgets them at trial," his grand jury testimony falls squarely within FRE 801(d)(1)(A).

United States v. Williams, 737 F.2d 594, 608 (7th Cir. 1984) (internal cites omitted). Under *Williams*, is Breen's position at trial inconsistent with his grand jury testimony?

2. California has lots of experience using prior inconsistent statements as substantive evidence because its Code permits this use of *all* such statements, whether or not given in a proceeding under oath. See California Evidence Code §1235. In applying this provision, California authority states that lack of memory at trial is inconsistent with a prior positive statement only if feigned. See People v. Simmons, 177 Cal. Rptr. 17, 19-20 (Cal. App. 1981) (a prior positive statement is inconsistent if the court finds the witness falsely claims not to recall facts to avoid testifying, but not if it finds he is "truly forgetful"). See also State v. Amos, 658 N.W.2d 201 (Minn. 2003) (defendant's daughter *M* testified "in some detail at her brother's trial," but in her father's trial she said she was "too emotional and confused" to remember the shooting incident; trial court properly admitted her prior testimony, since *M* was "obviously an evasive and reluctant witness" and these "dubious circumstances" made it reasonable to conclude that lack of memory was feigned). Federal cases agree that feigned lack of memory is inconsistent, but have not held that lack of memory must be feigned. See United States v. Bigham, 812 F.2d 943, 946-947 (5th Cir. 1987) (leaving for another day the question whether lack of memory justifies a finding of inconsistency only if feigned). What, if anything, is gained by saying only feigned and not genuine lack of memory is inconsistent with a prior statement?

3. If Breen says he cannot remember the robbery, is he "subject to cross-examination concerning" his prior statement under FRE 801(d) (1) (A)? What if he not only can't remember the robbery but can't remember testifying to the grand jury? Note that the exceptions for prior consistent statements and prior statements of identification, in clauses (B) and (C) of FRE 801(d) (1), are also subject to the cross-examination requirement. Consider these points:

(a) In United States v. Owens, 484 U.S. 554 (1988), the Supreme Court said the requirement can be satisfied even if the witness has forgotten the events. *Owens* involved the trial of a prison inmate for assaulting a correctional officer named Foster, who was hospitalized with serious injuries. At the trial of Owens, Foster remembered talking in the hospital with FBI Agent Mansfield and identifying Owens as his assailant, but Foster could not remember the assault, except for "feeling the blows to his head and seeing blood on the floor." Still the Supreme Court rejected the argument that Foster was not sufficiently cross-examinable, concluding that one may be "subject to cross-examination" under FRE 801(d) (1) (C) even if lack of memory about events makes him "unavailable" as a witness under FRE 804 for purposes of hearsay exceptions in the latter provision.

(b) At least one court has thought the cross-examination requirement means the witness must be able to give some kind of response to questions. See United States v. DiCaro, 772 F.2d 1314, 1323 (7th Cir. 1985) (cross-examination requirement should not be made "effectively meaningless," and in many if not most cases where witness suffers "total memory lapse concerning both the prior statement and its contents" he cannot be considered subject to cross). But see United States v. Keeter, 130 F.3d 297, 302 (7th Cir.) (admitting grand jury testimony by witness who feigned amnesia at trial, which did not block the necessary defense cross at trial), cert. denied, 523 U.S. 1034 (1997). It wouldn't be wise, would it, to interpret FRE 801(d)(1)(A) to mean only that the speaker must sit still long enough to answer questions, hence that one who remembers *neither* the events *nor* his statement is still "subject to cross-examination concerning" that statement?

4.   When you reach Chapter 4G, you will see that the Confrontation Clause of the Sixth Amendment, which guarantees the right of the accused to confront and cross-examine the "witnesses against" him, has considerable impact on the use of hearsay of the sort involved in *Smith* and Problem 4-A. Under the Supreme Court's 2004 decision in Crawford v. Washington, 124 S.Ct. 1354, prosecutors cannot offer "testimonial" statements against the accused, unless he has had an opportunity to cross-examine. In *Crawford,* the Court did not define "testimonial" comprehensively, but probably the term reaches "prior testimony that the defendant was unable to cross-examine" (which would include Breen's grand jury testimony) and statements to police (which would include Conlin's statement to the detective). In other words, it is not just the Rule that imposes a cross-examination requirement, but the Constitution. In light of the great stress that *Crawford* places on cross-examination, some have thought that the Constitution will one day offer more protection to defendants than *Owens* offered as a matter of construing the Rule. As you will see when you read *Crawford* and the materials on Confrontation, however, the Court has made many comments indicating that the Constitution does not guarantee more than the *Owens* construction of FRE 801(d)(1) guarantees.

5.   On the facts of Problem 4-A, should a court be more inclined to admit Breen's grand jury testimony if there is additional live testimony implicating Barlow? Suppose Zigler testifies to the essential facts in a manner that is consistent with Breen's account. Does such corroborating evidence relate only to the issue of sufficiency? Recall Senator Ervin's concern that one might be convicted by "an extra-judicial statement of a third person," see Chapter 3B3, supra. Also, look at footnote 3 of the Senate Report on FRE 801(d)(1)(A) (some opposition to the rule rests on "concern that a person could be convicted solely" on a statement admitted under this provision, but it addresses admissibility and "is not addressed to the question of sufficiency"; circumstances might arise "where, if this were the sole evidence, dismissal would be appropriate").

6.   While *DiCaro* and *Owens* suggest that the cross-examinability requirement of FRE 801(d)(1) can be easily satisfied, there are at least some cases that conclude that inability to cross-examine a forgetful or obstinate witness bars use of his prior statement as substantive evidence. See State v. Amos, 658 N.W.2d 201, 206 (Minn. 2003) (witness must be "testable about the statement, meaning that he must be reasonably responsive to questions on the circumstances in which he made it"); People v. Rios, 210 Cal. Rptr. 271, 280 (Cal. App. 1985) (observing demeanor of "totally recalcitrant witness" when questioned about

matters he refuses to address is meaningless, for there is "no way to test the truth" of his prior statement; admitting it would deny constitutional right to confrontation and cross-examination); People v. Simmons, 177 Cal. Rptr. 17 (Cal. App. 1981) (admitting unsworn statement by witness hospitalized for head injury and suffering retrograde amnesia violated defense confrontation rights, for observing demeanor of amnesiac witness "when questioned about that which he is incapable of recalling is as meaningless as attempting to gain information as to the truth of the unknown facts from his responses"). See also United States v. Torrez-Ortega, 184 F.3d 1128, 1132-1134 (10th Cir. 1999) (error to admit grand jury testimony by witness who "did not respond willingly to questions" at trial, and instead repeatedly claimed privilege against self-incrimination, refusing even to acknowledge that grand jury testimony was his).

2. Prior Consistent Statements   801 (d)(1)(B)

Prior consistent statements by a testifying witness are defined as "not hearsay" under some circumstances. FRE 801(d)(1)(B) sets out three conditions. First, the witness must be cross-examinable at trial "concerning the prior statement." Second, the statement must be "consistent" with his present testimony. Third, it must be offered to rebut a charge of "recent fabrication or improper influence or motive."

In one sense it is hard to get excited about this provision. To a large extent, a statement consistent with present testimony brings no new information and cannot be the only evidence on any point. Judgments are seldom reversed for error in admitting a prior consistency, which is largely "cumulative" of live testimony. In another sense, however, a prior consistent statement can be potent evidence, as you will discover as you read Tome (below).

Rule 801(d)(1)(B) contains limits that discourage resort to out-of-court statements as proof at trial. Those limits express the fear that deferred cross-examination is simply not as effective as contemporaneous cross-examination. In a sense, this fear is most acute with prior consistent statements, for it is here—where the witness sticks to his original story—that the danger seems real that any falsehood may "harden and become unyielding to the blows of truth" struck by the cross-examiner. State v. Saporen, 285 N.W. 898, 901 (Minn. 1939).

Rule 801(d)(2)(B) embraces any prior consistency, since there is no requirement that it be uttered under oath in a proceeding. But this provision raises two points of difficulty: First, what kind of attack on a witness raises a charge of "recent fabrication or improper influence or motive"? Second, what prior consistencies tend to "rebut" such an attack?

What kind of attack? Sometimes the cross-examiner suggests in so many words that the witness "just made it up" or "changed his story" because he was cajoled, paid, or frightened. Clearly FRE 801(d)(1)(B) reaches these easy cases where the charge of fabrication is express. But the Rule reaches further, giving the green light where charges of influence or motive are merely "implied." Professor Graham suggests these examples where "partiality" or "fabrication" is charged by implication: "You are the mother of the defendant, aren't you?" "You would do anything you could to help your son, wouldn't you?" "Didn't you talk with plaintiff's counsel shortly before testifying here today?"

"When did you first decide to change your testimony for trial?" See Graham, Prior Consistent Statements: Rule 801(d)(1)(B) of the Federal Rules of Evidence: Critique and Proposal, 30 Hastings L.J. 575, 586, 607 (1979).

When the cross-examiner attacks by asking the witness about a prior inconsistent statement, does the attack suggest that she fabricated her testimony or colored her story for "improper influence or motive"? Perhaps surprisingly, the answer is often no: We take up this subject in Chapter 8 on Impeachment.

What consistent statements rebut the charge? If an attack suggests fabrication or improper influence of motive, do *all* prior statements that are consistent with the testimony of the witness tend to repel the attack? Suppose that motorist David runs over pedestrian Paul, and that Paul sues David. Eyewitness Marian becomes involved in the pretrial skirmishing, and ultimately she testifies for motorist David:

PRETRIAL EVENTS

Day 1:   Marian comments, "David was driving within the speed limit."
Day 20:   David talks to Marian, perhaps pressures her to support him at trial (by cajolery, threat, bribe, or appeal to sympathy), but only David and Marian know.
Day 30:   Marian comments, "David was driving within the speed limit."

TRIAL TESTIMONY

On direct for David, Marian testifies: "David was driving within the speed limit."
On cross by Paul, Marian concedes: "On Day 20, I talked to David, and he insisted that he was driving within the speed limit. He pressed me to support him. I decided he was right."
Paul's lawyer says: "So what you told us here today about David driving within the speed limit—the source for that was David, wasn't it?"

Given this sequence, can counsel for David (calling party) ask Marian about her statements on Days 1 and 30, which are consistent with her direct testimony that David was driving within the speed limit? The hornbook answer is that a prior consistency tends to rebut such an attack ("repairing" or "rehabilitating" the witness) *only* if uttered *before* the supposed "influence or motive" came into play. On these facts, what Marian said on Day 1 would tend to refute the suggestion that her direct testimony was produced by influence or motive brought to bear on Day 20: After all, if she said the same thing on Day 1 that she says at trial, then whatever happened on Day 20 cannot account for her trial testimony.

On the other hand, Marian's utterance on Day 30 seems to *confirm* Paul's theory that the meeting with David on Day 20 is what led Marian to testify favorably for him. After all, her statement on Day 30 is consistent with her testimony, and she made the statement after talking to David, so her statement (like her testimony) reflects his influence. By pre-Rules tradition, courts often refused to let David prove such a statement because it would not repair Marian's credibility.

Effect of FRE 801(d)(1)(B). Following common law tradition, some modern decisions hold that FRE 801(d)(1)(B) does not embrace Marian's statement on Day 30. In its 1995 decision in *Tome* (below), the Supreme Court appears to have taken this position.

The question arises whether FRE 801(d)(1)(B) has any further effect. Where it applies, it permits *substantive* use of a prior consistent statement by a testifying witness, so the statement may be taken as proof of what it asserts: What Marian said on Day 1 can be taken as additional proof (along with her testimony) that David was driving within the speed limit. This consistent statement was made *before* David and Marian spoke, so it tends to refute any suggestion that his influence accounts for her testimony (she expressed the same view before she met with him, so his influence cannot account for her testimony).

As the separate opinion by Justice Breyer in *Tome* suggests, however, arguably consistent statements are relevant to rehabilitate an impeached witness even if the attacking party suggests something *other than* recent fabrication: Marian's consistent statement on Day 1 may, for instance, repel a suggestion that her testimony reflects lack of memory (if she said the same thing at the time of the accident that she says now, arguably her memory always carried the same version of events that her testimony reflects). So the question arises: Does FRE 801(d)(1)(B) mean such a statement *cannot be admitted at all,* or only that it cannot be given substantive effect?

TOME v. UNITED STATES
United States Supreme Court
513 U.S. 150 (1995)

JUSTICE KENNEDY announced the judgment of the Court and delivered the opinion of the Court with respect to Parts I, II-A, II-C, and III, in which JUSTICES STEVENS, SCALIA, SOUTER, and GINSBURG joined, and an opinion with respect to Part II-B, in which JUSTICES STEVENS, SOUTER, and GINSBURG joined.

. . . At issue is the interpretation of [FRE 801(d)(1)(B)] bearing upon the admissibility of statements, made by a declarant who testifies as a witness, that are consistent with the testimony and are offered to rebut a charge of a "recent fabrication or improper influence or motive." The question is whether out-of-court consistent statements made after the alleged fabrication, or after the alleged improper influence or motive arose, are admissible under the Rule.

I

Matthew Tome was convicted of sexually abusing his four-year-old daughter A.T. on the Navajo Reservation in New Mexico in summer 1990. A.T. had been staying with her father under a joint custody arrangement giving him primary physical custody after he and Beverly Padilla (A.T.'s mother) were divorced in 1988. In late August 1990, Beverly complained to authorities in Colorado (where she lived) that Matthew had sexually abused A.T.

The prosecutor sought to show that Matthew Tome abused A.T. while she was in his custody, and that she disclosed the crime when she vacationed with her mother in Colorado. A.T. was six and one-half years old at the time of trial, and most of her direct testimony consisted of one- or two-word answers to leading questions. During defense cross suggesting that she was motivated by her "desire to live with her mother," A.T. proved responsive on background subjects but reluctant to testify on conversations with the prosecutor and allegations of abuse, prompting the judge to comment on the "very difficult situation" facing the court.

801 (d)(1)(B)

Thereafter the government offered testimony by six witnesses describing seven statements by A.T. A babysitter described her statement that she did not want to return to her father because he "gets drunk and thinks I'm his wife." The babysitter also recounted other statements describing abuse, made while her mother Beverly listened from an adjacent room, and she too described these statements. A social worker described details that A.T. provided. Three pediatricians related statements by A.T. describing how and where Tome touched her. (They also testified to clinical evidence of vaginal penetration.)

The prior statements by A.T. were admitted under FRE 801(d)(1)(B) on the theory that they refuted the claim that wishing to live with her mother motivated her testimony. The Tenth Circuit affirmed the conviction, agreeing that A.T.'s statements fit FRE 801(d)(1)(B), even though made after her motive to fabricate arose.]

We granted certiorari, and now reverse.

II

The prevailing common-law rule for more than a century before adoption of the Federal Rules of Evidence was that a prior consistent statement introduced to rebut a charge of recent fabrication or improper influence or motive was admissible if the statement had been made before the alleged fabrication, influence, or motive came into being, but it was inadmissible if made afterwards. . . . The question is whether FRE 801(d)(1)(B) embodies this temporal requirement. We hold that it does.

A

FRE 801 defines prior consistent statements as nonhearsay only if they are offered to rebut a charge of "recent fabrication or improper influence or motive." Noting the "troublesome" logic of treating a witness' prior consistent statements as hearsay at all (because the declarant is present in court and subject to cross-examination), the Advisory Committee decided to treat those consistent statements, once the preconditions of the Rule were satisfied, as nonhearsay and admissible as substantive evidence, not just to rebut an attack on the witness' credibility. A consistent statement meeting the requirements of the Rule is thus placed in the same category as a declarant's inconsistent statement made under oath in another proceeding, or prior identification testimony, or admissions by a party opponent.

The Rules do not accord this weighty, nonhearsay status to all prior consistent statements. To the contrary, admissibility under the Rules is confined to those statements offered to rebut a charge of "recent fabrication or improper influence or motive," the same phrase used by the Advisory Committee in its description of the "traditiona[l]" common law of evidence, which was the background against which the Rules were drafted. Prior consistent statements may not be admitted to counter all forms of impeachment or to bolster the witness merely because she has been discredited. In the present context, the question is whether A.T.'s out-of-court statements rebutted the alleged link between her desire to be with her mother and her testimony, not whether they suggested that A.T.'s in-court testimony was true. The Rule speaks of a party rebutting an alleged motive, not bolstering the veracity of the story told.

This limitation is instructive, not only to establish the preconditions of admissibility but also to reinforce the significance of the requirement that the consistent statements must have been made before the alleged influence or motive to fabricate arose. That is to say, the forms of impeachment within the Rule's coverage are the ones in which the temporal requirement makes the most sense. Impeachment by charging that the testimony is a recent fabrication or results from an improper influence or motive is, as a general matter, capable of direct and forceful refutation through introduction of out-of-court consistent statements that predate the alleged fabrication, influence or motive. A consistent statement that predates the motive is a square rebuttal of the charge that the testimony was contrived as a consequence of that motive. By contrast, prior consistent statements carry little rebuttal force when most other types of impeachment are involved.

There may arise instances when out-of-court statements that postdate the alleged fabrication have some probative force in rebutting a charge of fabrication or improper influence or motive, but those statements refute the charged fabrication in a less direct and forceful way. Evidence that a witness made consistent statements after the alleged motive to fabricate arose may suggest in some degree that the in-court testimony is truthful, and thus suggest in some degree that that testimony did not result from some improper influence; but if the drafters of FRE 801(d)(1)(B) intended to countenance rebuttal along that indirect inferential chain, the purpose of confining the types of impeachment that open the door to rebuttal by introducing consistent statements becomes unclear. If consistent statements are admissible without reference to the time frame we find imbedded in the Rule, there appears no sound reason not to admit consistent statements to rebut other forms of impeachment as well. Whatever objections can be leveled against limiting the Rule to this designated form of impeachment and confining the rebuttal to those statements made before the fabrication or improper influence or motive arose, it is clear to us that the drafters of FRE 801(d)(1)(B) were relying upon the common-law temporal requirement. . . .

B

Our conclusion that FRE 801(d)(1)(B) embodies the common-law premotive requirement is confirmed by an examination of the ACN. We have relied on those well-considered Notes as a useful guide in ascertaining the meaning of the Rules. Where, as with FRE 801(d)(1)(B), "Congress did not amend the

Advisory Committee's draft in any way . . . the Committee's commentary is particularly relevant in determining the meaning of the document Congress enacted." Beech Aircraft Corp. v. Rainey, 488 U.S. 153, at 165-166, n.9 (1988). The Notes are also a respected source of scholarly commentary. Professor Cleary was a distinguished commentator on the law of evidence, and he and members of the Committee consulted and considered the views, criticisms, and suggestions of the academic community in preparing the Notes.

The Notes disclose a purpose to adhere to the common law in the application of evidentiary principles, absent express provisions to the contrary. Where the Rules did depart from their common-law antecedents, in general the Committee said so. [Court quotes ACN on FRE 804(b)(2)-(4).] The Notes give no indication, however, that FRE 801(d)(1)(B) abandoned the premotive requirement. [Court quotes ACN to FRE 801(d)(1)(B).]

Throughout their discussion of the Rules, the ACN rely on Wigmore and McCormick as authority for the common-law approach. In light of the categorical manner in which those authors state the premotive requirement, it is difficult to imagine that the drafters, who noted the new substantive use of prior consistent statements, would have remained silent if they intended to modify the premotive requirement. . . . Here, we do not think the drafters of the Rule intended to scuttle the whole premotive requirement and rationale without so much as a whisper of explanation. . . .

C

The Government's final argument in favor of affirmance is that the common-law premotive rule advocated by petitioner is inconsistent with the Federal Rules' liberal approach to relevancy and with strong academic criticism, beginning in the 1940s, directed at the exclusion of out-of-court statements made by a declarant who is present in court and subject to cross-examination. This argument misconceives the design of the Rules' hearsay provisions.

Hearsay evidence is often relevant. . . . That does not resolve the matter, however. Relevance is not the sole criterion of admissibility. Otherwise, it would be difficult to account for the Rule's general proscription of hearsay testimony (absent a specific exception), see FRE 802, let alone the traditional analysis of hearsay that the Rules, for the most part, reflect. That certain out-of-court statements may be relevant does not dispose of the question whether they are admissible. The Government's reliance on academic commentators critical of excluding out-of-court statements by a witness is subject to like criticism. To be sure, certain commentators in the years preceding the adoption of the Rules had been critical of the common-law approach to hearsay, particularly its categorical exclusion of out-of-court statements offered for substantive purposes. [Court quotes commentators.] As an alternative, they suggested moving away from the categorical exclusion of hearsay and toward a case-by-case balancing of the probative value of particular statements against their likely prejudicial effect. [Court cites commentators.] The Advisory Committee, however, was explicit in rejecting this balancing approach to hearsay: "The Advisory Committee has rejected this approach to hearsay as involving too great a measure of judicial discretion, minimizing the predictability of rulings, [and] enhancing the difficulties of preparation for trial." Advisory Committee's Introduction. Given the

Advisory Committee's rejection of . . . the general balancing approach to hearsay, . . . the Government's reliance on the views of those who advocated these positions is misplaced.

The statement-by-statement balancing approach advocated by the Government and adopted by the Tenth Circuit creates the precise dangers the Advisory Committee noted and sought to avoid: It involves considerable judicial discretion; it reduces predictability; and it enhances the difficulties of trial preparation because parties will have difficulty knowing in advance whether or not particular out-of-court statements will be admitted.

D

The case before us illustrates some of the important considerations supporting the Rule as we interpret it, especially in criminal cases. If the Rule were to permit the introduction of prior statements as substantive evidence to rebut every implicit charge that a witness' in-court testimony results from recent fabrication or improper influence or motive, the whole emphasis of the trial could shift to the out-of-court statements, not the in-court ones. The present case illustrates the point. In response to a rather weak charge that A.T.'s testimony was a fabrication created so the child could remain with her mother, the Government was permitted to present a parade of sympathetic and credible witnesses who did no more than recount A.T.'s detailed out-of-court statements to them. Although those statements might have been probative on the question whether the alleged conduct had occurred, they shed but minimal light on whether A.T. had the charged motive to fabricate. At closing argument before the jury, the Government placed great reliance on the prior statements for substantive purposes but did not once seek to use them to rebut the impact of the alleged motive. We are aware that in some cases it may be difficult to ascertain when a particular fabrication, influence, or motive arose. Yet, as the Government concedes, a majority of common-law courts were performing this task for well over a century, and the Government has presented us with no evidence that those courts, or the judicial circuits that adhere to the rule today, have been unable to make the determination. Even under the Government's hypothesis, moreover, the thing to be rebutted must be identified, so the date of its origin cannot be that much more difficult to ascertain. By contrast, as the Advisory Committee commented, the Government's approach, which would require the trial court to weigh all of the circumstances surrounding a statement that suggest its probativeness against the court's assessment of the strength of the alleged motive, would entail more of a burden, with no guidance to attorneys in preparing a case or to appellate courts in reviewing a judgment.

III

Courts must be sensitive to the difficulties attendant upon the prosecution of alleged child abusers. In almost all cases a youth is the prosecution's only eye witness. . . . When a party seeks to introduce out-of-court statements that contain strong circumstantial indicia of reliability, that are highly probative on the material questions at trial, and that are better than other evidence otherwise

use 803(24)
not
801(d)(1)(B)

available, there is no need to distort the requirements of FRE 801(d)(1)(B). If its requirements are met, FRE 803(24) exists for that eventuality. We intimate no view, however, concerning the admissibility of any of A.T.'s out-of-court statements under that section, or any other evidentiary principle. These matters, and others, are for the Court of Appeals to decide in the first instance.

Our holding is confined to the requirements for admission under FRE 801(d)(1)(B). The Rule permits the introduction of a declarant's consistent out-of-court statements to rebut a charge of recent fabrication or improper influence or motive only when those statements were made before the charged recent fabrication or improper influence or motive. These conditions of admissibility were not established here. The judgment of the Court of Appeals for the Tenth Circuit is reversed, and the case is remanded for further proceedings consistent with this opinion.

Reversed & Remanded

It is so ordered.

JUSTICE SCALIA, concurring in part and concurring in the judgment. [Admitting he had used the ACN to interpret the Rules, Justice Scalia now considers this approach wrong because the Notes "bear no special authoritativeness as the work of the draftsmen," and a Rule "says what it says, regardless of the intent of its drafters." Still "the merely persuasive force" of ACN suffices, and text of FRE 801(d)(1)(B) is also persuasive because it "tracks common-law cases and prescribes a result that makes no sense except on the assumption" that it adopts common law rule.]

JUSTICE BREYER, with whom THE CHIEF JUSTICE, JUSTICE O'CONNOR, and JUSTICE THOMAS join, dissenting.

The basic issue in this case concerns, not hearsay, but relevance. As the majority points out, the common law permitted a lawyer to rehabilitate a witness (after a charge of improper motive) by pointing to the fact that the witness had said the same thing earlier—but only if the witness made the earlier statement before the motive to lie arose. The reason for the time limitation was that, otherwise, the prior consistent statement had no relevance to rebut the charge that the in-court testimony was the product of the motive to lie. The treatises, discussing the matter under the general heading of "impeachment and support" (McCormick) or "relevancy" (Wigmore), and not "hearsay," make this clear. . . .

The majority believes that a hearsay-related rule, FRE 801(d)(1)(B), codifies this absolute timing requirement. I do not. FRE 801(d)(1)(B) has nothing to do with relevance. Rather, that Rule carves out a subset of prior consistent statements that were formerly admissible only to rehabilitate a witness (a non-hearsay use that relies upon the fact that the statement was made). It then says that members of that subset are "not hearsay." This means that, if such a statement is admissible for a particular rehabilitative purpose (to rebut a charge of recent fabrication, improper influence or motive), its proponent now may use it substantively, for a hearsay purpose (i.e., as evidence of its truth), as well.

The majority is correct in saying that there are different kinds of categories of prior consistent statements that can rehabilitate a witness in different ways, including statements (a) placing a claimed inconsistent statement in context; (b) showing that an inconsistent statement was not made; (c) indicating that the witness' memory is not as faulty as a cross-examiner has claimed; and (d) showing that the witness did not recently fabricate his testimony as a result of an improper influence or motive. But I do not see where, in the existence of several categories, the majority can find the premise, which it seems to think is important, that the reason the drafters singled out one category (category (d)) was that category's special probative force in respect to rehabilitating a witness. Nor, in any event, do I understand how that premise can help the majority reach its conclusion about the common-law timing rule.

I doubt the premise because . . . other categories of prior consistent statements (used for rehabilitation) also, on occasion, seem likely to have strong probative force. What, for example, about such statements introduced to rebut a charge of faulty memory (category (c) above)? . . . Would not such statements (received in evidence to rehabilitate) often turn out to be highly probative as well?

More important, the majority's conclusion about timing seems not to follow from its "especially probative force" premise. That is because probative force has little to do with the concerns underlying hearsay law. Hearsay law basically turns on an out-of-court declarant's reliability, as tested through cross-examination; it does not normally turn on the probative force (if true) of that declarant's statement. The "timing" circumstance (the fact that a prior consistent statement was made after a motive to lie arose) may diminish probative force, but it does not diminish reliability. Thus, from a hearsay perspective, the timing of a prior consistent statement is basically beside the point.

At the same time, one can find a hearsay-related reason why the drafters might have decided to restrict the Rule to a particular category of prior consistent statements. Juries have trouble distinguishing between the rehabilitative and substantive use of the kind of prior consistent statements listed in Rule 801(d)(1)(B). Judges may give instructions limiting the use of such prior consistent statements to a rehabilitative purpose, but, in practice, juries nonetheless tend to consider them for their substantive value. It is possible that the Advisory Committee made them "nonhearsay" for that reason, i.e., as a concession "more of experience than of logic." ACN on FRE 801(d)(1)(B) (also noting that the witness is available for cross-examination in the courtroom in any event). If there was a reason why the drafters excluded from FRE 801(d)(1)(B)'s scope other kinds of prior consistent statements (used for rehabilitation), perhaps it was that the drafters concluded that those other statements caused jury confusion to a lesser degree. On this rationale, however, there is no basis for distinguishing between pre and postmotive statements, for the confusion with respect to each would very likely be the same.

In sum, because the Rule addresses a hearsay problem and one can find a reason, unrelated to the premotive rule, for why it does so, I would read the Rule's plain words to mean exactly what they say: if a trial court properly admits a statement that is "consistent with the declarant's testimony" for the purpose of "rebut[ting] an express or implied charge . . . of recent fabrication or improper influence or motive," then that statement is "not hearsay," and the jury may also consider it for the truth of what it says.

Assuming FRE 801(d)(1)(B) does not codify the absolute timing requirement, I must still answer the question whether, as a relevance matter, the common-law statement of the premotive rule stands as an absolute bar to a trial court's admission of a postmotive prior consistent statement for the purpose of rebutting a charge of recent fabrication or improper influence or motive.

[Citing the example of a person already affected by a motive to fabricate who feels "a far more powerful motive to tell the truth" (perhaps because "only the truth will save his child's life") and the example of a postmotive spontaneous statement or one made when the motive to falsify was "weaker than it was at trial," Justice Breyer concludes that postmotive statements can "directly refute the charge of fabrication based on improper motive." Moreover, the common law premotive rule was "not so uniform as the majority suggests," and the Federal Rules changed common law traditions "in the direction of flexibility." Hence Justice Breyer would affirm.]

NOTES ON PRIOR CONSISTENT STATEMENTS AND FRE 801(d)(1)(B)

1. The decision in *Tome* brings difficulties of interpretation, perhaps because the whole area is confusing. The confusion stems from the fact that prior consistent statements can be used either to rehabilitate or as substantive evidence, or both. Recall that prior *inconsistent* statements may be used to impeach, and *sometimes* as substantive evidence under FRE 801(d)(1)(A), and that inconsistent statements may be used to impeach (on the theory that they show vacillation by the witness) even if they *cannot* be used as substantive evidence. At least in theory, similar possibilities arise with prior consistent statements: They could be used to rehabilitate (on the theory that they show constancy by the witness) or as substantive evidence. Sometimes *Tome* seems to be speaking of one use, and sometimes the other: Thus *Tome* speaks of using a consistent statement "to rebut a charge of recent fabrication" (rehabilitation), but toward the end *Tome* says its holding is "confined to the requirements" of FRE 801(d)(1)(B) (substantive evidence), and throughout the opinion the Court pays close attention to this provision. Hence the decision can be interpreted in at least two different ways:

(a) *Tome* might mean that a consistent statement must satisfy the premotive requirement if it is offered to refute a claim of improper influence or fabrication, and then it may be used *both* to rehabilitate and as substantive evidence under FRE 801(d)(1)(B). By this reading, *Tome* is a broad decision that addresses *both* possible uses of such statements. See State v. Veis, 962 P.2d 1153, 1156 (Mont. 1998) (in sexual assault trial, statement by victim identifying defendant did not satisfy premotive requirement, so it was "not admissible as a prior consistent statement" under *Tome* and state counterpart to federal rule); State v. Morris, 554 N.W.2d 627, 633 (Neb. 1996) (similar).

(b) *Tome* might mean that a consistent statement must satisfy the premotive requirement if it is offered to refute a claim of improper influence or fabrication, but only if it is to be used as substantive evidence as well. By this reading, *Tome* is a narrow decision that addresses only the use of prior consistent statements as substantive evidence. See People v. Eppens, 979 P.2d 14 (Colo. 1999) (in child abuse trial, error to exclude prior consistent statement by victim on ground that motive to fabricate already existed; such statements may be admitted for nonhearsay purpose of rehabilitation and need not satisfy premotive requirement); United States v. Simonelli, 237 F.3d 19, 25-28 (1st Cir.) (when prior consistent statement is offered solely to rehabilitate, FRE 801(d)(1)(B) and its restrictions do not apply), cert. denied, 534 U.S. 821 (2001); State v. Chew, 695 A.2d 1301, 1327-1328 (N.J. 1996) (in murder trial, admitting statements by witnesses suspected of complicity, despite fact that statements were made after motive to fabricate arose; declining to address difference between "substantive and supportive" use, court says jurors had heard that these witnesses had given statements exonerating defendant and concludes that "limited use of these prior consistent statements surely ought to have been permissible").

2. Justice Breyer is concerned that *Tome* might block the use of prior consistent statements to rehabilitate a witness impeached in other ways. Suppose, for example, an impeaching attack suggests the witness forgot what really happened (one of the situations Justice Breyer mentions), and consider again the example of Marian testifying about David driving within the speed limit. Suppose that in cross-examining Marian, Plaintiff Paul suggests that on other occasions she said David was speeding, asking her rhetorically "you've just forgotten what you once knew and reversed the truth, haven't you?" On redirect, David proposes to ask about her prior consistent statement on Day 1 he was driving within the speed limit. "Oh no, you can't do that," says Paul's lawyer in objection, "since *Tome* says prior consistent statements are admissible only if they refute claims of fabrication or undue influence, and all we've said is that she's forgotten the truth." In arguing for David, you'd stress that *Tome* is "confined to the requirements for admission under FRE 801(d)(1)(B)" (quoting language from the opinion), wouldn't you? And you'd wrap up like this (in your own rhetorical style): "*Tome* has nothing to say about nonsubstantive use of prior consistent statements to repair damage to credibility." Doesn't that sound about right?

3. The *Tome* majority is right to say many kinds of impeachment cannot be effectively answered by showing prior consistent statements: Attacks on "character for truth and veracity" suggest the witness is by disposition untruthful, and prior consistencies do not effectively rebut such suggestions.[1] Nor do prior consistencies hold much promise if the attack suggests simply that the witness is biased in favor of a party (she is his spouse, for example) or labors under some incapacity (poor eyesight, for example). Nor do prior consistencies hold much promise if the impeaching attack simply contradicts the testimony of the witness (unless the cross-examiner conveys by phrasing, innuendo, or argument that she has given in to improper motive or influence). In such cases, courts would likely exclude consistent statements because they lack relevance to repair credibility and are hearsay if offered for their truth. On this basic level, all nine Justices in *Tome* seem to agree.

4. Justice Breyer and the dissenters are right on at least two points: First, some pre-*Tome* decisions approve use of prior consistencies to repair credibility when the theory was that they added context necessary to understand inconsis-

---

1. In Chapter 8 you will study three ways to mount such an attack. One way is to call a second "character witness" to testify that the first witness (the "principal witness") has bad character for truth and veracity, as allowed by FRE 608(a). The second way is to cross-examine the principal witness on prior misconduct suggesting untruthfulness (lying on an employment form), as allowed by FRE 608(b). The third way is to cross-examine the principal witness on prior convictions, as allowed by FRE 609 (subject to restrictions).

tent statements, or suggested that such statements were never made or were not really inconsistent, or refuted claims that the witness changed her story because she had forgotten the truth. See, e.g., United States v. Castillo, 14 F.3d 802, 805-806 (2d Cir. 1994) (admitting prior consistent statement after witness was impeached by alleged inconsistent statements, to "aid the jury in determining whether the two statements meant the same thing") (standard for admitting consistent statement to rehabilitate is "less onerous" than standard for determining whether statement fits FRE 801(d)(1)(B) and qualifies as nonhearsay); United States v. Payne, 944 F.2d 1458, 1431 (9th Cir.) (admitting consistent statements by child victim to put prior statements into context and show that inconsistencies were minor part of otherwise consistent account), cert. denied, 503 U.S. 975 (1991); United States v. Coleman, 631 F.2d 908, 913-914 (D.C. Cir. 1980) (consistent statements are admissible where impeachment suggests lack of memory). Second, earlier decisions did not uniformly apply the premotive requirement, and post-Rules cases mostly abandoned this requirement for the practical reason that it may be impossible to figure out when a motive came into play. See generally 4 Mueller and Kirkpatrick, Federal Evidence §406 (1994).

5. Isn't it probable that the framers of FRE 801(d)(1)(B) wanted to pave the way for substantive use of any consistent statement that tends to repair credibility? After all, nothing *special* about consistent statements offered to refute claims of influence or fabrication qualifies them for substantive use. The problem is that the framers chose language that is not broad enough to reach every rehabilitating use of consistent statements. In *Tome*, the Court had two unattractive choices: One was to construe the Rule to achieve the most sensible result by allowing substantive use of all consistent statements that are relevant to rehabilitate the witness. This choice would do violence to language and discard the "plain meaning" jurisprudence that grew up around the Rules. The other choice was to hold that substantive use is possible only when a prior consistency is admitted on one particular ground, which would honor the language but disserve the purpose. *Tome* apparently took the latter course.

3. Prior Statements of Identification

At the dramatic moment of a criminal trial when an eyewitness is asked to point out, if she can, the person she saw commit the deed ("Do you see him in this courtroom?"), everybody knows the expected answer: "Yes, he is that man sitting over there." "Let the record show that the witness pointed to the defendant." No matter how the question is put, it is loaded and leading, for the circumstances are highly suggestive. The risk of false identification is obvious, and there is another less obvious risk—that alert jurors (perhaps affected by defense argument) will discount completely the courtroom identification because the setting renders it so suspect.

By comparison, pretrial identifications may be far more trustworthy. In a properly conducted lineup, for instance, the situation is less suggestive: The array does not single out the suspect, and it is possible through "blank" arrays to detect an overeager identifier or deflate any preconception that the suspect must be one of the ones before her. Often pretrial identifications are made close to the time of the offense, before pressure can be brought to bear upon the witness. And where the identifier appears in court, so that what she says there and what she said before can be compared, and she can be cross-examined on both statements, there is all the more reason for confidence.

For these reasons, FRE 801(d)(1)(C) creates what amounts to a hearsay exception for previous statements of identification, made by a witness "after perceiving" the subject, provided that the witness is subject at trial to cross-examination "concerning the statement." This exception was proposed by the Advisory Committee and the Court in the version of the Rules transmitted to Congress. There it was deleted before enactment, but within a year Congress reinstated the provision in an amendment correcting minor drafting errors introduced during the legislative process.

In criminal trials, eyewitness identification of the defendant brings serious risks of error or manipulation by police that transcend hearsay issues. The Supreme Court decided that pretrial identifications obtained by police (typically in lineups or "show-ups") require proper procedure. The Court also decided that later in-court identifications may be contaminated not merely by the inevitable suggestivity of physical arrangements in the courtroom, but by the ongoing influence of improper pretrial procedures. See generally United States v. Wade, 388 U.S. 218 (1967) (postindictment lineup is a "critical stage" where defendant is entitled to counsel); Gilbert v. California, 388 U.S. 263 (1967) (violation of *Wade* requires exclusion of pretrial identification).

The *Wade-Gilbert* doctrine, as it is known, is too elaborate to cover in detail, but can be summed up this way: *Wade-Gilbert* establishes a per se rule that blocks use of some pretrial statements of identification that might fit FRE 801(d)(1)(C)—those obtained in postindictment lineups where the defendant is denied counsel. Later decisions impose looser limits on the use of other pretrial statements that might fit this provision—those obtained in unnecessarily suggestive circumstances prior to indictment. Still other cases restrict later courtroom identifications that may have been influenced by improper pretrial procedures. See generally 4 Mueller and Kirkpatrick, Federal Evidence §410 (2d ed. 1994); 1 LaFave, Israel, and King, Criminal Procedure §§7.1-7.5 (1999).

Somewhat lost in the shuffle of constitutional issues is the hearsay question whether an out-of-court statement of identification should be admitted as proof of what it asserts. Since relatively few identifying statements are excluded on constitutional grounds, it is important to consider the question whether such statements satisfy FRE 801(d)(1)(C) and whether this provision adequately regulates the use of such statements.

STATE v. MOTTA
Hawaii Supreme Court
659 P.2d 745 (Haw. 1983)

Lum, C.J. . . .

On April 29, 1980 at about 11:30 P.M., Wendy Iwashita, a cashier on duty at Anna Miller's Coffee House in Pearlridge, was robbed at gunpoint by a man who demanded that she give him all the money she had in her cash register. Iwashita complied and the robber fled with approximately $300.00 in cash.

sketch
+
photo
lineup

Iwashita gave a description of the robber to the police who arrived at the scene soon thereafter. On May 6, 1980, Iwashita met with Joe Aragon, an artist for the Honolulu Police Department, who drew a composite sketch of the robbery suspect based on Iwashita's description.

On June 3, 1980, Iwashita picked appellant's photograph from a photographic array of about twenty-five to thirty pictures. On June 9, 1980, Iwashita positively identified appellant in a preliminary hearing. At trial, Iwashita confirmed her prior identifications and pointed out the appellant as the person who robbed her.

Appellant presented an alibi defense at trial. Appellant testified that he was at a nightclub at the time of the robbery. Appellant called several other witnesses to describe his physical appearance on the date of the robbery and to corroborate his alibi.

After considering the evidence presented, the jury found appellant guilty of the offense of robbery in the first degree. . . .

Appellant also contends that the trial court erred in admitting Aragon's composite sketch based on Iwashita's description of the robbery suspect. Appellant argues that the sketch was inadmissible hearsay under HRE 802 which provides that "[h]earsay is not admissible except as provided by these rules, or by other rules prescribed by the Hawaii supreme court, or by statute." Rule 801(3) defines "hearsay" as "a statement, other than one made by the declarant while testifying at the trial or hearing, offered in evidence to prove the truth of the matter asserted."

Other courts have admitted composite sketches into evidence under various rationales. One view, expressed by the Second Circuit Court of Appeals in United States v. Moskowitz, 581 F.2d 14 (2d Cir.), cert. denied, 439 U.S. 871 (1978), is that a police sketch is not even hearsay because it does not qualify as a statement which is defined in FRE 801(a) as "(1) an oral or written assertion or (2) nonverbal conduct of a person, if it is intended by him as an assertion." Under this view, since the sketch did not constitute hearsay, it merely had to satisfy the authentication requirements of FRE 901.

Another approach taken by some state courts is to view the police sketch as hearsay, but admissible under various common-law hearsay exceptions. The Pennsylvania Superior Court in Commonwealth v. Dugan, 381 A.2d 967 (Pa. Super. 1977) took this approach and found that a sketch made by a friend of the victim was properly admitted under the res gestae exception to the hearsay rule since the sketch had been made shortly after the victim had seen the suspect. The Illinois Supreme Court in People v. Rogers, 411 N.E.2d 223 (Ill. 1980) held that the hearsay rule did not bar admission of a composite sketch used as extra-judicial identification evidence to corroborate a witness' in-court identification.

A final alternative, which is available to those courts which have adopted rules similar to the Federal Rules of Evidence, is to allow the admission of composite sketches and other pretrial identifications under the prior identification exception to the general hearsay exclusionary rule under FRE 801(d)(1)(C). . . . The Senate Judiciary Committee which recommended the adoption of Rule 801(d)(1)(C) noted that

cts + sketch:
1. Not a statement
2. hear but admiss
3. prior identification
x exception

> Both experience and psychological studies suggest that identifications consisting of nonsuggestive lineups, photographic spreads, or similar identifications

made reasonably soon after the offense, are most [sic] reliable than in-court identifications. Admitting these prior identifications therefore provides greater fairness to both the prosecution and defense in a criminal trial. Their exclusion would thus be detrimental to the fair administration of justice.

Composite Sketches are hearsay

After careful review of the various alternatives, we find that the better approach is to recognize a composite sketch as hearsay but nevertheless admissible under the hearsay exception for prior identifications if it complies with HRE 802.1(3) (which is identical in substance to FRE 801(d)(1)(C)).

We recognize along with the majority of courts that a composite sketch is in fact hearsay. It has the same effect as if the victim had made a verbal description of the suspect's physical characteristics. Just because the sketch is in picture form does not change the fact that it is being offered as a statement made out of court to prove what the suspect looked like. See United States v. Moskowitz (Friendly, J., concurring); Commonwealth v. Dugan (Spaeth, J., concurring).

Although a composite sketch is hearsay, it may still be admissible as a prior identification under HRE 802.1(3) if (1) declarant testifies at trial and is subject to cross-examination concerning the subject matter of his statement and (2) the statement is one of identification of a person made after perceiving him. In the instant action, the admission of the sketch met the requirements of HRE 802.1(3): the declarant, Wendy Iwashita, testified at trial and was available for cross-examination regarding the subject matter of her description, and the sketch was an identification of the robbery suspect made after Iwashita had seen him.

Appellant contends that the composite sketch was admitted solely to corroborate Wendy Iwashita's in-court identification. Appellant consequently argues that since corroborating evidence is only admissible when offered to rebut testimony impeaching the witness and no such impeaching evidence was introduced, the sketch is inadmissible.

Appellant misapprehends the nature of the prior identification exception to the hearsay rule. Unlike the common-law extra-judicial identification exception. . . , the prior identification exception . . . allows the admission of pretrial identifications, not merely as corroborative evidence, but also as substantive proof of identity. . . . See also Gilbert v. California, 388 U.S. 263, 272, n.3 (1967) ("The recent trend . . . is to admit the prior identification under the exception that admits as substantive evidence a prior communication by a witness who is available for cross-examination at trial").

Thus . . . Rule 801(d)(1)(C) operates independently of the impeachment process and therefore the statement is admissible as substantive evidence even though it is not a prior inconsistent statement for impeachment purposes as required in FRE 801(d)(1)(A) nor a prior consistent statement for rehabilitation purposes as required in Rule 801(d)(1)(B).

The primary reason for excluding hearsay is the danger that the declarant is not available and her credibility therefore cannot be assessed by the trier of fact. That danger was not present in this case where both Joe Aragon, the police artist who made the sketch, and Wendy Iwashita, the eyewitness who provided the description, testified at trial and were subject to cross-examination by the defense. See also State v. Naeole, 617 P.2d 820, 826 (Haw. 1980) (testimony permitted with regard to photographic lineup where both the officer who conducted the lineup and the person making the identification were present at trial to testify about the prior identification and were subject to cross-examination). . . .

Given the fact that the jury was given the opportunity to judge the credibility of both the police artist and the eyewitness at trial, we find no reason to disturb the trial court's discretion in admitting the sketch into evidence. . . .

Affirmed.

NOTES ON APPLICATION OF FRE 801(d)(1)(C)

1. It was Wendy Iwashita, not sketch artist Joe Aragon, who saw the robber at Anna Miller's Coffee House, so only Iwashita can make a statement that fits within FRE 801(d)(1)(C). How can Aragon's sketch be viewed as Iwashita's statement?

2. Both Iwashita and Aragon testified at trial. If the sketch is to be received in evidence under FRE 801(d)(1)(C), *must* both testify and be cross-examinable? The decision suggests that an identification based on a photographic array ("mugshots") would satisfy the Rule too. Federal authority agrees. See United States v. Salameh, 152 F.3d 88, 125-126 (2d Cir. 1998). Can a mugshot be viewed as part of the identifier's out-of-court statement?

3. If David Motta had stood in a properly conducted lineup and Wendy Iwashita had picked him out as the robber, could the officer in charge testify to her statement at trial, or does FRE 801(d)(1)(C) require that she testify to it? See State v. Chinn, 1999 WL 317146 (Ohio 1999) (third party can testify). In this situation, the identifier too must take the stand, for FRE 801(d)(1)(C) requires that *she* be subject to cross. See also Mauet, Prior Identifications in Criminal Cases: Hearsay and Confrontation Issues, 24 Ariz. L. Rev. 29, 49 (1982) (officer may describe nature and circumstances of lineup, and identifier's words and manner, but officer's testimony cannot substitute for cross-examination of identifier going into his "ability to transfer accurately the mental images made during the commission of the crime to the place and time of the lineup").

4. FRE 801(d)(1)(C) contemplates statements by an eyewitness (like Wendy Iwashita) made "after perceiving" the subject. It clearly contemplates the situation in which the declarant saw the crime itself (or the subject in a situation that incriminates him), then later saw him again (typically in a lineup), and then says essentially, "He's the one who did it," thus identifying the person seen later as the perpetrator. What if the witness sees the crime, recognizes the culprit, and later comments to a friend (or to police at the stationhouse), "Tom Jones is the one who did it"? See United States v. Lopez, 271 F.3d 472, 484-485 (3d Cir. 2001) (exception embraces statements to police, made a day after the crime, indicating that declarant had seen three of the defendants in the area when crime was committed), cert. denied, 535 U.S. 908 and 962 (2002). What if the witness only hears the voice of the culprit and, hearing the voice of a person suspected (or a tape of that voice), comments, "Yes, that's the voice I heard before"? See United States v. Ayala, 289 F.3d 16, 25 (1st Cir. 2002) (admitting testimony that declarant "recognized four photographs" prosecutor showed him "as having been taken on April 28 in his presence," which identified defendants as people detained after demonstrations at naval base).

5.   The Rule contemplates that the identifier (someone like Wendy) will be "subject to cross-examination concerning" her statement. Suppose she cannot say at trial that "the man sitting over there is the one" (pointing to defendant), but instead says, "I don't know if he's the one, and I don't remember for sure what the guy looked like." Can an unremembering witness satisfy the cross-examination requirement? Suppose the same woman, who cannot identify defendant or remember what the culprit looked like, does remember going to a lineup or seeing a photo array and making an identification. Suppose she can be fully examined on this matter and on general credibility. Is that enough? See United States v. Owens, 484 U.S. 554 (1988) (cross-examination requirement of FRE 801(d)(1)(C) is satisfied despite "assertion of memory loss"); Crawford v. Washington, 124 S.Ct. 1354 (2004) (under Confrontation Clause, "testimonial" hearsay, including statements given to police, cannot be admitted unless the accused has a chance to cross-examine). If the best to be said for such statements is that they are more trustworthy than live trial identifications because the courtroom setting is suggestive, testing the prior statement at trial is vital, isn't it?

6.   What if Wendy Iwashita testified that defendant was *not* the one who robbed the coffee shop? Can her prior statement picking him still be admitted as positive proof that he did it? See United States v. O'Malley, 796 F.2d 891, 898-899 (7th Cir. 1986) (yes).

7.   Suppose Wendy Iwashita caught the eye of a police officer before the culprit got away, and watched the officer arrest him. She then tells the officer, "He's the one with the gun who took our money." Six months later she confronts David Motta at trial but is unsure that he's the one, testifying that "the man I pointed out did it; I saw him do it and never let him out of my sight." The officer testifies that "defendant is the man she pointed out." FRE 801(d)(1)(C) paves the way for this testimony, but do we even need a hearsay exception on these facts? Both Wendy and the police officer use her statement as a kind of "verbal marker" that gives meaning to their present testimony, don't they? Recall that this question was raised in Eagle's Nest Bar and Grill (Problem 3-G), where the barmaid was asked whether she had seen Nichols and Seaver together. Don't such audible spoken words help designate a person in about the same manner that the visible written words "Fighting Illini" help designate a mug in that problem? See United States v. Barbati, 284 F. Supp. 409 (E.D.N.Y. 1968) (barmaid's oral statement identifying people who passed counterfeit bills "can be classified as nonhearsay without doing violence to theory by analogizing it to proof of identification of objects"; in substance, barmaid testifies from present memory that "I was given a counterfeit bill by a man, X, and I saw the police arrest X," and police officer testifies, "The man we arrested was the defendant," and neither statement is hearsay).

B.   ADMISSIONS BY PARTY OPPONENT

Long before there was a hearsay doctrine, what a party said could be offered against him. Such statements continued to be admissible after the coming of the hearsay doctrine. In today's world a driver who runs over a pedestrian and comments about it afterwards ("I ran the red light") has made evidence against himself, and the same is true if he writes it down, or signs a statement prepared by another.

Sometimes admissions are viewed as nonhearsay. It is true that when a statement by a party is offered against him, usually it conflicts with his position at trial (the driver may claim the light was in his favor), so it has nonhearsay significance as evidence of vacillation. If he testifies, his admission is a "prior inconsistency" that directly undermines his credibility. In other words, an admission often has impeaching effect and could come in for that purpose even if there were no hearsay exception. But impeachment does not tell the whole story, for admissions come in as positive proof of what they assert (that indeed the driver ran the red light), which unavoidably raises the hearsay issue.

Hence it is understood that the hearsay doctrine needs some special wrinkle to account for the full use of admissions. Yet a formal hearsay exception for admissions would be a curiosity, since the other exceptions are grounded in notions of necessity and trustworthiness (as you will see), and admissions do not fit this pattern.

In the end, trying to classify admissions accurately in hearsay terminology seems to be a game that is not worth the candle. FRE 801(d)(2) just cuts the knot: By the same statutory magic we've seen before, it defines all admissions as "not hearsay." Once again, this solution is not an entirely happy one. If admissions actually lay beyond reach of the definition of hearsay (like verbal acts) there would be no need for such a provision. Maybe we should just say that admissions are statements with hearsay aspects that we treat as nonhearsay, or as hearsay exceptions.

Deciding to admit and resolving the hearsay issue by fiat leaves the real question unanswered. Why do admissions come in as proof of what they assert? The most persuasive explanation is that the admissions doctrine expresses the philosophy of the adversary system, in which each party is responsible for making or breaking, winning or losing, his own lawsuit—by his conduct both in and out of court. And a series of somewhat related reasons points in the same direction: The hearsay doctrine is designed to protect parties against uncross-examined statements, but a party can hardly complain that he didn't have a chance to cross-examine himself; admissions are a kind of conduct, amounting to behavior by a party that provides circumstantial evidence of what they assert;[2] admissions give rise to estoppel notions and should be usable against a party for similar reasons;[3] fairness suggests that one should simply not be allowed to complain that his words are proved against him.

When a statement comes in against a party as his admission, generally it is not "binding" in the sense of foreclosing him from taking a conflicting position at trial. A party may seek to explain away or reject what he said before. Indeed, the very fact that he takes such a position often induces the adverse

---

2.   Nonverbal nonassertive behavior comfortably fits this explanation. Consider cases where the accused fled the scene of the crime: Conduct suggests flight, which suggests guilty mind, which suggests guilt in fact (see Problem 2-B). Because Rule 801 rejects the doctrine of Wright v. Tatham (Chapter 3B1b), this use of defendant's conduct is not hearsay.

3.   Estoppel usually depends on elements of reliance by another party, however, while admissions may come in even if the other party did not rely on them. And estoppel ordinarily forecloses a party from taking certain positions, which goes well beyond the mere *evidential* effect given to admissions.

party to offer his admissions. Whether a party can succeed in avoiding the effect of his own prior statements is another matter: The trier may credit what he said before rather than his trial testimony, which is just a way of saying that admissions are potent evidence. (Recall from your civil procedure course that the rule is otherwise with pleadings filed in a pending civil suit, for averments in this form do constitute "judicial admissions," meaning that the party is foreclosed from offering evidence to the contrary. See FRCP 8(d), which provides in essence that what an answer does not deny is admitted.)

The modern admissions doctrine is elaborate, as a glance at the five subdivisions of FRE 801(d)(2) confirms. In a suit by or against an individual, the doctrine reaches his own statements offered against him, and it also sometimes reaches statements by others that a party makes his own by "adoption." Moreover, the doctrine reaches statements by a party's authorized agents, employees, and (usually in criminal cases) fellow conspirators. In short, admissions embrace many statements associated with the party against whom they are offered.

1. Individual Admissions

In the case of individual admissions, there are almost no limits. Some sense of the reach of the doctrine is suggested by a modern trial for bank fraud, in which a court admitted against a defendant an undelivered email that he had written to a radio personality, apparently conceding that he had "misappropriated" a large amount of money. See United States v. Sprick, 233 F.3d 845, 855 (5th Cir. 2000). It is true that occasional statutes restrict use of admissions and the Constitution protects the accused against the use of some things he says in some circumstances. And important principles bar or regulate certain lines of circumstantial evidence (like proof of character and safety measures taken after an accident), and these principles may incidentally require exclusion of admissions. But statements by a party are broadly admissible against him, and many plausible objections to proof in this form are routinely rejected.

PROBLEM 4-B. Fire in the Warehouse

Martin left his truck at Carter's Automotive Repair and Refinishing in Tupelo, Mississippi, because one of the brackets securing the gastank had broken. Carter himself was in Oxford, Mississippi, at the time. The shop is divided into three areas, one for repair and maintenance, another for body work, and a third for painting and refinishing. While the truck was being repaired, employee Dugan was working with a welding torch on a wrecked car, within five feet of the door to the paint storage room. Placing the flaming torch on the ground, he went around the side of the building to get a Coke from a vending machine. Moments later the fire alarm sounded, and Dugan returned to discover the paint shed burning out of control. The fire consumed the premises and destroyed Martin's truck.

Martin sues Carter to recover for loss of the truck. As proof that Dugan's negligence started the fire (hence that Carter is liable by respondeat superior), Martin calls an insurance adjuster named Esher. It turns out that Carter spoke to Esher after the fire in the course of advancing his insurance claim for loss of the building. If permitted, Esher will testify that Carter told him, "The fire started in the paint shed when Dugan put a flaming welding torch on the ground too close to the fumes."

Carter raises a hearsay objection, and Martin invokes the admissions doctrine and FRE 801(d)(2)(A). Should Carter's statement come in? Quite apart from what the Rule indicates, what is the sound result here?

NOTES ON INDIVIDUAL ADMISSIONS

1. Many cases reject the objection that declarant lacked personal knowledge when he spoke, and the Advisory Committee's Note to FRE 801 endorses this result. The dog-bite cases are typical: In a suit against a dog owner, plaintiff may introduce evidence that the latter, although he did not see the incident, said afterwards that his pet bit or attacked plaintiff. See Berkowitz v. Simone, 188 A.2d 665, 666 (R.I. 1963) (although she had not seen either incident, owner admitted that her dog had bitten two children; her statement was admissible); Janus v. Akstin, 20 A.2d 552 (N.H. 1941) (statement that dog "jumped on" woman and "knocked her down the steps" held admissible against pet owner even though he was not present at the time). Should such holdings be limited to situations in which declarant's presumed familiarity with the beast (or machine, or premises, if they cause injury) makes it reasonable to suppose he had a kind of "circumstantial knowledge" that enabled him to make an intelligent estimate of the likelihood of cause or fault?

2. Older cases sometimes refer to "admissions against interest" as if the doctrine reached only statements in which declarant "gave up" or conceded some point. Requiring an "against interest" element implies that the statement of a driver that he "ran a red light" would be admissible, but not one that "he honked his horn at me" (even though, later at trial, declarant's opponent might want to establish the point by proving his statement). But FRE 804(b)(3) carves out a separate exception for "declarations against interest," and it is crystal clear that the admissions doctrine carries no "against interest" requirement. People v. Meyer, 954 P.2d 1068 (Colo. 1999) (denials of wrongdoing fit admissions doctrine, which does not require against-interest element). Does it follow that a statement so obviously designed to *advance* the interest of the declarant (as in the example of Carter talking to Esher) should be admitted over his objection?

3. Consider a statement by a defendant in a personal injury suit that the accident "was all my fault" or one by an employee suing his employer for a job-related injury to the effect that working conditions were "safe and proper." Should the conclusory nature of such statements suffice to exclude? Does it matter that a witness testifying in this vein would likely be told to be more specific? See Strickland v. Davis, 128 So. 233 (Ala. 1930) (in suit arising out of auto accident, admitting statement by defendant that he was "at fault"; admissions "need not conform to statements the witness could make on the stand in his own behalf"); Owens v. Atchison, T.&S.F. Ry., 393 F.2d 77, 79 (5th Cir.) (admitting statement that plaintiff "considered the working conditions safe

and proper" and knew nothing that defendant "could have done to prevent the accident"; opinion rule "does not apply"), cert. denied, 393 U.S. 855 (1968). Why should we make concessions for out-of-court statements that we would not make for testifying witnesses?

4. What if declarant is drunk? Consider Commonwealth v. Walker, 456 N.E.2d 1154, 1156 (Mass. App. 1983) (rejecting claim by defendant that "he was too drunk to waive his *Miranda* rights in a knowing and intelligent fashion," despite testimony by police officer that he was "pretty loaded"; trial court could find that he "had his wits sufficiently about him"); Sutton v. State, 228 S.E.2d 815 (Ga. 1976) (in trial of father for murdering two daughters and setting fire to home to conceal crimes; admitting his incriminating remarks, where evidence conflicted on whether he was conscious or unconscious at the time).

5. What if declarant is severely injured and hospitalized? See Finnerty v. Darby, 138 A.2d 117, 126 (Pa. 1958) (admitting statement by plaintiff describing accident to police officer in hospital the morning after; yet at the time he "was so severely injured that his life was despaired of" and his tongue had been "sutured to his cheek to facilitate breathing"; moreover, "last rites were administered to him while unconscious" and for days following the accident "he was mostly in an unconscious or semi-conscious state"; his subsequent recovery was termed "most miraculous"; dissenting vigorously, Justice Musmanno notes that statement was written out by his wife at his bedside and witnessed by her, police officer, and nurse); Aide v. Taylor, 7 N.W.2d 757, 759-760 (Minn. 1943) (in personal injury suit by pedestrian struck by automobile, fact that plaintiff was "suffering from much pain," had taken "several hypos of morphine," and was "still semi-conscious" did not require exclusion of his statement indicating that he had run into the street without looking in the direction of defendant's car, for such facts affect "probative value and weight"; statements must be excluded where it "conclusively appears" that declarant is "incapacitated from making a rational admission, as where he was at the time in a coma"). In light of cases such as *Finnerty* and *Aide*, does it seem wise to enact statutes limiting or forbidding the use of statements from injured accident victims? See, e.g., Minn. Stat. Ann. §602.01 (statement by injured person obtained within 30 days after accident is presumed fraudulent in later suit; it may not be offered unless party obtaining it gives the injured person a copy within 30 days). See also Colo. Rev. Stat. §13-21-301 (barring hospitals and doctors from negotiating settlements with patients within thirty days after receiving treatment forming basis of later malpractice claim, and excluding statements obtained by doctors or hospitals from patients within fifteen days of such occurrence).

6. What if the party is asleep? Recall Iago's words from *Othello:*

> . . . I lay with Cassio lately,
> And being troubled with a raging tooth,
> I could not sleep.
> There are a kind of men so loose of soul
> That in their sleeps will mutter their affairs:
> One of this kind is Cassio.
> In sleep I heard him say 'Sweet Desdemona,
> Let us be wary, let us hide our loves';
> And then, sir, would he gripe and wring my hand,

> Cry 'O sweet creature!' then kiss me hard,
> As if he pluck'd up kisses by the roots,
> That grew upon my lips—then laid his leg
> Over my thigh—and sigh'd, and kiss'd, and then
> Cried 'Cursed fate that gave thee to the Moor!'

Shakespeare, Othello, Act III, Scene iii. Compare Flavell v. Flavell, 20 N.J. Eq. 211 (1869) (husband sought divorce for adultery, but wife claimed that he too was an adulterer; he admitted that he "met a girl named Ella" while in New York and intoxicated, but the evidence fell "far short" of proving adultery even though "he called out her name in his sleep, or when partly intoxicated and half asleep") with People v. Knatz, 428 N.Y.S.3d 709 (N.Y. App. Div. 1980) (in trial for manslaughter and arson, error to admit girlfriend's testimony concerning statements defendant made in his sleep; the fact that he slept detracted from their reliability; utterances were ambiguous and did not unequivocally relate to crime). Is sleeptalk more probative when it amorously names names than when it confesses to criminal acts? Or less so?

7. Probative worth apart, should it matter that the context is a criminal trial? There, "involuntary" confessions are barred under the Fifth Amendment, but only where an agent of the state plays some active role. See Colorado v. Connelly, 479 U.S. 157 (1986) (confession by defendant experiencing "command hallucinations" interfering with his "volitional abilities"—he was reacting to what he considered the "voice of God"—was voluntary for purposes of Fifth Amendment, and his waiver of *Miranda* rights was also voluntary, for *Miranda* protects only against "government coercion," and a "perception of coercion flowing from the 'voice of God,' . . . . is a matter to which the United States Constitution does not speak"). Confessions to police by severely injured or incapacitated defendants have been excluded. See Mincey v. Arizona, 437 U.S. 385 (1978) (defendant was seriously wounded during narcotics raid that resulted in death of police officer; he arrived at hospital "depressed almost to the point of coma," and was questioned by police detective while in intensive care, lying on his back encumbered by tubes, needles, and breathing apparatus; his confession, delivered bit by bit in written form because he was unable to speak, was involuntary and should have been excluded); Beecher v. Alabama, 389 U.S. 35 (1967) (murder confession signed when defendant was in a "kind of slumber" from morphine, and was feverish and in intense pain, was inadmissible because involuntary). See also Brock v. United States, 223 F.2d 681 (5th Cir. 1955) (admitting self-incriminating answers by defendant responding to questions asked while he was asleep violated Fifth Amendment rights).

8. What if declarant is a minor? Compare De Souza v. Barber, 263 F.2d 470 (9th Cir.) (admitting statements by alien resisting deportation, made approximately 28 years before proceedings while he was 19 and 20 years old; statutory definition of minority does not render statements inadmissible), cert. denied, 359 U.S. 989 (1959) with Fontaine v. Devonis, 336 A.2d 847, 852 (R.I. 1975) (statement by three-and-one-half-year-old child that he "just ran out into the street and got hit by the car" was inadmissible; such a child "could hardly be expected to elucidate upon the proper nuances to indicate his freedom from negligence").

PROBLEM 4-C.   *Street Skirmish*

Walking along a city street in a rough neighborhood, Parker exchanges words with a stranger who turns out to be Whalen. Tempers flare. The two scuffle. Whalen strikes Parker in the face with a liquor bottle, causing serious injuries. Police converge on the scene, break up the fight, and question both men. In the end, they arrest Whalen and charge him with third-degree assault.

Represented by counsel, Whalen pleads guilty. He does so after the judge explains the charges and the range of possible sentences and advises him that he has a right to a jury trial where the prosecutor would have to call witnesses and prove the charges and that he need not testify. The judge also advises Whalen that a plea of guilty waives his right to trial and leads to conviction. Still Whalen tells the court that he is "in fact guilty" of the offense, that he understands that his plea waives his rights and is "the same as a conviction," and he states that he assaulted Parker and "hit him with a liquor bottle."

Parker now brings a civil suit against Whalen, seeking money damages. Should Whalen's guilty plea be admissible in evidence in the trial of this civil action? Should it suffice for partial summary judgment on the issue of liability? Should Whalen's conviction have collateral estoppel effect on the question whether he struck Parker without justification?

NOTES ON PRIOR GUILTY PLEAS

1.   Ordinarily, pleading guilty to criminal charges involves facts like those set forth in the problem. The defendant has counsel, and the judge explains his situation. Usually such pleas are admitted in later damage suits arising from the incident.

2.   Consider a guilty plea to a traffic infraction, such as speeding, failure to yield right-of-way, or making an illegal lefthand turn. Should such a plea be admissible in a later civil damage action arising out of the same incident? See Jacobs v. Goodspeed, 429 A.2d 915 (Conn. 1980) (guilty plea to following too closely, admissible). Statutes in some states provide that pleas of guilty to traffic infractions are not admissions of guilt or fault, though the utility of these may be sharply limited by language disallowing protection if "another" person is killed or injured in an accident. See, e.g., Fla. Stat. §§318.14(4) and 318.19. If the ticketed person is injured and he sues the other party (who is not injured), can the latter offer the plea against the former? See MacNeil v. Singer, 389 So. 2d 232, 233-234 (Fla. App. 1980) (no). What if the offender, who got a citation permitting him to "waive" his appearance by sending a check for the fine to the court clerk, simply encloses a check and brings (or sends) it in? Hannah v. Ike Topper Structural Steel Co., 201 N.E.2d 63 (Ohio App. 1963) (exclude). Many state statutes provide that a "conviction" for a traffic infraction is inadmissible in any subsequent civil action for damages. Does such a statute mean that a guilty plea should also be excluded? See Jones v. Talbot, 394 P.2d 316, 319 (Idaho 1964) (exclude guilty plea, for admitting it would "achieve by indirection what the statute prohibits directly"). But see *McCormick* (note 3, infra). Some

statutes provide that drivers may pay for minor infractions without making an appearance, but that they must appear for a hearing if the infraction involves a serious accident inflicting death, personal injury, or significant property damage. Under that sort of statute, what happens if a driver commits an infraction causing significant property damage but mistakenly sends in a check for the fine rather than making the required appearance? See Carter v. Rukab, 437 So. 2d 761 (Fla. App. 1983) (through "bureaucratic misstep," driver used informal disposition procedure, and she should not be deemed to have acted under "entirely different procedure" where she would "more fully comprehend the significance of an incriminating admission").

3.   If a state statute excludes convictions for traffic infractions, should that statute be honored in a civil damage suit in federal court? See McCormick v. United States, 539 F. Supp. 1179, 1181-1182 (D. Colo. 1982) (suit under Federal Tort Claims Act, arising out of accident in which *G*, an employee of the USPS, collided with plaintiff's car at an intersection; *G*'s plea of guilty to running red light was admissible, despite state statute excluding convictions for traffic offenses; the evidence "may be inadmissible in state court under state law," but federal court was "required to follow federal procedural rules."). Should it matter that *McCormick* was a suit under a federal statute rather than a diversity suit? Is it relevant that the Federal Tort Claims Act specifies that state substantive law shall determine the liability of the federal government for the torts of its agents?

4.   What about a plea of nolo contendere? See FRE 410, and the discussion in Chapter 5D2, infra. *not admissible in other actions*

BRUTON v. UNITED STATES
United States Supreme Court
391 U.S. 123 (1968)

MR. JUSTICE BRENNAN delivered the opinion of the Court.

[In the federal trial of George Bruton and William Evans for armed postal robbery, a postal inspector testified that Evans made an oral confession indicating in effect that "Bruton and I committed the robbery." This confession was obtained in the course of interrogating Evans while he was in a St. Louis jail on state charges. The confession was admitted as evidence against Evans, but the judge told the jury it was hearsay against Bruton and could not be considered "in any respect" against him. At the close of trial, the judge told the jury that a confession by one defendant "may not be considered as evidence against" another who was "not present and in no way a party to" it. Each is entitled to have his case determined on "his own acts and statements," said the judge, so the jury should leave "out of consideration entirely any evidence admitted solely against" another defendant.

Bruton and Evans were convicted. The Eighth Circuit reversed the conviction of Evans on ground that his confession should not have been admitted against him. But the conviction of Bruton was affirmed, on the ground that the court's instructions kept him from any harm. The Eighth Circuit relied on Delli Paoli v. United States, 352 U.S. 232 (1957) (limiting instructions suffice to protect one defendant when another's confession is introduced). The Supreme Court reverses.]

Delli Paoli assumed that this encroachment on the right to confrontation could be avoided by the instruction to the jury to disregard the inadmissible hearsay evidence.[3] But, as we have said, that assumption has since been effectively repudiated. True, the repudiation was not in the context of the admission of a confession inculpating a codefendant but in the context of a New York rule which submitted to the jury the question of the voluntariness of the confession itself. Jackson v. Denno, 378 U.S. 368. Nonetheless the message of *Jackson* for *Delli Paoli* was clear. We there held that a defendant is constitutionally entitled at least to have the trial judge first determine whether a confession was made voluntarily before submitting it to the jury for an assessment of its credibility. More specifically, we expressly rejected the proposition that a jury, when determining the confessor's guilt, could be relied on to ignore his confession of guilt should it find the confession involuntary. Significantly, we supported that conclusion in part by reliance upon the dissenting opinion of Mr. Justice Frankfurter for the four Justices who dissented in *Delli Paoli*.

That dissent challenged the basic premise of *Delli Paoli* that a properly instructed jury would ignore the confessor's inculpation of the nonconfessor in determining the latter's guilt. "The fact of the matter is that too often such admonition against misuse is intrinsically ineffective in that the effect of such a nonadmissible declaration cannot be wiped from the brains of the jurors. The admonition therefore becomes a futile collocation of words and fails of its purpose as a legal protection to defendants against whom such a declaration should not tell." The dissent went on to say, as quoted in the cited note in *Jackson*, "The government should not have the windfall of having the jury be influenced by evidence against a defendant which, as a matter of law, they should not consider but which they cannot put out of their minds." To the same effect, and also cited in the *Jackson* note, is the statement of Mr. Justice Jackson in his concurring opinion in Krulewitch v. United States, 336 U.S. 440, 453: "The naive assumption that prejudicial effects can be overcome by instructions to the jury . . . all practicing lawyers know to be unmitigated fiction. . . ." . . .

In addition to *Jackson*, our action in 1966 in amending Rule 14 of the Federal Rules of Criminal Procedure also evidences our repudiation of *Delli Paoli*'s basic premise. Rule 14 authorizes a severance where it appears that a defendant might be prejudiced by a joint trial. The Rule was amended in 1966 to provide expressly that "[i]n ruling on a motion by a defendant for severance the court may order the attorney for the government to deliver to the court for inspection in camera any statements or confessions made by the defendants which the government intends to introduce in evidence at the trial." The Advisory Committee on Rules said in explanation of the amendment:

---

3.   We emphasize that the hearsay statement inculpating petitioner was clearly inadmissible against him under traditional rules of evidence, see Krulewitch v. United States, 336 U.S. 440; Fiswick v. United States, 329 U.S. 211, the problem arising only because the statement was . . . admissible against the declarant Evans. There is not before us, therefore, any recognized exception to the hearsay rule insofar as petitioner is concerned and we intimate no view whatever that such exceptions necessarily raise questions under the Confrontation Clause. See Pointer v. Texas, 380 U.S. 400; Barber v. Page, 390 U.S. 719; Mattox v. United States, 156 U.S. 237.

A defendant may be prejudiced by the admission in evidence against a co-defendant of a statement or confession made by that co-defendant. This prejudice cannot be dispelled by cross-examination if the co-defendant does not take the stand. Limiting instructions to the jury may not in fact erase the prejudice. . . .

The purpose of the amendment is to provide a procedure whereby the issue of possible prejudice can be resolved on the motion for severance. . . .

Those who have defended reliance on the limiting instruction in this area have cited several reasons in support. Judge Learned Hand, a particularly severe critic of the proposition that juries could be counted on to disregard inadmissible hearsay, wrote the opinion for the Second Circuit which affirmed Delli Paoli's conviction. In Judge Hand's view the limiting instruction, although not really capable of preventing the jury from considering the prejudicial evidence, does as a matter of form provide a way around the exclusionary rules of evidence that is defensible because it "probably furthers, rather than impedes, the search for truth. . . ." Nash v. United States, 54 F.2d 1006, 1007. Insofar as this implies the prosecution ought not to be denied the benefit of the confession to prove the confessor's guilt, however, it overlooks alternative ways of achieving that benefit without at the same time infringing the nonconfessor's right of confrontation.[10] Where viable alternatives do exist, it is deceptive to rely on the pursuit of truth to defend a clearly harmful practice.

Another reason cited in defense of Delli Paoli is the justification for joint trials in general, the argument being that the benefits of joint proceedings should not have to be sacrificed by requiring separate trials in order to use the confession against the declarant. Joint trials do conserve state funds, diminish inconvenience to witnesses and public authorities, and avoid delays in bringing those accused of crime to trial. But the answer to this argument was cogently stated by Judge Lehman of the New York Court of Appeals, dissenting in People v. Fisher, 164 N.E. 336, 341 (N.Y. Ct. App.):

> We still adhere to the rule that an accused is entitled to confrontation of the witnesses against him and the right to cross-examine them. . . . We destroy the age-old rule which in the past has been regarded as a fundamental principle of our jurisprudence by a legalistic formula, required of the judge, that the jury may not consider any admissions against any party who did not join in them. We secure greater speed, economy and convenience in the administration of the law at the price of fundamental principles of constitutional liberty. That price is too high.

Finally, the reason advanced by the majority in Delli Paoli was to tie the result to maintenance of the jury system. "Unless we proceed on the basis that the jury will follow the court's instructions where those instructions are clear

---

10. Some courts have required deletion of references to codefendants where practicable. [Court cites student notes criticizing such deletions (known as "redaction" as ineffective.] In this case Evans' confessions were offered in evidence through the oral testimony of the postal inspector. It has been said: "Where the confession is offered in evidence by means of oral testimony, redaction is patently impractical. To expect a witness to relate X's confession without including any of its references to Y is to ignore human frailty. Again, it is unlikely that an intentional or accidental slip by the witness could be remedied by instructions to disregard." Note, 3 Col. J. of Law & Soc. Prob. 80, 88 (1967). . . .

and the circumstances are such that the jury can reasonably be expected to follow them, the jury system makes little sense." We agree that there are many circumstances in which this reliance is justified. Not every admission of inadmissible hearsay or other evidence can be considered to be reversible error unavoidable through limiting instructions; instances occur in almost every trial where inadmissible evidence creeps in, usually inadvertently. "A defendant is entitled to a fair trial but not a perfect one." It is not unreasonable to conclude that in many such cases the jury can and will follow the trial judge's instructions to disregard such information. Nevertheless, as was recognized in Jackson v. Denno, supra, there are some contexts in which the risk that the jury will not, or cannot, follow instructions is so great, and the consequences of failure so vital to the defendant, that the practical and human limitations of the jury system cannot be ignored. Such a context is presented here, where the powerfully incriminating extrajudicial statements of a codefendant, who stands accused side-by-side with the defendant, are deliberately spread before the jury in a joint trial. Not only are the incriminations devastating to the defendant but their credibility is inevitably suspect, a fact recognized when accomplices do take the stand and the jury is instructed to weigh their testimony carefully given the recognized motivation to shift blame onto others. The unreliability of such evidence is intolerably compounded when the alleged accomplice, as here, does not testify and cannot be tested by cross-examination. It was against such threats to a fair trial that the Confrontation Clause was directed. . . .

Reversed.

[Justice Black concurred, and Justice Stewart filed a separate concurring opinion. Justice Marshall took no part.]

[Justice White dissented, arguing that a defendant's own confession is "probably the most and damaging evidence," which explains the rule requiring that they be absolutely excluded if coerced. White argued too that a coerced confession is excluded *not* because they are unreliable, but to serve "other ends" that juries would not understand, but that statements by co-offenders are "very different." Finally, White argued that the rule of *Bruton* will "severely limit" the circumstances in which co-offenders can be tried together, thus burden prosecutors unfairly.]

PROBLEM 4-D.   *His Master's Car*

Napton works for Ace Building Supplies, where his duties include making deliveries in a pickup truck. While working one day, Napton negligently runs over O'Brien. Napton has long been on thin ice with Ace, and a month later he loses his job for reasons unrelated to the accident. Six months later, Napton tells O'Brien that "the brakes on that truck just failed," and "I was speeding" at the time of the accident.

O'Brien sues both Napton and Ace for personal injuries.

At trial O'Brien offers Napton's statement in evidence as proof that the brakes were bad and that Napton was speeding, invoking the admissions doctrine. Ace objects that it is hearsay. (Assume that, as to Ace, Napton's statement is indeed inadmissible hearsay. Because Napton was not employed by Ace when he spoke, what he said does *not* fit FRE 801(d)(2)(D).) How should the court rule, and why?

NOTES ON *BRUTON* AND THE PROBLEM OF ADMISSIONS IN MULTIPARTY SITUATIONS

1. In both *Bruton* and *His Master's Car,* a statement by one defendant fits FRE 801(d)(2)(A) when offered against the person who spoke, but not when offered against a coparty. *Bruton* is a criminal case that addresses the common "spillover confession" problem, treating it as raising a constitutional issue under the Confrontation Clause. This issue is absent from *His Master's Car* because the Confrontation Clause does not apply in civil cases, and a civil defendant probably has no similar constitutional claim.

2. In *His Master's Car,* Ace surely does have a legitimate objection of some sort when O'Brien offers Napton's statement, even if the Constitution is not involved. What should Ace ask the court to do? The statement "I was speeding" seems to be relevant because it supports O'Brien's claim against both defendants, doesn't it? The statement "the brakes on that truck just failed" seems to support O'Brien's claim against Ace (assuming the company was responsible to maintain the brakes), but not O'Brien's claim against Napton (assuming he was *not* responsible for maintaining the brakes). Does this difference bear on what the court should do with the two elements in Napton's statement?

3. Would *Bruton* have been decided the same way if Evans' statement to the postal inspector had fit a hearsay exception *other than* the admissions doctrine? (On this point, look at footnote 3 in the Court's opinion.) Why should spillover confessions cause injury that is especially irreparable? Would it surprise you to learn that violations of the *Bruton* doctrine can be constitutionally harmless? See Harrington v. California, 395 U.S. 250 (1969) (where defendant's own confession placed him at the scene, error in admitting co-offender's confessions also placing him there was harmless beyond reasonable doubt); Schneble v. Florida, 405 U.S. 427 (1972) (confession by co-offender placing defendant at scene violated *Bruton;* error was harmless, despite lack of evidence "independent" of defendant's confession, which was perhaps coerced).

4. When *A* and *B* are charged with crimes, and *A* made a spillover confession to police implicating himself and *B* by name, *Bruton* poses a serious problem for prosecutors who want to prosecute *A* and *B* together. If *A* testifies, and *B* can cross-examine him about his confession, is *Bruton* satisfied? When you read the materials on confrontation, you will discover that "testimonial" statements like *A*'s confession are covered by a doctrine broader than *Bruton,* and that an opportunity to cross-examine declarants whose out-of-court statements to police are offered in evidence is one of the touchstones of modern confrontation law. See Crawford v. Washington, 124 S.Ct. 1354 (2004) (Chapter 4G, infra). Apart from the possibility that *A* will testify, a decision over which prosecutors have no control, what other choices are open to prosecutors wishing to prosecute two defendants?

5. Where several codefendants have made "interlocking" confessions that tie together in a consistent story, can one defendant raise a *Bruton* objection

if he is named (or his activities are described) in a confession by another, offered in evidence against the latter? See Cruz v. New York, 481 U.S. 186 (1987) (yes; a codefendant's confession is "enormously damaging if it confirms, in all essential respects, the defendant's alleged confession," though it might be different "if the defendant were *standing by* his confession") (5-4 decision).

6. Assume that defendant *X*'s confession describes criminal acts apparently committed by several people but makes no reference to defendant *Y*. If the confession is admitted against *X*, does *Y* have a *Bruton* objection? What if the confession describes criminal acts by *X* that bear on *Y*'s guilt as an accomplice? See Richardson v. Marsh, 481 U.S. 200 (1987) (admitting confession by *W* describing events culminating in robbery and murder, over codefendant *M*'s *Bruton* objection; *W*'s confession only incriminated *M* "when linked with evidence introduced later" in the form of *M*'s own testimony; when "such linkage" is necessary, "it is a less valid generalization that the jury will not likely obey the instruction to disregard the evidence") (6-3 decision).

7. *Bruton* endorses the technique of "redacting" a confession by one defendant to delete any reference to another. Suppose Anthony Bell and Kevin Gray are tried for the beating death of Stacey Williams, and that the prosecutor offers a redacted transcription of a statement by Bell to a police detective that contains the following:

Q: When Stacey was beaten on Wildwood Parkway, how was he beaten?
A: Hit, kicked.
B: Who hit and kicked Stacey?
C: I hit Stacey, he was kicked but I don't know who kicked him.
D: Who was in the group that beat Stacey?
A: Me,—,—, and a few other guys.
B: Do you have the other guys' names?
A: —,—, and me, I don't remember who was out there.

In each of the two places where the two blanks appear, one reference is to Kevin Gray, and the other is to a third person who had died. If Gray raises a *Bruton* objection, should it be sustained? Doesn't redaction comply with *Bruton*? And doesn't the suggestion in *Richardson* (supra, Note 6) apply here, meaning that the jury would have to link the blanks in the confession with "other evidence," which suggests that the *Bruton* concerns are "less valid"? See Gray v. Maryland, 523 U.S. 185 (1998) (concluding that *Richardson* does not control, and redactions that "simply replace a name with an obvious blank space or a word such as 'deleted' or a symbol or other similarly obvious indications of alteration" leave statements that "so closely resemble *Bruton*'s unredacted statements that, in our view, the law must require the same result"). *Gray* doesn't mean that redaction is dead as a technique for complying with *Bruton*, does it? When might redaction still work?

2. Adoptive Admissions

The heart of an admission by *X* need not be the words he speaks or writes: It may be a statement spoken or written by another. For if *X* "manifests his adoption or belief in its truth," then *X* becomes the "declarant" and the statement becomes his own. FRE 801(d)(2)(B).

This process of attribution is not mumbo jumbo, but common sense: "Were you speeding?" "Yes." A doctrine that would admit the yes if offered against the person uttering it but exclude the question that elicited the response would make no sense at all. The meaning in the words of inquiry is so absorbed in the meaning conveyed in the word of response that it is fair to conclude that the answering party conveyed the combined message of both statements.

Of course the attribution may be done well or badly. Close questions abound. Badly interpreted, the adoptive admissions doctrine may be a tool of oppression.

UNITED STATES v. HOOSIER
United States Court of Appeals for the Sixth Circuit
542 F.2d 687 (1976)

[Herman Hoosier was convicted of the armed robbery of a federally insured bank. Four witnesses identified him as the perpetrator.]

PER CURIAM.

Another witness, Robert E. Rogers, testified that he had been with the robbery defendant before and after the bank robbery, that before the bank robbery defendant told him that he was going to rob a bank, and that three weeks after the bank robbery, he saw defendant with money and wearing what he thought were diamond rings, and that in the presence of defendant, the defendant's girl friend said concerning defendant's affluence at that point, "That ain't nothing, you should have seen the money we had in the hotel room," and that she spoke of "sacks of money." Although both defendant and his girl friend disputed these facts in their testimony, obviously the resolution of that fact dispute was for the jury, and we must assume the jury resolved it in favor of the government by its verdict of "guilty."

Appellant's sole appellate argument to this court, however, is that the testimony elicited from the fifth witness concerning appellant's girl friend's statement was inadmissible hearsay, and that it was reversible error for the District Judge to fail to grant the objection to its admission.

[Court quotes FRE 801(d)(2)(B) and accompanying ACN.]

Our analysis of our present problem is made in the context of the Advisory Committee Note which is an appropriately guarded one. First, we note that the statement was made in appellant's presence, with only his girl friend and Rogers present. Since appellant had previously trusted Rogers sufficiently to tell him his plan to rob a bank, we see little likelihood that his silence in the face of these statements was due to "advice of counsel" or fear that anything he said might "be used against him." Under the total circumstances, we believe that probable human behavior would have been for appellant promptly to deny his girl friend's statement if it had not been true—particularly when it was said to a person to whom he had previously related a plan to rob a bank. While we agree with appellant's counsel that more is needed to justify admission of this statement than the mere presence and silence of the appellant, we observe that there was more in this record.

Finding no reversible error, the judgment of conviction is affirmed.

NOTES ON TACIT ADMISSIONS

1.   *Hoosier* seems rightly decided, but why? What "more" is there in the record to make it seem that Herman Hoosier adopted his girlfriend's statement? For another case admitting against a defendant a conversation in which he participated, see United States v. Robinson, 275 F.3d 371, 383-384 (4th Cir. 2001) (in carjacking trial with a fatal shooting, admitting *L*'s testimony describing conversation between defendants *R* and *O* even though *L* could not say who made any given statement; he could "discern two separate voices" and knew *R* and *O* were describing the crime; situation was such that, if one disagreed with the other, he would have said so), cert. denied, 535 U.S. 1006 and 1070 (2002).

2.   If a person receives in the mail an unsolicited offer that says that failure to reply will be deemed acceptance of the terms set forth, can nonreply bind *no* the recipient? Is it the law of evidence or the law of contracts that supplies the answer to this question? If plaintiff's lawyer sends to defense counsel a letter purporting to describe a conversation between the two and the latter makes no reply, does his inaction signal agreement with the substance of the letter? If a subcontractor sends to a contractor periodic invoices relating to a particular project, and the contractor makes periodic payments, do the invoices become admissions adopted by the contractor?

3.   Assume that a party makes some use of a statement by a third person, as happens, for example, when someone covered by insurance submits a physician's statement in support of a claim. Does such use mean that one "adopts" the third-person statement for purposes of the admissions doctrine? Compare Insurance Co. v. Newton, 89 U.S. (22 Wall.) 32, 35 (1874) (beneficiary "presented to the company" the findings of a coroner's jury that the insured had committed suicide, so the findings were "admissible as representations on the part of the party for whose benefit the policies were taken") with New York Life Insurance Co. v. Taylor, 147 F.2d 297, 299 (D.C. Cir. 1944) (physician's statement listing suicide as cause of death was properly excluded, where it had been made on a form submitted directly by the carrier to the physician and the beneficiary had not seen it; proofs of death are competent only where statements are authorized by the beneficiary).

4.   What if the government submits the affidavit of a law enforcement officer in support of a warrant application? Compare United States v. Warren, 42 F.3d 647, 655 (D.C. Cir. 1994) (affidavit that government submitted to federal magistrate constitutes admission by government) with United States v. Pena, 527 F.2d 1356, 1361 (5th Cir.) (raising but not deciding question whether informants "should be deemed agents of the United States for purposes of the rule as to vicarious admissions"), cert. denied, 426 U.S. 949 (1976). And see Chapter 4B4, infra. Can statements by government agents "bind the sovereign"?

5.   Consider this description of the elements and limits of the tacit admissions doctrine:

Tacit Admissions Doctrine

> At a minimum, it should be made to appear that (a) the party heard the statement, (b) the matter asserted was within his knowledge, and, perhaps most importantly, (c) the occasion and nature of the statement were such that he would likely have replied if he did not mean to accept what was said. Even if these conditions be satisfied, the statement should be excluded if it appears that (d) the party did not understand the statement or its significance, (e) some physical or psychological factor explains the lack of reply, (f) the speaker was someone whom the party would likely ignore, or (g) the silence came in response to questioning or comments by a law enforcement officer (or perhaps another) during custodial interrogation after *Miranda* warnings have been (or should have been) given. . . .

C. Mueller and L. Kirkpatrick, Evidence §8.29 (3d ed. 2003). Given that the admissions doctrine does not generally require personal knowledge, why should knowledge matter in the case of tacit admissions? The quoted description implies that items (a)-(c) should be proved by the proponent, but that (d)-(g) must be shown by the objecting party. Does this allocation of burdens make sense?

DOYLE v. OHIO
United States Supreme Court
426 U.S. 610 (1976)

MR. JUSTICE POWELL delivered the opinion of the Court.

[In separate state trials in Ohio, Jefferson Doyle and Richard Wood were convicted of selling ten pounds of marijuana to William Bonnell, a well-known street person acting as a local narcotics informant.

Evidence indicated that Bonnell told law enforcement agents he had arranged a "buy" of marijuana and needed $1,750. Agents gathered $1,320 in cash and gave it to Bonnell, who left for the rendezvous under surveillance. Bonnell met Doyle and Wood in a bar and took Wood in his truck to a nearby town while Doyle drove off for the marijuana. Arriving in his own car, Doyle met the other two as agreed, and a transaction occurred in a parking lot as agents watched. Doyle and Wood discovered they had been shortchanged by $430. They circled the neighborhood looking for Bonnell. Police stopped them, and agent Kenneth Beamer arrested them, delivering *Miranda* warnings. A search of Doyle's car turned up the $1,320 in cash.

In both trials, the defense tried to show the agents did not see what happened. They saw Bonnell standing next to Doyle's car with a package, and one agent said he saw the package passed through the window to Bonnell, but the agent had not mentioned this point in the preliminary hearing, and the defense argued that he changed his story. According to the defense, Bonnell framed Doyle and Wood since the arrangement had been *for him to sell them* marijuana. Doyle had gone off to get the money, the defense argued, but had decided to buy only one or two pounds instead of ten. When Bonnell reached Doyle's car, he was already carrying the marijuana, and Doyle tried to explain his change of mind. Bonnell got mad, threw the cash into Doyle's car, and took the marijuana back to his truck. Wood and Doyle then looked for Bonnell to find out what the money was for.

Wood testified at his own trial. On cross, the prosecutor asked whether Wood had told his story to agent Beamer:

Q: *[By the prosecutor.]* Mr. Beamer did arrive on the scene?
A: *[By Wood.]* Yes, he did.
Q: And I assume you told him all about what happened to you? . . .
A: No.
Q: You didn't tell Mr. Beamer? . . .
A: No.
Q: You didn't tell Mr. Beamer this guy put $1,300 in your car? . . .
A: No, sir.
Q: And we can't understand any reason why anyone would put money in your car and you were chasing him around town and trying to give it back? . . .
A: I didn't understand that.
Q: You mean you didn't tell him that? . . .
A: Tell him what? . . .
Q: Mr. Wood, if that is all you had to do with this and you are innocent, when Mr. Beamer arrived on the scene why didn't you tell him? . . .
Q: But in any event you didn't bother to tell Mr. Beamer anything about this?
A: No, sir.

Reviewing courts in Ohio affirmed the conviction. Concluding that use of post-*Miranda*-warning silence violates due process, the Supreme Court reverses.]

The State pleads necessity as justification for the prosecutor's action in these cases. It argues that the discrepancy between an exculpatory story at trial and silence at time of arrest gives rise to an inference that the story was fabricated somewhere along the way, perhaps to fit within the seams of the State's case as it was developed at pretrial hearings. Noting that the prosecution usually has little else with which to counter such an exculpatory story, the State seeks only the right to cross-examine a defendant as to post-arrest silence for the limited purpose of impeachment. In support of its position the State emphasizes the importance of cross-examination in general, and relies upon those cases in which this Court has permitted use for impeachment purposes of post-arrest statements that were inadmissible as evidence of guilt because of an officer's failure to follow *Miranda*'s dictates. Thus, although the State does not suggest petitioners' silence could be used as evidence of guilt, it contends that the need to present to the jury all information relevant to the truth of petitioners' exculpatory story fully justifies the cross-examination that is at issue.

Despite the importance of cross-examination, we have concluded that the *Miranda* decision compels rejection of the State's position. The warnings mandated by that case, as a prophylactic means of safeguarding Fifth Amendment rights, require that a person taken into custody be advised immediately that he has the right to remain silent, that anything he says may be used against him, and that he has a right to retained or appointed counsel before submitting to interrogation. Silence in the wake of these warnings may be nothing more than the arrestee's exercise of these *Miranda* rights. Thus, every post-arrest silence is insolubly ambiguous because of what the State is required to advise the person arrested. Moreover, while it is true that the *Miranda* warnings contain no express assurance that silence will carry no penalty, such assurance is implicit to any person who receives the warnings. In such circumstances, it would be fundamentally unfair and a deprivation of due process to allow the arrested person's silence to be used to impeach an explanation subsequently offered at trial. . . .

violated DP

We hold that the use for impeachment purposes of petitioners' silence, at the time of arrest and after receiving *Miranda* warnings, violated the Due Process Clause of the Fourteenth Amendment.[11] The State has not claimed that such use in the circumstances of this case might have been harmless error. Accordingly, petitioners' convictions are reversed and their causes remanded to the state courts for further proceedings not inconsistent with this opinion.

So ordered.

DISSENT

MR. JUSTICE STEVENS, with whom MR. JUSTICE BLACKMUN and MR. JUSTICE REHNQUIST join, dissenting.

[Stevens argues that the due process rationale has "characteristics of an estoppel theory," and the key point is that the *Miranda* warning is "deceptive unless we require the State to honor an unstated promise not to use the accused's silence against him." But "there is nothing deceptive or prejudicial" in the warning, nor does it lessen the probative value of silence or make it unfair to cross-examine about silence. Here silence was "graphically inconsistent" with testimony by defendants claiming they were framed because if that were so their failure to mention it at the time of arrest is "almost inexplicable." Indeed, the *Miranda* warning provides "the only plausible explanation" for their silence.

neither D claimed the privlege

If the warning really were the reason they were silent, they would have said so on cross. Instead they gave "quite a different jumble of responses." Since defendants did not rely on *Miranda* warning in failing to raise the point about being framed, the due process rationale "collapses."

Nor does use of silence violate the Fifth Amendment as interpreted by a footnote in *Miranda*, which says the state may not "use at trial the fact that the defendant stood mute or claimed the privilege in the face of accusations." *Doyle* did not remain silent, and neither he nor Wood claimed the privilege. And the footnote in *Miranda* is dictum that relies on Griffin v. California, 380 U.S. 609 (1965), which held that the Fifth Amendment (as incorporated in the Fourteenth) prohibits the prosecutor from commenting on defendant's failure to testify. But Raffel v. United States, 271 U.S. 494 (1926) lets the prosecutor use defendant's silence at a prior trial and recognizes a distinction between "affirmative use" of silence and use of silence for "impeachment purposes." Under *Raffel*, a state is "free to regard the defendant's decision to take the stand as a waiver of his objection to the use of his failure to testify at an earlier proceeding or his failure to offer his version of events prior to trial."]

In my judgment portions of the prosecutor's argument to the jury overstepped permissible bounds. In each trial, he commented upon the defendant's silence not only as inconsistent with his testimony that he had been "framed," but also as inconsistent with the defendant's innocence. Comment on the lack

11. It goes almost without saying that the fact of post-arrest silence could be used by the prosecution to contradict a defendant who testifies to an exculpatory version of events and claims to have told the police the same version upon arrest. In that situation the fact of earlier silence would not be used to impeach the exculpatory story, but rather to challenge the defendant's testimony as to his behavior following arrest. Cf. United States v. Fairchild, 505 F.2d 1378, 1383 (C.A.5 1975).

of credibility of the defendant is plainly proper; it is not proper, however, for the prosecutor to ask the jury to draw a direct inference of guilt from silence—to argue, in effect, that silence is inconsistent with innocence. But since the two inferences—perjury and guilt—are inextricably intertwined because they have a common source, it would be unrealistic to permit comment on the former but to find reversible error in the slightest reference to the latter. In the context of the entire argument and the entire trial, I am not persuaded that the rather sophisticated distinction between permissible comment on credibility and impermissible comment on an inference of guilt justifies a reversal of these state convictions.

Accordingly, although I have some doubt concerning the propriety of the cross-examination about the preliminary hearing and consider a portion of the closing argument improper, I would affirm these convictions.

NOTES ON SILENCE AS ADMISSION

1. *Doyle* condemns the use of postarrest postwarning silence by the accused where he testifies to an innocent version of events. The prosecutor's argument is that silence impeaches the testimonial explanation. But assume that defendant did not testify and offered instead testimony by another witness—one close enough to observe, hear what was said, and see who passed what to whom—and that this witness said Doyle tried to buy, not sell. The prosecutor might then elicit testimony by Agent Beamer that Doyle offered no such explanation after being *Mirandized,* hence that Doyle must have been the seller (and incidentally that his witness cannot be right). Is there any room to doubt that a Court that condemns the use of custodial post-*Miranda* silence to impeach Doyle's testimony would also condemn the use of such silence as substantive evidence (proof of guilt) if Doyle had not testified? Even Justice Stevens, though believing impeachment should be permitted, was disturbed at use of defendant's silence as substantive evidence.

2. The court later held that *Doyle* does not apply to prearrest silence. See Jenkins v. Anderson, 447 U.S. 231 (1980). *Jenkins* emphasizes that it is *Miranda* warning that makes it constitutionally unfair to use the silence of the accused against him. Why is it unfair? If the answer is that the warning advises the accused that what he says may be used against him, not what he doesn't say, could the problem be cured by amending the warning to say that what the accused does and what he does not say may *both* be used against him at trial? Would that be unfair? Would it deny the dignity of the individual defendant by subjecting him to the kind of cruel choice that the Fifth Amendment seeks to prevent? See Murphy v. Waterfront Commission, 378 U.S. 52, 55 (1964) (Fifth Amendment expresses "our unwillingness to subject those suspected of crime to the cruel trilemma of self-accusation, perjury or contempt"). Would a change in the warning be practical? Consider Kamisar, Police Interrogation and Confessions: Essays in Law and Policy 92 n.12 (1980): "Can a police officer be trusted to explain to a suspect how he can have 'a right to remain silent' and still have his silence used against him at trial? And even if an officer does his very best to explain, can the average person be expected to understand?"

3. If it is cruel to arrest a defendant and put him in a situation in which both what he says and what he does not say will later be usable in evidence against him, is it any less cruel to arrest and hold a defendant, refrain from giving *Miranda* warnings, and then use his silence against him? See Fletcher v. Weir, 455 U.S. 603 (1982) (per curiam) (upholding the use of postarrest silence where police neither question the defendant nor deliver *Miranda* warnings). But in Griffin v. California, 380 U.S. 609 (1965), the Court concluded that commenting on the failure of the accused to take the witness stand violated his Fifth Amendment rights. Can these holdings be squared?

4. What if defendants had testified at trial that they *did* tell arresting officers that Bonnell had "framed" them by throwing the money at them in an effort to make them look like sellers?

5. Reconsider Hoosier and his girlfriend. Assume both are arrested and charged with robbery, and in the squadcar she yells, "You idiot, I told you we'd never get away with it!" He makes no reply. Should her exclamation and his apparently acquiescent silence be provable against him? Should it matter whether *Miranda* warnings were given? Whether he already invoked his right to be silent or asked for a lawyer? See Illinois v. Perkins, 496 U.S. 292 (1990) (jail cell questioning by undercover agent produced incriminating answers; no warnings required because *Miranda* forbids coercion rather than "strategic deception," and coercion comes from "interaction of custody and official interrogation"); Arizona v. Mauro, 481 U.S. 520 (1987) (after being *Mirandized*, defendant declined to talk to police and demanded counsel; officer stayed in room and openly recorded conversation between defendant and his wife, where his responses to her desperation incriminated him; no *Miranda* violation because no interrogation); United States v. Harrison, 296 F.3d 994, 1001 (10th Cir. 2002) (in trial for child abuse, admitting statements by victim to FBI agent in presence of defendant, to which he replied that he was sorry and it wouldn't happen again; trial court found that defendant's response "admitted the truth"), cert. denied, 123 S.Ct. 919 (2003). Whatever *Doyle* means when arresting officers pose questions, *Perkins* and *Mauro* don't leave much for Hoosier in the way of a constitutional argument on our assumed facts, do they? If arresting officers give *Miranda* warnings, could Hoosier argue that the very fact of warning precludes later construing silence in the face of nonofficial comments as an admission? Can he distinguish his case from *Mauro* by arguing that in *Mauro* defendant chose to speak, while in his own case Hoosier had no choice (his girlfriend did the talking)? Could he avoid *Perkins* by arguing that in that case there was no coercion because the cops were not in sight? (In dissent, Justice Marshall complained that the *Perkins* majority would let police get informants to talk to people in jail while posing as priests or lawyers. Concurring in *Perkins*, Justice Brennan said that if defendant had *already* invoked his right to counsel or silence, the question would be whether he waived it later.)

PROBLEM 4-E.   *"Did You Rob That Bank?"*

Ivers is charged with armed bank robbery. At his trial, the prosecutor offers testimony by his friend Jessup that several days after the crime Jessup heard the following exchange between Ivers and another friend named Kerwin:

Kerwin: Are you the one who stuck up First Seacoast Bank the other day?
Ivers: Will you please leave me alone?

In deciding whether to admit Kerwin's statement and Ivers' reply, what role should the trial judge perform? Should she decide for herself whether the reply accepts the suggestion implicit in the question? Or should she admit the evidence if she thinks a reasonable jury could reach that conclusion?

This time assume that Jessup would testify to the following exchange:

Kerwin: You're the one who robbed First Seacoast Bank, aren't you? It just so happens that I was in the bank when the fellow came in, and it was you, wasn't it?
Ivers: Will you please leave me alone?

Is there a difference between the first and the second versions of the Kerwin-Ivers conversation that suggests a different role for the judge?

3. Admissions by Speaking Agents — Verbal Acts

Agency law defines conditions under which one person may act for another—a lawyer negotiating a contract for his client, a broker selling property by transmitting offer, counteroffer, and acceptance between buyer and seller, a corporate officer signing agreements for the company. In its own version of these principles, the admissions doctrine defines conditions in which a statement by one person is viewed as an admission by another.

When a person authorizes an agent actually to speak for him, as in arrangements between seller and broker, it seems obvious that what the one says may be offered in evidence against the other. Technically (although the point is often overlooked), what such a "speaking agent" says is not even hearsay in the common situation in which his words commit the principal and are offered to prove the commitment. The words are verbal acts. Principles of agency and notions of relevance indicate when and to what extent such words should be admissible. But sometimes words of a speaking agent are offered for a hearsay purpose, to prove that something they describe actually exists or happened.

If, for example, a seller's broker advises the buyer of Greenacre that there is a tractor in the barn that is included in the purchase price, those words are nonhearsay verbal acts if offered against the seller as proof that the deal includes the tractor (hence that the seller committed fraud if there was no tractor, or breached the agreement if he removed the tractor after the deal was struck). Substantive law and principles of relevancy would lead a court to admit those words even if there were no special exception in the hearsay doctrine, for the words are beyond the definition of hearsay. But the same words would be hearsay if offered against the seller to prove there actually was a tractor in the barn, for now they are used as proof of the physical reality that they depict.

Regardless whether the broker's words be used to prove the terms of the deal or the presence of the tractor in the barn, a court would likely cite FRE 801(d)(2)(C) in concluding that they are admissible against the seller (though only in the latter instance do we actually need a special provision to admit them). Why does the hearsay doctrine make the words admissible to prove the presence of the tractor. Again, it is the philosophy of the adversary system at work. When one person hires another to speak for him, it is fair to allow the words of the latter to establish facts at trial against the former.

PROBLEM 4-F.   *Couldn't He See the Boy?*

Eleven-year-old Albert Garment gets out of a school bus in front of the farm where he lives with his parents. He must cross to the other side of the highway to get home, so he walks around the front of the bus. In the meantime busdriver Martin Grider checks the traffic and, unaware that Albert is crossing in front, pulls forward. As the bus enters the traffic lane it runs over and kills Albert.

The parents of Albert Garment bring a wrongful death action against Martin Grider on a negligence theory. Shortly before the statute of limitations was to run, the Garments file an amended complaint that includes a second count stating a claim in strict liability against Standard Bus Sales. The new count alleges that Standard sold the bus to the School District and that the mirrors on the vehicle "were so positioned that a full and complete view of the area within the path of the bus was not discernible by a person positioned in the driver's seat."

But the Garments have named the wrong seller, and before trial Standard wins summary judgment on the ground that it did not sell the bus.

The case goes to trial against Martin Grider alone. Invoking FRE 801(d)(2)(C), Grider's lawyer seeks and obtains permission to read to the jury the allegations about the mirrors appearing in the now-dismissed second count. (Counsel for the Garments is also permitted to read Standard's denials of those allegations.) The jury returns a verdict for busdriver Martin Grider, and the Garments appeal, arguing that the trial court should not have permitted the superseded pleading to be read into evidence. Do they have a good argument? In defending the action of the trial judge, shouldn't Grider argue on appeal that the Garments' pleading entitled him to a directed verdict?

NOTES ON ADMISSIONS IN JUDICIAL PROCEEDINGS

1. Pleadings from prior lawsuits, as well as pleadings superseded by amendment in the pending suit, are generally admissible against the party who filed them. So are answers to interrogatories, whether filed in a prior suit or the pending action. Not so with an "admission" filed in response to requests to admit. Under FRCP 36(a), a matter admitted in this way is "conclusively established" in the pending suit, but FRCP 36(b) provides that such an admission is "for the purpose of the pending action only and is not an admission . . . for any other purpose" and may not "be used against him in any other proceeding." Why the difference in treatment?

2. Assume Grider has a defense to the negligence claim if the mirrors did not let him see in front of the bus. If Albert Garment's father or mother (plaintiffs in the case) had taken the stand and testified that they noticed that

the mirrors did not permit such a view, would they automatically lose their claim against Grider?

3.   What if the Garments offered testimony by an expert who had examined the bus, to the effect that the mirrors did not permit the necessary view of the front of the bus? Compare Fox v. Taylor Diving & Salvage Co., 694 F.2d 1349, 1354-1358 (5th Cir. 1983) ("central and explicit theme" of expert testimony presented by injured plaintiff stressed that he was "an onshore supervisory employee," and plaintiff did not question this assumption; potential for prejudice was too high to admit this testimony while instructing jury to assume that plaintiff was a seaman; facts justify inference of "silent adoption," and dismissal of Jones Act claim dependent on seaman status) with Kirk v. Raymark Industries, Inc., 61 F.3d 147, 163-164 (3d Cir. 1995) (experts are "supposed to testify impartially," and normally do not agree to be within party's control, which precludes invoking FRE 801(d)(2)(C) as the basis for admitting against a party in a later trial testimony given by expert who testified for that party in prior trial).

4.   Admissions by Employees and Agents

A company hiring a truck driver intends that he will operate the truck, not speak for the company. In this situation notions of relevancy and substantive principles of agency would not pave the way to admit against the company what the truck driver says, and for years the common law of evidence excluded such statements. But where such an employee injures another in the course of his duties, it came to be seen as unfair that an employer legally liable for the tort might remain evidentially immune from the statements of the tortfeasor. See Martin v. Savage Truck Line, 121 F. Supp. 417, 419 (D.D.C. 1954) (railing against the "legally untenable fiction" that permits a truck owner to hire another to drive as his agent, but not "truthfully" to describe an accident to police on the scene; it is as if a driver could make an admission usable against the company only if he were an officer or director, but "trucks are not operated that way") (excluding driver's statements denies an agency which "inherently exists").

FRE 801(d)(2)(D) addresses the situation of the truck driver and similar employees, resolving the issue in favor of admissibility against the principal or employer.

Multiple or "layered" hearsay. As you will discover when you reach the business records exception, statements made by employees (who are encompassed by the terms "agent or servant") often rest upon or repeat what *others* in the workplace have said. Suppose, for example, that Bob tells Arlo that Catherine as vice president for production "wants to reduce the production staff by ten people," and that all three work for the Digby Company. If, in a suit against Digby, Arlo testifies to what Bob said for the purpose of proving that Digby was reducing the production staff, this testimony involves multiple or layered hearsay. Bob's statement tends to prove what Catherine said, and her statement tends to prove Digby's intention or actions. Under FRE 805, multiple or layered hearsay is admissible if each statement fits an exception, and in this case it is

no personal knowledge req (handwritten margin note)

entirely possible that FRE 801(d)(2)(D) would reach both what Catherine said to Bob and what Bob said to Arlo, so a hearsay objection would not succeed.

Perhaps equally important in the setting of admissions, there is no personal knowledge requirement. Recall Problem 4-B (Fire in the Warehouse), where Carter's statements were admissible against him under FRE 801(d)(2)(A) even though Carter lacked personal knowledge. When you read the *Mahlandt* case (coming next), you will see how this principle plays out in the setting of FRE 801(d)(2)(D).

Government admissions. Arguably the logic of FRE 801(d)(2)(D) should apply to statements by agents and employees of the government. But the situations may not be quite the same, and anyway logic runs up against the counterforce of tradition here. Traditionally statements by public employees have not been admissible against the government, on the grounds that (1) such people do not have the same sort of personal stake in the outcome of any dispute as private employees have, and (2) agents cannot bind the sovereign. See United States v. Prevatte, 16 F.3d 767, 779 n.9 (7th Cir. 1994) (excluding statement by co-offender cooperating with government, offered by defense; court would not disturb longstanding rule against admitting statements by government employees as admissions, since "no individual can bind the sovereign"); United States v. Kampiles, 609 F.2d 1233, 1246 (7th Cir. 1979) (statements by CIA agent would not be admissible against government in espionage prosecution), cert. denied, 446 U.S. 954 (1980); United States v. Pandilidis, 524 F.2d 644, 650 (6th Cir. 1975) (in trial for failure to file tax returns, actions by IRS were not admissible to prove that government thought defendant was guilty of only a civil offense), cert. denied, 424 U.S. 933 (1976).

govt interest (handwritten margin note)

Are there better reasons to be cautious in admitting against the government statements by its agents? Consider the following points: The government must deal with its citizens evenhandedly. It should not accord preferential treatment and should administer policies and benefits uniformly. This overriding interest is threatened if statements by its agents are freely admissible. Government bureaucracy is massive, and the pertinent point is not so much the scope of an agent's employment but the authority of the agent to make policies and decisions. Do such concerns suggest that we should distinguish among statements by police officers in affidavits seeking warrants, statements by drivers of government vehicles involved in accidents, and statements by public servants within agencies such as the IRS or EPA?

Consider the context of the suit. An individual may sue a municipality under 42 U.S.C. §1983 for damages caused by civil rights violations, but the defendant is liable under the statute only for acts by its agents taken pursuant to policy, law, or regulation and not on the broader principle of respondeat superior. See Monell v. Department of Social Services, 436 U.S. 658 (1978). If plaintiff's recovery right is restricted by this standard, does it follow that statements by defendant's agents should be admissible only if they speak with express authorization?

There are no easy answers here, but modern decisions question the traditional result and point toward a wider rule of admissibility. See United States v. Kattar, 840 F.2d 118, 130-131 (1st Cir. 1988) (in criminal case, government is defendant's party-opponent; that does not necessarily mean "the entire federal government in all its capacities" fits this category, but Justice Department does;

on behalf of defendant, court should have admitted sentencing memorandum and brief filed in other cases) (invoking adoptive admissions doctrine); United States v. Morgan, 481 F.2d 933, 938 (D.C. Cir. 1978) (decisions like *Pandilidis* may not have survived; nothing in Rules indicates intent to put government beyond reach of agent's admission doctrine).

MAHLANDT v. WILD CANID SURVIVAL & RESEARCH CENTER
United States Court of Appeals for the Eighth Circuit
588 F.2d 626 (1978)

VAN SICKLE, J.

This is a civil action for damages arising out of an alleged attack by a wolf on a child. The sole issues on appeal are as to the correctness of three rulings which excluded conclusionary statements against interest. Two of them were made by a defendant, who was also an employee of the corporate defendant; and the third was in the form of a statement appearing in the records of a board meeting of the corporate defendant.

On March 23, 1973, Daniel Mahlandt, then 3 years, 10 months, and 8 days old, was sent by his mother to a neighbor's home on an adjoining street to get his older brother, Donald. Daniel's mother watched him cross the street, and then turned into the house to get her car keys. Daniel's path took him along a walkway adjacent to the Poos' residence. Next to the walkway was a five foot chain link fence to which Sophie had been chained with a six foot chain. In other words, Sophie was free to move in a half circle having a six foot radius on the side of the fence opposite from Daniel.

Sophie was a bitch wolf, 11 months and 28 days old, who had been born at the St. Louis Zoo, and kept there until she reached 6 months of age, at which time she was given to the Wild Canid Survival and Research Center, Inc. It was the policy of the Zoo to remove wolves from the Children's Zoo after they reached the age of 5 or 6 months. Sophie was supposed to be kept at the Tyson Research Center, but Kenneth Poos, as Director of Education for the Wild Canid Survival and Research Center, Inc., had been keeping her at his home because he was taking Sophie to schools and institutions where he showed films and gave programs with respect to the nature of wolves. Sophie was known as a very gentle wolf who had proved herself to be good natured and stable during her contacts with thousands of children, while she was in the St. Louis Children's Zoo.

Sophie was chained because the evening before she had jumped the fence and attacked a beagle who was running along the fence and yapping at her.

A neighbor who was ill in bed in the second floor of his home heard a child's screams and went to his window, where he saw a boy lying on his back within the enclosure, with a wolf straddling him. The wolf's face was near Daniel's face, but the distance was so great that he could not see what the wolf was doing, and did not see any biting. Within about 15 seconds the neighbor saw Clarke Poos, about seventeen, run around the house, get the wolf off of the boy, and disappear with the child in his arms to the back of the house. Clarke took the boy in and laid him on the kitchen floor.

Clarke had been returning from his friend's home immediately west when he heard a child's cries and ran around to the enclosure. He found Daniel lying within the enclosure, about three feet from the fence, and Sophie standing back from the boy the length of her chain, and wailing. An expert in the behavior of wolves stated that when a wolf licks a child's face that it is a sign of care, and not a sign of attack; that a wolf's wail is a sign of compassion, and an effort to get attention, not a sign of attack. No witness saw or knew how Daniel was injured. Clarke and his sister ran over to get Daniel's mother. She says that Clarke told her, "a wolf got Danny and he is dying." Clarke denies that statement. The defendant, Mr. Poos, arrived home while Daniel and his mother were in the kitchen. After Daniel was taken in an ambulance, Mr. Poos talked to everyone present, including a neighbor who came in. Within an hour after he arrived home, Mr. Poos went to Washington University to inform Owen Sexton, President of Wild Canid Survival and Research Center, Inc., of the incident. Mr. Sexton was not in his office so Mr. Poos left the following note on his door:

> Owen, would [you] call me at home, 727-5080? Sophie bit a child that came in our back yard. All has been taken care of. I need to convey what happened to you.

Denial of admission of this note is one of the issues on appeal.

Later that day, Mr. Poos found Mr. Sexton at the Tyson Research Center and told him what had happened. Denial of plaintiff's offer to prove that Mr. Poos told Mr. Sexton that, "Sophie had bit a child that day," is the second issue on appeal.

A meeting of the Directors of the Wild Canid Survival and Research Center, Inc., was held on April 4, 1973. Mr. Poos was not present at that meeting. The minutes of that meeting reflect that there was a "great deal of discussion . . . about the legal aspects of the incident of Sophie biting the child." Plaintiff offered an abstract of the minutes containing that reference. Denial of the offer of that abstract is the third issue on appeal.

Daniel had lacerations of the face, left thigh, left calf, and right thigh, and abrasions and bruises of the abdomen and chest. Mr. Mahlandt was permitted to state that Daniel had indicated that he had gone under the fence. Mr. Mahlandt and Mr. Poos, about a month after the incident, examined the fence to determine what caused Daniel's lacerations. Mr. Mahlandt felt that they did not look like animal bites. The parallel scars on Daniel's thigh appeared to match the configuration of the barbs or tines on the fence. The expert as to the behavior of wolves opined that the lacerations were not wolf bites or wounds caused by wolf claws. Wolves have powerful jaws and a wolf bite will result in massive crushing or severing of a limb. He stated that if Sophie had bitten Daniel there would have been clear apposition of teeth and massive crushing of Daniel's hands and arms which were not injured. Also, if Sophie had pulled Daniel under the fence, tooth marks on the foot or leg would have been present, although Sophie possessed enough strength to pull the boy under the fence.

The jury brought in a verdict for the defense.

The trial judge's rationale for excluding the note, the statement, and the corporate minutes, was the same in each case. He reasoned that Mr. Poos did not have any personal knowledge of the facts, and accordingly, the first two admissions were based on hearsay; and the third admission contained in the minutes of the board meeting was subject to the same objection of hearsay, and [also] unreliability because of lack of personal knowledge.

The Federal Rules of Evidence became effective in July 1975 (180 days after passage of the Act). Thus, at this time, there is very little case law to rely upon for resolution of the problems of interpretation.

The relevant rule here is . . . [FRE 801]. So the statement in the note pinned on the door is not hearsay, and is admissible against Mr. Poos. It was his own statement, and as such was clearly different from the reported statement of another. Example, "I was told that. . . ." See Cedeck v. Hamiltonian Fed. Sav. & L. Assn., 551 F.2d 1136 (8th Cir. 1977). It was also a statement of which he had manifested his adoption or belief in its truth. And the same observations may be made of the statement made later in the day to Mr. Sexton that, "Sophie had bit a child. . . ."

Are these statements admissible against Wild Canid Survival and Research Center, Inc.? They were made by Mr. Poos when he was an agent or servant of the Wild Canid Survival and Research Center, Inc., and they concerned a matter within the scope of his agency, or employment, i.e., his custody of Sophie, and were made during the existence of that relationship.

Defendant argues that Rule 801(d)(2) does not provide for the admission of "in house" statements; that is, it allows only admissions made to third parties.

The notes of the Advisory Committee on the Proposed Rules, discuss the problem of "in house" admissions with reference to Rule 801(d)(2)(C) situations. This is not a (C) situation because Mr. Poos was not authorized or directed to make a statement on the matter by anyone. But the rationale developed in that comment does apply to this (D) situation. Mr. Poos had actual physical custody of Sophie. His conclusions, his opinions, were obviously accepted as a basis for action by his principal. See minutes of corporate meeting. As the Advisory Committee points out in its note on (C) situations,

> . . . communication to an outsider has not generally been thought to be an essential characteristic of an admission. Thus a party's books or records are usable against him, without regard to any intent to disclose to third persons. J. Wigmore on Evidence §1557. . . .

After reciting a lengthy quotation which justifies the rule as necessary and suggests that such admissions are trustworthy and reliable, Weinstein states categorically [in Weinstein's Evidence §801(d)(2)(D)(01)] that although an express requirement of personal knowledge on the part of the declarant of the facts underlying his statement is not written into the rule, it should be. He feels that is mandated by Rules 805 and 403.

Rule 805 recites, in effect, that a statement containing hearsay within hearsay is admissible if each part of the statement falls within an exception to the hearsay rule. Rule 805, however, deals only with hearsay exceptions. A statement based on the personal knowledge of the declarant of facts underlying his statement is not the repetition of the statement of another, thus not hearsay.

It is merely opinion testimony. Rule 805 cannot mandate the implied condition desired by Judge Weinstein.

Rule 403 provides for the exclusion of relevant evidence if its probative value is substantially outweighed by the danger of unfair prejudice, confusion of the issues, or misleading the jury, or by consideration of undue delay, waste of time, or needless presentation of cumulative evidence. Nor does Rule 403 mandate the implied condition desired by Judge Weinstein.

Thus, while both Rule 805 and Rule 403 provide additional bases for excluding otherwise acceptable evidence, neither rule mandates the introduction into Rule 801(d)(2)(D) of an implied requirement that the declarant have personal knowledge of the facts underlying his statement. So we conclude that the two statements made by Mr. Poos were admissible against Wild Canid Survival and Research Center, Inc.

As to the entry in the records of a corporate meeting, the directors as primary officers of the corporation had the authority to include their conclusions in the record of the meeting. So the evidence would fall within 801(d)(2)(C) as to Wild Canid Survival and Research Center, Inc., and be admissible. The "in house" aspect of this admission has already been discussed, Rule 801(d)(2)(D), supra.

But there was no servant, or agency, relationship which justified admitting the evidence of the board minutes as against Mr. Poos.

None of the conditions of 801(d)(2) cover the claim that minutes of a corporate board meeting can be used against a non-attending, non-participating employee of that corporation. The evidence was not admissible as against Mr. Poos.

There is left only the question of whether the trial court's rulings which excluded all three items of evidence are justified under Rule 403. He clearly found that the evidence was not reliable, pointing out that none of the statements were based on the personal knowledge of the declarant.

Again, that problem was faced by the Advisory Committee on Proposed Rules. In its discussion of 801(d)(2) exceptions to the hearsay rule, the Committee said:

> The freedom which admissions have enjoyed from technical demands of searching for an assurance of trustworthiness in some against-interest circumstances, and from the restrictive influences of the opinion rule and the rule requiring first hand knowledge, when taken with the apparently prevalent satisfaction with the results, calls for generous treatment of this avenue to admissibility.

So here, remembering that relevant evidence is usually prejudicial to the cause of the side against which it is presented, and that the prejudice which concerns us is unreasonable prejudice; and applying the spirit of Rule 801(d)(2), we hold that Rule 403 does not warrant the exclusion of the evidence of Mr. Poos' statements as against himself or Wild Canid Survival and Research Center, Inc.

But the limited admissibility of the corporate minutes, coupled with the repetitive nature of the evidence and the low probative value of the minute record, all justify supporting the judgment of the trial court under Rule 403.

The judgment of the District Court is reversed and the matter remanded to the District Court for a new trial consistent with this opinion.

NOTES ON STATEMENTS BY AGENTS OR SERVANTS

1.   What made Kenneth Poos tell Owen Sexton that Sophie bit Daniel? Is the statement by Poos to Sexton admissible against the Center only because the Center acted on it? What action did it take?

2.   In *Mahlandt*, the court cites Cedeck v. Hamiltonian Federal Savings & Loan Association, 551 F.2d 1136, 1138 (8th Cir. 1977). There a woman working in a bank alleged sex discrimination in employment, and offered to testify that the branch manager (since deceased) told her that *he* had been told that she could not become a manager unless "she's flatchested and wears pants." The reviewing court concluded that what the branch manager told her was properly excluded because it "contained a reiteration of what someone told him" and was "hearsay within hearsay." Is *Mahlandt* really consistent with *Cedeck?* Should it matter whether the declarant quotes what another has told him? What if the person quoted is the declarant's superior? Should *Mahlandt* be decided the other way if Poos said, "My son told me Sophie bit the child"? Don't we often speak as if summarizing what another has said, when in reality we are conveying our own positions? Modern opinions split on the issue raised by *Cedeck.* Some come out the same way, but most cases take the view that references to statements by others in the organization do not matter. See EEOC v. HBE Corp., 135 F.3d 543, 552 (8th Cir. 1998) (in enforcement suit alleging race discrimination, admitting testimony that CEO did not like black employees; fact that "some of the statements came through multiple declarants does not matter," since all were agents of company speaking on activities within scope of their employment); Cook v. Arrowsmith Shelburne, Inc., 69 F.3d 1235, 1238 (2d Cir. 1995) (similar). See generally C. Mueller and L. Kirkpatrick, Evidence §8.32 (3d ed. 2003).

4.   Clearly FRE 801(d)(2)(D) applies only to statements by an "agent or servant." Sometimes questions arise as to whether the speaker really was an "agent or servant." Neither the Rule nor the accompanying ACN defines those operative terms, and leaves the matter to courts to resolve by applying agency principles. See City of Tuscaloosa v. Harcros Chemicals, Inc., 158 F.3d 548, 551-552 (11th Cir. 1998) (exception does not define "agent," leaving the matter to be resolved by "general common law principles of agency"), cert. denied, 528 U.S. 812 (1999). It seems that the intent of FRE 801(d)(2)(D) was to reach two classes of persons:

> One consists of people whose conduct produces liability for their employers or principals, sometimes on the theory of respondeat superior where the conduct looks like a personal tort for which the company is also liable, and sometimes because the people are actors whose conduct contributes significantly to organizational liability. The second category is comprised of people who are passive observers or bystanders rather than actors, but who make statements on matters within

the scope of their duties. People of this description are not always authorized spokespeople, and the reason to admit their statements is less compelling than the reasons to admit statements by liability-producing actors.

L. Kirkpatrick and C. Mueller, Evidence §8.32 (3d ed. 2003). In this environment, the question arises whether independent contractors are agents or servants under FRE 801(d)(2)(D). Under conventional principles of agency, independent contractors differ from agents or servants because the principal (entity or person who retains their services) exercises less control over what they do. See Murrey v. United States, 73 F.3d 1448, 1456 (7th Cir. 1996) (in suit against government alleging malpractice in government hospital, doctors retained as independent auditors were probably not agents or servants, so their statements were not admissions by the hospital).

5.   Even if independent contractors are not covered by FRE 801(d)(2)(D), sometimes the actions of the person who retains their services constitutes "adoption," so their statements become admissible against their principal. See the decision in *Murrey* (supra, note 4), which concluded that the action of Veterans Administration adopted the recommendations of independent auditors, and for that reason their statements were admissible against the government. The same principle can in effect sidestep questions of agency in other contexts. See, e.g., Pekelis v. Transcontinental & Western Air, 187 F.2d 122, 128 (2d Cir.) (after crash, airline sets up committee to investigate and recommend changes in procedures; committee makes recommendations that company implements; recommendations were admissions of company in suit by survivor of accident), cert. denied, 341 U.S. 951 (1951).

6.   Why aren't the minutes of the meeting of the directors of the Center admissible against Kenneth Poos? See, e.g., United States v. Wideyk, 71 F.3d 602, 605-606 (6th Cir. 1995) (in trial of Fund manager *W* for taking kickbacks, error to admit statements by *E* of DPS; while DPS was an agent of the Fund, it did not follow that *E* was an agent of *W*).

7.   FRE 801(d)(2)(D) applies only to statements by agents or servants that are "within the scope" of their duties. This phrase does *not* mean that the exception reaches only statements made while the speaker is, so to speak, "at work," nor does it require that the speaker have decision-making authority with respect to the matters of which he speaks. See, e.g., Aliotta v. National R.R. Passenger Corp., 315 F.3d 756, 761-763 (7th Cir. 2003) (declarant served in investigative capacity and "held no decisionmaking authority," but all that is required is that "the subject matter of the admission match the subject matter of the employee's job description," and declarant's job is "to investigate accidents"); Moore v. KUKA Welding Systems & Robot Corp., 171 F.3d 1073, 1081 (6th Cir. 1999) (admitting statements by *TM* recited by *DM* "at a social occasion," since *TM* told *DM* to pass his statement along). Still, a statement does not satisfy the criterion of relating to the scope of one's duties merely because it relates in some vague way to working conditions. See, e.g., Williams v. Pharmacia, Inc., 137 F.3d 944, 949-950 (7th Cir. 1998) (statements by employees claiming they were being discriminated against did not fit FRE 801(d)(2)(D) when offered against the company). And some statements, even though describing matters within the scope of one's duties, may be excludable for other

reasons. In *Aliotta,* supra this note, the court was willing to admit against a railroad statements by a "risk manager" about the causes of an accident, but not to admit his statement theorizing that a vacuum created by a passing train pulled a bystander into its path because the declarant had not been qualified as an expert and such a conclusion is admissible only if it is valid science under the *Daubert* standard. (You will read *Daubert* and study this standard in Chapter 9, infra.)

8.   The electronic age has brought email into the workplace, and there is no doubt that email messages, even though never intended for the eyes of anyone outside the company, are admissible against the company so long as the author of the email is speaking about matters within the scope of her duties. See, e.g., Sea-Land Service, Inc. v. Lozen International, L.L.C., 285 F.3d 808, 820-821 (9th Cir. 2002) ("internal company email" authored by plaintiff's employee and forwarded to defendant by another of plaintiff's employees, was admissible against plaintiff company) (email also qualified as adoptive admission because it was forwarded).

PROBLEM 4-G.   *"I Was on an Errand for My Boss"*

Driving a truck bearing the legend "Farmright Produce Corp.," Rogers collides with an automobile driven by Story. Neither is badly hurt, but the vehicles (especially the car) are damaged. Some 30 minutes after the accident, Rogers remarks to Story, "I'm sorry this happened. I was making a delivery for Farmright, and got distracted for a moment trying to read the purchase order on my clipboard."

Story sues Farmright Corp., which includes in its answer to the complaint an averment that "the driver Rogers was not acting within the scope of his employment at the time of the alleged accident." At trial, Story offers to testify to what Rogers said, invoking FRE 801(d)(2)(D). Farmright objects:

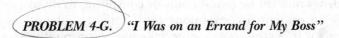

making a delivery not an employee of farmright

> Your Honor, that exception cannot be invoked unless plaintiff proves that Rogers was an agent of Farmright speaking of a matter within the scope of his employment. Plaintiff has not proved either point, and we are prepared to go forward with evidence that he was neither. In short, the necessary foundation for using that provision has not been laid. Moreover, Your Honor, they can't use the statement to prove the very facts which the Rule sets out as conditions of admissibility. That would be bootstrapping.

What result, and why? Check FRE 104(a) and (b).

5.   Coconspirator Statements

The coconspirator exception is a venerable feature of Anglo-American law. It first appeared during English conspiracy trials in the eighteenth century, and it appeared in this country shortly thereafter.

The elements in the exception have not changed, and they are set out in

FRE 801(d)(2)(E): Coconspirator statements are admissible if (1) declarant and defendant conspired ("coventurer" requirement), and the statement was made (2) during the course of the venture ("pendency" requirement) and (3) in furtherance thereof ("furtherance" requirement).

The coconspirator exception is available in civil and criminal cases alike, whether or not they involve charges of conspiracy. When the exception applies, it enables one party to introduce against another the statements made by persons who conspired with the latter. As a practical matter, however, proving conspiracy is an elaborate undertaking: Hence the exception seldom appears outside the context of prosecutions that include counts of criminal conspiracy, and as a practical matter most such prosecutions are brought in federal court.

Conspiracy prosecutions. It is worth pausing to consider why a conspiracy count is such a potent weapon in the arsenal of the federal prosecutor: It gives him an advantage in selecting venue (which can be laid where any part of the conspiracy transpired); it allows him to join multiple defendants who committed very different crimes at different times and places; it provides the possibility of conviction even if "substantive" counts fail (a defendant found innocent of importing drugs may yet be found guilty of conspiring to do so); and it brings into play useful evidential conventions (only "slight evidence" is needed to link a defendant to a conspiracy), especially the coconspirator exception.

Applying the exception. The prosecutor must establish the predicate facts, which means that she must show that the coventurer, pendency, and furtherance requirements are satisfied.

Applying the exception has proved exceptionally difficult for three reasons: First, proof of conspiracy is invariably circumstantial and diffuse. Second, the coventurer requirement introduces a problem of coincidence because conspiracy is both a predicate fact in the exception and (assuming defendant is charged with conspiring) an element of guilt or innocence, meaning that the question of conspiracy raises an ultimate issue for the jury to resolve. Third, often coconspirator statements assert or imply that declarant and defendant conspired, which introduces the problem of bootstrapping or circularity, for the statement asserts the very fact on which its admissibility depends.

Hearsay and nonhearsay uses. Almost invariably, coconspirator statements that satisfy the coconspirator exception are vital evidence of the existence and operation of the conspiracy, and in proving these points they have both hearsay and nonhearsay significance.

In a drug conspiracy case that reached the Supreme Court, for example, police acting with warrant had secretly confiscated some of the drugs in a search of an empty house, and in another house had arrested two partners of the defendant Inadi after they seemed to have acquired drugs from him (but they were released when no drugs were found in their possession). In later conversations, other alleged participants in the scheme discussed these events, one suggesting that Inadi may have "set them up" for the arrest, but another suggesting that he was not an informant. These somewhat cryptic comments seem indicative on their face of a conspiracy in process, and they also suggest that Inadi may have set up the police bust, thus suggesting implicitly that he was part of a conspiracy with the others. The trial court admitted these comments against Inadi under FRE 801(d)(2)(E). The Supreme Court rejected the argu-

ment that coconspirator statements should be admitted only where the declarant is unavailable as a witness, and spoke highly of the probative worth of such
statements:

> Because [coconspirator statements] are made while the conspiracy is in progress,
> such statements provide evidence of the conspiracy's context that cannot be
> replicated, even if the declarant testifies to the same matters in court. When the
> Government—as here—offers the statement of one drug dealer to another in
> furtherance of an illegal conspiracy, the statement will often derive its significance
> from the circumstances in which it was made. Conspirators are likely to speak
> differently when talking to each other in furtherance of their illegal aims than
> when testifying on the witness stand. Even when the declarant takes the stand,
> his in-court testimony seldom will reproduce a significant portion of the eviden-
> tiary value of his statements during the course of the conspiracy.
>
> In addition, the relative positions of the parties will have changed substantially
> between the time of the statements and the trial. The declarant and the defendant
> will have changed from partners in an illegal conspiracy to suspects or defendants
> in a criminal trial, each with information potentially damaging to the other. The
> declarant himself may be facing indictment or trial, in which case he has little
> incentive to aid the prosecution, and yet will be equally wary of coming to the
> aid of his former partners in crime. In that situation, it is extremely unlikely that
> in-court testimony will recapture the evidentiary significance of statements made
> when the conspiracy was operating in full force.

United States v. Inadi, 475 U.S. 387, 395 (1986).

Clearly the conversations in *Inadi* have nonhearsay significance: The fact
that alleged co-offenders had such a conversation, coupled with the tenor of
their comments, suggest a conspiracy in action, even without taking the assertions as proof of the facts they assert. As such they are nonhearsay "verbal
acts." But the conversations also have hearsay significance: One speaker asserts
a circumstantially relevant fact (Inadi set up the bust), which tends to implicate
him in the conspiracy. And arguably the other implies (intends to communicate)
that Inadi is one of their number (he is not an informant).

Because a conspiracy is a kind of agency arrangement, in which it is commonly said that all become criminally responsible for the acts of each member,
it is easy enough to account for the nonhearsay use of coconspirator statements:
The statement of each is an act of the conspiracy, and as such is relevant
evidence against all members. Accounting for the hearsay use of such statements
is somewhat more difficult. Analogies to the situation of statements by employees, now admitted under FRE 801(d)(2)(D), do not carry far in this setting,
for lines of authority and responsibility in conspiracies are not likely to be as
carefully drawn as in the business setting. Yet the coconspirator exception is
firmly settled and vitally important.

Procedure and substance. In what follows, we focus first on procedural issues
and then on substance. The Supreme Court's opinion in *Bourjaily* resolves some
procedural issues but leaves others untouched. In holding that the judge (rather
than the jury) decides whether the exception applies, *Bourjaily* seems clearly
correct, but this allocation raises issues of its own, explored in Notes after the
case. We then turn to substantive issues in applying the coconspirator exception.
Problem 4-H (Drugs Across the Border) illustrates the use and limits of the

exception and provides a setting in which to consider the procedural issues addressed in *Bourjaily.*

BOURJAILY v. UNITED STATES
United States Supreme Court
483 U.S. 171 (1987)

CHIEF JUSTICE REHNQUIST delivered the opinion of the Court. . . .

In May 1984, Clarence Greathouse, an informant working for the Federal Bureau of Investigation, arranged to sell a kilogram of cocaine to Angelo Lonardo. Lonardo agreed that he would find individuals to distribute the drug. When the sale became imminent, Lonardo stated in a tape-recorded telephone conversation that he had a "gentleman friend" who had some questions to ask about the cocaine. In a subsequent telephone call, Greathouse spoke to the "friend" about the quality of the drug and the price. Greathouse then spoke again with Lonardo, and the two arranged the details of the purchase. They agreed that the sale would take place in a designated hotel parking lot, and Lonardo would transfer the drug from Greathouse's car to the "friend," who would be waiting in the parking lot in his own car. Greathouse proceeded with the transaction as planned, and FBI agents arrested Lonardo and petitioner immediately after Lonardo placed a kilogram of cocaine into petitioner's car in the hotel parking lot. In petitioner's car, the agents found over $20,000 in cash.

Petitioner was charged with conspiring to distribute cocaine . . . and possession of cocaine with intent to distribute. . . . The Government introduced, over petitioner's objection, Angelo Lonardo's telephone statements regarding the participation of the "friend" in the transaction. The District Court found that, considering the events in the parking lot and Lonardo's statements over the telephone, the Government had established by a preponderance of the evidence that a conspiracy involving Lonardo and petitioner existed, and that Lonardo's statements over the telephone had been made in the course of and in furtherance of the conspiracy. Accordingly, the trial court held that Lonardo's out-of-court statements satisfied Rule 801(d)(2)(E) and were not hearsay. Petitioner was convicted on both counts and sentenced to 15 years. The United States Court of Appeals for the Sixth Circuit affirmed. The Court of Appeals agreed with the District Court's analysis and conclusion that Lonardo's out-of-court statements were admissible under the Federal Rules of Evidence. The court also rejected petitioner's contention that because he could not cross-examine Lonardo, the admission of these statements violated his constitutional right to confront the witnesses against him. We affirm.

Before admitting a co-conspirator's statement over an objection that it does not qualify under Rule 801(d)(2)(E), a court must be satisfied that the statement actually falls within the definition of the rule. There must be evidence that there was a conspiracy involving the declarant and the nonoffering party, and that the statement was made "in the course and in furtherance of the conspiracy." [The Court quotes FRE 104(a).] Petitioner and respondent agree that the existence of a conspiracy and petitioner's involvement in it are preliminary questions of fact that, under Rule 104, must be resolved by the court. The Federal Rules, however, nowhere define the standard of proof the court must observe in resolving these questions.

We are therefore guided by our prior decisions regarding admissibility determinations that hinge on preliminary factual questions. We have traditionally required that these matters be established by a preponderance of proof. Evidence is placed before the jury when it satisfies the technical requirements of the evidentiary Rules, which embody certain legal and policy determinations. The inquiry made by a court concerned with these matters is not whether the proponent of the evidence wins or loses his case on the merits, but whether the evidentiary Rules have been satisfied. Thus, the evidentiary standard is unrelated to the burden of proof on the substantive issues, be it a criminal case, see In re Winship, 397 U.S. 358 (1970), or a civil case. See generally Colorado v. Connelly, 479 U.S. 157 (1986). The preponderance standard ensures that before admitting evidence, the court will have found it more likely than not that the technical issues and policy concerns addressed by the Federal Rules of Evidence have been afforded due consideration. As in Lego v. Twomey, 404 U.S. 477, 488 (1972), we find "nothing to suggest that admissibility rulings have been unreliable or otherwise wanting in quality because not based on some higher standard." We think that our previous decisions in this area resolve the matter. See, e.g., Colorado v. Connelly, supra (preliminary fact that custodial confessant waived rights must be proved by preponderance of the evidence); Nix v. Williams, 467 U.S. 431, 444, n.5 (1984) (inevitable discovery of illegally seized evidence must be shown to have been more likely than not); United States v. Matlock, 415 U.S. 164 (1974) (voluntariness of consent to search must be shown by preponderance of the evidence); Lego v. Twomey, supra (voluntariness of confession must be demonstrated by a preponderance of the evidence). Therefore, we hold that when the preliminary facts relevant to Rule 801(d)(2)(E) are disputed, the offering party must prove them by a preponderance of the evidence.[1]

Even though petitioner agrees that the courts below applied the proper standard of proof with regard to the preliminary facts relevant to Rule 801(d)(2)(E), he nevertheless challenges the admission of Lonardo's statements. Petitioner argues that in determining whether a conspiracy exists and whether the defendant was a member of it, the court must look only to independent evidence—that is, evidence other than the statements sought to be admitted. Petitioner relies on Glasser v. United States, 315 U.S. 60 (1942), in which this Court first mentioned the so-called "bootstrapping rule." The relevant issue in Glasser was whether Glasser's counsel, who also represented another defendant, faced such a conflict of interest that Glasser received ineffective assistance. Glasser contended that conflicting loyalties led his lawyer not to object to statements made by one of Glasser's co-conspirators. The Government

---

1. We intimate no view on the proper standard of proof for questions falling under FRE 104(b) (conditional relevancy). We also decline to address the circumstances in which the burden of coming forward to show that the proffered evidence is inadmissible is appropriately placed on the nonoffering party. Finally, we do not express an opinion on the proper order of proof that trial courts should follow in concluding that the preponderance standard has been satisfied in an ongoing trial.

argued that any objection would have been fruitless because the statements were admissible. The Court rejected this proposition:

> [S]uch declarations are admissible over the objection of an alleged co-conspirator, who was not present when they were made, only if there is proof *aliunde* that he is connected with the conspiracy. . . . Otherwise, hearsay would lift itself by its own bootstraps to the level of competent evidence.

The Court revisited the bootstrapping rule in United States v. Nixon, 418 U.S. 683 (1974), where again, in passing, the Court stated, "Declarations by one defendant may also be admissible against other defendants upon a sufficient showing, *by independent evidence,* of a conspiracy among one or more other defendants and the declarant and if the declarations at issue were in furtherance of that conspiracy." . . . The Courts of Appeals have widely . . . held that in determining the preliminary facts relevant to co-conspirators' out-of-court statements, a court may not look at the hearsay statements themselves for their evidentiary value.

Both *Glasser* and *Nixon,* however, were decided before Congress enacted the Federal Rules of Evidence in 1975. . . . The question thus presented is whether any aspect of *Glasser*'s bootstrapping rule remains viable after the enactment of the Federal Rules of Evidence.

Petitioner concedes that Rule 104, on its face, appears to allow the court to make the preliminary factual determinations relevant to Rule 801(d)(2)(E) by considering any evidence it wishes, unhindered by considerations of admissibility. That would seem to many to be the end of the matter. Congress has decided that courts may consider hearsay in making these factual determinations. Out-of-court statements made by anyone, including putative co-conspirators, are often hearsay. Even if they are, they may be considered, *Glasser* and the bootstrapping rule notwithstanding. But petitioner nevertheless argues that the bootstrapping rule, as most Courts of Appeals have construed it, survived this apparently unequivocal change in the law unscathed and that Rule 104, as applied to the admission of co-conspirator's statements, does not mean what it says. We disagree.

Petitioner claims that Congress evidenced no intent to disturb the bootstrapping rule, which was embedded in the previous approach, and we should not find that Congress altered the rule without affirmative evidence so indicating. It would be extraordinary to require legislative history to *confirm* the plain meaning of Rule 104. The Rule on its face allows the trial judge to consider any evidence whatsoever, bound only by the rules of privilege. We think that the Rule is sufficiently clear that to the extent that it is inconsistent with petitioner's interpretation of *Glasser* and *Nixon,* the Rule prevails.[2]

Nor do we agree with petitioner that this construction of Rule 104(a) will allow courts to admit hearsay statements without any credible proof of the conspiracy, thus fundamentally changing the nature of the co-conspirator excep-

---

2. The Advisory Committee Notes show that the Rule was not adopted in a fit of absent-mindedness. [The Court quotes ACN to FRE 104.] We think this language makes plain the drafters' intent to abolish any kind of bootstrapping rule. Silence is at best ambiguous, and we decline the invitation to rely on speculation to import ambiguity into what is otherwise a clear rule.

tion. Petitioner starts with the proposition that co-conspirators' out-of-court statements are deemed unreliable and are inadmissible, at least until a conspiracy is shown. Since these statements are unreliable, petitioner contends that they should not form any part of the basis for establishing a conspiracy, the very antecedent that renders them admissible.

Petitioner's theory ignores two simple facts of evidentiary life. First, out-of-court statements are only *presumed* unreliable. The presumption may be rebutted by appropriate proof. See FRE 803(24) (otherwise inadmissible hearsay may be admitted if circumstantial guarantees of trustworthiness demonstrated). Second, individual pieces of evidence, insufficient in themselves to prove a point, may in cumulation prove it. The sum of an evidentiary presentation may well be greater than its constituent parts. Taken together, these two propositions demonstrate that a piece of evidence, unreliable in isolation, may become quite probative when corroborated by other evidence. A per se rule barring consideration of these hearsay statements during preliminary factfinding is not therefore required. Even if out-of-court declarations by co-conspirators are presumptively unreliable, trial courts must be permitted to evaluate these statements for their evidentiary worth as revealed by the particular circumstances of the case. Courts often act as factfinders, and there is no reason to believe that courts are any less able to properly recognize the probative value of evidence in this particular area. The party opposing admission has an adequate incentive to point out the shortcomings in such evidence before the trial court finds the preliminary facts. If the opposing party is unsuccessful in keeping the evidence from the factfinder, he still has the opportunity to attack the probative value of the evidence as it relates to the substantive issue in the case. See, e.g., FRE 806 (allowing attack on credibility of out-of-court declarant).

We think that there is little doubt that a co-conspirator's statements could themselves be probative of the existence of a conspiracy and the participation of both the defendant and the declarant in the conspiracy. Petitioner's case presents a paradigm. The out-of-court statements of Lonardo indicated that Lonardo was involved in a conspiracy with a "friend." The statements indicated that the friend had agreed with Lonardo to buy a kilogram of cocaine and to distribute it. The statements also revealed that the friend would be at the hotel parking lot, in his car, and would accept the cocaine from Greathouse's car after Greathouse gave Lonardo the keys. Each one of Lonardo's statements may itself be unreliable, but taken as a whole, the entire conversation between Lonardo and Greathouse was corroborated by independent evidence. The friend, who turned out to be petitioner, showed up at the prearranged spot at the prearranged time. He picked up the cocaine, and a significant sum of money was found in his car. On these facts, the trial court concluded, in our view correctly, that the Government had established the existence of a conspiracy and petitioner's participation in it.

We need not decide in this case whether the courts below could have relied solely upon Lonardo's hearsay statements to determine that a conspiracy had been established by a preponderance of the evidence. To the extent that *Glasser* meant that courts could not look to the hearsay statements themselves for any purpose, it has clearly been superseded by Rule 104(a). It is sufficient for today to hold that a court, in making a preliminary factual determination under Rule 801(d)(2)(E), may examine the hearsay statements sought to be admitted. As we have held in other cases concerning admissibility determinations, "the judge should receive the evidence and give it such weight as his judgment and experience counsel." United States v. Matlock, 415 U.S. 164, 175 (1974). The courts below properly considered the statements of Lonardo and the subsequent events in finding that the Government had established by a preponderance of the evidence that Lonardo was involved in a conspiracy with petitioner. We have no reason to believe that the District Court's factfinding of this point was clearly erroneous. We hold that Lonardo's out-of-court statements were properly admitted against petitioner.

[The Court also concludes that the coconspirator exception is "firmly enough rooted in our jurisprudence" so that the Confrontation Clause does not require an independent inquiry into reliability. Hence receipt of the statements here did not violate defendant's rights under the Confrontation Clause. This part of the decision is considered in Chapter 4G3, infra.]

The judgment of the Court of Appeals is affirmed.

[The concurring opinion of Justice Stevens is omitted.]

JUSTICE BLACKMUN, with whom JUSTICE BRENNAN and JUSTICE MARSHALL join, dissenting.

[The dissent says that the majority is wrong on three points. First, the Federal Rules do not change the requirement that "preliminary questions of fact, relating to admissibility of a nontestifying coconspirator's statement, must be established by evidence independent of that statement." Second, abandoning the independent evidence requirement eliminates "one of the few safeguards of reliability that this exemption from the hearsay definition possesses." Third, the coconspirator exception is not a "firmly rooted hearsay exception" for purposes of the Confrontation Clause.]

In order to understand why the Federal Rules of Evidence adopted without change the common-law co-conspirator exemption from hearsay, and why this adoption signified the Advisory Committee's intent to retain the exemption's independent-evidence requirement, it is useful to review briefly the contours of this exemption as it stood before enactment of the Rules. By all accounts, the exemption was based upon agency principles, the underlying concept being that a conspiracy is a common undertaking where the conspirators are all agents of each other and where the acts and statements of one can be attributed to all. . . .

Each of the components of this common-law exemption, in turn, had an agency justification. To fall within the exemption, the coconspirator's statement had to be made "in furtherance of" the conspiracy, a requirement that arose from the agency rationale that an agent's acts or words could be attributed to his principal only so long as the agent was acting within the scope of his employment. See Levie, Hearsay and Conspiracy: A Reexamination of the Co-Conspirators' Exception to the Hearsay Rule, 52 Mich. L. Rev. 1159, 1161 (1954) (Levie); 4 D. Louisell & C. Mueller, Federal Evidence §427, p. 348 (1980). The statement also had to be made "during the course of" the conspiracy. This feature necessarily accompanies the "in furtherance of" requirement, for there must be an employment or business relationship in effect between the agent and the principal, in accordance with which the agent is acting, for the principal to be bound by his agent's deeds or words.

The final feature of the co-conspirator hearsay exemption, the independent-evidence requirement, directly corresponds to the agency concept that an agent's statement cannot be used alone to prove the existence of the agency relationship.

Evidence of a statement by an agent concerning the existence or extent of his authority is not admissible against the principal to prove its existence or extent, unless it appears *by other evidence* that the making of such statement was within the authority of the agent or, as to persons dealing with the agent, within the apparent authority or other power of the agent (emphasis added).

Restatement (Second) of Agency §285 (1957). See Levie, 52 Mich. L. Rev., at 1161. The reason behind this concept is that the agent's authority must be traced back to some act or statement by the alleged principal. See 1 F. Mechem, Law of Agency §285, p. 205 (1914). . . .

Although, under common law, the reliability of the co-conspirator's statement was never the primary ground justifying its admissibility, there was some recognition that this exemption from the hearsay rule had certain guarantees of trustworthiness, albeit limited ones. This justification for the exemption has been explained:

> Active conspirators are likely to know who the members of the conspiracy are and what they have done. When speaking to advance the conspiracy, they are unlikely to describe non-members as conspirators, and they usually will have no incentive to misdescribe the actions of their fellow members.

Lempert & Saltzburg, [A Modern Approach to Evidence 395 (2d ed. 1982)]. See also 4 J. Wigmore, Evidence §1080a, p.199 (Chadbourn rev. 1972) ("the general idea of receiving vicarious admissions, is that where the third person was, at the time of speaking, in *circumstances that gave him substantially the same interest* to know something about the matter in hand as had the now opponent, and the *same motive* to make a statement about it, that person's statements have approximately the same testimonial value as if the now opponent had made them") (emphasis in original). And the components of the exemption were understood to contribute to this reliability. When making a statement "during the course of" and "in furtherance of" a conspiracy, a conspirator could be viewed as speaking from the perspective of all the conspirators in order to achieve the common goals of the conspiracy, not from self-serving motives. In particular, the requirement that a conspiracy be established by independent evidence also is seen to contribute to the reliability issue. Yet that requirement goes not so much to the reliability of the statement itself, as to the reliability of the process of admitting it: a statement cannot be introduced *until* independent evidence shows the defendant to be a member of an existing conspiracy. . . .

The Federal Rules of Evidence did not alter in any way this common-law exemption to hearsay.[5] . . . The Advisory Committee explained that the exclusion of admissions from the hearsay category is justified by the traditional

---

5. In codifying the common-law exemption, the Rules should be understood to adopt the Court's application in Glasser v. United States, 315 U.S. 60 (1942), of the exemptions independent-evidence requirement. The Court there examined the evidence apart from the co-conspirator's statement to see whether this evidence would establish Glasser's participation in an existing conspiracy. . . .

"adversary system" rationale, not by any specific "guarantee of trustworthiness" used to justify hearsay exceptions. . . .

Accordingly, when Rule 801(d)(2)(E) and Rule 104(a) are considered together—an examination that the Court neglects to undertake—there appears to be a conflict between the fact that no change in the co-conspirator hearsay exemption was intended by Rule 801(d)(2)(E) and the freedom that Rule 104(a) gives a trial court to rely on hearsay in resolving preliminary factual questions. Although one must be somewhat of an interpretative funambulist to walk between the conflicting demands of these Rules in order to arrive at a resolution that will satisfy their respective concerns, this effort is far to be preferred over accepting the easily available safety "net" of Rule 104(a)'s "plain meaning." The purposes of *both* Rules can be achieved by considering the relevant preliminary factual question for Rule 104(a) analysis to be the following: "whether a conspiracy that included the declarant and the defendant against whom a statement is offered has been demonstrated to exist on the basis of evidence *independent of the declarant's hearsay statements*" (emphasis added). Saltzburg & Redden, Federal Rules of Evidence Manual 735 (4th ed. 1986). This resolution sufficiently answers Rule 104(a)'s concern with allowing a trial court to consider hearsay in determining preliminary factual questions, because the only hearsay not available for its consideration is the statement at issue. The exclusion of the statement from the preliminary analysis maintains the common-law exemption unchanged. . . .

[D]espite the recognized need by prosecutors for co-conspirator statements, these statements often have been considered to be somewhat unreliable. It has long been understood that such statements in some cases may constitute, at best, nothing more than the "idle chatter" of a declarant or, at worst, malicious gossip. Moreover, when confronted with such a statement, an innocent defendant would have a difficult time defending himself against it, for, if he were not in the conspiracy, he would have no idea why the conspirator made the statement. . . . Even an experienced trial judge might credit an incriminatory statement that a defendant could not explain, precisely because the defendant had no ready explanation for it. Because of this actual "real world" experience with the possible unreliability of these statements, the Advisory Committee retained the agency rationale for this exemption in Rule 801(d)(2)(E), as well as the safeguards, albeit limited, against unreliability that this rationale provided the defendant. The independent-evidence requirement was one such safeguard. . . .

NOTES ON PROCEDURAL PROBLEMS

1. Under *Bourjaily*, the judge decides pursuant to FRE 104(a) whether the coventurer, pendency, and furtherance requirements are satisfied. The preponderance standard applies, and the court may consider the statement itself in determining the predicate facts. In fact, the preponderance standard applies more or less across the board to questions determined by the trial judge under FRE 104(a), whether they relate to hearsay exceptions, claims of privilege, or anything else. See also Lego v. Twomey, 404 U.S. 477 (1972) (preponderance

standard applies to decisions on question whether confession is voluntary). And see generally Mueller and Kirkpatrick, Evidence §1.12 (3d ed. 2003). From the facts given in the case, do you think there was enough evidence, independent of Lonardo's statements, to support a finding of the predicate? Do you think the Court would require exclusion of a coconspirator statement where there was *no* independent evidence? How *ought* such a case to be resolved?

2. The opinion in *Bourjaily* describes the situation as a "paradigm": Lonardo's statements themselves tend to establish that he and his friends were conventurers, and the conduct of Bourjaily and Lonardo in meeting at the appointed time corroborates what Lonardo said. If a court decides that one statement satisfies the conventurer exception, on the basis of other statements and conduct by the parties, isn't the court determining the predicate facts by evidence "independent" of the statement?

3. Since the trial judge alone determines the predicate facts under FRE 104(a), does it follow that in doing so he resolves credibility issues? See United States v. Nichols, 695 F.2d 86, 91 (5th Cir. 1982) (in determining predicate facts, "judging the credibility of the witness is a matter for the trial court").

4. The opinion in *Bourjaily* addresses the question *how* a court determines the predicate facts, but leaves open the question *when* it does so. Some eight years earlier, the Fifth Circuit addressed this matter and other procedural issues, concluding that the judge should hold what has come to be called a *James* hearing to resolve threshold issues, preferably before admitting coconspirator statements:

> [E]vidence [of coconspirator statements] endangers the integrity of the trial because the relevancy and apparent probative value of the statements may be so highly prejudicial as to color other evidence even in the mind of a conscientious juror, despite instructions to disregard the statements or consider them conditionally. . . .
>
> . . . Courts have on occasion allowed such statements to be heard by the jury upon the promise that the prosecutor will "connect it up" [by evidence proving the predicate facts]. Of course, if it is connected up, the defendant suffers no prejudice in the order of proof. If, however, the judge should conclude at the end of the trial that the proper foundation has not been laid, the defendant will have been prejudiced from the jury's having heard the inadmissible evidence. . . .
>
> Both because of the "danger" to the defendant if the statement is not connected and because of the inevitable serious waste of time, energy and efficiency when a mistrial is required in order to obviate such danger, we conclude that the present procedure warrants the statement of a preferred order of proof in such a case. The district court should, whenever reasonably practicable, require the showing of a conspiracy and of the connection of the defendant with it before admitting declarations of a coconspirator. If it determines it is not reasonably practical to require the showing to be made before admitting the evidence, the court may admit the statements subject to being connected up.

United States v. James, 590 F.2d 575, 579, 581-582 (5th Cir. 1979) (en banc). A previous panel opinion in the same case went even further:

> [T]he judge cannot allow the jury to hear a coconspirator's declaration until he has determined admissibility by a preponderance of the evidence.

United States v. James, 576 F.2d 1121, 1131 (5th Cir. 1978). Other courts have not even endorsed a "preferred order of proof," indicating that the trial judge can follow whatever sequence she prefers. See United States v. Smith, 320 F.3d 647, 654 (6th Cir.), cert. denied, 123 S.Ct. 1954 (2003). Why did the later en banc decision in *James* backtrack from the position taken by the panel? Why do *Smith* and similar cases refuse even to endorse a "preferred" order of proof?

5.   Because of the coincidence problem—the coventurer requirement raising both an issue of predicate fact for the coconspirator exception and an ultimate issue in a conspiracy prosecution—some have thought that the jury should be put in charge of applying the coconspirator exception. Under what came to be called the *Apollo* approach, the question whether the coconspirator exception applies would be treated as an issue of conditional relevancy under FRE 104(b), rather than admissibility under FRE 104(a). The jury would be told to consider a coconspirator statement as evidence against the defendant only if it found that declarant and defendant conspired. United States v. Apollo, 476 F.2d 156 (5th Cir. 1973). The decision in *Bourjaily* rejects this possibility, does it not?

6.   When it comes to handling the coincidence problem both the *Bourjaily* and the *Apollo* approaches have advantages and drawbacks:

a.   *Bourjaily* offers the advantage that it tends to assure that coconspirator statements are admitted only where proof of conspiracy is substantial. Consider a case in which the government's evidence is too weak to persuade the judge (under the preponderance standard) that declarant and defendant conspired, but is strong enough to block a defense motion for a judgment of acquittal (because the jury could conclude beyond a reasonable doubt that defendant and declarant conspired). Such a case is possible because the judge could disbelieve prosecution witnesses (and exclude coconspirator hearsay under *Bourjaily*) while acknowledging that the jury might believe them. The evidence might be such that the jury could reasonably convict on the basis of (i) other evidence alone or (ii) all the evidence, including the coconspirator statement. If the trial judge admitted the coconspirator statement under *Apollo* and the jury then convicted, we face the risk that the conviction rested on hearsay considered by the only competent authority in the tribunal (the judge) to fall outside the exception. But if the judge admitted the hearsay "subject to connection" under *Bourjaily,* he could tell the jury to disregard the coconspirator statement or grant a mistrial in situation (i), or take from the jury all charges dependent on the coconspirator statement in situation (ii).

b.   Unfortunately *Bourjaily* also has certain drawbacks. For one thing, *Bourjaily* is more likely than *Apollo* to send a case to the jury with instructions to disregard coconspirator statements. And under *Bourjaily,* judge and jury might reach conflicting decisions on a single factual issue—whether defendant and declarant conspired—which is common to the questions of guilt and admissibility. The conflict might take two forms: One arises where (i) the judge excludes the statement (finding that all the evidence fails to establish a conspiracy by a preponderance) but puts the case to the jury anyway and (ii) the jury convicts defendants of conspiring but acquits them of substantive charges. Here either the judge or the jury made a mistake on the conspiracy question, and the judge's view may have had decisive impact (leading to acquittal on substantive charges). The other arises where (i) the judge admits the statement (finding that all the evidence establishes the predicate facts by a preponderance) and puts the case to the jury and (ii) the jury acquits defendants of conspiring but convicts them on the substantive charges. Here perhaps judge or jury made a mistake on the conspiracy question, and the judge's opinion may have had decisive effect, this time producing conviction on the substantive charges.

PROBLEM 4-H.   *Drugs Across the Border*

Arlen and Bud decide to import cocaine from Colombia. They discuss the matter and agree that Bud will fly there with his friend Carol and acquire the stuff, while Arlen lines up customers. Bud recruits Carol to the conspiracy. Carol's friend Connie drives them to the airport, and the three share a beer before Carol and Bud board the plane:

Connie: So you guys are going into the import business?
Carol: Yeah, only thing I regret is Arlen. He's a real creep. Can he handle his end?
Bud: Yeah, he can talk good, and he knows how to set the price. Besides, he's fronted us the buy money for the trip, so what can you say?

Don, who works under cover for the Drug Enforcement Administration, approaches Arlen several days later:

Don: Looking for some coke. What can you do for me?
Arlen: How much you want to buy?
Don: Couple or three kilos.
Arlen: Hey man, that's a lot of bucks. You good for it?
Don: When can you produce and what's the price?
Arlen: Got some coming in on Monday. Hundred thou per kilo. First-rate stuff. Good price.
Don: I need to be able to count on it.
Arlen: Hey, you know Bud, don't you? He's gone south to make the buy, and he'll be back on Sunday. You can count on it. Meet you at the Alibi Club Monday at 3.
Don: OK.

At the airport on Sunday morning, other DEA agents (knowing nothing of Don's contact with Arlen) spot Carol on the basis of their drug courier profile and speak to her as she gets off the plane. Bud is on board too, but he and Carol are traveling separately, and he avoids detection. Finding nothing, the agents release but follow Carol, who finds Bud and tells him, "The feds let me go, and even apologized." On Sunday afternoon, Arlen (followed by Don's colleagues in the DEA) goes to see Bud. On Monday afternoon, Arlen keeps his engagement with Don at the Alibi, but immediately after the sale DEA agents arrest Arlen, and other agents simultaneously capture Bud and Carol at Bud's place. After receiving *Miranda* warnings, Carol implicates herself and tells the agents that "Bud made the buy in Colombia," and she "just helped carry the stuff past customs down there."

Arlen, Bud, and Carol are prosecuted together. All are charged with conspiracy to import and sell cocaine; Bud and Carol are charged with importation of cocaine; Arlen and Bud are charged with possession of cocaine; Arlen is charged with selling cocaine.

At trial, the prosecutor invokes the coconspirator exception in offering the following items of evidence: (1) testimony by Connie describing what Bud told her in the bar (Arlen "fronted us the buy money"), over Arlen's objection; (2) testimony by Don describing what Arlen said (Bud's "gone south to make the buy"), over Bud's objection; and (3) testimony by the DEA agent describing what Carol told him ("Bud made the buy"), over Bud's objection. Do any or all of these statements fit the coconspirator exception?

NOTES ON THE COCONSPIRATOR EXCEPTION

1. Many cases repeat the point that the coconspirator exception may be invoked even if no conspiracy is actually charged. Should the exception be available in a case in which charges of conspiracy are dropped on a defense motion to dismiss for insufficient evidence or in cases in which defendant is acquitted of conspiracy? See United States v. Xheka, 704 F.2d 974, 986 (7th Cir.) (although defendant was acquitted of conspiracy, coconspirator statement by another was properly admitted), cert. denied, 494 U.S. 993 (1983).

2. The exception does not reach statements made either before or after a conspiracy, and on the latter point the Supreme Court has been emphatic that statements made during what may be called the "concealment phase" of a conspiracy are not ordinarily within the exception. See Krulewitch v. United States, 336 U.S. 440 (1949) (in prosecution for transporting women across state lines for purpose of prostitution, statement by complaining witness more than a month after her arrival in Miami was not within the exception; conspirators "always expressly or implicitly agree to collaborate with each other to conceal facts in order to prevent conviction, detection and punishment," and "plausible arguments" could be made that most statements by one conspirator "tended to shield" another, but broadening the exception to reach such statements would "create automatically a further breach of the general rule against the admission of hearsay"). But in Grunewald v. United States, 353 U.S. 391 (1957), the Court made an exception for postconspiracy statements that further "the *main* criminal objectives of the conspiracy," suggesting that kidnappers "in hiding, waiting for ransom" commit acts of concealment "in furtherance of the objectives of the conspiracy itself, just as repainting a stolen car would be in furtherance of a conspiracy to steal," and such statements *are* within the exception. And in Dutton v. Evans, 400 U.S. 74 (1970), the Court concluded that the federal rule on this point is not constitutionally required, upholding the receipt of a postarrest statement under Georgia's version of the coconspirator exception.

3. Do all statements that satisfy the "furtherance" requirement amount to "verbal acts" that could be admitted without a coconspirator exception? What kinds of statements "further" a conspiracy, anyway?

4. The Supreme Court has repeatedly rejected constitutional challenges to the coconspirator exception, and it did so again in *Bourjaily* (in passages edited out of the book). When you get to the materials on confrontation, you will see that passages in Crawford v. Washington, 124 S.Ct. 1354 (2004), indicate

again that coconspirator hearsay does not offend the Confrontation Clause, although the involvement of an informant in generating the statement offered in *Bourjaily* may raise problems under the *Crawford* doctrine. See Chapter 4G, infra.

    5. Are coconspirator statements reliable? The admissions doctrine does not rest on reliability, and commentators have suggested that the coconspirator exception should require a showing of reliability. Would this revision be wise? See generally Mueller, The Federal Coconspirator Exception: Action, Assertion, and Hearsay, 12 Hofstra L. Rev. 323 (1984); Davenport, The Confrontation Clause and the Co-Conspirator Exception in Criminal Prosecutions: A Functional Analysis, 85 Harv. L. Rev. 1378 (1978).

C. UNRESTRICTED EXCEPTIONS

Most hearsay exceptions apply regardless whether declarant is available as a witness. Rule 803 sets out a daunting list of 23, almost all in this category. Two fall slightly outside the pattern, for Rule 803(5) paves the way for statements of past recollection recorded only if declarant testifies and lays a foundation, and Rule 803(18) reaches learned treatises only if an expert testifies as a witness.

1. Present Sense Impressions and Excited Utterances

Immediacy is the key to present sense impressions under FRE 803(1). Declarant describes what he sees as he sees it. Excitement is the key to the excited utterance exception in FRE 803(2). Declarant sees a startling event that rivets his attention, and then (then or later, but while still in its sway) he speaks in reaction.

    In practice, the two exceptions overlap. The one for present sense impressions is a recent arrival. It derives from the excited utterance exception, and both were distilled from the haze of a vague common law doctrine captured in the Latin term "res gestae" ("things that happened"). For present sense impressions and excited utterances, res gestae expressed the notion that the relationship between event and statement was so close that the happening impelled the words out of the declarant. Less poetically, the idea was that the connection was so close that declarant had no time to lie or forget, and that he focused his attention on what he described.

> ## NUTTALL v. READING CO.
> ### United States Court of Appeals for the Third Circuit
> ### 235 F.2d 546 (1956)

[Florence Nuttall, as executrix of the estate of Clarence Nuttall, sued the railroad (Reading) under the Federal Employers' Liability Act. Clarence Nuttall worked for Reading as an engineman, and in this suit his widow claimed that Reading required him to report to work despite his objection that he was ill.

The case was tried twice. In the first trial plaintiff recovered a verdict of $30,000, but the judge ordered a new trial (on the ground that an improper claim for damages on behalf of a minor child may have engendered "sympathetic emotion" in the jury).

In the second trial, the court directed a verdict against Florence Nuttall, from which she took this appeal. Here she urged error in the exclusion of evidence, including (1) two affidavits (one by Fireman John O'Hara, the other by Conductor James Snyder, both of whom worked with Nuttall on the occasion in question), (2) her own testimonial account of her husband's phone conversation with the yardmaster, and (3) testimony by the fireman about remarks Nuttall made in the trainyard on the day in question.

The affidavits were secured by the railroad after suit had been filed, but the judge excluded them as hearsay. The reviewing court here approves this ruling. Still, the affidavits tell the story that Mrs. Nuttall wanted the court to hear. They indicated that Clarence Nuttall did report to work, assuming his duties as engineman on the 7:00 A.M. Wilmington Yard shifter.

Fireman O'Hara's affidavit stated the following facts: Nuttall "did not look well," and "said he wasn't feeling too good." Nuttall was "coughing and couldn't seem to get his breath," and O'Hara relieved him after an hour while Nuttall "sort of propped himself on the Fireman's seat . . . perspiring and coughing" and having "trouble getting his breath." Nuttall "reported off until further notice" at about 1:00 P.M., declining O'Hara's offer of a lift home and driving off himself.

Conductor Snyder's affidavit confirmed O'Hara's version of events and commented that Nuttall looked "pretty ill" and "seemed choked up and his lips were blue."

Although failing on the affidavits, Florence Nuttall fared better with her claims that the judge erred in excluding testimony by herself and John O'Hara.]

GOODRICH, J.

If the plaintiff in this case can prove that management forced a sick employee, of whose illness they knew or should have known, into work for which he was unfitted because of his condition, a case is made out for the jury under the Federal Employers' Liability Act. As to this general proposition we think there is no dispute. . . .

Now we turn to the other vital piece of testimony. On the morning of January 5, 1952, Nuttall had a telephone conversation from his home with the yardmaster at Wilmington. This conversation took place in the presence of his wife and at the end there was an additional statement made to her after he had hung up the receiver. Here is [Florence Nuttal's account of] the conversation which plaintiff offered and the district judge refused. . . :

Q. Suppose you start again. He got on the phone and he dialed the office and he said something to George.
A. Yes. He said, "George," he said, "I am very sick, I don't think I will be able to come to work today."
Q. What was the next you heard your husband say?
A. I heard him say, "But I can't come to work today, I don't feel I can make it."
Q. What was the next thing you heard your husband say?
A. I heard him say, "but, George, why are you forcing me to come to work the way I feel?"

Q. Then did your husband say anything after that?
A. Well, he said, "I guess I will have to come out then."
Q. Was that the end of this conversation on the telephone?
A. It was.
Q. Then what did he do with the telephone?
A. He put the telephone back.
Q. Then did you help him? Then what happened? Did he go off, or go to work, or did he remain in the house, or what?
A. No, he went to work, he said to me, "I guess I will have to go."

[The court concludes that what Clarence Nuttall said to his wife was competent to prove that he was being forced to go to work. Moreover, what Nuttall said to O'Hara in the railroad yard (that he "was not feeling well, that he had requested to be off that day but was refused permission") was admissible to prove the same point.]

To hold the defendant responsible for sending a sick man into unsuitable work it must be shown that the man was not only under pressure but was under pressure to undertake the work by virtue of something the employer had done. The persecution complex is a well known psychiatric phenomenon; it would be highly unfair to hold an employer responsible for something the employee merely imagined without the employer inducing it.

Is the telephone conversation evidence of pressure by the employer? Unfortunately, both parties to the conversation are dead. Neither can minimize, enlarge, explain, or otherwise make any commentary upon the words Mrs. Nuttall heard her husband use on that morning of January 5.

We think that the conversation tends to show that Nuttall was being forced to do something by somebody. The "somebody" is identified without difficulty. He was Marquette the railroad employee in charge of operations in the yard. Knowing that Nuttall's superior was talking to him on the telephone we think that the words Nuttall used during the time and his statement immediately afterward tend to show that he was being forced to go to work. At this point we are assuming Nuttall's state of mind established and seeking probative evidence that his state of mind was induced by something his employer did. When a man talks as Nuttall did and acts as Nuttall did during and immediately following a conversation on the telephone with his boss, it has a tendency to show that the boss was requiring him to come to work against his will.

What Nuttall had to say during the telephone conversation was subject to Marquette's comment and response. In his statement to his wife following the conversation Nuttall merely reiterated what he had already said and in terms less accusatory. Mrs. Nuttall has no personal knowledge of what Marquette said and neither does anyone else for both parties to the conversation are dead. She did hear her husband characterize the statements of his boss at the very moment he heard what Marquette had to say and immediately thereafter. Such characterizations, since made substantially at the time the event they described was perceived, are free from the possibility of lapse of memory on the part of the declarant. And this contemporaneousness lessens the likelihood of conscious misrepresentation. All things considered, we think that Nuttall's statements during and immediately following the telephone conversation should be admitted into evidence to prove that he was being compelled to come to work.

[O'Hara's account of what Nuttall said in the trainyard, although admissible to prove compulsion, is not admissible to prove that Reading (acting through Marquette) was the force that created the compulsion.]

Mistakes on admissibility of evidence are almost inevitable during a hotly contested trial. Unless they seriously affect the case they are not a ground for reversal. But here the rejected evidence goes to the very heart of the plaintiff's case. It is unfortunate that this type of case must be tried three times. But that is necessary in this instance.

The judgment of the district court will be reversed and the case remanded with further proceedings not inconsistent with this opinion.

NOTES ON PRESENT SENSE IMPRESSIONS

1. *Nuttall* was decided almost twenty years before the Federal Rules took effect, but the case illustrates the utility of the exception for present sense impressions now embodied in FRE 803(1). Clarence Nuttall's words during his conversation with George Marquette, and immediately thereafter with his wife Florence, tend to prove that Nuttall felt pressured, don't they? If you look at his words ("I don't think I will be able to come to work" and "I guess I will have to come out then"), we *could* treat them as nonhearsay circumstantial evidence of state of mind (much like the words of Anna Sofer in Problem 3-H speaking of her being a "faithful and loving wife" while Ira reciprocated with "utter cruelty, disrespect, and indifference"). But absent peculiar facts present in Problem 3-H (wife publicizes her ill feelings about her husband), it seems wiser to treat words such as these as hearsay. One available exception is the one for state-of-mind statements, contained in FRE 803(3), which we will reach shortly. Another available exception is now provided by FRE 803(1).

2. Another thing suggested by Nuttall's words during and immediately after the phonecall is that "somebody" was applying that pressure, namely "George" (whom Nuttall calls by name on the phone). The court says that we can readily identify that "somebody" as George Marquette. If Nuttall's words are offered to prove this point (critical, in the court's mind, in view of the "well known" phenomenon of the "persecution complex"), the need for an exception is even greater, isn't it? Why?

3. What Nuttall said to O'Hara, upon arriving at the trainyard, tends once again to prove that Nuttall felt compelled to be there, doesn't it? But the court did not allow *those* words to prove that "someone" (namely Marquette, hence the railroad) had applied pressure. The result would be the same under FRE 803(1), wouldn't it? Why?

4. *Nuttall* bears close resemblance to later cases decided under FRE 803(1). See United States v. Portsmouth Paving Corp., 694 F.2d 312, 322-323 (4th Cir. 1982) (caller tells bystander what party on distant end had just said; immediacy requirement was satisfied because statement was made "no more than a few seconds" after call); United States v. Early, 657 F.2d 195, 197-198 (8th Cir. 1981) (immediately after hanging up phone, declarant said "Oh mom, what am I going to do? That sounded just like Butch"; admitted over defense objection that it was impossible to tell whether declarant meant Butch was

calling or that the caller was saying something Butch would say). These cases make it clear, don't they, that "perceiving" embraces not only what the declarant sees but what he hears? See also MCA, Inc. v. Wilson, 425 F. Supp. 443, 450-451 (S.D.N.Y. 1976) (in infringement action alleging wrongful appropriation of song "Boogie Woogie Bugle Boy," admitting "spontaneous reactions of cast and audience" to stage performance of allegedly infringing song during play).

5. Often the exception paves the way for statements identifying perpetrators of crime. In some dramatic cases, victims identify approaching assailants just before being killed and apparently before they know what is about to happen. See State v. Salgado, 974 P.2d 66, 664 (N.M. 1999) (admitting murder victim's statement "Hey, Timo, what's up?" uttered as victim greeted assailant just before being shot); Booth v. State, 508 A.2d 976 (Md. 1986) (murder victim tells caller that "some guy" had come to his door). In other cases, bystanders react to unfolding crimes, or notice critical facts, making comments to others that prove very useful in later trials. See, e.g., State v. Wright, 817 A.2d 600, 605 (R.I. 2003) (in murder trial, admitting statement by defendant's mother, was talking by phone to a friend about the killing shortly after the crime occurred, describing her sudden discovery of a purse, which turned out to be that of the victim); Cutchin v. State, 792 A.2d 359, 361-362 (Md. Spec. App. 2002) (in trial for vehicular manslaughter, admitting statement by unidentified speaker that defendant was driving car that struck tree).

6. In the age of the cellphone, people often call 911 and describe unfolding events that may include crimes. Such statements may satisfy the exception. See, e.g., Warren v. State, 774 A.2d 246, 250 (Del. 2001) (victim calls 911 and says defendant struck her in the face and broke into her neighbor's apartment through a window); State v. Hendrickson, 586 N.W.2d 906, 907 (Mich. 1998) (victim calls 911 and says "I have just had the living s— beat out of me"). It is not clear, doubtful, however, that this use of the exception can survive the decision in Crawford v. Washington, 124 S.Ct. 1354 (2004), which construes the Confrontation Clause as applying to "testimonial" statements, a category that includes statements to police describing crimes. See Chapter 4G, infra.

7. Even comments by defendants in the process of committing criminal acts have been found to qualify as present sense impressions. In one dramatic case from Oklahoma, for example, a defendant convicted of capital murder and sentenced to death won a new trial because the trial court erred in refusing to admit defendant's own statement, made after shooting two people, "it was them or me," offered in support of self-defense. See Williams v. State, 915 P.2d 371, 381 (Okla Crim. App. 1996). In another Oklahoma case, a comment by one defendant to another was admissible against both because it fit the exception. See Welch v. State, 968 P.2d 1231, 1239 (Okla. Crim. App. 1998) ("someone's getting a spanking over a deal"), cert. denied, 528 U.S. 829 (1999).

8. The exception is also useful when it comes to observations of vehicles prior to accidents, as illustrated in two classic precursors of FRE 803(1). See Claybrook v. Acreman, 373 S.W.2d 287, 291 (Tex. Civ. App. 1963) ("there goes Billy Joe Acreman" and "they won't last long at that rate of speed"); Houston Oxygen Co. v. Davis, 161 S.W.2d 474 (Tex. 1942) (referring to another car, automobile passenger said "they must have been drunk" and "we would find them somewhere on the road wrecked if they kept that rate of speed up").

9. Usually the testifying witness has seen (and can corroborate) whatever

is described in a present sense impression. ~~Some states applying similar exceptions require corroboration, most notably New York.~~ See People v. Vasquez, 670 N.E.2d 1328, 1334 (N.Y. 1996). Should FRE 803(1) be interpreted as requiring corroboration? Compare United States v. Ruiz, 249 F.3d 643, 646-647 (7th Cir. 2001) (FRE 803(1) does not require corroboration) with People v. Hendrickson, 586 N.W.2d 906, 909 (Mich. 1998) (identical state counterpart requires corroboration). *Without* a witness who was watching the declarant as he spoke, how does the court determine that he had firsthand knowledge? Can the content of the statement alone prove this point? Consider FRE 104(a), which provides that in determining admissibility the judge is not bound by the rules of evidence. See Miller v. Crown Amusements, Inc., 821 F.Supp. 703, 706 (S.D. Ga. 1993) (911 caller "noticed" truck as it "sideswiped" car parked on road; court relies on statement and circumstances in concluding that declarant observed the incident).

10.   Dying from a poisoned intravenous injection, declarant who suffered cardiac arrest at 4:30 P.M. wrote a note at 6:30 P.M. purporting to identify the person who administered the injection. Present sense impression? See United States v. Narciso, 446 F. Supp. 252, 284-288 (E.D. Mich. 1977) (no; statement "not made while the event or condition was being perceived by the declarant or even 'immediately thereafter' "). Alighting from a train in Chicago, defendant is accosted by police officers searching for drugs, who ask to question her. She walks with them 100 feet or so to a baggage area, and one of the officers asks a redcap following with a full cart whether he has any luggage belonging to defendant. "That's the bag she gave me," he replies, indicating a piece on the cart. Present sense impression? See United States v. Parker, 936 F.2d 950, 954 (7th Cir. 1991) (yes; statement was contemporaneous since interval between picking up bags and speaking was "extremely short"). Moments after accident, witness arrives and hears driver say that passenger "grabbed the wheel, causing the pickup to go into the ditch and overturn." Present sense impression? See Starr v. Morsette, 236 N.W.2d 183, 186-188 (N.D. 1975) (yes).

11.   Can a present sense impression be written? See State v. Hope, 33 P.3d 629, 631-632 (Mont. 2001) (in assault trial, admitting note written by victim saying that she and defendant "stopped at a friend's house," that defendant "got angry" and "yelled at me," adding that "I know there is going to be trouble and he'll blame it on me"); United States v. Ferber, 966 F. Supp. 90, 98 (D. Mass. 1997) (email message recounting phone conversation and "prepared shortly afterward" fit exception for present sense impressions when offered to prove substance of conversation).

UNITED STATES v. IRON SHELL
United States Court of Appeals for the Eighth Circuit
633 F.2d 77 (1980)

STEPHENSON, J.

Defendant, John Louis Iron Shell, appeals from a jury conviction of assault with intent to commit rape in violation of the Major Crimes Act, 18 U.S.C. §1153 (1970). Iron Shell raises ten issues on appeal. The . . . primary questions [include] two evidentiary rulings concerning hearsay. . . . We affirm the jury conviction.

The indictment in this case arose out of the defendant's acts on July 24, 1979, in the community of Antelope, which is within the Rosebud Indian Reservation and near Mission, South Dakota. The defense conceded at trial that Iron Shell had assaulted Lucy, a nine-year-old Indian girl. The key questions at trial concerned the nature of the assault and the defendant's intent.

At the time of the assault defendant Iron Shell was living in the Antelope community in the Beth Dillon home. He was staying there with his girlfriend, Jeanne Brave, who is Dillon's cousin. During the course of the day preceding the assault Iron Shell, in the company of friends, consumed considerable alcoholic beverages.

In the late afternoon William Burning Breast drove the defendant home. When they arrived at the Dillon house, the defendant was either asleep or had passed out. Breast and Mike Dillon, Beth Dillon's fifteen-year-old son, helped wake the defendant. Steve Mizner, a seventeen-year-old who also lived at Beth Dillon's house, helped the defendant out of the car and into the house. Mike and Steve testified that the defendant began to walk under his own power as he approached the front door. The defendant reached the Dillon house about 5:45 or 6:00 P.M. He talked and roughhoused briefly with Mike and Steve, and asked one of them to cook a hamburger. He then abruptly asked where his girlfriend Jeanne Brave was. When Mike said she was in St. Francis, the defendant was angered and left the house. He walked to his mother's home which is in the same neighborhood. He returned in about five minutes, ate the hamburger and again asked where Jeanne Brave was. When told again that she was not there, the defendant said you can tell her to go to hell and he kicked the door open and left for the second time.

Steve watched the defendant cross the highway in front of the Dillon house and enter the trail leading to his mother's house. The defendant staggered somewhat and retraced his steps several times. Because of his strange behavior, Steve called Mike to the window to watch the defendant. Both Mike and Steve testified that they saw the defendant approach Lucy who was near some cherry bushes just off the trail. Both saw the defendant grab Lucy and pull her down into some tall bushes. Steve testified he heard Lucy scream. Mike rode his bicycle to the spot where the defendant grabbed Lucy but couldn't see the girl and assumed she had escaped. Mike rode back to tell Steve, and the two returned to the bushes together. They then discovered that Lucy had not escaped. Mike testified that the defendant had his arm around Lucy and was trying to make her put her arm around him. The two boys alerted the neighbors.

Mae Small Bear was told by her granddaughter at about the same time that Lucy was "crying and hollering" in the bushes behind Small Bear's house. Small Bear walked to the bushes and saw Lucy lying on her back with the defendant lying beside her on his side. Lucy's jeans were down to her ankles and she was crying. Mae Small Bear testified that the defendant tried to hide Lucy by grabbing her legs. The defendant then ran to the end of the bushes, and when Small Bear returned to the house he ran across the highway.

At about this point Pam Lunderman arrived. She testified that she saw Lucy come out of the bushes pulling up her pants and crying. Lucy told Lunderman, "that guy tried to take my pants off." Lunderman testified that

Lucy had weeds on her back and head, that her hair was disheveled and that her face was swollen on one side. Both Steve and Mike saw Lucy come out of the bushes and confirmed Lunderman's testimony. Mike told the jury that Lucy was "crying hard," looked scared and that her jeans were down to her knees. Steve said he saw Lucy coming out of the bushes pulling up her pants and that she was crying. The time of the assault is uncertain, but it was somewhere between 6:00 and 6:30 P.M.

Lunderman took Lucy to the police station in Mission and was directed to the magistrate's office back in the Antelope community, where a complaint was signed. During this trip Lucy appeared scared and was still crying. A police car was dispatched from Rosebud, South Dakota, to Antelope, a distance of about eleven miles. Officer Noah Tucker, Bureau of Indian Affairs Law Enforcement, testified that his office received a report at about 6:45 P.M. Officer Tucker drove to the Dillon house to arrest the defendant. Another officer, Barbara Marshall, was sent to interview Lucy. Officer Tucker, along with a tribal policeman, found the defendant in the Dillon house asleep in his bedroom lying on his back. They noticed a knife underneath the defendant. They arrested him. The defendant was coherent and recognized Officer Tucker. He walked out under his own power.

Meanwhile, Officer Marshall conducted an interview with Lucy which began at about 7:15 P.M. in the magistrate's home and ended at about 7:30 P.M. Officer Marshall, according to her testimony, asked Lucy a single question: "What happened?" In response Lucy related the following. Lucy said her assailant grabbed her and held her around the neck and told her to be quiet or he would choke her. He told her to take her pants down and when she refused, he pulled them partially off. Lucy told Officer Marshall, "he tried to what you call it me."[4] Lucy also said that he had his hands between her legs. Officer Marshall recounted Lucy's statement in full at trial.[5]

Officer Marshall also testified that Lucy was not hysterical nor was she crying, but that her hair was messed and had leaves in it, that she appeared nervous and scared, and that her eyes were red. . . .

[Lucy's later statements to Dr. Hopkins, who examined Lucy at about 8:20 P.M., fit the medical statements exception in FRE 803(4) and were properly admitted.]

The defendant . . . asserts that it was prejudicial error to admit the hearsay testimony of Officer Marshall pursuant to 803(2). The rule allows admission of hearsay, otherwise competent, that is a "statement relating to a startling event or condition made while the declarant was under the stress of excitement caused by the event or condition." FRE 803(2). Officer Marshall interviewed Lucy at 7:15 P.M.; somewhere between forty-five minutes and one hour, fifteen minutes after the assault. The defense argues that Lucy was no longer "under the stress of excitement caused by the event" when she talked to Officer Marshall. The defendant emphasizes that Lucy was described as quiet and not crying, and that she had not made any spontaneous statements since immediately following the assault. He also asserts that Lucy's statements were not

_____
   4. This statement was revealed during cross-examination by defendant's counsel.
   5. Officer Marshall testified that Lucy did not spontaneously start to describe the incident but, in a halting manner, conveyed the facts as detailed above.

spontaneous because they were in response to an inquiry and were the product of reasoned reflection fostered by conversations between herself and her companions following the assault. The government, in response, stresses that Officer Marshall described Lucy as scared and nervous with her eyes still red from crying and her hair was still messed from the assault.

The lapse of time between the startling event and the out-of-court statement although relevant is not dispositive in the application of rule 803(2). . . . Nor is it controlling that Lucy's statement was made in response to an inquiry. . . . Rather, these are factors which the trial court must weigh in determining whether the offered testimony is within the 803(2) exception. Other factors to consider include the age of the declarant, the physical and mental condition of the declarant, the characteristics of the event and the subject matter of the statements. In order to find that 803(2) applies, it must appear that the declarant's condition at the time was such that the statement was spontaneous, excited or impulsive rather than the product of reflection and deliberation.

Determination of this issue is a close question. There is testimony that the declarant was calm and unexcited. In contrast the same witness described Lucy as nervous and scared. Testimony from other sources suggested that Lucy had struggled with the defendant, that he had threatened her with serious harm and that he had unsnapped and pulled down her jeans. The stress and fear that such an occurrence would impose upon a young girl cannot be discounted. Officer Marshall testified that Lucy did not give a detailed narrative but spoke in short bursts about the incident. The officer emphasized at trial that she did not ask Lucy suggestive questions but merely reported what Lucy said. The officer only asked Lucy, "What happened?"

We note at this point that our role is somewhat limited. We are not to substitute our judgment for that of the district court. We are only to reverse where we find that the admission of this testimony constituted an abuse of discretion. . . .

Applying this standard, we cannot say that the district court abused its discretion. The single question "what happened" has been held not to destroy the excitement necessary to qualify under this exception to the hearsay rule. A lapse of about one hour has also been held not to remove the evidence from the 803(2) exception, especially where the declarant is a young child. It also has been noted that the lack of recall may indicate that the declarant was under stress at the time of the statement. It is a truism to state that each of these cases must be decided on its own circumstances. We find that in these circumstances considering the surprise of the assault, its shocking nature and the age of the declarant, it was not an abuse of discretion for the trial court to find that Lucy was still under the stress of the attack when she spoke to Officer Marshall. It was not unreasonable, in this case, to find that Lucy was in a state of continuous excitement from the time of the assault.

Even if Officer Marshall's testimony concerning Lucy's statement was found to be inadmissible hearsay under 803(2), it is our view that the evidence was at most cumulative and therefore constituted harmless error. . . . In this case the defense presented no evidence to contradict the officer's testimony while it was supported, at least partially, by three other witnesses.

The defense also suggests that the admission of the two hearsay statements violates the confrontation clause. U.S. Const. Amend. VI. This case differs from the usual confrontation-hearsay case in that the declarant was a witness at trial and was subject to cross-examination. It has been recognized, however, that even though a declarant is available to testify, the confrontation clause protection may be called into question because the declarant is too young to be subjected to a thorough cross-examination as envisaged by the constitution. . . .

At trial Lucy was unable to repeat the statements she had made to Officer Marshall and Dr. Hopkins although she was able to provide some facts to support her earlier statements. Defense counsel cross-examined Lucy but did not ask about the assault or her statements shortly thereafter. It is difficult to conclude on this record that a more thorough cross-examination would not have provided the protections inherent in the confrontation clause. Nevertheless, assuming arguendo that Lucy was unavailable. . . , we conclude that the confrontation clause was not violated because the admitted hearsay statements, particularly those given to Dr. Hopkins, had sufficient indicia of reliability in order to afford the trier of fact a satisfactory basis for evaluating the truth of the prior statements. . . .[14]

We conclude that the defendant received a fair trial, no prejudicial error occurred, and that the jury's finding of guilt beyond a reasonable doubt is amply supported by the evidence.

Affirmed.

NOTES ON EXCITED UTTERANCES

1. What predicate facts bring FRE 803(2) into play? Who determines these facts, judge or jury? What evidence supports the necessary finding in *Iron Shell*? What other evidence might a court consider? If Lucy had been 27 instead of nine, would the outcome be the same? Could the exception reach the statement by Small Bear's granddaughter (Lucy was "crying and hollering")? See United States v. Bogan, 267 F.3d 614, 619 (7th Cir. 2001) (in trial of prisoners for assault on corrections officer, admitting exclamatory statement by eyewitness that defendants were trying to kill officer).

2. The involvement of Barbara Marshall, who worked in the area of law enforcement for the Bureau of Indian Affairs, in gathering Lucy's description of what happened, raises issues under the Confrontation Clause, as you will see when you read Crawford v. Washington, 2004 WL 413301 (2004) (Chapter 4G, infra). Essentially *Crawford* indicates that out-of-court "testimonial" statements (a category that includes descriptions of criminal acts given to police by victims) cannot be admitted into evidence unless the victim testifies and is subject to cross-examination. In this case, Lucy did testify and was subject to cross-examination by the defense, thus arguably satisfying the *Crawford* standard.

3. What if the time lapse had been 12 hours instead of 45 to 75 minutes? Compare People v. Smith, 581 N.W. 2d 654, 668 (Mich. 1998) (admitting statement by 16-year-old male describing sexual assault approximately nine

---

14. This conclusion would require a modification in our alternative holding concerning Officer Marshall's testimony. The assumed error would be elevated to a constitutional level. Our conclusion is the same, however. Any error is harmless beyond a reasonable doubt.

hours earlier; speaker's behavior between assault and statement was extraordinary, revealing "continuing level of stress arising from the assault that precluded any possibility of reflection") and State v. Stafford, 23 N.W.2d 832, 835 (Iowa 1946) (admitting statement by farm wife who spent the night wandering in the fields, naming her husband as her assailant, although she was speaking some 14 hours after the event) with United States v. Marrowbone, 211 F.3d 452, 454-456 (8th Cir. 2000) (error to admit statements by 16-year-old victim of sexual assault describing the crime, where these were made three hours after the event "by a teenager, not a small child," and "teenagers have an acute ability to fabricate") (harmless).

4. If someone drifts in and out of consciousness or lucidity for many hours after being injured in an accident, should we say the stress of the event and ensuing trauma endures, so what he first says on regaining his ability to speak coherently fits the exception? See Chestnut v. Ford Motor Co., 445 F.2d 967, 972-973 (4th Cir. 1971) (in product liability suit, plaintiff told his physician 20 hours after the fact that he sought to dim his lights on meeting a car but the headlight closure mechanism activated instead; in applying the exception, court on retrial should decide whether he had "regained his reflective powers"; apparently he spoke on earlier occasions, but record does not indicate whether these were rational statements or "merely the babblings of one in pain and in a state of severe shock"). Can excitement be rekindled long after the event, if declarant is suddenly reminded of a traumatic experience? See United States v. Tocco, 135 F.3d 116, 128 (2d Cir. 1998) (in prosecution of *F* for arson, admitting statement by alleged co-offender *T*, not on trial here, made three hours after lighting fire; if arson itself was not an exciting event, *T*'s later understanding that "people could be trapped inside the burning building" would be), cert. denied, 423 U.S. 1096 (1998); United States v. Napier, 518 F.2d 316, 317-318 (9th Cir.) (approving exclamation by kidnap victim hospitalized for seven weeks with head injuries, on seeing newspaper picture of defendant a week after her return home, "He killed me, he killed me"), cert. denied, 423 U.S. 895 (1975).

5. Would the exception embrace the statement by Lucy if she were only four years old? If a court would not permit her to testify because of youth or mental disturbance, should it admit her statement under the instant exception? Recall how the court finessed this issue in Betts v. Betts, 473 P.2d 403 (Wash. App. 1970) ("He killed my brother and he'll kill my mommie too"), Chapter 3E, supra.

6. The exception is most often invoked to admit statements by victims of criminal assault and people injured in accidents, such as Lucy in *Iron Shell* and plaintiff in *Chestnut* (Note 4, supra). For examples in the criminal context, see Commonwealth v. Carroll, 789 N.E.2d 1062, (Mass. 2003) ("Please help me. Help me. My eye. They beat me. They beat me"); Cromeans v. State, 2003 WL 21040217 (Ark. 2003) ("Mother, I've been raped"). In the civil sphere, see Simpson v. Wal-Mart Stores, Inc., 744 A.2d 625, 628 (N.H. 1999) (statement by slip-and-fall victim, "I went flying").

7. Emergency 911 calls often fit the exception, and recorded accounts of crimes or accidents as they occur or shortly afterwards are often admitted. See, e.g., Malloy v. United States, 797 A.2d 687, 689 (D.C. Ct. App. 2002) (witness describing screams of victim of kidnapping and assault); Davenport v.

State, 749 N.E.2d 1144, 1147 (Ind. 2001) (in murder trial, admitting 911 call placed by five-year-old, upon discovering body of his mother, saying that she had been beaten up and was dead); State v. Muscari, 807 A.2d 407, 414 (Vt. 2002) (assault victim's statements on 911 tape, uttered during attack); Clark v. State, 693 So. 2d 927, 932 (Miss. 1997) (hair-raising call by convenience store clerk as defendant batters door down before killing her; defendant's own voice audible on tape). For a criticism of these cases, see Richard D. Friedman and Bridget McCormack, Dial-In Testimony, 150 U. Pa. L. Rev. 1171 (2002). It is not clear that this use of the exception can survive the decision in Crawford v. Washington, 124 S.Ct. 1354 (2004), which construes the Confrontation Clause as applying to "testimonial" statements, a category that includes statements to police describing crimes. See Chapter 4G, infra.

8. Noting that such events present to the observer "a vast number of stimuli that far transcend the span of apperception," one critic suggests that the exception is "merely an artifice for the admission of highly unreliable evidence":

> Excitement is not a guarantee against lying, especially since the courts often hold that excitement may endure many minutes and even hours beyond the event. More important, excitement exaggerates, sometimes grossly, distortion in perception and memory especially when the observer is a witness to a nonroutine, episodic event such as occurs in automobile collision cases and crimes. The likelihood of inaccurate perception, the drawing of inferences to fill in memory gaps, and the reporting of nonfacts is high.

Stewart, Perception, Memory, and Hearsay: A Criticism of Present Law and the Proposed Federal Rules of Evidence, 1970 Utah L. Rev. 1, 8-22, 27-29. Convinced?

PROBLEM 4-I. *"I Felt This Sudden Pain"*

Fifty-five-year-old Eldon Sanders was employed as a pumper and well treater by Texas Oil (he was a 23-year veteran with the company). His job required him manually to load 30-gallon containers of chemicals onto a pickup truck and then drive around to wells in the field, unload the containers, and pour the contents down the wells. From time to time he also had to move pumps weighing 50 to 100 pounds, lifting them onto the truck and unloading them.

On the morning in question, Sanders had his usual coffee and doughnut at a cafe and drove the pickup into the fields at about 7:00 A.M. Two hours later he was seen en route to the "Chase Lease" to treat wells. At 10:00 A.M. he returned to town and went home, where he complained to his wife Eleanor, "I felt this sudden pain just a few minutes ago when I had to lift one of those 30-gallon cans out on the Chase."

Eleanor drove her husband to the office of their family physician Dr. Hillier, who took an electrocardiogram. There was no indication of heart damage, though Sanders' blood pressure was elevated. Hillier administered a tranquilizer and put Sanders to bed for observation. At first he rested easy and seemed better, but in the afternoon he became uncomfortable, and at 5:00 P.M. he died of acute myocardial infarction (heart attack).

Eleanor Sanders sues Liberty Insurance Company, the workers' compensation carrier for Texas Oil, seeking benefits as surviving widow. At trial, she testifies that she was surprised to see her husband come home at that hour of the morning and that he "never comes home at that time." She offers to testify to what Sanders told her, and her counsel invokes the excited utterance exception. Liberty objects, arguing that "there's no proof of an exciting event here, other than the statement itself, and letting the statement prove the condition on which admissibility depends would be bootstrapping." How should the court rule, and why?

NOTES ON PROVING EXCITEMENT FOR PURPOSES OF THE EXCEPTION

1. Should courts applying FRE 803(2) require independent evidence of an exciting event? Why or why not? Compare People v. Burton, 455 N.W.2d 133 (Mich 1989) (independent evidence required) with United States v. Brown, 254 F.3d 454, 459-460 (3d Cir. 2001) (independent evidence *not* required).

2. Widow sues to collect double indemnity payable on the accidental death of her husband (recovery otherwise limited to the face amount of the policy). The husband had died of a heart attack shortly after returning to bed at 3:00 A.M. Plaintiff wants to testify that just before her husband died, he had gotten out of bed and gone downstairs, and that he told her on his return that "he had taken a terrible fall on the stairs." Widow can also testify that on his return to bed her husband "seemed clammy to the touch, and was trembling all over." Her lawyer invokes the excited utterance exception, but the insurance carrier objects. What result, and why? Are there facts in Problem 4-I *other than the statement* that show that Eldon Sanders experienced an exciting event?

3. Reconsider Problem 4-G ("I Was on an Errand for My Boss"), but alter the facts slightly. This time declarant speaks immediately after the accident, obviously excited. If his statement comes in under FRE 803(2), could it prove that he was negligent (recall that he said he "got distracted for a moment trying to read the purchase order")? Could it prove he was employed by defendant and acting within the scope of his employment (recall that he said he was "making a delivery for Farmright")? See Murphy Auto Parts Co. v. Ball, 249 F.2d 508 (D.C. Cir. 1957) (yes to both questions), cert. denied, 355 U.S. 932 (1958). What issues do these uses raise?

2. *State of Mind*

The state-of-mind exception, as it is usually called, is another doctrine that emerged from the haze of res gestae. It is vitally important, often invoked, and in some respects difficult. As formulated in FRE 803(3), the exception has four distinct uses: To prove (a) declarant's then-existing physical condition, (b) his then-existing mental or emotional condition, (c) his later conduct, and (d) facts about his will.

On all but the third point, what declarant said is likely the best source of information, hence less suspect than the next-best alternative. That alternative (for points a and b) would be his own backward-looking testimonial account. On the first three points (a through c) his prior statement has the virtue of immediacy. On all four points, the risk of misperception is small, and the risk of faulty memory is virtually nonexistent.

But risks of candor and ambiguity remain, and some cases hold that the exception is unavailable where circumstances suggest insincerity, a risk that may seem considerable in the case of blame-avoiding statements. See United States v. Ponticelli, 622 F.2d 985, 991-992 (9th Cir.) (defendant had time enough "to concoct an explanation"), cert. denied, 449 U.S. 1016 (1980); Fla. Stat. Ann. §90.803(3)(b)(2) (1979) (authorizing exclusion where circumstances indicate "lack of trustworthiness"). But see United States v. DiMaria, 727 F.2d 265, 271-272 (2d Cir. 1984) ("truth or falsity was for the jury to determine," and statement within categorical exceptions "is admissible without any preliminary finding of probative credibility by the trial judge"). Judge for yourself as you proceed whether the exception should be subject to some general power in the trial judge to exclude on account of doubts over veracity of the declarant.

a. Then-Existing Physical Condition

In personal injury suits, the exception is regularly invoked for statements describing aches and pains. It matters not whether declarant speaks close in time to the injury or onset of ailment, so long as his words describe how he feels as he talks. The Supreme Court explained it this way in an early case:

> [T]he usual expressions of such feelings are original and competent evidence. Those expressions are the natural reflexes of what it might be impossible to show by other testimony. If there be such other testimony, this may be necessary to set the facts thus developed in their true light, and to give them their proper effect.

Insurance Co. v. Mosley, 75 U.S. 397, 404-405 (1869). These statements are admissible not only when spoken to treating physicians, but also when declarant talks to spouse or friend. In *Mosley*, he spoke to his son and wife. See also Mabry v. Travelers Insurance Co., 193 F.2d 497, 498 (5th Cir. 1952) (wife to husband); Casualty Insurance Co. v. Salinas, 333 S.W.2d 109, 116-118 (Tex. 1960) (worker to friends complaining of pain at various times after injury).

b. Then-Existing Mental or Emotional Condition

When mental state of a party is in issue (it often is), the exception paves the way for use of his own out-of-court statement. See United States v. Parry, 649 F.2d 292, 294-295 (5th Cir. 1981) (defendant claimed he thought he was leading undercover agents to drug sources; reversible error to exclude testimony by his mother that he said the person phoning him was an agent with whom he was working; court treats statement as nonhearsay circumstantial evidence of state of mind); Detroit Police Officers' Association v. Young, 608 F.2d 671, 693-694 (6th Cir. 1979) (in suit to enjoin affirmative action program, testimony describing reasons stated by former police supervisors for past discrimination was admissible in support of challenged program), cert. denied, 452 U.S. 938 (1981).

Sometimes the mental state of nonparties is in issue, and here too the exception is available, as in suits alleging loss of business good will. See Morris Jewelers v. General Electric Credit Corp., 714 F.2d 32, 33-34 (5th Cir. 1983) (admitting "complaints and expressions of anger" in letters from customers to prove their state of mind, which translates into loss of good will).

The exception reaches only statements of *present* mental state. Hence what the declarant says on Wednesday about his mental state on Monday does not fit the exception. See Bartlett & Co., Grain v. Merchants Co., 323 F.2d 501, 509-510 (5th Cir. 1963) (statement by grain inspector months after examining load did not fit exception when offered to prove his knowledge on the earlier occasion). But sometimes it is reasonable to assume that mental state persists over time, so what the declarant says on Wednesday about how he feels may shed light on his mental state both then *and* on the prior Monday and following Friday and can be admitted as proof of all these points. See Rayborn v. Hayton, 208 P.2d 133 (Wash. 1949) (woman said she would part with her deed only for money; she was thereafter murdered, and her husband appeared with deed in hand, claiming she delivered it to him in exchange for his promise to pay; her earlier statement was admissible to prove that she did not intend delivery); Mills v. Damson Oil Corp., 691 F.2d 715, 716-717 (5th Cir. 1982) (statement indicating that declarant knew about title to property reflected his knowledge at the time "and, by inference, prior thereto" when he dealt with grantor).

More often, however, courts refuse to draw inferences of continuity, particularly into the past. See Jackson v. State, 697 N.E.2d 53, 54 (Ind. 1998) (in murder trial, excluding defendant's statement two hours after the crime that he "didn't mean to kill"). And great care is warranted:

> The stream of consciousness has enough continuity so that we may expect to find the same characteristics for some distance up or down the current. But there is a point beyond which such evidence becomes irrelevant. Hudson River water at West Twenty-third St. Ferry is no proof of its quality above Fort Edward.

Chafee, The Progress of the Law—Evidence, 1919-1922, 35 Harv. L. Rev. 428, 444 (1922).

This application of the exception is complicated by the fact that often utterances indicating mental state are wholly or partially factual in nature. In what we can call "fact-laden statements," people may purposefully disclose state of mind by speaking in factual terms, choosing to communicate inclinations in that oblique way. Sometimes their main purpose is to communicate facts, but in doing so they also reveal something about inclinations, often consciously, but perhaps subconsciously or unconsciously.

Consider the following example of fact-laden statements communicating the speaker's inclination: Oberman sues Dun & Bradstreet, alleging that it issued a false credit report that caused Prudential Realty to refuse to lease a building to him. At trial, Oberman describes his telephone conversation with Rance of Prudential:

> I says,   "Well, if you are buying the building you will need a lessee, so I will lease the building. . . ."
> He [Rance] said,   "Well, you can't do that either."
> I said,   "Why?"
> He said,   "Well, I may as well give you the facts. I was trying to be nice to you. So I will give you the facts. I want to read a report to you I got here from Dun & Bradstreet. . . . You got a non-borrowing account at the bank. You got five thousand worth of receivables in your business. You are worth a thousand dollars. How are you going to pay one thousand four hundred thirty dollars a month for rent?"

At the end of the conversation Oberman offered to "get that corrected," but Rance replied: "Forget it. It is all over." Dun & Bradstreet objects that Rance was just "remembering a past decision" and that the state-of-mind exception does not embrace "statements of memory or belief." Should this objection be sustained? In the actual case, the reviewing court said no:

> Rance's statements . . . do not face backward. For present purposes, it is of no moment whether the facts which gave rise to Rance's declaration were true or actually occurred, because the concern here is only with the reason for Rance's refusal to lease the Hamlin Avenue property. Thus, there are no problems of memory and perception of the declarant to be tested, and therefore, as in the usual state of mind situation, Oberman's recollection of the statement is as likely to be correct as Rance's recollection.

Oberman v. Dun & Bradstreet, 507 F.2d 349, 351-352 (7th Cir. 1974).

Rance was surely stating facts, telling Oberman that he had in hand a credit report from Dun & Bradstreet and reciting what was in the report. Just as surely Rance consciously told Oberman why he couldn't lease the building, in effect saying "you're a poor credit risk." Thus Rance disclosed his (and presumably Prudential's) reasons for their decision—his own state of mind and Prudential's institutional judgment. Surely the reviewing court was right to apply FRE 803(3), even though on its face the statement recited facts rather than inclinations.

Recall that sometimes statements of fact are viewed as nonhearsay circumstantial evidence of state of mind. That was the route taken in the *Parry* case, supra (defendant told his mother that the caller was a narcotics agent with whom he was working). And remember the statements by Anna Sofer in Problem 3-H (Ira "reciprocated my tender feelings with utter cruelty, disrespect, and indifference") and Sharon in Problem 3-I (describing a bedroom with "a papier-mâché man").

Thus one challenge with fact-laden statements offered to prove state of mind is to decide whether they can reasonably be viewed as nonhearsay circumstantial evidence of state of mind. If not, another challenge is to decide whether to admit them under FRE 803(3): Obviously they also tend to prove the facts themselves, but FRE 803(3) says the exception does not embrace "a statement of memory or belief to prove the fact remembered or believed." In applying the latter provision, the problem is whether probative worth is "substantially outweighed" by the risk of "unfair prejudice" under FRE 403 (misuse of the statements as proof of the facts themselves).

PROBLEM 4-J.   *"He Says He'll Kill Me"*

The prosecutor has evidence that defendant Otto Neff was shaking down Paul Quade, who was found dead of knife wounds in a park. Neff is a smalltime tough guy, and the prosecutor thinks he was collecting "protection" money from Quade but that Quade balked and was killed for his resistance. At trial the prosecutor calls Quade's friend Roy Sarnak, who will testify (if permitted) that during the period in question Quade once told him:

> Neff is after me again. He says he'll kill me and my family if I don't pay protection. I've already paid him $5,000, and I'm trying to steer clear of him, and I need help but I just don't know what to do.

Neff raises a hearsay objection. The prosecutor invokes FRE 803(3).

If the charge against Neff is extortion, what arguments and counterarguments do you expect on the admissibility of what Quade said? What if the charge against Neff is murder? If it were, would it make a difference that Neff claims self-defense?

NOTES ON PROVING STATE OF MIND
BY FACT-LADEN UTTERANCES

1.   In an extortion case, fear on the part of the victim is an element in the prosecutor's case, isn't it? Does the victim's fear of the defendant have any *other* relevance in an extortion case? Quade's statement does suggest fear, doesn't it? Other things as well? What should the court do? See United States v. Collins, 78 F.3d 1021, 1036 (6th Cir.) (admitting statement by extortion victim indicating fear), cert. denied, 506 U.S. 1082 (1996).

2.   If Neff is charged simply with murder, is the victim's fear of the defendant still an element? Is such fear relevant? Should the court admit Quade's statement if murder is the only charge? Most courts do *not* admit such statements in this setting, and would not admit even pure statements indicating fear. Can you see why? Look at what Judge Ito said in the trial of O.J. Simpson for murdering Nicole Brown and Ronald Goldman, quoted in Note 5 on pages 255-256, infra. For modern examples of the prevailing view, see Commonwealth v. Laich, 777 A.2d 1057, 1061 (Pa. 2001) (in murder trial, reversible error to

admit victim's fact-laden statement indicating fear); United States v. Brown, 490 F.2d 758 (D.C. Cir. 1973) (state-of-mind exception does not generally apply to statement of fear by victim in homicide trial, especially when it describes another's conduct, unless victim's state of mind is itself an issue). And see generally C. Mueller and L. Kirkpatrick, Evidence §§8.38-8.39 (3d ed. 2003). But for another view, see Capano v. State, 781 A.2d 556, 612-615 (Del. 2001) (in kidnap-murder case, admitting statements of fear by victim as proof that she was seeking to end relationship, which tended to show motive), cert. denied, 536 U.S. 958 (2002).

3. In Shepard v. United States, 290 U.S. 96 (1933), the Supreme Court concluded that a statement by a dying wife accusing her husband of trying to kill her ("Dr. Shepard has poisoned me") did not fit the dying declaration exception. The prosecutor had another arrow for his bow, arguing that the statement should be admitted to prove Zenana Shepard's state of mind, in refutation of defendant's contention that she took her own life. But the trial court admitted her statement as a dying declaration, as proof that indeed Shepard poisoned her. The Supreme Court would not go along with the government's state-of-mind rationale:

> The defendant had tried to show by Mrs. Shepard's declarations to her friends that she had exhibited a weariness of life and a readiness to end it, the testimony giving plausibility to the hypothesis of suicide. By proof of these declarations evincing an unhappy state of mind the defendant opened the door to the offer by the Government of declarations evincing a different state of mind, declarations consistent with the persistence of a will to live. The defendant would have no grievance if the testimony in rebuttal had been narrowed to that point. What the Government put in evidence, however, was something very different. . . . It will not do to say that the jury might accept the declarations for any light that they cast upon the existence of a vital urge, and reject them to the extent that they charged the death to some one else. Discrimination so subtle is a feat beyond the compass of ordinary minds. The reverberating clang of those accusatory words would drown all weaker sounds. It is for ordinary minds, and not for psychoanalysts, that the rules of evidence are framed. They have their source very often in considerations of administrative convenience, of practical expediency, and not in rules of logic. When the risk of confusion is so great as to upset the balance of advantage, the evidence goes out. . . .
>
> The testimony now questioned faced backward and not forward. This at least it did in its most obvious implications. What is even more important, it spoke to a past act, and more than that, to an act by some one not the speaker. Other tendency, if it had any, was a filament too fine to be disentangled by a jury.

Shepard v. United States, 290 U.S. 96, 103-104, 106 (1933) (Cardozo). Would *Shepard* have been different if Zenana had said, "I don't want to die from poisoned liquor"?

4. In Problem 4-J, could defendant Neff turn the tables on the prosecutor by proving that *Quade* had been the one making threats, and that in fact *Quade* had threatened to kill *Neff*? In terms of hearsay and relevancy, would it matter whether Quade had *communicated* such threats to Neff, or would it be good enough to show that Quade uttered threats directed at Neff in the presence of third persons, even if they were never passed along to Neff? See Allison v.

United States, 160 U.S. 203, 215 (1895) (communicated threats by alleged victim against defendant were admissible); Griffin v. United States, 183 F.2d 990, 992 (App. D.C. 1950) (uncommunicated threats by alleged victim admissible when self-defense is claimed and there is substantial evidence that victim attacked defendant).

c. Subsequent Conduct

Did she embark on a journey? Her intent to go (or not to) bears on this question, and the instant exception permits use of her words to prove intent, so it is not surprising that what a person said is often admitted as proof of what she thereafter did (or did not do).

Two great difficulties attend this use of the exception:

One is that intent is a complicated matter. It comes to life in a tangle of beliefs and assumptions about conditions in the world and the expected behavior of other people. Consequently proof of intent often tends to prove other things as well. If Emily plans in November to take a January flight to Utah to go skiing, she likely believes or assumes there will be snow on the slopes and perhaps that discount tickets may be had and that she can stay with a friend. Proof that Emily harbored such intent, coupled with proof of even a few additional facts about her (that she is not wealthy, that she always stays in Utah with a particular friend, that she refuses to fly a certain airline), would tend not only to show that she went to Utah in January as planned but also to prove other things (that discount fares *are* available, that she has a friend with a place, that her friend is there and expects her to visit, that tickets may be had on airlines other than the one she dislikes, and so forth).

Another problem is that people often describe intent in statements that make factual assertions. Emily may speak of her plans by saying "Jan will let me stay at her house, and she's taking time off from work so we can both go skiing." Here Emily clearly intends to disclose her plans and some facts as well, including (implicitly) that she and Jan have been in touch and have agreed to get together.

MUTUAL LIFE INSURANCE CO. v. HILLMON
United States Supreme Court
145 U.S. 285 (1892)

[Sallie Hillmon sued Mutual Life Insurance Co. to recover $10,000 in proceeds payable under a policy on the life of her husband John Hillmon. She alleged that her husband, who was a 34-year-old cowboy and adventurer, had died in early March 1879 when accidentally shot by his companion John Brown at a campsite at Crooked Creek, Kansas, while the two were seeking out a place to start a ranch. At the same time Sallie Hillmon filed two other suits, for Hillmon had taken out two other policies on his life, each in the amount of $5,000, acquiring all of them less than four months prior to his disappearance. The three suits were consolidated for trial.

Evidence favorable to Sallie Hillmon included the deposition of Brown himself, who testified that indeed he had left Wichita with Hillmon in search of a ranch and that he did accidentally shoot Hillmon dead at Crooked Creek.

But the three insurance carriers resisted the claim, arguing that the body discovered at the campsite was not Hillmon's at all, but instead that of Adolph Walters. The defense theory was that Sallie Hillmon's suit was but the last step in a scheme by Hillmon and Brown to defraud the three carriers, and that in fact Hillmon had murdered Walters. And Brown, whose deposition supported the plaintiff, had previously signed an affidavit highly favorable to the defense position. In it Brown said that he and Hillmon had conspired to defraud the companies, that they had set out from Wichita and had thereafter met a man named "Berkley" or "Burgess" or "something like that" who joined them. Perhaps most important, Brown said that it was the latter (and not Hillmon) whose body was found at Crooked Creek, and that in fact Hillmon had fired the fatal shot.

In further support of the conspiracy theory, the defendants offered in evidence certain letters from Walters (who they claimed was the same man Brown had identified as "Berkley" or "Burgess"). In one, Walters wrote to his sister in Iowa that he intended "to leave Wichita on or about March 5th, with a certain Mr. Hillmon, a sheep-trader, for Colorado or parts unknown to me." In the other, Walters wrote to his fiancée in Iowa ("Dearest Alvina," it began), indicating his intent to leave Wichita "to see a part of the country that I never expected to see when I left home, as I am going with a man by the name of Hillmon, who intends to start a sheep ranch [and has] promised me more wages than I could make at anything else."

The trial court excluded the letters, and the jury returned verdicts favorable to Sallie Hillmon against all three carriers. Defendants appealed.]

MR. JUSTICE GRAY . . . delivered the opinion of the Court.

This question is of the admissibility of the letters written by Walters on the first days of March, 1879, which were offered in evidence by the defendants, and excluded by the court. In order to determine the competency of these letters it is important to consider the state of the case when they were offered to be read.

The matter chiefly contested at the trial was the death of John W. Hillmon, the insured; and that depended upon the question whether the body found at Crooked Creek on the night of March 18, 1879, was his body or the body of one Walters.

Much conflicting evidence had been introduced as to the identity of the body. . . .

The evidence that Walters was at Wichita on or before March 5th, and had not been heard from since, together with the evidence to identify as his the body found at Crooked Creek on March 18th, tended to show that he went from Wichita to Crooked Creek between those dates. Evidence that just before March 5th he had the intention of leaving Wichita with Hillmon would tend to corroborate the evidence already admitted, and to show that he went from Wichita to Crooked Creek with Hillmon. Letters from him to his family and his betrothed were the natural, if not the only attainable, evidence of his intention.

The position taken at the bar that the letters were competent evidence, . . . as memoranda made in the ordinary course of business, cannot be maintained, for they were clearly not such.

But upon another ground suggested they should have been admitted. A man's state of mind or feeling can only be manifested to others by countenance, attitude, or gesture, or by sounds or words, spoken or written. The nature of the fact to be proved is the same, and evidence of its proper tokens is equally competent to prove it, whether expressed by aspect or conduct, by voice or pen. When the intention to be proved is important only as qualifying an act, its connection with that act must be shown, in order to warrant the admission of declarations of the intention. But whenever the intention is of itself a distinct and material fact in a chain of circumstances, it may be proved by contemporaneous oral or written declarations of the party. The existence of a particular intention in a certain person at a certain time being a material fact to be proved, evidence that he expressed that intention at that time is as direct evidence of the fact as his own testimony that he then had that intention would be. After his death there can hardly be any other way of proving it, and while he is still alive his own memory of his state of mind at a former time is no more likely to be clear and true than a bystander's recollection of what he then said, and is less trustworthy than letters written by him at the very time and under circumstances precluding a suspicion of misrepresentation.

The letters in question were competent not as narratives of facts communicated to the writer by others, nor yet as proof that he actually went away from Wichita, but as evidence that, shortly before the time when other evidence tended to show that he went away, he had the intention of going, and of going with Hillmon, which made it more probable both that he did go and that he went with Hillmon than if there had been no proof of such intention. In view of the mass of conflicting testimony introduced upon the question whether it was the body of Walters that was found in Hillmon's camp, this evidence might properly influence the jury in determining that question.

The rule applicable to this case has been thus stated by this court: "Wherever the bodily or mental feelings of an individual are material to be proved, the usual expressions of such feelings are original and competent evidence. Those expressions are the natural reflexes of what it might be impossible to show by other testimony. If there be such other testimony, this may be necessary to set the facts thus developed in their true light, and to give them their proper effect. As independent, explanatory, or corroborative evidence it is often indispensable to the due administration of justice. Such declarations are regarded as verbal acts, and are as competent as any other testimony, when relevant to the issue. Their truth or falsity is an inquiry for the jury." Insurance Co. v. Mosley, 8 Wall. 397, 404, 405. . . .

Upon an indictment of one Hunter for the murder of one Armstrong at Camden, the court of errors and appeals of New Jersey unanimously held that Armstrong's oral declarations to his son at Philadelphia, on the afternoon before the night of the murder, as well as a letter written by him at the same time and place to his wife, each stating that he was going with Hunter to Camden on business, were rightly admitted in evidence. Chief Justice Beasley said:

In the ordinary course of things, it was the usual information that a man about leaving home would communicate, for the convenience of his family, the information of his friends, or the regulation of his business. At the time it was given, such declarations could, in the nature of things, mean harm to no one. He who uttered them was bent on no expedition of mischief or wrong, and the attitude of affairs at the time entirely explodes the idea that such utterances were intended to serve any purpose but that for which they were obviously designed. If it be said that such notice of an intention of leaving home could have been given without introducing in it the name of Mr. Hunter, the obvious answer to the suggestion, I think, is that a reference to the companion who is to accompany the person leaving is as natural a part of the transaction as is any other incident or quality of it. If it is legitimate to show by a man's own declarations that he left his home to be gone a week, or for a certain destination, which seems incontestable, why may it not be proved in the same way that a designated person was to bear him company? At the time the words were uttered or written they imported no wrongdoing to any one, and the reference to the companion who was to go with him was nothing more, as matters then stood, than an indication of an additional circumstance of his going. If it was in the ordinary train of events for this man to leave word or to state where he was going, it seems to me it was equally so for him to say with whom he was going.

Hunter v. State, 40 N.J. Law, 495, 534, 536-538.

Upon principle and authority, therefore, we are of opinion that the two letters were competent evidence of the intention of Walters at the time of writing them, which was a material fact bearing upon the question in controversy; and that for the exclusion of these letters, as well as for the undue restriction of the defendants' challenges, the verdicts must be set aside, and a new trial had. . . .

Judgment reversed, and case remanded to the circuit court, with directions to set aside the verdict and to order a new trial.

UNITED STATES v. PHEASTER
United States Court of Appeals for the Ninth Circuit
544 F.2d 353 (1976), cert. denied, 429 U.S. 1099 (1979)

[At about 9:15 P.M. on Saturday night, June 1, 1974, 16-year-old Larry Adell left his date Francine and a group of high school friends at a table in Sambo's North in Palm Springs, California, and disappeared. He had told Francine and Doug that he intended to meet "Angelo" in the parking lot to pick up some free marijuana. Larry never returned, and his family never saw him again. On the day after Larry disappeared, his father (a multimillionaire) got a phonecall making a ransom demand for $400,000 and a threat that he would never see his son alive again if he called police or FBI. Nevertheless he did immediately contact the FBI. Three attempts to pay the ransom failed—once because delivery instructions came after the deadline had passed, once because the father wanted assurance that Larry would be released, and once because the kidnappers apparently became aware that the pickup spot was under surveillance. In the end the kidnappers cut off communications, and attempts to renew contact failed.

Angelo Inciso and another are tried on federal charges of conspiracy to kidnap and related offenses of using the mail to demand money and convey threats. At trial, Francine and Doug are permitted over defense objection to testify to Larry's description of what he planned to do. Francine testifies that when Larry picked her up that evening he told her in substance that "he was going to meet Angelo at Sambo's North at 9:30 P.M." in order to "pick up a pound of marijuana that Angelo had promised him for free." Doug testifies that Larry "made similar statements to him in the afternoon and early evening" and that on leaving the table "to go into the parking lot" Larry said "he was going to meet Angelo and he'd be right back." Francine also testifies that while with Larry on an earlier occasion she met a man named Angelo, and she identifies defendant as that man.]

RENFREW, J. [sitting by designation].

The Government's position that Larry Adell's statements can be used to prove that the meeting with Inciso did occur raises a difficult and important question concerning the scope of the so-called "*Hillmon* doctrine," a particular species of the "state of mind" exception to the general rule that hearsay evidence is inadmissible. The doctrine takes its name from the famous Supreme Court decision in Mutual Life Insurance Co. v. Hillmon, 145 U.S. 285 (1892). That the *Hillmon* doctrine should create controversy and confusion is not surprising, for it is an extraordinary doctrine. Under the state of mind exception, hearsay evidence is admissible if it bears on the state of mind of the declarant and if that state of mind is an issue in the case. For example, statements by a testator which demonstrate that he had the necessary testamentary intent are admissible to show that intent when it is in issue. The exception embodied in the *Hillmon* doctrine is fundamentally different, because it does not require that the state of mind of the declarant be an actual issue in the case. Instead, under the *Hillmon* doctrine the state of mind of the declarant is used inferentially to prove other matters which are in issue. Stated simply, the doctrine provides that when the performance of a particular act by an individual is an issue in a case, his intention (state of mind) to perform that act may be shown. From that intention, the trier of fact may draw the inference that the person carried out his intention and performed the act. Within this conceptual framework, hearsay evidence of statements by the person which tend to show his intention is deemed admissible under the state of mind exception. Inciso's objection to the doctrine concerns its application in situations in which the declarant has stated his intention to do something *with another person,* and the issue is whether he did so. There can be no doubt that the theory of the *Hillmon* doctrine is different when the declarant's statement of intention necessarily requires the action of one or more others if it is to be fulfilled.

When hearsay evidence concerns the declarant's statement of his intention to do something with another person, the *Hillmon* doctrine requires that the trier of fact infer from the state of mind of the declarant the probability of a particular act not only by the declarant but also by the other person. Several objections can be raised against a doctrine that would allow such an inference to be made. One such objection is based on the unreliability of the inference but is not, in our view, compelling.[14] A much more significant and troubling objection is based on the inconsistency of such an inference with the state of mind exception. This problem is more easily perceived when one divides what is really a compound statement into its component parts. In the instant case, the statement by Larry Adell, "I am going to meet Angelo in the parking lot to get a pound of grass," is really two statements. The first is the obvious statement of Larry's intention. The second is an implicit statement of Angelo's intention. Surely, if the meeting is to take place in a location which Angelo does not habitually frequent, one must assume that Angelo intended to meet Larry there if one is to make the inference that Angelo was in the parking lot and the meeting occurred. The important point is that the second, implicit statement has nothing to do with Larry's state of mind. For example, if Larry's friends had testified that Larry had said, "Angelo is going to be in the parking lot of Sambo's North tonight with a pound of grass," no state of mind exception or any other exception to the hearsay rule would be available. Yet, this is in effect at least half of what the testimony did attribute to Larry.

Despite the theoretical awkwardness associated with the application of the *Hillmon* doctrine to facts such as those now before us, the authority in favor of such an application is impressive, beginning with the seminal *Hillmon* decision itself. . . .

Although *Hillmon* was a civil case, the Supreme Court cited with approval a number of criminal cases in support of its decision. One of them, Hunter v. State, 11 Vroom (40 N.J.L.) 495, involved facts remarkably similar to those before us here. . . .

The *Hillmon* doctrine has been applied by the California Supreme Court in People v. Alcalde, 24 Cal. 2d 177, 148 P.2d 627 (1944), a criminal case with facts which closely parallel those in *Hunter*. In *Alcalde* the defendant was tried and convicted of first degree murder for the brutal slaying of a woman whom he had been seeing socially. One of the issues before the California Supreme Court was the asserted error by the trial court in allowing the introduction of certain hearsay testimony concerning statements made by the victim on the day of her murder. As in the instant case, the testimony was highly incriminating, because the victim reportedly said that she was going out with Frank, the defendant, on the evening she was murdered. On appeal, a majority of the California Supreme Court affirmed the defendant's conviction, holding that *Hillmon* was "the leading case on the admissibility of declarations of intent to do an act as proof that the act thereafter was accomplished." Without purporting to "define or summarize all the limitations or restrictions upon the admissibility of" such evidence, the court did mention several prudential considerations not unlike those mentioned by Chief Justice Beasley in *Hunter*. Thus, the declarant

---

14. The inference from a statement of present intention that the act intended was in fact performed is nothing more than an inference. Even where no actions by other parties are necessary in order for the intended act to be performed, a myriad of contingencies could intervene to frustrate the fulfillment of the intention. The fact that the cooperation of another party is necessary if the intended act is to be performed adds another important contingency, but the difference is one of degree rather than kind. The possible unreliability of the inference to be drawn from the present intention is a matter going to the weight of the evidence which might be argued to the trier of fact, but it should not be a ground for completely excluding the admittedly relevant evidence.

declarant

should be dead or otherwise unavailable, and the testimony concerning his statements should be relevant and possess a high degree of trustworthiness. The court also noted that there was other evidence from which the defendant's guilt could be inferred. Applying these standards, the court found no error in the trial court's admission of the disputed hearsay testimony. "Unquestionably the deceased's statement of her intent and the logical inference to be drawn therefrom, namely, that she was with the defendant that night, were relevant to the issue of the guilt of the defendant."

In addition to the decisions in *Hillmon* and *Alcalde*, support for the Government's position can be found in the California Evidence Code and the new Federal Rules of Evidence, although in each instance resort must be made to the comments to the relevant provisions.

Section 1250 of the California Evidence Code carves out an exception to the general hearsay rule for statements of a declarant's "then existing mental or physical state." The *Hillmon* doctrine is codified in Section 1250(2) which allows the use of such hearsay evidence when it "is offered to prove or explain acts or conduct of the declarant." The comment to Section 1250(2) states that, "Thus, a statement of the declarant's intent to do certain acts is admissible to prove that he did those acts." Although neither the language of the statute nor that of the comment specifically addresses the particular issue now before us, the comment does cite the *Alcalde* decision and, therefore, indirectly rejects the limitation urged by Inciso.

Although the new Federal Rules of Evidence were not in force at the time of the trial below, we refer to them for any light that they might shed on the status of the common law at the time of the trial. The codification of the state of mind exception in Rule 803(3) does not provide a direct statement of the *Hillmon* doctrine. . . . Although Rule 803(3) is silent regarding the *Hillmon* doctrine, both the Advisory Committee on the Proposed Rules and the House Committee on the Judiciary specifically addressed the doctrine. After noting that Rule 803(3) would not allow the admission of statements of memory, the Advisory Committee stated broadly that

> The rule of Mutual Life Ins. Co. v. Hillmon [citation omitted] allowing evidence of intention as tending to prove the doing of the act intended, is, of course, left undisturbed.

Significantly, the Notes of the House Committee on the Judiciary regarding Rule 803(3) are far more specific and revealing:

> However, the Committee intends that the Rule be construed to limit the doctrine of Mutual Life Insurance Co. v. Hillmon [citation omitted] so as to render statements of intent by a declarant admissible *only to prove his future conduct, not the future conduct of another person* (emphasis added).

Although the matter is certainly not free from doubt, we read the note of the Advisory Committee as presuming that the *Hillmon* doctrine would be incorporated in full force, including necessarily the application in *Hillmon* itself. The language suggests that the Advisory Committee presumed that such a broad interpretation was the prevailing common law position. The notes of the

House Committee on the Judiciary are significantly different. The language used there suggests a legislative intention to cut back on what that body also perceived to be the prevailing common law view, namely, that the *Hillmon* doctrine could be applied to facts such as those now before us.

Although we recognize the force of the objection to the application of the *Hillmon* doctrine in the instant case,[18] we cannot conclude that the district court erred in allowing the testimony concerning Larry Adell's statements to be introduced. . . .

For the reasons set out above, we affirm the convictions.

NOTES ON STATE OF MIND AS PROOF OF CONDUCT

1. *Hillmon* recognizes, doesn't it, that what someone says he intends to do can be critically important in figuring out what he actually did? On this point, the *Hillmon* doctrine stands on firm footing. Courts regularly admit out-of-court statements indicating the intent of the declarant to do something, hence as proof that she acted accordingly. Particularly vivid are cases that admit

---

18. Criticism of the *Hillmon* doctrine has come from very distinguished quarters, both judicial and academic. However, the position of the judicial critics is definitely the minority position, stated primarily in dicta and dissent.

In his opinion for the Court in Shepard v. United States, 290 U.S. 96 (1933), Justice Cardozo indicated in dicta an apparent hostility to the *Hillmon* doctrine. . . . In his survey of the state of mind exception, Justice Cardozo appeared to suggest that the *Hillmon* doctrine is limited to "suits upon insurance policies," although the cases cited by the Court in *Hillmon* refute that suggestion.

The decision in *Shepard* was relied upon by Justice Traynor of the California Supreme Court in his vigorous dissent from the decision reached by the majority in People v. Alcalde. Justice Traynor argued that the victim's declarations regarding her meeting with Frank could not be used to "induce the belief that the defendant went out with the deceased, took her to the scene of the crime and there murdered her . . . without setting aside the rule against hearsay." Any other legitimate use of the declaration, in his opinion, was so insignificant that it was outweighed by the enormous prejudice to the defendant in allowing the jury to hear it.

Finally, the exhaustive analysis of a different, but related, hearsay issue by the Court of Appeals for the District of Columbia in United States v. Brown, 490 F.2d 758 (D.C. Cir. 1974), provides inferential support for the position urged by Inciso. The issue in that case was the admissibility of hearsay testimony concerning a victim's extrajudicial declarations that he was "[f]rightened that he may be killed" by the defendant. After surveying the relevant cases, the court stated a "synthesis" of the governing principles. One of the cases which was criticized by the court was the decision of the California Supreme Court in People v. Merkouris, 52 Cal. 2d 672, 344 P.2d 1 (1959), a case relied upon by the Government in the instant case. The court in *Merkouris* held that hearsay testimony showing the victim's fear of the defendant could properly be admitted to show the probable identity of the killer. The court in *Brown* expressed the following criticism of that holding, a criticism which might also apply to the application of the *Hillmon* doctrine in the instant case:

> Such an approach violates the fundamental safeguards necessary to the use of such testimony [citation omitted]. Through a circuitous series of inferences, the court reverses the effect of the statement so as to reflect on *defendant's* intent and actions rather than the state of mind of the declarant (victim). This is the very result that it is hoped the limiting instruction will prevent.

490 F.2d at 771 (emphasis in original).

For a frequently cited academic critique of the *Hillmon* doctrine, see Maguire, The *Hillmon* Case—Thirty-Three Years After, 38 Harv. L. Rev. 709 (1925).

statements indicating an intent to kill someone. The state-of-mind exception is not necessary for such statements when made by defendants on trial for homicide (they come in as admissions), but similar statements by others are sometimes important, and the state-of-mind exception paves the way. See, e.g., State v. Yarbrough, 767 N.E.2d 216, 224-225 (Oh. 2002) (in trial of *Y* for murdering *A* on behalf of *D*, admitting *D*'s statement that "he'd have [A] killed or kill her himself"), cert. denied, 123 S.Ct. 533 (2002). Also vivid are cases in which statements by a victim (later killed) describing an intent to break off a relationship are admitted against defendants in homicide cases to show that the victim later acted on such intent, provoking the crime or providing a motive for it. See, e.g., State v. Robinson, 903 P.3d 1289 (Hi. 1995) (admitting statements by murder victim, once to her friend, and once to both the friend and the defendant, that she wanted to break off her relationship with defendant).

2. In *Hillmon,* the Court says Walters' intent was "a distinct and material fact" even though it was *not* an ultimate issue (the question was whose body was at Crooked Creek), and the Court describes the contemporaneous expression (letters to sister and fiancée) as "direct evidence" of intent. The Court also says the letters tended to show Walters "had the intention of going, and of going with Hillmon, which made it more probable both that he did go and that he went with Hillmon." Does that mean the Court thinks the letters from Walters can prove what Hillmon did? Hadn't all parties agreed that Hillmon was at Crooked Creek? (Plaintiff claimed the body was Hillmon's; the carriers claimed Hillmon killed Walters there.) If a brother writes to his sister saying "I'm taking Amtrak to Chicago tomorrow," could his letter be admitted as proof that he went to Chicago the next day and took the train, but not as proof that Amtrak *actually ran* a train to Chicago the next day? Would such a limit make sense?

3. *Pheaster* forces the court to confront the question that could be slid by in *Hillmon,* doesn't it? The court in *Pheaster* approves the use of Larry Adell's words to prove what Angelo did, doesn't it? The trial in *Pheaster* was held before the Rules were adopted, and the reviewing court invokes common law tradition "for any light" it might shed on the Rules. Does *Pheaster* mean to *contrast* what would happen before the Rules took effect with what must happen now, or to *compare* the two in the course of concluding that nothing has changed?

4. Isn't it true that *before* any factfinder can take letters that Walters wrote on Monday as proof of what Hillmon did on Wednesday, and *before* it can take statements by Adell at 8:00 P.M. as proof of what Angelo did at 9:30 P.M., the factfinder must draw inferences about what Walters and Adell must have done before they wrote or spoke? What inferences? When FRE 803(3) says the state-of-mind exception does not authorize statements of "memory or belief to prove the fact remembered or believed," is it addressing these inferences? If you could write on a clean slate, would you admit for all purposes the letters by Walters and the statement by Adell? Would you, in deciding this point, be affected by the fact that both these men have vanished?

5. In *Pheaster,* there seems to have been no other evidence that Angelo went to the parking lot at Sambo's Restaurant that night. Would you be more comfortable admitting Adell's statement to show what Angelo did if there were corroborative evidence placing them together in the parking lot, or testimony that Angelo said he planned to meet Adell that evening? Several post-*Pheaster*

cases say state-of-mind statements can be used to prove a later meeting between the speaker and another if there is additional evidence of such a meeting. Compare United States v. Nersesian, 824 F.2d 1294, 1325 (2d Cir. 1987) (to prove M was in a drug conspiracy, admitting statement by A that he planned "to see other people with my kind of brochure," coupled with evidence that A and M then met in a restaurant, where "brochure" referred to narcotics; statements of "intention or future plans" are admissible against another person "when they are linked with independent evidence that corroborates the declaration") with United States v. Delvecchio, 816 F.2d 859, 862-863 (2d Cir. 1987) (error to admit statement by third person describing his intent to meet defendant and another on May 11th, absent independent evidence that defendant went to meeting). See also People v. James, 717 N.E.2d 1052, 1060 (N.Y. 1999) (statement of intent to act with others may be admitted if declarant is unavailable, statement "unambiguously contemplates some *future* action by the declarant," any past arrangement indicated by the statement was apparently made in the recent past, and there is "independent evidence of reliability" and proof that "the intended future acts were at least likely to have actually taken place"). For a modern case that *refuses* to admit statements by the victim indicating an intent to meet the defendant, see Brooks v. State, 787 S.2d 765, 770 (Fla. 2001) (statement admitted under state-of-mind exception can only be used to prove "the future act of the declarant, not the future act of another person") (reversing murder conviction and death sentence).

6. Cases like *Hunter* (described in *Hillmon*) and *Alcalde* (described in *Pheaster*) approve use of statements by victims in exactly the situation of *Pheaster*, where the purpose is really to prove that *defendant met* the victim. Despite the restrictive language in FRE 803(3), the doubt raised by the House Committee Report cited in *Pheaster*, and the corroborative evidence compromise suggested by the cases cited in Note 5, supra, some modern state cases applying state counterparts that are identical to FRE 803(3) continue to endorse the *Pheaster* result. See Lisle v. State, 941 P.2d 459, 467-468 (Nev. 1997) (in trial of *J* and *K* for murdering *L*, admitting *L*'s statement, made several hours before he was killed, that he was going out the door with "Vatos" to get drugs and would be back in fifteen minutes) ("Vatos" is what *L* called *K* and *J*), cert. denied, 525 U.S. 830 (1998); State v. Terrovona, 716 P.2d 295, 399-300 (Wash. 1986) (in trial of *T* for murder of *P*, admitting *P*'s statement telling girlfriend that *T* phoned and wanted *P* to meet him because he had run out of gas and needed), cert. denied, 499 U.S. 979 (1991).

7. In *Shepard*, Justice Cardozo seemed to be trying to build a dike to contain the *Hillmon* doctrine:

> There are times when a state of mind, if relevant, may be proved by contemporaneous declarations of feeling or intent. . . . [I]n suits upon insurance policies, declarations by an insured that he intends to go upon a journey with another, may be evidence of a state of mind lending probability to the conclusion that the purpose was fulfilled. Mutual Life Ins. Co. v. Hillmon. The ruling in that case marks the high water line beyond which courts have been unwilling to go. It has developed a substantial body of criticism and commentary. Declarations of intention, casting light upon the future, have been sharply distinguished from declarations of memory, pointing backwards to the past. There would be an end, or nearly that, to the rule against hearsay if the distinction were ignored.

[handwritten margin note: Cardozo on Hillmon]

Shepard v. United States, 290 U.S. 96, 104-106 (1933). Why would there be "an end" to the hearsay doctrine ("or nearly that") if statements of memory could be admitted to prove the fact believed? After *Pheaster,* is the level of the lake of admissible hearsay so high that it spills over the dike?

8. Salvatore Annunziato was a business agent for a labor union on a construction project. He was charged with taking an illegal payment from a contracting company. At trial the prosecutor introduced testimony by (a) Richard Terker that his father Harry (company president) told him over lunch that Annunziato called and requested "some money on the [Bridgeport] project," (b) the company comptroller that he drew $300 which he gave to Harry Terker in an envelope, and (c) project supervisor Mayhew that Terker gave him an envelope and told him "to deliver it to the business agent for the operating engineers" at the project. Eyewitnesses saw Annunziato meet Mayhew at the site and pick up an envelope. Harry Terker died before trial. Annunziato argued on appeal that what Harry told his son Richard should have been excluded as hearsay.

Writing for the Second Circuit, the late Judge Friendly disagreed. If the envelope "had popped out of Harry Terker's wallet as he was settling the luncheon check," he wrote, and if Harry had said it contained "money I'm sending up to Annunziato," this statement would be admissible because plans tend to show acts, and words are admissible to show plans. The question (said Judge Friendly) is whether the result should be different because Terker explained his plan by saying what prompted it. The answer (said Judge Friendly) was no:

> We do not think such nicety is demanded either by good sense or by authority . . . . *Shepard* does not hold that a declaration of design is rendered inadmissible because it embodies a statement why the design was conceived. In that case there was no relevant declaration of design. . . . Here the "most obvious implications" of Harry Terker's statement looked forward—he was going to send the money to Bridgeport. To say that this portion of his statement is sufficiently trustworthy for the jury to consider without confrontation, but that his reference to the telephone call from Annunziato which produced the decision to send money is not, would truly be swallowing the camel and straining at the gnat. The "vigorous leap" with respect to the hearsay exception . . . was taken when this was extended from cases where "it is material to prove the state of a person's mind, or what was passing in it, and what were his intentions," as to which the declaration may well be the most reliable evidence attainable, to cases where the state of mind is relevant only to prove other action, where it surely is not. True, inclusion of a past event motivating the plan adds the hazards of defective perception and memory to that of prevarication; but this does not demand exclusion or even excision, at least when, as here, the event is recent, is within the personal knowledge of the declarant and is so integrally included in the declaration of design as to make it unlikely in the last degree that the latter would be true and the former false. True also, the statement of the past event would not be admitted if it stood alone, as the *Shepard* case holds; but this would not be the only hearsay exception where the pure metal may carry some alloy along with it.

United States v. Annunziato, 293 F.2d 373, 377-378 (2d Cir.), cert. denied, 368 U.S. 919 (1961). Did *Annunziato* discard the limit that *Shepard* placed on *Hillmon?*

Was *Annunziato* rightly decided? Could it be decided the same way under FRE 803(3)?

9. On *Hillmon*, see Maguire, The *Hillmon* Case—Thirty-Three Years After, 38 Harv. L. Rev. 709 (1925); MacCracken, The Case of the Anonymous Corpse, 19 Am. Heritage 51 (1968). And see the modern analysis of the problems presented by these cases generally in McFarland, Dead Men Tell Tales: Thirty Times Three Years of the Judicial Process After *Hillmon*, 30 Vill. L. Rev. 1 (1985). On the general subject of applying FRE 803(3), see Weissenberger, Hearsay Puzzles: An Essay on Federal Evidence Rule 803(3), 64 Temp. L. Rev. 145 (1991).

PROBLEM 4-K. *Fright Points the Finger*

Donald is tried for the alleged murder of Virginia, who is found shot in the living room of the home they lived in. A kitchen knife is found on the floor close to her body, and the gun that fired the fatal shot is recovered. There is testimony from neighbors that the relationship between Donald and Virginia has been stormy, punctuated with loud fights and occasional violence. Other evidence points toward Donald's guilt, although all of it is circumstantial. The prosecutor wants to offer the following proofs to bolster his case:

1. Several weeks before her death Virginia told her neighbor, "I'm afraid Donald is going to kill me"; *does not speak to his intent*
2. Days before her death Virginia told her neighbor, "I'm going to take the train to Denver to stay with Mother for a while"; *her future conduct*
3. A few months before her death Virginia left home temporarily and took refuge in a shelter for battered women. *relevant not hearsay*

Should these items be excluded as hearsay? Does the state-of-mind exception apply? *yes*   *yes, #2*

NOTES ON STATEMENTS AND BEHAVIOR BY MURDER VICTIMS INDICATING FEAR

1. Recall in Problem 4-J ("He Says He'll Kill Me") that fear on the part of the victim was an element in the state's extortion case. But in the trial of Donald, Virginia's fear need not be proved to get a conviction—her fear is *not* an element in the state's case. Does that matter? *not according to Hillmon*
2. If Donald claimed self-defense, fear in Virginia might affect the likelihood that she attacked him on the occasion of her death. Does that increase the *relevance* of the statement to the neighbor (item 1) about her fear that Donald would kill her? How about *admissibility*?
3. If Virginia not only told her neighbor she was taking the train to Denver, but actually bought a train ticket, would that make it easier to admit the statement (item 2) going to Denver? Her *behavior* in buying a ticket isn't hearsay, is it? And the statement merely sheds light on her forward-looking

purpose in going to Denver, doesn't it? The inference backwards in time (Donald must have done something to scare her) is supported by buying the ticket *and* what she told her neighbor, isn't it?

4.   Virginia's flight to the shelter isn't hearsay, is it? It's just *conduct*, like driving forward into an intersection after the light changes to green. Recall Problem 2-D (The Battered Wife).

5.   In the trial of O.J. Simpson for the alleged murders of Nicole Brown and Ronald Goldman, Judge Ito excluded evidence that Ms. Brown told others she thought O.J. was going to kill her. In his ruling, Judge Ito made the following comment:

> To the man or woman on the street, the relevance and probative value of such evidence is both obvious and compelling, especially those statements made just days before the homicide. It seems only just and right that a crime victim's own words be heard, especially in the court where the facts and circumstances of her demise are to be presented. However, the laws and appellate court decisions that must be applied by the trial court hold otherwise. In factual situations distressingly similar to the assumed facts of this case, the California Supreme Court has given clear guidance to the trial court.

See Ruling on motion in limine, January 18, 1995, 1995 WL 21768, citing People v. Ireland, 450 P.2d 580 (Cal. 1969) (in trial of husband for murdering wife, reversible error to admit her statement to friend that she knew he was going to kill her and wished he would get it over with). One statement excluded in the Simpson case was apparently a call by one "Nicole" to a battered women's shelter, inquiring about the possibility of refuge, but the call could not be traced to Nicole Brown. Do words of that sort have a performative aspect that justifies treating them as nonhearsay? What if Nicole Brown had called police and sought advice or asked them for protection (as apparently she did on other occasions)?

d.   Facts About Declarant's Will

In a convoluted way, FRE 803(3) creates what might be treated as a separate exception for statements about declarant's will. (The language generally bars use of the exception to prove a "fact remembered or believed," but this restriction does not apply to statements relating to "execution, revocation, identification, or terms of declarant's will," so the exception *can* be used to prove this particular sort of "fact remembered or believed.")

Placing this subject within the ambit of the state-of-mind exception may be defended on ground that the mental state of the testator is of paramount importance in wills cases. Admitting what he has said on the subject also makes sense because (1) he is likely to be well informed on the subject, (2) he is likely to be dead when the matter is litigated, suggesting a strong need for evidence of what he has said, and (3) his own views on the subject may be as trustworthy as live testimony by interested parties disputing the disposition of the estate.

3. *Statements to Physicians*

When a person seeks treatment from a physician, life and health may hang in the balance. There is good reason to believe that he will be careful and accurate in describing his symptoms to his doctor and telling her what he thinks caused them. Hence Rule 803(4) recognizes an exception for such statements. Note that the exception embraces descriptions of both present and past symptoms, provided that they be pertinent to diagnosis or treatment, and in this temporal sense the exception is broader than the state-of-mind exception.

Consider some questions about the outer limits of the exception. Should it reach statements to physicians consulted simply to obtain a diagnosis and perhaps testimony at trial? Statements by persons other than the patient? Statements to persons such as nurses or intake clerks in hospitals or clinics? Statements to psychiatrists? On its face, Rule 803(4) is broad enough to reach all these, and on the first point the drafters clearly intended to open up the exception by rejecting a more cautious common law tradition.

803(4)

BLAKE v. STATE
Supreme Court of Wyoming
933 P.2d 474 (Wyo. 1997)

LEHMAN, JUSTICE.

David Alfred Blake (Blake) was convicted of two counts of second degree sexual assault of his stepdaughter. . . .

Responding to a report of alleged sexual abuse of a sixteen-year-old girl, an investigator from the Department of Family Services (DFS), together with an officer from the sheriff's office, interviewed the victim at a local high school. Following the interview, the victim was transported to the hospital emergency room for medical examination. During the course of the examination, and in response to questions by Dr. Mary Bowers, the victim stated that she had been forcibly subjected to sexual intercourse by her stepfather, Blake, numerous times over the previous several years. . . .

At trial, neither the State nor Blake called the victim to the witness stand. The State relied upon Blake's typed confession, Dr. Bowers' testimony, testimony of the nurse who assisted Dr. Bowers in the examination of the victim, testimony by the DFS investigator, testimony by the officer who interviewed the victim, and testimony by the officer who interviewed and obtained a confession from Blake. Over a continuing objection by defense counsel, the district court allowed Dr. Bowers to testify concerning what the victim stated to her during the sexual assault examination, including the victim's statements identifying Blake as the sexual assault perpetrator, pursuant to WRE 803(4) [which is identical to FRE 803(4)—Eds.]. The jury returned a verdict of guilty, convicting Blake of two counts of second degree sexual assault. Blake timely appeals. . . .

We acknowledge the general rule that statements attributing fault or identity usually are not admissible under rules identical to WRE 803(4). Goldade v. State, 674 P.2d 721, 725 (Wyo. 1983). However, we have held that in situations involving physical or sexual abuse of children, statements made by a child victim to a medical professional may be admitted.[2] Statements of identification in child abuse cases are admitted because of the special character of diagnosis and treatment in sexual abuse cases.

This court first had occasion to address this issue in *Goldade.* In that case, we upheld the admission of statements by a child victim to the treating physician under WRE 803(4). In so holding, we noted that child abuse is a unique and special problem encompassing more than physical injury. The State has expressed special concern for that problem in Wyoming's child protection statutes, and physicians and other medical personnel play a special role in detecting and dealing with the problem of child abuse.

In *Stephens* [v. State, 774 P.2d 60 (Wyo. 1989)], we emphasized that a proper foundation is essential to justify admission of identity statements under WRE 803(4). We cited with approval the two-part test set forth in United States v. Renville, 779 F.2d 430 (8th Cir. 1985), which encompasses the foundation requirement. The *Renville* test requires that, first, the declarant's motive in making the statement is consistent with the purposes of promoting treatment or diagnosis and, second, that the content of the statement is reasonably relied on by a physician in treatment or diagnosis. Because the case was remanded for a new trial, we did not decide whether the statements in *Stephens* were admissible.

More recently, this court applied the *Renville* test in *Betzle* [v. State, 847 P.2d 1010 (Wyo. 1993)] and *Owen* [v. State, 902 P.2d 60 (Wyo. 1995)]. In both those cases, we upheld the admission of hearsay testimony of an expert witness as to the identity of the perpetrator under the WRE 803(4) exception, finding the two-part test was met.

Our inquiry now turns to whether in this case the requirements of the *Renville* two-part test were fulfilled. At trial, Dr. Bowers testified as follows:

Q. What was the purpose of the examination?
A. The purpose of the examination was to provide health care because of an alleged sexual assault.
Q. Did you perform any specific examination on her?
A. Yeah. I performed a comprehensive physical examination on her, including a pelvic examination. . . .
Q. Okay. Could you please just describe generally what you normally would do, what you normally do, the procedure you normally follow in a rape kit examination.
A. The kit itself has specific instructions for the health care provider; and I usually begin by explaining what the purpose of the examination is to the patient and by taking a history from that patient about what has happened to them so that I can properly use the kit, collect specimens, so that I can also provide appropriate medical care. . . .
Q. Could you describe [victim's] condition at the time?
A. [Victim] was a very—very subdued, very quiet young lady. She was—we use the term "in no acute distress." She wasn't medically unstable; but she was quite withdrawn, seemed somewhat exhausted. . . .

2. [Court reports that "an overwhelming majority of jurisdictions, including at least 32 states and 4 federal circuits," admit statements by victims identifying the perpetrator in child physical or sexual assault cases. Many invoke the medical statements exception, but several jurisdictions admit such statements only in cases "where the perpetrator is a member of the immediate household or a relative, close family friend, or babysitter."]

Q. All right. Now, during the course of your examination did you have an opportunity to ask [victim] any questions?

A. Before proceeding with the exam, I asked her a number of questions to help direct my exam and determine what might be appropriate.

Q. Okay. Generally speaking, what types of questions would you have asked?

A. I ask general questions about what kinds of assault she may have been subjected to, what kind of sexual contact may have occurred, what she remembers of what had occurred, whether or not—whether or not she was aware of body fluids present in her, whether or not she had had any symptoms of vaginal discharge, itching, abdominal pain that might represent sexually-transmitted disease, what parts of her body had been violated.

Q. What is the purpose in asking those questions?

A. To determine where to collect certain kinds of specimens, what kinds of bacteriology studies to do, what kinds of treatment might be necessary to care for her and keep her healthy, restore her to health if she's ill. . . .

Q. Do you recall what the first question was that you asked her [victim]?

A. I asked her the nature of the assault, what had transpired that brought her to the emergency room.

Q. Okay. And why did you need to know that?

A. It was important for me to understand as a physician what her emotional state was; and I explained to her that I wanted to help her, that—because this is invariably an unpleasant experience, and I wanted to find out exactly why she was there.

Q. Was it important for your purposes of diagnosis or treatment?

A. It certainly is important. Who the alleged assailant might be in a sexual assault determines frequently the extent to which testing and treatment is given.

Q. In asking that question, what did she say?

A. She told me that she had been subjected to sexual intercourse forcibly by her stepfather numerous times over the previous several years.

Q. What did you ask her next?

A. I asked her when the most recent episode had been and what had happened, under what circumstances and if there was physical trauma. . . .

Q. How did she respond?

A. She responded that approximately a week prior to that she had been forced to the floor of the bathroom in their home and had had forcible genital sexual intercourse with her stepfather.

We conclude that the State laid the proper foundation and that the elements of the *Renville* two-part test were satisfied. The victim was examined by Dr. Bowers as a result of an investigation into allegations that she had been sexually abused. Dr. Bowers testified that in a rape kit examination, she takes a history from the patient about what has happened so as to properly collect specimens and provide appropriate medical care. The doctor also described the importance of understanding a victim's emotional state in a sexual assault case. The victim's statements were consistent with the purposes for which Dr. Bowers became involved with the victim, that is, to perform tests and treat the victim as necessary. Dr. Bowers' testimony indicates that she relied on the victim's account of the circumstances surrounding the sexual assault, including the abuser's identity, to determine how to properly treat the victim.

Blake asserts that because the victim was seventeen at the time of trial, her statements lack the reliability of statements made by a younger victim. Blake attempts to distinguish *Goldade, Betzle* and *Owen* on the ground that the victims in those cases were much younger than the victim here. We find no merit in this argument. The age of a child and her personal characteristics go toward the weight of the hearsay statements rather than their admissibility. United States v. George, 960 F.2d 97, 100 (9th Cir. 1992). Blake had the opportunity to attack the credibility of the victim but chose not to do so. The district court did not abuse its discretion by admitting the victim's hearsay statements into evidence pursuant to WRE 803(4). . . .

[The court rejects challenge to Dr. Bowers' testimony under the Confrontation Clause, finding the medical statements exception to be firmly rooted. It also finds that the state adequately proved that defendant was in a "position of authority" in the home of the victim. The court affirms the conviction.]

NOTES ON STATEMENTS TO PHYSICIANS

1. Dr. Bowers testified that she asked questions "to help direct my exam" and "understand as a physician what her [16-year-old patient's] emotional state was." Thus Bowers asked "what kind of sexual contact" might have occurred, and was interested in "who the alleged assailant might be." Apparently her young patient got the message, telling Bowers "she had been subjected to sexual intercourse forcibly by her stepfather numerous times," most recently about a week earlier, when she was "forced to the floor of the bathroom in her house." Note that *Blake* follows the breakthrough decision in United States v. Renville, 779 F.2d 430, 436 (8th Cir. 1985), which held that the exception requires courts to ask whether the patient's motive was "consistent with the purposes of promoting treatment" and whether the content of the statement is "such as is reasonably relied on by a physician in treatment or diagnosis." Are you satisfied that the questions put by Dr. Bowers, and the replies from her youthful patient, satisfy these standards? Wyoming and many other jurisdictions follow an expansive approach. Consider the following argument favoring this approach, advanced by Justice Castille in a Pennsylvania case:

> Child abuse . . . is one of the most devastating social ailments afflicting our society and the injuries suffered by an abused child differ dramatically from the types of injuries normally encompassed by the medical treatment exception to the hearsay rule. While most injuries are purely somatic, child abuse cases also often involve deep emotional and psychological injuries. In order to effectively treat child abuse victims, physicians must be attentive not only to the child's emotional and psychological injuries which result from this crime, but they must also take care to ensure the safety of the child when he or she is released from the physician's care, often back to the abusive situation that gave rise to the original injury. Effective treatment can only be provided for the child's physical and psychic injuries if the physician knows the identity of the abuser, especially when the abuser resides with the victim.

Justice Castille also addressed the question whether a youthful patient (five years old, in that case) is motivated to seek treatment:

While the child's motive here may not be readily apparent, a young child is generally aware of the emotional and physical pain that she is suffering and is able to comprehend that she is receiving medical treatment to alleviate that suffering. See [State v.] Nelson, 406 N.W.2d 385, 391 (Wis. 1987) (four year old child understood purpose of sessions with psychologist and thus passed motive prong of medical treatment hearsay exception); United States v. Nick, 604 F.2d 1199, 1201-02 (9th Cir. 1979) (statement by three year old to physician as to cause of injury admissible under FRE 803(4)). Moreover, there is nothing in the record to suggest an ulterior motive for the child to make the statement to the nurse other than to receive medical treatment.

Commonwealth v. Smith, 681 A.2d 1288, 1293 (Pa. 1996) (dissenting opinion). See also White v. Illinois, 502 U.S. 346 (1992) (in statement to doctor, small child identified intruder by name as assailant; Court assumes exception applies and holds that Confrontation Clause does not require showing that she was unavailable to testify).

2. There are two serious problems in the broad view. One is that the ACN says "statements as to fault" do not "ordinarily qualify." Thus a statement saying I "was struck by an automobile" would fit, but not a statement that the car "was driven through a red light." See also Roberts v. Hollocher, 664 F.2d 200, 204-205 (8th Cir. 1981) (in suit against police officers alleging that they beat plaintiff, excluding physician's diagnosis in hospital record indicating that injuries were "consistent with excessive force," noting that if conclusion rested on what plaintiff said, his statement would not fit FRE 803(4) because it concerned fault). You read the *Iron Shell* decision in connection with the excited utterance exception earlier in this chapter. In another part of the same opinion, the court applied the medical statements exception to admit statements by Lucy to a physician describing the assault. The court dismissed objections based on the fact that the doctor said her statements had "no effect" on the examination, noting that doctors regularly rely on such statements in treatment and diagnosis. In *Iron Shell*, however, the identity of the assailant was not in issue, and the court stressed that Lucy's statements "concern what happened rather than who assaulted her," referring to the limit against using the exception to prove fault. United States v. Iron Shell, 633 F.2d 77, 84 (8th Cir. 1980).

3. The other problem in the broad view is that "diagnosis" and "treatment" are not concepts that readily embrace steps like removing a child from an abusive home, and physicians (primary audience for statements offered under the exception) are not experts in remedies of this sort. In Commonwealth v. Smith, 681 A.2d 1288 (Pa. 1996) (opinion that generated the dissent by Justice Castille quoted above), the majority concluded that a statement by five-year-old Priscilla identifying her father as one who put her in a bathtub containing scalding hot water did not satisfy the medical statements exception (the father claimed he was asleep on the couch when Priscilla got into the tub, and that he was running cold water when the mother found the two in the bathroom together). Here is the majority's view on the point:

> We fail to see how the identity of the perpetrator of the physical abuse was pertinent to the treatment of Priscilla's scalding burns. What difference would it have made to the treatment of the burns whether a total stranger inflicted the burns or a close family relative? The Commonwealth simply fails to demonstrate

that the identity of the abuser is pertinent to medical treatment. See, e.g., United States v. Iron Shell, 633 F.2d 77, 81-85 (8th Cir. 1980), cert. denied, 450 U.S. 1001 (1981) (statements identifying assailant "would seldom if ever" be related to diagnosis or treatment); State v. Veluzat, 578 A.2d 93 (R.I. 1990) (statement to physician, identifying father as sexual abuser does not help physician to diagnose or treat); Cassidy v. State, 536 A.2d 666 (Md. Spec. App. 1988), cert. denied, 541 A.2d 965 (1988) ("[t]he identity of the person who inflicted the bruises, albeit perhaps of transcendent social importance, is not ordinarily of strictly medical importance"). Binder, Hearsay Handbook, §6.05 at p.184 ("[t]he general rule is that the identity of a person who inflicts harm on a patient is not reasonably pertinent to diagnosis or treatment of the patient's injuries.") Contra United States v. Renville, 779 F.2d 430 (8th Cir. 1985) and Goldade v. State, 674 P.2d 721 (Wyo. 1983), cert. denied, 467 U.S. 1253 (1984).

The Commonwealth argues that the statement as to identity of the perpetrator of abuse is of significance for psychological and emotional treatment of the victim as well as for the protection of the child from future abuse. . . . [W]e acknowledge that this goal is of utmost importance; however, this acknowledgement does not make the statements at issue admissible under the medical treatment exception. Protection from future abuse, as such, does not constitute medical treatment or diagnosis.

The Commonwealth's argument that the statement as to identity of a perpetrator is relevant to psychological and emotional treatment of the child is, at first blush, inviting. However, "[a]s a general rule all statements made in this context [of psychological treatment], regardless of their content, are relevant to diagnosis or treatment since experts in the field view everything relating to the patient as relevant to the patient's personality." Weinstein & Berger, Evidence, ¶803(4)[01]. Thus, were we to accept the Commonwealth's argument, everything said by the patient in the context of being questioned for the purposes of psychological treatment and diagnosis would be admissible under the medical treatment exception. This would destroy the "pertinent to medical treatment" requirement. The Commonwealth's position renders the "pertinent to medical treatment" requirement meaningless as a standard for judicial analysis. "The pertinency standard is intended to impose a true limit." Christopher B. Mueller and Laird C. Kirkpatrick, 4 Federal Evidence, §442 at p.461 (2d ed. 1994).

Commonwealth v. Smith, 681 A.2d 1288, 1292-1293 (Pa. 1996). Accord, State v. Huntington, 575 N.W.2d 268 (Wis. 1998). And see Mosteller, Child Sexual Abuse and Statements for the Purpose of Medical Diagnosis or Treatment, 67 N.C. L. Rev. 257 (1989) (rationale of exception cannot support its use in this context); Tuerkheimer, Convictions Through Hearsay in Child Sexual Abuse Cases: A Logic Progression Back to Square One, 72 Marq. L. Rev. 47 (1988) (arguing that statements to physicians or psychologists by child victims should not suffice to convict, that courts should require nonhearsay proof of defendant's guilt by a preponderance of the evidence, and that victim hearsay should be treated as corroborative proof).

4.   Note that the statements in *Blake* were gathered in a hospital after the Department of Family Services became involved. Suppose the investigator was present. Does the involvement of law enforcement personnel in collecting statements by crime victims raise special concerns? In Crawford v. Washington, 124 S.Ct. 1354 (2004), the Supreme Court said that the Confrontation Clause applies to "testimonial" statements, and that this category includes statements

describing crimes to police, at least where the defense does not have a chance to cross-examine. (Note that in *Blake* neither side called the victim. Why do you suppose the defendant did not call her?) The effect of confrontation jurisprudence on hearsay is taken up in Chapter 4G, infra. Obviously there are more concerns over making a very young child testify to abuse than there are when victims are older. In such cases, should we be more willing to accept hearsay by children who are 5 years old, or 16, than we are when the victim is 25? If so, could the exception embrace statements by five-year-old Priscilla to *a grandparent?* See State v. Smith, 337 S.E.2d 833 (N.C. 1985) (admitting statement by four- and five-year-old victims of sexual assault to their grandmother because "young children cannot independently seek out medical attention, but must rely on their caretakers to do so," and here the statements "immediately resulted in their receiving medical treatment and diagnosis"). Consider whether this problem could be better handled by a special hearsay exception or some other device for obtaining the story of child victims.

5.   Is it important in *Blake* that Dr. Bowers acted as a *treating* physician? Note that she said her purpose was "to provide health care," and she told her young patient that she "wanted to help her." The prosecuting attorney obviously had in mind the terms of the exception when he asked whether her interview with the child was important for "purposes of diagnosis or treatment." At common law, the exception reached only statements for purposes of *treatment*, not statements for purposes of *diagnosis*. Consider the arguments on either side of this point, advanced in another modern case: Josephine Tramutola emerged from a lung operation with a fragment of surgical needle in her chest. Suffering pain, she sued her physician, and the issue was whether her pain was caused by the metal fragment or the spreading of her ribs during surgery. At the request of her lawyer, she consulted Dr. Kaplan, a neuropsychiatrist who examined her in preparation for trial and testified that the needle fragment was the cause. Over defense objection, he also described the history that Tramutola had given him, but the reviewing court thought this testimony should have been excluded:

> [D]eclarations made to an examining physician to qualify him as an expert witness do not have the trustworthiness of declarations made to a treating physician because the self-interest of the declarant may become a motive for distortion, exaggeration and falsehood.

On this point a dissenting judge disagreed:

> Dr. Kaplan could not have formed an opinion as to plaintiff's mental state and psychiatric condition without being informed in at least some detail as to her prior history and complaints. His situation was not that of a treating doctor who can base an opinion on, at least, objective physical symptoms. Indeed, Dr. Kaplan said that his evaluation necessarily had to be based on his discussion with Mrs. Tramutola, and that discussion had to include her account of her past medical history.

Tramutola v. Bortone, 288 A.2d 863, 872 (N.J. Super. 1972).

6.   Who is right here? If an expert like Dr. Bowers or Dr. Kaplan is to testify, does it follow that what she learns from the person examined should

come out as part of her testimony? See Wise v. Monteros, 379 P.2d 116, 117-118 (Ariz. 1963) (yes, admissible on direct examination of physician, to "explain the basis" of her opinion but not "to prove the truth of the statements"); Continental Casualty Co. v. Jackson, 400 F.2d 285, 293 (9th Cir. 1968) (semble). Are cases like *Wise* futile in insisting that the statements may be admitted but only as proof of the basis? As amended in 2000, FRE 703 bars the proponent from mentioning to the jury of any inadmissible "facts or data" underlying an expert opinion "unless their probative value substantially outweighs their prejudicial effect." Does this language solve the problem? Is it consistent with the theory under which FRE 803(4) was extended to statements made for purposes of *diagnosis?*

7. Recall Problem 4-I ("I Felt This Sudden Pain"). Change the facts slightly. Assume that Eldon Sanders went straight to the office of Dr. Hillier and told *him* what had happened ("I felt this sudden pain, just a few minutes ago when I had to lift one of those 30-gallon cans out on the Chase"). Could Eleanor Sanders call Dr. Hillier to testify to this statement under FRE 803(4), as proof that Sanders felt the onset of pain at work—potentially a crucial point in her claim for worker's compensation? Why or why not? Clearly the exception reaches statements describing what the patient experienced, but it is less clear that it reaches statements saying that his pain began at work. See, e.g., Hansen v. Heath, 852 P.2d 977 (Utah 1993) (in suit arising out of accident, where the estate of the defendant was substituted after he died, admitting his statement to a physician indicating that "he suddenly lost consciousness without warning" prior to the accident) (diagnosed as coronary heart failure).

8. A Good Samaritan brings an unconscious accident victim to the hospital (or a parent brings a minor child). Does the exception reach statements by such third persons? See State v. Thompson, 707 P.2d 956, 962 (Ariz. App. 1985) (in trial of mother's boyfriend for manslaughter and reckless endangerment of child, after resuscitation efforts on 18-month-old victim were abandoned, admitting statement to emergency room doctor by child's father "that the children had bruises on them at previous times," which was "consistent with trauma rather than disease"); Leora v. Minneapolis Ry., 146 N.W. 520, 523-524 (Wis. 1914) (physician testifies to history of accident that he "got from some one else" when unconscious patient was brought in); Miller v. Watts, 436 S.W.2d 515, 519-521 (Ky. 1969) (admitting statement to physician by mother of infant describing accident).

9. What about statements by one physician to another concerning the patient? Compare O'Gee v. Dobbs Houses, Inc., 570 F.2d 1084, 1088-1089 (2d Cir. 1978) (approving testimony by consulting physician reciting what patient told him that other doctors had told her, where physician made it clear that he was also relying on actual reports by the other doctors) with Wilbanks v. Hartselle Hospital, 334 So. 2d 870, 872 (Ala. 1976) (testimony by one doctor that attending physician said that plaintiff was bitten by a spider while in the hospital was inadmissible, under circumstances indicating that plaintiff may have been source of the information and had earlier indicated uncertainty as to time and place of bite).

10. How about statements to psychiatrists and psychologists? See Wilson v. Zapata Off-Shore Co., 939 F.2d 260, 271-272 (5th Cir. 1991) (extending exception to statement by plaintiff's sister to social worker in hospital, made

several days after plaintiff was admitted for anxiety-related disorders, saying she is "a habitual liar and has been all her life"). Compare Capano v. State, 781 A.2d 556, 623-626 (Del. 2001) (in kidnap-murder case, admitting statements by victim to psychiatrist describing defendant's behavior toward her), cert. denied, 536 U.S. 958 (2002), with State v. Huntington, 575 N.W.2d 268 (Wis. 1998) (error to admit statements by 11-year-old child to counselor and social worker describing abuse; exception covers statements relating to treatment, not larger social remedies).

4.   *Past Recollection Recorded*

Sometimes a witness who fails to remember critical points has written down what he knew. Under certain conditions, what he wrote may be admitted as a substitute for his testimony. Typically the proponent tries to refresh recollection by reminding the witness of the statement, quoting relevant portions or showing him the document.

It is when these avenues lead nowhere that the proponent must try to get the statement itself into evidence. To do so, he must demonstrate that (1) the witness lacks present recollection of the matter, (2) the statement accurately reflects knowledge he once had, (3) he "made" or "adopted" the statement, and (4) he did so while the matter was "fresh" in his mind.

803(5)

| **OHIO v. SCOTT**
| **Ohio Supreme Court**
| **285 N.E.2d 344 (Ohio St. 1972)**

[Randy Scott was convicted of shooting at another with intent to kill, wound, or maim, and shooting at two police officers. Victim Willard Lee was blinded by a shotgun blast in the face when he opened his front door to investigate noises outside. A guest in his house then fled by car, only to be chased by defendant in a red Ford. The guest hailed police, who pursued the Ford, and defendant allegedly fired at them.]

LEACH, J.

The principal issue involved in this case is whether the rule of evidence, referred to as "past recollection recorded," is recognized in Ohio, whether it may be employed in a criminal trial, and whether, if so employed, such rule is violative of a defendant's Sixth Amendment right of confrontation, including the opportunity of cross-examination. Although such rule of evidence has been specifically approved by the highest courts of most of our sister states, it appears that this issue has not heretofore been directly passed upon by this court.

The problem of "past recollection recorded" arises in this case from the testimony of Carol Tackett, a witness for the state. Miss Tackett had been a friend of the defendant and had held a conversation with him at the theater just prior to his arrest. She gave a handwritten, signed statement to the police concerning this conversation the day after the arrest. A portion of the statement read as follows:

About 5 min. before the show was over Randy came in. I got up to talk to him. He had been drinking so I didn't really believe what he said. He had told me he wrecked a car and he shot a guy. I just looked [at] him and he asked me to help him. I then asked him if he was telling the truth. When he said he was I turned away from him and ran out of the theater and got in the car with my sister and we tried to find Gary [one of the policemen] to tell him.

This statement of Carol Tackett was admitted in evidence over the objection of the defendant. At the time of its admission Miss Tackett was on the witness stand. Prior to its admission she had testified, in part, as follows:

A.   Well, I sat through the whole show and, well, except for the last part of it. Randy was standing in the doorway inside the show and I got up and I was talking to him in the show. That was about five, ten minutes before the show ended or something like that.
Q.   All right. Now what was this conversation that you had with him at that time?
A.   Well, he wanted to know if I had a car and I told him no. And he wanted—I said that Linda had a car and he wanted to know if he could go with us and I said no that he couldn't go with us.
Q.   What else was said at that time?
A.   Why, he was kind of upset and everything and that's when we heard the sirens outside and stuff.
Q.   Did you have any other conversation with him?
A.   Well he said something about somebody being shot at that time and I left the show right after that with my sister and Linda.
Q.   Do you recall the police coming in the movie at that time?
A.   No. I wasn't there at that time.
Q.   You say you left before they came or you didn't see any police come in?
A.   Yes. I left before that.
Q.   Now, then, can you tell us what the words were that Randy used concerning somebody being shot?
A.   I can't remember exactly what they were, just that it was something about that.
Q.   Do you recall being interviewed by the police following this time?
A.   Yes.
Q.   Do you recall giving a statement to the police?
A.   Yes.
Q.   I will hand you what has been marked as state's Exhibit 17 and ask if you can identify what that is.
A.   That's the statement that I made out for the policeman.
Q.   Is this your handwriting on here?
A.   Yes.
Q.   According to this, this was made on the 24th day of November of 1969. Would that be correct?
A.   Yes.
Q.   And down here, this signature here, whose signature is that?
A.   It's mine.
Q.   Now then, at the time that you made this statement, Carol, did you make this statement according to what your knowledge was at that time?
A.   To the best that I remembered.
Q.   Then would you say that this was a true statement that you made at that time?
A.   Yes. . . .

Q. Now Carol, at the time that you made this statement which is identified as state's Exhibit 17, was your memory better than it is now?

A. Yes.

The state argues that the statement was properly admitted under the rule of "past recollection recorded." The defendant argues that the rule of "past recollection recorded" has not been recognized in Ohio, that the statement was "hearsay" and that its admission in evidence deprived the defendant of his constitutional right of confrontation and cross-examination. We hold that the statement was properly admitted as "past recollection recorded," and that its admission did not violate defendant's constitutional rights.

While the rule of "past recollection recorded" is historically an offshoot from the practice of permitting a witness to refresh or revive his memory by examination of his own written memorandum ("present recollection re-freshed"), it is fundamentally different in legal concept.

In the "present recollection refreshed" situation, the witness looks at the memorandum to refresh his memory of the events, but then proceeds to testify upon the basis of his present independent knowledge. However, in the "past recollection recorded" situation, the witness' present recollection is still absent or incomplete, but his present testimony is to the effect that his recollection was complete at the time the memorandum was written and that such recollection was accurately recorded therein.

[The court quotes four requirements for past recollection recorded proposed by McCormick, which found their way into FRE 803(5), noting that Wigmore endorsed the exception and suggested that the original record be used if available and shown to opposing counsel. And the court quotes the opinion by Justice Lockwood in *Kinsey v. State*, 49 Ariz. 201, 65 P.2d 1141 (1937). There Lockwood argues that recorded recollection should not be viewed as hearsay because it embodies a statement by a testifying witness, and that a witness who has made such a statement may be cross-examined on his honesty and integrity and ability to accurately. While he cannot be examined so well on his memory, it is "unnecessary" to do that because "he has already stated that he has *no* independent recollection of the event, which is all that could be brought out" on cross if he testified from present recollection.]

Thus, from the point of view of a procedural rule of evidence we are of the opinion that the rule of past recollection recorded is based upon sound logic and should be specifically recognized with approval in this state.

To the extent that appellant is asserting that the use of such rule in a criminal case would result in a violation of the defendant's Sixth Amendment right of confrontation, including the opportunity of cross-examination, we reject such assertion upon the basis of the holdings of the United States Supreme Court in *California v. Green* (1970), 399 U.S. 149 and *Nelson v. O'Neil* (1971), 402 U.S. 622. [The court presents a lengthy description of *Green*, which is described in Chapter 4G2, infra. It then concludes that "no constitutional inhibition" prevents use of statements of past recollection recorded against criminal defendants. *O'Neil* is also described in Chapter 4G2, infra.] . . .

The question remains as to whether the signed statement of Carol Tackett meets the requirements of past recollection recorded. We find that it does. The statement consisted of facts of which the witness had firsthand knowledge; the written statement was the original memorandum made near the time of the event while the witness had a clear and accurate memory of it; the witness lacked a present recollection of the words used by Randy Scott in the conversation; and the witness stated that the memorandum was accurate.

Thus, we find that the admission of the signed statement of Carol Tackett as past recollection recorded was proper, and that such did not amount to a denial of the defendant's right of confrontation or cross-examination. . . .

Judgment affirmed.

O'NEILL, C.J., and SCHNEIDER, HERBERT and STERN, JJ., concur.

CORRIGAN and BROWN, JJ., dissent.

It seems to this member of the court that a can of evidential worms is being opened and foisted into the soil of our trial procedure in Ohio with this innovative ruling adopting the precept of past recollection recorded into the criminal law of Ohio under the facts in this case. And, given time, they will emerge from that very soil in different fact situations and present problems of constitutional dimension to irk this court.

In the instant case, the written statement seems to me to be objectionable for at least four reasons:

1. the statement was not made in the presence of the defendant;
2. admitting the written paper as evidence results in it going to the deliberation room with the jury and a patent danger is that it will be given undue weight by the jury;
3. it places special emphasis on the facts recorded in the statement as against other facts testified to and contrary to the written statement; the written statement, likewise, gains an excessive value which ordinary testimony unreduced to available written form cannot have;
4. finally, under the traditional formulation of the rule, before a past recollection recorded could be received in evidence the witness who made it must testify that he lacks present memory of the events and therefore is unable to testify concerning them.

Here, the witness, Carol Tackett, testified for the state. She was the girlfriend of the defendant. She did not say, unambiguously, that she had no present memory of the events recorded in her statement. . . .

Certainly, in that state of the proof, the witness did not expressly say that any present memory of the facts recorded was absent or that she had no independent recollection of the event. More importantly, there was no effort made by the prosecutor to refresh her recollection from her prior written statement as to the facts therein. She was not asked if the written statement revived her memory.[3]

The admission of the statement under the facts in this criminal case was, in my view, prejudicially erroneous to the substantial rights of defendant, and I would reverse the judgment of the Court of Appeals and remand to the trial court for further proceedings.

_____

3. Russell v. Hudson River Rd. Co. (1858), 17 N.Y. 134, 140. It is "an indispensable preliminary to the introduction" of such memoranda as evidence "that the witness is unable with the aid of the memorandum to speak from [present] memory as to the facts." . . .

NOTES ON PAST RECOLLECTION RECORDED

1. *Scott* illustrates the lack-of-memory requirement. Had Carol Tackett forgotten what happened? Under FRE 104, who decides—judge or jury? What is the difference between past recollection recorded and refreshing recollection? *Scott* contrasts the two, and you will see the latter in Baker v. State, 371 A.2d 699 (Md. Spec. App. 1977) (Chapter 7A2, infra). In *Scott*, dissenting Judge Corrigan argues that the prosecutor should have tried to refresh the memory of Carol Tackett before resorting to her written statement. Why? Recall the exception for prior consistent statements in FRE 801(d)(1)(B). What are the differences between that provision and FRE 803(5)?

2. Since Carol Tackett gave her statement to a police officer, its use against the defendant raises constitutional issues under the Confrontation Clause. Under the approach taken in Crawford v. Washington, 124 S.Ct. 1354 (2004), however, it is likely that the use of such statements will pass constitutional muster, because the declarant could be cross-examined at trial. There is some question, however, whether a witness who does not remember the events described in her statement can be adequately cross-examined. *Crawford* is set forth in Chapter 4G, infra.

3. Consider the accuracy requirement. What does it mean for a witness who no longer recalls the critical facts to testify that his prior statement accurately reflects what he once knew? Should it suffice if he testifies that he would not sign a false statement? Compare Hodas v. Davis, 196 N.Y.S. 801 (N.Y. App. Div. 1922) (no; in testifying that "he never affixed his signature 'to any paper which did not contain the true facts,' " the witness "may have stated a sufficient premise" for believing that his statement was accurate, but "the conclusion that he so believed was not asserted") with Walker v. Larson, 169 N.W.2d 737, 741-743 (Minn. 1969) (admitting statement signed by passenger in car involved in accident, where he testified that "he would not have signed a statement without first reading it" and "would not have signed a record that was not true"; *Hodas* rule could "prevent an entirely correct and truthful statement from being presented to the trier of fact merely by showing a convenient loss of memory" at trial, "which would result in impeding justice"). Does FRE 803(5) require evidence of accuracy outside the statement itself, or would an "accuracy clause" be good enough?

4. Where one person writes a statement that another reads and signs, there is no doubt that the latter has "made" or "adopted" the statement for purposes of FRE 803(5). What if the signing party testifies that what he actually said was not "taken down word for word" and that the scrivener "wrote the statement in his own words"? See United States v. Williams, 571 F.2d 344, 346-348 (6th Cir.) ("signing and swearing to the statement" means he "adopted it"), cert. denied, 439 U.S. 841 (1978).

5. Freshness of memory is the fourth requirement in FRE 803(5), but there are no rules of thumb. One court found this requirement satisfied even where the statement was prepared three years after the event described. See United States v. Senak, 527 F.2d 129, 139-142 (7th Cir.) (statement "displayed no lapses of memory" and was "specific in detail"), cert. denied, 424 U.S. 907

(1975). Why have a freshness requirement if it is so easily satisfied? Consider the following suggestion:

> Gaps or qualifications on the face of a statement reflecting incomplete or uncertain memory suggest it is stale; relative importance of the matters described in the life of the speaker bears on how long memory is fresh; the nature of matters recorded may be such that they would likely be fresh in the mind for a longer time, or be of such complexity or detail that time is likely to wash them away quickly; indications of care and attention in the statements may indicate freshness, particularly if the maker personally and meticulously wrote it out, or (in the case of a writing prepared by another) if he made corrections or changes, while haste and vagueness or uncritical acceptance suggest the matter is stale. Wooden rules of thumb (memory stays fresh about two weeks) are not helpful.

C. Mueller and L. Kirkpatrick, Evidence §8.43 (2d ed. 1999).

6. As the bank robbers flee by car, a bystander comes to the front door of the bank (locked, now that the horses have bolted) and raps on the glass. A guard, shaken from the experience, goes to the door. "We're closed," he says, but the bystander replies, "The license number of that car that just drove off is WJF 6849." The guard fetches a deposit receipt, gets the bystander to repeat the number, and scribbles it down, taking also the bystander's name and address. At trial, the prosecutor can link the car to the defendant and wants to use what the bystander said to link the car to the crime. Can he get into evidence the license number that the guard wrote on the deposit slip? See United States v. Booz, 451 F.2d 719, 724-725 (3d Cir. 1971) (if the agent "can verify the accuracy of his transcription" and the observer "can testify [that] he related an accurate recollection of the number" to the agent, the evidence may come in). *Booz* reaches the right result, doesn't it? The ACN to FRE 803(5) seems to approve as well. That means, doesn't it, that "made or adopted" must be construed to embrace the acts of two persons—the first dictating and the second writing down what the first says—as long as both testify appropriately at trial?

7. Can testimony given by the witness in a prior proceeding get in under the present exception? See Isler v. United States, 824 A.2d 957, 960 (D.C. 2003) (in murder trial, admitting grand jury testimony by eyewitness as past recollection recorded). How about a business record comprising information orally conveyed by one to another, who writes it down, or a telephone message taken by one person and relayed orally to another who writes it down? See Curtis v. Bradley, 31 A. 591 (Conn. 1894) (business records); United States v. Allied Stevedoring Corp., 241 F.2d 925 (2d Cir.) (phone message), cert. denied, 353 U.S. 984 (1957). How about a tape-recorded statement? See Commonwealth v. Nolan, 694 N.E.2d 350 (Mass. 1998) (tape recording).

5. *Business Records*

The exception for business records is a blockbuster. The eyes glaze over at the mere thought of studying an exception of such prosaic title, but it is critical in litigation and astonishing in breadth.

Consider for a moment the variety of material[4] reached by the language "record, or data compilation, in any form" contained in FRE 803(6): Airline check-in and reservation records, report by soils testing laboratory; laundromat reconciliation sheets matching washer cycles with coins in pay boxes; internal corporate memoranda, minutes of trade group meetings, diaries describing business meetings; work orders and parts requisitions; telephone toll records; credit card receipts; truck driver's notebook recording deliveries; flight training records; drilling records describing operations of oil rig. Need more convincing?

In thinking about the exception, it is useful to have in mind the changes in language introduced by Congress. Set forth below are the terms of the exception, indicating in italics the words added by Congress and in brackets the words proposed by the Advisory Committee and Court but deleted by Congress:

A memorandum, report, record, or data compilation[,] in any form, of acts, events, conditions, opinions, or diagnoses, made at or near the time by, or from information transmitted by, a person with knowledge, [all] *if kept* in the course of a regularly conducted *business* activity, *and if it was the regular practice of that business activity to make the memorandum, report, record, or data compilation, all* as shown by the testimony of the custodian or other qualified witness, unless the source[s] of information or *the method or* [other] circumstances *of preparation* indicate lack of trustworthiness. *The term "business" as used in this paragraph includes business, profession, occupation, and calling of every kind.*

What were the apparent congressional purposes in amending the proposed language? Would regularly kept personal records fit the original language? The congressional rewording? See the pre-Rules decision in Sabatino v. Curtiss National Bank, 415 F.2d 632 (5th Cir.) (depositor's account book was within business records exception because "routinely entered" and "routinely checked" by a person having "no motive to falsify"), cert. denied, 396 U.S. 1057 (1969).

The four elements of the exception are as follows:

1. *Regular business; regularly kept record.* The exception embraces only records of a "business, institution, profession, occupation" or "calling" (though it need not generate profit), *and* only those records that it regularly generates. The more generous language preferred by the Advisory Committee and Court did not impose these requirements. Thus a record fits the exception only if each person involved in its preparation was acting in the regular course of her business activities. (Can you see why this requirement, which is clearer in the original language, survived in the amended version adopted by Congress?)

Even the congressional language is broad enough to reach records kept

---

4. The examples described in the text come, respectively, from United States v. Fuji, 301 F.3d 535 (7th Cir. 2002); Fortier v. Dona Anna Plaza Partners, 747 F.2d 1324 (10th Cir. 1984); State v. Evans, 932 P.2d 758 (Idaho 1997); In re Japanese Electronic Prods. Antitrust Litig., 723 F.2d 238 (3d Cir. 1983); Phoenix v. Com/Systems, 706 F.2d 1033 (9th Cir. 1983); United States v. Atchley, 699 F.2d 1055 (11th Cir. 1983); State v. Hager, 691 A.2d 1191, 1193 (Me. 1996); United States v. Cincotta, 689 F.2d 238 (1st Cir.), cert. denied, 459 U.S. 991 (1982); In re Aircrash in Bali, Indonesia, 684 F.2d 1301 (9th Cir. 1982); Matador Drilling Co. v. Post, 662 F.2d 1190 (5th Cir. 1981).

by a single person who is, so to speak, "in business for himself." See Keogh v. Commissioner, 713 F.2d 496 (9th Cir. 1983) (diary kept by Las Vegas casino dealer recording gains and losses fits exception; he kept it in course of his own business or occupation). It reaches too the records of such illegal enterprises as drug selling. See United States v. Foster, 711 F.2d 871, 882 (9th Cir. 1983). And language in the Conference Report makes clear the intent to cover "schools, churches and hospitals." No doubt it also reaches records of labor unions, political committees and parties, and charities like the Community Chest and Red Cross.

2. *Personal knowledge of source.* The source of the information must be someone with personal knowledge. Note that the person who makes the entry need not have such knowledge, so the exception contemplates multiple hearsay—one entry based on another, based on another, and so forth.

3. *Contemporaneity.* The exception contemplates that the information will be recorded (or at least gathered) at the time of the act or event, or when the condition was observed, but the requirement is not interpreted literally. It suffices that the record is made (or the information gathered) close to the time of the event.

4. *Foundation testimony.* Every hearsay exception requires a foundation, but this exception expressly contemplates testimony by the "custodian" of the records "or other qualified witness." The foundation witness need not have made the record nor observed its preparation or even have been employed by the business when the record was made. What is required is a witness (preferably the "custodian" of the records) with firsthand knowledge of the recordkeeping system who can describe the manner in which the records are prepared so as to satisfy the other three requirements of the exception. In short, the foundation witness may rely on a kind of "circumstantial" knowledge of the recordkeeping system, although a person lacking even this minimal knowledge cannot satisfy the requirement. Compare United States v. Evans, 572 F.2d 455, 490 (5th Cir.) (accountants could authenticate company records, regardless whether employed when records were made), cert. denied, 439 U.S. 870 (1978) with State v. Radley, 804 A.2d 1127, 1131 (Me. 2002) (credit union manager could not authenticate reports prepared by clearing house, since she was neither employed by the latter entity "nor in any way involved with creating, maintaining, or transmitting" those reports).

PETROCELLI v. GALLISON
United States Court of Appeals for the First Circuit
679 F.2d 286 (1982)

[James and Beverly Petrocelli sued Dr. Davis Gallison, alleging medical malpractice in connection with a hernia operation that Gallison performed on James on March 18, 1975. After the operation Petrocelli suffered intense pain in his groin area. Several months later he went to Massachusetts General Hospital and consulted Dr. Swartz. He diagnosed a recurrence of the hernia and did a second operation on September 25. This effort too failed to solve the problem, and Petrocelli underwent a third operation, suffering pain all the while.

At trial, Petrocelli described his pain after the operations. Beverly Petrocelli testified that she called Gallison after the first operation and asked whether there was anything she could do and that Gallison replied, "I could give him Darvon, but it is not going to do anything because I cut a nerve. What do you expect?" A consulting physician testified that in his opinion the ilioinguinal nerve was "injured" or "traumatized" in the first operation, although he could not say that it was severed. He neither examined nor treated Petrocelli and rested his opinion on complaints and the distribution of the pain. He had also looked at the hospital and medical records.

The defense attacked the plaintiff's expert, pointing out that he was a thoracic surgeon rather than a neurologist, that he had not performed a hernia operation in 16 years, and that he socialized occasionally with plaintiffs' attorney. Defendant also introduced evidence that a neurologist who had examined Petrocelli thought that "sensation appeared intact" in the ilioinguinal area. And Gallison himself testified that he neither severed the nerve nor told Beverly that he had.

From a jury verdict for Gallison, plaintiffs appeal, urging error in the exclusion of a sentence in Dr. Swartz's postoperative report and a surgical note by another physician.]

LEVIN H. CAMPBELL, J.

The first item of excluded evidence, noted below in italics, was contained in Dr. Swartz's report filed the day after he performed Petrocelli's second hernia operation. That report is divided into two sections, one labeled "Indications" and one labeled "Procedure." The first of these reads, in its entirety, as follows:

> INDICATIONS: This 37 year old man had a left inguinal hernia repair at an outside hospital 5 mos. prior to admission. *During the course of that surgical procedure, the left ilioinguinal nerve was severed.* A recurrence of the hernia was noted in the immediate postoperative period. He presented to this hospital for repair of the recurrence. [Emphasis added.]

There follows the section entitled "Procedure" which at great length details what Dr. Swartz himself did and observed during his repair operation. There is no mention whatever of the ilioinguinal nerve in this section.

The other excluded portion of the medical record was an entry made by a different physician at a Massachusetts General Hospital surgical clinic on October 28, 1975. In his report of Petrocelli's visit to the surgical clinic, this doctor noted, "Hernia well healed but very worried about pain from transected ilio femoral nerve. . . ." Plaintiffs assert on appeal that both of the above statements, while hearsay, should nevertheless have been admitted under the exception to the hearsay rule codified in FRE 803(6).

Rule 803(6), commonly called the business records exception, governs admissibility of "Records of regularly conducted activity." It provides that any report of "acts, events, conditions, opinions, or diagnoses, made at or near the time by, or from information transmitted by, a person with knowledge, if kept in the course of a regularly conducted business activity" should be admitted "even though the declarant is available as a witness." Plaintiffs argue that the notations describing the ilioinguinal nerve as having been "severed" at the earlier operation in a different hospital, and mentioning Petrocelli's worry about pain from "transected ilio femoral nerve," were both contained in reports kept by the hospital in the regular course, that they were made by doctors with knowledge of Petrocelli's condition, and that they should therefore have been admitted as the "opinions or diagnoses" of Petrocelli's attending physicians.

We think the district court did not abuse its discretion in excluding the parts of this hospital record which indicated that the nerve had earlier been severed. We reach this result primarily because of the complete absence of any indication as to where this information—relating to something that had happened six months ago in another hospital—came from. To be admissible as "business records" under Rule 803(6), the referenced notations would have to represent either the opinions or diagnoses of the Massachusetts General Hospital doctors who made the notations or the diagnoses of some other "person with knowledge" (such as a medical colleague) who reported to the maker of the record as part of the usual business or professional routine of Massachusetts General Hospital. If the entries were merely relaying what Mr. Petrocelli or his wife told the reporting physicians, when providing a medical history, the matter would not be admissible solely under Rule 803(6). . . . Rule 803(6) requires that information in a business record be "transmitted by a person with knowledge" acting "in the course of a regularly conducted business activity." The Advisory Committee Notes make clear that this encompasses only declarants—like nurses or doctors in the case of hospitals—who report to the recordkeeper as part of a regular business routine in which they are participants. Where the declarant is a hospital patient, his relating of his own history is not part of a "business" routine in which he is individually a regular participant.

Plaintiffs argued vigorously both here and below, that the notations concerning the severed nerve must be taken to reflect the medical opinions of the reporting doctors. But we think it entirely uncertain whether the reporting doctors themselves determined from ascertainable symptoms or observations, that the nerve had been "severed" or "transected" in the previous operation, or whether instead these doctors were simply recording what the patient or his wife had reported. The statements are not obviously diagnostic in quality. There is no mention of symptoms leading to a conclusion that the nerve had previously been cut. See Buckminster's Estate v. Commissioner, 147 F.2d 331 (2d Cir. 1944) (admitting medical report diagnosing party as exhibiting symptoms of cerebral hemorrhage). Nor are the statements in the nature of opinions based upon observations by the physicians. See Reed v. Order of United Commercial Travelers of America, 123 F.2d 252 (2d Cir. 1941) (statement by admitting physician in medical record that party was "still apparently well under the influence of alcohol" admitted to prove intoxication).

[The Petrocellis themselves might have been the source of the remark in the report by Dr. Swartz, and the trial court was in "no position to know" whether Dr. Swartz made an independent determination. Noting the testimony that detecting the severed nerve might be difficult during subsequent surgery because of scarring, and the absence of any mention of the point in the Procedure section of the Swartz report, the court concludes that one "bare" and "conclusory" sentence would be entitled to "no weight as reflecting the doctor's own opinion." The mention in the October 28 report is "even more cryptic" and might have rested on the report by Dr. Swartz, which may have been in the same file.]

In judging the reasonableness of exclusion under Rule 803(6), it is relevant that the excluded, elliptical reports could easily have been misconstrued by the jury as definitive opinion testimony on the most critical issue in the entire case—whether the nerve had, in fact, been severed. See FRE 403. Given the impossibility of determining from the records themselves whether these reports reflected medical judgments, and the lack of any corroborative evidence or testimony offered by the plaintiffs to assure the court that these were professional opinions, the district court could reasonably determine that the notations were simply too inscrutable to be admitted, bearing in mind that, if admitted under Rule 803(6), they would be admitted for their truth without any opportunity to cross-examine the physicians who made them. Pretrial discovery rules made it possible for plaintiffs to have deposed or otherwise sought clarification from the various physicians, including Dr. Swartz, which they apparently did not do. The trial court could thus entertain legitimate doubts as to whether the doctors who recorded these statements were actually rendering professional judgments. We emphasize that this case involves a rather narrow issue regarding the admissibility under Rule 803(6) of a business record which is so cryptic that pure guesswork and speculation is required to divine the source of the cited information. Under such circumstances the district judge acted within his discretion in determining that the hearsay statements could not be admitted as business records reflecting medical "opinions or diagnoses" under Rule 803(6).[3]

There is, to be sure, another basis for admission if we assume that Petrocelli himself or his spouse was the source of the "cut nerve" information. . . . Rule 803(4) provides for admission of patient or family statements "describing medical history, or past or present symptoms, pain, or sensations, or the inception or general character of the cause . . ." of a condition, provided the statements are "reasonably pertinent to diagnosis or treatment." Thus, if not admissible under Rule 803(6), the Petrocellis' recorded statements about the cut nerve were arguably admissible as part of patient history.[5] For the reasons which follow, however, we do not think such a theory warrants either a reversal or a new trial in this case.

First, the Petrocellis did not argue either to the court below or in their briefs on this appeal that the references in these medical records derived from statements made by Petrocelli or his wife to doctors at Massachusetts General Hospital and were, therefore, admissible as patient history. We do not ordinarily decide cases on the basis of theories never presented below nor argued to us.

One might surmise, moreover, that plaintiffs' reluctance to claim admissibility under Rule 803(4) was deliberate and strategic rather than inadvertent, making it even less appropriate for us to upset the lower court on the basis of a theory never advanced. The jury knew from the testimony of Petrocelli's wife

---

3. It may also be argued, although we need not decide the issue, that the patent ambiguity as to the true source of information in this hospital record created such a "lack of trustworthiness," see FRE 803(6), as to authorize the trial judge to exclude, on that separate ground, the references to the severed nerve.

5. Since the medical history arguably asserted here was recorded in a hospital record, the plaintiffs would actually have had to qualify the notations under a combination of Rule 803(6) (to admit the hospital record) and Rule 803(4) (to admit the patient history). See FRE 805.

that the Petrocellis believed the nerve had been severed by Dr. Gallison. A mere reiteration via the hospital record that Petrocelli or his wife had told Dr. Swartz that his nerve was cut during Dr. Gallison's operation would have added little beyond corroborating what Mrs. Petrocelli had already told the jury. Yet were these statements to have been admitted under Rule 803(4), fairness would have dictated that the judge instruct the jury, if requested, that the statements were admitted for their truth solely as matters related by the patient or a member of his family, not as professional opinion. Otherwise, the jury was open to the misimpression that the notations were admitted as the medical judgments of the two Massachusetts General Hospital doctors who wrote the entries or of the hospital itself. As it would have been manifestly improper for statements admitted as patient history under Rule 803(4) to be presented to the jury as something else[6] plaintiffs' attorney understandably sought admission exclusively under Rule 803(6). . . .

Affirmed.

NOTES ON MEDICAL RECORDS

1. The court in *Petrocelli* concludes that FRE 803(6) requires the source of information to be acting in the course of a regularly conducted business. Does the language of FRE 803(6) support this conclusion? Did Congress intend to include information supplied by an outsider to the business—like what a doctor gets from a patient?

2. Why isn't *Petrocelli* a perfect case to combine FRE 803(6) and 803(4)? If the statement in the record of Dr. Swartz that "the left ilioinguinal nerve was severed" rests on something James Petrocelli said, does his statement fit FRE 803(4)? See Merrow v. Bofferding, 581 N.W.2d 696, 702 (Mich. 1998) (in suit against landlord, admitting doctor's record indicating that plaintiff was hurt when his arm "went through the window").

3. Recall Problem 4-I ("I Felt This Sudden Pain"). This time assume that Eldon Sanders went to Dr. Hillier and told him what had happened ("I felt this sudden pain, just a few minutes ago when I had to lift one of those 30-gallon cans out on the Chase") *and* that Dr. Hillier recorded this information in his case history form ("Patient reports onset of pain while at work in the field"). Could Eleanor Sanders offer Hillier's form as a business record, combining FRE 803(6) with FRE 803(4)?

6. It may, of course, be urged that since it is fairly certain the information in the report came from one or the other of two sources—the doctors or the Petrocellis—either of which might have qualified the statements for admission under an applicable hearsay exception, the district court should have let the information in and allowed the *jury* to decide whether the statements were, in fact, the diagnoses of the attending physicians or the statements of the Petrocellis. No such theory was posed by plaintiffs, however, and such a procedure would run counter to FRE 104(a), which gives to the *judge* the preliminary duty of determining whether—and under what theory—an item of evidence is to be admitted. More importantly, where, as here, an item in a medical record is so ambiguous as to its source as to leave a jury with no clue as to how to evaluate it (other than the fact that it appears in an official record), a trial judge would be entitled in a case like this to exclude the evidence under FRE 403 on the ground that the danger of unfair prejudice from jury confusion substantially outweighed the record's probative value. . . .

4. Change some facts in *Petrocelli:*

a. Assume James Petrocelli tells Dr. Swartz he felt no pain until five months after the original operation, when he was doing weightlifting exercises, and that Dr. Swartz records this information. Couldn't Dr. Gallison offer the Swartz record against plaintiffs by combining FRE 803(6) and the admissions provision of FRE 801(d)(2)(A)? See Hansen v. Abrasive Engineering & Manufacturing, Inc., 526 P.2d 625, 630-631 (Or. 1993) (in product suit against maker of sanding machine, defense introduced record of psychiatrist reflecting statements by plaintiff; record fit business records exception, and statements by plaintiff were his admissions).

b. Assume that Dr. Swartz phoned Dr. Gallison about Petrocelli and wrote down that Gallison said the nerve was severed in the original surgery. Is there any doubt that James and Beverly Petrocelli could offer *this* Swartz record against Gallison, by combining FRE 803(6) with either FRE 801(d)(2)(A) or 803(4)? See O'Gee v. Dobbs Houses, Inc., 570 F.2d 1084, 1088-1089 (2d Cir. 1978).

c. What if Dr. Gallison forwarded to Dr. Swartz a copy of Petrocelli's patient files, and Swartz copied down the information into his own record?

Admitting the Swartz record in these changed situations would require a conclusion that he makes it a "regular practice" to record such data. Isn't it likely that he would? Before these exceptions can be combined, however, *Petrocelli* stands as a reminder that the proponent must show that *each level* of hearsay fits an exception.

5. Suppose that Dr. Swartz wrote in his report, "Examined patient—left ilioinguinal nerve severed or damaged, apparently in an earlier surgical procedure." Would it be admissible?

6. Suppose Petrocelli consulted Dr. Swartz after filing suit against Dr. Gallison, for purposes of getting Dr. Swartz to diagnose but not treat the injury. If Swartz recorded the "patient history" from what Petrocelli said, noting that "pain commenced five months after prior surgery," could Petrocelli offer this record in proof of that point? What if Petrocelli consulted Dr. Swartz pursuant to a discovery order obtained by Dr. Gallison under FRCP 35, specifically requiring Petrocelli to see Dr. Swartz? See Yates v. Bair Transport, 249 F. Supp. 681 (S.D.N.Y. 1965) (in personal injury suit, plaintiff could introduce reports by physicians who examined him on behalf of defendants, but not reports by physicians of his own choosing who examined him in anticipation of litigation).

NORCON, INC. v. KOTOWSKI
Supreme Court of Alaska
971 P.2d 158 (Alaska 1999)

[Mary Kotowski worked on the cleanup of the Exxon Valdez oil spill. Exxon retained Veco as general contractor on the project. Veco in turn subcontracted with Purcell Security to provide security and investigate allegations of rulebreaking, and with Norcon for other services. Veco and Norcon had a strict policy against alcohol consumption by anyone working on the project or living in company housing.

Kotowski was sent by her union in Fairbanks to work for Norcon on a shower barge attached to a ship called the Pacific Northwest Explorer (Pacific Northwest). There she worked 12-hour days for two weeks, and was quartered on the Pacific Northwest. Her supervisor reported to Mike Posehn, a Norcon foreman. On June 28, 1989, Posehn told Kotowski to pack and move to a barge called the Foss 280. Reporting there and checking with security, she was told she had not been assigned a room but was taken to a work station. Posehn appeared. Kotowski testified that "he came up to me, he kissed me, he kind of squeezed my bottom, asked me how's it going, babe?" She testified that she was distressed but she did not then complain. Later she asked Posehn if there was specific work for her. He told her to ask "one of the girls running around here . . . if they need help with anything."

At the end of the day Kotowski returned to her quarters on the Pacific Northwest. Back on the Foss 280 the next day, she asked Posehn for instructions, adding that if she were not needed there, she had work on the Pacific Northwest. Posehn invited her to his room. She went, and Posehn poured them both whisky. She took a sip, and he consumed his drink. He told her to calm down and go back to the Pacific Northwest for a nap, inviting her to return that evening for a party in his room and further discussion of her employment.

Back on the Pacific Northwest, Kotowski discussed events with Elmo Savell (Exxon executive in charge). She told Savell that Posehn was harassing her and that he "had a reputation for granting employment preferences in exchange for sex." She told him he had invited her to his room that evening, and she expected alcohol to be consumed. Savell gave her a tape recorder and (at her request) a note stating she had been assigned to help gather information on alcohol/drug abuse on the Foss 280, and was to have "amnesty from prosecution and from being fired."

Back on the Foss 280, Kotowski was told she had been transferred to the "beach" (a less desirable assignment). In Posehn's room she found the party, where she recorded the conversations. As reflected in the tape, many people were there, including identifiable Norcon managers. There was sexual banter and alcohol. Posehn told her she had been assigned to the beach, but he had changed it. As the party broke up, she told him she would see him the next day. He suggested she have another drink, and they would talk about her job. Later she went to the bathroom. She returned to find everyone gone but Posehn, who was in his underwear with the lights out. She said she was leaving. He asked her to spend the night and held the door closed, but she got it open and left, leaving her coat, life vest, and hard hat.

An Exxon executive who had been at the party asked a union steward to get Kotowski to sign a statement that she had been insubordinate. Told by the steward that her job would not be terminated, Kotowski signed the statement. The steward gave the statement to the Exxon executive while he was at lunch with other managers, and saw it being passed around the table, bringing laughter. Later a senior official with Norcon told Kotowski to pack and go to Valdez, where she was questioned by people working for Norcon, Veco, and Purcell.

She testified that the questioning was hostile, and she was concerned for her safety (she slept in a girlfriend's car instead of company barracks). The Exxon executive told her to "sit tight, relax, we'll figure something out."

Posehn was interviewed too. He denied drinking with Kotowski, but said that "if we had a drink that night it was after working hours."

Both Kotowski and Posehn were fired on July 10th. A never-delivered termination slip said Kotowski was terminated "for leaving work here [on the Foss 280] without permission." A second termination slip (issued and delivered) said she was terminated for "breaking camp rules" (apparently a reference to drinking). Posehn was fired for a sexual relationship with another Norcon employee. Only Kotowski was terminated for drinking.

A jury found Norcon liable for sexual harassment, and negligent and intentional infliction of emotional distress. Kotowski won $8,494 in lost earnings, $1,850 in emotional distress, and $3.8 million in punitive damages. The Alaska Supreme Court reduces the punitive award to $500,000 and deals with many issues.]

MATTHEWS, JUSTICE. . . .

Kotowski's Exhibit 7 is a three-page, handwritten memo from Bruce Ford, an investigator with Purcell Security, to Tom Varnell, his superior. Veco had contracted with Purcell to provide security for the cleanup, which included the investigation of allegations of rulebreaking on the cleanup vessels. The Ford memo summarizes the information Ford and fellow Purcell employee Mark Flechsing had gathered concerning Kotowski, Posehn, and other Norcon employees between July 2, 1989, and July 5, 1989. Kotowski offered the memo into evidence to prove the truth of the matters asserted in the following portion of the memo:

> Re: Mike Posehn. I talked with two roommates of Mike Posehn at the Foss 280 Rm. 235. The individuals were Jim Stampley and Mark Ruder and both Norcon employees. Stampley said that Posehn did have a lot of female visitors in his room and there was drinking of alcoholic beverages as a supervisor as a "springboard" for sexual activity with the females under his supervision.
>
> I also talked with Sgt. Mark Flechsing who is the head of security for Purcell at the Midway Barge. Flechsing said he had talked to Larry Coyle, one of the head supervisors for Norcon, concerning Posehn. Coyle told Flechsing that Posehn would do favors for some of his female crew in exchange for some sort of sexual activity. Coyle is now on R & R and is unavailable to be interviewed.

Norcon objected, arguing that this memo was inadmissible hearsay. Kotowski argued that the memo fell within the business records exception to the hearsay rule. See ARE 803(6) [which is identical to FRE 803(6)—Eds.]. Norcon also contested this, in part because the memo was an investigative report containing the hearsay statements of others. The superior court admitted the memo under the business records exception.

[Court quotes ARE 803(6).]

On appeal Norcon does not contest the superior court's implicit findings that Ford acquired his information as part of a regularly-conducted business activity, and that it was Purcell's regular practice to make and keep memoranda of this type. Instead, Norcon objects to the fact that the memo consisted of the "double and triple hearsay" of Coyle and Stampley, the informants who provided the information contained in the memo. According to Norcon, even if

Ford acted within the regular course of business in preparing the memo, no indication exists that these informants were acting within the regular course of their business. Norcon refers this court to the commentary on Rule 803(6), which reads in part:

> Sources of information present no substantial problem with ordinary business records. All participants, including the observer or participant furnishing the information to be recorded, are acting routinely, under a duty of accuracy, with employer reliance on the result, or in short "in the regular course of business." If, however, the supplier of the information does not act in the regular course, an essential link is broken; the assurance of accuracy does not extend to the information itself, and the fact that it may be recorded with scrupulous accuracy is of no avail.

ARE 803(6) commentary. [There is a substantially identical passage in the ACN to FRE 803(6)—Eds.]

Kotowski argues that Coyle and Stampley had business reasons, as employees of Norcon, to provide accurate and truthful responses. She argues alternatively that the testimony of these informants should be regarded as nonhearsay, as admissions of a party-opponent. ARE 801(d)(2). [In a footnote, court quotes ARE 801(8)(d)(2)(A)-(E), which are substantially identical to the corresponding federal provisions, except that the latter were later amended in ways not related to this case.]

In its reply brief, Norcon does not contest the admissibility of the Ford memo based on this alternative theory. In our view, the alternative argument has merit. To use the terms of Rule 801(d)(2), both Coyle and Stampley were agents speaking at a time that they were employed by Norcon. As supervisors and safety employees, alcohol use and sexual harassment are apparently matters which their jobs required them to report, especially in response to an employer-initiated investigation. We therefore conclude that it was not error to admit the Ford memo. . . .

NOTES ON INTERNAL REPORTS OFFERED
AS BUSINESS RECORDS

1. As *Norcon* reflects, private companies often investigate personnel disputes. Typically there is a human resources director, who might have a department and staff, and one of these persons interviews people and makes a report. In *Norcon*, the investigation was carried on by an outside firm hired to monitor compliance with workplace rules (Purcell), whose staff person Tom Varnell asked Bruce Ford to prepare the report. Ford spoke to people who worked for Norcon and Purcell. The court invokes the business records exception as the basis for admitting the Ford report to prove what was said by Stampley, Ruder, Coyle (Norcon employees) and Flechsing (a Purcell employee). The court invokes the admissions doctrine as the basis to take those statements as proof of what they assert (that Posehn engaged in misconduct). Would either exception be enough by itself to justify the result? Consider the following:

(a) Stampley, Ruder, and Coyle are in a sense outsiders to Purcell (they work for Norcon). Does this fact mean the business records exception would not justify admitting the Ford report for all purposes? In applying the exception, wouldn't it make sense to view the three companies as engaging in a single business, since Norcon and Purcell combined forces with Veco on the cleanup? Then could we view the various employees as though they all worked for one company?

(b)   One requirement of the business records exception is that each statement involved in the record be made in ordinary course of business. When Stampley spoke with Ford, and Coyle spoke with Flechsing (giving information about the drinking and sexual behavior of Posehn), do you think these men were performing normal duties?

(c)   If we follow the court's lead and invoke both the business records exception and the admissions doctrine, then presumably the statements of Stampley and Coyle must be viewed as "authorized admissions" by Norcon under FRE 801(d)(2)(C) or as statements on matters "within the scope of" their agency or employment under FRE 801(d)(2)(D). The latter doesn't apply, does it, unless the job responsibilities of these men include keeping an eye on Posehn? Does the former apply, on the ground that Norcon impliedly authorized them to speak on this matter to Ford and Flechsing? Is this approach preferable to invoking the business records exception alone?

2.   Suppose the facts were different. Suppose the Ford report exonerated Posehn, presenting Ford's conclusion that he did nothing amiss, and that statements by Stampley, Ruder, and Coyle support this conclusion. Could Norcon use this report as evidence in its favor? Consider a 1998 case, in which the Montana Supreme Court threw out a decision by the Board of Labor Appeals denying unemployment compensation to Mary Bean, a nurse who was dismissed from her job with the Village Health Care Center (Village). An Incident Report, prepared and offered by Village, indicated that Bean committed misconduct and had been fired for cause rather than laid off (hence that she was not entitled to compensation). The court thought this report did not even constitute "substantial evidence." It did not fit the business records exception because it was not prepared as part of the "routine business activity" of Village in "administering nursing services to elderly residents." Moreover, it was made "in anticipation of litigation," meaning it was untrustworthy. See Bean v. Montana Board of Labor Appeals, 965 P.2d 256, 261-262 (Mont. 1998). It's true, isn't it, that employers like Norcon and Village must anticipate trouble when they investigate employment issues like the ones involved in these cases? Are courts right to be suspicious when employers offer their own reports on these matters? Are they right to admit them in cases like *Norcon*, when they are offered *against* employers?

3.   Employers also investigate accidents that happen in the workplace or involve their products or services: Airlines investigate plane crashes, railroads investigate train accidents, and makers of consumer products investigate accidents with items like power tools. Long ago the Supreme Court decided in Palmer v. Hoffman that a railroad accident report could not be admitted under the statutory predecessor to FRE 803(6), which covered records "made in the regular course of any business" if it was "the regular course of such business to make" such records at the time of the transaction, occurrence or event recorded (28 U.S.C. §1732). In *Palmer,* a husband sued for the death of his wife

in a grade crossing accident, and defendant offered a statement by the engineer (since deceased), prepared for his signature after a question-and-answer interview with the assistant superintendent of the railroad. The Court in *Palmer* would have none of it:

> An accident report may affect [a] business in the sense that it affords information on which the management may act. It is not, however, typical of entries made systematically or as a matter of routine to record events or occurrences, to reflect transactions with others, or to provide internal controls. The conduct of a business commonly entails the payment of tort claims incurred by the negligence of its employees. But the fact that a company makes a business out of recording its employees' versions of their accidents does not put those statements in the class of records made "in the regular course" of the business within the meaning of the Act. . . . If the Act is to be extended to apply not only to a "regular course" of a business but also to any "regular course" of conduct which may have some relationship to business, Congress not this Court must extend it. Such a major change which opens wide the door to avoidance of cross-examination should not be left to implication. Nor is it an answer to say that Congress has provided in the Act that the various circumstances of the making of the record should affect its weight, not its admissibility. That provision comes into play only in case the other requirements of the Act are met.
>
> In short, it is manifest that in this case those reports are not for the systematic conduct of the enterprise as a railroad business. Unlike payrolls, accounts receivable, accounts payable, bills of lading and the like, these reports are calculated for use essentially in the court, not in the business. Their primary utility is in litigating, not in railroading.

Palmer v. Hoffman, 318 U.S. 109, 113-114 (1943) (per Douglas). It probably comes as no surprise to you that the Montana Supreme Court in *Bean* (Note 2, supra) cited and relied heavily on *Palmer.*

4. *Palmer* might have put an end to the whole idea that reports dealing with employment incidents (as illustrated in *Norcon* and *Bean*) or accidents (as illustrated in *Palmer* itself) could fit the business records exception. But it did not. See, e.g., Lewis v. Baker, 526 F.2d 470 (2d Cir. 1975), which admitted an accident report prepared and offered by a railroad in an FELA suit on behalf of a railroader killed in a yard accident. The reviewing court stressed that the report in *Palmer* was prepared by the engineer who was "personally involved" and knew he was likely to be charged with wrongdoing in a lawsuit, while in *Lewis* the report was prepared by men who were not involved and could not be "the target" of a suit. In *Lewis,* the court endorsed the view that a report need not be excluded merely because it "might ultimately be of some value" in a later suit, nor because it "embodies an employee's version" of events or "happens to work in favor of" the employer.

5. On balance, would you prefer a per se rule excluding reports dealing with employment incidents or accidents, or a case-by-case approach examining factors relating to trustworthiness? Does it serve the interests of justice to be more generous in admitting such reports when they are offered *for* the company that prepared them than when they are offered *against* that company?

6. Not surprisingly, government agencies are often involved in these investigations, particularly in the cases of railroad and aircraft accidents. The coopera-

tion of private parties is expected, but concerns arise that the prospect of litigation will affect both willingness to cooperate and the substance of information submitted. Hence statutes sometimes address questions of admissibility in these contexts. See, e.g., 49 U.S.C. §20903 (accident or incident reports filed by railroad with Secretary of Transportation may not be "used in a civil action for damages resulting from a matter mentioned in the report"); 10 U.S.C. §2254 (opinions on causation reflected in reports of military aircraft accidents prepared by secretary of department "may not be considered as evidence" in litigation). But see also 49 U.S.C. §1114 (with certain exceptions, providing for public disclosure of any "record, information, or investigation submitted or received" by the National Transportation Safety Board, and not restricting use of such material).

7. Some courts recognize a self-critical analysis privilege in related settings, offering some protection for employers who take constructive steps to address workplace issues. See, e.g., Kientzy v. McDonnell Douglas Corp., 133 F.R.D. 522, 527 (E.D. Mo. 1991) (in sex discrimination suit, recognizing corporate ombudsman's privilege covering some material plaintiff sought), rev'd on other grounds, 990 F.2d 1051 (8th Cir. 1993). Would it make sense to recognize such a privilege for reports of the sort generated in *Norcon?*

6. *Public Records*

The exception for public records rests mainly on the great responsibility that attends the discharge of government functions in a democracy. In effect, it is presumed that public servants go about their official tasks with care, without bias or corruption, and that the scrutiny and exposure surrounding government functions add assurance that public records are trustworthy. The repetitive routine involved in preparing many such documents adds some assurance against misstatement, though the idea of routine is not an element in this exception.

Necessity also plays a role: Public officials probably do not long remember much of what they record in the course of their duties. And public functions are so pervasive, and the importance of facts recorded this way is so great, that an exception may be necessary simply to keep litigation from interrupting public officials too often.

The range and variety of public documents is staggering, so the framers of FRE 803(8) found it necessary to make separate provision for various kinds of documents. They also included an escape hatch in the form of the last clause, which permits exclusion if circumstances "indicate lack of trustworthiness."

Clause (A) embraces mundane documents describing "activities of the office or agency." Examples[5] include court transcripts to prove testimony given, a marshal's return to indicate service of process, an order committing a criminal defendant, an "antidumping proceeding notice" by the Commissioner of Cus-

---

5. The examples described in the text come, respectively, from United States v. Arias, 575 F.2d 253 (9th Cir.), cert. denied, 439 U.S. 868 (1978); United States v. Union Nat. de Trabajadores, 576 F.2d 388 (1st Cir. 1978); United States v. Wilson, 690 F.2d 1267 (9th Cir. 1982), cert. denied, 464 U.S. 867 (1983); In re Japanese Electronic Prods. Antitrust Litig., 723 F.2d 238 (3d Cir. 1983); United States v. Stone, 604 F.2d 922 (5th Cir. 1979).

toms, and a "progress sheet" prepared by the Treasury Department describing the processing and mailing of numbered government checks.

Clause (B) covers "matters observed" by public officials, subject to certain restrictions taken up below. Examples[6] include IRS assessment liens indicating unpaid taxes, reports by building inspectors indicating code violations, cargo survey reports prepared for the Agency for International Development, and a legislative preamble from a state law enacted in 1807 indicating that the Housatonic River was navigable.

Clause (C) embraces "factual findings" from official investigations, subject again to certain restrictions taken up below. Examples[7] include findings of employment discrimination based on race and gender prepared by the Equal Economic Opportunity Commission, studies on toxic shock syndrome by the Centers for Disease Control, reports on power tool accidents prepared by the Consumer Products Safety Commission, and findings by a Coast Guard Hearing Examiner as to which of two crewmembers started a shipboard fight.

Note that other exceptions embrace other specific kinds of public records. FRE 803(9) creates an exception for records of vital statistics, such as birth and death; FRE 803(14) creates an exception for records of documents affecting interests in property; FRE 803(22) creates one for evidence of judgments of felony conviction; and FRE 803(23) creates one for judgments on matters of personal, family, or general history, or boundaries. In addition, FRE 803(10) creates an exception for proof of the *absence* of a public entry.

Difficulties in applying FRE 803(8) are of four varieties: First, the compartments are not watertight, and it often makes a difference which category is invoked. Second, the use restrictions in clauses (B) and (C) have required interpretation and have undergone what can only be called judicial modification: The one in clause (B) barring "in criminal cases matters observed by police officers and other law enforcement personnel" was added by Congress, but the one in clause (C) preventing its use against the accused in criminal cases was inserted by the drafters because of "the almost certain collision with confrontation rights." Third, these use restrictions may differ from constraining language found in other exceptions. Fourth, the "trustworthiness" clause is something of a wildcard, introducing necessary flexibility but consequent uncertainty.

BAKER v. ELCONA HOMES CORP.
United States Court of Appeals for the Sixth Circuit
588 F.2d 551 (1978), cert. denied, 441 U.S. 933 (1979)

[handwritten: admissibility of police accident report 803(5) v 803(8)]

ENGEL, J.

Early in the evening of June 7, 1973, a 1968 Plymouth Valiant automobile travelling southbound on State Route 4 and a Ford semi-tractor truck travelling

6. The examples described in the text come, respectively, from United States v. Fletcher, 322 F.3d 508, 518 (8th Cir. 2003) United States v. Hansen, 583 F.2d 325 (7th Cir.), cert. denied, 439 U.S. 912 (1978); United States v. Central Gulf Lines, 747 F.2d 315 (5th Cir. 1984); Connecticut Light & Power Co. v. Federal Power Commn., 557 F.2d 349 (2d Cir. 1977).

7. The examples described in the text come, respectively, from Chandler v. Roudebush, 425 U.S. 840 (1976); Ellis v. International Playtex, 745 F.2d 292 (4th Cir. 1984); Roth v. Black & Decker,

westbound on U.S. Route 20 collided at the intersection of the two routes, seriously injuring one and killing the other five occupants of the Valiant. The driver of the truck did not sustain serious injury. U.S. Route 20 at that intersection was a four-lane divided highway running generally east and west; State Route 4 was a two-lane highway running generally north and south. The intersection was controlled by a traffic light.[1]

The occupants of the automobile were returning home from a high school outing when their car was struck by the truck. Joseph Slabach, the driver of the truck, was returning home after making a delivery for his employer, Elcona Homes Corporation. It is not disputed that Slabach was operating the truck in the course of his employment for Elcona Homes Corporation.

A complaint invoking the diversity jurisdiction of the district court and filed by the administrators of the estates of the four deceased passengers of the Valiant was consolidated for trial with a similar complaint brought on behalf of the seriously injured passenger, Cindy Baker. Named as defendants were Slabach and Elcona Homes Corporation.

The plaintiffs' causes of action were based on the alleged negligence of the defendant Slabach. The primary factual issue in the lawsuit was which vehicle had the right-of-way at the time it entered the intersection. Since Slabach testified that he could not see the light because he was blinded by the sun, and since Cindy Baker had no recollection of the accident, there was no direct eyewitness testimony concerning this fact and the jury's resolution of the issue had to depend upon circumstantial evidence and such inferences as could be made from it. The burden of proof, of course, rested upon the plaintiffs. A jury trial resulted in a judgment in favor of the defendants; the plaintiffs appeal. We affirm.

I

The principal issue upon appeal concerns the admission into evidence of the police accident report prepared by Sgt. John N. Hendrickson, a twenty-eight

---

737 F.2d 779 (8th Cir. 1984); Lloyd v. American Export Lines, 580 F.2d 1179 (3d Cir.) (other parts of the same opinion set out in Chapter 4D2, infra), cert. denied, 439 U.S. 969 (1978).

1. The traffic light at the intersection was controlled by "sensors" or trip signals. Since U.S. Route 20 was the more heavily traveled highway, the signal system was designed so that if there was no traffic approaching the intersection on State Route 4, the signal controlling U.S. Route 20 would remain a constant green until a vehicle on State Route 4 crossed the sensors. Thus the signal's "rest" position was normally green for Route 20 and red for Route 4. According to the testimony, when a vehicle approaching the intersection southbound on State Route 4 crossed its sensor, and if no vehicle had crossed the sensor on U.S. Route 20 in the last six seconds, the traffic signal for U.S. Route 20 would immediately change from a green to an amber light and would remain amber for a period of four seconds while the signal for State Route 4 would remain red. Thereafter, the signal for U.S. Route 20 would change from amber to red so that both highways received red signals for a period of one second. After the expiration of one second, the signal controlling State Route 4 would change from red to green, while the signal for U.S. Route 20 remained red. Thus when the signal system is in the "rest" position, a minimum of four seconds would elapse between the moment that a vehicle on State Route 4 crossed its sensor until the signal controlling U.S. Route 20 changed to red. However, if a vehicle had crossed the sensor on U.S. Route 20 within six seconds prior to the time that the vehicle on State Route 4 passed its sensor, then a period of time, to a maximum of six seconds, would elapse between the crossing

year veteran of the Ohio State Highway Patrol. Hendrickson, as assistant post commander, was on duty at the Norwalk Post when the accident occurred and, upon receiving the accident report, sped directly to the scene, arriving approximately six minutes after the collision.

Sgt. Hendrickson was called as a witness by the defense, although he had been subpoenaed but not called by the plaintiffs. He testified at length about the physical circumstances at the accident scene, including the measurements taken and careful descriptions of the locations of the vehicles and physical markings, refreshing his recollection from time to time from the police accident report. He further testified to having visited the defendant Slabach at the hospital and to having taken a statement from him in which Slabach, while admitting that because of the sunlight he could not see the color of the traffic light controlling the intersection, described the location and speed of the Valiant when he first observed it emerging from behind a house located on the northeast corner of the intersection. Sgt. Hendrickson also identified a diagram of the accident scene on which were placed, on transparent overlays, the locations of the two vehicles at the point of impact and as they came to rest, calculated by the sergeant from his investigative materials and from his use of vector analysis.

While Sgt. Hendrickson was examined and cross-examined at length concerning the factual data which he incorporated in the accident report and the vector analysis he employed, he was not questioned concerning any opinion he might have as to who had the right-of-way, although he had qualified as an expert in accident reconstruction and although the plaintiffs had, in their case-in-chief, employed similarly an accident reconstruction expert who opined that the light was green for the Valiant at the time it entered the intersection.

After Sgt. Hendrickson had left the stand, however, the defense introduced the police accident report into evidence, over the hearsay objection of plaintiffs. Plaintiffs particularly objected to Sgt. Hendrickson's record of the statement of defendant Slabach[3] and to Sgt. Hendrickson's notations concerning the fault for the accident. The report included the observation that "apparently unit #2 [the Valiant] entered the intersection against a red light." Likewise, on the same page of the accident report under "contributing circumstances," Sgt. Hendrickson had checked the box provided on the form for failure of vehicle #2 [the Valiant] to yield the right-of-way and had also checked the boxes next to "driver preoccupation" for drivers of both the truck and the Valiant.

In admitting the accident report and the addenda to it, the district judge appears to have concluded that the report was admissible as a recorded recollection under FRE 803(5).[4] We conclude, however, that the report was more properly admissible as a public record under [FRE 803(8)].

---

of the sensor on State Route 4 [and] the instant that the signal for U.S. Route 20 changed to amber.

3. [Slabach said he was traveling west on U.S. 20 at a speed of fifty to fifty-five miles per hour and first saw the Valiant southbound on State Route 4 "when it came out from behind the house at the corner." It "looked just like a flash," moving "about 50-60 m.p.h." Slabach could not tell whether he had a green light because "the sun was in my eyes," but other traffic "was moving" eastbound on U.S. 20 and Slabach "saw no traffic stopped" and no cross-traffic on State Route 4 apart from the Valiant.—Eds.]

4. . . . Reliance upon Rule 803(5) is, in our opinion, insufficient here to support admissibility against the claim that it was hearsay. The parties dispute whether Sgt. Hendrickson in fact had

. . . A police report is, in our judgment, a "public record and report" within the meaning of the first part of Rule 803(8). The direct observations and recorded data of Sgt. Hendrickson in the course of his investigation which were placed upon the report clearly are "matters observed pursuant to duty imposed by law as to which matters there was a duty to report," under Rule 803(8)(B), and are thereby not inadmissible under the hearsay rule. The principal concerns, however, are whether Slabach's statement as recorded in the police report and whether the findings of Sgt. Hendrickson as to the color of the light at the time of the accident and his markings on the boxes relative to the contributing circumstances of the accident were properly allowed to be put before the jury as substantive evidence.

We address first the question of whether the finding that the Valiant ran the red light is a "factual finding" within the meaning of Rule 803(8)(C). We conclude that it is.

In enacting the Federal Rules of Evidence, the House Judiciary Committee adopted a narrow interpretation of "factual findings." . . . The Senate, however, disagreed with this narrow interpretation. . . . While the Conference Committee finally adopted the House's version of this Rule, both the House and Senate versions employed the term "factual findings," and the differing views as to the meaning of that term were not resolved. The Advisory Committee Notes, however, accept "evaluative reports" as being within the meaning of factual findings under Rule 803(8)(C).

Generally the courts have been liberal in determining admissibility under Rule 803(8). Thus in Melville v. American Home Assurance Company, 443 F. Supp. 1064 (E.D. Pa. 1977), the court allowed into evidence two FAA Air Worthiness directives, which impugned the mechanical safety of the model of plane which had been involved in that lawsuit. In admitting the reports, the district court took note of the conflict between the House and Senate interpretations of "factual findings," and agreed with the Senate Judiciary Committee that the Advisory Committee's methodology provided adequate guidance and safeguards for admissibility of such reports under Rule 803(8)(C).

In United States v. School District of Ferndale, Michigan, 577 F.2d 1339 (6th Cir. 1978), Judge Celebrezze reversed a determination of the district court that the findings of an HEW hearing examiner were inadmissible hearsay, untrustworthy and did not fall within the exception of Rule 803(8)(C) since they were not factual findings. There our court held that the district judge should have received under Rule 803(8) as evidence the findings of an HEW hearing examiner that a school had been established and maintained as a black school for segregatory purposes and that the district court had erred in excluding the findings as hearsay and as untrustworthy. The court stated: . . .

"insufficient recollection" within the meaning of the rule and a review of the record is convincing that Sgt. Hendrickson was able to remember basically what was in the report, although he refreshed himself from time to time. There was no testimony that he needed the report to testify fully and accurately as to its contents. More important, however, is the provision of Rule 803(5) that a memorandum or record may not itself be received as an exhibit unless offered by an adverse party. Since the record was introduced by the defendants who themselves called Sgt. Hendrickson, it would not have been admissible under this subsection.

We agree with the United States that the HEW findings come within the scope of Rule 803(8)(C) as they are "factual findings resulting from an investigation made pursuant to authority granted by law." The investigation vs. adjudication distinction fashioned by the district court finds no support in the rule or the cases interpreting it. The Supreme Court has construed Rule 803(8)(C) to apply in an analogous situation. Clearly, the HEW proceedings were an "investigation" into the state of affairs in the Ferndale schools within the plain meaning of that word. That the proceedings could also be labeled a "quasi-judicial hearing" is of no consequence in this regard.

Applying the rule and its background to the facts here, it is apparent that whether the light was red or green for one driver or the other at the time of the accident is distinctly a factual finding within the meaning of the rule, and certainly far more so than the HEW finding in *Ferndale*, which, we believe, is essentially an evaluative opinion resulting from evidence. It is also clear from the construction of the rule itself that factual findings admissible under Rule 803(8)(C) may be those which are made by the preparer of the report from disputed evidence, as contrasted to those facts which are "matters observed pursuant to duty imposed by law as to which matters there was a duty to report" called for under Rule 803(8)(B). The more conclusory nature of the HEW report, however, did not disturb our court in *Ferndale*, and it was concerned rather with the district judge's determination that the report lacked trustworthiness.

In determining whether the "sources of information or other circumstances" indicate lack of trustworthiness, the Advisory Committee Notes list four suggested factors for consideration: (1) the timeliness of the investigation; (2) the special skill or experience of the official; (3) whether a hearing was held on [and?] the level at which conducted, and (4) possible motivational problems. [Court quotes ACN to FRE 803(8).]

Because he did not rely on Rule 803(8), the trial judge did not make a specific finding of trustworthiness. We do not, however, consider the omission fatal. . . . The burden was upon the plaintiffs to show that the report was inadmissible because its sources of information or other circumstances indicated a lack of trustworthiness. That burden was not met here.

First, the report was timely because the police arrived at the scene of the accident minutes after it occurred. An investigation was begun immediately and although the final report was not issued for two months, a continuing effort was made to determine the facts.

Second, Sgt. Hendrickson, as a State Highway Patrolman with 28 years on the force, had investigated hundreds or even thousands of automobile accidents and his expertise and skill in accident reconstruction do not appear seriously to have been challenged. His attention to detail and his testimony concerning vector analysis make it apparent that he possessed special skill and experience in the investigation of automobile accidents.

The third factor concerns whether or not a hearing was held, and of course, no formal hearing was held in this case. The Rule, however, makes no reference to such a requirement; the factor appears only to be one of those suggested by the Advisory Committee. The evidence showed that Sgt. Hendrickson gathered all the evidence that he could from all sources. There is no indication that he neglected any one source or impermissibly preferred one over another. We do not believe that a formal hearing is a sine qua non of admissibility under Rule 803(8)(C) when other indicia of trustworthiness are present.

Finally, there is no indication that the report was made with any improper motive. Sgt. Hendrickson was completely independent of both parties and his testimony at the trial rather fully and convincingly demonstrated his impartiality.

We, therefore, conclude that the sergeant's own objective findings of fact, specifically his finding that the light was red for traffic approaching the intersection from the north, were admissible. The plaintiffs' objections go not so much to admissibility as to weight and credibility, matters which are essentially for the jury to consider. It is true, of course, that Sgt. Hendrickson was not directly questioned concerning the color of the light at the time of the accident. Nevertheless, examination and cross-examination did corroborate the accident report in most other respects and there is no showing that the plaintiffs' right of cross-examination was restricted in any way. That they did not choose to do so was no doubt a matter of proper trial strategy but cannot affect the admissibility of the report in the first place.

Likewise the trial judge carefully instructed the jury concerning the admissibility of opinion testimony and no complaint can be made that those instructions were unfair or inadequate.

The appellants also challenge the admissibility of the report insofar as it contained the statement of the driver Slabach. This would not, in our judgment, be admissible under Rule 803(8). The statement was neither an observation nor a factual finding of the police officer, although Slabach's statement, with other evidence, no doubt had a bearing upon the ultimate factual finding made by the officer. Nonetheless we need not determine to what extent, where factual findings are admissible, the underlying data considered by the investigating officer are also admissible under Rule 803(8). It appears that under Rule 801, Slabach's statement was not hearsay. [Court sets out FRE 801(d)(1)(B).]

Slabach was called for cross-examination by the plaintiffs in their case-in-chief. He was vigorously cross-examined about his recollection of the accident, particularly concerning when he had first seen the Valiant. The questioning of Slabach implied that his testimony in court differed from a statement he had made earlier, and therefore, it was proper under Rule 801 to introduce his prior statement given to the police officer as showing that, in fact, the testimony he gave at trial was consistent with prior statements and was not a recent fabrication or result of an improper influence or motive. Thus, Slabach's statement as appended to the police report was not hearsay, and thereby not inadmissible under Rule 802.

[Any error in allowing Hendrickson to testify that he issued no traffic citation to Slabach was harmless. The reviewing court rejects other claims of error and affirms the judgment below.]

NOTES ON PUBLIC RECORDS IN CIVIL CASES

1. To what extent does Officer Hendrickson's report fit FRE 803(8)(B)? To what extent does it fit FRE 803(8)(C)? What does the court mean toward

the end when it says that what Joseph Slabach said to Hendrickson "would not . . . be admissible" under FRE 803(8)? Isn't that what Elcona Homes and Slabach proved by Hendrickson's report? Did they need the report to prove that point? The court comments that Hendrickson was a "twenty-eight year veteran of the Ohio State Highway Patrol" and "qualified as an expert in accident reconstruction." What difference does that make?

2.   A famous New York decision held that a police report of an accident was not within the business records exception to the extent it rested on statements obtained by the officer from onlookers. See Johnson v. Lutz, 170 N.E. 517 (N.Y. 1930). The court reached that conclusion even though the statute said that circumstances like "lack of personal knowledge by the entrant or maker" of the report affect "weight" rather than "admissibility." *Baker* applies the public records exception rather than the one for business records. Could *Baker* be decided the same way under the business records exception contained in FRE 803(6)? Which exception properly applies here—FRE 803(6) or 803(8)?

3.   Should the term "factual findings" in FRE 803(8)(C) be construed to exclude interpretive conclusions like Officer Hendrickson's? The legislative material conflicts (compare the Advisory Committee's Note with the House and Senate Committee Reports). In its 1988 decision in a wrongful death suit against an aircraft manufacturer, the Supreme Court adopted a "broader interpretation" admitting "factually based conclusions or opinions." There the Court approved a report by a Navy Lieutenant Commander offered by the defense suggesting that the cause of a crash during a training mission was pilot error. See Beech Aircraft Corp. v. Rainey, 488 U.S. 153 (1988) (language of Rule yields "no clear answer" and legislative history is source of problem rather than solution; in view of "analytical difficulty" in separating facts from conclusions, concern over applying the provision too loosely may be answered by carefully considering trustworthiness and applying other safeguards relating to relevance and prejudice; ultimate safeguard is opponent's right "to present evidence tending to contradict or diminish the weight" of official conclusions; Court quotes *Elcona Homes* as approving reports resting on "disputed evidence"). See also Ellis v. International Playtex, 745 F.2d 292 (4th Cir. 1984), and Kehm v. Procter & Gamble Manufacturing Co., 724 F.2d 613 (8th Cir. 1983) (approving use of CDC findings on cause of toxic shock syndrome).

4.   Some states adopting rules based on the federal model either leave out the substance of FRE 803(8)(C) (Florida, Michigan, and Ohio) or add language that would bar use of reports such as that by Officer Hendrickson. Provisions adopted by Arkansas, Iowa, and Vermont, for example, state that "investigative reports by police and other law enforcement personnel" are "not within this exception." New York still excludes police accident reports based on eyewitness statements, and some decisions in other states do likewise. See Toll v. State, 299 N.Y.S.2d 589, 592 (N.Y. App. Div. 1969) (error to admit report by state trooper because he did not see accident; there was "no proof that whoever gave him the facts had a business duty to do so" and "no other hearsay exception" applies to statements by outsiders). See also Quaglio v. Tomaselli, 470 N.Y.S.2d 427 (App. Div. 1984) (error to permit plaintiff to offer in evidence a police accident report containing statements by eyewitness and officer's conclusion as to how accident occurred); Hewitt v. Grand Trunk Western R.R., 333 N.W.2d 264 (Mich. App. 1983) (police accident report concluding, on basis of

eyewitness statements, that decedent who was struck by train had committed suicide, not within FRE 803(8)); Belitz v. Suhr, 303 N.W.2d 284, 286-287 (Neb. 1981) (in auto accident case, error to permit defendant to adduce from police officer testimony as to statements by defendant which officer placed in accident report); Wallin v. Insurance Co. of North America, 596 S.W.2d 716 (Ark. Ct. App. 1980) (similar to *Hewitt,* where decedent was found dead of gunshot wound in motel room).

UNITED STATES v. OATES
United States Court of Appeals for the Second Circuit
560 F.2d 45 (1977)

WATERMAN, J.

This is an appeal from a judgment of the United States District Court for the Eastern District of New York convicting appellant, following a six-day jury trial, of possession of heroin with intent to distribute, and of conspiracy to commit that substantive offense. . . .

[In an incredibly prolix 39-page opinion, the court first upholds the denial of the defense motion to suppress a "certain white powdery substance" suspected to be heroin, which was seized from defendant's person at the time of his arrest. Then it considers the use of documents generated in a government laboratory as proof that the "white powdery substance" was in fact heroin.

At trial, the government sought to prove that the substance was heroin by means of a handwritten worksheet and an official report prepared by Milton Weinberg, whom the court describes as "a retired United States Customs Service chemist" who apparently did occasional work for the Service and performed laboratory tests on the powder found on the defendant. The government planned to call Mr. Weinberg to testify, but on the day of his scheduled appearance the assistant U.S. Attorney prosecuting the case explained to the trial court that Mrs. Weinberg had said that her husband was "very sick" with "some type of bronchial infection."

Hence the government introduced the worksheet and report indirectly, by means of testimony by Shirley Harrington, described as "another Customs chemist" acquainted with the "regular practices and procedures" employed by the Service in analyzing unknown substances. Harrington testified that she herself had conducted many tests to identify heroin, that she had testified many times before on such matters, that she did not know Weinberg personally but did recognize his handwriting, and that she could ascertain from the worksheet what steps Weinberg had taken in analyzing the substance. On this basis, the trial court admitted Weinberg's worksheet and report, which indicated that the substance was heroin.]

While the problem presented is not susceptible of any facile solution, we believe that, on balance, appellant's emphasis on the importance of FRE 803(8) is well-founded. . . . [A]lthough as a general rule there is no question that hearsay evidence failing to meet the requirements of one exception may nonetheless satisfy the standards of another exception, . . . we agree with appellant that both the language of Rule 803(8) and the congressional intent . . . have impact that extends beyond the immediate confines of exception (8) itself. We therefore regard FRE 803(8) as the proper starting point for our evidentiary analysis.

That the chemist's report and worksheet could not satisfy the requirements of the "public records and reports" exception seems evident merely from examining, on its face, the language of FRE 803(8). [The court quotes the Rule.] While there may be no sharp demarcation between the records covered by exception 8(B) and those referenced in exception 8(C), and indeed there may in some cases be actual overlap, we conclude without hesitation that surely the language of item (C) is applicable to render the chemist's documents inadmissible as evidence in this case, and they might also be within the ambit of the terminology of item (B), a claim appellant argues to us persuasively.

It is manifest from the face of item (C) that "factual findings resulting from an investigation made pursuant to authority granted by law" are not shielded from the exclusionary effect of the hearsay rule by "the public records exception" if the government seeks to have those "factual findings" admitted *against* the accused in a criminal case. It seems indisputable to us that the chemist's official report and worksheet in the case at bar can be characterized as reports of "factual findings resulting from an investigation made pursuant to authority granted by law." The "factual finding" in each instance, the conclusion of the chemist that the substance analyzed was heroin, obviously is the product of an "investigation," supposedly involving on the part of the chemist employment of various techniques of scientific analysis. Furthermore, in view of its reliance on the chemist's report at trial and its representation to the district court that "chemical analys[e]s of unidentified substances are indeed a regularly conducted activity of the Customs laboratory of Customs chemists," the government here is surely in no position to dispute the fact that the analyses regularly performed by United States Customs Service chemists on substances lawfully seized by Customs officers are performed pursuant to authority granted by law.

Though with less confidence, we believe that the chemist's documents might also fail to achieve status as public records under FRE 803(8)(B) because they are records of "matters observed by police officers and other law enforcement personnel." . . . If this characterization is justified, the difficult question would be whether the chemists making the observations could be regarded as "other law enforcement personnel." We think this phraseology must be read broadly enough to make its prohibitions against the use of government-generated reports in criminal cases coterminous with the analogous prohibitions contained in FRE 803(8)(C). We would thus construe "other law enforcement personnel" to include, at the least, any officer or employee of a governmental agency which has law enforcement responsibilities. Applying such a standard to the case at bar, we easily conclude that full-time chemists of the United States Customs Service are "law enforcement personnel." The chemist in this case was employed by the Customs Service, a governmental agency which had clearly defined law enforcement authority in the field of illegal narcotics trafficking; the officers who actually seized the suspected contraband were employed by the Customs Service, and the unidentified substance was delivered by them to a laboratory operated by the Customs Service. The unidentified substance was then subjected to analysis by a chemist, one of whose regular functions is to test substances seized from suspected narcotics violators. Chemists at the laboratory are, without question, important participants in the prosecutorial effort. As well as analyzing substances for the express purpose of ascertaining whether the substances are contraband, and if so, participating in eventual prosecution of narcotics offenders, the chemists are also expected to be familiar with the need for establishing the whereabouts of confiscated drugs at all times from seizure until trial. Moreover, the role of the chemist typically does not terminate upon completion of the chemical analysis and submission of the resulting report but participation continues until the chemist has testified as an important prosecution witness at trial. Indeed, Mrs. Harrington had herself testified "probably a hundred or so" times. Also of some interest perhaps is a remark made by Mrs. Harrington which indicates that the Customs chemists do not mentally disassociate themselves from those who undoubtedly are law enforcement personnel. After chemical analyses are performed, according to Mrs. Harrington, "the material [is] returned to the agent or *our* Customs officer." (Emphasis supplied.) In short, these reports are not "made by persons and for purposes unconnected with a criminal case [but rather they are a direct] result of a test made for the specific purpose of convicting the defendant and conducted by agents of the executive branch, the very department of government which seeks defendant's conviction." State v. Larochelle, 297 A.2d 223, 228 (N.H. 1972) (dissenting opinion). It would therefore seem that if the chemist's report and worksheet here can be deemed to set forth "matters observed," the documents would fail to satisfy the requirements of exception FRE 803(8) for the chemist must be included within the category of "other law enforcement personnel."

    Our conclusion that the chemist's report and worksheet do not satisfy the standards of FRE 803(8) comports perfectly with what we discern to be clear legislative intent not only to exclude such documents from the scope of FRE 803(8) but from the scope of FRE 803(6) as well. . . . [A]n overriding concern of the Advisory Committee was that the rules be formulated so as to avoid impinging upon a criminal defendant's right to confront the witnesses against him. . . . This preoccupation with preserving the confrontation rights of criminal defendants was shared by a Congress which established enhanced protection for those rights by substantially amending the proposed language . . . [to add the phrase] "excluding, however, in criminal cases matters observed by police officers and other law enforcement personnel." In the debate that followed the offer of this amendment, the accused's right to confront the witnesses against him was advanced as the impetus for the proposal. Speaking in support of the amendment, Representative Elizabeth Holtzman understood one of its purposes to be to "[reaffirm] the right of cross examination to the accused." In a similar vein, Representative Dennis . . . confirmed that this was the intent of the amendment by emphasizing that the amendment pertained to "criminal cases, and in a criminal case the defendant should be confronted with the accuser to give him the chance to cross examine." Following the addition of this language excluding reports reciting matters observed by law enforcement personnel, the Senate added to the pending legislation a proposed FRE 804(b)(5) which would have rendered the exclusion of such reports from the scope of FRE 803(8)(B) ineffective in the event the author of the report was "unavailable" to testify. This attempt to emasculate the Dennis amendment proved to be abortive, however, for the Committee of Conference removed it from the pending legislation.

The discussion in the preceding paragraphs describes *why* Congress decided to take the approach it did with regard to the use of "evaluative" reports under FRE 803(8)(C) and reports of law enforcement personnel under FRE 803(8)(B). The *result* Congress intended was the absolute inadmissibility of records of this nature, and that this was, indeed, the result which Congress believed it had achieved by Rules 803(8)(B) and (C), could not have been articulated with any more clarity than it was by Representative William L. Hungate. . . . He informed the House that the Committee of Conference had rejected the Senate's attempt to create a new hearsay exception which would have permitted admission of police reports authored by officers unavailable to testify. He explained the meaning of the remaining related provisions:

> As the rules of evidence now stand, police and law enforcement reports are not admissible against defendants in criminal cases. This is made quite clear by the provisions of rule 803(8)(B) and (C).

This unequivocal language shows that it was Representative Hungate's understanding, and he was as familiar with the legislation as anyone else in Congress, that the language retained in FRE 803(8)(B) and (C) meant that those provisions had the *effect* of rendering absolutely inadmissible against defendants in criminal cases the "police reports" of item (B) and the "evaluative reports" of item (C).

Representative Hungate's remarks would not be comprehensively all-encompassing, of course, if the police and evaluative reports denied the benefit of qualifying under FRE 803(8)(B) and (C) were considered eligible for qualification under FRE 803(6), the so-called business records exception, or under any other exception to the hearsay rule. In that event, such reports, upon qualifying under FRE 803(6) or any other exception, although they would not at that point be automatically admissible, see FRE 803, 402, would be one step closer to achieving admission, and would not be, contrary to Representative Hungate's understanding, definitely "not admissible against defendants in criminal cases."

Indeed, this very question of whether so-called police reports disqualified under FRE 803(8) could nonetheless gain eventual admission by first satisfying the standards of some other hearsay exception was expressly raised by Representative Elizabeth Holtzman. . . . She stated:

> [T]he conference committee rejected a proposed rule from the Senate which would have allowed police reports to be admitted as substantive evidence. However, by simultaneously adopting this open-ended hearsay exception, the conference report opens a "back door" to these police reports and negates the conference committee's prior prohibition against admission of such evidence. . . .

Representative David Dennis . . . responded, politely but bluntly:

> I would like to say in answer to my friend, the gentlewoman from New York, that this business of using a police report, if a policeman is unavailable, was not in the rules as they came to us. That was written in by the Senate, and we struck

it out in the conference, I am very happy to say. It was a terrible idea. But since we did take it out in the conference, and since it is gone, and since we insisted that it go, I cannot see how anybody could suggest that introducing such a report is possible or a thing that could be done under these rules; because the Senators put it in and we took it out in conference, and that is the legislative history.

While Representative Dennis did not specifically allude to evaluative reports or item (C), as did Representative Hungate, we think it clear that this was only because his response was tailored to the precise question propounded by Representative Holtzman. There is absolutely no reason to doubt that, if specifically asked, he would have answered that government-generated "evaluative reports" were similarly disqualified under *any* exception to the hearsay rule because, "as Representative Hungate's statement indicates, the prohibitory language of 803(8)(B), added on the floor of the House should be read in conjunction with the more carefully drafted parallel provision of 803(8)(C)."

It is, of course, of critical importance that it was with the explanations of Representatives Hungate and Dennis freshly in mind that the full House of Representatives on the very day these remarks were uttered finally approved the Federal Rules of Evidence. We thus think it manifest that it was the clear intention of Congress to make evaluative and law enforcement reports absolutely inadmissible against defendants in criminal cases. Just as importantly, it must have been the unquestionable belief of Congress that the language of FRE 803(8)(B) and (C) accomplished that very result.

Despite what we perceive to be clear congressional intent that reports not qualifying under FRE 803(8)(B) or (C) should, and would, be inadmissible against defendants in criminal cases, the government completely ignores those provisions, as well as FRE 803(24), another hearsay exception upon which it relied at trial,[30] and argues instead that the chemist's report and worksheet in the case at bar fall clearly within the literal terms of the modified business records exception to the hearsay rule contained in FRE 803(6), entitled "*Records of regularly conducted activity.*" . . .

In light of this paramount importance of legislative intent, we shall now attempt to ascertain the legislative intent underlying FRE 803(6). . . . In the case at bar our task is considerably facilitated by the presence of both explicit explanations of the *meaning* of relevant provisions of the Federal Rules of Evidence, and an abundant supply of information relating to one important *purpose* in drafting those provisions as they were drafted.

As already mentioned, Representative William Hungate, in presenting the

---

30. We agree with the government's appeal strategy. We think it clear that any reliance on FRE 803(24) or reliance on FRE 803(24)'s counterpart, FRE 804(b)(5), would be a mistaken reliance. Both of these hearsay exceptions, the first pertaining to the use of extra-judicial statements of available declarants, and the second concerning the use of extra-judicial statements made by unavailable declarants, [require pretrial notice]. Although we stress that it was through no fault of his own, the Assistant United States Attorney did not in advance of trial inform his adversary of the government's intention to offer the hearsay statements of the chemist Weinberg. Furthermore, our review of the relevant portions of the transcript leaves the distinct impression that prior to the calling of witness Harrington to the stand, the defense was unaware that the chemist's report and worksheet would be offered in lieu of the testimony of Weinberg himself. In other words, not only did the defense not receive notice in advance of trial, it did not receive any notice at all until the actual appearance of witness Harrington in the late afternoon of the fourth day of trial. . . .

report of the Committee of Conference to the House of Representatives, left no doubt that it was the belief of the Committee of Conference that under the new Federal Rules of Evidence the *effect* of FRE 803(8)(B) and (C) was to render law enforcement reports and evaluative reports inadmissible against defendants in criminal cases. It is thus clear that the only way to construe FRE 803(6) so that it is reconcilable with this intended effect is to interpret FRE 803(6) and the other hearsay exceptions in such a way that police and evaluative reports not satisfying the standards of FRE 803(8)(B) and (C) may not qualify for admission under FRE 803(6) or any of the other exceptions to the hearsay rule. That Congress must have understood that all the hearsay exceptions would be construed in light of the carefully drafted proscriptions of FRE 803(8) is also demonstrated, as discussed earlier in this opinion, by Representative Dennis' categorical remarks to that effect. . . .

[Court concludes that material within FRE 803(8)(B) and (C)] cannot satisfy the standards of any hearsay exception if those reports are sought to be introduced against the accused. . . .

NOTES ON USING LAB REPORTS IN CRIMINAL CASES

1. Does a report like the one prepared by Milton Weinberg describe a "matter observed" or a "factual finding"? Why is a chemist like Weinberg embraced in the phrase "law enforcement personnel"? Often law enforcement agencies retain private laboratories to perform ballistics tests, tissue and blood analysis, and chemical analysis of substances like the white powder found on Paul Oates. Does that bring a chemist in such a laboratory within the term "law enforcement personnel"? Or should a private laboratory report be analyzed under FRE 803(6)? For a modern decision following *Oates* in excluding crime lab reports, see State v. Sandoval-Tena, 71 P.3d 1075 (Idaho, 2003) (excluding lab report identifying substance seized from defendant as methamphetamine).

2. If Milton Weinberg had testified, do you think he would have remembered the analysis he ran on the bag of white powder? If not, does *Oates* mean his report could not come in under FRE 803(5) as past recollection recorded? See United States v. Sawyer, 607 F.2d 1190 (7th Cir. 1979) (IRS agent's report properly admitted under FRE 803(5) when he could not recall conversation, and use restrictions in FRE 803(8)(B) and (C) did not apply), cert. denied, 445 U.S. 943 (1980); United States v. Marshall, 532 F.2d 1279 (9th Cir. 1976) (police chemist's analysis of alleged heroin properly admitted under FRE 803(5)). Do the use restrictions in FRE 803(8) prevent the prosecutor from using FRE 803(9) or (10)? See United States v. Yakobov, 712 F.2d 20 (2d Cir. 1983) (certificate from Bureau of Alcohol, Tobacco, and Firearms could be admitted under FRE 803(10) despite *Oates*, to prove that defendant lacked a permit—but not in this case because certificate misspelled defendant's name). If the prosecutor can resort these other exceptions, what is left of the use restrictions in FRE 803(8)?

3. Many states have statutory provisions or rules relating to crime laboratory reports. Typically they require notice from the prosecutor, and then they provide that the defense is entitled to subpoena the technician, or they give

defendants a chance to object to the report (in which case apparently the technician is expected to testify). Oregon, for example, has a provision of the former kind that applies specifically in drug trials where the prosecutor must prove the chemical nature of controlled substances. See Or. Stat. §475.235. Kansas has a statute of the latter kind, providing that a certified forensic report prepared by the state bureau of investigation is admissible if the prosecutor satisfies a notice requirement, except that the defense may serve an objection to the use of the report, in which case it "shall [still] be admitted" unless it appears that the conclusions stated in it "will be contested at trial." Kan. Stat. §22-3437. Decisions in state courts conflict on the validity of such provisions. Compare State v. Crow, 974 P.2d 100, 111 (Kan. 1999) (upholding Kansas statute) with Miller v. State, 472 S.E.2d 74 (Ga. 1996) (striking down similar statute as unconstitutional). And compare State v. Hancock, 854 P.2d 926 (Or. 1993) (upholding Oregon provision) with State v. Clark, 964 P.2d 766 (Mont. 1998) (striking down similar Montana rule, as violating state constitutional right to confront witnesses and due process rights).

4. Should laboratory reports be admissible against the accused in criminal cases? Compare State v. Smith, 323 S.E.2d 316 (N.C. 1984) (approving use of report on blood alcohol content, offered in prosecution for drunk driving) with State v. Flynn, 494 A.2d 350 (N.J. Super. 1985) (such report inadmissible in that context). And see Giannelli, The Admissibility of Laboratory Reports in Criminal Trials: The Reliability of Scientific Proof, 49 Ohio St. L.J. 671 (1988); Imwinkelried, The Constitutionality of Introducing Evaluative Laboratory Reports Against Criminal Defendants, 30 Hast. L. J. 621 (1979).

5. Whether laboratory reports can be admitted against defendants in criminal cases without running afoul of the Confrontation Clause remains to be seen. Under a standard that stressed "reliability," it was sometimes plausible to argue that such reports pass muster, but under a constitutional standard that restricts use of out-of-court "testimonial" statements, it is possible that laboratory reports must be excluded, at least where the preparer does not testify. See Crawford v. Washington, 124 S.Ct. 1354 (2004), and the discussion of the constitutional standard in Chapter 4G, infra.

NOTES ON USING OTHER KINDS OF PUBLIC RECORDS IN CRIMINAL CASES

1. In a trial for possessing cocaine and heroin, the government offers computer data cards from the Treasury Enforcement Communications System (TECS), which were generated by a customs official at the San Ysidro border crossing between California and Mexico. The official punches into his computer the license numbers of cars crossing the border, and the data indicate that defendant's car crossed back and forth on the night when he told customs agents he was on a double date in Los Angeles. Admissible under FRE 803(8)? See United States v. Puente, 826 F.2d 1415, 1417-1418 (5th Cir. 1987); United States v. Orozco, 590 F.2d 789 (9th Cir.), cert. denied, 439 U.S. 1049 (1979) (both indicating yes). Can *Puente* and *Orozco* be squared with *Oates*? Should TECS records be admitted in such cases? For an extended critique of government information systems, see Garcia, "Garbage In, Gospel Out": Criminal Discovery,

Computer Reliability, and the Constitution, 38 UCLA L. Rev. 1043, 1087-1088 (1991) (arguing that *Orozco* should have asked whether agents double-check entries and whether anyone relies on such records on a regular basis). See also United States v. Brown, 315 F.3d 929, 931-932 (8th Cir. 2003) (in counterfeiting trial, admitting computerized database operated by Secret Service showing that bills with certain serial numbers appeared in Detroit; such information is "initially gathered" by law enforcement, and "routinely entered" by data entry personnel; database was not assembled "in anticipation of" defendant's trial).

2.   Are all public agents who secure public compliance with law included in the term "law enforcement personnel"? See United States v. Hansen, 583 F.2d 325 (7th Cir.) (city building inspector was not included, even though noncompliance with code may result in criminal conviction), cert. denied, 439 U.S. 912 (1978); United States v. Arias, 575 F.2d 253 (9th Cir.) (in perjury prosecution, reporter's transcript was properly admitted under FRE 803(8) to prove defendant's testimony and show that he was sworn), cert. denied, 439 U.S. 868 (1978).

3.   What if the accused offers a police report as defense evidence? See State v. Bertul, 664 P.2d 1181, 1185-1186 (Utah 1983) (under state exceptions for business records and public records, approving police booking sheet offered by defense to prove that defendant was intoxicated). What if the accused offers a police report under FRE 803(8)(B) as proof that the alleged victim made a statement to the investigating officer that is inconsistent with his trial testimony? See United States v. Smith, 521 F.2d 957 (D.C. App. 1975) (admit).

NOTES ON THE TRUSTWORTHINESS FACTOR

1.   The Advisory Committee's Note to FRE 803(8) lists the following factors affecting the assessment of trustworthiness under FRE 803(8)(C): timeliness of the investigation; use of hearing procedures; skill and motivation of investigator.

2.   What other factors affect trustworthiness? See Zenith Radio Corp. v. Matsushita Electric Industries Co., 505 F. Supp. 1125 (D.C. Pa.), aff'd in part, 723 F.2d 238 (3d Cir. 1983) (suggesting as additional criteria (1) the finality of the agency findings, (2) the extent to which findings rest on inadmissible evidence supplied by interested parties, (3) where hearings are employed, the extent to which appropriate safeguards are applied and observed, (4) the extent to which there is an ascertainable record on which findings are based, (5) the extent to which the findings express a policy judgment rather than a factual adjudication, (6) the extent to which findings rest upon findings by other bodies which may be suspect, and (7) where findings rest upon expert opinion, the extent to which the facts or data on which the opinion is based are reasonably relied on by experts in the field). See generally Note, The Trustworthiness of Government Evaluative Reports Under Federal Rules of Evidence 803(8)(C), 96 Harv. L. Rev. 492 (1982).

3.   Does the trustworthiness clause of FRE 803(8) apply to all public records or only to those in FRE 803(8)(C)?

4.   How should a court appraise the trustworthiness of an official report resting on conflicting statements gathered and considered by officials? See In

re Korean Air Lines Disaster, 932 F.2d 1475, 1482-1483 (D.C. Cir. 1991) (court properly admitted investigative report by international agency on what caused the Russian shoot-down of a commercial plane, despite defense claim that report was not trustworthy because it rested on Russian version of intercept); Moss v. Ole South Real Estate, Inc., 933 F.2d 1300, 1306-1308 (5th Cir. 1991) (in suit claiming racial discrimination in sale of real estate, magistrate over-stepped role in judging trustworthiness of public investigative report by considering credibility of information sources; court should focus on manner or "methodology," not credibility of sources; report may be excluded, however, if it lacks a reasonable basis, and court would *not* say bias of sources "may never render a report unreliable").

7. Learned Treatises

Traditionally learned treatises were usable only as impeaching evidence. Thus a party could cross-examine an expert about a treatise but not offer it as substantive evidence. Even this practice was restricted: Some courts permitted the cross-examiner only to ask about treatises on which the expert actually relied in his testimony; some permitted the cross-examiner to ask about the treatise of his choice if the expert relied on *any* treatise or to question him on treatises which he acknowledges as authoritative; some generously allowed the cross-examiner to ask about any treatise that could be established in some way as authoritative.

Under this scheme, even if the cross-examiner could point to a passage in a treatise tending to prove exactly what he wanted to prove at trial, he could use it only to argue that contrary testimony by the expert was wrong.

Four arguments supported the traditional approach. One was that technical material confuses jurors, who are likely to misread, misunderstand, and misapply it. Another was that such material may be too easily wrenched out of context, so that permitting substantive use would lead to unfair tactics. The third was that treatises are inferior to live testimony, meaning that live experts can shed more light on technical problems than authors. The fourth was that technical knowledge evolves so quickly that treatises are likely to convey obsolescent information.

Rule 803(18) rejects these arguments, permitting full use of a treatise where (1) it is shown to be "reliable authority" and (2) either the expert relies on it in direct examination or it is called to his attention on cross-examination.

NOTES ON LEARNED TREATISES

1. Why does FRE 803(18) permit treatises to be "read into evidence" but not "received as exhibits"? What exactly does the latter restriction mean?

2. To what extent should the exception be useful in medical malpractice cases? Compare Smith v. Knowles, 281 N.W.2d 653, 655-656 (Minn. 1979) (in suit against treating physician for wrongful death of pregnant woman and fetus after woman apparently went into eclamptic convulsions, passages from medical treatises offered during plaintiff's cross-examination of physician were "minimally sufficient" as substantive evidence "to establish the requisite standard of

care" but insufficient to prove departure from this standard or causation) with Heilman v. Snyder, 520 S.W.2d 321 (Ky. 1975) (in a malpractice suit against physician who failed to sterilize the skin of a patient before administering injections, approving receipt of treatise offered by defendant to prove that such sterilization is unnecessary).

3. Besides technical books, what does the exception embrace? See Alexander v. Conveyors & Dumpers, 731 F.2d 1221 (5th Cir. 1984) (safety codes); Dawson v. Chrysler Corp., 630 F.2d 950 (3d Cir. 1980) (crashworthiness reports prepared by private laboratory for Department of Transportation), cert. denied, 450 U.S. 959 (1981).

D. EXCEPTIONS—DECLARANT UNAVAILABLE

Continuing tradition, FRE 804 recognizes hearsay exceptions that may be invoked only if the declarant is unavailable as a witness. Statements within these exceptions are thought to be good enough to be admitted (certainly better than nothing), but not so good as live testimony by the declarant. FRE 804(b) sets out the five exceptions in this group. Most important are the ones for former testimony and declarations against interest, and these are taken up in this chapter in the order listed in the Rule.

Unavailability of the declarant alone does not by itself put an out-of-court statement into an exception. Recall that one approach to hearsay would reduce the doctrine to a rule of preference in which any statement by an unavailable declarant would be admissible if the only objection was that the statement was hearsay. But the Rules take another course, and unavailability helps a statement overcome a hearsay objection only if it fits one of the five exceptions in FRE 804(b).

Serious arguments are sometimes advanced that the unavailability requirement is either underbroad (more exceptions ought to require it) or overbroad (some that require it should not): In the *Inadi* case (quoted in Chapter 4B5, supra) the Supreme Court rejected a claim that the Constitution ought to require unavailability of the declarant as a condition of resorting to the coconspirator exception, and in People v. Spriggs, 389 P.2d 377 (Cal. 1964), the California Supreme Court said declarations against penal interest should be admissible regardless whether declarant is unavailable, but was overruled on this point by the California legislature. See Cal. Evidence Code §1230 (1965).

1. The Unavailability Requirement

As a glance at FRE 804(a) reveals, "unavailability as a witness" does not mean the declarant must be physically unobtainable—hiding or beyond reach of subpoena. The requirement is satisfied if his *testimony* is unobtainable. Even if someone is in court, he is unavailable for purposes of the Rule if he cannot remember, refuses to testify, or properly invokes a privilege.

The trial judge determines whether the declarant is unavailable under FRE 804(a), meaning that the question is one of "admissibility" under FRE 104(a). See United States v. Bell, 500 F.2d 1287, 1290 (2d Cir. 1974). Applying the unavailability criteria is usually straightforward, but not always. Some forms of unavailability have soft edges, and difficulties arise when the declarant is out of the jurisdiction, and when it appears that the prosecutor mishandled him. Unavailability has a constitutional dimension as well. (See the decision in *Barber*, infra.)

Claim of privilege. Under FRE 804(a)(1) a declarant is unavailable if exempted from testifying by court order on ground of privilege. In criminal cases, often witnesses invoke the Fifth Amendment privilege against self-incrimination.

The Rule contemplates an actual test: Declarant takes the stand, claims a privilege, and the court sustains his position. Generally a party hoping to take advantage of this form of unavailability cannot simply represent that the declarant would claim a privilege if called, see United States v. Pelton, 578 F.2d 701, 709-710 (8th Cir.), cert. denied, 439 U.S. 964 (1978). But sometimes this hardnosed approach is relaxed. Where one of several defendants wishes to offer a statement by another as a declaration against interest, for example, declarant's privilege against self-incrimination entitles him not even to be called as a witness. Hence he may be viewed as unavailable under FRE 804(a)(1) without being called to the stand for a ruling. United States v. Gossett, 877 F.2d 901, 907 (11th Cir.), cert. denied, 493 U.S. 1082 (1989).

Refusal to testify. FRE 804(a)(2) contemplates actual refusal: On the stand, declarant declines to answer and does not cooperate when ordered to answer. An effort to secure his cooperation is essential, and the Rule contemplates a threat of contempt. See United States v. MacCloskey, 682 F.2d 468, 478 n.19 (4th Cir. 1982). But see United States v. Boulahanis, 677 F.2d 586, 588 (7th Cir.) (court did not threaten contempt, but witness was unavailable where he refused to testify in fear of being killed, a fate that befell another involved in shakedown giving rise to this prosecution), cert. denied, 459 U.S. 1016 (1982).

Lack of memory. A declarant who testifies that he does not remember "the subject matter" of his prior statement is unavailable under FRE 804(a)(3). In United States v. DiCaro, 772 F.2d 1314 (7th Cir. 1985), for example, one Brown participated in a robbery leading to charges against DiCaro. At DiCaro's trial, Brown testified that he couldn't remember the robbery, although he had described it to a grand jury. The robbery was the "subject matter" of his grand jury testimony, so he was unavailable at trial.

DiCaro illustrates a paradox created by FRE 801(d)(1)(A) and 804(a)(3). Brown's grand jury testimony was held admissible under FRE 801(d)(1)(A), requiring the declarant to be "subject to cross-examination concerning [his prior] statement," for *DiCaro* found this requirement satisfied. Can it be that the same witness is at once "subject to cross-examination" under FRE 801(d)(1) and yet "unavailable" under FRE 804(a)? The answer appears to be yes. A person may remember making his statement well enough to be cross-examinable about it, thus satisfying FRE 801(d)(1), even though he has forgotten the underlying events. Yet the same person is "unavailable" under FRE 804(a)(3) *because* he has forgotten the events.[8]

---

8. In *DiCaro*, Brown testified that he had forgotten both the robbery and his prior statement. Still the court held that he was "subject to cross-examination concerning the statement." It seemed critical that he revealed on cross that he was in the Witness Protection Program when he gave his grand jury testimony, and so was at least thinly cross-examinable about that testimony. And the defense had a transcript of other testimony Brown had given, in which more impeaching data came out.

Death, illness, infirmity. Under FRE 804(a)(4), determining unavailability due to death has not posed problems, but the same is not always true of "illness or infirmity." A minor ailment from which speedy recovery is expected should not satisfy the requirement, even though the declarant cannot attend trial on a given day. In this situation it should be possible to adjourn the proceedings to allow time for recovery. But a serious illness of uncertain prognosis is likely to be enough. Context is important:

> [S]ince witness availability affects the court's ability to manage its cases, the trial court's decision to refuse an adjournment and to admit prior testimony must be treated with respectful deference. In exercising discretion a trial court must consider all relevant circumstances, including: the importance of the absent witness for the case; the nature and extent of cross-examination in the earlier testimony; the nature of the illness; the expected time of recovery; the reliability of the evidence of the probable duration of the illness; any special circumstances counseling against delay.

United States v. Faison, 679 F.2d 292, 297 (3d Cir. 1982).

In some settings, mental condition makes a witness unavailable to testify even though the modern view is that insanity does not disqualify one from giving evidence. Particularly in prosecutions for crimes against children involving sexual abuse or other physical mistreatment (like beatings), the victim may experience a level of apprehension, fear, or embarrassment that is so high that she cannot cope with testifying in court. In essence, these provisions recognize a form of "psychological or medical unavailability." Most states now have statutes that permit the use of depositions by children in this situation, and they may authorize children to testify from another room by use of video monitor. (Some of the statutes also create what amounts to catchall exceptions for child abuse victims, and sometimes these provisions are even more liberal if the child cannot testify for some reason.) Although few child abuse prosecutions are brought in federal court, Congress enacted a detailed statute on this subject. See 28 U.S.C. §3509 (in statutory supplement to this book), and see the discussion of Protected Witness Testimony in section G of this chapter, infra.

Unavoidable absence. Oversimplifying for the moment, a declarant is unavailable under FRE 804(a)(5) if her presence cannot be obtained at trial by subpoena or "other reasonable means."

Sometimes she is beyond reach of the subpoena power of the court. In state systems, usually the subpoena of a court of general jurisdiction runs the length and breadth of the state. In state criminal trials, usually the forum may invoke an interstate compact to obtain the assistance of another state in bringing in a needed witness. In civil litigation in the federal system, the subpoena power of the District Court reaches throughout the district, and the so-called bulge service provision extends to any point within 100 miles of the courthouse (even if outside the district). See FRCP 45(b). In isolated instances, a few statutes permit nationwide service of process. In federal criminal trials, the subpoena power runs nationwide. See FRCrimP 17(e). And in both civil and criminal cases litigated in federal court, it is sometimes possible to subpoena a citizen traveling abroad. See 28 U.S.C. §1783.

Even a witness beyond reach of subpoena is not necessarily unavailable, for "other reasonable means" may secure her presence. Occasionally courts expect parties simply to invite her to attend, and in the case of the government in criminal cases, to offer to pay travel expenses. See Government of Virgin Islands v. Aquino, 378 F.2d 540, 549-552 (3d Cir. 1967) (in trial for rape of stewardess on Norwegian vessel, court erred in admitting her preliminary hearing testimony; government did not show she had left the country; even if she had, government "would be required to reimburse her for her expenses of travel and subsistence" if necessary to secure her voluntary appearance).

Sometimes a witness who is physically within range of subpoena simply cannot be found, and the question arises whether the party seeking to offer her statement under FRE 804(b) has tried hard enough to serve her. See Perricone v. Kansas City S.R.R., 630 F.2d 317, 320-321 (5th Cir. 1980) (in suit arising out of grade crossing accident, plaintiff should not have introduced testimony by witness in prior trial; plaintiff did not subpoena witness, and defendant located him at his place of work in same town where accident occurred, only a mile from courthouse; he had recently moved from another town, but dialing his old telephone number would reach a recording giving his new number; plaintiff had not made a "diligent search").

The previous discussion oversimplifies slightly, for Congress saw fit to amend FRE 804(a)(5) by inserting the parenthetical phrase found there. In net effect, this addition puts pressure on parties to obtain deposition testimony by a declarant who might be unavailable at trial. The actual language says, in a somewhat convoluted way, that for purposes of the exceptions listed in FRE 804(b)(2) through (4), an unavailable witness is *not* one whose attendance cannot be procured if her "testimony" in some other form could be obtained. A deposition is what Congress had in mind.

Procurement or wrongdoing. A party who procures the absence of a declarant should not be allowed to invoke one of the exceptions that absence normally brings into play. The last sentence of FRE 804(a) so provides, though it is seldom invoked.

Should this principle prevent the government from resorting to one of the exceptions created by FRE 804(b) when the declarant claims her privilege against self-incrimination? The threat of prosecution can push the declarant to invoke the privilege, but if the government granted use immunity, her privilege claim would be overruled and she could be forced to testify. See Kastigar v. United States, 406 U.S. 441 (1972). Where the government threatens prosecution or refuses to immunize the witness, is it procuring her unavailability? Probably the answer is no, for the power to grant immunity is viewed as a government tool administered by the U.S. Attorney. But some decisions hint that sometimes a refusal to immunize might be viewed as abuse, United States v. Morrison, 535 F.2d 223, 225-229 (3d Cir. 1976), and that courts might play a role in deciding whether immunity should be granted, United States v. Herman, 589 F.2d 1191, 1204 (3d Cir. 1978), cert. denied, 441 U.S. 913 (1979).

PROBLEM 4-L.   *"The Government Let Her Go"*

Rick Masters is tried for importing cocaine when he and a 17-year-old Australian woman named Jane Shell are arrested as they arrive in Puerto Rico on a plane flight from Peru. Her name resulted in a "hit" during a computer check of debarking passengers, meaning that the Drug Enforcement Agency had information that she and an associate were suspected of smuggling drugs. A body search of Shell resulted in the discovery of ten packages of cocaine attached by tape inside her undergarments. Agents arrested Masters for the same reason, but a search of his person yielded no contraband.

Shell was arrested and detained in an adult prison facility, and she gave a statement that led to the indictment of Masters. Several weeks later, the U.S. Attorney sought permission to take Shell's deposition, suggesting that she might return to Australia and it would be impossible to bring her back to testify against Masters. The court permitted the deposition over defense objection, and defense counsel attended but did not question Shell. She incriminated Masters, testifying that he "hired me to carry the cocaine, which I was to turn over to him in exchange for $500 and my airline ticket to Australia when we arrived here in Puerto Rico." Shell also said she would not appear at the trial of Masters, and the U.S. Attorney returned her plane ticket and passport.

In the trial of Masters several months later, the government offers the deposition testimony of Shell, invoking the former testimony exception. The U.S. Attorney explains that "we checked with our Embassy in Australia and they found Shell, but she refuses to come back." The defense objects:

> If Shell is unavailable, your Honor, it's only because the government let her go. Indeed, they practically invited her to go by returning her ticket and passport. In the words of FRE 804(a), Shell is not unavailable because her absence is "due to the procurement or wrongdoing" of the government, and their purpose here was just what the Rule says—"preventing the witness from attending or testifying."

The U.S. Attorney rises to her feet and argues the other side:

> Your Honor, that provision contemplates at least negligent misbehavior and perhaps something worse, like deliberate scheming. We didn't do anything wrong. We couldn't just hold Shell in jail or deny her right to return home for two months. We knew she would likely leave, so we took her deposition with your permission. The defense was there and could cross-examine.

Should the court admit Shell's deposition? Why or why not?

NOTES ON PROCURED ABSENCE

1. Did the government behave properly on the facts of the Problem? Consider what else it might have done: It might have charged Shell with a crime and kept her in custody, or imprisoned her as a material witness, or kept her passport and ticket, or offered her money or a plane ticket to return to Puerto Rico. Should it have done any of those things?

2. Why shouldn't the government take the deposition of an important witness? In the Problem, defense counsel attended and could have questioned Shell. Should a deposition taken under these circumstances be any *less* admissible than testimony given by a prosecution witness in a preliminary hearing? See

Ohio v. Roberts, 448 U.S. 56 (1980) (admitting preliminary hearing testimony by a witness who had left the state and disappeared, where the defense had actually called her at the preliminary hearing and engaged in the "functional equivalent" of cross-examination). *Roberts* is set forth in section G of this chapter, infra.

3. Can the government detain a foreign national against whom no charges are pending? Confiscate her airline ticket? Could the government do so if she were a U.S. citizen? If the government behaved this way, must it pay for food and lodging for the period that the witness is delayed?

4. Consider the possibility of detaining Shell as a material witness. The relevant statute contemplates that a judge may impose conditions of release in such cases, but it forbids detention "if the testimony of such witness can adequately be secured by deposition." See 18 U.S.C. §3144. Yet in criminal cases depositions for "use in trial" are to be taken only in "exceptional cases." FRCrimP 15(a). Do these provisions mean Shell should be deposed? If so, do the provisions mean she should also be detained to testify at trial? If she leaves because the government does not take steps to keep her on the island (incarceration or taking her tickets or passport), do these provisions mean her deposition should be admissible?

> **BARBER v. PAGE**
> **United States Supreme Court**
> **390 U.S. 719 (1968)**

MR. JUSTICE MARSHALL delivered the opinion of the Court.

[Jack Barber and Charles Woods are tried for armed robbery in state court in Oklahoma. At a preliminary hearing, a lawyer named Parks had represented both defendants. There Woods waived his privilege against self-incrimination, and Parks withdrew as his attorney but continued to represent Barber. In his testimony at that hearing, Woods incriminated Barber, and Parks did not cross-examine, although a lawyer for another defendant did. When Barber was tried seven months later, Woods was in federal prison in Texas (about 225 miles away). Over Barber's objection, the state introduced a transcript of the testimony given by Woods at the preliminary hearing. Barber lost his appeals in the state system, and ultimately challenged his conviction in federal court by seeking a writ of habeas corpus, where he lost both at the District Court and on appeal.]

We start with the fact that the State made absolutely no effort to obtain the presence of Woods at trial other than to ascertain that he was in a federal prison outside Oklahoma. It must be acknowledged that various courts and commentators have heretofore assumed that the mere absence of a witness from the jurisdiction was sufficient ground for dispensing with confrontation on the theory that "it is impossible to compel his attendance, because the process of the trial Court is of no force without the jurisdiction, and the party desiring his testimony is therefore helpless." 5 Wigmore, Evidence §1404 (3d ed. 1940).

Whatever may have been the accuracy of that theory at one time, it is clear that at the present time increased cooperation between the States themselves and between the States and the Federal Government has largely deprived it of any continuing validity in the criminal law.[4] For example, in the case of a prospective witness currently in federal custody, 28 U.S.C. §2241(c)(5) gives federal courts the power to issue writs of habeas corpus ad testificandum at the request of state prosecutorial authorities. In addition, it is the policy of the United States Bureau of Prisons to permit federal prisoners to testify in state court criminal proceedings pursuant to writs of habeas corpus ad testificandum issued out of state courts.

In this case the state authorities made no effort to avail themselves of either of the above alternative means of seeking to secure Woods' presence at petitioner's trial. The Court of Appeals majority appears to have reasoned that because the State would have had to request an exercise of discretion on the part of federal authorities, it was under no obligation to make any such request. Yet as Judge Aldrich, sitting by designation, pointed out in dissent below, "the possibility of a refusal is not the equivalent of asking and receiving a rebuff." In short, a witness is not "unavailable" for purposes of the foregoing exception to the confrontation requirement unless the prosecutorial authorities have made a good-faith effort to obtain his presence at trial. The State made no such effort here, and, so far as this record reveals, the sole reason why Woods was not present to testify in person was because the State did not attempt to seek his presence. The right of confrontation may not be dispensed with so lightly.

The State argues that petitioner waived his right to confront Woods at trial by not cross-examining him at the preliminary hearing. That contention is untenable. Not only was petitioner unaware that Woods would be in a federal prison at the time of his trial, but he was also unaware that, even assuming Woods' incarceration, the State would make no effort to produce Woods at trial. To suggest that failure to cross-examine in such circumstances constitutes a waiver of the right of confrontation at a subsequent trial hardly comports with this Court's definition of a waiver as "an intentional relinquishment or abandonment of a known right or privilege." Johnson v. Zerbst, 304 U.S. 458, 464 (1938); Brookhart v. Janis, 384 U.S. 1, 4 (1966).

Moreover, we would reach the same result on the facts of this case had petitioner's counsel actually cross-examined Woods at the preliminary hearing. The right to confrontation is basically a trial right. It includes both the opportunity to cross-examine and the occasion for the jury to weigh the demeanor of the witness. A preliminary hearing is ordinarily a much less searching exploration into the merits of a case than a trial, simply because its function is the more limited one of determining whether probable cause exists to hold the accused for

---

4. For witnesses not in prison, the Uniform Act to Secure the Attendance of Witnesses from Without a State in Criminal Proceedings provides a means by which prosecuting authorities from one State can obtain an order from a court in the State where the witness is found directing the witness to appear in court in the first State to testify. The State seeking his appearance must pay the witness a specified sum as a travel allowance and compensation for his time. As of 1967 the Uniform Act was in force in 45 States, the District of Columbia, the Canal Zone, Puerto Rico, and the Virgin Islands. See 9 Uniform Laws Ann. 50 (1967 Supp.). For witnesses in prison, quite probably many state courts would utilize the common-law writ of habeas corpus ad testificandum at the request of prosecutorial authorities of a sister State upon a showing that adequate safeguards to keep the prisoner in custody would be maintained.

trial. While there may be some justification for holding that the opportunity for cross-examination of a witness at a preliminary hearing satisfies the demands of the confrontation clause where the witness is shown to be actually unavailable, this is not, as we have pointed out, such a case.

The judgment of the Court of Appeals for the Tenth Circuit is reversed and the case is remanded for further proceedings consistent with this opinion.

It is so ordered.

[The concurring opinion of JUSTICE HARLAN is omitted.]

NOTES ON UNAVAILABILITY AND THE CONSTITUTION

1.   Does *Barber* indicate that Shell's deposition testimony in Problem 4-L ("The Government Let Her Go") should not be admitted? In *Barber,* the Court says it would reach the same result even if lawyer Parks had cross-examined Woods in the preliminary hearing. That might suggest that the Confrontation Clause requires contemporaneous (as opposed to prior) cross-examination, but the Court has held that prior cross-examination suffices, at least sometimes. See California v. Green, 399 U.S. 149 (1970), and Ohio v. Roberts, 448 U.S. 56 (1980) (described in section G, infra). Why didn't Parks cross-examine Woods in the preliminary hearing?

2.   *Barber* implies that hearsay is inadmissible against the accused if the declarant is available as a witness. Modern confrontation doctrine, which changed substantially when the Supreme Court decided Crawford v. Washington, 124 S.Ct. 1354 (2004), concerns itself primarily with "testimonial" statements given prior to the trial in which they are offered, and this category clearly reaches the testimony by Woods in Barber's preliminary hearing. *Crawford* also indicates that cross-examination can satisfy the Clause, but it is not at all clear that a mere "opportunity" to cross-examine is enough. Indeed, *Crawford* cites *Barber* with apparent approval (along with other cases considering this matter), and it seems probable that *Barber* remains good law.

3.   Consider the possible effect of Mancusi v. Stubbs, 408 U.S. 204 (1972), where the unavailability requirement emerged in an attenuated setting. Stubbs was convicted of a felony in New York and sentenced as a second offender because of his prior murder conviction in Tennessee. The Tennessee conviction had come on retrial, in which testimony given in the first trial by Alex Holm (victim's husband) was introduced. Holm had returned to his native Sweden, becoming a "permanent resident" there, and the Tennessee prosecutor made no effort to bring him back. Stubbs challenged his conviction as a second offender in New York by contending that the Tennessee conviction was constitutionally infirm. The Supreme Court rejected the challenge. Noting that 28 U.S.C. §1783(a), as it read at the time, authorized a federal court to subpoena a citizen living abroad "for appearance before it," the Court thought that the statute "on its face does not appear to be designed for [the] purpose" of obtaining a federal subpoena for a witness to testify in state court. Hence there was no ready means to obtain Holm to testify on retrial of Stubbs in Tennessee:

The Uniform Act to secure the attendance of witnesses from without a State, the availability of federal writs of habeas corpus ad testificandum, and the established practice of the United States Bureau of Prisons to honor state writs of habeas corpus ad testificandum, all supported the Court's conclusion in *Barber* that the State had not met its obligations to make a good-faith effort to obtain the presence of the witness merely by showing that he was beyond the boundaries of the prosecuting State. There have been, however, no corresponding developments in the area of obtaining witnesses between this country and foreign nations. Upon discovering that Holm resided in a foreign nation, the State of Tennessee, so far as this record shows, was powerless to compel his attendance at the second trial, either through its own process or through established procedures depending on the voluntary assistance of another government. We therefore hold that the predicate of unavailability was sufficiently stronger here than in *Barber* that a federal habeas court was not warranted in upsetting the determination of the state trial court as to Holm's unavailability.

408 U.S. 204, at 212 (1972). In dissent, Justice Marshall argued that absence of a statute "reduced the likelihood that any effort would succeed" but did not "relieve[ ] the state of its obligation to make a good-faith effort" to obtain the witness.

4.   After Stubbs' second trial in Tennessee, the federal statute was amended to authorize a federal court to bring a witness "before a person or body designated by" the court. 28 U.S.C. §1783. Even under the original language (let alone the amended version), if a federal court can order a citizen located abroad to return to this country to testify, and can detain a material witness under 18 U.S.C. §3144, and can issue a writ of habeas corpus ad testificandum ordering release of a federal prisoner so that he may testify in state proceedings—if it can do all these things, can there be any doubt that it could have aided the Tennessee prosecutor to obtain Alex Holm for the second trial of Stubbs? Does the fact that it can do so now make the opinion in *Stubbs,* as Justice Marshall contended, a holding of "very limited significance"?

5.   Despite the holding in *Stubbs* that the Constitution did not require the prosecutor to do more, Rule 804(a) might be construed to require greater efforts, might it not? See State v. Smyth, 593 P.2d 1166 (Or. 1979) (under state constitution, prosecutor had to make a good-faith effort to bring the witness from Canada; *Stubbs* excuses the state from pursuing unavailable remedies but "does not relieve the prosecution from having to make any attempt whatever" to return the witness).

2.   *The Former Testimony Exception*

In some respects, former testimony is the closest thing to live testimony, and the exception here considered makes only a small inroad in the general bar against hearsay evidence. The easiest example is a case retried after a successful appeal, where a witness who testified at the first trial dies before the second. On retrial, a party wishing to make use of what the deceased witness had said may resort to the transcript of the prior proceedings, reading the original testimony as evidence: The prior statements were given under oath in a trial of the same issues, the declarant was cross-examinable, and the verbatim transcript of the earlier proceedings captures his exact words.[9]

But FRE 804(b)(1) reaches much further than the situation just described. It embraces depositions and testimony given in preliminary hearings in criminal cases, for example. And like the provision for prior inconsistent statements, the former testimony exception requires the statement to have been given in a "proceeding" but does not require a "judicial" proceeding, which opens the door to use of the former testimony exception for testimony given in administrative hearings as well.

The main limit in FRE 804(b)(1) is the cross-examination requirement. (Since the wording speaks of "an opportunity and similar motive to develop the testimony by direct, cross, or redirect examination," the term "cross-examination requirement" is an inexact but useful shorthand.) The language says the former testimony exception is available in civil cases if the party against whom it is offered or his "predecessor in interest" had a chance to cross-examine the declarant *in the prior proceedings*. In criminal cases, the requirement is stricter, since it will not do that a "predecessor in interest" had a chance to cross-examine before. Despite the language, however, one modern court has applied the "predecessor in interest" clause in a criminal case when the *defense* offered former testimony against the government. See United States v. McDonald, 837 F.2d 1287, 1290-1293 (5th Cir. 1988) (in RICO prosecution, testimony given in prior civil proceeding might be admissible against the government, although not in this case, since the strategy of the cross-examiner in the earlier case was "not sufficiently similar" to that of the government here). Presumably the government still may not offer former testimony against the accused if he himself did not have a previous chance to cross-examine, even if a predecessor in interest did.

As phrased in the Rule, it suffices that the party against whom the testimony is offered had "an opportunity and similar motive" to cross-examine the declarant. Often the objecting party argues that differences between the prior and the present proceedings show that on the earlier occasion there was less reason (or none) to go after the witness: The charges or issues were different in the earlier proceedings, or parties were added or dropped since then, or the purpose of the earlier hearing was narrower. Many such differences have no plausible effect, for it seems that the prior opportunity and motivation were much the same. See United States v. Licavoli, 725 F.2d 1040, 1048-1049 (6th Cir.) (against defendants in federal RICO trial, admitting testimony given in state murder trials; the issues "were nearly identical," despite the fact that the present case required proof of criminal enterprise; defendants "failed to point to any matter that they would have raised" on cross with respect to the enterprise element that they did not raise before), cert. denied, 467 U.S. 1252 (1984).

9. Almost always former testimony is proved by means of a transcript, which amounts to an out-of-court assertion by the reporter that the witness said thus-and-so at the prior proceedings. Hence we actually have two layers of hearsay, so we need an exception for each layer. See FRE 805. The former testimony exception paves the way to admit what the witness said as proof of what he asserts. The public records exception in FRE 803(8) paves the way to admit the transcript to prove the words uttered by the witness. See also 28 U.S.C. §753(b) (authorizing use of certified transcripts of court proceedings, as prima facie correct statements of testimony taken and proceedings which transpired). In effect we piggyback two exceptions.

Sometimes changes in parties or issues do matter. See United States v. Feldman, 761 F.2d 380, 385-386 (7th Cir. 1985) (deposition of codefendant *S*, taken in civil suit against corporation managed by *F* and *M*, was not admissible against them in criminal trial; they had "little personal or financial stake" in prior suit and pursued opposite strategies; the "naked opportunity" to cross-examine was not enough, absent an incentive to do so); United States v. Atkins, 618 F.2d 366, 372-373 (5th Cir. 1980) (excluding co-offender's testimony given in hearing on coconspirator statements and offered by defendant at trial; government "did not have the motivation" to examine witness on whether the "Robert" to whom he referred was the defendant, since government claimed defendant played different role in conspiracy). And sometimes other factors stifle cross-examination in the prior proceedings. See People v. Brock, 695 P.2d 209 (Cal. 1985) (in murder trial, woman dying of terminal cancer testified at preliminary hearing in hospital room; precarious condition and inability to follow and respond to questions undermined defense cross and precluded use of former testimony exception).

Note the difference between this exception and the one for prior inconsistent statements. While both require a chance for cross (and each exception rests heavily on this point), one requires a prior opportunity, and the other a present opportunity: The former testimony exception in FRE 804(b)(1) requires a *prior* chance to cross-examine the declarant; the exception for prior inconsistent statements in FRE 801(d)(1)(A) requires a *present* chance to cross-examine the declarant "concerning [his previous] statement."

LLOYD v. AMERICAN EXPORT LINES, INC.
United States Court of Appeals for the Third Circuit
580 F.2d 1179, cert. denied, 439 U.S. 969 (1978)

[Frank Lloyd, an electrician on the SS Export Commerce, was involved in a shipboard altercation with Roland Alvarez, a third assistant engineer. The incident occurred in Yokohama harbor on September 7, 1974. Lloyd sued shipowner American Export Lines, alleging negligence under the Jones Act and unseaworthiness under general maritime law. American Export impleaded Alvarez as third-party defendant, and Alvarez counterclaimed against American Export, alleging negligence and unseaworthiness.

Lloyd disappeared, and the claims of Alvarez against American Export came to trial. In essence, Alvarez contended that American Export was liable because Lloyd started the fight, while American Export argued no liability because Alvarez started it. At trial, Alvarez testified that Lloyd sneaked through the open door of a resistor house on deck without warning or provocation and viciously attacked him, striking him with an unidentified object and screaming that he wanted to "kill" him. During a life-threatening struggle, Alvarez picked up a turnbuckle and struck Lloyd, ending the fight.

To prove that Alvarez was the attacker, American Export resorted to the former testimony exception. It sought (unsuccessfully) to introduce a transcript of Lloyd's testimony, taken by a Coast Guard hearing examiner during proceedings to determine whether Lloyd's merchant mariner's documents should be suspended or revoked for misconduct. At that hearing both Lloyd and Alvarez were represented by counsel, and each testified under oath. In his testimony at the Coast Guard hearing—which the jury in the present case did not hear—Lloyd described his relationship to Alvarez. Coming to the September 7 incident, he said that he entered the resistor house, saw Alvarez, asked him what he was doing, "and that's the last thing I remember" because when "I woke up" two or three days later "I was in the hospital" bleeding and "spitting up blood."

The jury returned a verdict finding American Export negligent and awarding Alvarez $95,000, but rejecting the claim that American Export had breached its warranty of seaworthiness. American Export appealed, urging error in the exclusion of Lloyd's testimony from the Coast Guard hearing, and Alvarez cross-appealed, urging error in the refusal of the trial judge to enter judgment notwithstanding the verdict for "maintenance and cure" pursuant to the unseaworthiness claim.]

ALDISERT, J. . . .

In order for the hearsay exceptions of Rule 804 to apply, it is required that the declarant be "unavailable"—in this case, that he be "absent from the hearing and the proponent of his statement [be] unable to procure his attendance . . . by process or other reasonable means." Rule 804(a)(5). In preparation for trial, as has been noted, numerous attempts were made by Export to depose Lloyd, but he repeatedly failed to appear. Finally, on the day set for trial, Export learned that Lloyd would not appear to prosecute his case. Lloyd's counsel represented to the court that extensive efforts had been made to obtain his appearance, but they had failed, due at least in part to his seafaring occupation. We are satisfied that where Export and Lloyd's own counsel were unable to obtain his appearance in an action in which he had a formidable interest as a plaintiff, his unavailability status was sufficient to satisfy the requirement of Rule 804.

We turn now to the more difficult question: did Alvarez or a "predecessor in interest" have the "opportunity and similar motive to develop the testimony by direct, cross or redirect examination" as required by Rule 804(b)(1)? In rejecting the proffered evidence, the district court took a strict view of the new rule, one that we do not share.

We note at the outset that inasmuch as Congress did not define "predecessor in interest," that interpretive task is left to the courts. We find no definitive guidance in the reports accompanying language changes made as the Rules were considered, in turn, by the Supreme Court and the houses of Congress. As originally submitted by the Supreme Court, Rule 804(b)(1) would have allowed prior testimony of an unavailable witness to be received in evidence if the party against whom it was offered, or a person with "motive and interest similar," had an opportunity to examine the witness. The House of Representatives adopted the present language, the Committee on the Judiciary offering this rationale:

> Rule 804(b)(1) as submitted by the Court allowed prior testimony of an unavailable witness to be admissible if the party against whom it is offered or a person "with motive and interest similar" to his had an opportunity to examine the witness. The Committee considered that it is generally unfair to impose upon the party against whom the hearsay evidence is being offered responsibility for the manner

in which the witness was previously handled by another party. The sole exception to this, in the Committee's view, is when a party's predecessor in interest in a civil action or proceeding had an opportunity and similar motive to examine the witness. The Committee amended the Rule to reflect these policy determinations.

The Senate Committee on the Judiciary viewed the import of this change as follows:

> . . . The House amended the rule to apply only to a party's predecessor in interest. Although the committee recognizes considerable merit to the rule submitted by the Supreme Court, a position which has been advocated by many scholars and judges, we have concluded that the difference between the two versions is not great and we accept the House amendment.

We, too, fail to see a compelling difference between the two approaches.

In our analysis of this language change, we are aware of the basic thrust of subdivision (b) of Rule 804. It was originally designed by the Advisory Committee on Rules of Evidence of the Judicial Conference of the United States to strike a proper balance between the recognized risk of introducing testimony of one not physically present on a witness stand and the equally recognized risk of denying to the fact-finder important relevant evidence. Even in its slightly amended form as enacted by Congress, Rule 804 still serves the original intention of its drafters: "The rule expresses preferences: testimony given on the stand in person is preferred over hearsay, and hearsay, if of the specified quality, is preferred over complete loss of the evidence of the declarant."

Although Congress did not furnish us with a definition of "predecessor in interest," our analysis of the concept of interests satisfies us that there was a sufficient community of interest shared by the Coast Guard in its hearing and Alvarez in the subsequent civil trial to satisfy Rule 804(b)(1). Roscoe Pound has taught us that interests in law are "the claims or demands or desires which human beings, either individually or in groups or associations or relations, seek to satisfy. . . ."[8] The interest implicated here was a claim or desire or demand which Alvarez as an individual, and the Coast Guard as a representative of a larger group, sought to satisfy, and which has been recognized as socially valid by authoritative decision-makers in our society.

Individual interests, like those of Alvarez, are involved immediately in the individual life, in the Pound formulation, and asserted in title of that life. Public interests, like those of the Coast Guard, are involved in the life of a politically organized society, here the United States, and asserted in title of that entity. Thus, Alvarez sought to vindicate his individual interest in recovering for his injuries; the Coast Guard sought to vindicate the public interest in safe and unimpeded merchant marine service. Irrespective of whether the interests be considered from the individual or public viewpoints, however, the nucleus of operative fact[11] was the same—the conduct of Frank Lloyd and Roland Alvarez

---

8. Pound, A Survey of Social Interests, 57 Harv. L. R4ev. 1, 1943.

11. Karl Llewellyn has defined an interest as "a social fact or factor of some kind, existing [in]dependent of the law," with "value independent of the law." Llewellyn, A Realistic Jurisprudence—The Next Step, 30 Colum. L. Rev. 430, 441 (1930).

aboard the SS Export Commerce. And although the results sought in the two proceedings differed—the Coast Guard contemplated sanctions involving Lloyd's mariner's license, while Alvarez sought private substituted redress, i.e., monetary damages—the basic interest advanced by both was that of determining culpability and, if appropriate, exacting a penalty for the same condemned behavior thought to have occurred.[12] The Coast Guard investigating officer not only preferred charges against Lloyd but functioned as a prosecutor at the subsequent proceeding as well. Thus, he attempted to establish at the Coast Guard hearing what Alvarez attempted to establish at the later trial: Lloyd's intoxication, his role as the aggressor, and his prior hostility toward Alvarez. Dean Pound recognized that there can be such a community of individual and public interests as this: "It must be borne in mind that often we have here different ways of looking at the same claims or same type of claims as they are asserted in different titles."

Moreover, although our precise task is to decide whether the Coast Guard investigating officer was Alvarez' predecessor in interest, it is equally important to respect always the fundamentals that underlie the hearsay rule, and the reasons for the exceptions thereto. Any fact-finding process is ultimately a search for truth and justice, and legal precepts that govern the reception of evidence must always be interpreted in light of this. Whether it be fashioned by rules of decision in cases or controversies, or promulgated by the Supreme Court with the approval of Congress, or designed and adopted by Congress, every rule of evidence is a means to an end, not an end in itself. We strive to avoid interpretations that are wooden or mechanical, like obsolete common law pleadings, and to favor those that facilitate the presentation of a complete picture to the fact-finder. With this approach in mind, we are satisfied that there existed, in the language of Rule 804(b)(1), sufficient "opportunity and similar motive [for the Coast Guard investigating officer] to develop [Lloyd's] testimony" at the former hearing to justify its admission against Alvarez at the later trial.[14]

---

12. In this regard, McCormick takes the position that "insistence upon precise identity of issues, which might have some appropriateness if the question were one of res judicata or estoppel by judgment, are out of place with respect to former testimony where the question is not of binding anyone, but merely of the salvaging, for what it may be worth, of the testimony of a witness not now available in person. . . . It follows that neither the form of the proceeding, the theory of the case, nor the nature of the relief sought needs be the same." McCormick, Handbook of the Law of Evidence §257 at 261 (2d ed. 1972).

14. One can discern a confluence between the congressional policy determinations and our view of the interests in this case in an analysis offered by the Fourth Circuit in a case, also involving a prior Coast Guard proceeding, that predated the present rules.

> Chadwick's testimony was presented by use of a portion of the proceedings before the Coast Guard in its investigation of the catastrophe. In those proceedings Chadwick was sworn. There was a presiding officer who conducted the proceedings, ruled on the form of questions and ruled on the admissibility of evidence. The object of the inquiry was to fix responsibility for the fire—the object of these proceedings. Full cross-examination on the facts as then known by counsel for the Trexler estate, counsel for Crown and counsel for the barge and tug was permitted. The interests of those present and represented by counsel were substantially the same as those who are parties in these proceedings, but who did not appear in the Coast Guard proceedings.

Tug Raven v. Trexler, 419 F.2d 536, 542-543 (4th Cir. 1969), cert. denied sub nom. Crown Central Petroleum Corp. v. Trexler, 398 U.S. 938 (1970).

While we do not endorse an extravagant interpretation of who or what constitutes a "predecessor in interest," we prefer one that is realistically generous over one that is formalistically grudging. We believe that what has been described as "the practical and expedient view" expresses the congressional intention: "if it appears that in the former suit a party having a like motive to cross-examine about the same matters as the present party would have, was accorded an adequate opportunity for such examination, the testimony may be received against the present party."[15] Under these circumstances, the previous party having like motive to develop the testimony about the same material facts is, in the final analysis, a predecessor in interest to the present party. . . .

The judgment of the district court will be reversed and the cause remanded for a new trial.

Each side to bear its own costs.

STERN, J., concurring.

[Judge Stern would invoke the catchall to admit Lloyd's testimony, thus concurs in the result reached by the majority, but disagrees with the construction of "predecessor in interest" given by the majority.]

It is true that Congress nowhere defined "predecessor in interest," but it seems clear that this phrase, a term of art, was used in its narrow, substantive law sense. Although the commentators have expressed disapproval of this traditional and restrictive rule, they recognize that a "predecessor in interest" is defined in terms of a privity relationship.

The term "privity" denotes mutual or successive relationships to the same rights of property, and privies are distributed into several classes, according to the manner of this relationship. Thus, there are privies in estate, as donor and donee, lessor and lessee, and joint tenants; privies in blood, as heir and ancestor, and co-parceners; privies in representation, as executor and testator, administrator and intestate; privies in law, where the law, without privity of blood or estate casts the land upon another, as by escheat.

Metropolitan St. Ry. v. Gumby, 99 F. 192 (2nd Cir. 1900). . . .

The majority rejects the view that the Rule's wording signals a return to the common law approach requiring privity or a common property interest between the parties, and finds it sufficient that the Coast Guard investigator shared a community of interest with Alvarez. But community of interest seems to mean only that the investigating officer sought to establish the same facts as Alvarez attempted to prove in the instant suit. Used in this sense, community of interest means nothing more than similarity of interest or similarity of motive. But similar motive is a separate prerequisite to admissibility under 804(b)(1) and thus the majority's analysis which reads "predecessor in interest" to mean nothing more than person with "similar motive" eliminates the predecessor in interest requirement entirely.

Moreover, while I appreciate the fact that the Coast Guard investigator

15. McCormick, supra, §256 at 619-620. The approach of the Federal Rules of Evidence is to examine proffered former testimony in light of the prior opportunity and motive to develop the testimony, whether in the form of direct, redirect or cross-examination. This less restrictive approach finds support among commentators. See McCormick, supra, §255 at 617; Falknor, Former Testimony and the Uniform Rules: A Comment, 38 N.Y.U.L. Rev. 651 n.1 (1963).

sought to establish Lloyd's wrongdoing and that Alvarez sought to do the same, I do not believe that this establishes the kind of "common motive" sufficient to satisfy 804(b)(1).

A prosecutor or an investigating officer represents no ordinary party. He shoulders a peculiar kind of duty, even to his very adversary, a duty which is foreign to the adversarial process among ordinary litigants. The prosecutor, it is true, must seek to vindicate the rights of the alleged victim, but his interests go far beyond that. His interest in a prosecution is not that he shall win a case, but that justice shall be done.

The interests of an attorney representing the government surely overlap with those of the private litigant, but they do not coincide. The investigating officer was under no duty to advance every arguable issue against Lloyd in the vindication of Alvarez's interests, as Alvarez's own counsel would have been. He simply did not represent Alvarez.

Thus, even if I could agree that Congress intended to relax the common law requirement of actual privity between the parties before prior testimony could be admitted, I cannot endorse a rule which would automatically render admissible against a party evidence which was elicited in a different proceeding by an unrelated person merely because both shared an interest in establishing the same facts. The majority's holding makes admissible against Alvarez the testimony of all witnesses who appeared at the Coast Guard hearing—not just Lloyd—and this without any showing of necessity by the proponent of such evidence. Indeed under the majority view, all kinds of testimony adduced at all kinds of administrative hearings—hearings before the Civil Aeronautics Board on airplane disasters; hearings before the Federal Communications Commission on misuse of broadcast licenses; hearings before the Securities and Exchange Commission on securities fraud, just by way of example—would be admissible in subsequent civil suits, albeit that the parties were entirely different. With all due respect, I think this goes too far. The net result would be charging the party against whom the hearsay evidence is being offered with all flaws in the manner in which the witness was previously handled by another, and all flaws in another's choice of witnesses, the very result characterized by the House Judiciary Committee as "generally unfair."[2]

---

2. Alvarez derived no benefit from the Coast Guard proceeding against Lloyd. His private action for damages in no way derives from or is enhanced by the Coast Guard hearing convened for the purpose of determining whether Lloyd's papers should be revoked or suspended. This distinguishes the instant case from In re Master Key Antitrust Litigation, 72 F.R.D. 108 (D. Conn.), aff'd without published opinion, 551 F.2d 300 (2d Cir. 1976), the only case in which 804(b)(1) has been construed. In *Master Key*, a private class action antitrust suit, defendants sought to introduce testimony given in a prior governmental antitrust action which preceded and gave rise to the private suit. The question was whether the United States could be deemed predecessor in interest of the private plaintiffs for the purpose of Rule 804(b)(1). The court held that it could, but only after weighing "special considerations."

> The unique relationship between the Government's antitrust enforcement suits and the private actions which follow has Congressional recognition and ratification, which has in turn provided special benefits to the private plaintiffs. It has, for example, tolled the applicable statute of limitations, and thus allowed them to extend the period for which they may recover. . . . Furthermore, the judgment in the earlier decision will be admissible in evidence (although it too is hearsay) and serves to establish their prima facie case.

72 F.R.D. at 109 (citations omitted). No such special circumstances, no quid pro quo, exist here.

[Judge Stern then explains his view that the catchall can appropriately apply here.]

NOTES ON PRIOR CROSS-EXAMINATION REQUIREMENT

1. How's that again? Far from Judge Aldisert to distort congressional language by "extravagant interpretation," but the Coast Guard's investigating officer is a "predecessor in interest" to Alvarez? Could he have initiated proceedings against Lloyd to take away his seaman's license? For a discussion of the problem examined in *Lloyd*, see Weissenberger, The Former Testimony Exception: A Study in Rulemaking, Judicial Revisionism, and the Separation of Powers, 67 N.C. L. Rev. 295 (1989) (fairness to parties, not just accuracy in factfinding, underlay legislative judgment expressed in "predecessor in interest" clause; judicial interpretations conflict, and Supreme Court should grant review and restore meaning intended by Congress).

2. Before being too hard on Judge Aldisert, consider the following case: Partners JB and JC Wright lost their building to fire and sue their casualty carrier to recover for the loss. The carrier calls Eppler and Brown as witnesses, expecting that they would testify that JB Wright conspired with them to burn the building. But Eppler and Brown claim their privilege against self-incrimination and refuse to testify. In a prior prosecution of JB Wright for alleged arson, however, Eppler and Brown testified to a conspiracy, and the carrier offers a transcript of that testimony. In this case, the Oklahoma Supreme Court thought that the transcript was admissible against *both* JB and JC Wright:

> Is it important that JC Wright did not have an opportunity to cross-examine in the criminal case? JB Wright had the same motive and interest in cross-examining the witnesses in the criminal case as would JC Wright in the instant case. The issues were the same in both cases. . . . We conclude that JB Wright's opportunity to cross-examine the witness in the criminal case on the same issue, and with the same interest and motives that JC Wright would have in the instant case, satisfies the rule of substantial identity of issues and parties and opportunity for satisfactory cross-examination.
>
> From the foregoing it is seen that the question of substantial identity of parties is important only with regard to the parties as against whom such testimony is offered; therefore the fact that the state was JB Wright's adversary in the first case rather than the insurance companies is immaterial. Such fact has no bearing upon the question of whether there has been an adequate opportunity to thoroughly sift and test such testimony by cross-examination.

Travelers Fire Insurance Co. v. Wright, 322 P.2d 417 (Okla. 1958). Didn't *Wright* reach the best result? And putting aside FRE 804(b)(1), *Lloyd* reached an equally sound result, didn't it? If *Wright* arose today under FRE 804(b)(1), could the *Lloyd* interpretation justify admitting the former testimony of Eppler and Brown against JC Wright?

3. A Blue Lines bus collides with a car, and many bus passengers are killed or injured. Bus passenger Anne brings action 1 against Blue Lines and seeks to prove that excessive speed of the bus caused the accident. But eyewitness

Carl testifies for Blue Lines that the bus was traveling slowly in its own lane, and the car crossed the center line at the last minute, driving into the path of the bus. The jury returns a verdict for Blue Lines. Thereafter bus passenger Bart sues Blue Lines, alleging (like Anne) that the bus was speeding. Carl has died, and Blue Lines offers his testimony from action 1 against Bart. Does FRE 804(b)(1) permit this use of Carl's former testimony?

4.   Doug sues Emville Asbestos Corporation, alleging that he contracted asbestosis while installing Emville insulation products. At trial Dr. Gregory (physician employed by Emville) testifies to the state of medical knowledge regarding asbestos-related diseases. Then he dies. Now Eric, another insulation installer who suffers from asbestosis, sues Emville and Franklin Insulation Company, making similar allegations about products made by both companies. Can Eric offer against Emville and Franklin the testimony by Dr. Gregory in Doug's suit?

5.   The idea that a person may be bound or affected by what his "predecessor in interest" has done is central to the notion of "privity." In his concurring opinion in *Lloyd*, Judge Stern quotes a standard definition of privity. That concept was also central in explaining why a person not party to a lawsuit could nevertheless be bound by it—explaining, in other words, why the person was bound by res judicata or collateral estoppel. Is it appropriate, in deciding whether testimony from a prior suit may be admitted against a party who did not participate in the earlier suit, to apply the same test that determines whether the judgment in the earlier suit may have res judicata or collateral estoppel effect against that party?

6.   As noted in the opening discussion of the unavailability requirement, it is sometimes argued that the government has power to immunize a witness and that refusing to do so implicates the government in "procuring the availability of a witness who refuses to testify under a claim of his Fifth Amendment privilege. In 1995, a defendant made a similar argument that "adversarial fairness" should block the government from claiming it lacked the necessary motive to cross-examine a witness who gave testimony favorable to the defendant in grand jury proceedings but at trial claimed the Fifth Amendment and refused to repeat this testimony. If the government claim that it lacked the necessary motive were somehow blocked, the defense could offer the grand jury testimony under the former testimony exception. But the Supreme Court rejected this view, and the Second Circuit later held that the government lacked the necessary motive, hence the defense could not offer the grand jury testimony under FRE 804(b)(1). See United States v. Salerno, 505 U.S. 317 (1992) (rejecting "adversarial fairness" argument), on remand 974 F.2d 231 (2d Cir. 1992) (government lacked similar motive to cross-examine; exception unavailable).

3.   Dying Declarations

Where a person understands that his death is imminent and speaks of his circumstance, the hearsay doctrine has long recognized an exception for his words. The exception rests on a thought passed forward from a more godfearing age that a dying person will not meet his maker with a lie on his lips, and in the belief that psychological forces incline a dying person toward truthfulness.

There is also the point that dying declarations are likely to speak of facts in the forefront of memory.

The exception is most often invoked in criminal trials, paving way to admit the dying words of the victim identifying defendant as his assailant. See Commonwealth v. Moses, 766 N.E.2d 827, 830 (Mass. 2002) (in murder trial, admitting statement by victim to medical technician stating that "Prince" had shot him). These cases bring strong emotional appeal to listen to the last utterance of a helpless victim.

The exception embraces only those statements "concerning the cause and circumstances" of impending death. It reaches not only remarks identifying the assailant, but also descriptions of the accident or catastrophe that befell the declarant. See United States v. Mobley, 421 F.2d 345, 346-347 (5th Cir. 1970) (bank president shot during robbery describes the course of events); Connor v. State, 171 A.2d 699 (Md. 1960) (run over by husband, dying wife declares, "It was no accident"), cert. denied, 368 U.S. 906 (1961). Probably it also embraces descriptions of prior threats and quarrels, physical pain or sensations, and matters inhaled, injected, or ingested.

The federal language makes the exception available in civil cases as well, departing from common law tradition. See United Services Automobile Association v. Wharton, 237 F. Supp. 255, 257-260 (N.D.N.C. 1965) (breakthrough and colorful civil case rejecting the common law restriction and admitting hospital statement by woman fatally injured in head-on collision, to the effect that her husband said immediately before driving into left-hand lane that the two would "go to eternity together").

NOTES ON DYING DECLARATIONS

1.   Does the exception rest on a sound psychological premise? Consider the insight of Shakespeare, in the plea of the dying Melun:

> What in the world should make me now deceive,
>
> —*Salisbury* —
>
> May this be possible? May this be true?
>
> —*Melun*—
>
> Have I not hideous death within my view,
> Retaining but a quantity of life,
> Which bleeds away, even as a form of wax
> Resolveth from this figure 'gainst the fire?
> What in the world should make me now deceive,
> Since I must lose the use of all deceit?
> Why should I then be false, since it is true
> That I must die here and live hence by truth?

Shakespeare, King John, Act V, scene iv.

2.   How should we decide whether the declarant had a settled expectancy of imminent death? See Mattox v. United States, 146 U.S. 140, 151-152 (1892)

(relying on nature of wounds and advice by attending physician that declarant had no chance to survive); State v. Buggs, 581 N.W.2d 329, 335 (Minn. 1998) (shot six times in chest and abdomen, victim was found "lying on her back on the floor in a pool of blood, 'squirming,' and struggling to breathe"; seriousness of wounds, labored breathing, and fact of death within two hours were "sufficient circumstances from which the trial court could infer" that she had a firm belief in impending death).

3. Who should decide this point—judge or jury? Common law tradition included an instruction to the jury to consider the statement only if it believed that declarant knew death was imminent. See Freihage v. United States, 56 F.2d 127, 134 (9th Cir. 1932) (error to withdraw question from jury). But modern cases go the other way. See Commonwealth v. Cooley, 348 A.2d 103, 108 (Pa. 1975) (question whether statement qualifies as a dying declaration "is one of law" that is "not within the province of the jury," so court did not err in refusing to instruct jury "to assess for themselves whether the decedent believed he was about to die"). Which approach is correct under FRE 104?

4. How should we deal with the matter of personal knowledge? Compare Shepard v. United States, 290 U.S. 96, 100-102 (1933) (dying declaration admissible only if circumstances permit inference that declarant had knowledge and should be excluded if speaker expresses "suspicion or conjecture") and State v. Wilks, 213 S.W. 118 (Mo. 1919) (statement that certain people hired the assailant inadmissible as dying declaration because of lack of personal knowledge) with Soles v. State, 119 So. 791 (Fla. 1929) (admitting statement by declarant shot in the back of the head identifying defendant as his assailant, without discussion of the personal knowledge issue).

5. How imminent must the prospect of death be? Consider the trial of Charles Shepard, a doctor and army officer, for the murder of his wife Zenana. She was apparently poisoned with bichloride of mercury, her symptoms first appearing on May 20, and death following on June 15. Two days after falling ill, she asked the attending nurse to fetch a bottle of liquor from which she had drunk just before collapsing, asked whether enough was left to test for poison, adding that "the smell and taste were strange" and suggesting that "Dr. Shepard has poisoned me." In a famous opinion by Justice Cardozo, the Supreme Court concluded that the exception did not apply:

> We have said that the declarant was not shown to have spoken without hope of recovery and in the shadow of impending death. Her illness began on May 20. She was found in a state of collapse, delirious, in pain, the pupils of her eyes dilated, and the retina suffused with blood. The conversation with the nurse occurred two days later. At that time her mind had cleared up, and her speech was rational and orderly. There was as yet no thought by any of her physicians that she was dangerously ill, still less that her case was hopeless. To all seeming she had greatly improved, and was moving forward to recovery. There had been no diagnosis of poison as the cause of her distress. Not till about a week afterwards was there a relapse, accompanied by an infection of the mouth, renewed congestion of the eyes, and later hemorrhage of the bowels. Death followed on June 15.
>
> Nothing in the condition of the patient on May 22 gives fair support to the conclusion that hope had then been lost. She may have thought she was going to die and have said so to her nurse, but this was consistent with hope, which could not have been put aside without more to quench it. Indeed, a fortnight later, she said to one of her physicians, though her condition was then grave,

"You will get me well, won't you?" Fear or even belief that illness will end in death will not avail of itself to make a dying declaration. There must be "a settled hopeless expectation" (Willes, J. in Req. v. Peel, 2 F. & F. 21, 22) that death is near at hand, and what is said must have been spoken in the hush of its impending presence. Despair of recovery may indeed be gathered from the circumstances if the facts support the inference. There is no unyielding ritual of words to be spoken by the dying. Despair may even be gathered though the period of survival outruns the bounds of expectation. What is decisive is the state of mind. Even so, the state of mind must be exhibited in the evidence, and not left to conjecture. The patient must have spoken with the consciousness of a swift and certain doom.

What was said by this patient was not spoken in that mood. There was no warning to her in the circumstances that her words would be repeated and accepted as those of a dying wife, charging murder to her husband, and charging it deliberately and solemnly as a fact within her knowledge. To the focus of that responsibility her mind was never brought. She spoke as one ill, giving voice to the beliefs and perhaps the conjectures of the moment. The liquor was to be tested, to see whether her beliefs were sound. She did not speak as one dying, announcing to the survivors a definitive conviction, a legacy of knowledge on which the world might act when she had gone.

Shepard v. United States, 290 U.S. 96, 99-100 (1933). Are you persuaded? Are the words of Cardozo powerful enough to convince you of the validity of the exception? Are they just words, or do they capture a reality of the human condition?

4. Declarations Against Interest

a. Introduction and General Considerations

Declarations against interest are thought to be trustworthy on ground that a person is unlikely to state facts (or make statements) harming his own interest unless they are true.

Civil cases. Traditionally the exception embraced statements against financial or proprietary interest, and was invoked mostly in civil cases. If Sam says "I owe Tod $1,000," he concedes a debt, and the statement is against interest to that extent. It would likely be admissible to prove that he owed Tod that sum. (In a suit against Sam, Tod could offer the statement as Sam's admission— with no need for the against-interest exception. But if Sam has died and Tod presses a claim against his estate, resort to the exception may be necessary. You will discover in Chapter 6 that something called a Dead Man's Statute may bar Tod from testifying to what Sam said, but such statutes might not block testimony by others, or a document in which Sam acknowledges his debt.)

Similarly a statement acknowledging receipt of payment is likely to be against declarant's interest. If Tod said, "Sam paid me $200," the statement would be against Tod's interest in implying that Sam owes $200 less than before, and this same logic applies to a receipt for payment that Tod might give Sam[10]

---

10. Sometimes it is said that if the statute of limitations permits suit, his statement is against interest (it proves the date of payment, and might start a new limitations period, but it concedes payment); if the statute has run, his statement is self-serving (again it concedes payment but might begin a new limitations period, but this time it revives a previously barred claim for the unpaid balance).

Applying the exception is usually not so easy as this bare-bones example suggests. Even statements like Sam's can be difficult. Consider these factors:

1. *Context.* Here is a critical element. Imagine that Tod was hounding Sam to "pay back the $5,000 you owe me," and Sam said "I owe you $1,000." Sam's statement concedes a debt. But if his intent is to limit or reduce his obligation, it is not against interest, at least with respect to a claim above $1,000. Donovan v. Crisostomo, 689 F.2d 869, 876-877 (9th Cir. 1982) (statements by Philippine workers that they had not worked much were not against interest, when offered by employer in action by Secretary of Labor seeking back pay; a worker who might be sent back to the Philippines could feel that "it was in his interest to state he was paid properly to avoid the wrath of his employer").

2. *Conflicting interests.* Every person has multiple interests, and they are often complex rather than simple, conflicting rather than consistent. Not surprisingly, a statement may further one interest and impair another. In any such case, courts applying the exception could either (a) exclude the statement because conflicting interests cancel each other, or (b) determine whether the statement was predominantly disserving or self-serving, and admit or exclude accordingly.

Consider the dilemma of Mrs. Cosimo Demasi, an Italian immigrant who could neither read nor speak English. She and her husband operated a grocery in New Orleans, and just before the stock market crashed in 1929 she opened a savings account in a fictitious name, making her mark in the presence of a bank officer. At first the account held almost $700, but in 1932 her married daughter Carrie made a series of withdrawals, reducing the balance to about $70. Mr. and Mrs. Demasi sued the bank, alleging that the withdrawals were unauthorized, but the bank claimed Carrie had permission to draw from the account, and won. While an appeal was pending, the bank told Mrs. Demasi that she could take out the balance if she signed an affidavit conceding Carrie's authority. She did so and later died. On retrial Cosimo Demasi sought recovery for himself, arguing that the money was community property. The bank introduced Mrs. Demasi's affidavit and won again. But a reviewing court held that the affidavit was *not* a declaration against interest. The pertinent inquiry is whether the self-serving or the disserving interest preponderated:

Forasmuch as Mrs. Demasi at all times claimed ownership of the deposit and because of the pendency of this suit, the bank was only too willing to turn over to her this balance of $70.17, provided she consented to make a statement calculated to defeat her husband's recovery in these proceedings. She signed this document knowing that she would gain $70.17 by so doing and, from this point of view the affidavit must be considered as a statement tending to serve her interest. The disserving interest of the statement is her admission that the withdrawals from the savings account had been made by her or with her knowledge, approval, and consent. The problem is therefore: Which interest preponderated? Did she feel that she would obtain more by executing the document than she would lose in the event she failed to sign it? We cannot judge the disserving interest of the statement by what Mrs. Demasi would have gained in dollars and cents, had she not signed it, as it must be borne in mind that the suit . . . had already been tried in the district court and the judgment was adverse to his (and his wife's) interest. Hence it cannot fairly be said that, to the mind of Mrs. Demasi (for it is shown that she was an ignorant woman), she lost anything by signing the affidavit because it is probable that she felt (notwithstanding the appeal taken by her husband) there was little or no hope of success in maintaining the present suit for the recovery of the deposit. We believe that the interest which was uppermost in her mind (and which was the prevailing influence) was the fact that, by signing the document, she would receive $70.17 which she could not otherwise obtain. Moreover, it cannot be justly assumed that this woman realized that, by signing this affidavit, she was confessing that her testimony, given in this case, was false.

Demasi v. Whitney Trust & Savings Bank, 176 So. 703 (La. App. 1937).

3. *One-way interest.* A taxpayer fills out her return, stating taxable income for the year; an owner trying to sell his motel talks to a prospective buyer about gross receipts for a year. There are penalties for paying the government less than its due and for fraudulent sales, but the immediate interest of the taxpayer is to aim low, that of the owner to aim high. Each might speak against interest— she by overstatement, he by understatement. Does the instant exception play a role here?

Some courts have thought it might. If the taxpayer dies and suit is brought for wrongful death, decedent's tax return might be offered to show that decedent made *at least* as much as it says, for she would never declare more than she earned. If the motel owner dies and the property is condemned, the taking agency might offer the estimate of gross receipts as proof that the commercial value of the property is *no higher,* for declarant would never say the motel earned less than it did. See Plisco v. United States, 306 F.2d 784, 786-789 (App. D.C. 1962) (in IRS jeopardy assessment suit, admitting memoranda by taxpayers to show winnings but not losses; they "had no incentive to overstate their daily profit figures in order to increase their taxes," which the commissioner could accept as "minima," but "did have an incentive to overstate their daily loss," which commissioner could reject), cert. denied, 371 U.S. 948 (1963); Montgomery v. Fay, 80 S.E.2d 103, 111 (W. Va. 1954) (in wrongful death claim, what decedent told attorney to put on his tax return was admissible to show loss). Contra, Veach's Admr. v. Louisville & I. Ry., 228 S.W. 35 (Ky. 1921) (in wrongful death suit, tax return filed by decedent was not admissible to prove she earned at least the amount there stated, for return was "self-serving").

The exception is ill-designed for this situation, for nothing in statements or context shows that declarant spoke against interest. Yet we know the direction of her interest, and the statements seem reliable as proof of maximum or minimum. Although it might twist the exception (or show the need for another), here is a sensible outcome: Where the interest of declarant was to aim high, her statement should be admissible to show a maximum. Where the interest of declarant was to aim low, his statement should be admissible to show a minimum.

4. *Circumstantially adverse facts.* A statement may fit the exception without directly speaking of debts or property. Thus, a statement admitting fault in a context that might give rise to liability or loss to the declarant may satisfy the exception. In a suit by a building owner and insurance carrier against the tenant of a warehouse to recover for fire loss, for example, plaintiffs offered a statement made hours after the blaze by the tenant's employee Faulds to police officers and a fire inspector. There Faulds admitted that he and others had been drinking, and entered the warehouse at 3:00 A.M. and smoked cigarettes:

A statement is against pecuniary and proprietary interest when it threatens the loss of employment, or reduces the chances for future employment, or entails

> possible civil liability. . . . Here Faulds' statement is an important link in providing a basis for concluding that Faulds and the other nighttime visitors to the warehouse were responsible for starting the fire; the possibility of civil liability against him arising from the statement is thus evident. Indeed, an effort was made to make him a defendant in this case. . . . Further, even though [the tenant] did not have a rule against smoking on the premises, Faulds' admission that he had been there after hours, for a purpose unrelated to his employment, and while there did something which may have caused the destruction of his employer's stock in trade, reflects on his responsibility and trustworthiness, and can reasonably be said to jeopardize his standing with his employer.

Gichner v. Antonio Troiano Tile & Marble Co., 410 F.2d 238 (App. D.C. 1969) (case remanded to determine whether Faulds was unavailable).

5. *Declarant's understanding.* The exception only helps to pick out reliable statements if declarant understood his own interests and how the fact or statement could affect them. Hence courts exclude statements uttered by persons who lack the necessary information. See Filesi v. United States, 352 F.2d 339, 343-344 (4th Cir. 1965) (in suit by taxpayer to recover taxes previously assessed and paid, statement by deceased partner admitting that dancing went on in the bar they ran was not against his interest, partly because nothing indicated that he "realized the possible serious financial consequences to him which could arise from his admission that dancing was permitted"). Granting the soundness of the principle, can you believe that a tavern owner would be unaware of cabaret taxes?

6. *Effect of later events.* Some courts insist that the against-interest requirement is not satisfied where a statement becomes damaging in the light of later unexpected events. See Merritt v. Chonowski, 373 N.E.2d 1060, 1062-1063 (Ill. App. 1978) (in suit by car passenger alleging dramshop liability, driver coming out of bar said he "had consumed some six mixed drinks which were strong"; against-interest requirement not satisfied because he spoke "before the accident occurred at which time he had no reason to believe that he was going to become liable for an injury to another"). Can you believe someone about to drive a car would not know that admitting to drinking alcohol might be damaging?

7. *Conclusory remarks.* Two cars collide. One driver says to the other, "I'm sorry, lady, but you pulled right out in front of me," and she replies, "Yes, I know. It wasn't your fault." Is the woman's concession within the exception, though expressed as a conclusion? Some courts treat declarations against interest like admissions, allowing conclusions. Others disagree. Compare Ferrebee v. Boggs, 263 N.E.2d 574 (Ohio App. 1970) (truck driver's statement, "I didn't mean to kill your baby, it was all my fault," made to driver of car as ambulance took both to hospital, admissible against widow of truck driver in her suit for his wrongful death) with Carpenter v. Davis, 435 S.W.2d 382 (Mo. 1968) (admitting statement that declarant "pulled right out in front," but excluding statement that it "wasn't your fault"; opinions may be admissions, but not declarations against interest). Does it make sense to be stricter with conclusory statements when applying this exception than when applying the admissions doctrine?

Criminal cases. Traditionally the exception did not reach statements against "penal" interest. In a notorious prosecution of one Donnelly for the alleged murder of an Indian named Chickasaw, the Supreme Court found that a confession by Joe Dick (who had died of consumption) that he shot Chickasaw was inadmissible. The result moved Justice Holmes to protest that "no other statement is so much against interest as a confession of murder," which should be received as "far more calculated to convince than dying declarations, which would be let in to hang a man." Donnelly v. United States, 228 U.S. 243, 278 (1913). The argument against admitting confessions like Joe Dick's is that it invites defendants to offer perjured testimony describing third-party confessions that were never made, which are hard for prosecutors to investigate (let alone disprove) because necessarily the declarant is unavailable. The tide has turned, however, and modern authority extends the exception to statements against penal interest. What proved a surprise is the extent to which prosecutors use the exception for third-party confessions implicating the accused.

Statements against social interest. As originally proposed, FRE 804(b)(3) embraced statements tending to make the declarant "an object of hatred, ridicule, or disgrace," see F.R.D. 183, 321 (1972). But Congress balked, and courts either reject them outright or find that particular statements do not have this tendency. See United States v. Dovico, 380 F.2d 325, 327 (2d Cir.) (admission by prisoner that he and not defendant had committed the crime did not injure declarant's "penal or social interests"), cert. denied, 389 U.S. 944 (1967); United States v. Lemonakis, 485 F.2d 941, 956 (App. D.C. 1973) (prisoner admitted in suicide note that he lied about defendant; declarant's interest "against exposure to hatred, ridicule or disgrace, even if translated to his surviving family" was not sufficiently implicated), cert. denied, 415 U.S. 989 (1974). But see Timber Access Industries Co. v. U.S. Plywood-Champion Papers, 503 P.2d 482, 487-488 (Or. 1972) (admitting statement by operations manager admitting "disadvantageous deal" reflecting adversely upon his ability; against-interest exception would not apply, but declarant "was in a position to have knowledge" and "would not have made the statement unless it was the truth").

b. Criminal Cases—Statements Implicating the Accused

WILLIAMSON v. UNITED STATES
United States Supreme Court
512 U.S. 594 (1994)

JUSTICE O'CONNOR delivered the opinion of the Court, except as to Part IIC. In this case we clarify the scope of the hearsay exception for statements against penal interest. FRE 804(b)(3).

I

[Stopped for weaving on the highway, Reginald Harris was arrested after a search of the trunk led to the discovery of 19 kilograms of cocaine in two suitcases. DEA Agent Donald Walton interviewed him by phone. Harris said he got the cocaine from a Cuban in Fort Lauderdale, but it belonged to Fredel Williamson and was to be delivered at a dumpster that night. Later Walton spoke personally to Harris, who said he rented the car and drove to Fort Lauderdale to meet Williamson. Harris said he got the cocaine from a Cuban, who put it in the car with a note instructing Harris how to deliver the drugs.

Agent Walton tried to arrange a controlled delivery, but Harris then said he had lied about the Cuban, the note, and the dumpster. Actually, Harris said, he was taking the cocaine to Atlanta for Williamson, who had been driving in front in another car. Williamson saw that Harris had been stopped, doubled back and drove past, seeing the ongoing search. Hence a controlled delivery was impossible. Harris said he had lied because he was afraid of Williamson. He refused to let his statement be recorded or to sign a written version. Walton promised to report his cooperation to the U.S. Attorney.

Williamson and Harris were linked by other proof: The rental agreement listed Williamson as an additional driver; the luggage bore his sister's initials; the glove compartment held an envelope addressed to him and a receipt with his girlfriend's address.

Williamson was convicted of possessing cocaine with intent to distribute, conspiracy, and traveling interstate to promote distribution. Harris refused to testify, even when offered immunity and ordered to do so. The court admitted against Fredel Williamson what Reginald Harris told Agent Walton. On appeal Williamson claims the against-interest exception did not apply and that his rights under the Confrontation Clause were violated.]

II

A

. . . To decide whether Harris' confession is made admissible by FRE 804(b)(3), we must first determine what the Rule means by "statement," which FRE 801(a)(1) defines as "an oral or written assertion." One possible meaning, "a report or narrative," Webster's Third New International Dictionary 2229, definition 2(a) (1961), connotes an extended declaration. Under this reading, Harris' entire confession—even if it contains both self-inculpatory and non-self-inculpatory parts—would be admissible so long as in the aggregate the confession sufficiently inculpates him. Another meaning of "statement," "a single declaration or remark," definition 2(b), would make FRE 804(b)(3) cover only those declarations or remarks within the confession that are individually self-inculpatory. See also id. (defining "assertion" as a "declaration"); id. (defining "declaration" as a "statement").

Although the text of the Rule does not directly resolve the matter, the principle behind the Rule, so far as it is discernible from the text, points clearly to the narrower reading. FRE 804(b)(3) is founded on the commonsense notion that reasonable people, even reasonable people who are not especially honest, tend not to make self-inculpatory statements unless they believe them to be true. This notion simply does not extend to the broader definition of "statement." The fact that a person is making a broadly self-inculpatory confession does not make more credible the confession's non-self-inculpatory parts. One of the most effective ways to lie is to mix falsehood with truth, especially truth that seems particularly persuasive because of its self-inculpatory nature.

In this respect, it is telling that the non-self-inculpatory things Harris said in his first statement actually proved to be false, as Harris himself admitted during the second interrogation. And when part of the confession is actually self-exculpatory, the generalization on which FRE 804(b)(3) is founded becomes even less applicable. Self-exculpatory statements are exactly the ones which people are most likely to make even when they are false; and mere proximity to other, self-inculpatory, statements does not increase the plausibility of the self-exculpatory statements.

We therefore cannot agree with Justice Kennedy's suggestion that the Rule can be read as expressing a policy that collateral statements—even ones that are not in any way against the declarant's interest—are admissible. Nothing in the text of FRE 804(b)(3) or the general theory of the hearsay rules suggests that admissibility should turn on whether a statement is collateral to a self-inculpatory statement. The fact that a statement is self-inculpatory does make it more reliable, but the fact that a statement is collateral to a self-inculpatory statement says nothing at all about the collateral statement's reliability. We see no reason why collateral statements, even ones that are neutral as to interest, should be treated any differently from other hearsay statements that are generally excluded.

Congress certainly could, subject to the constraints of the Confrontational Clause, make statements admissible based on their proximity to self-inculpatory statements. But we will not lightly assume that the ambiguous language means anything so inconsistent with the Rule's underlying theory. In our view, the most faithful reading of FRE 804(b)(3) is that it does not allow admission of non-self-inculpatory statements, even if they are made within a broader narrative that is generally self-inculpatory. The district court may not just assume for purposes of FRE 804(b)(3) that a statement is self-inculpatory because it is part of a fuller confession, and this is especially true when the statement implicates someone else. "The arrest statements of a codefendant have traditionally been viewed with special suspicion. Due to his strong motivation to implicate the defendant and to exonerate himself, a codefendant's statements about what the defendant said or did are less credible than ordinary hearsay evidence." Lee v. Illinois, 476 U.S. 530, 541 (1986) (internal quotation marks omitted); see also Bruton v. United States, 391 U.S. 123, 136 (1968); Dutton v. Evans, 400 U.S. 74, 98 (1970) (Harlan, J., concurring in result).

[Quoting the ACN and the passage from McCormick that Justice Kennedy relies upon below, Justice O'Connor rejects the view that "an entire narrative, including non-self-inculpatory parts (but excluding the clearly self-serving parts)," fit the exception, finding that the ACN "is not particularly clear" and that its endorsement of McCormick "points the other way."] Without deciding exactly how much weight to give the ACN in this particular situation, we conclude that the policy expressed in the statutory text points clearly enough in one direction that it outweighs whatever force the Notes may have. And though Justice Kennedy believes that the text can fairly be read as expressing a policy of admitting collateral statements, for the reasons given above we disagree.

B

We also do not share Justice Kennedy's fears that our reading of the Rule "eviscerates the against penal interest exception," or makes it lack "meaningful effect." There are many circumstances in which FRE 804(b)(3) does allow the admission of statements that inculpate a criminal defendant. Even the confessions of arrested accomplices may be admissible if they are truly self-inculpatory, rather than merely attempts to shift blame or curry favor.

For instance, a declarant's squarely self-inculpatory confession—"yes, I killed *X*"—will likely be admissible under FRE 804(b)(3) against accomplices of his who are being tried under a coconspirator liability theory. Likewise, by showing that the declarant knew something, a self-inculpatory statement can in some situations help the jury infer that his confederates knew it as well. And when seen with other evidence, an accomplice's self-inculpatory statement can inculpate the defendant directly: "I was robbing the bank on Friday morning," coupled with someone's testimony that the declarant and the defendant drove off together Friday morning, is evidence that the defendant also participated in the robbery.

Moreover, whether a statement is self-inculpatory or not can only be determined by viewing it in context. Even statements that are on their face neutral may actually be against the declarant's interest. "I hid the gun in Joe's apartment" may not be a confession of a crime, but if it is likely to help the police find the murder weapon, then it is certainly self-inculpatory. "Sam and I went to Joe's house" might be against the declarant's interest if a reasonable person in the declarant's shoes would realize that being linked to Joe and Sam would implicate the declarant in Joe and Sam's conspiracy. And other statements that give the police significant details about the crime may also, depending on the situation, be against the declarant's interest. The question under FRE 804(b)(3) is always whether the statement was sufficiently against the declarant's penal interest "that a reasonable person in the declarant's position would not have made the statement unless believing it to be true," and this question can only be answered in light of all the surrounding circumstances.

C

In this case, however, we cannot conclude that all that Harris said was properly admitted. Some of Harris' confession would clearly have been admissible under FRE 804(b)(3). For instance, when he said he knew there was cocaine in the suitcase, he essentially forfeited his only possible defense to a charge of cocaine possession, lack of knowledge. But other parts of his confession, especially the parts that implicated Williamson, did little to subject Harris himself to criminal liability. A reasonable person in Harris' position might even think that implicating someone else would decrease his practical exposure to criminal liability, at least so far as sentencing goes. Small fish in a big conspiracy often get shorter sentences than people who are running the whole show, especially if the small fish are willing to help the authorities catch the big ones.

Nothing in the record shows that the District Court or the Court of Appeals inquired whether each of the statements in Harris' confession was truly self-inculpatory. As we explained above, this can be a fact-intensive inquiry, which would require careful examination of all the circumstances surrounding the criminal activity involved; we therefore remand to the Court of Appeals to conduct this inquiry in the first instance.

In light of this disposition, we need not address Williamson's claim that the statements were also made inadmissible by the Confrontation Clause, and in particular we need not decide whether the hearsay exception for declarations against interest is "firmly rooted" for Confrontation Clause purposes. We note, however, that the very fact that a statement is genuinely self-inculpatory—which our reading of FRE 804(b)(3) requires—is itself one of the "particularized guarantees of trustworthiness" that makes a statement admissible under the Confrontational Clause. See Lee v. Illinois, 476 U.S. 530, 543-545 (1986). We also need not decide whether, as some Courts of Appeals have held, the second sentence of FRE 804(b)(3) [quoting the language] also requires that statements inculpating the accused be supported by corroborating circumstances. The judgment of the Court of Appeals is vacated, and the case is remanded for further proceedings consistent with this opinion.

So ordered.

JUSTICE SCALIA, concurring. I join the Court's opinion, which I do not understand to require the simplistic view of statements against penal interest that Justice Kennedy attributes to it. . . .

Employing the narrower definition of "statement," so that FRE 804(b)(3) allows admission of only those remarks that are individually self-inculpatory, does not, as Justice Kennedy states, "eviscerate the against penal interest exception." A statement obviously can be self-inculpatory (in the sense of having so much of a tendency to subject one to criminal liability that a reasonable person would not make it without believing it to be true) without consisting of the confession "I committed X element of crime Y." Consider, for example, a declarant who stated: "On Friday morning, I went into a gunshop and (lawfully) bought a particular type of handgun and particular type of ammunition. I then drove in my 1958 blue Edsel and parked in front of the First City Bank with the keys in the ignition and the driver's door ajar. I then went inside, robbed the bank and shot the security guard." Although the declarant has not confessed to any element of a crime in the first two sentences, those statements in context are obviously against his penal interest, and I have no doubt that a trial judge could properly admit them.

Moreover, a declarant's statement is not magically transformed from a statement against penal interest into one that is inadmissible merely because the declarant names another person or implicates a possible codefendant. For example, if a lieutenant in an organized crime operation described the inner workings of an extortion and protection racket, naming some of the other actors and thereby inculpating himself on racketeering and/or conspiracy charges, I have no doubt that some of those remarks could be admitted as statements against penal interest. Of course, naming another person, if done, for example, in a context where the declarant is minimizing culpability or criminal exposure, can bear on whether the statement meets the FRE 804(b)(3) standard. The relevant inquiry, however—and one that is not furthered by clouding the waters with manufactured categories such as "collateral neutral" and "collateral self-serving"—must always be whether the particular remark at issue (and not the extended narrative) meets the standard set forth in the Rule.

JUSTICE GINSBURG, with whom JUSTICE BLACKMUN, JUSTICE STEVENS, and JUSTICE SOUTER join, concurring in part and concurring in the judgment. [Justice Ginsburg cites Lee as holding that a statement implicating another is inadmissible under the Confrontation Clause and stresses that an arrested person has "strong incentive to shift blame or downplay his own role" in hope of leniency and a shorter sentence. Hence none of the statements by Reginald Harris fit the exception, "even in part." She agrees in remanding, but only to let the government argue that admitting the statement was harmless error.]

JUSTICE KENNEDY, with whom the CHIEF JUSTICE and JUSTICE THOMAS join, concurring in the judgment.

I

. . . There has been a long-running debate among commentators over the admissibility of collateral statements. Dean Wigmore took the strongest position in favor of admissibility, arguing that "the statement may be accepted, not merely as to the specific fact against interest, but also as to every fact contained in the same statement." 5 J. Wigmore, Evidence §1465, p.271 (3d ed. 1940) (emphasis deleted). According to Wigmore, because "the statement is made under circumstances fairly indicating the declarant's sincerity and accuracy," the entire statement should be admitted. 5 J. Wigmore §1465, p.271 (3d ed. 1940). Dean McCormick's approach regarding collateral statements was more guarded. He argued for the admissibility of collateral statements of a neutral character, and for the exclusion of collateral statements of a self-serving character. For example, in the statement "John and I robbed the bank," the words "John and" are neutral (save for the possibility of conspiracy charges). On the other hand, the statement "John, not I, shot the bank teller" is to some extent self-serving and therefore might be inadmissible. See C. McCormick, Law of Evidence §256, pp.552-553 (1954) (hereinafter McCormick). Professor Jefferson took the narrowest approach, arguing that the reliability of a statement against interest stems only from the disserving fact stated and so should be confined "to the proof of the fact which is against interest." Jefferson, Declarations Against Interest: An Exception to the Hearsay Rule, 58 Harv. L. Rev. 1, 62-63 (1944). Under the Jefferson approach, neither collateral neutral nor collateral self-serving statements would be admissible. . . .

II

Because the text of FRE 804(b)(3) expresses no position regarding the admissibility of collateral statements, we must determine whether there are other authoritative guides on the question. In my view, three sources demonstrate that FRE 804(b)(3) allows the admission of some collateral statements. . . . :

[First, the ACN shows that some collateral statements are admissible, commenting that the exception reaches third-party confessions, including statements implicating the accused that come in as "related statements." Second, Congress intended that the principles and terms of the exception be applied "as they were at common law," which reached other facts contained in collateral statements connected with the disserving statement.]

There is yet a third reason weighing against the Court's interpretation, one specific to statements against penal interest that inculpate the accused. There is no dispute that the text of FRE 804(b)(3) contemplates the admission of those particular statements. Absent a textual direction to the contrary, therefore, we should assume that Congress intended the penal interest exception for inculpatory statements to have some meaningful effect. That counsels against adopting a rule excluding collateral statements. As commentators have recognized, "the exclusion of collateral statements would cause the exclusion of almost all inculpatory statements." Comment, 66 Calif. L. Rev., at 1207; see also Note, Inculpatory Statements Against Penal Interest and the Confrontation Clause, 83 Colum. L. Rev. 159, 163 (1983) ("most statements inculpating a defendant are only collateral to the portion of the declarant's statement that is against his own penal interest. The portion of the statement that specifically implicates the defendant is rarely directly counter to the declarant's penal interest") (footnote omitted); Davenport, The Confrontation Clause and the Co-Conspirator Exception in Criminal Prosecutions: A Functional Analysis, 85 Harv. L. Rev. 1378, 1396 (1972) ("the naming of another as a compatriot will almost never be against the declarant's own interest"). Indeed, as one commentator indicated, the conclusion that no collateral statements are admissible—the conclusion reached by the Court today—would "eviscerate the against penal interest exception." Comment, 66 Calif. L. Rev., at 1213.

To be sure, under the approach adopted by the Court, there are some situations where the Rule would still apply. For example, if the declarant said that he stole certain goods, the statement could be admitted in a prosecution of the accused for receipt of stolen goods in order to show that the goods were stolen. But as the commentators have recognized, it is likely to be the rare case where the precise self-inculpatory words of the declarant, without more, also inculpate the defendant. I would not presume that Congress intended the penal interest exception to the Rule to have so little effect with respect to statements that inculpate the accused.

I note finally that the Court's decision applies to statements against penal interest that exculpate the accused as well as to those that inculpate the accused. Thus, if the declarant said, "I robbed the store alone," only the portion of the statement in which the declarant said "I robbed the store" could be introduced by a criminal defendant on trial for the robbery. That seems extraordinary. The Court gives no justification for such a rule and no explanation that Congress intended the exception for exculpatory statements to have this limited effect.

III

Though I would conclude that FRE 804(b) (3) allows admission of statements collateral to the precise words against interest, that conclusion of course does not answer the remaining question whether all collateral statements related to the statement against interest are admissible; and if not, what limiting principles should apply. The ACN suggests that not all collateral statements are admissible. The ACN refers, for example, to McCormick's treatise, . . . [and McCormick stated that] within a declaration containing self-serving and disserving facts, he would "admit the disserving parts of the declaration, and exclude the self-serving parts" at least "where the serving and disserving parts can be severed." It thus appears that the ACN, by its reference to (and apparent incorporation of) McCormick, contemplates exclusion of a collateral self-serving statement, but admission of a collateral neutral statement.

In the criminal context, a self-serving statement is one that tends to reduce the charges or mitigate the punishment for which the declarant might be liable. See M. Graham, Federal Practice and Procedure §6795, p.810, n.10 (1992).

For example, if two masked gunmen robbed a bank and one of them shot and killed the bank teller, a statement by one robber that the other robber was the triggerman may be the kind of self-serving statement that should be inadmissible. By contrast, when two or more people are capable of committing a crime and the declarant simply names the involved parties, that statement often is considered neutral, not self-serving. See Graham, supra ("the statement 'John and I robbed the bank' is collateral neutral"); Note, 56 B.U. L. Rev., at 166, n.96 ("An examination of the decisions reveals that, with very few exceptions, collateral facts offered as part of a declaration against penal interest are neutral rather than self-serving").

Apart from that limit on the admission of collateral, self-serving statements, there is a separate limit applicable to cases in which the declarant made his statement to authorities; this limit applies not only to collateral statements but also to the precise words against penal interest. A declarant may believe that a statement of guilt to authorities is in his interest to some extent, for example as a way to obtain more lenient treatment, or simply to clear his conscience. The ACN takes account of that potentiality and states that courts should examine the circumstances of the statement to determine whether the statement was "motivated by a desire to curry favor with the authorities." That appears consistent with McCormick's recognition that "even though a declaration may be against interest in one respect, if it appears that the declarant had some other motive whether of self-interest or otherwise, which was likely to lead him to misrepresent the facts, the declaration will be excluded." McCormick §256, p.553.

Of course, because the declarant is by definition unavailable, see FRE 804(a), and therefore cannot be questioned to determine the exact motivation for his statement, courts have been forced to deviseadvise categories to determine when this concern is sufficient to justify exclusion of a statement as unreliable. It has been held, for example, that a statement to authorities admitting guilt, made after an explicit promise of dropped charges or of a reduction in prison time in exchange for the admission of guilt, may be so unreliable as to be inadmissible. See, e.g., United States v. Scopo, 861 F.2d 339, 348 (2d Cir. 1988) ("If . . . a pleading defendant had an agreement with the government or with the court that he would not be punished for the crimes to which he allocuted, then that allocution would not subject him to criminal liability and would not constitute a statement against his penal interest"). At the other extreme, when there was no promise of leniency by the government and the declarant was told that he had a right to remain silent and that any statements he made could be used against him, the courts have not required exclusion of the declarant's statement against interest. See United States v. Garcia, 897 F.2d 1413, 1421 (7th Cir. 1990) (declarant not motivated by desire to curry favor; he "voluntarily made his statement after being advised of his *Miranda* rights and did not enter into any plea agreements with the government"). This kind of line drawing is appropriate and necessary, lest the limiting principle regarding the declarant's possible desire to obtain leniency lead to the exclusion of all statements against penal interest made to police, a result the Rule and Note do not contemplate.

In sum, I would adhere to the following approach with respect to statements against penal interest that inculpate the accused. A court first should determine whether the declarant made a statement that contained a fact against penal interest. If so, the court should admit all statements related to the precise statement against penal interest, subject to two limits. Consistent with the ACN, the court should exclude a collateral statement that is so self-serving as to render it unreliable (if, for example, it shifts blame to someone else for a crime the defendant could have committed). In addition, in cases where the statement was made under circumstances where it is likely that the declarant had a significant motivation to obtain favorable treatment, as when the government made an explicit offer of leniency in exchange for the declarant's admission of guilt, the entire statement should be inadmissible. . . .

NOTES ON STATEMENTS AGAINST PENAL INTEREST THAT IMPLICATE THE ACCUSED

1. In substance, _Williamson_ holds that FRE 804(b)(3) does not reach associated (or "collateral") statements. Instead, Justice O'Connor's opinion for a six-member majority says a statement admitted under the exception must itself be against interest. Speaking for himself and two others, Justice Kennedy says the exception reaches statements that are neutral if they are related to against-interest statements. On this salient point of difference, O'Connor and Kennedy both stress legislative history and underlying purpose. Who has the better of the argument? Of course _Williamson_ does not bind states applying their own counterparts to FRE 804(b)(3). Some states have elected to follow _Williamson_. Others decline and go their own way. Compare State v. Keeton, 589 N.W.2d 85 (Minn. 1998) (following) with People v. Newton, 966 P.2d 563 (Colo. 1998) (declining).

2. The majority in _Williamson_ says, doesn't it, that a facially neutral statement may be against interest if context makes it so? Thus "Sam and I went to Joe's house" can be against interest "if a reasonable person in the declarant's shoes would realize that being linked to Joe and Sam would implicate the declarant in Joe and Sam's conspiracy." Assuming this condition is satisfied, the statement could be used to prove acts by Sam (he went with the speaker to Joe's house), couldn't it? That leads to the conclusion, doesn't it, that references to what others are doing need not be deleted from against-interest statements as "collateral"? Doesn't the majority confirm that a statement by one person (Harris, for instance) can be used against another person (Williamson, for instance) to prove what the latter did?

3. In _Williamson,_ the government offered statements by Reginald Harris referring to defendant Fredel Williamson. Forget for the moment what Harris initially said about the Cuban, and that Harris had been arrested and was talking to a DEA agent. In substance, Harris said the following:

I rented the car and went to Fort Lauderdale to meet Williamson. The cocaine in the suitcases in the trunk belonged to him, and I was transporting it to Atlanta for him. He was ahead of me in another rented car, but after I was stopped he turned around, came back and drove past, so he saw my car being searched. I lied about getting the drug from the Cuban because I'm afraid of Williamson.

What is most damaging to Williamson in this statement? Isn't it the claim that Williamson owned the cocaine, went on the drive to Atlanta (actively involved in transporting cocaine), and that Harris was acting for him? Don't these points implicate Harris in a conspiracy? Don't they do so as much as (if not more than) the statement cited by the majority as one that could fit the exception ("Sam and I went to Joe's house")? Then why does Justice O'Connor say the references to Williamson "did little to subject Harris himself to criminal liability"?

4.   Is the key point in *Williamson* the very one we put aside in Note 3 (Harris got himself caught red-handed with cocaine in his trunk and was talking to DEA agent Walton while under arrest)? What motivations affect someone in this situation? If Harris was "talking turkey," showing how helpful he could be in making a case against a cocaine distributor higher in the pecking order in a drug operation, his statements are profoundly untrustworthy, aren't they? This point animates the separate opinion by Justice Ginsburg for four Justices, who otherwise agree with Justice O'Connor. Indeed, all nine Justices acknowledge the force of this point, including the three Justices in Kennedy's concurrence. When someone speaks to authorities, Kennedy says, there is a limit that "applies not only to collateral statements but also to the precise words against penal interest" since the speaker may think admitting guilt "is in his interest to some extent" as a way of obtaining "more lenient treatment." In this setting, it is common to describe the motivation in terms of "currying favor," and "curry favor statements" are automatically suspect.

5.   Surely Reginald Harris had reason to curry favor with the DEA, since he had been arrested transporting drugs. Clearly a motive to curry favor arises when defendant and prosecutor engage in formal plea bargaining. See United States v. Bailey, 581 F.2d 341, 343-345 (3d Cir. 1978) (signed plea-bargaining statements made by co-offender with advice of counsel did not fit exception; he was motivated to help himself). Indeed, just being in custody triggers this concern. See United States v. Magana-Olvera, 917 F.2d 401, 407-409 (9th Cir. 1990) (statements naming defendant as drug source and claiming to be only middleman did not fit; speaker was in custody talking with federal authorities in attempt to curry favor).

6.   In the trial of Kim Schiappa for manslaughter in the death of her husband James, it appeared that she and her friend Stephen Staffy had sex, and that the two then attacked James, who had accosted them. The state offered testimony describing statements by Stephen, made shortly afterwards to his roommate in the presence of the defendant Kim, to the effect that he (Stephen) "just killed somebody," that "this stuff has to go" (referring to clothing and a knife), and that Kim "beat his ass too." Does the latter statement fit the exception? See State v. Schiappa, 728 A.2d 466 (Conn. 1999) (yes; state's theory was that Stephen bludgeoned James with a baseball bat and that Kim stabbed him with the knife). The court in *Schiappa* concluded that what it called "dual inculpatory statements" (meaning those that incriminate both speaker and defendant) can fit the exception. Would you be surprised to learn that *Schiappa* cites *Williamson* for the proposition that the question whether a statement is inculpatory can only be answered "in light of all the surrounding circumstances," and that there are "many circumstances" in which FRE 804(b)(3) reaches "statements that inculpate a criminal defendant"?

7.   In the *Lilly* case decided in 1999, the Court reached the constitutional issue it avoided in *Williamson*. *Lilly* involved a state conviction for robbery and murder, where the court admitted against Ben Lilly a confession by his brother Mark to police after his arrest, saying Ben murdered Alex. ("Ben shoots him," Mark said, answering "Pistol" when asked what Ben shot him with and "a couple of shots" when asked how many times Ben shot him.) A four-member plurality concluded that the against-interest exception was *not* "firmly rooted" for purposes of the Confrontation Clause, when applied to a confession implicating the accused, hence that the court had to determine on the basis of a particularized inquiry that the statement was trustworthy or reliable.[11] In *Lilly*, the Court concluded that this standard was not satisfied, even though Mark had been advised of his *Miranda* rights and had not been promised leniency. He had "a natural motive," the Court said, "to attempt to exculpate himself" and he would know that he may win leniency for himself by "placing blame on his cohorts." In short, *Lilly* involved another "curry favor" statement of the sort found in *Williamson*. See Lilly v. Virginia, 527 U.S. 116, 119 S. Ct. 1887 (1999) (reversing for constitutional error in admitting Ben's statement).

8.   As it turns out, *Lilly* did not dispose of the constitutional issue either, largely because the Court in *Lilly* was fractured, and five judges signed opinions that seemed to leave the door open to such statements under other circumstances. In this uncertainty, many state decisions continued to admit them, distinguishing *Lilly*. In 2004, however, everything changed: The Supreme Court handed down its decision in Crawford v. Washington, 124 S.Ct. 1354 (2004) (section G, infra). Of course the facts of *Crawford* are very different from those of *Lilly* and *Williamson*, but all three have in common the critical fact that the prosecutor offered in evidence a statement given to a law enforcement officer by someone involved with the defendant in the charged crime, in which the speaker talks about what the defendant did. Concluding that the Confrontation Clause bars the use against the accused of "testimonial" statements, the Court in *Crawford* reversed a state conviction for assault on this ground. The Court did not define "testimonial," but it said the term embraces *at least* statements "taken by police officers in the course of interrogations," and perhaps others too, such as statements that the declarant "would reasonably expect to be used" in prosecution. Consider the following points relating to *Crawford:*

(a) Clearly *Crawford* means that state courts cannot admit statements taken by police from alleged co-offenders that implicate the accused directly, like the statements in *Lilly* and *Williamson*.

(b) Perhaps *Crawford* does not reach statements made in conversations among friends, like the comments by Stephen Staffy to Kim Schiappa described in note 6, above, because they are "nontestimonial," although this conclusion is far from certain.

(c) Where *Crawford* does not apply, we cannot say with certainty whether the Confrontation Clause continues to require an individualized inquiry into

---

11.   Under the *Roberts* doctrine that prevailed when when *Lilly* was decided, hearsay fitting a "firmly rooted" exception satisfied the constitutional standard found in the Confrontation Clause of the Sixth Amendment. Hearsay not fitting such an exception, however, could be admitted only if specific factors indicate that it is trustworthy, and "corroborative evidence" does not count. See section G (Constitution as Bar Against Hearsay), infra.

reliability or trustworthiness. As you will see when you read *Crawford* and the *Roberts* case in section G, this question remains open.

(d) In this constitutional limbo, the *Williamson* gloss on FRE 804(b)(3) remains important.

9. Pending in 2004 are changes affecting FRE 804(b)(3). Those changes may be shelved for further consideration in light of *Crawford*. If they are adopted, however, they would seemingly tighten the requirements of the exception. For any statement "offered to inculpate an accused," the amendment requires that it be "supported by particularized guarantees of trustworthiness."

10.   In the trial of Tokars and Mason for racketeering, drug, and money laundering violations, evidence indicated that Tokars asked Lawrence to hire someone to kill his wife, Sara. Lawrence hired Rower, and he intercepted Sara as she returned from a trip and drove off with her in her car. Lawrence approached the car, and Sara was killed by the shotgun Rower was carrying. Police arrested Lawrence and Rower, but Rower claimed his shotgun went off accidentally when Lawrence grabbed it. In the later trial of Tokars and Mason, the prosecutor offered Rower's testimony from his bond hearing, where he said Sara had been kidnapped and that he (Rower) had agreed with Lawrence to kill her. Rower was unavailable at trial, and the court admitted his testimony from the bond hearing under the against-interest exception. The Court of Appeals affirmed the conviction. See United States v. Tokars, 95 F.3d 1520, 1534 (11th Cir. 1996) (stressing that Rowers did not directly implicate Tokars, and that what he said simply showed that Sara had been kidnapped). Does Rower's testimony fit the description offered in *Williamson* of a "squarely self-inculpatory confession" that would "likely be admissible" under FRE 804(b)(3) "against accomplices . . . who are being tried on a coconspirator liability theory"? Is it "testimonial" under *Crawford* even though it makes no mention of the persons against whom the statement is ultimately offered?

c.   Criminal Cases—Statements Exonerating the Accused

PROBLEM 4-M.   *"He Had Nothing to Do with It"*

While driving an 18-wheeler north on I-55 near Bloomington, Illinois, John Garvin is stopped by State Troopers Howard and Percy for a Motor Carrier Code violation. Garvin gets out of the cab and produces his license but does not have a logbook or bill of lading. On request, he lets Howard search the cab for these items, telling them he is traveling with co-driver Will Torrens, who is resting in the bunk behind the seat.

Officer Howard asks Torrens to get out of the cab and notes a strong smell of air freshener as Torrens emerges. Howard then looks through the cab as Percy watches the truckers. Once inside the cab, Howard smells a strong odor of marijuana and summons Percy, who notices it too. They see four brown suitcases, one with a sidepocket that is slightly unzipped. Howard sees duct tape through the opening and feels "bricklike objects" when he squeezes the bag. A trained dog is brought to the scene, leading to a search and the discovery of marijuana, both packed in the suitcases and hidden behind the bunk in the sleeping area.

Howard reads Garvin his *Miranda* rights, and Percy does the same with

Torrens. In one conversation Garvin tells Howard that the company assigned him to work with Torrens when Garvin's truck broke down, that the two drove from Milwaukee to Dallas to deliver a load of cheese, that on arrival in Dallas they got a hotel room, that Torrens left for several hours and on his return said the company wanted them to drive the cheese to Kansas City. Thereafter Garvin and Torrens took turns driving, and Torrens told Garvin the cheese had been delivered in Kansas City while Garvin was sleeping. Garvin said he never saw the bill of lading and knew nothing about any marijuana.

Meanwhile Torrens told Officer Percy: "The marijuana belongs to me, not Garvin. He had nothing to do with it. I just wanted to get rich quick. I took a chance and lost, and now I have to do the time. I'm ready for it."

Garvin and Torrens are charged in federal court with possessing marijuana with intent to distribute. Their motion to suppress the marijuana is rejected, and Torrens pleads guilty. Before Garvin is tried, the government successfully moves to suppress the statement by Torrens to Officer Percy exculpating Garvin. At trial the government proves the truck was empty and argues that Garvin must have known no cheese was ever carried or delivered and must have smelled the marijuana because its odor was apparent to Howard and Percy despite the air freshener. Garvin is convicted. On appeal, he argues that the court erred in excluding the statement by Torrens to Percy. What result, and why?

NOTES ON STATEMENTS AGAINST PENAL INTEREST THAT EXONERATE THE ACCUSED

1. Although Torrens is under arrest, he is not "currying favor" when he speaks to Officer Percy, is he? To put it another way, he is not blaming someone else while implicitly offering his services to help get a conviction, is he? Do the facts indicate that what Torrens said is trustworthy insofar as it tends to exonerate Garvin?

2. Was it against the interest of Torrens to tell Officer Percy that Garvin "had nothing to do with it"? Would a court following *Williamson* have to exclude this part of the statement? Some modern decisions admit statements exonerating defendants in this express manner. See, e.g., State v. White, 729 A.2d 31 (N.J. 1999) (statement exculpating defendant fits exception "if, when considered in the light of surrounding circumstances, they subject the declarant to criminal liability or if, as a related part of a self-inculpatory statement, they strengthen or bolster the incriminatory effect of the declarant's exposure to criminal liability"). Sometimes, however, courts come out the other way. See United States v. Vegas, 27 F.3d 773, 782 (2d Cir. 1994) (excluding proof that *J* said he knew "who gave me the drugs and who didn't" and that *M* and defendant "didn't give me" drugs). Does it matter whether the speaker says "the contraband is mine" or says instead "the contraband doesn't belong to the other guy; it's mine"? See United States v. Hilliard, 11 F.3d 618, 619 (6th Cir. 1993) (third party acknowledged "ownership of both the drugs and the money," which satisfied against-interest requirement).

3. In the trial of Bucky Barrett for crimes relating to the theft and sale of postage stamps from the Spellman Philatelic Museum, a coin dealer testified for the government that a gangster named Tilley asked him to appraise stamps

he and his gang had stolen. The dealer said he saw Bucky Barrett at the house to which he had been summoned, and another witness gave similar testimony. Then a man named Buzzy Adams testified that Bucky Barrett admitted his involvement. The defense offered testimony by James Melvin, who would (if allowed) testify that Tilley (who had died) told him over a poker game that he and Buzzy were "going to have some trouble" from California people over the stamp theft, that Melvin asked whether Tilley meant "Bucky or Buzzy" and Tilley said "No, Bucky wasn't involved. It was Buzzy." The trial court excluded Tilley's statement and Barrett was convicted. The reviewing court reversed, emphasizing that a reasonable person in Tilley's position would realize that his remark "strongly implied his personal participation in the stamp crimes." It conveyed the impression that he had "an insider's knowledge," and "the Bucky-Buzzy remark was sufficiently integral to the entire statement" that it should be admitted as "collateral" material that "actually tended to fortify the statement's disserving aspects." See United States v. Barrett, 539 F.2d 244, 251-253 (1st Cir. 1976). Would the reference to Bucky fit the exception after *Williamson?* Would the point about "insider knowledge" still justify admitting the statement? Does the reference to Bucky "fortify" other aspects of the statement enough to be against interest itself? Or is *Barrett* a good example of what Justice Kennedy warned about in *Williamson* in commenting that a court following the majority would have to delete "alone" from the statement "I robbed the store alone," if it were offered to exonerate a defendant charged with robbing the store?

4. *Barrett* approved use of the exception to admit a statement offered by the defense even though the speaker was talking with "acquaintances over cards" and might not have "expected his words to be repeated to the police." Another court applied the exception where the declarant was speaking to her daughter and an on "off-duty policeman friend." United States v. Goins, 593 F.2d 88, 90-91 (8th Cir.), cert. denied, 444 U.S. 827 (1979). It makes sense, doesn't it, to apply the exception to reach statements the speaker believes will not be reported to authorities? Even if disclosure to police seems improbable to the speaker, wouldn't ordinary caution and reluctance to create needless difficulties tend to assure truthfulness?

5. Sometimes application of the exception to statements exonerating the accused is easy: A third person confesses to having committed the deed, making no reference to defendant or others, in a setting in which the guilt of the declarant tends to exonerate the accused. See, e.g., Gray v. State, 796 A.2d 697, 534 (Md. 2002) (reversing conviction of husband for murdering wife; trial court erred in excluding statement by victim's lover to a friend to the effect that "I took care of her," which under the circumstances seemed to be a confession of murder).

d. Corroboration Requirement; Other Details

For statements offered to exonerate the accused, FRE 804(b) (3) requires corroboration. What does this mean? Consider the following account:

It is hard to say what is meant by "corroborating circumstances," but without them defendants in criminal cases cannot invoke the exception to admit third-party confessions. The requirement is satisfied by independent evidence that directly or circumstantially tends to prove the same points on which the statement is offered, and the requirement is almost certainly not met if the statement is demonstrably false in some important way. But the term seems broader and reaches evidence supporting the veracity of the speaker, including indications that the statement was against interest to an unusual degree or that he repeated the statement or could not be motivated to falsify for the benefit of the accused. The term should embrace other factors suggesting trustworthiness, such as spontaneity. A traditional concern was the risk of false reports of confessions, so it is plausible to suppose the corroboration requirement can be partly satisfied by additional proof that the statement was made. Some opinions mention the credibility of the testifying witness as a factor, but this one does not readily fit into the idea of corroboration, and it seems wiser to leave this matter to the testing process of direct and cross, and to the jury.

Mueller and Kirkpatrick, Evidence §8.74 (3d ed. 2003).

As written, FRE 804(b)(3) applies the corroboration requirement only to statements *exonerating* the accused, not statements *implicating* the accused. A proposal pending in 2004 to amend FRE 804(b)(3) would introduce more balance, although the proposal may be shelved in light of the decision in Crawford v. Washington, 124 S.Ct. 1354 (2004). If the amendment is adopted, statements exonerating the accused will continue to require corroboration, and statements implicating the accused will require "particularized guarantees of trustworthiness." The latter expression represents an attempt to tie the exception into the requirements of the confrontation clause and the doctrine of Ohio v. Roberts, 448 U.S. 56 (1980), which we take up in Chapter 4G, infra. With the decision in *Crawford*, the need for this change has diminished if not disappeared. *Crawford* is described briefly in the Notes after *Williamson*, supra, and is set forth in Chapter 4G, infra. Part of the reason that the corroboration requirement, in pre-amendment versions of the Rule, applies only to statements implicating the accused is that the framers did not expect prosecutors to use the exception very often.

If the amendment is shelved, FRE 804(b)(3) will continue to require corroboration for statements exonerating the accused but not for statements implicating the accused. Insofar as statements of the latter sort might still be admissible if they are "nontestimonial," the question of the imbalance in the Rule might still be an issue. Clearly the imbalance is constitutionally suspect, and some courts so they extend the requirement to statements implicating the accused. Here is the conclusion of one modern court:

[W]e agree with the parties that the requirement of corroborating circumstances clearly indicating the trustworthiness of a dual inculpatory statement [one that implicates the defendant and the declarant] greatly reduces the possibility of a confrontation clause violation, even though the statement properly may be admitted under rule 804(b)(3). "The admission of out-of-court statements by an unavailable declarant to inculpate a third party requires careful thought. Because the defendant has no opportunity to cross-examine the witness, the court must be thoroughly satisfied that the statements are accompanied by significant indicia of reliability. Absent factors that clearly indicate the trustworthiness of the statements, a confrontation clause problem arises." United States v. One Star, 979 F.2d 1319, 1322 (8th Cir. 1992). To the extent that rule 804(b)(3) is construed to permit only the use of those dual inculpatory statements that, in light of all the circumstances, carry strong indicia of reliability, such statements also are likely to satisfy the requirements of the confrontation clause. Essentially for this reason, and because "[t]he corroboration requirement of the [r]ule should be construed to effectuate its purpose of 'circumventing fabrication' " [United States v. Rodriguez, 706 F.2d 31, 40 (2d Cir. 1983), quoting ACN to FRE 804(b)(3)], a substantial number of the federal Circuit Courts of Appeals . . . have adopted the approach espoused by the parties.

In light of the significant confrontation clause issues presented by the use of a third-party statement offered to inculpate an accused, we believe that it would be incongruous to allow the admission of such a statement under a less restrictive standard than that employed for determining the admissibility of an exculpatory third party statement offered under rule 804(b)(3) "where [the] confrontation clause values at issue are minimal." [United States v. Sarmiento-Perez 633 F.2d 1092, 1099 (5th Cir. 1981), cert. denied, 459 U.S. 834 (1982).] Furthermore, the interpretation of rule 804(b)(3) that we approve today provides a uniform standard for statements against penal interest offered under the rule that either inculpate or exculpate the defendant.

State v. Schiappa, 728 A.2d 466, 477 (Conn. 1999). See also Tague, Perils of the Rulemaking Process: The Development, Application, and Unconstitutionality of Rule 804(b) (3)'s Penal Interest Exception, 69 Geo. L.J. 851, 890 (1981).

Sometimes defendants offer statements by already-incarcerated people in post-conviction attacks. Here courts are skeptical, especially where the speaker cannot be prosecuted for the criminal act because charges have been dropped or dismissed or the speaker is already convicted on charges relating to his statement. See United States v. Albert, 773 F.2d 386, 388-389 (1st Cir. 1985) (defense offered statement by co-offender at his sentencing hearing, but it did not fit exception because in that setting people speak "to help themselves, not to be sentenced to a longer term"); Witham v. Mabry, 596 F.2d 293, 296-298 (8th Cir. 1979) (rejecting challenge to murder conviction based on statement by incarcerated co-offender; absent proof that he was seeking post-conviction relief, his statement that defendant had nothing to do with killing was not against interest).

5. Statements of Personal or Family History

My mother told me I was born in West Virginia.
    Donald is my son.
    Dad told me that William was my uncle and that he sent for dad to join him in Texas.

These statements,[12] and others like them describing "family pedigree" and "family history," are admissible under FRE 804(b)(4) when the declarant is unavailable. The first statement would likely fit subdivision (A) of this exception

---

12. In order, the quoted statements above resemble those approved in Liacakos v. Kennedy, 195 F. Supp. 630, 633 (D.C. Dist. Col. 1961); Will of T., 86 Misc. 2d 452, 382 N.Y.S.2d 916, 919 (1976); Strickland v. Humble Oil & Rfg. Co., 140 F.2d 83, 86 (5th Cir.), cert. denied, 323 U.S. 712 (1944).

because declarant speaks mostly about herself. The second and third would likely fit subdivision (B) because she speaks mostly about "another person" related to her. Note that subdivision (B) would pave the way even for statements by a declarant who was "intimately associated" with the family of the person she describes, so statements by an intimate of the family conveying information of the sorts quoted above (where one was born, who was the son of whom, who was an uncle, and where he came from) would fit the exception.

Rule 804(b)(4) applies despite the fact that the declarant sometimes conveys what he heard from another and thus lacks personal knowledge (as is true in the first and third examples above). The exception is based on the assumption that pronouncements of this sort likely rest on adequate information, and in practice many are made before controversy arises and are thus untainted by the forces generating the litigation.

Where a statement is offered to prove facts about people other than the speaker, courts may require independent evidence that she belongs to the family (or is an intimate of the family) of the person described. See Fulkerson v. Holmes, 117 U.S. 389 (1886); United States v. Eng Suak Lun, 67 F.2d 307, 308-309 (10th Cir. 1933). But when her statement is offered to prove facts about herself (such as her marriage or children or the identity of her parents), other proof of the relationships in question is probably not required. See Morgan v. Susino Construction Co., 33 A.2d 607, aff'd, 36 A.2d 604 (N.J. 1943).

Courts applying the exception sometimes exclude self-serving statements, and those motivated by greed, ill will, or other forces suggesting untruthfulness. For example, in the prosecution of Puerto Rican immigrants Martha and Fernando Carvalho for alleged knowing use of false alien registration receipt cards, the government tried to prove that defendants, who married each other after meeting in the United States, were "sophisticated regarding the immigration laws." In support of this contention it offered affidavits from former spouses of each: One affiant said he married Martha "for love" several months earlier but planned "to terminate my marriage to this woman as soon as possible" and "to withdraw the application for permanent residence." The other said she married Fernando "because I felt sorry for him and out of anger because of what had happened to me" and because she "wanted to help him get his residence." The reviewing court concluded that these statements did not fit FRE 804(b)(4):

> While undoubtedly it is correct that for some purposes a statement regarding one's reasons for entering a marriage might well be a "statement concerning" one's marriage, it is also clear that evidence as to motive or purpose, highly debatable or controversial matters, is simply not within the scope of Rule 804(b)(4). . . .
>
> The propriety of a distinction between different types of facts concerning personal or family history relating to marriage is buttressed further by a comparison of marriage to the other items on the non-exhaustive list in Rule 804(b)(4). The list includes, for example, birth, adoption, divorce, legitimacy and ancestry. It is difficult to envision how issues similar to the frame of mind at the time of entering a marital relationship could arise regarding the other items on the list. More likely, the relevant issues instead would be a date of birth, existence of an adoption, or details of one's ancestry. Since "marriage" appears in Rule 804(b)(4) in the midst of a list of items unlikely to concern complex issues of motive, we

conclude that [affiants'] motives for marrying [defendants] was not a "fact" within the meaning of FRE 804(b)(4), and, accordingly, that the Rule does not provide a basis for admission of the affidavits.

United States v. Carvalho, 742 F.2d 146, 151 (4th Cir. 1984).

6. Statements Admissible Because of Forfeiture by Misconduct

Enacted in 1997, FRE 804(b)(6) paves the way to admit statements against a party who "engaged or acquiesced in wrongdoing that was intended to, and did," make the speaker unavailable as a witness. The intent is to deal with the problem of witness intimidation in criminal cases. One may speak of "waiver" in this setting, and decided cases often use this term. There is some merit in this practice, since "waiver" does suggest that the exception can only be invoked against a party who had the *intent* of keeping someone from testifying. But the caption in the new Rule speaks of "forfeiture," which seems a better term, since few people who intimidate witnesses are likely to know that what they are doing will cause loss of the protection of the hearsay doctrine at their eventual trial.

A handful of decisions, handed down before FRE 804(b)(6) was adopted, held that misconduct by a defendant that kept a grand jury witness from testifying at trial was enough to cause loss of protection of both the hearsay doctrine and the Confrontation Clause. See, e.g., United States v. Thevis, 665 F.2d 616, 627-628 (6th Cir.) (admitting grand jury testimony after finding that defendant was responsible for death of witness), cert. denied, 456 U.S. 1008 (1982). More importantly, the Supreme Court has commented that "the rule of forfeiture by wrongdoing (which we accept) extinguishes confrontation claims," seemingly clearing the way for the exception to operate. See Crawford v. Washington, 124 S.Ct. 1354 (2004) (Chapter 4G, infra).

PROBLEM 4-N. "If You Want to Stay Healthy"

Lanny Keeton is charged with armed robbery of Southside Quick Serve in St. Louis, and with assault and attempted murder. The crimes occurred at 2 A.M. when two masked men entered the store carrying sawed-off shotguns. The videotape shows that the two trained their guns on Nick Owens, the night-duty clerk in the cashier's cage behind bulletproof glass. Owens turned over the cash (as he was required to do in such situations), but the amount was small (less than $100) because he had just put most of the cash from the register into the safe, which could only be opened by dialing the combination and waiting ten minutes.

One perpetrator is seen on the videotape menacing a customer with the shotgun, and the customer is forced to lie face down on the floor. The videotape shows this perpetrator firing his shotgun through the change slot that scoops below the glass in the counter, injuring Owens who is struck by pellets that ricochet up inside the cage.

Ten days later, armed with minimal information supplied by the customer and Owens describing the getaway car, police arrest Marvin Spreigel in a routine traffic stop. (A search of the Police Information Network alerted the patrolman that Spreigel and his car might have been involved in the Quick Serve robbery.) Spreigel and Keeton are questioned separately. Spreigel acknowledges his participation in the robbery and says Keeton fired the shotgun at Owens and threatened the customer.

The prosecutor enters a plea bargain with Spreigel, who pleads guilty to aiding and abetting and agrees to testify against Keeton. When Keeton's case comes to trial, however, Spreigel refuses to testify. In a hearing in chambers attended by Spreigel and his lawyer, from which Keeton and his lawyer were excluded, Spreigel's lawyer reads a letter that he says Spreigel received from Keeton in jail while awaiting his sentencing hearing after entering his plea. The letter says "if you and that bitch of yours want to stay healthy, you know what you should do and what you shouldn't, so I better not see you as a stoolie at my trial." Spreigel's lawyer tells the judge that Lanny Keeton made oral threats targeting both Spreigel and his girlfriend.

The judge rules that statements Spreigel gave to police and prosecutors, as well as his later guilty plea allocutions, are admissible against Keeton under Rule 804(b)(6). Informed by the judge that the ruling rested on "conversations with Mr. Spreigel and his lawyer in chambers," the lawyer for Keeton raises a hearsay objection, and argues that "you can't find my client responsible for Spreigel's refusal to testify in an ex parte hearing on the basis of unsworn statements by a lawyer," and "besides, any finding that my client kept Spreigel off the stand must rest on proof beyond a reasonable doubt." Do these objections have merit?

NOTES ON THE FORFEITURE-BY-MISCONDUCT EXCEPTION

1. If you were the judge in this case, how would you feel about letting Keeton participate in a hearing designed to determine whether he threatened Spreigel? Why do you suppose Marvin Spreigel wanted his lawyer to do the talking? When the lawyer for Spreigel tells the judge that Keeton has threatened his client, the lawyer is accusing Keeton of another crime, isn't he? Doesn't that suggest that the judge should require proof beyond a reasonable doubt before finding Keeton in effect guilty of threatening witnesses or obstructing justice?

2. Recall from *Bourjaily* (page 215 supra) that the preponderance standard applies to decisions by the trial judge on the predicate facts of the coconspirator exception (one of which is that defendant and declarant must have conspired). See also United States v. Huddleston, 485 U.S. 681 (1988) (when prosecutor offers evidence that defendant committed some prior crime, in order to show things like intent at the time of the charged offense, preponderance standard applies) (pages 418-419, infra). Do *Bourjaily* and *Huddleston* support the view that the preponderance standard should apply to issues of waiver by misconduct under FRE 804(b)(6)?

3. Does Keeton have a due process right to be present in a hearing that

resolves the critical question whether hearsay statements can be admitted against him? See Kentucky v. Stincer, 482 U.S. 730 (1987) (in trial for sexual offenses against children, excluding defendant from a hearing to determine the competency of victims to testify did *not* violate due process or confrontation rights; his absence did not affect ability to cross-examine, and witnesses did not speak about the merits, so absence of defendant did not affect his opportunity to defend).

4. In a fair number of cases, what happens to a co-offender who "turns state's evidence" is that he gets killed. See United States v. White, 47 F.3d 909 (D.C. Cir. 1997) (defendant apparently shot Williams, his colleague-in-crime who was acting as government informant). Sometimes the trial itself involves criminal charges for the death of the victim. See United States v. Dhinsa, 243 F.3d 635, 653 (2d Cir.) (there is no "subject matter" limit on statements admissible under the exception; they can be used to prove that defendant murdered the declarant), cert. denied, 534 U.S. 897 (2001). If the court in such a case conducts a mini-hearing to determine whether to admit the out-of-court statements under FRE 804(b)(6), this mini-hearing can resemble a murder trial. In such cases, there is no reason to exclude the defendant from the hearing, is there? When the defendant is in effect accused of murdering the declarant, is there a stronger argument for applying the beyond reasonable doubt standard? In *White*, by the way, the reviewing court refused to adopt even a "clear and convincing" standard of proof, and approved a procedure in which a police detective read statements by unnamed witnesses who identified the defendant as the person who killed the informant Williams. The court noted that these same witnesses later testified in person on substantive issues in the case, so "in reality" the waiver determination "was not based on hearsay," but the court then pointedly commented that there was "no bar to partial reliance on hearsay" in determining the waiver issue.

5. Note that the prosecutor is offering statements that Marvin Spreigel made to police and prosecutors, and to the court in connection with his guilty plea. Stationhouse utterances and statements to prosecutors are sometimes written up and signed (even sworn to), and "guilty plea allocutions" are uttered in court on the record, but they are not testimony and usually they are not sworn (that's why they're called "allocutions" instead of testimony). If these statements were offered under the against-interest exception contained in FRE 804(b)(3), Spreigel's refusal to testify would satisfy the unavailability requirement. But wouldn't Spreigel be viewed as "currying favor" when he made his earlier statements, meaning that they wouldn't fit that exception? There is no trustworthiness requirement for statements offered under FRE 804(b)(6), is there?

6. As the Problem illustrates, coercive measures far short of murder can be effective in keeping a witness from testifying. See, e.g., Steele v. Taylor, 684 F.2d 1193, 1201 (6th Cir. 1982) (misconduct includes "persuasion and control by a defendant" and directing a witness "to exercise the fifth amendment privilege"), cert. denied, 469 U.S. 1053 (1983); United States v. Aguilar, 975 F.2d 45, 47 (2d Cir. 1992) (threats to tell other prisoners that witness is a murderer and an informer). Furthermore, it is often the case that defendants who want to discourage others from testifying are themselves in jail, and sometimes it is not the defendant personally, but others acting on his behalf who

kill or frighten (or "persuade") others so they don't testify. If the defendant simply *knows* that people "acting in his interests" are trying to frighten off a witness, is it enough that he takes no steps to discourage the attempt? See Friedman, Confrontation and the Definition of Chutzpa, 31 Israel L. Rev. 506, 520 (1997) (drafters of FRE 804(b)(6) wisely decided that forfeiture would occur "if, say, the defendant is in prison, knows about the illicit efforts about to be made on his behalf, and does nothing to stop them," but it might be as hard to prove knowledge as it is to prove direct intimidation).

7. What about out-of-court statements made by someone who was threatened not by the defendant, but by another with who the defendant was involved in criminal conspiracy of some kind? This issue arose in United States v. Cherry, 217 F.3d 811 (10th Cir. 2000), later appeal, 265 F.3d 1097 (10th Cir. 2001), cert. denied, 535 U.S. 1099 (2001), where Joshua and Teresa Price and three others were tried on drug conspiracy charges and Joshua apparently murdered a man named Lurks, who had made statements that were later offered in evidence against all five defendants. Lurks had been cooperating with the government, and his ex-wife told Joshua Price what Lurks was doing, apparently because she was angry at Lurks in connection with a child custody dispute. The approach outlined by *Cherry* merits close consideration:

(a) In *Cherry*, the trial court found that only Joshua Price had waived his confrontation rights, although circumstantial evidence suggested that Teresa Price had obtained a car, that she and Joshua drove to Lurks' home at the time of the murder, and that Teresa was present when Lurks was shot (a witness who spoke with Lurks by phone shortly before his death testified that she heard Teresa's voice "singing in the background").

(b) The Tenth Circuit thought that the trial court had applied the waiver doctrine too narrowly. Adopting in this setting the doctrine of Pinkerton v. United States, 328 U.S. 640 (1946), which defined the extent to which a conspirator could be liable for substantive crimes committed by other conspirators, the Tenth Circuit concluded that *Pinkerton* defines the appropriate reach of waiver. Under this approach, waiver of confrontation rights occurs if (i) a defendant "participated directly in planning or procuring the declarant's unavailability through wrongdoing," or (ii) the wrongful procurement "was in furtherance, within the scope, and reasonably foreseeable as a necessary or natural consequence of an ongoing conspiracy." 217 F.3d 811, at 820.

(c) The Tenth Circuit explained in *Cherry* that the scope of a conspiracy "is not necessarily limited to a primary goal—such as bank robbery—but can also include secondary goals relevant to the evasion of apprehension and prosecution for that goal—such as escape, or, by analogy, obstruction of justice." And a conspirator is responsible for the acts of colleagues unless he or she "meets the burden of proving that he or she took affirmative steps to withdraw from the conspiracy before those acts were committed." 217 F.3d 811, at 821.

(d) The Tenth Circuit stressed in *Cherry* that it was not adopting the *Pinkerton* scope-of-conspiracy doctrine for the purposes of imposing substantive liability for murder: Thus Teresa Price would not necessarily be guilty of the crime of murder on these facts, nor would the other three conspirators. But the *Pinkerton* test determines whether Teresa and the other three waived their confrontation rights.

(e) If you were the trial judge on remand in *Price*, would you find that

Teresa Price waived her confrontation rights? If she obtained the car and drove with Joshua to the murder scene, and was there when Joshua shot Lurks, wouldn't you find by a preponderance that Teresa "participated directly in the planning or procuring" of the unavailability of Lurks?

(f) The issue is much harder, so far as these facts reveal, for the other three, isn't it? If a drug conspiracy is threatened by exposure by a cooperating witness and one of the conspirators murders the witness, does that constitute "wrongful procurement in furtherance, within the scope, and reasonably foreseeable as a necessary or natural consequence" (to quote the *Price* standard)? See United States v. Thompson, 286 F.3d 950, 966 (7th Cir. 2002) (adopting *Cherry* standard but concluding that members of drug conspiracy neither knew nor had reason to know that informant would be murdered; hence they did not waive confrontation rights) (error harmless), cert. denied, 123 S.Ct. 918 (2003).

(g) Does it make sense to find that a defendant has waived or forfeited his confrontation rights, on account of the murder of an important witness by a colleague, if the facts are such that defendant could not be guilty of the crime of murder?

8. Suppose an intimidated witness actually takes the stand at defendant's trial, refusing to testify in a manner consistent with his pretrial statements to the prosecutor or to law enforcement officers. If the court concludes that defendant has forfeited his confrontation rights by frightening this witness to keep him from testifying, does it follow that the defense cannot cross-examine the witness after the prosecutor introduces his out-of-court statements under the exception? See Cotto v. Herbert, 331 F.3d 217, 251 (2d Cir. 2003) (granting habeas corpus relief from state murder conviction; reversible constitutional error to preclude defense cross-examination of declarant, who claimed not to have seen the crime but admitted that he had to think of his family).

E.   THE CATCHALL EXCEPTION

1.   *Origin of the Catchall*

Last of the exceptions in Article VIII is the so-called catchall that is now codified in FRE 807. When the Rules were enacted, there were two catchalls, one set out as 803(24) and the other as 804(b)(5). They were identical, although the latter required the declarant to be unavailable as a witness. In 1997, they were consolidated in FRE 807, which did away with the redundancy but made no substantive change in wording. This provision authorizes courts to admit hearsay that does not fit any of the other ("categorical") exceptions if it is nevertheless trustworthy and necessary.

Origin: The Dallas County case. The catchall descends from occasional pre-Rules cases recognizing that sometimes reliable and necessary hearsay simply does not fit any established exception. The classic case, cited by the Advisory Committee and the Senate Report on the original catchall provisions, is Dallas County v. Commercial Union Assurance Co., 286 F.2d 388 (5th Cir. 1961). There, Dallas County sued an insurance carrier after the wooden clock tower above the courthouse in Selma, Alabama, collapsed on a Sunday morning in July. The County claimed that lightning had caused the collapse, but the carrier claimed that the charred timbers came from a fire that happened while the tower was under construction many years earlier. The trial judge admitted an old newspaper clipping to prove the earlier fire. In an eloquent opinion by Judge Wisdom, the reviewing court affirmed:

> There is no procedural canon against the exercise of common sense in deciding the admissibility of hearsay evidence. In 1901 Selma, Alabama, was a small town. Taking a common sense view of this case, it is inconceivable to us that a newspaper reporter in a small town would report there was a fire in the dome of the new courthouse—if there had been no fire. He is without motive to falsify, and a false report would have subjected the newspaper and him to embarrassment in the community. The usual dangers inherent in hearsay evidence, such as lack of memory, faulty narration, intent to influence the court proceedings, and plain lack of truthfulness are not present here. To our minds, the article published in the Selma Morning-Times on the day of the fire is more reliable, more trustworthy, more competent evidence than the testimony of a witness called to the stand fifty-eight years later.

286 F.2d 388, at 391-392, 397.

The Rules. In early drafts, the framers of the Rules wanted to follow the lead of Judge Wisdom in *Dallas County,* so those drafts *began* with broad-brush provisions. Under proposed Rule 8-03, a statement by an available declarant was not excludable hearsay "if its nature and the special circumstances under which it was made offer assurances of accuracy not likely to be enhanced by calling the declarant as a witness," and proposed Rule 8-04 did the same thing for a statement by an unavailable declarant if circumstances offered "strong assurances of accuracy." Both provisions then hammered home the main point by setting out lists of "examples" that basically track what we call the categorical exceptions (business records, excited utterances, and so forth), only these were offered "[b]y way of illustration only, and not by way of limitation." See the Preliminary Draft of March, 1969, 46 F.R.D. 161, 345, 377 (1969).

The legal profession was uncomfortable with such broad provisions and strenuously opposed this approach. Before the Rules reached Congress, the Committee sensed the direction of the wind and changed course. It abandoned its lists of "examples" in favor of categorical exceptions that were prescriptive rather than exemplary. It moved the broad-brush provisions out of the opening lines of Rules 803 and 804, and put them at the bottom instead. But the Committee did not abandon those provisions, for the final lines of both Rules continued to authorize courts to admit any statement "not specifically covered by any of the foregoing exceptions but having comparable circumstantial guarantees of trustworthiness." See 51 F.R.D. 315, 419-422, 439 (1971).

Congress made changes, however, which are now visible in FRE 807. It was Congress that added requirements framed in terms of (1) material fact, (2) probativity and diligence, (3) interest of justice, and (4) notification to the adversary. Consider these detailed (almost forbidding) words that squeeze and hedge the exception. Consider too its placement *after* lists of more categorical exceptions. What is the message here?

2. *The Catchall and Proof of Exonerating Facts*

| STATE v. WEAVER
| Supreme Court of Iowa
| 554 N.W.2d 240 (1996)

McGIVERIN, CHIEF JUSTICE.

[Mary Weaver was charged with first degree murder and child endangerment in the death of 11-month-old Melissa Mathes. Her first trial resulted in a hung jury. She then requested a court trial, and was convicted by Judge Peterson of first degree murder.

Mary Weaver had picked up Melissa at the Mathes home at 10:20 A.M. on Friday, January 22, 1993. At 11:14 A.M., Weaver called 911 and reported that Melissa was not breathing. The child died of respiratory arrest the next day.

An autopsy showed that Melissa had old and recent injuries, including a skull fracture, subdural hematoma, bleeding in the brain, and bilateral retinal hemorrhages, which were "consistent with shaken baby syndrome." Doctors Robinson, Folberg, and Schelper thought the skull fracture was seven-ten days old. Dr. Robinson thought the subdural hemorrhage was one to two weeks old, and that cell death and a blood clot in the brain were seven-ten days old. Melissa also suffered "acute injuries," including "diffuse subarachnoid hemorrhage, contusion (frontal cortex), bilateral retinal hemorrhage, and bilateral anterior chamber hemorrhage." These conditions "would have been nonsubtle and immediate," and occurred shortly before Melissa arrived at the hospital.

After her conviction, Mary Weaver moved for a new trial on the basis of affidavits by Robin McElroy and Mistry Lovig, who reportedly did not know each other, but said that Melissa's mother Tessia Mathes had said that Weaver "had not hurt Melissa" and that Melissa "had hit her head on a coffee table at the Mathes home" on the morning of January 22 before being placed in Mary Weaver's care. Judge Peterson denied the motion, concluding that the affidavits contained hearsay that fit no exception and lacked "circumstantial guarantees of trustworthiness."

The Court of Appeals affirmed the conviction, but the Iowa Supreme Court remanded the case to consider a second new trial motion based on new affidavits by three other women recounting another statement by Tessia Mathes. Chief Judge Ronald Schechtman referred the matter to Judge Alan Goode, from a nearby judicial district.[5] At the hearing on this motion, Mary Weaver adduced live testimony by all five women describing statements by Tessia Mathes. The Supreme Court, however, limits its consideration to the new affidavits by the three women, which it quotes:

---

5. Chief Judge Schechtman gave the following reasons for the special assignment: Due to the nature and circumstances of the limited remand, the nature of the motion, the fact that the original trial court was the factfinder, without a jury, and the availability of a complete transcript of the trial, the undersigned concludes that the matter warrants the assignment of a special judge, who has not been a previous trial court herein, to hear the merits of the motion for new trial. Counsel for each of the parties, as well as the defendant, have no objection to this administrative assignment. [This is the Court's footnote—Eds.]

(1)   Affidavit by Evelyn Braack (age 68) dated 10/20/95:

>   Some friends of ours and my husband and I have coffee every
>   Wednesday afternoon around 2:30 P.M. at Hardees in Marshalltown.
>   The women sit together and the men do the same. We knew Tessia
>   Mathes as she worked there. Shortly after the baby died (2-3 weeks)
>   Tessia told the women present that she had been putting on the baby's
>   snowsuit and she had thrown her head back and hit her head on a
>   table injuring her head but she did not say how bad. . . .

(2)   Affidavit by Flossie Wall (age 67) dated 10/24/95:

>   My husband and I meet at Hardees every Wednesday for coffee
>   with several couples. Tessia Mathes worked there. Shortly after her
>   baby died and was buried she came back to work and came over to
>   talk to us. She told us that one morning as she was dressing the baby
>   to leave the house she was putting on the baby's snowsuit, [the baby]
>   was fussing and moving around. The baby hit her head on the coffee
>   table and was knocked unconscious. . . .

(3)   Affidavits by Elaine Kail (age 68) dated 10/20/95 and 10/24/95:

>   Several friends including our husbands meet on Wednesday after-
>   noons at about 2:30 P.M. at Hardees. A short time after the baby died,
>   her mother Tessia told myself and Evelyn Braack, Flossie Wall, Donna
>   Parsons, that one morning as she was dressing Melissa, the baby had
>   hit her head on the coffee table. She did not elaborate any further. . . .
>
>   This statement [is] in addition to the statement I provided on
>   October 20, 1995. That night I thought about this further and remem-
>   bered that Tessia had told us the baby had went limp after she had
>   hit her head on the coffee table and became unconscious. My impres-
>   sion was that Tessia was telling us how the baby had died. It was my
>   impression that the baby struck her head on the coffee [table] on the
>   morning that she died.

None of the affiants "could absolutely identify the date" on which Tessia
Mathes said the coffee table incident occurred, but the reviewing court does
not consider this "determinative," and it notes that Judge Goode thought it
was "reasonable to assume" that the affidavits referred to an incident that
occurred on January 22, 1993 "some time prior to the time defendant picked
up Melissa." The State and the defense agree that if she were called as a witness,
Tessia Mathes would testify that Melissa "neither struck her head against a
coffee table" on the fateful morning nor "ever lost consciousness for any reason
while in Tessia's care," and that she (Tessia) "never described" to Braack, Wall,
or Kail any "fall" against a coffee table that would have resulted in a loss of
consciousness.

One question on appeal is whether Tessia Mathes' statements would be
admissible in a new trial.]

After a careful consideration of the record in this matter including the
findings of the district court, we believe the court did not abuse its discretion
in ruling that the affidavits and testimony of Braack, Wall and Kail at the hearing
on the motion were admissible hearsay evidence. Therefore, the district court

properly considered that evidence in ruling on defendant's second motion for new trial.[10]

As the State contests only the trustworthiness prong of admissibility under IRE 803(24), we consider the merits of that factor only and deem the other factors waived in the State's appeal. . . .

Factors to consider in making a trustworthiness determination under rule 803(24) include: the declarant's (Tessia Mathes') propensity to tell the truth, whether the alleged statements by Tessia Mathes were made under oath, assurance of Tessia Mathes' personal knowledge, the time lapse between the alleged event and the statement by Tessia Mathes concerning the event, and the motivations of Tessia Mathes to make the alleged statements. Additional circumstances to consider include corroboration, reaffirming or recanting the statement by the declarant, credibility of the witness reporting the statement, and availability of the declarant for cross-examination.[11]

In concluding that the affidavits and testimony were trustworthy for purposes of admissibility under rule 803(24), the district court made the following findings based on the facts and trustworthiness factors to be considered:

1. The witnesses reporting the statement are very credible.
2. The declarant, Tessia Mathes, is available to testify.
3. The statement was made shortly after the incident in close proximity to events the declarant could be expected to remember.
4. The declarant had firsthand knowledge of the substance of the statement and was not relying on potentially erroneous secondary information.
5. The statement was unambiguous and explicit that the event occurred.
6. The statement was in response to an open-ended question, and was not the result of interrogation or investigation by the accused or others on her behalf.
7. The statement was made to more than one person, who agree on the substance of what was said.
8. A similar account of the episode of trauma was made on other separate occasions.
9. The statement is corroborated by objective medical evidence showing a contusion on the left occiput which has not been otherwise explained.

In addition to the above findings, several other facts convince us that the affidavits and testimony were sufficiently trustworthy to constitute admissible hearsay under IRE 803(24) under this record. The three affiants were acquaintances of Tessia Mathes, the declarant, only through her employment at Hardees. The affiants did not socialize with Tessia Mathes and only saw and spoke to her when they would go to Hardees for coffee with their friends. None of

10. In retrial on the merits, the evidence of the witnesses Braack, Wall, and Kail must be offered in the usual way, will be subject to objection anew, and must be ruled on by the court as to admissibility. The affidavits alone of those witnesses would not be admissible at trial without agreement of both the State and the defendant.

11. We do not believe the above factors are an exclusive list to be considered in any one given trustworthiness analysis.

the affiants are alleged to have had a personal vendetta against Tessia Mathes and, perhaps more importantly, none of the affiants personally knew the defendant.

In opposition to the above findings, the State asserts the information provided in the affidavits is not trustworthy for several reasons, including: (1) the passage of time, nearly three years from the time Tessia Mathes allegedly offered the statements to the affiants; (2) the affiants' exposure to extensive media coverage over Melissa's death and the resulting trials; and (3) the affiants' admitted collective memory efforts regarding the statements allegedly made to them by Tessia Mathes a couple of weeks after Melissa's death.

As we believe the above contentions go to the weight to be given to the evidence and not admissibility, we find the State's attempt to bar the admissibility of the affidavits to be without merit for the purposes of the hearing on the motion.

Based on the findings of the district court and additional facts herein stated which are supported by substantial evidence, we cannot conclude the court's decision to admit the evidence under IRE 803(24) was an abuse of discretion. There are facts in the record that establish the trustworthiness of the affidavits; therefore, we cannot conclude the court's ruling was clearly unreasonable or was based on clearly untenable grounds.

As the State does not contend on appeal that defendant has not satisfied the other factors required to prove admissibility under rule 803(24) at the hearing on the motion, we find those are met.

[Reaching the question whether this evidence "probably would have changed the result at trial," the court notes the State's claim that nobody believes that the retinal hemorrhages and the bilateral anterior chamber hemorrhages could have been caused by a fall against the coffee table. But the court concludes otherwise.]

One of defendant's medical experts, Dr. Blackbourne, testified at the hearing on defendant's second motion for new trial that Melissa's bilateral retinal hemorrhages could have been attributable to chronic edema that the child may have had from the alleged cookie monster chair incident on January 22, 1993. Dr. Earl Rose opined that Melissa's respiratory arrest was caused when a previously existing subdural hematoma re-bled. Based on the newly-discovered evidence, Dr. Rose believed the alleged coffee table incident caused the rebleed to occur and resulting respiratory arrest. On cross-examination, Dr. Rose agreed that the existing subdural hematoma could have either been caused by Melissa's alleged fall from the cookie monster chair on January 22, 1993 (as maintained by Tessia Mathes), or from the alleged coffee table incident on the morning of January 22, 1993 (as alleged by the three affiants).

Although the State and its medical experts vigorously challenge [these] theories concerning the cause of death, we believe the district court's conclusion that the newly-discovered evidence probably would change the result at trial was not clearly unreasonable or untenable. The State's case advocating shaken or slammed baby syndrome as the cause of death was disputed by the defendant's experts based in part on the newly-discovered evidence. There is a factual basis in the record to support the court's grant of defendant's second motion for new trial. The district court in an extensive ruling evaluated the newly-discovered evidence and assessed the credibility and weight of the new witnesses' testimony against the complete trial record and thus was in a good position to determine what evidence would and would not probably change the result at trial.

NOTES ON PROVING EXONERATING FACTS WITH THE CATCHALL

1. Three times the court in *Weaver* speaks in terms of admitting the "affidavits and testimony" of Evelyn Braack, Flossie Wall, and Elaine Kail, but isn't it clear that the court expects these women to testify? Using their affidavits to prove Tessia made the crucial statement, which in turn indicates that Melissa hit her head on a table, would involve *double* hearsay, wouldn't it? There is but one layer of hearsay if the three women testify to what Tessia Mathes said. Are you satisfied that the statement by Tessia Mathes to the three women was trustworthy? Are you bothered by the fact that the affidavits were prepared more than two and one-half years after Melissa died? How important is it that Tessia Mathes was expected to testify? How important is it that the fact asserted (Melissa hit her head) was corroborated by medical evidence? The court comments that Mathes made similar statements to others (a reference to her conversations with Robin McElroy and Mistry Lovig). Why does this count?

2. After this opinion, Mary Weaver was tried a third time. Tessia Mathes testified for the state, indicating that nothing untoward happened to Melissa that morning and denying that she made statements describing a fall. All five of the women mentioned above testified, and said Tessia Mathes told them that Melissa fell. Was the catchall exception necessary in this case? The prior statements by Tessia Mathes would have been admissible to impeach her testimony. Iowa has a rule identical to FRE 801(d)(1)(A), which would *not* reach the statements by Tessia Mathes to the five women because they were not made under oath in proceedings. So they could *only* be used to impeach. What difference does that make in this case, if any?

3. Would the statements by Tessia Mathes fit the against-interest exception? She didn't say *she* had done anything to Melissa—only that Melissa hit her head while Tessia was putting her into her snowsuit. But an adult in charge is always responsible to some extent for injuries suffered by infants (a concept recognized in the child endangerment charges brought against Mary Weaver), and the possibility that Melissa sustained an earlier untreated skull fracture plus a head-bumping incident at home raises questions about the nature of parental care. Is there any doubt that if the state had prosecuted the mother instead, her statement would be offered to show she didn't take proper care of Melissa? But Tessia Mathes testified in the trials of Mary Weaver, so the against-interest exception could not apply. Some courts subscribe to the "near miss" theory, under which a statement that *almost* fits one of the categorical exceptions cannot be admitted under the catchall. See United States v. Vigoa, 656 F. Supp 1149, 1504 (D.C. N.J. 1987) (refusing to admit grand jury testimony that did not fit former testimony exception because there was no opportunity to cross-examine, and concluding that catchall could not apply to statements that were "covered" but excluded by other exceptions). Most courts reject this theory. See, e.g., United States v. Clarke, 2 F.3d 81, 83 (4th Cir. 1993) (admitting

testimony from suppression hearing in related case, and rejecting near miss theory). Is the unavailability requirement of the against-interest exception so crucial that using the catchall in *Weaver* would undermine important policy concerns? The "near miss" theory is different, isn't it, from the theory adopted in the *Oates* case (page 292, supra), under which the use restriction in FRE 803(8)(B) would bar a court from admitting a police report under the business records exception?

4.   Suppose now a case in which someone on trial for a crime wants to offer a third-party statement that not only asserts facts that exculpate the defendant (as in *Weaver*) but actually *confesses* to the crime (unlike *Weaver*). And suppose that the against-interest exception can't do the job alone, either because the person who confesses is available or because the person who heard him confess won't testify, but did tell others about the confessions. In such cases courts are only sometimes willing to apply the catchall. Compare United States v. Hall, 165 F.3d 1095, 1110-1111 (7th Cir. 1999) (in kidnap-rape-murder trial, excluding confession by *G*, which did not fit catchall; *G* appeared to be psychotic, confessing to any crime about which he was questioned, lacked knowledge of pertinent facts, and there was no corroboration) and State v. Walker, 691 A.2d 1341 (Md. 1997) (refusing to apply catchall to statement by girlfriend of defendant indicating that he confessed to armed robbery; the two had married, and she refused to testify against him; her unavailability was not an extraordinary circumstance justifying use of catchall) with Demby v. State, 695 A.2d 1152 (Del. 1997) (in murder trial, error to exclude videotaped statement by Lehman reciting confession in which Flonnory said he, and not defendant, shot victim; Lehman and Flonnory invoked privilege against self-incrimination and refused to testify; Flonnory's statement fit against-interest exception, and Lehman's videotaped recitation of Flonnory's statement fit catchall).

5.   Mary Weaver was acquitted of all charges in her third trial. Do you think the catchall was put to good use here?

3.   The Catchall and Child Abuse Prosecutions

Recall that the exceptions for excited utterances and medical statements are often used in child abuse cases as the basis to admit statements by young victims. You saw the excited utterance exception at work in that setting in the *Iron Shell* case (page 232, supra), and the medical statements exception being used in the *Blake* case (page 256, supra).

Here is an area where the catchall played (indeed continues to play) an important role, as courts often use it to admit statements by child victims describing abuse.[13] Courts have developed lists of factors that bear on the determination of trustworthiness, including the following: Precocious knowledge and age-appropriate language (the former gives new expression to an old

---

13.   See, e.g., United States v. Dunford, 148 F.3d 385, 392-394 (4th Cir 1998) (admitting statements by daughters of defendant describing abuse; court stresses "serious nature" of statements and notes that they were repeated and consistent); State v. Rojas, 524 N.W.2d 659 (Iowa 1994) (admitting videotaped interview between ten-year-old victim and social worker under state catchall).

idea that a statement may be trusted if it is unlikely that the speaker could say what she said without experiencing something close to what she describes; the latter means that a statement on difficult or delicate matters is more likely to be trustworthy if phrased in terms one would expect of a child); behavioral changes (often fearfulness of men, regression in toilet habits, sleep disturbances, new problems at home or school); general demeanor and affect, and particular indications of pain or emotional upset; spontaneity; the presence or absence of bias or other motives on the part of the speaker or the reporting witnesses; signs of tension or disagreement between the child and the person accused of abuse; the training and techniques of people who talk to the child; the number and consistency of repetitions of the basic story make a difference; the character of the child. See generally Mueller and Kirkpatrick, Evidence §8.83 (3d ed. 2003). And see Graham, Indicia of Reliability and Face to Face Confrontation: Emerging Issues in Child Sexual Abuse Prosecutions, 40 U. Miami L. Rev. 19 (1985); MacFarlane, Diagnostic Evaluations and the Use of Videotapes in Child Sexual Abuse Cases, 40 U. Miami. L. Rev. 135 (1985); Note, The Testimony of Child Victims in Sex Abuse Prosecutions, 98 Harv. L. Rev. 806 (1985).

So frequent and compelling are such cases that statutory reforms in many states provide multiple means for putting before the factfinder what the young victims of abuse have to say. One simple reform involves what amounts to a rifle-shot exception paving the way for statements by children describing abuse.[14] For one typical example of such provisions, see Minnesota Stat. Ann §595.02:

> An out-of-court statement made by a child under the age of ten years . . . alleging, explaining, denying, or describing any act of sexual contact or penetration performed with or on the child or any act of physical abuse of the child . . . is admissible as substantive evidence if:
>
> (a) the court . . . finds, in a hearing conducted outside of the presence of the jury, that the time, content, and circumstances of the statement and the reliability of the person to whom the statement is made provide sufficient indicia of reliability; and
>
> (b) the child . . . either:
>
> (i) testifies at the proceedings; or
>
> (ii) is unavailable as a witness and there is corroborative evidence of the act; and
>
> (c) the proponent of the statement notifies the adverse party of the proponent's intention to offer the statement and the particulars of the statement sufficiently in advance of the proceeding at which the proponent intends to offer the statement into evidence to provide the adverse party with a fair opportunity to prepare to meet the statement.

In a way, of course, such rifle-shot hearsay exceptions are just new wine in an old flask (or perhaps old wine in a new flask): These exceptions do not state specific criteria relating to trustworthiness in the manner typical of the categorical exceptions, but simply define a subject area (abuse) and a declarant

---

14. Another involves videotaped depositions, where a child can testify in a setting that is more comfortable than the witness stand in a courtroom, and her videotaped testimony can be offered at trial. A third involves special procedures for taking the testimony of the child from a remote setting, with a television monitoring system. See the discussion in Chapter 4G5, infra.

(the child victim), and then direct courts to admit trustworthy statements. Hence the trustworthiness criteria described above, that developed in connection with the catchall exception, are now applied in cases applying the rifle-shot child abuse exceptions, and these are routinely upheld against constitutional challenge. See, e.g., Thomas v. Delaware, 725 A.2d 424 (Del. 1999) (rejecting constitutional challenge to statute similar to Minnesota's, quoted above).

In another way, of course, these exceptions really are new: The Minnesota provision acknowledges, for instance, that "the reliability of the person to whom the statement is made" counts in the calculus. And the exception requires corroboration in the event that the child does not testify. And of course there is a notice provision, reminiscent of the catchall itself.

Apart from the general problem of trustworthiness, the new child abuse exceptions have brought two new issues:

One is constitutional in nature, and it arises because these exceptions are almost always invoked as the basis to admit hearsay against defendants in criminal cases, which means that the Confrontation Clause applies. This subject is taken up later, but briefly the Supreme Court has decided that statements offered under the catchall and similar new exceptions must satisfy a constitutional standard of trustworthiness before they may be used against defendants, and the trustworthiness of such statements must be determined without reference to "corroborative evidence." See Idaho v. Wright, 497 U.S. 805 (1990) (set out in Chapter 4G4, infra). Note, however, that the statute quoted above *requires* corroboration for statements admitted under it if the declarant does not testify, and the obvious belief of the framers of those provisions is that corroborative evidence does count in the trustworthiness calculus.

The other is an issue of statutory meaning, and essentially the question is whether the existence of these special rifle-shot exceptions forecloses resort to other more traditional exceptions that might apply. In at least some cases, courts have concluded that resort to certain other exceptions, including the catchall, is inappropriate because the specific exception was meant to be the primary (or sole) means to deal with such statements. See, e.g., State v. Jones, 625 So. 2d 821 (Fla. 1993) (statements by child abuse victims to physicians are to be appraised under special exception for statements by child victims, and not under state's medical statements exception).

F. THE MINOR EXCEPTIONS

You have looked at some 21 hearsay exceptions, including the categorical exceptions set out in FRE 803 and 804, the catchall exception, and eight categories of statements that are "not hearsay" under FRE 801. There are 15 more exceptions in FRE 803 that are less important in practice, though well established and necessary in particular cases. Three of these minor provisions are worthy of particular mention:

1. *Ancient documents.* FRE 803(16) creates an exception for statements in documents that have been around for 20 years or more. Age does not improve accuracy, but suggests three reasons to be lenient. First, forces generating the litigation are unlikely to have affected whatever was said long ago, so one major

source of concern over trustworthiness is absent. Second, better evidence about events long ago may be hard to come by. Third, such events are unlikely to be pivotal in litigation. See Dallas County v. Commercial Union Assurance Co., 286 F.2d 388 (5th Cir. 1961). This hearsay exception connects with a special authentication provision in FRE 901(b)(8), which authorizes courts to accept such documents as genuine on the basis of how they look and where they came from (easing foundation requirements).

2. *Market reports, commercial lists.* FRE 803(17) paves the way for a variety of data "published" and "generally used and relied upon by the public or by persons in particular occupations." The notion here is that widespread circulation and reliance create pressures ensuring reliability. Hence price lists published in catalogues, stock market quotations appearing in newspapers, mortality and morbidity tables used in the insurance industry, and city directories are admissible to prove the various facts they reflect. Specialty periodicals in astonishing number circulate among interested persons on subjects ranging from the marketing and servicing of rubber tires to the raising of livestock to modern commercial and banking practices, and all these are potentially within the exception. See McMillen Feeds v. Harlow, 405 S.W.2d 123 (Tex. Civ. App. 1966) (growth statistics for turkeys published in Turkey World).

It is harder to say whether the exception reaches credit ratings. These seem to fall within the literal wording of the exception, and they are widely relied on by lenders of all description, but reports are highly judgmental and cautious in the sense of overincluding unchecked information. The greater number of cases seem to approve such documents, though often for the non-hearsay purpose of showing the information available to the creditor rather than proving the matters reported. Compare United States v. Beecroft, 608 F.2d 753, 760-761 (9th Cir. 1979) (in mail fraud prosecution, Dun & Bradstreet report properly admitted under business records exception as proof of information available to defendant) with Phillip Van Heusen, Inc. v. Korn, 460 P.2d 549 (Kan. 1969) (Dun & Bradstreet reports not admissible against third parties but may be received against person whose statements appear therein).

3. *Felony convictions.* Evidence of felony convictions is admissible in carefully limited circumstances under FRE 803(22) to prove facts "essential to sustain the judgment." In the *Lloyd* case (Chapter 4D2, supra), for example, the question was who started a shipboard fight. The court (in an omitted portion of the opinion) held that the trial judge erred in excluding a Japanese judgment convicting Roland Alvarez of injuring Frank Lloyd, a crime punishable in Japan by imprisonment for more than a year. The court found that Japanese law recognizes self-defense, while permitting the accused to be held criminally liable to the extent he used "excessive force." Lloyd v. American Export Lines, 580 F.2d 1179, 1188 (3d Cir.), cert. denied, 439 U.S. 969 (1978).

Notably, FRE 803(22) contains a restriction for criminal prosecutions reminiscent of the use restrictions in FRE 803(8). Thus in criminal cases the prosecutor cannot introduce prior convictions of third persons "for purposes other than impeachment." This language is responsive to a constitutional pronouncement by the Supreme Court in Kirby v. United States, 174 U.S. 47 (1899). There the accused was charged with receiving stolen property, and the Court concluded that using against him a conviction of others for theft, offered to prove that the property was indeed stolen, violated defendant's rights under the Confrontation Clause. As is true of FRE 803(8)(B) and (C), here too it seems that the restrictive language seeks not only to limit application of FRE 803(22) but to block resort to other exceptions in offering such judgments.

Several difficulties of construction lurk behind FRE 803(22). The phrase quoted above envisions the use of convictions of witnesses for impeachment purposes, but FRE 803(22) itself embraces only felonies and not misdemeanor convictions. Yet FRE 609(a)(2) authorizes use of both felony and misdemeanor convictions to impeach both government and defense witnesses.[15] And the restrictive language in FRE 803(22) bars use of felony convictions based on pleas of nolo contendere, which seems right in some situations but not in others, a point taken up further in the discussion of FRE 410 (see Chapter 5D2, infra).

Perhaps the greatest difficulty posed by FRE 803(22) is that it is hard to imagine giving merely evidentiary (as opposed to conclusive collateral estoppel) effect to a judgment that says that so-and-so was convicted of thus-and-such. Where a party *can* obtain the benefit of collateral estoppel effect from a prior judgment, pretty clearly he would prefer to use the judgment in this way.[16] But evidentiary effect is what the exception contemplates, and the reviewing court in *Lloyd* concluded that the judgment should be admitted under FRE 803(22) rather than given collateral estoppel effect to bar recovery by Alvarez. See Motomura, Using Judgments as Evidence, 70 Minn. L. Rev. 979 (1986).

The other "minor exceptions" cover scattered territory:

Absence of record. Two provisions authorize proof of the *absence* of entries in business and public records, as evidence of the "nonoccurrence or nonexistence of a matter" that one would expect to see recorded in such places if it occurred or existed. See FRE 803(7) and (10). In a criminal trial, for example, the government was refuted evidence that defendant loaned his car to one Dale Olson by evidence that an FBI agent checked credit records, city directories, and various public records and found no trace of such a person. United States v. Rich, 580 F.2d 929, 937-939 (9th Cir.) (court assumed testimony by custodian of such records is required and approved agent's testimony only because defendant did not argue failure of foundation), cert. denied, 439 U.S. 935 (1978).

Birth, marriage, death. Several provisions authorize proof of "milestones" and assorted family matters. One paves the way to prove vital statistics (births, fetal deaths, deaths, marriage) by means of public records. See FRE 803(9). Another authorizes use of religious records as proof of matters of personal and

---

15. The special phrase in FRE 803(22) with its double negative ("not including" third-party convictions offered by the government in criminal cases "for purposes other than impeachment") seems designed to ensure that felony convictions of third parties *may* be used to impeach. The supposition underlying the phrase (reasonable in itself) is that this use of such felonies implicates the hearsay doctrine (for the convictions are offered to prove what the witness did). But if convictions are hearsay when used in this way, they must be hearsay whether the charge is a felony or a misdemeanor. Yet there is no hearsay exception for misdemeanor convictions, so how do *they* overcome a hearsay objection when offered to impeach?

16. The ability of a party to obtain this larger benefit may turn upon whether the jurisdiction still observes the traditional "mutuality" doctrine (a party can benefit from collateral estoppel only if he would have been bound by the judgment, if the case had been decided the other way). FRE 803(22) reaches potentially much further than collateral estoppel ever could because it permits evidential use of a prior judgment against a party who could *not* be bound by the judgment, subject to the restriction described in the text.

family history, such as marriage, divorce, ancestry, and relationship by blood or marriage. FRE 803(11). Yet another paves the way for "family records" as proof of matters of personal or family history (including that infamous example of legal obscurity and butt of jokes on the lore of hearsay—"engravings on urns, crypts, or tombstones"). FRE 803(13).

Real property. Four provisions relate to real property. The content of documents of conveyance may be proved by the records of the land office under FRE 803(14). Old land office records contain descriptions of conveyances, handwritten by public clerks, so the instant exception is needed if these are to be admissible to prove what the originals contain. But the modern hall of records contains mechanical reproductions of the originals, and the issue is one of Best Evidence rather than hearsay. (Can the original be proved by the mechanical copy? The answer, given in Best Evidence terms by FRE 1007, is yes.) The more difficult hearsay issue is whether documents of conveyance may be used to prove the truth of matters they assert, such as source and condition of title. FRE 803(15) says yes, relying on the serious nature of such transactions as providing some assurance of trustworthiness. Yet another provision authorizes receipt of "reputation" as to "boundaries of or customs affecting lands" in the community. FRE 803(20). The purpose of the latter is to authorize use of such hearsay to show where boundaries lie and who has what rights in the land.

Reputation evidence. Two provisions authorize evidence of personal reputation. One covers reputation of a person within his family concerning matters such as his birth, marriage, death, and relationship by blood and marriage. FRE 803(19).

The other authorizes proof of reputation within the "community" as to "character." FRE 803(21). In this context hearsay issues are complicated. You will see that evidence of the character of a person is commonly admitted to prove his out-of-court behavior (FRE 404 and 405) and in-court veracity or lack of it (FRE 608). Often the proof takes the form of testimony as to his "reputation." When reputation is offered for this purpose, clearly it is multiple hearsay. Somewhere, someone has said "*X* is a belligerent fellow" or "*X* is honest and truthful." In due course another repeats it. The word spreads, and reputation takes shape. Then comes litigation, and the question arises whether *X* started a fight or whether he should be believed as a witness. A character witness is called, and she says she knows *X*'s reputation, which indicates that he is "belligerent" or "truthful." Here the immediate aim is to prove exactly that, and the ultimate aim is to convince the trier that *X* started a fight or told the truth. Testimony by the character witness conveys hearsay—multiple hearsay, in fact— and FRE 803(21) lets it in.

Sometimes, however, reputation itself is the issue. In a libel case, for example, defendant might hope to prove that plaintiff's reputation was bad before the allegedly libelous statement was uttered. The point is not to prove what plaintiff is really like, but how he is reputed to be. "Reputation" in this sense could be viewed in either of two ways. Probably the more realistic view is that it shows "what people think": Seen this way, reputation is hearsay because it sums up a multitude of statements as proof of what various people think and say that others think. Somewhat less realistically, reputation is simply "what people say": So viewed, it amounts simply to the "noise" generated in the community, making it in effect multiple "verbal acts" and not hearsay at all.

The exception created by FRE 803(21) chops through this thicket and permits receipt of "what people say" as proof of "what they (in aggregate) think" even if it is hearsay.

Complementing the provisions for "reputation" evidence is one for "judgments" as proof of "matters of personal, family or general history, or boundaries," where the finding is "essential to the judgment." FRE 803(23). This provision in effect assumes that such matters are carefully litigated and that the outcome is to be trusted as much as reputation evidence, hence that judgments may be admitted to prove any point that "would be provable by evidence of reputation."

G.   CONSTITUTION AS BAR AGAINST HEARSAY

1.   Introduction

The Sixth Amendment of the United States Constitution provides in part:

> In all criminal prosecutions, the accused shall enjoy the right . . . to be confronted with the witnesses against him; to have compulsory process for obtaining witnesses in his favor, and to have the Assistance of Counsel for his defense.

These three clauses protect the right of the accused to defend criminal charges. The first (Confrontation Clause) bears directly on using hearsay against the accused, but the relationship between the Clause and the hearsay doctrine took years to work out, and large areas of uncertainty remain.

To begin with some points of certainty, it is settled that the Confrontation Clause entitles the accused to be there when witnesses testify against him, and to cross-examine. In 1988, the Court held that the Clause entitles the defendant not only to be present, and to see and hear the witnesses against him, but also *to be in view of* them. See Coy v. Iowa, 487 U.S. 1012 (1988) (condemning use of translucent screen separating teen-aged girl from defendant in sexual assault case, designed to let defendant see her but shielding her from seeing him). But the accused may *lose* the right to be present by misbehaving, see Illinois v. Allen, 397 U.S. 337 (1970), and a court may let youthful assault victims testify from another room, their image and words conveyed into court by one-way video circuit, on the basis of a case-specific finding that this step is necessary to protect the child, see Maryland v. Craig, 497 U.S. 836 (1990), discussed in Chapter 4G5, infra.

Obviously the use of hearsay can be seen as infringing defendant's right to face and cross-examine witnesses. If "witness against" includes anyone who makes an out-of-court statement offered against the accused, the infringement is obvious. Even if "witness against" embraces only people who testify, letting them recite statements by others seems to undercut the right to cross-examine, since witnesses are not accountable for what others say. Even using prior statements by one who testifies might be seen in this light, since cross-examination envisions "striking while the iron is hot," rather than testing later.

These possibilities raise questions: Does the Confrontation Clause entitle the accused to exclude hearsay? Always? If it blocks some hearsay but not all, how do we separate what is allowed from what is not? What if the declarant is dead or otherwise unavailable? Do the hearsay doctrine and its exceptions control or affect the meaning of the Clause? If so, in what way? Or does the Confrontation Clause drive the hearsay doctrine, at least in criminal cases?

Origins: Sir Walter Raleigh's case. As you will see when you read Crawford v. Washington, 124 S.Ct. 1354 (2004), most accounts of the Confrontation Clause cite the trial of Sir Walter Raleigh for treason in 1603, though it is not clear that this example inspired the American framers. Raleigh was charged with conspiring against King James (raising money abroad to distribute among malcontents in England, to put Arabella Stuart on the throne).[17] He was convicted on what we would call "rank hearsay," despite his claim of right to confront his accusers "face to face." The most damning evidence was an out-of-court statement by alleged coconspirator Lord Cobham, given during an "examination" (questioning by officers of the Crown in the Tower, under pressure if not torture), naming Raleigh as instigator and claiming he was fomenting an insurrection.

Raleigh offered explanations for his borrowing and showed that Cobham recanted. He argued that the statute required two witnesses and urged the court to "call my Accuser" so they might stand "face to face." He conceded that a witness need not be called where he "is not to be had conveniently," but pointed out that Cobham was "alive, and in the house." The judges rejected Raleigh's position: One argued that the law permits conviction without witnesses (three may be convicted of conspiracy if "they all confess," so "here is never a Witness, yet they are condemned"!); another said "Many horse-stealers may escape, if they may not be condemned without witnesses"; yet another intoned that the law "presumes a man will not accuse himself to accuse another."

Early forays. In several nineteenth-century decisions, the Court seemed to say the Clause preserved common law protections but was not an instrument of reform. Thus the Court approved hearsay that fit standard exceptions in Mattox v. United States, 156 U.S. 237, 244-250 (1895) (testimony from first trial), and 146 U.S. 140 (1892) (dying declarations). It also intimated that the Clause accommodates evolving doctrine. See Snyder v. Massachusetts, 291 U.S. 97, 107 (1934) (dying declarations and documentary evidence are recognized exceptions to the Clause, which are not static and "may be enlarged from time to time if there is no material departure").

Once, however, the Court came out the other way. See Kirby v. United States, 174 U.S. 47 (1899) (conviction of third party for theft amounted to hearsay statement of jury in earlier proceeding that could not be used in this case to prove that property, which defendant was charged with possessing, had been stolen). *Kirby* inspired the limiting language in FRE 803(22) preventing

---

17. The quoted passages from the Raleigh trial are reported in 2 Howell's State Cases 15-20 (1803). See also Stephen, The Trial of Sir Walter Raleigh, 2 Trans. Royal Hist. Soc. 172 (4th Series 1919). Raleigh was sentenced to die, but King James found use for his talents and sent him to Guyana for gold. The expedition became an embarrassment because Raleigh attacked Spanish settlements, and executing him became convenient (gesture of good will toward Spain). He was beheaded 15 years after his trial, at the age of 66. Most historians think he was not plotting against the crown.

third-party felony convictions from being used against the defendant "to prove any fact essential" to the earlier judgment.

Beginning of the modern era. In 1965, during the Warren Court reforms, the Confrontation Clause attained greater importance. The Court decided that the Due Process Clause of the Fourteenth Amendment makes the Confrontation Clause binding on the states. The Court also disapproved some hearsay that courts usually admit, but declined to block use of other hearsay that courts usually exclude. These cases called into question any assumption that hearsay within standard exceptions has smooth sledding.

The modern era begins with Pointer v. Texas, 380 U.S. 400 (1965). There, defendant was convicted in state court of armed robbery, and the judge admitted testimony from a preliminary hearing where the accused was not represented. Justice Black wrote for the Court that the right of confrontation is "fundamental" and "obligatory on the States" under the Fourteenth Amendment. Admitting the preliminary hearing testimony under the former testimony exception violated defendant's rights, but the Court said it would be "different" if he "had been represented by counsel who had been given a complete and adequate opportunity to cross-examine."

It is with *Pointer* that interpretive difficulties begin. The quoted comment suggests that *prior* cross (or just an opportunity) would satisfy the Clause. The only reason it did not in *Pointer* was that the accused did not have a lawyer. Three years later the Court said preliminary hearing testimony could not come in even if defense counsel "actually cross-examined" on the earlier occasion, because the witness was not shown to be unavailable. See Barber v. Page, 390 U.S. 719, 725 (1968) (Chapter 4D1, supra). In a companion case to *Pointer,* the Court condemned the practice of smuggling in, under the guise of cross-examination by the prosecutor, out-of-court statements by a testifying witness who refuses to be cross-examined by the defense. The case was Douglas v. Alabama, 380 U.S. 415 (1965), where defendant was tried for assault with intent to commit murder. The prosecutor questioned co-offender Loyd (already convicted separately) on *his* confession, and read parts accusing Douglas of firing the gun. But Loyd refused to answer defense questions, and the Court concluded that the rights of Douglas were violated because he could not cross-examine ("effective" confrontation would be possible if Loyd "affirmed the statement as his," which he did not do).

Douglas suggests that the Clause might be satisfied by deferred cross-examination (questioning at trial on an earlier statement) *if* declarant affirms the statement as his. If the inference is right, the next question is whether acknowledging the statement suffices no matter how uncooperative the witness is otherwise.

After *Pointer* and *Douglas* came the holding in *Barber,* supra, that the state has a constitutional obligation to produce a declarant in preference to offering his testimony from a preliminary hearing, and the holding in *Bruton* that admitting a confession by one defendant incriminating another by name violates the Clause despite limiting instructions, see Bruton v. United States, 391 U.S. 123 (1968). These narrow holdings led to distinct lines of authority that we explored earlier (see Chapter 4B and 4D1).

Modern era arrives. In 1970 two decisions announced the modern era. One was California v. Green, 399 U.S. 149 (1970), rejecting challenges to the use of statements by a witness who seemed conveniently forgetful at trial but who previously incriminated defendant in a conversation with a police officer and in a preliminary hearing. Broadly read, *Green* suggests that two kinds of statements pass muster—those subject to *prior* cross-examination because they were made in proceedings where defendant had a lawyer who tested them, and those subject to *deferred* cross-examination at trial because defendant can *then* question the witness about what he said *before*.

The next decision was Dutton v. Evans, 400 U.S. 74 (1970), which rejected a challenge to an out-of-court statement that was never tested by cross-examination because declarant never testified. The statement came in under a state coconspirator exception, which (unlike counterparts in the federal system and elsewhere) reached utterances by a conspirator who was already imprisoned. Broadly read, *Dutton* says the Confrontation Clause is satisfied if a statement possesses "indicia of reliability," similar to the factors underlying traditional hearsay exceptions. The Court stressed that the speaker had "no apparent reason to lie" and that his statement was "spontaneous" and "against his penal interest." Yet the message of *Dutton* is blurred because the Court stressed other factors: The speaker had participated in the crime and could not have had "faulty recollection," and he only obliquely incriminated the defendant ("If it hadn't been for that dirty son-of-a-bitch Alex Evans," said Williams, "we wouldn't be in this now"), so there was "no express assertion about past fact" and the statement "carried on its face a warning to the jury" against giving it "undue weight." Finally, defendant could have subpoenaed Williams, but decided not to do so.

2.   Modern Doctrine: Roberts, Crawford, and the Ascendance of Two Theories

What had not emerged, even as Warren Era reforms brought renewed interest in the confrontation, was a larger theory. At least four theories might explain how the Confrontation Clause operates on hearsay:

1. *Minimalist theory.* The Clause speaks only to live testimony and has nothing to say about out-of-court statements. It entitles the accused to be present and cross-examine witnesses who testify but does not stop the prosecutor from offering testimonial accounts of what others have said. In other words, "witness against" means someone who testifies at trial, not someone who makes an out-of-court statement. Wigmore took this position, see 5 Wigmore, Evidence §1397 (Chadbourn rev. 1974), and Justice Harlan once endorsed it too, see Dutton v. Evans, 400 U.S. 74 (1970) (concurring opinion), but the Supreme Court itself never adopted this view.

2. *Production theory.* The Clause requires the prosecutor to produce an available declarant in preference to his out-of-court statement, but has nothing to say about statements by people who are unavailable—whose presence or testimony the prosecutor cannot obtain. Professor Westen advanced this view in an elegant article, see Westen, Confrontation and Compulsory Process: A Unified Theory of Evidence for Criminal Cases, 91 Harv. L. Rev. 567, 596 (1978) (arguing that Confrontation and Compulsory Process Clauses protect

procedural rights and should be read together; the latter does not compel the prosecutor to perform the impossible task of producing unavailable witnesses for the defense; the former should not exclude statements by declarants who cannot be produced). The Court partially adopted this view in *Roberts*, infra, and in *Barber*, supra (both stressing the duty of the prosecutor to produce declarants).

Roberts

3. *Reliability theory.* The Clause sets a constitutional standard of reliability for hearsay offered against the accused, although concerns over reliability may be satisfied by circumstances similar to the ones associated with hearsay exceptions, and reliability is unimportant (or less so) if the accused can cross-examine. As you will see in reading *Roberts*, the Court also adopted this approach.

4. *Testimonial theory.* A variant of the first theory, another approach holds that the Clause applies to "testimonial" statements (at least where the declarant cannot be cross-examined), and "testimonial" refers *at least* to statements to law enforcement officers describing crimes, where the purpose is to aid in prosecuting or trying the alleged culprit. You are about to see that the Supreme Court embraced this theory in the *Crawford* case. More than a decade earlier, Justices Thomas and Scalia were interested in this approach, see White v. Illinois, 502 U.S. 346 (1992) (concurring opinion), and Justice Breyer expressed interest in this approach in Lilly v. Virginia, 527 U.S. 116 (1999) (separate opinion favors reexamining confrontation jurisprudence and severing its connection to hearsay doctrine). Professor Richard Friedman developed this approach, and helped persuade the Court to go this way. See Friedman, Confrontation: The Search for Basic Principles, 86 Geo. L. J. 1011 (1998).

Sup Ct ↓ Crawford

OHIO v. ROBERTS
United States Supreme Court 448 U.S. 56 (1980)

MR. JUSTICE BLACKMUN delivered the opinion of the Court.

[In the trial of Herschel Roberts for possessing stolen credit cards and checks, the state offered preliminary hearing testimony by Anita Isaacs, daughter of Bernard and Amy Isaacs. Anita Isaacs had testified at the earlier hearing when called by the defense. Then, Anita Isaacs said she knew Roberts and let him use her apartment for several days while she was away. Despite defense efforts, Isaacs did not admit that she gave him the checks and credit cards without telling him she did not have permission, and in fact she denied doing so.

unavailable at trial

More than a year later the case went to trial. Five times the prosecutor tried to serve a subpoena on Amy Isaacs at the home of her parents Bernard and Amy Isaacs, but she was not found, and she did not telephone or appear at trial.

Roberts testified that she gave him the checkbook and credit cards "with the understanding that he could use them." The trial court admitted Anita Isaacs' preliminary hearing testimony, and Roberts was convicted. He won a reversal. The Ohio Supreme Court thought that the preliminary hearing testimony was inadmissible even though Isaacs was unavailable, because "the mere opportunity to cross-examine" at that time did not satisfy the Confrontation Clause.]

II

A

The Court here is called upon to consider once again the relationship between the Confrontation Clause and the hearsay rule with its many exceptions. The basic rule against hearsay, of course, is riddled with exceptions developed over three centuries. These exceptions vary among jurisdictions as to number, nature, and detail. But every set of exceptions seems to fit an apt description offered more than 40 years ago: "an old-fashioned crazy quilt made of patches cut from a group of paintings by cubists, futurists and surrealists." Morgan & Maguire, Looking Backward and Forward at Evidence, 50 Harv. L. Rev. 909, 921 (1937).

The Sixth Amendment's Confrontation Clause, made applicable to the States through the Fourteenth Amendment, provides: "In all criminal prosecutions, the accused shall enjoy the right . . . to be confronted with the witnesses against him." If one were to read this language literally, it would require, on objection, the exclusion of any statement made by a declarant not present at trial. But, if thus applied, the Clause would abrogate virtually every hearsay exception, a result long rejected as unintended and too extreme.

The historical evidence leaves little doubt, however, that the Clause was intended to exclude some hearsay. Moreover, underlying policies support the same conclusion. The Court has emphasized that the Confrontation Clause reflects a preference for face-to-face confrontation at trial, and that "a primary interest secured by [the provision] is the right of cross-examination." Douglas v. Alabama, 380 U.S. 415, 418 (1965).[6] In short, the Clause envisions

> a personal examination and cross-examination of the witness, in which the accused has an opportunity, not only of testing the recollection and sifting the conscience of the witness, but of compelling him to stand face to face with the jury in order that they may look at him, and judge by his demeanor upon the stand and the manner in which he gives his testimony whether he is worthy of belief.

Mattox v. United States, 156 U.S., at 242-243. These means of testing accuracy are so important that the absence of proper confrontation at trial "calls into question the ultimate 'integrity of the fact-finding process.'" Chambers v. Mississippi, 410 U.S. 284, 295 (1973).

6. . . . Of course, these purposes are interrelated, since one critical goal of cross-examination is to draw out discrediting demeanor to be viewed by the factfinder. Confrontation at trial also operates to ensure reliability in other ways. First, "[t]he requirement of personal presence . . . undoubtedly makes it more difficult to lie against someone, particularly if that person is an accused and present at trial." 4 J. Weinstein & M. Berger, Weinstein's Evidence Par 800[01], pp. 800-810 (1979). Second, it "insures that the witness will give his statements under oath—thus impressing him with the seriousness of the matter and guarding against the lie by the possibility of a penalty for perjury." California v. Green, 399 U.S., at 158.

The Court, however, has recognized that competing interests, if "closely examined," Chambers v. Mississippi, may warrant dispensing with confrontation at trial. See Mattox v. United States, 156 U.S., at 243 ("general rules of law of this kind, however beneficent in their operation and valuable to the accused, must occasionally give way to considerations of public policy and the necessities of the case"). Significantly, every jurisdiction has a strong interest in effective law enforcement, and in the development and precise formulation of the rules of evidence applicable in criminal proceedings.

This Court, in a series of cases, has sought to accommodate these competing interests. True to the common-law tradition, the process has been gradual, building on past decisions, drawing on new experience, and responding to changing conditions. The Court has not sought to "map out a theory of the Confrontation Clause that would determine the validity of all . . . hearsay 'exceptions.'" California v. Green. But a general approach to the problem is discernible.

B

The Confrontation Clause operates in two separate ways to restrict the range of admissible hearsay. First, in conformance with the Framers' preference for face-to-face accusation, the Sixth Amendment establishes a rule of necessity. In the usual case (including cases where prior cross-examination has occurred), the prosecution must either produce, or demonstrate the unavailability of, the declarant whose statement it wishes to use against the defendant. See Mancusi v. Stubbs, 408 U.S. 204 (1972); Barber v. Page, 390 U.S. 719 (1968). See also Motes v. United States, 178 U.S. 458 (1900); California v. Green, supra.[7]

[margin note: ① Prosecution must produce (or demonstrate the unavailability of the witness]

The second aspect operates once a witness is shown to be unavailable. Reflecting its underlying purpose to augment accuracy in the factfinding process by ensuring the defendant an effective means to test adverse evidence, the Clause countenances only hearsay marked with such trustworthiness that "there is no material departure from the reason of the general rule." The principle recently was formulated in Mancusi v. Stubbs:

> The focus of the Court's concern has been to insure that there "are indicia of reliability which have been widely viewed as determinative of whether a statement may be placed before the jury though there is no confrontation of the declarant," Dutton v. Evans, and to "afford the trier of fact a satisfactory basis for evaluating the truth of the prior statement," California v. Green. It is clear from these statements, and from numerous prior decisions of this Court, that even though the witness be unavailable his prior testimony must bear some of these "indicia of reliability."

[margin note: ② witness' prior testimony must bear "indicia of reliability"]

The Court has applied this "indicia of reliability" requirement principally by concluding that certain hearsay exceptions rest upon such solid foundations that admission of virtually any evidence within them comports with the "sub-

---

7.   A demonstration of unavailability, however, is not always required. In Dutton v. Evans, 400 U.S. 74 (1970), for example, the Court found the utility of trial confrontation so remote that it did not require the prosecution to produce a seemingly available witness.

stance of the constitutional protection." Mattox v. United States.[8] This reflects the truism that "hearsay rules and the Confrontation Clause are generally designed to protect similar values," California v. Green, and "stem from the same roots," Dutton v. Evans. It also responds to the need for certainty in the workaday world of conducting criminal trials.

CC requirements

✳

In sum, when a hearsay declarant is not present for cross-examination at trial, the Confrontation Clause normally requires a showing that he is unavailable. Even then, his statement is admissible only if it bears adequate "indicia of reliability." Reliability can be inferred without more in a case where the evidence falls within a firmly rooted hearsay exception. In other cases, the evidence must be excluded, at least absent a showing of particularized guarantees of trustworthiness.

III

[The Court rejects an argument that *Green* suggests only in "dictum" or "alternative" that cross-examined testimony from a preliminary hearing may be admitted consistently with the Confrontation Clause. The Court declines to say whether "mere opportunity to cross-examine" at that hearing suffices to make such testimony admissible at trial, quoting a remark by Professor Westen that this issue is "truly difficult to resolve under conventional theories of confrontation."

The Court also concludes that defense questioning of Anita Isaacs at the preliminary hearing amounted to cross-examination as a matter of both form and substance, since it was "replete with leading questions" and challenged the truth of her story by attempting to show that she and Roberts shared an apartment, and that she gave him credit cards to get a television. Finally, the Court concludes that Anita Isaacs was unavailable "in the constitutional sense," citing evidence that her parents last heard from Anita during the previous summer, that she had left San Francisco and was traveling outside of Ohio, and that neither the parents nor their other children had any way to contact Anita, even in an emergency.

Hence the state did not breach its duty to make a good faith effort to obtain Anita Isaacs, even though the prosecutor might have tried to locate the social worker in San Francisco to whom Mrs. Isaacs spoke many months before and might have tried other steps. The "great improbability that such efforts would have resulted in locating" her and bringing her to trial "neutralizes any intimation that a concept of reasonableness required their execution."]

The judgment of the Supreme Court of Ohio is reversed. . . .

[The dissenting opinion of Justice Brennan, joined by Justices Marshall and Stevens, is omitted.]

---

8. See, e.g., Pointer v. Texas, 380 U.S., at 407 (dying declarations); Mattox v. United States, 156 U.S., at 243-244 (same); Mancusi v. Stubbs, 408 U.S. 204, 213-216 (1972) (cross-examined prior-trial testimony); Comment, 30 La. L. Rev. 651, 668 (1970) ("Properly administered the business and public records exceptions would seem to be among the safest of the hearsay exceptions").

NOTES ON THE *ROBERTS TWO-PRONGED APPROACH*

1.   Couldn't *Roberts* have been decided on the ground that (a) defendant cross-examined Anita Isaacs, or (b) she was unavailable as a witness?

2.   If narrower grounds were available, why does the Court speak more broadly? Is it because the Court sees a broader role for the Confrontation Clause in assuring the reliability of hearsay? Doesn't *Roberts* speak to situations like the one in *Dutton,* where defendant never had a chance to cross-examine the declarant? To deal with this situation, the Court adopts a two-pronged approach, but adds qualifiers to both prongs: Under the first prong, the prosecutor must produce witnesses rather than offering their out-of-court statements, but an escape clause in the footnote says unavailability "is not always required"! Under the second prong, statements must carry "indicia of reliability" (a phrase that first appeared in *Dutton*), but the next sentence says reliability "can be inferred without more" if the statement fits "a firmly rooted hearsay exception." What do you think of a two-pronged approach containing two standards, each of which is qualified by open-ended language?

3.   You are about to read the 2004 opinion in *Crawford,* which displaces *Roberts* in part, and raises doubts as to whether *Roberts* survives at all. But *Roberts* may not yet be a dead letter, so you should know that the escape clause in the first *Roberts* prong proved important. Recall that the *Roberts* footnote says the prosecutor need not show unavailability if the "utility" of trial confrontation is "remote." In 1985 the Court held that *Roberts* did not require unavailability for the coconspirator exception, and implied that this prong applies only to statements offered as prior testimony. See United States v. Inadi, 475 U.S. 387, 394 (1985) (*Roberts* "must be read consistently with the question it answered, the authority it cited, and its own facts"). In 1992 the Court hinted that the other *Roberts* qualifier—statements are reliable if they fit a "firmly rooted" exception—trumps the unavailability requirement. See White v. Illinois, 502 U.S. 346 (1992) (statements fitting firmly rooted exceptions for excited utterances and medical statements have "sufficient guarantees of reliability" to satisfy the Clause). Should the constitutional unavailability prong have been narrowed so far? Consider Kirkpatrick, Confrontation and Hearsay: Exemptions from the Constitutional Unavailability Requirement, 70 Minn. L. Rev. 665 (1986) (whether to require unavailability should turn on centrality of statement, reliability, likelihood that cross could realistically test it, and adequacy of alternative means of challenge).

4.   You must be curious to know which exceptions are "firmly rooted" under *Roberts,* and which are not. Here are the important exceptions labeled as "firmly rooted," by the Supreme Court or other appellate courts: Coconspirator statements, excited utterances, statements for medical diagnosis or treatment, business records, dying declarations, agent's admissions and public records.[18]

---

18.   See White v. Illinois, 502 U.S. 346 (1992) (excited utterances; statements for medical diagnosis or treatment); Bourjaily v. United States, 483 U.S. 171 (1987) (coconspirator statements); Ohio v. Roberts, 448 U.S. 56 (1980) (former testimony; mentioning business records and dying declarations as firmly rooted exceptions). And see United States v. De Water, 846 F.2d 528, 530 (9th Cir. 1988) (public records); United States v. McLean-Davis, 785 F.2d 1534, 1536-1537 (11th Cir. 1986) (speaking agency exception).

Most important among exceptions found *not* "firmly rooted" are the catchall and the against-interest exception. As you are about to see, however, *Crawford* goes far to take the against-interest exception off the table.

CRAWFORD v. WASHINGTON
United States Supreme Court 2004 WL 413301 (2004)

Scalia, J., delivered the opinion of the Court, in which Stevens, Kennedy, Souter, Thomas, Ginsburg, and Breyer, JJ., joined. Rehnquist, C.J., filed an opinion concurring in the judgment, in which O'Connor, J., joined.

JUSTICE SCALIA delivered the opinion of the Court.

Petitioner Michael Crawford stabbed a man who allegedly tried to rape his wife, Sylvia. At his trial, the State played for the jury Sylvia's tape-recorded statement to the police describing the stabbing, even though he had no opportunity for cross-examination. The Washington Supreme Court upheld petitioner's conviction after determining that Sylvia's statement was reliable. The question presented is whether this procedure complied with the Sixth Amendment's guarantee that, "in all criminal prosecutions, the accused shall enjoy the right . . . to be confronted with the witnesses against him."

I

On August 5, 1999, Kenneth Lee was stabbed at his apartment. Police arrested petitioner later that night. After giving petitioner and his wife *Miranda* warnings, detectives interrogated each of them twice. Petitioner eventually confessed that he and Sylvia had gone in search of Lee because he was upset over an earlier incident in which Lee had tried to rape her. The two had found Lee at his apartment, and a fight ensued in which Lee was stabbed in the torso and petitioner's hand was cut.

Petitioner gave the following account of the fight:

Q. Okay. Did you ever see anything in [Lee's] hands?
A. I think so, but I'm not positive.
Q. Okay, when you think so, what do you mean by that?
A. I coulda swore I seen him goin' for somethin' before, right before everything happened. He was like reachin', fiddlin' around down here and stuff . . . and I just . . . I don't know, I think, this is just a possibility, but I think, I think that he pulled somethin' out and I grabbed for it and that's how I got cut . . . but I'm not positive. I, I, my mind goes blank when things like this happen. I mean, I just, I remember things wrong, I remember things that just doesn't, don't make sense to me later.

Sylvia generally corroborated petitioner's story about the events leading up to the fight, but her account of the fight itself was arguably different—particularly with respect to whether Lee had drawn a weapon before petitioner assaulted him:

Q. Did Kenny do anything to fight back from this assault?
A. (pausing) I know he reached into his pocket . . . or somethin' . . . I don't know what.
Q. After he was stabbed?
A. He saw Michael coming up. He lifted his hand . . . his chest open, he might [have] went to go strike his hand out or something and then (inaudible).
Q. Okay, you, you gotta speak up.
A. Okay, he lifted his hand over his head maybe to strike Michael's hand down or something and then he put his hands in his . . . put his right hand in his right pocket . . . took a step back . . . Michael proceeded to stab him . . . then his hands were like . . . how do you explain this . . . open arms . . . with his hands open and he fell down . . . and we ran (describing subject holding hands open, palms toward assailant).
Q. Okay, when he's standing there with his open hands, you're talking about Kenny, correct?
A. Yeah, after, after the fact, yes.
Q. Did you see anything in his hands at that point?
A. (pausing) um um (no).

The State charged petitioner with assault and attempted murder. At trial, he claimed self-defense. Sylvia did not testify because of the state marital privilege, which generally bars a spouse from testifying without the other spouse's consent. See Wash. Rev. Code §5.60.060(1)(1994). In Washington, this privilege does not extend to a spouse's out-of-court statements admissible under a hearsay exception, so the State sought to introduce Sylvia's tape-recorded statements to the police as evidence that the stabbing was not in self-defense. Noting that Sylvia had admitted she led petitioner to Lee's apartment and thus had facilitated the assault, the State invoked the hearsay exception for statements against penal interest, WRE 804(b)(3)(2003).

[handwritten margin note: marital privilege 804(b)(3)]

Petitioner countered that, state law notwithstanding, admitting the evidence would violate his federal constitutional right to be "confronted with the witnesses against him." According to our description of that right in Ohio v. Roberts, 448 U.S. 56 (1980), it does not bar admission of an unavailable witness's statement against a criminal defendant if the statement bears "adequate 'indicia of reliability.'" To meet that test, evidence must either fall within a "firmly rooted hearsay exception" or bear "particularized guarantees of trustworthiness." The trial court here admitted the statement on the latter ground, offering several reasons why it was trustworthy: Sylvia was not shifting blame but rather corroborating her husband's story that he acted in self-defense or "justified reprisal"; she had direct knowledge as an eyewitness; she was describing recent events; and she was being questioned by a "neutral" law enforcement officer. The prosecution played the tape for the jury and relied on it in closing, arguing that it was "damning evidence" that "completely refutes [petitioner's] claim of self-defense." The jury convicted petitioner of assault.

[The Washington Court of Appeals reversed, but the Washington Supreme Court reinstated Michael's conviction.

The Court of Appeals thought Sylvia's statement lacked guarantees of trustworthiness. Her statement contradicted something she said earlier, was given in response to questions, and she admitted that she "shut her eyes during the stabbing." Michael and Sylvia agreed about events up to that point, but differed on the crucial question whether Lee "had something in his hand" when Michael stabbed him. Michael's statement seemed to say yes, but Sylvia's seemed to say Lee was "grabbing for something only after" being stabbed.

The Washington Supreme Court thought Sylvia's statement was trustworthy even though it did not fit a "firmly rooted" exception. What Sylvia said was "virtually identical" with what Michael said, so her statement "interlocks with" his. Both thought Lee "was possibly grabbing for a weapon," but neither was sure when. The Washington Supreme Court rejected arguments that defendant "waived his confrontation rights" because he kept Sylvia off the stand by invoking the spousal testimony privilege. Noting this point, and also noting that the State did not challenge the view that if error was committed, the error was not harmless, Justice Scalia comments "We express no opinion" on these points.]

We granted certiorari to determine whether the State's use of Sylvia's statement violated the Confrontation Clause.

II

The Sixth Amendment's Confrontation Clause provides that, "in all criminal prosecutions, the accused shall enjoy the right . . . to be confronted with the witnesses against him." We have held that this bedrock procedural guarantee applies to both federal and state prosecutions. Pointer v. Texas, 380 U.S. 400, 406 (1965). As noted above, *Roberts* says that an unavailable witness's out-of-court statement may be admitted so long as it has adequate indicia of reliability—*i.e.*, falls within a "firmly rooted hearsay exception" or bears "particularized guarantees of trustworthiness." Petitioner argues that this test strays from the original meaning of the Confrontation Clause and urges us to reconsider it.

A

The Constitution's text does not alone resolve this case. One could plausibly read "witnesses against" a defendant to mean those who actually testify at trial, those whose statements are offered at trial, or something in-between. We must therefore turn to the historical background of the Clause to understand its meaning.

The right to confront one's accusers is a concept that dates back to Roman times. The founding generation's immediate source of the concept, however, was the common law. English common law has long differed from continental civil law in regard to the manner in which witnesses give testimony in criminal trials. The common-law tradition is one of live testimony in court subject to adversarial testing, while the civil law condones examination in private by judicial officers. See 3 W. Blackstone, Commentaries on the Laws of England 373-374 (1768).

Nonetheless, England at times adopted elements of the civil-law practice. Justices of the peace or other officials examined suspects and witnesses before trial. These examinations were sometimes read in court in lieu of live testimony, a practice that "occasioned frequent demands by the prisoner to have his 'accusers,' *i.e.*, the witnesses against him, brought before him face to face." 1

J. Stephen, History of the Criminal Law of England 326 (1883). In some cases, these demands were refused.

Pretrial examinations became routine under two statutes passed during the reign of Queen Mary in the 16th century. These Marian bail and committal statutes required justices of the peace to examine suspects and witnesses in felony cases and to certify the results to the court. It is doubtful that the original purpose of the examinations was to produce evidence admissible at trial. See J. Langbein, Prosecuting Crime in the Renaissance 21-34 (1974). Whatever the original purpose, however, they came to be used as evidence in some cases, resulting in an adoption of continental procedure.

The most notorious instances of civil-law examination occurred in the great political trials of the 16th and 17th centuries. One such was the 1603 trial of Sir Walter Raleigh for treason. Lord Cobham, Raleigh's alleged accomplice, had implicated him in an examination before the Privy Council and in a letter. At Raleigh's trial, these were read to the jury. Raleigh argued that Cobham had lied to save himself: "Cobham is absolutely in the King's mercy; to excuse me cannot avail him; by accusing me he may hope for favour." 1 D. Jardine, Criminal Trials 435 (1832). Suspecting that Cobham would recant, Raleigh demanded that the judges call him to appear, arguing that "the Proof of the Common Law is by witness and jury: let Cobham be here, let him speak it. Call my accuser before my face . . . ." 2 How. St. Tr., at 15-16. The judges refused, and, despite Raleigh's protestations that he was being tried "by the Spanish Inquisition," the jury convicted, and Raleigh was sentenced to death.

One of Raleigh's trial judges later lamented that " 'the justice of England has never been so degraded and injured as by the condemnation of Sir Walter Raleigh.' " Through a series of statutory and judicial reforms, English law developed a right of confrontation that limited these abuses. For example, treason statutes required witnesses to confront the accused "face to face" at his arraignment. Courts, meanwhile, developed relatively strict rules of unavailability, admitting examinations only if the witness was demonstrably unable to testify in person. Several authorities also stated that a suspect's confession could be admitted only against himself, and not against others he implicated.

One recurring question was whether the admissibility of an unavailable witness's pretrial examination depended on whether the defendant had had an opportunity to cross-examine him. In 1696, the Court of King's Bench answered this question in the affirmative, in the widely reported misdemeanor libel case of King v. Paine, 5 Mod. 163, 87 Eng. Rep. 584. The court ruled that, even though a witness was dead, his examination was not admissible where "the defendant not being present when [it was] taken before the mayor . . . had lost the benefit of a cross-examination.". . . .

Paine had settled the rule requiring a prior opportunity for cross-examination as a matter of common law, but some doubts remained over whether the Marian statutes prescribed an exception to it in felony cases. The statutes did not identify the circumstances under which examinations were admissible, and some inferred that no prior opportunity for cross-examination was required. Many who expressed this view acknowledged that it meant the statutes were in derogation of the common law. Nevertheless, by 1791 (the year the Sixth Amendment was ratified), courts were applying the cross-examination rule even to examinations by justices of the peace in felony cases. When Parliament amended the statutes in 1848 to make the requirement explicit, the change merely "introduced in terms" what was already afforded the defendant "by the equitable construction of the law." Queen v. Beeston, 29 Eng. L. & Eq. R. 527, 529 (Ct. Crim. App. 1854) (Jervis, C. J.).

B

Controversial examination practices were also used in the Colonies. Early in the 18th century, for example, the Virginia Council protested against the Governor for having "privately issued several commissions to examine witnesses against particular men *ex parte*," complaining that "the person accused is not admitted to be confronted with, or defend himself against his defamers." A Memorial Concerning the Maladministrations of His Excellency Francis Nicholson, reprinted in 9 English Historical Documents 253, 257 (D. Douglas ed. 1955). A decade before the Revolution, England gave jurisdiction over Stamp Act offenses to the admiralty courts, which followed civil-law rather than common-law procedures and thus routinely took testimony by deposition or private judicial examination. Colonial representatives protested that the Act subverted their rights "by extending the jurisdiction of the courts of admiralty beyond its ancient limits." Resolutions of the Stamp Act Congress §8th (Oct. 19, 1765), reprinted in Sources of Our Liberties 270, 271 (R. Perry & J. Cooper eds. 1959). John Adams, defending a merchant in a high-profile admiralty case, argued: "Examinations of witnesses upon Interrogatories, are only by the Civil Law. Interrogatories are unknown at common Law, and Englishmen and common Lawyers have an aversion to them if not an Abhorrence of them." Draft of Argument in Sewall v. Hancock (1768-1769), in 2 Legal Papers of John Adams 194, 207 (K. Wroth & H. Zobel eds. 1965).

Many declarations of rights adopted around the time of the Revolution guaranteed a right of confrontation. [Court cites Declarations from Virginia, Pennsylvania, Delaware, Maryland, North Carolina, Vermont, Massachusetts, and New Hampshire.] The proposed Federal Constitution, however, did not. At the Massachusetts ratifying convention, Abraham Holmes objected to this omission precisely on the ground that it would lead to civil-law practices: "The mode of trial is altogether indetermined; . . . whether [the defendant] is to be allowed to confront the witnesses, and have the advantage of cross-examination, we are not yet told . . . . We shall find Congress possessed of powers enabling them to institute judicatories little less inauspicious than a certain tribunal in Spain, . . . the *Inquisition*." 2 Debates on the Federal Constitution 110-111 (J. Elliot 2d ed. 1863). Similarly, a prominent Antifederalist writing under the pseudonym Federal Farmer criticized the use of "written evidence" while objecting to the omission of a vicinage right: "Nothing can be more essential than the cross examining [of] witnesses, and generally before the triers of the facts in question . . . . Written evidence . . . [is] almost useless; it must be frequently taken ex parte, and but very seldom leads to the proper discovery of truth." R. Lee, Letter IV by the Federal Farmer (Oct. 15, 1787). The First Congress responded by including the Confrontation Clause in the proposal that became the Sixth Amendment.

Early state decisions shed light upon the original understanding of the common-law right. State v. Webb, 2 N.C. 103 (1794) (per curiam), decided a mere three years after the adoption of the Sixth Amendment, held that depositions could be read against an accused only if they were taken in his presence. Rejecting a broader reading of the English authorities, the court held: "It is a rule of the common law, founded on natural justice, that no man shall be prejudiced by evidence which he had not the liberty to cross examine."

. . .

Many other decisions are to the same effect. Some early cases went so far as to hold that prior testimony was inadmissible in criminal cases *even if* the accused had a previous opportunity to cross-examine. See Finn v. Commonwealth, 26 Va. 701, 708 (1827); State v. Atkins, 1 Tenn. 229 (1807) (per curiam). Most courts rejected that view, but only after reaffirming that admissibility depended on a prior opportunity for cross-examination. Nineteenth-century treatises confirm the rule.

III

This history supports two inferences about the meaning of the Sixth Amendment.

A

First, the principal evil at which the Confrontation Clause was directed was the civil-law mode of criminal procedure, and particularly its use of *ex parte* examinations as evidence against the accused. It was these practices that the Crown deployed in notorious treason cases like Raleigh's; that the Marian statutes invited; that English law's assertion of a right to confrontation was meant to prohibit; and that the founding-era rhetoric decried. The Sixth Amendment must be interpreted with this focus in mind.

Accordingly, we once again reject the view that the Confrontation Clause applies of its own force only to in-court testimony, and that its application to out-of-court statements introduced at trial depends upon "the law of Evidence for the time being." 3 Wigmore §1397, at 101; accord, Dutton v. Evans, 400 U.S. 74, 94 (1970) (Harlan, J., concurring in result). Leaving the regulation of out-of-court statements to the law of evidence would render the Confrontation Clause powerless to prevent even the most flagrant inquisitorial practices. Raleigh was, after all, perfectly free to confront those who read Cobham's confession in court.

This focus also suggests that not all hearsay implicates the Sixth Amendment's core concerns. An off-hand, overheard remark might be unreliable evidence and thus a good candidate for exclusion under hearsay rules, but it bears little resemblance to the civil-law abuses the Confrontation Clause targeted. On the other hand, *ex parte* examinations might sometimes be admissible under modern hearsay rules, but the Framers certainly would not have condoned them.

The text of the Confrontation Clause reflects this focus. It applies to

English History

"witnesses" against the accused—in other words, those who "bear testimony." 1 N. Webster, An American Dictionary of the English Language (1828). "Testimony," in turn, is typically "[a] solemn declaration or affirmation made for the purpose of establishing or proving some fact." An accuser who makes a formal statement to government officers bears testimony in a sense that a person who makes a casual remark to an acquaintance does not. The constitutional text, like the history underlying the common-law right of confrontation, thus reflects an especially acute concern with a specific type of out-of-court statement.

Various formulations of this core class of "testimonial" statements exist: "*ex parte* in-court testimony or its functional equivalent—that is, material such as affidavits, custodial examinations, prior testimony that the defendant was unable to cross-examine, or similar pretrial statements that declarants would reasonably expect to be used prosecutorially"; "extrajudicial statements . . . contained in formalized testimonial materials, such as affidavits, depositions, prior testimony, or confessions"; "statements that were made under circumstances which would lead an objective witness reasonably to believe that the statement would be available for use at a later trial." These formulations all share a common nucleus and then define the Clause's coverage at various levels of abstraction around it. Regardless of the precise articulation, some statements qualify under any definition—for example, *ex parte* testimony at a preliminary hearing.

Statements taken by police officers in the course of interrogations are also testimonial under even a narrow standard. Police interrogations bear a striking resemblance to examinations by justices of the peace in England. The statements are not *sworn* testimony, but the absence of oath was not dispositive. Cobham's examination was unsworn, yet Raleigh's trial has long been thought a paradigmatic confrontation violation. Under the Marian statutes, witnesses were typically put on oath, but suspects were not. Yet Hawkins [Court refers to W. Hawkins, Pleas of the Crown (T. Leach 6th ed. 1787)] and others went out of their way to caution that such unsworn confessions were not admissible against anyone but the confessor.

That interrogators are police officers rather than magistrates does not change the picture either. Justices of the peace conducting examinations under the Marian statutes were not magistrates as we understand that office today, but had an essentially investigative and prosecutorial function. England did not have a professional police force until the 19th century, so it is not surprising that other government officers performed the investigative functions now associated primarily with the police. The involvement of government officers in the production of testimonial evidence presents the same risk, whether the officers are police or justices of the peace.

In sum, even if the Sixth Amendment is not solely concerned with testimonial hearsay, that is its primary object, and interrogations by law enforcement officers fall squarely within that class.[4]

The historical record also supports a second proposition: that the Framers

---

4. We use the term "interrogation" in its colloquial, rather than any technical legal, sense. Just as various definitions of "testimonial" exist, one can imagine various definitions of "interrogation," and we need not select among them in this case. Sylvia's recorded statement, knowingly given in response to structured police questioning, qualifies under any conceivable definition.

Framers' intent

would not have allowed admission of testimonial statements of a witness who did not appear at trial unless he was unavailable to testify, and the defendant had had a prior opportunity for cross-examination. The text of the Sixth Amendment does not suggest any open-ended exceptions from the confrontation requirement to be developed by the courts. Rather, the "right . . . to be confronted with the witnesses against him," is most naturally read as a reference to the right of confrontation at common law, admitting only those exceptions established at the time of the founding. See Mattox v. United States, 156 U.S. 237, 243 (1895). As the English authorities above reveal, the common law in 1791 conditioned admissibility of an absent witness's examination on unavailability and a prior opportunity to cross-examine. The Sixth Amendment therefore incorporates those limitations. The numerous early state decisions applying the same test confirm that these principles were received as part of the common law in this country.

We do not read the historical sources to say that a prior opportunity to cross-examine was merely a sufficient, rather than a necessary, condition for admissibility of testimonial statements. They suggest that this requirement was dispositive, and not merely one of several ways to establish reliability. This is not to deny, as the Chief Justice notes, that "there were always exceptions to the general rule of exclusion" of hearsay evidence. Several had become well established by 1791. But there is scant evidence that exceptions were invoked to admit *testimonial* statements against the accused in a *criminal* case.[6] Most of the hearsay exceptions covered statements that by their nature were not testimonial—for example, business records or statements in furtherance of a conspiracy. We do not infer from these that the Framers thought exceptions would apply even to prior testimony. Cf. Lilly v. Virginia, 527 U.S. 116, 134 (1999) (plurality opinion) ("Accomplices' confessions that inculpate a criminal defendant are not within a firmly rooted exception to the hearsay rule").[7]

IV   *Case law*

Our case law has been largely consistent with these two principles. Our leading early decision, for example, involved a deceased witness's prior trial testimony. Mattox v. United States, 156 U.S. 237 (1895). In allowing the statement to be

---

6. The one deviation we have found involves dying declarations. The existence of that exception as a general rule of criminal hearsay law cannot be disputed. See, e.g., Mattox v. United States, 156 U.S. 237, 243-244 (1895); [Court cites an English case and treatises from 18th and 19th centuries]; see also F. Heller, The Sixth Amendment 105 (1951) (asserting that this was the *only* recognized criminal hearsay exception at common law). Although many dying declarations may not be testimonial, there is authority for admitting even those that clearly are. We need not decide in this case whether the Sixth Amendment incorporates an exception for testimonial dying declarations. If this exception must be accepted on historical grounds, it is *sui generis*.

7. We cannot agree with [the concurring and dissenting opinion of] the Chief Justice that the fact "that a statement might be testimonial does nothing to undermine the wisdom of one of these [hearsay] exceptions." Involvement of government officers in the production of testimony with an eye toward trial presents unique potential for prosecutorial abuse—a fact borne out time and again throughout a history with which the Framers were keenly familiar. This consideration does not evaporate when testimony happens to fall within some broad, modern hearsay exception, even if that exception might be justifiable in other circumstances.

admitted, we relied on the fact that the defendant had had, at the first trial, an adequate opportunity to confront the witness . . . .

Our later cases conform to *Mattox*'s holding that prior trial or preliminary hearing testimony is admissible only if the defendant had an adequate opportunity to cross-examine. See Mancusi v. Stubbs, 408 U.S. 204 (1972); California v. Green, 399 U.S. 149 (1970); Pointer v. Texas, 380 U.S. 400 (1965), cf. Kirby v. United States, 174 U.S. 47 (1899). Even where the defendant had such an opportunity, we excluded the testimony where the government had not established unavailability of the witness. See Barber v. Page, 390 U.S. 719 (1968); cf. Motes v. United States, 178 U.S. 458 (1900). We similarly excluded accomplice confessions where the defendant had no opportunity to cross-examine. See Roberts v. Russell, 392 U.S. 293 (1968) (*per curiam*); Bruton v. United States, 391 U.S. 123 (1968); Douglas v. Alabama, 380 U.S. 415 (1965). In contrast, we considered reliability factors beyond prior opportunity for cross-examination when the hearsay statement at issue was not testimonial. See Dutton v. Evans, 400 U.S., at 87-89 (plurality opinion).

Even our recent cases, in their outcomes, hew closely to the traditional line. *Roberts* admitted testimony from a preliminary hearing at which the defendant had examined the witness. *Lilly* excluded testimonial statements that the defendant had had no opportunity to test by cross-examination. And Bourjaily v. United States, 483 U.S. 171 (1987), admitted statements made unwittingly to an FBI informant after applying a more general test that did *not* make prior cross-examination an indispensable requirement.[8]

Lee v. Illinois, 476 U.S. 530 (1986), on which the State relies, is not to the contrary. There, we *rejected* the State's attempt to admit an accomplice confession. The State had argued that the confession was admissible because it "interlocked" with the defendant's. We dealt with the argument by rejecting its premise, holding that "when the discrepancies between the statements are not insignificant, the codefendant's confession may not be admitted." Respondent argues that "the logical inference of this statement is that when the discrepancies between the statements *are* insignificant, then the codefendant's statement *may* be admitted." But this is merely a possible inference, not an inevitable one, and we do not draw it here. If *Lee* had meant authoritatively to announce an exception—previously unknown to this Court's jurisprudence—for interlocking confessions, it would not have done so in such an oblique manner. Our only precedent on interlocking confessions had addressed the entirely different question whether a limiting instruction cured prejudice to codefendants from admitting a defendant's *own* confession against him in a joint trial. See Parker v. Randolph, 442 U.S. 62, 69-76 (1979) (plurality opinion), abrogated by Cruz v. New York, 481 U.S. 186 (1987).

Our cases have thus remained faithful to the Framers' understanding:

---

8.   One case arguably in tension with the rule requiring a prior opportunity for cross-examination when the proffered statement is testimonial is White v. Illinois, *502 U.S. 346 (1992)*, *which involved, inter alia*, statements of a child victim to an investigating police officer admitted as spontaneous declarations. . . . [T]he only question presented in *White* was whether the Confrontation Clause imposed an unavailability requirement on the types of hearsay at issue. The holding did not address the question whether certain of the statements, had to be excluded *even if* the witness was unavailable. We "[took] as a given . . . that the testimony properly falls within the relevant hearsay exceptions."

Testimonial statements of witnesses absent from trial have been admitted only where the declarant is unavailable, and only where the defendant has had a prior opportunity to cross-examine.[9]

V

Although the results of our decisions have generally been faithful to the original meaning of the Confrontation Clause, the same cannot be said of our rationales. *Roberts* conditions the admissibility of all hearsay evidence on whether it falls under a "firmly rooted hearsay exception" or bears "particularized guarantees of trustworthiness." This test departs from the historical principles identified above in two respects. First, it is too broad: It applies the same mode of analysis whether or not the hearsay consists of *ex parte* testimony. This often results in close constitutional scrutiny in cases that are far removed from the core concerns of the Clause. At the same time, however, the test is too narrow: It admits statements that *do* consist of *ex parte* testimony upon a mere finding of reliability. This malleable standard often fails to protect against paradigmatic confrontation violations.

Members of this Court and academics have suggested that we revise our doctrine to reflect more accurately the original understanding of the Clause. See, *e.g.*, *Lilly* (Breyer, J. concurring); *White* (Thomas, J., joined by Scalia, J., concurring in part and concurring in judgment); A. Amar, The Constitution and Criminal Procedure 125-131 (1997); Friedman, Confrontation: The Search for Basic Principles, 86 Geo. L. J. 1011 (1998). They offer two proposals: First, that we apply the Confrontation Clause only to testimonial statements, leaving the remainder to regulation by hearsay law—thus eliminating the overbreadth referred to above. Second, that we impose an absolute bar to statements that are testimonial, absent a prior opportunity to cross-examine—thus eliminating the excessive narrowness referred to above.

In *White*, we considered the first proposal and rejected it. Although our analysis in this case casts doubt on that holding, we need not definitively resolve whether it survives our decision today, because Sylvia Crawford's statement is testimonial under any definition. This case does, however, squarely implicate the second proposal.

A

Where testimonial statements are involved, we do not think the Framers meant to leave the Sixth Amendment's protection to the vagaries of the rules of evidence, much less to amorphous notions of "reliability." Certainly none

9. . . . Finally, we reiterate that, when the declarant appears for cross-examination at trial, the Confrontation Clause places no constraints at all on the use of his prior testimonial statements. See California v. Green, 399 U.S. 149 (1970). It is therefore irrelevant that the reliability of some out-of-court statements "'cannot be replicated, even if the declarant testifies to the same matters in court'" (quoting United States v. Inadi, 475 U.S. 387, 395 (1986)). The Clause does not bar admission of a statement so long as the declarant is present at trial to defend or explain it. (The Clause also does not bar the use of testimonial statements for purposes other than establishing the truth of the matter asserted. See Tennessee v. Street, 471 U.S. 409 (1985).)

Procedural Guarantee

of the authorities discussed above acknowledges any general reliability exception to the common-law rule. Admitting statements deemed reliable by a judge is fundamentally at odds with the right of confrontation. To be sure, the Clause's ultimate goal is to ensure reliability of evidence, but it is a procedural rather than a substantive guarantee. It commands, not that evidence be reliable, but that reliability be assessed in a particular manner: by testing in the crucible of cross-examination. The Clause thus reflects a judgment, not only about the desirability of reliable evidence (a point on which there could be little dissent), but about how reliability can best be determined. Cf. 3 Blackstone, Commentaries, at 373 ("This open examination of witnesses . . . is much more conducive to the clearing up of truth"); M. Hale, History and Analysis of the Common Law of England 258 (1713) (adversarial testing "beats and bolts out the Truth much better").

Roberts ↓ judicial determination of reliability

The *Roberts* test allows a jury to hear evidence, untested by the adversary process, based on a mere judicial determination of reliability. It thus replaces the constitutionally prescribed method of assessing reliability with a wholly foreign one. In this respect, it is very different from exceptions to the Confrontation Clause that make no claim to be a surrogate means of assessing reliability. For example, the rule of forfeiture by wrongdoing (which we accept) extinguishes confrontation claims on essentially equitable grounds; it does not purport to be an alternative means of determining reliability. See Reynolds v. United States, 98 U.S. 145, 158-159 (1879).

The Raleigh trial itself involved the very sorts of reliability determinations that *Roberts* authorizes. In the face of Raleigh's repeated demands for confrontation, the prosecution responded with many of the arguments a court applying *Roberts* might invoke today: that Cobham's statements were self-inculpatory, that they were not made in the heat of passion, and that they were not "extracted from [him] upon any hopes or promise of Pardon." It is not plausible that the Framers' only objection to the trial was that Raleigh's judges did not properly weigh these factors before sentencing him to death. Rather, the problem was that the judges refused to allow Raleigh to confront Cobham in court, where he could cross-examine him and try to expose his accusation as a lie.

Dispensing with confrontation because testimony is obviously reliable is akin to dispensing with jury trial because a defendant is obviously guilty. This is not what the Sixth Amendment prescribes.

B

The legacy of *Roberts* in other courts vindicates the Framers' wisdom in rejecting a general reliability exception. The framework is so unpredictable that it fails to provide meaningful protection from even core confrontation violations.

Reliability is an amorphous, if not entirely subjective, concept. There are countless factors bearing on whether a statement is reliable; the nine-factor balancing test applied by the Court of Appeals below is representative. See, *e.g.,* People v. Farrell, 34 P. 3d 401, 406-407 (Colo. 2001) (eight-factor test). Whether a statement is deemed reliable depends heavily on which factors the judge considers and how much weight he accords each of them. Some courts wind up attaching the same significance to opposite facts. For example, the

Colorado Supreme Court held a statement more reliable because its inculpation of the defendant was "detailed," while the Fourth Circuit found a statement more reliable because the portion implicating another was "fleeting," United States v. Photogrammetric Data Servs., Inc., 259 F.3d 229, 245 (2001). The Virginia Court of Appeals found a statement more reliable because the witness was in custody and charged with a crime (thus making the statement more obviously against her penal interest), see Nowlin v. Commonwealth, 579 S. E. 2d 367, 371-372 (Va. App. 2003), while the Wisconsin Court of Appeals found a statement more reliable because the witness was *not* in custody and *not* a suspect, see State v. Bintz, 650 N.W.2d 913, 918 (Wis. App. 2002). Finally, the Colorado Supreme Court in one case found a statement more reliable because it was given "immediately after" the events at issue, *Farrell*, while that same court, in another case, found a statement more reliable because two years had elapsed, Stevens v. People, 29 P. 3d 305, 316 (2001).

The unpardonable vice of the *Roberts* test, however, is not its unpredictability, but its demonstrated capacity to admit core testimonial statements that the Confrontation Clause plainly meant to exclude. Despite the plurality's speculation in *Lilly* that it was "highly unlikely" that accomplice confessions implicating the accused could survive *Roberts*, courts continue routinely to admit them. [Court cites modern decisions from a federal Court of Appeals, and from the states of Colorado, Kentucky, Ohio, Wisconsin, Michigan, and Illinois.] One recent study found that, after *Lilly*, appellate courts admitted accomplice statements to the authorities in 25 out of 70 cases—more than one-third of the time. Kirst, Appellate Court Answers to the Confrontation Questions in Lilly v. Virginia, 53 Syracuse L. Rev. 87, 105 (2003). Courts have invoked *Roberts* to admit other sorts of plainly testimonial statements despite the absence of any opportunity to cross-examine. [Court cites federal and state decisions admitting plea allocutions, grand jury testimony, and prior trial testimony.]

To add insult to injury, some of the courts that admit untested testimonial statements find reliability in the very factors that *make* the statements testimonial. As noted earlier, one court relied on the fact that the witness's statement was made to police while in custody on pending charges—the theory being that this made the statement more clearly against penal interest and thus more reliable. Other courts routinely rely on the fact that a prior statement is given under oath in judicial proceedings. That inculpating statements are given in a testimonial setting is not an antidote to the confrontation problem, but rather the trigger that makes the Clause's demands most urgent. It is not enough to point out that most of the usual safeguards of the adversary process attend the statement, when the single safeguard missing is the one the Confrontation Clause demands.

C

Roberts' failings were on full display in the proceedings below. Sylvia Crawford made her statement while in police custody, herself a potential suspect in the case. Indeed, she had been told that whether she would be released "depended on how the investigation continues." In response to often leading questions from police detectives, she implicated her husband in Lee's stabbing and at least arguably undermined his self-defense claim. Despite all this, the trial court admitted her statement, listing several reasons why it was reliable. In its opinion reversing, the Court of Appeals listed several *other* reasons why the statement was *not* reliable. Finally, the State Supreme Court relied exclusively on the interlocking character of the statement and disregarded every other factor the lower courts had considered. The case is thus a self-contained demonstration of *Roberts'* unpredictable and inconsistent application.

Each of the courts also made assumptions that cross-examination might well have undermined. The trial court, for example, stated that Sylvia Crawford's statement was reliable because she was an eyewitness with direct knowledge of the events. But Sylvia at one point told the police that she had "shut [her] eyes and . . . didn't really watch" part of the fight, and that she was "in shock." The trial court also buttressed its reliability finding by claiming that Sylvia was "being questioned by law enforcement, and, thus, the [questioner] is . . . neutral to her and not someone who would be inclined to advance her interests and shade her version of the truth unfavorably toward the defendant." The Framers would be astounded to learn that *ex parte* testimony could be admitted against a criminal defendant because it was elicited by "neutral" government officers. But even if the court's assessment of the officer's motives was accurate, it says nothing about Sylvia's perception of her situation. Only cross-examination could reveal that.

The State Supreme Court gave dispositive weight to the interlocking nature of the two statements—that they were both ambiguous as to when and whether Lee had a weapon. The court's claim that the two statements were *equally* ambiguous is hard to accept. Petitioner's statement is ambiguous only in the sense that he had lingering doubts about his recollection: "A. I coulda swore I seen him goin' for somethin' before, right before everything happened . . . . But I'm not positive." Sylvia's statement, on the other hand, is truly inscrutable, since the key timing detail was simply assumed in the leading question she was asked: "Q. Did Kenny do anything to fight back from this assault?" Moreover, Sylvia specifically said Lee had nothing in his hands after he was stabbed, while petitioner was not asked about that.

The prosecutor obviously did not share the court's view that Sylvia's statement was ambiguous—he called it "damning evidence" that "completely refutes [petitioner's] claim of self-defense." We have no way of knowing whether the jury agreed with the prosecutor or the court. Far from obviating the need for cross-examination, the "interlocking" ambiguity of the two statements made it all the more imperative that they be tested to tease out the truth.

We readily concede that we could resolve this case by simply reweighing the "reliability factors" under *Roberts* and finding that Sylvia Crawford's statement falls short. But we view this as one of those rare cases in which the result below is so improbable that it reveals a fundamental failure on our part to interpret the Constitution in a way that secures its intended constraint on judicial discretion. Moreover, to reverse the Washington Supreme Court's decision after conducting our own reliability analysis would perpetuate, not avoid, what the Sixth Amendment condemns. The Constitution prescribes a procedure for determining the reliability of testimony in criminal trials, and we, no less than the state courts, lack authority to replace it with one of our own devising.

We have no doubt that the courts below were acting in utmost good faith when they found reliability. The Framers, however, would not have been content to indulge this assumption. They knew that judges, like other government officers, could not always be trusted to safeguard the rights of the people . . . . They were loath to leave too much discretion in judicial hands. By replacing categorical constitutional guarantees with open-ended balancing tests, we do violence to their design. Vague standards are manipulable, and, while that might be a small concern in run-of-the-mill assault prosecutions like this one, the Framers had an eye toward politically charged cases like Raleigh's—great state trials where the impartiality of even those at the highest levels of the judiciary might not be so clear. It is difficult to imagine *Roberts* providing any meaningful protection in those circumstances.

. . .

Where nontestimonial hearsay is at issue, it is wholly consistent with the Framers' design to afford the States flexibility in their development of hearsay law—as does *Roberts*, and as would an approach that exempted such statements from Confrontation Clause scrutiny altogether. Where testimonial evidence is at issue, however, the Sixth Amendment demands what the common law required: unavailability and a prior opportunity for cross-examination. We leave for another day any effort to spell out a comprehensive definition of "testimonial."[10] Whatever else the term covers, it applies at a minimum to prior testimony at a preliminary hearing, before a grand jury, or at a former trial; and to police interrogations. These are the modern practices with closest kinship to the abuses at which the Confrontation Clause was directed.

In this case, the State admitted Sylvia's testimonial statement against petitioner, despite the fact that he had no opportunity to cross-examine her. That alone is sufficient to make out a violation of the Sixth Amendment. *Roberts* notwithstanding, we decline to mine the record in search of indicia of reliability. Where testimonial statements are at issue, the only indicium of reliability sufficient to satisfy constitutional demands is the one the Constitution actually prescribes: confrontation.

The judgment of the Washington Supreme Court is reversed, and the case is remanded for further proceedings not inconsistent with this opinion.

It is so ordered.

[The opinion of chief Justice Rehnquist, with whom Justice O'Connor joins, concurring in the judgment, is omitted.]

NOTES ON *CRAWFORD*'S "TESTIMONIAL" APPROACH

1. *Crawford* represents a new departure, doesn't it? *Crawford* recasts the Confrontation Clause as a provision that blocks the use against the accused of "testimonial" statements made out of court, and as a provision with a "procedural" purpose of insuring that "reliability be assessed" by "testing in the

---

10. We acknowledge the Chief Justice's objection that our refusal to articulate a comprehensive definition in this case will cause interim uncertainty. But it can hardly be any worse than the status quo. The difference is that the *Roberts* test is *inherently*, and therefore *permanently*, unpredictable.

crucible of cross-examination." Under *Crawford,* what Sylvia said to police after the crime can't come in even if is found reliable, can it?

2.   The key element in *Crawford* is the word "testimonial," and the Court quotes some definitions, but doesn't offer its own. We know, however, that "testimonial" means at least a statement to a police officer by an eyewitness to a crime, where the statement describes the crime and both parties know the statement will prove useful in prosecution or trial. Should the result be the same if Sylvia spoke to an undercover officer and did not know he was trying to build a case? What if she was talking to a friend? If, in the latter case, the statement is *not* testimonial, would it be testimonial if a police officer overheard it? Consider these suggestions by Professor Friedman:

> A statement made knowingly to the authorities that describes criminal activity is almost always testimonial. A statement made by a person claiming to be the victim of a crime and describing the crime is usually testimonial, whether made to the authorities or not. In the case of a crime committed over a short period of time, if a statement is made before the crime is committed, it almost certainly is not testimonial. A statement made by one participant in a criminal enterprise to another, intended to further the enterprise, is not testimonial. And neither is a statement made in the course of going about one's ordinary business, made before the criminal act has occurred or with no recognition that it relates to criminal activity.

Richard D. Friedman, Confrontation: The Search for Basic Principles, 86 Geo. L.J. 1011, 1040-43 (1998).

3.   Consider what *Crawford* might mean in situations you've already seen:

(a) In a situation like the one in Problem 3-K ("My Husband is in Denver"), in which someone lies to police to throw them off the scent, should such a statement be viewed as "testimonial"? Note the comment in *Crawford* that the Confrontation clause "does not bar the use of testimonial statements for purposes other than" proving the matter asserted.

(b) In cases involving several defendants, *Bruton* disapproved use of a confession by one naming another. *Crawford* cites *Bruton* with approval, and the rationale of *Crawford* reinforces this safeguard, in the usual situation in which the confession is given to a law enforcement officer, doesn't it?

(c) In a conspiracy trial, *Bourjaily* approved use of a statement by a member of the venture to an informant identifying defendant as a conspirator and potential drug buyer. *Crawford* puts "statements in furtherance of a conspiracy" in the nontestimonial category, and Professor Friedman (in the passage quoted above) says a statement "by one participant in a criminal enterprise to another, intended to further the enterprise," is not testimonial. What do you think? Does the involvement of the informant, as in *Bourjaily,* make the statement testimonial?

(d) In situations like the one in *Tome* (Chapter 4A2, supra), where a child is asked to describe sexual abuse that she has recounted in more private settings earlier, *Crawford* reinforces the message of caution, doesn't it? The ground of decision in *Tome* was that FRE 801(d)(1)(B) only reaches statements made before the motive to fabricate arose, but an additional problem in such cases is that a child may not really be cross-exminable about the events in issue, and the jury may instead rely on the child's out-of-court statements. *Crawford*'s stress on cross-examination emphasizes this concern, doesn't it?

(e) 911 calls describing criminal acts have been admitted as present sense impressions or excited utterances. If offered against criminal defendants, are they testimonial? See Richard D. Friedman & Bridget McCormack, Dial-In Testimony, 150 U. Pa. L. Rev. 1171, 1240 (2002): "If a statement is made in circumstances in which a reasonable person would realize that it likely would be used in investigation or prosecution of a crime, then the statement should be deemed testimonial." Do you agree?

(f) *Oates* excluded an official lab report that a powdery substance was cocaine, offered under FRE 803(8). But recall that some cases admit routine official records, such as those noting license numbers of cars crossing the border or serial numbers of bills. How would such material fare under *Crawford?*

(g) What about dying declarations? *Crawford* refers to cases admitting them even if they are testimonial. Does that mean they still come in, even if made by a crime victim to an officer naming defendant as the culprit?

(h) Cases like *Williamson* and *Lilly* become easier, don't they? Doesn't *Crawford* bar use of co-offender statements to police—like the statement that the cocaine belonged to Williamson, and the statement that "Ben shoots him"?

(i) *Crawford* clears the way for the forfeiture-by-misconduct provision in FRE 804(b)(6), doesn't it? So in situations like the one described in Problem 4-N ("If You Want to Stay Healthy"), prosecutors can use testimonial hearsay, right?

4.   After *Crawford,* is *Roberts* a dead letter? Recalling Problem 3-A (Three See a Robbery), suppose Plaintalk tells his friend Lissner excitedly, "My God, that fellow Higgins is robbing the bank." Or suppose Plaintalk conveys his present sense impression to Officer Jones, "That's Higgins' car, parked by the bank." In the first case, it's friend talking to friend, but the statement describes a crime. In the second, it's citizen talking to police, but it's an everyday observation about a fact with no apparent criminal significance. Arguably both these statements are nontestimonial (although it's hard to be sure *Crawford* will play out this way). If so, *Crawford* is not a barrier, is it? Then *Roberts* could apply, couldn't it? But *Crawford* is critical of *Roberts.* After labeling the earlier decision "*inherently,* and therefore *permanently,* unpredictable," can the Court return to the *Roberts* standard for nontestimonial statements? If *Roberts* is a dead letter, would it follow that the Confrontation Clause has no application to nontestimonial hearsay?

3.   What About Statements Subject to Prior or
Later Cross-Examination?

Cross-examination is not *all* that the Confrontation Clause protects, but it seems the most important thing. So two questions naturally arise: First, is it enough that the accused could cross-examine the declarant *before trial* on the statement that is offered against her? Second, is it enough that the accused can cross-examine the declarant *at trial* on a prior statement that is offered against her? In other words, does previous or deferred cross-examination suffice?

To put it bluntly, the Court has given mixed signals, but the indications are that deferred cross-examination does suffice, and that previous cross-examination *may* suffice, at least in some circumstances. More precisely, in the latter instance the strongest signals suggest that *previous* cross-examination is enough (perhaps merely a prior *opportunity* to cross-examine, although this point is less clear), if the witness is unavailable at the time of trial. The pathbreaking opinion is California v. Green, 399 U.S. 149 (1970), which supports both these conclusions, while leaving room for defendants to argue that in special situations neither prior nor later cross-examination is enough (meaning that nothing but live testimony, subject to contemporaneous cross-examination, would do).

a. Prior Cross-Examination

Recall the prior testimony exception in FRE 804(b)(1). That provision paves the way for testimony previously given by someone who is now unavailable, provided that the party against whom the testimony is offered (or in civil cases his "predecessor in interest") had motive and opportunity "to develop the testimony by direct, cross, or redirect examination."

Now consider what happened in *Green*. There, 16-year-old Melvin Porter testified in a preliminary hearing that John Green asked him to sell some marijuana ("stuff" or "grass") and pick up a sack containing baggies of it in the bushes at the house of Green's parents. Porter did, and sold some to undercover officer Wade. Counsel for Green extensively cross-examined Porter. At Green's trial, Porter became evasive. He said Green called and asked him to sell some stuff, that he got baggies of marijuana thereafter, but did not know whether Green had supplied it because he was on LSD. He said he could not remember what happened after Green called, and could not distinguish fact from fantasy. The prosecutor read excerpts from Porter's preliminary hearing testimony, and Green was convicted. The California Supreme Court reversed, finding that prior cross did not satisfy the Confrontation Clause (and later cross at trial did not make up the deficit). The United States Supreme Court disagreed:

> Porter's preliminary hearing testimony was admissible as far as the Constitution is concerned wholly apart from the question of whether [Green] had an effective opportunity for confrontation at the subsequent trial. For Porter's statement at the preliminary hearing had already been given under circumstances closely approximating those that surround the typical trial. Porter was under oath; [Green] was represented by counsel—the same counsel in fact who later represented him at the trial; [Green] had every opportunity to cross-examine Porter as to his statement; and the proceedings were conducted before a judicial tribunal, equipped to provide a judicial record of the hearings.

California v. Green, 399 U.S. 149, 165 (1970).

In a jurisdiction governed by the Federal Rules, the prosecutor might invoke FRE 804(b)(1) to get in what Melvin Porter said at John Green's preliminary hearing, raising two issues:

First, is Porter "unavailable" for purposes of FRE 804(a) and the Confrontation Clause? It seems that indeed Porter *would* be unavailable under FRE 804(a)(3) because he testified to "a lack of memory concerning the subject matter" of his prior testimony (he doesn't remember whether Green was his supplier). Probably this lack of memory would make him unavailable for purposes of the Confrontation Clause too. Recall that cases construing this constitutional dimension of unavailability focus on the question whether the prosecutor made adequate efforts to obtain the testimony of the witness. See Barber v. Page, 390 U.S. 719 (1968); Mancusi v. Stubbs, 408 U.S. 204 (1972) (see Chapter 4D1, supra). On our supposed facts, there is no reason to "blame" the prosecutor for Porter's claimed lack of memory.

Great for Essay Practice

Second, did the opportunity provided to Green to cross-examine Porter at the preliminary hearing satisfy FRE 804(b)(1) and the Confrontation Clause? Here we have to be careful.

If Green's lawyer *did* cross-examine Porter on substance, then probably Green had the "opportunity and similar motive" required by FRE 804(b)(1). Arguably this cross-examination means that the Confrontation Clause is satisfied too. The Court thought so in *Roberts*, and *Crawford*'s statement about "adequate opportunity to cross-examine" points in the same direction.

If Green's lawyer did *not* cross-examine Porter at the preliminary hearing, the questions are whether the opportunity he passed up was enough to satisfy (a) FRE 804(b)(1), and (b) the Confrontation Clause. There are no easy answers: Defense lawyers usually think the best strategy is to *forego* cross-examination at the preliminary hearing, on the theory that tipping their hand to the witness (whom they expect to see at trial) is worse than forging ahead on the slim chance that they can get the case thrown out. *Roberts* avoids answering this question, noting that it is hard to construe such conduct as waiver. Despite the sweeping language in *Crawford* that a prior "opportunity" is enough, the better view is that the question remains open. See generally the discussion in Mueller and Kirkpatrick, Evidence §8.68 (3d ed. 2003).

b.   Deferred Cross-Examination

Recall standard exceptions that require the declarant to be cross-examinable at trial about something he said earlier, or *assume* that such cross can occur. FRE 801(d)(1) creates three exceptions for a prior statement that fits any one of three different categories, provided that declarant is "subject [at trial] to cross-examination concerning the statement." The first covers inconsistent statements given under oath in a proceeding or deposition; the second covers consistent statements; the third covers statements of identification. There is also the exception for past recollection recorded in FRE 803(5), which assumes that the declarant testifies and is (for that reason) subject to cross-examination. Beyond these provisions, many exceptions *can* apply in situations in which the declarant testifies, thus being cross-examinable.

In *Green*, the state offered another statement by Melvin Porter. Arrested for selling marijuana to undercover officer Wade, Porter talked to officer Wade four days later. At trial, after Porter's evasive behavior and vagueness about what happened, the state called Wade. According to him, Porter said Green called and asked him to sell marijuana ("stuff" or "grass"). Then Green personally delivered a sack containing 29 baggies of marijuana—the source of what Porter sold to Wade. Under a statute allowing full use of prior inconsistent statements by testifying witnesses, the California court admitted Porter's out-of-court statement to Wade. Ultimately the United States Supreme Court concluded that this procedure did not violate Green's confrontation rights.

The Court said that the question was not whether a jury would be better able to evaluate Porter's statement if it had heard him originally, but whether it could adequately evaluate his statement at trial. Confrontation provides for an oath, cross-examination, and demeanor evidence. On the oath, the Court said:

> [T]he witness must now affirm, deny, or qualify the truth of the prior statement under the penalty of perjury; indeed, the very fact that the prior statement was not given under a similar circumstance may become the witness' explanation for its inaccuracy—an explanation a jury may be expected to understand and take into account in deciding which, if either, of the statements represents the truth.

On the matter of cross-examination, the Court in *Green* concluded:

> [T]he inability to cross-examine the witness at the time he made his prior statement cannot easily be shown to be of crucial significance as long as the defendant is assured of full and effective cross-examination at the time of trial. The most successful cross-examination at the time the prior statement was made could hardly hope to accomplish more than has already been accomplished by the fact that the witness is now telling a different, inconsistent story, and—in this case—one that is favorable to the defendant. We cannot share the California Supreme Court's view that belated cross-examination can never serve as a constitutionally adequate substitute for cross-examination contemporaneous with the original statement. The main danger in substituting subsequent for timely cross-examination seems to lie in the possibility that the witness' "[f]alse testimony is apt to harden and become unyielding to the blows of truth in proportion as the witness has opportunity for reconsideration and influence by the suggestions of others, whose interest may be, and often is, to maintain falsehood rather than truth." State v. Saporen, 285 N.W. 898, 901 (Minn. 1939). That danger, however, disappears when the witness has changed his testimony so that, far from "hardening," his prior statement has softened to the point where he now repudiates it.

On the matter of demeanor, the Court in *Green* concluded:

> The witness who now relates a different story about the events in question must necessarily assume a position as to the truth value of his prior statement, thus giving the jury a chance to observe and evaluate his demeanor as he either disavows or qualifies his earlier statement. The jury is alerted by the inconsistency in the stories, and its attention is sharply focused on determining either that one of the stories reflects the truth or that the witness, who has apparently lied once, is simply too lacking in credibility to warrant its believing either story.

California v. Green, 399 U.S. 149, 159-160 (1970).

In explaining why deferred cross-examination is good enough, *Green* assumed that the declarant would acknowledge making the prior statement. *Green* also left open the possibility that deferred cross-examination would *not* be enough if a lack of memory blocked the attempt to test what he said before. Later, however, the Court all but closed the door against claims that such problems undercut the right of cross-examination.

In one case, the Court held that even a witness who denies making a statement can be adequately cross-examined. There defendant *R*, whose confession to police implicated codefendant *O*, took the stand and denied making the statement. (Recall that *Bruton* generally blocks use of "spillover" confessions in joint trials, but *Bruton* problems go away if the confessing defendant takes the stand, and the other can cross-examine.) The case was Nelson v. O'Neil, 402 U.S. 622, 628-630 (1971), and the Court said *O* would be *worse* off if *R* admitted making the confession. The fact that he denied it was "more favorable" for *O* than anything cross-examination could do if he "affirmed the statement as his."

In another case, the Court concluded that even an unremembering witness is adequately cross-examinable. The case involved the trial of an inmate arising out of an attack on correctional counselor John Foster, who was beaten with a metal pipe and suffered a skull fracture and memory impairment. Three weeks later, FBI Agent Mansfield interviewed Foster in the hospital, and Foster described the attack, named Owens and picked his photograph from an array. At trial, Foster again described the attack (feeling the blows, seeing his blood on the floor) and recalled talking to Mansfield and naming Owens, but admitted he couldn't remember "seeing his assailant" and couldn't remember other hospital visitors or whether they suggested Owens' name. The trial court let Mansfield testify to Foster's hospital statement under the exception for statements of identification in FRE 801(d)(1)(C), and the Supreme Court approved:

[The] opportunity [to cross-examine] is not denied when a witness testifies as to his current belief but is unable to recollect the reason for that belief. It is sufficient that the defendant has the opportunity to bring out such matters as the witness's bias, his lack of care and attentiveness, his poor eyesight, and even (what is often a prime objective of cross-examination) the very fact that he has a bad memory. If the ability to inquire into these matters suffices to establish the constitutionally requisite opportunity for cross-examination when a witness testifies as to his current belief, the basis for which he cannot recall, we see no reason why it should not suffice when the witness's past belief is introduced and he is unable to recollect the reason for that past belief. In both cases the foundation for the belief (current or past) cannot effectively be elicited, but other means of impugning the belief are available. Indeed, if there is any difference in persuasive impact between the statement "I believe this to be the man who assaulted me, but can't remember why" and the statement "I don't know whether this is the man who assaulted me, but I told the police I believed so earlier," the former would seem, if anything, more damaging and hence give rise to a greater need for memory-testing, if that is to be considered essential to an opportunity for effective cross-examination. We conclude . . . that it is not. The weapons available to impugn the witness's statement when memory loss is asserted will of course not always achieve success, but successful cross-examination is not the constitutional guarantee. They are . . . realistic weapons, as is demonstrated by defense counsel's summation in this very case, which emphasized Foster's memory loss and argued that his identification of respondent was the result of the suggestions of people who visited him in the hospital.

United States v. Owens, 484 U.S. 554, at 559-560 (1988).

In a third case, the question what kind of cross-examination is adequate under the Clause arose in a different setting. There the Court concluded that expert testimony could be admitted *even though* the expert could not recall, when cross-examined about his conclusion, what it rested on. In language that the Court later quoted in *Owens*, the Court said: "Generally speaking, the Confrontation Clause guarantees an *opportunity* for effective cross-examination, not cross-examination that is effective in whatever way, and to whatever extent, the defense might wish." Delaware v. Fensterer, 474 U.S. 15, 19 (1985).

Here are some concluding points: If *Green* arose today under the Rules, the prosecutor probably could not use, as substantive evidence against Green, Porter's statement to Wade. Unlike California law, the Rules do not permit substantive use of all prior inconsistent statements by testifying witnesses. You read State v. Smith, 651 P.2d 207 (Wash. 1982) (Chapter 4A1, supra), admitting a stationhouse affidavit under the state counterpart to FRE 801(d)(1)(A), but most decisions do not agree that such a statement was made in a "proceeding." Porter did not sign an affidavit, so even *Smith* would not help the prosecutor on the facts of *Green*.

In sum, the situation for defendants is about what Justice Scalia implies in *Crawford:* The Clause "does not bar admission of a statement so long as the declarant is present at trial to defend or explain it." But maybe there remains some glimmer of an argument that defendants can make. After all, the exceptions in Rule 801(d)(1) only exist because the declarant "testifies" and is "subject to cross-examination concerning the statement" being offered. If a witness stonewalls and answers no questions whatsoever, can it *still* be said that he is cross-examinable? In the *Owens* case the Court left the door slightly ajar, commenting that "limitations on the scope of examination by the trial court or assertions of privilege by the witness" might "undermine the process" so far that "meaningful cross-examination" for purposes of FRE 801(d)(1)(C) "no longer exists." Arguably this point supports a similar argument under the Confrontation Clause, particularly in light of the stress on cross-examination found in *Crawford* as the central focus on the Confrontation Clause.

4.   "New Hearsay"

IDAHO v. WRIGHT
United States Supreme Court 497 U.S. 805 (1990)

JUSTICE O'CONNOR delivered the opinion of the Court:

[Laura Wright and Robert Giles were tried for abusing the two-and-one-half-year-old daughter of both and the five-and-one-half-year-old daughter of Laura and her former husband Louis. The crime came to light when the older daughter told a woman friend of Louis that Giles and Laura abused both her and her sister. Both children were taken to a hospital for medical examinations. At trial, the older child testified that Robert and Laura victimized both children, and that Robert had intercourse with the younger child while Laura held her.

Dr. Jambura, the examining physician, testified that both children had bruises and other physical symptoms consistent with sexual abuse, and that the injuries to the younger child were strongly suggestive of abuse.

The younger child (three at trial) did not testify because the judge concluded on the basis of voir dire that she could not communicate with the jury (lawyers for both sides concurred). But the judge let Dr. Jambura describe what she said, invoking the Idaho catchall exception, which tracks FRE 807. Dr. Jambura testified that he asked her questions, including this one: "Does daddy touch you with his pee-pee?" According to him, the child "did admit to that," adding that "daddy does do this with me, but he does it a lot more with my sister."

The Idaho Supreme Court concluded that admitting these statements violated the Confrontation Clause, and the United States Supreme Court agrees.]

We note at the outset that Idaho's residual hearsay exception, under which the challenged statements were admitted, is not a firmly rooted hearsay exception for Confrontation Clause purposes. Admission under a firmly rooted hearsay exception satisfies the constitutional requirement of reliability because of the weight accorded longstanding judicial and legislative experience in assessing the trustworthiness of certain types of out-of-court statements. The residual hearsay exception, by contrast, accommodates ad hoc instances in which statements not otherwise falling within a recognized hearsay exception might nevertheless be sufficiently reliable to be admissible at trial. Hearsay statements admitted under the residual exception, almost by definition, therefore do not share the same tradition of reliability that supports the admissibility of statements under a firmly rooted hearsay exception. Moreover, were we to agree that the admission of hearsay statements under the residual exception automatically passed Confrontation Clause scrutiny, virtually every codified hearsay exception would assume constitutional stature, a step this Court has repeatedly declined to take. . . .

The State responds that a finding of "particularized guarantees of trustworthiness" should instead be based on a consideration of the totality of the circumstances, including not only the circumstances surrounding the making of the statement, but also other evidence at trial that corroborates the truth of the statement. We agree that "particularized guarantees of trustworthiness" must be shown from the totality of the circumstances, but we think the relevant circumstances include only those that surround the making of the statement and that render the declarant particularly worthy of belief. [The Court quotes Wigmore's account of the rationale of hearsay exceptions.] In other words, if the declarant's truthfulness is so clear from the surrounding circumstances that the test of cross-examination would be of marginal utility, then the hearsay rule does not bar admission of the statement at trial. The basis for the "excited utterance" exception, for example, is that such statements are given under circumstances that eliminate the possibility of fabrication, coaching, or confabulation, and that therefore the circumstances surrounding the making of the statement provide sufficient assurance that the statement is trustworthy and that cross-examination would be superfluous. Likewise, the "dying declaration" and "medical treatment" exceptions to the hearsay rule are based on the belief that persons making such statements are highly unlikely to lie. "The circumstantial guarantees of trustworthiness on which the various specific exceptions to the hearsay rule are based are those that existed at the time the statement was made and do not include those that may be added by using hindsight." Huff v. White Motor Corp., 609 F.2d 286, 292 (7th Cir. 1979).

We think the "particularized guarantees of trustworthiness" required for admission under the Confrontation Clause must likewise be drawn from the totality of circumstances that surround the making of the statement and that render the declarant particularly worthy of belief. Our precedents have recognized that statements admitted under a "firmly rooted" hearsay exception are so trustworthy that adversarial testing would add little to their reliability. Because evidence possessing "particularized guarantees of trustworthiness" must be at least as reliable as evidence admitted under a firmly rooted hearsay exception, we think that evidence admitted under the former requirement must similarly be so trustworthy that adversarial testing would add little to its reliability. Thus, unless an affirmative reason, arising from the circumstances in which the statement was made, provides a basis for rebutting the presumption that a hearsay statement is not worthy of reliance at trial, the Confrontation Clause requires exclusion of the out-of-court statement.

The state and federal courts have identified a number of factors that we think properly relate to whether hearsay statements made by a child witness in child sexual abuse cases are reliable. [The Court cites cases stressing "spontaneity and consistent repetition," the "mental state of the declarant," and the "use of terminology unexpected of a child of similar age."] Although these cases (which we cite for the factors they discuss and not necessarily to approve the results that they reach) involve the application of various hearsay exceptions to statements of child declarants, we think the factors identified also apply to whether such statements bear "particularized guarantees of trustworthiness" under the Confrontation Clause. These factors are, of course, not exclusive, and courts therefore have considerable leeway in their consideration of appropriate factors. We therefore decline to endorse a mechanical test for determining "particularized guarantees of trustworthiness" under the Clause. Rather, the unifying principle is that these factors relate to whether the child declarant was particularly likely to be telling the truth when the statement was made.

As our discussion above suggests, we are unpersuaded by the State's contention that evidence corroborating the truth of a hearsay statement may properly support a finding that the statement bears "particularized guarantees of trustworthiness." To be admissible under the Confrontation Clause, hearsay evidence used to convict a defendant must possess indicia of reliability by virtue of its inherent trustworthiness, not by reference to other evidence at trial. "[T]he Clause countenances only hearsay marked with such trustworthiness that 'there is no material departure from the reason of the general rule.'" Ohio v. Roberts, 448 U.S. 56 (1980). A statement made under duress, for example, may happen to be a true statement, but the circumstances under which it is made may provide no basis for supposing that the declarant is particularly likely to be telling the truth—indeed, the circumstances may even be such that the declarant is particularly unlikely to be telling the truth. In such a case, cross-examination at trial would be highly useful to probe the declarant's state-of-mind when he made the statements; the presence of evidence tending to corroborate the truth of the statement would be no substitute for cross-examination of the declarant at trial.

In short, the use of corroborating evidence to support a hearsay statement's "particularized guarantees of trustworthiness" would permit admission of a presumptively unreliable statement by bootstrapping on the trustworthiness of other evidence at trial, a result we think at odds with the requirement that hearsay evidence admitted under the Confrontation Clause be so trustworthy that cross-examination of the declarant would be of marginal utility. Indeed, although a plurality of the Court in [Dutton v. Evans, 400 U.S. 74 (1970),] looked to corroborating evidence as one of four factors in determining whether a particular hearsay statement possessed sufficient indicia of reliability, we think the presence of corroborating evidence more appropriately indicates that any error in admitting the statement might be harmless, rather than that any basis exists for presuming the declarant to be trustworthy. . . .

The trial court in this case, in ruling that the Confrontation Clause did not prohibit admission of the younger daughter's hearsay statements, relied on the following factors:

> In this case, of course, there is a physical evidence to corroborate that sexual abuse occurred. It would also seem to be the case that there is no motive to make up a story of this nature in a child of these years. We're not talking about a pubescent youth who may fantasize. The nature of the statements themselves as to sexual abuse are such that they fall outside the general believability that a child could make them up or would make them up. This is simply not the type of statement, I believe, that one would expect a child to fabricate.
>
> We come then to the identification itself. Are there any indicia of reliability as to identification? From the doctor's testimony it appears that the injuries testified to occurred at the time that the victim was in the custody of the Defendants. The [older daughter] has testified as to identification of [the] perpetrators. Those— the identification of the perpetrators in this case—are persons well known to the [younger daughter]. This is not a case in which a child is called upon to identify a stranger or a person with whom they would have no knowledge of their identity or ability to recollect and recall. Those factors are sufficient indicia of reliability to permit the admission of the statements.

Of the factors the trial court found relevant, only two relate to circumstances surrounding the making of the statements: whether the child had a motive to "make up a story of this nature," and whether, given the child's age, the statements are of the type "that one would expect a child to fabricate." The other factors on which the trial court relied, however, such as the presence of physical evidence of abuse, the opportunity of respondent to commit the offense, and the older daughter's corroborating identification, relate instead to whether other evidence existed to corroborate the truth of the statement. These factors, as we have discussed, are irrelevant to a showing of the "particularized guarantees of trustworthiness" necessary for admission of hearsay statements under the Confrontation Clause.

We think the Supreme Court of Idaho properly focused on the presumptive unreliability of the out-of-court statements and on the suggestive manner in which Dr. Jambura conducted the interview. Viewing the totality of the circumstances surrounding the younger daughter's responses to Dr. Jambura's questions, we find no special reason for supposing that the incriminating statements were particularly trustworthy. The younger daughter's last statement regarding the abuse of the older daughter, however, presents a closer question. According to Dr. Jambura, the younger daughter "volunteered" that statement "after she sort of clammed-up." Although the spontaneity of the statement and the change in demeanor suggest that the younger daughter was telling the truth when she made the statement, we note that it is possible that "[i]f there is evidence of prior interrogation, prompting, or manipulation by adults, spontaneity may be an inaccurate indicator of trustworthiness." State v. Robinson, 735 P.2d 801, 811 (Ariz. 1987). Moreover, the statement was not made under circumstances of reliability comparable to those required, for example, for the admission of excited utterances or statements made for purposes of medical diagnosis or treatment. Given the presumption of inadmissibility accorded accusatory hearsay statements not admitted pursuant to a firmly rooted hearsay exception, we agree with the court below that the State has failed to show that the younger daughter's incriminating statements to the pediatrician possessed sufficient "particularized guarantees of trustworthiness" under the Confrontation Clause to overcome that presumption.

The State does not challenge the Idaho Supreme Court's conclusion that the Confrontation Clause error in this case was not harmless beyond a reasonable doubt, and we see no reason to revisit the issue. We therefore agree with that court that respondent's conviction involving the younger daughter must be reversed and the case remanded for further proceedings. Accordingly, the judgment of the Supreme Court of Idaho is affirmed.

It is so ordered.

[In a dissenting opinion, Justice Kennedy, Chief Justice Rehnquist, and Justices White and Justice Blackmun argue that the statements in this case were reliable and that it is a mistake to bar consideration of corroborating evidence in making this determination.]

NOTES ON CONSTITUTIONAL LIMITS ON NEW HEARSAY

1. Do you suppose the Court that decided *Crawford* would say the statements offered in *Wright* are "testimonial"? If the answer is "no" where such children speak to a treating physician, even if their father brings the children in because of concern that they have been abused, would the answer change if someone from a state protective agency attends the session with the doctor? If the doctor is required to report suspected crimes, does that bear on the question?

2. If such statements *are* testimonial, should prosecutors try harder to get such children to testify and endure cross-examination? You will see in the next section ("New Hearsay") that accommodations are often made for children, letting them testify from remote locations less forbidding than a courtroom. Before *Crawford*, the Court approved such measures under some circumstances.

3. Surely the future of *Wright* is open to question:

(a) *Wright* is an application of the *Roberts* doctrine, and it is not clear whether *Roberts* continues to apply to nontestimonial statements, or is a dead letter. If *Roberts* drops from the picture, and statements like those in *Wright* are not testimonial, one possibility is that there will be no constitutional standard against which to measure such statements. Would that be an improvement?

(b) Perhaps equally important, *Wright* was a 5-4 decision, and four Justices have been replaced (two each from the majority and the dissent). Even if *Wright* is the law, its days may be numbered.

4.   There is nothing new about admitting trustworthy hearsay that falls outside standard exceptions, but the catchall is unbounded in that it lacks specific criteria. Experience applying the catchall produces lines of doctrine that develop hard-edged tests similar in specificity to categorical exceptions. But the idea of the catchall is to let courts be flexible. Arguably excluding the catchall from the "firmly rooted" category is good because it lets reviewing courts engage in closer scrutiny. Do trial judges lack the wisdom that reviewing courts can bring to bear? Should trial judges not be trusted with ad hoc decisions in the very cases in which they preside?

5.   Many states have statutes paving the way for statements by children describing sexual abuse. To the extent that such statutes reach "testimonial" statements within the meaning of the *Crawford* case, their use is subject to constitutional challenge. Almost certainly, statements by children to prosecutors, or to the staff of social service agencies acting as adjuncts to the office of the prosecutor, must be viewed as testimonial. It would seem to follow that such statements cannot be used unless the child also testifies in the case and is cross-examinable about the statements.

6.   These statutes can also apply to statements given by children describing abuse to caregivers (parents, teachers, babysitters, perhaps even doctors or nurses), and these may or may not be viewed as testimonial. If such statements are not testimonial, then the question is whether the Confrontation Clause plays any role. Like traditional or categorical exceptions, these rifle-shot provisions aim at a particular kind of hearsay. But like the catchall in *Wright*, these exceptions set out general criteria, telling courts to consider such factors as "trustworthiness" and "time, content, and circumstances." See, e.g., Colo. Rev. Stat. §13-25-129. Clearly, then, such exceptions are not "firmly rooted." If *Wright* continues in force, then, nontestimonial statements admitted under these exceptions are subject to strict scrutiny for reliability under *Roberts*, and might even be subject to an unavailability requirement. Given these realities, do you suppose caregivers who suspect abuse will try to obtain such statements before involving law enforcement? Would that work?

7.   Recall that in White v. Illinois, 502 U.S. 346 (1992), the trial court admitted a statement by a child to a physician under the exception for medical statements, and the Court (which considered only whether to require unavailability) didn't blink. Does it make sense to admit such statements with little or no constitutional scrutiny while giving strict scrutiny to statements admitted under the catchall?

5.   Protected-Witness Testimony

Child-abuse trials have not only generated new hearsay exceptions and new uses of traditional ones, but led to new ways to get live testimony.

Most states have statutes authorizing depositions of child victims, allowing their use at trial if the child is unavailable, and defining unavailability to include immaturity (too young to communicate or deal with the courtroom) and medical reasons (trauma from court appearance). Many states authorize child victims to give live testimony from outside the courtroom, with voice and image transmitted to the court by one-way video (people in court can see and hear child on monitor) or two-way (child can also see and hear courtroom on monitor).

Coy decision. In the first case to consider the general issue, the Court threw cold water on such measures. The case was Coy v. Iowa, 487 U.S. 1012 (1988), which involved a trial for sexual assault in which a screen was placed between the witness stand and the defense table so the complaining witnesses (13-year-old girls) could not see defendant while testifying, though he could see them. (The girls were assaulted while camping in the back yard next door to defendant's house. The assailant wore a stocking over his head and shined a flashlight in their eyes, so they could not describe his face and did not try to identify defendant as the one.) The screen was authorized by an Iowa statute, which also provided for testimony by closed-circuit television, with the parties in the same room. In an opinion by Justice Scalia, the Supreme Court disapproved: The Confrontation Clause guarantees defendant "a face-to-face meeting with witnesses." The interest of fairness is served because a witness may feel different when he repeats his story looking at the person he will harm if he distorts or mistakes facts, and because it is harder to lie about someone "to his face" than "behind his back." While the witness need not look at defendant, the trier will "draw its own conclusions" if she "studiously look[s] elsewhere." Some rights secured by the Clause are not absolute, but it has an "irreducible literal meaning" that guarantees a face-to-face encounter. If there *are* exceptions, they must rest on "individualized findings" (not statutory categories).

Craig decision. After *Coy,* several courts approved remote testimony by child-abuse victims, in which the child sat in another room and her image and words were transmitted to court through closed-circuit television (both lawyers being with the child, while defendant remained in the courtroom in voice contact with his lawyer). In the *Craig* decision in 1990, the Supreme Court approved this technique, under certain circumstances. In *Craig,* the Maryland Court of Appeals thought *Coy* required a face-to-face courtroom encounter between victim and defendant before a judge could decide to use this device. The Supreme Court disagreed, concluding that the state's interest in "physical and psychological well-being" of such victims is important enough to outweigh the defense right to face accusers in court. The state must make a "case-specific" finding that this procedure is "necessary to protect the welfare of the particular child" and must find that "emotional distress" is "more than mere nervousness or excitement or some reluctance to testify," but can do so without bringing the child into defendant's presence. Maryland v. Craig, 497 U.S. 805 (1990).

NOTES ON PROTECTED-WITNESS TESTIMONY

1. Assume a child is capable of entering the courtroom and describing acts of abuse in the presence of the very person who (allegedly) committed it, but that doing so would be traumatic. Can a judge, or for that matter a psycholo-

gist or psychiatrist, distinguish between the fear and nervousness that would grip *anyone* in this setting and a reaction that would cause severe psychological damage? In *Coy*, the court thought the former was a good thing, didn't it?

2.   Do you think that such procedures survive the decision in *Crawford?* Statements by children utilizing such procedures are testimonial, aren't they? And *Crawford* lays great stress on the importance of cross-examination, doesn't it?

3.   Do you think there a constitutional distinction between using a child's videotaped deposition and using a child's live testimony from another room through closed-circuit television? Should the "unavailability" criterion be the same for each? Should it matter, in the case of a deposition, whether the court is immediately available to rule on questions or procedural matters that the parties cannot amicably resolve? Does "live testimony" from another room guarantee a kind of immediacy or spontaneity that makes it better or more reliable, or that helps a jury in its evaluative task?

Five

RELEVANCE REVISITED

A. CHARACTER EVIDENCE

1. Relevancy and Form

"Character" is a loaded term. In its broadest sense it suggests a particular combination of human qualities that defines the essence (and in a sense measures the worth) of a person. He is good or kind or caring, or perhaps awful or vicious or selfish. Even talking about character in this sense is awkward, for doing so casts the speaker in a judgmental role and trenches hard on the privacy of the person in question.

But "character" also carries a narrower meaning, describing specific inclinations of a person and suggesting their innateness in him. We speak of someone as being "by nature" cautious or careless, brave or fearful, combative or affable, and so forth, meaning that these traits shape his natural tendencies.

Character as evidence of conduct. It is in the narrower sense that "character" has its great evidential significance, for specific inclinations are not only descriptive but predictive, suggesting probable patterns of behavior and thus telling us something about the likelihood that a person would or would not do certain acts. Emphasizing the predictive aspect of character traits, we may say that a person is "by disposition" tricky or deceitful, or that he is "disposed" in the opposite direction, toward fairness and honesty. If the question is whether X knowingly made a false statement in selling his car, proof he is honest is some indication he did not make the statement or (if he did) he thought it to be true, while proof he is tricky or deceitful is some indication he made the statement *and* knew it was false. When proof of character is used in this way, we speak of the "propensity argument," which justifies using proof of character as "substantive evidence of conduct on a particular occasion."

Obviously the probative worth of such proof cannot be measured with precision. Its weight turns in part on the inclination in question and the point to be proved: If, for example, we have in one case evidence of a fair and honest disposition and in another evidence of treachery and dishonesty, the former seems more persuasive as proof that the person did *not* utter the falsehood in issue than the latter in proving that he *did*. The reason is that fairness and honesty seem to lessen the likelihood that a person uttered any falsehood (hence necessarily the one at issue), while treachery and dishonesty seem only to increase the likelihood that the person utters falsehoods (but *not necessarily* the one in issue).

In the end the assessment of probative worth must be left to intuition and judgment. It is hard to know how strong or deep run the currents of any trait, or to be sure that a person truly has one rather than the other, or indeed to understand what those inclinations portend in the particular soul or psyche under the circumstances confronting the person at the crucial moment.

Form of the evidence. If character (or a trait of character) is to be proved, how should it be done? There are three ways, all involving testimony by what we may call "character witnesses." Such a witness might describe acts by the person that indicate the existence of the trait—that he falsified a document, for example, or rendered a correct account of moneys entrusted to him. Or she might give her opinion that the person has the trait in question—she thinks him "honest" or "deceitful." Or she might describe his reputation—"the shadow his daily life has cast in his neighborhood," as the Supreme Court called it in Michelson v. United States, 335 U.S. 469, 477 (1948). In our example, she might testify that he is by reputation "honest" or "deceitful."

By longstanding common law tradition, only reputation testimony was allowed when the purpose was to prove character as circumstantial evidence of conduct on a particular occasion. Reputation evidence has been praised in eloquent terms as

> the slow growth of months and years, the resultant picture of forgotten incidents, passing events, habitual and daily conduct, presumably honest because disinterested, and safer to be trusted because prone to suspect. . . . It sums up a multitude of trivial details. It compacts into the brief phrase of a verdict the teaching of many incidents and the conduct of years. It is the average intelligence drawing its conclusion.

Finch, J., in Badger v. Badger, 88 N.Y. 546, 552 (1882), quoted in *Michelson*, supra.

But many chafed at the common law restriction, mounting strong arguments that opinion too should be allowed:

> Put any one of us on trial for a false charge, and ask him whether he would not rather invoke in his vindication, as Lord Kenyon said, "the warm, affectionate testimony" of those few whose long intimacy and trust has made them ready to demonstrate their faith to the jury, than any amount of colorful assertions about reputation. Take the place of a juryman, and speculate whether he is helped more by the witnesses whose personal intimacy gives to their belief a first and highest value, or by those who merely repeat a form of words in which the term "reputation" occurs. . . . The Anglo-American rules of evidence have . . . never done anything so curious in the way of shutting out evidential light as when they decided to exclude the person who knows as much as humanly can be known about the character of another, and have still admitted the secondhand, irresponsible product of multiplied guesses and gossip which we term "reputation."

7 J. Wigmore, Evidence §1986 (3d ed. 1940).

But the common law restriction (which allowed only reputation testimony) persevered, for reasons perhaps best summed up in these words:

> The answer to [Wigmore's] argument is found in overwhelming considerations of practical convenience. If a witness is to be permitted to testify to the character of an accused person, basing his testimony solely on his own knowledge and observation, he cannot logically be prohibited from stating the particular incidents affecting the defendant and the particular actions of the defendant which have led him to his favorable conclusion. In most instances it would be utterly impossible for the prosecution to ascertain whether occurrences narrated by the witness as constituting the foundation of his conclusion were or were not true. They might be utterly false, and yet incapable of disproof at the time of trial. Furthermore, even if evidence were accessible to controvert the specific statements of the witness in this respect, its admission would lead to the introduction into the case of innumerable collateral issues which could not be tried out without introducing the utmost complication and confusion into the trial, tending to distract the minds of the jurymen and befog the chief issue in litigation.

People v. Van Gaasbeck, 82 N.E. 718 (N.Y. 1907).

As a glance at FRE 405(a) reveals, the Federal Rules authorize both reputation and opinion evidence, but sharply restrict evidence of specific instances.

The regulating scheme. FRE 404 and 405 largely restate the rules that had evolved at common law. As you will discover, those principles are somewhat complicated and full of compromise. In the *Michelson* case, the Supreme Court took note of the common law scheme but declined to change it:

> [M]uch of this law is archaic, paradoxical and full of compromises and compensations by which an irrational advantage to one side is offset by a poorly reasoned counterprivilege to the other. But somehow it has proved a workable even if clumsy system when moderated by discretionary controls in the hands of a wise and strong trial court. To pull one misshapen stone out of the grotesque structure is more likely simply to upset its present balance between adverse interests than to establish a rational edifice.

Michelson v. United States, 335 U.S. 469, 486 (1948).

In the material that follows, concentrate on the following issues: In what way (if at all) is character evidence relevant? Is it admissible under FRE 404 or 405? What reasons underlie the answers given by the Rules? If character evidence is admissible, what form should it take?

2. *Character to Prove Conduct on a Particular Occasion*

a. **Character of Criminal Defendant**

First consider evidence of defendant's character—which has long presented the most common problem and acute difficulty.

PROBLEM 5-A.   Fight in the Red Dog Saloon

Don and Vince come to blows in a local watering hole known as the Red Dog Saloon. Both suffer serious injuries, although Vince gets the worst of it: Wineglass in hand, Don takes a wild swing, and the glass shatters as it strikes Vince in the mouth, inflicting lacerations leading to permanent scars on his face. Don is charged with assault and battery. He pleads self-defense. Testimony conflicts as to who struck the first blow, though it appears that Don was seated at the bar enjoying his Chablis when Vince muttered something snide about what "real men" drink.

In the trial of Don, the prosecutor calls Coach Jones as a witness during the state's case-in-chief, offering his testimony that Don is "one mean aggressive physical man, quick tempered and prone to violence." Don objects that the proffered testimony is "irrelevant" and "barred by the character rule."

During the defense case-in-chief, Don calls Reverend Gram, offering his testimony that Don is "peaceably disposed toward all people, gentle and nonviolent, more likely to run from a fight than to defend himself, and certainly not likely to initiate violence." The prosecutor objects that the proffered testimony is "irrelevant" and "barred by the character rule."

What result on these objections and why? If the court lets Gram testify for Don, can the prosecutor call Coach Jones during the state's case-in-rebuttal? See FRE 404(a).

NOTES ON EVIDENCE OF DEFENDANT'S CHARACTER

1.   Why should it make a difference whether evidence of a defendant's character is first offered by the defendant or by the prosecutor?

2.   What is a "pertinent" character trait? That depends largely on the nature of the charges. In a battery prosecution, a court would likely exclude evidence that defendant is "honest" but admit proof that he is "peaceable" or "nonviolent." See United States v. Jackson, 588 F.2d 1046, 1055 (5th Cir.) (in drug trial, evidence of defendant's reputation for truth and veracity was not admissible under FRE 404(a)(1) because truthfulness was "not pertinent to the criminal charges of conspiracy to distribute heroin or possession of heroin"), cert. denied, 442 U.S. 941 (1979).

3.   What level of specificity is required? Rule 404(a)(1) and (2) speaks of a "pertinent trait" of character, and the ACN speaks of limiting the evidence to such traits rather than proving "character generally." Compare State v. Blake, 249 A.2d 232, 234-235 (Conn. 1968) (alleged indecent assault; on retrial, defendant should be permitted to prove "specific traits" of "sexual morality and decency," but not "general good character") with United States v. John, 309 F.3d 298, 303 (5th Cir. 2002) (in trial for sexual assault against minor, admitting testimony by (a) wife of defendant indicating that the two "had a good marriage and a normal sexual relationship," (b) social service worker who placed eight foster children with defendant and his wife, indicating that she considered them "very good parents [who were] willing to do whatever needs to be done for the children," (c) defendant himself indicating that he

was "fifty-one years old and had never been accused of sexual misconduct," and (d) defendant's 33-year-old daughter indicating that defendant had a "good" reputation in the community for "sexual morality and decency"). But general proof that defendant is "law abiding" seems at least marginally relevant in all contexts, and courts seem disposed to admit it. See United States v. Diaz, 961 F.2d 1417 (9th Cir. 1992) (in drug trial, error to block defense from asking pastor about defendant's "character traits for being prone to criminal activity" since traits need not be specific and may include general traits such as being law abiding) (but "being prone to large-scale drug dealing" was not a character trait, and court properly blocked government cross raising this point).

4. If evidence of defendant's good character is admitted, should the jury be told anything? Can the jury properly acquit a defendant on the basis of proof of good character alone, or should it be told to consider character evidence in the context of all the proof in the case? Compare Edgington v. United States, 164 U.S. 361, 366 (1896) and United States v. Pujana-Mena, 949 F.2d, 24, 29-32 (2d Cir. 1991) (both implying that jury should be told to consider defense evidence of good character in the context of all the evidence) with United States v. John, 309 F.3d 298, 304-305 (5th Cir. 2002) (reversible error to refuse to instruct jury that evidence of defendant's good character may create reasonable doubt).

5. It may be that the best that defendant can offer is someone to testify that he "has heard nothing ill" of the defendant. Should such a lukewarm endorsement be permitted? See Michelson v. United States, 335 U.S. 469, 478 (1948) (yes).

b. Character of Crime Victim

PROBLEM 5-B. Red Dog Saloon—Part II

In the trial of Don for the assault on Vince described above, Don calls Ernie, offering his testimony that Vince is "a belligerent, fight-picking, aggressive fellow with a real short fuse." The prosecutor objects that the proffered testimony is "irrelevant" and "barred by the rule against character evidence." Is this objection well taken on either ground? Spell out Don's argument that Ernie's testimony is relevant. If the judge overrules the prosecutor's objection, what exactly should Ernie be permitted to testify to? See FRE 404(a) and 405.

NOTES ON EVIDENCE OF THE VICTIM'S CHARACTER

1. If Don can introduce evidence that Vince is violent, can the prosecutor introduce evidence that Don is also violent? In 2000, FRE 404(a)(1) was amended to permit the prosecutor to introduce "evidence of a pertinent trait" of the accused if the latter introduces evidence of a trait of the victim under FRE 404(a)(2). Is this change wise?

2. Assume that instead of calling Ernie to describe the character of Vince, Don calls an eyewitness to testify that Vince struck the first blow without provoca-

tion. Could the prosecutor then introduce evidence that Vince is by disposition peaceable? What if Don had killed Vince and was charged with his murder?

3.   Sometimes a defendant like Don, who is accused of assault and related crimes, offers evidence that the alleged victim has made threats to attack or kill the defendant. Is such evidence relevant? What does it tend to show? Do FRE 404 and 405 apply to such proof? See Torres v. State, 71 S.W.3d 758, 761 (Tex. Crim. App. 2002) (threats to harm defendant are not excludable as character evidence; they are admissible because they shed direct light on victim's state of mind).

c.   Methods of Proving Character

PROBLEM 5-C.   Red Dog Saloon—Part III

In Don's trial, if the judge lets Ernie testify about the character of Vince, should Ernie be permitted to testify as described above (Vince is "a belligerent, fight-picking fellow with a real short fuse")? What kind of testimony is that? If the judge lets Reverend Gram testify that Don is "peaceably disposed," and lets Coach Jones testify that Don is "quick tempered and prone to violence," is such testimony similar in nature? (See FRE 405.) What foundation should the proponent lay?

Suppose Ernie testified that Vince was "known in the community" as a belligerent person, or that he "has a reputation" for aggressiveness. What kind of testimony would that be? (Again, see FRE 405.) What kind of foundation would be required? Could Reverend Gram and Coach Jones, in describing the character of Don, cast their testimony in similar form?

In support of his conclusion that Vince is "belligerent, fight-picking," and "aggressive," could Ernie describe past fights that he had seen Vince involved in? In support of his conclusion that Don is "quick-tempered and prone to violence," could Coach Jones describe specific acts by Don? What would be wrong with that?

NOTES ON OPINION AND REPUTATION

1.   How well must a character witness know the defendant or victim to testify to his reputation? Is a college student qualified to give either positive or negative testimony as to the character of the accused if the witness has known defendant for two months around campus or in a dormitory, sorority, or fraternity? What about a business associate who has no social contact with the defendant and knows nothing of his home life? See United States v. Parker, 447 F.2d 826, 831 (7th Cir. 1971) (error to exclude positive testimony as to defendant's reputation among coworkers). How about an investigator hired to interview members of the community? See United States v. Perry, 643 F.2d 38, 52 (2d Cir.) (excluding testimony by private investigator hired by defendant's wife), cert. denied, 454 U.S. 835 (1981).

2.   When Don claims that Vince was the first aggressor, does that mean that the character of Vince is an element in Don's defense?

(a)   If the character of Vince *were* an element in Don's defense, couldn't Don prove specific instances of aggressive behavior by Vince? See FRE 405(b). But the correct answer is that the character of Vince is *not* an element in Don's defense. Why is that correct? See State v. Hutchinson, 959 P.2d 1061, 1071 (Wash. 1998) (in murder trial, where defendant claimed self-defense, limiting defendant to opinion or reputation evidence relating to character of victim).

(b)   Suppose Don makes the somewhat different claim that *his* behavior was reasonable because *he knew that* Vince had committed violent acts in similar situations, hence that special self-protective measures were necessary. *Now* can Don offer proof relating to prior acts by Vince? See United States v. Burks, 470 F.2d 432, 434-435 (D.C. Cir. 1972) (violent acts by the victim were admissible, when known by the defendant, on the question whether the defendant "reasonably feared he was in danger of imminent great bodily injury"). Do FRE 404 and 405 apply here?

3.   Should the prosecutor be permitted to ask a character witness about the reputation of the defendant *after* the crime was committed? See United States v. Curtis, 644 F.2d 263, 268-269 (3d Cir. 1981) (no), cert. denied, 459 U.S. 1018 (1982). Why not?

4.   Should FRE 405 be amended to bar reputation evidence now that opinion is admissible? See Uviller, Evidence of Character to Prove Conduct: Illusion, Illogic, and Injustice in the Courtroom, 130 U. Pa. L. Rev. 845, 885 (1982) (reputation is the least trustworthy and least testable form of character evidence, and should be disallowed).

5.   Should a defendant be permitted to offer the "expert" opinion of a psychologist or psychiatrist to the effect that defendant is by disposition nonviolent? Compare United States v. MacDonald, 688 F.2d 224, 227-228 (4th Cir. 1982) (excluding psychiatric testimony that defendant's "personality configuration" is inconsistent with "outrageous and senseless murders" charged against him) with United States v. Staggs, 553 F.2d 1073, 1075-1076 (7th Cir. 1977) (in trial for armed threats against federal officer, reversible error to exclude testimony by psychologist that defendant "was more likely to hurt himself than to direct his aggression toward others"). We approach this question from another perspective in Chapter 9C2, infra (expert testimony on behavioral and psychological patterns).

d.   Cross-Examination and Rebuttal

PROBLEM 5-D.   *What Price Truth?*

In Don's trial, the judge excludes the testimony of Coach Jones during the prosecutor's case-in-chief and admits the testimony of Reverent Gram during the defense case-in-chief. After Gram has told the trier of fact that Don is a "peaceable nonviolent fellow," the prosecutor rises for cross-examination:

Q: Reverend Gram, you tell us that Don is not a violent man, is that right?
A: Yes, sir.

Q: And that he is not in the habit of striking his fellow man?
A: No, indeed.
Q: But that doesn't go for women, does it?
A: I beg your pardon—
Ms. Davenport: Your honor, I object to that last question and move that it be struck from the record. The question is whether the defendant starts fights, and the Reverend here has said he doesn't. The question is not proper cross-examination under Rule 405 and is beyond the scope of the direct besides.
Court: Overruled. It's a preliminary question, and I think maybe he's leading up to something. Go ahead, Mr. Irwin.
Mr. Irwin: Did you know, Reverend, that two weeks ago Don's wife was treated in the emergency room of the Crosbie Clinic, suffering multiple bruises, lacerations, and two cracked ribs, all at the hands of the defendant, who you say wouldn't harm anyone?

Is the question proper, or did the court err in rejecting the defense objection? Can Mr. Irwin ask Reverend Gram whether he knows Don was fired for embezzling from his employer? Whether he knows Don was convicted of tax evasion? Whether he knows Don was arrested for brawling after a football game?

NOTES ON CROSS-EXAMINATION OF CHARACTER WITNESSES

1.   When the accused calls a character witness to testify to his good character, the prosecutor may cross-examine about incidents from defendant's past that could not be proved otherwise. Recognizing that merely *asking* such questions may "waft an unwarranted innuendo into the jury box," the Supreme Court nevertheless concluded:

> A defendant . . . is powerless to prevent his cause from being irretrievably obscured and confused; but, in cases such as the one before us, the law foreclosed this whole confounding line of inquiry, unless defendant thought the net advantage from opening it up would be with him. Given this option, we think defendants . . . have no valid compliant at the latitude which existing law allows to the prosecution to meet by cross-examination an issue voluntarily tendered by the defense.

Michelson v. United States, 335 U.S. 469, 484-485 (1948).
2.   What's going on with such cross-questions, anyway? Does this form of counterattack permit the prosecutor to argue that the accused is a person of bad character who must have committed the deed? The Supreme Court in *Michelson* said the accused was entitled to limiting instructions even though the jury will likely "find them unintelligible." What sort of unintelligible instruction should the court give?
3.   What if Mr. Irwin simply dreams up the nastiest question he can think of and asks it: "Did you know, Reverend Gram, that Don beats up derelicts for kicks and throws rocks at little children?" Should we require the prosecutor to prove that he has a good faith basis for his questions, so that if the jury misuses them, at least it will be misusing fact rather than fiction? How?

4. Can *Don's* lawyer ask Coach Jones on cross-examination whether Jones knows about the times Don "refused to fight back when attacked," and "intervened to prevent violence among his teammates"? Is the defense likely to follow this tactic?

5. Reverend Gram gave his opinion of Don's good character. Then the cross-examiner asked "Did you know" of specific instances of misbehavior. In casting the question in that form, the prosecutor did exactly the right thing. Why? How should the question be put if Reverend Gram testified to Don's *reputation* for peacefulness?

e. Civil Cases

FRE 404(a) states a general rule excluding character when offered to prove conduct, and then sets out three exceptions. Putting aside the third, character of the witness (taken up in Chapter 8), no provision touches civil cases.

It follows that character evidence, when offered to prove behavior in a particular instance, is *never* admissible in civil cases. Despite this fact, however, courts sometimes admit character evidence in civil cases where the underlying conduct is criminal in nature. See Perrin v. Anderson, 784 F.2d 1040, 1043-1045 (10th Cir. 1986) (despite "literal language" of exceptions in FRE 404(a), civil defendant may invoke exceptions when central issue "is in nature criminal"). Some state counterparts make limited provision for character evidence in civil cases. See Oregon Evidence Rule 404(2)(d) (allowing character evidence in support of claim of self-defense in civil assault and battery cases). And at least one modern commentator has argued for expanded admissibility of character evidence in civil cases. See Leonard, The Use of Character to Prove Conduct: Rationality and Catharsis in the Law of Evidence, 58 Colo. L. Rev. 1, 56-57 (1987) (favoring more general rule that would not limit character evidence to criminal cases but would admit such evidence unless it would waste time, confuse or mislead, or be unfairly prejudicial).

FRE 415 carves out an exception to the ban on character evidence in civil cases where the claimant seeks damages for sexual assault or child molestation. In this setting, claimants can prove that the defendant committed other offenses of sexual assault, which may be considered for any relevant purpose. Does it make sense to carve out a special exemption from the character rules in these cases? If such an exemption is to be made, shouldn't we *also* allow the defending party to offer evidence of *good* character? Should we allow the defending party to offer good character evidence even if the claimant *does not* offer proof of prior offenses? We do so in criminal cases, don't we?

3. Character as an Element of a Charge, Claim, or Defense

a. Criminal Cases

We have seen that evidence of character is usually inadmissible to prove conduct on a particular occasion. In criminal cases, the prosecutor may not offer such evidence during his case-in-chief to persuade the jury that defendant committed the crime. But exceptions created by FRE 404(a) sometimes allow character evidence to prove conduct. For example, the accused may resort to such proof to show he did *not* commit the charged crime.

We have also seen that *when* character evidence is admitted as proof of conduct, the proof must take the form of opinion or reputation evidence (rather than proof of specific instances). Finally, we have seen that specific instances may be raised on cross. Thus the cross-examiner may ask a character witness about acts by the person whose character he has described. Rule 405(a) makes that much clear.

Now look at something new. Rule 404 does *not* bar evidence of character when it is offered for *other reasons* than to prove conduct on a particular occasion. And note that Rule 405(b) provides that "proof" of "specific instances" of conduct is admissible whenever character is an "essential element" of a charge or defense.

So we have a new question: When is character an "element" of a charge or defense?

In criminal cases the answer is "almost never." The Advisory Committee tried to think of an example and could only come up with one that is obscure and archaic—"the chastity of the victim under a statute specifying her chastity as an element of the crime of seduction"! Hard as it is to imagine a trial for such a crime in the twenty-first century, assume for a moment that such charges are brought and forget how appalling it might seem to admit defense evidence of every "unchaste" act committed by the victim (offered as proof that she was "unchaste"). In such a trial, however, the accused would have to resort to Rule 405(b) if he wanted to prove such acts. Otherwise he would be limited by Rule 405(a) to offering opinion or reputation evidence.

Now check your understanding, bearing in mind that the accused often does try to show his innocence by proving his own good character. It is no exaggeration to say that the jury's opinion of his character may be his most important asset. But it does not follow that his character is "an essential element" of a charge or defense under FRE 405(b). In more common parlance, character itself is not "in issue" regardless how vigorously it may be disputed or how important it may be in the jury's deliberations. Put yet another way, we do not (or should not) convict a person because he is "bad" (unless it also happens that he committed the charged offense) or acquit him because he is "good" (unless it also happens that he did not commit the charged offense).

Consider for a moment the character of the alleged victim. It would be possible to make the victim's character an element of a charge or defense. We could, for example, define the crime of battery as beating up a good person, which would mean that someone who beat up a bad person would be innocent of this crime. But the criminal law has not taken this direction, and constitutional principles such as equal protection and substantive due process would likely block this approach.

PROBLEM 5-E.   *"She's a Known Thief"*

Gretta is charged with shoplifting from Bloomingdeal's. Helen, a plain-clothes security guard in the woman's clothing department, stopped her after she had visited the changing room and as she was leaving the store. On conducting a search of Gretta's purse, Helen discovered a blouse and skirt that appeared to be new and matched items carried by the store. There were no store markings on the items, however, and Gretta said she was carrying them "as a change of clothing because I'm meeting a friend for a drink after work."

Gretta pleaded innocent and advanced the same explanation at trial. During his case-in-chief, the prosecutor offered Helen's testimony that "I watched Gretta closely that day because I had learned by watching videotapes that Gretta stole other clothing items from the department in recent weeks, including a sweater, some gloves, and some lingerie." Helen would also testify (if allowed) that Gretta had a reputation among the security guards in the store as a shoplifter of small items from many departments, from electronics to homewares to cosmetics and jewelry. The prosecutor also offered evidence that Gretta had been convicted of shoplifting (at other stores) four times in the last five years.

Gretta objected that this evidence was "barred by the rule against character evidence." The prosecutor replied, "Your honor, she's a known thief, and being a thief is what she's charged with. She denies it. We're entitled to prove otherwise." What result, and why?

NOTES ON CHARACTER AS AN "ELEMENT" IN CRIMINAL CASES

1. The prosecutor has a point, doesn't he? Either Gretta is a thief or she isn't, and she says she isn't. But Gretta entered a plea of innocence and offered an explanation. The real question isn't whether she is a thief, but whether she was stealing the blouse and skirt. If FRE 404(a) doesn't apply, when would it ever apply? Compare State v. Demeritt, 813 A.2d 393 (N.H. 2002) (alleged vehicular manslaughter; defendant claimed victim caused accident by reckless driving; victim's "recklessness" was not an essential element of the defense; trial court properly excluded victim's specific acts).

2. Do the prior thefts of clothing that Helen would describe support an inference that Gretta *intended* to steal something on the day she was apprehended? If so, do those thefts do so only because they suggest that Gretta is by disposition a thief? That's still "character evidence," isn't it?

3. Suppose the prosecutor offers Helen's testimony on what the guards at Bloomingdeal's thought of Gretta in order to "explain why Helen followed Gretta and searched her purse." Should this argument overcome the "character" objection that Gretta raises?

4. Consider criminal prosecutions in which defendant claims "insanity" or "diminished capacity." Do FRE 404 and 405 apply in this context, or do these defenses involve something apart from "character"? See United States v. Emery, 682 F.2d 493, 496-501 (5th Cir.) (admitting prior offense evidence as part of government's proof that defendant was sane), cert. denied, 459 U.S. 1044 (1982).

5. Consider trials under repeat offender statutes in which a prior conviction is an element in the present charges (as in prosecutions for illegal possession of a firearm by a convicted felon). How about cases in which prior offenses may affect the punishment imposed? Do FRE 404 and 405 apply in these situations? Recall that the Supreme Court held in *Old Chief* that in this setting a defense offer to stipulate requires the court to exclude proof of prior crimes (see Chapter 2, supra).

6.   When defendants claim entrapment, they are essentially saying government action induced them to commit crimes they would not otherwise commit. Thus it becomes plausible to say character is an element in the defense. Typically, however, the response of the prosecution is not to introduce opinion or reputation evidence but to offer proof that defendant committed similar crimes on other occasions. Usually courts admit such evidence under FRE 404(b) rather than to refute an element of the defense under FRE 404(a)(1) or to prove an element of the crime under 405(b).

b.   Civil Cases

In civil litigation (unlike criminal cases) there are several common situations in which character is an ultimate issue. Here the evidence is not offered as a predicate fact supporting an inference of behavior on a particular occasion, but as an end in itself.

Defamation. The most obvious example is the defamation suit in which truth is raised as a defense: If a basketball player sues the local newspaper on account of a story reporting that he "shaves points for cash," then defense evidence that in fact plaintiff did exactly that would be admissible. The proof would likely take the form of evidence of point-shaving in particular games. If the alleged libel is more general (accusing plaintiff of being a "thief"), a defense of truth would pave the way for evidence of particular thefts, or even opinion or reputation testimony that plaintiff is indeed a thief. Sometimes reputation as such bears on damages. Defendant in a libel suit might allege that what was said did not damage plaintiff, simply because plaintiff suffered a bad reputation even before the defamatory utterance, in which case evidence of such bad reputation is admissible. See Schafer v. Time, Inc., 142 F.3d 1361, 1370 (11th Cir. 1998) (in libel suit, admitting evidence of specific acts by plaintiff, since his character was substantively at issue under FRE 405).

Negligent entrustment. Another obvious example is the negligent entrustment action, where plaintiff alleges that defendant was negligent in permitting another to operate his equipment (typically a car or truck) and that the other negligently injured plaintiff. Here plaintiff must prove that the latter was by disposition careless, in order to prevail on the point that defendant should not have entrusted the equipment to him. On this point it is clear that evidence of specific instances of prior negligence with such equipment may be proved. See Scroggins v. Yellow Freight Systems, Inc., 98 F.Supp 928, 930 (E.D. Tenn. 2000) (truck driver); In re Aircrash in Bali, 684 F.2d 1301, 1315 (9th Cir. 1982) (airline pilot); Breeding v. Massey, 378 F.2d 171, 181 (8th Cir. 1967) (car driver). In these cases, of course, plaintiff must also prove the person entrusted with the equipment was negligent at the time of the accident. Can you see why plaintiffs sometimes seek recovery on a theory of negligent entrustment even though this theory may require them to prove everything they must prove to recover in respondeat superior, plus one more thing?

Child custody. Yet another example is the child custody dispute, in which relative parental fitness of mother and father is assessed in order to serve the "best interests" of the child. Here character, in the sense of being a good parent, is the ultimate issue in the case. See Berryhill v. Berryhill, 410 So. 2d 416, 418-419 (Ala. 1982) (specific acts and reputation evidence admissible).

Wrongful death. A common instance of such use of character evidence is the wrongful death action in which the amount of recoverable damages may turn on the "worth" of the decedent to the plaintiff. Whatever tactical difficulties may confront the defense in "speaking ill of the dead," in theory the bereaved plaintiff should recover less if it can be shown that the deceased was an "alcoholic" or "compulsive gambler" than would be recoverable if the deceased was a hardworking, dedicated, and loving spouse, parent, or child. See Perkins v. United Transport Co., 219 F.2d 422, 423 (2d Cir. 1955) (approving reputation evidence).

NOTES ON CHARACTER AS AN "ELEMENT" IN CIVIL CASES

1. In libel cases where the alleged defamatory statement was broad or general, can defendant support a claim of truth by reputation or opinion evidence? If the statement charges specific acts of wrongdoing, can defendant support a defense of truth by evidence of *other* specific acts of a similar nature? See Roper v. Mabry, 551 P.2d 1381 (Wash. App. 1976) (no). Cf. Reynolds v. Pegler, 223 F.2d 429, 435 (2d Cir.) (excluding letters linking plaintiff with other subversive organizations, offered in support of defense of truth of statements associating plaintiff with communism), cert. denied, 350 U.S. 846 (1955).

2. Could defendant use proof of such different acts to show that plaintiff's reputation was not injured by the allegedly defamatory statements? See Meiners v. Moriarity, 563 F.2d 343, 351 (7th Cir. 1977) (court should have let party charged with libel cross-examine claimant on "relevant specific instances of conduct" that might have produced adverse publicity, including "events other than the . . . incident" mentioned in statement). What if plaintiff has engaged in other misconduct but that misconduct has not become known to the public or the business community? See Shirley v. Freunscht, 735 P.2d 600 (Or. 1987) (in defamation suit, defendant tried to show that plaintiff had bad reputation beforehand; error to let witnesses relate specific instances of "business misconduct," which are irrelevant "unless they were generally known in the business community," which wasn't shown here).

3. In a wrongful death action against the maker of a household spray product purposefully inhaled by the 14-year-old decedent, can defendant prove that the boy also smoked marijuana? See Harless v. Boyld-Midway Division, American Home Products, 594 F.2d 1051, 1057-1058 (5th Cir. 1979) (no). Why not? How about evidence, in a suit for wrongful death of plaintiff's husband, that plaintiff and decedent had begun living together before decedent divorced his first wife? See St. Clair v. Eastern Air Lines, 279 F.2d 119, 121 (2d Cir.) (no), cert. denied, 364 U.S. 882 (1960). Why not? In a suit for alleged wrongful death of a wage-earning spouse, should evidence be admitted that decedent was honest or dishonest? See Perkins v. United Transport Co., 219 F.2d 422, 423 (2d Cir. 1955) (yes). How about evidence that he is or is not well regarded in his trade or calling? See *St. Clair,* supra (yes). Wouldn't these uses of such evidence amount to character to prove probable conduct? As such, why doesn't FRE 404 bar the proof?

4. Prior Acts as Proof of Motive, Intent, Plan, and Related Points

a. General Considerations

So elaborate and settled are the restrictions against using character evidence to prove conduct that it may come as a surprise that prosecutors often get in evidence of previous "bad acts" by the defendant. FRE 404(b), paving the way for such proof, sets out a lengthy (and nonexclusive) list of specific points on which it may be admitted, one of the most important being "intent." Nothing is more common in federal courts than drug cases in which the government offers evidence that on some other occasion defendant sold drugs, as proof that *on this* occasion he *intended* to sell similar drugs found in his possession. And specific acts are admitted on many other points, like knowledge, motive, and plan.

Yet in such cases the risk of prejudice to the defendant is manifest: Obviously the court must carefully analyze probative worth and risks of unfair prejudice and confusion of issues, and often the proof is excludable under FRE 403 even though it is marginally relevant on some point. Many courts endorse a four-part test or process under which the judge (a) decides whether the evidence is offered for a proper purpose, (b) decides whether it is relevant for that purpose, (c) decides whether its probative worth is outweighed by the risk of unfair prejudice, and (d) gives a limiting instruction on request. See Huddleston v. United States, 485 U.S. 681 (1988).

So common are such cases that a glance at the reporters yields hundreds of appellate decisions on point, usually rejecting defense arguments that the proof should have been excluded under FRE 403 or 404(a). Indeed, it sometimes seems that the basic rule against "character evidence" is a sham. It might better depict reality if reformulated as a narrow bar against the propensity inference: Prior offense evidence may be admitted in criminal cases on any issue to which it is relevant unless probative value is substantially outweighed by the risk of unfair prejudice, except that it is not admissible if its only relevance is to show a propensity on the part of the accused.

Viewing the cases in this way can be misleading. Consider the fact that defendants take most appeals in criminal cases, and the times they successfully exclude such proof at trial are largely hidden from view. And prior acts seem especially relevant in drug cases, which are a staple in federal courts, and less often relevant in trials for offenses like theft and homicide, which are common in state courts. There is at least some reason to think that trial judges are not quite as receptive to prior crimes evidence as appellate opinions seem to suggest, and to suppose such evidence is admitted somewhat less often in state than in federal court.

b. Proving Intent

PROBLEM 5-F.   Drug Sale or Scam?

Rhoda Smith once lived with Ronald Moore, but after a quarrel she moves out and approaches the police, offering to act as a paid informant. After she tells them Moore "deals large quantities of cocaine," the police ask her to arrange for undercover officer Hardy to buy cocaine from Moore.

Smith tells Moore she has "a buyer from Virginia" who wants four ounces of cocaine. They arrange a sale to occur in Smith's motel room. At the appointed time Moore arrives, and Smith introduces Hardy as "the drug dealer from Virginia whose sources have run dry." Moore first offers Hardy a small amount of hashish, which Hardy buys for $100. Then Moore agrees to sell Hardy the four ounces of cocaine, but first asks to inspect the cash. Holding it up to the light, he complains that it is "dusty" and walks out, telling Smith "I won't do business with this turkey." (In fact the cash had been dusted to pick up fingerprints.)

Police intercept Moore and recover a small vial of cocaine from his coat pocket, but not enough to suggest that he came to deal. A search of Moore's home and car turns up nothing useful. Still Moore is prosecuted for distribution of hashish and conspiracy to sell cocaine.

At trial Moore argues that the proposed cocaine transaction was "a scam to dupe the buyer," and that he planned to collect the money and depart without turning over any cocaine. The prosecutor offers testimony by Smith describing numerous hashish and cocaine sales by Moore during the 18 months the two lived together. Moore vigorously objects.

Relevant

Should Smith be allowed to testify to the prior hashish sales? To the prior cocaine sales? What if Moore claims the government entrapped him by using Smith as its agent to induce him to commit the charged criminal acts?

NOTES ON PRIOR ACTS AS PROOF OF INTENT AND RELATED POINTS IN CRIMINAL CASES

1. On what point is Rhoda Smith's testimony (Problem 5-F) describing prior hashish and cocaine sales by Ronald Moore relevant? Does this use of such testimony involve a propensity argument, or something else? Does the proper inference flow from prior sales of both drugs?

2. After some states included language requiring the prosecutor to give pretrial notice of intent to offer evidence of prior acts under state counterparts to FRE 404(b), the Supreme Court amended the federal version in 1991. Now FRE 404(b) requires the prosecutor to give notice, before trial if the defense requests (which should be routine) "or during trial if the court excuses pretrial notice on good cause shown," of "the general nature" of evidence of prior acts or wrongs that it intends to introduce. Suppose the prosecutor *does* give notice of intent to offer evidence of a prior offense and defendant seeks a pretrial ruling that would exclude such evidence. Does the notification requirement imply that courts should resolve such issues in advance of trial? If the answer is no, what good does pretrial notification do?

3. Should courts, in resolving the admissibility issue, spell out their reasoning and findings in balancing the relevant factors? Reviewing courts comment that they would prefer such findings, but are reluctant to reverse simply because such findings do not appear in the record. Compare *United States v. Osum*, 943 F.2d 1394, 1403 (5th Cir. 1991) (when expressly asked, court must make on-

the-record findings, but objecting is not the same thing as requesting findings; if no request is made, reviewing court may still remand for findings if relevant factors are not apparent in record or there is doubt over ruling) with United States v. Smith, 292 F.3d 90, 98 (1st Cir. 2002) (absence of express findings in ruling under FRE 404(b) and 403 would not inhibit appellate review; reviewing court would assume that trial judge undertook required balancing), cert. denied, 123 S. Ct. 332 (2003). How effective do you suppose it is to remand to the trial judge a case that has already produced a conviction for a finding on the record of probative value versus prejudice?

4. Would it be sensible (at least sometimes) to exclude prior crimes evidence offered to show intent during the prosecutor's case-in-chief but admit it (if necessary) during the prosecutor's case-in-rebuttal? Should it make a difference whether intent is something that can be inferred from action (as is often true when the action is selling drugs) or requires extrinsic proof (as is often true in fraud cases)? Compare United States v. Colon, 880 F.2d 650, 660-662 (2d Cir. 1989) (in drug trial, reversible error to admit other transactions during government's case-in-chief since defendant's claim that he did not engage in the transaction removed issue of intent) with United States v. Parziale, 947 F.2d 123, 128-129 (5th Cir. 1991) (in drug conspiracy case, plea of not guilty raised issue of intent sufficiently to justify admitting other acts).

5. If the defense offers to stipulate to such points, should that block the use of prior crimes? Recall the decision in *Old Chief* (Chapter 2, supra), which held (in federal courts as a matter of federal law, but not as a constitutional principle) that a defense stipulation requires exclusion of the names of prior convictions, in the setting of a felon-in-possession trial where the convictions are elements of the charged offense. In *Old Chief*, however, the Court carefully said its holding did not apply to prior crimes offered in FRE 404(b) to show intent and similar points. On this point, state courts may take a different course. See State v. Glodgett, 749 A.2d 283, 286 (N.H. 2000) (reversible error to admit other crimes where defendant offered to stipulate that if jury found that he committed sexual assault, he had requisite intent; to be relevant under Rule 404(b), "proffered evidence must be pertinent to an issue that is actually in dispute"), appeal after new trial, 813 A.2d 444 (N.H. 2002). Federal courts have taken the hint and have declined to require exclusion in this setting. See United States v. Cassell, 292 F.3d 788, 794 (D.C. Cir. 2002) (in felon-in-possession trial, fact that defense did not contest knowledge or intent did not prevent government from showing other instances to prove these points); United States v. Tan, 254 F.3d 1204, 1212 (10th Cir. 2001) (in second degree murder trial arising out of accident involving truck driven by defendant while intoxicated, *Old Chief* did not require exclusion of prior drunk driving convictions despite willingness of defendant to stipulate that he knew it was dangerous to drink and drive). See generally Mueller and Kirkpatrick, Evidence §4.16 (3d ed. 2003).

6. While intent is a central mental element in many prosecutions, it is not the only one that bears on guilt. Evidence of prior crimes often sheds light on other relevant mental conditions. See United States v. Loera, 933 F.2d 725, 729 (9th Cir. 1991) (on question of malice, admitting misdemeanor convictions for drunk driving, which showed that defendant had reason to know the risk his drinking and driving pose to others); United States v. Ramirez, 894 F.2d

565, 568-569 (2d Cir. 1990) (defendant claimed lack of knowledge of drugs; court properly admitted later cocaine offense to rebut this claim); United States v. Dornhofer, 859 F.2d 1195, 1198-1199 (4th Cir. 1988) (in trial for possession of child pornography, admitting evidence that defendant had other similar material as proof of "intent and lack of mistake or accident"), cert. denied, 490 U.S. 1005 (1990).

7. The entrapment defense raises the question of intent in its largest sense. The heart of this defense is that government action induced a crime the defendant would not otherwise commit, and the prosecutor's usual response is to offer proof that defendant committed similar crimes on other occasions. Courts admit such proof typically citing FRE 404(b). See Sorrells v. United States, 287 U.S. 435, 451-452 (1932) (defendant who raises entrapment defense "cannot complain of an appropriate and searching inquiry into his own conduct and predisposition as bearing upon that issue"); United States v. Van Horn, 277 F.3d 48, 57-58 (1st Cir. 2002) (defense of entrapment meant prosecutor could cross-examine defendant about his involvement in prior similar crimes).

c. Identity, Modus Operandi

PROBLEM 5-G. *"He Came Running in All Hunched Over"*

Danzey and Gore are charged with bank robbery. The prosecutor calls eyewitnesses who describe the crime. One who was outside saw two men in ski masks and gloves emerge from a white car and enter the bank. Another in the bank said one of the men "came running in all hunched over" and vaulted the counter, taking the money trays from the teller and stuffing them into a bag. A third witness in an apartment two blocks away saw the perpetrators arrive at about 9:00 a.m. in separate cars, one white and the other brown. They returned a short time later, got into the brown car, and left the scene.

An eyewitness can identify Danzey as one of the robbers, but nobody can identify the other. As proof that the other was Gore, the government introduces his confession of involvement in eight similar robberies, all committed between 9:00 a.m. and 11:00 a.m., all using stolen cars of contrasting light and dark colors (one to drive to the bank, the other parked some blocks away to be used after a "switch" as the getaway car). In his confession Gore said that he always wears a ski mask and gloves and always "runs hunched over and jumps over the counter."

Should Gore's confession of similar robberies be admitted? What if there is no confession, but Gore was convicted of the other offenses? What if the government has neither a confession nor convictions but eyewitness testimony identifying Gore as the robber on the other occasions?

NOTES ON PRIOR ACTS TO PROVE MODUS OPERANDI

1. On what point is evidence of prior bank robberies by Gore (Problem 5-G) relevant? Does this use of such evidence involve a propensity argument

or something else? Do the features common to what Gore did before and the charged offense amount to a "signature" or distinctive modus operandi suggesting that he probably committed the latter since he committed the former? Compare United States v. Robinson, 161 F.3d 463, 467 (7th Cir. 1998) (in trial for bank robbery on April 8th, admitting proof of defendant's involvement in April 18th robbery, to prove modus operandi; prior act must bear singular strong resemblance to charged offense, and similarities must be sufficiently idiosyncratic to permit inference of pattern; here both robbers entered bank "carrying a distinctive duffel bag in one hand and brandishing a handgun in the other," and "vaulted over the teller counter and demanded money"; in both cases robber emptied drawers by himself after putting gun down; in both cases getaway car was blue Chevrolet Cavalier; robberies occurred within ten days and 25 miles of each other) with United States v. Lail, 846 F.2d 1299, 1300-1302 (11th Cir. 1988) (reversible error to admit evidence that defendant committed a prior robbery as proof of modus operandi; both robberies involved lone gunman, handgun, lack of disguise, and proximity, but common elements did not make a "signature" in light of striking differences, since earlier crime involved dynamite and culprit who posed as businessman and took hostage).

2. Suppose defendant wants to prove other crimes by a third person, sometimes called "reverse" 404(b) evidence. By its terms FRE 404(b) applies to such proof, doesn't it? Typically defendant argues that offenses by another so strikingly resemble the charged crime that the proof suggests that the other must be guilty of the offense charged to the defendant, too. Compare United States v. Stevens, 935 F.2d 1380 1401-1406 (3d Cir. 1991) (alleged aggravated sexual assault and robbery on military base; defense claimed mistaken identity and offered testimony by another victim that a different man who looked like defendant committed similar crime on same base; reversible error to exclude this testimony) (the two offenses took place within a few hundred yards; both were armed robberies involving a handgun; both happened between 9:30 and 10:30 p.m.; both were committed against military personnel; both involved a black assailant described similarly by his victims) with United States v. Perkins, 937 F.2d 1397, 1400-1401 (9th Cir. 1991) (in bank robbery trial, excluding evidence of four other robberies, offered on theory that these "signature" crimes showed defendant could not be culprit here because he was at work during two of the others; all, including the one charged here, involved a man wearing disguises like fake moustache, beard, and glasses, but two of the others involved someone using tennis racket cover to carry the money; defendant stressed this feature as unique, but it was not part of charged offense).

d. Plan, Design

PROBLEM 5-H.   The Corrupt Judge

In 1995 John Murdock, an associate judge of the Caleb County Circuit Court, is indicted in federal court on 27 counts of accepting bribes to fix the outcomes of cases in his courtroom, from drunken driving to battery to felony theft. Every count but one is based on the Hobbs Act, which prohibits extortion affecting interstate commerce. In this case, the indictment alleges that Murdock committed extortion by soliciting and taking bribes. The remaining count rested on the Racketeer Influenced and Corrupt Organizations Act (RICO), which prohibits operating an "enterprise" in interstate commerce through a "pattern" (two or more events) of "racketeering" (violating state or federal laws). The "enterprise" here was the Caleb County Circuit Court.

In addition to evidence of the bribes specified in the indictment, the prosecutor offers testimony by Rupert, a former court employee, that Murdock received envelopes full of cash on a monthly basis for the last eight years. But Rupert could not link these payments to Judge Murdock's rulings. The prosecutor offered testimony by Neely (a local lawyer who had been granted immunity) that he had paid bribes to Judge Murdock to fix criminal cases on dozens of occasions between 1989 and the end of 1994. On cross, Murdock's lawyer asked Neely to specify "just one case by name," but he could not.

Murdock's lawyer objects to this "anonymous case" evidence, arguing that "Clarence Darrow couldn't defend against that, and he wouldn't have been asked to." How should the court rule and why?

NOTES ON PRIOR ACTS OFFERED TO PROVE PLAN OR DESIGN

1. Does the RICO count strengthen the government's argument that the testimony by Rupert and Neely should be admitted? If the RICO count were not there, could this testimony still come in under FRE 404(b)? If so, should it be excluded under FRE 403 as unfairly prejudicial?

2. Suppose Judge Murdock takes the stand during the defense case and testifies on direct that he's never taken bribes in his life. Would the prosecutor then have an additional reason to prove he took uncharged bribes?

3. How do you distinguish the permissible use of other crimes' evidence to prove a plan from the impermissible use of such evidence to prove conduct on a particular occasion? See Mendez and Imwinkelried, People v. Ewoldt: The California Supreme Court's About-Face on the Plan Theory for Admitting Evidence of an Accused's Uncharged Misconduct, 28 Loyola L.A. L. Rev. 473, 480-485 (1995) (in true plan cases, the accused "formulates a single, overall grand design that encompasses both the charged and uncharged offenses" where the design is "overarching" and all the crimes are "integral components or portions of the same plan" so each amounts to a "step or stage" in executing the plan; to be contrasted with these are "spurious" or "unlinked" plans where the prosecutor shows only that the charged offense and prior acts are "similar and temporally proximate" without showing a "common objective").

4. In sexual abuse cases, evidence that defendant also abused the victim's sibling is sometimes offered as evidence of plan or design. Should it be admissible for such purposes? Compare People v. Ewoldt, 867 P.2d 757 (Cal. 1994) (in trial of man for sexual assaults over three-year-period against wife's daughter *J* when she was 11-14 years old, involving touching and attempted penetration in bedrooms at home, admitting proof of other acts with *J* and other acts with her sister *N*; acts may prove common design or plan if "similar" to charged offense even if not part of "single, continuing conception or plot") with Government of Virgin Islands v. Pinney, 967 F.2d 912, 916-917 (3d Cir. 1992) (in trial

for rape of seven-year-old girl in apartment, error to admit evidence that seven years earlier defendant raped victim's older sister in same apartment; insufficient temporal connection to establish "common plan"). How about admitting proof of sexual misconduct toward others in the extended family? See State v. Wermerskirchen, 497 N.W.2d 235 (Minn. 1993) (in trial for sexual abuse of eight-year-old daughter, admitting proof that defendant abused 12-year-old stepdaughter *and* engaged in sexual touching and conversation with nieces years earlier, to show "design or intent" and "opportunistic fondling of young girls within the family context").

e.   Other Purposes

PROBLEM 5-I.   "It Was an Accident"

Late one night Tim Valence, a three-year-old boy, was brought into the emergency room by his mother Donna. He was unconscious and suffering from severe head injuries and three broken ribs. Despite the best efforts of the hospital staff, he died the next day. Donna claimed that Tim's injuries were the result of a fall down the stairs of the family home, but the treating doctor suspected abuse and notified police. After a brief investigation, Donna was indicted for manslaughter.

At trial, to show that the injuries were unlikely to have been accidental, the prosecutor offers evidence of two incidents in the last year: In both, Donna brought Tim to the hospital, once with broken bones and once with a concussion. Both time she said the injuries resulted from accidents. Admissible? What if such things had happened five times in the same period? Would it make a difference whether a doctor familiar with the previous injuries thought they were caused by child abuse? Would it make a difference whether Donna or someone else was with Tim at the time?

NOTES ON OTHER USES OF PRIOR CRIMES EVIDENCE

1.   Increasing concern to catch and deter child abuse has led courts to admit proof of previous abuse. A significant difficulty is that the testifying physician cannot say who inflicted the injuries or exactly when or how they happened. Often, however, circumstances indicate that one or another adult-in-charge must be the source or must be aware of the child's condition, and sometimes the nature or extent of the injuries suggests that they must have been intentionally inflicted. See Estelle v. McGuire, 502 U.S. 62 (1991) (rejecting due process challenge to state conviction of father for murdering six-month-old daughter Tori, where court admitted evidence that she had rectal tearing and fractured ribs; there was no proof that defendant caused the injuries, but the evidence could be taken to prove that Tori died at the hands of another, and not by accident, and that whoever inflicted the injuries did so intentionally) (defendant and his wife were the only two people caring for her); United States v. Bowers, 660 F.2d 527, 528-529 (5th Cir. 1981) (admitting doctor's testimony

that deceased child suffered numerous previous injuries, as proof that parent's explanation of other injuries was a fabrication, permitting inference that parent in sole custody deliberately harmed child). The term "battered child syndrome" has come to mean a string of suspicious injuries, and it is also used to describe behavior patterns seen in children who suffer repeated sexual or physical abuse (see Chapter 9C).

2. Five defendants are charged with interstate transportation of a stolen Chevrolet, and the government offers testimony that (1) all five drove the Chevrolet from Tennessee to Illinois to rob a bank, (2) in the presence of the other defendants, two of them disarmed two policemen after the Chevrolet got stuck and drove off with a third defendant in a police car, (3) these three defendants abandoned the police car and stole a Pinto at gunpoint, (4) a gun and ammunition were found in the trunk of the Chevrolet and more ammunition was found in one defendant's apartment, and (5) the remaining two defendants kidnapped the two policemen and a tow truck driver and tried unsuccessfully to escape. Since the five were charged only with transporting a stolen Chevrolet, is there any justification for admitting all this other evidence? *No ?* See United States v. Miller, 508 F.2d 444, 449 (7th Cir. 1974) (approving all but the last two items because other crimes may be proved when they are so blended or connected with the charged offense that one tends incidentally to involve or explain the other). Can you see why the court thought the last two items were improper?

3. Other uses of prior crimes expressly contemplated in FRE 404(b) include proving motive and opportunity (often in the sense of skill or capacity to do criminal acts). See United States v. Palmer, 809 F.2d 1504, 1505 (11th Cir. 1987) (in tax evasion case, admitting proof that defendant trafficked in drugs as evidence of his motive in using currency and failing to keep records); United States v. Maravilla, 907 F.2d 216, 222 (1st Cir. 1990) (as proof that defendant "had the ability" to get victim through customs, admitting evidence that previously he did something similar).

4. Beyond the listed uses are others seemingly not mentioned in the Rule but within its contemplation (the list is exemplary rather than exhaustive). See United States v. Scarfo, 850 F.2d 1015, 1019-1020 (3d Cir. 1988) (in trial of organized crime boss for extortion, admitting proof of his involvement in murders to show "tight control over an organization capable of executing those who incurred his displeasure"); United States v. Mendez-Ortiz, 810 F.2d 76, 78-79 (6th Cir. 1986) (admitting evidence that defendant sought to bribe a witness, to show consciousness of guilt). Perhaps especially noteworthy is the fact that a defendant who makes the mistake of testifying falsely that he has "never been in trouble before" may be contradicted by proof of his prior crimes. This subject is examined in Chapter 8B2 infra.

f. Proving the Prior Act

PROBLEM 5-J. *"I Didn't Know They Were Stolen"*

After he was arrested in possession of 5,000 stolen blank video cassette tapes, Huddleston is tried for knowingly receiving stolen property. He was trying to sell them at less than cost, but he denied knowing that they were stolen. As proof that he did know, the prosecutor offers evidence that Huddleston had been involved in selling stolen property before—testimony of a store owner that defendant recently sold him 48 new 17-inch color television sets for $35 apiece.

Defendant argues that the trial court (1) should not admit this testimony without a preliminary finding by the judge under FRE 104(a) that the televisions were stolen and defendant knew it, and (2) should apply a standard requiring the prosecutor to prove these points by clear and convincing evidence, or at least a preponderance. The prosecutor contends that (a) the question is for the jury under FRE 104(b) rather than the court under FRE 104(a), and (b) there is enough evidence for a jury to find that the televisions were stolen and defendant knew it (as shown by the unreasonably low price).

Who is right about these points?

NOTES ON PROVING PRIOR ACTS

1. In United States v. Huddleston, 485 U.S. 681 (1988), the Supreme Court answered these questions in favor of the prosecutor. *Huddleston* announced two conclusions: First, the Rules do *not* require a "preliminary finding" by the court that the government proved a prior act by a preponderance. Instead the judge makes a "threshold" decision whether the evidence is "probative of a material issue other than character." Second, admitting evidence of prior acts raises a question of relevance conditioned on a fact under FRE 104(b), which is for *the jury* to decide under the preponderance standard. By this approach, proof of a prior crime is relevant if the jury "can reasonably conclude" by a preponderance that "the act occurred and that defendant was the actor."

2. *Huddleston* is not a constitutional decision, so it is not binding on the states, and some have adopted the holding while others have rejected it. Compare State v. Wheel, 587 A.2d 933, 943 (Vt. 1990) (adopting *Huddleston*) with People v. Garner, 806 P.2d 366, 370-374 (Colo. 1991) (rejecting *Huddleston* sufficiency standard and adopting preponderance requirement; whether prior crime occurred is for court to decide under Rule 104(a)).

3. Was *Huddleston* right in holding that prior acts raise fact questions for the jury to decide under FRE 104(b)? Of course the episode with the televisions could easily be split into three questions (Did defendant possess them? Were they stolen? Did he know they were?), but *that* isn't an argument against an enhanced standard of proof and a stronger role for the trial judge, is it? Isn't it obvious that nobody but the judge can prevent or minimize the effect of prejudicial evidence, and that requiring "clear and convincing" proof has the virtue of limiting prejudice, since defendant is exposed to this inevitable risk only when we are at least confident that he committed the prior act? In a remarkable footnote, *Huddleston* agreed "that the strength of the evidence establishing the similar act is one of the factors the court may consider when conducting the Rule 403 balancing." Does it follow that courts can, if they want, reintroduce the clear-and-convincing standard?

4. In *Huddleston,* the Court said defendant "conceded" that his original argument for a clear-and-convincing standard was "untenable" under Bourjaily v. United States, 483 U.S. 171 (1987), which held that the preponderance standard applies to proof of the predicate facts underlying the coconspirator exception (see Chapter 4B5). Is it so clear that the same standard should apply to prior crimes evidence? Coconspirator statements do not pose a risk that the jury will conclude that defendant is a bad person or should be penalized regardless whether he is guilty as charged, do they?

5. Although *Huddleston* was a unanimous opinion, many academic commentators and practitioners favor measures that would make it harder for prosecutors to offer evidence of prior crimes. Consider the following proposals: (1) amend FRE 404 to restore the clear-and-convincing standard, see 120 F.R.D. 299, at 330 (1988) (American Bar Association); (2) amend FRE 404(b) to burden prosecutors with showing that probative value outweighs prejudice, see Imwinkelried, The Need to Amend Federal Rule of Evidence 404(b): The Threat to the Future of the Federal Rules of Evidence, 30 Vill. L. Rev. 1465, 1497 (1985); (3) pay more attention to the issue of fairness to the accused since the general propensity argument cannot be effectively refuted even though it may not be right in any particular case, see Weissenberger, Making Sense of Extrinsic Act Evidence: Federal Rule of Evidence 404(b), 70 Iowa L. Rev. 607-611 (1985); (4) admit only those prior acts that are distinguished by their "unusual nature" or "regular occurrence" so they really do show "predisposition to behave in a similar fashion under similar circumstances," see Uviller, Evidence of Character to Prove Conduct: Illusion, Illogic, and Injustice in the Courtroom, 130 U. Pa. L. Rev. 845, 886-889 (1982). Would you favor any or all of these reforms?

6. What if defendant was charged but acquitted of a prior crime in a trial on the merits? In Dowling v. United States, 493 U.S. 342 (1990), the Court approved testimony describing a crime that led to acquittal. *Dowling* was a prosecution for bank robbery in which the culprit wore a ski mask and carried a pistol. The trial court let Vena Henry testify that defendant and a man named Christian assaulted her at home two weeks after the bank robbery, and that defendant was wearing a knit mask with cutout eyes and carrying a handgun (she could identify him because the man who assaulted her was unmasked in a struggle). But Dowling had been acquitted of charges arising out of the assault, and in the later bank robbery trial the government offered Henry's testimony to strengthen the identification of Dowling as the bank robber and link him with Christian (getaway driver). The Court held that the acquittal did not block Henry's testimony under a concept of collateral estoppel found in the Double Jeopardy Clause, pointing out that the assault on Henry was not an ultimate issue in *both* the prior and the present case and that *Huddleston* requires only that the prosecutor prove the prior crime by a preponderance (not beyond reasonable doubt, as required in the prior proceeding). *Dowling* also rejected a due process argument that admitting Henry's testimony put defendant to the unfair burden of spending time and money relitigating points resolved before, replying that the Rules provide adequate protection.

(a) Do you agree that collateral estoppel should not apply to a point that was an ultimate issue in the prior proceeding if it is not an ultimate issue in the later proceeding?

(b)   The Court in *Dowling* is right, isn't it, in holding that acquittal on earlier charges is consistent with a later finding by a preponderance that defendant committed the earlier offense? Even if the reformers throw out *Huddleston*, wouldn't the earlier acquittal be consistent with a later finding that Henry's testimony is clear and convincing evidence that Dowling committed the earlier offense?

(c)   In a second prong of the *Dowling* opinion, the Court stressed that defendant failed to show that the acquittal indicated he "was not one of the men" in the assault (because the jury might have agreed with his claim that the intruders were trying to retrieve money, not commit robbery), and declined to make the prosecutor prove this point. Even if the Court decides collateral estoppel applies, the second prong of *Dowling* will still make things pretty hard on defendants, won't it, because of the difficulty of knowing the basis for the jury's verdict?

5.   *Character in Sex Offense Cases*

a.   Sexual History of Victim (Rape Shield Statutes)

Sex offense cases present a peculiarly difficult challenge for many reasons. The offense is serious, the punishment severe; the behavior is offensive and the psychological (and sometimes physical) injury to the victim may be serious; the charge alone may damage the defendant, and pressing the charge may hurt the complainant; the subject of sex provokes strong emotions and gender-related reactions; often there are no "neutral" observers, and the complainant and defendant contradict each other, each having strong self-interested motivations.

Should evidence of the past sexual conduct of the complaining witness be admitted in such cases? Unfortunately the common law tradition answered that question with an emphatic across-the-board yes, which meant that women who brought charges of rape were fair game for cross-examination on their sexual behavior. This sorry sexist tradition had it that such cross-examination bore upon both the credibility of the woman as a witness and the issue of consent. The underlying hypocrisy was exposed by the facts that such cross-examination was not thought to bear on the credibility of women testifying in other settings, and that in rape trials such cross-examination was permitted even where clinical evidence of physical injury made any suggestion of consent ridiculous.

Against this backdrop, "rape shield" statutes were enacted in nearly every state. Congress did likewise by enacting FRE 412, which qualifies FRE 404(a)(2) by restricting the use of evidence relating to the sexual history of a sex crime victim.

That evidence of sexual behavior has no bearing on credibility standing by itself seems beyond reasonable dispute. That such evidence *often* has little or no bearing on the question whether a person consented to engage in sex on a particular occasion seems also to be true. But it is not clear that such evidence is never relevant in sexual assault cases, and the operation of rape shield rules and statutes presents some difficulties. Consider now, not the case in which a woman is suddenly assaulted on the street or in her home by a person she has never seen before, but the one in which circumstances lend at least some credibility to defense claims of consent and in which the woman was a "victim" only if she is speaking the truth and defendant is lying.

PROBLEM 5-K. *Ordeal of Leslie or Fred*

Leslie returns to her sorority sometime after midnight on Homecoming Saturday, earlier than most celebrants. She has been to a luau at the Beta Theta Sigma House, and a few of her more serious friends (who generally avoid such things) discover Leslie sometime later. She is in bed under the covers but not asleep, having taken off coat and shoes but leaving the rest of her clothes on. She seems tense and sullen but flat in emotional affect and looks at her friends without expression.

Ultimately Leslie tells her roommate and a few others that she met a fellow named Fred at the luau. She says she met him several times in the previous summer while she worked at a pool as a lifeguard where he was a swimming instructor. She says she made the mistake of accepting Fred's offer of a ride home from the luau and that he took her to a lonely spot and made advances. At first she "didn't mind," but he "got completely out of hand" and finally raped her. Leslie is persuaded to go to the clinic, where she is clinically examined. Bruises are observed on her legs and forearms, and semen is found in her vagina.

As it turns out, Fred is an outsider (a casual acquaintance of Greg, one of the fraternity brothers) who had no business being at the luau.

Fred is charged with rape. He pleads innocent. At his trial Fred claims that Leslie consented, and he testifies that he and Leslie had consensual sexual relations once during the previous summer. He also offers testimony by Greg that "Leslie is sexually very active" and "known as an easy mark." And he offers testimony by Thomas (another friend at Beta Theta Sigma) that *he* had sex with Leslie earlier that same night.

The prosecutor objects that the proffered testimony of Fred, Greg, and Thomas is "irrelevant" and "barred by the rape shield" law.

Is the objection well taken on either ground? See FRE 412. Spell out Fred's argument that the evidence is relevant and the prosecutor's response that it is not. *Should* such evidence be excluded?

NOTES ON EVIDENCE OF COMPLAINANT'S PRIOR SEXUAL CONDUCT

1. Does Rule 412 rest on modern ideas of relevancy or something else? What else? See Sandoval v. Acevedo, 996 F.2d 145, 149 (7th Cir. 1993) (Posner, J.) (noting "essential insight behind the rape shield statute," which is that in post-Victorian age "in which most unmarried young women are sexually active," sexual activity by a woman on specific occasions "does not provide appreciable support for an inference that she *consented* to engage in this activity with the defendant").

2.   Is the defendant constitutionally entitled to introduce evidence of the victim's sexual history to show a motive for making a false charge against the defendant? See Olden v. Kentucky, 488 U.S. 227 (1988) (reversible error to refuse to let defendant ask complainant whether she claimed rape in order to preserve relationship with boyfriend with whom she was cohabiting); Commonwealth v. Black, 487 A.2d 396 (Pa. Super. 1985) (unconstitutional to preclude sexual history evidence of victim's incestuous relationship with brother "which may logically demonstrate" complainant's "bias, interest or prejudice" against defendant father for stopping relationship).

3.   What other evidence may a defendant be constitutionally entitled to introduce under FRE 412(b)(1)(C)? See Galvin, Shielding Rape Victims in the State and Federal Courts: A Proposal for the Second Decade, 70 Minn. L. Rev. 763, 893, 903-905 (1986) (criticizing "constitutionally required" exception of FRE 412 because of its uncertain scope; proposing list of more specific exceptions where sexual history evidence would be allowed). See generally C. Mueller and L. Kirkpatrick, Evidence §4.33 (3d ed. 2003).

4.   If defendant is charged with attempted rape, should he be permitted to introduce evidence that he had been told beforehand that the woman in question would say no but mean yes? Could he do so under FRE 412? See Doe v. United States, 666 F.2d 43, 46-48 (4th Cir. 1981) ("We are not prepared to state that extraordinary circumstances will never justify admission of [reputation and opinion] evidence to preserve a defendant's constitutional rights"; approving evidence of defendant's "state of mind as a result of what he knew of her reputation").

5.   If a male defendant is charged with sexual assault against another male, should rape-shield rules or statutes block proof that the complainant is homosexual, offered in support of the claim of consent? See generally Peter Nicholas, "They Say He's Gay": The Admissibility of Evidence of Sexual Orientation, 37 Ga. L. Rev. 793, 821 (2003) (reporting that most statutes hold that rape shield legislation blocks such proof).

6.   FRE 412 contemplates that preliminary hearings on the admissibility of evidence of complainant's sexual conduct will be held out of public view. Does this procedure violate defense or public rights to an "open" trial? See Globe Newspaper Co. v. Superior Court, 457 U.S. 596, 606-609 (1982) (holding unconstitutional state rule requiring mandatory exclusion of the public from trial of sex offense cases involving minor victims). If the court overrules the prosecutor's objection to evidence of sexual conduct by the complainant, should she be permitted to appeal? See Doe v. United States, 666 F.2d 43, 46 (4th Cir. 1981) (allowing interlocutory appeal by complainant).

7.   In 1994, FRE 412 was extended to civil cases. The extension was recommended by the Evidence Advisory Committee and the Judicial Conference, but the Supreme Court refused to approve it. See 154 F.R.D. 509 (1994). Congress had the last word and added the extension to civil cases as part of the Violent Crime Control and Enforcement Act of 1994. FRE 412 is important in sexual harassment suits. What type of evidence about the complainant in such suits is now likely to be excluded? Note that FRE 412(a) excludes evidence of both the alleged victim's sexual behavior and her "sexual predisposition." What does that mean? Are there ever situations where such evidence will be admitted? See FRE 412(b)(2) (establishing a balancing test).

b. Prior Offenses by Defendants in Sex Crime Trials

In 1994 Congress enacted three provisions (FRE 413-415) inviting prosecutors to prove sexual assault or child molestation by means of evidence that defendant assaulted or molested others. These sparked controversy and their effective date was delayed, but ultimately they took effect in July 1995. It is worth noting that relatively few sexual assault or child molestation cases are prosecuted in federal court. For the most part, federal courts try such cases only when they arise in federal enclaves such as national parks and military bases, or on Indian Reservations. (Offenses committed on military bases by military personnel are tried in military courts under the Military Rules of Evidence, not in federal courts under the Federal Rules of Evidence.) In large measure, FRE 413-415 were enacted as examples for states to consider and perhaps adopt as part of their own Rules. (The same is true of FRE 412, the federal rape shield statute.)

FRE 413-415 came as part of a politically charged crime bill, apparently added at the last minute in a Conference Committee in order to win votes in the House crucial to passage. These provisions did not go through the rulemaking processes, and professional reaction was strongly negative. For an early and useful review of these provisions, see Duane, The New Federal Rules of Evidence on Prior Acts of Accused Sex Offenders: A Poorly Drafted Version of a Very Bad Idea, 157 F.R.D. 95 (1994). But see Cassell and Strassberg, Evidence of Repeated Acts of Rape and Child Molestation: Reforming Utah Law to Permit the Propensity Inference, 1998 Utah L. Rev. 145 (favoring generous rule of admissibility for prior rapes and acts of child abuse); Park, The Crime Bill of 1994 and the Law of Character Evidence: Congress Was Right About Consent Cases, 22 Fordham Urban L.J. 271 (1995) (supporting FRE 413-415 in sex crime prosecutions where consent defense is asserted).

The advisory committees of the Federal Judicial Conference opposed the new provisions, as did the Standing Committee of the Judicial Conference. In its report to Congress, the Conference urged Congress to reconsider FRE 413-415 and noted the strong opposition to these provisions. Even the ABA House of Delegates adopted a resolution opposing them.

Consider the substance of these provisions. Briefly, FRE 413 provides where a defendant is accused of sexual assault, evidence of other sexual assault offenses "is admissible, and may be considered" on any matter to which it is relevant. In parallel language, FRE 414 provides that trials for child molestation, evidence of other child molestation offenses "is admissible and may be considered for its bearing" on any matter to which it is relevant. And FRE 415 extends the doctrines of FRE 413 and 414 to civil cases raising issues of sexual assault or child molestation.

As part of the compromise that produced these provisions, Congress invited the Judicial Conference to make alternative recommendations. The Conference did so, in the form of a suggested amendment to FRE 404(b) that would have allowed *some* use of prior assaults or child molestation, but with specific criteria directing courts to consider such factors as proximity in time between prior and charged offense, degree of resemblance, frequency of other acts, and so forth. Congress ignored this proposal in the end, however, and FRE 413-415 took effect as proposed.

PROBLEM 5-L.   "I Told Him to Stop"

In his federal trial for the alleged rape of Karin on Fort Linden Air Force Base at 1:30 a.m. on Sunday, Craig raises the defense of consent. Craig is 32 years old, and he works at Fort Linden as a civilian avionics technician and instructor. He resides in an apartment in town near the base. Karin is a 27-year-old Air Force enlisted woman in the avionics training program. She is enrolled in a training course that Craig teaches, and she lives in a women's barracks on Fort Linden.

Government proof shows that Craig and Karin met at the Aero Squad Bar, which is located in town near Fort Linden. While at the Aero Squad, Karin and Craig consumed gin and tonics for several hours. Karin had come to the bar with other women from the base, but they left on the understanding that Craig would drive her back to Fort Linden.

Karin testified that on arriving at the base Craig suggested that they "go up the hill" to a secluded area of trees and grass that was maintained as a picnic ground for base personnel. Once there, the two sat on a blanket that Craig produced from the trunk of his car and continued to drink gin from a pint bottle Craig had bought at the package store before the two left the Aero Squad. Karin testified that Craig "put his arm around me and we kissed," but that she "physically resisted" when "he began touching me through my blouse and started to unbutton my blouse and skirt." She continued, "I told him to stop and that I didn't want to have sex with him tonight," but he "kept pressing himself against me and trying to reach up my blouse which had come untucked," until "I finally stood up and told him I was going to walk back to the barracks, and I proceeded to run as fast as I could." At that point, according to Karin, Craig grabbed her and dragged her back to the blanket, where he held her arms down with his knees, ripped off her clothes, and raped her.

On cross, counsel for Craig tries to get Karin to admit that she was "laughing and responding in kind" when Craig kissed her, that she wasn't "resisting in any way" and in fact "co-operated in taking off" her clothes. Karin agrees that they were "laughing at first" and that she kissed him, and even helped unfasten her blouse and bra because she was "afraid he was going to rip the fabric," but she emphatically denies "helping him take my skirt off," and denies "cooperating when he raped me," saying instead that she "told him to stop" and "tried to get him off me, but he was too heavy, and held my arms down by my wrists."

Anticipating that Craig was likely to testify in a manner consistent with the tenor of the cross-examination of Karin, the government proposes to offer two further proofs that what happened was rape rather than consensual sex:

First, the prosecutor calls Laura. In aid of an offer of proof, Laura testifies outside the jury's hearing that she "dated Craig for several weeks" about a year earlier while they were living in another state, and that once when they returned to her apartment after a movie, Craig "tried to rape me." She says she "made the mistake" of letting him touch her, that he "kept coming on after I told him to stop," and "tried to rape me," except that she "screamed and kicked him in the privates" so hard that he "cried out in pain" and ran away.

Second, the prosecutor offers a certified copy of a judgment of conviction for sexual assault on a minor obtained against Craig in another state three years earlier. According to the record, the victim was 13-year-old N, daughter of a woman named Rita, with whom Craig was living in a trailer at the time. The record indicates that Craig encouraged N to drink beer one afternoon while Rita was at work, that the two then played "strip poker," and that Craig fondled and sodomized N. He served a year in prison and was on probation at the time of the charged offense at Fort Linden.

Counsel for Craig objects to these proofs:

> Laura's proposed testimony and the prior conviction amount to character assassination. Laura's testimony cannot be admitted to prove intent or modus operandi because it's too dissimilar from what supposedly happened at Fort Linden between Craig and Karin. And the conviction for abusing N shows acts of a totally different nature that cannot be relevant in any way to what the government claims here. If this evidence is admitted, the jury will be invited to convict the defendant just because it thinks Craig is "that sort of person." These proofs will inflame the jury, inviting it to convict Craig out of anger at what he may have done before, which is classic unfair prejudice.

How should the court rule on this objection under FRE 413 and FRE 403, and why?

NOTES ON PROVING DEFENDANT'S PRIOR SEXUAL
CONDUCT IN TRIALS FOR SEXUAL ASSAULT AND
CHILD ABUSE

1. If Craig did to Laura what she says he did, his act may have been the crime of "abusive sexual contact" under 18 U.S.C. §2244 (a provision in chapter 109A of title 18, to which FRE 413 refers). What Craig was convicted of doing to N amounts to "sexual abuse of a minor" under 18 U.S.C. §2243 (another provision in chapter 109A of title 18). Does FRE 413 mean these specific instances of Craig's past conduct may be considered to prove he raped Karin? FRE 413 says proof of other offenses "may be considered for its bearing on any matter to which it is relevant" in sexual assault cases. Doesn't it follow that the jury may consider Craig's past conduct as evidence of character (disposition toward sexual assault), hence as proof that he committed the crime charged? FRE 404 would bar such reasoning, wouldn't it, so FRE 413 must amend FRE 404 by necessary implication?

2. Note the firm language in the broad admissibility provision: FRE 413 says evidence of other sexual offenses "is admissible" in sexual assault trials and "may be considered for its bearing on any matter to which it is relevant."

(a) Does this language authorize courts to exclude such evidence if it is irrelevant? Or does this language mean such evidence is *always deemed* relevant in such cases?

(b) Does this language mean proof of other sexual offenses may not be excluded for "unfair prejudice" under FRE 403? Some comments during floor debate in Congress indicate that FRE 413 *is* subject to FRE 403.[1] Under the

---

1. See the statement by Representative Susan Molinari (New York) that the reform "allows" but does not "mandate" such evidence if the judge thinks "the cases are similar and relevant

"plain meaning" approach endorsed by the Supreme Court in cases like *Daubert, Williamson,* and *Tome,* will such comments count?

(c)   Theoretically relevancy is one thing, and risk of prejudice is another. But sometimes the two seem almost to meet. Compare Blind-Doan v. Sanders, 291 F.3d 1079 (9th Cir. 2002) (in suit by prisoner alleging that jailer sexually abused her, error to exclude testimony by 17 others describing other "relevant" acts; trial court may exclude under FRE 403, and may consider "similarity of the prior acts to the acts charged," but judge did not indicate how he "evaluated the factors," and some excluded testimony tended to answer the claim that defendant would not have abused plaintiff because "the presence of a police witness" deprived him of opportunity) (judgment for defendant reversed) with Johnson v. Elk Lake School District, 283 F3d 138, 155 (3rd Cir. 2002) (despite "absolutist tone," Congress thought FRE 403 would apply; in suit alleging sexual harassment of student by guidance counselor *S,* excluding testimony by former colleague *R* that *S* touched *R*'s crotch while lifting her onto his shoulders; *R* was "equivocal" as to whether touching was intentional, and differences between "bizarre incident" with *R* and misconduct in issue here was such that "dissimilarities reduced significantly the probative value" of *R*'s testimony).

3.   Does the episode with Laura suggest that Craig raped Karin? If the answer is yes, is it because that episode suggests (as the defense argues) that Craig is "that sort of person"? FRE 413 incorporates what is sometimes called a "lustful disposition" doctrine, holding in effect that specific acts may be proved by evidence of general sexual disposition. See generally E. Imwinkelried, Uncharged Misconduct §§4.11-4.16 (1994); Reed, Reading Gaol Revisited: Admission of Uncharged Misconduct Evidence in Sex Offender Cases, 21 Am. J. Crim. L. 127 (1993) (describing this and other doctrines). States vary in their approach to this issue. Compare People v. Donoho, 788 N.E.2d 707, 716-717 (Ill. 2003) (reporting that only four states have added "a propensity exception in sexual offense cases by statute or court rule," but that 25 other states recognize an exception to the bar against proving other offenses when they show "lustful disposition or tendency toward sexual predation"; also reporting that some states limit the doctrine to cases involving same victim, to cases in which victim is a minor, or to incest cases) (upholding statute admitting evidence of lustful disposition in cases alleging predatory sexual assault against child) with State v. Morgan, 791 S.2d 100 (La. 2001) (reversing conviction for aggravated rape where prosecutor made "lustful disposition" argument based on other assaults against other victims; state does not recognize lustful disposition exception to bar against character evidence).

---

enough," 140 Cong. Rec. H5,437 (June 29, 1994). Several years earlier she made a similar point, indicating that FRE 413-415 "would not eliminate the power of judges to exclude evidence of similar offenses when the prejudicial effect of that evidence on the defendant exceeds the probative value of that evidence," 147 Cong. Rec. H3,504 (Oct. 22, 1991). See also comments by Representative Kyl (Arizona) that admissibility is "not automatic," and courts have "discretion to admit" while retaining "total discretion to exclude the evidence of its probative value is substantially outweighed by the danger of unfair prejudice." 140 Cong. Rec. H5,438 (June 29, 1994). Finally, see comments by Senator Robert Dole (Kansas) that the "practical effect" of FRE 413-415 is to put proof of other offenses of sexual assault and child molestation "on the same footing as other types of relevant evidence," and referring to a "presumption" that such evidence is relevant and that "probative value is not outweighed by any risk of prejudice." 140 Cong. Rec. S12,991 (daily ed. Sept. 20, 1994).

4. In sexual assault trials, is admitting evidence of a defendant's character or propensity to engage in sexual assaults a good thing? Should we admit such proof because otherwise it is so often "her word against his"? Because in the area of sex (or sexual aggression), such a disposition or propensity is peculiarly reliable as a predictor of future behavior? Is it true that lots of men who commit one or two rapes commit more rapes, but that only a few men who commit one or two robberies commit more robberies? Is there empirical evidence that the correlation between one or two rapes and further rapes is stronger than the correlation between one or two robberies and further robberies? See E. Imwinkelried, Uncharged Misconduct §4.16 (1994) (citing studies showing that recidivism is *not* higher among those convicted of sexual assault than among those convicted of other crimes).

5. Suppose Craig calls others working at Fort Linden who frequent the Aero Squad Bar, and that five of them would testify that "Karin is a regular there" and has often been seen "arriving alone or with women friends and departing with men she met at the bar." Suppose two of these witnesses are men who would each testify that he "picked up Karin at the Aero Squad," that he had "never met her before," and that he had "consensual sex with her after leaving the bar." Under FRE 412, such testimony would not be admitted in support of Craig's claim of consent, would it? Is it right to admit evidence of sexual *misconduct* by the accused while excluding evidence of sexual *conduct* by the complaining witness? Consider Bryden and Park, "Other Crimes" Evidence in Sex Offense Cases, 78 Minn. L. Rev. 529, 568 (1994) (favoring admissibility of prior offenses by the accused in acquaintance rape cases; arguing that "the basic notion of a rape shield law [excluding sexual history of the complainant] does not conflict with admission of evidence of the rape defendant's prior crimes").

6. Is the episode with Laura "another offense" under FRE 413, or does this language require *convictions* for sexual offenses? Congressional comments indicate that the term "offense" does *not* require a conviction (raising the question how much these comments count in applying the Rule).[2] Should the judge in Problem 5-L determine that Laura's account proves a crime? This question is one of "admissibility" under FRE 104(a), isn't it? And the jury should be excluded during any such inquiry under FRE 104(c), shouldn't it? Should Craig have a chance to refute Laura's account? If Craig testifies, could the prosecutor cross-examine about what happened with Karin? On the latter point, see FRE 104(d). Should the judge decide whether a crime was committed before by looking to the law of the other state where Craig and Laura were, or to the law of the forum state? If Craig offers evidence that he didn't do what Laura says, should the judge decide this point under FRE 104(a) by applying the preponderance standard, or must this question go to the jury under FRE 104(b)? See Johnson v. Elk Lake School District, 283 F3d 138, 153 (3rd Cir. 2002) (jury determines this point under FRE 104(b); court reluctantly follows *Huddleston* doctrine here).

---

2. See comments by Representative Susan Molinari (New York) that FRE 413-415 mean that "Evidence of offenses for which the defendant has not previously been prosecuted or convicted will be admissible, as well as evidence of prior convictions" and observing that "No time limit is imposed," 140 Cong. Rec. H5,437 (June 29, 1994).

B.   HABIT AND ROUTINE PRACTICE

In contrast to "character" evidence, proof of personal habit is freely admitted. Indeed, Rule 406 stands out among the provisions of Article IV in stating a rule of admissibility rather than limits. On its face it rejects limits by providing that habit is viewed as "relevant" to prove conduct (hence generally "admissible" according to FRE 402) "whether corroborated or not and regardless of the presence of eyewitnesses." The same liberality extends to proof of the routine practice of an organization.

Whence comes this difference, the cold shoulder for character and cordiality toward habit evidence? Partly the answer lies in the moral overtones of the former and neutral quality of the latter. Partly it lies in the conviction that habit is simply more probative of conduct.

How should we distinguish between character and habit? Consider the following attempts:

> "Character" is a generalized description of one's disposition in respect to a general trait such as honesty, temperance, or carefulness, while "habit" is more specific. The latter designates a regular practice of meeting a particular kind of situation with a certain type of conduct, or a reflex behavior in a specific set of circumstances. Evidence of habit or custom is relevant to an issue of behavior on a specific occasion because it tends to prove that the behavior on such occasion conformed to the habit or custom.

Frase v. Henry, 444 F.2d 1228, 1232 (10th Cir. 1971).

> [Habit] denotes one's regular response to a repeated situation. If we speak of a character for care, we think of the person's tendency to act prudently in all the varying situations of life—in business, at home, in handling automobiles and in walking across the street. A habit, on the other hand, is a person's regular practice of responding to a particular kind of situation with a specific type of conduct. Thus, a person may be in the habit of bounding down a certain stairway two or three steps at a time, of patronizing a particular pub after each day's work, or of driving his automobile without using a seatbelt. The doing of the habitual act may become semi-automatic, as with a driver who invariably signals before changing lanes.

McCormick, Evidence §195 (J. Strong 4th ed. 1992).

> Why is such a sharp distinction drawn between character evidence, which is generally excluded, and habit evidence, which is generally admitted? The primary reason is that habit describes particular behavior in a specific setting, and it is by nature at least regular if not invariable, so it has greater probative value in proving conduct on a particular occasion than does evidence of more general propensities. Also, habit evidence is less likely to carry moral overtones or to present serious dangers of unfair prejudice or confusion.

2 C. Mueller and L. Kirkpatrick, Federal Evidence §124 (2d ed. 1994).

Perhaps most often evidence of habit is offered in civil negligence cases, but occasionally it appears in criminal cases as well. See Derring v. State, 619

S.W.2d 644, 646-647 (Ark. 1981) (in trial for murder, where body was never found, admitting evidence that victim was "very dependable in his routine, kept a fairly rigid schedule, always had breakfast with the same person each day, attended school regularly, had no bad habits, and returned home to his apartment at the same time each evening," to prove he "did not disappear on his own volition").

So how does one prove habit, and what is it, anyway?

PROBLEM 5-M.   *Death on the Highway*

Lance Teel and his wife Judy were driving westbound on Highway 46 when they collided with a car driven by Paul Finney, in which his wife Lena was riding as a passenger. All four were killed immediately, and no eyewitness saw the accident. The cars collided at the intersection of the highway and a county road, and the highway patrolman who examined the scene concluded that the Finney vehicle was entering the highway from the north and was in the process of turning left (eastward) when it was struck. The accident occurred at 8:00 a.m. on a cool cloudy gray September morning, when visibility was only about one-quarter of a mile.

The Teel estate sues the Finney estate for wrongful death. The highway patrolman testifies to the appearance of the scene, and the court lets him testify as an expert in accident reconstruction, stating his conclusions as to probable speed and positions of the vehicles at the time of impact.

Because the accident looked like one that could happen only if one of the two drivers was at fault, and because there was no direct proof on this point, the Teel estate seeks to prove that Lance Teel was exercising due care. It calls witnesses Budge and Frese, who are prepared to testify that Lance Teel was "a good, careful driver." The Finney estate objects that the proffered evidence "is just proof of character, which cannot be admitted to show conduct on a particular occasion."

How should the court rule, and why?

PROBLEM 5-N.   *The Exploding Can*

Forest Halleck worked as a mechanic who specialized in the repair and maintenance of automobile air conditioning systems. One day after replacing the compressor unit in a vehicle, he began to charge the new unit in the usual way by injecting a pressurized liquid refrigerant (Freon). After two cans flowed into the unit without difficulty, he encountered problems with the third and fourth cans. He filled an empty two-pound coffee can with warm water to raise the temperature and pressure of the smaller can of refrigerant, but as he warmed the fourth can it exploded and injured him seriously.

Halleck sued Lorton Chemicals (maker of the Freon), which defended on the basis that Halleck was negligent in ignoring warning labels on the can.

At trial, Lorton sought to prove that Halleck habitually used an immersion heater to raise the temperature of the water in the coffee can and that the explosion was caused when the temperature went above 130 degrees (the maximum safe temperature, as noted on the can). It called Mike Newsome, a fellow worker who was prepared to testify that he had often seen Halleck use an immersion coil to heat water, and thus to heat cans of Freon.

Halleck objects that the evidence is "barred by the rule against character evidence." Should Newsome be allowed to testify?

NOTES ON HABIT EVIDENCE IN NEGLIGENCE CASES

1. The commentators quoted in the text above describe habit as "reflex behavior" which is "semi-automatic" or "mechanistic." Can being a careful driver be described in those terms? How about always wearing (or not wearing) a seatbelt? See Sharpe v. Bestop, 730 A.2d 285 (N.J. 1999) (admitting evidence of plaintiff's "habitual disregard" of warnings to wear seatbelts, but excluding proof of "occasional disregard of warnings not to drink and drive"). How about always going to church on Sunday morning? Physically abusing or threatening someone? Compare Brett v. Berkowitz, 706 A.2d 509, 516 (Del. 1998) (in sexual misconduct and malpractice suit against lawyer, excluding proof that he had "prior relations with clients") with State v. Huerta, 947 P.2d 483, 490 (Mont. 1997) (in trial of boyfriend of victim's mother, evidence that *she* abused child, offered to show she was source of his injuries, qualified as habit, but court could exclude under FRE 403) and State v. Brown, 543 S.E.2d 552 (S.C. 2001) (in trial of *B* for murdering his nephew, proof that he became violent when angry was not habit). How about carrying a gun? See Ware v. State, 759 A.2d 764, 777 (Md. 2000) (yes).

2. If you were counsel for the Teel estate (Problem 5-M), what further description would you hope that Budge and Frese might provide concerning Lance Teel's "driving habits"? See Barton v. Plaisted, 256 A.2d 642, 647 (N.H. 1969) (admitting testimony on decedent's "customary driving speed over a period of years, along the 'flat' leading southerly into the curve where the accident occurred," offered to prove that car driven by him crossed center stripe there).

3. If a pedestrian often crosses a certain street, does evidence that she stays in a crosswalk amount to habit evidence? See Charmley v. Lewis, 729 P.2d 567, 570 (Or. 1986) (yes; it tended to prove her "specific response to going to the grocery store"); Glatt v. Feist, 156 N.W.2d 819, 828 (N.D. 1968) (approving testimony that plaintiff "had been in the habit of crossing Main Street in returning from church at the point east of the crosswalk," as proof that she was not in the crosswalk when struck by a car).

4. In Problem 5-N, if Newsome testifies that he saw Halleck use an immersion heater "several" times, would that suffice to show habit? Short of testimony that he saw Halleck do so "all the time," how much is enough? Six times? A dozen? Should Newsome be permitted to give what amounts to his opinion that Halleck used an immersion heater "routinely" or "customarily" or "as a matter of habit"? Compare Henry v. Cline, 626 S.W.2d 958 (Ark. 1982) (excluding testimony that defendant drove on this road "a dozen times" and "was speeding half of those times," which was "not sufficient to establish a mode of behavior that has become nearly or completely involuntary") with Sams v.

Gay, 288 S.E.2d 822, 823 (Ga. App. 1982) (admitting testimony that "it was the decedent's custom and habit to chain-smoke while drinking and that 'many times' he had passed out under such circumstances while holding a lighted cigarette and had burned holes in the furniture"). Who decides whether specific instances suffice to show habit under FRE 406, judge or jury?

5. How should courts deal with evidence of drug or drinking "habits"? If defendant can show that plaintiff was convicted four times for public intoxication in the previous three and one-half years, should he be able to offer such evidence as proof that plaintiff was intoxicated on the occasion in question? Compare Reyes v. Missouri Pacific Ry., 589 F.2d 791, 794 (5th Cir. 1979) (no) with Hooker v. State, 716 So. 2d 1104 (Miss. 1998) (in murder trial, where victim had passed out in his car from drunkenness, admitting proof that he habitually parked in that spot, to show that defendant "knew where to look to find" him). And see Burchett v. Commonwealth, 98 S.W.2d 492 (Ky. 2003) (reversing conviction for reckless homicide; trial court should not have admitted proof that defendant smoked marijuana on daily basis) (habit evidence is not admissible in Kentucky; such evidence is problematic and unreliable). What if plaintiff's employer can testify that he routinely carries a cooler of beer on his truck, drinks on the job to the point of generating complaints from customers, and admits to drinking beer at some time during a normal day? See Loughan v. Firestone Tire & Rubber Co., 749 F.2d 1519, 1523-1524 (11th Cir. 1985) (admit). But see generally Donald v. Triple S. Well Service, Inc., 708 So. 2d 1318 (Miss. 1998) (canvassing cases and counseling caution).

PROBLEM 5-O. *Was He Served?*

Manuel Gutierrez is charged with illegal entry after previous deportation. At trial, the government must prove that defendant was served with the warrant of deportation and a letter in his native language warning him of the penalties of reentry.

As part of its proof on this point, the government calls Agent Lesher, of the Immigration and Naturalization Service (INS). Lesher did not himself serve Gutierrez, but he has worked for INS in a variety of positions for the last 12 years, serving on traffic check, line watch, and as a warrant officer. If permitted, he would describe the procedures followed by detention officers in carrying out deportations and the preparation and service of the forms involved. He would testify that in the ordinary course of deportation proceedings an immigration officer picks up the "deportee," fills in blanks on the back of the warrant, signs it as witness to the deportation, obtains the right thumb print of the deportee on the back of the warrant, and hands him the letter and a copy of the warrant. In this case, no signature appears on the warrant, although it is otherwise filled out and has defendant's thumb print.

During defense voir dire, Agent Lesher testifies that he has never executed such a warrant and that his knowledge of the procedures comes from "what I have been told by detention officers" and from knowing "the normal rule of things and the normal processes of deportation."

Defendant then objects that Agent Lesher's testimony cannot establish service in this case. Should Lesher be permitted to testify?

NOTES ON ORGANIZATIONAL CUSTOM AND PRACTICE

1. Should proof of organizational routine to show the doing of an act be more readily admitted than proof of individual habit? Why or why not?

2. If the question is whether a physician or dentist warned her patient of the hazards of a dental or medical procedure, should the court admit evidence that she always gives such warnings? Does proof of this sort amount to "the habit of a person," or is it "routine practice of an organization"? Can such proof be rebutted by testimony by particular patients indicating in their case she did *not* give such warnings? See Arthur v. Zearley, 292 S.W.2d 67 (Ark. 1999) (testimony by doctor about "what he told all of his patients" during informed consent conference qualified as "habit and routine") (but other patients could testify that he did not give them such warnings).

3. The issue is whether a letter rescinding an agreement was posted. The author testifies that he dictated and signed the letter, that he saw an appropriately addressed envelope in the "out" box on his secretary's desk, and that a clerk in the office periodically collects the contents of this box and posts letters or hand delivers interoffice material. Should testimony of this sort suffice to prove mailing? Receipt in due course? See Wells Fargo Business v. Ben Kozloff, Inc., 695 F.2d 940, 944 (5th Cir.) (yes), cert. denied, 464 U.S. 818 (1983). Should it matter whether the witness personally carries out the routine he describes?

4. Can organizational routine prove the presence of terms in an agreement? Compare Amoco Production Co. v. United States, 619 F.2d 1383, 1390 (10th Cir. 1980) (admitting evidence of "routine practice" of Federal Farm Mortgage Corporation "to reserve a one-half mineral interest in all property transferred," as proof of term in lost deed) and Joseph v. Krull Wholesale Drug Co., 147 F. Supp. 250, 258 (E.D. Pa. 1956) (evidence that company had entered into certain kinds of contracts with officers of company was admissible to show a practice "not to make written contracts or contracts for definite periods of time"), aff'd, 245 F.2d 231 (3d Cir. 1957) with C.F.W. Construction Co. v. Travelers Insurance Co., 363 F.2d 557 (6th Cir. 1966) (evidence that whenever endorsement was required, practice was to submit contract to insurance company could not prove it was done in this instance).

5. Should proof of industry practice be admitted on the question of standard of care? See Avena v. Clauss & Co., 504 F.2d 469, 472 (2d Cir. 1974) (custom of moving bales by inserting longshoremen's hooks under the bands to move packages, admissible to prove intended use, hence dangerous condition). And sometimes it bears on the interpretation of contracts. See M/V American Queen v. San Diego Marine Construction Co., 708 F.2d 1483, 1491 (9th Cir. 1983) (custom and practice regarding limits of liability in ship repair). Are these uses regulated by FRE 406?

C. REMEDIAL MEASURES

Often it happens that someone involved in an accident takes later steps to avoid future mishaps. These may involve physical modifications of the machine or premises, changes in labels or instructions, modification of procedures, firing of employees thought to be responsible, or reorganization of the department or unit involved. At common law, evidence of such "subsequent remedial measures" has long been excludable, when offered to prove that the person in question was somehow at fault before, and FRE 407 continues tradition on this point.

The exclusionary doctrine rests on policy, relevance, and confusion of issues. As a matter of policy, it is thought wise to avoid discouraging efforts to make things better or safer (hence furthering an aim completely "extrinsic" to the conduct of litigation). Also it is considered unfair to introduce against a person, over his objection, evidence that he behaved responsibly after the fact. Concerns over relevancy arise because efforts to prevent future accidents may not show or even indicate that past practice or conditions amounted to negligence or fault. Concerns over confusion of issues arise partly because of the relevancy problem and partly because it may be impossible even to show that changes that follow an accident were made *because* of the accident.

Three major issues arise in the application of FRE 407. First, does the exclusionary doctrine apply in product liability cases? (Any question on that point was resolved by a 1997 amendment to FRE 407, which expressly says the exclusionary doctrine *does* apply here, but many states do *not* apply the exclusionary doctrine in this setting.) Second, does the *Erie* doctrine require federal courts to follow state practice on subsequent measures? (The bulk of modern authority says no, but the matter is still open to debate. And as noted above, federal law conflicts with many state rules in product liability cases.) Third, when may subsequent measures be shown to prove "feasibility"? (FRE 407 so permits if that point is "controverted," but what does "controverted" mean?)

TUER v. McDONALD
Court of Appeals of Maryland
701 A.2d 1101 (1997)

WILNER, Judge.

[Mary Tuer brought a medical malpractice suit against St. Joseph's Hospital in Baltimore, along with cardiac surgeons Garth McDonald and Robert Brawley, after her husband Eugene Tuer died of cardiac arrest on November 3, 1992, while awaiting coronary artery bypass graft surgery (CABG).

Eugene Tuer was 63, and had suffered angina for 16 years. Originally scheduled for surgery on Monday November 9th, he was admitted to St. Joseph's on Friday October 30th after suffering chest pains Thursday night. His surgery was rescheduled for 9 a.m. on Monday November 2nd, and he was put on Atenolol (beta blocker that reduces pressure on the heart) and Heparin (anticoagulant). His angina stabilized over the weekend, and he suffered no further pains or shortness of breath.

Following hospital protocol, an anesthesiologist stopped the Heparin at 5:30 a.m. on Monday morning, to allow the drug to be metabolized so Tuer would not have an anticoagulant in his blood during surgery. Drs. McDonald and Brawley prepared him, but an emergency involving another patient, more critically ill than Tuer, required Tuer's operation to be postponed. Tuer was placed in the Coronary Surgery Unit and monitored. At 1:30 p.m., Dr. McDonald found Tuer short of breath and suffering arrhythmia and low blood pressure. He went into cardiac arrest. Resuscitation efforts and seven hours of surgery kept him alive, but he died the next day.

After Tuer's death, and apparently because of it, St. Joseph changed its protocol with respect to discontinuing Heparin for patients with stable angina. Under the new protocol, Heparin is continued until the patient is taken into the operating room.

Defendants made a motion in limine to exclude any reference to the change in protocol under Maryland Rule 5-407. Plaintiff countered that (a) the change was not a remedial measure because the defense claimed the prior protocol was correct, and (b) she was entitled to prove the change to show that continuing Heparin was "feasible." The trial court rejected the first argument (saying that defendants did not have to admit wrongdoing in order to claim that a change was remedial), but ruled that it would admit the proof if defendants denied feasibility.

Called by plaintiff as an adverse witness, Dr. McDonald testified that he approved discontinuing the Heparin to minimize the risk of excessive bleeding that would occur in the event of inadvertent puncture of the carotid artery. CABG requires puncturing the jugular vein with a needle, inserting a guide wire, then making an incision and inserting a catheter. The jugular is close to the carotid artery (high-pressure vessel bringing blood from the heart to the brain), and in 5 to 10 percent of the cases the anesthesiologist inadvertently punctures the artery when trying to insert the needle into the jugular, causing bleeding and sometimes death. Plaintiff got Dr. McDonald to say that under no circumstances would a patient in Tuer's condition (unstable angina stabilized by Heparin) continue on Heparin to the time of surgery. He considered restarting the Heparin when surgery was postponed, but decided against it. The court sustained a defense objection to the question whether it was "feasible to restart Heparin," but plaintiff got McDonald to say that restarting it would have been unsafe.

Plaintiff argued that she was entitled to prove the change in protocol, to impeach and to show it was not unsafe to restart Heparin, but the court disagreed. On cross, McDonald testified that he would have restarted Heparin if Tuer had developed new chest pains indicating unstable angina, pointing out that Heparin is used later in CABG surgery to prevent clotting as blood circulates through a heart-lung machine.

Two doctors testified for plaintiff that Tuer had unstable angina, and that failing to restart Heparin departed from the customary standard. Three testified for defendant that it was right not to restart Heparin, since Tuer had stabilized.

The Court traces the law on subsequent measures in Maryland, describing the adoption of Maryland Rule 5-407, which is substantially identical to FRE 407 (before the 1997 amendment of the latter, which made changes not pertinent to this case).]

The Federal Advisory Committee on Rules of Evidence, which drafted FRE 407, offered two justifications for excluding evidence of subsequent remedial measures to prove culpability: first, that the subsequent conduct "is not in fact an admission, since the conduct is equally consistent with injury by mere accident or through contributory negligence," and second, the "social policy of encouraging people to take, or at least not discouraging them from taking, steps in furtherance of added safety." Although some commentators have since questioned the efficacy of the "social policy" argument, it was . . . sufficiently persuasive to cause the Federal rule to be proposed by the Supreme Court and adopted by Congress.[8]

These grounds and the commentary on them were considered by both the Rules Committee and this Court in deciding whether to adopt an analog to FRE 407. . . . The discussion at the open hearing held by this Court [on proposed Maryland Rule 407 shows that the Court agreed] that evidence of subsequent remedial measures should no longer be admissible to show either what the applicable standard of care was at the time of the occurrence or a deviation from that standard of care. In that regard, the exclusionary aspect of the Rule is broader than the common law it replaced. . . .

[Plaintiff argues that proof of the change in protocol is admissible to show feasibility and impeach the testimony that restarting Heparin would be unsafe.]

FEASIBILITY

Rule 5-407(b) exempts subsequent remedial measure evidence from the exclusionary provision of Rule 5-407(a) when it is offered to prove feasibility, if feasibility has been controverted. That raises two questions: what is meant by "feasibility" and was feasibility, in fact, controverted? These two questions also tend to overlap and are often dealt with together; whether a defendant has controverted feasibility may well depend on how one defines the term.

The exception allowing subsequent conduct evidence to show feasibility has been a troublesome one, especially in negligence cases, for, as Judge Weinstein points out, "negligence and feasibility [are] often indistinct issues. The feasibility of a precaution may bear on whether the defendant was negligent not to have taken the precaution sooner." 2 Weinstein's Federal Evidence §407.04[3]. The Court of Special Appeals noted [in this case] that two seemingly divergent approaches have been taken in construing the feasibility exception. Some courts have construed the word narrowly, disallowing evidence of subsequent remedial measures under the feasibility exception unless the defendant has essentially contended that the measures were not physically, technologically, or economically possible under the circumstances then pertaining. Other courts have swept into the concept of feasibility a somewhat broader spectrum of motives and explanations for not having adopted the remedial measure earlier, the effect of which is to circumscribe the exclusionary provision.

Courts in the first camp have concluded that feasibility is not contro-

---

8. Criticism of the "social policy" argument centers on the notion that an exclusionary rule is not necessary to impel corrective action—that a defendant who is able to do so would likely take corrective action even in the absence of such a rule. [Court notes what it calls a "modified social policy argument" for the rule, which is that "people who take post-accident safety measures are doing exactly what good citizens should do" and that courts should not penalize behavior that seems "praiseworthy," at least so long as the probative worth of evidence of their behavior is small. Court notes as well the argument that the rule rests on relevancy, meaning that the "marginal relevance" of subsequent measures is "almost always substantially outweighed by the risk of jury confusion."]

verted—and thus subsequent remedial evidence is not admissible under the Rule—when a defendant contends that the design or practice complained of was chosen because of its perceived comparative advantage over the alternative design or practice ([citing cases]); or when the defendant merely asserts that the instructions or warnings given with a product were acceptable or adequate and does not suggest that additional or different instructions or warnings could not have been given ([citing cases]); or when the defendant urges that the alternative would not have been effective to prevent the kind of accident that occurred ([citing cases]).

Courts announcing a more expansive view have concluded that "feasible" means more than that which is merely possible, but includes that which is capable of being utilized successfully. In Anderson v. Malloy, 700 F.2d 1208 (8th Cir. 1983), for example, a motel guest who was raped in her room and who sued the motel for failure to provide safe lodging, offered evidence that, after the event, the motel installed peep holes in the doors to the rooms. The appellate court held that the evidence was admissible in light of the defendant's testimony that it had considered installing peepholes earlier but decided not to do so because (1) there were already windows next to the solid door allowing a guest to look out, and (2) based on the advice of the local police chief, peepholes would give a false sense of security. Although the motel, for obvious reasons, never suggested that the installation of peepholes was not possible, the court, over a strident dissent, concluded that, by inferring that the installation of peepholes would create a lesser level of security, the defendant had "controverted the feasibility of the installation of these devices." [Court describes other cases.]

The apparent divergence indicated by these cases may, at least to some extent, be less of a doctrinal division than a recognition that the concept of practicability is implicit in the notion of feasibility and allows some leeway in the application of the rule. [Court notes that dictionary definitions connote "practicability," but that some stress that which can be done "physically, technologically, or economically" and some stress "value, effectiveness, and overall utility."]

To some extent, the problem may be driven by special considerations arising from application of the rule to product liability cases, especially those grounded on strict liability. When the plaintiff is obliged to establish that there were feasible alternatives to the design, manufacturing method, or warnings used by the defendant, he or she necessarily injects the question of feasibility into the case, to which the defendant ordinarily responds by showing why those alternatives were not used. As [commentators] point out, if a remedial measure has, in fact, been taken that could have been taken earlier, the defendant is not likely to claim that the measure was not possible or practicable, and, indeed, defendants often are willing to stipulate to feasibility in order to avoid having the subsequent remedial evidence admitted. The issue arises when the defendant offers some other explanation for not putting the measure into effect sooner—often a judgment call as to comparative value or a trade-off between cost and benefit or between competing benefits—and the plaintiff characterizes that explanation as putting feasibility into issue.[9] To the extent there can be

9. Wright and Graham note that many of the cases in which the feasibility exception has been invoked are product liability cases, and that "it may be that courts had intuitive appreciation

said to be a doctrinal split among the courts, it seems to center on whether that kind of judgment call, which is modified later, suffices to allow the challenged evidence to be admitted.

That is essentially what occurred in this case. At no time did Dr. McDonald or any of his expert witnesses suggest that the Heparin could not have been restarted following the postponement of Mr. Tuer's surgery. Indeed, they indicated quite the opposite; Dr. McDonald, in fact, made clear that, had Mr. Tuer exhibited signs of renewed unstable angina, he would have restarted the Heparin. The only fair reading of his testimony and that of his supporting experts is that the protocol then in effect was the product of a professional judgment call that the risk to Mr. Tuer of having CABG surgery commence while there was a significant amount of Heparin in his blood outweighed the prospect of harm accruing from allowing him to remain Heparin-free for several hours.

Dr. McDonald's brief response to one question that, at the time, he regarded it as "unsafe" to restart the Heparin cannot be viewed in isolation but has to be read in the context of his whole testimony. Under any reasonable view of the meaning of feasibility, a flat assertion by a physician that the remedial measure was inappropriate because it was medically "unsafe" would ordinarily be tantamount to asserting that the measure was not feasible and would thus suffice to controvert the feasibility of the measure. In a medical context at least, feasibility has to include more than mere physical possibility; as we have so sadly learned from history, virtually anything can physically be done to the human body. The practice of medicine is quintessentially therapeutic in nature. Its purpose is to comfort and to heal, and a determination of whether a practice or procedure is feasible has to be viewed in that light. The assertion that a given course would be unsafe, in the sense that it would likely cause paramount harm to the patient, necessarily constitutes an assertion that the course would not be feasible. Dr. McDonald was not asserting, however, in any absolute sense, that restarting the Heparin would have been unsafe but only that, given the complications that could have arisen, and that, in other cases had arisen, from an inadvertent puncture of the carotid artery, weighed against Mr. Tuer's apparently stable condition at the time and the intensive monitoring he would receive during the waiting period, there was a relative safety risk that, at the time, he and the hospital believed was not worth taking. That does not, in our view, constitute an assertion that a restarting of the Heparin was not feasible. It was feasible but, in their view, not advisable.

IMPEACHMENT

The exception in the Rule for impeachment has created some of the same practical and interpretive problems presented by the exception for establishing feasibility. As Saltzburg, Martin, and Capra point out, "almost any testimony given by defense witnesses could be contradicted at least in some minimal way by a subsequent remedial measure. If the defendant's expert testifies that the

---

of the inappropriateness of the traditional rule in that context and were using the 'exception' as an alternative to holding the rule inapplicable in strict liability." 23 Wright and Graham, Federal Practice and Procedure §5288 (footnote omitted) (1980 and 1997 Supp.).

product was safe, a subsequent remedial measure could be seen as contradicting that testimony. If the defendant is asked on cross-examination whether he thinks that he had taken all reasonable safety precautions, and answers in the affirmative, then a subsequent remedial measure can be seen as contradicting that testimony." 1 Saltzburg, Martin, and Capra, [Federal Rules of Evidence Manual 487 (6th ed. 1994)].

The prevailing, and pragmatically necessary, view is that the impeachment exception cannot be read in so expansive a manner. As Wright and Graham note, even at common law it would likely have been impermissible for the plaintiff to "have called the defendant to the stand, asked him if he thought he had been negligent, and impeached him with evidence of subsequent repairs if he answered 'no.' " 23 Wight and Graham, supra, §5289, at 145 (1980).[10] Thus, as Saltzburg, Martin, and Capra point out, most courts have held that subsequent remedial measure evidence is not ordinarily admissible for impeachment "if it is offered for simple contradiction of a defense witness' testimony." 1 Saltzburg, Martin and Capra, supra, at 487.

To some extent, that begs the question; whether the evidence is allowed for impeachment seems to depend more on the nature of the contradiction than on the fact of it. In Muzyka v. Remington Arms Co., 774 F.2d 1309, 1313 (5th Cir. 1985), for example, where a defense witness asserted that the challenged product constituted "perhaps the best combination of safety and operation yet devised," a design change made after the accident but before the giving of that testimony was allowed as impeachment evidence, presumably to show either that the witness did not really believe that to be the case or that his opinion should not be accepted as credible. In Dollar v. Long Mfg., N.C., Inc., 561 F.2d 613 (5th Cir. 1977), the court allowed evidence of a post-accident letter by the manufacturer to its dealers warning of "death dealing propensities" of the product when used in a particular fashion to impeach testimony by the defendant's design engineer, who wrote the letter, that the product was safe to operate in that manner. In these circumstances, the subsequent remedial measure falls neatly within the scope of classic impeachment evidence and directly serves the purpose of such evidence—to cast doubt on the credibility of the witness's testimony; it is not a mere pretext for using the evidence to establish culpability.

Consistent with the approach taken on the issue of feasibility, however, subsequent remedial measure evidence had been held inadmissible to impeach testimony that, at the time of the event, the measure was not believed to be as practical as the one employed, or that the defendant was using due care at the time of the accident.

---

10. The plaintiff has not made a separate issue of the court's disallowance of her question to Dr. McDonald and Dr. Fortuin of whether restarting the Heparin would have been feasible, although she has asked rhetorically what harm would have ensued from allowing the answer if feasibility was not being controverted. [Court does not answer this question, but notes the view of another court that "to impeach the credibility of a witness through the introduction of a subsequent remedial measure, the testimony providing grounds for impeachment must have been initiated by the witness," since the impeachment exception was created "to protect a plaintiff from an aggressive defendant attempting to manipulate the exclusionary nature of the rule for his own advantage." Hence "a plaintiff who is on the offensive should not be allowed to manipulate the impeachment exception in order to introduce evidence for purposes otherwise inadmissible."]

Largely for the reasons cited with respect to the feasibility issue, we do not believe that the change in protocol was admissible to impeach Dr. McDonald's brief statement that restarting the Heparin would have been unsafe. As we observed, that statement must be read in context, and, when so read, would not be impeached by the subsequent change in protocol. It is clear that Dr. McDonald made a judgment call based on his knowledge and collective experience at the time. . . . The only reasonable inference from his testimony . . . was that Dr. McDonald and his colleagues reevaluated the relative risks in light of what happened to Mr. Tuer and decided that the safer course was to continue the Heparin. That kind of reevaluation is precisely what the exclusionary provision of the Rule was designed to encourage.

[The judgment is affirmed.]

NOTES ON SUBSEQUENT REMEDIAL MEASURES

1. How does the court in *Tuer* read "feasibility" in FRE 407? How does it read "impeachment"? In effect, does the court in *Tuer* take a narrow view of both terms in order to achieve a broad protective purpose? Do you think a large urban hospital would hesitate to change its protocol requiring the cessation of anticoagulants prior to CABG surgery if proof of such change were admissible in cases like *Tuer?* For other cases raising the impeachment question, see MacDonald v. B.M.D. Golf Associates, Inc., 813 A.2d 488 (N.H. 2002) (in suit against golf course for injuries occurring when golf cart tipped over, testimony that area was safe without warning sign did not pave way for proof that sign was later installed, but testimony that signs just create a lot of chaos *did* pave the way for such proof); Doe v. Wal-Mart Stores, 558 S.E.2d 663 (W.Va. 2001) (in suit by kidnap victim alleging that lack of lighting in parking lot was to blame, article stating that Wal-Mart was using roving golf carts to cut crime in parking lots would be admissible if defendant claimed that lot was as safe as it could be).

2. Nobody doubts that FRE 407 applies in negligence cases like *Tuer,* but the question whether the exclusionary principle *does or should* apply in product liability cases has divided courts. The policy issue is complicated, and the original wording of FRE 407 left room to argue either way.

(a) On the question whether the exclusionary principle *should* reach product liability cases, consider what the California Supreme Court said in the *Ault* case, which declined to apply a state provision (the model for original FRE 407) in that setting. *Ault* involved a Scout vehicle that plunged 500 feet to the bottom of a canyon, leading to a claim that the accident was caused by failure of a gearbox from metal fatigue. The court concluded that plaintiff should have been permitted to prove that afterwards the manufacturer changed the metal in gearboxes from aluminum to malleable iron:

Historically, the common law rule . . . was developed with reference to the usual negligence action, in which a pedestrian fell into a hole in a sidewalk or a plaintiff was injured on unstable stairs; in such circumstances, it may be realistic to assume that a landowner or potential defendant might be deterred from making repairs if such repairs could be used against him in determining liability for the initial accident.

When the context is transformed from a typical negligence setting to the modern products liability field, however, the "public policy" assumptions justifying this evidentiary rule are no longer valid. The contemporary corporate mass producer of goods, the normal products liability defendant, manufactures tens of thousands of units of goods; it is manifestly unrealistic to suggest that such a producer will forego making improvements in its product, and risk innumerable additional lawsuits and the attendant adverse effect upon its public image, simply because evidence of adoption of such improvement may be admitted in an action founded on strict liability for recovery on an injury that preceded the improvement. In the products liability area, the exclusionary rule . . . does not affect the primary conduct of the mass producer of goods, but serves merely as a shield against potential liability. In short, the purpose . . . is not applicable to a strict liability case and hence its exclusionary rule should not be gratuitously extended to that field.

Ault v. International Harvester Co., 528 P.2d 1148 (Cal. 1974). In effect, *Ault* argues that the *reason* for the exclusionary principle is to *affect out-of-court conduct* by encouraging responsible behavior, but that the exclusionary principle *won't have that effect* in product liability cases. Note also the argument mentioned in *Tuer* that notions of feasibility are bound to come up in conversation about what constitutes a defective product, hence it is impossible to avoid the subject in this setting, and excluding evidence of design changes means the conversation will be incomplete and distorted. See generally C. Mueller and L. Kirkpatrick, Federal Evidence §131 (2d ed. 1994). But see Flaminio v. Honda Motor Co., Ltd., 733 F.2d 463 (7th Cir. 1984) (rejecting *Ault* and arguing that "effects of scale are symmetrical" because exposure for *future* accidents if the defect is *not* fixed is offset by exposure for *past* accidents if the defect *is* fixed and the change is then provable in litigation).

(b) On the question whether FRE 407 *does or does not apply* to strict liability claims, all doubt was removed in 1997 by the addition of language covering proof of defective "product" or "design" or the need for "warning or instruction." Before the amendment, FRE 407 reached only proof of "negligence or culpable conduct," and it was arguable that strict liability cases involved *neither.* Strict liability, after all, came along because negligence principles seemed inadequate in product cases. And "culpable conduct" could refer to "deliberate" or "intentional" or "wanton" misconduct. That's how *Ault* read the California provision that was the model for original FRE 407.

(c) On the matter of conflicting state rules, and the conflict between the federal rule and what some states do, consider these points: For years, states have disagreed on the question whether to apply their counterparts to FRE 407 in this setting. Compare Minton v. Honda of America, 684 N.E.2d 648 (Ohio 1997) and Jeep Corp. v. Murray, 708 P.2d 297 (Nev. 1985) (declining to apply their state counterparts to product liability claims) with Dutchess v. Langston Corp., 769 A.2d 1131 (Pa. 2001), and Hyjek v. Anthony Industries, 944 P.2d 1036 (Wash. 1997) (their state counterparts do apply in strict liability suits). It is not at all certain that states that have already gone in the direction of Ohio and Nevada in refusing to apply the exclusionary principle in product liability cases will follow the federal lead. The California provision construed in *Ault* is statutory, and *Ault* is still the law in that state. And the Colorado Supreme Court, knowing about the change in FRE 407 extending it to strict liability cases, declined to apply CRE 407 in this setting, making it unlikely that the state rules committee will recommend any change on this point. See Forma Scientific, Inc. v. Biosera, Inc., 960 P.2d 108 (Colo. 1998) (CRE 407 does not apply in design defect cases).

3. Suppose an Ohio citizen sues an out-of-state automaker alleging a defect in the design of a gearbox, and the automaker removes the suit to federal court. It is possible that plaintiff would win in state court because he can show the design change, but lose in federal court because the proof is excluded. If so, the *reason* he would lose is that federal and state law conflicts on the matter of how best to affect out-of-court behavior by automakers. This disagreement sounds like a matter of substantive law rather than procedural law, doesn't it? Doesn't the *Erie* doctrine seek *precisely* to avoid differences in outcome, as between state and federal court, when these are caused by conflicts in substantive law? Of course federal law *could* properly control on all substantive issues relating to product liability. But FRE 407 is part of the *Federal Rules of Evidence,* not part of some "Federal Product Liability Law," which doesn't exist. Wouldn't it be better to apply the *state* law on subsequent measures in product cases until and unless we adopt federal law governing the whole subject comprehensively?

4. Plaintiff has an accident in a 1984 car in 1988. The accident was caused by a defective steering mechanism, and the automaker corrected the defect by design change in its 1985 model. Assume that a court applies FRE 407 to product liability suits. Is evidence of the 1985 design change admissible at trial? Does "event" in FRE 407 refer to the making of the car or the accident? See Van Gordon v. Portland General Electric Co., 693 P.2d 1285, 1289 (Or. 1985) ("event" means accident).

D. SETTLEMENT NEGOTIATIONS

1. Civil Settlements

FRE 408 bars proof of civil settlements, offers to settle, and "conduct or statements made" during settlement negotiations, when offered to prove "liability for or invalidity of the claim or its amount." In part this exclusionary principle rests on concerns of relevancy: Payment of a small sum (or willingness to do so) does not tend strongly to prove liability; acceptance of a large sum (or willingness to do so) does not tend strongly to prove that a claim is weak. But relevancy alone would not likely produce such rule, for payment of a large sum *would* tend strongly to suggest liability, and acceptance of a small sum *would* tend strongly to suggest that a claim lacks merit.

The major underlying reason for the rule is public policy: The system would grind to a halt if every case filed were tried, yet lawyers would not be able to risk negotiating if what they said or did in trying to settle were later provable if the attempt to settle failed.

PROBLEM 5-P.   Two Potato, One Potato

Potato farmer Amos Perrin purchased from salesman Evan Sosbee an herbicide marketed under the name Perquod and made by the Cheron Chemical Company, for application on his potato crop. Sosbee was an agronomist by training, and his job for Cheron was not only to sell its chemical products, but also to deal with customers by offering suggestions on application and processing any complaints.

Appearing at the Perrin farm at the initial application of the Perquod, Sosbee advises Perrin that "Cheron will back up its recommendation of the product."

Midway through the growing season, Sosbee again appears on the farm, and Perrin comments that "the stuff we put on killed the weeds alright, but my potato plants don't look as healthy as they should." Sosbee replies, "Don't worry. We'll take care of you."

At harvest time, Perrin again sees Sosbee on the farm, at which time Perrin, clearly unhappy, advises Sosbee that "my yield isn't half what it was last year." Sosbee replies, "You just tell us the damages you're claiming, and we'll bill Cheron."

Cheron doesn't pay. Perrin sues the company. At trial, he offers to testify to the various statements by Sosbee. Assume that Sosbee's comments fit within FRE 801(d)(2)(D), but Cheron objects that "Sosbee's statements were offers to settle Perrin's claim, and as such they are excludable under FRE 408."

How should the court rule and why?

NOTES ON SETTLEMENT OFFERS

1. By nature a cautious bunch, lawyers usually conduct settlement talks by couching their factual remarks in terms of "let us assume for sake of discussion that" or "just suppose" or "what if, hypothetically now." Is such caution still required?

2. While driving in a car, Plaintiff and Passenger are struck by a car driven by Defendant, causing injuries all around. Plaintiff and Passenger come forward with claims against Defendant, but Passenger settles his claim while Plaintiff presses her claim forward to trial. Can Plaintiff seek to prove that Defendant was negligent by offering proof that he paid Passenger money to settle his claim? If Defendant calls Passenger as a witness, can Plaintiff cross-examine Passenger on the fact of settlement? For what purposes?

3. Assume that Contractor and Owner enter into an agreement under which the former is to build a motel for the latter, but the two have a falling out concerning performance and payment. They sit down to discuss their differences, and Contractor hires Architect to prepare a report identifying possible defects in the construction and evaluating Owner's complaints. A lawsuit ensues, and Owner offers the report in evidence. Contractor objects that the report embodies statements made in pursuit of settlement under FRE 408, but Owner replies that the next-to-last sentence in FRE 408 applies ("This rule does not require the exclusion of any evidence . . ."), hence that the

report should be admitted. Should it? See Ramada Development Co. v. Rauch, 644 F.2d 1097, 1106-1107 (5th Cir. 1981) (no, report should be excluded). What does that sentence mean, anyway? Doesn't FRE 408 in fact do precisely what that sentence says it does not do?

4. Betty Peed sought to purchase a valuable collection of dolls from Louise Stasko through the mail. Stasko sent the dolls in cartons to Peed, who apparently opened the bottoms, removed the dolls, resealed the boxes, and then sought indemnity from the U.S. Postal Service, claiming that the dolls had been stolen. Suspecting that Peed was the thief, postal inspectors arranged for Stasko to record a later conversation in which Peed indicated that she would return the dolls if Stasko would "drop the charges" against her. In her prosecution for alleged mail fraud and related offenses, the government offers this incriminating remark. Peed objects that her statement was an attempt to compromise Stasko's civil claim, but the government contends that it was "an effort to obstruct a criminal investigation or prosecution" within the meaning of the last sentence of FRE 408. Which is it? See United States v. Peed, 714 F.2d 7, 9-10 (4th Cir. 1983) (admit the statement). If one drinking buddy takes an unprovoked swing at another and criminal battery charges are filed, can an offer by the slugger to pay medical expenses be admitted against him in the criminal action? Does it become admissible if the understanding is that criminal charges will be dropped? Shouldn't we encourage people in this setting to resolve their differences in this way without invoking the criminal process?

2. Plea Bargaining in Criminal Cases

Plea bargaining statements are excludable for many of the same reasons that apply to civil settlement negotiations. Present policy strongly favors plea bargaining as a way of disposing of criminal cases, and without protection such bargaining could not occur. Moreover, sometimes what is said during such bargaining does not tend to prove guilt of the accused or any weakness in the government's case, although it "looks bad" for one side or the other. FRE 410(4) requires exclusion of plea bargaining statements by the accused, and other subdivisions of the Rule similarly exclude withdrawn pleas of guilty, pleas of nolo contendere, and courtroom statements by the accused in entering such pleas.

PROBLEM 5-Q. "I Used His Stuff"

Martin Rackly is charged with passing counterfeit bills. His lawyer Kent Slavin sets up an appointment with Assistant U.S. Attorney Amy Norton to discuss the situation. Slavin meets Norton and two Secret Service agents in the Federal Building, where Norton advises Slavin, "I'm not prepared to enter into any plea bargain because I haven't yet had a chance to study the case." Slavin replies that "Rackly's involvement in the counterfeiting operation is marginal at best, but he can help you get the guys you really want. So if you think you're interested in a deal, I think Rackly will cooperate with you."

Thereafter Slavin calls Norton's office and sets up another meeting in the

Federal Building. He and Rackly both attend, as do the two Secret Service agents, but nobody from the U.S. Attorney's Office is there. The agents deliver *Miranda* warnings, but Slavin protests that "We're here to talk about a plea, not a confession." On Slavin's advice, Rackly refuses to sign a Waiver of Rights Form (which would acknowledge receipt of *Miranda* warnings and state that "no promises have been made" and that Rackly "waives his right against self-incrimination"). He then makes a detailed statement, which includes the following crucial points: "Brody was my source. He had the bills, and I passed quite a few of them. I used his stuff at Wolf Brothers and Champion Electronics in Kansas City."

Ensuing telephone conversations between Slavin and Norton result in a draft plea agreement, but in the end Rackly does not sign. He is tried for passing bills at Wolf Brothers and Champion Electronics.

The prosecutor offers in evidence Rackly's statements admitting those transactions, but the defense objects: "Those are plea bargaining statements, and they should be excluded under Rule 410." What result, and why?

PROBLEM 5-R. *"Just Keep Them out of It"*

Executing a search warrant at the home of Bill Bragen in El Paso, DEA agents seize chemicals and laboratory equipment apparently used to manufacture methamphetamine. They also encounter and arrest Bragen and his wife Ann Bragen, as well as Al Roberts and his companion Judy Stall.

Thereafter Bill Bragen and Al Roberts, each represented by counsel, meet in the Federal Building with the DEA Agents and U.S. Attorney George Kendall. The lawyers for Bragen and Roberts advise Kendall that their clients "want to get the women out of this thing because they are not involved." During ensuing discussions, both Bragen and Roberts make incriminating statements. Referring to Ann Bragen and Judy Stall, both men say in substance, "Just keep them out of it, they had nothing to do with this whole nasty business."

Kendall directs the two women to be released and obtains indictments against Bragen and Roberts. At trial, Kendall calls the DEA agents in support of the government's case. They describe the results of their search, and Kendall then asks them to "describe what defendants said when we all met in the Federal Building." Bragen and Roberts object. Outside the hearing of the jury, they argue that "what was said in that room was plea bargaining, and it is excludable under Rule 410."

NOTES ON PLEA BARGAINING STATEMENTS AND NOLO CONTENDERE PLEAS

1. In Problem 5-Q, is it critical that the first meeting did not lead to serious discussions? Can plea bargaining occur even if no formal offer is made on either side? What if the Secret Service agents announced in the second meeting that Norton "would go for a plea to a one-count indictment for passing the bill at Wolf Brothers"? See United States v. Grant, 622 F.2d 308, 313-315 (8th Cir. 1980) (FRE 410 applies).

2. In Problem 5-R, should the meeting with Bragen and Roberts be characterized as (a) an exchange in which the men confessed to get the release of the women or (b) an attempt to bargain a plea, which led to release of the women because Kendall recognized they were innocent? If the first version is correct, the government should be able to use the statements of Bragen and Roberts, shouldn't it? (The government did its part by releasing the women; if the confessions are excluded it got nothing in return.) But if the second version is correct, the incriminating statements should be excluded under Rule 410, shouldn't they? Does Rule 410 address attempts by the accused to help other people? See United States v. Robertson, 582 F.2d 1356 (5th Cir. 1978) (on similar facts, defendants were making "independent" confessions rather than engaging in plea negotiations; court applies earlier version of Rule 410); United States v. Brooks, 670 F.2d 625, 626-628 (5th Cir. 1982) (postarrest statements to agents in effort to "work something out" for defendant's girlfriend were not excludable).

3. Originally Rule 410 required exclusion of "an offer to plead guilty" and statements "made in connection with, and relevant to" such an offer. That language did not confine the exclusionary doctrine to discussions with the prosecutor. Since the accused has a constitutional right to represent himself at trial, see Faretta v. California, 422 U.S. 806 (1975), it became plausible to argue that he might conduct his own "plea bargaining" by talking to arresting officers in the field or stationhouse. What if he tells a police officer he "wants to work something out" and the officer does nothing to discourage him? See United States v. Herman, 544 F.2d 791, 798 (5th Cir. 1977) (defendant made incriminating remarks in conversation with postal inspectors during recess in a hearing in which he requested appointment of a lawyer for his defense; the remarks were excludable, for Congress did not want plea bargaining to be "formalized, ritualized or structured," and the government, "as one of the dancing partners, should not be able to lead its partner to a trap door on the dance floor").

4. Concern that Rule 410 was too broad led to amendment in 1980. Now the Rule reaches plea bargaining statements only when made "in the course of plea discussions with an attorney for the prosecuting authority." Under this language, can statements by a defendant to an arresting agent *ever* be excluded as plea bargaining? Consider the following comment by the Criminal Rules Advisory Committee:

> This change, it must be emphasized, does not compel the conclusion that statements made to law enforcement agents, especially when the agents purport to have authority to bargain, are inevitably admissible. Rather, the point is that such cases are not covered by the per se rule of [FRCrimP] 11(e)(6) [which was and is identical to FRE 410] and thus must be resolved by that body of law dealing with police interrogations.

Does this comment mean statements to an arresting officer might still be excluded as plea bargaining if, for example, defendant says he wants to "work things out, like a lawyer would," and the officer promises "to help you out any way I can"? Many decisions endorse a "two-tiered" approach, turning on (a) whether defendant "exhibited an actual subjective expectation to negotiate a plea," and (b) whether that expectation "was reasonable given the totality of the objective circumstances." United States v. Robertson, 582 F.2d 1356, 1366 (5th Cir. 1978). But even courts following this approach have so far let the statements in. See United States v. Sebetich, 776 F.2d 412, 421-422 (3d Cir. 1985) (defendant could not have expected to bargain in "unplanned encounter" in parking lot during investigative stage); United States v. Karr, 742 F.2d 493, 496 (9th Cir. 1984) (any subjective belief unreasonable).

5. Assume that a conversation between the accused and the prosecutor amounts to plea bargaining, but that no bargain is reached (or that a plea is entered and then withdrawn) and the accused goes to trial. If he takes the stand and gives testimony contradicting his earlier plea-bargaining statements, should they be admissible to impeach? Legislative history makes it clear that FRE 410 blocks this use of plea-bargaining statements. But what if defendant waives his right to exclude his statements in the event of trial? See United States v. Mezzanatto, 513 U.S. 196, 202 (1995) (defendant engaged in plea bargaining in meeting in which prosecutor said they could talk only if defendant was "completely truthful" and only if he agreed that "any statements he made during the meeting could be used to impeach any contradictory testimony" he might give at trial; protections of FRE 410 may be waived); United States v. Burch, 156 F.3d 1315 (D.C. Cir. 1998) (upholding waiver allowing government to introduce defendant's plea-bargaining statements as substantive evidence during its case-in-chief; waiver was obtained as part of plea agreement, rather than being imposed as a condition at the beginning). Given *Mezzanatto*, how often do you think plea bargaining goes forward *without* a defense waiver?

6. Consider the last sentence in FRE 410, which makes some such statements admissible "in a criminal proceeding for false statement." What situation is that provision aimed at, anyway? See FRCrimP 11(c)(5) and (d) (the former contemplates that in considering a plea of guilty or nolo contendere the court may "question the defendant under oath, on the record, and in the presence of counsel"; the latter provides that the court shall not accept such a plea "without first, by addressing the defendant personally in open court, determining that the plea is voluntary and not the result of force or threats or of promises apart from a plea agreement").

7. FRE 410(2) makes inadmissible a plea of nolo contendere. Why should such a plea be excluded? Does that provision mean that in proceedings for deportation or license revocation on account of a prior felony conviction, such a conviction is inadmissible if it is based on a plea of nolo contendere?

8. FRE 410 prohibits only introduction of plea bargaining statements against the defendant. What if the defense wants to suggest that the prosecutor lacks confidence in his own case, hence that it must be weak, by introducing evidence that the prosecutor offered to let defendant plead guilty to a lesser charge? See United States v. Verdoorn, 528 F.2d 103, 107 (8th Cir. 1976) (invoking FRE 408 rather than 410, court concludes that "government proposals concerning pleas should be excludable").

E.   PROOF OF PAYMENT OF MEDICAL EXPENSES

Where a person pays for injuries or other expenses incurred by another, in the belief that he is responsible or even simply as a Good Samaritan (believing himself to be without blame but anxious to help another in need), FRE 409 provides that proof of such behavior is excludable if offered to prove "liability." The bases for this exclusionary principle are similar to those underlying FRE 407 and 408: Responsible behavior after the fact does not necessarily prove legal fault, and the system should encourage such behavior.

The provision is particularly useful in making it possible for an insurance carrier, which anticipates both liability and a possible dispute over amount, to advance sums necessary to compensate the claimant while still maintaining the position that it is not liable for the full amount claimed. A number of state statutes authorize advance payments of such sums, while providing for exclusion of evidence of payment.

By its terms, FRE 409 excludes only "furnishing or offering or promising to pay" medical and similar expenses, which seems narrower than the coverage of FRE 408. The latter excludes not only settlement offers, but "conduct or statements made in compromise negotiations." This difference in wording suggests that statements accompanying an offer to pay medical expenses might not be excludable under FRE 409, although such statements would be excludable if the context suggests that the parties were trying to settle the case.

F. PROOF OF INSURANCE COVERAGE

Does having or not having liability coverage affect the exercise of care? There once was a time when litigants could argue either that (1) a person who purchased insurance was buying a license to be careless, hence that proof of coverage tended to show that he was negligent on the occasion, or that (2) a person who bought insurance was displaying special caution, hence that proof of coverage tended to show that he was careful on the occasion. The speculative and contradictory nature of those arguments could not survive the growth of insurance to become commonplace in modern life. Thus concerns over relevance alone would justify Rule 411, which bars evidence of coverage offered in support of arguments such as these.

Rule 411 also serves the purpose of preventing the jury from deciding cases or adjusting damage estimates in the belief that insurance will pay the judgment.[3] Does this policy also justify excluding evidence of the *absence* of insurance?

The exclusionary principle has not gone without criticism. Auto accident cases provide what may be the most common circumstance in which insurance plays a role, and many jurisdictions require motorists to carry insurance coverage. Jurors likely believe that most people carry coverage and are likely aware of any requirement to do so. Arguably there are greater risks in keeping juries in the dark about coverage than in letting them know of the existence and limits of coverage.

---

3. This aspect of Rule 411 dovetails with the "collateral source" doctrine, which generally holds that a party who carries casualty coverage, medical insurance, or life insurance is entitled to collect not only from the carrier but from an alleged tortfeasor as well. In other words, ordinarily the party at fault cannot "take advantage of the thrift" of the insured party, and the insured sometimes obtains "double recovery."

For several reasons, Rule 411 does not always succeed in keeping the involvement of insurance from the jury. For one thing, lawyers often insinuate the fact of insurance into the case in other ways—during voir dire, for instance, where they put screening questions theoretically designed to prevent persons connected with the insurance industry from sitting in cases where insurance coverage is involved. And where an insurance carrier retains counsel for plaintiff or defendant, lawyers on the other side have been known to refer to the carrier by a "slip of the tongue" heard by the jury.

Occasionally various procedural and substantive principles also inject the fact of insurance into the case. Consider these three: First, it is often true (even where the collateral source doctrine applies) that any "second recovery" by the injured party actually belongs to the insurance carrier under principles of subrogation. Those may arise from the terms of the insurance contract or by law, as is most often true with casualty insurance and medical coverage (though it is seldom true in the context of life insurance). Second, in subrogation cases the insurance carrier is sometimes the "real party in interest." That is true in some states and the federal system, which consider the carrier to be the real party in interest to the extent of its subrogation rights. (Other states still consider the insured to be the real party in interest, even though recovery goes to the carrier.) Third, a few states (notably Wisconsin and Arkansas) have "direct action" statutes that permit injured claimants formally to name the alleged tortfeasor's insurance carrier as defendant.

Finally, Rule 411 is not "airtight," for it recognizes several situations where the fact of insurance is admissible. Consider the situations mentioned in the Notes below.

NOTES ON EVIDENCE OF INSURANCE COVERAGE

1. Insurance investigators sometimes gather pretrial statements from eye-witnesses, and these may be admissible for impeachment purposes. If a party uses such a statement in this way and the witness contests its accuracy, should the fact that an investigator prepared it be admissible? See Complete Auto Transit v. Wayne Broyles Engineering Corp., 351 F.2d 478, 481-482 (5th Cir. 1965) (yes).

2. Plaintiff sues the alleged owner of a truck for personal injuries suffered when the truck ran into her car. Defendant denies ownership of (and responsibility for) the truck. Should plaintiff be permitted to show that defendant carried insurance covering the operation of the truck? See Newell v. Harold Shaffer Leasing Co., 489 F.2d 103, 110 (5th Cir. 1974) (yes).

3. Recall Problem 2-F ("My Insurance Will Cover It"). If a person admits fault by suggesting that his insurance will pay the damages, should FRE 411 block receipt of his admission? Compare Reid v. Owens, 93 P.2d 680, 685 (Utah 1939) (reference to insurance admissible in evidence because "freighted with admission") with Cameron v. Columbia Builders, 320 P.2d 251, 254 (Or. 1958) (sever reference to insurance whenever possible).

Six | COMPETENCY OF WITNESSES

A. HISTORICAL NOTE

One of the striking contrasts between the early common law and modern rules of evidence is in the area of competency of witnesses. The common law imposed a number of disabilities that rendered many potential witnesses incompetent to testify in court. Often in fact, the most knowledgeable people could not testify.

Mental incapacity. Those who were insane or mentally impaired were incompetent to be witnesses at common law. "It makes no difference from what cause this defect of understanding may have arisen; nor whether it be temporary and curable, or permanent; whether the party be hopelessly an idiot or maniac, or only occasionally insane, as a lunatic. . . . While the deficiency of understanding exists, be the cause of what nature soever, the person is not admissible to be sworn as a witness." S. Greenleaf, Evidence §365 (1883).

Religious belief. At common law, belief in a deity who would punish false swearing, either in this life or the hereafter, was an essential component of the oath. Belief in a Christian faith was not required, and members of most major religions were regarded as competent to take such an oath. But atheists, agnostics, and members of certain sects could not satisfy this religious test and were disqualified as witnesses. This disqualification has been repudiated everywhere, and affirmations are now allowed as an alternative to the oath. This ground of incompetency is expressly prohibited by a number of state constitutions. See, e.g., Cal. Const. 1879, art. I, 14 (nobody is "incompetent to be a witness or juror" on account of "opinions on matters of religious belief").

Criminal conviction. A principle of law extending back to Greek and Roman times held that persons convicted of certain "infamous" crimes were rendered "civilly dead." They could not vote, hold office, serve on a jury, or exercise similar rights of citizenship. One aspect of "civil death" incorporated by the common law was that persons convicted of felonies or crimen falsi were disqualified as witnesses. Such persons were viewed as having demonstrated such disregard for morality and the laws of society that any testimony they might give could not be trusted. This ground of incompetency has been abolished by statute in England and virtually all states. A few state statutes still make a person convicted of perjury incompetent to testify.

Infancy. The common law was much more strict than modern evidence law in disqualifying children as witnesses. The issue was generally approached as a disputable presumption of incompetency, in contrast to criminal law doctrines that conclusively presumed that children below a certain age were incapable of committing a crime. In evaluating the competency of child witnesses, courts tended to focus more on their ability to understand the oath than on their capacities of perception and recollection. Wigmore comments:

> In the earlier common-law precedents, . . . the paramount question has been the eligibility of children to take the oath; and the religious sense required for this has usually been the sole subject of argument, to the neglect of the question whether, independently of the oath, any particular degree of intelligence is necessary as a purely testimonial element.

2 J. Wigmore, Evidence §505 at 711 (J. Chadbourn ed. 1979).

Parties. The general rule of the common law was that a party could not be a witness for himself or a coparty in the case. According to an early treatise writer,

> This rule of the common law is founded, not solely in the consideration of interest, but partly also in the general expediency of avoiding the multiplication of temptations to perjury. In some cases at law, and generally by the course of proceedings in equity, one party may appeal to the conscience of the other, by calling him to answer interrogatories upon oath. . . . But where the party would volunteer his own oath, or a co-suitor, identified in interest with him, would offer it, this reason for the admission of the evidence totally fails: "and it is not to be presumed that a man, who complains without cause, or defends without justice, should have honesty enough to confess it."

S. Greenleaf, Evidence §329 (1892).

This ground of incompetency has today been abandoned by all jurisdictions.

Spouses of parties. At one time, a spouse was considered incompetent to testify either for or against the other, although an exception was developed for testimony pertaining to offenses against the family. The rationale for barring favorable testimony was that it was likely to be biased by interest and affection. The rationale for barring adverse testimony was to prevent marital discord and to preserve the unity of the family. Also a husband and wife were viewed as one by the common law. Today a spouse is no longer incompetent to give favorable testimony, and the rules on adverse spousal testimony have been narrowed and incorporated into a spousal testimonial privilege (see Chapter 12, infra). Usually the privilege is recognized only in criminal cases, and often the holder is the *witness* rather than the defendant (meaning that he cannot block testimony by a spouse who is willing to give it).

Accomplices. The common law barred the testimony of accomplices either for or against a criminal defendant if they were parties of record to the same charge. This disability continued in a number of states until the mid-twentieth century. Finally, in Washington v. Texas, 388 U.S. 14 (1967), the United States

Supreme Court declared the practice of barring accomplices from testifying for each other to be unconstitutional.

Other interested persons. As an extension of the disability of parties, spouses of parties, and accomplices, the common law also disqualified as a witness any other person having a direct interest in the litigation. Here is an early statement of the justification:

> It is founded on the known infirmities of human nature, which is too weak to be generally restrained by religious or moral obligations, when tempted and solicited in a contrary direction by temporal interests. There are, no doubt, many whom no interests could seduce from a sense of duty, and their exclusion by the operation of this rule may in particular cases shut out the truth. But the law must prescribe general rules; and experience proves that more mischief would result from the general reception of interested witnesses than is occasioned by their general exclusion.

T. Starkie, Evidence 83 (1824). This disqualification is now virtually obsolete in all jurisdictions, with the exception of the continuing existence of state Dead Man's Statutes (discussed in Section F of this chapter).

NOTES ON HISTORICAL GROUNDS OF INCOMPETENCY

1. Do you agree with the modern view generally rejecting the grounds of incompetency described above? To what extent should it be an objective of evidence law to ensure trustworthy testimony? Is there any relationship between competency standards and the extent of perjury in the courtroom?

2. Even though these old grounds of incompetency have been repudiated, most remain available for another purpose under modern evidence law. See FRE 609 (convictions may be used to impeach credibility). But see FRE 610 (religious beliefs may *not* be used to impeach credibility).

B. COMPETENCY: THE MODERN VIEW

UNITED STATES v. LIGHTLY
United States Court of Appeals for the Fourth Circuit
677 F.2d 1027 (1982)

ERVIN, J.

On December 19, 1979, Terrance McKinley, an inmate at Lorton Reformatory in northern Virginia, sustained serious stab wounds from an assault in his cell. Two of McKinley's fellow inmates, Randy Lightly and Clifton McDuffie, were investigated, but only Lightly was formally charged. McDuffie was not indicted by the grand jury because a court appointed psychiatrist found him incompetent to stand trial and criminally insane at the time of the offense. He is presently confined in a mental hospital.

On May 22, 1980, Lightly was convicted of assault with intent to commit murder, and sentenced to ten years imprisonment to run consecutively with the sentence he already was serving. Lightly had also been charged with conspiracy to commit murder, but this charge was dropped.

At trial two different accounts of the stabbing developed. The government's case included testimony from the victim, Terrance McKinley, inmates Harvey Boyd and Robert Thomas, and McKinley's treating physician, Dr. Lance Weaver, which indicated that McDuffie and Lightly cornered McKinley in his cell and repeatedly stabbed him with half pairs of scissors. Lightly received a severe cut on his hand in the assault. Lightly's account of the stabbing was that he was walking along cell block three when he saw McDuffie and McKinley fighting in McKinley's cell. Lightly said he went into the cell to stop the fight and while he was pulling McDuffie off of McKinley, McDuffie turned around and cut him. His testimony was corroborated by three other inmates.

The defense also attempted to have McDuffie testify. McDuffie would have testified that only he and not Lightly had assaulted McKinley. The court ruled McDuffie incompetent to testify because he had been found to be criminally insane and incompetent to stand trial, and was subject to hallucinations.[1] We believe this was error and that Lightly is entitled to a new trial.

Every witness is presumed competent to testify, FRE 601, unless it can be shown that the witness does not have personal knowledge of the matters about which he is to testify, that he does not have the capacity to recall, or that he does not understand the duty to testify truthfully. This Rule applies to persons considered to be insane to the same extent that it applies to other persons. In this case, the testimony of McDuffie's treating physician indicated that McDuffie had a sufficient memory, that he understood the oath, and that he could communicate what he saw. The district judge chose not to conduct an in camera examination of McDuffie. On this record, it was clearly improper for the court to disqualify McDuffie from testifying. . . .

McDuffie's potential testimony would have substantially corroborated Lightly's testimony. His disqualification from testifying, therefore, cannot be considered harmless error. In finding Lightly entitled to a new trial on this ground, we decline to rule on the other issues he raised in this appeal.

Reversed and remanded.

NOTES ON THE MODERN VIEW OF COMPETENCY

1. Would this case have been decided differently if McDuffie's treating physician had not testified?

2. When the mental capacity of a proposed witness is questioned, does the trial judge have authority to order a psychiatric examination? See United States v. Gutman, 725 F.2d 417, 420 (7th Cir.), cert. denied, 469 U.S. 860 (1984)

---

1. McDuffie believed that "Star Child" told him to kill McKinley because McKinley and Hodge, who apparently was a prison administrator, were going to kill him.

(court "has the power, and in an appropriate case the duty, to hold a hearing to determine whether a witness should not be allowed to testify because insanity has made him incapable of testifying" competently). But see United States v. Raineri, 670 F.2d 702, 709 (7th Cir.), cert. denied, 459 U.S. 1035 (1982) (court "must consider the infringement on a witness's privacy, the opportunity for harassment, and the possibility that an examination will hamper law enforcement by deterring witnesses").

3. The ACN to FRE 601 states that "[a] witness wholly without [mental] capacity is difficult to imagine." Can you imagine such a witness? In extreme cases of insanity or mental incapacity, could the witness's testimony be excluded under other Rules, such as FRE 401, 403, 602, or 611(a)?

4. What if the witness is shown to be a drug addict or an alcoholic? See United States v. Jackson, 576 F.2d 46 (5th Cir. 1978) (fact that witness is a narcotics user goes not to his competency but to his credibility). What if the witness is under the influence of drugs or alcohol while testifying? See United States v. Van Meerbeke, 548 F.2d 415 (2d Cir.) (witness found competent who, while on the stand, consumed opium taken from a trial exhibit), cert. denied, 430 U.S. 974 (1976).

C. THE OATH REQUIREMENT

UNITED STATES v. FOWLER
United States Court of Appeals for the Fifth Circuit
605 F.2d 181 (1979)

GEE, J.

This cause provides eloquent testimony, albeit negative, to the value of counsel's assistance to criminal defendants. Appellant Fowler, a dealer in gravestones and an apparent tax protester among other things, ceased filing federal income tax returns in 1953. A wheel that did not squeak, Fowler's practices at last attracted Revenue's notice in time to result in his indictment for willful failure to file returns for the years 1971-75. During the investigation, he cooperated with investigating revenue agents no further than by providing them with partial records for the years in question. A trial at which the government employed the "bank-deposits" mode of proof resulted in his conviction on all counts, and he appeals.

Fowler, who conducted his own defense at trial but is represented by counsel here, advances seven points of error. Six present little of merit and may be dealt with rather briefly, but the seventh is of slight difficulty. Upon a careful consideration of all, however, we affirm his convictions. We treat his contentions in the order in which he presents them. . . .

Fowler next complains that the court erred in refusing to allow him to testify after he refused either to swear or affirm that he would tell the truth or submit to cross-examination. At one point in their extended colloquy on the point, the judge offered to accept the simple statement, "I state that I will tell the truth in my testimony." Fowler was willing to do no more than laud himself in such remarks as, "I am a truthful man," and "I would not tell a lie to stay out of jail." Rule 603, Federal Rules of Evidence, is clear and simple: "Before testifying, every witness shall be required to declare that he will testify truthfully, by oath or affirmation . . ." No witness has the right to testify but on penalty of perjury and subject to cross-examination. This contention is frivolous. . . .

We cannot doubt that Fowler has derived substantial financial benefit from a long refusal to carry his share of the common burdens of citizenship. Sad to say, for he is a man no longer young, he must now respond not only in currency but in another coin: incarceration. Counsel's efforts on his behalf are commendable, but they came too late.

Affirmed.

NOTES ON THE OATH REQUIREMENT

1. What if a witness under subpoena refuses to be sworn? If refusal to testify may be punished as contempt, may refusal to take an oath or affirmation also be punished? See Note, A Reconsideration of the Sworn Testimony Requirement: Securing Truth in the Twentieth Century, 75 Mich. L. Rev. 1681, 1698 n.89 (1977) (collecting state and foreign cases holding refusal to be sworn to be contempt of court).

2. An affirmation differs from an oath by eliminating reference to swearing and to divine power. The words and ceremony that must be used in administering an oath or affirmation are not specified by FRE 603 or by most state rules on the subject. It has been held that neither raising the hand nor using the word "solemn" is required. Flexibility in the wording of oaths or affirmations is often mandated by state constitutional provisions that prohibit religious tests for witnesses. With respect to the flexibility that should be allowed, see United States v. Looper, 419 F.2d 1405, 1407 n.4 (4th Cir. 1969) (English courts "have permitted Chinese to break a saucer, a Mohammedan to bow before the Koran and touch it to his head and a Parsee to tie a rope around his waist to qualify them to tell the truth").

3. One purpose of the oath is to impress on the mind of the witness a duty to speak only the truth. A less obvious purpose is to make him amenable to criminal prosecution if perjured testimony is given. Given their possible criminal liability, should witnesses be warned of the penalties for perjury before beginning their testimony? See United States v. Mandujano, 425 U.S. 564 (1976) (no requirement to warn witness not to commit perjury or to tell the truth, once he has been sworn). Consider Oregon Rule of Evidence 603(2) (suggesting but not requiring the following form of oath: "Under penalty of perjury, do you solemnly swear that the evidence you shall give in the issue (or matter) now pending between _____ and _____ shall be the truth, the whole truth and nothing but the truth, so help you God?").

4. Are there other factors, apart from the words in an oath or affirmation, that may have even greater effect in impressing on a witness the duty to tell the truth?

5. The typical oath or affirmation requires the witness to tell the "whole" truth. From what you have learned thus far in the course, do you think that

witnesses are being asked to make a commitment that they may not be allowed to fulfill?

D.   THE CHILD WITNESS

> **RICKETTS v. DELAWARE**
> **Delaware Supreme Court**
> **488 A.2d 856 (1985)**

MOORE, J.

This is an appeal from a conviction of first degree rape of a five year old girl. The sole issue is whether the trial court committed reversible error in allowing the minor victim, then six years old, to testify without an adequate foundation to determine her competency as a witness. We find that under Rules 601 and 603 of the Delaware Rules of Evidence, the trial court did not err in permitting the child to testify. Accordingly, we affirm.

The defendant, Darrell Ricketts was indicted, tried and convicted on one count of first degree rape of a five year old girl. The child was the daughter of a woman the defendant was dating. At a bench trial, the victim, then six years old, testified with the use of anatomically correct dolls and drawings that Ricketts had anally raped her while her mother slept in an adjacent room.

Before testifying, a voir dire examination was conducted during which the child stated that she went to church, that a lie was a thing that is not true, and that it was a bad thing to tell a lie. She testified further that if you tell a lie you sometimes get a spanking. She also promised to tell the truth about everything that she was asked in court. However, in response to questions by the defense attorney and the court, the witness indicated that she was not sure what heaven was.

The court ruled that the child was competent to testify because, although she did not understand the concept of perjury, she knew the difference between truth and falsehood, which was the only test of competency.

The sole issue is whether the trial court erred in permitting the six year old to testify. A determination by the trial court that a witness is competent to testify pursuant to DRE 601 and 603 will be reversed only if the determination was an abuse of the trial judge's discretion. Thompson v. State, 399 A.2d 194, 198-99 (Del. Supr. 1979).

Under DRE 601 "[e]very person is competent to be a witness except as otherwise provided in these rules."[1] The Advisory Committee's Note[2] to the Federal Rules of Evidence makes the following observations about Rule 601:

---

1.   The only rules specifically providing for the disqualification of a witness are those precluding the presiding judge or a member of the jury from testifying in the trial in which they are sitting. DRE 605, 606.

2.   As the comment to DRE 601 points out, this rule tracks URE 601 and the first sentence of FRE 601. The Delaware Study Committee, which drafted the DRE has stated that the historical materials surrounding the promulgation of the Federal Rules and the FRE official notes and comments, "should be considered as being part of the comments prepared by the Delaware Study

[n]o mental or moral qualifications for testifying as a witness are specified. . . . Discretion is regularly exercised in favor of allowing the testimony. A witness wholly without capacity is difficult to imagine. The question is one particularly suited to the jury as one of weight and credibility, subject to judicial authority to review the sufficiency of the evidence.

ACN to FRE 601.

Thus, Rule 601 adopts the position that almost anyone is competent to testify, letting the concerns of mental or moral capacity go to the issues of credibility or weight given to the evidence.

Accordingly, under the Delaware Rules of Evidence the six year old rape victim is presumed competent to testify once the trial judge is satisfied by voir dire that the child understood her obligation to tell the truth, and the difference between truth and falsehood.

The defendant further argues that the child should not have been permitted to testify in this case because the voir dire examination demonstrated that she did not understand the oath. DRE 603 provides that "[b]efore testifying, every witness shall be required to declare that he will testify truthfully, by oath or affirmation administered in a form calculated to awaken his conscience and impress his mind with his duty to do so." DRE 603. We once again turn to the Federal Rules of Evidence Advisory Committee's Note, which states: "[t]he rule is designed to afford the flexibility required in dealing with . . . children."

Here, the child testified that she promised not to tell a lie and to tell the truth about everything that was asked of her in court. The trial court was correct in concluding that this was a sufficient affirmation that she would testify truthfully.

Therefore, we conclude that this six year old was properly found to be competent to testify, and that her promise to "tell the truth" was an affirmation sufficient to impress on her mind her duty to be truthful as required by DRE 603.[3]

NOTES ON CHILDREN AS WITNESSES

1. Is a voir dire examination of a child witness always necessary? On what authority? What questions should be asked of the child at such an examination?
2. A number of states do not follow the "presumption of competency" approach of FRE 601 and continue to presume incompetency of children below a certain age. See, e.g., N.Y. Crim. Proc. Law §60.20 (Consol. 1979) (12 years).
3. What if a child satisfies the competency requirement, but because of her age and the subject of her expected testimony the experience of testifying

---

Committee and a court should refer to these materials in construing these rules." DRE, Delaware Study Committee Prefatory Note.

3. Because all witnesses (except those specifically excluded by the rules) are competent to testify under DRE 601, we note it is no longer necessary to go through the guidelines for determining competency of a child witness set forth in Kelluem v. State, 396 A.2d 166, 168 (Del. Super. 1978).

would be traumatic? Should the child be forced to testify? Does it depend on other factors? Who should make the decision?

4.   Could a child be found competent for purposes of direct examination but of insufficient maturity to withstand cross-examination? Could the testimony of such a child be admitted? In criminal cases, is the determination of competency partly a constitutional matter that requires the trial judge to consider the defendant's right to confront and cross-examine adverse witnesses?

5.   Sometimes courts overlook competency issues or deliberately override objections on that ground when out-of-court statements by children are offered pursuant to a hearsay exception. See, e.g., United States v. Nick, 604 F.2d 1199 (9th Cir. 1979) (excited utterance); People v. Wilkins, 349 N.W.2d 815 (Mich. App. 1984) (statement for medical diagnosis). Many states have created a new hearsay exception for statements of a child sex crime victim. See generally Comment, A Comprehensive Approach to Child Hearsay Statements in Sex Abuse Cases, 83 Colum. L. Rev. 1745 (1983). Should the hearsay statement of a child be received if the child would not be competent to testify?

6.   States are experimenting with procedures in sexual abuse prosecutions to facilitate the testimony of child witnesses and reduce the trauma of testifying. These innovations include use of interdisciplinary teams from law enforcement and social services agencies, appointment of a special advocate to provide support for the child before and during trial, and assignment of the same prosecutor to all stages of the case. See Bulkley, Background and Overview of Child Sexual Abuse: Law Reforms in the Mid-1980's, 40 U. Miami L. Rev. 5, 9 (1985). Some states authorize presentation of the child's testimony by closed-circuit television or videotaped deposition. However, a "case specific" finding that such a procedure is necessary to protect the welfare of the child is constitutionally required in order to override the defendant's right to face his accuser. See Maryland v. Craig, 497 U.S. 836 (1990). See generally Graham, Indicia of Reliability and Face to Face Confrontation: Emerging Issues in Child Sexual Abuse Prosecutions, 40 U. Miami L. Rev. 19 (1985). Anatomical dolls are being used with increasing frequency to assist children to overcome verbal inhibitions in describing sexual activity.

E.   PREVIOUSLY HYPNOTIZED WITNESSES

ROCK v. ARKANSAS
United States Supreme Court
483 U.S. 44 (1987)

JUSTICE BLACKMUN delivered the opinion of the Court.

The issue presented in this case is whether Arkansas' evidentiary rule prohibiting the admission of hypnotically refreshed testimony violated petitioner's constitutional right to testify on her own behalf as a defendant in a criminal case.

Petitioner Vickie Lorene Rock was charged with manslaughter in the death of her husband, Frank Rock, on July 1, 1983. A dispute had been simmering about Frank's wish to move from the couple's small apartment adjacent to Vickie's beauty parlor to a trailer she owned outside town. That night a fight erupted when Frank refused to let petitioner eat some pizza and prevented her from leaving the apartment to get something else to eat. When police arrived on the scene they found Frank on the floor with a bullet wound in his chest. Petitioner urged the officers to help her husband, and cried to a sergeant who took her in charge, "please save him" and "don't let him die." The police removed her from the building because she was upset and because she interfered with their investigation by her repeated attempts to use the telephone to call her husband's parents. According to the testimony of one of the investigating officers, petitioner told him that "she stood up to leave the room and [her husband] grabbed her by the throat and choked her and threw her against the wall and . . . at that time she walked over and picked up the weapon and pointed it toward the floor and he hit her again and she shot him."

Because petitioner could not remember the precise details of the shooting, her attorney suggested that she submit to hypnosis in order to refresh her memory. Petitioner was hypnotized twice by Doctor Betty Back, a licensed neuropsychologist with training in the field of hypnosis. Doctor Back interviewed petitioner for an hour prior to the first hypnosis session, taking notes on petitioner's general history and her recollections of the shooting. Both hypnosis sessions were recorded on tape. Petitioner did not relate any new information during either of the sessions, but, after the hypnosis, she was able to remember that at the time of the incident she had her thumb on the hammer of the gun, but had not held her finger on the trigger. She also recalled that the gun had discharged when her husband grabbed her arm during the scuffle. As a result of the details that petitioner was able to remember about the shooting, her counsel arranged for a gun expert to examine the handgun, a single action Hawes .22 Deputy Marshal. That inspection revealed that the gun was defective and prone to fire, when hit or dropped, without the trigger's being pulled.

When the prosecutor learned of the hypnosis sessions, he filed a motion to exclude petitioner's testimony. The trial judge held a pretrial hearing on the motion and concluded that no hypnotically refreshed testimony would be admitted. The court issued an order limiting petitioner's testimony to "matters remembered and stated to the examiner prior to being placed under hypnosis." At trial, petitioner introduced testimony by the gun expert, but the court limited petitioner's own description of the events on the day of the shooting to a reiteration of the sketchy information in Doctor Back's notes. The jury convicted petitioner on the manslaughter charge and she was sentenced to 10 years imprisonment and a $10,000 fine.

On appeal, the Supreme Court of Arkansas rejected petitioner's claim that the limitations on her testimony violated her right to present her defense. The court concluded that "the dangers of admitting this kind of testimony outweigh whatever probative value it may have," and decided to follow the approach of States that have held hypnotically refreshed testimony of witnesses inadmissible per se. Although the court acknowledged that "a defendant's right to testify is fundamental," it ruled that the exclusion of petitioner's testimony did not violate her constitutional rights. Any "prejudice or deprivation" she suffered "was minimal and resulted from her own actions and not by any erroneous ruling of the court." We granted certiorari, to consider the constitutionality of Arkansas' per se rule excluding a criminal defendant's hypnotically refreshed testimony.

Petitioner's claim that her testimony was impermissibly excluded is bottomed on her constitutional right to testify in her own defense. At this point in the development of our adversary system, it cannot be doubted that a defendant in a criminal case has the right to take the witness stand and to testify in his or her own defense. . . .

The question now before the Court is whether a criminal defendant's right to testify may be restricted by a state rule that excludes her post-hypnosis testimony. This is not the first time this Court has faced a constitutional challenge to a state rule, designed to ensure trustworthy evidence, that interfered with the ability of a defendant to offer testimony. In Washington v. Texas, 388 U.S. 14 (1967), the Court was confronted with a state statute that prevented persons charged as principals, accomplices, or accessories in the same crime from being introduced as witnesses for one another. . . . [T]he Court found that the mere presence of the witness in the courtroom was not enough to satisfy the Constitution's Compulsory Process Clause. By preventing the defendant from having the benefit of his accomplice's testimony, "the State *arbitrarily* denied him the right to put on the stand a witness who was physically and mentally capable of testifying to events that he had personally observed, and whose testimony would have been relevant and material to the defense." (Emphasis added.)

Just as a State may not apply an arbitrary rule of competence to exclude a material defense witness from taking the stand, it also may not apply a rule of evidence that permits a witness to take the stand, but arbitrarily excludes material portions of his testimony. In Chambers v. Mississippi, 410 U.S. 284 (1973), the Court invalidated a State's hearsay rule on the ground that it abridged the defendant's right to "present witnesses in his own defense." Chambers was tried for a murder to which another person repeatedly had confessed in the presence of acquaintances. The State's hearsay rule, coupled with a "voucher" rule that did not allow the defendant to cross-examine the confessed murderer directly, prevented Chambers from introducing testimony concerning these confessions, which were critical to his defense. This Court reversed the judgment of conviction, holding that when a state rule of evidence conflicts with the right to present witnesses, the rule may "not be applied mechanistically to defeat the ends of justice," but must meet the fundamental standards of due process. In the Court's view, the State in *Chambers* did not demonstrate that the hearsay testimony in that case, which bore "assurances of trustworthiness" including corroboration by other evidence, would be unreliable, and thus the defendant should have been able to introduce the exculpatory testimony.

Of course, the right to present relevant testimony is not without limitation. The right may, in appropriate cases, bow to accommodate other legitimate interests in the criminal trial process.[11] But restrictions of a defendant's right

---

11.   Numerous state procedural and evidentiary rules control the presentation of evidence and do not offend the defendant's right to testify. See, e.g., Chambers v. Mississippi, 410 U.S. 284,

to testify may not be arbitrary or disproportionate to the purposes they are designed to serve. In applying its evidentiary rules a State must evaluate whether the interests served by a rule justify the limitation imposed on the defendant's constitutional right to testify.

The Arkansas rule enunciated by the state courts does not allow a trial court to consider whether posthypnosis testimony may be admissible in a particular case; it is a per se rule prohibiting the admission at trial of any defendant's hypnotically refreshed testimony on the ground that such testimony is always unreliable. Thus, in Arkansas, an accused's testimony is limited to matters that he or she can prove were remembered *before* hypnosis. This rule operates to the detriment of any defendant who undergoes hypnosis, without regard to the reasons for it, the circumstances under which it took place, or any independent verification of the information it produced.

In this case, the application of that rule had a significant adverse effect on petitioner's ability to testify. It virtually prevented her from describing any of the events that occurred on the day of the shooting, despite corroboration of many of those events by other witnesses. Even more importantly, under the court's rule petitioner was not permitted to describe the actual shooting except in the words contained in Doctor Back's notes. The expert's description of the gun's tendency to misfire would have taken on greater significance if the jury had heard petitioner testify that she did not have her finger on the trigger and that the gun went off when her husband hit her arm.

In establishing its per se rule, the Arkansas Supreme Court simply followed the approach taken by a number of States that have decided that hypnotically enhanced testimony should be excluded at trial on the ground that it tends to be unreliable. Other States that have adopted an exclusionary rule, however, have done so for the testimony of *witnesses,* not for the testimony of a *defendant.* The Arkansas Supreme Court failed to perform the constitutional analysis that is necessary when a defendant's right to testify is at stake.

Although the Arkansas court concluded that any testimony that cannot be proved to be the product of prehypnosis memory is unreliable, many courts have eschewed a per se rule and permit the admission of hypnotically refreshed testimony. Hypnosis by trained physicians or psychologists has been recognized as a valid therapeutic technique since 1958, although there is no generally accepted theory to explain the phenomenon, or even a consensus on a single definition of hypnosis. See Council on Scientific Affairs, Scientific Status of Refreshing Recollection by the Use of Hypnosis, 253 J.A.M.A. 1918, 1918-1919 (1985) (Council Report).[17] The use of hypnosis in criminal investigations, how-

---

302 (1973) ("In the exercise of this right, the accused, as is required of the State, must comply with established rules of procedure and evidence designed to assure both fairness and reliability in the ascertainment of guilt and innocence"); Washington v. Texas, 388 U.S. 14, 23 n.21 (1967) (opinion should not be construed as disapproving testimonial privileges or nonarbitrary rules that disqualify those incapable of observing events due to mental infirmity or infancy from being witnesses).

17.   Hypnosis has been described as "involving the focusing of attention; increased responsiveness to suggestions; suspension of disbelief with a lowering of critical judgment; potential for altering perception, motor control, or memory in response to suggestions; and the subjective experience of responding involuntarily." Council Report, 253 J.A.M.A. at 1919.

ever, is controversial, and the current medical and legal view of its appropriate role is unsettled.

Responses of individuals to hypnosis vary greatly. The popular belief that hypnosis guarantees the accuracy of recall is as yet without established foundation and, in fact, hypnosis often has no effect at all on memory. The most common response to hypnosis, however, appears to be an increase in both correct and incorrect recollections.[18] Three general characteristics of hypnosis may lead to the introduction of inaccurate memories: the subject becomes "suggestible" and may try to please the hypnotist with answers the subject thinks will be met with approval; the subject is likely to "confabulate," that is, to fill in details from the imagination in order to make an answer more coherent and complete; and, the subject experiences "memory hardening," which gives him great confidence in both true and false memories, making effective cross-examination more difficult. Despite the unreliability that hypnosis concededly may introduce, however, the procedure has been credited as instrumental in obtaining investigative leads or identifications that were later confirmed by independent evidence.

The inaccuracies the process introduces can be reduced, although perhaps not eliminated, by the use of procedural safeguards. One set of suggested guidelines calls for hypnosis to be performed only by a psychologist or psychiatrist with special training in its use and who is independent of the investigation. See Orne, The Use and Misuse of Hypnosis in Court, 27 Intl. J. Clinical & Experimental Hypnosis 311, 335-336 (1979). These procedures reduce the possibility that biases will be communicated to the hypersuggestive subject by the hypnotist. Suggestion will be less likely also if the hypnosis is conducted in a neutral setting with no one present but the hypnotist and the subject. Tape or video recording of all interrogations, before, during, and after hypnosis, can help reveal if leading questions were asked. Such guidelines do not guarantee the accuracy of the testimony, because they cannot control the subject's own motivations or any tendency to confabulate, but they do provide a means of controlling overt suggestions.

The more traditional means of assessing accuracy of testimony also remain applicable in the case of a previously hypnotized defendant. Certain information recalled as a result of hypnosis may be verified as highly accurate by corroborating evidence. Cross-examination, even in the face of a confident defendant, is an effective tool for revealing inconsistencies. Moreover, a jury can be educated to the risks of hypnosis through expert testimony and cautionary instructions. Indeed, it is probably to a defendant's advantage to establish carefully the extent of his memory prior to hypnosis, in order to minimize the decrease in credibility the procedure might introduce.

We are not now prepared to endorse without qualifications the use of

18.   "When hypnosis is used to refresh recollection, one of the following outcomes occurs: (1) hypnosis produces recollections that are not substantially different from nonhypnotic recollections; (2) it yields recollections that are more inaccurate than nonhypnotic memory; or, most frequently, (3) it results in more information being reported, but these recollections contain both accurate and inaccurate details. . . . There are no data to support a fourth alternative, namely, that hypnosis increases remembering of only accurate information." [Court cites Council Report, supra.]

hypnosis as an investigative tool; scientific understanding of the phenomenon and of the means to control the effects of hypnosis is still in its infancy. Arkansas, however, has not justified the exclusion of *all* of a defendant's testimony that the defendant is unable to prove to be the product of prehypnosis memory. A State's legitimate interest in barring unreliable evidence does not extend to per se exclusions that may be reliable in an individual case. Wholesale inadmissibility of a defendant's testimony is an arbitrary restriction on the right to testify in the absence of clear evidence by the State repudiating the validity of all posthypnosis recollections. The State would be well within its powers if it established guidelines to aid trial courts in the evaluation of posthypnosis testimony and it may be able to show that testimony in a particular case is so unreliable that exclusion is justified. But it has not shown that hypnotically enhanced testimony is always so untrustworthy and so immune to the traditional means of evaluating credibility that it should disable a defendant from presenting her version of the events for which she is on trial.

In this case, the defective condition of the gun corroborated the details petitioner remembered about the shooting. The tape recordings provided some means to evaluate the hypnosis and the trial judge concluded that Doctor Back did not suggest responses with leading questions. Those circumstances present an argument for admissibility of petitioner's testimony in this particular case, an argument that must be considered by the trial court. Arkansas' per se rule excluding all posthypnosis testimony infringes impermissibly on the right of a defendant to testify on his or her own behalf.

[The dissenting opinion of CHIEF JUSTICE REHNQUIST, joined by three other Justices, is omitted.]

NOTES ON HYPNOSIS IN THE COURTROOM

1. Is *Rock* limited to criminal defendants, or does it also bar a per se rule excluding testimony by defense witnesses whose memory has been hypnotically refreshed? What about prosecution witnesses? What about witnesses in a civil case?

2. What are the dangers of hypnotically refreshed testimony that most concern courts and legislatures? The problem of "confabulation" has been described as follows:

> The hypnotic suggestion to relive a past event, particularly when accompanied by questions about specific details, puts pressure on the subject to provide information for which few, if any, actual memories are available. This situation may jog the subject's memory and produce some increased recall, but it will also cause him to fill in details that are plausible but consist of memories or fantasies from other times. It is extremely difficult to know which aspects of hypnotically aided recall are historically accurate and which aspects have been confabulated.

Orne, The Use and Misuse of Hypnosis in Court, 27 Intl. J. Clinical & Experimental Hypnosis 311, 317-318 (1979).

3. As the Court observes in *Rock,* many states besides Arkansas also have a per se rule barring the admission of hypnotically refreshed testimony, although not necessarily that of criminal defendants. See, e.g., Contreras v. State, 718

P.2d 129 (Alaska 1986); State ex rel. Collins v. Superior Court, 644 P.2d 1266, 1293-1294 (Ariz. 1982); Bundy v. State, 471 So. 2d 9, 18-19 (Fla. 1985), cert. denied, 479 U.S. 894 (1986); Commonwealth v. Nazarovitch, 436 A.2d 170, 177 (Pa. 1981); State v. Martin, 684 P.2d 651 (Wash. 1984). Some of these jurisdictions hold that hypnosis fails to satisfy the general standard for the admissibility of scientific evidence established in Frye v. United States, 293 F. 1013 (D.C. Cir. 1923), because the use of hypnosis to enhance memory is not generally accepted as reliable by the scientific community.

4.   Some jurisdictions take the opposite view, and have adopted a per se rule of admissibility for hypnotically refreshed testimony, holding that the fact of hypnosis affects only credibility, not admissibility. See, e.g., Beck v. Norris, 801 F.2d 242, 244-245 (6th Cir. 1986); United States v. Awkard, 597 F.2d 667, 669 (9th Cir.), cert. denied, 444 U.S. 885 (1979); State v. Wren, 425 So. 2d 756 (La. 1983); State v. Brown, 337 N.W.2d 138, 151 (N.D. 1983); State v. Glebock, 616 S.W.2d 897, 903-904 (Tenn. Crim. App. 1981). In these jurisdictions, parties are often allowed to offer expert testimony on the reliability of hypnotically refreshed testimony and to request cautionary instructions to the jury that will enable the jury to assess the proper weight to be given to the evidence.

5.   Some courts balance the probative value of the evidence against its prejudicial effect on a case-by-case basis. See, e.g., McQueen v. Garrison, 814 F.2d 951, 958 (4th Cir. 1987); Wicker v. McCotten, 783 F.2d 487, 492-493 (5th Cir.), cert. denied, 478 U.S. 1010 (1986); State v. Iwakiri, 682 P.2d 571, 578 (Idaho 1984) (weigh "totality of circumstances").

6.   Finally, some courts will admit hypnotically refreshed testimony, provided proper procedural safeguards were followed. See Sprynczynatyk v. General Motors, 771 F.2d 1112 (8th Cir. 1985), cert. denied, 475 U.S. 1046 (1986):

> We adopt a rule which requires the district court, in cases where hypnosis has been used, to conduct pretrial hearings on the procedures used during the hypnotic session in question and assess the effect of hypnosis upon the reliability of the testimony before making a decision on admissibility. The proponent of the hypnotically enhanced testimony bears the burden of proof during this proceeding.

In making the determination whether the hypnotically refreshed testimony is sufficiently reliable, the *Sprynczynatyk* court instructed trial judges to consider the following safeguards:

> (1) The hypnotic session should be conducted by an impartial licensed psychiatrist or psychologist trained in the use of hypnosis and thus aware of its possible effects on memory so as to aid in the prevention of improper suggestions and confabulation. Appointment of the psychiatrist or psychologist should first be approved by the trial court. . . . (2) Information given to the hypnotist by either party concerning the case should be noted, preferably in written form, so that the extent of information the subject received from the hypnotist may be determined. (3) Before hypnosis, the hypnotist should obtain a detailed description of the facts from the subject, avoiding adding new elements to the subject's description. (4) The session should be recorded so a permanent record is available to ensure against suggestive procedures. Videotape is a preferable method of recordation. (5) Preferably, only the hypnotist and subject should be present during any phase of the hypnotic session, but other persons should be allowed

to attend if their attendance can be shown to be essential and steps are taken to prevent their influencing the results of the session.

771 F.2d, at 1112 n.14.

7.   For a sampling the law review literature on hypnosis in the courtroom, see Beaver, Memory Restored or Confabulated by Hypnosis—Is It Competent?, 6 U. Puget Sound L. Rev. 155 (1983); Diamond, Inherent Problems in the Use of Pretrial Hypnosis on a Prospective Witness, 68 Calif. L. Rev. 313 (1980); Falk, Post-Hypnotic Testimony—Witness Competency and the Fulcrum of Procedural Safeguards, 57 St. John's L. Rev. 30 (1982); Mickenberg, Mesmerizing Justice: The Use of Hypnotically Induced Testimony in Criminal Trials, 34 Syracuse L. Rev. 927 (1983); Perry, The Trend Toward Exclusion of Hypnotically Refreshed Testimony—Has the Right Question Been Asked?, 31 U. Kan. L. Rev. 579 (1983); Sies and Webster, Judicial Approaches to the Question of Hypnotically Refreshed Testimony: A History and Analysis, 35 DePaul L. Rev. 77 (1985).

F.   DEAD MAN'S STATUTES

When state legislatures repeal statutes rendering a witness incompetent because of interest, there is continuing concern about an interested witness testifying on a transaction with a person now deceased. Not only does the survivor have an incentive to testify falsely, but the death of the other makes it hard to expose or rebut false testimony. As a surviving remnant of incompetency by reason of interest, most states retain what are commonly referred to as Dead Man's Statutes, which limit in differing ways testimony about transactions with deceased persons.

In a number of states, such statutes apply to torts involving the deceased as well as contractual transactions. See, e.g., Zeigler v. Moore, 335 P.2d 425 (Nev. 1959) (survivor may not testify to manner in which automobile collision occurred when the other party is deceased). In their most extreme form, they bar testimony by the survivor on *any* fact occurring prior to the other's death, even facts that could not be personally disputed by the other if she had lived. See, e.g., Topkins v. DeLeon, 595 P.2d 242 (Colo. 1979) (plaintiffs who survived automobile accident barred from testifying regarding their pain and suffering that occurred prior to decedent's death).

Scholars have long criticized the Dead Man's Statute as a crude legislative device that unfairly casts suspicion on all who pursue claims against estates of decedents. Consider this strong criticism by Dean Mason Ladd:

Dead man statutes in different states continue to mystify able courts and good lawyers in their endless complexities of interpretation and application to the ever changing facts requiring proof to establish transactions and communications had with a person since deceased. Statutes vary greatly as do the interpretations of similar statutes. The basic objective of all statutes is the same. Survivors of a deceased person are looked upon with suspicion as persons ready on first opportunity to fabricate false claims against the decedent's estate because the deceased is unable to repudiate them. The right of living claimants to establish honest claims is sacrificed because of the danger that a substantially greater number of the survivors would take advantage of the situation and give perjured testimony for their gain. The existence of the dead man statutes represents the judgment of legislative bodies that the general honesty and truthfulness of people in modern society is at a pretty low ebb and that all it takes is the motive of interest plus a good chance created by death of one of the parties to cause the majority of people to concoct false claims to plunder the estates of deceased persons.

Ladd, The Dead Man Statute: Some Further Observations and a Legislative Proposal, 26 Iowa L. Rev. 207 (1941). See also Coker, Competency of a Defendant to Testify When Sued Under the Wrongful Death Statute, 29 Miss. L.J. 2558 (1958); Ford, Deadman's Statute in Auto Collision Cases, 24 Ala. Law. 138 (1963); Ray, The Dead Man's Statute—A Relic of the Past, 10 Sw. L.J. 390 (1956); Ray, Dead Man's Statutes, 24 Ohio St. L.J. 89 (1963); Stout, Should the Dead Man's Statute Apply to Automobile Collisions?, 38 Tex. L. Rev. 14 (1959).

A few states have repealed their Dead Man's Statute entirely. See, e.g., Ariz. R. Evid. 601; Nev. Rev. Stat. §50.015. Many other states have narrowed the scope of testimony excluded by their statutes or have adopted approaches other than restricting the competency of witnesses. What is your assessment of the following state statutes?

TESTIMONY OF INTERESTED PERSONS
Florida Statutes §90.602
(West, 1999)

(1) No person interested in an action or proceeding against the personal representative, heir at law, assignee, legatee, devisee, or survivor of a deceased person, or against the assignee, committee, or guardian of a mentally incompetent person, shall be examined as a witness regarding any oral communication between the interested person and the person who is deceased or mentally incompetent at the time of the examination.

(2) This section does not apply when:

(a) A personal representative, heir at law, assignee, legatee, devisee, or survivor of a deceased person, or the assignee, committee, or guardian of a mentally incompetent person, is examined on his or her own behalf regarding the oral communication.

(b) Evidence of the subject matter of the oral communication is offered by the personal representative, heir at law, assignee, legatee, devisee, or survivor of a deceased person, or the assignee, committee, or guardian of a mentally incompetent person.

TRANSACTIONS WITH LUNATIC OR DECEDENT; PROOF REQUIRED
New Jersey Statutes Annotated §2A:81-2
(West, 1983)

When 1 party to any civil action is a lunatic suing or defending by guardian or when 1 party sues or is sued in a representative capacity, any other party who asserts a claim or an affirmative defense against such lunatic or representative, supported by oral testimony of a promise, statement or act of the lunatic while of sound mind or of the decedent, shall be required to establish the same by clear and convincing proof.

**STATEMENT OF DECEDENT OFFERED IN ACTION
AGAINST HIS ESTATE
California Evidence Code §1261
(West, 1995)**

(a)   Evidence of a statement is not made inadmissible by the hearsay rule when offered in an action upon a claim or demand against the estate of the declarant if the statement was made upon the personal knowledge of the declarant at a time when the matter had been recently perceived by him and while his recollection was clear.

(b)   Evidence of a statement is inadmissible under this section if the statement was made under circumstances such as to indicate its lack of trustworthiness.

NOTES ON DEAD MAN'S STATUTES

1.   The second sentence of FRE 601 was not included in the Rule as originally promulgated but was added by Congress. Is the second sentence mandated by the *Erie* doctrine? If not, what are the arguments that can be made for and against this policy of deferral to state rules of witness competency, including state Dead Man's Statutes, in cases where state law provides the rule of decision?

2.   Will state rules of competency always control in a diversity or pendant jurisdiction case? What if testimony by a single witness is relevant to both state and federal claims?

3.   Note that the California statute, quoted in the text above, "opens the mouth" of both parties. It permits the survivor to testify (simply because it does not restrict testimony by the survivor), and it does the next best thing for the decedent, which is to create a hearsay exception paving the way to admit much of what he said on the subject while he was alive. The California provision is an obvious attempt to help people with claims against estates, while accommodating the basic policy of protecting estates against fraudulent claims. Since this statute is a substitute for the traditional Dead Man's Statute, should it be viewed as a "State law" governing "competency of a witness" under FRE 601? If not, wouldn't a federal court in California likely *admit* the survivor's testimony and *exclude* many statements by the decedent as hearsay, thus undermining California's modern legislative solution to this problem?

G.   LAWYERS AS WITNESSES

At common law, attorneys were incompetent as witnesses in cases they were trying only if they had a direct pecuniary interest in the subject of the litigation. Although modern cases generally recognize the competency of attorneys to testify in cases where they are acting as counsel, many decisions hold that the judge has discretion to exclude such testimony or to condition it on withdrawal by the attorney from the case.

The problem is that testimony by an attorney who is acting as counsel violates the Code of Professional Responsibility, unless the testimony falls into one of several narrow exceptions. DR 5-101(B) provides:

> A lawyer shall not accept employment in contemplated or pending litigation if he knows or it is obvious that he or a lawyer in his firm ought to be called as a witness, except that he may undertake the employment and he or a lawyer in his firm may testify: (1) If the testimony will relate solely to an uncontested matter. (2) If the testimony will relate solely to a matter of formality and there is no reason to believe that substantial evidence will be offered in opposition to the testimony. (3) If the testimony will relate solely to the nature and value of legal services rendered in the case by the lawyer or his firm to the client. (4) As to any matter, if refusal would work a substantial hardship on the client because of the distinctive value of the lawyer or his firm as counsel in the particular case.

See also DR 5-102(A) (requiring a lawyer to withdraw as counsel when "it is obvious that he or a lawyer in his firm ought to be called as a witness on behalf of his client").

The Code of Professional Responsibility explains the rationale for this ethical proscription as follows:

> Occasionally a lawyer is called upon to decide in a particular case whether he will be a witness or an advocate. If a lawyer is both counsel and witness, he becomes more easily impeachable for interest and thus may be a less effective witness. Conversely, the opposing counsel may be handicapped in challenging the credibility of the lawyer when the lawyer also appears as an advocate in the case. An advocate who becomes a witness is in the unseemly and ineffective position of arguing his own credibility. The roles of an advocate and of a witness are inconsistent; the function of an advocate is to advance or argue the cause of another, while that of a witness is to state facts objectively.

Model Code of Professional Responsibility, EC 5-9 (1980).

NOTES ON LAWYERS AS WITNESSES

1. The ABA Model Rules of Professional Conduct contain a similar proscription. See Rule 3.7, which provides:

> (a) A lawyer shall not act as advocate at a trial in which the lawyer is likely to be a necessary witness except where:
> (1) The testimony relates to an uncontested issue;
> (2) The testimony relates to the nature and value of legal services rendered in the case; or
> (3) Disqualification of the lawyer would work substantial hardship on the client. . . .
> (b) A lawyer may act as advocate in a trial in which another lawyer in the lawyer's firm is likely to be called a witness unless precluded from doing so by Rule 1.7 or Rule 1.9.

Rules 1.7 and 1.9 deal with conflict of interest situations.

2.   It would be a simple matter to codify Disciplinary Rule 5-101(B) or Model Rule of Professional Conduct 3.7 as a ground of incompetency in an evidence code. What are the merits of such an approach?

3.   Sometimes in a trial an attorney seeks to impeach a witness by inquiring about a prior inconsistent statement made to the attorney. What tactical and ethical issues are presented by such attempted impeachment? Is there a way these issues can be satisfactorily resolved?

H. JURORS AS WITNESSES

1. *Preverdict Testimony by Jurors*

The common law did not disqualify a juror from testifying before a jury of which he was a member. There was concern that a juror whose testimony was excluded would simply relate the information to other jurors without cross-examination or impeachment and that it would be preferable to have such sharing of information in open court. Today the issue rarely arises because jurors who might be called as witnesses are usually identified in voir dire and excused from serving. Nonetheless, even where the potential of a juror to be called as a witness has been overlooked, FRE 606(a) prohibits testimony by that juror before the jury panel on which he serves.

PROBLEM 6-A.   *Outside Influence*

In a highly publicized criminal prosecution of Volstad, a leading political figure, the jury is given strict instructions not to read newspaper accounts of the trial or discuss the case with anyone. During the trial, the judge receives information that one juror read newspaper accounts of the trial and discussed those accounts with others at lunch. The judge also hears that an associate of the defendant talked with the same juror outside of court and offered what may have been a bribe. During a recess in trial, after other jurors had been excused, the judge questions the juror about both matters. Does FRE 606(a) bar such inquiry?

2. *Postverdict Testimony By Jurors*

| TANNER v. UNITED STATES
| United States Supreme Court
| 483 U.S. 107 (1987)

JUSTICE O'CONNOR delivered the opinion of the Court.

Petitioners William Conover and Anthony Tanner were convicted of conspiring to defraud the United States in violation of 18 U.S.C. §371, and of committing mail fraud in violation of 18 U.S.C. §1341. The United States Court of Appeals for the Eleventh Circuit affirmed the convictions. Petitioners argue that the District Court erred in refusing to admit juror testimony at a post-verdict hearing on juror intoxication during the trial. . . .

The day before petitioners were scheduled to be sentenced, Tanner filed a motion, in which Conover subsequently joined, seeking continuance of the sentencing date, permission to interview jurors, an evidentiary hearing, and a new trial. According to an affidavit accompanying the motion, Tanner's attorney had received an unsolicited telephone call from one of the trial jurors, Vera Asbul. Juror Asbul informed Tanner's attorney that several of the jurors consumed alcohol during the lunch breaks at various times throughout the trial, causing them to sleep through the afternoons. The District Court continued the sentencing date, ordered the parties to file memoranda, and heard argument on the motion to interview jurors. The District Court concluded that juror testimony on intoxication was inadmissible under FRE 606(b) to impeach the jury's verdict. The District Court invited petitioners to call any nonjuror witnesses, such as courtroom personnel, in support of the motion for new trial. Tanner's counsel took the stand and testified that he had observed one of the jurors "in a sort of giggly mood" at one point during the trial but did not bring this to anyone's attention at the time. . . .

Following the hearing the District Court filed an order stating that "[o]n the basis of the admissible evidence offered I specifically find that the motions for leave to interview jurors or for an evidentiary hearing at which jurors would be witnesses is not required or appropriate." The District Court also denied the motion for new trial.

While the appeal of this case was pending before the Eleventh Circuit, petitioners filed another new trial motion based on additional evidence of jury misconduct. In another affidavit, Tanner's attorney stated that he received an unsolicited visit at his residence from a second juror, Daniel Hardy. Despite the fact that the District Court had denied petitioners' motion for leave to interview jurors, two days after Hardy's visit Tanner's attorney arranged for Hardy to be interviewed by two private investigators. The interview was transcribed, sworn to by the juror, and attached to the new trial motion. In the interview Hardy stated that he "felt like . . . the jury was on one big party." Hardy indicated that seven of the jurors drank alcohol during the noon recess. Four jurors, including Hardy, consumed between them "a pitcher to three pitchers" of beer during various recesses. Of the three other jurors who were alleged to have consumed alcohol, Hardy stated that on several occasions he observed two jurors having one or two mixed drinks during the lunch recess, and one other juror, who was also the foreperson, having a liter of wine on each of three occasions. Juror Hardy also stated that he and three other jurors smoked marijuana quite regularly during the trial. Moreover, Hardy stated that during the trial he observed one juror ingest cocaine five times and another juror ingest cocaine two or three times. One juror sold a quarter pound of marijuana to another juror during the trial, and took marijuana, cocaine and drug paraphernalia into the courthouse. Hardy noted that some of the jurors were falling asleep during the trial, and that one of the jurors described himself to Hardy as "flying." Hardy stated that before he visited Tanner's attorney at his residence, no one had contacted him concerning the jury's conduct, and Hardy had not been offered anything in return for his statement. Hardy said that he came forward "to clear my conscience" and "[b]ecause I felt . . . . that the people on the jury didn't have no business being on the jury. I felt . . . that Mr. Tanner should have a better opportunity to get somebody that would review the facts right."

The District Court, stating that the motions "contain supplemental allegations which differ quantitatively but not qualitatively from those in the April motions," denied petitioners' motion for a new trial. . . . Petitioners argue that the District Court erred in not ordering an additional evidentiary hearing at which jurors would testify concerning drug and alcohol use during the trial. Petitioners assert that, contrary to the holdings of the District Court and the Court of Appeals, juror testimony on ingestion of drugs or alcohol during the trial is not barred by FRE 606(b). Moreover, petitioners argue that whether or not authorized by Rule 606(b), an evidentiary hearing including juror testimony on drug and alcohol use is compelled by their Sixth Amendment right to trial by a competent jury.

By the beginning of this century, if not earlier, the near-universal and firmly established common-law rule in the United States flatly prohibited the admission of juror testimony to impeach a jury verdict.

Exceptions to the common-law rule were recognized only in situations in which an "extraneous influence" was alleged to have affected the jury. . . . The Court allowed juror testimony on influence by outsiders in Parker v. Gladden, 385 U.S. 363, 365 (1966) (bailiff's comments on defendant), and Remmer v. United States, 347 U.S. 227, 228-230 (1954) (bribe offered to juror). In situations that did not fall into this exception for external influence, however, the Court adhered to the common-law rule against admitting juror testimony to impeach a verdict. . . .

Lower courts used this external/internal distinction to identify those instances in which juror testimony impeaching a verdict would be admissible. The distinction was not based on whether the juror was literally inside or outside the jury room when the alleged irregularity took place; rather, the distinction was based on the nature of the allegation. Clearly a rigid distinction based only on whether the event took place inside or outside the jury room would have been quite unhelpful. For example, under a distinction based on location a juror could not testify concerning a newspaper read inside the jury room. Instead, of course, this has been considered an external influence about which juror testimony is admissible. Similarly, under a rigid locational distinction jurors could be regularly required to testify after the verdict as to whether they heard and comprehended the judge's instructions, since the charge to the jury takes place outside the jury room. Courts wisely have treated allegations of a juror's inability to hear or comprehend at trial as an internal matter.

Most significant for the present case, however, is the fact that lower federal courts treated allegations of the physical or mental incompetence of a juror as "internal" rather than "external" matters. . . .

Substantial policy considerations support the common-law rule against the admission of jury testimony to impeach a verdict. As early as 1915 this Court explained the necessity of shielding jury deliberations from public scrutiny:

> [L]et it once be established that verdicts solemnly made and publicly returned into court can be attacked and set aside on the testimony of those who took part

in their publication and all verdicts could be, and many would be, followed by an inquiry in the hope of discovering something which might invalidate the finding. Jurors would be harassed and beset by the defeated party in an effort to secure from them evidence of facts which might establish misconduct sufficient to set aside a verdict. If evidence thus secured could be thus used, the result would be to make what was intended to be a private deliberation, the constant subject of public investigation—to the destruction of all frankness and freedom of discussion and conference.

McDonald v. Pless, 238 U.S. at 267-268. . . .

There is little doubt that post-verdict investigation into juror misconduct would in some instances lead to the invalidation of verdicts reached after irresponsible or improper juror behavior. It is not at all clear, however, that the jury system could survive such efforts to perfect it. Allegations of juror misconduct, incompetency, or inattentiveness, raised for the first time days, weeks, or months after the verdict, seriously disrupt the finality of the process. Moreover, full and frank discussion in the jury room, jurors' willingness to return an unpopular verdict, and the community's trust in a system that relies on the decisions of laypeople would all be undermined by a barrage of post verdict scrutiny of juror conduct.

FRE 606(b) is grounded in the common-law rule against admission of jury testimony to impeach a verdict and the exception for juror testimony relating to extraneous influences. . . .

Petitioners have presented no argument that Rule 606(b) is inapplicable to the juror affidavits and the further inquiry they sought in this case, and, in fact, there appears to be virtually no support for such a proposition. See 3 D. Louisell & C. Mueller, Federal Evidence §287, pp. 121-125 (1979) (under Rule 606(b), "proof to the following effects is excludable . . . that one or more jurors was inattentive during trial or deliberations, sleeping or thinking about other matters"). . . . [P]etitioners argue that substance abuse constitutes an improper "outside influence" about which jurors may testify under FRE 606(b). In our view the language of the Rule cannot easily be stretched to cover this circumstance. However severe their effect and improper their use, drugs or alcohol voluntarily ingested by a juror seems no more an "outside influence" than a virus, poorly prepared food, or a lack of sleep.

In any case, whatever ambiguity might linger in the language of Rule 606(b) as applied to juror intoxication is resolved by the legislative history of the Rule. . . .

[T]he legislative history demonstrates with uncommon clarity that Congress specifically understood, considered, and rejected a version of Rule 606(b) that would have allowed jurors to testify on juror conduct during deliberations, including juror intoxication. This legislative history provides strong support for the most reasonable reading of the language of Rule 606(b)—that juror intoxication is not an "outside influence" about which jurors may testify to impeach their verdict.

Finally, even if Rule 606(b) is interpreted to retain the common-law exception allowing post verdict inquiry of juror incompetence in cases of "substantial if not wholly conclusive evidence of incompetency," the showing made by the petitioners falls far short of this standard. The affidavits and testimony presented in support of the first new trial motion suggested, at worst, that several of the jurors fell asleep at times during the afternoons. The District Court judge appropriately considered the fact that he had "an unobstructed view" of the jury, and did not see any juror sleeping. The juror affidavit submitted in support of the second new trial motion was obtained in clear violation of the District Court's order and the court's local rule against juror interviews; on this basis alone the District Court would have been acting within its discretion in disregarding the affidavit. In any case, although the affidavit of juror Hardy describes more dramatic instances of misconduct, Hardy's allegations of *incompetence* are meager. Hardy stated that the alcohol consumption he engaged in with three other jurors did not leave any of them intoxicated. ("I told [the prosecutor] that we would just go out and get us a pitcher of beer and drink it, but as far as us being drunk, no we wasn't"). The only allegations concerning the jurors' ability to properly consider the evidence were Hardy's observation that some jurors were "falling asleep all the time during the trial," and that Hardy's own reasoning ability was affected on one day of the trial. These allegations would not suffice to bring this case under the common-law exception allowing post verdict inquiry when an extremely strong showing of incompetency has been made.

Petitioners also argue that the refusal to hold an additional evidentiary hearing at which jurors would testify as to their conduct "violates the sixth amendment's guarantee to a fair trial before an impartial and *competent* jury."

This Court has recognized that a defendant has a right to "a tribunal both impartial and mentally competent to afford a hearing." Jordan v. Massachusetts, 225 U.S. 167, 176 (1912). In this case the District Court held an evidentiary hearing in response to petitioners' first new trial motion at which the judge invited petitioners to introduce any admissible evidence in support of their allegations. At issue in this case is whether the Constitution compelled the District Court to hold an additional evidentiary hearing including one particular kind of evidence inadmissible under the Federal Rules.

As described above, long-recognized and very substantial concerns support the protection of jury deliberations from intrusive inquiry. Petitioners' Sixth Amendment interests in an unimpaired jury, on the other hand, are protected by several aspects of the trial process. The suitability of an individual for the responsibility of jury service, of course, is examined during voir dire. Moreover, during the trial the jury is observable by the court, by counsel, and by court personnel. Moreover, jurors are observable by each other, and may report inappropriate juror behavior to the court *before* they render a verdict. Finally, after the trial a party may seek to impeach the verdict by nonjuror evidence of misconduct. Indeed, in this case the District Court held an evidentiary hearing giving petitioners ample opportunity to produce nonjuror evidence supporting their allegations.

In light of these other sources of protection of the petitioners' right to a competent jury, we conclude that the District Court did not err in deciding, based on the inadmissibility of juror testimony and the clear insufficiency of the nonjuror evidence offered by petitioners, that an additional post-verdict evidentiary hearing was unnecessary.

[The dissenting opinion of JUSTICE MARSHALL, joined by three other Justices, is omitted.]

NOTES ON TANNER v. UNITED STATES

1.   The Court suggests that evidence of a juror reading a newspaper would constitute "external influence" about which juror testimony is admissible. Could one juror testify that she saw another juror reading a newspaper? If so, why cannot one juror testify that she saw another drinking, smoking marijuana, or ingesting cocaine to the point of being impaired?

2.   Would the evidence of juror intoxication have been received if it could have been established by nonjuror testimony? See United States v. Taliaferro, 558 F.2d 724, 725-726 (4th Cir. 1977) (court considered records of club where jurors dined, and testimony of marshal who accompanied jurors, to determine whether jurors were intoxicated during deliberations), cert. denied, 434 U.S. 106 (1978).

3.   If the affidavit of Hardy had been received, would it have justified granting Tanner a new trial? In ruling on whether juror affidavits or testimony are admissible under FRE 606(b), to what extent should a judge consider the question whether the evidence, if believed, provides a sufficient basis for a new trial?

4.   What if the verdict were challenged on the ground that one juror was a neighbor of Tanner and told other jurors that "he has been in trouble with the law since he was a kid"? Is this statement an "outside influence" or "extraneous prejudicial information"? What if on voir dire the juror had falsely denied knowing Tanner? Does FRE 606(b) block inquiry into possible perjury on voir dire that could be the basis for granting a new trial? See Urseth v. City of Dayton, 680 F. Supp. 1084, 1089 (S.D. Ohio 1987) (no). See generally Crump, Jury Misconduct, Jury Interviews, and the Federal Rules of Evidence: Is the Broad Exclusionary Doctrine of Rule 606(b) Justified?, 66 N.C. L. Rev. 509 (1988); Diehm, Impeachment of Jury Verdicts: *Tanner v. United States* and Beyond, 65 St. John's L. Rev. 389 (1991).

PROBLEM 6-B.   *Refusal to Take the Stand*

Adkins is convicted of unlawful possession of narcotics at a trial in which he did not testify in his own defense. A week after trial, the judge receives a letter from a juror expressing concern that the jury violated the judge's instructions because it considered Adkins' refusal to take the stand as an admission of guilt. The judge informs both counsel of the letter, and the attorney for Adkins files a motion for a new trial based on juror misconduct. May the juror be called to testify on the matters in the letter? May the letter be considered?

PROBLEM 6-C.   *The $800,000 Jury Error*

When Baker loses his farm to the bank in a foreclosure, he turns against his lawyer Henderson and brings a malpractice suit alleging that Henderson failed properly to advise him on the matter of redeeming the farm. In a bifurcated proceeding, the jury returns a verdict that Henderson was negligent, and the court then delivers the following instruction on the proper measure of damages:

> Damages are the difference between fair market value of the farm and the redemption cost plus the mortgage balance on the property.

The evidence indicates that fair market value was about $500,000, that costs of redemption would have been about $10,000, and that the outstanding balance on the mortgage was about $400,000. During deliberations, the jury foreman sends a note to the judge asking whether the jury must follow this formula in calculating damages. With approval by both lawyers, the judge answers in the affirmative. After returning a verdict for Baker in the amount of $890,000, the jury is dismissed. The court enters judgment on the verdict.

Immediately Henderson's lawyer gets permission from the court to interview jurors. Within days, he obtains affidavits from all 12, saying that they understood that they were to add the mortgage balance to fair market value (rather than subtracting the former from the latter). Henderson seeks a new trial, arguing that the jury made an $800,000 mistake.

If the judge agrees that the jury erred, should she grant a new trial? Does FRE 606(b) allow such affidavits? Could Henderson have asked the trial judge, at the time the jury announced its verdict, to ask the jury how it understood the instruction?

PROBLEM 6-D.   The Jury View

In a personal injury action arising out of an automobile accident, a verdict is returned for the plaintiff. After trial, counsel for defendant receives information that two jurors went to the accident scene one evening during the period of deliberations, apparently on a "factfinding" mission. At a hearing on a motion for a new trial, may the defense attorney make inquiry of the two jurors regarding the truth of this report?

PROBLEM 6-E.   The Bomber

Jones is convicted of detonating an explosive device in a public building. Afterwards her lawyer is told that one juror is willing to testify that another informed the jury he was a demolitions expert in the Army and that the type of bomb Jones used was powerful enough to kill anyone within 20 feet, even though no injuries were inflicted by the explosion. If Jones moves for a new trial, may she offer such testimony in support of the motion? If so, may the prosecutor call other jurors to testify that this information had no influence on their votes?

I. JUDGES AS WITNESSES

Somewhat surprisingly, the common law did not consider a judge incompetent to testify in a trial over which the judge was presiding. FRE 605 is explicit in making this one of the few federal grounds of incompetency. Note that FRE 605 does not prohibit calling a judge as a witness in another trial or hearing, even a post-trial proceeding in the same case. Does it follow that any question may be asked of the judge at such a subsequent hearing? See Washington v. Strickland, 673 F.2d 879, 902-906 (5th Cir. 1982) (holding that trial judge could not be questioned regarding his reasons for giving the death sentence to defendant; rationale of FRE 606(b) barring testimony by jurors on mental processes "applies equally here"), on reh'g, 693 F.2d 1243 (5th Cir. 1982), rev'd on other grounds, 466 U.S. 668 (1984).

FRE 614 authorizes the court to question witnesses. Does this provision potentially conflict with FRE 605? In one pre-Rules criminal prosecution, the accused testified, and the judge asked him about their prior conversation:

> [D]idn't I say to you at that time that if you wanted to do what was right you would tell the truth about it, no matter who it involved, and that I felt sure you had been selling liquor, and that you replied that you would not tell the truth, because you felt that it would involve so many people, and that you would rather take your punishment than tell the truth?

Doesn't such questioning improperly cast the judge as a witness in the case in which he presides? The reviewing court thought so, for it reversed the conviction:

> It is the right and duty of a federal judge to elicit by questions the relevant facts when they have not been brought out by counsel. But a judge cannot testify in the form of questions. If a judge has in his possession evidences of a defendant's guilt or innocence they can be adduced for or against him only by examination and cross-examination of the judge on the witness stand at a trial presided over by another judge.

Terrell v. United States, 6 F.2d 498, 499 (4th Cir. 1925).

J. THE PERSONAL KNOWLEDGE REQUIREMENT

FRE 602 provides that "[a] witness may not testify to a matter unless evidence is introduced sufficient to support a finding that he has personal knowledge of the matter." Is this requirement a component of competency or merely a means of regulating the subjects about which the witness may testify? Note that a distinction is made between competency and the personal knowledge requirement by FRE 104. Competency pertains to the "qualification of a person to be a witness" and is a matter for the court under FRE 104(a). Who decides whether the personal knowledge requirement is satisfied, the judge under FRE 104(a) or the jury under FRE 104(b)?

The personal knowledge requirement is usually satisfied by preliminary questions showing that the witness personally perceived certain facts before the witness is asked to relate those facts to the jury. In an automobile accident case, for example, a witness may be asked preliminary questions showing that she was walking along the street at the time and place of the accident and that she observed the accident, before she is asked any questions regarding the accident itself.

How does the personal knowledge requirement apply to hearsay testimony? Even if the hearsay is admissible, the witness relating the out-of-court statement often has no personal knowledge of the facts asserted in the statement. But is that the knowledge that is required of a witness who testifies regarding a hearsay statement? In assessing the overlap between the hearsay doctrine and the personal knowledge requirement, consider the following problem.

PROBLEM 6-F.   The Peacock's Tale

Brown, a part-time tax preparer, is charged with preparing and presenting fraudulent and false income tax returns on behalf of his clients. At trial, the government offers the testimony of an IRS agent named Adrienne Peacock that she audited 160 returns prepared by Brown and that between 90 and 95 percent of them contained substantially overstated itemized deductions. She based this conclusion on information received from the individuals for whom the returns were prepared. Is her testimony objectionable? On what grounds?

Seven

DIRECT AND CROSS-EXAMINATION REVISITED

A. DIRECT EXAMINATION

1. Nonleading Questions

Recall that litigants ordinarily present testimony by means of direct examination. Remember too the beginnings of the process: The lawyer develops background information about the witness; she places him at the scene and establishes personal knowledge; in the case of the expert witness, she develops the basis of his expertise. Only then does the focus shift to substantive matters.

Particularly when it comes to substance, recall that direct examination means (for the most part) nonleading questions, as FRE 611(c) makes clear. The aim is to bring out what *the witness* has to say, and the attorney should not put words in his mouth or testify for him. But the system is not rigid, and the bar against leading the witness on direct is not absolute. Consider now the exceptions to the pattern.

2. Exceptions—Leading Questions Allowed

Under FRE 611(c), trial judges have discretion to permit leading questions, even during direct examination. By longstanding tradition, which changed little if any when the Rules were adopted, it is considered expedient to permit leading on direct in four situations:

1. *When necessary to develop testimony.* FRE 611(c) contemplates direct examination of a witness by leading questions when these "may be necessary to develop his testimony." Thus, usually the questioner is permitted to lead a witness who is (a) very young, hence apprehensive, uncomprehending, or confused, (b) timid, reticent, reluctant, or frightened, (c) ignorant, uncomprehending, or unresponsive, or (d) infirm. Of course the danger of leading seems especially great for people of such description, but where the choice is to run the risks posed by this form of examination or to do without the knowledge

of such witnesses, the risks become acceptable. See United States v. Nabors, 762 F.2d 642, 650-651 (8th Cir. 1985) (rejecting defense objection that prosecutor improperly led a 12-year-old boy, who hesitated in repeating "naughty" word allegedly used by defendant; trial court "was in the best position to evaluate the emotional condition of the child witness and his hesitancy to testify").

2. *When the witness is uncooperative.* FRE 611(c) also contemplates direct examination by leading questions when the witness is "hostile" or "an adverse party" or "identified with an adverse party." Here the idea is that when a witness refuses to cooperate, the trial lawyer may need a little coercive power to get at what the witness knows. Leading questions enable the lawyer to press and may be the only way to bring out what the witness knows. Adverse parties and their agents or associates are likely to be in this category, as are others generally described by the term "hostile." See United States v. Hicks, 748 F.2d 854, 859 (11th Cir. 1984) (prosecutor led defendant's girlfriend, who was "identified with an adverse party").

3. *When the Rule is more trouble than it is worth.* Sometimes requiring non-leading questions on direct is simply not worth the trouble. On preliminary matters, for example, leading questions save time and are allowed:

Q *(Phillips).*   You are Doctor Martin J. Young, are you not, and you reside at 1873 La
     Vista Drive in Atlanta?
A *(Dr. Young).*   That is correct.
Q.   And you are the chief surgeon at Brady Memorial Hospital in Atlanta, specializing
     in abdominal surgery?
A.   Yes.

The same is true of matters that are not contested. Even though there may be no formal stipulation between the parties, all participants may know that certain points will not be seriously disputed, and on such matters leading questions may be allowed simply to save time. Finally, most courts give short shrift to any objection to leading a witness who has qualified as an expert by virtue of formal professional training, on the theory that such witnesses simply "won't be led" in matters within their expertise while being examined by lawyers, who are from their perspective laypersons. Physicians, for example, are unlikely to cave in to the pressure of leading questions on subjects within their area of professional competence.

4. *When memory seems exhausted.* Perhaps the most important and potentially troublesome instance in which leading questions are permissible on direct is the situation in which the memory of the witness seems exhausted. Like all mortals, witnesses forget. When questioning is stymied by the inability of the witness to recollect the matters at hand, the lawyer is generally permitted to attempt to "refresh his recollection." Usually that means that the lawyer gently reminds the witness of something he has said before, perhaps in a written statement or affidavit or in a deposition, and FRE 612 expressly recognizes this technique: In time-honored tradition, the lawyer hands the statement to the witness, asks him to read it, and then asks whether "his memory is now refreshed." If he says yes, the lawyer proceeds with questioning on the subject at hand and elicits the desired information.

BAKER v. STATE
Maryland Court of Appeals
371 A.2d 699 (Md. App. 1977)

MOYLAN, J.

This appeal addresses the intriguing question of what latitude a judge should permit counsel when a witness takes the stand and says, "I don't remember." What are the available keys that may unlock the testimonial treasure vaults of the subconscious? What are the brush strokes that may be employed "to retouch the fading daguereotype of memory?" The subject is that of Present Recollection Revived.

The appellant, Teretha McNeil Baker, was convicted by a Baltimore City jury of both murder in the first degree and robbery. Although she raises two appellate contentions, the only one which we find it necessary to consider is her claim that the trial judge erroneously refused her the opportunity to refresh the present recollection of a police witness by showing him a report written by a fellow officer.

The ultimate source of most of the evidence implicating the appellant was the robbery and murder victim himself, Gaither Martin, a now-dead declarant who spoke to the jury through the hearsay conduit of Officer Bolton.[3] When Officer Bolton arrived at the crime scene, the victim told him that he had "picked these three ladies up . . . at the New Deal Bar"; that when he took them to their stated destination, a man walked up to the car and pulled him out; that "the other three got out and proceeded to kick him and beat him." It was the assertion made by the victim to the officer that established that his money, wallet and keys had been taken. The critical impasse, for present purposes, occurred when the officer was questioned, on cross-examination, about what happened en route to the hospital. The officer had received a call from Officer Hucke, of the Western District, apparently to the effect that a suspect had been picked up. Before proceeding to the hospital, Officer Bolton took the victim to the place where Officer Hucke was holding the appellant. The appellant, as part of this cross-examination, sought to elicit from the officer the fact that the crime victim confronted the appellant and stated that the appellant was not one of those persons who had attacked and robbed him. To stimulate the present memory of Officer Bolton, appellant's counsel attempted to show him the police report relating to that confrontation and prepared by Officer Hucke.

The record establishes loudly and clearly that appellant's counsel sought to use the report primarily to refresh the recollection of Officer Bolton and that he was consistently and effectively thwarted in that attempt:

By Mr. Harlan:
Q. Do you have the report filed by Officer Hucke and Officer Saclolo?
A. Right, I have copies.

---

3. The exception to the Hearsay Rule urged by the State and utilized by the court to make the out-of-court assertion admissible was the "excited utterance" exception and not the "dying declaration" exception. We are not here considering the admissibility of this hearsay, but are rather assuming it to have been admissible.

Q. Okay.

Mr. Doory: I would object to that, Your Honor.

The Court: I will sustain the objection. This is not his report. . . .

By Mr. Harlan:

Q.   All right. Would you consult your report and maybe it will refresh your recollection.

The Court: I think the response is he doesn't know who—

Mr. Harlan: He can refresh his recollection if he looks at the report.

The Court: He can't refresh his recollection from someone else's report, Mr. Harlan.

Mr. Harlan: I would object, Your Honor. Absolutely he can.

The Court: You might object, but—

Mr. Harlan: You are not going to permit the officer to refresh his recollection from the police report?

The Court: No. It is not his report. . . . He says he does not know who it was before. So, he can't refresh his recollection if he does not know simply because someone else put some name in there.

Mr. Harlan: He has to read it to see if it refreshes his recollection, Your Honor.

The Court: We are reading from a report made by two other officers which is not the personal knowledge of this officer.

Mr. Harlan: I don't want him to read from that report. I want him to read it and see if it refreshes his recollection.

On so critical an issue as possible exculpation from the very lips of the crime victim, appellant was entitled to try to refresh the memory of the key police witness. She was erroneously and prejudicially denied that opportunity. The reason for the error is transparent. Because they both arise from the common seedbed of failed memory and because of their hauntingly parallel verbal rhythms and grammatical structures, there is a beguiling temptation to overanalogize Present Recollection Revived and Past Recollection Recorded. It is a temptation, however, that must be resisted. The trial judge in this case erroneously measured the legitimacy of the effort to revive present recollection against the more rigorous standards for the admissibility of a recordation of past memory.

It is, of course, hornbook law that when a party seeks to introduce a record of past recollection, he must establish 1) that the record was made by or adopted by the witness at a time when the witness did have a recollection of the event and 2) that the witness can presently vouch for the fact that when the record was made or adopted by him, he knew that it was accurate. . . . Had the appellant herein sought to offer the police report as a record of past recollection on the part of Officer Bolton, it is elementary that she would have had to show, *inter alia,* that the report had either been prepared by Officer Bolton himself or had been read by him and that he can now say that at that time he knew it was correct. Absent such a showing, the trial judge would have been correct in declining to receive it in evidence.

When dealing with an instance of Past Recollection Recorded, the reason for the rigorous standards of admissibility is quite clear. Those standards exist to test the competence of the report or document in question. Since the piece of paper itself, in effect, speaks to the jury, the piece of paper must pass muster in terms of its evidentiary competence.[4]

---

4.   . . . Maryland is in the minority position (preferred, however, by Wigmore) that where a proper foundation is laid, a past recollection recorded is admissible without regard to the state of declarant's recollection at the time of trial.

Not so with Present Recollection Revived! By marked contrast to Past Recollection Recorded, no such testimonial competence is demanded of a mere stimulus to present recollection, for the stimulus itself is never evidence. Notwithstanding the surface similarity between the two phenomena, the difference between them could not be more basic.[5] *It is the difference between evidence and non-evidence.* Of such mere stimuli or memory-prods, McCormick says, "[T]he cardinal rule is that they are not evidence, but only aids in the giving of evidence." When we are dealing with an instance of Present Recollection Revived, the only source of evidence is the testimony of the witness himself. The stimulus may have jogged the witness's dormant memory, but the stimulus itself is not received in evidence. Dean McCormick makes it clear that even when the stimulus is a writing, when the witness "speaks from a memory thus revived, his testimony is what he says, not the writing." McCormick describes the psychological phenomenon in the following terms:

It is abundantly clear from everyday observation that the latent memory of an experience may be revived by an image seen, or a statement read or heard. It is a part of the group of phenomena which the classical psychologists have called the law of association. The recall of any part of a past experience tends to bring with it the other parts that were in the same field of awareness, and a new experience tends to stimulate the recall of other like experiences.

The psychological community is in full agreement with the legal community in assessing the mental phenomenon. See Cairn, Law and the Social Sciences 200 (1935). . . .

The catalytic agent or memory stimulator is put aside, once it has worked its psychological magic, and the witness then testifies on the basis of the now-refreshed memory. The opposing party, of course, has the right to inspect the memory aid, be it a writing or otherwise, and even to show it to the jury. This examination, however, is not for the purpose of testing the competence of the memory aid (for competence is immaterial where the thing in question is not evidence) but only to test whether the witness's memory has in truth been refreshed. . . . And he cannot be allowed to read the writing in the guise of refreshment, as a cloak for getting in evidence an inadmissible document."[6] One of the most thorough reviews of this aspect of evidence law is found in United States v. Riccardi, 174 F.2d 883 (3d Cir., 1949), where the court said at 888:

In the case of present recollection revived, the witness, by hypothesis, relates his present recollection, and under oath and subject to cross-examination asserts that it is true; his capacities for memory and perception may be attacked and tested; his determination to tell the truth investigated and revealed; protestations of lack of memory, which escape criticism and indeed constitute a refuge in the situation of past recollection recorded, merely undermine the probative worth of his testimony.

In solid accord with both the psychological sciences and the general common law of evidence, Maryland has long established it that even when a writing

5. "Under the guidance of Wigmore, we now recognize this as quite a different process. In the one instance, the witness stakes his oath on his present memory; in the other, upon his written recital of things remembered in the past." McCormick, Law of Evidence (1st Ed., 1954), p. 15.

6. McCormick, Law of Evidence (2nd Ed., 1972), 19 n.66.

of some sort is the implement used to stir the embers of cooling memory, the writing need not be that of the forgetful witness himself, need not have been adopted by him, need not have been made contemporaneously with or shortly after the incident in question, and need not even be necessarily accurate. The competence of the writing is not in issue for the writing is not offered as evidence but is only used as a memory aid. . . .

When the writing in question is to be utilized simply "to awaken a slumbering recollection of an event" in the mind of the witness, the writing may be a memorandum made by the witness himself, 1) even if it was not made immediately after the event, 2) even if it was not made of firsthand knowledge and 3) even if the witness cannot now vouch for the fact that it was accurate when made. It may be a memorandum made by one other than the witness, even if never before read by the witness or vouched for by him. It may be an Associated Press account. It may be a highly selective version of the incident at the hands of a Hemingway or an Eliot. All that is required is that it ignite the flash of accurate recall—that it accomplish the revival which is sought. . . .

Not only may the writing to be used as a memory aid fall short of the rigorous standards of competence required of a record of past recollection, the memory aid itself need not even be a writing. What may it be? It may be anything.[10] It may be a line from Kipling or the dolorous refrain of "The Tennessee Waltz"; a whiff of hickory smoke; the running of the fingers across a swatch of corduroy; the sweet carbonation of a chocolate soda; the sight of a faded snapshot in a long-neglected album. All that is required is that it may trigger the Proustian moment.[11] It may be anything which produces the desired testimonial prelude, "It all comes back to me now."[12]

Of just such possibilities did Learned Hand speak in United States v. Rappy, 157 F.2d 964, 967 (2d Cir. 1946):

> Anything may in fact revive a memory: a song, a scent, a photograph, an allusion, even a past statement known to be false.

The United States Court of Appeals for the Ninth Circuit addressed the same issue in Jewett v. United States, 15 F.2d 955 (1926), and concluded, at 956:

> [I]t is quite immaterial by what means the memory is quickened; it may be a song, or a face, or a newspaper item, or a writing of some character. It is sufficient that by some material operation, however mysterious, the memory is stimulated to recall the event, for when so set in motion it functions quite independently of the actuating cause. . . .

10. Limited only, in the wise discretion of the trial judge, by such questions as time investment, logistics, and a sense of courtroom decorum or taste.

11. Marcel Proust, in his monumental epic In Remembrance of Things Past, sat, as a middle-aged man, sipping a cup of lime-flavored tea and eating a madeleine, a small French pastry. Through both media, two long-forgotten tastes from childhood were reawakened. By association, long-forgotten memories from the same period of childhood came welling and surging back. Once those floodgates of recall were opened, seven volumes followed.

12. Generally speaking, the process of refurbishing a witness' memory will take place as a part of astute counsel's trial preparation. It is only when memory, through courtroom fear or otherwise, unexpectedly bogs down on the witness stand (or when the witness whose memory needs refreshing is one other than counsel's own) that the courtroom becomes the arena for the refurbishing. . .

Although the use of a memorandum of some sort will continue quantitatively to dominate the field of refreshing recollection, we are better able to grasp the process conceptually if we appreciate that the use of a memorandum as a memory aid is not a legal phenomenon unto itself but only an instance of a far broader phenomenon. In a more conventional mode, the process might proceed, "Your Honor, I am about to show the witness a written report, ask him to read it and then inquire if he can now testify from his own memory thus refreshed." In a far less conventional mode, the process could just as well proceed, "Your Honor, I am pleased to present to the court Miss Rosa Ponselle who will now sing 'Celeste Aida' for the witness, for that is what was playing on the night the burglar came through the window." Whether by conventional or unconventional means, precisely the same end is sought. One is looking for the effective elixir to revitalize dimming memory and make it live again in the service of the search for truth.

Even in the more conventional mode, it is quite clear that in this case the appropriate effort of the appellant to jog the arguably dormant memory of the key police witness on a vital issue was unduly and prejudicially restricted.

Judgments reversed; case remanded for a new trial; costs to be paid by Mayor and City Council of Baltimore.

NOTES ON REFRESHING RECOLLECTION

1. Should defense counsel have been required to establish the genuineness of Officer Hucke's report before using it to refresh the recollection of Officer Bolton? Should the technique of refreshing recollection be limited to writings made by the witness himself? What would have happened in *Baker* if Officer Bolton's memory had not been refreshed? Surely refreshing recollection amounts to witness-coaching. Does FRE 612 contain safeguards sufficient to overcome the risk of abuse?

2. After inspecting a document used to refresh recollection, can the cross-examiner offer it in evidence? Does FRE 612 create a new hearsay exception?

3. In one sense *Baker* is an exceptional case, for usually the instrument used in an attempt to refresh recollection contains a prior statement by the witness himself. In this common setting, consider how refreshing recollection relates to other devices—some of which you have seen already:

a. *Past recollection recorded.* The attempt to refresh memory may fail, in which case the document itself may be admitted. See FRE 803(5) (but the document does not go to the jury room during deliberations). Recall the *Scott* case (Chapter 4C4, supra).

b. *Prior inconsistent statement as substantive evidence.* The attempt to refresh recollection may succeed only too well, reviving a memory of events very much at odds with what the witness said before. If the prior statement was given under oath in proceedings, and if the witness is now cross-examinable about the statement, then the examining lawyer may be allowed to use the statement as substantive evidence (that is, as proof of whatever it asserts) under FRE 801(d)(1)(A). Even if witness *does not* regain his memory of events, his seeming forgetfulness may persuade the court that his prior statement is inconsistent with his present position. Here too FRE 801(d)(1)(A) might be available.

c.   *Prior inconsistent statement as impeaching proof.* Once again, the attempt to refresh memory may succeed only in bringing out a story that conflicts with what the witness said earlier, or it may fail, but the persistent forgetfulness may seem evasive and inconsistent with what was said earlier. Even if the prior statement does *not* fit a hearsay exception, it may be used to impeach.

B.   CROSS-EXAMINATION

1.   *Leading Questions*

Recall that, in the process of presenting testimony, cross-examination follows direct. Here the adverse party (against whom the direct testimony is offered) begins the process of testing, limiting, and rebuttal. Here the lawyer rather than the witness is the focus; here the substantive points are largely contained in the questions themselves, as the answers confirm or acknowledge what the questions in effect assert.

Recall too that the mode of questioning is cross-examination, which means (for the most part) leading questions under FRE 611(c). Only in rare instances must the cross-examiner avoid leading the witness: She cannot lead when the witness is her own client (or aligned with her client), as happens when (for example) plaintiff in a civil case calls the defendant to testify and defense counsel then "cross-examines."

One aim of cross-examination is to develop the substance of the story as the adverse party hopes that the jury will see it—to recast the story presented by the calling party. Another is to limit or confine the impact of the testimony of the witness. Yet another is to impeach the credibility of the witness. The line between these functions sometimes disappears, but in what follows the focus is on tactics that generally aim to confine and limit the effect of adverse testimony.

2.   *Cross-Examining on Witness Preparation Material*

In *Baker* you saw the process of refreshing memory on the witness stand, and the safeguards that FRE 612 provides for the cross-examining party. But witness preparation ("woodshedding," in the occasional lingo of the trade) begins well before trial, and almost invariably the cross-examiner tries to show that this pretrial process affected the testimony of the witness. In reading *James Julian,* consider the tension between this process and the protection accorded to attorney work product.

JAMES JULIAN, INC. v. RAYTHEON CO.
United States District Court for the District of Delaware
93 F.R.D. 138 (1982)

[Plaintiff James Julian, Inc. (Julian) seeks injunctive relief and damages under the Sherman Act and National Labor Relations Act, naming as defendants several labor organizations and union officers, as well as Raytheon Co. (Raytheon) and Raytheon Service Co. (RSC). Here defendants Raytheon and RSC seek return of certain documents turned over during discovery under a court order that provided disclosure would not waive privilege claims, as well as production of a binder of materials prepared by counsel for Julian for purposes of review by Julian's officers in preparation for their deposition testimony.]

MURRAY M. SCHWARTZ, J.

In the course of preparing witnesses for depositions plaintiff's counsel assembled a binder which was reviewed by current principals, officers and employees of Julian who were being deposed by the Raytheon defendants. The binder, which was not reviewed by the Court, contains: 1) selected documents obtained from RSC through discovery; 2) documents obtained by Julian from the public records of the Delaware Solid Waste Authority through a Freedom of Information Act request; and 3) documents prepared by Julian during the course of the project.

Julian does not object to defendants' obtaining the documents contained in the binder; indeed, Julian has represented that many of the documents were already turned over during the course of discovery. Rather, plaintiff objects to the production of the binder itself, arguing that the selection and ordering of documents constitute privileged work product reflecting counsel's opinions, mental impressions, conclusions or legal theories and is therefore entitled to special protection under Rule 26(b)(3) of the Federal Rules of Civil Procedure. The Raytheon defendants argue first, that production of the binder would not reveal the thought processes of plaintiff's counsel and second, that even if the binder was at one time entitled to special protection, plaintiff waived that entitlement by using the binder to prepare witnesses for deposition.

The threshold issue can be dispensed with quickly. The binder contains a small percentage of the extensive documents reviewed by plaintiff's counsel. In selecting and ordering a few documents out of thousands counsel could not help but reveal important aspects of his understanding of the case. Indeed, in a case such as this, involving extensive document discovery, the process of selection and distillation is often more critical than pure legal research. There can be no doubt that at least in the first instance the binders were entitled to protection as work product.

Even assuming the binder was once entitled to protection, the Raytheon defendants argue that plaintiff waived that protection. Relying on Rule 612 of the Federal Rules of Evidence, they argue that if a party uses protected documents to prepare a witness for deposition, those documents become discoverable. . . . [The provisions of FRE 612] are made applicable to depositions by virtue of Rule 30(c) of the Federal Rules of Civil Procedure. The legislative history and case law both discuss Rule 612 in terms of privilege without clearly distinguishing the attorney work product doctrine. As a result the following analysis will discuss the Rule's effect on protected documents generally before considering the effect, if any, of the fact that in this case plaintiff claims the protection of the work product doctrine.

There is no doubt that Rule 612(2) constituted a major departure from the settled rule that the use of a privileged document to refresh a witness' memory only constituted a waiver of the privilege if it occurred at the time of testimony. The precise issue presented by the Raytheon defendants' motion is whether in extending the rule to include documents used to refresh a witness' memory before testifying Congress intended to include all such documents or only those not subject to claims of privilege.

The legislative history of Rule 612 is ambiguous. It can be read to indicate a congressional intent to leave the decision as to privileged documents to the sound discretion of the district courts for resolution on a case by case basis. It is also possible to view the record as reflecting an intent to exempt privileged documents from the operation of the expanded rule.

As noted, prior case law required disclosure of privileged documents used to refresh memory at the time of testimony. Plaintiff argues, based largely on legislative history, that Congress intended to limit Rule 612's expansion of prior law to nonprivileged documents used to refresh witness' memory prior to testimony. As enacted, Rule 612 does limit the expansion of prior law, not, as plaintiff suggests, by exempting privileged documents, but by conditioning disclosure on the discretionary approval of the district court. It would thus appear that Congress left the task of striking a balance between the competing interests of full disclosure and the maintenance of confidentiality for case by case determination.

Those courts which have considered the issue have generally agreed that the use of protected documents to refresh a witness' memory prior to testifying constitutes a waiver of the protection. In what is perhaps the leading case, Berkey Photo, Inc. v. Eastman Kodak Co., 74 F.R.D. 613 (S.D.N.Y. 1977) (Frankel, J.), defendant's attorneys used four notebooks to prepare expert witnesses for deposition. The court noted that:

> [Given the] modern views favoring broad access to materials useful for effective cross-examination, embodied in rules like 612 [and the Jencks Act], it is disquieting to posit that a lawyer may "aid" a witness with items of work product and then prevent totally the access that might reveal and counteract the effects of such assistance. There is much to be said for a view that a party or its lawyer, meaning to invoke the privilege, ought to use other, and different materials, available later to a cross-examiner, in the preparation of witnesses. When this simple choice emerges the decision to give the work product to the witness could well be deemed a waiver of the privilege.

The court's actual holding that the notebook which had "the sound and quality of materials appropriate 'to promote the search of credibility and memory,' " need not be produced was based not on its reading of Rule 612 but on its perception that an order compelling discovery would work undue hardship on defendant, whose counsel were unaware of the scope of the then recently adopted rule. Indeed, the court was at pains to put the bar on notice that in the future a contrary result would obtain.

Judge Frankel's prediction has proved largely accurate. Thus, for example, the court in Wheeling-Pittsburgh Steel Corp. v. Underwriters Laboratories, Inc., 81 F.R.D. 8 (N.D. Ill. 1978), held that the use of privileged documents to refresh a witness' recollection prior to testimony served as an effective waiver of the privilege. Plaintiff attempts to distinguish *Wheeling* by arguing that because the witness had left the party's employ by the time of his deposition, his review of the documents destroyed their confidentiality. The *Wheeling* Court did hold that the use of the documents to refresh the witness' recollection constituted a waiver of the attorney-client privilege, but any notion that it was relying on concepts of publication to noncorporate personnel must be dispelled by its reliance on Bailey v. Meister Brau, Inc., 57 F.R.D. 11 (N.D. Ill. 1972), a pre-Rule 612 case. In *Bailey* privileged documents were used to refresh a witness's recollection at his deposition. In rejecting plaintiff's claim that privileged documents are excepted from the general rule that a party is entitled to inspect any document used to refresh recollection the court held that:

> To adopt such an exception would be to ignore the unfair disadvantage which could be placed upon the cross-examiner by the simple expedient of using only privileged writings to refresh recollection.

The *Bailey* court also considered the applicability of the attorney work product doctrine to the requested documents and concluded that the use of the documents to refresh recollection constituted a waiver of that doctrine for the same reasons that it constituted a waiver of the attorney-client privilege. [A]ccord, Marshall v. United States Postal Service, 88 F.R.D. 348 (D.D.C. 1980) (unsigned affidavit prepared by attorney from interview notes used to refresh recollection at deposition); Williamson v. Puritan Chemical Corp., 80 Civ. 1698 (S.D.N.Y. March 6, 1981) (statement made to counsel and reviewed prior to testifying); Peck & Peck, Inc. v. Jack La Lanne, 76 Civ. 4020 (S.D.N.Y. Jan. 12, 1978) (use of privileged investigative report to refresh recollection prior to testimony).

Aside from *Berkey* the only case Court or counsel have discovered in which the court denied production of privileged documents reviewed prior to testimony is Jos. Schlitz Brewing Co. v. Muller & Phipps (Hawaii) Ltd., 85 F.R.D. 118 (W.D. Mo. 1980). In *Schlitz* the witness, an attorney, testified that he had reviewed his correspondence file consisting of thirty-nine documents in preparation for his deposition. Although the Court did state that language and history of Rule 612 indicated that the Rule's adoption occasioned "little if any widening of disclosure obligations," the court's actual holding was simply that "there was insufficient establishment of actual use of any of the various documents [contained in the file], so as to authorize [the invocation of] Rule 612."

Plaintiff attempts to distinguish the above cited cases by asserting that, with the exception of *Bailey*, a pre-Rule 612 case, and *Berkey*, which is dismissed as containing mere dicta, none involved a claim of attorney opinion work product, the disclosure of which the court is obligated to protect against. FRCP 26(b)(3). Plaintiff's argument is not without merit. Each case must, of course, be evaluated on its own facts. In a given case the fact that the privileged documents contained attorneys' mental impressions might cause the Court to strike the balance in favor of nondisclosure. However, this is not that case. The binder at issue contains various documents selected and arranged by plaintiff's counsel and given to various witnesses prior to their depositions. Without reviewing those binders defendants' counsel cannot know or inquire into the extent to which the witnesses' testimony has been shaded by counsel's presentation of the factual background. The instant request constitutes neither a fishing expedition into plaintiff's files nor an invasion of counsel's "zone of privacy." Plaintiff's counsel made a decision to educate their witnesses by supplying them with the binders, and the Raytheon defendants are entitled to know the content of that education.

Based on the foregoing the Court concludes that the binders are properly within the scope of Rule 612(2) and in the interests of justice should be disclosed. An appropriate order will issue.

NOTES ON APPLYING RULE 612

1.   Why did the defense want to discover what plaintiff's corporate officers reviewed in preparation for their testimony? Is there anything wrong in what plaintiff's counsel did? If defense counsel already has the documents, what more can he reasonably request?

2.   Pre-Rules practice drew a bright line between documents that a witness reviews before testifying and those he reviews on the stand to refresh memory, for the cross-examiner was entitled to production of the latter but not the former. *James Julian* reads FRE 612 as requiring production of the former as well, subject only to judicial discretion to disallow production. Isn't that a backward reading? The "discretion" clause *broadens* discovery, doesn't it? Documents reviewed before testifying must be produced only if the trial judge in his "discretion" so requires: Couldn't a judge decline to require production of such documents even though they are neither privileged nor protected by work product? How likely is it that Congress intended by that clause to enable a judge to override the protection otherwise afforded by privilege or the work product doctrine? See the House Judiciary Committee's Note following FRE 612. (In practice, attorneys routinely take advantage of any "recess" or "adjournment" in order to go over expected testimony with witnesses, seeking privacy in the nearest alcove, closet, or restroom if all else fails. The cross-examiner does not always bother to inquire about such informal preparatory sessions, particularly if he is not sure they even occurred.)

3.   Quite apart from the question of interpreting FRE 612, does the result endorsed in *James Julian* make sense? Should a client who reviews a document before testifying waive his claim of attorney-client privilege for that document? Should an attorney who uses his work product to prepare a witness before testifying thereby lose the protection of the work product doctrine for the document?

4.   If the cross-examiner is entitled to see hardcopy material provided by counsel to witnesses for review, does prudence suggest that counsel should coach witnesses orally as much as possible? Or would doing so evade a basic principle of fairness and rob the cross-examiner of necessary information? See IBM Corp. v. Edelstein, 526 F.2d 37 (2d Cir. 1975) (overturning order directing transcription of witness interviews).

5.   Do other procedural concerns justify limiting contact between trial counsel and potential witnesses? In a class suit, what about contact between defense counsel and potential members of the plaintiff class?

6.   The Jencks Act (18 U.S.C. §3500) entitles criminal defendants to obtain certain statements by government witnesses, but only after they testify. Does use

of such statements by the prosecutor to prepare witnesses waive the protection otherwise provided by the statute? What policy underlies the statute?

7. Disclosure of materials protected by the work product doctrine or attorney-client privilege ordinarily results in loss of further protection. But modern decisions have been more generous in permitting continuing protection after limited disclosure. Do such cases undercut the logic and result in *James Julian?*

Consider what happened in a massive antitrust suit by MCI against AT&T. There AT&T turned over to MCI seven million pages of documents, under a protective order preserving confidentiality. The government had brought a parallel enforcement action, charging AT&T with monopolizing and conspiring to monopolize markets for telecommunication services and equipment, and the order in the MCI suit was modified to permit MCI to turn over to the government one and one-half million of the AT&T documents. MCI *also* gave the government its computerized database consisting of "abstracts of documents, deposition transcripts, and exhibits received from AT&T." Counsel for AT&T quickly realized that the MCI database might reveal which of the AT&T documents MCI "might consider important, why counsel might consider them to be important, and what portions of those documents counsel might think are most important." Thus AT&T sought the MCI database from the government, arguing that counsel for MCI had waived work product protection by disclosure. But the reviewing court disagreed:

> *The attorney-client privilege exists* to protect confidential communications, to assure the client that any statements he makes in seeking legal advice will be kept strictly confidential between him and his attorney; in effect, *to protect the attorney-client relationship.* Any voluntary disclosure by the holder of such a privilege is inconsistent with the confidential relationship and thus waives the privilege.
>
> By contrast, the *work product privilege* does not exist to protect a confidential relationship, but rather *to promote the adversary system by safeguarding the fruits of an attorney's trial preparations from the discovery attempts of the opponent.* The purpose of the work product doctrine is to protect information against opposing parties, rather than against all others outside a particular confidential relationship, in order to encourage effective trial preparation. . . . A disclosure made in the pursuit of such trial preparation, and not inconsistent with maintaining secrecy against opponents, should be allowed without waiver of the privilege. We conclude, then, that *while the mere showing of a voluntary disclosure to a third person will generally suffice to show waiver of the attorney-client privilege, it should not suffice in itself for waiver of the work product privilege.*

United States v. AT&T, 642 F.2d 1285, 1299 (D.C. Cir. 1980).

The protections of the work product doctrine and attorney-client privilege may survive disclosure to private parties too. See United States v. Gulf Oil Corp., 760 F.2d 292, 295-296 (Temp. Emer. Ct. App. 1985) (documents prepared by counsel for Cities Service in preparation for litigation with Department of Energy, and turned over to counsel for Gulf Oil pursuant to merger agreement between the companies, were still covered by work product doctrine; transfer "to a party with 'strong common interests in sharing the fruit of trial preparation efforts,' " or transfer "concurrently with a guarantee of confidentiality," does not necessarily waive work product protection).

8.   If *James Julian* had upheld plaintiff's claim of work product protection for documents reviewed prior to testimony, consider whether the adverse party might get just about what he wants by a slightly different tactic. On cross he could ask, couldn't he, what documents the witness had reviewed in preparation for his testimony? If the witness has reviewed documents covered by work product or attorney-client privilege, could the calling party block questions about the content of those documents or a request that the documents be produced? If not, does it follow that *at this point* the documents must be produced, even though production could be resisted during discovery? Cf. Sporck v. Peil, 759 F.2d 312, 317-319 (3d Cir. 1985) (in securities fraud suit, plaintiff's attorney tried to find out, during deposition of defendant, which documents he reviewed in preparation; selection of documents used in this way was indeed protected by work product, and conditions set by FRE 612 were not satisfied, because counsel "failed to establish either that petitioner relied on any documents in giving his testimony, or that those documents influenced his testimony," and "[w]ithout first eliciting the testimony, there existed no basis for asking petitioner the source of that testimony"; yet if counsel does elicit testimony, he may then ask "which, if any, documents informed that testimony," and work product doctrine would not be implicated), cert. denied, 474 U.S. 903 (1985).

3.   Cross-Examination as an Entitlement

In civil and criminal cases alike, each party has virtually an unassailable *right* to cross-examine witnesses called by the other side. Recall that absence of cross-examination is the main reason why the hearsay doctrine so often requires exclusion of out-of-court statements. Hence it is no surprise that where cross-examination is cut short by the death or illness of the witness, this curtailment of the opponent's right is viewed as so serious that the direct testimony must often be stricken, and sometimes a mistrial is required. See United States v. Panza, 612 F.2d 432, 436-437 (9th Cir. 1979) (striking testimony by defendant when he refused to be cross-examined), cert. denied, 447 U.S. 925 (1980).

Consider the following discussion by the appellate court in a civil suit brought by a widow against an insurance carrier on account of an accident in which a car driven by her son Lyle collided head-on with another vehicle, causing the death of his passenger—the man who had been father to Lyle and husband to plaintiff. The trial court ruled that plaintiff could not cross-examine Lyle (since she had called him as a witness), but the reviewing court disagreed:

> The process of truth-telling as is the process of truth-ascertainment is seldom the simple question whether there has been conscious, willful falsity. Nor is it even the simpler one of resolving the matter in terms of likely hostility *against* or friendliness *for* one party or the other. Thus, for every factor here tending Lyle toward the Plaintiff, there was one tugging in the opposite direction. Not the least of the latter was the suggestion hammered home by defense counsel that a finding of negligence was equivalent to a finding that Lyle had killed his father.
>
> Just what Lyle's real interests might be was not a matter for the District Judge, nor for us in the way of binding ex post facto parenthetical observations made

from our remote position. That was for the jury to appraise in the light of a full and searching revelation. Our system of justice rests necessarily on the historic assumption that civilized moral people try their dead level best to tell the truth no matter how much it hurts or helps. But being a mechanism for the resolution of man's disputes, the instrument of cross examination is an integral part of that system in order to penetrate all of the conflicting impulses or obstacles to lay bare the whole truth. And yet from the nature of the strict procedural limitation imposed by the Judge, this could not be effectively done.

Real cross examination was entirely missing. The Plaintiff's counsel was forbidden by the Court's ruling to engage either in it, or in the indigenous but powerful tool of leading questions. The Defendants, while having the nominal right to cross examine, did not for perfectly obvious reasons do so in fact. By this procedural ruling the defense was put in the fortunate position of being able to argue that the witness (Lyle)—for whose truthfulness and reliability the Plaintiffs generally vouched—by his court-testimony and a written statement given to an insurance adjuster, had made contradictory statements on his knowledge of the existence of the Stop Sign. This physical-mental fact was at the very heart of the reasonableness of his conduct in thinking (or in not thinking) that the oncoming car would or would not stop. And as to this issue, the jury may have taken the easy way out—the Plaintiff's failure to satisfy a preponderance of the evidence—simply because it could not ascertain for sure just when Lyle had stated the truth.

This was not, therefore, the case of admission or exclusion of some bit of testimony asserted on appellate review to have been erroneous. This was the denial of the use of a tool of advocacy which our long judicial heritage marks as one of the most effective in the quest for truth. This was a substantial right. The experience of the bar is that it has substantial value. Indeed, the District Court recognized that by the very ruling under attack. Were it not effective, did he not think it would give the Plaintiff a substantial benefit (to which he thought the Plaintiff was not legally entitled) there is no reason for the Judge to have made the pretrial decision and order. As it was the denial of an important weapon in the arsenal of advocacy, the concept of FRCP 61 does not require that the record developed without its assistance affirmatively pinpoint the harm in so many words. It is sufficient if we can see, as we readily do here, that the development of this record and the development of the testimony of Lyle as a witness might well have been quite different had the Plaintiff been accorded the right to put Lyle through all of the rigors of a sharp, relentless, pressing, vigorous cross examination as he verbally retraced foot-by-foot, second-by-second the crucial moments during which the two vehicles pursued their tragic fatal collision course.

Degelos v. Fidelity & Casualty Co., 313 F.2d 809, 814 (5th Cir. 1963).

In criminal cases the Sixth Amendment entitles the accused to "confront the witnesses against him," and cross-examination is the single most critical aspect of this constitutional right. This entitlement applies in state as well as federal prosecutions, see Pointer v. Texas, 380 U.S. 400 (1965), and the Supreme Court has found that a variety of trial court rulings that cut into this entitlement abridge defense confrontation rights. See Smith v. Illinois, 390 U.S. 129, 131-132 (1968) (requiring new trial where court let witness use alias instead of real name and refuse to state address); Davis v. Alaska, 415 U.S. 308, 316 (1974) (requiring new trial where court let state witness refuse to answer questions on juvenile record). Recall that the Confrontation Clause also bears on the use of hearsay against the accused and his use of hearsay for the defense.

Sometimes events apparently beyond control of the parties or the court cut short or deny completely the right to cross-examine a witness. He may fall ill or die or claim a privilege or simply refuse to cooperate despite the threat of contempt. In any such case the problem arises in a different guise: What should be done about testimony that he has already given?

Generally the solutions have been either the draconian sanction of striking the direct testimony completely when no cross-examination could be had, or the more moderate sanction of striking portions of the direct if the interruption came after cross-examination had begun, thus keeping portions of the direct as to which cross-examination had occurred. Often the decisions are affected by an aroma of suspicion, particularly where the witness is a party or clearly allied with a party, or where the impediment to cross-examination arises from apparent illness or a claim of privilege, and in such cases completely striking the testimony is more likely.

C.   EXCLUDING WITNESSES

1.   The General Principle

Common sense calls out that matching independent accounts of an event are more to be trusted than versions in which the narrators may have been affected by what others say about the same acts, events, or conditions. Police routinely interview suspects and witnesses separately, and in their questioning avoid disclosing what others have said, except when it becomes useful to do otherwise. And courts routinely exclude ("sequester") witnesses, directing them to remain outside the courtroom before testifying, to minimize the risk that they will "shape" their later testimony in order to agree with (or supplement or refute) what others testify to. Consider the modern embodiment of the "Witness Rule" in FRE 615. And consider the following illustration of the general principle, in the story of Susanna and the Elders, an apocryphal addition to the Old Testament book of Daniel.

> **SUSANNA AND THE ELDERS**
> from N. deLange, Apocrypha: Jewish Literature
> of the Hellenistic Age 130-132 (1978)

That year two elders of the people were appointed judges, and cases were brought before them even from other towns. These two both conceived a violent passion for the wife of one of their brother-Israelites, a certain Joakim. The woman's name was Susanna, the daughter of Helkiah. She was a beautiful woman, and she was in the habit of taking a walk in her husband's gardens toward evening. The elders' passion got the better of their good sense and made them forget all thought of Heaven or of justice. . . .

"We must have her," one of them said. So they agreed on a plan and made advances to her and tried to force her to do what they wanted. But Susanna

. . . said to them, "I know that if I give in to you I shall be killed, and I also know that if I refuse I won't escape unharmed. Still, it's better that I should reject you and face the consequences than sin before the Lord."

So the two lechers left her, bent on revenge and determined to bring about her death. They went to the assembly of the town, where all the Jews were gathered in session, and there they stood up and said, "Send for Susanna, the daughter of Helkiah, the wife of Joakim." . . .

Susanna was a very attractive woman, and the two scoundrels ordered her to be unveiled so that they could feast their eyes on her beauty. At this her family and friends burst into tears. The two elder-judges came forward and put their hands on her head. Susanna, trusting in the Lord, looked up to heaven and said through her tears, "Lord, eternal God, who knows all things before they happen, you know that I have not done what these vicious men accuse me of."

The two elders said, "We were walking in her husband's garden, and as we were going past the stadium we saw this woman with a man. We stood and watched them making love, and they did not realize we were there. We decided we must find out who they were and moved closer. We recognized her, but the young man, who was masked, escaped. We seized the woman and asked her who the man was but she refused to tell us. This is our solemn testimony."

The whole assembly believed them because they were elders and judges of the people.

As Susanna was being led off to be executed, an angel of the Lord inspired a young man [Daniel], who parted the crowd and stood in their way.

"Are you such fools, you Israelites," he said, "as to condemn a Jewish woman to death without investigating the charge and discovering the truth? Separate these men and let me cross-examine them."

When they were separated, [Daniel] addressed the assembly. "Don't think," he said, "that these men can't be liars just because they are elders. I am going to confront them both now with a question that has been put in my mind."

He summoned one of the elders, and . . . said, "Listen to me, you hardened sinner. The sins you have committed in the past have finally found you out. You were empowered to try capital cases and you convicted the innocent and acquitted the guilty, even though the Lord says, 'You shall not put the innocent and the guiltless to death.'"

"Where were you in the garden, what kind of tree were you standing under, when you saw them together?"

"It was an ash tree," said the wretched man.

"Your perjury rebounds on your own head," replied [Daniel]. "This very day the angel of the Lord will burn you to a fine ash!"

[Daniel] told them to take him away and fetch the other one. "You are more like a lewd Sidonian than a Jew. You were infatuated by beauty and dragged down by your lust. You had your way, no doubt, with Israelite women; they submitted to you out of fear. But this daughter of Judah was too proud to give in to your disgusting demands. Tell me, now, where exactly were you in the park, what tree were you standing under, when you saw them carrying on together?"

"It was a pear tree," said the elder.

"Sinner!" replied [Daniel]. "At this very moment the angel of the Lord is standing with his sword drawn, waiting for the people to finish with you so that he can pare you to the quick!"

The whole assembly began to shout and cheer the young man because he had convicted them of perjury out of their own mouths. They punished them, in accordance with the law, with the same penalty they had planned to inflict on their sister-Israelite. They gagged them and led them off and hurled them into a chasm, and there the angel of the Lord burned them with flames. And so an innocent life was saved that day.

NOTES ON EXCLUDING WITNESSES

1. If Susanna were tried under modern procedure with Daniel as her lawyer, he could invoke FRE 615. What could he ask the court to do?

2. The testimony of the elders differ on what one might call a "minor" point (under what kind of tree did the events transpire): Of course we are essentially told that the charges were made up, that the elders were guilty of what we would call rape or sexual assault, and that their stories of Susanna's adultery were false. In an ordinary setting, more congenial to our modern sense that criminalizing adultery is appalling, would such a discrepancy prove decisive? Suppose a man were tried for sexual assault against Susanna, and that the state's principal witnesses gave matching accounts except that one said the event occurred under an ash tree, and the other said under a pear tree. Is there some truth to the idea that concocted stories are likely to match in what one might ordinarily call their "essential" points and differ only on what one might call "marginal" points? Does it follow that "impeachment on collateral points" should be more freely allowed when the situation suggests that two witnesses have cooperated in preparing their testimony?

PROBLEM 7-A. *Daily Transcripts*

On the first day of the trial of Excel's claim against Mentor for patent infringement, counsel for plaintiff obtains a court order excluding all witnesses. Novick is the key expert witness for the defense, and he complies with the order. Just before Mentor calls Novick to testify, however, plaintiff learns that defense counsel has purchased daily transcripts of the trial, through private (and entirely proper) arrangement with the court reporter. Counsel for Excel suspects that defense counsel has at least gone over the pertinent portions of this transcript in preparing Novick for his time on the stand, and that in all likelihood Novick has actually read critical passages containing testimony given by witnesses for Excel.

Plaintiff's counsel seeks to bar Novick from testifying, arguing that any sharing of transcripts violates the order of exclusion. How should the court rule, and why?

NOTES ON BREADTH OF FRE 615

1. FRE 615 authorizes exclusion of witnesses "so that they cannot hear the testimony of other witnesses." Does the Rule authorize exclusion during opening statements? See United States v. Brown, 547 F.2d 36, 37 (3d Cir. 1976) (no), cert. denied, 431 U.S. 905 (1977).

2. Does FRE 615 authorize the court to direct witnesses not to confer privately? See United States v. Greschner, 802 F.2d 373, 375-376 (10th Cir. 1986) (yes), cert. denied, 480 U.S. 908 (1987). Does it authorize the court to direct counsel not to convene meetings with several witnesses at once, in preparation for their testimony? What about an order directing counsel not to convey to one witness the substance of testimony given by another?

2. Traditional Exemptions from the Witness Rule

Under FRE 615(1), a person who is party to an action cannot be excluded. Nor can an "officer or employee" who is "designated as its representative." Parties are as likely as witnesses, aren't they, to shape their testimony to make it align better with what others say?

How about requiring parties to testify first? In a civil case, that would solve any problem of a *plaintiff* shaping her testimony, but what about the defendant (who presumably gets to hear the whole of the plaintiff's case before testifying)? Does the fact that parties are exempt from sequestration mean judges should not try to accommodate concerns over "tailored testimony" by requiring a certain sequence in calling witnesses? See FRE 611(a) (courts may control "mode and order" of interrogating witnesses).

Also exempt from exclusion by FRE 615(3) is a person shown to be "essential to the presentation" of a cause. Wouldn't the elders in the trial of Susanna be essential to the presentation of the prosecutor's case?

More generally, what kinds of witnesses likely qualify under the language in exemption 3? In criminal trials, investigative agents generally qualify. See United States v. Parodi, 703 F.2d 768, 773-775 (4th Cir. 1983) (rejecting arguments that an investigator should be (a) excluded because he coached other witnesses by nodding or shaking his head, and (b) required to testify first). Experts also commonly fit exemption 3, though not always. Compare United States v. Burgess, 691 F.2d 1146, 1157 (4th Cir. 1982) (psychiatrists for defense and prosecution both allowed to remain in court) with Miller v. Universal City Studios, 650 F.2d 1365, 1372-1374 (5th Cir. 1981) (doubting that expertise provides "automatic basis" for exemption, and suggesting that literary expert in copyright infringement suit might not qualify), and with United States v. Farnham, 791 F.2d 331, 335 (4th Cir. 1986) ("singular phrasing" in exemption 3 means that only one of two FBI agents remain in courtroom).

Suppose a witness excluded from the proceedings violates the order and *does* listen to other testimony (or talk to other witnesses). When the disadvantaged party learns of this violation of the court's order, what is the appropriate remedy? In an old case, the Supreme Court addressed the matter thus:

> If a witness disobeys the order of withdrawal, while he may be proceeded against for contempt and his testimony is open to comment to the jury by reason of his conduct, he is not thereby disqualified, and the weight of authority is that he cannot be excluded on that ground merely, although the right to exclude under particular circumstances may be supported as within the sound discretion of the trial court.

Holder v. United States, 150 U.S. 91, 92-93 (1893). Modern authority makes it clear that violating a sequestration order does not automatically call for excluding the testimony of the witness. See Government of Virgin Islands v. Edinborough, 625 F.2d 472, 474 (3d Cir. 1980).

Should an aggrieved party have to demonstrate that violating the order prejudiced the outcome, or should such prejudice be presumed? Compare United States v. Ell, 718 F.2d 291, 293-294 (9th Cir. 1983) (FRE 615 could be read as (a) requiring a showing of prejudice, (b) requiring automatic reversal, or (c) raising a presumption of prejudice; choosing the latter, court comments that "prejudice is presumed and reversal is required unless it is manifestly clear" that the error was harmless or prosecutor proves harmless error by a preponderance) with United States v. Greschner, 802 F.2d 373, 375-376 (10th Cir. 1986) (defendant must show "probable prejudice or an abuse of discretion" when witness violates sequestration order and trial court lets him testify).

3. The Special Case of Crime Victims

In our system, crime victims are not parties. The state or federal government as prosecuting authority acts on behalf of "the people" or "the State" or "the United States" on behalf of all citizens and the larger body politic. Hence victims are not covered by FRE 615's exemption for "parties." Nor are victims normally categorized as persons "essential to the presentation of a case," and this exemption in FRE 615 is far more often applied to case agents and experts.

People who are personally and directly victimized by crime, such as those who suffer sexual or physical assault or robbery, are likely to be the first witnesses called by the prosecutor—or at least the first witnesses called to describe the crime itself. At least to this extent, concerns over "tailored" testimony can be accommodated without sequestering them. There are also victims who do not see what has happened, as is typically true in larceny and burglary cases, and people like these usually testify (if at all) about such things as the conditions of the premises or the items stolen, where once again concerns over tailored testimony are not great.

In the closing decade of the twentieth century, however, growing social and political concern led to enactment of statutes that create and protect certain important rights for crime victims. Among these are the right to be treated with fairness and dignity, the right to be notified of important court proceedings, and to attend and be heard in such proceedings. See, e.g., Utah Constitution, Art. I §§12 and 28. The movement to guarantee such rights regained momentum when, in the Oklahoma City bombing trial of Timothy McVeigh in 1996, Judge Matsch excluded from the courtroom, during the "guilt phase" of trial, all survivors of the bombing who were to give "victim impact" testimony during the punishment phase (in the event of conviction). Judge Matsch invoked FRE 615, which at the time had no exemption covering victims, and the reviewing court refused to disturb this ruling, even though the Victim Compensation and Assistance Act was already part of federal law, and it includes a provision entitling victims "to be present at all public court proceedings related to the offense" unless the court determines that their testimony "would be materially affected" by other testimony. See 42 U.S.C. §10606(a) and United States v. McVeigh, 106 F.3d 325 (10th Cir. 1997). Congress reacted by enacting another statute, which provides that federal courts shall not exclude "any victim of an offense" from a trial merely because he may testify during sentencing. See 18 U.S.C. §3510. Judge Matsch acquiesced in the obvious legislative message and did *not* thenceforth exclude survivors of the Oklahoma City bombing, although he did conduct his own voir dire of these witnesses during the sentencing phase to satisfy himself that their testimony would not be affected by what they had heard.

In 1997, the fourth exemption was added to FRE 615, making it clear that people "authorized by statute" to be present at trial are not to be sequestered, and the intent was to accommodate the victim's right statutes.

PROBLEM 7-B. "Neither Victims nor Parents of a Victim"

In the Arkansas trial of Robert Salmon for murder in the shooting death of his wife Janice, defendant asked the court to exclude the victim's daughters Jennifer, Peggy, and Teresa (all women in their 20s) from the courtroom. The judge declined, citing the principle that crime victims should be allowed to remain and noting that none of these women was present when Janice was shot. Witnesses testified that Janice had sought a divorce from Robert shortly before she was shot, and on her deathbed in the hospital Janice told two nurses and two doctors that she and Robert had quarreled about the divorce, that he had shot her, and that it was not accidental.

Jennifer testified that she went to the hospital because Robert phoned her and said she was needed. She said Robert told her that he and Janice had been target shooting when she "just stepped in front of me as I was shooting my gun." Jennifer also testified that her sister Peggy came to the emergency room, that the two of them went to the waiting room where they found Robert, and that Jennifer heard Robert tell the County Sheriff that "I told Janice I'd blow her head off."

Peggy testified that Janice said, as she lay dying, "tell them we were arguing and Bob shot me on purpose." Peggy also testified that defendant told her that "Janice and I argued about a credit card bill."

Teresa testified that defendant told her that "we were arguing about a bill, and I got out the gun and we argued about that, and I shot her but didn't mean to."

The jury convicted Robert of first degree murder, and he was sentenced to imprisonment for 40 years. On appeal, Robert argues that the trial court erred in allowing Jennifer, Peggy, and Teresa to remain in the courtroom prior to testifying. The defense points out that Arkansas Rule 615 is identical to FRE 615, except that the Arkansas provision lacks an exemption for people "authorized by statute" to be present (it was not amended in 1997 to match its federal counterpart). Arkansas Rule 616 does exempt crime victims from sequestration, but it reaches only "the victim of a crime, and in the event that the victim of a crime is a minor child under eighteen (18) years of age, that minor victim's parents, guardian, [or] custodian." Thus, argues the defense, the court erred in failing to exclude Jennifer, Peggy, and Teresa because "they're neither victims nor parents of a victim." The prosecutor argues that the court "made no mistake," and in any event there "was no prejudice."

Did the trial court err? If so, should defendant get a new trial?

NOTES ON EXEMPTING CRIME VICTIMS

1.   Is it possible to read "victim of a crime" in Arkansas Rule 616 to reach the children of a murdered parent? Would it make a difference if the children witnessed the crime? If they were toddlers in the care of her mother when she was murdered? If you conclude that the Arkansas exemption does *not* apply to Jennifer, Peggy, and Teresa, should the defendant get a new trial? Do the facts suggest that he suffered any prejudice from the fact that they were not excluded?

2.   Should crime victims be exempt from sequestration orders? Even if the prosecutor doesn't *need* their continual presence in order to present a coherent case? If victims should be exempt, should we exempt *only* those who directly suffer injury or loss, rather than extending the concept to parents or spouses? See Utah Stat. §77-38-2 (defining victim to mean, for the most part, any person "against whom the charged crime or conduct is alleged to have been perpetrated or attempted").

3.   It seems that most people would willingly extend the principle to *parents* of minor victims. Should the principle extend to *children* of victims? *Emancipated* children? How about the spouse of a victim (where the spouse is not the defendant)? In Arizona, the applicable rule defines "victim" as a person "against whom a criminal offense" has allegedly been committed, "or the spouse, parent, lawful representative, or child of someone killed or incapacitated by the alleged criminal offense" (unless that spouse, parent, lawful representative, or child is the accused). See Ariz. RCrimP 39. See also ARE 615 (victims as defined in Ariz. RCrimP 39 are exempt from sequestration). The Arizona rule would cover Jennifer, Peggy, and Teresa, wouldn't it? How about brothers and sisters? How about intimate companions? Friends? In Colorado, the relevant statute divides the category between "primary victims" (meaning those who suffer "property damage, economic loss, injury, or death") and other "victims" (meaning anyone "who attempts to assist or assists a primary victim" or "a relative of the primary victim"). Seemingly the Colorado statute would reach not only spouses, parents and children, but brothers and sisters (among others). See Colo. Rev. Stat. §14-4.1-102.

4.   Would it be a good idea to vest in prosecutors the power to *withhold* an exemption from a crime victim? See Utah Rule 615(d) (exempting victim from sequestration "where the prosecutor agrees with the victim's presence"). And see Cassell, Balancing the Scales of Justice: The Case for and the Effects of Utah's Victim's Rights Amendment, 1994 Utah L. Rev. 1373, 1392 (prosecutors

obtained this provision to deal with "circumstances in which, if a victim was present during trial, a defense attorney might convince a jury that the victim's testimony was irretrievably tainted from hearing the testimony of other witnesses").

5. A court must have the power, must it not, to exclude a victim who becomes disruptive, even if he is exempt from the general sequestration power? See Utah Rule 615(d) (court may exclude if victim "becomes disruptive").

6. Suppose three armed robbers enter and rob a bank at gunpoint while eight customers and 12 bank clerks and officers are present, and that the perpetrators order everyone to lie on the floor, brandishing weapons and yelling threats. All 20 of these people are now "victims," are they not? Is it clear that exempting these people from sequestration is a good thing? See Mosteller, Victims' Rights and the United States Constitution: An Effort to Recast the Battle in Criminal Litigation, 85 Geo. L.J. 1691, 1698 (1997) (there is a "substantial danger" that testimony by such witnesses "will be influenced by their presence during the testimony of others concerning the same set of facts").

Eight | IMPEACHMENT OF WITNESSES

INTRODUCTION

Methods of impeachment. There are five ways to impeach a witness. Three focus on bringing out reasons to doubt his word in general, without pinpointing a particular error or lie in his testimony. The other two target particular misstatements or lies, but without suggesting reasons.

The first three methods are definite but nonspecific: They are definite in telling the trier why to doubt the witness, but nonspecific in not showing what testimony to doubt. They include (1) showing that the witness has some bias, animus, motivation, or corruption that might lead him to fabricate or shade his testimony to help or hurt one of the parties, (2) showing a defect in his sensory or mental capacity (perception or memory) that undercuts his testimony, and (3) showing that he is by disposition untruthful. A party may mount this third attack in three different ways, including (a) cross-examining the target witness about nonconviction misconduct casting doubt on his honesty (Rule 608(b)), (b) cross-examining him about convictions for certain kinds of criminal acts (Rule 609), and (c) testimony by a character witness that the target witness is untruthful (Rule 608(a)).

The fourth and fifth methods are specific but indefinite: They are specific in calling into doubt particular points in the testimony of the witness (hence suggesting the possibility of error or falsehood on other points) but indefinite because they do not necessarily reveal the underlying cause. These include (4) showing that the witness has made a prior inconsistent statement (meaning one that conflicts with his current testimony), and (5) contradicting the witness—showing that he is just plain wrong on one or another point in his testimony.

Usually these attacks are mounted during cross-examination of the target witness. However, most may also be made by means of extrinsic evidence (generally testimony by another witness) after the target witness has left the stand. In one instance (attacking the character of the target by nonconviction misconduct), the Rules actually *limit* the attacking party to cross-examination of the target witness. In another (attacking the character of the target by means of convictions), the Rule was amended to allow extrinsic evidence without any restriction on timing. (Originally FRE 609 allowed use of a "public record" to show prior convictions, but only "during cross-examination.") And in a third instance (prior inconsistent statements), the attack may be mounted during cross-examination (and it usually is), but extrinsic evidence is also admissible, and Rule 613 regulates some aspects of the subject. Most importantly, it imposes a requirement that the witness be permitted to explain her prior statements.

Repairing credibility. Usually the adversary of the attacking party has an interest in repelling the attack or otherwise repairing the credibility of the witness. Subject to the discretion of the court under FRE 611 to limit excursions into side issues, the "supporting party" may examine the witness in an effort to refute points suggested during the attack or explain away any aspersions cast upon his veracity.

Sometimes the supporting party mounts an offensive of his own. Under certain conditions, he may offer proof of the good character of the witness for truth and veracity or evidence of prior consistent statements by the witness (which harmonize with his direct testimony).

The regulating scheme. The drafters of the Federal Rules chose to regulate the subjects of impeaching and repairing witness credibility only in part. Thus the Rules make no mention of bias or mental or sensory capacity, no mention of contradiction, and only refer indirectly to the use of prior consistent statements to repair credibility.

A. NONSPECIFIC IMPEACHMENT

1. Bias and Motivation

So active and motivated is the imagination of counsel, and so many and varied are the relationships that give rise to favor or animus, that the range of points the attacking party may raise in an attempt to impeach for bias or influence is wide indeed. There are few hard-edged rules, and the extent of permissible cross-examination for bias is very much a matter for the discretion of the trial judge. But it is clear that the court cannot properly cut off all apparently legitimate attempts to show that a witness is biased, and some subjects (like plea bargains affecting prosecution witnesses, or fees paid to experts) are so clearly proper that at least some questions are always allowed.

Of course much depends on the circumstance, so a question proper in one case might be improper in another. But bearing that warning in mind, consider the following questions, all of which have been upheld as means of indicating bias:[1]

---

1. The examples set out here rest on opinions in United States v. Coviello, 225 F.3d 54, 68 (1st Cir. 2000) (lawyer being paid), cert. denied, 531 U.S. 602 (2001); United States v. Leja, 568 F.2d 493, 495-499 (6th Cir. 1977) (work as informer); Collins v. Wayne Corp., 621 F.2d 777, 783-784 (5th Cir. 1980) (expert fees); United States v. Kerr, 464 F.2d 1367, 1372 (6th Cir. 1972) (grocery bills); United States v. Jones, 766 F.2d 412, 413-414 (9th Cir. 1985) (homosexual advance); and United States v. Garza, 754 F.2d 1202, 1206 (5th Cir. 1985) (arrests).

Q (government to turncoat government witness): Defendants are paying your lawyer, aren't. they?

Q (defense to government witness): Isn't it true, sir, that your livelihood depends entirely on government payment for your work as an informer and that you made up your testimony about my client in order to collect government bounty?

Q (plaintiff to defendant's expert in product liability case): Will you tell us, sir, what hourly rate you charge for testifying in cases such as this one?

Q (prosecutor to defense witness, an alleged co-offender): Isn't it true that defendant has been paying your wife's grocery and light bills since you were incarcerated?

Q (defense to government witness): Isn't it true, sir, that my client rebuffed your homosexual advance?

Q (defendant sheriff, charged with civil rights violations, to prosecution witness): Isn't it true that you were arrested on an earlier occasion by defendant's deputies?

So important is the defense right to develop bias on the part of prosecution witnesses that the Supreme Court has held that denying cross-examination on such a point can violate defense confrontation rights and due process. See Olden v. Kentucky, 488 U.S. 227 (1988) (confrontation rights violated by blocking defense effort to show complainant was living with boyfriend; theory was that rape charges were concocted to explain why she was driving with him and other men in car after meeting them at bar, to protect relationship with boyfriend); Davis v. Alaska, 415 U.S. 308 (1974) (confrontation rights violated by preventing defense from cross-examining youthful witness under state statute blocking use of juvenile adjudications for impeachment purposes; probationer status might reveal "biases, prejudices, or ulterior motives"). Partly because of the importance of this impeaching mechanism, the Supreme Court has held that the trial judge must permit defendant to uncover basic identifying facts about government witnesses, such as name and address, and place of employment. See Smith v. Illinois, 390 U.S. 129 (1968) (where witness used pseudonym "James Jordan," sustaining objection to defense question seeking his true identity violated confrontation rights); Alford v. United States, 282 U.S. 687 (1931) (error to disallow defense question as to "place of residence" of government witness).

Still, the court may impose reasonable limits on efforts to show bias and cut off questioning when the point has been made.

UNITED STATES v. ABEL
United States Supreme Court
469 U.S. 45 (1984)

JUSTICE REHNQUIST delivered the opinion of the Court.

A divided panel of the Court of Appeals for the Ninth Circuit reversed respondent's conviction for bank robbery. The Court of Appeals held that the District Court improperly admitted testimony which impeached one of respondent's witnesses. We hold that the District Court did not err, and we reverse.

Respondent John Abel and two cohorts were indicted for robbing a savings and loan in Bellflower, Cal. . . . The cohorts elected to plead guilty, but respondent went to trial. One of the cohorts, Kurt Ehle, agreed to testify against respondent and identify him as a participant in the robbery.

Respondent informed the District Court at a pretrial conference that he would seek to counter Ehle's testimony with that of Robert Mills. Mills was not a participant in the robbery but was friendly with respondent and with Ehle, and had spent time with both in prison. Mills planned to testify that after the robbery Ehle had admitted to Mills that Ehle intended to implicate respondent falsely, in order to receive favorable treatment from the government. The prosecutor in turn disclosed that he intended to discredit Mills' testimony by calling Ehle back to the stand and eliciting from Ehle the fact that respondent, Mills, and Ehle were all members of the "Aryan Brotherhood," a secret prison gang that required its members always to deny the existence of the organization and to commit perjury, theft, and murder on each member's behalf.

Rebuttal testimony

Defense counsel objected to Ehle's proffered rebuttal testimony as too prejudicial to respondent. After a lengthy discussion in chambers the District Court decided to permit the prosecutor to cross-examine Mills about the gang, and if Mills denied knowledge of the gang, to introduce Ehle's rebuttal testimony concerning the tenets of the gang and Mills' and respondent's membership in it. The District Court held that the probative value of Ehle's rebuttal testimony outweighed its prejudicial effect, but that respondent might be entitled to a limiting instruction if his counsel would submit one to the court.

At trial Ehle implicated respondent as a participant in the robbery. Mills, called by respondent, testified that Ehle told him in prison that Ehle planned to implicate respondent falsely. When the prosecutor sought to cross-examine Mills concerning membership in the prison gang, the District Court conferred again with counsel outside of the jury's presence, and ordered the prosecutor not to use the term "Aryan Brotherhood" because it was unduly prejudicial. Accordingly, the prosecutor asked Mills if he and respondent were members of a "secret type of prison organization" which had a creed requiring members to deny its existence and lie for each other. When Mills denied knowledge of such an organization the prosecutor recalled Ehle.

Ehle testified that respondent, Mills, and he were indeed members of a secret prison organization whose tenets required its members to deny its existence and "lie, cheat, steal [and] kill" to protect each other. The District Court sustained a defense objection to a question concerning the punishment for violating the organization's rules. Ehle then further described the organization and testified that "in view of the fact of how close Abel and Mills were" it would have been "suicide" for Ehle to have told Mills what Mills attributed to him. Respondent's counsel did not request a limiting instruction and none was given.

The jury convicted respondent. On his appeal a divided panel of the Court of Appeals reversed. The Court of Appeals held that Ehle's rebuttal testimony was admitted not just to show that respondent's and Mills' membership in the same group might cause Mills to color his testimony; the court held that the contested evidence was also admitted to show that because Mills belonged to a perjurious organization, he must be lying on the stand. This suggestion of perjury, based upon a group tenet, was impermissible. The court reasoned:

> It is settled law that the government may not convict an individual merely for belonging to an organization that advocates illegal activity. Scales v. United

States, 367 U.S. 203, 219-24; Brandenburg v. Ohio, 395 U.S. 444. Rather, the government must show that the individual knows of and personally accepts the tenets of the organization. Neither should the government be allowed to impeach on the grounds of mere membership, since membership, without more, has no probative value. It establishes nothing about the individual's own actions, beliefs, or veracity. 707 F.2d 1013, 1016 (1983) (citations omitted).

The court concluded that Ehle's testimony implicated respondent as a member of the gang; but since respondent did not take the stand, the testimony could not have been offered to impeach him and it prejudiced him "by mere association."

We hold that the evidence showing Mills' and respondent's membership in the prison gang was sufficiently probative of Mills' possible bias towards respondent to warrant its admission into evidence. Thus it was within the District Court's discretion to admit Ehle's testimony, and the Court of Appeals was wrong in concluding otherwise.

Both parties correctly assume, as did the District Court and the Court of Appeals, that the question is governed by the Federal Rules of Evidence. But the Rules do not by their terms deal with impeachment for "bias," although they do expressly treat impeachment by character evidence and conduct, Rule 608, by evidence of conviction of a crime, Rule 609, and by showing of religious beliefs or opinion, Rule 610. Neither party has suggested what significance we should attribute to this fact. Although we are nominally the promulgators of the Rules, and should in theory need only to consult our collective memories to analyze the situation properly, we are in truth merely a conduit when we deal with an undertaking as substantial as the preparation of the Federal Rules of Evidence. In the case of these Rules, too, it must be remembered that Congress extensively reviewed our submission, and considerably revised it.

Before the present Rules were promulgated, the admissibility of evidence in the federal courts was governed in part by statutes or rules, and in part by case law. This Court had held in Alford v. United States, 282 U.S. 687 (1931) that a trial court must allow some cross-examination of a witness to show bias. This holding was in accord with the overwhelming weight of authority in the state courts as reflected in Wigmore's classic treatise on the law of evidence. Our decision in Davis v. Alaska, 415 U.S. 308 (1974) holds that the Confrontation Clause of the Sixth Amendment requires a defendant to have some opportunity to show bias on the part of a prosecution witness.

With this state of unanimity confronting the drafters of the Rules, we think it unlikely that they intended to scuttle entirely the evidentiary availability of cross-examination for bias. One commentator, recognizing the omission of any express treatment of impeachment for bias, prejudice, or corruption, observes that the Rules "clearly contemplate the use of the above-mentioned grounds of impeachment." E. Cleary, McCormick on Evidence, §40 p. 85 (3d ed. 1984). Other commentators, without mentioning the omission, treat bias as a permissible and established basis of impeachment under the Rules. 3 D. Louisell & C. Mueller, Federal Evidence §341 p. 470 (1979); 3 J. Weinstein & M. Berger, Weinstein's Evidence §607[03] (1981).

We think this conclusion is obviously correct. Rule 401 defines as "relevant evidence" evidence having any tendency to make the existence of any fact that is of consequence to the determination of the action more probable or less probable than it would be without the evidence. Rule 402 provides that all relevant evidence is admissible, except as otherwise provided by the United States Constitution, Act of Congress, or by applicable rule. A successful showing of bias on the part of a witness would have a tendency to make the facts to which he testified less probable in the eyes of the jury than it would be without such testimony.

The correctness of the conclusion that the Rules contemplate impeachment by showing of bias is confirmed by the references to bias in the Advisory Committee Notes to Rules 608 and 610, and by the provisions allowing any party to attack credibility in Rule 607, and allowing cross examination on "matters affecting the credibility of the witness" in Rule 611(b). The Courts of Appeals have upheld use of extrinsic evidence to show bias both before and after the adoption of the Federal Rules of Evidence.

We think the lesson to be drawn from all of this is that it is permissible to impeach a witness by showing his bias under the Federal Rules of Evidence just as it was permissible to do so before their adoption. In this connection, the comment of the Reporter for the Advisory Committee which drafted the Rules is apropos:

> In principle, under the Federal Rules no common law of evidence remains. "All relevant evidence is admissible, except as otherwise provided. . . ." In reality, of course, the body of common law knowledge continues to exist, though in the somewhat altered form of a source of guidance in the exercise of delegated powers.

Cleary, Preliminary Notes on Reading the Rules of Evidence, 57 Neb. L. Rev. 908, 915 (1978) (footnote omitted).

Ehle's testimony about the prison gang certainly made the existence of Mills' bias towards respondent more probable. Thus it was relevant to support that inference. Bias is a term used in the "common law of evidence" to describe the relationship between a party and a witness which might lead the witness to slant, unconsciously or otherwise, his testimony in favor of or against a party. Bias may be induced by a witness' like, dislike, or fear of a party, or by the witness' self-interest. Proof of bias is almost always relevant because the jury, as finder of fact and weigher of credibility, has historically been entitled to assess all evidence which might bear on the accuracy and truth of a witness' testimony. The "common law of evidence" allowed the showing of bias by extrinsic evidence, while requiring the cross-examiner to "take the answer of the witness" with respect to less favored forms of impeachment.

Mills' and respondent's membership in the Aryan Brotherhood supported the inference that Mills' testimony was slanted or perhaps fabricated in respondent's favor. A witness' and a party's common membership in an organization, even without proof that the witness or party has personally adopted its tenets, is certainly probative of bias. We do not read our holdings in *Scales* and *Brandenburg* to require a different conclusion. Those cases dealt with the constitutional requirements for convicting persons under the Smith Act and state syndicalism laws for belonging to organizations which espoused illegal aims and engaged in illegal conduct. Mills' and respondent's membership in the Aryan Brotherhood was not offered to convict either of a crime, but to impeach Mills' testimony. Mills was subject to no sanction other than that he might be disbelieved. Under these circumstances there is no requirement that the witness must be shown to have subscribed to all the tenets of the organization, either casually or in a manner sufficient to permit him to be convicted under laws such as those involved in *Scales* and *Brandenburg*. For purposes of the law of evidence the jury may be permitted to draw an inference of subscription to the tenets of the organization from membership alone, even though such an inference would not be sufficient to convict beyond a reasonable doubt in a criminal prosecution under the Smith Act.

Respondent argues that even if the evidence of membership in the prison gang were relevant to show bias, the District Court erred in permitting a full description of the gang and its odious tenets. Respondent contends that the District Court abused its discretion under Federal Rules of Evidence 403, because the prejudicial effect of the contested evidence outweighed its probative value. In other words, testimony about the gang inflamed the jury against respondent, and the chance that he would be convicted by his mere association with the organization outweighed any probative value the testimony may have had on Mills' bias.

Respondent specifically contends that the District Court should not have permitted Ehle's precise description of the gang as a lying and murderous group. Respondent suggests that the District Court should have cut off the testimony after the prosecutor had elicited that Mills knew respondent and both may have belonged to an organization together. This argument ignores the fact that the *type* of organization in which a witness and a party share membership may be relevant to show bias. If the organization is a loosely knit group having nothing to do with the subject matter of the litigation, the inference of bias arising from common membership may be small or nonexistent. If the prosecutor had elicited that both respondent and Mills belonged to the Book of the Month Club, the jury probably would not have inferred bias even if the District Court had admitted the testimony. The attributes of the Aryan Brotherhood—a secret prison sect sworn to perjury and self-protection—bore directly not only on the *fact* of bias but also on the *source* and *strength* of Mills' bias. The tenets of this group showed that Mills had a powerful motive to slant his testimony towards respondent, or even commit perjury outright.

A district court is accorded a wide discretion in determining the admissibility of evidence under the Federal Rules. Assessing the probative value of common membership in any particular group, and weighing any factors counseling against admissibility is a matter first for the district court's sound judgment under Rules 401 and 403 and ultimately, if the evidence is admitted, for the trier of fact.

Before admitting Ehle's rebuttal testimony, the District Court gave heed to the extensive arguments of counsel, both in chambers and at the bench. In an attempt to avoid undue prejudice to respondent the court ordered that the name "Aryan Brotherhood" not be used. The court also offered to give a limiting instruction concerning the testimony, and it sustained defense objections to the prosecutor's questions concerning the punishment meted out to unfaithful members. These precautions did not prevent *all* prejudice to respondent from Ehle's testimony, but they did in our opinion ensure that the admission of this highly probative evidence did not *unduly* prejudice respondent. We hold there was no abuse of discretion under Rule 403 in admitting Ehle's testimony as to membership and tenets.

Respondent makes an additional argument based on Rule 608(b). That Rule allows a cross-examiner to impeach a witness by asking him about specific instances of past conduct, other than crimes covered by Rule 609, which are probative of his veracity or "character for truthfulness or untruthfulness." The Rule limits the inquiry to cross-examination of the witness, however, and prohibits the cross-examiner from introducing extrinsic evidence of the witness' past conduct.

Respondent claims that the prosecutor cross-examined Mills about the gang not to show bias but to offer Mills' membership in the gang as past conduct bearing on his veracity. This was error under Rule 608(b), respondent contends, because the mere fact of Mills' membership, without more, was not sufficiently probative of Mills' character for truthfulness. Respondent cites a second error under the same Rule, contending that Ehle's rebuttal testimony concerning the gang was extrinsic evidence offered to impugn Mills' veracity, and extrinsic evidence is barred by Rule 608(b).

The Court of Appeals appears to have accepted respondent's argument to this effect, at least in part. It said:

> Ehle's testimony was not simply a matter of showing that Abel's and Mills' membership in the same organization might "cause [Mills], consciously or otherwise, to color his testimony." . . . Rather it was to show as well that because Mills and Abel were members of a gang whose members "will lie to protect the members," Mills must be lying on the stand.

It seems clear to us that the proffered testimony with respect to Mills' membership in the Aryan Brotherhood sufficed to show potential bias in favor of respondent; because of the tenets of the organization described, it might also impeach his veracity directly. But there is no rule of evidence which provides that testimony admissible for one purpose and inadmissible for another purpose is thereby rendered inadmissible; quite the contrary is the case. It would be a strange rule of law which held that relevant, competent evidence which tended to show bias on the part of a witness was nonetheless inadmissible because it also tended to show that the witness was a liar.

We intimate no view as to whether the evidence of Mills' membership in an organization having the tenets ascribed to the Aryan Brotherhood would be a specific instance of Mills' conduct which could not be proved against him by extrinsic evidence except as otherwise provided in Rule 608(b). It was enough that such evidence could properly be found admissible to show bias.

The judgment of the Court of Appeals is reversed.

NOTES ON SHOWING BIAS

1. In the view of the Ninth Circuit, the prosecutor's proof of Mills' membership in the "secret type of prison organization" had "no probative value"

and prejudiced defendant "by mere association." Does "mere membership" in the Aryan Brotherhood tell nothing about Mills' inclinations as a witness? How does the Supreme Court deal with that point? Who is right, and why? If membership in such a group cannot be a crime, does it follow that membership has little (or no) bearing on Mills' credibility?

2. The Court (relying on Professor Cleary, principal draftsman of the Rules) reaches a sensible resolution of the problem of the Rules' failure to mention bias, doesn't it? How *does* it resolve this matter?

3. Often it happens that key prosecution witnesses are themselves involved in crimes giving rise to prosecution. The prosecutor must disclose information about deals and promises of leniency affecting such witnesses, see Giglio v. United States, 405 U.S. 150 (1972), and defendants always follow up at trial by asking them about these points. See United States v. Maloof, 205 F.3d 819, 829 (5th Cir. 2000) (defense questioned alleged co-offender extensively about her plea agreement), cert. denied, 531 U.S. 873 (2000); United States v. Roberts, 618 F.2d 530, 535 (9th Cir. 1980) (court should allow defense questions about plea agreements between government and its witnesses), cert. denied, 452 U.S. 942 (1981). What if the witness lies about promises or deals? See Annunziato v. Manson, 566 F.2d 410 (2d Cir. 1977). What if defendant asks him not only about the deal, but about his involvement in the criminal acts, and he claims his right against self-incrimination? See United States v. Gray, 626 F.2d 494, 499-500 (5th Cir. 1980), cert. denied, 449 U.S. 1091 (1981).

4. Typically a deal takes the form of a written agreement that commits the witness to plead guilty to a lesser offense and testify against his cohorts in their upcoming trials, in exchange for the prosecutor's agreement to recommend that his plea be accepted and that a particular sentence be imposed. Given the inevitability of defense cross-examination on this subject, what should the prosecutor do on direct? See United States v. Gaev, 24 F.3d 473, 478-479 (3d Cir. 1994) (on direct, government properly asked drug conspirator about plea agreement; otherwise jury would learn he was involved and might infer that he had not been punished). And see generally United States v. Smith, 232 F.3d 344 (D.C. 2000) (defense cross-examined government witness on plea agreement, and government showed previous truthful cooperation; court avoids deciding whether this tactic is proper because defense did not preserve claim).

5. Although the Supreme Court held (in the *Alford* and *Smith* cases described above prior to the *Abel* case) that the defense should be able to uncover basic identifying facts about government witnesses, a concurring opinion by Justices White and Marshall in *Smith* sought to limit the reach of the principle:

> In *Alford* . . . the Court recognized that questions which tend merely to harass, annoy, or humiliate a witness may go beyond the bounds of proper cross-examination. I would place in the same category those inquiries which tend to endanger the personal safety of the witness. But in these situations, if the question asked is one that is normally permissible, the State or the witness should at the very least come forward with some showing of why the witness must be excused from answering the question.

Smith v. Illinois, 390 U.S. 129, 133-134 (1968). Where risks to the safety of the witness appear, trial judges frequently disallow defense cross-examination on such basic facts. What sort of inquiry should the trial judge conduct if the prosecutor objects to such basic questions? See United States v. Varella, 692 F.2d 1352, 1355-1356 (11th Cir. 1982), cert. denied, 463 U.S. 1210 (1983); United States v. Mesa, 660 F.2d 1070, 1075-1076 (5th Cir. 1981).

6. Often bias is indicated by something the witness has said. When a party uses prior statements by a witness to impeach on the theory that they are *inconsistent with* his present testimony, you will see that FRE 613(b) allows extrinsic evidence of such statements (testimony by another person) only if the witness under attack has a chance to explain. Does the same requirement apply when a statement by a witness is offered on the different theory that it shows bias? Courts sometimes say or imply that the answer is yes. See United States v. Betts, 16 F.3d 748, 764 (7th Cir. 1994) (although FRE 613 does not apply, still attacking party must show statement to witness first).

PROBLEM 8-A.   The Hired Gun

In a product liability suit, defendant General Motors has called Dr. Norbert Riley as an expert witness. Riley is a professor of engineering design, holding a Ph.D. and an endowed chair at the University of Michigan. General Motors intends to elicit Riley's testimony that the accident could not have happened in the manner alleged because the design of the automatic shift mechanism made it impossible for the car to go into reverse unattended. On direct examination, counsel for the defendant broaches the subject of the fee arrangement between General Motors and Riley:

Q [defense counsel]:   Now Professor Riley, of course you're here because General Motors has paid for your assistance in this case. Will you please advise the jury how you are paid?

A [Riley]:   Our arrangement, I believe, is that I will receive $400 per day for my appearances here in court.

Q: Thank you, sir. Now Professor Riley, you examined the vehicle involved in the accident, did you not?

Ensuing questioning go to substance, and no further mention was made of the fee arrangements. On cross-examination, plaintiff's counsel raises the subject anew:

Q [plaintiff's counsel]:   Professor Riley, you mentioned that you are being paid here today. $400 a day, is that right?

A [Riley]:   That's correct.

Q: All right, sir, now could you tell us please how much you expect to be paid for your work on this case in total?

[Defense counsel]:   Your Honor, we have nothing to hide here, but plaintiff's counsel clearly wants to browbeat this witness. The professor has said how much he gets paid, and it's a lot of money because he's a highly trained expert. There's no reason to go into great detail here. It just wastes time and distracts us all from what's really at stake here.

[Plaintiff's counsel]: Your Honor, the jury should know how much this man expects to get paid. I want them to know some other things too, including (1) how much he made testifying for GM last year, (2) whether he expects to testify for GM again, (3) how much he made, all told, in court appearances last year testifying for automakers, and (4) approximately what proportion of his total income comes from such appearances.

Q *[defense counsel]:* Well, Your Honor, I have to object to that outburst. He's obviously grandstanding here, and it's well settled that inquiries of the sort he proposes are collateral. I'm going to have to ask you to advise the jury not to consider the implications in any of those last remarks as evidence and to understand that GM is paying this man $400 a day, just as we said in the beginning.

What should the judge do, and why?

NOTES ON CROSS-EXAMINING THE PAID WITNESS

1. Of course it is proper to cross-examine an expert on fees paid by the calling party, for the fact that a witness is on retainer bears directly on bias. Invariably the calling party does pay for the services of any expert who testifies, and brings out the fact of payment during the initial phases of direct examination. The harder questions are the ones posed above: How far can the cross-examiner go before we reach the point of diminishing returns? Compare Collins v. Wayne Corp., 621 F.2d 777, 784 (5th Cir. 1980) (approving cross-examination of expert as to fees earned in other cases; a pattern of compensation suggests possibility that witness "slanted his testimony in those cases so he would be hired to testify in future cases") with United States v. 412.93 Acres of Land, 455 F.2d 1242, 1247 (3d Cir. 1972) (proper to cross-examine expert on per diem fee for testifying, while disallowing cross as to compensation for whole project). See also Graham, Impeaching the Professional Expert Witness by a Showing of Financial Interest, 53 Ind. L.J. 35 (1977-1978).

2. Witnesses are sometimes paid special fees in criminal cases too—and the practice reaches not only experts but lay witnesses (informants) who would not cooperate otherwise. See United States v. Gray, 626 F.2d 494, 499 (5th Cir. 1980) (rejecting claim of prosecutorial misconduct, where one government witness was paid $37,000, and another got $25,000; while "high informant fees" are suspicious, an informant's testimony is not excluded "unless there is evidence that he was promised payment contingent upon conviction"), cert. denied, 449 U.S. 1091 (1981). Should such witnesses be cross-examinable on fees they expect for their services in other cases? As to yearly compensation for such services?

3. If a witness for the prosecution is in the Witness Protection Program (making him beholden to the government to protect his "new identity" and pay monthly support), should the defendant be able to bring out this fact? See United States v. Harris, 210 F.3d 165, 166 (3d Cir. 2000) (defense is entitled to be informed, and to cross-examine witness on this point). What are the dangers in this strategy?

2.   *Sensory and Mental Capacity*

The attacking party may seek to show that a witness had only a brief chance to see or hear what she has described in her testimony, or that she labors under defects in sensory capacity that may affect her observation, or that human perceptive processes work in ways suggesting that her testimony is not so persuasive as it seems. Sometimes the attack proceeds by cross-examination, but such points may also be proved by extrinsic evidence when the attacking party presents his case.

It is settled that the attacking party may show that the witness was under the influence of drugs or alcohol at the time of the events or even during trial. See Williams v. State, 749 N.E.2d 1139,1142 (Ind. 2001). Cross-examination on mental afflictions or illness is also proper, including questioning about treatment or stays in mental institutions. See United States v. Lindstrom, 698 F.2d 1154,1159-1194 (11th Cir. 1983) (rulings restricting defense cross on psychiatric history violated confrontation rights; defense sought to show that witness was motivated by "hatred" and was "carrying out a vendetta" that "resulted from a continuing mental illness, for which she had been periodically treated and confined").

Occasionally courts order production of medical records to assist in cross, United States v. Honneus, 508 F.2d 566, 573 (1st Cir. 1974), cert. denied, 421 U.S. 948 (1975), and sometimes they admit psychiatric testimony when it bears on capacity to observe or report, United States v. Partin, 493 F.2d 750 (5th Cir.), (error to exclude expert testimony that government witness suffered from undifferentiated schizophrenic reaction, which bore on his "ability to see and hear accurately"), cert. denied, 434 U.S. 903 (1974).

NOTES ON PROVING LACK OF CAPACITY

1.   The Rules make no express mention of impeachment directed at showing limits or impairment of sensory or mental capacity. Should this topic have been covered? What provisions would you cite if you sought to cross-examine a witness on such matters?

2.   As you recall, no witness is incompetent because of mental illness. If you believe a critical witness for the other side is seriously afflicted, can you get a court-ordered mental examination? See United States v. Gutman, 725 F.2d 417, 420 (7th Cir.) (trial judge has power and sometimes duty to hold hearing to determine whether witness should be permitted to testify only if he agrees to psychiatric examination), cert. denied, 105 U.S. 244 (1984), and United States v. Martino, 648 F.2d 367, 384-385 (5th Cir. 1981) (court-appointed psychiatrist examined key government witness, finding him competent to testify; no error to refuse defense request to determine his competency at time of alleged offenses as well).

3.   By what authority does a court order a witness to undergo psychiatric examination? What if the witness refuses? Doesn't a witness have some legitimate concern over invasion of privacy? In one case, defendant sought to cross-

examine a government witness over a psychiatric report that had found him competent, but the trial judge refused to permit it. In an instructive opinion by Judge Russell, the reviewing court affirmed:

> One's psychiatric history is an area of great personal privacy which can only be invaded in cross-examination when required in the interests of justice. This is so because cross-examination of an adverse witness on matters of such personal privacy, if of minimal probative value, is manifestly unfair and unnecessarily demeaning of the witness. Moreover, such cross-examination will generally introduce into the case a collateral issue, leading to a large amount of testimony substantially extraneous to the essential facts and issues of the controversy being tried. . . . [M]any psychiatric problems or fixations which a witness may have had are without any relevancy to the witness' credibility, concerned as it is with whether the witness' mental impairment is related to "his capacity to observe the event at the time of its occurrence, to communicate his observations accurately and truthfully at trial, or to maintain a clear recollection in the meantime." It follows that the witness' mental impairment, to constitute a proper subject for cross-examination, must have been "at a time probatively related to the time period about which he was attempting to testify," must go to the witness' qualification to testify and ability to recall, and must not "introduce into the case a collateral issue which would confuse the jury and which would necessitate allowing the Government to introduce testimony explaining the matter."
>
> Whether the cross-examination is to be permitted under the above principles is an issue committed to the discretion of the trial court, which, in its determination, is "entitled to weigh the potential unfairness of a free wheeling inquiry intended to stigmatize the witness against whatever materiality the evidence might have." To enable the trial court to make that determination, the party seeking to engage in the determination should make an offer of proof of the evidence it seeks to develop on the witness' mental impairment. The decision of the trial court, finally, on the allowability of such cross-examination may be reversed only for abuse of discretion.

United States v. Lopez, 611 F.2d 44, 45-46 (4th Cir. 1979) (court relies on FRE 403). See also Velasquez v. United States, 801 A.2d 72, 79 (D.C. Ct. App. 2002) (in trial for sexual assault, defense was not entitled to cross-examine complainant on her mental breakdown and hospitalization three years after offense; no showing that she suffered mental illness that would affect her testimony).

4. Should experts testify on the reliability of eyewitness identification? Testimony by experimental psychologists is sometimes offered to show that (a) memory diminishes exponentially (quickly losing its edge, then gradually fading), (b) stress causes inaccuracies in perception and recall, (c) observers assimilate or incorporate new and potentially inaccurate information they learn afterward and confuse or conflate this data with their original memory, (d) later conversations reinforce opinions about identification (feedback factor), (e) accuracy bears little or no relationship with certainty, and (f) cross-racial identifications contain more mistakes. Courts sometimes exhibit some sympathy toward such proof, United States v. Downing, 753 F.2d 1224 (3d Cir. 1985) (error to apply per se rule of exclusion; court should assess scientific basis and utility), and sometimes even reverse judgments or criticize rulings excluding it, see People v. Innis, 564 N.E. 2d 1155 (Ill. 1990); People v. McDonald, 690 P.2d 709 (Cal. 1984). Most courts, however, remain unconvinced, and appellate

opinions either find such testimony inadmissible or defer to the discretion of the trial judge. Compare State v. Butterfield, 27 P.3d 1133, 1146 (Utah 2001) (trial judge must give cautionary instruction; whether to admit expert testimony is discretionary); Johnson v. State, 526 S.E.2d 549 (Ga. 2000) (court has discretion; no error to exclude here).

3. Character for "Truth and Veracity"   608 § 609

Proving "bad character for truth and veracity" (in the catchphrase of the profession) is a standard impeaching strategy, long a feature of Anglo-American law. The Rules continue this tradition, recognizing three means of proving untruthfulness: Cross-examination on nonconviction misconduct, cross-examination on convictions, and use of character witnesses.

Recall that FRE 404 generally bars the use of character evidence to prove conduct outside of court. Showing that a person is untruthful involves character evidence to show a particular kind of conduct in court—lying on the witness stand—and FRE 404(a)(3) makes an exception permitting this strategy. FRE 608 and 609 authorize (and regulate) this means of attack.

The restrictions that apply to this impeachment mechanism protect both witnesses and parties. It is embarrassing, even humiliating, for a witness to have his veracity called into question, and FRE 611 authorizes judges to "protect witnesses from harassment or undue embarrassment." When the witness is a party, such impeachment raises a risk of prejudice similar to that which FRE 404 guards against.

It is worth noting that a party may lose much of the protection that FRE 404 provides if he decides to testify, for doing so opens him up to the kind of impeachment by evidence of bad character that FRE 608 and 609 permit. Yet testifying does not sacrifice all the protection of FRE 404, since an impeaching attack must focus on traits relating to veracity. If defendant in a murder trial testifies, for example, FRE 608 and 609 entitle the prosecutor to try to suggest that he is by disposition "dishonest," but FRE 404 continues to bar evidence that he is by disposition violent. Cf. United States v. Fountain, 768 F.2d 790, 795 (7th Cir.) (improper to ask defendant whether he was a "peaceable man" because violent men "are not necessarily liars"), reh'g denied, 777 F.2d 345 (1985).

a.   Cross-Examination on Nonconviction Misconduct

One way to suggest that the witness is disposed to be untruthful is to bring out on cross instances of nonconviction misconduct that seem to bear on veracity. You may decide for yourself whether such instances indicate untruthfulness, but bear in mind that it is a long-cherished belief that they do, and for most people this belief makes intuitive sense. FRE 608(b) endorses cross-examination on such points if the court in its discretion decides that they tend to suggest this conclusion.

Consider the following lines of inquiry, all approved[2] in appellate opinions:

Q (prosecutor to defendant):   Isn't it a fact that you lied on two employment applications nine years ago, when you replied no to the question whether you had ever been convicted, fined, imprisoned, or placed on probation?

Q (prosecutor to defendant):   Weren't you involved in persuading ineligible voters to fill out false registration forms? Didn't you even steal forms for them to fill out? Didn't you misrepresent to the registrar that persons you found in the park were the persons named in the registration forms? Didn't you tell falsely registered voters to lie if questioned?

Q (prosecutor to defendant):   Didn't you give false information on a bank loan application and your tax returns?

Q (defense counsel to government witness):   Isn't it a fact, ma'am, that you used false names or aliases?

Q (defense counsel to undercover officer):   Sir, have you ever made an oath rejecting the power of God and Christ and accepting Satan as omnipotent?

Q (defense counsel to government IRS agent):   Isn't it a fact, ma'am, that you have accepted bribes in the performance of your official duties?

Just putting such questions can impeach, no matter how the witness replies, for the odor raised by the question may linger after any denial. If there were no regulating mechanism, the cross-examining lawyer could inflict damage by just coming up with the nastiest question he can think of (taking care to link it to some actual condition or event so it doesn't sound like a shot in the dark): "You lied to your spouse about what you were doing on that trip to Orlando, didn't you?" or "You inflated your credentials on your resume when you applied for that job at Northern Bell, didn't you?" You don't need much imagination to see the mischief such questions can cause, and the Supreme Court suggested long ago that lawyers cannot ask such questions without adequate basis. See Michelson v. United States, 335 U.S. 469, 481 (1948) (judge properly ascertained that defendant, testifying as witness, had actually been arrested before cross-examiner was permitted to ask about underlying deeds, so "groundless question" would not "waft an unwarranted innuendo into the jury box").

The modern attitude is even more cautious: The thinking is that *even if* the cross-examiner has a factual basis for such questions, they can be damaging beyond their power to shed light on veracity. Hence trial judges have discretion to block even well-founded questions. In somewhat convoluted language, FRE 608(b) takes this position by indicating that specific instances of conduct relating to truthfulness or untruthfulness "may . . . in the discretion of the trial court"

---

2. The examples set out here rest on opinions in United States v. Howard, 774 F.2d 838, 844-845 (7th Cir. 1985) (answer was that defendant understood that application referred only to convictions in the last ten years; nature of any conviction was not disclosed); United States v. Girdner, 773 F.2d 257, 260 (10th Cir. 1985) (defendant himself was charged with giving false testimony in prosecution for absentee ballot fraud), cert. denied, 475 U.S. 1066 (1986); United States v. Zandi, 769 F.2d 229, 236 (4th Cir. 1985); United States v. Mansaw, 714 F.2d 785, 789 (8th Cir.) (asking witness about her use of aliases was proper; defendant not entitled to bring out that witness worked as prostitute), cert. denied, 464 U.S. 964 (1983); State v. Zobel, 222 N.W.2d 570, 572 (Neb. 1974) (defense also offered to prove that officer was a priest of Satan who had forsworn truth and accepted evil; reviewing court approves exclusion of extrinsic evidence of these points, but approves the basic question put on cross-examination); United States v. Irwin, 354 F.2d 192, 198 (2d Cir. 1965), cert. denied, 383 U.S. 967 (1966).

be raised on cross. Here is the way one modern court described the appropriate caution:

> "[A] witness may be cross-examined on a prior bad act that has not resulted in a criminal conviction only where (1) the examiner has a factual predicate for the question, and (2) the bad act bears directly upon the veracity of the witness in respect to the issues involved [i]n the trial." Portillo v. United States, 609 A.2d 687, 690-691 (D.C. 1992) (citations and internal quotation marks omitted). The second prong of this test [asks whether the prior bad acts are probative of truthfulness or untruthfulness]. . . . [T]his court has looked to decisions of the federal courts applying FRE 608(b) in determining whether a bad act "bears directly upon the veracity of the witness in respect to the issues involved in the trial." Woodward & Lothrop v. Hillary, 598 A.2d 1142, 1150 (D.C. 1991).
>
>   In ruling on proposed inquiry into specific prior acts, the trial court "is vested with broad discretion" in two ways. "First, notwithstanding the fact that a party proposing cross-examination claims to have a 'factual predicate' for inquiry into prior bad acts, the trial court may assess the questioner's offer of proof to determine whether such a factual predicate exists." Second, the court (a) may "impose reasonable limits" on cross-examination to prevent, among other things, "harassment, prejudice, confusion of the issues," physical harm to the witness, "or interrogation that is repetitive or only marginally relevant," *Roundtree* [*v. United States*, 581 A.2d 315, 320 (D.C. App. 1990)] (quoting Delaware v. Van Arsdall, 475 U.S. 673, 679 (1986)); or (b), "[w]ith regard to prejudice, . . . may preclude a proposed line of cross-examination 'if it appears that the danger of unfair prejudice will outweigh its probative value.'" *Roundtree* (quoting Lee v. United States, 454 A.2d 770, 775 (D.C. 1982), cert. denied, 464 U.S. 972 (1983)).

Murphy v. Bonanno, 663 A.2d 505, 508 (D.C. Ct. App. 1995). See also State v. Gomez, 63 P.3d 72, 79 (Utah 2002) (in rape trial, not allowing defense to ask victim whether she used false identification card to gain entry into bars; probative value was "fairly low" when compared with potential to "inflame the jury").

     Notice, however, that FRE 608 does not require pretrial notice that such questions are to be asked. A responsible lawyer, if there is any doubt whatsoever that a question is proper (and such doubt usually does exist), advises the court so the matter can be aired in advance. Some judges insist that lawyers warn them, and one state supreme court simply grafted a notice requirement onto the Rule. See State v. Fallin, 540 N.W.2d 518 (Minn. 1995).

     Most modern cases disapprove cross-examination about behavior that does not directly involve lies or deception. Thus questioning about drug use, violence, or sexual relationships is generally disapproved,[3] although occasionally such points come out in attacks that show bias or motivation on the part of the witness.

---

     3.   See United States v. Fountain, 768 F.2d 790, 795 (7th Cir. 1985) ("[v]iolent men are not necessarily liars"); United States v. Rubin, 733 F.2d 837, 841-842 (11th Cir. 1984) (drug overdose "unrelated to truthfulness"); United States v. Cox, 536 F.2d 65, 71 (5th Cir. 1976) (illicit sex "totally immaterial to credibility").

UNITED STATES v. MANSKE
United States Court of Appeals for the Seventh Circuit
186 F.3d 770 (1999)

Before FLAUM, RIPPLE, and ROVNER, Circuit Judges.
  FLAUM, Circuit Judge.
  [In his trial for conspiracy to distribute cocaine, Thomas Manske sought to cross-examine two alleged co-offenders, Stephen Pszeniczka and Daniel Knutowski, who had "fingered Manske as their drug source." Pszeniczka and Knutowski both testified that Manske was their primary supplier of cocaine between 1993 and 1996, and that he delivered one to two ounces to them every Wednesday at various locations. Over the three-year period, Manske sold them 5.78 kilograms of cocaine. This testimony made up "the bulk" of the government's case.
  Thomas Manske testified that he knew Pszeniczka and Knutowski, and admitted engaging in illegal sports betting and bookmaking with them. He also testified that the weekly Wednesday meetings and phonecalls involved gambling.
  Manske attacked the credibility of Pszeniczka and Knutowski and two other government witnesses (Mary Colburn and Jacky Campbell), bringing out that they were receiving leniency in exchange for their testimony, and that they had extensive histories of drug use and drug dealing.
  The government made a motion in limine to block the defense from cross-examining Pszeniczka about threats he had made to witnesses testifying in a related case, and from cross-examining Colburn and Campbell on this subject. Jeffrey Matter, for example, had told police that Pszeniczka was involved in drug dealing, and Matter gave a sworn statement that Pszeniczka threatened him by phone, telling him "if you don't change your statement you might as well be dead" because "Either I'll kill you or my friends will." Matter changed his story, and Pszeniczka (on learning of the switch) told Matter that "if you go back to what you first said, I'll put a cap in your head." A witness testified in a previous trial that Pszeniczka confronted and threatened her for talking to police, and another witness told a Wisconsin law enforcement officer that Pszeniczka had come looking for Mary Colburn and said, on learning that Colburn had left town, that it was "good" because "if [Colburn] hadn't [she'd] be dead." Yet another witness testified that he lied to a grand jury when Pszeniczka urged him to do so and made "thinly veiled threats."
  Manske also wanted to question Jackie Campbell about things that Pszeniczka had said to her about "mob connections" and his willingness to use violence against people who "crossed him." Colburn and her boyfriend (who testified against Manske) were prepared to describe an incident in which they found "dolls with ropes around their necks hanging from a tree" on Colburn's front yard and a sign saying "Narcs Live Here" and "You're dead."
  In its motion in limine, the government argued that the threats amounted to "conduct not probative of truthfulness or untruthfulness" because they tended only to show "propensity for violence." Manske argued that "threats calculated to encourage people to break the law" are probative of truthfulness or untruthfulness, and that the threats supported the defense theory that the

government's case rested on an "elaborate set-up" depending on testimony by Pszeniczka and others who were afraid to contradict him. The trial court granted the government's motion. Manske was convicted, and he appeals.]

THE PSZENICZKA CROSS-EXAMINATION

FRE 608(b) is a rule of limited admissibility. Other than certain criminal convictions allowed into evidence by FRE 609, a witness's specific instances of conduct may only be raised on cross-examination if they are probative of truthfulness or untruthfulness. . . . The defendant argues that these threats deal with more than mere violence—Pszeniczka's willingness to threaten violence was a means to achieve an end of dissuading people from testifying truthfully in legal proceedings—and thus clearly implicates Pszeniczka's truthfulness.

As a leading treatise notes, there are three ways of looking at 608(b): a broad one, a narrow one, and a middle one. See Christopher B. Mueller & Laird C. Kirkpatrick, Federal Evidence, 154-155 (2d ed.1994). The broad view holds that "virtually any conduct indicating bad character indicates untruthfulness, including robbery and assault." *Id.* This view is untenable, as it would open the door to a potentially mind-numbing array of questions on every cross-examination. It would also "pave the way to an exception [to 608(b)'s limitations] that swallows the rule . . . [because it] adopts the hypothesis that all bad people are liars, which is an unverifiable conclusion." Joseph M. McLaughlin, Weinstein's Federal Evidence, §608.12[4][c] 608-639 (2d ed.1999). The narrow reading of the rule, which the government essentially urges on us, considers a crime as bearing on veracity only if it involves falsehood or deception, such as forgery or perjury. Mueller & Kirkpatrick at 154. The middle view "is that behavior seeking personal advantage by taking from others in violation of their rights reflects on veracity." *Id.* While this generally does not cover "personal crimes" involving violence, it does not necessarily exclude all such acts. The threat evidence would clearly be allowed in under the broad view, and probably excluded under the narrow one. Whether it would fit under the middle view is a more vexing question.

Mueller and Kirkpatrick note that "[u]nder some circumstances, it seems wise to allow questions that would not be embraced by the more focused view but would pass muster under the middle view, and there appears to be a trend in this direction [among courts]." *Id.* at 159-160. Their treatise discusses a circumstance nearly identical to this one, where although the specific instance of conduct may not facially appear relevant to truthfulness, closer inspection reveals that it bears on that issue. "[W]hen [a party's question is] specific and well-founded, the cross-examiner should be allowed to ask . . . questions on acts better described as dishonest than false . . . [including questions related to] *concealing or frightening off witnesses* or suborning perjury (even in unrelated cases.)" *Id.* at 160-161 (emphasis added).

We have not had many occasions to address the scope of 608(b); however, when we have, our approach has been closest to the middle view. For example, in Varhol v. National RR Pass. Corp., 909 F.2d 1557, 1566 (7th Cir.1990) (en banc) (per curiam), we rejected the plaintiff's contention that 608(b) only allowed questioning about acts involving fraud or deceit, such as perjury, subornation of perjury, false statements, embezzlement and false pretenses. We held that although "receiving stolen goods [fell] into a gray area," the plaintiff could be questioned about buying stolen railroad tickets because "people generally regard stealing (and receiving and using stolen property) as acts that 'reflect adversely on a [person's] honesty and integrity.' " Id. *(quoting* Gordon v. United States, 383 F.2d 936, 940 (D.C.Cir.1967)); see also United States v. Smith, 80 F.3d 1188, 1193 (7th Cir.1996) (under FRE 608(b), witness could be cross-examined regarding prior thefts for which he was not charged because "acts of theft . . . are, like acts of fraud or deceit, probative of a witness's truthfulness or untruthfulness"); United States v. Zizzo, 120 F.3d 1338, 1355 (7th Cir.1997) (cross-examination about defendant's receipt of stolen tires not precluded under FRE 608(b)); United States v. Wilson, 985 F.2d 348, 351 (7th Cir.1993) (allowing questions on defendant's failure to file federal income tax returns and bribery as probative of untruthfulness under FRE 608(b)); United States v. Fulk, 816 F.2d 1202, 1206 (7th Cir.1987) (improper for district court to prevent questioning on whether defendant lost his chiropractor's license because of deceptive practices). In *Varhol,* the full court observed that "if the witness has no compunctions against stealing another's property . . . it is hard to see why he would hesitate to obtain an advantage for himself or a friend in trial by giving false testimony. . . . As a practical matter, it is difficult to distinguish between untruthfulness and dishonesty."

Although the factual context of *Varhol* differs, the relationship between the specific acts of misconduct and truthfulness is, if anything, more compelling in this case. Threatening to cause physical harm to a person who proposes to testify against you is at least as probative of truthfulness as receiving stolen tires or a stolen railroad ticket. Also, because Stephen Pszeniczka had no compunction about intimidating potential witnesses in previous legal proceedings, "it is hard to see" why he would hesitate to obtain an advantage for himself in Manske's trial by giving false testimony against Manske. The advantage he hoped to obtain, it appears, was leniency from the government in return for his testimony. Pszeniczka had already been given ten years off of his sentence for cooperation in a prior prosecution, and acknowledged that if the remaining thirty years of his sentence was not reduced, he would likely die in prison. Because of the sum of these facts, we conclude it was legally erroneous for the district court to conclude that the threat evidence was irrelevant under 608(b).

The government urges us to reject the defendant's argument that this was error because the district court is entitled to great deference. See FRE 608(b) (specific instances of conduct may be inquired into "in the discretion of the court"). Recognizing that a district court's decision as to 608(b) is ordinarily reviewed for an abuse of discretion, United States v. Nelson, 39 F.3d 705, 709-710 (7th Cir.1994), does not change our view of this matter. The usual deference does not apply when a district court incorrectly categorizes the nature of the evidence. Here, the trial court construed the threat evidence too narrowly: its error was in perceiving the threats as probative only of violence (which − if correct—would have been a proper reason to grant the government's motion in limine). However, because the threat evidence also implicated Pszeniczka's truthfulness, the government's motion should have been denied. Thus, this is not the prototypical case where we give deference to a district court's decision to exclude evidence because it was repetitive, unfairly prejudicial, or might cause confusion.[8]

The government maintains that even if the district court's decision was erroneous, the error was harmless. While we might have accepted this argument if 608(b) was the only issue the defendant raised on appeal, because of the inter-relatedness of Manske's two claims, we cannot assess the level of harm this error caused in a vacuum. Instead, we can only determine whether it was harmless in conjunction with our discussion of the district court's ruling prohibiting the defendant from using the threat evidence to probe the biases of other witnesses.

LIMITATIONS ON ESTABLISHING WITNESS BIAS

The defendant's theory of the case was that Pszeniczka fabricated his testimony to frame him, and that other witnesses—including Mary Colburn and Jackie Campbell—corroborated this false story because they feared what Pszeniczka or his associates would do to them if they contradicted him. Had the district court not barred him from doing so, Manske hoped to probe this matter through cross-examination, thus undermining these other witnesses' testimony.

Unlike the FRE 608(b) issue discussed above, no federal rule of evidence is directly pertinent. However, it is well established that a witness may be cross-examined for bias. We have noted that "bias is one of five acceptable methods of attacking a witness's credibility." United States v. Lindemann, 85 F.3d 1232, 1243 (7th Cir.), cert. denied, 519 U.S. 966 (1996); see United States v. Abel, 469 U.S. 45, 50 (1984) (despite absence of explicit mention of bias in federal rules, bias is "permissible and established basis of impeachment"). Indeed, it is the "quintessentially appropriate topic for cross-examination." Bachenski v. Malnati, 11 F.3d 1371, 1375 (7th Cir.1993). Bias is always relevant, and parties should be granted reasonable latitude in cross-examining target witnesses. United States v. Frankenthal, 582 F.2d 1102, 1106 (7th Cir.1978). This latitude is wide enough, we believe, to encompass the case before us, where the defendant's theory was that the witnesses were biased against him because they feared for their personal safety, even though the incidents upon which they based that fear arose outside the context of this case. . . . See Mueller and Kirkpatrick, Federal Evidence, 401-402 (2d ed. 1994) ("[P]arties should be given considerable leeway, by wide-ranging inquiry on cross. . . . Proof of bias may properly show the following . . . fear by the witness for his [or her] personal safety or the safety of friends or family, relating to the parties or issues in suit"). See also Abel, 469 U.S. at 52, 105 S.Ct. 465 ("Bias may be induced by a witness's likes, dislikes, [or] fear . . . or by the witness's self-interest.") . . . In reaching our conclusion, we emphasize how closely this point and the FRE 608(b) issue

---

8. We also note that the questions Manske sought to ask were not part of a broad fishing expedition. The district court, government, and defense were all familiar with the threat subject matter. This is salient, in light of Mueller & Kirkpatrick's point referenced above—which we endorse—that questions such as those asked by Manske should be allowed when they are "specific and well founded."

are entwined. If the bias question arose alone and was not, in combination, so central to the case, we might not consider it relevant.

[The government argues that the trial court's ruling is reviewable only for abuse of discretion. Indeed, trial courts do have "wide latitude" in setting reasonable limits on the scope and extent of cross, and trial courts may act to prevent harassment, confusion of issues, and prejudice. But deferential review is appropriate for those areas on the periphery of the right of cross-examination, and de novo review is appropriate for rulings affecting the core value of the right to confront witnesses, which includes aspects of exploring bias.] In this case the district court entirely prevented the defendant from asking Colburn and Campbell about their fear of Pszeniczka and its relationship, if any, to their testimony against Manske. This complete ban cut off an important avenue for the defendant to expose those individual's alleged bias and motive to testify as they did, leaving the jury short of potentially essential information.

As an alternative argument, the government asserts that the district court's ruling was correct because Manske did not lay a "proper foundation" for asking the bias-related questions. At trial, when Manske renewed his objection to the district court's limitations on his cross-examination of Colburn and Campbell, the trial judge reaffirmed his earlier decision, noting that because the defendant had not established a clear nexus between the threats and his theory of the case by asking specific kinds of questions, cross-examination could not proceed into this area. However, we find no support for such a requirement in our case law.

Indeed, one commentator has expressly noted "[t]here are no special foundational requirements for bias evidence; the [party] may prove any fact or event logically relevant to show bias." Edward J. Imwinkelreid, Evidentiary Foundations 164 (4th ed.1998). As we have already noted, the questions Manske sought to ask were "logically relevant to show bias." Thus, the only "necessary" questions the defendant need ask are the "who, what, why, where, and when" of the specific incidents he claims give rise to bias.[9] If accepted, the government's argument in its brief that the defendant needed to explicitly ask questions like: "are you presently afraid of Steve Pszeniczka?" or "do you feel pressured to testify a certain way because of Steve Pszeniczka?" would dramatically limit the effectiveness of many cross-examinations. See Id. at 164-165 (Most experienced counsel avoid attempts to obtain a direct concession from a witness that he is biased, because the witness rarely makes the concession, and "in the attempt to force the concession, the counsel might become argumentative. Experienced counsel prefer to invite the jury to draw the inference of bias during closing arguments."); see also Thomas A. Mauet, Fundamentals of Trial Techniques 254-259 (2d ed.1988) (cross-examiner should not ask directly about bias, but instead should make point through suggestion that a witness has a motive or bias to lie). Thus, since such a "foundation" was not required, its absence

---

9. Of course, a district court may require some showing that the answers the cross-examination hopes to elicit are relevant, but the "who, what, why" questions are designed to achieve this result. Moreover, in this case, the relevance of Pszeniczka's prior threats seems readily apparent.

cannot be used as a reason to deny the defendant the opportunity to ask these questions about bias.

[The court rejects the government's argument that the errors were harmless. In answering the question whether error is harmless, the court considers "the importance" of the testimony, "the presence or absence of corroborating or contradictory evidence," the extent of cross-examination, and the strength of the government's case. Here the errors "impacted the cross-examination of three of the government's key witnesses," and assessing Pszeniczka's credibility was "critical" because of the lack of physical evidence. In Crivens v. Roth, 172 F.3d 991, 998 (7th Cir.1999), this court concluded that a propensity to lie to police officers, prosecutors, and judges is "especially damaging" to credibility. A bent toward "threats and intimidation of potential witnesses" is just as serious as the tendencies described in *Crivens.* In this case, the only corroborating evidence was testimony by witnesses whom Manske could not adequately cross-examine. The quality was kept from cross-examining fully. The strength of the government's case is a function of all these factors. Finally, the threat evidence is so important that the blocking the area off cannot be harmless.]

While it is a most unusual case in which we order a new criminal trial based on a district court's evidentiary rulings, this is such a case. Accordingly, for the reasons we have discussed, the defendant's conviction is REVERSED and this case is Remanded to the district court for a new trial consistent with this opinion.

NOTES ON CROSS-EXAMINATION ON NONCONVICTION MISCONDUCT

1. *Manske* describes a broad, narrow, and middle view of the breadth of questioning under FRE 608(b). The broad view allows questioning on almost any misconduct; the narrow view confines the cross-examiner to acts that are themselves false or misleading. The middle view reaches conduct "seeking personal advantage by taking from others in violation of their rights." Courts applying FRE 608(b) have rejected the broad view, and generally they allow questions that satisfy the narrow view by asking directly about deceptive statements or behavior. Compare United States v. Geston, 299 F.3d 1130, 1137 (9th Cir. 2002) (cannot ask about violent behavior while intoxicated) with United States v. Simonelli, 237 F.3d 19, 23 (1st Cir. 2001) (can ask about altering time cards and inflating bills). It is in settings like *Manske,* where the conduct has a wrongful and exploitive aspect but is not false or deceptive in itself that courts come out either way. Compare United States v. Alaniz, 148 F.3d 968, 1006-1007 (8th Cir. 1998) (can't ask jailer whether he "turned his head" to allow several inmates to beat another inmate) with United States v. Zidell, 323 F.3d 412, 426 (6th Cir. 2003) (can ask defendant whether he attempted to secure perjured testimony). *Manske* clearly approves impeachment by questioning on such matters, doesn't it? Does the outcome seem right? And see Unmack v. Deaconess Medical Center, 967 P.2d 783, 785 (Mont. 1998) (cannot ask expert, who happened to be both doctor and lawyer, about being disciplined as a lawyer for "having improperly initiated contact" with prospective clients to obtain their

business, where disciplinary board concluded that there was "no dishonest or selfish motive").

2.   In asking Stephen Pszeniczka (pronounced "Zen eek a") about his threatening behavior, Thomas Manske was actually trying to impeach him in two different ways: One involved suggesting that Pszeniczka was simply untruthful, and the other involved suggesting that he was "framing" Manske, which is a form of bias or influence. (Apparently Pszeniczka himself was under investigation for money laundering and other offenses, and there was some logic behind the strategy of Manske in suggesting that Pszeniczka couldn't be trusted because he was in trouble with authorities.) If this latter theory dropped out of the case—if the *only* argument for questioning Pszeniczka about threatening witnesses was that it showed an untruthful disposition, would you still think the questions proper under FRE 608(b)?

3.   When *Manske* was decided, FRE 608(b) covered cross-examination on specific instances of conduct "for the purpose of attacking or supporting the witness' credibility." Since December 1, 2003, FRE 608(b) has covered cross-examination on specific instances of conduct "for the purpose of attacking or supporting the witness' character for truthfulness." The change attempts to make express what was always intended—FRE 608(b) covers attacks on veracity or truthfulness (attacks on *character*), and nothing else. *Manske* gets this point right, doesn't it? That is to say, *Manske* is right to say that FRE 608(b) does *not* apply to questioning that aims to show bias. Confusion on this point is commonplace in Rules jurisdictions, where we also find decisions mistakenly invoking this provision in dealing with impeachment by contradiction. See State v. Martinez, 824 A.2d 443, 449 (R.I. 2003) (invoking state rule 608 in blocking defense effort to offer testimony contradicting complaining witness on "collateral" points). Hopefully the amended language will cut down the numbers of mistakes on this point. For a decision from the same state that got this point right, see Sweet v. Pace Membership Warehouse, 795 A.2d 524, 528 n. 6 (R.I. 2002) (reversing judgment in personal injury suit for exclusion of videotape indicating that plaintiff was not injured as seriously as he claimed; videotape was not barred by FRE 608 as extrinsic evidence indicating untruthfulness because it was offered to impeach by contradiction). You will read about impeachment by contradiction in Chapter 8B2, infra.

4.   When it *does* apply (that is to say, when the questioner seeks to show that the witness is by character or disposition untruthful), FRE 608(b) allows for cross-examination, but not "extrinsic evidence." Thus in *Manske,* if the only relevance of Pszeniczka's efforts to scare witnesses into lying was to show that Pszeniczka was an untruthful person, the defendant would have to "take the answer of the witness," and could not call people like Jeffrey Matter to testify to the threats. Why does FRE 608(b) block resort to "extrinsic evidence" in this setting? *Manske* doesn't mention this point, but focuses on the larger question whether the proposed impeachment should be allowed at all. Since the threats tended also to prove bias or influence on the part of Pszeniczka, Thomas Manske has a pretty good argument that Jeffrey Matter and the others should be allowed to testify, doesn't he? (Recall from *Abel* and ensuing notes in Chapter 8A1 that bias *may be* proved by extrinsic evidence.)

5.   There are fewer cases applying FRE 608 than you might think. Probably the reason is that litigants do not always uncover acts of deception committed

by witnesses. In contrast, there are many cases applying FRE 609 (cross-examination on convictions) because the information is more readily available from public records. When opposing litigants know each other, however, as happens in lawsuits arising in the aftermath of relationships that have gone sour, clients can give their lawyers lots of ammunition that becomes the basis for impeaching the opposing party. See, for example, Murphy v. Bonanno, 663 A.2d 505 (D.C. Ct. App. 1995) (in suit by defendant *B*'s estranged wife *E* and a woman friend *D*, with whom *E* was staying, plaintiffs alleged that *B* forced his way into *E*'s home and assaulted them; *B* sought to cross-examine *E* about alleged false statements on a financial statement *E* submitted in connection with a loan application, about alleged "false and fraudulent" claims *E* submitted after an automobile accident, and *E*'s tactics in extorting a settlement from a doctor who loaned her money, whom *E* accused of sexual harassment). Cases like *Murphy* suggest that litigants sometimes use FRE 608(b) in efforts to enlarge the fight and take out their frustrations. Deceptive behavior in personal relationships sometimes crops up as the subject for cross-examination in other settings. See Garden v. Sutton, 683 A.2d 1041, 1044 (Del. 1996) (in suit against police officer and city arising out of traffic accident, plaintiff could ask officer whether he had lied to a woman with whom he was having an affair in order to gain access to her car for purposes of setting it afire, leading to dismissal from police force); State v. Bishop, 488 S.E.2d 769, 391 (N.C. 1997) (in murder-arson trial, prosecutor properly asked defendant whether she took money from boyfriend by forging his signature on loan application using his life insurance as collateral, and by forging his name on check). How about asking a witness whether he has engaged in adultery? See States v. Moses, 726 A.2d 250, 252-253 (N.H. 1999) (cannot ask about adulterous relationship; adultery does not relate directly to truthfulness, and marital infidelities are generally not proper basis for impeachment).

6.   Sometimes it is simply unclear whether prior statements by a witness, which an adverse party wants to raise on cross in an effort to impeach, were or were not false. They may, for instance, have been subject to doubts at the time they were made, but the doubts were never resolved. Or they may have led to charges that were dismissed or resulted in acquittal. Should questioning be allowed to proceed in settings of this kind? See United States v. Crowley, 318 F.3d 401, 417 (2d Cir. 2003) (in trial for sexual abuse, blocking defense effort to cross-examine complainant *V* about her prior allegedly false charges of abuse; claimant would deny that charges were false, leaving for jury only *V*'s "denial of falsehood," producing "little of probative value"), cert. denied, 124 S.Ct. 239 (2003); State v. Leggett, 664 A.2d 271, 272 (Vt. 1995) (in sexual assault trial, blocking defense attempt to cross-examine 14-year-old complaining witness on prior claim of sexual assault that was not prosecuted because victim's mother did not believe incident occurred; defense "failed to make a sufficient showing that the victim's prior allegations were, in fact, false" and mere fact of nonprosecution does not suffice).

7.   Can a cross-examiner ask whether the witness has ever stolen anything (even if he was not charged with a crime)? How many people can truthfully say that they have never stolen anything? Doesn't such a question put almost any witness completely on the spot? How about asking the witness about a particular theft (assuming there is a basis for the question)? Professor Lilly

suggests leaving it to the discretion of the trial judge: "Common observation probably supports the conclusion that a thief's veracity is somewhat suspect. At least, admissibility presents a close enough question so that the trial judge's decision should not be overturned on appeal." Lilly, Introduction to the Law of Evidence 407 (3d ed. 1996). Courts reach different conclusions on such points. Some say that theft is simply not probative of truthfulness, or that it is probative only if it involves actual deception. See Riddick v. United States, 806 A.2d 631, 637 (D.C. Ct. App. 2002) (cannot ask about being expelled from neighborhood stores for theft, absent a showing that "acts of stealing involved an element of deceit or falsification"); State v. Bashaw, 785 A.2d 897, 900 (N.H. 2001) (cannot ask about stealing police badge; petty theft does not suggest untruthfulness); State v. McDaniel, 560 S.E.2d 484, 489 (W.Va. 2001) (can ask about misdemeanor conviction for complicity in theft; witness "unlawfully and fraudulently converted to her own use goods that belonged to her employer," which was "a crime of dishonesty"); State v. Bell, 450 S.E.2d 710, 720-721 (N.C. 1994) (thefts were "not necessarily probative" on truthfulness; can ask whether witness tried to lure acquaintance away from home so accomplices could break in and steal property). Others appear to allow inquiry only when the theft leads to conviction, or when the questioner has a specific basis and focuses on particular instances of theft. Compare Brent v. State, 632 So. 2d 936, 942-945 (Miss. 1994) (after getting child to admit he took his grandmother's ring, and that his mother "had to whip" him for taking things, trial judge properly blocked counsel from asking "what things" he had taken; counsel offered no specific instances and was engaged in "no more than a fishing expedition" and may not ask "open-ended questions" such as whether a witness has "ever stolen or lied"); Robinson v. State, 468 A.2d 328, 332 (Md. 1983) (defense could ask about conviction for theft, but not whether witness "had in fact stolen property," since value of "groundless inquiry" would be outweighed by prejudicial effect; conviction "conclusively establishes the underlying misconduct").

b. Proving Prior Convictions

A second means of suggesting that a witness is untruthful involves his prior convictions. Almost invariably this form of attack is accomplished on cross-examination. FRE 609(a) states the basic principle: It lets the cross-examiner ask about (1) convictions for crimes "punishable by death or imprisonment in excess of one year" (in the federal system that description embraces felonies, and the same is true in many states too), but for witnesses other than a criminal defendant the admissibility of such convictions is subject to FRE 403, and such convictions can be used to impeach a criminal defendant only where their probative value "outweighs" their "prejudicial effect" to the defendant (a "reverse 403" standard because it favors excluding rather than admitting evidence), and (2) convictions for either felonies or misdemeanors involving "dishonesty or false statement."

Note three important points here: First, convictions are matters of public record, so counsel is more likely to know about them than to know about other misdeeds. Particularly in a criminal case, both prosecutor and defense counsel are likely to know about prior convictions of the defendant—the former because defendant's "rap sheet" is likely to bear on the charges brought in the present case, and the latter because defense counsel always wants to know whether his client has a "record" of past convictions, if only because that affects the decision whether he should take the stand. Second, convictions are far more often used to impeach witnesses in criminal than in civil cases and seem most often to be used to impeach the accused when he testifies in his own defense. (Why is that so?) Third, a conviction is compelling evidence not only that the person committed the deed, but that the deed was a serious crime for which he bears criminal culpability, which alone magnifies and dramatizes the impact of the deed itself.

Note the dual approach of FRE 609(a): What counts is either the seriousness of the offense or the nature of the deed, for the Rule endorses use of serious convictions and those for crimes of "dishonesty or false statement," no matter how trivial. People of good will differ on the question whether felonies such as murder or drug-dealing tell anything about veracity. They differ as well on the question whether crimes like petty theft tell us anything useful. Would you be surprised to learn that many courts think crimes of theft do not involve "dishonesty or false statement"? See United States v. Givens, 767 F.2d 574, 579 n.1 (9th Cir.) ("crimes of violence, theft crimes, and crimes of stealth do not involve dishonesty or false statement within the meaning of Rule 609(a)(2)"), cert. denied, 474 U.S. 953 (1985). Reacting to earlier rulings similar to that in *Givens,* the principal architect of the Rules commented that the author of Alice in Wonderland "would have been pleased" at this conclusion! Cleary, Preliminary Notes on Reading the Rules of Evidence, 57 Neb. L. Rev. 908, 919 (1978).

For these reasons, the use of prior convictions for impeachment engenders much variety in approach,[4] brings problems of interpretation, raises many issues in trial, and generates many appeals. And there is room to doubt whether this particular game is worth the candle—whether this form of impeachment is fair or just. A salient fact, and one often advanced by those favoring abolition of this method of impeachment, is that defendants in many criminal cases avoid taking the witness stand if they have a prior record that may come out during cross-examination. See generally the criticism of this form of impeachment in Spector, Impeaching the Defendant by His Prior Convictions and the Proposed Federal Rules of Evidence: A Half Step Forward and Three Steps Backward, 1 Loyola U. Chi. L. Rev. 247 (1970); Nichol, Prior Crime Impeachment of Criminal Defendants: A Constitutional Analysis of Rule 609, 82 W. Va. L. Rev. 391 (1980).

Legislative background. Recognizing the explosive impact of convictions used to impeach, both the ACN and Congress struggled in drafting FRE 609. They

---

4. States adopting codes based on the Federal Rules differ sharply in this area. Consider these examples: Alaska Rule 609 permits use of a conviction to impeach only if the crime involves "dishonesty or false statement." Colorado has no counterpart to FRE 609 but has a statute providing that any felony conviction "may be shown for the purpose of affecting the credibility" of a witness, either by cross-examination or "other competent testimony," except that convictions more than five years old are inadmissible in civil cases. Colo. Rev. Stat. §13-90-101 (2003). Hawaii Rule 609 permits only the use of convictions for crimes involving "dishonesty." Montana Rule 609 disallows the use of all convictions for impeachment purposes, while Maryland Rule 609 permits use of convictions for any crime that is "infamous" or "relevant to the witness's credibility."

considered no fewer than five drafts before settling on the one that was finally enacted.

The Preliminary Draft would have permitted impeachment by convictions for felonies or crimes involving dishonesty or false statement, making no provision for the exercise of discretion. A second draft sought to incorporate the holding in Luck v. United States, 348 F.2d 763 (D.C. Cir. 1965), that a judge has discretion to exclude prior convictions out of concern for prejudice to the accused.[5] The draft language authorizing discretion was cast in favor of *admissibility* (exclude if probative worth is "substantially outweighed" by the danger of prejudice, as FRE 403 also provides). This second draft also blocked use of any conviction based "on a plea of nolo contendere."

A third draft of FRE 609 deleted the restriction against proving convictions based on *nolo* pleas and limited the discretion clause (as revised, the clause referred only to felony convictions, not those for crimes of dishonesty or false statements). The fourth draft would have admitted *only* convictions for crimes involving dishonesty or false statement and would have eliminated the discretionary language. Both these drafts were proposed in the House of Representatives.

A fifth draft appearing in the Senate would have given the green light to convictions for dishonesty or false statement but restricted use of felony convictions to witnesses other than the defendant. And the Senate draft included a discretion clause that would apply to felony convictions, but would have reversed the cast of the clause to favor exclusion (felony convictions of witnesses other than the accused could be used, but only if probative value "outweighed" prejudicial effect).

Finally came the enacted version of FRE 609(a):

> For the purpose of attacking the credibility of a witness, evidence that he has been convicted of a crime shall be admitted if elicited from him or established by public record during cross-examination but only if the crime (1) was punishable by death or imprisonment in excess of one year under the law under which he was convicted, and the court determines that the probative value of admitting this evidence outweighs its prejudicial effect to the defendant, or (2) involved dishonesty or false statement, regardless of the punishment.

In light of the legislative history, this enacted version presented three important ambiguities:

First, FRE 609(a)(1) said courts may exclude felony convictions on account of prejudice "to the defendant" without referring to criminal cases or saying anything about other parties or nonparty witnesses. Clearly the *intent* was to authorize courts to protect criminal defendants only: This form of impeachment is far more common in criminal than in civil cases. All the attention was focused on criminal cases, and it made no sense to distinguish between civil *plaintiffs* and *defendants*. In 1989, however, the Court decided that FRE 609 meant what

---

5. The court in *Luck* was interpreting a statute that said such convictions "may" be admitted, but the Advisory Committee rejected *Luck* as "subject to deficiencies" that appear with any particular restrictive doctrine in this area. See 46 F.R.D. 161, 299 (1969). Its proposed language said evidence of conviction "is admissible," which stimulated Congress itself to repudiate the *Luck* doctrine by amending the District of Columbia Statute to say such a conviction "shall be admitted."

it said, and that it *did not permit* a court to block cross-examination of a civil plaintiff on his prior conviction. See Green v. Bock Laundry Machine Co., 490 U.S. 504 (1989).

Second, the absence of language in the enacted version authorizing courts to consider the risk of prejudice and perhaps exclude convictions for crimes of dishonesty or false statement under FRE 609(a)(2) created uncertainty. On the one hand, because (a)(1) expressly authorizes exclusion of felonies for this reason, the silence of (a)(2) seemed significant. On the other hand, FRE 403 normally applies across the board, and judges invoke it with respect to much evidence that is addressed by other provisions that are similarly silent on this general subject.

Third, the enacted version of FRE 609 authorized impeachment by convictions only during "cross-examination" (although it also referred to use of the record to establish such convictions), which left open the question whether such impeachment could go forward during direct examination or (less probably) at a time after the witness has left the stand.

In 1990, FRE 609(a) was amended in an effort to solve these problems. For witnesses other than criminal defendants, the amended version provides that impeachment by convictions for crimes punishable by death or imprisonment for more than one year is subject to FRE 403 (a standard that favors admissibility, since exclusion is warranted only if risk of prejudice substantially outweighs probative worth). For criminal defendants testifying as witnesses, amended FRE 609(a) provides greater protection, allowing use of such convictions only if probative value outweighs prejudicial effect (a reverse 403 standard that favors exclusion). Amended FRE 609(a) also deletes the language limiting impeachment to "cross-examination," suggesting that it may go forward on direct and perhaps after the witness has left the stand.

Time limit. FRE 609(b) recognizes a ten-year time limit, which in effect creates a presumption that convictions older than that are excludable, as measured from the later of the date of final release (which ordinarily *is* later) or the date of conviction (which is later if defendant is sentenced to time served). Sometimes older convictions are admitted, pursuant to the notice provision in the second sentence, but ordinarily they are excluded. If the person convicted flees when released on parole, should the ten-year period be extended? See United States v. McClintock, 748 F.2d 1278, 1288 (9th Cir. 1984) (yes), cert. denied, 474 U.S. 822 (1985).

Pardon, annulment. FRE 609(c) disallows the use of convictions to impeach in some circumstances where formal procedures indicate that the witness has been rehabilitated (pardon, annulment, certification) if there have been no later felony convictions, or where a formal procedure concludes that the witness is innocent. These escapes have not been expansively interpreted. See Wilson v. Attaway, 757 F.2d 1227, 1244-1246 (11th Cir. 1985) (first offender statute authorizes judge to place defendant on probation without entering judgment of guilt, if he pleads guilty; statute also provides that on fulfilling terms of probation defendant is to be discharged, that this completion of probation exonerates him, signifying rehabilitation, and that he is then to be considered rehabilitated and as if he did not have a conviction; still a sentence under this statute is a conviction for purposes of FRE 609).

Juvenile adjudications. FRE 609(d) provides that youthful brushes with the law are "generally" inadmissible, but that in criminal cases such adjudications may be raised in the case of "witnesses other than the accused." In effect this provision expresses the philosophy that transgressions by young people are not as serious as adult crimes and not as probative of credibility. What counts is not the age of the offender but the nature of the proceedings against him: Convictions under statutory schemes permitting prosecution of youthful offenders as adults but providing alternate penalties fall outside the restrictive language of FRE 609(d), which embraces only special juvenile offense schemes. See United States v. Ashley, 569 F.2d 975, 978 (5th Cir.) (sentence under Youth Corrections Act was not within FRE 609(d)'s protection, which reaches only findings of delinquency under Juvenile Delinquency Act and equivalent state schemes), cert. denied, 439 U.S. 853 (1978).

The second sentence was placed in FRE 609(d) in response to the Supreme Court's decision in Davis v. Alaska, 415 U.S. 308 (1974), where defendant was convicted of burglary largely on the basis of testimony by one Green, who was on probation after a juvenile adjudication for burglary. On cross-examination, the defense asked Green whether he might have been under suspicion for the charged offense and whether he had "ever been questioned" before on such subjects (Green answered no, apparently untruthfully). But the trial court disallowed further efforts to bring out that Green had been found delinquent in connection with a similar offense and was now on probation. The Supreme Court reversed, noting Green may have been biased because of his "vulnerable status as a probationer" and his "possible concern that he might be a suspect." The Court was careful to distinguish between the use of prior crimes to suggest untruthful disposition, and the "more particular attack" aimed at "revealing possible biases, prejudices, or ulterior motives" directly related to the case.

Thus *Davis* does not necessarily mean that defendant has a constitutional right to cross-examine prosecution witnesses on prior juvenile adjudications in all cases, see United States v. Jones, 557 F.2d 1237, 1238-1239 (8th Cir. 1977). Arguably FRE 609 does not always entitle the defense to cross-examine on such matters either, for juvenile adjudications remain "generally inadmissible" under the Rule and "may" become the proper subject of defense cross-examination if "necessary for a fair determination" on the merits of the case.

Pendency of appeal. FRE 609(e) permits cross-examination on convictions despite pendency of an appeal, a result justified by the fact that convictions are so much more often affirmed than reversed. The principle suggests that an actual judgment may not be necessary and that the cross-examiner may ask about both pleas and verdicts of guilty (even though these have not yet led to judgment and sentence). See United States v. Klein, 560 F.2d 1236, 1241 (5th Cir. 1977) (upholding cross-examination on guilty verdict, but warning that guilty pleas might be treated differently because they are not as reliable an indication of actual guilt), cert. denied, 434 U.S. 1073 (1978); United States v. Smith, 623 F.2d 627, 630-631 (9th Cir. 1980) (permitting cross-examination on guilty plea).

Permitting in a later case the impeaching use of an earlier conviction that is being appealed can hardly be error (given FRE 609(e)), but the later reversal of the earlier conviction creates argument for a new trial in the second case, on the basis of new evidence. See United States v. Soles, 482 F.2d 105, 107-108 (2d Cir.), cert. denied, 414 U.S. 1027 (1973).

UNITED STATES v. LIPSCOMB   *Pre-rules case*
United States Court of Appeals for the District
of Columbia Circuit
702 F.2d 1049 (1983)

[In his second jury trial for possession of heroin with intent to distribute, Michael Lipscomb was convicted. He had testified in his first trial (ending in a hung jury), and was impeached by cross-examination about his robbery conviction eight years earlier.

Lipscomb made a motion in limine to prevent such cross-examination on retrial, but Judge Oberdorfer ruled that the prosecutor could ask about the robbery conviction pursuant to FRE 609(a)(1), and Lipscomb did not testify. The judge also let the prosecutor bring out prior convictions of three defense witnesses—Floyd Little (convicted of armed robbery five years earlier), Daryl Smith (convicted of armed robbery one year earlier), and Robert Green (convicted of accessory after the fact to manslaughter five years earlier).

Trial court's balancing process. In the case of Smith's prior conviction, Judge Oberdorfer concluded that "the desperate person who would commit an armed robbery would also lie under oath." In the case of the convictions of Little and Green, he thought probative value outweighed prejudicial effect. Apparently troubled by the ruling on Lipscomb's own prior conviction, Judge Oberdorfer invited the prosecutor to present further evidence during a post-trial hearing on Lipscomb's motion for a new trial.

In that hearing, the government produced additional evidence on the prior convictions of Lipscomb *and* the three defense witnesses: On Lipscomb, the evidence showed that (1) in 1973 he and two others robbed a man on the street by threatening him with a B-B gun, taking from him $13 and his hat and coat, (2) he "pled guilty while maintaining his innocence" under the *Alford* doctrine,[a] (3) he was sentenced to three years' probation, then spent four months in a halfway house but was evicted for "disruptive behavior," including smuggling in a gun, and was shortly thereafter arrested for burglary, though charges were dropped and the only outcome was revocation of probation and an indeterminate sentence on the original conviction to six years in prison, (4) in 1976 he failed to return from an unescorted furlough, was placed on "escape status," but turned himself in, (5) while in a community care center he was arrested and convicted for several burglaries and reincarcerated, and (6) he was finally released when his robbery sentence expired in November 1979.

The conviction of Smith for robbery followed his plea of not guilty. The

---

a.   [Under North Carolina v. Alford, 400 U.S. 25 (1970), a defendant may sometimes plead guilty even though continuing to assert his innocence in fact. Ordinarily FRCrimP 11(f) requires the judge to determine that a guilty plea has a "factual basis," and the *Alford* doctrine represents an exception to this practice. The motive behind an *Alford* plea is to enable the defendant, by agreement with the prosecutor, to plead to lesser charges and thus reduce his exposure to penalty when he is not confident in his ability to obtain an acquittal. In *Alford* itself, a defendant charged with murder in the first degree pleaded guilty to murder in the second degree, avoiding a possible death penalty and limiting his risk to a maximum sentence of thirty years' imprisonment. See generally 2 LaFave and Israel, Criminal Procedure §20.4(f) (1984).]

evidence indicated that he robbed a man at gunpoint and stole his car. The conviction of Little followed his plea of not guilty, and the evidence indicated that he and his brother had robbed a man at gunpoint, with Little stating "I've got a gun, punk, give me your money." The conviction of Green, on a plea of guilty to being an accessory after the fact to manslaughter, arose from an incident in which he and others robbed an 18-year-old boy, after which some of the others stabbed and killed the boy and then fled with Green to Green's house. Green "expressed no regret" and explained his plea by saying that "all of my witnesses stood up for the government."]

WALD, J.

[A]ll felony convictions are probative of credibility to some degree. However, evidence that a witness is a convicted criminal can also seriously prejudice the defense, especially when the witness is the defendant himself.

The jury is told to consider the defendant's prior conviction only on the issue of credibility and not on the overall issue of guilt. But limiting instructions of this type require the jury to perform "a mental gymnastic which is beyond, not only their powers, but anybody's else." Nash v. United States, 54 F.2d 1006, 1007 (2d Cir.) (L. Hand, J.), cert. denied, 285 U.S. 556 (1932). In the words of Justice Jackson: "The naive assumption that prejudicial effects can be overcome by instructions to the jury, all practicing lawyers know to be unmitigated fiction." Krulewitch v. United States, 336 U.S. 440, 453 (1949) (Jackson, J., concurring). The transcript in this case ironically confirms these observations. It includes the following interchange between the trial judge and the prosecutor:

The Court: Say again why [Lipscomb's prior robbery conviction] is probative of his guilt in this case.
Mr. Cornell: It is not probative. If it was probative of his guilt—
The Court: Probative of his credibility. Why is it probative of his credibility?

When the defendant is impeached by a prior conviction, the question of prejudice, as Congress well knew, is not *if*, but how much. Congress in Rule 609(a)(1) therefore instructed the courts to admit evidence of a prior felony conviction "only if . . . the court determines that the probative value of admitting this evidence outweighs its prejudicial effect to the defendant."

In this part, we consider how much information the trial judge needs to perform this balance. To meet its burden of justifying admission of the conviction, the government at a minimum must furnish the district court with the name of the crime (to show that it is a felony) and the date of the conviction (to show that the conviction is less than 10 years old). At issue here is when the district court can or must seek additional information, and how much. Lipscomb argues that the district court must usually inquire into the underlying facts and circumstances, while the government argues that the district court should not be permitted to do so.

We note preliminarily that the district court must carefully and thoughtfully consider the information before it to determine if probativeness outweighs prejudice to the defendant. This balancing must not become a ritual leading inexorably to admitting the prior conviction into evidence. Rather, the final version of Rule 609(a)(1) must be understood as a compromise between the House preference for excluding all prior convictions unless the crime involved "dishonesty or false statement" and the Senate preference for admitting all prior felony convictions. In particular, there can be no legal presumption of admissibility. To the contrary, as noted earlier, the burden is on the government to show that the probative value of a conviction outweighs its prejudicial effect to the defendant.

There is less risk of prejudice when a defense witness other than the defendant is impeached through a prior conviction because the jury cannot directly infer the defendant's guilt from someone else's criminal record. The jury may, however, still presume guilt or lack of credibility of the defendant by association or may unduly discount the defense witness' testimony. . . .

A. PLAIN MEANING

A comparison of Rule 609(a)(1) with Rule 609(b) strongly suggests that Rule 609(a)(1) does not require the district court always to inquire into the facts and circumstances underlying a prior felony conviction. Under Rule 609(b), a felony conviction more than 10 years old can be admitted only if "the probative value of the conviction *supported by specific facts and circumstances* substantially outweighs its prejudicial effect." (Emphasis added.) Rule 609(a)(1), in contrast, does not require that the probative value of the conviction be supported by specific facts and circumstances. We must presume that the omission was intentional.

On the other hand, Rule 609(a)(1) is broadly phrased to require balancing of probativeness against prejudice, with no specific instructions as to how the balance is to be performed. The language of the Rule gives no hint that Congress intended to preclude the district court from considering all relevant evidence. And Rule 609(b) shows Congress' belief that the "specific facts and circumstances" of the prior crime are relevant to the balancing inquiry.

In addition, Rule 609(b) controls admission of convictions for which more than 10 years have elapsed "since the date of the conviction or of the release of the witness from the confinement imposed for that conviction, whichever is the later date." To determine if the defendant was released from confinement less than 10 years ago even though the conviction occurred more than 10 years ago, the trial judge must inquire into some of the background facts; in particular, the sentence imposed and the release date.

Moreover, Rule 609(a)(2) creates a per se rule that probativeness outweighs prejudice for crimes "involv[ing] dishonesty or false statement." Often, however, the trial judge will not be able to determine from the name of a crime whether the defendant's conduct involved dishonesty or false statement. All circuits that have considered the question, including our own, have held that the prosecution may adduce specific facts to bring a prior conviction within Rule 609(a)(2).[b] It seems equally appropriate to permit the district court to elicit such facts in balancing probativeness against prejudice under Rule 609(a)(1).

b.   [The Court cites United States v. Smith, 551 F.2d 348 (D.C. Cir. 1976), which held that a conviction for attempted robbery did not involve "dishonesty or false statement" for purposes of FRE 609(a)(2). In a footnote, however, the court in *Smith* delivered a considered dictum: "Of course, if a statutory petty larceny offense is committed not by stealth, but by fraudulent or deceitful means, e.g., taking by false pretenses, it may qualify as a crime involving dishonesty or

We conclude from the language of Rule 609, then, that the district court can inquire into the background facts and circumstances, but need not always do so. Because the Rule does not indicate when the district court should seek this additional information, we further conclude that the district court has discretion to decide when it should do so. . . .

C. POLICY CONSIDERATIONS

The government argues that even if the district court *can* look into the facts and circumstances underlying a prior conviction, we should discourage the court from doing so because the inquiry would be burdensome and time consuming and "is likely to yield nothing more than the fact, for example, that a larceny was a typical larceny." A sufficient response is that Congress did not discourage such inquiry. But we are also unconvinced as a policy matter that we ought to discourage the district court from inquiring into the underlying facts.

First, the facts of this case contradict the government's assertion that the additional information will generally be of little help to the district court in assessing probative value. Smith's and Little's robberies seem fairly typical robberies. However, the extra information requested by the trial court and belatedly furnished by the government shows that both pled not guilty and were convicted after trial. The record does not indicate whether either Smith or Little testified in his own defense, but if the government had shown that to be so, "the jury's verdict . . . is in a sense a de facto finding that the accused did not tell the truth when sworn to do so." *Gordon* [*v. United States,* 383 F.2d 936, at 940 n.8 (D.C. Cir. 1967), cert. denied, 390 U.S. 1029 (1967)].

Moreover, the extra information on Lipscomb—in particular, his more recent burglary conviction—shows that he has not been rehabilitated since his robbery conviction, and therefore enhances the probativeness of the robbery conviction. And Green, although convicted only for accessory after the fact to manslaughter, had in fact been part of a group, another member of which had robbed and stabbed an 18-year-old boy; the group members then fled to Green's home.

The reported cases supply numerous other examples of the relevance of background information. In some cases, the specific facts will make a conviction automatically admissible under Rule 609(a)(2).[64] In others, one specific fact—the date of release from confinement—will determine whether the district court rules on admissibility under Rule 609(a)(1) or under the much stricter standards of Rule 609(b).[65] In yet others, specific facts will simply prove relevant to the

---

false statement. Where the formal title of an offense leaves room for doubt, automatic admissibility under Rule 609(a)(2) will normally not be permitted, unless the prosecution first demonstrates to the court, outside the jury's hearing, that a particular prior conviction rested on facts warranting the dishonesty or false statement description."]

64. . . . The government, unsurprisingly, wants to retain the option of introducing specific facts to bring a prior conviction under Rule 609(a)(2).

65. See, e.g., United States v. Portillo, 633 F.2d 1313, 1323 & n.6 (9th Cir. 1980) (remanding for findings on specific facts and circumstances under Rule 609(b), but noting that the record showed only the date of conviction, not the date of release from prison), cert. denied, 450 U.S. 1043 (1981), on appeal after remand, 699 F.2d 461, 463 (9th Cir. 1982) (conviction admissible

Rule 609(a)(1) balancing. The cases suggest the broad range of potentially relevant information. See, e.g., *Jackson,* 627 F.2d at 1210 n.28 (manslaughter conviction; defendant had shot his wife and "the man who was with his wife at the time"); United States v. Rosales, 680 F.2d 1304, 1307 (10th Cir. 1981) (defense witnesses were serving substantial prison terms, hence would have "some motivation to testify falsely in a dispute with prison guards"); United States v. Jones, 647 F.2d 696, 700 (6th Cir.) (prior crime was committed when defendant was only 20 years old), cert. denied, 454 U.S. 898 (1981); United States v. Hayes, 553 F.2d 824, 828 (2d Cir.) (defendant had been convicted after testifying in own defense), cert. denied, 434 U.S. 867 (1977).[66]

Nor do we consider the burden on the government or possible delay of the trial to be serious problems. First, the district court is fully capable of taking possible burden or delay into account in deciding how much information it needs.[67] Second, in many cases, the district court may be satisfied with readily available information—perhaps the witness' case jacket or presentence report, if available. Such information was sufficient to satisfy the district court in this case. The burden on the government to obtain this information is slight, and may well be outweighed by the possibility that—as for Lipscomb and Green—the extra information will strengthen the government's argument for admitting the convictions. Also, there need be no delay at all if the government makes a regular practice of obtaining this basic information before trial. We join the district court in urging the government to do so.

Third, extra information is most likely to be important for the defendant because prejudice is far greater when the defendant himself is impeached. But we find it hard to imagine a conscientious prosecutor not making a reasonable effort to obtain at least some details of the defendant's past convictions before deciding whether to seek an indictment, which charges to bring, or what sort of a plea bargain to offer.[68] Finally, we are unwilling to tell the trial judge to

---

under Rule 609(a)(1) because less than 10 years had elapsed since the defendant's release from prison); United States v. Ball, 547 F. Supp. 929, 933 (E.D. Tenn. 1981) (government seeks to introduce conviction under Rule 609(b), district court "notices judicially from its own records" that the defendant was released from prison less than 10 years ago and admits the conviction under Rule 609(a)(1)).

66. See also United States v. Solomon, 686 F.2d 863, 873 (11th Cir. 1982) (proper for defendant to point out that coconspirator who testified for the government had struck a favorable plea bargain).

Some circuits allow one piece of background information—length of sentence—to be introduced at trial as relevant to a witness' credibility, despite possible prejudice to the defendant. See United States v. Bogers, 635 F.2d 749, 751 (8th Cir. 1980). . . . But see United States v. Tumblin, 551 F.2d 1001, 1004 (5th Cir. 1977) (defendant must give answers only as to the name of the felony and the date of conviction). One circuit allows more extensive background information to be introduced. See *Bogers,* supra, 635 F.2d at 751 (currently incarcerated; shotgun involved in prior assault). Cf. United States v. Harding, 525 F.2d 84, 89-90 (7th Cir. 1975) (prosecutor could have brought out the fact that the police seized 80 pounds of marijuana from defendant, but it was plain error to inquire further into the details of the prior crime).

67. The trial court's discretion in this regard is, we believe, adequate rebuttal to the government's concern that it may not know until shortly before trial who the defense witnesses will be.

68. Knowledge of the details of a past conviction may also prove helpful in impeaching specific testimony by the defendant. See, e.g., United States v. Clemente, 640 F.2d 1069, 1082 (2d Cir.), cert. denied, 454 U.S. 820 (1981) (defendant, a longshoremen's union official, denied receiving loans by reason of his union position, government then impeached him with a prior conviction for receiving such a loan from a waterfront businessman).

decide without adequate information the important question of whether to admit a prior conviction, simply because the government finds it a nuisance to gather the information.

D. SUMMARY

In sum, we hold, based on the language of Rule 609, the legislative history, and sound policy, that the district court has discretion to determine when to inquire into the facts and circumstances underlying a prior conviction and how extensive an inquiry to conduct. We decline at this time to establish general guidelines for determining when inquiry beyond the name and date of a conviction is necessary. . . . We will review the district court's decision as part of our overall deferential review of whether a decision to admit or exclude evidence is an abuse of discretion.

[The conviction is affirmed.]

PROBLEM 8-B.   "Hit the Deck"

On May 16, 1999, a man wearing a Halloween mask and carrying a sawed-off shotgun entered the Franklin First Bank in Little Rock, ordered all customers to "hit the deck," and at gunpoint forced the tellers in each cage to put their cash in a canvas sports bag that he was carrying. He then fled the scene. Two weeks later Dan Dennet is arrested and charged with robbery.

Ray Elmo is the star witness for the prosecution, testifying that Dennet confessed the robbery to him and sought his help in hiding the money and escaping to Mexico. Dennet asserts an alibi defense, testifying that he and an old friend George Farr were on a fishing trip together in the Ozarks at the time of the robbery, and Farr corroborates his story.

Assume Dennet, Elmo, and Farr each have a prior conviction for bank robbery arising out of independent incidents occurring within the last five years. May Elmo be impeached by evidence of his prior conviction? May Farr? What about Dennet? Does the same balancing test apply to the defendant as to Elmo and Farr? How do they differ?

NOTES ON APPLYING FRE 609(a)(1)

1. *Lipscomb* was decided under the pre-1990 version of FRE 609(a), but the amendments made that year do not change the principles examined and applied in the case. Note that both the real Michael Lipscomb and the fictional Dan Dennet (Problem 8-B) faced impeachment by convictions for robbery. Do you think such a conviction tells much about truthfulness? Does the fact that Dennet is charged with robbery make it easier or harder to justify using his *prior* robbery conviction to impeach his veracity? More generally, how should a court in cases like *Lipscomb* and Problem 8-B ("Hit the Deck") approach the problem of balancing probative worth and unfair prejudice? In a pre-Rules decision, Gordon v. United States, 383 F.2d 936 (D.C. Cir.), cert. denied, 390

U.S. 1029 (1967), the same court addressed this problem and set out a list of factors to consider. *Lipscomb* itself treated *Gordon* as authoritative in applying FRE 609, and made the following comments about probativity and prejudice:

> Robbery is generally less probative than crimes that involve deception or stealth. But it does involve theft and is a serious crime that shows conscious disregard for the rights of others. Such conduct reflects more strongly on credibility than, say, crimes of impulse, or simple narcotics or weapons possession. The age of the conviction (eight years ago) and Lipscomb's age when it was committed (16) reduce the probativeness of the conviction. On the other hand, credibility was central to the trial, and prejudice was not especially great because the prior conviction was not similar to the present one. Cf. *Gordon* ("convictions which are for the same crime should be admitted sparingly"). . . . Any possible doubt on the propriety of admitting Lipscomb's prior robbery conviction is eliminated by the underlying facts that were submitted to the district court at the close of trial. This additional information shows that Lipscomb, although convicted eight years ago, had been released from prison only a year-and-a-half ago, and was a repeat offender with a more recent burglary conviction which the government had not proffered to impeach his credibility. This subsequent conviction enhances the probativeness of Lipscomb's earlier robbery conviction because it shows that the robbery was not merely an isolated criminal episode from which Lipscomb has since been rehabilitated. Cf. *Gordon* (subsequent "legally blameless life" affects probativeness of prior conviction).

702 F.2d at 1070. In sum, the *Gordon* factors include (1) the nature of the conviction, (2) its recency or remoteness, (3) whether it is similar to the charged offense, (4) whether defendant's record is otherwise clean (convictions are presumably more probative of credibility if they show a continuing pattern rather than isolated instances), (5) the importance of credibility issues, and (6) the importance of getting the defendant's own testimony. Both *Lipscomb* and *Gordon* are careful to say that these factors don't exhaust the possibilities. Are you persuaded by the suggestion in *Lipscomb*, advanced in connection with defense witnesses Smith and Little, that convictions are more probative of credibility if they follow a plea of innocence in a trial in which the alleged offender testifies and is convicted anyway?

2.   Cases like *Lipscomb* give defendants only cold comfort, don't they? Although Michael Lipscomb prevailed in his argument that courts can look behind the record of conviction, it did him no good to focus the court's attention on the broader factual picture, and his conviction here is affirmed. Can you think of the factors that would help someone in a similar situation? For a contrasting view stressing that the trial judge should not look into underlying facts, see Hopkins v. State, 768 A.2d 89, 91 (Md. Spec. App. 2001) (in deciding whether conviction is for "an infamous crime or other crime relevant to the witness's credibility" under Rule 609, the court "must limit its focus to 'the name of the crime'" and should never conduct a mini-trial by examining the underlying circumstances").

3.   In a case like Problem 8-B ("Hit the Deck"), is there any doubt that defendant may be prejudiced when a *defense witness* is impeached by *his* prior felony conviction? Why is that so? FRE 609 authorizes courts to consider this point, doesn't it? When defendant *himself* is impeached by a prior felony, the

standard differs from the one that applies when *defense witnesses* are impeached. What is the difference in the two standards? Clearly FRE 609 authorizes a court to block impeachment of *government* witnesses by balancing risk of prejudice against probative worth. In "Hit the Deck," does the risk of prejudice to the prosecutor differ in any important way from risk of prejudice to the defense?

4. In Problem 8-B ("Hit the Deck"), suppose the *government* decided to bring out Ray Elmo's prior conviction on direct examination. Wouldn't that actually tend to *enhance* Elmo's credibility, since a man with a robbery record seems especially likely to know something about robberies? Generally courts let the calling party "disarm an expected attack" by bringing out prior convictions during direct examination.

5. Most courts allow the cross-examining party to bring out only limited information about the prior conviction—usually only the fact of conviction, name of the crime, date, and sentence. Sometimes courts restrict the cross-examiner even further. Compare State v. Robb, 723 N.E.2d 1019, 1036 (Oh. 2000) (trial court has discretion to limit cross-examination under Rule 609 to name of crime, time and place of conviction, and punishment imposed) with State v. Montano, 65 P.3d 61, 74 (Az. 2003) (in murder trial, "sanitizing" conviction of state witness by allowing defense to bring out only fact of conviction, and not that it was for child pornography, to minimize prejudice). Almost all courts agree that the cross-examiner may not go into details of the underlying offense. See Banks v. State, 761 N.E.2d 403, 405 (Ind. 2002) (defense could bring out that state witness was convicted of robbery, but could not question him "about the details of the conviction"); Acevedo v. State, 467 So. 2d 220, 225-226 (Miss. 1985) (cross-examination should not "go into the details of the former crime nor the punishment given"). But see United States v. Bogers, 635 F.2d 749, 751 (8th Cir. 1980) (approving cross-examination that brought out terms of sentence, fact that defendant was currently incarcerated, and fact that shotgun "was involved in the assault for which he was previously convicted").

6. When a witness is cross-examined on a prior conviction under FRE 609, should he be permitted on redirect to offer some explanation? Why or why not? See United States v. Jackson, 627 F.2d 1198, 1208-1210 (D.C. Cir. 1980) (on redirect, defendant "presumably could have brought out" certain facts that might "mitigate somewhat the 'bad man' image" that the conviction might have suggested). *Jackson* was a drug trial. Defendant had been convicted of manslaughter for "shooting and killing his wife" and "had also shot the man who was with his wife at the time." If Jackson believed, in the context of his drug trial, that these additional facts lessened the impact of his prior conviction, should he be permitted to bring them out? If they undercut the probative worth of the conviction as impeaching evidence, wouldn't it make more sense to bar all mention of it? If the evidence in the earlier trial indicated that defendant and his wife had a stormy marriage, that he long knew about her involvement with the other man, and that he had beaten her in repeated quarrels, should the prosecutor be able to bring out *these* facts on recross? Where does it end?

7. Other than exclusion, are there any measures a court can take to minimize the prejudice of impeachment by a prior conviction involving a crime similar to the one presently charged? What about limiting the proof to the fact

that defendant was convicted of a prior felony on a particular date but not telling the jury its nature? See State v. Demeritt, 813 A.2d 393, 399 (N.H. 2002) (in trial for vehicular homicide, allowing state to bring out fact of defendant's prior convictions for "felony assaults" but not mentioning that they were in fact "sexual" assaults); United States v. Beahm, 664 F.2d 414, 418-419 (4th Cir. 1981) (where defendant was accused of taking indecent liberties with children, error to impeach him with prior conviction for similar offenses; under balancing test of FRE 609(a)(1), trial court should have refused to admit the evidence "or at the very least limited disclosure to the fact of conviction without revealing its nature"). Can a jury appraise the conviction in trying to assess truthfulness if it does not know what the conviction was for? See Bells v. State, 759 A.2d 1149, (Md. Sp. App. 2000) (in drug trial, reversible error to impeach defendant with sanitized prior conviction which was "totally undefined" because it would leave the jury "completely unable to assess what, if any, impact" the conviction should have on credibility) (prior drug convictions should have been excluded altogether).

PROBLEM 8-C. "The Plaintiff Is an Ex-Con"

Adrian Pratt sues George Denko for damages sustained when Pratt, while crossing a street, was struck by Denko's car and suffered severe injuries. After Pratt testifies in support of his claim, Denko proposes to impeach Pratt by asking him about two prior felony convictions—one for manslaughter seven years earlier and one for forgery nine years earlier. Before the jury hears this evidence, Pratt's attorney vigorously objects. Denko's attorney argues at a bench conference that "the jury is entitled to know that the plaintiff is an ex-con." Should impeachment by either or both convictions be permitted?

NOTES ON APPLYING FRE 609(a)(2)

1. Unless there are special and unusual facts underlying Pratt's manslaughter conviction (Problem 8-C), probably it did *not* involve "dishonesty or false statement" and could *not* be admitted under FRE 609(a)(2). But crimes like perjury, fraud, and forgery seem to involve dishonesty or false statement, don't they? For the most part, courts take the position that crimes involving violence, prostitution, drunkenness, and narcotics do not involve dishonesty or false statement.[6] What about smuggling? Counterfeiting? Failure to file a tax return? Embezzlement?

6. Cases approving resort to FRE 609(a)(2) include United States v. Bay, 762 F.2d 1314, 1317-1318 (9th Cir. 1984) (forgery); United States v. Williams, 642 F.2d 136, 140 (5th Cir. 1981) (bribery); United States v. Lester, 749 F.2d 1288, 1300 (9th Cir. 1984) (filing false police report); United States v. McClintock, 748 F.2d 1278, 1288 (9th Cir. 1984) (mail fraud). Cases disapproving resort to FRE 609(a)(2) include United States v. Mansaw, 714 F.2d 785, 789 (8th Cir.) (prostitution), cert. denied, 464 U.S. 986 (1983); Czajka v. Hickman, 703 F.2d 317, 319 (8th Cir. 1983) (rape); United States v. Mehrmanesh, 689 F.2d 822, 833-834 (9th Cir. 1982) (narcotics); Reyes v. Missouri P. R.R., 589 F.2d 791, 795 (5th Cir. 1979) (public intoxication); United States v. Harvey, 588 F.2d 1201, 1203 (8th Cir. 1978) (assault).

2.   Is there a difference between the operation of FRE 609(a)(1) and 609(a)(2)? The former modifies the phrase "shall be admitted" by empowering judges to disallow the impeaching attack in certain situations where concerns over prejudice warrant exclusion of the convictions. FRE 609(a)(2) contains no modifying language, and most courts have concluded that trial judges lack discretion to disallow impeachment for crimes involving "dishonesty and false statement" and that FRE 403 does not operate in this context. See SEC v. Sargent, 229 F.3d 68, 79 (1st Cir. 2000) (no discretion to exclude). See also Green v. Bock Laundry Machine Co., 490 U.S. 504 (1989) (strongly implying same conclusion).

3.   It has been especially hard to apply FRE 609(a) where the conviction involves a crime of theft. Many courts exclude theft from FRE 609(a)(2). See, e.g., State v. Pacheco, 26 P.3d 572, 587 (Hi. 2001) (under state rule allowing cross-examination only on convictions for "crime of dishonesty," petty theft did not qualify); United States v. Owens, 145 F.3d 923, 927 (7th Cir. 1998) (excluding conviction for stealing car stereo, leading to plea of guilty for misdemeanor retail theft; implying that this conviction was not for crime of dishonesty or false statement). Other courts disagree. See, e.g., McHenry v. Chadwick, 896 F.2d 184, 188-189 (6th Cir. 1990) (convictions for shoplifting and concealing stolen property involved dishonesty or false statement). Not surprisingly, the actual facts surrounding many theft crimes clearly *do* involve dishonesty or false statement. Do particular facts *count* for purposes of applying FRE 609(a) if the elements in the crime do not include them? Most courts have said the facts do count. See, e.g., United States v. Payton, 159 F.3d 49, 56-57 (2d Cir. 1998) (third degree larceny conviction of defendant's mother, arising out of false statements in her application for food stamps, fit second prong; court would "look beyond the elements of the offense" to determine this point). And see Altobello v. Borden Confectionery Products, Inc., 872 F.2d 215, 216-217 (7th Cir. 1989) (misdemeanor theft fit FRE 609(a)(2) where facts showed that defendant tampered with electric meter, which was *"necessarily* a crime of deception") (opinion by Judge Posner, in his inimitable style).

4.   Looking behind a theft conviction to decide whether the particular facts involve dishonesty or false statement under FRE 609(a)(2) is consistent with the mandate of *Lipscomb* to consider background information in applying FRE 609(a)(1), isn't it? But it's *not* consistent, is it, with the tradition of letting the jury hear only the bare bones facts (name of the offense, time, and sometimes place of conviction, and punishment imposed)? If it is the particular facts that bring a conviction within FRE 609(a)(2), shouldn't the jury learn about them? Note that looking behind a conviction to see whether FRE 609(a)(2) applies is likely to be bad news for defendants since the question is whether to apply an automatic rule of admissibility to a conviction that (on its face) doesn't fit the automatic rule.

5.   What if the witness has been convicted of petty larceny (a misdemeanor) on a guilty plea, but in the present proceedings the prosecutor offers to demonstrate for the trial judge that in fact the witness was at the time employed in a position of trust and was taking money from his employer. That misdeed amounts to embezzlement, which is a felony. Could the prosecutor argue that even though petty larceny does not fit FRE 609(a)(2) (because most courts believe it is *not* a crime of "dishonesty or false statement"), nevertheless

the conviction should be admitted under FRE 609(a)(1) because the underlying deed was a felony? See United States v. Lane, 708 F.2d 1394, 1398 (9th Cir. 1983) (government witness was charged with felony arson, but pleaded guilty to a misdemeanor lesser included; excluding prior conviction, for misdemeanor does not fit FRE 609(a)(2) "unless it involved dishonesty or false statement").

PROBLEM 8-D. Five-Time Loser

On August 1, 2004, Durston is charged with armed assault against Vincent, which allegedly occurred on June 10, 2004. Trial commences on October 1, 2004. The defense claims that Durston was elsewhere at the time of the alleged crime and that Vincent has made a mistaken identification. Durston testifies that he traveled alone to a nearby town on a personal errand, returning only after the alleged crime. He has no corroborative witnesses and no documentary or circumstantial evidence to support his story.

On cross-examination the prosecutor proposes to ask him about the following prior convictions:

1. A conviction six months earlier for falsifying a motel register (a misdemeanor violation of city ordinance), leading to a fine; *dishonesty*
2. A conviction two years earlier for unlawful sale of marijuana (a felony punishable by up to six years' imprisonment), leading to a suspended sentence;
3. A conviction four years earlier for grand larceny (a felony punishable by up to ten years' imprisonment), leading to a two-year sentence served in its entirety;
4. A conviction eight years earlier for first degree armed assault (a felony punishable by up to 15 years' imprisonment), leading to a five-year sentence and release on parole after two years; and
5. A conviction entered 12 years earlier (on September 1, 1992) for forging a bank application (a felony punishable by up to ten years' imprisonment), leading to a two-year sentence served in its entirety (Durston having been released on September 1, 1994).

Anticipating these questions, Durston seasonably objects. Which of these convictions, if any, should the court permit the prosecutor to pursue on cross-examination?

PROBLEM 8-E. Faker, Thug?

Allen is charged with burglary, arising out of an incident in which a masked intruder allegedly gained entrance at night through the ground floor window of a condominium owned by Beatrice and stole jewelry and silverware. State witnesses place Allen in the neighborhood at the time of the offense. Beatrice testifies that she returned home on the occasion in question and surprised the intruder, and in court she identifies Allen as the culprit. But defense cross-examination shakes her testimony, bringing out that in pretrial statements she said the perpetrator wore a "class ring" on his right hand and a "silver banded watch" on his left. (Allen has testified that he wears neither a ring nor a watch, and acquaintances from his place of employment support him on these points.)

During cross-examination of Allen, the prosecutor proposes to ask him about an incident four years earlier in which he allegedly falsified his federal income tax return. That event led to a tax fraud prosecution, a conviction on a felony count after a trial, and incarceration for one and one-half years. In the present burglary proceedings, the trial judge holds an in camera hearing in aid of the defense objection. There the prosecutor asks permission to bring out on cross-examination of Allen that

1. He claimed an exemption on his tax return for a child, though he has no children;
2. He claimed a deduction in the amount of $4,000 for mortgage interest, though he lived in a rented house and was entitled to no such deduction; and
3. He claimed a deduction in the amount of $800 for "charitable contributions," for which he "possessed receipts," when in fact he had no proof of any charitable contributions.

Allen objects, arguing that cross-examination under FRE 609 "is restricted to bringing out the fact of conviction, the date and place, and the sentence imposed." The prosecutor replies in this vein:

I have no intention of mentioning any conviction. I just want to ask about the acts under FRE 608(b). There is no doubt that Allen did precisely what the questions imply, for the record of the proceedings against him establishes all these points. There is nothing in Rule 609 that says I must proceed under that provision, and FRE 608(b) authorizes the court to permit cross-examination about "[s]pecific instances of the conduct of a witness" that bear upon "his credibility," as these "instances" certainly do. This man is asking the jury to believe him when he says he did not commit the burglary, and I think the jury is entitled to know that he lied repeatedly on his tax return.

How should the judge rule and why? *Should* the specific limits developed in cases applying FRE 609 apply when the misbehavior of the witness has resulted in conviction, even if the prosecutor proposes to make no mention of the conviction?

NOTES ON CO-ORDINATING FRE 608 WITH 609

1. Obviously it is possible to read FRE 608 and 609 just as the prosecutor in Problem 8-E suggests. But it is also possible, isn't it, to conclude that FRE 609 governs whenever the conduct in question has led to conviction, and that the limits observed in cross-examining on convictions should apply in such cases? Consider the following argument in favor of this view:

[Q]uestioning about criminal acts without mentioning a conviction would generate a distorted and incomplete picture, inviting the factfinder to believe, for instance, that the witness not only misbehaved but "got away with it." And arguably the purpose of the various specific restrictions in FRE 609, including the ten-year rule and the provision on juvenile adjudications, is not only to bar questions on convictions but to limit all reference to the whole subject and to put certain aspects of it out of bounds. Hence allowing resort to FRE 608 would essentially evade the restrictions.

Mueller and Kirkpatrick, Evidence §6.34 (3d ed. 2003).

2. Courts have been surprisingly unconcerned over this matter, but occasionally the issue arises, and at least sometimes the outcomes seem to reach an appropriate accommodation of conflicting policies. See State v. Clark, 24 P.3d 1006 (Wash. 2001) (in capital murder trial, defense invoked Rule 608 in seeking to cross-examine jailhouse informant *H* about "specific instances of conduct underlying his 1993 convictions for theft and forgery," but trial court did not allow it; noting that cross-examination under Rule 609 cannot go into "details of the acts leading to the prior convictions," reviewing court comments that this restriction is "limited to" Rule 609, and that trial judge could have allowed questioning on the misconduct itself, but had discretion to decide otherwise; since *H* was cross-examined on each of his 36 prior convictions, ruling was not erroneous), cert. denied, 534 U.S. 1000 (2001).

| **LUCE v. UNITED STATES**
| **United States Supreme Court**
| **469 U.S. 38 (1984)**

CHIEF JUSTICE BURGER delivered the opinion of the Court.

We granted certiorari to resolve a conflict among the Circuits as to whether the defendant, who did not testify at trial, is entitled to review of the District Court's ruling denying his motion to forbid the use of a prior conviction to impeach his credibility.

I

Petitioner was indicted on charges of conspiracy, and possession of cocaine with intent to distribute, in violation of 21 U.S.C. §§846 and 841(a)(1). During his trial in the United States District Court for the Western District of Tennessee, petitioner moved for a ruling to preclude the Government from using a 1974 state conviction to impeach him if he testified. There was no commitment by petitioner that he would testify if the motion were granted, nor did he make a proffer to the court as to what his testimony would be. In opposing the motion, the Government represented that the conviction was for a serious crime—possession of a controlled substance.

The District Court ruled that the prior conviction fell within the category of permissible impeachment evidence under Federal Rule of Evidence 609(a). The District Court noted, however, that the nature and scope of petitioner's trial testimony could affect the court's specific evidentiary rulings; for example, the court was prepared to hold that the prior conviction would be excluded if petitioner limited his testimony to explaining his attempt to flee from the arresting officers. However, if petitioner took the stand and denied any prior involvement with drugs, he could then be impeached by the 1974 conviction. Petitioner did not testify, and the jury returned guilty verdicts.

II

The United States Court of Appeals for the Sixth Circuit affirmed. The Court of Appeals refused to consider petitioner's contention that the District Court abused its discretion in denying the motion in limine without making an explicit finding that the probative value of the prior conviction outweighed its prejudicial effect. The Court of Appeals held that when the defendant does not testify, the court will not review the District Court's in limine ruling.

Some other Circuits have permitted review in similar situations;[3] we granted certiorari to resolve the conflict. We affirm.

III

It is clear, of course, that had petitioner testified and been impeached by evidence of a prior conviction, the District Court's decision to admit the impeachment evidence would have been reviewable on appeal along with any other claims of error. The Court of Appeals would then have had a complete record detailing the nature of petitioner's testimony, the scope of the cross-examination, and the possible impact of the impeachment on the jury's verdict.

A reviewing court is handicapped in any effort to rule on subtle evidentiary questions outside a factual context.[4] This is particularly true under Rule 609(a)(1), which directs the court to weigh the probative value of a prior conviction against the prejudicial effect to the defendant. To perform this balancing, the court must know the precise nature of the defendant's testimony, which is unknowable when, as here, the defendant does not testify.[5]

Any possible harm flowing from a district court's in limine ruling permitting impeachment by a prior conviction is wholly speculative. The ruling is subject to change when the case unfolds, particularly if the actual testimony differs from what was contained in the defendant's proffer. Indeed even if nothing unexpected happens at trial, the district judge is free, in the exercise of sound judicial discretion, to alter a previous in limine ruling. On a record such as here, it would be a matter of conjecture whether the District Court would have

---

3. . . . The Ninth Circuit allows review if the defendant makes a record unequivocally announcing his intention to testify if his motion to exclude prior convictions is granted, and if he proffers the substance of his contemplated testimony. See United States v. Cook, 608 F.2d 1175, 1186 (1979) (en banc), cert. denied, 444 U.S. 1034 (1980).

4. Although the Federal Rules of Evidence do not explicitly authorize in limine rulings, the practice has developed pursuant to the district court's inherent authority to manage the course of trials. See generally Fed. Rule Evid. 103(c); cf. Fed. Rule Crim. Proc. 12(e).

5. Requiring a defendant to make a proffer of testimony is no answer; his trial testimony could, for any number of reasons, differ from the proffer.

allowed the Government to attack petitioner's credibility at trial by means of the prior conviction.

When the defendant does not testify, the reviewing court also has no way of knowing whether the Government would have sought to impeach with the prior conviction. If, for example, the Government's case is strong, and the defendant is subject to impeachment by other means, a prosecutor might elect not to use an arguably inadmissible prior conviction.

Because an accused's decision whether to testify "seldom turns on the resolution of one factor," New Jersey v. Portash, 440 U.S. 450, 467 (1979) (Blackmun, J., dissenting), a reviewing court cannot assume that the adverse ruling motivated a defendant's decision not to testify. In support of his motion a defendant might make a commitment to testify if his motion is granted; but such a commitment is virtually risk free because of the difficulty of enforcing it.

Even if these difficulties could be surmounted, the reviewing court would still face the question of harmless error. Were in limine rulings under Rule 609(a) reviewable on appeal, almost any error would result in the windfall of automatic reversal; the appellate court could not logically term "harmless" an error that presumptively kept the defendant from testifying. Requiring that a defendant testify in order to preserve Rule 609(a) claims, will enable the reviewing court to determine the impact any erroneous impeachment may have had in light of the record as a whole; it will also tend to discourage making such motions solely to "plant" reversible error in the event of conviction.

Petitioner's reliance on Brooks v. Tennessee, 406 U.S. 605 (1972), and New Jersey v. Portash, supra, is misplaced. In those cases we reviewed Fifth Amendment challenges to state-court rulings that operated to dissuade defendants from testifying. We did not hold that a federal court's preliminary ruling on a question not reaching constitutional dimensions—such as a decision under Rule 609(a)—is reviewable on appeal.

However, Justice Powell, in his concurring opinion in *Portash,* stated essentially the rule we adopt today:

> The preferred method for raising claims such as [petitioner's] would be for the defendant to take the stand and appeal a subsequent conviction. . . . Only in this way may the claim be presented to a reviewing court in a concrete factual context.

440 U.S., at 462.

We hold that to raise and preserve for review the claim of improper impeachment with a prior conviction, a defendant must testify. Accordingly, the judgment of the Court of Appeals is affirmed.

[JUSTICE STEVENS did not participate. JUSTICES BRENNAN and MARSHALL joined in a separate concurring opinion, which is omitted.]

NOTES ON PRESERVING ERROR FOR REVIEW

1. Why do defendants like Edward Luce make pretrial motions to bar impeachment under FRE 609? Would the Court have reached the merits of

the Luce claim of error if defense counsel had indicated that Luce would testify (if his conviction could not be used against him) and described in detail the tenor of the expected testimony?

2.   In New Jersey v. Portash, 440 U.S. 450, 454-455 (1979), defendant was prosecuted for misconduct and extortion in office. He twice sought a ruling that his prior grand jury testimony, given under a grant of use immunity, would not be admissible if he testified. The trial judge ruled that the testimony would be admissible to impeach if he contradicted what he said before, and defendant did not testify. Still the Supreme Court reached the merits of his claim, holding that immunized testimony was involuntary, hence inadmissible under the Fifth Amendment. It resolved this question over the state's objection that it was "abstract and hypothetical" because defendant did not testify. The Court replied that the trial judge "did rule on the merits" and that the "case or controversy" requirement was satisfied. Should the Court reach the merits of a constitutional issue in cases like *Portash* but not evidence issues in cases like *Luce*?

3.   In its decision in *Cook* (cited in *Luce*), the Ninth Circuit held that a defendant who does not testify may nevertheless challenge an adverse ruling in limine under FRE 609 if he "establishes on the record that he will in fact take the stand and testify if his challenged prior convictions are excluded" and "sufficiently outlines the nature of his testimony so that the trial court, and the reviewing court, can do the necessary balancing." The court argued:

> [I]t is unrealistic to continue to refuse to review these rulings unless the defendant takes the stand. The effect of the preliminary ruling can substantially change the course of the trial, and any ruling which so changes the course of a trial ought to be subject to judicial review.
>
> Defendants and their counsel make many tactical choices during a trial. Ordinarily, these choices are binding upon the defendant. However, assuming only for the purpose of argument that the trial court erred in announcing its application of Rule 609, the error may cause a defendant to make a choice that he might otherwise not have made. The government must admit that the tactical choice to remain silent is more likely a product of the court's ruling than of the defendant's free selection among strategic options.
>
> It pushes the doctrine of waiver beyond its usual criminal-law application to say that a defendant responding to an erroneous ruling by the trial court by remaining silent has waived his right to testify. And waiver becomes even less convincing if we say that by remaining silent under the constraints of an erroneous ruling on a point of law the defendant has waived his right to challenge that ruling on appeal.

United States v. Cook, 608 F.2d 1175, 1183-1184, 1186 (9th Cir. 1979), cert. denied, 444 U.S. 1304 (1980). Decisions from at least eight circuits similarly allowed review, despite defendant's failure to testify, although not all required a commitment and proffer. Did the court in *Luce* adequately answer the points made in *Cook*?

4.   Note that *Luce* establishes only the procedure to be followed in federal criminal prosecutions. States remain free to follow the procedure endorsed in *Cook*, allowing defense appeals from adverse rulings applying state counterparts to Rule 609 despite defendant's failure to testify. Decisions in a number of states reject *Luce*. See People v. Moore, 156 A.2d 394, 346 (N.Y. 1989); Common-

wealth v. Jackson, 561 A.2d 335 (Pa. Super. 1988); State v. McClure, 692 P.2d 579, 583-584 & n.4 (Or. 1984) (all declining to follow *Luce* doctrine). In one state, the Rule expressly provides that defendant need not take the stand to preserve the claim of error. See Tennessee Rules of Evidence, Rule 609(e) (in the case of criminal defendants, "reasonable written notice" of intent to impeach by prior convictions must be given in advance of trial, and court "may rule" on admissibility prior to the trial "but in any event shall rule prior to the testimony of the accused," who "need not actually testify at the trial to later challenge the propriety" of admitting the conviction). Other states, however, have elected to follow *Luce.* See Walker v. State, 790 A.2d 1214 (Del. 2002); State v. Wickham, 796 P.2d 1354, 1356 (Alaska, 1990); People v. Finley, 431 N.W.2d 19, 24 (Mich. 1988) (all following *Luce*).

5.   If a defendant makes and loses a motion in limine to exclude his convictions, then testifies and brings them out on direct in order to minimize the expected damage from the impeachment, can he claim error in the trial court's ruling? See Ohler v. United States, 529 U.S. 753 (2000) (no). Between them, *Luce* and *Ohler* put the accused in a very difficult position, don't they? Some states have fallen in line behind *Ohler,* but some have not. Compare Brown v. State, 817 A.2d 241 (Md. 2003) (following *Ohler*) with State v. Daly, 623 N.W.2d 799 (Iowa 1999) (declining to follow *Ohler*).

c.   Character Witnesses

The third way of suggesting lack of veracity is to introduce testimony by a character witness that the witness in question (we may call him the "principal witness") is untruthful. FRE 608(a) authorizes testimony of this sort. Here too the Rules expand common law tradition by permitting "opinion" as well as "reputation" testimony (FRE 405 does likewise in the case of character evidence used to prove out-of-court conduct), meaning that the character witness may say what he personally thinks of the veracity of the principal witness.

In either case of course a foundation is necessary, and at least some minimal elaboration is typically allowed:

Q (to character witness):   Coach Jones, are you acquainted with the reputation of [principal witness] Grace Gardner in the community of Riverdale for truth and veracity?
A (Coach Jones):   Yes sir, I am.
Q: And what is that reputation?
A: It is very bad.
Q: And knowing what you know of that reputation, would you believe Grace Gardner in a serious matter?
A: Well, not exactly.
Q: Would you believe her under oath?
A: No, I honestly would not.

The foundation for opinion testimony is substantially the same, except that what is needed is a period of personal acquaintance.

Usually the character witness has resided in the same community with the principal witness and knows him personally or knows his reputation in that

setting. But the character witness need not satisfy a formal residency requirement. One modern case put it this way:

> We also think there should be no restriction necessarily limited to the community
> in which the witness sought to be impeached lives, and that the realities of our
> modern, mobile, impersonal society should also recognize that a witness may have
> a reputation for truth and veracity in the community in which he works and may
> have impressed on others in that community his character for truthfulness or
> untruthfulness. Therefore, we believe the community in which the witness worked,
> the law office of [character witness] Cory in this instance, was a proper locality
> in which to prove [principal witness] O'Toole's reputation or character for truth-
> fulness or untruthfulness. We do not imply that such character in the community
> in which she lived might not have been proved.

United States v. Mandel, 591 F.2d 1347, 1350 (4th Cir. 1979), cert. denied, 445
U.S. 961 (1980).

Admitting opinion testimony suggests at least the possibility that experts
might testify—perhaps psychiatrists or psychologists. But such testimony is seldom admitted, and modern cases repeatedly uphold trial court rulings excluding proffered psychiatric testimony. See Nichols v. American National Insurance
Co., 154 F.3d 875, 882-884 (8th Cir. 1998) (in suit alleging sexual harassment
and constructive discharge, error to let psychiatrist testify to plaintiff's "poor
psychiatric credibility," and describe her supposed "recall bias, secondary gain,
and malingering"; record does not show testimony satisfied *Daubert*, and witness
"sought to answer the very question at the heart of the jury's task," which is
whether plaintiff could be believed; this testimony created "a serious danger
of confusing or misleading the jury" and might cause jury to "substitute the
expert's credibility assessment for its own common sense"); United States v.
Cecil, 836 F.2d 1431, 1440-1441 (4th Cir.) (in drug trial, excluding psychiatrist's
out-of-court statement that government witness was incapable of telling the
truth, partly because credibility is strictly for jury), cert. denied, 487 U.S. 1205
(1988). But there are exceptions to this pattern. One outstanding exception
to the pattern is an old and famous case—the prosecution of Alger Hiss for
perjury. See United States v. Hiss, 88 F. Supp. 559 (S.D.N.Y. 1950) (admitting
defense psychiatric testimony on mental condition of main prosecution witness
Whittaker Chambers; his credibility was "one of the major issues upon which
the jury must pass," and insanity bears importantly on question of credibility).

NOTES ON EXPERT OPINION RELATING
TO CREDIBILITY

1. Are you surprised that courts disallow expert testimony on witness
credibility? Why shouldn't such testimony get in?

2. Do cases that permit experts to testify on the accuracy of eyewitness
identification (see Notes on Proving Lack of Capacity in Section 8A2, supra)
suggest that experts should be permitted to testify on lack of veracity too? Some
courts admit expert testimony concerning the trauma suffered by victims of
rape or child abuse, and such testimony sometimes has the effect of bolstering

credibility. See Notes on Proving Truthfulness: Character and Behavioral Syndrome Evidence (Chapter 8C2, infra).

3.   Suppose that the party who calls Grace Gardner wants to cross-examine Coach Jones about particular instances of good conduct in Gardner's life, reflective of truthfulness. "Coach Jones," counsel might say, "have you heard that Grace Gardner has for years acted as faculty treasurer in the school where you both teach and that she has rendered scrupulously correct accounts year after year?" Is such a question proper under FRE 608? Why do you suppose that such questions are seldom asked?

B.   SPECIFIC IMPEACHMENT

1.   *Prior Inconsistent Statements*

Almost always a witness has made previous statements on the subject of her testimony, if only because a lawyer seldom calls someone without talking to her first. If her testimony differs on some point from her prior statements, the attacking party may cross-examine on these statements and (subject to some conditions) prove them by "extrinsic evidence" (testimony by other witnesses).

Depending on the situation and his forensic skills, the attacking lawyer may be able to make devastating use of this "self-contradiction." He can argue that the prior statement has the specific effect of refuting testimony by the witness on the point in question. And while the mere fact of the prior inconsistent statement is indefinite in that it does not explain *why* the witness has changed her view, the cross-examiner may be able to draw from the larger setting all sorts of theories on this point: The witness changed her story out of bias for the calling party, or because she has been "bought" or "frightened" off, or because her memory is poor, and so forth. And with theories of this sort the cross-examiner may take a small blot on the credibility of the witness and make it spread, arguing thus: "If she has contradicted herself on this one point, how can we rely on anything else she says?"

A moment's reflection explains why prior statements are so commonly known to the attacking party. In civil cases many witnesses give depositions that produce a permanent record of what they have said; in criminal cases key witnesses for the prosecution testify before grand juries or in preliminary hearings; insurance investigators regularly (often promptly) seek out witnesses and obtain formal written or recorded statements, and careful lawyers often send investigators out for the same purpose; the prosecuting attorney follows a similar practice, and statements obtained in this way must be turned over to the defense.[7] Moreover, in life it often happens that witnesses have written letters

---

7.   Under the Supreme Court's decision in Brady v. Maryland, 373 U.S. 83 (1963), the prosecutor has a constitutional obligation, if asked by the defense, to turn over evidence tending to exculpate the defendant. But FRCrimP 16(a)(2) in effect delays defense discovery of prior statements by "government witnesses or prospective government witnesses," for the Jencks Act (18 U.S.C. §3500) provides that such statements are discoverable by the defense only after "said witness has testified on direct examination." (Do you understand the purpose of this provision?) In practice, pretrial statements by witnesses called by the prosecutor are commonly turned over

or made business records or notes, or have spoken to others on the transactions in issue, and all these matters may be unearthed during discovery or pretrial investigation.

Procedural fairness. By longstanding common law tradition, the attacking lawyer observed certain delicate conventions when raising the issue of prior inconsistencies. First, during cross-examination he was expected to lead the witness gently into the subject of her inconsistency. The lawyer was to show the statement to the witness, if written, and in other cases to remind her of its substance; the lawyer was to draw her attention to the time of the statement and the surrounding circumstances; only after these preliminaries was he to ask whether the witness in fact wrote the statement or spoke the words and to suggest that they undercut her credibility.

Second, the attacking lawyer was not permitted to prove the statement by extrinsic evidence (offering the writing into evidence, or adducing testimony by another witness as to what the first had said) unless he had first raised the matter on cross-examination.

These conventions, which were known as The Rule in Queen Caroline's Case, 2 Brod. & Bing. 284, 129 Eng. Rep. 976, 977 (1820), came to be seen as a nuisance. However "fair" they may be in civil discourse, they seemed out of place in an adversary trial. They blunted the impeaching attack by providing the witness an opportunity to explain away the inconsistency even before the attacker could "spring" it on her, and they blocked extrinsic evidence if the cross-examiner forgot to lay the foundation properly.

Modern revision. FRE 613 changes that common law practice. The message of FRE 613(a) is simple. No longer need the cross-examiner worry about approaching the subject gently. Instead, he may go straight to the point: "You just testified that the light was red for the blue car, but didn't you tell the adjuster that the blue car had the green light?" The only restriction is that "opposing counsel" (usually the lawyer for the party who called the witness) is entitled on request to see the statement or learn its contents, the purpose being to enable him to repair, if possible, the damage done by the attacker if he distorted the statement or wrenched it out of context.

The message of FRE 613(b) is more complicated. If a prior inconsistency is proved by "extrinsic evidence," generally the witness must have an opportunity "to explain or deny" it (unless "the interests of justice otherwise require"), and the adverse party (usually the one who called the witness) must have a chance to interrogate her. Note that sequence is not specified: The Rule does not say that the chance to explain must *come before* extrinsic evidence is admitted, as *Queen Caroline's Case* would require, and it is clear that if a witness *later* has a chance to explain, the Rule is satisfied. See Wilmington Trust Co. v. Manufacturers Life Insurance, 749 F.2d 694, 699 (11th Cir. 1985) (FRE 613(b) contains "no specification of any particular time or sequence"; defendant could have requested that the witness be permitted to take the stand in surrebuttal but made no such request).

---

to the defense at the start of trial, in order to avoid the delay that would result if the proceedings had to be halted in order to permit defense counsel to read the statement as he rises to commence cross-examination.

PROBLEM 8-F.   "He's Trying to Sandbag Us!"

In his civil suit seeking recovery for injuries sustained during an assault, Plimpton claims that Dirk struck him in the chest with a shovel, causing severe injuries. During plaintiff's case-in-chief, Welch testifies for Plimpton that Dirk struck the blow without provocation. Counsel for Dirk then cross-examines Welch, but does not ask whether Welch made any prior statement about the event.

During the defense case, Dirk calls Murphy, the police officer who investigated the incident. Murphy testifies that Welch told him that he did not actually see the blow being struck, and thinks Plimpton may have thrown a rock at Dirk.

Plaintiff's counsel is immediately on her feet:

> Your Honor, he's trying to sandbag us. Mr. Welch is gone, and he has had no opportunity to respond to the suggestion that he's changed his story. Defendant had a chance to put the same question to Welch, and deliberately did not. He should have laid a foundation back then. Rule 613(b) requires that Welch have a chance to explain.

How should the court rule, and why? Does it matter whether Welch has left the courtroom? What if he was told that he may go home and not told that he remains subject to recall? What if it is learned that he joined the French Foreign Legion and is beyond reach of subpoena?

NOTES ON APPLYING FRE 613(b)

1. Does Problem 8-F suggest that the trial judge should advise all witnesses that they are subject to recall after they have been examined on direct and cross, just to take care of this contingency? Or does FRE 611(a) authorize the trial judge to require the attacking party to raise any prior inconsistency on cross, so FRE 613(b) is satisfied, even though the latter does not require this sequence? If the witness has been excused, should the burden fall on the attacking party to obtain and serve a new subpoena, or should this burden be put on the calling party?

2. Rule 613 is silent on the appropriate treatment of such problems. The cases have been pragmatic. Compare Jones v. Collier, 762 F.2d 71, 72 (8th Cir. 1985) (trial court properly refused to admit extrinsic evidence of prior statement by witness who had testified the day before and returned to his place of incarceration 300 miles away, for plaintiff "did not lay any foundation for his rebuttal," apparently as "part of trial strategy") with United States v. McLaughlin, 663 F.2d 949, 953-954 (9th Cir. 1981) (defense properly allowed to offer extrinsic evidence of prior statement, after reminding declarant of the meeting in question on cross; government was free to recall witness to give him further opportunity to explain).

3. Recall from Problem 3-C ("The Blue Car Ran a Red Light") that the impeaching use of prior inconsistent statements is considered a nonhearsay use. Traditionally such statements were almost always admitted for the impeaching

(nonhearsay) purpose of proving vacillation, even where the hearsay doctrine prohibited their substantive (hearsay) use to prove what they asserted. This tradition persisted despite serious doubts that juries would consider such statements only as impeachment. Recall too that the Advisory Committee wanted to define all prior inconsistent statements as nonhearsay, but that Congress refused to go along. So we live still in a world in which many prior inconsistencies may be admitted to impeach, but not as substantive evidence. Consider this point as you read the *Webster* case, infra.

4.   Concern that a prior inconsistent statement will be taken as proof of what it asserts is perhaps the most obvious reason that might persuade a court to exclude it (this "substantive" use of a statement admitted only to "impeach" the declarant is a form of "misuse" that could lead to exclusion under FRE 403). There are other reasons why such statements might be excluded: For example, statements made during plea bargaining are also excludable (FRE 410), as are statements made during settlement negotiations (FRE 408). If a litigant who has made statements covered by these Rules testifies, may such statements be used to impeach his credibility? Pretty clearly the answer is "no" in the case of plea bargaining statements, for legislative history of FRE 410 makes clear that Congress intended to exclude such statements, even when offered only to impeach (Chapter 5D2, supra). But defendant can waive the right to exclude plea-bargaining statements when offered for this purpose. In civil cases, the history of FRE 408 sheds no light on this question. What of the constitutional exclusionary principles? Recall from Doyle v. Ohio, 426 U.S. 610 (1976) (Chapter 4B2, supra), that the Court said a defendant would lose his protection against impeachment by postwarning silence if he testifies that he gave police the same version of events that he presents at trial. Bear this decision in mind as you read *Harris*, infra.

UNITED STATES v. WEBSTER
United States Court of Appeals for the Seventh Circuit
734 F.2d 1191 (1984)

607

POSNER, J.
The defendant, Webster, was convicted of aiding and abetting the robbery of a federally insured bank and receiving stolen bank funds, was sentenced to nine years in prison, and appeals. Only one issue need be discussed. The government called the bank robber, King (who had pleaded guilty and been given a long prison term), as a witness against Webster. King gave testimony that if believed would have exculpated the defendant, whereupon the government introduced prior inconsistent statements that King had given the FBI inculpating Webster. Although the court instructed the jury that it could consider the statements only for purposes of impeachment, Webster argues that this was not good enough, that the government should not be allowed to get inadmissible evidence before the jury by calling a hostile witness and then using his out-of-court statements, which would otherwise be inadmissible hearsay, to impeach him.
. . . [I]t would be an abuse of [FRE 607], in a criminal case, for the

prosecution to call a witness that it knew would not give it useful evidence, just so it could introduce hearsay evidence against the defendant in the hope that the jury would miss the subtle distinction between impeachment and substantive evidence—or, if it didn't miss it, would ignore it. The purpose would not be to impeach the witness but to put in hearsay as substantive evidence against the defendant, which Rule 607 does not contemplate or authorize. We thus agree that "impeachment by prior inconsistent statement may not be permitted where employed as a mere subterfuge to get before the jury evidence not otherwise admissible." United States v. Morlang, 531 F.2d 183, 190 (4th Cir. 1975). Although *Morlang* was decided before the Federal Rules of Evidence became effective, the limitation that we have quoted on the prosecutor's rights under Rule 607 has been accepted in all circuits that have considered the issue. We agree with these decisions.

But it is quite plain that there was no bad faith here. Before the prosecutor called King to the stand she asked the judge to allow her to examine him outside the presence of the jury, because she didn't know what he would say. The defendant's counsel objected and the voir dire was not held. We do not see how in these circumstances it can be thought that the prosecutor put King on the stand knowing he would give no useful evidence. If she had known that, she would not have offered to voir dire him, as the voir dire would have provided a foundation for defense counsel to object, under *Morlang,* to the admission of King's prior inconsistent statements.

Webster urges us, on the authority of Graham, Handbook of Federal Evidence §607.3 (1981 and Supp. 1983), to go beyond the good-faith standard and hold that the government may not impeach a witness with his prior inconsistent statements unless it is surprised and harmed by the witness's testimony. But we think it would be a mistake to graft such a requirement to Rule 607, even if such a graft would be within the power of judicial interpretation of the rule. Suppose the government called an adverse witness that it thought would give evidence both helpful and harmful to it, but it also thought that the harmful aspect could be nullified by introducing the witness's prior inconsistent statement. As there would be no element of surprise, Professor Graham would forbid the introduction of the prior statements; yet we are at a loss to understand why the government should be put to the choice between the Scylla of forgoing impeachment and the Charybdis of not calling at all a witness from whom it expects to elicit genuinely helpful evidence. The good-faith standard strikes a better balance; and it is always open to the defendant to argue that the probative value of the evidence offered to impeach the witness is clearly outweighed by the prejudicial impact it might have on the jury, because the jury would have difficulty confining use of the evidence to impeachment. See FRE 403.

The judgment of conviction is affirmed.

NOTES ON "ABUSE" OF FRE 607

1.   Under *Webster,* how does the court distinguish between abuse of FRE 607 and legitimate impeachment by the calling party? Assume that King told investigators that he and Webster planned and did the robbery. Assume that

King testifies on voir dire (outside the hearing of the jury) that the two planned the robbery, but Webster begged off and did not go to the bank. Assume that the jury returns and the prosecutor adduces from King that he and Webster planned the robbery. *Now* is it an abuse for her to ask about the robbery itself (Webster did not come along, says King), then to attack King by raising his prior contrary statement implicating Webster? If the prosecutor only asked King about the planning, would she be misleading the jury? If she stopped there and *defendant* got King to say that Webster did not go to the bank, would it then be an abuse for the prosecutor to ask about the prior statement?

2. The court in *Webster* refers to an earlier Fourth Circuit opinion in *Morlang*. There the prosecutor called Wilmoth to the stand, ostensibly to adduce his testimony that Morlang admitted participating in a scheme to divert federal funds to private ends. But Wilmoth had told the prosecutor before trial that he would not testify in this way, and (true to his latest word) he denied the conversation on the stand. Then the prosecutor called a fellow named Crist (Wilmoth's cellmate), who testified that Wilmoth attributed to Morlang the statement, "One of us had to take the rap so the other one could stay out and take care of the business." Concluding that the prosecutor called Wilmoth in order to elicit his denial of the conversation with Morlang, the reviewing court decided that refuting this denial by the testimony of Crist was improper:

> While it is the rule in this circuit that a party calling a witness does not vouch for his credibility, it has never been the rule that a party may call a witness where his testimony is known to be adverse for the purpose of impeaching him. To so hold would permit the government, in the name of impeachment, to present testimony to the jury by indirection which would not otherwise be admissible. The courts have consistently refused to sanction such a practice. . . .
>
> We . . . recognize that the strict rule against impeaching one's own witness has long been discredited. . . . The overwhelming weight of authority is, however, that impeachment by prior inconsistent statement may not be permitted where employed as a mere subterfuge to get before the jury evidence not otherwise admissible.
>
> Witnesses may, of course, sometimes fail to come up to the expectations of counsel and in such situations there is an understandable temptation to get before the jury any prior statement made by the witness. And it may be that in certain instances impeachment might somehow enhance the truth-finding process. Yet, whatever validity this latter assertion may have, it must be balanced against the notions of fairness upon which our system is based. Foremost among these concepts is the principle that men should not be allowed to be convicted on the basis of unsworn testimony.

United States v. Morlang, 531 F.2d 183, 189-190 (4th Cir. 1975). Accord, United States v. Gomez-Gallardo, 915 F.2d 553, 555 (9th Cir. 1990) (impeachment improper when used as guise for submitting to jury otherwise inadmissible substantive evidence; question is whether government examined witness for "primary purpose" of doing that); United States v. Johnson, 802 F.2d 1459, 1466 (D.C. Cir.) (prosecutor inappropriately called witness for "sole purpose" of getting in his prior statement, knowing his live testimony would favor defendant and that his prior statement was not independently admissible), cert. denied, 488 U.S. 1004 (1986).

Does *Webster* leave the *Morlang* doctrine intact?

3.   Recall that the drafters of the Rules proposed to let all prior inconsistencies be used as substantive evidence and do away with the voucher principle. Congress balked at the first proposal but went along with the second, and FRE 607 sailed through in the form proposed by the Advisory Committee. To sum it up: At common law, prior inconsistent statements were often admitted only to impeach, but usually not at the behest of the party who called the witness; under the Advisory Committee's proposal, prior inconsistencies could be used for all purposes and could be offered by either party; under the system Congress enacted, prior inconsistent statements are often admissible only to impeach, but FRE 607 implies that any party can offer them. When Congress refused to permit full use of all prior inconsistencies, should it have considered retaining the voucher principle in some form? Does the *Morlang* doctrine mean that sometimes the calling party will be restricted in much the same way that the voucher principle would restrict him? See generally Graham, Employing Inconsistent Statements for Impeachment and as Substantive Evidence: A Critical Review and Proposed Amendments of Federal Rules of Evidence 801(d)(1)(A), 613, and 607, 75 Mich. L. Rev. 1565 (1977); Ordover, Surprise! That Damaging Turncoat Witness Is Still with Us: An Analysis of Federal Rules of Evidence 607, 801(d)(1)(A) and 403, 5 Hofstra L. Rev. 65 (1976).

4.   Recall that *some* prior inconsistencies *are* admissible as substantive evidence—namely, those that fit FRE 801(d)(1)(A) because they were given in proceedings under oath and the declarant is now cross-examinable about them. As we saw in Problem 4-A ("I Got Amnesia"), prior grand jury testimony can fit FRE 801(d)(1)(A), and so can testimony given at preliminary hearings, and for that matter in suppression motions, depositions, or other trials. If the calling party offers a prior inconsistent statement that fits this (or some other) exception, doesn't the *Morlang* issue disappear? No longer can it be said that the calling party is offering inconsistent statements in hope that the jury will misuse them as substantive evidence: The reason is that making substantive use of such statements *simply isn't* misuse anymore.

5.   *Webster* is not the only case that seems to restrict the *Morlang* doctrine. Another important opinion seems to say that *Morlang* cannot apply to witnesses who are in some sense crucial to the calling party's case. In that case, the government sought to prove that Vincent DeLillo installed substandard concrete pipes and conspired with others to hide leaks. The government offered testimony by Gorman (a participant in the scheme) that Vincent directed a subordinate to hide the leaks, but it also called Monahan (another participant), who testified that Vincent said no such thing. Then the government introduced a taped statement in which Monahan said that Vincent *had* told them to hide the leaks, after all. Abuse? The reviewing court thought not:

> Beyond doubt, Monahan was not called . . . as a subterfuge with the primary aim of getting to the jury a statement impeaching him. Monahan's corroborating testimony was essential in many areas of the government's case. Once there, the government had the right to question him, and to attempt to impeach him, about those aspects of his testimony which conflicted with Gorman's account of the same events. *Morlang* itself explicitly recognizes the propriety of impeachment where it is "necessary to alleviate the harshness of subjecting a party to the mercy

of a witness who is recalcitrant or may have been unscrupulously tampered with." To the extent that defendants rely on *Morlang* for the principle that a witness cannot be put on the stand if the side calling him knows that he will give testimony that it will have to impeach, it seems clear to us that the effect of [FRE] 607 . . . is to nullify the plausibility of such a reading.

United States v. DeLillo, 620 F.2d 939, 946-947 (2d Cir.), cert. denied, 449 U.S. 835 (1980). Does *DeLillo* undercut *Morlang?* If there are to be "exceptions" to the *Morlang* doctrine, does *Webster* or *DeLillo* represent the sounder approach, or do we need both?

6. Should the *Morlang* doctrine (and any necessary exceptions) apply equally to defense impeachment of defense witnesses? See United States v. MacDonald, 688 F.2d 224, 233-234 (4th Cir. 1982) (approving exclusion of testimony by defense witnesses about earlier statement by defense witness *S,* who corroborated the defense version of events in some ways but contradicted it in others; invoking *Morlang* doctrine; reviewing court notes that the proffered testimony was "unduly confusing and not proper as impeachment since its substance already had been ruled inadmissible for its truth"; where jury is likely to be "confounded by" statements that witness cannot remember, exclusion under FRE 403 is proper).

HARRIS v. NEW YORK
United States Supreme Court
401 U.S. 222 (1971)

[handwritten: Miranda barred statements used to impeach]

[Harris was charged with selling heroin in transactions on January 4 and 6. On both occasions the buyer was an undercover police officer who became the state's principal witness. Taking the stand in his own defense, Harris testified that he knew the police officer, but he denied engaging in any transaction with him on January 4. He further testified that on January 6 he had sold the officer two glassine bags containing what appeared to be heroin, but he contended that in reality they contained only baking powder and that his motive in making the sale was to gain the sum of $12.

On cross-examination, the prosecutor asked defendant about certain statements he had apparently made after his arrest on January 7. (At that time, Harris had not gotten *Miranda* warnings, and the state conceded that his statements were inadmissible under the rule in that case. The prosecutor had made no reference to those statements during the state's case-in-chief. The Supreme Court opinion comments that Harris "makes no claim that the statements made to the police were coerced or involuntary.")

Defendant replied that he could not remember much about what he said in the stationhouse, (and) the prosecutor essentially read the statements to the defendant and (at defense request, for purposes of appeal) included the transcript of the statements in the record. Those statements "partially contradicted" Harris's direct testimony. (In his dissenting opinion, Justice Brennan says that in those statements Harris said that on January 4 "the officer had used [Harris] as a middleman to buy some heroin from a third person with money furnished

[handwritten margin note: not Hearsay? → prior uncons. statement]

by the officer" and that on January 6 Harris "had again acted for the officer in buying two bags of heroin from a third person for which [Harris] received $12 and a part of the heroin.") The trial judge told the jury that the statements "could be considered only in passing on [Harris's] credibility and not as evidence of guilt," and both the prosecutor and the defense commented on the statements in closing argument.]

MR. CHIEF JUSTICE BURGER delivered the opinion of the Court.

Some comments in the *Miranda* opinion can indeed be read as indicating a bar to use of an uncounseled statement for any purpose, but discussion of that issue was not at all necessary to the Court's holding and cannot be regarded as controlling. *Miranda* barred the prosecution from making its case with statements of an accused made while in custody prior to having or effectively waiving counsel. It does not follow from *Miranda* that evidence inadmissible against an accused in the prosecution's case in chief is barred for all purposes, provided of course that the trustworthiness of the evidence satisfies legal standards.

In Walder v. United States, 347 U.S. 62 (1954), the Court permitted physical evidence, inadmissible in the case in chief, to be used for impeachment purposes.

> It is one thing to say that the Government cannot make an affirmative use of evidence unlawfully obtained. It is quite another to say that the defendant can turn the illegal method by which evidence in the Government's possession was obtained to his own advantage, and provide himself with a shield against contradiction of his untruths. Such an extension of the *Weeks* doctrine would be a perversion of the Fourth Amendment.
>
> [T]here is hardly justification for letting the defendant affirmatively resort to perjurious testimony in reliance on the Government's disability to challenge his credibility.

It is true that Walder was impeached as to collateral matters included in his direct examination, whereas petitioner here was impeached as to testimony bearing more directly on the crimes charged. We are not persuaded that there is a difference in principle that warrants a result different from that reached by the Court in *Walder*. Petitioner's testimony in his own behalf concerning the events of January 7 contrasted sharply with what he told the police shortly after his arrest. The impeachment process here undoubtedly provided valuable aid to the jury in assessing petitioner's credibility, and the benefits of this process should not be lost, in our view, because of the speculative possibility that impermissible police conduct will be encouraged thereby. Assuming that the exclusionary rule has a deterrent effect on proscribed police conduct, sufficient deterrence flows when the evidence in question is made unavailable to the prosecution in its case in chief. Every criminal defendant is privileged to testify in his own defense, or to refuse to do so. But that privilege cannot be construed to include the right to commit perjury. Having voluntarily taken the stand, petitioner was under an obligation to speak truthfully and accurately, and the prosecution here did no more than utilize the traditional truth-testing devices of the adversary process.[2] Had inconsistent statements been made by the accused

---

2. If, for example, an accused confessed fully to a homicide and led the police to the body of the victim under circumstances making his confession inadmissible, the petitioner would have us allow that accused to take the stand and blandly deny every fact disclosed to the police or

to some third person, it could hardly be contended that the conflict could not be laid before the jury by way of cross-examination and impeachment.

The shield provided by *Miranda* cannot be perverted into a license to use perjury by way of a defense, free from the risk of confrontation with prior inconsistent utterances. We hold, therefore, that petitioner's credibility was appropriately impeached by use of his earlier conflicting statements.

Affirmed.

MR. JUSTICE BLACK dissents.

MR. JUSTICE BRENNAN, with whom MR. JUSTICE DOUGLAS and MR. JUSTICE MARSHALL join, dissenting.

It is conceded that the question-and-answer statement used to impeach petitioner's direct testimony was, under Miranda v. Arizona, 384 U.S. 436 (1966), constitutionally inadmissible as part of the State's direct case against petitioner. I think that the Constitution also denied the State the use of the statement on cross-examination to impeach the credibility of petitioner's testimony given in his own defense. The decision in Walder v. United States, 347 U.S. 62 (1954), is not, as the Court today holds, dispositive to the contrary. Rather, that case supports my conclusion.

[Justice Brennan summarizes the facts.]

Walder v. United States was not a case where tainted evidence was used to impeach an accused's direct testimony on matters directly related to the case against him. In *Walder* the evidence was used to impeach the accused's testimony on matters *collateral* to the crime charged. Walder had been indicted in 1950 for purchasing and possessing heroin. When his motion to suppress use of the narcotics as illegally seized was granted, the Government dismissed the prosecution. Two years later Walder was indicted for another narcotics violation completely unrelated to the 1950 one. Testifying in his own defense, he said on direct examination that he had never in his life possessed narcotics. On cross-examination he denied that law enforcement officers had seized narcotics from his home two years earlier. The Government was then permitted to introduce the testimony of one of the officers involved in the 1950 seizure, that when he had raided Walder's home at that time he had seized narcotics there. The Court held that on facts where "the defendant went beyond a mere denial of complicity in the crimes of which he was charged and made the sweeping claim that he had never dealt in or possessed any narcotics," the exclusionary rule of Weeks v. United States, 232 U.S. 383 (1914), would not extend to bar the Government from rebutting this testimony with evidence, although tainted, that petitioner had in fact possessed narcotics two years before. The Court was careful, however, to distinguish the situation of an accused whose testimony, as in the instant case, was a "denial of complicity in the crimes of which he was charged," that is, where illegally obtained evidence was used to impeach the accused's direct testimony on matters directly related to the case against him. As to that situation, the Court said:

> Of course, the Constitution guarantees a defendant the fullest opportunity to meet the accusation against him. He must be free to deny all the elements of the

---

discovered as a "fruit" of his confession, free from confrontation with his prior statements and acts. The voluntariness of the confession would, on this thesis, be totally irrelevant. We reject such an extravagant extension of the Constitution.

case against him without thereby giving leave to the Government to introduce by way of rebuttal evidence illegally secured by it, and therefore not available for its case in chief.

From this recital of facts it is clear that the evidence used for impeachment in *Walder* was related to the earlier 1950 prosecution and had no direct bearing on "the elements of the case" being tried in 1952. The evidence tended solely to impeach the credibility of the defendant's direct testimony that he had never in his life possessed heroin. But that evidence was completely unrelated to the indictment on trial and did not in any way interfere with his freedom to deny all elements of that case against him. In contrast, here, the evidence used for impeachment, a statement concerning the details of the very sales alleged in the indictment, was directly related to the case against petitioner.

While *Walder* did not identify the constitutional specifics that guarantee "a defendant the fullest opportunity to meet the accusation against him . . . [and permit him to] be free to deny all the elements of the case against him," in my view *Miranda* identified the Fifth Amendment's privilege against self-incrimination as one of those specifics. That privilege has been extended against the States. Malloy v. Hogan, 378 U.S. 1 (1964). It is fulfilled only when an accused is guaranteed the right "to remain silent unless he chooses to speak in the *unfettered* exercise of his own will" (emphasis added). The choice of whether to testify in one's own defense must therefore be "unfettered," since that choice is an exercise of the constitutional privilege, Griffin v. California, 380 U.S. 609 (1965). *Griffin* held that comment by the prosecution upon the accused's failure to take the stand or a court instruction that such silence is evidence of guilt is impermissible because it "fetters" that choice—"[i]t cuts down on the privilege by making its assertion costly." For precisely the same reason the constitutional guarantee forbids the prosecution to use a tainted statement to impeach the accused who takes the stand: The prosecution's use of the tainted statement "cuts down on the privilege by making its assertion costly." Thus, the accused is denied an "unfettered" choice when the decision whether to take the stand is burdened by the risk that an illegally obtained prior statement may be introduced to impeach his direct testimony denying complicity in the crime charged against him. We settled this proposition in *Miranda* where we said:

> The privilege against self-incrimination protects the individual from being compelled to incriminate himself in *any* manner. . . . [S]tatements merely intended to be exculpatory by the defendant are often *used to impeach his testimony at trial. . . . These statements are incriminating in any meaningful sense of the word and may not be used without the full warnings and effective waiver required for any other statement.*

This language completely disposes of any distinction between statements used on direct as opposed to cross-examination. "An incriminating statement is as incriminating when used to impeach credibility as it is when used as direct proof of guilt and no constitutional distinction can legitimately be drawn." People v. Kulis, 221 N.E.2d 541, 543 (N.Y. 1966) (dissenting opinion).

The objective of deterring improper police conduct is only part of the larger objective of safeguarding the integrity of our adversary system. The "essential mainstay" of that system is the privilege against self-incrimination, which for that reason has occupied a central place in our jurisprudence since before the Nation's birth. Moreover, "we may view the historical development of the privilege as one which groped for the proper scope of governmental power over the citizen. . . . All these policies point to one overriding thought: the constitutional foundation underlying the privilege is the respect a government . . . must accord to the dignity and integrity of its citizens." *Miranda*. These values are plainly jeopardized if an exception against admission of tainted statements is made for those used for impeachment purposes. Moreover, it is monstrous that courts should aid or abet the law-breaking police officer. It is abiding truth that "[n]othing can destroy a government more quickly than its failure to observe its own laws, or worse, its disregard of the charter of its own existence." Mapp v. Ohio, 367 U.S. 643, 659 (1961). Thus, even to the extent that *Miranda* was aimed at deterring police practices in disregard of the Constitution, I fear that today's holding will seriously undermine the achievement of that objective. The Court today tells the police that they may freely interrogate an accused incommunicado and without counsel and know that although any statement they obtain in violation of *Miranda* cannot be used on the State's direct case, it may be introduced if the defendant has the temerity to testify in his own defense. This goes far toward undoing much of the progress made in conforming police methods to the Constitution. I dissent.

NOTES ON IMPEACHMENT BY *MIRANDA*-BARRED STATEMENTS

1. If *Harris* had been decided the other way, would the prosecutor lose the best mechanism to keep testifying defendants honest? As it was decided, does *Harris* significantly increase police incentive to violate the *Miranda* rights of an arrested suspect? Does *Miranda* also establish a moral principle? If it offends a moral standard for the state to offer *Miranda*-barred statements, what weight (if any) should we assign to the fact that the accused takes the stand and apparently commits perjury? Did *Harris* reach an appropriate adjustment of competing principles and needs?

2. *Miranda* discloses that the Court was concerned with the "interrogation atmosphere and the evils it can bring," emphasizing that the Fifth Amendment protects personal "dignity and integrity," requiring the state "to respect the inviolability of the human personality." 384 U.S. 436, at 456 & 460 (1967). The Court notes that abuses in interrogation procedures "may even give rise to a false confession" and that the presence of counsel during interrogation "can mitigate the dangers of untrustworthiness," 384 U.S. 436, at 455 n.24 & 470 (1967). Still, reliability of stationhouse confessions seems not to have been the main concern, and the Court said that confessions "remain a proper element in law enforcement" and that police need not "stop a person" from making voluntary statements, 384 U.S. 436, at 478 (1967). Does an assumption of reliability of stationhouse confessions underlie the decision in *Harris*?

3. In *Harris,* does it matter that the statement was offered to impeach

direct testimony by the accused, as opposed to testimony adduced on cross-examination? Long before *Harris,* the Court considered this point in a related context. In a drug conspiracy trial, the accused testified on direct that he received packages but did not know they contained cocaine. On cross-examination, the prosecutor asked whether he had ever seen cocaine before, and he replied that he "never" had. The government then offered in evidence a can of cocaine, illegally seized in violation of the Fourth Amendment on an unrelated occasion, but the Supreme Court disapproved. It quoted the principle that the "essence of a provision forbidding the acquisition of evidence in a certain way is not merely that evidence so acquired shall not be used before the court but that it shall not be used at all," and commented that defendant "did not testify [on direct] concerning the can of cocaine," hence that he "did nothing to waive his constitutional protection." Agnello v. United States, 269 U.S. 20 (1925).

Are you surprised that *Harris* did not cite *Agnello?* Doesn't the last-quoted passage point toward the outcome reached in *Harris?* Should *Agnello* be distinguished because it involved the Fourth Amendment rather than the Fifth? Reconsider this point after *Havens,* infra.

4. *Miranda* requires police not only to warn the arrested suspect but to cease interrogation if he claims his right to counsel. If he does so but police continue to question him, does *Harris* permit the use for impeachment purposes of what he says thereafter? See Oregon v. Hass, 420 U.S. 714 (1975) (yes). Is *Hass* different enough from *Harris* that it should have been decided the other way even if *Harris* is right?

5. Rufus Mincey was hospitalized after an exchange of gunfire with an arresting officer. While in the emergency room with an intravenous feeding tube, a catheter in his bladder, and tubes in his throat and nose, he was questioned by a police detective. Since he could not speak, he wrote his answers on pieces of paper. The interrogation continued despite his repeated requests for a lawyer, and his replies were admitted to impeach him at his murder trial. The Supreme Court distinguished *Harris* and reversed Mincey's conviction, concluding that this use of an "*involuntary* statement" by a "seriously wounded" defendant in his "debilitated and helpless condition . . . on the edge of consciousness" violated due process. Mincey v. Arizona, 437 U.S. 385, 398-401 (1978). Why the difference in outcome between *Harris* and *Mincey?*

6. Local official Joseph Portash was subpoenaed to testify before a grand jury, and he invoked his privilege against self-incrimination. Through counsel, Portash then negotiated an immunity agreement, under which his testimony and any evidence derived from it could not be used in any later proceedings against him (apart from a perjury prosecution). Portash was later indicted for misconduct in office and extortion. He sought a pretrial ruling that would bar the use against him for impeachment purposes of his immunized grand jury testimony, but the motion was denied. Portash did not testify and was convicted. The Supreme Court reversed, distinguishing *Harris* and *Hass* on the ground that no contention was made there that the statements were "involuntary," while in this case

Testimony given in response to a grant of legislative immunity is the essence of coerced testimony. In such cases there is no question whether physical or psychological pressures overrode the defendant's will; the witness is told to talk or face the government's coercive sanctions, notably, a conviction for contempt. The information given in response to a grant of immunity may well be more reliable than information beaten from a helpless defendant, but it is no less compelled. The Fifth and Fourteenth Amendments provide a privilege against *compelled* self-incrimination, not merely against unreliable self-incrimination.

New Jersey v. Portash, 440 U.S. 450, 459 (1979). Can *Portash* be reconciled with *Harris?*

7.   Daryl James is tried for murder, arising out of the events in a nighttime street confrontation between eight boys returning from a party and three others demanding money. The defense suppressed statements Daryl made at the time of his arrest to the effect that his hair was reddish brown, long, and combed straight back on the day of the crime, and that he went to his mother's beauty salon to get his hair dyed black and curled to change his appearance. At trial, state witnesses described the assailant as having reddish hair worn shoulder length in a slicked-back "butter" style, and remembered seeing Daryl several weeks earlier wearing his hair that way. The defense called a family friend named Jewel Henderson, who testified that on the day of the crime she took Daryl to register for school and that his hair was black. Can the state now introduce Daryl's suppressed statements on the theory that *Harris* allows use of these statements to contradict Henderson's testimony? See James v. Illinois, 493 U.S. 307 (1990) (no) (threat of perjury prosecution deters witnesses from lying, but not defendants faced with other charges; expanding impeachment exception would "chill some defendants from presenting their best defense" and "significantly weaken" deterrent effect of exclusionary rule).

JENKINS v. ANDERSON
United States Supreme Court
447 U.S. 231 (1980)

— prearrest silence to impeach & 5th Amendment [handwritten annotation]

Mr. Justice Powell delivered the opinion of the Court.

The question in this case is whether the use of prearrest silence to impeach a defendant's credibility violates either the Fifth or Fourteenth Amendment to the Constitution.

I

On August 13, 1974, the petitioner stabbed and killed Doyle Redding. The petitioner was not apprehended until he turned himself in to governmental authorities about two weeks later. At his state trial for first-degree murder, the petitioner contended that the killing was in self-defense.

The petitioner testified that his sister and her boyfriend were robbed by Redding and another man during the evening of August 12, 1974. The petitioner, who was nearby when the robbery occurred, followed the thieves a short distance and reported their whereabouts to the police. According to the

*"killed in self defense"
but didn't report to
police until 2 weeks later*

petitioner's testimony, the next day he encountered Redding, who accused him of informing the police of the robbery. The petitioner stated that Redding attacked him with a knife, that the two men struggled briefly, and that the petitioner broke away. On cross-examination, the petitioner admitted that during the struggle he had tried "[t]o push that knife in [Redding] as far as [I] could," but maintained that he had acted solely in self-defense.

During the cross-examination, the prosecutor questioned the petitioner about his actions after the stabbing:

> Q. And I suppose you waited for the Police to tell them what happened?
> A. No, I didn't.
> Q. You didn't?
> A. No.
> Q. I see. And how long was it after this day that you were arrested, or that you were taken into custody?

After some discussion of the date on which petitioner surrendered, the prosecutor continued:

prearrest silence for 2 weeks!

> Q. When was the first time that you reported the things that you have told us in Court today to anybody
> A. Two days after it happened.
> Q. And who did you report it to?
> A. To my probation officer.
> Q. Well, apart from him?
> A. No one.
> Q. Who?
> A. No one but my—
> Q. (Interposing) Did you ever go to a Police Officer or to anyone else?
> A. No, I didn't.
> Q. As a matter of fact, it was two weeks later, wasn't it?
> A. Yes.

In closing argument to the jury, the prosecutor again referred to the petitioner's prearrest silence. The prosecutor noted that petitioner had "waited two weeks, according to the testimony—at least two weeks before he did anything about surrendering himself or reporting [the stabbing] to anybody." The prosecutor contended that the petitioner had committed murder in retaliation for the robbery the night before.

The petitioner was convicted of manslaughter and sentenced to 10 to 15 years' imprisonment in state prison. . . . [Federal habeas corpus relief is denied, and the Supreme Court here affirms.]

prosecutor impeachment of self defense

II

At trial the prosecutor attempted to impeach the petitioner's credibility by suggesting that the petitioner would have spoken out if he had killed in self-defense. The petitioner contends that the prosecutor's actions violated the Fifth Amendment as applied to the States through the Fourteenth Amendment. The

Fifth Amendment guarantees an accused the right to remain silent during his criminal trial and prevents the prosecution from commenting on the silence of a defendant who asserts the right. . . . In this case, of course, the petitioner did not remain silent throughout the criminal proceedings. Instead, he voluntarily took the witness stand in his own defense.

This Court's decision in Raffel v. United States, 271 U.S. 494 (1926), recognized that the Fifth Amendment is not violated when a defendant who testifies in his own defense is impeached with his prior silence. The defendant in *Raffel* was tried twice. At the first trial, a Government agent testified that Raffel earlier had made an inculpatory statement. The defendant did not testify. After the first trial ended in deadlock the agent repeated his testimony at the second trial, and Raffel took the stand to deny making such a statement. Cross-examination revealed that Raffel had not testified at the first trial. . . . The Court held that inquiry into prior silence was proper because "[t]he immunity from giving testimony is one which the defendant may waive by offering himself as a witness. . . . When he takes the stand in his own behalf, he does so as any other witness, and within the limits of the appropriate rules he may be cross-examined. . . ." Thus, the *Raffel* Court concluded that the defendant was "subject to cross-examination impeaching his credibility just like any other witness." Grunewald v. United States, 353 U.S. 391 (1957).[2]

It can be argued that a person facing arrest will not remain silent if his failure to speak later can be used to impeach him. But the Constitution does not forbid "every government-imposed choice in the criminal process that has the effect of discouraging the exercise of constitutional rights." Chaffin v. Stynchcombe, 412 U.S. 17, 30 (1973). . . . The " 'threshold question is whether compelling the election impairs to an appreciable extent any of the policies behind the rights involved.' " Chaffin v. Stynchcombe, supra [quoting another authority]. The *Raffel* Court explicitly rejected the contention that the possibility of impeachment by prior silence is an impermissible burden upon the exercise of Fifth Amendment rights. "We are unable to see that the rule that [an accused who] testified . . . must testify fully, adds in any substantial manner to the inescapable embarrassment which the accused must experience in determining whether he shall testify or not."

This Court similarly defined the scope of the Fifth Amendment protection in Harris v. New York, 401 U.S. 222 (1971). There the Court held that a statement taken in violation of Miranda v. Arizona, 384 U.S. 436 (1966), may be used to impeach a defendant's credibility. Rejecting the contention that such impeachment violates the Fifth Amendment, the Court said:

> Every criminal defendant is privileged to testify in his own defense, or to
> refuse to do so. But that privilege cannot be construed to include the right to
> commit perjury. . . . Having voluntarily taken the stand, petitioner was under
> an obligation to speak truthfully and accurately, and the prosecution here did no

2. In *Raffel*, the defendant's decision not to testify at his first trial was an invocation of his right to remain silent protected by the Fifth Amendment. In this case, the petitioner remained silent before arrest, but chose to testify at his trial. Our decision today does not consider whether or under what circumstances prearrest silence may be protected by the Fifth Amendment. We simply do not reach that issue because the rule of *Raffel* clearly permits impeachment even if the prearrest silence were held to be an invocation of the Fifth Amendment right to remain silent.

more than utilize the traditional truth-testing devices of the adversary process. . . .

In determining whether a constitutional right has been burdened impermissibly, it also is appropriate to consider the legitimacy of the challenged governmental practice. . . . Attempted impeachment on cross-examination of a defendant, the practice at issue here, may enhance the reliability of the criminal process. Use of such impeachment on cross-examination allows prosecutors to test the credibility of witnesses by asking them to explain prior inconsistent statements and acts. A defendant may decide not to take the witness stand because of the risk of cross-examination. But this is a choice of litigation tactics. Once a defendant decides to testify, "[t]he interests of the other party and regard for the function of courts of justice to ascertain the truth become relevant, and prevail in the balance of considerations determining the scope and limits of the privilege against self-incrimination." Brown v. United States, 356 U.S. 148 (1958).

Thus, impeachment follows the defendant's own decision to cast aside his cloak of silence and advances the truth-finding function of the criminal trial. We conclude that the Fifth Amendment is not violated by the use of prearrest silence to impeach a criminal defendant's credibility.

III

The petitioner also contends that use of prearrest silence to impeach his credibility denied him the fundamental fairness guaranteed by the Fourteenth Amendment. We do not agree. Common law traditionally has allowed witnesses to be impeached by their previous failure to state a fact in circumstances in which that fact naturally would have been asserted. . . . Each jurisdiction may formulate its own rules of evidence to determine when prior silence is so inconsistent with present statements that impeachment by reference to such silence is probative. For example, this Court has exercised its supervisory powers over federal courts to hold that prior silence cannot be used for impeachment where silence is not probative of a defendant's credibility and where prejudice to the defendant might result. See United States v. Hale, 422 U.S. 171, 180-181 (1975).[5]

Only in Doyle v. Ohio, 426 U.S. 610 (1976), did we find that impeachment by silence violated the Constitution. In that case, a defendant received the warnings required by Miranda when he was arrested for selling marihuana. . . .

In this case, no governmental action induced petitioner to remain silent before arrest. The failure to speak occurred before the petitioner was taken into custody and given Miranda warnings. Consequently, the fundamental unfairness present in Doyle is not present in this case. We hold that impeachment by use of prearrest silence does not violate the Fourteenth Amendment.

5. Mr. Justice Marshall contends that the petitioner's prearrest silence is not probative of his credibility. In this case, that is a question of state evidentiary law. In federal criminal proceedings the relevance of such silence, of course, would be a matter of federal law. . . . Mr. Justice Marshall's further conclusion that introduction of the evidence in this trial violated due process relies upon the Court's reasoning in Doyle and Hale. But the Court's decision in Hale rested upon nonconstitutional grounds, and Doyle is otherwise distinguishable.

IV

Our decision today does not force any state court to allow impeachment through the use of prearrest silence. Each jurisdiction remains free to formulate evidentiary rules defining the situations in which silence is viewed as more probative than prejudicial. We merely conclude that the use of prearrest silence to impeach a defendant's credibility does not violate the Constitution. The judgment of the Court of Appeals is affirmed.

[The concurring opinion of JUSTICE STEWART and the dissenting opinion of JUSTICES MARSHALL and BRENNAN are omitted.]

NOTES ON THE USE OF SILENCE TO IMPEACH

1.   If Jenkins had fled after the killing, taking the nearest flight to Florida, would proof of this fact at trial violate his right to travel? Would it impose a duty not to travel? Can it be seriously argued that the use against him of his silence violates his privilege against compelled self-incrimination or imposes on him a duty to confess?

2.   Jenkins was a black resident of inner city Detroit, apparently on parole, and it was there that he killed Redding. Do you think that the fact that he did not seek out police to explain what happened tends to refute his testimony at trial that he acted in self-defense? Wasn't the reticence of Jenkins as "insolubly ambiguous" as defendant's silence in *Doyle* (Chapter 4B2 supra)?

3.   Eric Weir stabbed Ronnie Buchanan to death in a parking lot near a poolhall. Weir left the scene in his truck, and the next afternoon (17 hours after the event) police came to his trailer with a warrant for his arrest on murder charges. They advised him of the warrant, and for five to ten minutes nothing more was said, as Weir put on his socks and boots. After placing him in the police cruiser, arresting officers gave him *Miranda* warnings. At trial, the evidence suggested that Buchanan pinned Weir to the ground. Weir testified that Buchanan attacked him, that Weir drew a knife from a scabbard at his waist, and that Buchanan "fell on it." Weir testified that he put the knife in a toolbox on the back of his truck, but it was never found. On cross-examination, the prosecutor suggested that Weir had fled and asked why he had not told various friends what happened. The prosecutor also asked these questions:

The next day when the State Police came to your house and searched it, why didn't you just tell them, "I lost it"?
    Why didn't you tell the State Police where the knife was?
    Why didn't you go to the police department?

Weir v. Fletcher, 658 F.2d 1126, 1127-1128 nn.3 & 4 (6th Cir. 1980). Weir challenged his conviction, and ultimately the Supreme Court concluded that questioning about postarrest but prewarning silence did not violate the Fifth Amendment:

[W]e have consistently explained *Doyle* as a case where the government had induced silence by implicitly insuring the defendant that his silence would not be used against him. . . . In *Jenkins,* we noted that the failure to speak involved in that case occurred before the defendant was taken into custody and was given his *Miranda* warnings, commenting that no governmental action induced the defendant to remain silent before his arrest. . . .

In the absence of the sort of affirmative assurances embodied in the *Miranda* warnings, we do not believe that it violates due process of law for a State to permit cross-examination as to post-arrest silence when a defendant chooses to take the stand. A State is entitled, in such situations, to leave to the judge and jury under its own rules of evidence the resolution of the extent to which post-arrest silence may be deemed to impeach a criminal defendant's own testimony.

Fletcher v. Weir, 455 U.S. 603, 606-607 (1982). Does *Weir* mean that police may arrest a suspect, sit with him in an interview room for 30 minutes, then Mirandize him, and in this way provide the prosecutor with the benefit of the impeaching use of both his prewarning silence (if he refuses to cooperate later) and his postwarning statements (if he talks after being warned)?

4.　Suppose that in the next case a suspect asks a police officer, after his arrest but before he receives *Miranda* warnings, "Do I have to talk to you?" or "Can I discuss the situation with a lawyer before talking about it?" If he is going to be truthful, the officer would have to answer the first question no and the second question yes, wouldn't he? In either of these cases, should the prosecutor be permitted to ask defendant on cross why he didn't tell arresting officers the story he tells at trial? If the arresting officer maintains his own silence in the face of such questions, could the prosecutor ask the accused at trial why he didn't tell his story at the time of his arrest? If the arresting officer doesn't answer these questions and the suspect decides to talk, should his confession be admissible at trial?

5.　Can post-*Miranda* silence by the accused be offered as evidence against him in a hearing to determine his sanity at the time of the alleged crime? See Wainright v. Greenfield, 474 U.S. 284 (1986) (no; *Doyle* indicates that it is "fundamentally unfair to promise an arrested person that his silence will not be used against him and thereafter to breach that silence to impeach his trial testimony," and it is "equally unfair" to break the promise by using silence to overcome a claim of insanity).

6.　Glenn Charles was charged with first degree murder after being found with the victim's car and other personal effects. After receiving *Miranda* warnings, Charles told the arresting officer that he stole the car after finding it unattended in the vicinity of Washtenaw and Hill Streets, about two miles from the local bus station. At trial, however, Charles testified that he stole the car from the parking lot of Kelly's Tire Co. in Ann Arbor (right next to the bus station). On cross, the prosecutor brought out that the bus station and Kelly's Tire were next to the jail and asked whether that was where he "got the idea to come up with the story that you took a car from that location." The defendant protested that he was telling the truth, and the prosecutor then asked:

Don't you think it's rather odd that if it were the truth that you didn't come forward and tell anybody at the time you were arrested, where you got the car? . . .

Well, you told Detective LeVanseler back when you were first arrested, you stole the car back on Washtenaw and Hill Street?

Does the former question violate *Doyle*, or is the prosecutorial attack saved by the latter? See Anderson v. Charles, 447 U.S. 404, 406-407 (1980) (*Doyle* "does not apply to cross-examination that merely inquires into prior inconsistent statements," for such questioning "makes no unfair use of silence"; cross-examination cannot be "bifurcated . . . neatly," and any "ambiguity" in the initial question was "quickly resolved" by later reference to what defendant told the arresting officer).

2. *Contradiction* — *Counterproof*

Impeaching a witness by contradiction entails a showing that something he said in his testimony is not so. Sometimes the impeachment is done by cross-examination, as questions force the witness to admit that he erred (even lied) on some point, but often it is accomplished by extrinsic evidence (testimony or something else, like a writing or recording), which for convenience we may call counterproof.

Assume that George is a witness for defendant Florence in a suit for property damage and personal injuries brought by Ernie, arising out of a collision in which Florence allegedly drove her car into the rear of Ernie's at an intersection stop. On direct examination, George testifies that (1) Ernie caused the accident by suddenly backing up into the car driven by Florence after she had come to a full stop, (2) he (George) saw the accident from the curb and first met Florence when she spoke to him afterward about what he had seen, and (3) he was returning from making a purchase at Jason's Drugs when he saw the accident. During his case-in-rebuttal Ernie offers testimony (a) by Hal that Ernie's car was standing still when Florence ran into him, (b) by Ike (who is acquainted with George) that Florence and George had been seeing each other socially for at least a year prior to the accident, and (c) by Jason that his drugstore was closed for remodeling on the day of the accident.

If any one of Ernie's rebuttal witnesses is believed, his testimony is counterproof that contradicts George. Like inconsistent statements, the counterproof refutes him on specific points, though standing alone it is indefinite in failing to explain why George erred or lied. But the forensic skill of counsel and the psychology of the moment, taken in the larger factual setting of the case, may allow for lots of theories that explain why George should not be believed, and once these theories are expounded the stain on credibility may spread to other points in his testimony.

Setting a limit. Few witnesses testify so perfectly that nothing they say can be challenged, and no trial lawyer worth her salt would chase after a witness at every opportunity. But lawyers sometimes push too far, and courts react by setting limits, barring contradiction on trivial points.

In doing so, courts generally recognize that *all* contradicting counterproof has some impeaching effect but letting it in only if it has *additional* relevance in the case—some relevance *independent* of its contradicting effect. Three kinds of counterproof may be discerned in the cases:

three kinds of
counterproof
① merits
of the
case

The first is counterproof that not only contradicts but also tends to prove a substantive point, as is true of Hal's testimony that Ernie's car was standing still at the time of the accident. Here the counterproof ordinarily gets in, as it would even if it did not have contradicting effect, for it goes to the merits of the case. Its impeaching (contradicting) effect is often forgotten, being overshadowed by the struggle of each party to establish one version of the facts and to destroy the competing version. (In the example, Ernie is more intent on having Hal's version of events accepted as the truth than in persuading the jury through Hal's testimony that George is not a believable witness.)

② showing bias

The second is counterproof that not only contradicts but tends to prove some other impeaching point, as is true of Ike's testimony that Florence and George have been seeing each other. Here too the counterproof usually gets in, as would be true once again even if it did not have contradicting effect, for it tends to show bias. (Recall that bias may be proved by extrinsic evidence, so the attacking party is not limited to cross-examination.) The fact that it also catches George in a lie (if he has been seeing Florence socially, he is unlikely to be *merely mistaken* in saying he first met her at the time of the accident) adds a second impeaching dimension to the counterproof.

③ only contradicts

The third is counterproof that *only* contradicts, as is true of Jason's testimony that the drugstore was closed on the day of the accident. Here the evidence is usually excluded, for it has no relevancy *apart* from contradicting the witness. The fact that it catches George in an error or lie (who knows whether he has forgotten about the errand he was on that day or lied about it?) would not be viewed as reason enough to admit the evidence. It contradicts on what courts usually call a "collateral" point and would usually be excluded. Sometimes, however, courts admit counterproof on such a point where it seems that a witness could not be innocently mistaken. After all, even a point that seems collateral from the perspective of a trial may be a telltale point, perhaps the linchpin in the story, from the perspective of the witness. In other words, what is collateral in the suit may not be collateral in the life of the witness, so counterproof contradicting him on the point may convincingly suggest that he must be lying.

To sum up: Courts generally exclude counterproof that contradicts only on a collateral point. In effect, they require a dual relevancy of evidence offered to contradict a witness, for such proof must tend not only to prove that he lied or erred, but also to prove some other point that could make a difference in the case.

Why contradiction? Reconsider what you've just read. Doesn't it suggest that counterproof gets in to contradict only if it could get in anyway? Then why recognize "contradiction" as a fifth method of impeachment, rather than just an opportunity for making arguments to the jury?

There are two reasons.

One is that the contradicting effect of counterproof justifies departing from normal trial sequence. Thus Hal testified during the case-in-rebuttal of plaintiff Ernie, rather than during his case-in-chief, simply because the *occasion* to prove that Ernie did not suddenly drive backwards arose most strongly after defendant Florence presented her case. Though Hal's testimony went to substantive issues, Ernie was properly allowed to delay offering that testimony until after George had testified for Florence.

The other is that the contradicting effect of counterproof justifies admitting some evidence that would otherwise be excluded. If, for example, Florence had taken the witness stand and testified that she never had an accident before, Ernie would be allowed to prove (if he had the evidence) that in fact Florence had been involved in several prior accidents. Normally such proof would not get in: Even if Ernie could prove, for instance, that Florence was negligent in having other accidents, such evidence would not be admissible to show she was a bad driver, hence careless on the occasion in question, for proving this point in that way would be disallowed by FRE 404 and 405. But if Florence "opens the door" by testifying to her accident-free past (which suggests that she is a careful driver, hence careful on the occasion in question), counterproof of her prior accidents (especially if they were her fault) would be admitted to impeach her by contradiction.

Otherwise-excludable counterproof. Ponder for a moment the destination we have reached. It is paradoxical.

To avoid wasting time on trivia, we bar impeachment on collateral matters, admitting only counterproof that has dual relevancy in the case. But then counterproof gets in that would not otherwise come in at all, just *because* it contradicts. When Florence testifies to her accident-free past, counterproof of prior accidents comes in: It is admissible because it contradicts Florence (thus impeaches her) and bears on the question whether she is a careful driver, hence careful or negligent at the time of the accident. But the evidence comes in only to contradict her, not to prove she was negligent at the time, because the bar against character evidence makes it incompetent (though relevant) to prove negligence. So we insist that counterproof be relevant on some point other than contradiction, then let in counterproof that is incompetent on that other point, just because it contradicts!

And consider this point: When otherwise-excludable counterproof is admitted to contradict a witness, usually the testimony being contradicted *could itself* have been excluded. If counsel for Florence had asked her on direct whether she considered herself a careful driver, for example, counsel for Ernie might plausibly have objected in this vein:

> Your honor, whether Florence is or is not generally careful when she drives is beside the point. The issue in this case is whether she was negligent in colliding with Ernie. She cannot prove that she exercised due care on that occasion by testifying that she is normally careful. In the first place, her own testimony on that point is so hopelessly self-serving that it is unworthy of belief. In the second place, even if she had another witness who was willing to testify to that point, that testimony would not be admissible. It would be barred by the rule against character evidence—Rules 404 and 405. And it could not get in as habit either, because it's too general to qualify under Rule 406.

Isn't that objection entirely sound? Isn't it clear that it should be sustained? Why do you suppose counsel for Ernie would not likely make the objection? Can you imagine the glee in Ernie's camp if counsel knew that Florence has had other accidents (as he likely would if he took her deposition before trial or obtained the public record of her motor vehicle infractions), when Florence is foolish enough to suggest in her testimony that she has never been in an accident before?

Procedural morass. If you look through the Federal Rules, you will find that the subject here discussed is hardly mentioned at all. No provision governs impeachment by contradiction or suggests that it is proper or that it should be limited in any way. Yet such impeachment goes on every day, and the scheme of limitation sketched above is more or less understood almost instinctively by courts and litigators. It is probable that if a party someday challenges this impeaching technique, a court will resolve the matter very much the way the Supreme Court resolved the question of impeachment by showing bias in *Abel.*

The concerns that lead to exclusion of counterproof that contradicts on collateral points are very much the concerns that find expression in FRE 403 and 611, and these can be and are read to limit this form of impeachment.

You can see that the question whether the attacking lawyer can contradict by otherwise-excludable evidence raises questions of procedural fairness. If Florence testifies *on direct examination* that she has never been in an accident before, then it seems fair to permit cross-examination and extrinsic evidence which prove the contrary. See Atkinson v. Atchison, Topeka & Santa Fe Ry., 197 F.2d 244 (10th Cir. 1952) (approving cross-examination of plaintiff similar to that set out above after she testified *on direct* to her usually cautious driving habits). But imagine a case in which Florence makes no reference to her driving history on direct, and *Ernie* first raises the matter on cross-examination:

Q *(Ernie's counsel):*   Now can you tell me, ma'am, whether you consider yourself to be a careful driver.

A *(Florence):*   Yes, sir, I do.

Q: Well isn't it a fact, ma'am, that last year you were involved in a collision with another car while you were in the wrong lane of the highway?

Should Ernie be permitted to "open his own door" for otherwise-excludable counterproof, contradicting a denial that he himself elicits? See Nesbit v. Cumberland Contracting Co., 75 A.2d 339 (Md. 1950) (disapproving cross-examination of plaintiff on prior convictions for reckless driving and similar infractions, after defendant elicited on cross that plaintiff considered himself a good driver, for this line of questioning "was not directed at any testimony of general competence developed in direct examination"). Reconsider this question after reading *Havens* and the accompanying Notes, infra.

A point of confusion? Note that FRE 608(b) provides that an attacking party may cross-examine a witness on nonconviction misconduct "if probative of . . . untruthfulness" but that such misconduct "may not be proved by extrinsic evidence." Doesn't that mean that if the witness denies the misconduct, the attacking party is simply stuck with the answer? Wouldn't extrinsic evidence of the misconduct contradict the denial? Doesn't FRE 608(b) in effect tell us that we cannot engage in contradiction in this situation?

Why doesn't FRE 608(b) prevent Ernie's lawyer from offering extrinsic evidence that Florence has had previous accidents, after she has testified that she never had an accident before? The reason is that FRE 608(b) regulates only one mechanism of impeachment, not others: It speaks to impeachment by showing untruthful disposition, not impeachment by contradiction. Recall what the Court said in United States v. Abel, 469 U.S. 45 (1984), to the effect that FRE 608(b) applies only to attacks aiming to show untruthful character, and does not block extrinsic evidence of statements or acts indicating bias (Chapter 8A1, supra).

In one cocaine prosecution, defendant *O* argued that she had been entrapped, which permitted the government to try to prove that she had dealt in cocaine on other occasions. (The entrapment defense essentially argues that defendant was not predisposed to commit the charged offense, and other crimes are then admissible under FRE 404(b) or 405(b) to show that he was predisposed, after all.) Government witness *P* described the prior crimes and testified that he worked at a beauty salon with *O* at the time, but *O* contended otherwise and sought to establish the point by cross-examination. *P* stuck to his story, and *O* then offered business records suggesting that *P* did not work in the salon during that period. Invoking FRE 608(b), the trial court excluded the business records, but the reviewing court reversed:

> The application of Rule 608(b) to exclude extrinsic evidence of a witness's conduct is limited to instances where the evidence is introduced to show a witness's general character for truthfulness. . . . We consider Rule 608(b) to be inapplicable in determining the admissibility of relevant evidence introduced to contradict a witness's testimony as to a material issue. So long as otherwise competent, such evidence is admissible. This was long the rule in this Circuit prior to the enactment of the Federal Rules of Evidence. We find no reason to reach a different result today.

United States v. Opager, 589 F.2d 799, 801-802 (5th Cir. 1979).

Does *Opager* explain why counsel for Ernie can cross-examine Florence about her prior accidents after she testifies on direct that she has a clean driving record?

 PROBLEM 8-G.   "That's Just Collateral, Your Honor"

Oswald is charged with a robbery that occurred in Seattle at 7:00 p.m. on July 14. Defendant claims alibi. Ardiss testifies to this point as principal witness during the defense case-in-chief.

Ardiss testifies that he operates the Jolly Roger Restaurant in Portland, that Oswald is a regular customer, and that he was there for the entire evening on July 14. The prosecutor cross-examines:

Q [prosecutor]:   To the best of your knowledge, Mr. Ardiss, would you say that Oswald was in the Jolly Roger in Portland every day during the weeks prior to July 14, or was he gone for occasional periods of three or four days, or what?

A [Ardiss]:   No, it would be my testimony that Mr. Oswald was in there every day during that time.

During the state's case-in-rebuttal, the prosecutor calls Police Detective Kinney of Seattle. Kinney testifies that he saw Oswald in Seattle on June 27 and that "Mr. Oswald told me that he had been there, in Seattle I mean, for the last couple of days before I ran into him." The prosecutor also calls Samuels, a waiter who worked at the Jolly Roger in Portland during the period in question, and elicits his testimony that "I never laid eyes on Mr. Oswald in the Jolly Roger."

counterproof?

Oswald has raised timely objection to the testimony of both Kinney and Samuels: "We have to object to this whole approach. He's just trying to distract the jury here. That's just collateral, Your Honor, what he's going into now. We strenuously object to these delaying and distracting tactics. It's just not proper impeachment."

How should the court rule, and why?

NOTES ON "COLLATERAL MATTERS" AND THE RELEVANCY OF COUNTERPROOF OFFERED TO CONTRADICT

1.   In Problem 8-G, there is little doubt that Detective Kinney and Samuels contradicted what Ardiss said. But did Kinney's rebuttal testimony contradict Ardiss on a point that was relevant in the case? Could the prosecutor properly have offered Detective Kinney's testimony during the state's case-in-chief to establish that Oswald was present in Seattle on June 27? Was Samuels' testimony relevant on a substantive point? What if Samuels had not been at the Jolly Roger on July 14?

2.   Now consider some cases that raise both the question whether the proffered counterproof contradicts and the question whether it contradicts on a collateral point:

a.   In her trial for the alleged shooting murder of her husband Jack, Ivy Kelly claims self-defense. She calls an expert who describes the battered woman syndrome and suggests that defendant fits the profile. The characteristics include frustration, stress disorders, depression, economic and emotional dependence, hope that the relationship will improve, poor self-image, and (most important) "isolation" and "learned helplessness." Should the prosecutor be permitted to rebut this testimony by proof that Ivy threatened injury to a trespasser, beat on the back door of her house with a shovel while Jack was inside, and became "verbally abusive" with a neighbor trying to clean an easement between their properties? See State v. Kelly, 685 P.2d 564, 569-571 (Wash. 1984) (no, for this proof "has no bearing upon [defendant's] inability to extricate herself from the marital relationship" and does not tend to refute "evidence explaining her gradual loss of contact with her family and friends"). Is the court right? Or does the counterproof tend to contradict testimony that defendant suffered from "learned helplessness"? If so, does the counterproof also escape the "collateral matters" bar because "learned helplessness" is relevant to self-defense?

b.   Bobbie Beavers, a coach in a public school, is prosecuted for allegedly taking indecent liberties with two girls, aged ten and eleven, as he drove them home from a basketball game. Defendant and his wife testify. On cross-examination, the prosecutor asks defendant why he left three prior teaching positions in Kansas, insinuating that there were other "complaints of sexual misconduct with students," and also asks whether he "knew of other complaints against him" at his present job. Are such questions proper? See Beavers v. State, 709 P.2d 702, 705 (Okla. Crim. App. 1985) (yes; since defendant "raised the issue of the reasons for his resignations," prosecutor was properly permitted "to attempt to impeach his testimony"). Is the court right? If Beavers testified on direct that he left other jobs for professional reasons, seeking better position or salary, does the counterproof tend to contradict? If so, does it contradict on a relevant point, or only on a collateral point?

UNITED STATES v. HAVENS
United States Supreme Court
446 U.S. 620 (1980)

MR. JUSTICE WHITE delivered the opinion of the Court.

The petition for certiorari filed by the United States in this criminal case presented a single question: whether evidence suppressed as the fruit of an unlawful search and seizure may nevertheless be used to impeach a defendant's false trial testimony, given in response to proper cross-examination, where the evidence does not squarely contradict the defendant's testimony on direct examination.

I

Respondent was convicted of importing, conspiring to import, and intentionally possessing a controlled substance, cocaine. According to the evidence at his trial, Havens and John McLeroth, both attorneys from Ft. Wayne, Ind., boarded a flight from Lima, Peru, to Miami, Fla. In Miami, a customs officer searched McLeroth and found cocaine sewed into makeshift pockets in a T-shirt he was wearing under his outer clothing. McLeroth implicated respondent, who had previously cleared customs and who was then arrested. His luggage was seized and searched without a warrant. The officers found no drugs but seized a T-shirt from which pieces had been cut that matched the pieces that had been sewn to McLeroth's T-shirt. The T-shirt and other evidence seized in the course of the search were suppressed on motion prior to trial.

Both men were charged in a three-count indictment, but McLeroth pleaded guilty to one count and testified against Havens. Among other things, he asserted that Havens had supplied him with the altered T-shirt and had sewed the makeshift pockets shut. Havens took the stand in his own defense and denied involvement in smuggling cocaine. His direct testimony included the following:

Q. And you heard Mr. McLeroth testify earlier as to something to the effect that this material was taped or draped around his body and so on, you heard that testimony?
A. Yes, I did.
Q. Did you ever engage in that kind of activity with Mr. McLeroth and Augusto or Mr. McLeroth and anyone else on that fourth visit to Lima, Peru?
A. I did not.

On cross-examination, Havens testified as follows:

Q. Now, on direct examination, sir, you testified that on the fourth trip you had absolutely nothing to do with the wrapping of any bandages or tee shirts or anything involving Mr. McLeroth; is that correct?
A. I don't—I said I had nothing to do with any wrapping or bandages or anything,

yes. I had nothing to do with anything with McLeroth in connection with this cocaine matter. . . .

Q. And your testimony is that you had nothing to do with the sewing of the cotton swatches to make pockets on that tee shirt?

A. Absolutely not.

Q. Sir, when you came through Customs, the Miami International Airport, on October 2, 1977, did you have in your suitcase Size 38-40 medium tee shirts?

An objection to the latter question was overruled and questioning continued:

Q. On that day, sir, did you have in your luggage a Size 38-40 medium man's tee shirt with swatches of clothing missing from the tail of that tee shirt?

A. Not to my knowledge. . . .

Q. Mr. Havens, I'm going to hand you what is Government's Exhibit 9 for identification and ask you if this tee shirt was in your luggage on October 2nd, 1975 [sic]?

A. Not to my knowledge. No.

Respondent Havens also denied having told a Government agent that the T-shirts found in his luggage belonged to McLeroth.

On rebuttal, a Government agent testified that Exhibit 9 had been found in respondent's suitcase and that Havens claimed the T-shirts found in his bag, including Exhibit 9, belonged to McLeroth. Over objection, the T-shirt was then admitted into evidence, the jury being instructed that the rebuttal evidence should be considered only for impeaching Havens' credibility.

The Court of Appeals reversed relying on Agnello v. United States, 269 U.S. 20 (1925), and Walder v. United States, 347 U.S. 62 (1954). The court held that illegally seized evidence may be used for impeachment only if the evidence contradicts a particular statement made by a defendant in the course of his direct examination. We reverse.

II . . .

These cases were understood by the Court of Appeals to hold that tainted evidence, inadmissible when offered as part of the Government's main case, may not be used as rebuttal evidence to impeach a defendant's credibility unless the evidence is offered to contradict a particular statement made by a defendant during his direct examination; a statement made for the first time on cross-examination may not be so impeached. This approach required the exclusion of the T-shirt taken from Havens' luggage because, as the Court of Appeals read the record, Havens was asked nothing on his direct testimony about the incriminating T-shirt or about the contents of his luggage; the testimony about the T-shirt, which the Government desired to impeach, first appeared on cross-examination, not on direct.

It is true that *Agnello* involved the impeachment of testimony first brought out on cross-examination and that in *Walder, Harris,* and *Hass,* the testimony impeached was given by the defendant while testifying on direct examination. In our view, however, a flat rule permitting only statements on direct examination to be impeached misapprehends the underlying rationale of *Walder, Harris,* and *Hass.* These cases repudiated the statement in *Agnello* that no use at all may be made of illegally obtained evidence. Furthermore, in *Walder,* the Court said that in *Agnello,* the Government had "smuggled in" the impeaching opportunity in the course of cross-examination. The Court also relied on the statement in *Agnello* that Agnello had done nothing "to justify cross-examination in respect of the evidence claimed to have been obtained by the search." The implication of *Walder* is that *Agnello* was a case of cross-examination having too tenuous a connection with any subject opened upon direct examination to permit impeachment by tainted evidence.

In reversing the District Court in the case before us, the Court of Appeals did not stop to consider how closely the cross-examination about the T-shirt and the luggage was connected with matters gone into in direct examination. If these questions would have been suggested to a reasonably competent cross-examiner by Havens' direct testimony, they were not "smuggled in"; and forbidding the Government to impeach the answers to these questions by using contrary and reliable evidence in its possession fails to take account of our cases, particularly *Harris* and *Hass.* In both cases, the Court stressed the importance of arriving at the truth in criminal trials, as well as the defendant's obligation to speak the truth in response to proper questions. We rejected the notion that the defendant's constitutional shield against having illegally seized evidence used against him could be "perverted into a license to use perjury by way of a defense, free from the risk of confrontation with prior inconsistent utterances." Both cases also held that the deterrent function of the rules excluding unconstitutionally obtained evidence is sufficiently served by denying its use to the government on its direct case. It was only a "speculative possibility" that also making it unavailable to the government for otherwise proper impeachment would contribute substantially in this respect.

Neither *Harris* nor *Hass* involved the impeachment of assertedly false testimony first given on cross-examination, but the reasoning of those cases controls this one. There is no gainsaying that arriving at the truth is a fundamental goal of our legal system. We have repeatedly insisted that when defendants testify, they must testify truthfully or suffer the consequences. This is true even though a defendant is compelled to testify against his will. It is essential, therefore, to the proper functioning of the adversary system that when a defendant takes the stand, the government be permitted proper and effective cross-examination in an attempt to elicit the truth. The defendant's obligation to testify truthfully is fully binding on him when he is cross-examined. His privilege against self-incrimination does not shield him from proper questioning. He would unquestionably be subject to a perjury prosecution if he knowingly lies on cross-examination. In terms of impeaching a defendant's seemingly false statements with his prior inconsistent utterances or with other reliable evidence available to the government, we see no difference of constitutional magnitude between the defendant's statements on direct examination and his answers to questions put to him on cross-examination that are plainly within the scope of the defendant's direct examination. Without this opportunity, the normal function of cross-examination would be severely impeded.

We also think that the policies of the exclusionary rule no more bar impeachment here than they did in *Walder, Harris,* and *Hass.* In those cases, the ends of the exclusionary rules were thought adequately implemented by denying the government the use of the challenged evidence to make out its

case in chief. The incremental furthering of those ends by forbidding impeachment of the defendant who testifies was deemed insufficient to permit or require
that false testimony go unchallenged, with the resulting impairment of the
integrity of the factfinding goals of the criminal trial. We reaffirm this assessment
of the competing interests, and hold that a defendant's statements made in
response to proper cross-examination reasonably suggested by the defendant's
direct examination are subject to otherwise proper impeachment by the government, albeit by evidence that has been illegally obtained that is inadmissible
on the government's direct case, or otherwise, as substantive evidence of guilt.

In arriving at its judgment, the Court of Appeals noted that in response
to defense counsel's objection to the impeaching evidence on the ground that
the matter had not been "covered on direct" the trial court had remarked
that "[i]t does not have to be covered on direct." . . . [W]e cannot accept
respondent's suggestions that because of the illegal search and seizure, the
Government's questions about the T-shirt were improper cross-examination.
McLeroth testified that Havens had assisted him in preparing the T-shirt for
smuggling. Havens, in his direct testimony, acknowledged McLeroth's prior
testimony that the cocaine "was taped or draped around his body and so
on" but denied that he had "ever engage[d] in that kind of activity with Mr.
McLeroth. . . ." This testimony could easily be understood as a denial of
any connection with McLeroth's T-shirt and as a contradiction of McLeroth's
testimony. Quite reasonably, it seems to us, the Government on cross-examination called attention to his answers on direct and then asked whether he had
anything to do with sewing the cotton swatches on McLeroth's T-shirt. This was
cross-examination growing out of Havens' direct testimony; and, as we hold
above, the ensuing impeachment did not violate Havens' constitutional rights.

We reverse the judgment of the Court of Appeals and remand the case to
that court for further proceedings consistent with this opinion.

So ordered.

MR. JUSTICE BRENNAN, joined by MR. JUSTICE MARSHALL and joined in Part
I by MR. JUSTICE STEWART and MR. JUSTICE STEVENS, dissenting.

The Court upholds the admission at trial of illegally seized evidence to
impeach a defendant's testimony deliberately elicited *by the Government* under
the cover of impeaching an accused who takes the stand in his own behalf. I
dissent. Criminal defendants now told that prosecutors are licensed to insinuate
otherwise inadmissible evidence under the guise of cross-examination no longer
have the unfettered right to elect whether or not to testify in their own behalf.
Not only is today's decision an unwarranted departure from prior controlling
cases, but, regrettably, it is yet another element in the trend to depreciate the
constitutional protections guaranteed the criminally accused. . . .

The Court's opinion attempts to discredit *Agnello* by casting a strawman as
its holding, and then demolishing the pitiful scarecrow of its own creation. . . .
[T]he actual principle of *Agnello,* as discerned by *Walder,* is that the Government
may not employ its power of cross-examination to predicate the admission of
illegal evidence. In other words, impeachment by cross-examination about—or
introduction of—suppressible evidence must be warranted by defendant's statements upon direct questioning. That principle is not at all inconsistent with
later cases holding that the defendant may not take advantage of evidentiary
suppression to advance specific perjurious claims as part of his direct case.

Nor is it correct to read *Agnello* as turning upon the tenuity of the link between the cross-examination involved there and the subject matter of the direct examination. The cross-examination about Agnello's previous connection with cocaine was reasonably related to his direct testimony that he lacked knowledge that the commodity he was transporting was cocaine. For "[t]he possession by Frank Agnello of the can of cocaine which was seized tended to show guilty knowledge and criminal intent on his part. . . ." Thus, the constitutional flaw found in *Agnello* was that the introduction of the tainted evidence had been prompted by statements of the accused first elicited upon cross-examination. And the case was so read in Walder v. United States. That decision specifically stated that a defendant "must be free to deny all the elements of the case against him without thereby giving leave to the Government to introduce by way of rebuttal evidence illegally secured by it, and therefore not available for its case in chief." Since as a matter of the law of evidence it would be perfectly permissible to cross-examine a defendant as to his denial of complicity in the crime, the quoted passage in *Walder* must be understood to impose a further condition before the prosecutor may refer to tainted evidence—that is, some particular direct testimony by the accused that relies upon "the Government's disability to challenge his credibility."

In fact, the Court's current interpretation of *Agnello* and *Walder* simply trivializes those decisions by transforming their Fourth Amendment holdings into nothing more than a constitutional reflection of the common-law evidentiary rule of relevance.

Finally, the rationale of Harris v. New York and Oregon v. Hass does not impel the decision at hand. The exclusionary rule exception established by *Harris* and *Hass* may be fairly easily cabined by defense counsel's willingness to forgo certain areas of questioning. But the rule prescribed by the Court in this case passes control of the exception to the Government, since the prosecutor can lay the predicate for admitting otherwise suppressible evidence with his own questioning. To be sure, the Court requires that cross-examination be "proper"; however, traditional evidentiary principles accord parties fairly considerable latitude in cross-examining opposing witnesses. In practical terms, therefore, today's holding allows even the moderately talented prosecutor to "work in . . . evidence on cross-examination [as it would] in its case in chief. . . ." Walder v. United States, 347 U.S., at 66. To avoid this consequence, a defendant will be compelled to forgo testifying on his own behalf. . . .

The foregoing demonstration of its break with precedent provides a sufficient ground to condemn the present ruling—unleashing, as it does, a hitherto relatively confined exception to the exclusionary rule. But I have a more fundamental difference with the Court's holding here, which culminates the approach taken in Harris v. New York and Oregon v. Hass. For this sequence of decisions undercuts the constitutional canon that convictions cannot be procured by governmental lawbreaking. . . .

Ultimately, I fear, this ad hoc approach to the exclusionary rule obscures the difference between judicial decisionmaking and legislative or administrative policymaking. More disturbingly, by treating Fourth and Fifth Amendment privileges as mere incentive schemes, the Court denigrates their unique status as *constitutional* protections. Yet the efficacy of the Bill of Rights as the bulwark of our national liberty depends precisely upon public appreciation of the special character of constitutional prescriptions. The Court is charged with the responsibility to enforce constitutional guarantees; decisions such as today's patently disregard that obligation.

Accordingly, I dissent.

NOTES ON CONTRADICTING A WITNESS BY CONSTITUTIONALLY EXCLUDABLE COUNTERPROOF

1. Given the decision in *Harris,* are you surprised at the outcome in *Havens?* Which is harder—justifying use of *Miranda*-barred statements to impeach, or justifying similar use of evidence seized in violation of the Fourth Amendment? Is *Havens* likely to have an impact on the way in which police search for evidence?

2. In *Havens,* did the T-shirt only contradict what J. Lee Havens said on cross-examination, or did it also contradict his direct testimony? If it contradicted also the direct, why does the Court take such pains to say that the prosecutor may offer constitutionally excludable evidence to contradict testimony elicited on cross-examination? Justice Brennan is right in his dissent in *Havens,* isn't he, in arguing that allowing the government to impeach testimony elicited *on cross* by illegally seized evidence "passes control" of this powerful impeaching mechanism to the prosecutor?

3. *Havens* says that in *Agnello* the government " 'smuggled in' the impeaching opportunity." In that case, recall that defendant testified that he did not know what certain packages contained (cocaine), and was asked on cross whether he had ever seen cocaine before (he replied, essentially, "never"). If a case identical to *Agnello* arose today, would such cross-examination be "reasonably suggested" by the direct, so a denial paves the way to admit illegally seized evidence? In a case remarkably similar to *Agnello,* one court indicates that the answer is yes (the cross is related; the illegally seized evidence comes in). It was another drug prosecution, and defendant testified on direct that he didn't know the packages he delivered contained Quaaludes (he thought they were "Greek statues"). On cross, the government asked whether he was "familiar with Quaaludes." Defendant said no, and the government contradicted the denial by showing that at the time of the offense agents seized Quaaludes from defendant's car (the search was illegal). See United States v. Hernandez, 646 F.3d 970 (5th Cir. 1981) (although never overruled, *Agnello* has been "practically eviscerated," and *Havens* controls), cert. denied, 454 U.S. 1082 (1981). Cases like *Havens* and *Hernandez* suggest, don't they, that if a case identical to *Havens* arose today, defendant could not avoid paving the way to admit the T-shirt by confining his direct testimony to an assertion that he "knew nothing about what McLeroth was carrying"? Doesn't this outcome make Justice Brennan's point (that "control" has passed to the government)?

4. One small consolation for defendants. As some decisions from Illinois illustrate, modern cases sometimes *do* conclude that the prosecutor has "pushed things too far" by expanding cross-examination into new areas. See People v. Lawson, 762 N.E.2d 633 (Ill. App. 2001) (defendant testified on direct that he was going from a pool hall to a store at time of robbery; prosecutor asked on

cross whether he told detective, in suppressed statement, that he "had witnesses" who saw him at the pool hall but "couldn't name them," since this question was "not related to any specific statements that defendant made on direct") (conviction reversed), app. denied, 770 N.E.2d 222 (2002); People v. Williams, 564 N.E.2d 168 (Ill. App. 1990) (defendant described his military service on direct; on cross, prosecutor asked whether he had "ever" seen a .38 caliber weapon or bullet, and defendant said no; prosecutor should not then have introduced .38 caliber bullet illegally seized from defendant at time of arrest) (conviction for armed robbery reversed), app. denied, 567 N.E.2d 341 (1991).

5. Of course state courts remain free to fashion rules giving more protection to defendants. See, e.g., State v. Brunelle, 534 A.2d 198 (Vt. 1987) (refusing to follow *Havens,* and rejecting even *Harris* in holding that suppressed evidence may not be introduced to impeach criminal defendants; even if defendant did not testify, but stayed off the stand because the trial court ruled that the evidence could be used to impeach if it tended to contradict his testimony, defendant could still raise the point on appeal).

PROBLEM 8-H. *"Have You Ever Sold Narcotics Before?"*

Young is charged with selling narcotics. He testifies on direct that he did not commit the charged offense and that he was elsewhere at the time. On cross-examination, the prosecutor asks, "Have you ever sold narcotics before?" The defense timely objects. Is the question improper? On what ground?

What if defendant answers before counsel interposes an objection: "No, sir, I never have sold narcotics, not this time and not before either." During the state's case-in-rebuttal, the prosecutor offers testimony by undercover agents to the effect that they saw defendant sell narcotics on three previous unrelated occasions. The defense raises timely objection. Should this testimony be excluded? Why or why not?

NOTES ON CONTRADICTING A WITNESS BY COUNTERPROOF EXCLUDABLE UNDER THE RULES

1. Does *Havens* suggest that the tactic pursued by the prosecutor in Problem 8-H is proper? In theory, the answer is no because both the rule in *Havens* and the rationale behind it differ from the rule involved in Problem 8-H and the rationale behind it.

(a) The rule involved in *Havens* amounts to a constitutional principle (in effect, a limit on the exclusionary doctrine, under which illegally seized evidence can be used to contradict testimony by the defendant). In contrast, the rule involved in Problem 8-H amounts to a principle of evidence law (in effect, a limitation on the protective policy in FRE 404).

(b) The reason behind the constitutional principle has to do with balancing incentives—encouraging police to respect individual rights while discouraging defendants from lying on the witness stand. The reason behind the evidence rule has to do with fairness (it is unfair to ask defendants to defend their whole lives, as opposed to specific charges) and sound verdicts (we don't want juries thinking about other crimes when the question is guilt of the *charged* crime).

(c) Still, the bad news for defendants is that decisions on constitutional points announced by the United States Supreme Court sometimes affect other areas, and *Havens* is sometimes cited as authority for the point that cross-examination and contradiction are proper because testimony elicited on cross is reasonably related to the direct, even if the counterproof raises no constitutional issue of the sort examined in *Harris* and *Havens*. See, for example, United States v. Sotomayor-Vazquez, 249 F.3d 1, 11 (1st Cir. 2001) (sweeping denial of involvement in schemes like the one charged paved the way for proof that defendant engaged in such a scheme on a prior occasion; court invokes *Havens* even though the rebuttal evidence raised no constitutional issue).

(d) More bad news for defendants: Often the facts raise *both* a constitutional issue and an evidence issue, but the bright glare of the constitutional issue distracts courts from seeing or paying attention to related issues of evidence law. See, e.g., United States v. Martinez, 967 F.2d 1343, 1346 (9th Cir. 1992) (defendant denied knowing about cocaine in house; on cross, government asked whether he "ever used or sold cocaine," then contradicted his denial by proving that earlier he engaged in illegally intercepted conversation about cocaine transaction; cross reasonably suggested by direct); Ware v. United States, 579 A.2d 701 (D.C. Ct. App. 1990) (defendant testified on direct that he did not sell dilaudid to *B* or "to anyone else" that day; government properly showed 17 dilaudid tablets recovered from his car in illegal search).

2. Assume in Problem 8-H that Young testified on direct that he had "never been involved with narcotics before." Then it should be all right, shouldn't it, for the prosecutor to raise on cross-examination (or show by extrinsic evidence) defendant's prior narcotics convictions? United States v. Gaertner, 705 F.2d 210, 214-216 (7th Cir. 1983) (yes, for "defendant himself had raised the issue of his lack of prior involvement in drug trafficking" and thus "opened the door on the question of his prior or present drug involvement"), cert. denied, 464 U.S. 1071 (1984). Should the prosecutor be permitted to call undercover agents to testify that they saw him engaging in other drug transactions? See United States v. Paulsen, 645 F.2d 13, 14-15 (8th Cir.) (admitting "collateral evidence" of drug run after defendant testified on direct that he "had never been involved with drugs or drug dealing"), cert. denied, 454 U.S. 848 (1981).

3. Some good news for defendants is that not all modern courts apply the logic of *Havens* to evidence excludable under the Rules. Consider the trial of Gerald Simpson for possession with intent to distribute cocaine, and possession of dilaudid and marijuana. Simpson testified on his own behalf, apparently sticking to the facts underlying the charges against him. On cross, the government tried to broaden the inquiry, asking whether he had "ever seen these yellow pills before" (referring to the dilaudid) and defendant admitted that he had and said he was familiar with the pills, but he denied knowing how the drug is commonly packaged. To undermine the claim of unfamiliarity with packaging, the prosecutor then asked whether defendant had been carrying dilaudid when he was arrested some six years before the charged offense (he denied it). The reviewing court disapproved. Evidence of prior possession was not "relevant to any permissible purpose," and the initial question served

only "to demonstrate Simpson's criminal propensities," which is forbidden by FRE 404. The government's claim that it could contradict his denial by proving the prior conviction was "circular." It might have been proper to ask whether Simpson had dilaudid when arrested *this* time, but the government "may not use impermissible means" to get at this point by asking about defendant's general knowledge of dilaudid packaging. See United States v. Simpson, 992 F.2d 1224, 1225-1226 (D.C. Cir. 1993) (reversing conviction as product of plain error), cert. denied, 510 U.S. 906 (1993).

C. REPAIRING CREDIBILITY

When a witness has been impeached, ordinarily some party (generally the one who called the witness) has an interest in repairing the damage, if possible. The Rules allow for this strategy, but two conditions are paramount: First, generally courts disallow any attempt to repair credibility before the attack has come. In the specific context of character witnesses, FRE 608(a) states this principle directly. Second, the repair should be made at the point of attack. Both these limits bring some difficulties in application, as you will see.

1. Rebutting Impeaching Attacks

Generally courts have held that the first of these conditions is not violated when a party anticipating an attack seeks to deflect it by bringing out on direct examination the points he expects the cross-examiner to raise. Thus, it is permissible on direct (1) for any party to adduce testimony by his expert to the effect that she is being paid for her services, (2) for the prosecution or the defense to bring out that its witness has been convicted of crimes, (3) for the prosecutor to bring out that its witness has entered into a plea bargain, and (4) for the calling party to bring out any connection or affinity that she has with the witness (obvious grounds of bias that the other side would raise).

NOTES ON REBUTTING IMPEACHING ATTACKS

1. In the prosecution of Andre Maltais for alleged murder, the state calls his girlfriend Robin Murphy, who saw the crime being committed. On cross-examination, defense counsel brings out that Murphy was "totally drunk" at the time, that she has been a longtime drug user, that she "lied to police" about the murder, and that she is "a prostitute, a lesbian, and an alcoholic." On redirect examination of Murphy, should the prosecutor be permitted to bring out that defendant introduced her to drug use when "she was eleven years old and he picked her up hitchhiking"? Commonwealth v. Maltais, 438 N.E.2d 847, 854 (Mass. 1982) (yes). Do these questions rehabilitate the witness, or only prejudice the defense? Are they justifiable because defendant somehow "opened the door" to them?

2.   If defendant testifies, and counsel brings out his prior convictions in an effort to deflate an expected impeachment, should the prosecutor be permitted to go over the ground once again? See Acevedo v. State, 467 So. 2d 220, 225 (Miss. 1985) (where defendant "fails to fully enumerate all of his prior convictions," prosecutor "is entitled to ask the defendant of what crimes or misdemeanors he has been convicted," and to ask whether defendant "denies being convicted of a particular crime on a particular date in a particular court"). What if defendant has listed every past conviction?

3.   If a defendant brings out that a prosecution witness has entered into a plea agreement, should the government be permitted on redirect to bring out that the witness promised to testify "truthfully and completely" and that the deal is "null and void" if he does not do so? Usually courts say yes, though some modern opinions see dangers in this practice. What dangers can there be? See United States v. Hilton, 772 F.2d 783, 785-787 (11th Cir. 1985); United States v. Roberts, 618 F.2d 530, 535 (9th Cir. 1980), cert. denied, 452 U.S. 942 (1981).

2.   *Evidence of Good Character*

Recall the example of witness Grace Gardner, whose credibility was attacked through testimony by Coach Jones that she has a bad reputation in Riverdale for truth and veracity (Chapter 8A3c, supra). After such attack, the calling party might seek to repair the damage by offering testimony that in fact she is truthful:

Q *(to character witness):*   Reverend Gram, are you acquainted with Grace Gardner?
A *(Reverend Gram):*   Yes, sir, I am.
Q: She is a member of your Riverdale congregation, is she not?
A: Yes, she is.
Q: And you have had occasion to work with her on church projects?
A: Yes, sir, I did. She served as chair of our building committee several years ago and did a superb job, I might add.
Q: Yes, and you got to know her quite well during that period, did you not?
A: Yes, sir.
Q: How would you estimate her character for truth and veracity?
A: Oh, it is of the very highest order, sir, the very highest order. She is a scrupulously honest woman.
Q: And you would believe her under oath?
A: Oh, yes, absolutely. I would believe her whether she is under oath or not.
Q: Thank you, Reverend. Your witness, counsel.

Such supporting testimony is allowed under FRE 608(a), which authorizes courts to admit "opinion or reputation" testimony supporting credibility after "character for truthfulness has been attacked." See, e.g., United States v. Bonner, 302 F.3d 776, 780 (7th Cir. 2002) (after defense suggested that *A* gained by cooperating with government, prosecutor could ask *G* "what kind of woman" *A* was, eliciting *G*'s answer that *A* was "an honest mother" and "a good wife" and "a friend of mine") (defense objected, and court required a "more precise question").

Note that the supporting party laid a foundation for Reverend Gram's good opinion, and of course the supporting party hopes very much that any stature and esteem that the character witness might bring with him to the stand will "rub off" a little on the witness being supported, and generally on the cause of the supporting party.

   Cross-examination. Of course there are risks in this strategy. If Coach Jones harbors a bad opinion of Grace Gardner, presumably he has some particular reasons, perhaps arising out of specific instances of behavior by Gardner herself. And the attacking party (who called Coach Jones) may learn of these reasons and is entitled (if he can) to turn these to good use in cross-examining Reverend Gram:

Q *(attacking party):* Now Reverend Gram, you say that Grace Gardner is an honest
     woman, is that right?
A *(Reverend Gram):* Yes, sir.
Q: And you would believe her, regardless whether she is sworn to tell the truth or
     not?
A: Yes, sir.
Q: Well, sir, did you know that she embezzled money from her employer the Seacoast
     Bank? Did you know that?
A: No sir, and I don't know it now. Whatever people may have said—
Q: And that she pleaded guilty to embezzlement charges, did you know that?
A: No.

Here as in the case of cross-examination of character witnesses under FRE 405, the ostensible purpose is to test the knowledge and judgment of the good character witness. With questions as damning as those suggested here, the attacking party comes out ahead regardless how the character witness replies. If Gram did not know of the incidents, then he lacked important information about Gardner; if he did know of them, then his good opinion of her honesty is hard to understand.

   Here as before, the cross-examiner must have a reasonable basis for the questions, or they amount to gross misconduct.

UNITED STATES v. MEDICAL THERAPY SCIENCES
United States Court of Appeals for the Second Circuit
583 F.2d 36 (1978)

[Stanley Berman and his Connecticut company, Medical Therapy Sciences, were convicted of filing false claims for Medicare payments, and related charges. Government proof suggested that Berman devised a scheme to obtain payment from insurance carriers in Connecticut and New York, using Medical Therapy and its New York branch, Respiratory Specialties, to double bill for the same patients, and to charge for more expensive equipment than was provided and for supplies neither delivered nor needed. Barbara Russell, a trusted employee and personal intimate of Berman, was an unindicted coconspirator who testified for the government. She supervised much of the billing and testified that she and Berman often discussed the applicable rules and practices of the companies, suggesting that both knew they were obtaining funds to which they were not entitled. On appeal, Berman contended that the trial judge erred in permitting the prosecutor to call character witnesses to bolster Russell's credibility, and that this error was crucial in light of Berman's claim that Russell alone perpetrated the frauds.]

MOORE, J.

Rule 608(a) . . . provides that character evidence may be used to support a witness, but limits its use so that "evidence of truthful character is admissible only after the character of the witness for truthfulness has been attacked by opinion or reputation evidence or otherwise." Berman's claim is that the foundation for character evidence was not present in this case because Russell's character for truthfulness had not been attacked within the meaning of the Rule. He argues that cross examination elicited only matters of Russell's bias in favor of the Government and against Berman and that, in any event, the Government itself initially brought to the jury's attention, on its direct examination of Russell, the facts that she had had two prior convictions and that she had been accused by Berman of having embezzled money from Medical Therapy. Berman contends that the Government should not thereafter have been allowed to bolster her credibility when the defense cross examined only as to matters brought out on direct.

The Government's argument is that, in questioning Russell on direct as to her prior convictions, the prosecutor was only anticipating defense impeachment, as it had the right to do, so that the jury would not gain the impression that the Government was attempting to hide information from them. Because Russell's truthfulness was "attacked" on cross examination, the Government argues that Rule 608(a) by its terms permits it the use of character evidence, notwithstanding its own elicitation of Russell's background.[2] Although the issue is a close one, we believe that the decision to permit the evidence in question was one within the trial judge's discretion.

As to the point that the Government first elicited the impeaching facts, we agree that the Government had the right to proceed as it did. Rule 608 itself contains no limitation that precludes a party from offering character evidence under circumstances where it anticipates impeachment; rather, the event that triggers the applicability of the Rule is an "attack" on the witness' veracity. While under the Federal Rules, a party *may* impeach his own witness, FRE 607, there is a vast difference between putting that witness' veracity in issue by eliciting the impeaching facts and merely revealing the witness' background. Indeed, even in jurisdictions where a party may not discredit his own witness, it has been held that the fact of prior convictions may be brought out on direct examination for non-impeachment purposes. As stated by the New York Court of Appeals,

> The law does not limit a party to witnesses of good character, nor does it compel a party to conceal the bad record of his witnesses from the jury, to have it afterwards revealed by the opposing party with telling effect. Such a rule would

---

2. The Government also argues that Berman waived any objection on the ground that the Government had been the first to elicit the "impeachment facts" from its own witness. While it is true that this precise point was not raised below, defense counsel did interpose an objection to the character witnesses pursuant to Rule 608(a), and we think that the issue is properly before us.

be unfair alike to the party calling the witness and the jury. . . . [W]hen a disreputable witness is called and frankly presented to the jury as such, the party calling him represents him for the occasion and the purposes of the trial as worthy of belief.

People v. Minsky, 124 N.E. 126, 127 (N.Y. 1919).

While we do not think that Rule 608(a) should make supporting character evidence available to a party who elicits impeachment material on direct examination for impeaching purposes, we do believe that, when the tenor of the direct examination does not suggest an "attack" on veracity, and when cross examination *can* be characterized as such an attack, the trial judge should retain the discretion to permit the use of character witnesses. His proximity to the situation allows him to make the determination of when, and by whom, an attack is made. Were the rule to be otherwise, a party would have to choose between revealing, on direct, the background of a witness and its right to use character evidence if the witness' veracity is subsequently impugned.

In the instant case, the Government's direct questioning of Russell was brief and to the point. She was simply asked whether, when she left Medical Therapy to establish a business which was in competition with Berman's, she had taken patients from Berman's operation; she answered in the negative. This questioning covered about one page. The prosecutor also elicited the fact that, near the end of Russell's employment with Berman, at a time when relations between the two were strained, Berman had accused Russell of taking $70 from him, and that she had denied the charge (claiming, in fact, that Berman had owed her and her husband for past loans), but had repaid the money to avoid any further problem. Finally, she admitted her two prior convictions for obtaining amphetamines by fraudulent practices, but explained that she had committed the acts at a time when she had been addicted to the drug for weight control purposes and that she had sought help after her second conviction. Even this interchange covered only five pages of transcript. At least on the basis of the cold record before us, it appears that, in a very real sense, the Government did not put Russell's veracity in issue. Thus, though we believe that the trial judge should retain discretion to disallow the use of character evidence under circumstances such as this, we think he must also be permitted to allow it when, subsequent to the revelation of a witness' problems on direct, the opponent paints the witness with more accusatory strokes—especially where, as here, wrongdoing which implicates veracity is alleged and denied.

In this case, however, Berman argues that his counsel did not open the door to character evidence because his cross examination of Russell did not constitute an "attack on veracity." We conclude, however, that Judge Carter could have properly characterized the defense's treatment of Russell as an attack within the meaning of Rule 608(a).

In this case, cross examination of Russell included sharp questioning about her prior convictions, which were predicated on activities characterized as fraudulent. When such convictions are used for impeachment purposes, as they were on cross examination here, we think that the door is opened to evidence in support of truthfulness.[3]

---

3. Indeed, under Rule 609(a)(2), a witness may always be impeached by proof of a prior conviction if the crime involved "dishonesty or false statement." . . . Since the attack on Russell was predicated in part on convictions for fraud, which are deemed to have a bearing on a witness'

Russell's character was also attacked by "specific act" evidence, to wit, allegations that she had embezzled money and stolen patients from Berman's company. While Berman argues that such evidence, because it involved her efforts to set up a competing business, bore solely on her bias against him, and, as such, did not constitute an attack on character, we do not think that the implications were so limited. As noted by the commentators, evidence of bias can take many forms. Some types of bias, for example bias stemming from a relationship with a party, do not necessarily involve any issue relating to the moral character of the witness, but suggest only that the witness' testimony may perhaps unwittingly be slanted for reasons unrelated to general propensity for untruthfulness. As such, character evidence is not relevant to meet such an attack. On the other hand, alleged partiality based on hostility or self-interest may assume greater significance if it is sought to be proven by conduct rising to the level of corruption.[4] Certainly, the embezzlement and theft of which Russell was accused can be said to fall within the category of corrupt conduct, within the contemplation of Rule 608(a).[5] Furthermore, Russell consistently denied the larceny that was ascribed to her by the defense attack.[6] Under such a circumstance, the commentators again agree that "rehabilitating evidence should be allowed in the judge's discretion if he finds the witness' denial has not erased the jury's doubts." [3 J. Weinstein and M. Berger, Weinstein's Evidence ¶608[05], at 608-41-42 (1977).]

We think, in sum, that the decision to permit the character evidence must be affirmed on the facts. We emphasize, however, that discretion in this area must be exercised with circumspection so that the jury's attention is not diverted from the main issues to be tried. It is not every cross examination that should trigger the authority of Rule 608(a)'s provision for supporting character evidence. However, since the attack in this case went even beyond cross examina-

---

truthfulness, supporting character evidence would be relevant under Rule 608(a) to meet the impeachment.

4. Here, Berman did attempt to prove Russell's embezzlement by extrinsic evidence—i.e., the testimony of defense witness Spyek. Further, defense witness Menti testified that Russell had suggested that he "steal" from Medical Therapy to supply her competing business with equipment, contrary to Russell's denials; he also testified that he had seen Medical Therapy equipment at Russell's company. While this evidence may have suggested bias, and while it was admissible pursuant to the defense theory that Russell had falsified claims in order to obtain money for her own purposes, it also served to attack Russell's veracity in a severe manner by suggesting that she had lied when she denied the embezzlement and theft.

5. Embezzlement convictions are treated by the Conference Report as relevant to truthfulness. See n.3 supra. If embezzlement is alleged, but it never was the subject of a conviction, logically the accusation does not lose its character as an attack on truthfulness.

6. See n.4 supra, to the effect that the defense attack here went far beyond mere accusation by cross-examination and denial. Other witnesses were called to contradict Russell's denials in order to support the defense's theory that Russell had the motive to commit the frauds, on her own, and for her own purposes—that she could have submitted false claims to cover up for her embezzlement. Though contradiction cannot usually be characterized as an "attack" on character, here the contradiction specifically implicated Russell's veracity.

We think that trial judges should be permitted, under Rule 608, to exercise sound discretion to permit or deny a party the use of character evidence to support veracity. As is always the case, the balancing test under Rule 403 must be considered before any such evidence is permitted over objection. Furthermore, it is always open to the trial judge to deny a party the opportunity to present only cumulative evidence bearing solely on credibility.

tion, and since Berman's guilt was established not only by Russell's testimony, but also by ample supporting evidence, both documentary and in the form of testimony from the Blue Cross specialist and from other employees of Medical Therapy, we affirm.

Judgment affirmed.

| NOTES ON PROVING TRUTHFULNESS: CHARACTER AND
| BEHAVIORAL SYNDROME EVIDENCE

1.   Did the prosecutor succeed in "suckering" the defense into an attack that paved the way for supporting evidence? Does the strategy of the prosecution amount to advance (and hidden) support that should be disallowed?

2.   Should courts admit expert testimony that a person is telling the truth? Generally courts exclude such testimony and express suspicion when an expert even gets close to endorsing the truthfulness of one of the litigants. See United States v. Muckala, 303 F.3d 1207, 1217 (10th Cir. 2002) (in suit by nurse alleging sexual harassment at hospital, allowing treating psychiatrist to describe her psychological condition but not to give his opinion on her truthfulness in bringing the complaint or to say whether he believes she was harassed). Often courts raise two objections: One is that experts do not know how to distinguish truthful from untruthful tendencies or dispositions in people; the other is that juries can resolve credibility issues, and expert testimony might even infringe on the prerogatives of the jury. The latter ground is obsolete, see FRE 704 (abolishing "ultimate issue" objection), but courts continue to express apprehension that expert testimony on credibility issues will discourage juries from making their own independent judgment.

3.   The deluge of prosecutions for child sexual abuse that began in the 1980s put pressure on courts to relax this attitude and make room for such proof. Often experts now give social framework testimony describing familial or other settings in which abuse occurs, or syndrome testimony focusing on behavioral patterns of the actors. Parallel developments appear in sexual assault cases, where experts sometimes testify to Rape Trauma Syndrome, and in homicide prosecutions in which women being tried for killing men raise the defense that they were battered, hence justifiably acting in self-defense (Battered Woman Syndrome). See generally C. Mueller and L. Kirkpatrick, Evidence §7.22 (3d ed. 2003) (describing child sexual abuse accommodation syndrome, rape trauma syndrome, and battered woman syndrome). And see Chapter 9, pages 645-650, infra. Such testimony occasionally draws close to commenting directly on the veracity or "believability" of particular witnesses, and some modern opinions approve. See State v. Bachman, 446 N.W.2d 271, 276 (S.D. 1989) (expert testified that allegations were truthful); State v. Kim, 645 P.2d 1330, 1338-1339 (Haw. 1982) (expert found 13-year-old daughter of defendant believable). But most modern opinions insist that experts should not testify that the child is truthful or that her story is believable. See State v. Keller, 844 P.2d 195, 201 (Or. 1993) (reversible error to let expert testify that five-year-old child was telling truth); People v. Fasy, 829 P.2d 1314, 1318 (Colo. 1992) (expert did not comment on

truthfulness); State v. Sims, 608 A.2d 1149, 1153-1154 (Vt. 1991) (error to let expert convey impression that she believed victim).

4. Testimony describing child abuse and rape trauma syndromes differs from standard testimony supporting veracity, doesn't it? An expert who describes syndromes and ventures the opinion that the story of the complaining witness fits a pattern is actually saying the story is plausible, isn't she? Is she also saying that people who give such accounts fit a pattern in which truthfulness is a common element? Doesn't that mean such testimony is covered by FRE 608? See State v. Grecinger, 569 N.W.2d 189 (Minn. 1997); State v. Rimmasch, 775 P.2d 388 (Utah 1989); People v. Snook, 745 P.2d 647 (Colo. 1987) (all applying FRE 608 to such testimony). If so, it would seem at the very least that an expert should not give such testimony about the complaining witness unless she testifies and her character for veracity is attacked. And arguably the effect of FRE 608 is to bar any direct comment on the truthfulness or believability of a particular story, since the Rule contemplates far more generalized testimony about the disposition of the witness toward truthfulness.

5. Whatever reservations a court might have on the question of admitting expert testimony based on someone's apparent mental or emotional condition, a court should let experts testify on the basis of physical symptoms, shouldn't it? See United States v. Bowers, 660 F.2d 527, 528-529 (5th Cir. 1981) (approving testimony by pediatrician describing "battered child syndrome," which "may show that the parent's explanation of the child's injuries is a fabrication" and let jury infer not only that child's injuries were not accidental but that parent deliberately caused them), and State v. Taylor, 663 S.W.2d 235, 239-240 (Mo. 1984) (disapproving testimony by psychologist that seemed to vouch for credibility of complaining witness in rape case, but indicating that physician may opine that victim's wounds "were caused by forcible sexual intercourse"). Are psychological scars and reactions so closely analogous to physical bruises, tears, ruptures, or abrasions that the two should be similarly treated as the basis for expert testimony aimed at verification?

6. If expert testimony on child abuse and rape trauma syndromes indicates that a particular story is plausible, does it have a bearing on the case that goes beyond credibility issues? Does it shed light on all the proof in the case, typically tending to support the contention that abuse or rape occurred by suggesting that what happened fits a broader pattern? Putting aside for a moment those cases where experts base conclusion on physical injuries, do you think they know enough about human nature to know whether abuse or rape has occurred? Do they know enough to know when a particular person is being truthful? These questions bring into play the legal doctrines governing expert testimony, and the subject is revisited in Chapter 9 (Opinion and Expert Testimony).

7. Much has been written on the subjects of child abuse and rape trauma syndromes. Among the best articles in the legal literature are Mosteller, Legal Doctrines Governing the Admissibility of Expert Testimony Concerning Social Framework Evidence, 52 L. & Contemp. Probs. 85 (1989); McCord, Expert Psychological Testimony About Child Complainants in Sexual Abuse Prosecutions: A Foray into the Admissibility of Novel Psychological Evidence, 77 J. Crim. L. & Criminology 1 (1986); Massaro, Experts, Psychology, Credibility, and Rape: The Rape Trauma Syndrome Issue and Its Implications for Expert Psychological

Testimony, 69 Minn. L. Rev. 395 (1985); McCord, The Admissibility of Expert Testimony Regarding Rape Trauma Syndrome in Rape Prosecutions, 26 B.C.L. Rev. 1143 (1985).

3. Prior Consistent Statements

At common law, prior consistent statements were admissible to rehabilitate a witness, provided that the attacking party had suggested that her testimony was tainted by recent fabrication or undue influence or motive. In this situation a prior statement by the witness, consistent with her direct testimony, might tend to refute the attack. This rehabilitating effect was clearest if the witness had made her prior consistent statement before the alleged motive or influence came into play: Evidence that she previously said the same thing that she says at trial suggests that her testimony should *not* be rejected as a fabrication or discounted on account of supposed improper motive.

Sometimes the attacking party clearly suggests that the witness is fabricating or allowing improper motives to affect her testimony. Recall the examples suggested in the discussion of FRE 801(d)(1)(B) in Chapter 4A2, supra. But an attack for bias may convey this message subtly (improper influence being simply a particular kind of bias): *Something* is fishy here, we don't know what, but this witness has been frightened or cajoled or "bought off" so she now favors one side. See United States v. Sutton, 732 F.2d 1483, 1493-1494 (10th Cir. 1984) (government witness testified on direct that he phoned defendant and got instructions; defense counsel then asked him on cross to identify the first person to whom he mentioned the call; prosecutor properly called wife of witness to say that he told her the same thing, as the trial judge "reasonably concluded" that the defense was trying to suggest that "no conversation . . . ever took place," hence that the testimony was "recently fabricated"), cert. denied, 469 U.S. 1157 (1985).

Attack by prior inconsistent statement. A perennially difficult situation arises when the cross-examiner asks the witness about prior inconsistent statements. Does such an attack suggest that she fabricated her present testimony or colored her story on account of "improper influence or motive"? Not necessarily, according to common law tradition, for vacillation might simply reflect confusion arising from problems in perception or memory. Professor Lilly put it this way:

> [E]ven if evidence of the prior consistencies were received, the trier still would be left with inconsistent versions of the witness's story. Hence, the accrediting evidence fails to dissipate either the impeaching fact or its associated inference.

G. Lilly, Introduction to the Law of Evidence 432 (3d ed. 1996).

But recall now the example considered in Chapter 4A2, supra, where Marian testified on direct that David was driving within the speed limit. Change the facts slightly. Assume this time that pedestrian Paul's lawyer cross-examines Marian on a prior inconsistent statement, in this vein:

Q (Paul's lawyer to Marian):   Didn't you say, some ten days after the accident, that the Ford was speeding?

A (Marian):   Yes, sir, I did.

Q: Isn't it true, ma'am, that your testimony today is just a fabrication—you're just hiding what you've known from the beginning to be the truth?

A: No, not at all—

Q: Did David tell you what to say here in court?

A: No, he didn't—

Q: Thank you, ma'am. No further questions.

Here Marian's prior inconsistent statement on Day 10 *could* represent simply vacillation born of inattentiveness or bad memory. But Paul's lawyer has implied something very different: The likely explanation, he implies, is that Marian was (as they say) "reached" or "gotten to" sometime *after* Day 10 when she said David was speeding—maybe at some later date (perhaps Day 20) when she met with David and he insisted that he was driving within the speed limit. It is for that reason that she changed her story. Thus, depending on the way in which the cross-examiner plays his hand, argues his point, and perhaps on the degree to which other circumstances come to light, an attack predicated on a prior inconsistent statement *may be interpreted* as raising charges of fabrication or improper motive.

What consistent statements rebut the charge? Assuming that the inconsistency between a prior statement and trial testimony suggests that the witness fabricated her testimony (or was affected by improper influence), do *all* prior statements that are consistent with her testimony tend to refute the charge? Referring again to Marian, recall that she said on Days 1 and 30 that David "was driving within the speed limit," but we learn that on Day 10 she said that David "was speeding." By tradition, the statement on Day 1 would tend to rehabilitate Marian. *That* one indicates that she believed from the beginning that David was not at fault. See G. Lilly, Introduction to the Law of Evidence 432 (3d ed. 1996) ("a prior consistent statement *that predates* the alleged recent fabrication or the motive to falsify has sufficient probative value to be admitted because it tends to rebut the cross-examiner's charge of recent contrivance") (original emphasis). But the statement by Marian on Day 30 would not rehabilitate her: On Day 10 she apparently said that David "was speeding," and Paul argues that she changed her tune thereafter (perhaps when she met with David on Day 20?), so what she said on Day 30 actually reinforces the attack (she was "reached").

A procedural muddle. Recall that FRE 801(d)(1)(B) defines as "not hearsay" a prior consistent statement offered to rebut "an express or implied charge . . . of recent fabrication or improper influence or motive." When that provision applies, it permits use of the prior statement to prove what it asserts: On the facts of our example, Marian's statement (David "was driving within the speed limit") could be used to prove that David was indeed driving within the speed limit.

On its face, however, FRE 801(d)(1)(B) does not speak to the use of prior consistent statements considered here. The reason is that rehabilitating a witness by a prior consistent statement involves a nonhearsay use, analogous to the nonhearsay use made by prior *inconsistent* statements to impeach. (Recall

Problem 3-C, "The Blue Car Ran the Red Light," where using a prior *inconsistent* statement to prove vacillation did not involve hearsay.) In the example above, the rehabilitating party (David) argues in this vein: "When Marian said before that I was within the speed limit, that shows that she long held the view to which she testified here at trial, and this showing does not involve a hearsay use." Arguably, then, the restrictions in FRE 801(d)(1)(B) do not apply when the rehabilitating party offers the prior statement for this limited purpose.

Broader use of prior consistencies. If FRE 801(d)(1)(B) does not regulate the rehabilitating process, the question arises whether a prior statement may be admitted to rehabilitate even if it does *not* qualify as substantive proof under that provision. If the attacking party suggests, for instance, that the present testimony of the witness is wrong simply because she *does not remember the events,* then a prior consistency might refute this suggestion because her consistent statement suggests that she *has always seen matters the same way.* And if she claims never to have made an inconsistent statement, then a prior consistency might support the notion that she has always said approximately what she says in court, never something else. And there may be other instances when rehabilitating use of a prior consistency would seem appropriate even though the conditions in FRE 801(d)(1)(B) are not met.

Recall the Supreme Court's 1995 decision in *Tome* (page 169, supra), which holds that FRE 801(d)(1)(B) continues the common law premotive requirement. As suggested in the Notes following *Tome,* it seems better to interpret the decision to mean that a prior consistent statement *offered to refute claims of improper motive or fabrication* is only admissible if it was made before the motive to fabricate arose, which means that other rehabilitating uses are not regulated by FRE 801(d)(1)(B).

PROBLEM 8-I.   *"She Handed Me the Heroin"*

Clair and Arla are suspected of conspiring to distribute heroin. An informant introduces undercover FBI Agent Turner to the two women, and during lunch at a restaurant Clair agrees to sell Turner 100 grams of heroin. Turner suggests that Clair go to the women's restroom to put a sample of the heroin in a paper towel so Turner can test it. Both women go to the restroom and later return with the heroin, and the sale is made.

Clair and Arla are arrested and charged. Matrons do a search and discover that Clair (not Arla) is carrying a large quantity of heroin. Thereafter Clair pleads guilty to a drug offense.

Arla is charged with selling heroin, arising out of the transaction in the restaurant. Turner testifies for the government that when Clair and Arla returned from the women's restroom, it was Arla who produced the heroin sample from her purse, wrapped in a paper towel. Counsel for Arla vigorously cross-examines:

Q: Isn't it a fact, Mr. Turner, that you don't really remember which woman was carrying the heroin?

A: No, sir, I remember very well. It was the woman in the black and white dress.

Q: What you're really trying to do here, and have been trying all along to do, is to put *two* women in jail, on the basis of mere guilt by association?
A: No, sir.

During the defense case-in-chief, however, both Clair and defendant Arla testify that it was *Clair* who carried the heroin back and handed it to Turner.

During the government's case-in-rebuttal, the prosecutor offers a tape recording of a statement by Turner, made outside the restaurant only moments after Clair and Arla were arrested, in which Turner said: "The woman in the black and white dress had the stuff in her purse. She took the heroin out of her purse after she came out of the restroom and handed it to me." It is undisputed that Arla was wearing the black-and-white dress, while Clair wore slacks and a blouse.

Arla raises a hearsay objection, and argues in addition that the prosecutor is engaging in "improper rehabilitation." How should the court rule, and why?

NOTES ON PRIOR CONSISTENCIES

1. Since Arla's lawyer implies that Turner forgot who produced the heroin sample in the restaurant, does that suggest that what Turner said into the recorder outside the restaurant should be admitted to repair his credibility? If *Tome* means that FRE 801(d)(1)(B) authorizes substantive use *only* when a consistent statement is offered to refute a claim of improper influence or motive, then using the statement to refute the claimed lack of memory would not pave the way for its use as substantive evidence, would it? Of course Arla's lawyer also implies that Turner was trying to do at trial the same thing he was trying to do at the time of the arrest, which is to railroad Arla into jail. If Arla's lawyer was making *this* argument, and if the prior statement is offered to refute it, then *Tome* probably means the court must decide whether the motive to fabricate had arisen by the time Turner spoke. Had it?

2. It often happens in criminal cases that prosecution witnesses have been actors in the alleged offense. When defendant cross-examines such a witness on his prior inconsistent statements, should the prosecutor be permitted on redirect to bring out prior consistent statements that the witness made to law enforcement officers? Does it matter whether such statements were made after arrest, or before or during plea bargaining? Compare United States v. Awon, 135 F.3d 96, 99-100 (1st Cir. 1998) (error to admit prior consistent statements by two brothers hired to set fires, made in conversations in which police promised not to prosecute if they cooperated; they had same "desire for leniency" that they had at trial, so premotive requirement was not satisfied) with United States v. Prieto, 232 F.3d 816, 819-822 (11th Cir. 2000) (admitting post-arrest statements as prior consistencies; such statements "are not automatically and necessarily contaminated by a motive to fabricate in order to curry favor"), cert. denied, 534 U.S. 950 (2001).

D. FORBIDDEN ATTACKS

FRE 610 disallows impeaching attempts that attack credibility on the basis of "beliefs or opinions . . . on matters of religion." The idea is that religious belief is intensely personal, that religious attitudes may evoke strong feelings in jurors, that our society tolerates diversity of religious conviction, and that in the end the subject brings great risk of prejudice and little prospect of developing anything that helps.

Note that FRE 603 requires a witness to declare "by oath or affirmation" that he will speak the truth. Here too it is clear that some sensitivity to religious diversity is required, and that a person who objects to an "oath" must be allowed to commit himself to the truth by some other means. See Chapter 6C, supra.

NOTES ON RELIGIOUS BELIEF AND IMPEACHMENT

1.   Does FRE 610 bar cross-examination aiming to uncover bias on account of the affiliation of a witness with a religious organization having an interest in the case?

2.   Recall that in United States v. Abel (Chapter 8A1, supra), the Supreme Court upheld cross-examination by the prosecutor that uncovered the common membership of the defendant and a defense witness in the Aryan Brotherhood. Would the result have been different if the Aryan Brotherhood were a "religious" organization? Cf. Government of Virgin Islands v. Petersen, 553 F.2d 324, 328 (3d Cir. 1977) (in murder trial, disallowing defense effort to establish that defendant and alibi witness were Rastafarians who "reject violence," for FRE 610 "prohibits such testimony when it is used to enhance the witness' credibility").

3.   Recall the *Zobel* case (footnote 2 in this chapter), approving questions asking a police officer whether he had forsworn God and Christ and accepted evil. The defense contended that he was a priest of Satan. Would FRE 610 block this attack? Cf. United States v. Sampol, 636 F.2d 621, 666 (D.C. App. 1980) (cutting off defense inquiry aiming to establish that government witness adhered to "Luceme religion," where witness testified on voir dire that "he faithfully adhered to the teaching of that sect and consulted with spirits of his religion before taking certain actions," but that his religious belief would not cause him to violate his oath to testify truthfully).

OPINION AND EXPERT TESTIMONY; SCIENTIFIC EVIDENCE

Nine

A. LAY OPINION TESTIMONY

By longstanding tradition, lay witnesses testify to facts, not opinions based on facts. They did so before the Rules were adopted, and they do so in modern practice. Yet lay witnesses *do* give opinion testimony and always have. And while the Rules did not bring a day-and-night change, they significantly altered the approach to lay testimony, and are more generous than the common law in allowing lay opinions.

The common law approach. Many pre-Rules cases tried to draw a bright line between fact and opinion, welcoming factual testimony by lay witnesses and rejecting their opinions. Yet you know already how difficult (even futile) it is to maintain this dichotomy. Ask any of us to estimate the height of a person. Is our answer fact or opinion? Consider the redness of a barn, the speed of a car, the intoxication of a driver. If we testify to such points, are we giving fact or opinion?

Still, courts long tried to separate "fact" from "opinion," for three reasons:

First was a misreading of old English precedents, which sometimes expressed the (entirely sound) requirement of firsthand knowledge by rejecting opinion testimony. American courts seemed to overlook the purpose of the distinction and rejected opinions even where the witness had firsthand knowledge.

Second was the emergence of the idea that an expert witness (one trained in matters of science) should be allowed to state his "opinion," in the sense of analyzing and interpreting underlying data so as to paint a picture understandable by a lay trier of fact. It came to be understood that lay opinions were improper simply because, by definition, lay witnesses lacked special training.

Third was the notion that the trier of fact should draw its own conclusions, and that lay opinion testimony would "invade the province of the jury." See the account of these points in 7 Wigmore on Evidence §1917 (J. Chadbourn rev. 1978).

The Rules approach. The modern view recognizes that "facts" and "opinions" are regions in a continuum, and they differ in degree rather than kind:

Facts are more specific or concrete, opinions more general or conclusory. While most courts would instinctively agree that testimony by lay witnesses should be specific rather than general, concrete rather than conclusory, Rule 701 does not try to preserve a fact-opinion dichotomy. Instead it speaks functionally. It provides that a lay witness may give opinion testimony, speaking in generalities or conclusions, when these are "rationally based" on his "perception" and "helpful" to the trier of fact in understanding his testimony or determining a fact in issue. In net effect, FRE 701 is more generous than common law tradition, allowing more latitude to admit lay opinion testimony.

The Rules address the underlying concerns in other ways. Thus, Rule 602 requires lay witnesses to have "personal knowledge," treating this matter as an aspect of witness competency rather than testimonial form. On the issue of invading the province of the jury, FRE 704 says simply that lay opinion testimony is "not objectionable because it embraces an ultimate issue." The fact is that *any* relevant testimony speaks to issues that the jury must resolve, so the old objection was overbroad, even simplistic. (You will see, however, that more refined concerns remain: Opinion testimony may still be "too conclusory," and FRE 704(b) restricts expert testimony on the "mental state or condition" of a defendant in a criminal case. Moreover, there remains a fear that some kinds of testimony may confuse or overwhelm a lay jury, and such testimony may be rejected for that reason.)

Finally, the Rules cover the expert testimony separately in FRE 702 and 703. As you will see, the modern approach (at least in the federal system) is to require that scientific and technical testimony satisfy a reliability standard. This standard covers people like doctors and geologists, where nobody is likely to imagine that FRE 701 applies (because FRE 701 covers only the witness who "is not testifying as an expert"). However, the boundary line between lay opinions and expert and technical opinions is not always clear, since people like police officers and auto mechanics often give opinion testimony on points lying well beyond everyday experience. Clause (c) was added to FRE 701 in 2000, in an effort to insure that the liberal standard of FRE 701 is applied only to testimony that is "*not* based on scientific, technical, or other specialized knowledge within the scope of Rule 702."

Modern practice. Even common law tradition recognized that lay opinions should be welcomed on many points, and courts applying Rule 701 continue to admit such testimony. The so-called collective facts doctrine makes the point that certain ideas well within common experience can best be expressed, and reliably so, by means of a shorthand word or phrase. One court put it this way:

> If it is impossible or difficult to reproduce the data observed by the witnesses, or the facts are difficult of explanation, or complex, or are of a combination of circumstances and appearances which cannot be adequately described and presented with the force and clearness as they appeared to the witness, the witness may state his impressions and opinions based upon what he observed. It is a means of conveying to the jury what the witness has seen or heard. If the jury can be put into a position of equal vantage with the witness for drawing the opinion, then the witness may not give an opinion. Because it is sometimes difficult to describe [various matters,] witnesses may relate their opinions or conclusions of what they observed.

United States v. Skeet, 665 F.2d 983, 985 (9th Cir. 1982) (listing as examples "the mental or physical condition of a person, his character or reputation, the emotions manifest by his acts," and "speed of a moving object," as well as matters like "size, heights, odors, flavors, color, heat").

An early opinion provides an even longer list, with which courts applying FRE 701 would likely be equally comfortable. Lay opinions should be admissible

upon a great variety of unscientific questions arising every day, and in every judicial inquiry. These are questions of identity, handwriting, quantity, value, weight, measure, time, distance, velocity, form, size, age, strength, heat, cold, sickness, and health; questions also concerning various mental and moral aspects of humanity, such as disposition and temper, anger, fear, excitement, intoxication, veracity, general character, and particular phases of character, and other conditions and things, both moral and physical, too numerous to mention.

Hardy v. Merrill, 56 N.H. 227, 22 Am. Rep. 441 (1878).

Another notion, first expressed by able common law judges, has proved equally durable, and it animates Rule 701: A witness should not be so closely confined by rules of legal diction that, in the end, he is effectively muzzled. As Judge Learned Hand put it:

Every judge of experience in the trial of causes has again and again seen the whole story garbled, because of insistence upon a form with which the witness cannot comply, since, like most men, he is unaware of the extent to which inference enters into his perceptions. He is telling the "facts" in the only way that he knows how, and the result of nagging and checking him is often to choke him altogether, which is, indeed, usually its purpose.

Central Ry. v. Monahan, 11 F.2d 212, 214 (2d Cir. 1926). Consider this elaboration of that thought, in an opinion approving testimony describing the understanding of another:

The question ought always to be whether it is more convenient to insist that the witness disentangle in his own mind—which, much more often than not, he is quite unable to do—those constituent factors on which his opinion is based; or to let him state his opinion and leave to cross examination a searching inquisition to uncover its foundations. . . . To require him to unravel that nexus will, unless he is much practiced in self scrutiny, generally make him substitute an utterly unreal—though honest—set of constituents, or will altogether paralyze his powers of expression.

United States v. Petrone, 185 F.2d 334, 336 (2d Cir. 1950) (per curiam, before Judges Hand, Swan, and Frank), cert. denied, 340 U.S. 931 (1951).

In the spirit of these comments, modern reviewing courts have approved opinion testimony of the following sorts:[1]

---

1. The ensuing passages are not direct quotations, but they fairly describe testimony approved, respectively, by the decisions in Torres v. County of Oakland, 758 F.2d 147, 149-150 (6th Cir. 1985); Kurczy v. St. Joseph Veterans Association, 820 A.2d 929, 940 (R.I. 2003); Young v. Illinois C.G. Ry., 618 F.2d 332, 337 (5th Cir. 1980); Singletary v. Secretary of Health, Educ. & Welfare, 623 F.2d 217, 219 (2d Cir. 1980); Virginia Ry. & Power Co. v. Burr, 133 S.E. 776 (Va. 1926).

1. In deciding not to promote *T, M* did not base his decision on her national origin;
2. After accidental fall in stairwell, 10-year-old boy underwent "personality change" and his physical, behavioral, and educational performance in school declined;
3. The railroad crossing was in poor condition and difficult to get across;
4. Claimant was an alcoholic unable to work;
5. It seemed that plaintiff had time to get out of the way.

Still, courts are not always so generous or flexible in their approach to these matters. Despite its apparently accommodating attitude, for example, the reviewing court in *Skeet* saw fit to approve a ruling by the trial court excluding, in an assault trial, testimony by defense witnesses opining that "the shooting was accidental"!

PROBLEM 9-A. "It Was My Impression"

In the trial of Cox for unlawful detonation of explosives, arising from the apparent firebombing of motor vehicles, the prosecutor calls defendant's former girlfriend Carter. She testifies that Cox told her twice that he knew someone who would blow up cars for $50 and that he showed her a newspaper account of one of the bombings giving rise to the present charges. During the state's case-in-chief, the following exchange occurs:

Q [prosecutor]:   Did Mr. Cox admit being involved in this bombing?
A [Carter]:   He never actually said that, you know, he had blown it up, but it was my understanding by his mentioning that he had a friend and showing me the article that it was my impression when we were done talking that he was involved in having blown it up.
Ms. Dreeves: The defense objects to that, your Honor. It calls for opinion and speculation, and nothing she says can be helpful in understanding her testimony or determining the facts in issue in this case.

How should the court rule, and why?

PROBLEM 9-B. The Watchful Neighbor

A pickup truck driven by defendant Al Davis collides with a car driven by Sandy Pinkston, seriously injuring her child Amy, who is in the right front seat. In the ensuing lawsuit by Sandy Pinkston against Al Davis, plaintiff calls Luke Hanson as a witness.

Peruse the following transcript of Hanson's testimony on direct and cross-examination. Consider whether either side has proper objections under FRE 701. Consider too how you would avoid or cure any problems in Hanson's testimony.

Direct Examination

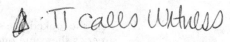 *TT calls witness*

Q [plaintiff's counsel]:   Please state your name and address for the court reporter.
A: Luke Hanson, 1623 Elm Street, in Fayetteville.
Q: Mr. Hanson, directing your attention now to the afternoon of June 12 of last year, did you see an automobile accident in the 1600 block of Elm Street, near your home?
A [Mr. Hanson]:   Yes, sir. I was sitting outside on my front porch swing. It happened practically in front of me.
Q: Please tell the jury what you saw.
A: Well, the lady across the street, Mrs. Pinkston, was backing her car out of the driveway to take her daughter to ballet lessons when a pickup truck plowed right into the side of her.   → *collateral / need foundation to support opinion*
Q: Did you see the driver of the pickup?
A: I did.
Q: Do you see him here today?
A: I'm really not sure. It's been almost a year. The driver had a beard and that fellow is clean-shaven. But I would guess that's him over there [pointing to the defendant].
Q: Let the record show that the witness pointed to the defendant. Now Mr. Hanson, how fast was the pickup going at the time of the collision?
A: I would say he was going at least 35 miles per hour.
Q: And what is the speed limit on that street?
A: Well, generally it's 35 miles per hour, but the law says you can go only 20 if you're within 500 feet of a school, and we are. So he was breaking the speed limit, no question about it.
Q: Did you go over to the pickup after the accident?
A: Yes, sir.
Q: Did you notice any unusual odor coming from the truck?
A: Yes, sir. There was a strong smell of pot. I'm sure the driver was smoking a joint—had been, anyway.
Q: Would you say he was stoned?
A: I really can't say.
Q: Well, how did he seem?
A: It's hard to say, but he had a real guilty look, like he was afraid he was going to lose his license or get sued.
Q: What was Mrs. Pinkston doing after the accident?
A: She was crying, real hard.
Q: What about?
A: I think she was upset about her little girl Amy, who got hurt the worst of anyone.
Q: What injuries did Amy and her mother suffer?
A: Well, Amy looked like she had a broken back, but Mrs. Pinkston only had a dislocated shoulder.
Q: How extensive was the damage to the station wagon?
A: The whole right side was caved in. The car was totaled.
Q: And do you know the approximate value of the car?
A: I'd say about $5,000.
Q: No further questions. Thank you, Mr. Hanson.

Cross-Examination

Q: Mr. Hanson, isn't it true that Mrs. Pinkston barreled out of her driveway without stopping or looking to see whether anyone was coming?

A: Well, she looked like she was in a hurry, and she didn't turn around to look at the street as she came out.

Q: And Mr. Davis, in the pickup, did everything he could to avoid a collision, isn't that so?

A: Yes, he couldn't have stopped in that short a space. Mrs. Pinkston just backed out right in front of him. It was sad to see.

Q: Now Mr. Hanson, let's assume that we can identify the most careful driver in the world. If he or she had been driving along Elm Street on that fateful afternoon, could that hypothetical perfect driver have avoided Mrs. Pinkston's car, backing out the way she did?

A: No, I don't believe so.

NOTES ON LAY OPINION TESTIMONY

1.   Consider the testimony interpreting what Cox said (Problem 9-A). When it comes to understanding the meaning, intention, or comprehension of another on the basis of what he says, it would be a hard rule indeed that either barred all testimony or required a witness to sort out the particulars underlying his conclusion. In *Petrone* (quoted prior to Problem 9-A), the Second Circuit recognized this difficulty:

> Nothing is less within the powers of the ordinary witness than to analyze the agglomerate of sensations which combine in his mind to give him an "impression" of the contents of another's mind.

United States v. Petrone, 185 F.2d 334, 336 (2d Cir. 1950) (per curiam) (alleged possession of counterfeit bills; federal agent testified that defendant "had not given 'the impression . . . that he did not know those bills were in that room'"), cert. denied, 340 U.S. 931 (1951). See also United States v. Davis, 787 F.2d 1501, 1505 (11th Cir. 1986) (alleged drug conspiracy; *V* testified that in asking *V* whether he "wanted to make a trip," *L* "was referring to an illegal act" and that in telling *V* that "you don't have to worry about" *M, L* meant that *M* "must have known about the 'dope business' "), cert. denied, 479 U.S. 852 (1986). Do *Petrone* and *Davis* support a ruling that would let Carter testify that Cox was admitting his involvement in the car bombing? Or did Carter go too far beyond the ordinary meaning of the words she heard Cox speak?

2.   What about interpreting what another thinks or feels on the basis of nonverbal behavior? In a suit on an accidental death policy, arising on the death of a husband killed in a fight he started with his wife, liability turned upon whether the husband thought he would be killed in the fight. The trial court permitted the daughter to testify that he "did not believe his wife would ever kill him," and the reviewing court approved:

> When . . . the witness observes first hand the altercation in question, her opinions on the feelings of the parties are based on her personal knowledge and rational perceptions and are helpful to the jury. The Rules require nothing more for admission of the testimony.

John Hancock Mutual Life Insurance Co. v. Dutton, 585 F.2d 1289, 1294 (7th Cir. 1978). See also Bohannon v. Pegelow, 652 F.2d 729, 731-732 (7th Cir. 1981) (in suit alleging that police officer violated civil rights in arresting plaintiff for pandering, admitting testimony by plaintiff's girlfriend, whose favors plaintiff allegedly offered to sell to defendant, that "the arrest was motivated by racial prejudice," for she "observed" it).

3. Should a lay witness be allowed to testify that a person is sane or insane? At common law, laypersons could describe conduct bearing on the assessment of sanity but could venture an opinion on sanity only on the basis of longer observation. United States v. Alden, 476 F.2d 378, 385 (7th Cir. 1973) (trial court should be "liberal in admission" of lay testimony describing "any acts, conduct, declarations, spoken words, appearance, and manner of speech," but an opinion "can only be expressed where the witness has been qualified by sufficient association with an opportunity to observe the subject"). A post-Rules decision suggests that FRE 701 opens the door even further. The government offered testimony by three FBI agents that defendant Lawson was "sane" at the time of the offense, based on their investigation of the alleged extortion scheme leading to the charges being tried, and on dealings with him at a rendezvous where they met and arrested him as he sought to collect the money:

> The [Federal Rules] permit the introduction of substantially more evidence than was formerly admissible. They place great reliance on cross-examination, for much more evidence is now admissible subject to cross-examination as a means of verification. It is then up to the fact finder to determine the weight to be attached to that evidence. No more foundation was necessary in this case to admit the opinion testimony of the FBI agents. On cross-examination of each of them, defense counsel pointed out that each had had the opportunity to observe Lawson on only one occasion. The jury was free to give that testimony, particularly in light of the expert testimony that was also heard, whatever weight it felt appropriate.

United States v. Lawson, 653 F.2d 299, 303 (7th Cir. 1981), cert. denied, 454 U.S. 1150 (1982).

4. Consider the questions to Hanson on the "hypothetical perfect driver." Do they smack too much of speculation and guesswork? In a personal injury case arising out of a collision between a pickup truck and a semi-tanker, the defense offered lay testimony by one Highlan (driver of another car) that Welsch (driver of the tanker) "did everything he could to avoid this accident" and that plaintiff Gorby "could have avoided" it. The trial court excluded this testimony, and the reviewing court affirmed:

> Highlan . . . was not present in the truck's cab with Welsch. Highlan could only observe the semi-tanker truck from a car in the opposite lane of traffic and thus could not know the exact measures Welsch took to avoid the accident. More significantly, Highlan could not know when Welsch perceived Gorby's truck. Furthermore, even if Highlan had been present in the cab with Welsch, we would still find that the opinion was not based upon first-hand knowledge or observation. Appellant never established that Highlan was familiar with the Schneider semi-tanker truck. In particular, appellant never established that Highlan was familiar with the safety equipment semi-tanker trucks carry, the distances over which trucks may safely stop, the load the Schneider truck carried, or the brake and steering

equipment of such trucks. The mere fact that Highlan was a motorist with twenty-nine years of experience did not give him the personal knowledge necessary to formulate an admissible lay opinion. . . .

Gorby v. Schneider Tank Lines, 741 F.2d 1015, 1021-1022 (7th Cir. 1984).

B.   EXPERT WITNESSES

1.   Who Is an Expert?

Expertise in astonishing variety finds its way into the courtroom. Physicians and psychiatrists are familiar figures, as are real estate appraisers and engineers. And these represent only the tip of the iceberg.

Under Rule 702, as at common law, an expert is essentially someone with specialized knowledge.

Clearly FRE 702 embraces experts who have formal education or training, such as physicians, engineers, and geologists. The standard is intended to be lenient. A person with suitable training or education may qualify even if he is not a specialist or not renowned, and even if he lacks a certification or experience. See Garrett v. Desa Industries, 705 F.2d 721, 724-725 (4th Cir. 1983) (though he lacked "prior experience," a person holding a master's in engineering qualified as expert); Payton v. Abbott Laboratories, 780 F.2d 147, 155-156 (1st Cir. 1985) (physicians properly testified about injuries resulting from use of DES during pregnancy, even though neither was a "research scientist[ ]" or a "specialist in the field").

Rule 702 reaches much further, embracing people with practical experience but no formal training. See United States v. Thomas, 676 F.2d 239, 245 (7th Cir. 1980) (testimony by person who had worked in car repair shop and had rebuilt cars as a hobby, to the effect that defendant was not operating such a shop, since he only had tools for "taking apart" cars and none for "assembling, repairing or painting"), cert. denied, 450 U.S. 931 (1981).

The ACN to FRE 702 also refers to "skilled" witnesses, listing "bankers or landowners testifying to land values." Thus property owners should be allowed to testify to the value of their holdings; people operating businesses may describe their financial picture (estimating profits or losses); farmers and ranchers may estimate the values of crops or livestock. See United States v. 79.20 Acres of Land, 710 F.2d 1352, 1357 (8th Cir. 1983) (landowner testifies to value of property); Rossi v. Mobil Oil Corp., 710 F.2d 821, 830 (Emer. Ct. App. 1983) (bookkeeper employed by gasoline retailer testifies to gallonage and profitability figures); Greenwood Ranches v. Skie Construction Co., 629 F.2d 518, 522-523 (8th Cir. 1980) (rancher testifies to probable value at maturity that failed crop would have had).

2.   When Can Experts Testify?

Under Rule 702, an expert may testify only if what he says will "assist the trier of fact to understand the evidence or to determine a fact in issue." This standard—for it is too vague to be a test—is also intended to be generous, and under it courts have admitted a wide range of testimony.

Consider the following modern examples, all approved as proper:[2]

1. Testimony in a mail fraud prosecution describing "the typical structure of mail fraud schemes";
2. Testimony by fire marshals, in a suit to recover for fire loss, that arson started the blaze;
3. Testimony by a professor of management and marketing, in an employment discrimination suit, that plaintiff "was terminated because of his age";
4. Testimony by a DEA agent in a drug prosecution describing the purity of heroin commonly sold on the street;
5. Testimony, in a product liability suit against an automaker, describing hammer tests in which one person struck the outer handle of a car door while another pushed against the inside of the door with his feet, offered in support of plaintiff's theory that the door popped open during a sideswipe accident; and
6. Testimony that hairs recovered from articles used by the robbers were microscopically like hair samples taken from defendants.

The question has arisen whether the helpfulness requirement means that experts should testify only on subjects beyond the ken of lay juries (as common law courts often held). Modern decisions conflict. Compare In re Japanese Electric Products Antitrust Litigation, 723 F.2d 238, 278-279 (3d Cir. 1983) (FRE 702 does not limit expert testimony to matters "beyond the jury's sphere of knowledge") with K-Mart Corporation v. Honeycutt, 24 S.W.3d 357 (Tex. 2000) (in suit by patron of store who was injured while sitting on lower rail of shopping-cart corral when employee pushed other carts into corral, error to let "human factors and safety expert" testify that missing top rail presented unreasonable risk of injury; where subject is within common knowledge of jurors, expert testimony should be excluded).

The *Japanese Products* case reaches the preferable result. Experts may well help the jury understand even familiar matters, in virtue of experience or training that provides a more thorough or refined understanding than ordinary experience provides. See Garbincius v. Boston Edison Co., 621 F.2d 1171, 1174-1175 (1st Cir. 1980) (approving testimony by civil engineer as to adequacy in number and placement of devices warning motorists of excavation). Where expertise is only marginally helpful because the subject is simple or familiar, special education or experience may not add much to common understanding. If so, a decision excluding such testimony better rests on FRE 403. Where the

---

2. The ensuing passages are not direct quotations, but they fairly describe testimony approved, respectively, by the decisions in United States v. McCollum, 802 F.2d 344, 345-346 (9th Cir. 1986); American Home Assur. Co. v. Sunshine Supermarket, 753 F.2d 321, 325 (3d Cir. 1985); Davis v. Combustion Eng., 742 F.2d 916, 919 (6th Cir. 1984); United States v. Pugliese, 712 F.2d 1574, 1582 (2d Cir. 1983); Bauman v. Volkswagenwerk Aktiengesellschaft, 621 F.2d 230, 233-234 (6th Cir. 1980); United States v. Cyphers, 553 F.2d 1064, 1071-1072 (7th Cir.), cert. denied, 434 U.S. 843 (1977).

subject *is* beyond the understanding of a lay jury, testimony by someone with special knowledge likely will be helpful—in other words, the notion works better as a basis to admit testimony than to exclude it.

3. Bases for Expert Testimony — *FRE 703*

Rule 703 lets an expert witness base his testimony on facts or data of three sorts, provided that they are "of a type reasonably relied upon by experts in the particular field," even if not admitted (nor even "admissible") in evidence. First, an expert may rely on facts or data that he learns by firsthand observation "before the hearing." Second, an expert may rely on facts or data that he learns "at the hearing." Third, an expert may rely on what amounts to outside data, meaning information he gleans before trial by consulting other sources.

(1) *Firsthand knowledge.* The first category embraces essentially the kind of personal knowledge (firsthand experience) that Rule 602 always requires of lay witnesses. Often an expert personally observes, examines, or tests the very place, object, or person to be described in his testimony. Routinely, for example, a doctor examines an injured claimant and testifies at trial to the diagnosis of ailment or injury and the prognosis for future difficulties or recovery. In these cases, the question is whether he has sufficient data to support an opinion, and on this point the expert himself is likely to have a view worth hearing.

(2) *Facts learned at trial.* The second category is unique to experts. It embraces information "perceived by or made known to" the expert at trial. For all practical purposes, this category means (1) testimony heard by the expert while sitting in the courtroom listening to other testimony before taking the stand himself and (2) information conveyed in hypothetical questions summing up evidence previously admitted. (Note that Rule 602 contains a clause making the personal knowledge principle "subject to the provisions of rule 703, relating to experts," which accommodates these techniques.)

(3) *Outside data.* The third category, again unique to experts, is broad and somewhat problematic. Rule 703 lets experts rely on facts or data "reasonably relied upon" by other experts in the field. This category amounts to formal recognition, not openly sanctioned until adoption of the Rules, of what has long been the reality: *Necessarily* experts rely on facts and data that are not mentioned at trial.[3] Here too the intent of Rule 703 is to be generous in

---

3. Prior to adoption of the Rules, American courts indulged a kind of Puritan fiction that acknowledged only the first two categories (personal knowledge or information provided at trial). But it came to be understood that experts—and especially those with formal training, like physicians, engineers, and similar professional people—rely on a great deal of "background" data gleaned from books and articles, conversations and conferences with colleagues, courses, and experiments, and that it is impractical or impossible to introduce such material in evidence at trial. Most such information amounts to "hearsay," and much would be inadmissible at trial even if it could be offered. For early recognition of this truth, see Jenkins v. United States, 307 F.2d 637, 641-642 & n.21 (D.C. Cir. 1962) ("better reasoned authorities admit opinion testimony based, in part, upon reports of others which are not in evidence but which the expert customarily relies upon"; still, the expert diagnosis cannot "rest solely" on unintroduced reports, for "[s]uch reliance would amount to offering an opinion of another in violation of the hearsay rule").

admitting expert testimony, as illustrated in the following examples approved by modern reviewing courts:[4]

1. Testimony by an expert from the Bureau of Alcohol, Tobacco, and Firearms concerning origin of firearm, on the basis of markings on the gun, trade publications, and company catalogues;
2. Testimony by psychologist that injuries suffered by railroad employee, while working in control tower on account of nearby lightning strike, could have caused hearing and psychological damage and impaired ability to work;
3. Testimony of a biomechanical engineer, based on a seminar sponsored by automaker, papers on car accidents prepared by the Society of Automotive Engineers, and "a whole body of literature in the area of biomechanics," to the effect that an infant car seat was improperly designed;
4. Testimony by a fire marshal, based in part on information from other marshals on fire inspection team, to the effect that the fire was caused by a person; and
5. Psychiatric testimony concerning the sanity of the accused, based in part on conversations of the psychiatrist with IRS agents recounting their dealings with the accused.

But courts have not always accepted expert opinions as reasonably based. Consider the following opinions, both rejected by reviewing courts:[5]

1. Testimony by an investigative agent, based on results of a psychological stress evaluation (voice stress analysis), that plaintiff knew about and authorized setting the fire;
2. Testimony by an expert, based on accident information compiled by assistant safety director for truck company summarizing some 3,000 accident reports, to the effect that a fuel system fire probably did not cause the crash.

Use at trial of outside information. The relationship between expert opinion testimony and outside data is a matter of exquisite subtlety. On one important point we can be clear. The intent of Rule 703, in authorizing expert testimony based on outside information, is *not* to make underlying data admissible for all purposes or to create a new hearsay exception. As indicated above, the framers of Rule 703 had nearly the opposite purpose in mind—simply recognizing that inevitably experts rely on outside data, that doing so is proper, hence that it is foolish (even risky) to ignore this reality.

On a second point we can also be clear. The framers assumed (and made

---

4. United States v. Harper, 802 F.2d 115, 121 (5th Cir. 1986); Cashman v. Allied Prod. Corp., 761 F.2d 1250, 1254-1255 (8th Cir. 1985); Walker v. Soo Line R. Co., 208 F.3d 581, 586 (7th Cir. 2000), cert. denied 591 U.S. 930; American Universal Ins. Co. v. Falzone, 644 F.2d 65, 66-67 (1st Cir. 1981); United States v. Sims, 514 F.2d 147, 149 (9th Cir.), cert. denied, 423 U.S. 845 (1975).
5. Barrel of Fun, Inc. v. State Farm Fire & Cas. Co., 739 F.2d 1028, 1033 (5th Cir. 1984); Soden v. Freightliner Corp., 714 F.2d 498, 503-504 (5th Cir. 1983).

it express in Rule 705) that sometimes the outside data would come before the trier of fact, if only because the adverse party will cross-examine the expert on the bases of his opinion in hopes of showing it to be ill-founded. (On this point, more below.) The framers also may have assumed, although not so visibly, that the calling party might ask questions about the underlying data on direct: The justification for doing so is to make the opinion-to-come more convincing by explaining its underlying basis. But the risk of abuse seemed too great, and in 2000 FRE 703 was amended to block the proponent from disclosing to the jury "otherwise inadmissible" facts or data underlying expert testimony (unless the court rules otherwise, in cases where probative value "substantially outweighs" prejudicial effect).

Here is the rub. These impeaching and supporting uses of the data do not mean that the data themselves are admissible for all purposes. Hence we face a paradox: In effect, Rule 703 envisions a category of outside data that experts may reasonably rely upon, but not the trier of fact. In other words, some pretty refined distinctions are in order. And we also face the difficulty of admitting evidence susceptible of misuse, and of tempting the parties to exploit the opening thus provided. In other words, Rule 403 has a role to play.

Consider first the paradox. It is commonplace for experts to rely on out-of-court statements, which would be hearsay if introduced to prove what they assert. But Rule 703 does not obviate the hearsay objection to this use of such statements, even where a testifying witness relies upon them. Here is a description of what we are doing:

> The rationale . . . is that the expert is fully capable of judging for himself what is, or is not, a reliable basis for his opinion. This relates directly to one of the functions of the expert witness, namely to lend his special expertise to the issue before him. . . . In a sense, the expert synthesizes the primary source material—be it hearsay or not—into properly admissible evidence in opinion form. The trier of fact is then capable of judging the credibility of the witness as it would that of anyone else giving expert testimony. This rule respects the functions and abilities of both the expert witness and the trier of fact, while assuring that the requirement of witness confrontation is fulfilled.

United States v. Sims, 514 F.2d 147, 149 (9th Cir.), cert. denied, 423 U.S. 845 (1975). Are those just brave words, or do they convince? How true is it that experts like physicians and engineers acquire the ability "to separate the wheat from the chaff," as the court in *Sims* later remarked?

Now consider the difficulty of jury misuse and party exploitation of underlying data. In one post-Rules case, a reviewing court approved, in the trial of Wright and Moss, testimony by Wright's psychiatrist, who referred (during government cross) to something that Wright said about Moss. Understandably, Moss was disturbed by the risk that the jury might make hearsay use of Wright's statement. But giving more weight to the philosophy of Rule 703 than to the dangers of exploitation and misuse, the reviewing court upheld the ruling below:

> Moss does not argue on appeal that psychiatrists do not reasonably rely on conversations with their patients in arriving at a diagnosis. Rule 705 . . . provides that an

expert may be required on cross-examination to disclose the facts or data underlying his opinion. Read together, Rules 703 and 705 reveal that the data underlying
an expert's opinion which is elicited on cross-examination does [sic] not come in
as substantive evidence. The data is [sic] admitted for the limited and independent
purpose of enabling the jury to scrutinize the expert's reasoning.

United States v. Wright, 783 F.2d 1091, 1100 (D.C. Cir. 1986).

In another post-Rules case, however, the reviewing court was more troubled
by the risk of abuse. Charged with attempted bank robbery, defendant McCollum called Dr. Jorgensen (a "forensic hypnotist") in support of his claim that
he had been drugged, threatened, and hypnotized before entering the bank.
Jorgensen described his interview with McCollum, and repeated some of what
he had said, but other experts called by both sides gave conflicting testimony
as to whether McCollum was under hypnosis during his session with Jorgensen.
In this context, the defense sought to introduce a videotape of the session. The
trial court refused to allow the tape, and the reviewing court approved:

> In this circumstance, the court possessed broad discretion to exclude the video-
> tape, which was merely cumulative evidence of the basis for the expert's opinion.
> The attempt to introduce the tape essentially amounted to an effort to put the
> defendant's testimony directly before the jury without subjecting him to the cross-
> examination and impeachment that would have followed had he taken the witness
> stand.

United States v. McCollum, 732 F.2d 1419, 1423 (9th Cir.), cert. denied, 469
U.S. 920 (1984).

PROBLEM 9-C. "The Tube Came Out"

After an operation that replaced his aortic valve, Paul Richards experiences
neurological difficulties. After consulting counsel and medical experts, he
brings a malpractice suit against St. Cecelia's Hospital in Minneapolis and his
operating physician, Dr. Norlan.

Evidence at trial shows that Richards' condition was caused by an embolus
(air bubble) introduced into the bloodstream during surgery. Dr. Joan Key
testifies for Richards as an expert. Her credentials established, Key testifies that
the embolus could have been caused by (1) residual air trapped in the chambers
of the heart or aorta, (2) air introduced into the heart through a monitoring
line, or (3) air introduced through the aortic cannula (tube attached to heart-
lung machine helping to circulate blood while the heart is bypassed during
surgery), either when the tube was initially inserted, or if it leaked, became
disconnected, or came out during surgery:

Q: Dr. Key, can you determine what happened in this instance?
A: Well, Dr. Nirmel was the attending neurologist, and I know what he wrote on the
    chart. He wrote that the cannula came out during surgery. Relying on that note,
    I would say that the tube came out, causing the embolus.
Q [defense counsel]: Your Honor, I object and move to strike the answer. What a resident

wrote on a postoperative report is not a proper basis for speculation as to the cause of the embolus.

Q *[plaintiff's counsel]:*   Well, Your Honor, certainly Dr. Key can rely on the hospital record in forming her opinion. Would you permit me to ask one further question, by way of foundation?

Court: Proceed, counsel.

Q *[plaintiff's counsel]:*   Thank you, Your Honor. Dr. Key, you examined Paul Richards shortly after surgery, did you not?

A *[Dr. Key]:*   I did, yes.

Q: And you read the chart first?

A: Yes. I had no doubt what the chart meant, and I accepted what it said as true.

Q *[defense counsel]:*   Your Honor, I renew the objection and move to strike Dr. Key's testimony that the embolus was caused by the cannula falling out. I also ask that all reference to the chart be stricken from the record.

How should the court rule, and why?

NOTES ON BASES FOR EXPERT TESTIMONY

1.   Should the judge alone decide, pursuant to FRE 104(a), whether an expert such as Dr. Key in Problem 9-C has an adequate basis for giving her opinion, or should the judge simply act as screening agent and pass the ultimate decision to the jury under FRE 104(b)? What about a third possibility—that the expert herself might be the sole judge of the reasonableness of relying upon the underlying data? Compare In re Japanese Electric Products Antitrust Litigation, 723 F.2d 238, 276-277 (3d Cir. 1983) (when experts testified that underlying data "were of a type reasonably relied upon by experts in their respective fields," trial court erred in "substituting its own opinion as to what constitutes reasonable reliance") with Soden v. Freightliner Corp., 714 F.2d 498, 505 (5th Cir. 1983) (experts have "wide latitude in picking and choosing the sources on which to base opinions," but FRE 703 "requires courts to examine the reliability of those sources").

2.   Does it matter that the notation on the chart is hearsay? Does it matter whether the chart would satisfy FRE 803(6)—the business records exception? What if Dr. Nirmel, who entered the notation, lacked personal knowledge and instead relied on what he learned from attending nurses and staff?

3.   Should an expert be permitted to rely on statements by interested witnesses? See Dallas & Mavis Forwarding Co. v. Stegall, 659 F.2d 721, 722 (6th Cir. 1981) (excluding testimony by state trooper that defendant's car had moved into the left lane before the accident, because this opinion "was based on no physical evidence" and came "primarily from the story of a biased eyewitness," who should be "required to testify directly and to be subject to cross-examination"). But recall Baker v. Elcona Homes, 588 F.2d 551 (6th Cir. 1978), set forth in Chapter 4C6, supra.

4.   Does FRE 703 permit a witness to report the opinion of others whom she considers reliable, or must she offer *her own* opinion? What if she bases her own opinion *entirely* on what others say? On the first point, one modern opinion seems correctly to answer in the negative. See United States v. Tomasian, 784

F.2d 782, 785-786 (7th Cir. 1986) (trial court properly excluded defense expert testimony on value of ivory tusks, where witness indicated that he "consulted outside sources to ascertain the price per pound of ivory and then multiplied that figure by the weight of the tusks"; it would have been "different" if the expert had given "an opinion based on hearsay facts," but this expert "could only relay another's opinion of the price per pound of ivory" and "had no opinion of his own on the matter" or on whether "price per pound . . . is any measure of a tusk's value").

5. In a criminal case, does the Confrontation Clause bar expert opinion testimony against the accused when it rests on out-of-court statements by others? What if the hearsay would *not* fit within a "firmly rooted hearsay exception" (in the words of the *Roberts* opinion, see Chapter 4G3, supra)? Or does the Confrontation Clause only bar use of the statements themselves and not opinions based on them? Consider the following approach:

> In criminal cases, a court's inquiry under Rule 703 must go beyond finding that hearsay relied on by an expert meets these standards [of reasonable reliance by other experts in the field]. An expert's testimony that was based entirely on hearsay reports, while it might satisfy Rule 703, would nevertheless violate a defendant's constitutional right to confront adverse witnesses. The Government could not, for example, simply produce a witness who did nothing but summarize out-of-court statements made by others. A criminal defendant is guaranteed the right to an effective cross-examination. . . .
>
> In addition to the reasonable reliance requirement of Rule 703, a criminal defendant must therefore also have access to the hearsay information relied upon by an expert witness. Without such access, effective cross-examination would be impossible. Rule 705, which provides that an expert need not disclose the facts or data underlying his opinion prior to his testimony unless the court orders otherwise, recognizes this requirement.

United States v. Lawson, 653 F.2d 299, 302 (7th Cir. 1981) (testimony by government psychiatrist, based in part on FBI and hospital reports supplied to the defense prior to trial, was properly admitted), cert. denied, 454 U.S. 1150 (1982).

6. When experts openly parrot the opinions of others, or claim that other nontestifying experts have endorsed their opinions, some modern courts have reversed. See State v. Towne, 453 A.2d 1133 (Vt. 1982) (forensic psychiatrist called by prosecutor testified that he consulted physician who wrote book containing "the best description" of psychosexual disorders and that the latter was "in concurrence with my opinion in this case"; in summation, prosecutor reminded jury that witness had gone "to the man who wrote the book, so to speak"; despite defense failure to object, this testimony and argument violated defense confrontation rights) (reversing).

7. Does the risk of reliance on facts or data not proved in evidence persuade you to tighten up Rule 703? Consider the Michigan counterpart:

> The facts or data in the particular case upon which an expert bases an opinion or inference may be those perceived by or made known to him at or before the hearing. The court may require that underlying facts or data essential to an opinion or inference be in evidence.

Michigan Rules of Evidence, Rule 703. And see Ohio Rule 703 ("The facts or data in the particular case upon which an expert bases an opinion or inference may be those perceived by him or admitted in evidence at the hearing").

8.   On the problems of inadmissible evidence as the basis for expert opinion testimony, see generally Carlson, Policing the Bases of Modern Expert Testimony, 59 Vand. L. Rev. 577 (1986); Carlson, Collision Course in Expert Testimony: Limitations on Affirmative Introduction of Underlying Data, 36 U. Fla. L. Rev. 234 (1984).

PROBLEM 9-D.   ".24 Percent Alcohol"

While driving her car late one night, Brenda Ditmer leaves the road and strikes a telephone pole, sustaining serious injuries. At the hospital, Emmet Fuller (the attending physician) draws a blood sample and orders a test for alcohol.

The laboratory reports a blood alcohol content of .24 percent, and Ditmer is charged with driving while intoxicated. Before trial she successfully moves to suppress the results of the test, on ground that they were illegally taken in violation of the state's implied consent law.

At trial, the prosecutor calls Dr. Fuller. In a sidebar conference, Ditmer objects that Dr. Fuller "should not be allowed to testify concerning any conclusions he may have reached on the basis of the suppressed blood test." The prosecutor replies that "under Rule 703, expert opinion testimony need not rest on admissible evidence." Over Ditmer's continuing objection, Fuller then testifies (1) that in his opinion Ditmer was under the influence of alcohol at the time of the accident, (2) that his opinion rests upon a blood alcohol test, and (3) that the test disclosed a concentration of .24 percent in Ditmer's blood. Should the trial court have sustained Ditmer's objection on any of these three points? Why or why not?

4.   Formal Problems—Ultimate Issues, Legal Elements, and So Forth

Common law tradition restricted expert testimony in various ways that seem more formal than substantive. Rule 704 abolishes one such restriction—the one barring testimony on "ultimate issues." But in 1984 Congress amended Rule 704 to reinstate the old restriction when it comes to expert testimony on the mental conditions amounting to elements of charges or defenses in criminal cases. And some of the underlying traditional concerns persist in modern cases.

The ultimate issue restriction. By common law tradition, witnesses (both experts and laypeople) could not testify to ultimate issues in the case, lest they "invade the province of the jury." This quaint phrase can be read as expressing a fear that certain testimony might push the jury into abandoning its responsibility to weigh evidence and determine facts, adopting uncritically whatever a witness might say.

But much relevant and useful testimony addresses ultimate facts in the case, and there is no particular reason to think that it is just such testimony that might overwhelm the jury. Rule 704 abolishes this old saw, and nobody has missed it.

One aspect of the old thought remains. Modern courts continue to reject expert testimony concerning the proper application of legal standards. The Advisory Committee's Note to Rule 704 suggests that courts ought to disallow questions phrased "in terms of inadequately explored legal criteria," but permit more specific questions, apparently phrased in readily understood terms. Thus an expert could not testify that decedent had "capacity to make a will" but could testify that he knew "the nature and extent of his property and the natural objects of his bounty."

Mental condition as element of claim or defense. In 1984 Congress amended Rule 704(b) to prevent an expert in a criminal prosecution from stating an opinion that defendant had or lacked a mental state or condition "constituting an element of the crime charged or of a defense."[6] There is little doubt of the purpose. The accompanying Senate Report indicates an intent to limit psychiatrists to "presenting and explaining their diagnoses," and to prevent them from being asked to speak in terms of "legal or moral constructs."

Long before this change in the law, an opinion in the District of Columbia Circuit argued for much the same result:

> [T]here is no justification for permitting psychiatrists to testify on the ultimate issue. Psychiatrists should explain how defendant's disease or defect relates to his alleged offense, that is, how the development, adaptation and functioning of defendant's behavioral processes may have influenced his conduct.

Washington v. United States, 390 F.2d 444, 456 (D.C. Cir. 1967) (applying then-current test, in which insanity was established if crime was a "product" of mental illness).

NOTES ON FORMAL RESTRICTIONS

1. Can you distinguish between adequately explained and inadequately explained criteria in a legal standard? Courts have had trouble in this area. Compare United States v. Burton, 737 F.2d 439, 443 (5th Cir. 1984) (excluding opinion of tax professor that taxpayer's theory "was not implausible," for evidence as to "uncertainty of the controlling law" is excludable under FRE 403) and Owen v. Kerr-McGee Corp., 698 F.2d 236, 239-240 (5th Cir. 1983) (excluding expert opinion testimony as to "legal" as opposed to "factual" cause of the accident; FRE 704 does not pave the way for such testimony) with

---

6. At the same time Congress also codified the insanity defense, apparently in dissatisfaction over the acquittal of John Hinckley for alleged attempted assassination of President Reagan. Hinckley was acquitted on grounds that he was insane. The statute defines insanity to mean that "defendant, as a result of a severe mental disease or defect, was unable to appreciate the nature and quality or the wrongfulness of his acts." It also places on defendant the burden of proving insanity "by clear and convincing evidence," and it provides that mental disease or defect "does not otherwise constitute a defense." 18 U.S.C. §17.

United States v. Gold, 743 F.2d 800, 817 (11th Cir. 1984) (approving expert testimony that particular claims were reimbursable under Medicare), cert. denied, 469 U.S. 1217 (1985).

2. Consider whether FRE 704(b) should apply in the following cases:

(a) In the trial of John Bennett on fraud charges arising out of an alleged ponzi scheme, in which Bennett encouraged charities and charitable donors to deposit money with New Era by promising that after a holding period such deposits would be matched by other wealthy donors, defendant offers psychiatric testimony that he suffered mental disorders that prevented him from forming an intent to defraud, or made it unlikely that he would have such a purpose. Admit under FRE 704(b), or exclude? See United States v. Bennett, 161 F.3d 171, 183 (3d Cir. 1998) (exclude; expert proposed to "go beyond merely assisting the jury, explaining the nature" of defendant's mental disease or describing the "typical effect" of such disease, "to state expressly whether Bennett possessed the requisite mental intent").

(b) In a case like *Bennett,* can the proponent convey the substance of an opinion going directly to defendant's mental state by using "mirroring hypotheticals"? Imagine the lawyer asking "whether a person who suffers from the disorder attributed to the defendant would intend to defraud people if he set up the scheme that the defendant set up?" In *Bennett,* the court indicated its awareness of such techniques, citing United States v. Levine, 80 F.3d 129, 134 (5th Cir.1996) for the proposition that "a majority of circuits find that 'hypothetical questions mirroring the fact patterns of the evidence in the trial case [violate FRE 704(b)] when the answering testimony contains a necessary inference as to whether the defendant did or did not have the mental state or condition constituting an element of the crime charged or of a defense thereto.' "

(c) In his trial for attempted bank fraud, arising out of scheme involving phony instruments resembling bank checks submitted in payment of a mortgage loan along with a demand to refund the difference between the amount of the supposed check and the amount of the debt, Joseph Finley offers a psychologist's testimony that he suffers from an "atypical belief system" that is "fixed and rigid," in support of his claim that he lacked the requisite intent to defraud. Admit under FRE 704(b), or exclude? See United States v. Finley, 301 F.3d 1000, 1007-1013 (9th Cir. 2002) (admit; FRE 704(b) "allows expert testimony on a defendant's mental state so long as the expert does not draw the ultimate inference or conclusion for the jury," and here the expert did not cross line; jury could accept the proffered diagnosis and still find that defendant "knowingly defrauded the banks").

3. Can a *lay* witness testify in the manner described in these cases? Rule 704(b) poses no barrier to lay testimony, does it? But note that FRE 701, as amended in 2000, blocks *lay* testimony based on "scientific, technical or other specialized knowledge within the scope of Rule 702," in effect preventing (or seeking to prevent) any "end run" around the restrictions on expert testimony.

Testimony of the sort described above *would* rest on "scientific, technical, or other specialized knowledge," wouldn't it?

4.   Should the judge admit expert testimony only if the witness states her conclusions to a "reasonable certainty"? Or should experts be permitted to testify that the underlying data suggest something that "could be" or "might be" so? See State v. Hebert, 480 A.2d 742, 749 (Me. 1984) (no "special degree of certainty" required). But see In re Air Disaster at Lockerbie, Scotland, on December 21, 1988, 37 F.3d 804, 824-825 (2d Cir. 1994) (excluding defense evidence suggesting alternative explanations to government claim that bombing was work of terrorists, as "speculative and conjectural" since there was no foundation for such alternate theories). See Breidor v. Sears, Roebuck & Co., 722 F.2d 1134, 1138 (3d Cir. 1983) (court should not have excluded testimony pointing to refrigerator icebox as source of blaze, where fire investigator identified cause "in terms of probabilities (as opposed to mere possibilities) by eliminating all but one reasonable potential cause," and mere fact that he could not identify a specific defect did not mean he was "speculating").

5.   *Presentation of Expert Testimony*

When a party calls an expert witness, usually the first questions establish that the matter at hand could benefit from expertise. Then comes the foundation. In the case of a professional person (such as a physician or engineer), usually the calling party brings out (1) educational background, including degree and perhaps certificate or license to practice, (2) experience, such as employment or practice in the area to be covered by the questioning, and (3) familiarity with the subject in suit. The pattern is similar (usually less elaborate) with skilled people having informal expertise resting on experience.

Qualifying the witness. Before the witness can testify to matters of substance, typically the calling party asks the court to "qualify the witness as an expert." Sometimes initial questioning establishes qualifications beyond reasonable dispute, and the court grants the request. (Indeed, the adverse party may be all too willing to stipulate on this point, hoping that the preliminaries can be dispensed with, before the jury becomes *too* impressed. But if credentials are impressive, ordinarily the calling party declines this generous invitation and is allowed to go through the motions of qualifying the witness out of his own mouth.)

Sometimes quite the opposite happens. The adverse party may think he has a shot at undercutting the credentials, perhaps even denying qualification. Hence the adverse party not only refuses to stipulate but requests an opportunity to voir dire the witness—meaning essentially, to cross-examine him on his credentials and familiarity with the subject at hand. After completion of voir dire, the court rules. (The question is governed by FRE 104(a), meaning that the court alone resolves this point and does not ask the jury to decide for itself.) If the expert qualifies, the calling party proceeds to substance. By far the most important point achieved by qualifying the witness as an expert is that he then will be allowed to state his opinion on technical points.[7]

voir dire

7.   Several lesser advantages flow from qualifying the witness as an expert. The court is likely to allow the calling party greater latitude in phrasing questions. (The objection against "leading the witness" gets short shrift, at least in the case of accomplished professional people, who are

Bringing out expert opinion. Recall the three bases for expert testimony—firsthand knowledge, facts learned at trial, and the newly recognized basis of outside information (facts reasonably relied upon by others in the field). How does the calling party get into evidence an opinion resting upon one or more of these sources?

In somewhat elliptical fashion, Rule 705 provides the answer. The calling party may ask directly for the "opinion or inference" of the expert (and the underlying reasons) "without prior disclosure" of the basis. Of course establishing the basis first is not *prohibited* either, and a party may well choose to do so, typically by resort to the hypothetical question. The point here is that he need not. Before looking more closely at these two approaches, be advised that in the apparently mild language of Rule 705, which speaks only to order of proof, lies an extraordinary change. (To be sure, the Rule contains qualifiers: The court may yet "require[ ] otherwise"—it may force the proponent to bring out the underlying facts or data first. And "in any event" the expert may be required to yield up the basis for his opinion "on cross-examination.")

1. *Asking directly.* Consider it a minute. Essentially Rule 705 permits a party to call a witness, qualify him as an expert, then go straight to the heart of the matter:

Q: Doctor Kirsten, do you have an opinion as to what caused Linda McMartin's nervous condition?
A *(Kirsten):* I do.
Q: What caused it?
A: The accident in May, in which her stationary car was struck from behind and rammed into the stopped car in front of her. The effect of the first impact was to ram her body sharply forward, which in turn snapped her neck and head sharply backward. The effect of the second impact, when her car struck the one in front, was just the reverse: Her body struck the steering wheel while her head and neck snapped forward. Essentially she suffered what we call severe whiplash, and that led to physical pain and dislocation of vertebra, then to nervous shock, and finally to what we call traumatic neurosis or anxiety, which was aggravated by her pregnancy and her natural fear over the health and life of her baby.

Testimony by a lay witness would never come out so directly, even assuming a subject within his competence. The proponent would be expected first to "lay the foundation"—to show that the witness has personal knowledge. The proponent would place him at the scene, show that he saw what happened, and then bring out what he saw. Of course laying the foundation for a physician to testify in the manner of Dr. Kirsten would differ somewhat. He would not have seen the impact, and he would have acquired his knowledge long after the fact. But analogy to the lay witness suggests that the proponent should

unlikely actually to be led by a lawyer.) Qualifying the witness as an expert also paves the way to compute witness "costs" at whatever statutory rate applies to experts. (In civil suits, the prevailing party normally recovers such costs as part of the judgment.) But most jurisdictions do not permit out-of-pocket costs of hiring an expert to be taxed to the losing party, and the statutory rate is set at a much lower level than experts actually charge, so this point is less important than it might seem. In the federal system, the statutory fee for both lay and expert witnesses is $40 per day. 28 U.S.C. §1821(b). See also Crawford Fitting Co. v. J.T. Gibbons, Inc., 482 U.S. 437 (1987) (expert fees taxed to losing party may not exceed amount authorized by §1821).

establish that Dr. Kirsten examined and diagnosed Linda McMartin and should bring out whatever facts might be essential to support his opinion that McMartin suffered a whiplash injury. Yet FRE 705 permits a qualified physician to testify *without* first establishing such points. Why?

There are two somewhat related reasons:

First is the frustration felt by lawyers, courts, and experts alike with the clumsiness of eliciting opinions by hypothetical questions. Experts traditionally based their testimony on information laid out for them in the form of questions summarizing that portion of the evidence that supported the answer sought by the questioning lawyer. But hypothetical questions became long and complex, taking up pages of trial record and requiring as much as 15 minutes (or longer) to recite. Suffice it to say here that Rule 705 takes the position that there must be a better way.

Second is the great stride made by Rule 703 in permitting the expert to base his opinion on outside information ("facts reasonably relied upon"). To the extent that it is reasonable to anticipate that an expert will be wise and responsible in sifting outside data, drawing on what is trustworthy and ignoring what is not, the risk in letting him state his opinion at the outset is not great—and there is not much risk, then, of a mistrial or a need to strike his testimony.

2. *Hypothetical questions.* Rule 705 leaves open the more traditional approach, which proceeded by hypothetical questions. Imagine for a moment how the examination of Dr. Kirsten might have gone if plaintiff's counsel had embodied the necessary factual basis in a hypothetical question:

Q: Doctor Kirsten, I want to ask you what you think caused Linda McMartin's present nervous condition. Please assume the following facts to be true:

First, Linda McMartin was sitting in the driver's seat of her car at a full stop;

Second, her car was struck from behind by another car traveling at a speed on impact of ten to fifteen miles per hour;

Third, the force of that impact impelled Linda McMartin's car forward so that it struck another stopped car approximately eight feet in front of it;

Fourth, Linda McMartin was in good general health at the time, experiencing no particular anxiety, nervousness, or other disability;

Fifth, she was seven months pregnant at the time of the accident;

Sixth, Linda McMartin immediately experienced great pain in her neck and head;

Seventh, it was later discovered that she had suffered two dislocated vertebra; and finally

Eighth, from that time forward she became extremely nervous and anxious, suffering fears and constant worries, nightmares, and emotional distress leading to frequent crying and depression.

Now Doctor Kirsten, based on the foregoing facts, which I ask you to assume to be true, can you tell us what caused Linda McMartin's present physical and emotional condition?

A: Yes, sir. I would say that the accident caused Linda McMartin to suffer what we call severe whiplash injury. That in turn led to physical pain, dislocation of vertebra, to nervous shock, and finally to what we call traumatic neurosis or anxiety, aggravated by her pregnancy and natural fear for the health and life of her baby.

There can be little doubt that eliciting expert opinion in this manner is cumbersome. The question is long and clumsy, and the supposing takes on a surreal quality—why should one have to suppose anything, when actual evidence has been presented? Besides, the focus is all wrong: When the point is to get at what the expert knows, the lawyer does most of the talking, and the answer, when finally given, seems almost an anticlimax.

And there is more. The hypothetical question generated objection and argument: Opposing counsel would contend (if for no other reason than to disrupt the process), that the question did not accurately sum up the evidence, or omitted crucial facts, or that the facts recited could not support the opinion sought, and so forth. So customary are such objections that typically the court instructs the witness please to wait and not to answer until the other party has a chance to object. While FRE 705 much reduces the need to resort to the hypothetical question, lawyers still sometimes use it. Better reasoned modern decisions are more flexible, holding that the hypothetical question need not embody all pertinent facts, as long as it is reasonably complete and not misleading. See Iconco v. Jensen Construction Co., 622 F.2d 1291, 1301 (8th Cir. 1980).

Implications of the new approach. Allowing the calling party to ask the expert directly for his opinion has greatly increased the importance of cross-examination as a means of testing that opinion. The Advisory Committee anticipated this result, commenting in its Note to Rule 705 that the cross-examiner may bring out data "unfavorable to the opinion," while acknowledging that the effectiveness of this approach depends upon "advance knowledge" that should be acquired (in civil cases at least) through discovery under FRCP 26.

Recall the expanded civil discovery authorized by the 1994 amendments to the Federal Rules. And recall that many states follow the federal model, but that states are free to adopt or reject the amendments. Briefly, here is the discovery scheme outlined in the amended Federal Rules (with reference to prior practice, which many states still follow):

1. Under amended FRCP 26(a)(2), each party must automatically supply the names of anyone "who may be used at trial to present expert testimony." And for any witness "retained or specially employed" to provide expert testimony "or whose duties as an employee" involve regularly giving expert testimony, each party must supply a written report setting forth "all opinions to be expressed" along with the "basis and reasons" and "data or other information" used in forming such opinions, the "exhibits to be used as a summary" and a description of qualifications and publication record. Prior to 1994, discovery proceeded by interrogatories, which could seek names of experts whom the adversary "expects to call," plus descriptions of subject matter, the "substance" of facts and opinions and a "summary of the grounds" for the expected testimony.

2. Under amended FRCP 26(b)(4), each party may depose any person "identified as an expert whose opinions may be presented at trial" (depositions to proceed *after* reports are provided), and generally the party taking the deposition must pay for the expert's time in responding. Prior to 1994, such depositions required court permission.

3. Under FRCP 35, which did *not* change in 1994, the parties exchange medical reports that come out of court-ordered examinations, and a

party examined at the request of his adversary must, if he obtains a copy of the report, provide his adversary similar reports by other physicians on the same condition.

4. Under FRCP 26(b)(4)(B), a party may seek discovery of "facts known or opinions held" by an expert "retained or specially employed" in anticipation of litigation or preparation for trial, but who is *not* expected to testify at trial, only by showing "exceptional circumstances" making it "impracticable" to obtain opinions on the subject by other means, and the discovering party normally pays for the time of the expert in responding and pays "a fair portion" of fees and expenses incurred by the other side in obtaining facts and opinions from such experts.

In a scheme that so readily admits expert opinion testimony by direct questioning, clearly the capacity of counsel at trial to engage in effective cross-examination depends upon effective use of discovery. Once the names of the experts have been exchanged, and their reports have been turned over to the other side, the question whether to pursue further discovery by means of depositions is up to the parties. Clearly the 1994 amendments substantially increase pretrial discovery opportunities relating to experts.

NOTES ON PRESENTING EXPERT TESTIMONY

1. Assume that you are counsel for Linda McMartin, and that you know that Dr. Kirsten is well qualified and well prepared. Pretty clearly you will prefer to elicit Kirsten's testimony in the direct manner, rather than by hypothetical questions. You might even hope that the lawyer for the other side will bring out, on cross-examination, the truly solid basis for Kirsten's opinion. But what if your adversary, knowing that Kirsten is qualified and well prepared, asks only a few questions probing at weak spots, or asks none at all? Would it be wise for the proponent, even if she elicits an expert opinion directly, to bring out the underlying basis by further questions?

2. Are there circumstances in which eliciting opinion testimony by means of hypothetical questions might still be useful? What if your expert has *not* made a thorough investigation before trial? What if the expert is called by another party? In the latter case, how often will a lawyer *dare* to ask hypothetical questions?

3. In common law tradition, the adverse party was routinely allowed to conduct a voir dire examination, as described in the text above, before an expert was permitted to give his opinion. Voir dire provided a chance at the outset (a) to challenge the credentials of the witness, and thus block (or overturn) a ruling that qualified him as an expert, and (b) to try to show that the expert lacked sufficient foundation for his expected testimony. A moment's reflection will suggest that voir dire could rapidly expand into a full-fledged impeaching attack. Doesn't the approach authorized by Rule 705 produce a new tension with the voir dire process? Maine's counterpart to FRE 705 includes an additional subdivision that addresses this point:

(b) *Objection.* An adverse party may object to the testimony of an expert on the ground that he does not have a sufficient basis for expressing an opinion. He may before the witness gives his opinion be allowed to conduct in the absence of the jury a voir dire examination directed to the underlying facts or data on which the opinion is based. If a prima facie case is made that the expert does not have sufficient basis for his opinion, the opinion is inadmissible unless the party offering the testimony first establishes the underlying facts or data.

Maine Rules of Evidence, Rule 705. See also Alaska Rule 705(b) and Delaware Rule 705(b), containing similar provisions. Is such language a good idea? See also Hawaii Rule 705 (permitting expert to give opinion testimony without first disclosing basis "if the underlying facts or data have been disclosed in discovery proceedings").

4.   Is a lawyer, cross-examining a professional person on a technical subject, really up to the task of discrediting testimony already given? Some lawyers and judges have entertained doubts on this score. One experienced federal trial judge (who has since retired from the bench) used to require experts to testify by means of prepared scripts, exchanged with opposing counsel in advance:

> [A]dvance knowledge is so important that in civil cases I require an expert's direct testimony to be written out, in full, and provided to the other side well in advance of trial. Whether the testimony is presented in narrative or in question and answer form is optional with the attorney. In the courtroom, when the expert appears, I read or summarize her qualifications to the jury, clarify how an expert's testimony differs from that of an ordinary witness, and explain why her testimony will be different in form. I further caution the jury not to draw an inference from the fact that the expert will read the testimony. After the expert reads her direct testimony to the jury, the opposing attorney cross-examines her, and any loose ends are then picked up on redirect examination.

Pratt, A Judicial Perspective on Opinion Evidence Under the Federal Rules, 39 Wash. & Lee L. Rev. 313, 322 (1982). What benefits do you see from this approach? What drawbacks? Are you satisfied that a federal judge has authority to require the calling party to "stick to a script" in presenting expert opinion testimony? That the judge has authority automatically to order exchanges of scripts among parties? What about the limits in the discovery rules, as described above?

5.   Most states following the federal model have gone along with Rule 705, but Ohio balked. See Ohio Rule 705:

> The expert may testify in terms of opinion or inference and give his reasons therefor after disclosure of the underlying facts or data. The disclosure may be in response to a hypothetical question or otherwise.

Would you prefer the Ohio approach?

6.   Does the extra burden placed on the cross-examiner by Rule 705 justify strict enforcement, against parties offering expert opinion testimony, of discovery and pretrial obligations? The reviewing court in at least one post-Rules decision thought so. There, it reversed an $800,000 judgment in a suit against an automaker for internal injuries sustained in an accident, allegedly

caused by improperly designed seatbelts. In that case plaintiff had given notice, two and one-half months before trial, of his intent to call Dr. Freston to testify concerning "medical treatment of the Plaintiff" and "his prognosis." At trial Dr. Freston described plaintiff's injuries and opined in addition that "the seat belt was involved in that injury." The reviewing court noted (a) that two other experts, called by plaintiff and deposed by defendant before trial, stated that they had no opinion as to the cause of the injuries, (b) that plaintiff "failed to provide any information, in the form of interrogatory responses," concerning Dr. Freston's expected testimony, (c) that plaintiff did not indicate, during discovery or in the pretrial statement, that Dr. Freston would testify to cause, and (d) that Ford obtained only at trial a copy of an article that Dr. Freston heavily relied upon in his direct, and had "only eleven minutes" to prepare for cross-examination. Under these circumstances, the court concluded:

> [T]he Federal Rules of Evidence contemplate that the "full burden of exploration of the facts and assumptions underlying the testimony of an expert witness [falls] squarely on the shoulders of opposing counsel's cross-examination." [Court cites Graham, Discovery of Experts Under Rule 26(b)(4) of the Federal Rules of Civil Procedure: Part One, An Analytical Study, 1976 U. Ill. L.F. 895, 897.] "Before an attorney can even hope to deal on cross-examination with unfavorable expert opinion he must have some idea of the basis of that opinion and the data relied upon. If the attorney is required to await examination at trial to get this information, he often will have too little time to recognize and expose vulnerable spots in the testimony." [Court cites Friedenthal, Discovery and Use of an Adverse Party's Expert Information, 14 Stan. L. Rev. 455, 486 (1962).] Finally, proper impeachment or rebuttal may have required advance knowledge so that Ford's own experts could have been consulted.

Smith v. Ford Motor Co., 626 F.2d 784, 799 (10th Cir. 1980), cert. denied, 450 U.S. 918 (1981).

6. *Court-Appointed Experts*   — FRE 706 *independent experts*

Perennially trial lawyers and commentators complain that expert testimony has become a cottage industry, that experts can be hired to advance nearly any cause, and that trials become "battles of experts" that bewilder lay juries. Some have thought that the way out of this dilemma is to permit the court itself to appoint "independent" experts, and Rule 706 authorizes this procedure.

Perhaps not surprisingly, segments of the trial bar vigorously oppose court appointment of experts, raising objections that Rule 706 seeks to solve, or at least ameliorate. Worries over surprise are answered by a provision that the expert will "advise the parties of his findings" and submit to a deposition "taken by any party." The fear that a court-appointed expert will be viewed as the responsibility of one party or another is answered in part by language allowing any party actually to call the expert and entitling all to cross-examine. Finally, the converse fear that the court-appointed expert will bask in a special aura of respectability is answered (at least in part) by language in Rule 706(c) implying that the source of the expert's appointment need not always be disclosed (the actual language states that the court may "authorize disclosure to the jury of the fact that the court appointed the expert").

Yet court appointment of experts continues to be a rarity in American practice, perhaps for two reasons:

First is the adversary tradition. For the most part, judges are reluctant to interfere in the presentation of evidence. Moreover, trial lawyers tend deeply to resent judicial participation, worrying that the judge does not adequately understand the issues, strengths, or dynamics of the unfolding trial, or for that matter the weak points in each side, with the result that the judge will only "mess up the case" by meddling. They worry too over the erosion of party control that judicial appointment of experts represents.

Second is the awkward problem of compensation. Rule 706(b) does address the point, for it enables the court to fix compensation "from funds which may be provided by law" in criminal cases and condemnation actions, and in civil cases to tax the parties for paying court-appointed experts "in like manner as other costs." But courts have some reluctance to draw upon public funds for such purposes, and in civil cases the power to tax costs at the end of the proceedings may not satisfy an expert who is accustomed to being paid as he works. (Taxing costs earlier is awkward because the losing party usually pays.)

In the end, courts appoint experts only rarely, and Rule 706 is one of the least-used provisions in the Federal Rules.

C. RELIABILITY STANDARD FOR SCIENTIFIC AND OTHER TECHNICAL EVIDENCE

1. *Defining a Standard*

For many years American courts required evidence offered as science to satisfy a special standard: Such evidence must be "generally accepted" in the pertinent scientific community. There were many fears, but the heart of the concern was that false and unreliable evidence would be offered and that juries would be unable to appraise it wisely. Universally the standard was known as the *Frye* standard, after the two-page decision in Frye v. United States, 293 F. 1013, 1014 (D.C. Cir. 1923) (rejecting lied detector evidence).

In the last decade of the twentieth century, things changed. First, the Supreme Court decided the *Daubert* case in 1993, discarding *Frye* for federal courts in favor of a more flexible approach designed to insure the reliability of scientific evidence. Second, the Supreme Court decided *Kumho Tire* in 1999, extending the *Daubert* standard to *all* expert testimony presenting technical or specialized material. Third, FRE 702 was amended in 2002 "in response to" *Daubert* (as the ACN says), so that it formally requires expert testimony to rest upon sufficient facts or data, to reflect reliable principles and methods, and to embody a reliable application of these principles and methods.

With the coming of *Daubert* in the federal system, about half the states have followed suit, while at least 16 states (including major jurisdictions such as California and New York) continue to follow their own versions of the old

Frye rule. In a number of other states, the matter is still up in the air. For a sampling of opinions adopting *Daubert,* see Springfield v. State, 860 P.2d 435 (Wyo. 1993); Commonwealth v. Lanigan, 641 N.E.2d 1342 (Mass. 1994). For a sampling of post-*Daubert* opinions adhering to state versions of the *Frye* standard, see People v. Leahy, 882 P.2d 321 (Cal. 1994); Brim v. State, 695 So. 2d 268 (Fla. 1997); State v. Carter, 524 N.W.2d 763 (Neb. 1994). See generally, Mueller and Kirkpatrick, Evidence §7.17, n.29 (3d ed. 2003) (listing jurisdictions following *Frye* and jurisdictions following *Daubert*).

As you read *Daubert,* consider its reasons for rejecting the *Frye* standard. Bear in mind that *Frye* was recognized almost universally as the rule for 70 years. Consider as you read *Daubert* why you might find the *Frye* approach attractive if you were a judge. Suppose you were presiding in a modern toxic tort case where the claimants offered proof of causation in the form of expert testimony describing epidemiological studies indicating a statistical correlation between exposure (or taking medication) and observed outcome (serious ailments or birth defects). Suppose further that the defendants offered expert testimony that these studies were flawed because the reported correlations were not "statistically significant" and because variables ignored by the claimant's experts might account for the observed outcomes.

As trial judge, you might find yourself drawn to one or another of the following three approaches: First, admit the evidence because the experts are qualified and let the jury resolve the dispute. Second, decide for yourself whether the plaintiff's proof is valid science and admit or exclude accordingly. Third, defer to the broader scientific community for its judgment on the validity of the science, asking the proponent to show not only what the proof is and what it means, but also to show that scientists generally agree with it. The *Frye* standard most clearly resembles the third of these approaches. As trial judge, can you imagine being glad to have a way out? *Frye* would let you say to yourself, "I'm not going to let everything in and I'm not going to resolve scientific disputes myself; if I exclude anything I'll do it because other scientists don't accept the proof and I can tell the expert it's not my opinion that counts, but the verdict of other scientists."

Even before *Daubert* was decided, many able courts were beginning to reject *Frye* as being vague, manipulable, and too restrictive in excluding the fruits of cutting-edge (unestablished) scientific learning. In 1985 Judge Becker wrote an influential opinion for the Third Circuit rejecting *Frye*. See United States v. Downing, 753 F.2d 1224 (3d Cir. 1985). As you will see, *Daubert* drew so heavily on *Downing* that the new federal standard might well be called the *Daubert-Downing* standard.

DAUBERT v. MERRELL DOW PHARMACEUTICALS
United States Supreme Court
509 U.S. 579 (1993)

JUSTICE BLACKMUN delivered the opinion of the Court.

In this case we are called upon to determine the standard for admitting expert scientific testimony in a federal trial.

I

Petitioners Jason Daubert and Eric Schuller are minor children born with serious birth defects. They and their parents sued respondent in California state court, alleging that the birth defects had been caused by the mothers' ingestion of Bendectin, a prescription anti-nausea drug marketed by respondent. Respondent removed the suits to federal court on diversity grounds.

After extensive discovery, respondent moved for summary judgment, contending that Bendectin does not cause birth defects in humans and that petitioners would be unable to come forward with any admissible evidence that it does. In support of its motion, respondent submitted an affidavit of Steven H. Lamm, physician and epidemiologist, who is a well-credentialed expert on the risks from exposure to various chemical substances.[1] Doctor Lamm stated that he had reviewed all the literature on Bendectin and human birth defects—more than 30 published studies involving over 130,000 patients. No study had found Bendectin to be a human teratogen (i.e., a substance capable of causing malformations in fetuses). On the basis of this review, Doctor Lamm concluded that maternal use of Bendectin during the first trimester of pregnancy has not been shown to be a risk factor for human birth defects.

Petitioners did not (and do not) contest this characterization of the published record regarding Bendectin. Instead, they responded to respondent's motion with the testimony of eight experts of their own, each of whom also possessed impressive credentials.[2] These experts had concluded that Bendectin can cause birth defects. Their conclusions were based upon "in vitro" (test tube) and "in vivo" (live) animal studies that found a link between Bendectin and malformations; pharmacological studies of the chemical structure of Bendectin that purported to show similarities between the structure of the drug and that of other substances known to cause birth defects; and the "reanalysis" of previously published epidemiological (human statistical) studies.

The District Court granted respondent's motion for summary judgment. The court stated that scientific evidence is admissible only if the principle upon which it is based is "sufficiently established to have general acceptance in the field to which it belongs." The court concluded that petitioners' evidence did not meet this standard. Given the vast body of epidemiological data concerning Bendectin, the court held, expert opinion which is not based on epidemiological evidence is not admissible to establish causation. Thus, the animal-cell studies, live-animal studies, and chemical-structure analyses on which petitioners had

---

1. Doctor Lamm received his master's and doctor of medicine degrees from the University of Southern California. He has served as a consultant in birth-defect epidemiology for the National Center for Health Statistics and has published numerous articles on the magnitude of risk from exposure to various chemical and biological substances.

2. For example, Shanna Helen Swan, who received a master's degree in biostatistics from Columbia University and a doctorate in statistics from the University of California at Berkeley, is chief of the section of the California Department of Health and Services that determines causes of birth defects, and has served as a consultant to the World Health Organization, the Food and Drug Administration, and the National Institutes of Health. Stewart A. Newman, who received his master's and a doctorate in chemistry from Columbia University and the University of Chicago, respectively, is a professor at New York Medical College and has spent over a decade studying the effect of chemicals on limb development. The credentials of the others are similarly impressive.

relied could not raise by themselves a reasonably disputable jury issue regarding causation. Petitioners' epidemiological analyses, based as they were on recalculations of data in previously published studies that had found no causal link between the drug and birth defects, were ruled to be inadmissible because they had not been published or subjected to peer review.

The United States Court of Appeals for the Ninth Circuit affirmed. Citing Frye v. United States, 293 F. 1013, 1014 (D.C. Cir. 1923), the court stated that expert opinion based on a scientific technique is inadmissible unless the technique is "generally accepted" as reliable in the relevant scientific community. The court declared that expert opinion based on a methodology that diverges "significantly from the procedures accepted by recognized authorities in the field . . . cannot be shown to be 'generally accepted as a reliable technique.' "

The court emphasized that other Courts of Appeals considering the risks of Bendectin had refused to admit reanalyses of epidemiological studies that had been neither published nor subjected to peer review. Those courts had found unpublished reanalyses "particularly problematic in light of the massive weight of the original published studies supporting [respondent's] position, all of which had undergone full scrutiny from the scientific community." Contending that reanalysis is generally accepted by the scientific community only when it is subjected to verification and scrutiny by others in the field, the Court of Appeals rejected petitioners' reanalyses as "unpublished, not subjected to the normal peer review process and generated solely for use in litigation." The court concluded that petitioners' evidence provided an insufficient foundation to allow admission of expert testimony that Bendectin caused their injuries and, accordingly, that petitioners could not satisfy their burden of proving causation at trial.

We granted certiorari, in light of sharp divisions among the courts regarding the proper standard for the admission of expert testimony.

II

A

In the 70 years since its formulation in the *Frye* case, the "general acceptance" test has been the dominant standard for determining the admissibility of novel scientific evidence at trial. Although under increasing attack of late, the rule continues to be followed by a majority of courts, including the Ninth Circuit. The *Frye* test has its origin in a short and citation-free 1923 decision concerning the admissibility of evidence derived from a systolic blood pressure deception test, a crude precursor to the polygraph machine. In what has become a famous (perhaps infamous) passage, the then Court of Appeals for the District of Columbia described the device and its operation and declared:

> Just when a scientific principle or discovery crosses the line between the experimental and demonstrable stages is difficult to define. Somewhere in this twilight zone the evidential force of the principle must be recognized, and while courts will go a long way in admitting expert testimony deduced from a well-recognized scientific principle or discovery, the thing from which the deduction is made must

be sufficiently established to have gained general acceptance in the particular field in which it belongs.

Because the deception test had "not yet gained such standing and scientific recognition among physiological and psychological authorities as would justify the courts in admitting expert testimony deduced from the discovery, development, and experiments thus far made," evidence of its results was ruled inadmissible.

The merits of the *Frye* test have been much debated, and scholarship on its proper scope and application is legion.[4]

Petitioners' primary attack, however, is not on the content but on the continuing authority of the rule. They contend that the *Frye* test was superseded by the adoption of the Federal Rules of Evidence.[5] We agree.

We interpret the legislatively-enacted Federal Rules of Evidence as we would any statute. Beech Aircraft Corp. v. Rainey, 488 U.S. 153 (1988). Rule 402 provides the baseline [Court quotes Rule]. "Relevant evidence" is defined as that which has "any tendency to make the existence of any fact that is of consequence to the determination of the action more probable or less probable than it would be without the evidence." FRE 401. The Rule's basic standard of relevance thus is a liberal one.

Frye, of course, predated the Rules by half a century. In United States v. Abel, 469 U.S. 45 (1984), we considered the pertinence of background common law in interpreting the Rules of Evidence. We noted that the Rules occupy the field, but, quoting Professor Cleary, the Reporter, explained that the common law nevertheless could serve as an aid to their application:

> In principle, under the Federal Rules no common law of evidence remains. "All relevant evidence is admissible, except as otherwise provided. . . ." In reality, of

---

4. See, e.g., Green, Expert Witnesses and Sufficiency of Evidence in Toxic Substances Litigation: The Legacy of Agent Orange and Bendectin Litigation, 86 Nw. U.L. Rev. 643 (1992) (hereinafter Green); Becker & Orenstein, The Federal Rules of Evidence After Sixteen Years—The Effect of "Plain Meaning" Jurisprudence, the Need for an Advisory Committee on the Rules of Evidence, and Suggestions for Selective Revision of the Rules, 60 Geo. Wash. L. Rev. 857, 876-885 (1992); Hanson, "James Alphonso Frye Is Sixty-Five Years Old; Should He Retire?," 16 W. St. U. L. Rev. 357 (1989); Black, A Unified Theory of Scientific Evidence, 56 Ford. L. Rev. 595 (1988); Imwinkelried, The "Bases" of Expert Testimony: The Syllogistic Structure of Scientific Testimony, 67 N.C. L. Rev. 1 (1988); Proposals for a Model Rule on the Admissibility of Scientific Evidence, 26 Jurimetrics J. 235 (1986); Gianelli, The Admissibility of Novel Scientific Evidence: Frye v. United States, A Half-Century Later, 80 Colum. L. Rev. 1197 (1980); the Supreme Court, 1986 Term, 101 Harv. L. Rev. 7, 119, 125-127 (1987).

Indeed, the debates over *Frye* are such a well-established part of the academic landscape that a distinct term—"Frye-ologist"—has been advanced to describe those who take part. See Behringer, Introduction, Proposals for a Model Rule on the Admissibility of Scientific Evidence, 26 Jurimetrics J., at 239, quoting Lacey, Scientific Evidence, 24 Jurimetrics J. 254, 264 (1984).

5. Like the question of *Frye's* merit, the dispute over its survival has divided courts and commentators. Compare, e.g., United States v. Williams, 583 F.2d 1194 (CA2 1978), cert. denied, 439 U.S. 1117 (1979) (*Frye* is susperseded by the Rules of Evidence), with Christophersen v. Allied-Signal Corp., 939 F.2d 1106, 1111, 1115-1116 (CA5 1991) (en banc) (*Frye* and the Rules coexist), cert. denied, 112 S. Ct. 1280 (1992), 3 J. Weinstein & M. Berger, Weinstein's Evidence ¶ 702[03], pp.702-36 to 702-37 (1988) (hereinafter Weinstein & Berger) (*Frye* is dead), and M. Graham, Handbook of Federal Evidence §703.2 (2d ed. 1991), (*Frye* lives). See generally P. Gianelli & E. Imwinkelried, Scientific Evidence §1-5, pp.28-29 (1986 & Supp. 1991) (citing authorities).

course, the body of common law knowledge continues to exist, though in the somewhat altered form of a source of guidance in the exercise of delegated powers.

We found the common-law precept at issue in the *Abel* case entirely consistent with Rule 402's general requirement of admissibility, and considered it unlikely that the drafters had intended to change the rule. In Bourjaily v. United States, 483 U.S. 171 (1987), on the other hand, the Court was unable to find a particular common-law doctrine in the Rules, and so held it superseded.

Here there is a specific Rule that speaks to the contested issue. Rule 702, governing expert testimony, provides: "If scientific, technical, or other specialized knowledge will assist the trier of fact to understand the evidence or to determine a fact in issue, a witness qualified as an expert by knowledge, skill, experience, training, or education, may testify thereto in the form of an opinion or otherwise." Nothing in the text of this Rule establishes "general acceptance" as an absolute prerequisite to admissibility. Nor does respondent present any clear indication that FRE 702 or the Rules as a whole were intended to incorporate a "general acceptance" standard. The drafting history makes no mention of *Frye,* and a rigid "general acceptance" requirement would be at odds with the "liberal thrust" of the Federal Rules and their "general approach of relaxing the traditional barriers to 'opinion' testimony." Beech Aircraft Corp. v. Rainey (citing Rules 701 to 705). See also Weinstein, Rule 702 of the Federal Rules of Evidence is Sound; It Should Not Be Amended, 138 F.R.D. 631, 631 (1991) ("The Rules were designed to depend primarily upon lawyer-adversaries and sensible triers of fact to evaluate conflicts"). Given the Rules' permissive backdrop and their inclusion of a specific rule on expert testimony that does not mention "general acceptance," the assertion that the Rules somehow assimilated *Frye* is unconvincing. *Frye* made "general acceptance" the exclusive test for admitting expert scientific testimony. That austere standard, absent from and incompatible with the Federal Rules of Evidence, should not be applied in federal trials.

B

That the *Frye* test was displaced by the Rules of Evidence does not mean, however, that the Rules themselves place no limits on the admissibility of purportedly scientific evidence.[7] Nor is the trial judge disabled from screening such evidence. To the contrary, under the Rules the trial judge must ensure that any and all scientific testimony or evidence admitted is not only relevant, but reliable.

The primary locus of this obligation is FRE 702, which clearly contemplates some degree of regulation of the subjects and theories about which an expert may testify. "*If scientific,* technical, or other specialized *knowledge will assist the trier of fact* to understand the evidence or to determine a fact in issue" an expert "may testify *thereto.*" The subject of an expert's testimony must be "scientific

---

7. The Chief Justice "does not doubt that FRE 702 confides to the judge some gatekeeping responsibility," but would neither say how it does so, nor explain what that role entails. We believe the better course is to note the nature and source of the duty.

. . . knowledge."[8] The adjective "scientific" implies a grounding in the methods and procedures of science. Similarly, the word "knowledge" connotes more than subjective belief or unsupported speculation. The term "applies to any body of known facts or to any body of ideas inferred from such facts or accepted as truths on good grounds." Webster's Third New International Dictionary 1252 (1986). Of course, it would be unreasonable to conclude that the subject of scientific testimony must be "known" to a certainty; arguably, there are no certainties in science. See, e.g., Brief for Nicolaas Bloembergen et al. as Amici Curiae 9 ("Indeed, scientists do not assert that they know what is immutably 'true'—they are committed to searching for new, temporary theories to explain, as best they can, phenomena"); Brief for American Association for the Advancement of Science and the National Academy of Sciences as Amici Curiae 7-8 ("Science is not an encyclopedic body of knowledge about the universe. Instead, it represents a *process* for proposing and refining theoretical explanations about the world that are subject to further testing and refinement") (emphasis in original). But, in order to qualify as "scientific knowledge," an inference or assertion must be derived by the scientific method. Proposed testimony must be supported by appropriate validation—i.e., "good grounds," based on what is known. In short, the requirement that an expert's testimony pertain to "scientific knowledge" establishes a standard of evidentiary reliability.[9] FRE 702 further requires that the evidence or testimony "assist the trier of fact to understand the evidence or to determine a fact in issue." This condition goes primarily to relevance. "Expert testimony which does not relate to any issue in the case is not relevant and, ergo, non-helpful." 3 Weinstein & Berger Par 702[02], pp.702-18. See also United States v. Downing, 753 F.2d 1224, 1242 (CA3 1985) ("An additional consideration under FRE 702—and another aspect of relevancy—is whether expert testimony proffered in the case is sufficiently tied to the facts of the case that it will aid the jury in resolving a factual dispute"). The consideration has been aptly described by Judge Becker as one of "fit." "Fit" is not always obvious, and scientific validity for one purpose is not necessarily scientific validity for other, unrelated purposes. See Starrs, Frye v. United States Restructured and Revitalized: A Proposal to Amend Federal Evidence Rule 702, and 26 Jurimetrics J. 249, 258 (1986). The study of the phases of the moon, for example, may provide valid scientific "knowledge" about whether a certain night was dark, and if darkness is a fact in issue, the knowledge will

---

8. FRE 702 also applies to "technical, or other specialized knowledge." Our discussion is limited to the scientific context because that is the nature of the expertise offered here.

9. We note that scientists typically distinguish between "validity" (does the principle support what it purports to show?) and "reliability" (does application of the principle produce consistent results?). See Black, A Unified Theory of Scientific Evidence, 56 Ford. L. Rev. 595, 599 (1988). Although "the difference between accuracy, validity, and reliability may be such that each is distinct from the other by no more than a hen's kick," Starrs, Frye v. United States Restructured and Revitalized: A Proposal to Amend Federal Evidence Rule 702, 26 Jurimetrics J. 249, 256 (1986), our reference here is to evidentiary reliability—that is, trustworthiness. Cf., e.g., ACN on FRE 602 (" 'The rule requiring that a witness who testifies to a fact which can be perceived by the senses must have had an opportunity to observe, and must have actually observed the fact' is a 'most pervasive manifestation' of the common law insistence upon 'the most reliable sources of information.' "); ACN on Art. VIII of the Rules of Evidence (hearsay exceptions will be recognized only "under circumstances supposed to furnish guarantees of trustworthiness"). In a case involving scientific evidence, evidentiary reliability will be based upon scientific validity.

assist the trier of fact. However (absent creditable grounds supporting such a link), evidence that the moon was full on a certain night will not assist the trier of fact in determining whether an individual was unusually likely to have behaved irrationally on that night. FRE 702's "helpfulness" standard requires a valid scientific connection to the pertinent inquiry as a precondition to admissibility.

That these requirements are embodied in FRE 702 is not surprising. Unlike an ordinary witness, see FRE 701, an expert is permitted wide latitude to offer opinions, including those that are not based on first-hand knowledge or observation. See FRE 702 and 703. Presumably, this relaxation of the usual requirement of first-hand knowledge—a rule which represents "a 'most pervasive manifestation' of the common law insistence upon 'the most reliable sources of information,' " ACN on FRE 602 (citation omitted)—is premised on an assumption that the expert's opinion will have a reliable basis in the knowledge and experience of his discipline.

C

Faced with a proffer of expert scientific testimony, then, the trial judge must determine at the outset, pursuant to FRE 104(a),[10] whether the expert is proposing to testify to (1) scientific knowledge that (2) will assist the trier of fact to understand or determine a fact in issue.[11] This entails a preliminary assessment of whether the reasoning or methodology underlying the testimony is scientifically valid and of whether that reasoning or methodology properly can be applied to the facts in issue. We are confident that federal judges possess the capacity to undertake this review. Many factors will bear on the inquiry, and we do not presume to set out a definitive checklist or test. But some general observations are appropriate.

Ordinarily, a key question to be answered in determining whether a theory or technique is scientific knowledge that will assist the trier of fact will be whether it can be (and has been) tested. "Scientific methodology today is based on generating hypotheses and testing them to see if they can be falsified; indeed, this methodology is what distinguishes science from other fields of human inquiry." Green, at 645. See also C. Hempel, Philosophy of Natural Science 49 (1966) ("The statements constituting a scientific explanation must be capable of empirical test"); K. Popper, Conjectures and Refutations: The Growth of Scientific Knowledge 37 (5th ed. 1989) ("The criterion of the scientific status of a theory is its falsifiability, or refutability, or testability").

Another pertinent consideration is whether the theory or technique has been subjected to peer review and publication. Publication (which is but one element of peer review) is not a sine qua non of admissibility; it does not necessarily correlate with reliability, see S. Jasanoff, The Fifth Branch: Science

---

10. [Court quotes FRE 104(a).] These matters should be established by a preponderance of proof. See Bourjaily v. United States, 483 U.S. 171, 175-176 (1987).

11. Although the *Frye* decision itself focused exclusively on "novel" scientific techniques, we do not read the requirements of FRE 702 to apply specially or exclusively to unconventional evidence. Of course, well-established propositions are less likely to be challenged than those that are novel, and they are more handily defended. Indeed, theories that are so firmly established as to have attained the status of scientific law, such as the laws of thermodynamics, properly are subject to judicial notice under FRE 201.

Advisors as Policymakers 61-76 (1990), and in some instances well-grounded but innovative theories will not have been published, see Horrobin, The Philosophical Basis of Peer Review and the Suppression of Innovation, 263 J. Am. Med. Assn. 1438 (1990). Some propositions, moreover, are too particular, too new, or of too limited interest to be published. But submission to the scrutiny of the scientific community is a component of "good science," in part because it increases the likelihood that substantive flaws in methodology will be detected. See J. Ziman, Reliable Knowledge: An Exploration of the Grounds for Belief in Science 130-133 (1978); Relman and Angell, How Good Is Peer Review?, 321 New Eng. J. Med. 827 (1989). The fact of publication (or lack thereof) in a peer-reviewed journal thus will be a relevant, though not dispositive, consideration in assessing the scientific validity of a particular technique or methodology on which an opinion is premised.

Additionally, in the case of a particular scientific technique, the court ordinarily should consider the known or potential rate of error, see, e.g., United States v. Smith, 869 F.2d 348, 353-354 (7th Cir. 1989) (surveying studies of the error rate of spectrographic voice identification technique), and the existence and maintenance of standards controlling the technique's operation. See United States v. Williams, 583 F.2d 1194, 1198 (CA2 1978) (noting professional organization's standard governing spectrographic analysis), cert. denied, 439 U.S. 1117 (1979).

Finally, "general acceptance" can yet have a bearing on the inquiry. A "reliability assessment does not require, although it does permit, explicit identification of a relevant scientific community and an express determination of a particular degree of acceptance within that community." Downing. Widespread acceptance can be an important factor in ruling particular evidence admissible, and "a known technique that has been able to attract only minimal support within the community," Downing, may properly be viewed with skepticism.

The inquiry envisioned by FRE 702 is, we emphasize, a flexible one.[12] Its overarching subject is the scientific validity—and thus the evidentiary relevance and reliability—of the principles that underlie a proposed submission. The focus, of course, must be solely on principles and methodology, not on the conclusions that they generate.

Throughout, a judge assessing a proffer of expert scientific testimony under FRE 702 should also be mindful of other applicable rules. FRE 703 provides that expert opinions based on otherwise inadmissible hearsay are to be admitted only if the facts or data are "of a type reasonably relied upon by experts in the particular field in forming opinions or inferences upon the subject." FRE 706 allows the court at its discretion to procure the assistance of an expert of its own choosing. Finally, FRE 403 permits the exclusion of relevant evidence "if

---

12.   A number of authorities have presented variations on the reliability approach, each with its own slightly different set of factors. See, e.g., Downing, 753 F.2d 1238-1239 (on which our discussion draws in part); 3 Weinstein & Berger, Weinstein's Evidence Par. 702[03] (on which the Downing court in turn partially relied); McCormick, Scientific Evidence: Defining a New Approach to Admissibility, 67 Iowa L. Rev. 879, 911-912 (1982); and Symposium on Science and the Rules of Evidence, 99 F.R.D. 187, 231 (1983) (statement by Margaret Berger). To the extent that they focus on the reliability of evidence as ensured by the scientific validity of its underlying principles, all these versions may well have merit, although we express no opinion regarding any of their particular details.

its probative value is substantially outweighed by the danger of unfair prejudice, confusion of the issues, or misleading the jury. . . ." Judge Weinstein has explained: "Expert evidence can be both powerful and quite misleading because of the difficulty in evaluating it. Because of this risk, the judge in weighing possible prejudice against probative force under FRE 403 of the present rules exercises more control over experts than over lay witnesses." Weinstein, 138 F.R.D., at 632.

III

We conclude by briefly addressing what appear to be two underlying concerns of the parties and amici in this case. Respondent expresses apprehension that abandonment of "general acceptance" as the exclusive requirement for admission will result in a "free-for-all" in which befuddled juries are confounded by absurd and irrational pseudoscientific assertions. In this regard respondent seems to us to be overly pessimistic about the capabilities of the jury, and of the adversary system generally. Vigorous cross-examination, presentation of contrary evidence, and careful instruction on the burden of proof are the traditional and appropriate means of attacking shaky but admissible evidence. See Rock v. Arkansas, 483 U.S. 44, 61 (1987). Additionally, in the event the trial court concludes that the scintilla of evidence presented supporting a position is insufficient to allow a reasonable juror to conclude that the position more likely than not is true, the court remains free to direct a judgment, FRCP 50(a), and likewise to grant summary judgment, FRCP 56. Cf., e.g., Turpin v. Merrell Dow Pharmaceuticals, Inc., 959 F.2d 1349 (CA6) (holding that scientific evidence that provided foundation for expert testimony, viewed in the light most favorable to plaintiffs, was not sufficient to allow a jury to find it more probable than not that defendant caused plaintiff's injury), cert. denied, 506 U.S. 826 (1992); Brock v. Merrell Dow Pharmaceuticals, Inc., 874 F.2d 307 (CA5 1989) (reversing judgment entered on jury verdict for plaintiffs because evidence regarding causation was insufficient), modified, 884 F.2d 166 (CA5 1989), cert. denied, 494 U.S. 1046 (1990); Green 680-681. These conventional devices, rather than wholesale exclusion under an uncompromising "general acceptance" test, are the appropriate safeguards where the basis of scientific testimony meets the standards of FRE 702.

Petitioners and, to a greater extent, their amici exhibit a different concern. They suggest that recognition of a screening role for the judge that allows for the exclusion of "invalid" evidence will sanction a stifling and repressive scientific orthodoxy and will be inimical to the search for truth. See, e.g., Brief for Ronald Bayer et al. as Amici Curiae. It is true that open debate is an essential part of both legal and scientific analyses. Yet there are important differences between the quest for truth in the courtroom and the quest for truth in the laboratory. Scientific conclusions are subject to perpetual revision. Law, on the other hand, must resolve disputes finally and quickly. The scientific project is advanced by broad and wide-ranging consideration of a multitude of hypotheses, for those that are incorrect will eventually be shown to be so, and that in itself is an advance. Conjectures that are probably wrong are of little use, however, in the project of reaching a quick, final, and binding legal judgment—often of great consequence—about a particular set of events in the past. We recognize that in practice, a gatekeeping role for the judge, no matter how flexible, inevitably on occasion will prevent the jury from learning of authentic insights and innovations. That, nevertheless, is the balance that is struck by Rules of Evidence designed not for the exhaustive search for cosmic understanding but for the particularized resolution of legal disputes.[13]

IV

To summarize: "general acceptance" is not a necessary precondition to the admissibility of scientific evidence under the Federal Rules of Evidence, but the Rules of Evidence—especially FRE 702—do assign to the trial judge the task of ensuring that an expert's testimony both rests on a reliable foundation and is relevant to the task at hand. Pertinent evidence based on scientifically valid principles will satisfy those demands.

The inquiries of the District Court and the Court of Appeals focused almost exclusively on "general acceptance," as gauged by publication and the decisions of other courts. Accordingly, the judgment of the Court of Appeals is vacated and the case is remanded for further proceedings consistent with this opinion.

It is so ordered.

CHIEF JUSTICE REHNQUIST, with whom JUSTICE STEVENS joins, concurring in part and dissenting in part.

The petition for certiorari in this case presents two questions: first, whether the rule of *Frye* remains good law after the enactment of the Federal Rules of Evidence; and second, if *Frye* remains valid, whether it requires expert scientific testimony to have been subjected to a peer-review process in order to be admissible. The Court concludes, correctly in my view, that the *Frye* rule did not survive the enactment of the Federal Rules of Evidence, and I therefore join Parts I and II-A of its opinion. The second question presented in the petition for certiorari necessarily is mooted by this holding, but the Court nonetheless proceeds to construe FRE 702 and 703 very much in the abstract, and then offers some "general observations."

"General observations" by this Court customarily carry great weight with lower federal courts, but the ones offered here suffer from the flaw common to most such observations—they are not applied to deciding whether or not particular testimony was or was not admissible, and therefore they tend to be not only general, but vague and abstract. This is particularly unfortunate in a case such as this, where the ultimate legal question depends on an appreciation of one or more bodies of knowledge not judicially noticeable, and subject to different interpretations in the briefs of the parties and their *amici*. Twenty-two *amicus* briefs have been filed in the case, and indeed the Court's opinion contains no less than 37 citations to *amicus* briefs and other secondary sources.

---

13. This is not to say that judicial interpretation, as opposed to adjudicative factfinding, does not share basic characteristics of the scientific endeavor: "The work of a judge is in one sense enduring and in another ephemeral. . . . In the endless process of testing and retesting, there is a constant rejection of the dross and a constant retention of whatever is pure and sound and fine." B. Cardozo, The Nature of the Judicial Process 178, 179 (1921).

The various briefs filed in this case are markedly different from typical briefs, in that large parts of them do not deal with decided cases or statutory language—the sort of material we customarily interpret. Instead, they deal with definitions of scientific knowledge, scientific method, scientific validity, and peer review—in short, matters far afield from the expertise of judges. This is not to say that such materials are not useful or even necessary in deciding how FRE 703 should be applied; but it is to say that the unusual subject matter should cause us to proceed with great caution in deciding more than we have to, because our reach can so easily exceed our grasp.

But even if it were desirable to make "general observations" not necessary to decide the questions presented, I cannot subscribe to some of the observations made by the Court. In Part II-B, the Court concludes that reliability and relevancy are the touchstones of the admissibility of expert testimony. FRE 402 provides, as the Court points out, that "evidence which is not relevant is not admissible." But there is no similar reference in the Rule to "reliability." The Court constructs its argument by parsing the language "if scientific, technical, or other specialized knowledge will assist the trier of fact to understand the evidence or to determine a fact in issue . . . an expert . . . may testify thereto." FRE 702. It stresses that the subject of the expert's testimony must be "scientific . . . knowledge," and points out that "scientific" "implies a grounding in the methods and procedures of science," and that the word "knowledge" "connotes more than subjective belief or unsupported speculation." From this it concludes that "scientific knowledge" must be "derived by the scientific method." Proposed testimony, we are told, must be supported by "appropriate validation." Indeed, in footnote 9, the Court decides that "in a case involving scientific evidence, evidentiary reliability will be based upon scientific validity."

Questions arise simply from reading this part of the Court's opinion, and countless more questions will surely arise when hundreds of district judges try to apply its teaching to particular offers of expert testimony. Does all of this dicta apply to an expert seeking to testify on the basis of "technical or other specialized knowledge"—the other types of expert knowledge to which FRE 702 applies—or are the "general observations" limited only to "scientific knowledge"? What is the difference between scientific knowledge and technical knowledge; does FRE 702 actually contemplate that the phrase "scientific, technical, or other specialized knowledge" be broken down into numerous subspecies of expertise, or did its authors simply pick general descriptive language covering the sort of expert testimony which courts have customarily received? The Court speaks of its confidence that federal judges can make a "preliminary assessment of whether the reasoning or methodology underlying the testimony is scientifically valid and of whether that reasoning or methodology properly can be applied to the facts in issue." The Court then states that a "key question" to be answered in deciding whether something is "scientific knowledge" "will be whether it can be (and has been) tested." Following this sentence are three quotations from treatises, which speak not only of empirical testing, but one of which states that "the criterion of the scientific status of a theory is its falsifiability, or refutability, or testability."

I defer to no one in my confidence in federal judges; but I am at a loss to know what is meant when it is said that the scientific status of a theory depends on its "falsifiability," and I suspect some of them will be, too.

I do not doubt that FRE 702 confides to the judge some gatekeeping responsibility in deciding questions of the admissibility of proffered expert testimony. But I do not think it imposes on them either the obligation or the authority to become amateur scientists in order to perform that role. I think the Court would be far better advised in this case to decide only the questions presented, and to leave the further development of this important area of the law to future cases.

KUMHO TIRE COMPANY, LTD. v. CARMICHAEL
United States Supreme Court
526 U.S. 137 (1998)

JUSTICE BREYER delivered the opinion of the Court.

[The right rear steel-belted radial tire of a minivan driven by Patrick Carmichael blew out, causing an accident that killed one passenger and severely injured others. The Carmichaels sued Kumho Tire (maker and distributor) in federal court. Plaintiffs relied on deposition testimony by Dennis Carlson, an expert in tire failure analysis.

Carlson in turn relied on certain features of tire technology: A steel-belted radial has a "carcass" containing layers of flexible cords ("plies"), and steel strips ("belts") that are laid between the plies and outer tread. Steel wire loops ("beads") hold the plies together along the inner circumference. The outer layer ("tread") encases the carcass, and the whole is bound together in rubber by the use of heat and chemicals. The tire rests on the "bead seat" of the wheel assembly, which contains a "rim flange" extending over the bead and holding the side of the tire.

Carlson assumed that the tire had traveled far. It had been made in 1988 and installed before the Carmichaels bought the minivan in March 1993. They had driven it about 7,000 miles before the tire blew out in July 1993. The tread depth (11/32 of an inch when new) was worn to depths ranging from 3/32 of an inch to nothing. The tire tread had punctures that had been inadequately repaired.

Nevertheless, Carlson concluded that a manufacturing or design defect caused the blowout. He relied in part on three premises, not disputed: First, the carcass should stay bound to the inner side of the tread, even after the tread is worn. Second, in this case the tread separated from its carcass prior to the accident. Third, this separation caused the blowout.

Carlson's conclusions rested on other propositions that are in dispute. First, if misuse in the form of "overdeflection" does *not* cause tire failure, then usually the cause is a tire defect. (Overinflection means underinflating the tire or putting too much weight on it, generating heat that can undo the bond between the tread and the carcass.) Second, a tire misused in this way will reveal (a) greater tread wear on the shoulder than the center, (b) a "bead groove" where the bead pushes too hard against the bead seat inside the rim, (c) signs of deterioration on the sidewalls, such as discoloration, and (d) marks on the rim flange. The *absence* of two or more of these signs means that a defect caused the separation.

On inspecting the tire, Carlson found greater tread wear on the shoulder than the center, signs of a bead groove, discoloration, marks on the rim flange, and inadequately filled puncture holes (which cause heat leading to separation). Carlson thought these symptoms were not significant and did not show overdeflection. The extra shoulder wear, for example, appeared mostly on one shoulder (an overinflected tire shows wear on both shoulders). Hence the tire did not reveal two of the four symptoms, so a defect caused the blowout.

The trial court ruled Carlson's testimony inadmissible because his methodology failed the reliability requirement of FRE 702 and *Daubert,* and granted summary judgment for the defense. Plaintiffs appealed, and the Eleventh Circuit reversed, concluding that *Daubert* applies only to scientific evidence, not to expert testimony more generally. The Supreme Court granted certiorari.]

II

A

In *Daubert,* this Court held that FRE 702 imposes a special obligation upon a trial judge to "ensure that any and all scientific testimony . . . is not only relevant, but reliable." The initial question before us is whether this basic gatekeeping obligation applies only to "scientific" testimony or to all expert testimony. We, like the parties, believe that it applies to all expert testimony.

[Court quotes FRE 702, which then consisted only of the first sentence of present FRE 702.]

This language makes no relevant distinction between "scientific" knowledge and "technical" or "other specialized" knowledge. It makes clear that any such knowledge might become the subject of expert testimony. In *Daubert,* the Court specified that it is the Rule's word "knowledge," not the words (like "scientific") that modify that word, that "establishes a standard of evidentiary reliability." Hence, as a matter of language, the Rule applies its reliability standard to all "scientific," "technical," or "other specialized" matters within its scope. We concede that the Court in *Daubert* referred only to "scientific" knowledge. But as the Court there said, it referred to "scientific" testimony "because that [wa]s the nature of the expertise" at issue.

Neither is the evidentiary rationale that underlay the Court's basic *Daubert* "gatekeeping" determination limited to "scientific" knowledge. *Daubert* pointed out that FRE 702 and 703 grant expert witnesses testimonial latitude unavailable to other witnesses on the "assumption that the expert's opinion will have a reliable basis in the knowledge and experience of his discipline" (pointing out that experts may testify to opinions, including those that are not based on firsthand knowledge or observation). The Rules grant that latitude to all experts, not just to "scientific" ones.

Finally, it would prove difficult, if not impossible, for judges to administer evidentiary rules under which a gatekeeping obligation depended upon a distinction between "scientific" knowledge and "technical" or "other specialized" knowledge. There is no clear line that divides the one from the others. Disciplines such as engineering rest upon scientific knowledge. Pure scientific theory itself may depend for its development upon observation and properly engineered machinery. And conceptual efforts to distinguish the two are unlikely to produce clear legal lines capable of application in particular cases. Cf. Brief for National Academy of Engineering as *Amicus Curiae* (scientist seeks to understand nature while the engineer seeks nature's modification); Brief for Rubber Manufacturers Association as *Amicus Curiae* (engineering, as an " 'applied science,' " relies on "scientific reasoning and methodology"); Brief for John Allen et al. as *Amici Curiae* (engineering relies upon "scientific knowledge and methods").

Neither is there a convincing need to make such distinctions. Experts of all kinds tie observations to conclusions through the use of what Judge Learned Hand called "general truths derived from . . . specialized experience." Hand, Historical and Practical Considerations Regarding Expert Testimony, 15 Harv. L. Rev. 40, 54 (1901). And whether the specific expert testimony focuses upon specialized observations, the specialized translation of those observations into theory, a specialized theory itself, or the application of such a theory in a particular case, the expert's testimony often will rest "upon an experience confessedly foreign in kind to [the jury's] own." The trial judge's effort to assure that the specialized testimony is reliable and relevant can help the jury evaluate that foreign experience, whether the testimony reflects scientific, technical, or other specialized knowledge.

We conclude that *Daubert*'s general principles apply to the expert matters described in Rule 702. The Rule, in respect to all such matters, "establishes a standard of evidentiary reliability." It "requires a valid . . . connection to the pertinent inquiry as a precondition to admissibility." And where such testimony's factual basis, data, principles, methods, or their application are called sufficiently into question, the trial judge must determine whether the testimony has "a reliable basis in the knowledge and experience of [the relevant] discipline."

B

Petitioners ask more specifically whether a trial judge determining the "admissibility of an engineering expert's testimony" *may* consider several more specific factors that *Daubert* said might "bear on" a judge's gatekeeping determination. These factors include:

1. Whether a "theory or technique . . . can be (and has been) tested";
2. Whether it "has been subjected to peer review and publication";
3. Whether, in respect to a particular technique, there is a high "known or potential rate of error" and whether there are "standards controlling the technique's operation"; and
4. Whether the theory or technique enjoys "general acceptance" within a "relevant scientific community."

Emphasizing the word "may" in the question, we answer that question yes.

Engineering testimony rests upon scientific foundations, the reliability of which will be at issue in some cases. In other cases, the relevant reliability concerns may focus upon personal knowledge or experience. As the Solicitor General points out, there are many different kinds of experts, and many different kinds of expertise. See Brief for United States as *Amicus Curiae* (citing cases involving experts in drug terms, handwriting analysis, criminal *modus operandi*, land valuation, agricultural practices, railroad procedures, attorney's fee valuation, and others). Our emphasis on the word "may" thus reflects *Daubert's* description of the Rule 702 inquiry as "a flexible one." *Daubert* makes clear that the factors it mentions do *not* constitute a "definitive checklist or test." And *Daubert* adds that the gatekeeping inquiry must be "tied to the facts" of a particular "case" (quoting United States v. Downing, 753 F.2d 1224, 1242 (C.A.3 1985)). We agree with the Solicitor General that "[t]he factors identified in *Daubert* may or may not be pertinent in assessing reliability, depending on the nature of the issue, the expert's particular expertise, and the subject of his testimony." Brief for United States as *Amicus Curiae*. The conclusion, in our view, is that we can neither rule out, nor rule in, for all cases and for all time the applicability of the factors mentioned in *Daubert*, nor can we now do so for subsets of cases categorized by category of expert or by kind of evidence. Too much depends upon the particular circumstances of the particular case at issue.

Daubert itself is not to the contrary. It made clear that its list of factors was meant to be helpful, not definitive. Indeed, those factors do not all necessarily apply even in every instance in which the reliability of scientific testimony is challenged. It might not be surprising in a particular case, for example, that a claim made by a scientific witness has never been the subject of peer review, for the particular application at issue may never previously have interested any scientist. Nor, on the other hand, does the presence of *Daubert's* general acceptance factor help show that an expert's testimony is reliable where the discipline itself lacks reliability, as, for example, do theories grounded in any so-called generally accepted principles of astrology or necromancy.

At the same time, and contrary to the Court of Appeals' view, some of *Daubert's* questions can help to evaluate the reliability even of experience-based testimony. In certain cases, it will be appropriate for the trial judge to ask, for example, how often an engineering expert's experience-based methodology has produced erroneous results, or whether such a method is generally accepted in the relevant engineering community. Likewise, it will at times be useful to ask even of a witness whose expertise is based purely on experience, say, a perfume tester able to distinguish among 140 odors at a sniff, whether his preparation is of a kind that others in the field would recognize as acceptable.

We must therefore disagree with the Eleventh Circuit's holding that a trial judge may ask questions of the sort *Daubert* mentioned only where an expert "relies on the application of scientific principles," but not where an expert relies "on skill- or experience-based observation." We do not believe that Rule 702 creates a schematism that segregates expertise by type while mapping certain kinds of questions to certain kinds of experts. Life and the legal cases that it generates are too complex to warrant so definitive a match.

To say this is not to deny the importance of *Daubert's* gatekeeping requirement. The objective of that requirement is to ensure the reliability and relevancy of expert testimony. It is to make certain that an expert, whether basing testimony upon professional studies or personal experience, employs in the courtroom the same level of intellectual rigor that characterizes the practice of an expert in the relevant field. Nor do we deny that, as stated in *Daubert*, the particular questions that it mentioned will often be appropriate for use in determining the reliability of challenged expert testimony. Rather, we conclude that the trial judge must have considerable leeway in deciding in a particular case how to go about determining whether particular expert testimony is reliable. That is to say, a trial court should consider the specific factors identified in *Daubert* where they are reasonable measures of the reliability of expert testimony.

C

The trial court must have the same kind of latitude in deciding *how* to test an expert's reliability, and to decide whether or when special briefing or other proceedings are needed to investigate reliability, as it enjoys when it decides *whether or not* that expert's relevant testimony is reliable. Our opinion in *General Electric Co. Joiner*, 522 U.S. 166 (1997), makes clear that a court of appeals is to apply an abuse-of-discretion standard when it "review[s] a trial court's decision to admit or exclude expert testimony." That standard applies as much to the trial court's decisions about how to determine reliability as to its ultimate conclusion. Otherwise, the trial judge would lack the discretionary authority needed both to avoid unnecessary "reliability" proceedings in ordinary cases where the reliability of an expert's methods is properly taken for granted, and to require appropriate proceedings in the less usual or more complex cases where cause for questioning the expert's reliability arises. Indeed, the Rules seek to avoid "unjustifiable expense and delay" as part of their search for "truth" and the "jus[t] determin[ation]" of proceedings. FRE 102. Thus, whether *Daubert's* specific factors are, or are not, reasonable measures of reliability in a particular case is a matter that the law grants the trial judge broad latitude to determine. And the Eleventh Circuit erred insofar as it held to the contrary.

III

We further explain the way in which a trial judge "may" consider *Daubert's* factors by applying these considerations to the case at hand, a matter that has been briefed exhaustively by the parties and their 19 *amici*. The District Court did not doubt Carlson's qualifications, which included a masters degree in mechanical engineering, 10 years' work at Michelin America, Inc., and testimony as a tire failure consultant in other tort cases. Rather, it excluded the testimony because, despite those qualifications, it initially doubted, and then found unreliable, "the methodology employed by the expert in analyzing the data obtained in the visual inspection, and the scientific basis, if any, for such an analysis." After examining the transcript in "some detail," and after considering respondents' defense of Carlson's methodology, the District Court determined that Carlson's testimony was not reliable. It fell outside the range where experts might reasonably differ, and where the jury must decide among the conflicting views of different experts, even though the evidence is "shaky." In our view, the doubts that triggered the District Court's initial inquiry here were reasonable, as was the court's ultimate conclusion.

For one thing, and contrary to respondents' suggestion, the specific issue before the court was not the reasonableness *in general* of a tire expert's use of a visual and tactile inspection to determine whether overdeflection had caused the tire's tread to separate from its steel-belted carcass. Rather, it was the reasonableness of using such an approach, along with Carlson's particular method of analyzing the data thereby obtained, to draw a conclusion regarding *the particular matter to which the expert testimony was directly relevant.* That matter concerned the likelihood that a defect in the tire at issue caused its tread to separate from its carcass. The tire in question, the expert conceded, had traveled far enough so that some of the tread had been worn bald; it should have been taken out of service; it had been repaired (inadequately) for punctures; and it bore some of the very marks that the expert said indicated, not a defect, but abuse through overdeflection. The relevant issue was whether the expert could reliably determine the cause of *this* tire's separation.

Nor was the basis for Carlson's conclusion simply the general theory that, in the absence of evidence of abuse, a defect will normally have caused a tire's separation. Rather, the expert employed a more specific theory to establish the existence (or absence) of such abuse. Carlson testified precisely that in the absence of *at least two* of four signs of abuse (proportionately greater tread wear on the shoulder; signs of grooves caused by the beads; discolored sidewalls; marks on the rim flange), he concludes that a defect caused the separation. And his analysis depended upon acceptance of a further implicit proposition, namely, that his visual and tactile inspection could determine that the tire before him had not been abused despite some evidence of the presence of the very signs for which he looked (and two punctures).

For another thing, the transcripts of Carlson's depositions support both the trial court's initial uncertainty and its final conclusion. Those transcripts cast considerable doubt upon the reliability of both the explicit theory (about the need for two signs of abuse) and the implicit proposition (about the significance of visual inspection in this case). Among other things, the expert could not say whether the tire had traveled more than 10, or 20, or 30, or 40, or 50 thousand miles, adding that 6,000 miles was "about how far" he could "say with any certainty." The court could reasonably have wondered about the reliability of a method of visual and tactile inspection sufficiently precise to ascertain with some certainty the abuse-related significance of minute shoulder/center relative tread wear differences, but insufficiently precise to tell "with any certainty" from the tread wear whether a tire had traveled less than 10,000 or more than 50,000 miles. And these concerns might have been augmented by Carlson's repeated reliance on the "subjective[ness]" of his mode of analysis in response to questions seeking specific information regarding how he could differentiate between a tire that actually had been overdeflected and a tire that merely looked as though it had been. They would have been further augmented by the fact that Carlson said he had inspected the tire itself for the first time the morning of his first deposition, and then only for a few hours. (His initial conclusions were based on photographs.)

Moreover, prior to his first deposition, Carlson had issued a signed report in which he concluded that the tire had "not been . . . overloaded or underinflated," not because of the absence of "two of four" signs of abuse, but simply because "the rim flange impressions . . . were normal." That report also said that the "tread depth remaining was 3/32 inch," though the opposing expert's (apparently undisputed) measurements indicate that the tread depth taken at various positions around the tire actually ranged from .5/32 of an inch to 4/32 of an inch, with the tire apparently showing greater wear along *both* shoulders than along the center.

Further, in respect to one sign of abuse, bead grooving, the expert seemed to deny the sufficiency of his own simple visual-inspection methodology. He testified that most tires have some bead groove pattern, that where there is reason to suspect an abnormal bead groove he would ideally "look at a lot of [similar] tires" to know the grooving's significance, and that he had not looked at many tires similar to the one at issue.

Finally, the court, after looking for a defense of Carlson's methodology as applied in these circumstances, found no convincing defense. Rather, it found (1) that "none" of the *Daubert* factors, including that of "general acceptance" in the relevant expert community, indicated that Carlson's testimony was reliable; (2) that its own analysis "revealed no countervailing factors operating in favor of admissibility which could outweigh those identified in *Daubert*"; and (3) that the "parties identified no such factors in their briefs." For these three reasons *taken together*, it concluded that Carlson's testimony was unreliable.

Respondents now argue to us, as they did to the District Court, that a method of tire failure analysis that employs a visual/tactile inspection is a reliable method, and they point both to its use by other experts and to Carlson's long experience working for Michelin as sufficient indication that that is so. But no one denies that an expert might draw a conclusion from a set of observations based on extensive and specialized experience. Nor does anyone deny that, as a general matter, tire abuse may often be identified by qualified experts through visual or tactile inspection of the tire. As we said before, the question before the trial court was specific, not general. The trial court had to decide whether this particular expert had sufficient specialized knowledge to assist the jurors "in deciding the particular issues in the case." 4 J. McLaughlin, Weinstein's Federal Evidence ¶702.05[1], p. 702-733 (2d ed. 1998); see also ACN on Proposed FRE 702, Preliminary Draft of Proposed Amendments to the Federal Rules of Civil Procedure and Evidence: Request for Comment 126 (1998) (stressing that district courts must "scrutinize" whether the "principles and methods" employed by an expert "have been properly applied to the facts of the case").

The particular issue in this case concerned the use of Carlson's two-factor test and his related use of visual/tactile inspection to draw conclusions on the basis of what seemed small observational differences. We have found no indication in the record that other experts in the industry use Carlson's two-factor test or that tire experts such as Carlson normally make the very fine distinctions about, say, the symmetry of comparatively greater shoulder tread wear that were necessary, on Carlson's own theory, to support his conclusions. Nor, despite the prevalence of tire testing, does anyone refer to any articles or papers that validate Carlson's approach. Indeed, no one has argued that Carlson himself, were he still working for Michelin, would have concluded in a report to his employer that a similar tire was similarly defective on grounds identical to those upon which he rested his conclusion here. Of course, Carlson himself claimed that his method was accurate, but, as we pointed out in *Joiner*, "nothing in either *Daubert* or the Federal Rules of Evidence requires a district court to admit opinion evidence that is connected to existing data only by the *ipse dixit* of the expert."

Respondents additionally argue that the District Court too rigidly applied *Daubert's* criteria. They read its opinion to hold that a failure to satisfy any one of those criteria automatically renders expert testimony inadmissible. The District Court's initial opinion might have been vulnerable to a form of this argument. There, the court, after rejecting respondents' claim that Carlson's testimony was "exempted from *Daubert*-style scrutiny" because it was "technical analysis" rather than "scientific evidence," simply added that "none of the four admissibility criteria outlined by the *Daubert* court are satisfied." Subsequently, however, the court granted respondents' motion for reconsideration. It then explicitly recognized that the relevant reliability inquiry "should be 'flexible,' " that its " 'overarching subject [should be] . . . validity' and reliability," and that "*Daubert* was intended neither to be exhaustive nor to apply in every case." And the court ultimately based its decision upon Carlson's failure to satisfy either *Daubert's* factors *or any other* set of reasonable reliability criteria. In light of the record as developed by the parties, that conclusion was within the District Court's lawful discretion.

In sum, Rule 702 grants the district judge the discretionary authority, reviewable for its abuse, to determine reliability in light of the particular facts and circumstances of the particular case. The District Court did not abuse its discretionary authority in this case. Hence, the judgment of the Court of Appeals is

Reversed.

JUSTICE SCALIA, with whom JUSTICE O'CONNOR and JUSTICE THOMAS join, concurring. [Trial judges have discretion to "choose among *reasonable* means" of appraising science; they do not have discretion to perform the gatekeeping responsibility "inadequately."]

JUSTICE STEVENS, concurring in part and dissenting in part. [The question whether Dennis Carlson should have been allowed to testify should be decided by the trial court under the correct standard, as set forth in this opinion.]

NOTES ON *DAUBERT, KUMHO TIRE,* AND THE RELIABILITY STANDARD

1.   There was a longstanding debate on the question whether *Frye's* "general scientific acceptance" standard survived enactment of the Rules. Are you convinced by *Daubert's* analysis of this point? Recall United States v. Abel, 469 U.S. 45 (1984) (page 503, supra), where the Court said the failure of the Rules to mention bias did not put an end to this method of impeachment: Citing the "state of unanimity" on bias as a proper method, the Court in *Abel* said it was "unlikely" that the drafters of the Rules "intended to scuttle entirely" this method of attack. Wasn't the *Frye* doctrine universal too?

2.   Does *Daubert* discard *Frye?* If not, what is left of it? Clearly *Daubert* does not say the only question is whether the expert is qualified by training or experience. Doesn't *Daubert* hold that the expert, in addition to being qualified,

must present valid science? Where in the Rules does the Court find a requirement for valid science?

3.   *Daubert* refines the method of scrutinizing scientific evidence, doesn't it? What factors does *Daubert* emphasize? Could a court, consistently with *Daubert,* also take into account the types of error, the existence of a professional literature appraising the process or technique, nonjudicial uses and experience with it, its newness and relationship to more established processes or techniques, and the qualifications or stature of the witnesses? See generally United States v. Downing, 753 F.2d 1224 (3d Cir. 1985) (mentioning these factors).

4.   One criticism of *Frye* was that it excluded too much evidence, but a new concern had arisen by the time *Daubert* was decided, which was that courts were being flooded with "junk science," and were taking more responsibility for risk management than they could handle. The term "junk science" was popularized in Peter Huber, Galileo's Revenge: Junk Science in the Courtroom (1991), which the Ninth Circuit cited in *Daubert.*[8] Huber's argument is that technology has made our environment safer, but that popular fears over toxicity and risk combine with lax evidentiary and legal standards to produce counterproductive court judgments that burden and stifle technology without crediting its contributions. Does *Daubert* respond more to the view that *Frye* kept too much expert testimony out, or to the view that lax standards let too much in? On remand, the Ninth Circuit again found that the plaintiff's proof was not valid science. See Daubert v. Merrell Dow Pharmaceuticals, 43 F.3d 1311 (9th Cir. 1995) (without peer reviews, proponent must show validity another way, including testimony by experts explaining "how they went about reaching their conclusions" and showing that they "followed the scientific method" as practiced by at least a recognized minority; proof that Bendectin caused limb reduction defects must also satisfy criterion of "fit," which means it must show that "children whose mothers took Bendectin are more than twice as likely" to suffer defects as children of mothers who did not) (neither showing was made).

5.   Before *Kumho Tire* was decided, nobody could say for sure whether the *Daubert* standard applied to experts in such technical fields as engineering, medicine, psychiatry, and economics. *Kumho Tire* put an end to those doubts, didn't it? Are you convinced that *Daubert* is as broad as *Kumho Tire* said? Apart from that, is it wise for *Daubert* to extend as far as *Kumho Tire* says? Suppose a slip-and-fall injury sustained in a "big-box" retail store leads to a suit, and that plaintiff calls *C* as "a psychologist and expert in vocational rehabilitation" to testify that plaintiff suffers permanent 50 to 60% vocational disabilities as a result of the fall. How should plaintiff and defendant argue the *Daubert* issue here? What factors should the court consider in deciding whether the *Daubert* standard is met? See Elcock v. KMart Corp., 233 F.3d 734, 746-748 (3d Cir. 2000) (*C* gave plaintiff IQ and aptitude tests, considered her work history, and consulted Directory of Occupational Titles in reaching conclusion; *C* used combined procedures drawn from Fields and Gamboa, but did not explain in detail how he reached the 50 to 60% figure or why he changed from prior

---

8.   For more scholarly developments of these themes, see Huber, Safety and the Second Best: The Hazards of Public Risk Management in the Courts, 85 Colum. L. Rev. 277 (1985); Epstein, The Legal and Insurance Dynamics of Mass Tort Litigation, 13 J. Legal Stud. 475 (1984).

assessment of 50 to 75% disability; Fields and Gamboa developed "accepted methodologies," but "novel synthesis of the two methodologies" paved the way for a subjective judgment; *Daubert* hearing would have provided better opportunity to probe particulars and assess methods) (reversing judgment for plaintiff).

6.   Consider the task that *Daubert* sets for trial judges, and the "discretion" that finds such emphasis in *Kumho Tire:*

(a)   *Daubert* says the trial judge should look not only at "reasoning or methodology," but *application* of reasoning and methodology. The focus is the "task at hand," not the broad contours of scientific theory or methods. *Kumho Tire* stresses the same point: There the question "was not the reasonableness in general of a tire expert's use of visual and tactile inspection," but the reasonableness of the method and approach "regarding the *particular matter*" to which the expert testified. That means that the trial judge is supposed to take a pretty close look, doesn't it?

(b)   *Kumho Tire* also stresses that the trial judge has discretion—not only in deciding whether any particular criterion is satisfied, but also in deciding *what criteria* to apply in the first place. *Kumho Tire* was not the first Supreme Court follow-up on *Daubert*. The first was General Electric Co. Joiner, 522 U.S. 166 (1997), 509 U.S. 579 (1993), which rejected the view that a decision *excluding* scientific evidence was subject to a "particularly stringent" standard of review. Instead, the Court held that an ordinary "abuse of discretion" standard applies. The emphasis on "discretion" really began in *Joiner,* and the term is hardly mentioned at all in *Daubert*. In effect, *Joiner* endorsed a discretionary standard to insure that *Daubert* would actually require courts to take a "close look" at science. Is it really wise to interpret *Daubert* as creating a rule of judicial discretion?

(c)   That concept is usually invoked in connection with the most general principles, such as those embodied in FRE 403 (weighing probative value against unfair prejudice) and 611 (controlling the mode and order of presentation in order to make it effective and efficient, and to protect witnesses). And the concept of discretion is invoked where we think trial judges can do as well or better than reviewing courts. But *Daubert* sets out a multifactor standard that is more detailed and particular than FRE 403 and 611, doesn't it? Don't *Daubert* and *Kumho Tire*, taken together, tell trial judges that "you must be very careful, but we won't look too hard at what you do?"

(d)   Consider the possibility that it was necessary in *Kumho Tire* to construe *Daubert* as a discretionary standard in order to explain how *Daubert* can be applied across the board to technical expertise. Note the example of "a perfume tester able to distinguish among 140 odors at a sniff," where it would seem futile to ask for much peer reviews, technical standards, or information about error rates. Does broadening *Daubert* require diluting its rigor? Surely *Kumho Tire* does not mean, does it, that when an epidemiologist testifies on causation issues (as in *Daubert* itself), the trial judge is free to decide not to ask about peer reviews, technical standards, or error rates?

7.   Not surprisingly, modern federal opinions reviewing *Daubert* stress that they will reverse only for abuse of discretion. In many states, the practice is similar, but not universal. Decisions in at least nine states and the District of Columbia endorse far more searching appellate review. See, e.g., Schultz v.

States, 664 A.2d 60, 64 (Md. App. 1994) (question of reliability of scientific technique "does not vary according to the circumstances of each case," so it is inappropriate to apply abuse of discretion standard on review). There is no reason, is there, to think trial judges can better appraise the validity of science than appellate judges? For an argument that appellate courts should exercise more scrutiny over what trial judges do, see Christopher Mueller, Daubert Asks the Right Questions: Now Appellate Courts Should Help Find the Right Answers, 33 Seton Hall L. Rev. 987 (2003).

8. Consider amended FRE 702. Paraphrasing, the new language says expert testimony must be "sufficiently based upon reliable facts or data," and must be "the product of reliable principles and methods" that are "applied reliably to the facts." Does this amendment capture the tasks described in *Daubert* and *Kumho Tire*? The idea of a sufficient basis is at best implicit in *Daubert*, but it is reasonable, isn't it, to require a sufficient basis as part of an overall assessment of reliability? *Daubert* holds that trial judges perform the "gatekeeping" role under FRE 104(a), and the new language in FRE 702 looks very much like specifications of admissibility. Hence it seems that trial judges determine these matters, and not juries under FRE 104(b) (describing conditional relevancy). The question whether technicians followed laboratory protocol determines whether principles and methods were "reliably applied to the facts," doesn't it? That means that trial judges determine this point as a matter affecting "admissibility," rather than juries determining it as a matter of "weight." Although the ACN does not reflect this point, modern cases had split on this point. Compare United States v. Martinez, 3 F.3d 1191, 1197 (8th Cir. 1993) (under *Daubert*, court should require expert to show that he "properly performed the protocols involved in DNA profiling") with United States v. Chischilly, 30 F.3d 1144, 1154 (9th Cir. 1994) (questions relating to conduct of lab procedures go to weight, not admissibility). For an argument that indeed *courts* rather than juries should perform this roll, see Edward J. Imwinkelried, The Debate in the DNA Cases Over the Foundation for the Admission of Scientific Evidence: The Importance of Human Error as a Cause of Forensic Misanalysis, 69 Wash. U. L. Q. 19 (1991) (matters of laboratory protocol should affect admissibility, not just weight).

9. When cutting-edge science is offered, *Daubert* means the trial judge should determine issues of validity in a pretrial hearing, doesn't it? Such hearings can be major undertakings. In United States v. Bonds, 12 F.3d 540, 558-560 (6th Cir. 1993), the trial judge assigned to a magistrate the task of appraising DNA testing of blood in an FBI laboratory. The hearing took six weeks. The magistrate issued a 120-page report recommending in favor of the evidence, and the reviewing court affirmed a conspiracy conviction and approved the evidence under *Daubert*. Isn't it clear that such a mammoth inquiry cannot be undertaken every time the government wants to offer this kind of proof? Must the next court undertake a similar inquiry?

10. When scientific evidence is statistical, does it matter whether the results would be viewed as significant in the scientific community? The convention in this community is to insist on results that are so strong that there is only a 5 percent likelihood that the observed correlation, which itself might be large (like a 50 percent increase in ailment from exposure) or slight (like an 8 percent increase in ailment from exposure), is the result of chance or accident. Should courts content themselves with less persuasive evidence be-

cause courts, unlike scientists and scholars, must answer today's questions today and cannot wait for better results? Professor Cohen argues that a scientist should be allowed to testify that, although the correlation would not satisfy the usual required level of statistical significance (p = .05), still the scientist herself finds the reported correlation persuasive, and might base her own personal decision on that finding. See Neil Cohen, The Gatekeeping Role in Civil Litigation and the Abdication of Legal Values in Favor of Scientific Values, 33 Seton Hall L. Rev. 943 (2003). In thinking about this question, don't equate the conventional level of statistical significance with the certainty of the conclusion:

> [T]he conventional standard does *not* mean that science usually accepts only results that are 95% certain. Statistical significance at the level of p = .05 means that there is but one chance in 20 that the observed results could happen by chance. *Satisfying* the standard means that there is one chance in 20 (or less) that mere accidental variation would produce such a result, not that we can be 95% certain that the outcome (22 out of 42 observed ailments were caused by exposure, or 16 out of 36, as Examples 1 and 3 indicate) is correct. We do not and cannot know that. All we know is that the observed outcome would rarely be produced by chance alone, which gives us *some reason* to believe that the indicated correlation is correct. Any suggestion, however, that the conventional standard produces results of which we are 95% certain is false.

Christopher Mueller, Daubert Asks the Right Questions: Now Appellate Courts Should Help Find the Right Answers, 33 Seton Hall L. Rev. 987, 1013 (2003) (acknowledging that "we should consider carefully the possibility of accepting results in lawsuits that scientists are not yet prepared to accept," but stating reservations). In yet another Bendectin case, the same court that decided *Downing* refused to endorse the conventional academic standard of statistical significance. See DeLuca v. Merrell Dow Pharmaceuticals, Inc., 911 F.2d 941, 955 (3d Cir. 1990) (court erred in excluding testimony by pediatric pharmacologist based on analysis of epidemiological evidence, that Bendectin is teratogenic; while p-value in studies exceeds .05 and it is common to reject such results as statistically insignificant, confidence levels and statistical significance "is but a part of a meaningful evaluation" of the validity of scientific evidence). And see generally Nesson, Agent Orange Meets the Blue Bus: Factfinding at the Frontier of Knowledge, 66 B.U. L. Rev. 521, 529-530 (1986) (scientist exploring hypothesis that toxic agent causes cancer is "likely to suspend scientific judgment" until testing or study can eliminate alternative hypotheses; doctor, lawyer, or judge "often does not have the luxury of postponing a decision" and juries are expected to reach conclusions "without insisting or waiting for scientific demonstration"). But see Allen, Rationality, Mythology, and the "Acceptability of Verdicts" Thesis, 66 B.U. L. Rev. 541, 561-562 (1986) (judicial decisions should not be allowed to depart from reality as best we can reconstruct it; judicial system "should continue to strive for rationality").

2. Modern Science in the Courtroom

Even to survey the field of scientific evidence with a sample of cases from each area would make this book much too long. Standard and useful technical sources address these areas in detail, offering both scientific and legal insights.[9] Suffice it to say that forensic evidence relating to ballistics, fingerprints, blood typing, intoxication, footprints, analysis of hair and human tissue, testing of matter by neutron activation analysis, and innumerable other subjects have become staples in the trial process.

Outside such settled areas, however, scientific evidence sometimes presents great challenge to courts. Questions of causation in toxic tort cases like *Daubert* have proven very difficult. The same is true of "syndrome" evidence developed by psychologists working with the techniques of social science, which has become commonplace in prosecutions for child abuse, sexual assault, and sometimes domestic violence cases. A third area of considerable challenge is the presentation and assessment of DNA evidence in criminal cases as illustrated by the closely watched murder trial of O.J. Simpson in 1995. And with DNA evidence comes statistics (which play a role in toxic tort cases too), which in turn can lead to Bayesian estimates of the likelihood that important propositions are true, as is most visible in paternity cases. (See the discussion of Bayesian analysis in pages 659-666, infra.) To these areas we now briefly turn.

a. Toxic Tort Cases

In toxic tort cases like *Daubert*, part of the problem is that science often has no answer to the crucial question. Proof of causation usually takes the form of cluster studies (people in the exposed area experience higher rates of illness), short-term screening assays (testing the effects of chemicals on bacteria or cells in culture dishes), "differential diagnosis" (by process of elimination, doctor concludes that only exposure to the agent in question could account for the ailment), animal studies, and epidemiology (statistical analyses of disease incidence). The first three kinds of proof can be obtained relatively quickly and cheaply, but the latter two are expensive and take a long time to develop.

The strength of epidemiological evidence, which is in some respects the most persuasive kind, varies widely in ways requiring the skills of a statistician to explain. One great difficulty in all such proof is that it typically leaves the question of causation in any particular case unanswered. The problem for the factfinder is compounded when issues of multiple or synergistic causation appear (did asbestos cause lung cancer, or was smoking the cause, or both?). Another difficulty in such proof is that it often shows only an increase in ailments from exposure (20 out of 1,000 unexposed people suffer the ailment; 35 out of 1,000 exposed people suffer the ailment), which suggests "general" or "possible" cause, but cannot support an inference of cause in any particular case. To support an inference that a particular person caught the ailment from the exposure, the proof must show at least a "doubling" of risk (20 out of

---

9.   See D. Faigman, D. Kaye, M. Saks and J. Sanders, Modern Scientific Evidence (1997); P. Gianelli and E. Imwinkelried, Scientific Evidence (2d ed. 1993); A. Moenssens, F. Inbau and J. Starrs, Scientific Evidence in Criminal Cases (3d ed. 1986); Jane Campbell Moriarty, Psychological and Scientific Evidence in Criminal Trials (2002). For a brief account of issues of scientific proof, see also Reference Manual on Scientific Evidence (Federal Judicial Center 1994).

1,000 unexposed people suffer the ailment; 50 out of 1,000 exposed people suffer the ailment).

The increased scrutiny of such proof, which *Daubert* clearly invites, has led to increased use of motions for summary judgment to throw out cases that depend on unproven science. Some have criticized this development; see Margaret A. Berger, Upsetting the Balance Between Adverse Interests: The Impact of the Supreme Court's Trilogy on Expert Testimony in Toxic Tort Litigation, 64 L. & Contemp. Problems 289 (2001) (opinions applying *Daubert* mistakenly require epidemiological evidence to prove a doubling of risk; federal courts should look to state requirements for proving causation); Lucinda Finley, Guarding the Gate to the Courthouse: How Trial Judges are Using their Evidentiary Screening Role to Remake Tort Causation Rules, 49 DePaul L. Rev. 335 (1999) (courts should not place burden of scientific uncertainty on plaintiffs). For a defense of *Daubert* in this setting, see Joseph Sanders, The Paternalistic Justification for Restrictions on the Admissibility of Expert Evidence, 33 Seton Hall L. Rev. 881 (2003) (judges can better appraise science than juries); Christopher Mueller, Daubert Asks the Right Questions: Now Appellate Courts Should Help Find the Right Answers, 33 Seton Hall L. Rev. 987, 993 (2003) (*Daubert* is wise to place this decision in the hands of judges).

Proposals to address these problems are varied and imaginative, and they often involve procedural mechanisms like class actions to consolidate claims, the use of statistics to prove general causation, some form of proportional recovery, and the creation of funds to compensate victims. But the road has been rocky, and the more innovative reforms have not been adopted. Several times the Supreme Court has warned that class suits may not be capable of reaching global solutions to these problems. See, e.g., Ortiz v. Fibreboard Corp., 527 U.S. 815 (1999) (in asbestos, disapproving proposed settlement because, among other things, interests of claimants covered by settlement were too disparate); Amchem Products, Inc. v. Windsor, 521 U.S. 591 (1997) (disapproving relaxation of requirements for class suit in connection with "settlement class"). Congress has not yet stepped into the picture, although legislative proposals to resolve massive cases routinely appear.

Modest reform of civil discovery rules has at least made expert testimony more readily discoverable than it had previously been. Now FRCP 26(a)(2) requires every civil litigant automatically to identify "any person who may be used at trial" as an expert witness. In most cases, each litigant is also to supply "a written report prepared and signed" by the expert containing "a complete statement of all opinions to be expressed and the basis and reasons therefor," along with "data or other information" considered by the witness, exhibits used to summarize or support the opinions, "a list of all publications" written by the witness within the last ten years, details on compensation, and a list of other cases where the witness has testified as an expert within the previous four years.

b. Syndrome and Social Framework Evidence

In the 1990s, expert testimony describing behavioral syndromes and social frameworks came of age. In at least three settings such proof has become commonplace, although controversy and disagreement continue on points of detail.

In child abuse prosecutions, courts often admit testimony describing battered child syndrome (BCS) or child sexual abuse accommodation syndrome (CSAAS). In the sexual abuse cases, experts describe delays in reporting and initial reporting of only part of what happened, behavioral problems at school, vomiting, sexualized play, and regression in toilet training (among younger children), disclosure to a friend, withdrawal and daydreaming, and low self-esteem (among older children). See L.C.H. v. T.S., 28 P.3d 915 (Alaska 2001) (in victim's civil suit against step-grandfather, admitting profile testimony in child sexual abuse case, but only to refute defense claims that conduct of child was inconsistent with abuse); State v. Edelman, 593 N.W.2d 419, 423 (S.D. 1999) (testimony on CSAAS satisfied *Daubert* standard; here witness described the following symptoms: initial disclosure of only part of what happened; changes in later accounts; sense of helplessness and entrapment). Less often, similar testimony is offered in prosecutions of children for killing parents. See, e.g., State v. Nemeth, 694 N.E.2d 1332, 1335 (Ohio 1998) (in trial of 16-year-old boy for killing his mother with bow and arrow, admitting expert testimony on battered child syndrome, which shed light on question whether he acted with requisite state of mind). Courts often comment, however, that such experts should not say either that the child was abused in this particular case or that the child's account is truthful or correct. See State v. Huntington, 575 N.W.2d 268, 278 (Wis. 1998) (expert cannot testify that child is telling the truth, but may testify that delayed disclosure, as happened here, is to be expected); Commonwealth v. Federico, 683 N.E.2d 1035 (Mass. 1997) (reversing conviction for sexual abuse of child for error in letting expert testify in effect that abuse had occurred).

In sexual assault trials, courts often admit evidence of "rape trauma syndrome" (RTS) to help assess conduct by the victim after the fact and evaluate defense claims of consent. See People v. Hampton, 746 P.2d 947, 951-954 (Colo. 1987) (psychologist describes pattern of emotional adjustment in rape victims, which could help jury assess delay in reporting) (should not argue that reaction "paralleled" typical victims, but could use it to "corroborate her testimony"). Courts have tended not to allow use of RTS to prove that an attack (or criminal penetration) occurred. See People v. Taylor, 552 N.E.2d 131 (N.Y. 1990); People v. Bledsoe, 681 P.2d 291 (Cal. 1984).

Finally, in trials of men for beating women in intimate relationships and in trials of women for killing men in such relationships (where the issue is typically self-defense), courts often admit evidence of battered woman syndrome (BWS) to shed light on the behavior of the woman. See State v. Vega, 788 A.2d 1221, 1234 (Conn. 2001) (in trial of man for kidnapping and assaulting his girlfriend, admitting testimony on BWS), cert. denied, 537 U.S. 836 (2002); Truhillo v. State, 953 P.2d 1182 (Wyo. 1998) (in trial of man for kidnapping and aggravated assault against girlfriend, admitting testimony on BWS to explain her behavior); State v. Grecinger, 569 N.W.2d 189, 194-195 (Minn. 1997) (admitting BWS in trial of husband for attempted murder and assault against wife, to explain her behavior in remaining in relationship, telling contradictory stories, and waiting three years before going to police).

When such testimony describes generalized behavioral patterns based on observing many people, the term "social framework" seems an appropriate description. In terms of the criteria in FRE 702, the important questions are whether the expert has an adequate basis in observation and theory and whether the jury needs the kind of help an expert can provide.

When such testimony describes the behavior of a crime victim or criminal defendant, the term "social framework" is no longer accurate, and syndrome evidence draws close to being character evidence of the sort regulated by FRE 404 and 405. As you recall, the latter restrict the use of character to prove conduct, although they are generous in allowing defendants to try to show their innocence by proof of good character. Unlike typical character witnesses, however, where the testifying witness learned what she knows before the events in suit, expert witnesses usually glean what they know afterward and are usually looking for (even expecting to find) confirmation of alleged events.

When expert testimony comments on the credibility of crime victims or criminal defendants, it draws close to being character evidence of the sort regulated by FRE 608. See State v. Grecinger, 569 N.W.2d 189, 193-194 (Minn. 1997) (in trial of man for attempted murder and battery against intimate companion, admitting expert testimony on BWS under MRE 608 as bearing on her veracity). While the latter allows opinion evidence, it typically blocks proof of *good* character until the other side has brought credibility into question. And once again, the expert who describes syndromes with specific reference to a criminal defendant or victim has typically gleaned what she knows after the fact and not by being acquainted with the subject for some period before the events in suit.

Consider now what such testimony may look like in a child sexual abuse case.

PROBLEM 9-E. *"They Become Anxious and Guilt-Ridden"*

Art Milton is charged with sexual assault on his 14-year-old daughter Sandra, which allegedly took place on the morning of December 22, 2002, in the family home. Jean Milton (Art's wife and Sandra's mother) was out at the time, as was Sandra's sister Terri (age 16). Art Milton has pleaded innocent.

At trial Sandra testifies that Art Milton ordered her to hold still while he removed her clothes and touched her between her legs and "did what I know he does to mom." Under questioning by the district attorney, Sandra states that Milton had touched her similarly on other occasions and describes what seems to have been rape or attempted rape, although she is not entirely sure whether penetration was accomplished.

During defense cross-examination, Sandra concedes that in February 2003 she wrote out a statement indicating that she had lied about the incident. At that time she explained her accusations as having been motivated by her desire "to be able to stay out at night like other girls my age," and she added that "after I reported it to the social worker and the prosecutor, everybody has been pushing me really hard to stick to the story, which isn't true."

Art Milton testifies that Sandra had gotten in trouble in school for truancy and for stealing money and shoplifting, and that she had run away from home several times. He also testifies to facts suggesting that Terri too resents "the

10:00 curfew we insist on during the week, and 11:30 on weekends," and that Terri may have pressured Sandra "to get me in trouble."

During its case-in-rebuttal, the prosecutor calls a Dr. Clara Burton, a clinical psychologist:

Q [prosecutor]:   Dr. Burton, how long have you worked with domestic sex abuse?
A [Burton]:   A little over 12 years.
Q: And how many sexually abused children have you seen in that time?
A: Between three and four hundred.
Q: So you are familiar with the behavior patterns of such children?
A: Oh yes, very much so.
Q: Could you describe it, please?
Q [defense]:   Objection, Your Honor. May we approach the bench?

The jury is excused, and the following discussion takes place:

Defense counsel: Your Honor, we object to Dr. Burton's testimony for many reasons:
    First, there is no model of behavior for sexually abused children that is accepted by psychologists or reliable enough for use in a criminal prosecution. In short, this testimony cannot satisfy the *Daubert* standard.
    Second, if Dr. Burton is allowed to testify, she will be taking the case away from the jury, invading the jury's province and testifying on the very question which the jury has to decide—who is telling the truth here.
    Third, the jury doesn't need help appraising Sandra's behavior, and what Dr. Burton has to say cannot help. Either she's going to talk in generalities about how *most* abused children behave or she's going to speculate about what did or did not happen to Sandra.
    Fourth, it is axiomatic that credibility issues are for the jury to decide. Juries don't need help deciding who to believe.
    Fifth, if we let Dr. Burton testify, the jury won't know how to evaluate what she has to say. She'll snow them with her expertise, and they, the common people on the jury, will just throw in the sponge.
Prosecutor: Your Honor, the question is whether Dr. Burton is a qualified expert, and whether the underlying theories and technique are reliable under *Daubert.* Dr. Burton is qualified, and she can help. The defense has suggested in lots of ways that Sandra is just lying, and the jury doesn't know how to evaluate that. Could we just put Dr. Burton on the stand now, and make a proffer of what she would testify to?
Court: Go ahead.
Dr. Burton: Well, I would say that what Sandra did in this case is characteristic of sexually abused children. What happens is that they become anxious and guilt-ridden. They actually carry a heavy burden of guilt, thinking that it was somehow their fault. They often retract what they say at first because they realize that the guilty party is their parent, and they still care for them. Sandra fits the pattern exactly. Another thing is that children in Sandra's position worry that they might be blamed or punished, and that they might break up the family. Often children like Sandra don't trust their mother. I can also say that it's extremely rare for children to make up stories of this sort. We have many studies that confirm all these points, and they are reliable and generally accepted in the professional community.

How should the judge rule in this case, and why?

NOTES ON SYNDROME AND FRAMEWORK EVIDENCE

1. Do jurors need help understanding battered or sexually abused children? See People v. McAlpin, 812 P.2d 563, 570-571 (Cal. 1991) (describing myths surrounding child abuse). Is the same true of battered women? See State v. Vega, 788 A.2d 1221, 1234 (Conn. 2001) ("although battered women's syndrome has become known to the public more widely than it was in the past, much of the subject still remains beyond the ken of the average juror"), cert. denied, 537 U.S. 836 (2002); State v. Koss, 551 N.E.2d 970, 974 (Ohio 1990) (describing general misconceptions relating to battered women). Rape victims? See People v. Taylor, 552 N.E.2d 131, 136 (N.Y. 1990) (describing cultural myths relating to rape). If jurors need help, is it because they lack experience in human relationships generally? In abuse, or battering, or rape? In arson or murder trials, should jurors be brought up to speed on the effects of these crimes on victims or on the social factors that lead arsonists or murderers toward committing such crimes? On the pressures of inner city life when gang members are charged with violent crimes?

2. If experts give syndrome evidence in child abuse cases, should they use terms like "battered child syndrome"? Should they say the victim suffers from (or exhibits) this syndrome? In the other settings described above, should experts use the terms "battered woman syndrome" and "rape trauma syndrome"? Should experts say the particular woman suffers from (or exhibits) the syndrome? Courts have tended to say no. Why? See Commonwealth v. Craig, 783 S.W.2d 387, 389 (Ky. 1990) (should not say whether shooting was "result" of BWS); State v. Gettier, 438 N.W.2d 1, 5-6 (Iowa 1989) (should not use RTS label).

3. Absent clinical symptoms, do experts understand children well enough to know whether they were likely beaten or sexually abused? Compare United States v. St. Pierre, 812 F.2d 417, 419-420 (8th Cir. 1987) (scientific community recognizes "certain emotional and psychological characteristics" in sexually abused children) with Miller v. Commonwealth, 77 S.W.2d 566 (Ky. 2002) (CSAAS is not a diagnosis generally accepted in the relevant scientific community, and may invade province of jury; one may not introduce "evidence of the habit of a class of individuals either to prove that another member of the class acted the same way under similar circumstances or to prove that the person was a member of that class because he/she acted the same way"). Do experts understand women well enough to know whether they were likely raped? See People v. Bledsoe, 681 P.2d 291 (Cal. 1984) (RTS was devised as "therapeutic tool" to identify and treat emotional problems; counselors try to help rape victims deal with trauma, and accuracy of their descriptions is not "vital" to the task; rape counselors try to avoid credibility judgments and do not probe inconsistencies) (RTS inadmissible to show rape). If Bledsoe is right that RTS is a therapeutic rather than an investigative technique, does it follow that such evidence should be excluded altogether?

4. As the cases illustrate, syndrome evidence can help the prosecution or the defense. In trials for abuse of children or battery against women, usually the evidence relates to the behavior of the victim. In trials of women for killing intimate male companions, syndrome evidence often describes the defendant

and supports the claim of self-defense. See State v. Koss, 551 N.E.2d 970, 974-975 (Ohio 1990). Should similar evidence be admitted when it relates to behavioral patterns of the defendant and supports the claim that he did the deed? See, e.g., United States v. Long, 328 F.3d 655, 667-669 (D.C. Cir. 2003) (in trial for transporting a minor for purposes of engaging in criminal sexual activity, admitting expert testimony on modus operandi of "preferential sex offenders," describing their "typology, identification, characteristics, and strategies," as well as "characteristics and behavior of child victims of sexual abuse"). In the 1995 trial of O.J. Simpson for the double homicide of Nicole Brown and Ronald Goldman, the prosecutor contemplated offering expert testimony describing patterns of domestic abuse. The trial court reserved its ruling, and the evidence was not offered. Should such proof be allowed?

5. In 1974 the California Evidence Code was amended to add language making expert testimony on "battered women's syndrome" admissible for the state or the defense "except when offered against a criminal defendant to prove the occurrence of the act or acts of abuse which form the basis of the criminal charge." See Cal. Evid. Code §1107. This provision means, doesn't it, that expert testimony of this sort is inadmissible in the setting of the Simpson trial? The statute describes BWS as including "physical, emotional or mental effects upon the beliefs, perceptions, or behavior of victims of domestic violence." Does the statute cover "battering man syndrome" evidence (BMS) if such proof relates to patterns of behavior observed in men who beat or abuse women in intimate relationships? To the extent that BWS evidence is admissible, does it follow that BMS evidence is admissible?

6. Isn't it clear, at least after *Kumho Tire*, that syndrome evidence must satisfy the scientific validity standard of *Daubert*? On this point, compare United States v. Hadley, 918 F.2d 848, 852-853 (9th Cir. 1990) (psychiatric testimony on behavioral patterns in sexually abused children need not satisfy pre-*Daubert* standard of *Frye*) and Cal. Evid. Code §1107 (BWS "shall not be considered a new scientific technique whose reliability is unproven" if expert is properly qualified) with United States v. Amador-Galvan, 9 F.3d 1414, 1417-1418 (9th Cir. 1993) (remanding so trial court can apply *Daubert* in ruling on motion to admit expert testimony on reliability of eyewitness identification). If syndrome evidence rested on common observation, there would be no need for expert testimony, would there? If it rests on knowledge that only trained social scientists have, isn't it science?

7. How about admitting other kinds of psychological profiles to aid the defense? See State v. Davis, 645 N.W.2d 913 (Wis. 2002) (in trial for illegal sexual contact with a minor, defendant may offer expert testimony that he lacks the psychological characteristics typical of such offenders, but must give pretrial notice, and prosecutor may seek to compel an examination of the accused by its own expert; privilege against self-incrimination may be waived to the extent necessary to enable prosecutor to meet the defense evidence); United States v. Rahm, 993 F.2d 1405, 1409-1410 (9th Cir. 1993) (in trial for possessing counterfeit currency, error to exclude defense expert testimony based on Wechsler Adult Intelligence Scale and Minnesota Multiphasic Personality Inventory that defendant's intelligence was average but her scores on subtests were below average and indicated a tendency to overlook visual details). How about admitting such proof to help the state? See United States v. Gillespie, 852 F.2d 475,

479-481 (9th Cir. 1988) (in trial for sexual assault of minor, error to admit testimony describing "characteristics common to child molesters").

c. DNA Evidence

Courts in most states now admit scientific evidence based on analysis of deoxyribonucleic acid (DNA). DNA evidence, sometimes popularly described as genetic profiling (or "gene mapping" or "genetic fingerprinting"), offers the possibility of finding a "match" or "nonmatch" between tissue or fluid samples of unknown origin and known exemplars. In forms that are highly variable and individualized, DNA is found in most human tissue and fluids, from saliva to blood to semen, and in fingernails, skin, and hair. In any one person, DNA extracted from *any* and *all* such samples shows a pattern that differs from the pattern that would be seen in similar samples from most other people.

In criminal trials, especially rape and homicide prosecutions, DNA evidence can be powerfully incriminating (or exculpatory). In the California murder trial of O.J. Simpson in 1995, DNA linked the defendant to the scene and the victims to the defendant (blood found in his car and on a glove at his residence matched that of the victims'). In the typical clinical setting of a paternity suit, analyzing DNA extracted from blood samples taken from the child and from the mother can yield precise information on the nature of the DNA that the child's father must have.[10]

The technical and evidentiary challenges to proof in this form are daunting. In 1992, the National Research Council published a report prepared by a committee of scientists and jurists, see DNA Technology in Forensic Science (1992) (*NRC Report*). This study made numerous recommendations for handling DNA Evidence, and the Report had considerable impact on modern decisions. In 1996 the NRC published a followup study that revisits areas of difficulty, see The Evaluation of Forensic DNA Evidence (1996) (*NRC Update*). This study too has had considerable impact.

The following excerpt from the landmark Montana decision in *Moore* presents a lucid description of technical concepts. Read this account to get your sea legs. Then use Problem 9-F ("We Found a Match") and the following Notes on DNA Evidence in Criminal Cases to consider the evidentiary issues that come with such proof.

STATE v. MOORE
Supreme Court of Montana
885 P.2d 457 (1994)

[Larry Moore was charged with the murder of Brad Brisbin, who disappeared without trace on the morning of November 9, 1990. No body was recovered,

---

10. Analyzing HLA (human leucocyte antigen) in blood drawn from the child and blood drawn from the mother yields similar information (HLA pattern that the father must have). Both HLA and DNA analysis can exclude a man from fatherhood to a scientific certainty. Since particular

but Brad Brisbin's wife Rene testified that Brad had said Moore had called and asked to meet him at a truckstop. There was proof that Brisbin headed up Gallatin Canyon toward West Yellowstone, and that Moore returned from that direction in his truck sometime later. Moore made inconsistent statements about Brisbin, commenting at first that he had seen Brisbin climb into a car with a woman on the morning he disappeared, and that Brisbin and Moore had been together, that Brisbin had an accident with a gun in Moore's truck, and that Moore had then driven off with an unknown woman.

Before trial the defense moved to exclude all DNA evidence, but the court denied the motion. The defense then moved to exclude testimony describing statistical calculations "which would have presented a probability that any alleged match between the tissue samples and the Brisbin children is not coincidental." The trial court granted this motion.

The court admitted DNA analyses of human blood and small pieces of human muscle and brain tissue found in the cab of the defendant's truck. Cellmark Diagnostics conducted RFLP analysis ("restriction fragment length polymorphism") on a muscle fragment and the Analytic Genetic Testing Center (AGTC) performed PCR analysis ("polymerase chain reaction") on another muscle fragment and the cerebellum tissue. An expert from AGTC testified that the samples it analyzed "could not be excluded as having come from the biological father" of Brad Brisbin's children. An expert from Cellmark testified that DNA in the muscle tissue was "consistent with" that of Brad Brisbin's mother.

The Montana Supreme Court provides the following account of the theory and some aspects of the testing process:]

DNA is a fundamental material, which determines the genetic properties of all living things. All nucleated cells of every human being contain DNA, and every cell of a particular individual contains the same configuration of DNA. The significance of DNA for forensic purposes is that, with the exception of identical twins, no two individuals have identical DNA. Another important fundamental aspect of human genetics is that, except for unusual but recognized occurrences of mutation, offspring inherit genes from their parents, receiving one-half from the mother and one-half from the father.

The DNA molecule is composed of a long double helix, which looks like a twisted ladder. The sides of the ladder are made up of alternating units of phosphate and sugar. Attached to the sides of the ladder are the rungs, which are made up of four types of organic bases: adenine, guanine, cytosine, and thymine. Due to their chemical compositions, adenine will only bond with thymine, and cytosine will only bond with guanine. Thus, the bases on one side of the rung will determine the order on the other side. For the purpose of DNA profiling, these base pairs are the critical components of the ladder. It is the order or sequence of the base pairs (the rungs) that determines the genetic

patterns of HLA and DNA are often very rare, a "match" between the pattern that a child must have inherited from his father and the pattern observed in a particular man can suggest very strongly that the man is the father, but cannot prove the point to a certainty. Both HLA and DNA analysis can produce a "paternity index" (or "probability of paternity"), and the use of such evidence in that way is examined below in subsection d.

traits of an individual life form and each human being. A specific sequence of base pairs that is responsible for a particular trait is called a gene.

Genetically, humans are more alike than dissimilar. Approximately 99 percent of human DNA molecules, i.e., base pair sequences, are the same, creating such shared features as arms and legs. Other sections of the DNA ladder, however, vary distinctly from one person to another. It is these variable regions, called "polymorphisms," which make it possible to establish identity and differences between individuals.

The length of each polymorphism is determined by the number of repeat core sequences of base pairs. The core sequence is called a Variable Number Tandem Repeat (VNTR) while the total fragment length is called a Restriction Fragment Length Polymorphism (RFLP). Alternative forms of RFLP's are called alleles.

A particular region on the DNA molecule where a specific VNTR occurs is called a "locus." A locus is considered polymorphic when the number of VNTR's varies from one person to another. Of the approximately three billion base pairs contained in one DNA molecule, roughly three million are thought to be polymorphic. DNA profiling focuses on several highly polymorphic or hypervariable segments of the DNA. Different people will have the same VNTRs in a particular hypervariable locus, but the loci will differ in length because varying numbers of the VNTRs are linked together. Although a person may not have a unique polymorphic area at any one locus, the frequency with which two people will exhibit eight or ten of these alleles at four or five different locations is extremely low. Thus DNA analysis attempts to detect these highly variable regions and distinguish among the alleles that exist there.

At the time the testing was conducted in this case, there were two technologies generally used in forensic DNA analysis to detect the polymorphic regions: restriction fragment length polymorphism (RFLP), and polymerase chain reaction (PCR). Both methods were employed in this case.

RFLP ANALYSIS

As is explained in [several cases], RFLP analysis involves several steps.

1. Extraction of DNA. The DNA must be extracted from the evidentiary sample by using chemical enzymes. An enzyme is then added to digest cellular material that is not DNA, thereby providing a purer sample.

2. Restriction or Digestion. The DNA is then mixed with restriction enzymes which cut the DNA molecules into fragments at specific base sequences. The restriction enzymes recognize particular sequences of base pairs. The enzymes sever the DNA molecule at targeted locations within the sequence. The process severs the DNA molecule at all sites targeted at locations along the three billion base pair length of the molecule. Therefore, some of the resulting "restriction fragments" will contain polymorphic DNA segments, although most will not. Because the alleles differ markedly in length from one person to the next, the restriction fragments containing the alleles will also differ in length.

3. Gel Electrophoresis. This technique entails placing the DNA fragments into an agarose gel which has a negative and positive electrode at either end. An electrical current is then run through the gel. The restriction fragments,

which are negatively charged in their natural state, travel toward the positive charge. The process is able to sort the restriction enzymes by length, as the shorter fragments—which are lighter and less bulky—will travel further in the gel. Several samples are run on the gel but in different tracks or lanes which run parallel to each other. In addition to the samples, fragments of known base-pair lengths are placed in separate lanes to facilitate measurement.

4.   Southern Transfer. This procedure transfers the fragments to a more functional surface. A nylon membrane is placed over the gel and, through capillary action, the DNA fragments attach themselves to the membrane while occupying the same position relative to one another as they had on the gel. The restriction fragments are then treated with a chemical which cuts the fragments of DNA lengthwise along each base pair, by sawing through the middle of each rung. The result is a collection of single stranded restriction fragments.

5.   Hybridization. The nylon membrane is dipped into a solution containing various "genetic probes," which are single stranded DNA fragments of known length and sequence designed to link with identified polymorphic alleles. The probes will link only to those DNA fragments which contain base pair sequences that are complementary to the base sequences of the probe. The genetic probes are tagged with a radioactive marker so that after the probe links with a particular allele, its position relative to the other restriction fragments can be observed.

6.   Autoradiography. The nylon membrane is placed on an x-ray film and exposed by the radioactively charge probes. The result is a pattern of bands called an "autoradiograph," or "autorad." Each band represents a different polymorphic allele, and its position indicates the length of the restriction fragment in which that allele occurs. Because individuals differ in length of their polymorphic alleles, the position of the bands on the DNA prints will tend to differ from person to person.

7.   Interpretation of the DNA Print. The DNA print of the crime sample and the DNA print of the defendant are then compared both visually and with a machine to determine if both samples of DNA came from the same person. A match will be declared if the samples fall within a certain distance of one another. Cellmark Diagnostics, the laboratory conducting the RFLP analysis in this case, will declare a match if the bands from two DNA prints fall within one millimeter of each other.

8.   Statistical Analysis. Statistical analysis is used in both RFLP and PCR analysis. If the two DNA samples match, then population geneticists determine the likelihood that the match is unique. The scientists determine the frequency with which a particular allele is found in the population, then by using a multiplication or product rule, compute an aggregate estimate of the statistical probability that the suspect's combination of alleles would be found in the relevant racial population.

[The trial court properly admitted the DNA testimony. By requesting exclusion of statistics, the defense waived the claim that DNA evidence should not be admitted without statistical correlations, the question whether such proof should be presented without statistics in other cases is reserved. DNA evidence satisfies the *Daubert* standard. Problems with missing bands in the autorads for the wife and children did not require exclusion of the evidence, nor did inconsistencies in the test results for defendant's mother, nor did alleged problems with the "thermal cycler" used in the PCR process.]

PROBLEM 9-F. *"We Found a Match"*

Donald Vanbart is charged with first degree murder in the slaying of Kim Gosberg, whose body was found three days after she disappeared, partially buried under leaves and forest debris in a wooded area about 200 yards from the home where she lived with her husband and children. The autopsy indicates that Gosberg died of strangulation and had been raped. (An athletic sock was tied around her neck; her hands were tied behind her with shoelaces and pantyhose; semen stains were found on her body and clothing.) The prosecutor proposes to offer evidence of a match between DNA isolated from semen found on the clothing and body of the victim and DNA isolated from a blood sample obtained from the defendant.

In a pretrial hearing on evidence issues, the prosecutor shows that the case against Vanbart is strong. Shortly after the murder of Karen Gosberg was generally reported, he told his sister in reference to her, "this time I went too far." A neighbor of Gosberg was prepared to testify that he heard a woman scream in the woods where the body was later discovered (the time being close to that later determined to be the probable time of death); another neighbor would testify that he saw the defendant driving away from the neighborhood in a blue sedan; another neighbor noted the license number, and the car was shown to be a blue sedan registered to Vanbart. Two other women were prepared to testify that on separate occasions within the last six months Vanbart had assaulted them in separate incidents, by dragging them into wooded areas, tying them up with shoelaces and undergarments, choking them with an athletic sock, and raping them. (The court ruled in favor of admitting this evidence under FRE 404(b) as proof of "modus operandi and identity.")

In the evidence hearing, the prosecutor calls Dr. Lawrence Mullens, who holds advanced degrees in biochemistry and human genetics. Mullens is employed by Lifemark Laboratories, a private firm specializing in DNA analysis, and he describes the underlying theory and technique of RFLP analysis in substantially the terms outlined in the quoted passage from the Montana decision in *Moore*. Mullens is prepared to say "we found a match" in the DNA taken from the semen sample found at the crime scene and the DNA extracted from the blood of the defendant (also that DNA from the semen sample did *not* match DNA from the blood of Karen Gosberg's husband). If allowed, Mullens would say "only one Hispanic person in 187,000 would produce such a match" (Vanbart being Hispanic).

After cross-examining Dr. Mullens, counsel for Vanbart makes the following objections:

1. Your Honor, *Daubert* requires you to find the underlying science to be valid, and the theory behind this proof is new and untested.
2. Quite apart from underlying theory, your honor, is the question of valid laboratory technique. How do we know what Lifemark does is reliable? *Daubert* speaks of industry standards and peer review literature.

Has the Lifemark technique been peer reviewed? Is Lifemark subject to any industry standards that could give us confidence in the work they do?

3. Your Honor, *Daubert* requires you as gatekeeper to determine whether Lifemark followed accepted laboratory protocols in this particular case. Before admitting this evidence, the prosecutor has to produce all its records of this test, along with competent testimony by the chemists who did the work, showing that they didn't slip up by contaminating the sample or misreading or misinterpreting the autorads.

4. Your Honor, *Daubert* requires you as gatekeeper to determine the validity of the underlying statistical analysis that produced the one in 187,000 figure mentioned by Dr. Mullens. That figure appears to relate specifically to the Hispanic population, and my client is Hispanic, but the NSC Study recognizes that there may well be population substructures in which the combination of alleles seen here is far more common, so the figure may be grossly exaggerated. And nobody knows whether the NSC's "ceiling principle" really works to remove the risk of overestimation.

5. Your honor, why compare the semen samples with data from "Hispanics" specifically? Again, my client is Hispanic, but we can't assume his guilt in making such comparisons. We should compare the "matching alleles" here with *all* subgroups in the population, taking the basis of comparison to be the subgroup in which the allele is most common. That's what they did in the O.J. Simpson case, and after all, the true assailant might be anyone.

6. Finally, your honor, I object that this proof is prejudicial and misleading. Presenting these astronomical numbers and the fancy labels and apparatus of science will distract the jury from what it should be doing, which is considering the real evidence of guilt or innocence. *Without* the numbers, the proof of "match" will be assumed to be conclusive evidence of guilt, which is not correct at all. *With* the numbers, the jury will forget about all the other proof, including *our* defense evidence that others were seen leaving the neighborhood at the time of the crime, and the culprit may well be among those.

How should the judge handle these various objections, and why?

| NOTES ON DNA EVIDENCE

1. A court applying *Daubert* and *Kumho Tire,* and following the directives of FRE 702, must decide whether the underlying genetic theory is reliable or valid. Clearly it is the judge who must make this decision under FRE 104(a) as a matter of "admissibility." In states like Montana, where *Moore* outlines and accepts this underlying theory or model, surely courts need not take testimony and make findings on this point every time DNA evidence is offered. They can take judicial notice based on *Moore,* can't they? Insofar as the first objection raised by counsel for Vanbart (theory is "new and untested") raises this point,

the objection would be overruled in Montana, wouldn't it? What if the jurisdiction has no decision like *Moore?* Could the judge take judicial notice of similar decisions from other states?

2. Doesn't the judge *also* have to decide whether the laboratory *techniques* are scientifically valid? Vanbart's second objection raises this point. The RFLP process varies in detail from laboratory to laboratory and changes over time, but the basics are described above in the passage from *Moore.* Assuming the judge in the Problem recognized *Moore* as authoritative, could *Moore* be used in some way as authority that the Lifemark RFLP process is valid (recall that *Moore* approved Cellmark RFLP process)? How about using *Moore* as a baseline, then putting the burden on the proponent to show the Lifemark process is substantially similar to Cellmark's? Or should the burden be on the objecting party to prove the contrary? *Moore* illustrates the point that other techniques are sometimes used: A common alternative is PCR ("polymerase chain reaction"), which extends or amplifies small samples that otherwise could not be analyzed, but later testing is less powerful in identifying or excluding sources. Presumably proponents must establish the validity of new processes. See State v. Russell, 882 P.2d 747, 759-769 (Wash. 1994) (admitting PCR evidence in murder case).

3. It seems clear now, under the language of amended FRE 702, that judges must *also* resolve objections that the laboratory did not correctly perform the tests in the particular case or got results that are unreliable because something went wrong during the process (Vanbart's third objection), doesn't it? Many things can go wrong, including the following: Technicians can mistakenly put DNA from a single sample in two lanes of gel, obtaining a perfect (but false) band match; restriction enzymes can cut DNA in the wrong places (producing "star activity"); the gel can vary in consistency, producing band-shifting, hence possible false matches or nonmatches (reportedly band-shifting is more likely to prevent matches than to cause false matches, and corrective measures are sometimes applied, including test lanes with material from a single sample); occasionally tagged probes do not bond properly to unzipped fragments (those that have been "restricted" or "digested" in the second phase of the process described in the *Moore* case), producing autorads that are hard to interpret. Even if it is better to ask judges to resolve these issues than to expect juries to do so, we are putting a pretty heavy burden on judges' aren't we?

4. The *Daubert* validity standard applies, doesn't it, to the statistical method used to determine a match and describe the probability of finding it in a relevant populace (Vanbart's fifth objection)? In a 1991 scientific article, two respected scholars suggested that information in data banks supporting frequency estimates might produce misleading results. Essentially these estimates depend on use of the product rule (see *Collins* case, page 90, supra): If one match were found in 1/10 of the relevant populace and another were found in 1/20 of the populace, and *if these matches are mutually independent* (Hardy-Weinberg equilibrium), the product rule suggests that both matches would be found in 1/100 of the populace.[11] The 1991 article advanced the

---

11. The computation is $2(1/10 \times 1/20) = 1/100$. "The factor of 2 arises in the heterozygous case [where the subject carries different alleles at one or more genetic loci, and the autorad shows two bands at any one locus], because one must consider the case in which allele a1 was contributed by the father and allele a2 by the mother and vice versa: each of the two cases has a probability $p_{a1}p_{a2}$." NRC Report, at 78.

population substructure thesis, which holds that subgroups within larger populations contain band matches that are *not* mutually independent because mating patterns are not truly random, and also that some combinations of matches might not be mutually independent. So powerful was this thesis that some courts began to exclude DNA evidence or bar frequency estimates. See State v. Bible, 858 P.2d 1152 (Ariz. 1993) (statistical estimates inadmissible); Commonwealth v. Curnin, 565 N.E.2d 440 (Mass. 1991) (excluding DNA evidence because of doubt over statistical independence). Others did not let this objection stand in the way, see United States v. Bonds, 12 F.3d 540, 564-566 (6th Cir. 1993) (population substructure controversy goes to weight, not admissibility).

The 1992 NRC Report took the substructure thesis seriously and suggested that estimates should employ an interim conservative "ceiling principle" (using the higher of 10 percent or the highest frequency for any observed match in any population group) until the issue could be resolved either by discovery that there is no significant substructure variation or by developing more refined data. The intended result of applying the ceiling principle is a conservative estimate that gives defendant the benefit of a doubt for matches that are incriminating. Instead of $2(1/10 \times 1/20) = 1/100$, the ceiling principle might lead to $2(1/5 \times 1/8) = 1/20$. Actual competing interpretations of match data exhibit even more disparity. See United States v. Bonds, 12 F.3d 540, 552 (6th Cir. 1993) (government claims probability was 1 in 35,000; using ceiling method, defense claims probability is 1 in 17 and government claims it is 1 in 6,200). Some decisions accepted the ceiling method. See State v. Streich, 658 A.2d 38 (Vt. 1995); Commonwealth v. Lanigan, 641 N.E.2d 1342 (Mass. 1994); State v. Vandebogart, 652 A.2d 671 (N.H. 1994). But later research, including findings published in the 1996 NRC Update, led experts to conclude that the feared disparities and variations due to population substructuring did not significantly affect the underlying statistics or calculations. Some modern decisions now say the precautions are no longer required. See Commonwealth v. Blasioli, 713 A.2d 1117, 1125 (Pa. 1998) (substructuring does not significantly affect frequency estimates, so controversy over use of the product rule has abated) (collecting cases); Lempert, DNA, Science and the Law: Two Cheers for the Ceiling Principle, 34 Jurimetrics Journal 41 (1993).

If one estimate is admitted, isn't it clear that the court must admit competing estimates? Must it admit estimates that are not supported by good science? Do differences of this magnitude mean something is wrong with the whole process?

5. What about Vanbart's fifth objection that the relevant comparison is not the population subgroup of the defendant, but a population group that contains all possible suspects? For each observed match, should the prosecutor choose the highest observed frequency in *all* population groups—an approach that would, like the ceiling principle, produce an estimate benefiting the defendant? Instead of conveying that only one person in three million would display such a match, the more conservative estimate might say only one person in three hundred would display such a match. See State v. Carter, 524 N.W.2d 763 (Neb. 1994) (reversing murder conviction of black defendant, partly because state introduced probabilities based on comparison with black and Caucasian databases; method did not account for possibility that perpetrator might come from some other racial or ethnic group).

6.   What about Vanbart's last objection that the proof is prejudicial and misleading? Recall that in *Collins* the California Supreme Court complained that the astronomical numbers might distract and hypnotize the jury. In *Collins*, of course, some confusion may have come from the fact that there was no actual *proof* of underlying probabilities. But some of it surely came as well from the very magnitude of the numbers, and some of it came from the fact that the individual probabilities did not satisfy the independence requirement on which the product rule depends. Similar problems arise in the DNA cases, don't they? See State v. Pierce, 597 N.E.2d 107 (Ohio 1992) (admitting testimony that "only one in forty billion blacks would have the same DNA composition"). Note that in *Moore* the court rejected the claim that admitting proof of a match was misleading without probability estimates, concluding that the defense has waived this objection by objecting to the estimates themselves. Vanbart has a point, doesn't he, when he says admitting proof of "a match" *without* numbers may lead the jury to accept the proof as conclusive and that admitting proof *with* the numbers may overwhelm the jury? How about a "compromise" in which the testimony is limited to saying that DNA tests "place the defendant in a group of people who might have left" the semen or blood observed at the scene? Doesn't this drastically *understate* the probative force of such proof? See State v. Bloom, 516 N.W.2d 159 (Minn. 1994) (approving expert testimony that goes beyond reporting that DNA tests are "consistent" with defendant's being source of blood; expert should be allowed to say that "given a reliable multi-locus match, the probability that the match is random or coincidental is extremely low," and should be allowed to say "that, to a reasonable scientific certainty," defendant is the source, and may "give an opinion as to random match probability" using NRC approach).

d.   Serologic and DNA Testing and Paternity

In paternity suits, scientific evidence plays a critical role. Here modern serologic and DNA testing combines with probabilistic analysis, despite doubts expressed in *Collins* about distraction and distortion that can come with the numbers, to produce something called a "Paternity Index" that usually suggests a very high probability that the defendant in the case is the biological father.

Until the 1970s standard "blood tests" were useful but often inconclusive. Such tests could be categorical in establishing nonpaternity, but could weed out only about 15 percent of nonfathers falsely accused (meaning that for most people who might be mistakenly named as the father, the test would not eliminate them). The tests were even less effective in the other direction, identifying defendant as the father, because they could only place him in a group of about one-fifth to one-third of the population who would have the appropriate blood type to be the father. In the 1970s, however, immunologic systems became testable by blood or tissue sample, and these more powerful serologic tests could exclude about 98 percent of nonfathers falsely accused. HLA tests (the letters stand for human leucocite antigen) attained a power exceeding 95 percent and can reduce the pool of potential fathers to as little as 2 percent of the male population. It came to be recognized that these tests could support a positive (but less than certain) inference that a particular man was the father.

In the 1990s, DNA evidence brought the promise of even greater power to identify a particular man as the father. One day, DNA profiling (or "gene mapping") may become for all intents and purposes conclusive, producing a kind of unique profile for each person. But that point has not yet been reached, and in the closing years of the twentieth century DNA and HLA tests are both still used to produce a Paternity Index that expresses the scarcity of indicators common to the father of the child (indicators present in the child that he must have gotten from his father) and the defendant.

The Paternity Index leads to an application of something called Bayesian analysis, which employs a standard equation in wide use that was originally developed in the nineteenth century by Reverend Thomas Bayes. Essentially Bayes' Theorem describes the degree to which a new item of evidence, when it can be expressed as a datum of known frequency, affects our prior assessment of an issue on which the new evidence bears. Suppose X stands for the proposition to be proved (such as biological fatherhood), E stands for the evidence (such as lab tests placing defendant in a small group of possible fathers), and the notation | stands for "given" or "assuming." Then Odds $(X \mid E)$ stands for the odds of X given evidence E. Bayes' Theorem says *these* odds (the odds of X, given E) are equal to the *prior* odds of X (without evidence E) multiplied by something called the Likelihood Ratio (LR). In other words, Odds $(X \mid E) =$ P(X) × LR. The Likelihood Ratio is a fraction in which the numerator is the probability that evidence E would exist if X were so, and the denominator is the probability that Evidence E would exist if X were *not* so. Hence:

$$\textbf{(1)} \ \text{Odds} \ (X \mid E) \ = \ \frac{P(E \mid X)}{P(E \mid \text{not-}X)} \times \text{Odds} \ (X)$$

Bayes' Theorem may also be cast in numeric form to yield likelihood expressed as a fraction or decimal number (probability), which is easier for some people to use, although the equation in this form is more complicated.[12] In what follows, the expression $P(X \mid E)$ stands for the probability of X, given evidence E:

$$\textbf{(2)} \ P(X \mid E) \ = \ \frac{P(E \mid X) P(X)}{P(E \mid X) \ P(X) \ + \ P(E \mid \text{not-}X) \ P(\text{not-}X)}$$

Equation (1), which expresses the Theorem in odds form, makes the idea close to intuitively obvious because the Likelihood Ratio expresses an idea that is easy to grasp. Remember that the equation in odds form tells us our new assessment of X [Odds $(X \mid E)$] equals likelihood that evidence E would exist

---

12. The probability of getting heads on a coin flip is one half, usually written 1/2 or .5. The odds of getting heads are one to one, usually written 1:1. Probability converts to odds by this equation: Odds = P/(1–P). Thus, the probability of one-half converts this way to odds: Odds = .5/(1–.5) = 1:1. Odds convert to probability by treating the number to the left of the colon as the numerator in a fraction whose denominator is the *sum* of the numbers on each side of the colon. Thus, odds of 1:1 convert in this way to probability: Probability = 1/(1+1) = 1/2 or .5.

if we knew the matter to be proved *were so* $[P(E \mid X)]$ divided by the likelihood that such evidence would exist if we knew it was *not* so $[P(E \mid \text{not-}X)]$, multiplied by our *prior assessment* of X, before getting the new evidence [Odds (X)]. Try using the Theorem with a simple card problem. Suppose we want to know whether a card drawn from a hat containing a full mixed deck is the Queen of Hearts. If asked for an initial estimate of the likelihood of drawing that card, knowing only that the hat contains a full mixed deck, we would say the odds are 1:51 (one chance of drawing that card against 51 chances of drawing some other), and that the probability is 1/52 (or .019). If we were told a red card was drawn and asked how this datum affects the likelihood that this card is a Queen of Hearts, we would say the new odds are 1:25 (one chance of getting the Queen of Hearts against 25 chances of getting other red cards), and the probability is 1/26 (or .03846).

Bayes' Theorem expresses the same reasoning mathematically. For X, substitute QH to mean drawing the Queen of Hearts; for E, substitute R to mean drawing a red card. The equation shows how to modify our original estimate of the odds of drawing the Queen of Hearts, given the datum that the card drawn is red. Using the in odds form, we have:

$$\text{Odds } (QH \mid R) = \frac{P(R \mid QH)}{P(R \mid \text{not-}QH)} \times \text{Odds } (QH) = \frac{(1)}{(25/51)} \times 1{:}51$$

$$= 2.04{:}51 \text{ (probability of .03846)}$$

Dividing the number on each side of the colon by 2.04 yields odds of 1:25 (as we expect). The calculations are harder, but we reach the probability of .03846 by applying Equation (2)—the Theorem in numeric form.

PROBLEM 9-G. *Paternity Index 624*

In her paternity suit, Lisa claims Richard is the father of her child Jason. Lisa testifies that she had an ongoing relationship with Richard during the probable time of conception and that they had frequent intercourse. Richard testifies that he saw Lisa only occasionally during the time, and they had intercourse twice. He also testifies that thereafter Lisa turned down his overtures, telling him she wanted to see other men, and that she was seeing four other men that Richard knew about.

Important to Lisa's case is a report prepared by Lifemark Diagnostics, a private laboratory specializing in DNA and HLA testing. The report analyzes blood samples taken from Lisa, Jason, and Richard. It contains the following statements:

> On the attached protocol are results obtained in our laboratory on blood specimens from the mother Lisa, the child Jason, and Richard. The samples were tested for both serologic and genetic factors to determine whether Richard might be or is not the biological father. Shown on the protocol are certain serologic and genetic characteristics of these persons and the combined probability, based on estimates of the frequency of these characteristics in the Caucasian population,

that Richard, as compared to a random Caucasian man, could be the source of the paternal genes and antigens observed in Jason.

From the testing performed here, falsely accused males would be excluded in 95% of the cases. The results do not provide evidence of nonpaternity for Richard. Since parentage cannot be excluded for him, the test results have been used to calculate a Paternity Index (PI), which reflects the number of unrelated random Caucasian men who would have to be tested to find another with the appropriate genes and antigens to be the father of Jason. Here the index is 624, which converts to a probability of paternity of 99.84%. These figures indicate the plausibility of Richard being the father of Jason. The significance of this evidence must be weighed with other factors, such as access to the mother by Richard or other men at the time of conception.

Signed,

Hilston K. Pool, Ph.D.
Certified Pathologist
Lifemark Laboratories

The attached protocol shows that Lifemark performed HLA and DNA tests on the blood samples and describes the findings in detail. Dr. Pool testifies and is prepared to explain the report and, in substance, to testify from present memory on what it says and means.

Richard objects. He concedes the relevance and admissibility of evidence of (1) the genotypes and serologic factors found in the blood of Lisa, Jason, and himself, (2) the fact that Jason's father must have certain serologic and genetic characteristics, and (3) the fact that Richard has them too, and could pass them to his child. But he argues that the numeric data, including the Paternity Index and probability of paternity, should be excluded. How should the court rule, and why?

NOTES ON SEROLOGIC AND GENETIC TESTS IN PATERNITY CASES

1. Testing laboratories routinely produce reports like the one described above, complete with a Paternity Index expressed as a number (624) and a "probability of paternity" expressed as a percentage (99.84 percent). The number in the Paternity Index indicates how many men would probably have to be tested to find another who could be the father. The probability of paternity is found by doing the division in a fraction in which the numerator is the Paternity Index and the denominator is that number plus one, and converting the result to a percentage (in the Problem, $624/625 = .9984$ or 99.84 percent). Both the Paternity Index and the probability of paternity are routinely admitted in paternity cases. Both the number and the percentage are likely to be high, and both usually go to the jury. See Child Support Enforcement Agency v. Doe, 51 P.3d 366, 367 (Hawai'i 2002) (2542 to 1 or 99.96%); El Dorado v. Misura, 38 Cal. Rptr. 2d 908 (Cal. App. 1995) (index 970 yielding percentage 99.69 percent). See generally Peterson, A Few Things You Should Know about Paternity

Tests (But Were Afraid to Ask), 22 Santa Clara L. Rev. 667 (1982); Reisner and Bolk, A Layman's Guide to the Use of Blood Group Analysis in Paternity Testing, 20 J. Fam. L. 657 (1982); Ellman and Kaye, Probabilities and Proof: Can HLA and Blood Group Testing Prove Paternity, 54 N.Y.U. L. Rev. 1131 (1979).

2. Suppose Hilston Pool testifies that the Lifemark test has the power to exclude 95 percent of all men falsely accused. Since the test did not exclude Richard, does it follow that the probability is 95 percent that he is the father? That only 5 percent of the men in the general populace could be the father? The answer to both questions is no. Do you see why? Suppose the question is whether a card drawn at random from a mixed full deck is the Queen of Hearts. Suppose we have a test that recognizes all red face cards and the test is run and yields a positive result (a red face card was drawn). Among the possible "wrong" cards (all that are not the Queen of Hearts), this test has the power to exclude 45/51, or 88.2 percent. The positive result on the test means the drawn card is one out of six red face cards, so the odds are 1:5 that the card is the Queen of Hearts (a probability of 1/6, or 16.7 percent, not 88.2 percent). The percentage of cards that is a Queen of Hearts is 1.9 percent (not 11.8 percent, which is the difference between 88.2 percent and 100 percent). It is easy for a layperson to misinterpret the power of a test, and some courts have cautioned against careless use of such information. See Commonwealth v. Beausoleil, 490 N.E.2d 788, 792 n.5, and 795 (Mass. 1986) (incorrect to equate probability of exclusion with probability that nonexcluded man is father; in some cases, probability of exclusion ranged from 80 percent to 96 percent but probability of paternity for a nonexcluded male ranged between 4.4 percent and 44 percent; jury is apt to confuse these probabilities, so they should not be presented); Reisner and Bolk, A Layman's Guide to the Use of Blood Group Analysis in Paternity Testing, 20 J. Fam. L. 657, 670-671 (1982).

3. Consider the Paternity Index, which actually comes from the Likelihood Ratio that is an element in Bayes' Theorem. The number, given in the Problem as 624, is derived by carrying out the division in the fraction that makes up the Likelihood Ratio. In the Problem, the numerator is the probability that Richard, if he were the father, would pass to his child the observed genetic characteristics Jason got from his father. The denominator is the probability that a random man in the populace would pass these characteristics to Jason. For nonexcluded males, the numerator might be .4486—a probability that is realistically substantial but less than half.[13] The denominator might be .000719—a probability that is realistically tiny since any particular combination of observed markers is likely to be rare in the general population. These figures produce the Paternity Index given in the problem (.4486/.000719 = 624). The higher the Index, the stronger the indication of paternity, and the number is likely to *be* high for *any* nonexcluded male. See Koehler, DNA Matches and Statistics, 76 Judicature 222, 224 (1993) (Paternity Index measures "the strength of the genetic evidence, where higher numbers are more probative of paternity

13. Half the genetic information in a child comes from each parent. However, the genetic markers a father passes to his offspring combine in innumerable different ways, so any *particular* combination of paternal genes will not likely appear in half his children. Of course the same comment applies on the mother's side.

than lower numbers"). Consider this explanation of the Paternity Index, offered by one modern court:

> [T]he denominator of the paternity index will be the same for every putative father. This is because the denominator is the gene frequency in the population. The numerator, however, will vary from putative father to putative father because their phenotypes will vary. . . . Because the numerator varies from putative father to putative father, the paternity index will also vary. Thus, even though all men not excluded by a paternity test are capable of fathering the child, they will have different paternity indexes and thus different relative likelihoods of having fathered the child.

Plemel v. Walker, 735 P.2d 1209, 1214 (Or. 1987) (expert must explain this point to jury). Do you think a jury can understand such explanations?

4. Suppose Lisa is a 32-year-old woman who lives in a metropolitan area containing 100,000 unmarried men within 12 years of Lisa's age (20–44 years). Can Richard reasonably argue that the test evidence suggests there are likely to be 72 men who could be Jason's father?

5. Consider the probability of paternity, stated in the problem as 99.84 percent. If we take this figure as describing the probability that Richard is the father, given the test results, it reflects an application of Bayes' Theorem *with a hidden assumption*. From Note 1, recall that the percentage is computed by dividing the Paternity Index by that number plus one (624/625 = .9984, or 99.84 percent). The same idea can be expressed as Odds 624:1, meaning the odds that Richard is the father are 624 to 1. Recall from Note 3 that the Index itself comes from dividing (a) the probability that Richard (if he were the father) would pass to his child the observed paternal genetic markers by (b) the probability that a random man would do so. Using the realistic assumptions in Note 3, the larger figure (.4476) provides the numerator in the Likelihood Ratio in Equation (1), which is $P(E \mid X)$—the probability that Jason would have the observed paternal genetic markers (E) if we knew Richard was his father (X). The smaller figure (.000719) provides the denominator, which is $P(E \mid$ non-X)—the probability that Jason would have the observed paternal genetic markers (E) if we knew Richard was *not* his father (non-X) because someone else is (a "random man"). Doing the arithmetic gives us the Index as well as the probability (99.84 percent) and Odds (624:625). But Equation (1) says that estimating the odds that Richard is the father *given* the test data [Odds ($X \mid E$)] requires a *prior* independent estimate of the odds [Odds (X)]. Note well: *The hidden assumption in presenting the probability of paternity is that the prior odds are 1:1.* See Plemel v. Walker, 735 P.2d 1209, 1217 n.9 (Or. 1987) ("standard assumption" in calculating probability of paternity is that "prior probability of paternity is 50 percent"). In effect, converting an estimate of the scarcity of Jason's paternal genes in the population into an estimate of the odds or probability of Richard's paternity involves a prior assumption of a substantial probability that he is the father—the odds are already 1:1 (probability .5). Where does this prior estimate come from? What does it reflect? Are there special problems with using such an assumption in *criminal* cases in which proving paternity would show guilt of a crime? See State v. Skipper, 637 A.2d 1101 (Conn. 1994) (in trial for sexual assault allegedly resulting in pregnancy, proving probability

of paternity infringed right to be presumed innocent because it assumed prior probability of .5).

6.   Suppose the jury thinks Lisa was intimate with four other men during the probable period of conception. Would it make sense to take the prior odds of Richard's paternity to be 1:4 (probability 20 percent)? If we did, applying Bayesian logic and using the same figures set out above would lead us to new odds 156:1 (probability 99.36 percent) favoring the conclusion that Richard is the father. A reduction from 99.84 percent to 99.36 percent leaves the probability overwhelmingly high in favor of Richard's paternity, doesn't it? If you experimented with the numbers, you would discover that the paternity index would have to be in the neighborhood of 36 (Richard's was 624) before proof of relations with four other men would reduce the new calculation to odds of 9:1 (probability 90 percent). See County of El Dorado v. Misura, 38 Cal. Rptr. 2d 908 (Cal. App. 1995) (compute new probability by dividing paternity index of defendant by sum of his index and indices of untested men, assumed to be 1); State v. Pressler, 1994 WL 677593 (Tenn. App. 1994) (adjust prior odds proportionately to reflect sexual relations between plaintiff and other men). At least in the common situation where the paternity index for the defendant is very high, then, even multiple relationships have little effect on the final probability.

7.   Would it be wise to describe inclusionary impact without numbers? How about translating an impressive number like 99.84 percent into a statement that tests "put defendant in a small group of men who might be the father" or mean he is "very likely" to be the father or "much more likely to be the father" than a man selected at random? How about telling the jury there is a likelihood of "more than 40 percent" that Richard would pass to his child the paternal genetic markers found in Jason, and fewer than "one man in a thousand" would do so? See Joint AMA-ABA Guidelines: Present Status of Serologic Testing in Problems of Disputed Parentage, 10 Fam. L.Q. 247, 262 (1976) (suggesting "practically proved" for PI 99.8-99.9, "extremely likely" for PI 99.1-99.75, "very likely" for PI 95-99, "likely" for PI 90-95, "undecided" for PI 80-90, and "not useful" for PI less than 80). But see County of El Dorado v. Misura, 38 Cal. Rptr. 2d 908, 911 n.1 (Cal. App. 1995); Plemel v. Walker, 735 P.2d 1209, 1219 (Or. 1987) (both disapproving use of these verbal predicates).

8.   How about having the expert apply the Paternity Index to a range of prior estimates, perhaps using a chart like this one:

	1	2
Select from column 1 a prior estimate of the	0	0
likelihood that defendant is the father, without	.1	.48
considering the laboratory evidence. The ap-	.2	.67
propriate new estimate, given the laboratory,	.3	.78
is set out directly across in Column 2.	.4	.85
	.5	.89
	.6	.93
	.7	.95
	.8	.97
	.9	.99
	1.0	1.0

See Plemel v. Walker, 735 P.2d 1209, 1219 (Or. 1987) (on request, expert must "calculate the probability that the defendant is the father by using more than a single assumption about the strength of the other evidence" so results are shown "without overstating the information that can be derived from them").

9.   Some statutes create a "presumption of paternity" when genetic evidence is convincing. See California Family Code §7555 (presumption arises when paternity index is "100 or greater" and may be rebutted by a preponderance of the evidence); New York Family Court Act §532 (DNA test indicating at least 95 percent probability raises rebuttable presumption of paternity). Given the probative force of tests producing high indices and probabilities, why have a presumption? Should proof that plaintiff had relations with other men dislodge the presumption? How about testimony by the defendant that he was not intimate with plaintiff? How about evidence that he had a vasectomy? See County of El Dorado v. Misura, 38 Cal. Rptr. 2d 908, 913-914 (Cal. App. 1995) (showing untested other men had access does not dislodge presumption) (but if test was improperly conducted or wrong tables were used, index might be too low to trigger presumption; defendant might show nonaccess or infertility, which would establish prior probability of zero, proving nonpaternity; defendant might show another man with high paternity index had access).

Regardless whether a presumption is deployed, a test showing a high paternity index should suffice, shouldn't it, to take the issue of paternity to a jury if there is proof of intimacy *despite* defense denials or counterproof? See Brooks v. Rogers, 445 S.E.2d 725 (Va. App. 1994) (despite claim that defendant had vasectomy and that his son had relations with plaintiff, affirming judgment of paternity) (absent medical record, judge did not believe vasectomy; no evidence of sexual relations between plaintiff and son of defendant). What if tests foreclose paternity? See Pondexter v. Washington, 1995 WL 57224 (Ohio App. 1995) (dismissing where HLA test indicated exclusion *despite* affidavit that plaintiff had relations with no other man before or after conception); State v. Pressler, 1994 WL 677593 (Tenn. App. 1994) (dismissing where DNA tests excluded defendant, although less sensitive HLA test did not exclude). If powerful test evidence is presented and is met only by denials of intimacy or proof that other men had access, can a court or jury reasonably find *against* paternity? Compare Matter of Debra L. v. William J., 594 N.Y.S.2d 810 (App. Div. 1993) (reversing dismissal of petition based on proof of intimacy and test showing 99 percent probability of paternity, and directing court to enter judgment of paternity despite testimony denying intercourse) with Zearfoss v. Frattaroli, 646 A.2d 1238 (Pa. Super. Ct. 1994) (where plaintiff and defendant offered conflicting evidence on crucial question of timing, error to award summary judgment to plaintiff based on test results indicating 99.99 percent probability of paternity) (test evidence is not conclusive).

10.   Perhaps not surprisingly, sometimes DNA test evidence is offered to advance an alleged father's claim of parental rights. See Matter of Leon L. v. Carole H., 621 N.Y.S.2d 93 (App. Div. 1994) (in claim to establish parental rights for child born to defendant during her marriage to another, ordering DNA tests of plaintiff, defendant, and child); Matter of Gregory F.W. v. Lori Anne B., 617 N.Y.S.2d 276 (Fam. Ct. 1994) (in petition by parents of alleged father, since deceased, ordering DNA tests of decedent, mother, and child).

Ten | BURDENS OF PROOF AND PRESUMPTIONS

A. BURDENS AND PRESUMPTIONS IN CIVIL CASES

Courts normally act only when parties ask them to do so and "prove their case," so it comes naturally to think that litigants must carry "burdens" or lose if they fail. Unfortunately the subject of burdens is among the most slippery in the larger areas of procedure and evidence, and attempts to refine what we know lead quickly to difficulty. No thoughtful person emerges from considering the subject without feeling great apprehension that the various devices that define and impose burdens are easily misunderstood and misapplied, that they may disguise what is happening, and that they gloss over real problems.

Bear in mind these points in approaching this subject. First, the various burdens are functionally related, as are the concerns and policies that underlie them. Second, every burden raises questions of allocation (who bears it?) and weight or degree (how much must a party do in order to carry it?). Third, the various burdens, despite their similarities, have vastly different consequences in the lawsuit.

With respect to trial burdens, bear in mind too these questions: Is it appropriate, when the evidence leaves a matter in doubt, to act *as if* we know the answer? If doubt is unresolvable, in a case or category of cases, would it be wise to redefine what is in issue? Should a burden-imposing device always impose *the same* burden, or should its weight or consequences be adjustable to the particular case or category of cases?

1. Pretrial Burdens (Pleading, Pretrial Statement)

In some ways, the burden of pleading is least important and least problematic. Recall the trend toward reducing the impact of pleadings in litigation. Parties set out claims and defenses in a short and plain manner; amendments are allowed as of course; motions to dismiss for failure to state a claim or for judgment on the pleadings seldom succeed. Pleadings no longer have much impact on the shape of trial, which is more a function of discovery and pretrial.

And many pleading conventions are clear and settled, some by express provision in Rules or statute, others by judicial holding. In a suit for breach of contract, plaintiff normally pleads agreement, consideration, performance, breach, and resultant damages (with particular allegations if she seeks "consequential" damages). Obviously these are not all the points that might affect the right to recover (others include capacity to contract, legality, modification, and accord and satisfaction), but they suffice in a complaint.

Yet figuring out what to plead is not easy in actions that rest on modern remedial statutes or assert new rights. Resolving uncertainties by "overpleading" is not entirely satisfactory, because it tempts all participants uncritically to assume that the pleader bears the burden of persuasion on the points pleaded.

It is a challenging task (and largely thankless) to develop a coherent rationale explaining the assignment of pleading burdens—a system for assigning pleading burdens when no rule, statute, or case provides the answer. Courts sometimes grasp at straws. They look to the grammar of statutes for clues (even where phrasing seems accidental), and resort to shibboleths as if they provide guidance (plaintiff pleads everything in the "affirmative" case; defendant pleads "denials"). See generally Cleary, Presuming and Pleading: An Essay on Juristic Immaturity, 12 Stan. L. Rev. 5 (1959).

Sometimes pleading burdens are allocated out of concerns peculiar to the process of pleading. The purpose may be to help the pleadings make sense: In a suit on a promissory note, usually plaintiff must plead nonpayment; in a defamation action, usually plaintiff must plead untruth (think how odd such complaints would seem if these allegations were missing). In these instances the burden of pleading does not match the later trial burdens. That is, usually at trial a defendant sued on a promissory note must prove payment, and a defendant sued for defamation must prove truth. Another purpose peculiar to pleading is simply to provide certainty, so litigators know what to do at the beginning of the lawsuit. Cf. Palmer v. Hoffman, 318 U.S. 109 (1943) (FRCP 8 requires defendant to plead contributory negligence in a diversity case, even though state law puts the burden of persuasion on this point upon plaintiff).

2. Trial Burdens (Production and Persuasion)

The term "burden of proof" embraces two related but different concepts that come into play in the trial of an action. One is the burden of producing evidence; the other is the burden of persuasion.

Burden of production. To say a party bears the burden of producing evidence is to say she runs the risk of losing automatically (on motion for judgment as a matter of law, before or after the verdict) if she does not offer sufficient evidence to enable a reasonable person to find in her favor. At the outset, usually the party who bears the burden of persuasion also bears the burden of production. If Agnes sues Burt for personal injuries arising from an automobile accident, for example, she would ordinarily bear the burden of producing evidence of Burt's negligence. If she carries that burden, she is assured that the trier will consider and weigh her evidence, a benefit most visible in a jury-tried case.

Success in carrying the burden of production does not necessarily shift that burden to the adversary. If Agnes offers sufficient evidence to support a finding that Burt was negligent, the trier of fact ordinarily remains free to reject her proof. Hence the burden of production does not pass to Burt, and he might win even if he produces no counterproof, though the risk that the trier will find against him may be higher if he stands silent rather than offering credible counterproof.

If the party bearing the burden of production carries it very well, however, the burden does shift to her opponent. That means he loses automatically if he does not offer rebuttal evidence. Jurisdictions vary in defining proof that shifts the burden of production to the opponent. As a convenient shorthand, we use the term "cogent and compelling," but remember that the concept is not uniform. (Most jurisdictions agree that testimonial proof cannot have this burden-shifting effect if a reasonable person could disbelieve the witnesses. Jurisdictions vary as to whether all the evidence may be considered, or only that offered by the opponent.) Agnes might well shift the burden to Burt if she offers unequivocal testimony by neutral observers that Burt rear-ended her car while she was stopped at the intersection for a red light, and if Burt fails to make any headway in discrediting the witnesses by cross-examination. At this juncture, Burt must offer *some* counterproof—such as evidence that he did not run into Agnes from behind, or did so only because *he* was struck by another car from his rear. Failing to produce such counterproof puts him at risk of a partial judgment as a matter of law on negligence, leaving only damages to be determined by the jury.

Burden of persuasion. To say that a party bears the burden of persuasion (or risk of nonpersuasion) is to say that she can win only if the evidence persuades the trier of the existence of the facts that she needs in order to prevail. (Ordinarily that means that she wins only if, on the basis of the evidence, the facts seem more likely true than not.) Perhaps because this burden operates at the end of trial, courts often say it never "shifts." Usually it is actually mentioned only in jury trials, in argument and instructions.

Elements in these burdens. Parties need not produce evidence on every element that might bear on liability, any more than they must plead them. The best reason to ignore many potential elements is that ordinarily they do not affect outcome. As Professor Cleary put it, requiring plaintiff in a contract suit "to establish the existence or nonexistence . . . of every concept treated in Corbin and Williston" would indeed be burdensome, and would force the lawsuit to cover "unnecessary territory." Cleary, supra at 7.

Thus, evidence sufficient to enable the trier to find agreement, consideration, performance, breach, and damages normally satisfies the burden of production in a contract suit. In the absence of defense evidence, plaintiff prevails if the trier is persuaded on these points. Yet the right to recover might turn on matters such as the fulfillment of conditions, legality of the agreement or contemplated performance, modification of terms, waiver, estoppel, or accord and satisfaction. If such issues are raised (normally defendant must do so), the outcome might turn on how they are resolved.

Allocating the burdens. On any particular point, ordinarily burdens of pleading, producing evidence, and persuading the trier of fact are all cast upon the same party. Unfortunately, even modern textwriters give confusing signals on the relationship between the pretrial burden of pleading and the trial burdens.

They imply that one burden impels the others, but apparently disagree as to which is in the driver's seat.[1] And (as is true of the burden of pleading) it is easy enough to discern the custom on such matters, but hard to explain *why* the trial burdens are allocated as they are, or to come up with rules of general application.

In the typical contract suit, plaintiff bears the burdens of production and persuasion on agreement, consideration, performance, breach, and damages. If nonfulfillment of a condition (including non performance by plaintiff) is an issue, plaintiff bears the burdens on this point too. (Normally it becomes an issue only if defendant pleads it with specificity under FRCP 8(c), so here is a place where pleading and trial burdens do not match.) If failure of consideration becomes an issue, the burdens of production and persuasion usually fall upon defendant. (Here too the point usually becomes an issue only if he pleads it; it is an "affirmative defense," which is but another way of saying that defendant bears all the burdens—pleading, production, persuasion.)

Reasons for allocating burdens. Precedent aside, the reasons that account for the allocation of burdens can be given only in general terms, by reference to four broad concerns:

First and perhaps most important, burdens are allocated to serve substantive policy, making it easier or harder for plaintiffs to recover or defendants to avoid liability. In negligence cases, plaintiffs will more likely recover if defendants bear the burdens on the issue of contributory negligence. In a suit against an insurance carrier on a double indemnity life insurance policy, seeking recovery for alleged accidental death, the beneficiary will more likely recover the full sum if the carrier bears the burdens on the question whether suicide was the cause of death.[2]

Second, we allocate burdens so as to recognize what is most probably true. In a contract suit, for example, it is unlikely that *none* of the conditions precedent to defendant's obligations have occurred, for few plaintiffs would waste time and money bringing suit in such cases. It is more likely that most conditions have occurred. In light of this reality, the Rules put on defendant the burden of specifically alleging that certain conditions have not occurred. (Recall, however, that when a defendant does allege that conditions have not occurred, plaintiff bears the burden of persuading the trier of fact that the conditions have occurred.) In similar vein, we all know that a properly posted letter is

---

1. Compare McCormick on Evidence §337, at 509 (J. Strong 5th ed. 1999) (usually "the party who has the burden of pleading a fact will have the burdens of producing evidence and of persuading the jury of its existence") with J. Cound, J. Friedenthal, A. Miller and J. Sexton, Civil Procedure Cases and Materials 527 (8th ed. 2001) (burden of pleading an issue "usually is assigned to the party who has the burden of producing evidence on that issue at trial"). The evidence people seem to want the procedure people to bear the laboring oar, and vice versa. For the most part, we believe that the burden of pleading should follow the burden of persuasion.

2. On a life insurance policy with a double indemnity feature, the carrier pays the face amount of the policy if the insured died of natural causes, and twice that sum if accident was the cause of death. But if death resulted from suicide, the carrier generally owes nothing if the policy is new, or owes the face amount if the policy has existed for a minimum statutory period (such as two years). If the carrier takes the position that suicide was the cause of death, usually it bears the burden of persuasion on this issue. See 10 Couch on Insurance 2d §41:49 (1982); 19 id. §79:386; 21A J. Appleman, Insurance Law and Practice §12571 (rev. ed. 1981).

almost always delivered to the addressee in due course, so we have a presumption to this effect.

Third, we allocate burdens so as to place them on the party most likely to have access to the necessary proof. In a suit against a bailee for damage to goods, for example, defendant is more likely than plaintiff to be able to show (if such be the case) that something other than its own negligence was the cause, and typically such defendant bears the burdens on this issue. Similarly, it is easier for a debtor to prove payment of an obligation than for the creditor to prove nonpayment, and for this reason usually the burden of proving payment is allocated to the defendant.

Fourth, we allocate burdens to help resolve cases where definitive proof is unavailable. Thus, absence for seven years without tidings raises a presumption of death, unless someone offers proof that the person in question is still alive.

Weight of the burdens. In civil cases, the burden of pleading a point requires the party to include necessary allegations in the appropriate complaint, answer, or reply. You likely spent weeks on this subject in the basic procedure course.

The burdens of production and persuasion are related: The first requires a party to produce sufficient evidence to permit reasonable persons on the jury to find the point with the requisite measure of certainty, as defined by the burden of persuasion. The second means, in most civil actions,[3] proof by a preponderance—that is, evidence that persuades the jury (acting as reasonable persons) that the points to be proved are more likely so than not.

3. A Special Device for Shifting and Allocating Burdens: The Presumption

a. Sources and Nature of Presumptions

Burdens in civil cases may be allocated by a presumption: In a suit against a bailee for damage to goods placed in his care and custody, for example, it is usually "presumed" that if the goods were in good shape when turned over to the bailee, but damaged on retrieval, then the bailee caused the damage by his negligence. Normally the bailor bears the burdens (pleading, production, persuasion) on the "basic facts" (delivery of undamaged goods; retrieval of damaged goods), but if the bailor succeeds on the basic facts, he gets the benefit of a presumption that the bailee was negligent and that his negligence caused the damage.

The term "presumption" describes a device that *requires* the trier to draw a particular conclusion when the basic facts are established, in the absence of

---

3. In some civil actions (such as suits for fraud or reformation of a contract), the party bearing those burdens can prevail only on the basis of "clear and convincing evidence." This standard seems to enhance both burdens. That is, a particular body of evidence might suffice to carry the burden of coming forward in an ordinary case, but would not do so under the "clear and convincing" standard. And such a body of evidence might persuade the jury in an ordinary case, but fail to persuade if the instruction calls for "clear and convincing" proof. In assorted other special cases, similar heavy burdens are imposed. See, e.g., Addington v. Texas, 441 U.S. 418 (1979) (in civil commitment proceedings, due process requires burden of persuasion "equal to or greater than" clear and convincing standard).

evidence tending to disprove the fact presumed ("counterproof"). Thus, in the bailor's suit (if the basic facts are proved) the trier *must* conclude that negligence by the bailee caused the damage unless he offers counterproof of some other cause—such as earthquake, crime, or fire spreading from nearby property. Here is the essence of it: A presumption unopposed controls decision on the point in question.

There are many presumptions. Some (like the bailed goods presumption) apply again and again in a particular setting; they are context specific. Others are unattached. They roam the terrain of procedural conventions like Don Quixote—out to do good and operating in random and independent fashion. Consider the mailed letter presumption: If it is shown that a letter was properly posted (addressed, stamped, placed in the mailbox), a presumption directs the trier to conclude that it was delivered to the addressee in due course (three days or so for domestic mail), unless there is counterproof that the addressee never got it. Here is a presumption of obvious utility (mailers are seldom in a position to show that what they sent was delivered at the distant end), and it is definitely unattached: It can arise in a suit against an insurance carrier, where it might help the claimant to prove renewal of the policy or the carrier to prove cancellation; it can arise in an infringement action to prove the date or fact of registration of a patent. In short, this presumption comes into play whenever a party bears a burden to prove delivery of a mailed letter.

Some presumptions grew out of common law. They appear as courts wrestle with recurrent problems, and devise ways to deal with them. See, e.g., Owens v. Publix Supermarkets, Inc., 802 So.2d 315, 330 (Fla. 2001) (creating a presumption, arising on proof of a slip-and-fall on business premises where some "transitory foreign substance" is found on the floor, that the condition was "not safe" and the owner "did not maintain the premises in a reasonably safe condition") (presumption shifts burden of persuasion to owner). A full list of such presumptions would be long indeed. Other presumptions are statutory: The one for bailed goods is embodied in the UCC, which contains many provisions on matters of burden, although these sometimes lead to interpretive difficulties. Presumptions also grow out of efforts to implement remedial statutes, as you will see in *Burdine,* infra. Here is a sampling:

1. In a suit against the owner of an automobile involved in an accident, upon proof of ownership, a presumption that the driver had the owner's permission (the "loaned auto" presumption); also a presumption, arising upon proof that defendant owned the car and employed the driver, that the driver was acting within the scope of his duties (the "scope-of-employment" presumption);

2. In a suit on an accidental death policy or a life insurance policy with a double indemnity feature, upon proof that decedent came to a sudden violent end, a presumption that accident (as opposed to suicide or crime) caused the death;[4]

4. In many poignant cases, the cause of sudden death is hard to determine because circumstances suggest accident or suicide (other alternatives may appear—death while committing a crime, or a natural cause like heart attack): When the beneficiary sues under such an insurance policy, generally she bears the burden of persuasion on the question of accident. The presumption comes to her aid, and it determines either (1) *the way* her case is conveyed to the jury in the

3. In a suit for death benefits, upon proof that the insured has been absent without tidings for a period of seven years, a presumption that he is dead; and

4. In a suit for death benefits, upon proof that plaintiff and decedent entered into a ceremonial marriage, a presumption that the marriage is valid and ongoing.

Presumptions such as these resolve recurring problems of proof without the need for extended debate: If a party seeking to prove delivery of a document shows that it was properly posted and the adversary offers no counterproof, the matter is settled, without need for extended argument or additional evidence.

Unfortunately, talking about presumptions quickly bogs down in a mire of verbiage comprised of redundant and conflicting terms with shifting meanings and interpretation. Here are some of the more common:

1. *Conclusive or irrebuttable presumption.* Rules of substantive law sometimes borrow the language of presumptions.

Under the Coal Mine Health and Safety Act of 1969, for example, a miner shown by X-ray or other clinical evidence to have pneumoconiosis (black lung disease) is "irrebuttably presumed" to be totally disabled, and the presumption "operates conclusively to establish entitlement to benefits." Usery v. Turner Elkhorn Mining Co., 428 U.S. 1, 11 (1976). And it was once true in California that a husband was irrebuttably presumed to be the father of a child born to his wife during marriage (absent proof that they did not cohabit or that he was impotent). The presumption still cannot be rebutted by ordinary evidence (testimony denying intercourse or evidence that the wife had intercourse with another), but the statute now requires a finding of nonpaternity if blood tests so indicate. Cal. Evid. Code §621. These legal rules are not presumptions at all, as the term is ordinarily used. They are principles of substantive law, expressed in the language of presumptions.

2. *Mandatory presumption or presumption of law.* Generally these terms refer to the true presumption—the device that is the principal focus of this section. It controls decision if unopposed, so in jury-tried cases an instruction is in order and in bench trials the judge has no option but to find the presumed fact. "Mandatory" is redundant, for "presumption" by itself conveys this meaning.

3. *Permissive presumption, inference, presumption of fact.* These terms usually refer to conclusions that are permitted but not required. The term "inference" adequately captures the central meaning here, and using the word "presump-

---

court's instructions or (2) *whether* her case gets to the jury at all, if the facts seem strongly to suggest suicide.

The presumption dislodges any assumption that death came from natural causes (which is unlikely if the insured died in a collision or is found with a bullet in his head), and sometimes it is phrased as a presumption *against* suicide. The insurance carrier normally bears the burden of persuasion when it claims that the insured committed suicide (see footnote 2, supra), and the presumption of accidental death is sometimes viewed as the *source* of this burden or as playing some role in it. Generally the carrier also bears the burden of proving that some other exclusion in the policy applies (such as death while committing a crime), and the presumption of accidental death sometimes plays a role in this matter too. Problem 10-B (The Death of Mason Parnell) illustrates this presumption in operation. See page 679, infra.

tion" in this context simply clouds the message (since an inference never controls decision, the term "presumption" is inapposite).

Of course jurors draw inferences on their own from the evidence in the case, viewed in the light of their own lifetime experiences. We expect them to do so. In this sense, inferences are simply conclusions drawn by reasonable persons on the basis of information provided to them.

But there is another kind of inference. We mean the kind that the judge mentions to the jury in formal instructions—a conclusion permissible on the basis of the evidence, to which the judge openly draws the jury's attention. Inference instructions amount to judicial comment on the evidence, and they almost "nudge" or invite the jury to draw a conclusion.[5] They are discouraged in many states, used sparingly in others, and sometimes particular instructions are disallowed altogether. Even federal judges may be reluctant to give inference instructions, though traditionally they have more latitude than their state counterparts to comment on the evidence.

Probably the best known inference is the "res ipsa loquitur" device from tort law. Under certain conditions, it permits a finding of negligence to rest upon circumstantial evidence, even though the defense might otherwise hope for a directed verdict. This particular inference is special in expressing an important policy that certain plaintiffs should be allowed to recover, if the jury chooses to find in their favor. It is special too in that it is conveyed to the jury in careful and explicit instructions, which (in most jurisdictions) are given even in the face of counterproof offered by the defense.

4. *Prima facie case.* This supremely ambiguous term is used in two very different ways. It means either that the evidence *requires* a particular conclusion (like a presumption unanswered) or that the evidence *permits* that conclusion (like an inference). You will see this term in operation in the *Burdine* case, infra.

b.   How They Work in One-Sided and Contingent Situations

The operation of presumptions is easily understood on the two ends of the continuum of situations arising at trial. The matter becomes more complicated in what we call "contingent cases." (And things become almost unmanageable, and fraught with continuing controversy, in what we call the "in-between" case, separately taken up below.)

The one-sided situations. On one end of the spectrum, the unopposed presumption controls. Thus, if the basic facts are established by cogent and compelling evidence or stipulation and there is no counterproof indicating that the presumed fact is not so, then the trier must find the presumed fact. (In the example of the bailor's suit, the unopposed presumption requires the trier to

---

5. The question whether to instruct a civil jury that it may draw an inference gets mixed up in the analysis of presumptions. It is sometimes hard to figure out whether anything remains when a presumption is met by counterproof indicating the nonexistence of the presumed fact. One possibility is that an inference remains. If so, the next question is whether to mention the inference to the jury.

find that bailee's negligence caused the damage.) At the other end of the spectrum, the presumption disappears. Thus, if the party opposing the presumption offers cogent and compelling proof that the presumed fact is not so, the presumption drops from the case. (The bailee might win a directed verdict, despite the presumption, if he offers cogent and compelling evidence that the goods were undamaged on their return, for instance, or that any damage resulted from fire or earthquake or other "act of God.") In each of these one-sided situations, at opposite ends of the spectrum of possibilities, we can be confident of full and complete answers.

The contingent case. Sometimes there is enough proof of the basic facts to support a finding that they exist, but not enough to require such a finding, so the trier might find against the basic facts, disbelieving witnesses or resolving a conflict of proof by concluding that the basic facts are just not so. In this intermediate situation—between the case in which there is no proof of the basic facts (or insufficient evidence to support a finding) and the case in which the basic facts are established, by conclusive proof or stipulation—the presumption affects decision only if the trier finds the basic facts to be so. In this situation in a jury-tried case the judge must give a contingent (or conditional) instruction that *if* the jury finds the basic facts, *then* it must find the presumed fact.

PROBLEM 10-A.   *The Unhappy Harpsichordist*

Atlas Moving Company advertises as follows: "We are the ones who care. Trust our people to move your most cherished possessions as carefully as you would."

Glen, a professional pianist and harpsichordist, is famed for his modern interpretation of Bach's Goldberg Variations. On moving from New Haven to Los Angeles to become pianist in residence at the University of Southern California, Glen hired Atlas to move his valued antique harpsichord, along with other household furniture. The month was April, and one Larson (an experienced mover for Atlas) picked up and loaded Glen's possessions on the 12th and drove straight to Los Angeles, arriving there on the 16th. When the shipment arrived, Glen discovered a deep crack in the inner casing of the harpsichord, which severely impaired its tonal quality.

Glen sues Atlas for $20,000, supporting his damage claim with expert testimony. Glen himself testifies that he plays the instrument nearly every day and that it was in perfect condition when Atlas picked it up in New Haven.

Atlas introduces the deposition of Keenan, another accomplished keyboard artist in New Haven. The transcript contains Keenan's testimony that he played Glen's harpsichord in New Haven and noticed the crack in the casing at the time, along with impaired tonality.

At the close of the evidence, Glen requests the court to instruct the jury that if it finds that the harpsichord was undamaged when Larson picked it up, it must find Atlas responsible for damage to the instrument. Should the instruction be given?

NOTE ON PRESUMPTIONS IN THE CONTINGENT SITUATION

1.   Is the jury free to believe or reject Glen's testimony? Keenan's deposition testimony? What if Larson, in preparing the freight list, had described the harpsichord in these terms: "Item 16. One antique harpsichord. Good condition."

2.   Language originally proposed by the Advisory Committee would have told courts and lawyers how to handle the contingent situation:

> *Determination on Evidence of Basic Facts.* When no evidence is introduced contrary to the existence of the presumed fact, the question of its existence depends upon the existence of the basic facts and is determined as follows:
>
> (A) If reasonable minds would necessarily agree that the evidence renders the existence of the basic facts more probable than not, the judge shall direct the jury to find in favor of the existence of the presumed fact; or
>
> (B) If reasonable minds would necessarily agree that the evidence does not render the existence of the basic fact more probable than not, the judge shall direct the jury to find against the existence of the presumed fact; or
>
> (C) If reasonable minds would not necessarily agree as to whether the evidence renders the nonexistence of the basic facts more probable than not, the judge shall submit the matter to the jury with an instruction to find in favor of the existence of the presumed fact if they find from the evidence that the existence of the basic facts is more probable than not, but otherwise to find against the existence of the presumed fact.

Preliminary Draft, Rules of Evidence, Rule 3-03(2), 46 F.R.D. 161, 212-213 (1969). See St. Mary's Honor Center v. Hicks, 509 U.S. 502, 506 and n.3 (1993) (in setting of statutory presumption of discrimination, basic facts make out a prima facie case; court comments that if "reasonable minds could *differ* as to whether a preponderance of the evidence establishes the facts of a prima facie case" *and* if the factfinder "finds that the prima facie case *is*" made out, *then* the factfinder "*must* find the existence of the presumed fact" of discrimination) (original emphasis). In the absence of counterproof that the presumed fact does not exist, does its existence always "depend[ ] upon the existence of the basic facts"? Might there not be direct evidence of the presumed fact (such as testimony that a letter was delivered)? If so, then counterproof tending to show the nonexistence of the *basic facts* (such as testimony that the letter was not stamped) could not justify the instruction required by subsection (B). Do these possibilities explain why the above-quoted language was dropped?

c.   How They Work in the "In-Between" Situation

Sometimes the party hurt by the presumption offers counterproof that the presumed fact is not so—in the bailed goods case, that means evidence that the bailor was not negligent or that his negligence was not the cause of damage. Here is the "in-between" case: We are no longer in the one-sided situation where the presumption controls decision because there is no counterproof, but neither are we in the opposite one-sided situation where the presumption is routed because the counterproof is so "cogent and compelling" that victory goes automatically to the adverse party. Rather, we are in the middle, and the difficulties become serious. A debate has long raged between what has come to be called the "bursting bubble" approach (associated with the name of Thayer) and the reformist approach (associated with Morgan). The tension between these two views greatly affected Rule 301.

1. *The bursting bubble.* Common law had it that the presumption vanished from sight in this "in-between" situation. Courts and commentators waxed poetic (though sometimes in mixed metaphors): Presumptions "smoke out" the opponent, making him produce sufficient counterproof that the presumed fact is not so; when he does produce, the presumption is "put to flight"; hence presumptions are like "bursting bubbles"; also "like bats of the law, flitting in the twilight, but disappearing in the sunshine of actual facts"; and like "Maeterlinck's male bee" ("having functioned they disappear").[6] Thayer endorsed this traditional view, and it is associated with his name.

Less poetically, common law tradition meant that the presumption shifted, to the party against whom it operated, the burden of coming forward with evidence (burden of production) and *not* the burden of persuasion. In its pure form, the traditional approach meant the bailor could lose automatically if the bailee offered evidence that fire damaged the goods. Even though the bailor had a presumption working for him, the bailee's counterproof caused it to burst and the jury never got the case.

2. *The reformist approach.* The bursting bubble effect seemed absurd to able commentators. Most astute among the critics of the traditional approach was Professor Edmund Morgan, who argued that a presumption should shift the burden of persuasion. How, he asked, can a presumption be strong enough to *require* a finding in the absence of counterproof, yet so weak that it vanishes in the face of counterproof which the jury could reject? He had in mind the poignant circumstance in which only a presumption can take the case to the jury, which means that if counterproof "bursts" the presumption, then indeed the case fails, even though a jury would remain free (if only it got the chance) to disbelieve the counterproof. Here is his argument:

MR. MORGAN . . . In McIver v. Schwartz, [145 A. 101 (R.I. 1929),] the basic fact was the general employment of a servant by the defendant to drive the defendant's automobile. The presumed fact was that the servant . . . was in the scope of his employment at the time of the collision with the plaintiff. . . . The only evidence in the case on this point was testimony by the defendant himself who got on the stand and said that the boy was not authorized to drive the car at this particular hour. He had been driving the car in the morning. He had the keys to the car, and the employer explained [that] this was because he had neglected to turn the keys back. The boy was not called as a witness. The Supreme Court of Rhode Island assumed that both the trial judge and the jury positively

6. E.L. Cheeney Co. v. Gates, 346 F.2d 197, 202 (5th Cir. 1965) ("smoke out" the opponent); Cleary, Presuming and Pleading: An Essay in Juristic Immaturity, 12 Stan. L. Rev. 5, 16-17 (1959) ("bursting bubble"); Mackowik v. Kansas City, St. J. & C.B.R.R., 94 S.W. 256, 262 (Mo. 1906) ("bats of the law"); Bohlen, The Effect of Rebuttable Presumptions of Law Upon the Burden of Proof, 68 U. Pa. L. Rev. 307, 314 (1920) ("Maeterlinck's male bee").

disbelieved the testimony of the defendant. The plaintiff had a verdict; the defendant appealed on the ground that there was no question for the jury. . . . because the only testimony on scope of employment was the testimony as to the general employment of the servant by the defendant to drive the defendant's automobile. The plaintiff as respondent said: "That is true under previous Rhode Island decisions, but I had a presumption to help me." The Supreme Court of Rhode Island answered, "Yes, you had a presumption to help you, until the defendant introduced that testimony; it was testimony which a jury might have believed, and if the jury had believed the testimony, it would have justified them in finding no scope of employment. So your presumption was destroyed by the mere introduction of the evidence, and the fact that neither the jury nor the trial judge believed the testimony is entirely immaterial. The mere introduction of the evidence wipes out the total effect of the presumption." That is straight Thayer. . . . Mr. Thayer says in so many words that the sole effect of the presumption is to put on the opposing party the burden of producing evidence which would justify a trier in finding [against] the presumed fact.

. . . What I object to in the Thayerian rule is this: the creation of a presumption for a reason that the court deems sufficient, a rule of law [that] if this basic fact stands by itself [unrebutted] there must be a finding of a presumed fact, whether the jury would ordinarily find it from the basic fact or not; but some testimony is put in which anybody can disbelieve, which comes from interested witnesses, and which is of a sort that is usually disbelieved. It seems to me it is futile to create a presumption if it is to be so easily destroyed. . . . I say that the slightest definite weight you can give [to presumptions] . . . is to [let them] fix the burden of persuasion because the burden of persuasion is important . . . where the mind of the jury or the trier of fact is in equilibrium.

18 American Law Institute Proceedings 201-221 (1940-1941). Morgan lost the battle on that point, but his view prevailed in other times and other places, and the war is not over yet.

3. *FRE 301 and modern practice.* The drafters of the Rules were persuaded by the Morgan argument. In all three preenactment versions, the Committee included the following language:

[A] presumption imposes on the party against whom it is directed the burden of proving that the nonexistence of the presumed fact is more probable than its existence.

See 46 F.R.D. 161, 212 (1969) (Preliminary Draft); 51 F.R.D. 315, 336 (1971) (Revised Draft); 56 F.R.D. 183, 208 (1972) (draft sent to Congress).

Congress was not persuaded. The House of Representatives sought a compromise between the bursting bubble and the Morgan approach, and proposed treating civil presumptions as evidence. By this view, a presumption would not shift the burden of persuasion, but would not burst like a bubble either. Here is the critical language in the House proposal: "[E]ven though met with contradicting evidence, a presumption is sufficient evidence of the fact presumed, to be considered by the trier of the facts." See House Judiciary Print of H.R. 6453, November 15, 1973. But this approach had long been discredited and had been tested in only a few jurisdictions. The problem is that a presumption is *not* evidence, but a way of looking at evidence—so telling a jury that a presumption is evidence can only confuse.

The Senate rejected both the Committee's proposal and the House version, and settled on the language ultimately adopted. That language seems ever so much like a straight adoption of the bursting bubble approach. The crucial passage is as follows:

> [A] presumption imposes on the party against whom it is directed the burden of going forward with evidence to rebut or meet the presumption, but does not shift to such party the burden of proof in the sense of the risk of nonpersuasion, which remains throughout the trial upon the party on whom it was originally cast.

Here is an instance in which the Federal Rules did not carry their usual influence. The framers of the new Uniform Rules of Evidence (URE) preferred the Morgan approach, so Uniform Rule 301 follows the Advisory Committee's initial proposal rather than the congressional revision. And states adopting codes based on the federal model are badly split on this point.[7]

PROBLEM 10-B. *The Death of Mason Parnell*

Mason Parnell was a wheat farmer. At age 49, he died of a head wound inflicted by discharge of a 30.06 rifle while alone in the spare sleeping room in the basement of his house.

His widow Vera Parnell sues Midcontinent Casualty Company on an accidental death policy covering her husband, seeking recovery in the amount of $100,000. Midcontinent claims that suicide was the cause of death and denies all liability. In such cases claimant bears the burden of pleading that death came by accident, and also the burdens of production and persuasion on that point.

Physical evidence shows that Mason Parnell was flat on his back on the bed when the gun discharged and that the muzzle was close to his chin at the time.

There is other circumstantial evidence. Vera Parnell introduces testimony that (1) Mason Parnell did not shoot himself intentionally because no soot pattern or flash burn was found on his face (indicating that the muzzle was more than 12 inches away), (2) a rifle owned by Parnell accidentally discharged during an earlier hunting trip, (3) Parnell died clutching a cigarette lighter (hence he may have had only one hand free to hold the rifle and pull the trigger), and (4) Parnell was in good financial condition, healthy, happily married, and not moody or morose.

---

7. Out of 42 states adopting codes based on the Rules, 12 provide expressly that civil presumptions shift the burden of persuasion (Arkansas, Delaware, Maine, Mississippi, Montana, Nebraska, Nevada, North Dakota, Oregon, Utah, Wisconsin, and Wyoming). Another 17 states follow FRE 301 to the extent of providing expressly that civil presumptions affect the burden of production but not the burden of persuasion (Alaska, Colorado, Idaho, Indiana, Kentucky, Maryland, Michigan, Minnesota, New Hampshire, New Jersey, New Mexico, North Carolina, Ohio, South Carolina, South Dakota, Vermont, and West Virginia). Eight other states, unwilling to enter the fray, either omit provision for civil presumptions or omit any directive on their effect (Arizona, Connecticut, Iowa, Louisiana, Pennsylvania, Tennessee, Texas, and Washington). The other five states provide that *some* presumptions shift the burden of persuasion, while others shift only the burden of production (Alabama, Florida, Hawaii, Oklahoma, and Rhode Island).

But Midcontinent also introduces evidence that (a) the rifle that caused Parnell's death was in perfect order and was not the one that had accidentally discharged earlier, (b) some nasal hairs were found on the front gunsight, and (c) Parnell had experienced marital difficulties and may have been suffering from Alzheimer's disease.

At the close of the evidence, Vera requests that the jury be instructed on the presumption, arising from proof of sudden violent death, that death resulted from accident rather than suicide. Midcontinent argues that no such instruction is proper under the circumstances and moves for a directed verdict. The jurisdiction has adopted Rule 301, in the form enacted by Congress. What should the court do, and why?

NOTES ON PRESUMPTIONS IN THE "IN-BETWEEN" CASES

1. Almost all American jurisdictions recognize the presumption that Vera Parnell has invoked. Why? If that presumption were not recognized, do you think that a reasonable person could think, on the facts described in the problem, that the evidence establishes by a preponderance that Mason Parnell died an accidental death?

2. Courts in the "in-between" situation have sought in numerous ways to avoid the bursting bubble effect. Consider these approaches:

a. *"Substantial" or "uncontradicted" evidence.* A presumption survives the introduction of counterproof, and is rebutted only by counterproof of high quality—"substantial" or "uncontradicted" evidence, or counterproof that is "undisputed" or "clear and positive" or "unimpeached." One message of decisions taking this approach is that even counterproof sufficient to support a finding for the adverse party does not burst the presumption altogether, so satisfying the burden of production does not get the adversary out from under. Apparently another message is that the presumption, reduced in force, now protects an inference from extinction—in other words, it takes the case to the jury and allows it to find the presumed fact. This approach is most often seen with the loaned automobile and scope-of-employment presumptions. See Bieszck v. Avis Rent-A-Car System, Inc., 583 N.W.2d 691, 696 (Mich. 1998) (loaned auto presumption does not shift burden of persuasion, but can only be overcome by "positive, unequivocal, strong and credible" evidence, which "high threshold" serves the "legislative purpose underlying the statute and helps promote public safety") (this standard was met here); Gaither v. Myers, 404 F.2d 216 (D.C. Cir. 1968) (owner denied driving car, but his testimony "was not so consistent and conclusive" as to "overcome the presumption and permit a directed verdict"); E.L. Cheeney Co. v. Gates, 346 F.2d 197, 201-204 (5th Cir. 1965) (employee testified that he was supposed to drive the truck only to and from home and he had been visiting a friend, but "his credibility was attacked by a prior inconsistent statement" that he "had been working in an oilfield south of Dayton"; while this statement "would not carry the day on agency," there was a presumption which "alone suffices until it is rebutted by clear, positive, uncontradicted testimony," and in this case the counterproof did not "conclusively overcome the presumption").

b. *"Believe the evidence."* A presumption survives the introduction of counterproof challenging the presumed fact, and the jury should be told to find the presumed fact unless it "believes" the counterproof. See Sutphen v. Hagelin, 344 A.2d 270 (Conn. 1975) ("family car" presumption that driver had owner's permission does not disappear in the face of counterproof, and jury should be told that presumption applies if it disbelieves the counterproof).

c. *"Equipoise."* A presumption survives the introduction of counterproof, and the trier must find the presumed fact unless the counterproof makes the nonexistence of the presumed fact as likely as its existence. This "equipoise" approach is best expounded in an opinion by the Maine Supreme Court in Hinds v. John Hancock Mutual Life Insurance Co., 155 A.2d 721 (Me. 1959). There the court decided that presumptions should have "maximum coercive force short of shifting the burden of persuasion," and so endorsed a rule that the presumption controls "until the contrary evidence persuades the factfinder that the balance of probabilities is in equilibrium, or, stated otherwise, until the evidence satisfies the jury or factfinder that it is as probable that the presumed fact does not exist as that it does exist." (*Hinds* involved a presumption against suicide similar to that involved in Problem 10-B. Years later Maine adopted Uniform Rule 301, providing that presumptions shift the burden of persuasion.)

d. *"Shift burden of persuasion."* A presumption shifts to the party against whom it operates the burden of persuasion. Some common law decisions adopted Professor Morgan's approach. See, e.g., Knowles v. Gilchrist Co., 289 N.E.2d 879 (Mass. 1972) (bailed goods presumption shifts to bailee the burden of persuasion on the issue of its due care). Recall that the Advisory Committee did likewise in its original version of FRE 301 and that many states adopted that version of Rule 301. Others reach this result in some particular situations. See, e.g., Frederick v. Shankle, 785 A.2d 749, 751 (Md. 2001) (in context of statutory presumption that police officer suffering heart condition or hypertension contracted that disease at work, applying rule that policy-based presumptions shift burden of persuasion); Smith v. Atkinson, 771 So.2d 429, 435 (Ala. 2000) (in context of presumption that plaintiff would have prevailed but for destruction of evidence by spoliation, applying similar rule).

Apart from the Morgan view, do any of these alternatives appeal to you? Why or why not? See generally C. Mueller and L. Kirkpatrick, Evidence §3.8 (3d ed. 2003).

3. Sometimes courts avoid deciding how much counterproof is required before the presumption disappears, and instead focus on instructing the jury. Like Morgan's favorite example of *McIver*, the case of Grier v. Rosenberg, 131 A.2d 737 (Md. 1957) involved the presumption, arising on proof of car ownership, that the driver was the owner's agent. Here, however, plaintiff had been a passenger on a bus, which allegedly braked hard to avoid defendant's car when it carelessly cut in front of the bus. As in *McIver*, defendant testified that he did not remember the incident and had checked with others who sometimes used his car, learning that none of them recalled any such incident either. The Maryland Supreme Court concluded that the trial judge should "mention the presumption, so that the jury may appreciate the legal recognition of a slant

of policy or probability." See also Murphy v. 24th Street Cadillac Corp., 727 A.2d 915, 920 (Md. 1999) (under Maryland law, presumption "operates conclusively" if opposing party presents no evidence, but burden of production shifts back to party for whom presumption operates if opposing party produces conclusive evidence, and opposing party may be entitled to directed verdict; in the "final and perhaps most likely scenario," the opposing party produces "some evidence," and the existence of the presumed fact is submitted to the jury, which is "informed of the presumption"). Should a court use the word "presumption" in such instructions? Does that term oversell the force of the underlying policy, or undersell it? Or just confuse?

4.   Alaska Rule 301(a) includes the following:

> When the burden of producing evidence to meet a presumption is satisfied, the court must instruct the jury that it may, but is not required to, infer the existence of the presumed fact from the proved fact, but no mention of the word "presumption" may be made to the jury.

See Alaska Rules of Evidence (2002). Similar language appears in some other provisions. See, e.g., Maryland Rule 5-301(a) (when counterproof is offered, "the presumption will retain the effect of creating a question to be decided by the trier of fact" unless presumption has been rebutted "as a matter of law"); North Carolina Rule 301 (similar to Alaska provision, but with no admonition about the word "presumption"). Does this suggestion solve anything? Do the "proved fact[s]" in Problem 10-B support an inference that Mason Parnell died accidentally? How about providing that these cases should get to the jury without *any* instruction? A provision in Vermont seems to adopt this approach. It states that where the opponent has carried its burden of production, "the court shall submit the question of the existence of the presumed fact to the jury on the evidence as a whole without reference to the presumption," unless a reasonable juror could not find the presumed fact on all the evidence. Vermont Rules of Evidence, Rule 301(c)(2) (1983).

5.   Consider an instruction that tells the jury something about the underlying basis of presumptions. The Oregon Supreme Court endorsed this approach in a pre-Rules case similar to Problem 10-B. There the court concluded:

> The jury should be told that there is a presumption against suicide. The basis for the presumption should be explained, i.e., the normal human revulsion against taking one's own life. It would be proper to explain to the jury that it may infer that because people normally do not take their own lives because of this instinct for self-preservation, the deceased did not take his own life in the case before it. The jury should be told that the improbability of suicide is to be treated as any other evidentiary fact and that the presumption does not endow the fact upon which it is based with any special value for evidentiary purposes.

United States National Bank v. Underwriters at Lloyd's, London, 396 P.2d 765, 775 (Or. 1964). This approach has the virtue of reassuring the jury that it may apply common sense in evaluating the evidence, and that the law permits the jury to take into account the normal and expected patterns of life in reaching its decision. Thus the approach is better, isn't it, than telling the jury that the presumption itself is evidence, as some courts did in the past? But why tell the jury not to treat the inference as having "any special value"? And how, if at all, could this approach be adapted to the situation of the bailed goods presumption?

6. Some modern commentators endorse the bursting bubble approach. See Lansing, Enough Is Enough: A Critique of the Morgan View of Rebuttable Presumptions in Civil Cases, 62 Or. L. Rev. 485 (1983). Some modern cases do likewise. See O'Brien v. Equitable Life Assurance Society, 212 F.2d 383, 388-389 (8th Cir.) (while in bed with a woman, decedent was shot by woman's husband; decedent's widow sued the insurance carrier, invoking the presumption of accidental death, which could apply if decedent died as *victim* of a criminal assault; but the woman testified that decedent had forced her onto the bed and that she could not remember anything further; the presumption was "destroyed" because her testimony suggested that decedent died while *perpetrating* an assault), cert. denied, 348 U.S. 835 (1954). Was the purpose of the presumption of accidental death adequately served in *O'Brien?*

d. Operation of Rule 301

Consider again the language in Rule 301, which (we said above) "seems ever so much like a straight adoption of the bursting bubble approach." There is no doubt that the naked language of the provision is susceptible of that interpretation—the bursting bubble in pure form. But recall too how common law courts struggled to avoid this outcome, and consider post-Rules developments.

TEXAS DEPARTMENT OF COMMUNITY AFFAIRS v. BURDINE
United States Supreme Court
450 U.S. 248 (1981)

JUSTICE POWELL delivered the [unanimous] opinion of the Court.

This case requires us to address again the nature of the evidentiary burden placed upon the defendant in an employment discrimination suit brought under Title VII of the Civil Rights Act of 1964, 42 U.S.C. §2000e et seq. The narrow question presented is whether, after the plaintiff has proved a prima facie case of discriminatory treatment, the burden shifts to the defendant to persuade the court by a preponderance of the evidence that legitimate, nondiscriminatory reasons for the challenged employment action existed.

I

Petitioner, the Texas Department of Community Affairs (TDCA), hired respondent, a female, in January 1972, for the position of accounting clerk in the Public Service Careers Division (PSC). PSC provided training and employment opportunities in the public sector for unskilled workers. When hired, respondent possessed several years' experience in employment training. She was promoted to Field Services Coordinator in July 1972. Her supervisor resigned in November of that year, and respondent was assigned additional duties. Although she applied for the supervisor's position of Project Director, the position remained vacant for six months.

PSC was funded completely by the United States Department of Labor. The Department was seriously concerned about inefficiencies at PSC.[1] In February 1973, the Department notified the Executive Director of TDCA, B. R. Fuller, that it would terminate PSC the following month. TDCA officials, assisted by respondent, persuaded the Department to continue funding the program, conditioned upon PSC's reforming its operations. Among the agreed conditions were the appointment of a permanent Project Director and a complete reorganization of the PSC staff.

After consulting with personnel within TDCA, Fuller hired a male from another division of the agency as Project Director. In reducing the PSC staff, he fired respondent along with two other employees, and retained another male, Walz, as the only professional employee in the division. It is undisputed that respondent had maintained her application for the position of Project Director and had requested to remain with TDCA. Respondent soon was rehired by TDCA and assigned to another division of the agency. She received the exact salary paid to the Project Director at PSC, and the subsequent promotions she has received have kept her salary and responsibility commensurate with what she would have received had she been appointed Project Director.

Respondent filed this suit in the United States District Court for the Western District of Texas. She alleged that the failure to promote and the subsequent decision to terminate her had been predicated on gender discrimination in violation of Title VII. After a bench trial, the District Court held that neither decision was based on gender discrimination. The court relied on the testimony of Fuller that the employment decisions necessitated by the commands of the Department of Labor were based on consultation among trusted advisers and a non-discriminatory evaluation of the relative qualifications of the individuals involved. He testified that the three individuals terminated did not work well together, and that TDCA thought that eliminating this problem would improve PSC's efficiency. The court accepted this explanation as rational and, in effect, found no evidence that the decisions not to promote and to terminate respondent were prompted by gender discrimination.

The Court of Appeals for the Fifth Circuit reversed in part. . . . It rejected the District Court's finding that Fuller's testimony sufficiently had rebutted respondent's prima facie case of gender discrimination in the decision to terminate her employment at PSC. The court reaffirmed its previously announced views that the defendant in a Title VII case bears the burden of proving by a preponderance of the evidence the existence of legitimate nondiscriminatory reasons for the employment action and that the defendant also must prove by objective evidence that those hired or promoted were better qualified than the plaintiff. The court found that Fuller's testimony did not carry either of these evidentiary burdens. It, therefore, reversed the judgment of the District Court

1. Among the problems identified were overstaffing, lack of fiscal control, poor bookkeeping, lack of communication among PSC staff, and the lack of a full-time Project Director.

and remanded the case for computation of backpay. Because the decision of the Court of Appeals as to the burden of proof borne by the defendant conflicts with interpretations of our precedents adopted by other Courts of Appeals, we granted certiorari. We now vacate the Fifth Circuit's decision and remand for application of the correct standard.

II

In McDonnell Douglas Corp. v. Green, 411 U.S. 792 (1973), we set forth the basic allocation of burdens and order of presentation of proof in a Title VII case alleging discriminatory treatment.[5] First, the plaintiff has the burden of proving by the preponderance of the evidence a prima facie case of discrimination. Second, if the plaintiff succeeds in proving the prima facie case, the burden shifts to the defendant "to articulate some legitimate, nondiscriminatory reason for the employee's rejection." Third, should the defendant carry this burden, the plaintiff must then have an opportunity to prove by a preponderance of the evidence that the legitimate reasons offered by the defendant were not its true reasons, but were a pretext for discrimination.

The nature of the burden that shifts to the defendant should be understood in light of the plaintiff's ultimate and intermediate burdens. The ultimate burden of persuading the trier of fact that the defendant intentionally discriminated against the plaintiff remains at all times with the plaintiff. See generally 9 J. Wigmore, Evidence §2489 (3d ed. 1940) (the burden of persuasion "never shifts"). The *McDonnell Douglas* division of intermediate evidentiary burdens serves to bring the litigants and the court expeditiously and fairly to this ultimate question.

The burden of establishing a prima facie case of disparate treatment is not onerous. The plaintiff must prove by a preponderance of the evidence that she applied for an available position for which she was qualified, but was rejected under circumstances which give rise to an inference of unlawful discrimination.[6] The prima facie case serves an important function in the litigation: it eliminates

---

5. We have recognized that the factual issues, and therefore the character of the evidence presented, differ when the plaintiff claims that a facially neutral employment policy has a discriminatory impact on protected classes.

6. In *McDonnell Douglas*, we described an appropriate model for a prima facie case of racial discrimination. The plaintiff must show:

> (i) that he belongs to a racial minority; (ii) that he applied and was qualified for a job for which the employer was seeking applicants; (iii) that, despite his qualifications, he was rejected; and (iv) that, after his rejection, the position remained open and the employer continued to seek applicants from persons of complainant's qualifications.

We added, however, that this standard is not inflexible, as

> [t]he facts necessarily will vary in Title VII cases, and the specification above of the prima facie proof required from respondent is not necessarily applicable in every respect in differing factual situations.

In the instant case, it is not seriously contested that respondent has proved a prima facie case. She showed that she was a qualified woman who sought an available position, but the position was left open for several months before she finally was rejected in favor of a male, Walz, who had been under her supervision.

the most common nondiscriminatory reasons for the plaintiff's rejection. . . . [T]he prima facie case "raises an inference of discrimination only because we presume these acts, if otherwise unexplained, are more likely than not based on the consideration of impermissible factors." Establishment of the prima facie case in effect creates a presumption that the employer unlawfully discriminated against the employee. If the trier of fact believes the plaintiff's evidence, and if the employer is silent in the face of the presumption, the court must enter judgment for the plaintiff because no issue of fact remains in the case.[7]

The burden that shifts to the defendant, therefore, is to rebut the presumption of discrimination by producing evidence that the plaintiff was rejected, or someone else was preferred, for a legitimate, nondiscriminatory reason. The defendant need not persuade the court that it was actually motivated by the proffered reasons. It is sufficient if the defendant's evidence raises a genuine issue of fact as to whether it discriminated against the plaintiff.[8] To accomplish this, the defendant must clearly set forth, through the introduction of admissible evidence, the reasons for the plaintiff's rejection.[9] The explanation provided must be legally sufficient to justify a judgment for the defendant. If the defendant carries this burden of production, the presumption raised by the prima facie case is rebutted,[10] and the factual inquiry proceeds to a new level of specificity. Placing this burden of production on the defendant thus serves simultaneously to meet the plaintiff's prima facie case by presenting a legitimate reason for the action and to frame the factual issue with sufficient clarity so that the plaintiff will have a full and fair opportunity to demonstrate pretext. The sufficiency of the defendant's evidence should be evaluated by the extent to which it fulfills these functions.

The plaintiff retains the burden of persuasion. She now must have the opportunity to demonstrate that the proffered reason was not the true reason

---

7. The phrase "prima facie case" not only may denote the establishment of a legally mandatory, rebuttable presumption, but also may be used by courts to describe the plaintiff's burden of producing enough evidence to permit the trier of fact to infer the fact at issue. *McDonnell Douglas* should have made it apparent that in the Title VII context we use "prima facie case" in the former sense.

8. This evidentiary relationship between the presumption created by a prima facie case and the consequential burden of production placed on the defendant is a traditional feature of the common law. "The word 'presumption' properly used refers only to a device for allocating the production burden." F. James & G. Hazard, Civil Procedure §7.9, p. 255 (2d ed. 1977) (footnote omitted). See FRE 301. Usually, assessing the burden of production helps the judge determine whether the litigants have created an issue of fact to be decided by the jury. In a Title VII case, the allocation of burdens and the creation of a presumption by the establishment of a prima facie case is intended progressively to sharpen the inquiry into the elusive factual question of intentional discrimination.

9. An articulation not admitted into evidence will not suffice. Thus, the defendant cannot meet its burden merely through an answer to the complaint or by argument of counsel.

10. See generally J. Thayer, Preliminary Treatise on Evidence 346 (1898). In saying that the presumption drops from the case, we do not imply that the trier of fact no longer may consider evidence previously introduced by the plaintiff to establish a prima facie case. A satisfactory explanation by the defendant destroys the legally mandatory inference of discrimination arising from the plaintiff's initial evidence. Nonetheless, this evidence and inferences properly drawn therefrom may be considered by the trier of fact on the issue of whether the defendant's explanation is pretextual. Indeed, there may be some cases where the plaintiff's initial evidence, combined with effective cross-examination of the defendant, will suffice to discredit the defendant's explanation.

for the employment decision. This burden now merges with the ultimate burden of persuading the court that she has been the victim of intentional discrimination. She may succeed in this either directly by persuading the court that a discriminatory reason more likely motivated the employer or indirectly by showing that the employer's proffered explanation is unworthy of credence.

III

In reversing the judgment of the District Court that the discharge of respondent from PSC was unrelated to her sex, the Court of Appeals adhered to two rules it had developed to elaborate the defendant's burden of proof. First, the defendant must prove by a preponderence of the evidence that legitimate, nondiscriminatory reasons for the discharge existed. Second, to satisfy this burden, the defendant "must prove that those he hired . . . were somehow *better* qualified than was plaintiff; in other words, comparative evidence is needed."

A

The Court of Appeals has misconstrued the nature of the burden that *McDonnell Douglas* and its progeny place on the defendant. We stated in [Board of Trustees of Keene State College v.] Sweeney [439 U.S. 24 (1978)] that "the employer's burden is satisfied if he simply 'explains what he has done' or 'produc[es] evidence of legitimate nondiscriminatory reasons.' " It is plain that the Court of Appeals required much more: it placed on the defendant the burden of persuading the court that it had convincing, objective reasons for preferring the chosen applicant above the plaintiff.

The Court of Appeals distinguished *Sweeney* on the ground that the case held only that the defendant did not have the burden of proving the absence of discriminatory intent. But this distinction slights the rationale of *Sweeney* and of our other cases. We have stated consistently that the employee's prima facie case of discrimination will be rebutted if the employer articulates lawful reasons for the action; that is, to satisfy this intermediate burden, the employer need only produce admissible evidence which would allow the trier of fact rationally to conclude that the employment decision had not been motivated by discriminatory animus. The Court of Appeals would require the defendant to introduce evidence which, in the absence of any evidence of pretext, would *persuade* the trier of fact that the employment action was lawful. This exceeds what properly can be demanded to satisfy a burden of production.

The court placed the burden of persuasion on the defendant apparently because it feared that "[i]f an employer need only *articulate*—not prove—a legitimate, nondiscriminatory reason for his action, he may compose fictitious, but legitimate, reasons for his actions." We do not believe, however, that limiting the defendant's evidentiary obligation to a burden of production will unduly hinder the plaintiff. First, as noted above, the defendant's explanation of its legitimate reasons must be clear and reasonably specific. This obligation arises both from the necessity of rebutting the inference of discrimination arising from the prima facie case and from the requirement that the plaintiff be afforded "a full and fair opportunity" to demonstrate pretext. Second, although the defendant does not bear a formal burden of persuasion, the defendant nevertheless retains an incentive to persuade the trier of fact that the employment decision was lawful. Thus, the defendant normally will attempt to prove the factual basis for its explanation. Third, the liberal discovery rules applicable to any civil suit in federal court are supplemented in a Title VII suit by the plaintiff's access to the Equal Employment Opportunity Commission's investigatory files concerning her complaint. Given these factors, we are unpersuaded that the plaintiff will find it particularly difficult to prove that a proffered explanation lacking a factual basis is a pretext. We remain confident that the *McDonnell Douglas* framework permits the plaintiff meriting relief to demonstrate intentional discrimination.

B

The Court of Appeals also erred in requiring the defendant to prove by objective evidence that the person hired or promoted was more qualified than the plaintiff. *McDonnell Douglas* teaches that it is the plaintiff's task to demonstrate that similarly situated employees were not treated equally. The Court of Appeals' rule would require the employer to show that the plaintiff's objective qualifications were inferior to those of the person selected. If it cannot, a court would, in effect, conclude that it has discriminated.

The court's procedural rule harbors a substantive error. Title VII prohibits all discrimination in employment based upon race, sex, and national origin. . . . Title VII, however, does not demand that an employer give preferential treatment to minorities or women. . . . It does not require the employer to restructure his employment practices to maximize the number of minorities and women hired.

The views of the Court of Appeals can be read, we think, as requiring the employer to hire the minority or female applicant whenever that person's objective qualifications were equal to those of a white male applicant. But Title VII does not obligate an employer to accord this preference. Rather, the employer has discretion to choose among equally qualified candidates, provided the decision is not based upon unlawful criteria. The fact that a court may think that the employer misjudged the qualifications of the applicants does not in itself expose him to Title VII liability, although this may be probative of whether the employer's reasons are pretexts for discrimination.

IV

In summary, the Court of Appeals erred by requiring the defendant to prove by a preponderance of the evidence the existence of nondiscriminatory reasons for terminating the respondent and that the person retained in her stead had superior objective qualifications for the position. When the plaintiff has proved a prima facie case of discrimination, the defendant bears only the burden of explaining clearly the nondiscriminatory reasons for its actions. The judgment of the Court of Appeals is vacated, and the case is remanded for further proceedings consistent with this opinion.

It is so ordered.

NOTES ON *BURDINE* AND FRE 301 IN
"IN-BETWEEN" CASES

1.   *Burdine* was a Title VII suit for purposeful discrimination, and before 1991 a claim based on that statute was tried to a court without a jury. The Supreme Court recognized as much in footnote 8, where it commented that the presumption helps "sharpen the inquiry into the elusive factual question of intentional discrimination" rather than playing its more usual role in helping determine whether plaintiff produced enough evidence to take her case to a jury. But in 1991 Congress amended the statute. In suits claiming "unlawful intentional discrimination" (as opposed to disparate impact), the amended statute says plaintiffs may recover "compensatory and punitive damages" (previously only back pay and injunctive relief could be had under Title VII). And it says plaintiffs seeking compensatory or punitive damages "may demand a trial by jury." See 42 U.S.C. §1981a. Hence *Burdine*'s interpretation of "prima facie case" now applies in jury trials.

2.   *Burdine* says a plaintiff in a Title VII suit makes out a "prima facie case" by showing she was a member of a protected class, that she applied for a job, that she was qualified, that the job remained open, and that the job went to one who was not in a protected class. Surely proof of those points would not suffice, as a matter of pure logic, to take a case to a jury or to permit a judge to find in claimant's favor. If the facts underlying the prima facie case are established and defendant offers no counterproof, what should happen in a jury-tried case, according to *Burdine*? In a judge-tried case?

3.   Suppose a new case similar to *Burdine:* This time defendant offers proof sufficient to support a finding that the man promoted to supervisor in preference to plaintiff was better qualified. But plaintiff vigorously attacks this proof by cross-examining defense witnesses, and in the end the factfinder could reasonably conclude that the man was *not* better qualified, or that his qualifications were *not* the reason he was preferred. Finally, suppose plaintiff seeks compensatory damages. If there were a jury, could the defense win a motion seeking judgment as a matter of law? (On this point, consider what effect a "bursting bubble" theory would have.) Could she ask for a conditional instruction directing the jury to find in her favor, in accord with the concept of the "prima facie case" developed in *Burdine,* if the jury rejects the defense explanation? In St. Mary's Honor Center v. Hicks, 509 U.S. 502 (1993), a five-Justice majority answered the first question yes (plaintiff survives) and the second question no (she does not get a favorable instruction). *St. Mary's* was a judge-tried race discrimination case, and there the Court concluded that rejecting the counterproof *did not mean* the judge had to find for the plaintiff. Once a defendant carries its burden of production, the *McDonnell Douglas* framework (with its "presumptions and burdens") was "no longer relevant" and "resurrect[ing] it later . . . flies in the face of *Burdine*." But if plaintiff could not *win* automatically, it did not follow that she must *lose* automatically either. Here is the important language in *St. Mary's:*

The presumption, having fulfilled its role of forcing the defendant to come forward with some response, simply drops out of the picture. The defendant's "production" (whatever its persuasive effect) having been made, the trier of fact proceeds to decide the ultimate question: whether plaintiff has proven "that the defendant intentionally discriminated against [him]" because of his race. The factfinder's disbelief of the reasons put forward by the defendant (particularly if disbelief is accompanied by a suspicion of mendacity) may, together with the elements of the prima facie case, suffice to show intentional discrimination. Thus, rejection of the defendant's proffered reasons, will *permit* the trier of fact to infer the ultimate fact of intentional discrimination, and the Court of Appeals was correct when it noted that, upon such rejection, "no additional proof of discrimination is *required*." But the Court of Appeals' holding that the rejection of the defendant's proffered reasons *compels* judgment for the plaintiff disregards the fundamental principle of Rule 301 that a presumption does not shift the burden of proof, and ignores our repeated admonition that the Title VII plaintiff at all times bears the "ultimate burden of persuasion."

St. Mary's Honor Center v. Hicks, 509 U.S. 502, 511 (1993).

4.   In *Burdine*, plaintiff apparently had no "direct evidence" of discrimination, but relied on circumstantial evidence—she belonged to a protected class, was qualified, made timely application for an open position, and was turned down. This "prima facie case" gave rise to the presumption that shifted the burden of production to the defendant. In Price Waterhouse v. Hopkins, 490 U.S. 228 (1990), Justice Brennan wrote for a plurality of four Justices that if plaintiff shows by a preponderance that an improper motive (like gender) was a factor in the employer's decision, the defendant then bears the burden of persuasion on the question whether it would have made the same decision solely on the basis of proper motives. In *Price Waterhouse* (unlike *Burdine*), plaintiff had some direct evidence that her employer considered gender in its decision. There was a comment that she should "walk more femininely, talk more femininely, dress more femininely, wear make-up, have her hair styled, and wear jewelry." There was also evidence of proper motivation: She was faulted for "abrasiveness" and "brusqueness" and related deficiencies in "interpersonal skills." Putting on an employer the burden of persuasion on the question whether the employer's decision would have been the same without considering gender "casts no shadow on *Burdine*," wrote Justice Brennan, because the situation "is not the one of 'shifting burdens' " that *Burdine* addressed, and the employer's burden in this mixed motive case "is most appropriately deemed an affirmative defense." (Three dissenters would have put on the plaintiff the burden of persuasion on the question whether improper motive like gender was the "but-for" basis of the decision, arguing that under *Burdine* the plaintiff bears the ultimate burden of persuasion on this point.) In separate concurring opinions, Justices White and O'Connor agreed with the Brennan plurality that after plaintiff offers sufficient evidence of mixed motives, defendant bears the burden of persuading the factfinder that the same decision would have been made in the absence of the improper motive. Both White and O'Connor thought this approach was consistent with *Burdine*, and Justice O'Connor added this explanation:

The structure of the presentation of evidence in an individual treatment case should conform to the general outlines we established in *McDonnell Douglas* and *Burdine*. First, the plaintiff must establish the *McDonnell Douglas* prima facie case by showing membership in a protected group, qualification for the job, rejection for the position, and that after rejection the employer continued to seek applicants of complainant's general qualifications. The plaintiff should also present any direct evidence of discriminatory animus in the decisional process. The defendant should then present its case, including its evidence as to legitimate, nondiscriminatory reasons for the employment decision. . . . Once all the evidence has been received, the court should determine whether the *McDonnell Douglas* or *Price Waterhouse* framework properly applies to the evidence before it.

490 U.S. 228, at 278. *Price Waterhouse* means, doesn't it, that plaintiffs in Title VII cases are in a *much better position* if they offer "direct evidence" of discrimination than they are if they must rely on the presumption?

5.   *Burdine* cites FRE 301 but doesn't actually say the scheme mapped for Title VII suits is the one FRE 301 would impose. In *St. Mary's,* the passage quoted above in Note 3 referring to "the fundamental principle of Rule 301" suggests again that the Title VII scheme is an application of FRE 301, doesn't it? A similar attitude is visible in a decision involving two "black lung" presumptions, which are designed to help coal miners and their families recover benefits when miners contract or die of pneumoconiosis: One is a presumption, arising on proof that miner was employed in the mines for ten years and suffered from pneumoconiosis, that the ailment was contracted in the mines; another is a presumption, arising on proof that a miner employed for ten years died from a respiratory ailment, that this disease caused his death. Here again the Court cited FRE 301 and said that each presumption is "explicitly rebuttable, and the effect of each is simply to shift the burden of going forward with evidence from the claimant to the [mine] operator." See Usery v. Turner Elkhorn Mining Co., 428 U.S. 1, 27 (1976). Why is the Court, in two discrimination cases and a black lung case, so coy on the question whether FRE 301 actually applies?

6.   Recall that Congress was responsible for the direction taken in FRE 301: The Advisory Committee endorsed the Morgan position, but Congress rejected it. Does the enacted version of FRE 301 mandate the bursting bubble approach? Consider the Report of the House-Senate Conference Committee, which says that if the adverse party offers "evidence contradicting the presumed fact," the jury should be told "that it may infer the existence of the presumed fact from proof of the basic facts." Does that sound like a bursting bubble? When the logical probative force of the basic facts would support an inference of the presumed fact, such an inference should remain possible even if counterproof against the presumed fact is offered and the presumption is treated as having burst like a bubble and disappeared. But the same cannot be said if the probative force of the basic facts would not support such an inference, as is the case with the presumption of discrimination involved in *Burdine* and *St. Mary's.* The comment in the Report does not distinguish between these situations, does it? Not surprisingly, modern authority is split on the effect that FRE 301 prescribes for civil presumptions in the "in-between" case where there is some counterproof but not enough to require a decision favoring the party against whom the presumption operates. Compare Rice v. Office of Servicemembers' Group Life Insurance, 260 F.3d 1240 (10th Cir. 2001) (declining to accept bursting bubble interpretation, and approving instruction conveying to jury a presumption of competency despite proof of incompetency) and United States

v. Jessup, 757 F.2d 378, 380-384 (1st Cir. 1985) (rejecting bursting bubble approach for statutory bail presumption applied by magistrate, and seeking "middle ground" where magistrate or judge should "still keep in mind" that Congress found that major drug offenders "pose special risks of flight") with A.C. Aukerman Co. v. R.L. Chaides Construction Co., 960 F.2d 1020, 1037-1038 (Fed. Cir. 1992) (FRE 301 embodies bursting bubble theory, under which presumption "completely vanishes upon introduction of evidence sufficient to support a finding of the nonexistence of the presumed fact") and In re Yoder Co., 758 F.2d 1114, 1119-1120 (6th Cir. 1985) (FRE 301 adopts bursting bubble theory).

7. Note that the same congressional report says that if no counterproof is offered, the court should instruct the jury that "it may presume the existence of the presumed fact." Does that mean a presumption governed by FRE 301 never *controls* decision? In *St. Mary's*, the Court commented that a presumption means that "a finding of the predicate fact (here, the prima facie case) produces 'a required conclusion in the absence of explanation' (here, the finding of unlawful discrimination)," adding that the Title VII presumption "operates like all presumptions, as described in Rule 301." See St. Mary's Honor Center v. Hicks, 509 U.S. 502, 1747 (1993) (quoting a commentator). The congressional notes are confused about the nature of presumptions, aren't they? The Court in *St. Mary's* rejects the view that presumptions never control decisions, and in fact the Court in *St. Mary's* has a far better grasp of the subject, doesn't it?

8. Modern commentators have been critical of FRE 301. See generally Allen, Presumptions, Inferences and Burden of Proof in Federal Civil Actions—An Anatomy of Unnecessary Ambiguity and a Proposal for Reform, 76 Nw. L. Rev. 892 (1982); Mueller, Instructing the Jury Upon Presumptions in Civil Cases, 22 Land & Water L. Rev. 219 (1977).

FURTHER NOTES ON *BURDINE* AND APPLICATION OF FRE 301

1. Long ago the Supreme Court held that a "legislative presumption" could pass muster under the Due Process and Equal Protection Clauses if there were "some rational connection between the fact proved and the ultimate fact presumed," such that finding the latter on the basis of the former is not "so unreasonable as to be a purely arbitrary mandate." Mobile, J. & K.C. Ry. v. Turnipseed, 219 U.S. 35, 43 (1910). The decision in *Turner Elkhorn* quotes another opinion to the effect that courts judging rationality should give "significant weight" to the capacity of Congress "to amass the stuff of actual experience and cull conclusions from it," and quickly concludes that the black lung presumptions are valid. Usery v. Turner Elkhorn Mining Co., 428 U.S. 1, 28 (1976). Given *Turner Elkhorn*, it seems clear that the prima facie case in *Burdine* satisfies the "rational basis" standard. That means, doesn't it, that Congress may enact statutory civil presumptions serving substantive policy even where the basic facts would not, as a matter of mere logic, suffice to prove the presumed fact?

2. It seems clear that *Turner Elkhorn's* "black lung" presumptions express an important policy favoring recovery for coal miners and their families. Surely

those presumptions also help resolve cases where positive and particularized proof cannot be had. Can the same things be said of the prima facie case in *Burdine?* Don't these points suggest that bursting bubble treatment is singularly inappropriate for the presumptions in both cases? What do these points suggest about FRE 301?

3. Federal law (the Carmack Amendment to the Interstate Commerce Act) makes common carriers liable to shippers "for any loss, damage or injury" to property they receive for transportation, and the Supreme Court has held that under this statute the shipper makes out a "prima facie case" by showing "delivery in good condition, arrival in damaged condition, and the amount of damages," and that thereafter "the burden of proof is upon the carrier to show both that it was free from negligence and that the damage to the cargo was due to one of the excepted causes relieving the carrier of liability." Missouri Pacific R.R. v. Elmore & Stahl, 377 U.S. 134, 137 (1964). In a judge-tried post-Rules suit by the shipper of 198,568 aerosol cans of Solarcaine spray, seeking recovery because the plastic caps in the top two layers of cartons were "discolored" (apparently road dirt came through a hole in the truck), the trial court gave judgment for defendant. The Sixth Circuit reversed, concluding that the Carmack Amendment as interpreted in *Missouri Pacific* shifts "not the burden of going forward" but the burden of persuasion, and that the trial court erred in placing that burden on plaintiff shipper. The reviewing court rejected defendant's contention that the trial judge did right under FRE 301:

> It is immediately apparent that Rule 301 does not affect the burden of proof in Carmack Amendment cases. For well-articulated reasons Congress chose to place the burden of proof on a carrier in whose hands goods are damaged rather than on the shipper. This is more than a burden of going forward with the evidence. It is a true burden of proof in the sense of the risk of nonpersuasion and it remains on the carrier once the prima facie showing has been made.

Plough, Inc. v. Mason & Dixon Lines, 630 F.2d 468, 472 (6th Cir. 1980). How can we tell that FRE 301 does not control the effect of a "prima facie case" under the Carmack Amendment? What are the "well-articulated reasons" that justify putting on defendant carrier the burden of persuasion when plaintiff shipper makes his "prima facie case"? See also Tenneco Chemical v. William T. Burnett & Co., 691 F.2d 658, 663-664 (4th Cir. 1982) (statutory presumption of validity of patent shifts burden of persuasion, and FRE 301 does not apply).

4. Does the phrase "otherwise provided for" embrace a presumption established by statute that is entirely silent on its procedural ramifications? Presbyterian/St. Luke's Medical Center v. NLRB, 653 F.2d 450 (10th Cir. 1981) (presumption favoring "single facility [bargaining] units" entertained by NLRB in applying National Labor Relations Act is controlled by FRE 301). How about a presumption evolving entirely as a matter of federal common law? See James v. River Parishes Co., 686 F.2d 1129, 1132-1133 (5th Cir. 1982) (when drifting vessel causes damage, presumption of negligence arises, under which custodian of vessel "bears the burden of disproving fault by a preponderance of the evidence"; FRE 301 does not apply to this presumption arising from "substantive principles of admiralty and maritime law" that "long antedated" the Rules); accord City of Boston v. S.S. Texaco Texas, 773 F.2d 1396, 1398 (1st Cir. 1985).

5. Do you sense in *Burdine* and *Turner Elkhorn* a certain reticence to say

whether FRE 301 applies? Do you see in *Plough* and *James* a downright reluctance to apply FRE 301? What accounts for such resistance?

e. The "In-Between" Situation Reconsidered

Recall Morgan and the *McIver* case. Morgan complained about the outcome there (plaintiff's case taken from jury on defendant's testimony that the boy was not authorized to drive the car). But in the same speech, he suggested that the "bursting bubble" approach would not be so bad "where the evidence would ordinarily take the case to the jury anyhow" because the evidence of the basic fact "would ordinarily justify a finding of the presumed fact" even without the aid of a presumption. 18 American Law Institute Proceedings 221 (1940-1941). It turns out that what Morgan had in mind was not one rule for civil presumptions, but two, and the idea of a bifurcated approach has scored several successes.

Many years later, the National Commissioners on Uniform State Laws followed the Morgan suggestion, at least in creating two rules for presumptions. Under the original Uniform Rules, adopted by the Commissioners in 1953, where the basic facts have "any probative value as evidence of the existence of the presumed fact," the presumption shifts the burden of persuasion, but where they have "no probative value as evidence of the existence of the presumed fact," the presumption shifts only the burden of production, disappearing when counterproof is adduced. See Uniform Rules of Evidence, Rule 14 (1953). See also Oklahoma Evidence Code, Rule 303 (1978) (similar). These codifications, however, seemed to turn Morgan on his head, giving *more effect* to presumptions based "merely" on logic than to presumptions based on policy.

Several other major jurisdictions also take a bifurcated approach, and appear to follow Morgan more closely. In California, Florida, and Hawaii, for example, a presumption designed to further a "public policy" shifts the burden of persuasion, but a presumption designed "to facilitate the determination of the particular action" shifts only the burden of production. See Cal. Evid. Code §§603-606 (West, 1995); Fla. Stat. Ann. §§90.301-90.303 (1999); Haw. Rules of Evidence, Rules 301-303 (1983). California and Florida provide further help, with statutory lists of presumptions in each category. In both states, the presumption of validity of a ceremonial marriage and the presumption of death of a person not heard from for seven years belong in the public policy category (affecting the burden of persuasion), and the mailed letter presumption only facilitates determination of the action (affecting only burden of production).

Surely Morgan and the last-mentioned jurisdictions taking a dual approach are on to something. Not all presumptions are created equal, and some should have greater effect than others. Unfortunately it is hard to decide which presumption belongs in which category and even to define the scope of the categories. In a dual scheme, how should we treat the bailed goods presumption? The presumption that accident rather than suicide caused the death? The presumption of discrimination in employment? The black lung presumption?

The problem may be that we have no rank ordering of presumptions and might never agree upon one. The common law failed to develop a comprehensive approach; the few jurisdictions that tackle the problem by code disagree on the categories and offer only incomplete lists for each one. If we are going to have a one-rule world, which one should we choose for all presumptions, URE 301 or FRE 301?

f. State Presumptions in Diversity Cases

Rule 302 provides that in federal courts state law controls the "effect" of presumptions relating to "a fact which is an element of a claim or defense as to which State law supplies the rule of decision." Clearly this provision expresses the judgment that presumptions are "substantive" for *Erie* purposes, in obvious expectation that *Erie* requires federal courts to apply state presumptions.

Many state counterparts to Rule 302 similarly require state courts to recognize federal presumptions in the relatively unusual case in which state courts apply federal law in civil litigation.

NOTES ON FRE 302

1. Note that the ACN to FRE 302 distinguishes between mere "tactical" presumptions, which a federal court may ignore, and presumptions that "operate[ ]" on an "element of the claim or defense." Imagine a diversity suit on an open account, in which a merchant seeks to prove that a buyer tacitly agreed with the amount stated in monthly bills by failing to protest. If the merchant seeks to prove delivery of such bills by proving that he posted them, does FRE 302 require the federal court to give the same "effect" to this presumption that applicable state law would give? Why not require application of state "tactical" presumptions?

2. For purposes of FRE 302, "presumption" should be read to embrace res ipsa loquitur. It is settled that in diversity cases the state doctrine of res ipsa applies. See Travelers Insurance Co. v. Riggs, 671 F.2d 810 (4th Cir. 1982). Probably "presumption" in FRE 302 also embraces such devices as the prima facie case, at least when sophisticated statutory schemes such as the Uniform Commercial Code employ them in an obvious effort to regulate burdens in litigation. See UCC §2-719(3) (with respect to consumer goods, contractual limitations on consequential damages is prima facie unconscionable).

3. The Federal Tort Claims Act authorizes suit against the government for tortious injury inflicted by its agents. The statute requires federal courts to apply the law of the state "where the act or omission occurred." 18 U.S.C. §1346(b). Certainly Congress could, if it chose, enact substantive tort principles to govern such claims, so here state law applies only because Congress wisely chose not to go in that direction, and instead *provided* that state law governs. Here, in other words, is a place in which state law is made part of a federal standard. Should FRE 302 require application of state presumptions in this instance, or only where (as in diversity cases) state law applies of its own accord under *Erie*? See Pacheco v. United States, 409 F.2d 1234, 1238 (3d Cir. 1969) (applying state presumption in suit brought under Federal Tort Claims Act).

4. Sometimes federal courts face a challenge in applying state presumptions. Consider a diversity suit in Pennsylvania on an accidental death policy, arising out of the crash of a private plane in Delaware. Defendant American

Home claims that Scott committed suicide by interfering with the controls, killing himself and the pilot. Scott got the policy from a Philadelphia broker, who obtained an oral binder (and policy itself) from American in New York. All three states recognize a presumption against suicide but give it different effects. Which version should a federal court in Pennsylvania choose? Under FRE 302, should a federal court look to the state choice-of-law rule to decide which state's presumption applies, or devise a federal choice-of-law rule? Absent federal statute (none applied here), it is settled by Klaxon v. Stentor Electric Manufacturing Co., 313 U.S. 487 (1941), that in a diversity case *Erie* requires a federal court to apply the choice-of-law rule of the state where it sits. See Melville v. American Home Assurance Co., 584 F.2d 1306 (3d Cir. 1978) (apply Delaware rule because a Pennsylvania state court would do so).

B. BURDENS, PRESUMPTIONS, AND INFERENCES IN CRIMINAL CASES

1. *Burden of Persuasion*

It is settled that the Due Process Clauses of the Fifth and Fourteenth Amendments require the prosecutor to prove beyond a reasonable doubt every element in the crime charged against the accused, in state and federal court alike. In re Winship, 397 U.S. 358 (1970); Mullaney v. Wilbur, 421 U.S. 684 (1975) (described in *Patterson,* infra). It would be possible to take an all-inclusive approach to this proposition: That would mean that every fact bearing upon guilt is an element in the prosecutor's case, including sanity, absence of justification (self-defense or defense of others), and even entrapment. But that is not the approach taken.

Hence the constitutional requirement of proof beyond a reasonable doubt requires us to answer two questions: What are the elements in the prosecutor's case? How (if at all) does the Constitution limit legislative power to determine that a certain factor should be an "affirmative defense" on which the accused bears the burden of persuasion, as opposed to an "element" of the offense on which the prosecutor bears that burden? Usually the answer to the first question is easy, for the elements are established by statute with some precision, and many are noncontroversial. Modern statutes (such as the Model Penal Code) provide direct and explicit instruction on the elements for each offense. And such statutes often expressly provide for certain defenses, defining the burden that the defendant must carry on these. But the answer to the second question is not so easy.

| PATTERSON v. NEW YORK
| United States Supreme Court
| 432 U.S. 197 (1977)

MR. JUSTICE WHITE delivered the opinion of the Court.

The question here is the constitutionality under the Fourteenth Amendment's Due Process Clause of burdening the defendant in a New York State

murder trial with proving the affirmative defense of extreme emotional disturbance as defined by New York law.

I

After a brief and unstable marriage, the appellant, Gordon Patterson, Jr., became estranged from his wife, Roberta. Roberta resumed an association with
John Northrup, a neighbor to whom she had been engaged prior to her marriage to appellant. On December 27, 1970, Patterson borrowed a rifle from an
acquaintance and went to the residence of his father-in-law. There, he observed
his wife through a window in a state of semiundress in the presence of John
Northrup. He entered the house and killed Northrup by shooting him twice
in the head.

Patterson was charged with second-degree murder. In New York there are
two elements of this crime: (1) "intent to cause the death of another person";
and (2) "caus[ing] the death of such person or of a third person." N.Y. Penal
Law §125.25 (McKinney 1975). Malice aforethought is not an element of the
crime. In addition, the State permits a person accused of murder to raise an
affirmative defense that he "acted under the influence of extreme emotional
disturbance for which there was a reasonable explanation or excuse."

New York also recognizes the crime of manslaughter. A person is guilty of
manslaughter if he intentionally kills another person "under circumstances
which do not constitute murder because he acts under the influence of extreme
emotional disturbance." Appellant confessed before trial to killing Northrup,
but at trial he raised the defense of extreme emotional disturbance.[4]

The jury was instructed as to the elements of the crime of murder. Focusing
on the element of intent, the trial court charged:

> Before you, considering all of the evidence, can convict this defendant or
> anyone of murder, you must believe and decide that the People have established
> beyond a reasonable doubt that he intended, in firing the gun, to kill either the
> victim himself or some other human being. . . .
>
> Always remember that you must not expect or require the defendant to prove
> to your satisfaction that his acts were done without the intent to kill. Whatever
> proof he may have attempted, however far he may have gone in an effort to
> convince you of his innocence or guiltlessness, he is not obliged, he is not obligated
> to prove anything. It is always the People's burden to prove his guilt, and to prove
> that he intended to kill in this instance beyond a reasonable doubt.[5]

---

4.   Appellant also contended at trial that the shooting was accidental and that therefore he
had no intent to kill Northrup. It is here undisputed, however, that the prosecution proved beyond
a reasonable doubt that the killing was intentional.

5.   The trial court's instructions to the jury focused emphatically and repeatedly on the
prosecution's burden of proving guilt beyond a reasonable doubt.

> The burden of proving the guilt of a defendant beyond a reasonable doubt rests at all
> times upon the prosecution. A defendant is never obliged to prove his innocence.
>
> Before you can find a defendant guilty, you must be convinced that each and every
> element of the crime charged and his guilt has been established to your satisfaction by
> reliable and credible evidence beyond a reasonable doubt.

The jury was further instructed, consistently with New York law, that the defendant had the burden of proving his affirmative defense by a preponderance of the evidence. The jury was told that if it found beyond a reasonable doubt that appellant had intentionally killed Northrup but that appellant had demonstrated by a preponderance of the evidence that he had acted under the influence of extreme emotional disturbance, it had to find appellant guilty of manslaughter instead of murder.

The jury found appellant guilty of murder. Judgment was entered on the verdict, and the Appellate Division affirmed. While appeal to the New York Court of Appeals was pending, this Court decided Mullaney v. Wilbur, 421 U.S. 684 (1975), in which the Court declared Maine's murder statute unconstitutional. Under the Maine statute, a person accused of murder could rebut the statutory presumption that he committed the offense with "malice aforethought" by proving that he acted in the heat of passion on sudden provocation. The Court held that this scheme improperly shifted the burden of persuasion from the prosecutor to the defendant and was therefore a violation of due process. In the Court of Appeals appellant urged that New York's murder statute is functionally equivalent to the one struck down in *Mullaney* and that therefore his conviction should be reversed.

The Court of Appeals rejected appellant's argument, holding that the New York murder statute is consistent with due process. The Court distinguished *Mullaney* on the ground that the New York statute involved no shifting of the burden to the defendant to disprove any fact essential to the offense charged since the New York affirmative defense of extreme emotional disturbance bears no direct relationship to any element of murder. This appeal ensued, and we noted probable jurisdiction. We affirm.

II

It goes without saying that preventing and dealing with crime is much more the business of the States than it is of the Federal Government, and that we should not lightly construe the Constitution so as to intrude upon the administration of justice by the individual States. Among other things, it is normally "within the power of the State to regulate procedures under which its laws are carried out, including the burden of producing evidence and the burden of persuasion," and its decision in this regard is not subject to proscription under the Due Process Clause unless "it offends some principle of justice so rooted in the traditions and conscience of our people as to be ranked as fundamental." Speiser v. Randall, 357 U.S. 513, 523 (1958).

In determining whether New York's allocation to the defendant of proving the mitigating circumstances of severe emotional disturbance is consistent with due process, it is therefore relevant to note that this defense is a considerably expanded version of the common-law defense of heat of passion on sudden provocation and that at common law the burden of proving the latter, as well as other affirmative defenses—indeed, "all . . . . circumstances of justification, excuse or alleviation"—rested on the defendant. 4 W. Blackstone, Commentaries *201; M. Foster, Crown Law 255 (1762). This was the rule when the Fifth

Amendment was adopted, and it was the American rule when the Fourteenth Amendment was ratified.

In 1895 the common-law view was abandoned with respect to the insanity defense in federal prosecutions. Davis v. United States, 160 U.S. 469 (1895). This ruling had wide impact on the practice in the federal courts with respect to the burden of proving various affirmative defenses, and the prosecution in a majority of jurisdictions in this country sooner or later came to shoulder the burden of proving the sanity of the accused and of disproving the facts constituting other affirmative defenses, including provocation. *Davis* was not a constitutional ruling, however, as Leland v. Oregon, [343 U.S. 790 (1952)] made clear.[9]

At issue in Leland v. Oregon was the constitutionality under the Due Process Clause of the Oregon rule that the defense of insanity must be proved by the defendant beyond a reasonable doubt. Noting that *Davis* "obviously establish[ed] no constitutional doctrine," the Court refused to strike down the Oregon scheme, saying that the burden of proving all elements of the crime beyond reasonable doubt, including the elements of premeditation and deliberation, was placed on the State under Oregon procedures and remained there throughout the trial. To convict, the jury was required to find each element of the crime beyond a reasonable doubt, based on all the evidence, including the evidence going to the issue of insanity. Only then was the jury "to consider separately the issue of legal sanity per se. . . ." This practice did not offend the Due Process Clause even though among the 20 States then placing the burden of proving his insanity on the defendant, Oregon was alone in requiring him to convince the jury beyond a reasonable doubt.

In 1970, the Court declared that the Due Process Clause "protects the accused against conviction except upon proof beyond a reasonable doubt of every fact necessary to constitute the crime with which he is charged." In re Winship, 397 U.S. 358 (1970). Five years later, in *Mullaney,* the Court further announced that under the Maine law of homicide, the burden could not constitutionally be placed on the defendant of proving by a preponderance of the evidence that the killing had occurred in the heat of passion on sudden provocation. The Chief Justice and Mr. Justice Rehnquist, concurring, expressed their understanding that the *Mullaney* decision did not call into question the ruling in *Leland* with respect to the proof of insanity.

Subsequently, the Court confirmed that it remained constitutional to burden the defendant with proving his insanity defense when it dismissed, as not raising a substantial federal question, a case in which the appellant specifically challenged the continuing validity of *Leland*. This occurred in Rivera v. Delaware, 429 U.S. 877 (1976), an appeal from a Delaware conviction which, in reliance on *Leland,* had been affirmed by the Delaware Supreme Court over the claim

9. Meanwhile, the Court had explained that although the State could go too far in shifting the burden of proof to a defendant in a criminal case, the Due Process Clause did not invalidate every instance of burdening the defendant with proving an exculpatory fact. In Morrison v. California, 291 U.S. 82 (1934), a state law made it illegal for an alien ineligible for citizenship to own or possess land. Initially, in a summary dismissal for want of a substantial federal question, Morrison v. California, 288 U.S. 591 (1933), the Court held that it did not violate the Due Process Clause for the State to place on the defendant "the burden of proving citizenship as a defense," once the State's evidence had shown that the defendant possessed the land and was a member of a race barred from citizenship. . . .

that the Delaware statute was unconstitutional because it burdened the defendant with proving his affirmative defense of insanity by a preponderance of the evidence. The claim in this Court was that *Leland* had been overruled by *Winship* and *Mullaney*. We dismissed the appeal as not presenting a substantial federal question.

III

We cannot conclude that Patterson's conviction under the New York law deprived him of due process of law. The crime of murder is defined by the statute, which represents a recent revision of the state criminal code, as causing the death of another person with intent to do so. The death, the intent to kill, and causation are the facts that the State is required to prove beyond a reasonable doubt if a person is to be convicted of murder. No further facts are either presumed or inferred in order to constitute the crime. The statute does provide an affirmative defense—that the defendant acted under the influence of extreme emotional disturbance for which there was a reasonable explanation—which, if proved by a preponderance of the evidence, would reduce the crime to manslaughter, an offense defined in a separate section of the statute. It is plain enough that if the intentional killing is shown, the State intends to deal with the defendant as a murderer unless he demonstrates the mitigating circumstances.

Here, the jury was instructed in accordance with the statute, and the guilty verdict confirms that the State successfully carried its burden of proving the facts of the crime beyond a reasonable doubt. Nothing in the evidence, including any evidence that might have been offered with respect to Patterson's mental state at the time of the crime, raised a reasonable doubt about his guilt as a murderer; and clearly the evidence failed to convince the jury that Patterson's affirmative defense had been made out. It seems to us that the State satisfied the mandate of *Winship* that it prove beyond a reasonable doubt "every fact necessary to constitute the crime with which [Patterson was] charged."

In convicting Patterson under its murder statute, New York did no more than *Leland* and *Rivera* permitted it to do without violating the Due Process Clause. Under those cases, once the facts constituting a crime are established beyond a reasonable doubt, based on all the evidence including the evidence of the defendant's mental state, the State may refuse to sustain the affirmative defense of insanity unless demonstrated by a preponderance of the evidence.

The New York law on extreme emotional disturbance follows this pattern. This affirmative defense, which the Court of Appeals described as permitting "the defendant to show that his actions were caused by a mental infirmity not arising to the level of insanity, and that he is less culpable for having committed them," does not serve to negative any facts of the crime which the State is to prove in order to convict of murder. It constitutes a separate issue on which the defendant is required to carry the burden of persuasion; and unless we are to overturn *Leland* and *Rivera*, New York has not violated the Due Process Clause, and Patterson's conviction must be sustained.

We are unwilling to reconsider *Leland* and *Rivera*. But even if we were to hold that a State must prove sanity to convict once that fact is put in issue, it would not necessarily follow that a State must prove beyond a reasonable doubt every fact, the existence or nonexistence of which it is willing to recognize as an exculpatory or mitigating circumstance affecting the degree of culpability or the severity of the punishment. Here, in revising its criminal code, New York provided the affirmative defense of extreme emotional disturbance, a substantially expanded version of the older heat-of-passion concept; but it was willing to do so only if the facts making out the defense were established by the defendant with sufficient certainty. The State was itself unwilling to undertake to establish the absence of those facts beyond a reasonable doubt, perhaps fearing that proof would be too difficult and that too many persons deserving treatment as murderers would escape that punishment if the evidence need merely raise a reasonable doubt about the defendant's emotional state. It has been said that the new criminal code of New York contains some 25 affirmative defenses which exculpate or mitigate but which must be established by the defendant to be operative.[10] The Due Process Clause, as we see it, does not put New York to the choice of abandoning those defenses or undertaking to disprove their existence in order to convict of a crime which otherwise is within its constitutional powers to sanction by substantial punishment.

The requirement of proof beyond a reasonable doubt in a criminal case is "bottomed on a fundamental value determination of our society that it is far worse to convict an innocent man than to let a guilty man go free." *Winship* (Harlan, J., concurring). The social cost of placing the burden on the prosecution to prove guilt beyond a reasonable doubt is thus an increased risk that the guilty will go free. While it is clear that our society has willingly chosen to bear a substantial burden in order to protect the innocent, it is equally clear that the risk it must bear is not without limits; and Mr. Justice Harlan's aphorism provides little guidance for determining what those limits are. Due process does not require that every conceivable step be taken, at whatever cost, to eliminate the possibility of convicting an innocent person. Punishment of those found guilty by a jury, for example, is not forbidden merely because there is a remote possibility in some instances that an innocent person might go to jail.

It is said that the common-law rule permits a State to punish one as a murderer when it is as likely as not that he acted in the heat of passion or under severe emotional distress and when, if he did, he is guilty only of manslaughter. But this has always been the case in those jurisdictions adhering to the traditional rule. It is also very likely true that fewer convictions of murder would occur if New York were required to negative the affirmative defense at issue here. But in each instance of a murder conviction under the present law New York will have proved beyond a reasonable doubt that the defendant has intentionally killed another person, an act which it is not disputed the State may constitutionally criminalize and punish. If the State nevertheless chooses

---

10.   [A 1977 study indicates that after completion of the Model Penal Code in 1962, 22 states codified or reformed their criminal laws. Of these, at least 12 employ the concept of an "affirmative defense" that defendant must prove by a preponderance. Other jurisdictions do not use that term, but nevertheless shift to the defendant the burden of proof on particular issues. Still the trend favors requiring the prosecutor to disprove affirmative defenses beyond a reasonable doubt. Some 22 jurisdictions place on the defendant the burden of proving insanity, while 28 place on the prosecutor the burden of disproving insanity.]

to recognize a factor that mitigates the degree of criminality or punishment, we think the State may assure itself that the fact has been established with reasonable certainty. To recognize at all a mitigating circumstance does not require the State to prove its nonexistence in each case in which the fact is put in issue, if in its judgment this would be too cumbersome, too expensive, and too inaccurate.[11]

We thus decline to adopt as a constitutional imperative, operative countrywide, that a State must disprove beyond a reasonable doubt every fact constituting any and all affirmative defenses related to the culpability of an accused. Traditionally, due process has required that only the most basic procedural safeguards be observed; more subtle balancing of society's interests against those of the accused have been left to the legislative branch. We therefore will not disturb the balance struck in previous cases holding that the Due Process Clause requires the prosecution to prove beyond a reasonable doubt all of the elements included in the definition of the offense of which the defendant is charged. Proof of the nonexistence of all affirmative defenses has never been constitutionally required; and we perceive no reason to fashion such a rule in this case and apply it to the statutory defense at issue here.

This view may seem to permit state legislatures to reallocate burdens of proof by labeling as affirmative defenses at least some elements of the crimes now defined in their statutes. But there are obviously constitutional limits beyond which the States may not go in this regard. "[I]t is not within the province of a legislature to declare an individual guilty or presumptively guilty of a crime." McFarland v. American Sugar Rfg. Co., 241 U.S. 79 (1916). The legislature cannot "validly command that the finding of an indictment, or mere proof of the identity of the accused, should create a presumption of the existence of all the facts essential to guilt." Tot v. United States, 319 U.S. 463, 469 (1943).

Long before *Winship*, the universal rule in this country was that the prosecution must prove guilt beyond a reasonable doubt. At the same time, the long-accepted rule was that it was constitutionally permissible to provide that various affirmative defenses were to be proved by the defendant. This did not lead to such abuses or to such widespread redefinition of crime and reduction of the prosecution's burden that a new constitutional rule was required. This was not the problem to which *Winship* was addressed. Nor does the fact that a majority of the States have now assumed the burden of disproving affirmative defenses—for whatever reasons—mean that those States that strike a different balance are in violation of the Constitution.

IV

It is urged that Mullaney v. Wilbur necessarily invalidates Patterson's conviction. In *Mullaney* the charge was murder, which the Maine statute defined as the unlawful killing of a human being "with malice afore-thought, either express

---

11. [The Model Penal Code puts on the prosecutor the burden of proving the nonexistence of most affirmative defenses, including extreme emotional disturbance. But the drafters would put the burden on the defense in "some exceptional circumstances," citing situations in which the prosecutor would have trouble obtaining the evidence.]

or implied." The trial court instructed the jury that the words "malice afore-thought" were most important because "malice aforethought is an essential and indispensable element of the crime of murder." Malice, as the statute indicated and as the court instructed, could be implied and was to be implied from "any deliberate, cruel act committed by one person against another suddenly . . . or without a considerable provocation," in which event an intentional killing was murder unless by a preponderance of the evidence it was shown that the act was committed "in the heat of passion, on sudden provocation." The instructions emphasized that " 'malice aforethought and heat of passion on sudden provocation are two inconsistent things'; thus, by proving the latter the defendant would negate the former."

Wilbur's conviction, which followed, was affirmed. The Maine Supreme Judicial Court held that murder and manslaughter were varying degrees of the crime of felonious homicide and that the presumption of malice arising from the unlawful killing was a mere policy presumption operating to cast on the defendant the burden of proving provocation if he was to be found guilty of manslaughter rather than murder—a burden which the Maine law had allocated to him at least since the mid-1800's.

The Court of Appeals for the First Circuit then ordered that a writ of habeas corpus issue, holding that the presumption unconstitutionally shifted to the defendant the burden of proof with respect to an essential element of the crime. . . . This Court . . . unanimously agreed with the Court of Appeals that Wilbur's due process rights had been invaded by the presumption casting upon him the burden of proving by a preponderance of the evidence that he had acted in the heat of passion upon sudden provocation.

Mullaney's holding, it is argued, is that the State may not permit the blame-worthiness of an act or the severity of punishment authorized for its commission to depend on the presence or absence of an identified fact without assuming the burden of proving the presence or absence of that fact, as the case may be, beyond a reasonable doubt.[15] In our view, the *Mullaney* holding should not be so broadly read. The concurrence of two Justices in *Mullaney* was necessarily contrary to such a reading; and a majority of the Court refused to so understand and apply *Mullaney* when *Rivera* was dismissed for want of a substantial federal question.

Mullaney surely held that a State must prove every ingredient of an offense beyond a reasonable doubt, and that it may not shift the burden of proof to the defendant by presuming that ingredient upon proof of the other elements of the offense. This is true even though the State's practice, as in Maine, had been traditionally to the contrary. Such shifting of the burden of persuasion

---

15. There is some language in *Mullaney* that has been understood as perhaps construing the Due Process Clause to require the prosecution to prove beyond a reasonable doubt any fact affecting "the degree of criminal culpability." It is said that such a rule would deprive legislatures of any discretion whatsoever in allocating the burden of proof, the practical effect of which might be to undermine legislative reform of our criminal justice system. Carried to its logical extreme, such a reading of *Mullaney* might also, for example, discourage Congress from enacting pending legislation to change the felony-murder rule by permitting the accused to prove by a preponderance of the evidence the affirmative defense that the homicide committed was neither a necessary nor a reasonably foreseeable consequence of the underlying felony. The Court did not intend *Mullaney* to have such far-reaching effect.

with respect to a fact which the State deems so important that it must be either proved or presumed is impermissible under the Due Process Clause.

It was unnecessary to go further in *Mullaney.* The Maine Supreme Judicial Court made it clear that malice aforethought, which was mentioned in the statutory definition of the crime, was not equivalent to premeditation and that the presumption of malice traditionally arising in intentional homicide cases carried no factual meaning insofar as premeditation was concerned. Even so, a killing became murder in Maine when it resulted from a deliberate, cruel act committed by one person against another, "suddenly without any, or without a considerable provocation." Premeditation was not within the definition of murder; but malice, in the sense of the absence of provocation, was part of the definition of that crime. Yet malice, i.e., lack of provocation, was presumed and could be rebutted by the defendant only by proving by a preponderance of the evidence that he acted with heat of passion upon sudden provocation. In *Mullaney* we held that however traditional this mode of proceeding might have been, it is contrary to the Due Process Clause as construed in *Winship.*

As we have explained, nothing was presumed or implied against Patterson; and his conviction is not invalid under any of our prior cases. The judgment of the New York Court of Appeals is affirmed.

MR. JUSTICE REHNQUIST took no part in the consideration or decision of this case.

MR. JUSTICE POWELL, with whom MR. JUSTICE BRENNAN and MR. JUSTICE MARSHALL join, dissenting.

In the name of preserving legislative flexibility, the Court today drains *Winship* of much of its vitality. Legislatures do require broad discretion in the drafting of criminal laws, but the Court surrenders to the legislative branch a significant part of its responsibility to protect the presumption of innocence.

I . . .

New York's present homicide laws had their genesis in lingering dissatisfaction with certain aspects of the common-law framework that this Court confronted in *Mullaney.* Critics charged that the archaic language tended to obscure the factors of real importance in the jury's decision. Also, only a limited range of aggravations would lead to mitigation under the common-law formula, usually only those resulting from direct provocation by the victim himself. It was thought that actors whose emotions were stirred by other forms of outrageous conduct, even conduct by someone other than the ultimate victim, also should be punished as manslaughterers rather than murderers. Moreover, the common-law formula was generally applied with rather strict objectivity. Only provocations that might cause the hypothetical reasonable man to lose control could be considered. And even provocations of that sort were inadequate to reduce the crime to manslaughter if enough time had passed for the reasonable man's passions to cool, regardless of whether the actor's own thermometer had registered any decline. . . .

[The American Law Institute sought to remedy these problems. It proposed replacing "heat of passion" with the concept of "extreme mental or emotional disturbance," and New York adopted the ALI formula. Thus it replaced the "rigid objectivity" of the traditional approach in favor of a more subjective appraisal and permitted mitigation even where disturbance comes from circumstances other than provocation by the victim. The New York statute is "framed in lean prose" favoring "operative descriptions" rather than "classical labels." Still, the major factor distinguishing murder from manslaughter in New York is the modern equivalent of "heat of passion." In one important respect, however, New York departed from the ALI recommendation. New York placed on defendant the burdens of production and persuasion on the issue of extreme emotional disturbance.]

Mullaney held invalid Maine's requirement that the defendant prove heat of passion. The Court today, without disavowing the unanimous holding of *Mullaney,* approves New York's requirement that the defendant prove extreme emotional disturbance. The Court manages to run a constitutional boundary line through the barely visible space that separates Maine's law from New York's. It does so on the basis of distinctions in language that are formalistic rather than substantive.

This result is achieved by a narrowly literal parsing of the holding in *Winship:* "[T]he Due Process Clause protects the accused against conviction except upon proof beyond a reasonable doubt of every fact necessary to constitute the crime with which he is charged." The only "facts" necessary to constitute a crime are said to be those that appear on the face of the statute as a part of the definition of the crime. Maine's statute was invalid, the Court reasons, because it "defined [murder] as the unlawful killing of a human being 'with malice aforethought, either express or implied.' " "[M]alice," the Court reiterates, "in the sense of the absence of provocation, was part of the definition of that crime." *Winship* was violated only because this "fact"—malice—was "presumed" unless the defendant persuaded the jury otherwise by showing that he acted in the heat of passion. New York, in form presuming no affirmative "fact" against Patterson, and blessed with a statute drafted in the leaner language of the 20th century, escapes constitutional scrutiny unscathed even though the effect on the defendant of New York's placement of the burden of persuasion is exactly the same as Maine's.

This explanation of the *Mullaney* holding bears little resemblance to the basic rationale of that decision. But this is not the cause of greatest concern. The test the Court today establishes allows a legislature to shift, virtually at will, the burden of persuasion with respect to any factor in a criminal case, so long as it is careful not to mention the nonexistence of that factor in the statutory language that defines the crime. The sole requirement is that any references to the factor be confined to those sections that provide for an affirmative defense. . . .

With all respect, this type of constitutional adjudication is indefensibly formalistic. A limited but significant check on possible abuses in the criminal law now becomes an exercise in arid formalities. What *Winship* and *Mullaney* had sought to teach about the limits a free society places on its procedures to safeguard the liberty of its citizens becomes a rather simplistic lesson in statutory draftsmanship. Nothing in the Court's opinion prevents a legislature from applying this new learning to many of the classical elements of the crimes it punishes.[8] It would be preferable, if the Court has found reason to reject the rationale of *Winship* and *Mullaney,* simply and straightforwardly to overrule those precedents.

The Court understandably manifests some uneasiness that its formalistic approach will give legislatures too much latitude in shifting the burden of persuasion. And so it issues a warning that "there are obviously constitutional limits beyond which the States may not go in this regard." The Court thereby concedes that legislative abuses may occur and that they must be curbed by the judicial branch. But if the State is careful to conform to the drafting formulas articulated today, the constitutional limits are anything but "obvious." This decision simply leaves us without a conceptual framework for distinguishing abuses from legitimate legislative adjustments of the burden of persuasion in criminal cases.[9]

II

It is unnecessary for the Court to retreat to a formalistic test for applying *Winship*. Careful attention to the *Mullaney* decision reveals the principles that should control in this and like cases. *Winship* held that the prosecution must bear the burden of proving beyond a reasonable doubt "the existence of every fact necessary to constitute the crime charged." In *Mullaney* we concluded that heat of passion was one of the "facts" described in *Winship*—that is, a factor as to which the prosecution must bear the burden of persuasion beyond a reasonable doubt. We reached that result only after making two careful inquiries. First, we noted that the presence or absence of heat of passion made a substantial difference in punishment of the offender and in the stigma associated with the conviction. Second, we reviewed the history, in England and this country, of the factor at issue. Central to the holding in *Mullaney* was our conclusion that heat of passion "has been, almost from the inception of the common law of homicide, the single most important factor in determining the degree of culpability attaching to an unlawful homicide."

Implicit in these two inquiries are the principles that should govern this case. The Due Process Clause requires that the prosecutor bear the burden of persuasion beyond a reasonable doubt only if the factor at issue makes a substan-

---

8.   For example, a state statute could pass muster under the only solid standard that appears in the Court's opinion if it defined murder as mere physical contact between the defendant and the victim leading to the victim's death, but then set up an affirmative defense leaving it to the defendant to prove that he acted without culpable *mens rea*. The State, in other words, could be relieved altogether of responsibility for proving *anything* regarding the defendant's state of mind, provided only that the fact of the statute meets the Court's drafting formulas.

To be sure, it is unlikely that legislatures will rewrite their criminal laws in this extreme form. The Court seems to think this likelihood of restraint is an added reason for limiting review largely to formalistic examination. But it is completely foreign to this Court's responsibility for constitutional adjudication to limit the scope of judicial review because of the expectation—however reasonable—that legislative bodies will exercise appropriate restraint.

9.   I have no doubt that the Court would find some way to strike down a formalistically correct statute as egregious as the one hypothesized in n.8, supra. But today's ruling suggests no principled basis for concluding that such a statute falls outside the "obvious" constitutional limits the Court invokes.

tial difference in punishment and stigma. The requirement of course applies a fortiori if the factor makes the difference between guilt and innocence. But a substantial difference in punishment alone is not enough. It also must be shown that in the Anglo-American legal tradition the factor in question historically has held that level of importance.[11] If either branch of the test is not met, then the legislature retains its traditional authority over matters of proof. But to permit a shift in the burden of persuasion when both branches of this test are satisfied would invite the undermining of the presumption of innocence, "that bedrock 'axiomatic and elementary' principle whose 'enforcement lies at the foundation of the administration of our criminal law.' " In re Winship, 397 U.S., at 363. This is not a test that rests on empty form, for "*Winship* is concerned with substance rather than . . . formalism." Mullaney v. Wilbur, 421 U.S., at 699.

I hardly need add that New York's provisions allocating the burden of persuasion as to "extreme emotional disturbance" are unconstitutional when judged by these standards. "Extreme emotional disturbance" is, as the Court of Appeals recognized, the direct descendant of the "heat of passion" factor considered at length in *Mullaney*. I recognize, of course, that the differences between Maine and New York law are not unimportant to the defendant; there is a somewhat broader opportunity for mitigation. But none of those distinctions is relevant here. The presence or absence of extreme emotional disturbance makes a critical difference in punishment and stigma, and throughout our history the resolution of this issue of fact, although expressed in somewhat different terms, has distinguished manslaughter from murder. See 4 W. Blackstone, Commentaries *190-193, 198-201.

III

The Court beats its retreat from *Winship* apparently because of a concern that otherwise the federal judiciary will intrude too far into substantive choices concerning the content of a State's criminal law. The concern is legitimate, but misplaced. *Winship* and *Mullaney* are no more than what they purport to be: decisions addressing the procedural requirements that States must meet to comply with due process. They are not outposts for policing the substantive boundaries of the criminal law.

The *Winship/Mullaney* test identifies those factors of such importance, historically, in determining punishment and stigma that the Constitution forbids shifting to the defendant the burden of persuasion when such a factor is at issue. *Winship* and *Mullaney* specify only the procedure that is required when a State elects to use such a factor as part of its substantive criminal law. They do not say that the State must elect to use it. For example, where a State has chosen to retain the traditional distinction between murder and manslaughter, as have New York and Maine, the burden of persuasion must remain on the prosecution with respect to the distinguishing factor, in view of its decisive

11.   As the Court acknowledges, the clear trend over the years has been to require the prosecutor to carry the burden of persuasion with respect to all important factors in a criminal case, including traditional affirmative defenses.

historical importance. But nothing in *Mullaney* or *Winship* precludes a State from abolishing the distinction between murder and manslaughter and treating all unjustifiable homicide as murder.[13] In this significant respect, neither *Winship* nor *Mullaney* eliminates the substantive flexibility that should remain in legislative hands.

Moreover, it is unlikely that more than a few factors—although important ones—for which a shift in the burden of persuasion seriously would be considered will come within the *Mullaney* holding. . . . New ameliorative affirmative defenses,[14] about which the Court expresses concern, generally remain undisturbed by the holdings in *Winship* and *Mullaney*—and need not be disturbed by a sound holding reversing Patterson's conviction.[15]

Furthermore, as we indicated in *Mullaney*, even as to those factors upon which the prosecution must bear the burden of persuasion, the State retains an important procedural device to avoid jury confusion and prevent the prosecution from being unduly hampered. The State normally may shift to the defendant the burden of production,[16] that is, the burden of going forward

13. Perhaps under other principles of due process jurisprudence, certain factors are so fundamental that a State could not, as a substantive matter, refrain from recognizing them so long as it chooses to punish given conduct as a crime. But substantive limits were not at issue in *Winship* or *Mullaney*, and they are not at issue here.

Even if there are no constitutional limits preventing the State, for example, from treating all homicides as murders punishable equally regardless of mitigating factors like heat of passion or extreme emotional disturbance, the *Winship/Mullaney* rule still plays an important role. The State is then obliged to make its choices concerning the substantive content of its criminal laws with full awareness of the consequences, unable to mask substantive policy choices by shifts in the burden of persuasion. The political check on potentially harsh legislative action is then more likely to operate.

[United States v.] Romano [382 U.S. 136 (1965)] involved a challenge to a federal statute that authorized the jury to infer possession, custody, and control of an illegal still from mere presence at the site. The Government contended that the statute should be sustained since it was merely Congress' way of broadening the substantive provisions in order to make a crime of mere presence. The Court rejected this argument, serving notice that Congress could not work a substantive change of that magnitude in such a disguised form.

14. Numerous examples of such defenses are available: New York subjects an armed robber to lesser punishment than he would otherwise receive if he proves by a preponderance of the evidence that the gun he used was unloaded or inoperative. A number of States have ameliorated the usual operation of statutes punishing statutory rape, recognizing a defense if the defendant shows that he reasonably believed his partner was of age. Formerly the age of the minor was a strict-liability element of the crime. The Model Penal Code also employs such a shift in the burden of persuasion for a limited number of defenses. For example, a corporation can escape conviction of an offense if it proves by a preponderance of the evidence that the responsible supervising officer exercised due diligence to prevent the commission of the offense.

15. A number of commentators have suggested that the Constitution permits the States some latitude in adjusting the burden of persuasion with respect to new ameliorative affirmative defenses that result from legislative compromise, but not with respect to other factors.

16. There are outer limits on shifting the burden of production to a defendant, limits articulated in a long line of cases in this Court passing on the validity of presumptions. Most important are the "rational connection" requirement . . . , and also the "comparative convenience" criterion. . . .

Caution is appropriate, however, in generalizing about the application of any of these cases to a given procedural device, since the term "presumption" covers a broad range of procedural mechanisms having significantly different consequences for the defendant.

with sufficient evidence "to justify [a reasonable] doubt upon the issue."[17] If the defendant's evidence does not cross this threshold, the issue—be it malice, extreme emotional disturbance, self-defense, or whatever—will not be submitted to the jury. Ever since this Court's decision in Davis v. United States, federal prosecutors have borne the burden of persuasion with respect to factors like insanity, self-defense, and malice or provocation, once the defendant has carried this burden of production. I know of no indication that this practice has proven a noticeable handicap to effective law enforcement.[19]

To be sure, there will be many instances when the *Winship/Mullaney* test as I perceive it will be more difficult to apply than the Court's formula. Where I see the need for a careful and discriminating review of history, the Court finds a brightline standard that can be applied with a quick glance at the face of the statute. But this facile test invites tinkering with the procedural safeguards of the presumption of innocence, an invitation to disregard the principles of *Winship* that I would not extend.

NOTES ON BURDEN OF PERSUASION IN CRIMINAL CASES

1. What is the difference between the crime of first degree murder in New York and the crime of murder in Maine? In *Mullaney* as described in *Patterson*, did the Maine trial judge put on the state the burden of proving all elements in the charged crime? Describe the relationship between "intentional" killing and "emotional disturbance" under New York law, and the relationship between "malice aforethought" and "heat of passion" under Maine law. Which state has the more realistic view of those relationships?

2. Most states recognize a "presumption of sanity," which means only that the accused bears one or more burdens if he hopes to be acquitted on that ground. In some states, he need only plead insanity (then the prosecutor bears the burdens of producing evidence and persuading the jury); in others, he must plead and produce evidence of insanity (though the burden of persuasion rests with the state); in still others, he must plead, offer evidence, and persuade. See 18 U.S.C. §17 (defendant must establish insanity by clear and convincing evidence). In Leland v. Oregon, 343 U.S. 790 (1952), the Court upheld a state scheme imposing on the accused the burden of persuasion on this issue beyond a reasonable doubt. *Leland* survived *Patterson*, didn't it? If so, surely all these approaches pass constitutional muster.

3. To what extent can a legislature affect criminal sanctions by directing

---

17. This does not mean that the defendant must introduce evidence in every case. In some instances the prosecution's case may contain sufficient evidence in support of the defendant's position to generate a jury issue.

19. Dean McCormick emphasized that the burden of production is "a critical and important mechanism in a jury trial." In his view, "this mechanism has far more influence upon the final outcome of cases than does the burden of persuasion, which has become very largely a matter of the technique of the wording of instructions to juries." C. McCormick, Evidence §307, pp. 638-639, and n.2 (1st ed. 1954).

courts to impose higher sentences if certain factors appear, and authorizing judges to determine such factors during sentencing under the preponderance standard? See McMillan v. Pennsylvania, 477 U.S. 79 (1986) (approving scheme requiring five years imprisonment if judge determines during sentencing that perpetrator visibly possessed firearm); Almendez-Torres v. United States, 523 U.S. 224 (1998) (approving scheme allowing judge to impose 20-year sentence because defendant, convicted of crime of illegal entry carrying penalty of two years, was previously convicted of aggravated felonies). But see Apprendi v. New Jersey, 530 U.S. 466 (2000) (finding due process violation where defendant was convicted of illegal possession of firearm, carrying penalty of 5-10 years, but judge imposed 12-year sentence under statute increasing penalties for hate crimes; "any fact that increases the penalty for a crime beyond the prescribed statutory maximum," apart from prior convictions, "must be submitted to a jury, and proved beyond a reasonable doubt").

4.   Some commentators read *Patterson* as a necessary retreat from *Winship-Mullaney*. Under what may be called a "purely procedural" interpretation, *Winship-Mullaney* required prosecutors to prove beyond a reasonable doubt everything relating to culpability. But that reading threatened to destroy every affirmative defense. Assume that the Piedmont legislature decides that consensual intercourse with an underage female is not a crime if defendant made a reasonable mistake as to age. Under a "purely procedural" interpretation, the legislature could modify the definition of the crime by requiring the state to prove beyond reasonable doubt that defendant could not have made such a mistake. But the legislature could not create an "affirmative defense," burdening defendant with proving mistake. Would you defend this approach? See Underwood, The Thumb on the Scales of Justice: Burdens of Persuasion in Criminal Cases, 86 Yale L.J. 1299, 1317-1325 (1977). Hasn't something gone wrong when concern over procedure makes it harder for legislatures to soften the criminal sanction? Does *Patterson* put an end to that worry?

5.   Does *Patterson* throw the baby out with the bath? At the opposite extreme from the "purely procedural" interpretation of *Winship-Mullaney* is a "no-holds-barred" interpretation inspired by *Patterson*. Assume that the state of Albany defines murder as "causing the death of a person" (see Justice Powell's *Patterson* dissent) and provides an "affirmative defense," in the form of proof by a preponderance that defendant "lacked an intent to kill or cause injury." Could we tolerate such a statute? Hasn't something gone wrong if procedural safeguards are subject to boundless substantive manipulation by the legislature?

6.   Is there a middle ground between the "purely procedural" and "no-holds-barred" approaches? Consider what we might call a "final check" approach suggested by Professors Jeffries and Stephan. They argue that the Eighth Amendment (barring "cruel and unusual punishments") limits legislative capacity to define criminality in three different ways, by requiring an act ("actus reus"), a blameworthy mental attitude ("mens rea"), and proportionality in punishment.[8] Assume that the state of Plymouth has a statute making it a felony

8. See, e.g., Enmund v. Florida, 458 U.S. 782 (1982) (where defendant only drove getaway car used in robbery and killing, death penalty was cruel and unusual under proportionality analysis); Robinson v. California, 370 U.S. 660 (1962) (punishment for the status of drug addiction

to transfer narcotics. The legislature wants to amend the statute by exempting anyone who transfers narcotics to accommodate a friend, without trying to make a profit or encourage addiction. The Constitution does not require accommodation suppliers to be exempt from punishment. Thus exempting them is "gratuitous," and Plymouth can amend its statute, tempering its laws against trafficking in narcotics by making proof of "accommodation" an affirmative defense. Under this approach, what would you do with "statutory rape" in Piedmont (Note 4)? Could Albany define murder as "causing death," with lack of intent as an affirmative defense (Note 5)? See Jeffries and Stephan, Defenses, Presumptions, and Burden of Proof in the Criminal Law, 88 Yale L.J. 1325 (1979). Does the *Patterson* majority hint that it prefers the "final check" approach in remarking that there are "constitutional limits beyond which states may not go"?

PROBLEM 10-C.   *Killing by "Calculation and Design"?*

Esther Marlin is prosecuted for alleged aggravated murder of her husband Wilbur. The offense is defined as "purposefully killing another with prior calculation and design." The evidence indicates that Esther and Wilbur quarreled over grocery money in the kitchen of their home, that Wilbur struck Esther in the head, that she went upstairs, donned a robe, and then returned with Wilbur's pistol. Wilbur saw that Esther was carrying something, asked her about it, and then came at her. She fired six shots, three of which struck and killed Wilbur.

At trial, Esther claims that she acted in self-defense.

Applying state law, the trial judge advises the jury that Esther bears the burden of proving self-defense. He instructs that self-defense requires that defendant (1) be not at fault in creating the situation giving rise to the argument and (2) have an honest belief that she was in imminent danger of death or great bodily harm and that only such force could provide a means of escape.

The jury finds Esther guilty. In the United States Supreme Court, she argues that the instruction putting on her the burden of persuasion on self-defense violates *Winship-Mullaney-Patterson*. Specifically, she argues that requiring her to prove that she believed that she was in "imminent danger of death or great bodily harm" unconstitutionally relieved the state of its burden to prove that she acted with "prior calculation and design."

What result, and why?

---

is cruel and unusual punishment); Morissette v. United States, 342 U.S. 246 (1952) (implying that mens rea is essential in defining criminality); United States v. Weems, 217 U.S. 349 (1910) (punishment of 15 years' hard labor, imposed on Coast Guard disbursing officer for minor falsifications which harmed no one, was cruel and unusual). But see Tison v. Arizona, 481 U.S. 137 (1987) (upholding death sentence for participant in prison escape leading to murder, where defendant's state of mind was one of reckless indifference); Rummel v. Estelle, 445 U.S. 263 (1980) (upholding imposition of life sentence under Texas habitual offender statute, where defendant had been convicted on three occasions for fraudulently obtaining money and goods worth a total of $229.11).

2.   Presumptions and Inferences

Presumptions and inferences present greater difficulty in criminal than in civil cases.[9]

Both the constitutional entitlement to a jury trial and considerations of due process restrict use of these devices in criminal cases. Probably *no* presumption operating against the accused on an element in the offense can *control* decision, even if he offers no counterproof. The reason is that directed verdicts against the accused are not allowed, and a presumption instruction binding the jury amounts to a partial directed verdict. (The jury in criminal cases has the power to acquit the defendant, no matter what. Arguably it lacks authority to do so, but the distinction is theoretical, for the jury cannot be forced to convict.) A binding directive is improper even where the evidence is so cogent and compelling that any reasonable person would conclude beyond reasonable doubt that defendant is guilty.

The Supreme Court has addressed criminal presumptions in different ways:

1. Sometimes it focuses on jury instructions, asking whether the jury was misled on its prerogative to determine the facts, or proper allocation of the burden of persuasion. The Court has found that instructions are ambiguous where they suggest, on the one hand, that defendant may be convicted only on proof beyond a reasonable doubt, but, on the other hand, that he may be convicted on the strength of a presumption alone. The Court has reversed convictions following such "double track" instructions where the jury may have relied on a presumption that could not satisfy the beyond-reasonable-doubt standard. See United States v. Romano, 382 U.S. 136 (1965) (in trial for being in possession, custody, or control of illegal still, jury was told that presence at still was "sufficient evidence to authorize conviction"; reversal required even though there was enough other evidence to convict, for jury "may have disbelieved or disregarded the other evidence" and convicted defendants for "presence alone," and inferring possession or control from presence was "arbitrary").

2. Often the Court appraises the logical relationship between the predicate fact of a presumption and the conclusion. Does the one support an inference of the other beyond reasonable doubt? Or does the one only make the other more probable than not? Or is the connection looser still, so that the predicate

---

9. The presumptions that concern us here have nothing to do with the "presumption of innocence," which is a hallmark of Anglo-American criminal jurisprudence. The latter gives positive expression to the truth that the prosecutor bears the burden of persuasion on each element of the offense, and it amounts to a symbol of freedom and respect for human rights and dignity. See Taylor v. Kentucky, 436 U.S. 478 (1978) (failure to instruct on presumption of innocence violates due process).

What does concern us is the array of presumptions that operate in favor of the prosecutor on points that may be critical. There are more such presumptions (most statutory) than you might suspect. Consider United States v. Gainey, 380 U.S. 63 (1965), where the Court approved a statutory presumption, arising from proof that defendant was present at a still, that he was "carrying on" the business of a distillery. And consider Leary v. United States, 395 U.S. 6 (1969), where a former Harvard professor was tried for importing marijuana, after he was stopped entering the United States from Mexico at Laredo, Texas. There the Court upheld a statutory presumption, arising upon proof of possession of marijuana, that the marijuana was imported, but struck down a presumption that defendant *knew* the marijuana was imported and so reversed the conviction.

alone could not reasonably support the conclusion? By this approach, some presumptions fail because they cannot satisfy even the preponderance standard. See Leary v. United States, 395 U.S. 6 (1969) (striking down presumption, arising from proof of possession of marijuana, that defendant knew it was imported; most marijuana is imported, but much is grown domestically, so possession does not make it more probable than not that defendant knew the marijuana was imported). Other presumptions have survived because they satisfy the beyond-reasonable-doubt standard. See Turner v. United States, 396 U.S. 398 (1970) (upholding presumption, arising from proof of possession of heroin, that defendant knew it was imported: "To possess heroin *is* to possess imported heroin," for "little if any heroin is made in the United States," and defendant "doubtless knew [it] came from abroad"; presumption satisfies reasonable doubt standard). Interestingly, the Court never clearly resolved the problem of the intermediate situation, where the presumption satisfies the lower but fails the higher standard. (The *Allen* case, infra, may present that situation, and the holding points toward *requiring* the higher standard only where the judge invites the jury to make a critical finding based on the presumption alone, and otherwise *permitting* the lower standard.)

3. Occasionally the Court considers arguments that criminal presumptions violate other constitutional safeguards, including the rights (a) to a *trial* of guilt or innocence, (b) to be *tried by a jury*, both of which are arguably infringed by a *legislative* enactment prescribing that one fact supports a finding of another, see Leary v. United States, 395 U.S. 6 (1969) (Black, concurring), (c) against self-incrimination (a presumption instruction may state that the basic fact permits a finding of the presumed fact unless the defendant gives a satisfactory explanation, which arguably amounts to a comment about the failure of the accused to refute the invited inference by testifying), see United States v. Gainey, 380 U.S. 63 (1965) (Black, dissenting), and (d) to be presumed innocent, which seems inoperable with respect to any "presumed" fact. See Ashford and Risinger, Presumptions, Assumptions, and Due Process in Criminal Cases: A Theoretical Overview, 79 Yale L.J. 165, 176 (1969). So far these arguments have not commanded a majority on the Court.

The Court has struggled to reconcile presumptions and inferences with the constitutional rights of criminal defendants. The opinions are not always clear, but basic issues have been resolved. Most of the modern thinking is reflected in *Sandstrom* and *Allen*, infra.

SANDSTROM v. MONTANA
United States Supreme Court
442 U.S. 510 (1979)

MR. JUSTICE BRENNAN delivered the opinion of the Court.

The question presented is whether, in a case in which intent is an element of the crime charged, the jury instruction, "the law presumes that a person intends the ordinary consequences of his voluntary acts," violates the Fourteenth Amendment's requirement that the State prove every element of a criminal offense beyond a reasonable doubt.

I

On November 22, 1976, 18-year-old David Sandstrom confessed to the slaying of Annie Jessen. Based upon the confession and corroborating evidence, petitioner was charged on December 2 with "deliberate homicide," in that he "purposely or knowingly caused the death of Annie Jessen." At trial, Sandstrom's attorney informed the jury that, although his client admitted killing Jessen, he did not do so "purposely or knowingly," and was therefore not guilty of "deliberate homicide" but of a lesser crime. The basic support for this contention was the testimony of two court-appointed mental health experts, each of whom described for the jury petitioner's mental state at the time of the incident. Sandstrom's attorney argued that this testimony demonstrated that petitioner, due to a personality disorder aggravated by alcohol consumption, did not kill Annie Jessen "purposely or knowingly."

The prosecution requested the trial judge to instruct the jury that "[t]he law presumes that a person intends the ordinary consequences of his voluntary acts." Petitioner's counsel objected, arguing that "the instruction has the effect of shifting the burden of proof on the issue of" purpose or knowledge to the defense, and that "that is impermissible under the Federal Constitution, due process of law." He offered to provide a number of federal decisions in support of the objection, including this Court's holding in Mullaney v. Wilbur, 421 U.S. 684 (1975), but was told by the judge: "You can give those to the Supreme Court. The objection is overruled." The instruction was delivered, the jury found petitioner guilty of deliberate homicide, and petitioner was sentenced to 100 years in prison.

Sandstrom appealed to the Supreme Court of Montana, again contending that the instruction shifted to the defendant the burden of disproving an element of the crime charged, in violation of Mullaney v. Wilbur, supra, In re Winship, 397 U.S. 358 (1970), and Patterson v. New York, 432 U.S. 197 (1977). The Montana court conceded that these cases did prohibit shifting the burden of proof to the defendant by means of a presumption, but held that the cases "do not prohibit allocation of *some* burden of proof to a defendant under certain circumstances." Since in the court's view, "[d]efendant's sole burden under instruction No. 5 was to produce *some* evidence that he did not intend the ordinary consequences of his voluntary acts, not to disprove that he acted 'purposely' or 'knowingly,' . . . the instruction does not violate due process standards as defined by the United States or Montana Constitution . . ." (emphasis added).

Both federal and state courts have held, under a variety of rationales, that the giving of an instruction similar to that challenged here is fatal to the validity of a criminal conviction. We granted certiorari to decide the important question of the instruction's constitutionality. We reverse.

II

The threshold inquiry in ascertaining the constitutional analysis applicable to this kind of jury instruction is to determine the nature of the presumption it describes. That determination requires careful attention to the words actually spoken to the jury, for whether a defendant has been accorded his constitutional rights depends upon the way in which a reasonable juror could have interpreted the instruction.

Respondent argues, first, that the instruction merely described a permissive inference—that is, it allowed but did not require the jury to draw conclusions about defendant's intent from his actions—and that such inferences are constitutional. These arguments need not detain us long, for even respondent admits that "it's possible" that the jury believed they were required to apply the presumption. Sandstrom's jurors were told that "[t]he law presumes that a person intends the ordinary consequences of his voluntary acts." They were not told that they had a choice, or that they might infer that conclusion; they were told only that the law presumed it. It is clear that a reasonable juror could easily have viewed such an instruction as mandatory.

In the alternative, respondent urges that, even if viewed as a mandatory presumption rather than as a permissive inference, the presumption did not conclusively establish intent but rather could be rebutted. On this view, the instruction required the jury, if satisfied as to the facts which trigger the presumption, to find intent *unless* the defendant offered evidence to the contrary. Moreover, according to the State, all the defendant had to do to rebut the presumption was produce "some" contrary evidence; he did not have to "prove" that he lacked the required mental state. Thus, "[a]t most, it placed a *burden of production* on the petitioner," but "did not shift to petitioner the *burden of persuasion* with respect to any element of the offense . . ." (emphasis added). Again, respondent contends that presumptions with this limited effect pass constitutional muster.

We need not review respondent's constitutional argument on this point either, however, for we reject this characterization of the presumption as well. Respondent concedes there is a "risk" that the jury, once having found petitioner's act voluntary, would interpret the instruction as automatically directing a finding of intent. Moreover, the State also concedes that numerous courts "have differed as to the effect of the presumption when given as a jury instruction without further explanation as to its use by the jury," and that some have found it to shift more than the burden of production, and even to have conclusive effect. Nonetheless, the State contends that the only authoritative reading of the effect of the presumption resides in the Supreme Court of Montana. And the State argues that by holding that "[d]efendant's sole burden under instruction No. 5 was to produce *some* evidence that he did not intend the ordinary consequences of his voluntary acts, not to disprove that he acted 'purposely' or 'knowingly,' " the Montana Supreme Court decisively established that the presumption at most affected only the burden of going forward with evidence of intent—that is, the burden of production.[5]

5.   For purposes of argument, we accept respondent's definition of the production burden when applied to a defendant in a criminal case. We note, however, that the burden is often described quite differently when it rests upon the prosecution. We also note that the effect of a failure to meet the production burden is significantly different for the defendant and prosecution. When the prosecution fails to meet it, a directed verdict in favor of the defense results. Such a consequence is not possible upon a defendant's failure, however, as verdicts may not be directed against defendants in criminal cases.

The Supreme Court of Montana is, of course, the final authority on the legal weight to be given a presumption under Montana law, but it is not the final authority on the interpretation which a jury could have given the instruction. If Montana intended its presumption to have only the effect described by its Supreme Court, then we are convinced that a reasonable juror could well have been misled by the instruction given, and could have believed that the presumption was not limited to requiring the defendant to satisfy only a burden of production. Petitioner's jury was told that "*[t]he law presumes* that a person intends the ordinary consequences of his voluntary acts." They were not told that the presumption could be rebutted, as the Montana Supreme Court held, by the defendant's simple presentation of "some" evidence; nor even that it could be rebutted at all. Given the common definition of "presume" as "to suppose to be true without proof," Webster's New Collegiate Dictionary 911 (1974), and given the lack of qualifying instructions as to the legal effect of the presumption, we cannot discount the possibility that the jury may have interpreted the instruction in either of two more stringent ways.

First, a reasonable jury could well have interpreted the presumption as "conclusive," that is, not technically as a presumption at all, but rather as an irrebuttable direction by the court to find intent once convinced of the facts triggering the presumption. Alternatively, the jury may have interpreted the instruction as a direction to find intent upon proof of the defendant's voluntary actions (and their "ordinary" consequences), unless *the defendant* proved the contrary by some quantum of proof which may well have been considerably greater than "some" evidence—thus effectively shifting the burden of persuasion on the element of intent. Numerous federal and state courts have warned that instructions of the type given here can be interpreted in just these ways. And although the Montana Supreme Court held to the contrary in this case, Montana's own Rules of Evidence expressly state that the presumption at issue here may be overcome only "by a preponderance of evidence contrary to the presumption." Montana Rule of Evidence 301(b)(2). Such a requirement shifts not only the burden of production, but also the ultimate burden of persuasion on the issue of intent.[7]

We do not reject the possibility that some jurors may have interpreted the challenged instruction as permissive, or, if mandatory, as requiring only that the defendant come forward with "some" evidence in rebuttal. However, the fact that a reasonable juror could have given the presumption conclusive or

---

7. The potential for these interpretations of the presumption was not removed by the other instructions given at the trial. It is true that the jury was instructed generally that the accused was presumed innocent until proved guilty, and that the State had the burden of proving beyond a reasonable doubt that the defendant caused the death of the deceased purposely or knowingly. But this is not rhetorically inconsistent with a conclusive or burden-shifting presumption. The jury could have interpreted the two sets of instructions as indicating that the presumption was a means by which proof beyond a reasonable doubt as to intent could be satisfied. For example, if the presumption were viewed as conclusive, the jury could have believed that, although intent must be proved beyond a reasonable doubt, proof of the voluntary slaying and its ordinary consequences constituted proof of intent beyond a reasonable doubt. Cf. *Mullaney* ("These procedural devices require (in the case of a presumption) . . . the trier of fact to conclude that the prosecution has met its burden of proof with respect to the presumed . . . fact by having satisfactorily established other facts").

persuasion-shifting effect means that we cannot discount the possibility that Sandstrom's jurors actually did proceed upon one or the other of these latter interpretations. And that means that unless these kinds of presumptions are constitutional, the instruction cannot be adjudged valid. It is the line of cases urged by petitioner, and exemplified by *Winship*, that provides the appropriate mode of constitutional analysis for these kinds of presumptions.

III

In *Winship*, this Court stated:

> Lest there remain any doubt about the constitutional stature of the reasonable-doubt standard, we explicitly hold that the Due Process Clause protects the accused against conviction except upon proof beyond a reasonable doubt *of every fact* necessary to constitute the crime with which he is charged.

Id., at 364 (emphasis added). Accord, *Patterson*. The petitioner here was charged with and convicted of deliberate homicide, committed purposely or knowingly. It is clear that under Montana law, whether the crime was committed purposely or knowingly is a fact necessary to constitute the crime of deliberate homicide. Indeed, it was the lone element of the offense at issue in Sandstrom's trial, as he confessed to causing the death of the victim, told the jury that knowledge and purpose were the only questions he was controverting, and introduced evidence solely on those points. Moreover, it is conceded that proof of defendant's "intent" would be sufficient to establish this element. Thus, the question before this Court is whether the challenged jury instruction had the effect of relieving the State of the burden of proof enunciated in *Winship* on the critical question of petitioner's state of mind. We conclude that under either of the two possible interpretations of the instruction set out above, precisely that effect would result, and that the instruction therefore represents constitutional error.

We consider first the validity of a conclusive presumption. This Court has considered such a presumption on at least two prior occasions. In Morissette v. United States, 342 U.S. 246 (1952), the defendant was charged with willful and knowing theft of Government property. Although his attorney argued that for his client to be found guilty, "the taking must have been with felonious intent," the trial judge ruled that "[t]hat is presumed by his own act." After first concluding that intent was in fact an element of the crime charged, and after declaring that "[w]here intent of the accused is an ingredient of the crime charged, its existence is . . . a jury issue," *Morissette* held:

> It follows that the trial court may not withdraw or prejudge the issue by instruction that the law raises a presumption of intent from an act. It often is tempting to cast in terms of a "presumption" a conclusion which a court thinks probable from given facts. . . . [B]ut [w]e think presumptive intent has no place in this case. A conclusive presumption which testimony could not overthrow would effectively eliminate intent as an ingredient of the offense. A presumption which would permit but not require the jury to assume intent from an isolated fact would prejudge a conclusion which the jury should reach of its own volition. A

presumption which would permit the jury to make an assumption which all the evidence considered together does not logically establish would give to a proven fact an artificial and fictional effect. In either case, this presumption would conflict with the overriding presumption of innocence with which the law endows the accused and which extends to every element of the crime. (Emphasis added.)

Just last Term, . . . we reaffirmed the holding of *Morissette*. . . .

As in *Morissette*. . . , a conclusive presumption in this case would "conflict with the overriding presumption of innocence with which the law endows the accused and which extends to every element of the crime," and would "invade [the] factfinding function" which in a criminal case the law assigns solely to the jury. The instruction announced to David Sandstrom's jury may well have had exactly these consequences. Upon finding proof of one element of the crime (causing death), and of facts insufficient to establish the second (the voluntariness and "ordinary consequences" of defendant's action), Sandstrom's jurors could reasonably have concluded that they were directed to find against defendant on the element of intent. The State was thus not forced to prove "beyond a reasonable doubt . . . every fact necessary to constitute the crime . . . charged," and defendant was deprived of his constitutional rights as explicated in *Winship*. A presumption which, although not conclusive, had the effect of shifting the burden of persuasion to the defendant, would have suffered from similar infirmities. If Sandstrom's jury interpreted the presumption in that manner, it could have concluded that upon proof by the State of the slaying, and of additional facts not themselves establishing the element of intent, the burden was shifted to the defendant to prove that he lacked the requisite mental state. Such a presumption was found constitutionally deficient in *Mullaney*. In *Mullaney*, the charge was murder, which under Maine law required proof not only of intent but of malice. The trial court charged the jury that "malice aforethought is an essential and indispensable element of the crime of murder." However, it also instructed that if the prosecution established that the homicide was both intentional and unlawful, malice aforethought was to be implied unless the defendant proved by a fair preponderance of the evidence that he acted in the heat of passion on sudden provocation. As we recounted just two Terms ago in *Patterson*, "[t]his Court . . . unanimously agreed with the Court of Appeals that Wilbur's due process rights had been invaded by the presumption casting upon him the burden of proving by a preponderance of the evidence that he had acted in the heat of passion upon sudden provocation." And *Patterson* reaffirmed that "a State must prove every ingredient of an offense beyond a reasonable doubt, and . . . may not shift the burden of proof to the defendant" by means of such a presumption.

Because David Sandstrom's jury may have interpreted the judge's instruction as constituting either a burden-shifting presumption like that in *Mullaney*, or a conclusive presumption like those in *Morissette* . . . and because either interpretation would have deprived defendant of his right to the due process of law, we hold the instruction given in this case unconstitutional. . . .

Accordingly, the judgment of the Supreme Court of Montana is reversed, and the case is remanded for further proceedings not inconsistent with this opinion.

It is so ordered.

[A concurring opinion by JUSTICE REHNQUIST, joined by CHIEF JUSTICE BURGER, is omitted.]

NOTES ON THE SIGNIFICANCE OF *SANDSTROM*

1. The *Sandstrom* majority considers four interpretations of the instruction given by the trial judge. One suggested by the state is that the instruction created "a permissive inference." Assume that the trial judge instructed the jury thus:

> You may find that defendant acted purposefully or knowingly only if you conclude that the evidence proves that point beyond a reasonable doubt. Depending on the circumstances, it is sometimes possible to reach that conclusion on the basis of proof that a person acted voluntarily.

Would such an instruction be proper under *Sandstrom?*

2. The other three interpretations involve a so-called mandatory presumption. If a properly worded inference instruction is acceptable but one or more versions of the mandatory presumption are not, then *Sandstrom* presents a "double track" (or "multiple track") problem similar to *Romano* (described in the text, supra). What are the three possible interpretations of the "mandatory presumption" discussed in *Sandstrom?* Try to imagine three different "water-tight" instructions, each delivering a message consistent with only one of these interpretations. Does *Sandstrom* condemn all three of these instructions?

3. A "mild" form of "mandatory presumption" would impose a burden of production upon the defendant. Not surprisingly, Montana urged such an interpretation in *Sandstrom.* Consider an *even milder* form of instruction, in which the trial judge tells the jury:

> If you find that defendant acted voluntarily, you should find that he acted purposefully or knowingly unless there is other evidence in the case that indicates that he did not.

Would such an instruction be improper under *Sandstrom?*

4. Would the problems in *Sandstrom* be cured if the trial judge had emphasized to the jury that the prosecutor bears the burden of persuasion beyond a reasonable doubt on intent? See Francis v. Franklin, 471 U.S. 307 (1985) (no). But see United States v. Nelson, 277 F.3d 164, 197 (2d Cir. 2002) (instruction that jury "may infer and find that defendants intended all consequences that a person, standing in circumstances and posing like knowledge, should have expected to result from acts he knowingly committed" does not violate *Sandstrom;* it merely let jury infer that accused intends consequences of actions), cert. denied, 537 U.S. 835 (2002).

5. David Sandstrom was charged with "deliberate homicide," a crime punishable by death or imprisonment for life or a term of two to 100 years. Montana law defined the crime as "purposely or knowingly" causing the death of another, and recognized a crime of "mitigated deliberate homicide," defined

as deliberate homicide "committed under the influence of extreme mental or emotional stress for which there is reasonable explanation or excuse," punishable by imprisonment for not less than two nor more than 40 years. See Montana Code §§94-5-102 and 94-5-103 (1973).

Change the facts slightly: This time Sandstrom claims he was under the influence of "extreme mental or emotional stress," and the state offers sufficient evidence that he acted "purposely or knowingly." Assume that Montana (like New York in *Patterson*) takes the view that a person can "purposely or knowingly" kill another while being under "extreme mental or emotional stress," but that Montana recognizes a presumption that a person acting on such purpose or knowledge is *not* under extreme mental or emotional stress. Accordingly, the trial judge tells the jury:

> The law presumes that a person acting purposefully or knowingly is not under the influence of extreme mental or emotional stress. If you find beyond a reasonable doubt that defendant acted purposefully or knowingly, you should conclude, if you believe it to be the case, that he was not acting under the influence of extreme mental or emotional stress, unless other evidence persuades you to the contrary.

Under *Patterson,* couldn't Montana allocate to the defendant the burden of proving extreme mental or emotional stress? Under *Sandstrom,* could Montana do something similar by means of a presumption? See generally Harris, Constitutional Limits on Criminal Presumptions as an Expression of Changing Concepts of Fundamental Fairness, 77 J. Crim. L. & Criminology 308, 335 (1986) (concluding that *Sandstrom* "tends to encourage the legislature to express in more straightforward ways what the state must prove to justify punishing a person").

COUNTY OF ULSTER v. ALLEN
United States Supreme Court
442 U.S. 140 (1979)

MR. JUSTICE STEVENS delivered the opinion of the Court.

A New York statute provides that, with certain exceptions, the presence of a firearm in an automobile is presumptive evidence of its illegal possession by all persons then occupying the vehicle.[1] The United States Court of Appeals

---

1. New York Penal Law §265.15(3) (McKinney 1967):

The presence in an automobile, other than a stolen one or a public omnibus, of any firearm, defaced firearm, firearm silencer, bomb, bombshell, gravity knife, switchblade knife, dagger, dirk, stiletto, billy, blackjack, metal knuckles, sandbag, sandclub or slingshot is presumptive evidence of its possession by all persons occupying such automobile at the time such weapon, instrument or appliance is found, except under the following circumstances:

> (a) if such weapon, instrument or appliance is found upon the person of one of the occupants therein; (b) if such weapon, instrument or appliance is found in an automobile which is being operated for hire by a duly licensed driver in the due, lawful and proper pursuit of his trade, then such presumption shall not apply to the driver; or (c) if the weapon so found is a pistol or revolver and one of the occupants, not present under duress, has in his possession a valid license to have and carry concealed the same.

In addition to the three exceptions delineated in §§265.15(3)(a)-(c) above as well as the stolen-vehicle and public-omnibus exception in §265.15(3) itself, §265.20 contains various exceptions that

for the Second Circuit held that respondents may challenge the constitutionality of this statute in a federal habeas corpus proceeding and that the statute is "unconstitutional on its face." We granted certiorari to review these holdings and also to consider whether the statute is constitutional in its application to respondents.

Four persons, three adult males (respondents) and a 16-year-old girl (Jane Doe, who is not a respondent here), were jointly tried on charges that they possessed two loaded handguns, a loaded machinegun, and over a pound of heroin found in a Chevrolet in which they were riding when it was stopped for speeding on the New York Thruway shortly after noon on March 28, 1973. The two large-caliber handguns, which together with their ammunition weighed approximately six pounds, were seen through the window of the car by the investigating police officer. They were positioned crosswise in an open handbag on either the front floor or the front seat of the car on the passenger side where Jane Doe was sitting. Jane Doe admitted that the handbag was hers.[2] The machinegun and the heroin were discovered in the trunk after the police pried it open. The car had been borrowed from the driver's brother earlier that day; the key to the trunk could not be found in the car or on the person of any of its occupants, although there was testimony that two of the occupants had placed something in the trunk before embarking in the borrowed car.[3] The jury convicted all four of possession of the handguns and acquitted them of possession of the contents of the trunk.

Counsel for all four defendants objected to the introduction into evidence of the two handguns, the machinegun, and the drugs, arguing that the State had not adequately demonstrated a connection between their clients and the contraband. The trial court overruled the objection, relying on the presumption of possession created by the New York statute. Because that presumption does not apply if a weapon is found "upon the person" of one of the occupants of the car, the three male defendants also moved to dismiss the charges relating to the handguns on the ground that the guns were found on the person of

---

apply when weapons are present in an automobile pursuant to certain military, law enforcement, recreational, and commercial endeavors.

2. The arrest was made by two state troopers. One officer approached the driver, advised him that he was going to issue a ticket for speeding, requested identification, and returned to the patrol car. After a radio check indicated that the driver was wanted in Michigan on a weapons charge, the second officer returned to the vehicle and placed the driver under arrest. Thereafter, he went around to the right side of the car and, in "open view," saw a portion of a .45-caliber automatic pistol protruding from the open purse on the floor or the seat. He opened the car door, removed that gun, and saw a .38-caliber revolver in the same handbag. He testified that the crosswise position of one or both of the guns kept the handbag from closing. After the weapons were secured, the two remaining male passengers, who had been sitting in the rear seat, and Jane Doe were arrested and frisked. A subsequent search at the police station disclosed a pocketknife and marihuana concealed on Jane Doe's person.

3. Early that morning, the four defendants had arrived at the Rochester, N.Y., home of the driver's sister in a Cadillac. Using her telephone, the driver called their brother, advised him that "his car ran hot" on the way there from Detroit and asked to borrow the Chevrolet so that the four could continue on to New York City. The brother brought the Chevrolet to the sister's home. He testified that he had recently cleaned out the trunk and had seen no weapons or drugs. The sister also testified, stating that she saw two of the defendants transfer some unidentified item or items from the trunk of one vehicle to the trunk of the other while both cars were parked in her driveway.

Jane Doe. Respondents made this motion both at the close of the prosecution's case and at the close of all evidence. The trial judge twice denied it, concluding that the applicability of the "upon the person" exception was a question of fact for the jury.

At the close of the trial, the judge instructed the jurors that they were entitled to infer possession from the defendants' presence in the car. He did not make any reference to the "upon the person" exception in his explanation of the statutory presumption, nor did any of the defendants object to this omission or request alternative or additional instructions on the subject.

[Defendants sought relief by post-trial motion and appeal in the state courts in New York, arguing that apart from the presumption there was not enough evidence to convict. They lost. Then they sought and obtained a writ of habeas corpus in the United States District Court, which concluded that the presence of two guns in a woman's handbag in a car could not reasonably support an inference that the guns were in the possession of three other persons in the car. The Second Circuit Court of Appeals affirmed, but on a different ground, finding that the statute creating the presumption was unconstitutional on its face because it "sweeps within its compass (1) many occupants who may not know they are riding with a gun (which may be out of their sight), and (2) many who may be aware of the presence of the gun but not permitted access to it." The Supreme Court granted certiorari. Before reaching the presumption itself, the Court concluded that the District Court had jurisdiction to entertain the constitutional challenge, since the New York state courts had themselves reached the constitutional question, and had not ruled against defendants on the basis of any "independent and adequate state procedural ground" that would foreclose adjudication of the constitutional challenge.]

In this case, the Court of Appeals undertook the task of deciding the constitutionality of the New York statute "on its face." Its conclusion that the statutory presumption was arbitrary rested entirely on its view of the fairness of applying the presumption in hypothetical situations—situations, indeed, in which it is improbable that a jury would return a conviction,[14] or that a prosecution would ever be instituted. We must accordingly inquire whether these respondents had standing to advance the arguments that the Court of Appeals considered decisive. An analysis of our prior cases indicates that the answer to this inquiry depends on the type of presumption that is involved in the case.

Inferences and presumptions are a staple of our adversary system of fact-finding. It is often necessary for the trier of fact to determine the existence of an element of the crime—that is, an "ultimate" or "elemental" fact—from the existence of one or more "evidentiary" or "basic" facts. The value of these evidentiary devices, and their validity under the Due Process Clause, vary from case to case, however, depending on the strength of the connection between the particular basic and elemental facts involved and on the degree to which the device curtails the factfinder's freedom to assess the evidence independently.

---

14. Indeed, in this very case the permissive presumptions in §265.15(3) and its companion drug statute, N.Y. Penal Law §220.25(1), were insufficient to persuade the jury to convict the defendants of possession of the loaded machinegun and heroin in the trunk of the car notwithstanding the supporting testimony that at least two of them had been seen transferring something into the trunk that morning. . . .

Nonetheless, in criminal cases, the ultimate test of any device's constitutional validity in a given case remains constant: the device must not undermine the factfinder's responsibility at trial, based on evidence adduced by the State, to find the ultimate facts beyond a reasonable doubt.

The most common evidentiary device is the entirely permissive inference or presumption, which allows—but does not require—the trier of fact to infer the elemental fact from proof by the prosecutor of the basic one and which places no burden of any kind on the defendant. In that situation the basic fact may constitute prima facie evidence of the elemental fact. When reviewing this type of device, the Court has required the party challenging it to demonstrate its invalidity as applied to him. Because this permissive presumption leaves the trier of fact free to credit or reject the inference and does not shift the burden of proof, it affects the application of the "beyond a reasonable doubt" standard only if, under the facts of the case, there is no rational way the trier could make the connection permitted by the inference. For only in that situation is there any risk that an explanation of the permissible inference to a jury, or its use by a jury, has caused the presumptively rational factfinder to make an erroneous factual determination.

A mandatory presumption is a far more troublesome evidentiary device. For it may affect not only the strength of the "no reasonable doubt" burden but also the placement of that burden; it tells the trier that he or they *must* find the elemental fact upon proof of the basic fact, at least unless the defendant has come forward with some evidence to rebut the presumed connection between the two facts.[16] In this situation, the Court has generally examined the

16.   This class of more or less mandatory presumptions can be subdivided into two parts: presumptions that merely shift the burden of production to the defendant, following the satisfaction of which the ultimate burden of persuasion returns to the prosecution; and presumptions that entirely shift the burden of proof to the defendant. The mandatory presumptions examined by our cases have almost uniformly fit into the former subclass, in that they never totally removed the ultimate burden of proof beyond a reasonable doubt from the prosecution.

To the extent that a presumption imposes an extremely low burden of production—e.g., being satisfied by "any" evidence—it may well be that its impact is no greater than that of a permissive inference, and it may be proper to analyze it as such. See generally Mullaney v. Wilbur, 421 U.S. 684, 703 n.31 (1975).

In deciding what type of inference or presumption is involved in a case, the jury instructions will generally be controlling, although their interpretation may require recourse to the statute involved and the cases decided under it. Turner v. United States [319 U.S. 463 (1970)] provides a useful illustration of the different types of presumptions. It analyzes the constitutionality of two different presumption statutes (one mandatory and one permissive) as they apply to the basic fact of possession of both heroin and cocaine, and the presumed facts of importation and distribution of narcotic drugs. The jury was charged essentially in the terms of the two statutes.

The importance of focusing attention on the precise presentation of the presumption to the jury and the scope of that presumption is illustrated by a comparison of United States v. Gainey, 380 U.S. 63 (1965), with United States v. Romano [382 U.S. 136 (1965)]. Both cases involved statutory presumptions based on proof that the defendant was present at the site of an illegal still. In *Gainey* the Court sustained a conviction "for carrying on" the business of the distillery in violation of 26 U.S.C. §5601(a)(4), whereas in *Romano*, the Court set aside a conviction for being in "possession, or custody, or . . . control" of such a distillery in violation of §5601(a)(1). The difference in outcome was attributable to two important differences between the cases. Because the statute involved in *Gainey* was a sweeping prohibition of almost any activity associated with the still, whereas the *Romano* statute involved only one narrow aspect of the total undertaking, there was a much higher probability that mere presence could support an inference of guilt in the former case than in the latter.

presumption on its face to determine the extent to which the basic and elemental facts coincide. To the extent that the trier of fact is forced to abide by the
presumption, and may not reject it based on an independent evaluation of
the particular facts presented by the State, the analysis of the presumption's
constitutional validity is logically divorced from those facts and based on the
presumption's accuracy in the run of cases.[17] It is for this reason that the Court
has held it irrelevant in analyzing a mandatory presumption, but not in analyzing
a purely permissive one, that there is ample evidence in the record other than
the presumption to support a conviction.

Without determining whether the presumption in this case was mandatory,[18] the Court of Appeals analyzed it on its face as if it were. In fact, it was
not, as the New York Court of Appeals had earlier pointed out.

The trial judge's instructions make it clear that the presumption was merely

---

Of perhaps greater importance, however, was the difference between the trial judge's instructions to the jury in the two cases. In *Gainey*, the judge had explained that the presumption was
permissive; it did not require the jury to convict the defendant even if it was convinced that he
was present at the site. On the contrary, the instructions made it clear that presence was only "a
circumstance to be considered along with all the other circumstances in the case." As we emphasized, the "jury was thus specifically told that the statutory inference was not conclusive." In
Romano, the trial judge told the jury that the defendant's presence at the still "shall be deemed
sufficient evidence to authorize conviction." Although there was other evidence of guilt, that
instruction authorized conviction even if the jury disbelieved all of the testimony except the proof
of presence at the site. This Court's holding that the statutory presumption could not support
the *Romano* conviction was thus dependent, in part, on the specific instructions given by the trial
judge. Under those instructions it was necessary to decide whether, regardless of the specific
circumstances of the particular case, the statutory presumption adequately supported the guilty
verdict.

17.   In addition to the discussion of *Romano* in n.16, supra, this point is illustrated by Leary
v. United States [395 U.S. 6 (1969)]. In that case, Dr. Timothy Leary, a professor at Harvard
University, was stopped by customs inspectors in Laredo, Tex., as he was returning from the
Mexican side of the international border. Marihuana seeds and a silver snuffbox filled with
semirefined marihuana and three partially smoked marihuana cigarettes were discovered in his
car. He was convicted of having knowingly transported marihuana which he knew had been
illegally imported into this country in violation of 21 U.S.C. §176a (1964 ed.). That statute included
a mandatory presumption: "possession shall be deemed sufficient evidence to authorize conviction
[for importation] unless the defendant explains his possession to the satisfaction of the jury."
Leary admitted possession of the marihuana and claimed that he had carried it from New York
to Mexico and then back.

Mr. Justice Harlan for the Court noted that under one theory of the case, the jury could
have found direct proof of all of the necessary elements of the offense without recourse to the
presumption. But he deemed that insufficient reason to affirm the conviction because under
another theory the jury might have found knowledge of importation on the basis of either direct
evidence or the presumption, and there was accordingly no certainty that the jury had not relied
on the presumption. The Court therefore found it necessary to test the presumption against the
Due Process Clause. Its analysis was facial. Despite the fact that the defendant was well educated
and had recently traveled to a country that is a major exporter of marihuana to this country, the
Court found the presumption of knowledge of importation from possession irrational. It did so,
not because Dr. Leary was unlikely to know the source of the marihuana, but instead because "a
majority of possessors" were unlikely to have such knowledge. Because the jury had been instructed
to rely on the presumption even if it did not believe the Government's direct evidence of knowledge
of importation (unless, of course, the defendant met his burden of "satisfying" the jury to the
contrary), the Court reversed the conviction.

18.   Indeed, the court never even discussed the jury instructions.

a part of the prosecution's case,[19] that it gave rise to a permissive inference available only in certain circumstances, rather than a mandatory conclusion of possession, and that it could be ignored by the jury even if there was no affirmative proof offered by defendants in rebuttal. The judge explained that possession could be actual or constructive, but that constructive possession could not exist without the intent and ability to exercise control or dominion over the weapons. He also carefully instructed the jury that there is a mandatory presumption of innocence in favor of the defendants that controls unless it, as the exclusive trier of fact, is satisfied beyond a reasonable doubt that the defendants possessed the handguns in the manner described by the judge. In short, the instructions plainly directed the jury to consider all the circumstances tending to support or contradict the inference that all four occupants of the car had possession of the two loaded handguns and to decide the matter for itself without regard to how much evidence the defendants introduced.

Our cases considering the validity of permissive statutory presumptions such as the one involved here have rested on an evaluation of the presumption as applied to the record before the Court. None suggests that a court should pass on the constitutionality of this kind of statute "on its face." It was error for the Court of Appeals to make such a determination in this case.

As applied to the facts of this case, the presumption of possession is entirely rational. Notwithstanding the Court of Appeals' analysis, respondents were not "hitchhikers or other casual passengers," and the guns were neither "a few inches in length" nor "out of [respondents'] sight." The argument against possession by any of the respondents was predicated solely on the fact that the guns were in Jane Doe's pocketbook. But several circumstances—which, not surprisingly, her counsel repeatedly emphasized in his questions and his argument—made it highly improbable that she was the sole custodian of those weapons.

Even if it was reasonable to conclude that she had placed the guns in her purse before the car was stopped by police, the facts strongly suggest that Jane Doe was not the only person able to exercise dominion over them. The two guns were too large to be concealed in her handbag. The bag was consequently open, and part of one of the guns was in plain view, within easy access of the driver of the car and even, perhaps, of the other two respondents who were riding in the rear seat.

Moreover, it is highly improbable that the loaded guns belonged to Jane

---

19. "It is your duty to consider all the testimony in this case, to weigh it carefully and to test the credit to be given to a witness by his apparent intention to speak the truth and by the accuracy of his memory to reconcile, if possible, conflicting statements as to material facts and in such ways to try and get at the truth and to reach a verdict upon the evidence."

"To establish the unlawful possession of the weapons, again the People relied upon the presumption and, in addition thereto, the testimony of Anderson and Lemmons who testified in their case in chief."

"Accordingly, you would be warranted in returning a verdict of guilt against the defendants or defendant if you find the defendants or defendant was in possession of a machine gun and the other weapons and that the fact of possession was proven to you by the People beyond a reasonable doubt, and an element of such proof is the reasonable presumption of illegal possession of a machine gun or the presumption of illegal possession of firearms, as I have just before explained to you."

Doe or that she was solely responsible for their being in her purse. As a 16-year-old girl in the company of three adult men she was the least likely of the four to be carrying one, let alone two, heavy handguns. It is far more probable that she relied on the pocketknife found in her brassiere for any necessary self-protection. Under these circumstances, it was not unreasonable for her counsel to argue and for the jury to infer that when the car was halted for speeding, the other passengers in the car anticipated the risk of a search and attempted to conceal their weapons in a pocketbook in the front seat. The inference is surely more likely than the notion that these weapons were the sole property of the 16-year-old girl.

Under these circumstances, the jury would have been entirely reasonable in rejecting the suggestion—which, incidentally, defense counsel did not even advance in their closing arguments to the jury—that the handguns were in the sole possession of Jane Doe. Assuming that the jury did reject it, the case is tantamount to one in which the guns were lying on the floor or the seat of the car in the plain view of the three other occupants of the automobile. In such a case, it is surely rational to infer that each of the respondents was fully aware of the presence of the guns and had both the ability and the intent to exercise dominion and control over the weapons. The application of the statutory presumption in this case therefore comports with the standard laid down in *Tot* and restated in *Leary*. For there is a "rational connection" between the basic facts that the prosecution proved and the ultimate fact presumed, and the latter is "more likely than not to flow from" the former.

Respondents argue, however, that the validity of the New York presumption must be judged by a "reasonable doubt" test rather than the "more likely than not" standard employed in *Leary*. Under the more stringent test, it is argued that a statutory presumption must be rejected unless the evidence necessary to invoke the inference is sufficient for a rational jury to find the inferred fact beyond a reasonable doubt. Respondents' argument again overlooks the distinction between a permissive presumption on which the prosecution is entitled to rely as one not necessarily sufficient part of its proof and a mandatory presumption which the jury must accept even if it is the sole evidence of an element of the offense.[29]

In the latter situation, since the prosecution bears the burden of establishing guilt, it may not rest its case entirely on a presumption unless the fact proved is sufficient to support the inference of guilt beyond a reasonable doubt. But in the former situation, the prosecution may rely on all of the evidence in the record to meet the reasonable-doubt standard. There is no more reason to require a permissive statutory presumption to meet a reasonable-doubt standard before it may be permitted to play any part in a trial than there is to require

---

29. The dissenting argument rests on the assumption that "the jury [may have] rejected all of the prosecution's evidence concerning the location and origin of the guns." Even if that assumption were plausible, the jury was plainly told that it was free to disregard the presumption. But the dissent's assumption is not plausible; for if the jury rejected the testimony describing where the guns were found, it would necessarily also have rejected the only evidence in the record proving that the guns were found in the car. The conclusion that the jury attached significance to the particular location of the handguns follows inexorably from the acquittal on the charge of possession of the machinegun and heroin in the trunk.

that degree of probative force for other relevant evidence before it may be admitted. As long as it is clear that the presumption is not the sole and sufficient basis for a finding of guilt, it need only satisfy the test described in *Leary*.

The permissive presumption, as used in this case, satisfied the *Leary* test. And, as already noted, the New York Court of Appeals has concluded that the record as a whole was sufficient to establish guilt beyond a reasonable doubt.

The judgment is reversed.

So ordered.

[The concurring opinion of CHIEF JUSTICE BURGER is omitted.]

MR. JUSTICE POWELL, with whom MR. JUSTICE BRENNAN, MR. JUSTICE STEW-ART and MR. JUSTICE MARSHALL join, dissenting. . . .

In the criminal law, presumptions are used to encourage the jury to find certain facts, with respect to which no direct evidence is presented, solely because other facts have been proved.[1] The purpose of such presumptions is plain: Like certain other jury instructions, they provide guidance for jurors' thinking in considering the evidence laid before them. Once in the juryroom, jurors necessarily draw inferences from the evidence—both direct and circum-stantial. Through the use of presumptions, certain inferences are commended to the attention of jurors by legislatures or courts.

Legitimate guidance of a jury's deliberations is an indispensable part of our criminal justice system. Nonetheless, the use of presumptions in criminal cases poses at least two distinct perils for defendants' constitutional rights. The Court accurately identifies the first of these as being the danger of interference with "the factfinder's responsibility at trial, based on evidence adduced by the State, to find the ultimate facts beyond a reasonable doubt." If the jury is instructed that it must infer some ultimate fact (that is, some element of the offense) from proof of other facts unless the defendant disproves the ultimate fact by a preponderance of the evidence, then the presumption shifts the burden of proof to the defendant concerning the element thus inferred.[2]

But I do not agree with the Court's conclusion that the only constitutional difficulty with presumptions lies in the danger of lessening the burden of proof the prosecution must bear. As the Court notes, the presumptions thus far reviewed by the Court have not shifted the burden of persuasion; instead, they either have required only that the defendant produce some evidence to rebut the inference suggested by the prosecution's evidence, or merely have been suggestions to the jury that it would be sensible to draw certain conclusions

---

1. Such encouragement can be provided either by statutory presumptions, or by presump-tions created in the common law. Unless otherwise specified, "presumption" will be used herein to "permissible inferences," as well as to "true" presumptions.

2. The Court suggests that presumptions that shift the burden of persuasion to the defendant in this way can be upheld provided that "the fact proved is sufficient to support the inference of guilt beyond a reasonable doubt." As the present case involves no shifting of the burden of persuasion, the constitutional restrictions on such presumptions are not before us, and I express no views on them.

It may well be that even those presumptions that do not shift the burden of persuasion cannot be used to prove an element of the offense, if the facts proved would not permit a reasonable mind to find the presumed fact beyond a reasonable doubt. My conclusion makes it unnecessary for me to address this concern here.

on the basis of the evidence presented.[3] Evolving from our decisions, therefore, is a second standard for judging the constitutionality of criminal presumptions which is based—not on the constitutional requirement that the State be put to its proof—but rather on the due process rule that when the jury is encouraged to make factual inferences, those inferences must reflect some valid general observation about the natural connection between events as they occur in our society. . . . In sum, our decisions uniformly have recognized that due process requires more than merely that the prosecution be put to its proof.[6] In addition, the Constitution restricts the court in its charge to the jury by requiring that, when particular factual inferences are recommended to the jury, those factual inferences be accurate reflections of what history, common sense, and experience tell us about the relations between events in our society. Generally, this due process rule has been articulated as requiring that the truth of the inferred fact be more likely than not whenever the premise for the inference is true. Thus, to be constitutional a presumption must be at least more likely than not true.

In the present case, the jury was told:

> Our Penal Law also provides that the presence in an automobile of any machine gun or of any handgun or firearm which is loaded is presumptive evidence of their unlawful possession. In other words, [under] these presumptions or this latter presumption upon proof of the presence of the machine gun and the hand weapons, you may infer and draw a conclusion that such prohibited weapon was possessed by each of the defendants who occupied the automobile at the time when such instruments were found. The presumption or presumptions is effective only so long as there is no substantial evidence contradicting the conclusion flowing from the presumption, and the presumption is said to disappear when such contradictory evidence is adduced.

Undeniably, the presumption charged in this case encouraged the jury to draw a particular factual inference regardless of any other evidence presented: to infer that respondents possessed the weapons found in the automobile "upon proof of the presence of the machine gun and the hand weapon" and proof that respondents "occupied the automobile at the time such instruments were found." I believe that the presumption thus charged was unconstitutional because it did not fairly reflect what common sense and experience tell us about passengers in automobiles and the possession of handguns. People present in automobiles where there are weapons simply are not "more likely than not" the possessors of those weapons. . . .

In another context, this Court has been particularly hesitant to infer possession from mere presence in a location, noting that "[p]resence is relevant and admissible evidence in a trial on a possession charge; but absent some showing of the defendant's function at the [illegal] still, its connection with possession

---

3. The Court suggests as the touchstone for its analysis a distinction between "mandatory" and "permissive" presumptions. I have found no recognition in the Court's prior decisions that this distinction is important in analyzing presumptions used in criminal cases.

6. The Court apparently disagrees, contending that "the factfinder's responsibility . . . to find the ultimate facts beyond a reasonable doubt" is the only constitutional restraint upon the use of criminal presumptions at trial.

is too tenuous to permit a reasonable inference of guilt—'the inference of the one from proof of the other is arbitrary. . . .' " United States v. Romano. We should be even more hesitant to uphold the inference of possession of a handgun from mere presence in an automobile, in light of common experience concerning automobiles and handguns. Because the specific factual inference recommended to the jury in this case is not one that is supported by the general experience of our society, I cannot say that the presumption charged is "more likely than not" to be true. Accordingly, respondents' due process rights were violated by the presumption's use.

As I understand it, the Court today does not contend that in general those who are present in automobiles are more likely than not to possess any gun contained within their vehicles. It argues, however, that the nature of the presumption here involved requires that we look, not only to the immediate facts upon which the jury was encouraged to base its inference, but to the other facts "proved" by the prosecution as well. The Court suggests that this is the proper approach when reviewing what it calls "permissive" presumptions because the jury was urged "to consider all the circumstances tending to support or contradict the inference."

It seems to me that the Court mischaracterizes the function of the presumption charged in this case. As it acknowledges was the case in *Romano*, the "instruction authorized conviction even if the jury disbelieved all of the testimony except the proof of presence" in the automobile.[7] The Court nevertheless relies on all of the evidence introduced by the prosecution and argues that the "permissive" presumption could not have prejudiced defendants. The possibility that the jury disbelieved all of this evidence, and relied on the presumption, is simply ignored. . . .

NOTES ON THE SIGNIFICANCE OF *ALLEN*

1. In *Allen,* the Court concludes that the "presumption" was "permissive." (You know that using this term is at best confusing and misleading and that it would better be described as an "inference.") What made the Court conclude that it was "permissive"? Do you agree that it was?

2. *Allen* also refers to a "mandatory presumption" that "tells the trier that he or they *must* find the elemental fact" unless defendant comes forward with counterproof. (You know that in this context "presumption" is indeed the proper term.) Could a presumption operate in that way against the accused

---

7. In commending the presumption to the jury, the court gave no instruction that would have required a finding of possession to be based on anything more than mere presence in the automobile. Thus, the jury was not instructed that it should infer that respondents possessed the handguns only if it found that the guns were too large to be concealed in Jane Doe's handbag; that the guns accordingly were in the plain view of respondents; that the weapons were within "easy access of the driver of the car and even, perhaps, of the other two respondents who were riding in the rear seat"; that it was unlikely that Jane Doe was solely responsible for the placement of the weapons in her purse; or that the case was "tantamount to one in which the guns were lying on the floor or the seat of the car in the plain view of the three other occupants of the automobile."

on elements in the offense? Doesn't *Sandstrom,* which was decided only two weeks after *Allen,* make it clear that the answer is no?

3. If Justice Stevens simply misspoke in implying that a "mandatory presumption" could operate to *require* a finding in a criminal case, how else could it operate? How would it differ from a "permissive" presumption (or inference, to use the right term)? What standard must it satisfy?

PROBLEM 10-D.   *Presence of a Firearm*

College student Sam Alden returns to home in Rochester, New York, for a Christmas visit with his family. During his visit he encounters his former high school classmate Burnell, and late one evening the two drive around town in Burnell's car. Police stop them, and it turns out that the car matches the description of a getaway car used in a nearby liquor store holdup in which the salesperson was killed 20 minutes earlier.

The arresting officers direct Burnell to open the trunk, where they discover a sawed-off shotgun and three Uzi automatic rifles. Alden and Burnell are charged with unlawful possession of firearms.

At trial, the prosecutor offers evidence of the facts outlined above. He also calls Clayton as a witness, and he testifies that he and Burnell belong to a gun club and that Burnell once bragged that "I have a bunch of Uzis, and a modified shotgun."

At the close of the evidence, the prosecutor requests that the court instruct the jury as follows:

> The presence in an automobile of a loaded firearm is presumptive evidence of unlawful possession. On proof of the presence of guns in the car, you may infer that each defendant in the car possessed them. The presumption is effective only so long as there is no substantial evidence contradicting that conclusion, and the presumption disappears when such contradictory evidence is adduced. To establish unlawful possession of the weapon, the prosecutor relied on the presumption as well as testimony. Accordingly, you would be warranted in returning a verdict of guilty if you find beyond a reasonable doubt that possession is proved, and an element of such proof is the presumption of illegal possession.

Alden and Burnell both object, claiming the instruction violates due process. The prosecutor replies that the Supreme Court in *Allen* has approved such an instruction. On these facts, is the instruction proper as against Alden? As against Burnell?

NOTES ON INFERENCES IN CRIMINAL CASES

1. Doesn't the requested instruction in Problem 10-D fairly paraphrase the instruction approved in *Allen?* Can the court and the parties know before all the evidence is in whether such an instruction is proper in any given case?

2. The legislative device in *Allen* might be described as a "nudging inference" because it encourages the jury to infer one fact on the basis of another,

where the inference is plausible but less than certain. Why do we have (and permit) the use of such a nudging instruction relating to the elements of an offense in criminal cases?

Consider what courts tell jurors about the prosecutor's burden: Invariably they learn that the state must prove its case beyond a reasonable doubt. But trial courts often advise juries as well that the prosecutor need not prove guilt "beyond all possible doubt," see Kevin F. O'Malley, Jay E. Grenig & Hon. William C. Lee, Federal Jury Practice and Instructions §12.10 (2000). Sometimes they add that "reasonable doubt" does not mean "a mere possible doubt or a speculative, imaginary, or forced doubt, because everything relating to human affairs is open to some possible or imaginary doubt." See United States v. Muckenstrum, 515 F.2d 568, 571 (5th Cir.) (rejecting challenge to this language, but also criticizing instruction that reasonable doubt means "substantial rather than speculative doubt"), cert. denied, 423 U.S.1032 (1975).

Does the "nudging" inference sabotage the reasonable doubt standard? Or serve as a constructive reminder to a lay factfinder that it need not abandon common sense? Can the "nudging" inference be justified as a way of telling the jury that circumstantial evidence can suffice to convict and that reasonable doubt does not mean "speculative" or "imaginary" doubt?

3. Is there a reason, *apart* from the "nudging" effect of those words, to be uncomfortable with a conviction that follows such an instruction? On the facts of Problem 10-D, wouldn't Burnell likely be convicted even without the instruction? Usually a criminal trial is decided on the basis of conflicting testimony, circumstantial evidence, questions of witness credibility, or combinations of these. Is there a reason to prefer convictions resting on such proof over convictions resting on the weight that the jury gives to a presumption instruction? Recall the arguments made against use of probabilistic evidence in criminal cases in Chapter 9C2b, supra. See also Nesson, Reasonable Doubt and Permissive Inferences: The Value of Complexity, 92 Harv. L. Rev. 1187 (1979).

4. Look again at the presumption instruction given in *Allen* and paraphrased in Problem 10-D. Do you like this language? Professor Nesson suggests telling the jury that "it is often possible to infer" the conclusion from the basic fact. In *Allen*, for example, the judge could say:

It is often possible to infer from the presence of loaded firearms in an automobile that the occupants of the automobile possessed the weapons. You must decide whether, in the context of this case, such a conclusion is justified as to each defendant. You should consider all the facts. For example, consider where the guns were found, whether they were in plain sight, how easy they were to reach. Based on your consideration of all the evidence, you must decide whether the prosecution has proved beyond reasonable doubt that each defendant is guilty as charged.

Nesson, Rationality, Presumptions, and Judicial Comment: A Response to Professor Allen, 94 Harv. L. Rev. 1574, 1589 (1981). What do you think of this suggestion?

5. In federal court Timothy Leary was charged, inter alia, with possession and concealment of imported marijuana. See Leary v. United States, 395 U.S. 6 (1969). Does the element of importation relate to culpability or to federal-

ism—the proper division of responsibility between federal government and states? Sometimes Congress can properly decide for itself that certain kinds of acts affect "interstate commerce," and if the finding is reasonable Congress can criminalize those acts. The statute will be upheld as a proper exercise of congressional power to regulate interstate commerce. See Perez v. United States, 402 U.S. 146 (1970) (upholding federal statute criminalizing extortionate credit transactions because Congress could reasonably conclude that extortion is a problem affecting interstate commerce). Suppose Congress finds that traffic in cocaine affects interstate commerce, so it enacts criminal penalties for possessing cocaine, but only if it is imported or taken across state lines. Can Congress determine that these latter points "affect only federal jurisdiction," thus avoid the constitutional restraints that ordinarily apply in criminal prosecutions? Consider (1) allocating to the court (rather than the jury) the responsibility for deciding them, (2) authorizing decision on such points by only a preponderance of the evidence, (3) giving such questions to the jury to decide under that lesser standard, (4) burdening *the defense* with the task of proving by a preponderance that the cocaine did *not* come from abroad or cross state lines. Should Congress be permitted to choose any or all of these procedures?

Eleven | JUDICIAL NOTICE

A. INTRODUCTION

Judicial notice describes the process by which a court determines certain matters without need of formal proof. Judicial notice covers four areas: Adjudicative facts, which is the *only* area governed by FRE 201, evaluative facts, legislative facts, and law. Notice of legislative and evaluative facts is unregulated; judicial notice of law is regulated by a different set of rules and conventions.

Adjudicative facts are not defined in FRE 201, but the ACN quotes the suggestion by Professor Davis that they are "the facts that normally go to the jury in a jury case." It is also said that adjudicative facts are those that would have to be proved by evidence if notice were not taken. Judicial notice of adjudicative facts thus serves as a substitute for evidence. It is a doctrine that relieves a party of the burden of producing evidence on indisputable issues, furthering trial efficiency. In a nonjury trial, the judge takes judicial notice merely by making an announcement or ruling, and she might or might not use the term "judicial notice." In a jury trial, judicial notice requires an instruction informing the jury that notice has been taken and explaining what that means. See FRE 201(g).

Evaluative facts include matters of common knowledge that judges and jurors bring to their deliberations. These facts amount to background information, appearing "inconspicuously and interstitially in [the] elementary processes of understanding and reasoning." McNaughton, Judicial Notice— Excerpts Relating to the Morgan-Wigmore Controversy, 14 Vand. L. Rev. 779, 789 (1961). Because no evidence is usually offered to prove evaluative facts, they are also known as "nonevidence" facts. When jurors consider such matters, we sometimes refer to the process as "jury notice."

The most basic evaluative facts are those that help judge and jury understand testimony and other evidence, such as the usual meaning of words, idioms, and slang expressions and what is meant by various forms of assertive conduct. When a witness says "fire engine," it is assumed that the jury understands what is meant without a dictionary or other evidence being offered. When a witness testifies that the defendant nodded after being asked whether he was the person driving the car, again it is assumed that the jury understands the usual meaning of a nod.

Other evaluative facts help the trier assess formal evidence. Such facts are likely to be comprised of arrays of factual data that underlie ordinary judgments about the world, which are captured in terms like "human nature" and "physical laws." When a witness is impeached, for example, by a showing that he has a close romantic or economic relationship with one of the parties, it is assumed that the jury understands how and why such relationships might affect his credibility. And when evidence is offered that an airplane crashed to the ground after its engine failed in flight, it is assumed that the jury understands the connection between the two events, without the need for testimony describing principles of Newtonian physics.

Because an evaluative fact is normally a matter of general knowledge, there is usually no need to instruct the jury to take notice of such a fact. If a party seeks an instruction, it is an indication that she views the matter as an adjudicative fact rather than an evaluative fact. But a general instruction on evaluative facts is sometimes given, telling jurors they may use their experience in the affairs of life, their general knowledge of the natural tendencies and inclinations of human beings, and their common sense in evaluating formal evidence.

Legislative facts are those that are considered by a trial or appellate court in ruling on a question of law. The legal question may be the interpretation of a statute or constitutional provision or the creation, modification, or repeal of a common law rule. As Professor Davis has stated: "When a court . . . develops law or policy, it is acting legislatively; the courts have created the common law through judicial legislation, and the facts which inform the tribunal's legislative judgment are called legislative facts." Davis, Judicial Notice, 55 Colum. L. Rev. 945, 952 (1955). Although legislative facts may include the legislative history of a relevant statute or similar legal matters, they are much broader. They also encompass all nonlegal matters, whether scientific, sociological, historical, or otherwise, considered by a court in making a legal ruling. No jury instruction is given on judicial notice of legislative facts because legal rulings are beyond the province of the jury.

Judicial notice of law refers to the process by which the court determines controlling law. To the extent judicial notice is taken, parties are relieved of the burden of proving law, although they generally help the court in this task. If judicial notice of law is not taken, responsibility for proving the applicable law rests with the parties. Federal courts traditionally take judicial notice not only of federal law, but also of the law of the forum state and sister states. State courts traditionally take judicial notice of federal law and the law of the forum state, but until relatively recently, many have been unwilling to notice the law of sister states. There is a strong trend toward expanding the scope of judicial notice of law. Although the Federal Rules of Evidence do not address the issue, most states specify the scope of judicial notice of law by statute or rule.

The four categories of judicial notice are easy to describe, but there is sometimes confusion on the question how a particular matter should be classified. Sometimes a fact overlaps two or more categories (meaning essentially that it is used for more than one purpose in the case). Classification is important because the restrictions and procedures of FRE 201 apply only if the matter noticed is an adjudicative fact.

B. JUDICIAL NOTICE OF ADJUDICATIVE FACTS

PROBLEM 11-A. Dry Pavement

Paulsen sues Davis for injuries sustained in an automobile accident at an intersection in Indianapolis on September 8, 1999. Paulsen asks the court to take judicial notice that it did not rain in Indianapolis on that date and that the pavement at the intersection was dry. In support of this request, Paulsen furnishes the court with a copy of the official weather bureau record for Indianapolis on September 8, 1999, which clearly indicates that no precipitation was recorded. Davis objects on grounds that the record is hearsay and has not been properly authenticated. Should the request for judicial notice be granted, in whole or in part? Is FRE 104(a) applicable?

PROBLEM 11-B. The Subpoena

West is cited to show cause why he should not be held in contempt for failure to appear as a witness at a trial after being served a subpoena. West denies getting the subpoena. The petitioning party asks the court to take judicial notice that West was served, directing court's attention to a properly executed return of service filed by the sheriff and included as part of the record of the case. The petitioning party also asks the court to take judicial notice that West had been held in contempt for failure to appear at an earlier trial of the same case, and had also been held in contempt for refusing to testify in related cases in two other states. What ruling?

PROBLEM 11-C. Interstate Call

Lauro is charged with knowingly using the telephone in interstate commerce for purposes of transacting bets or wagers. Telephone records show the call was placed interstate from Baborian in New Haven, Connecticut to Lauro in Rhode Island, but Lauro denies knowing that it was an interstate call. At trial the only evidence of knowledge was testimony that Lauro, who admittedly was in Rhode Island, spoke to Baborian's father in New Haven, Connecticut at 6:36 p.m., and the father said Baborian was with him in New Haven at that time, but was driving to Rhode Island and would be calling Lauro shortly. At 6:51 p.m., Lauro got Baborian's call. The prosecutor asks the court to take judicial notice (1) that the driving time from New Haven, Connecticut, to Rhode Island is more than 15 minutes and (2) that therefore Lauro must have known Baborian's call was from out of state. What ruling?

PROBLEM 11-D. The Football Fan

Rogers is charged with armed robbery. He asserts an alibi defense, claiming that he was watching a professional football game on television with friends at the time of the robbery. To rebut this defense, the prosecutor supplies the

court with a copy of TV Guide and asks the court to take judicial notice that
there was no football game of any type being televised at the time of the robbery.
What ruling?

PROBLEM 11-E. The Arab Oil Embargo

Shell Oil sues Mainland Shipping Company for failure to deliver an oil
shipment on schedule in the fall of 1973. Mainland asserts the defense of
impossibility of performance, claiming the delay was caused by the political
action of Iraq in refusing to allow the oil to leave the country.

Mainland asks the court to take judicial notice of the Arab oil embargo of
October 1973. What ruling?

PROBLEM 11-F. Asbestos and Cancer

Plaintiffs who contracted cancer after exposure to asbestos file a product
liability action against a leading asbestos manufacturer. Plaintiffs request that
the court take judicial notice that asbestos causes cancer. What ruling? Assume
the request is granted. Is defendant then barred from trying to prove the
contrary? Is defendant barred from arguing to the jury that asbestos does not
cause cancer?

GOVERNMENT OF THE VIRGIN ISLANDS v. GEREAU
United States Court of Appeals for the Third Circuit
523 F.2d 140 (1975)

Defendants-appellants contend that the District Court of the Virgin Islands,
Division of St. Croix, erred in denying their motion for a new trial. Rejecting
this contention, we affirm the district court.

On August 13, 1973, defendants were found guilty of first degree murder,
first degree assault, and robbery. The jury which returned the verdicts had
deliberated for nine days. The jurors were polled individually and each acknowledged the verdict as his own. Two days later, defendants filed a motion requesting a new trial on the ground that the verdict had not been freely assented
to by all the jurors. . . .

Juror Agneta Cappin testified that one of the jury attendants, Matron Foye,
spoke to her about the case.

> She just asked me how everything is going and I tell her not so good. And I say
> two of them that don't understand, they don't come in yet. And she say to me
> she want them to hurry up so she can get to go home, that is all.

Matron Foye denied the conversation. The trial judge, finding both women
to be credible witnesses, chose to believe Foye rather than Cappin because he

knew that Foye "was grateful for the opportunity to earn extra income as a jury matron." We do not consider these credibility findings to lack adequate support in the record. However, we do hold that the trial judge's reliance on his personal, subjective belief about the needs and motive of Matron Foye was an improper ground for rejecting Cappin's concededly credible testimony.

In basing his fact-finding on personal knowledge, the trial judge was, in effect, taking judicial notice of extra-record, adjudicative facts. "With respect to judicial notice of adjudicative facts, the tradition has been one of caution in requiring that the matter be beyond reasonable controversy." Advisory Committee's Notes to FRE 201(b); cf. FRE 201(a) and (b). A second hallmark of facts properly the subject of judicial notice is that they be either matters of common knowledge or "capable of immediate and accurate determination by resort to easily accessible sources of indisputable accuracy.. . ." Weaver v. United States, 298 F.2d 496, 498 (5th Cir. 1962). Facts possessing these characteristics are entitled to be considered by a judge without first being proved through the routine processes of introducing evidence. The necessary cachet is not, however, bestowed merely by a judge's knowledge of a particular fact.

> There is a real but elusive line between the judge's *personal knowledge* as a private man and these matters of which he takes judicial notice as a judge. The latter does not necessarily include the former; as a judge, indeed, he may have to ignore what he knows as a man, and contrariwise. . . .
>
> It is therefore plainly accepted that the judge is not to use from the bench, under the guise of judicial knowledge, that which he knows *only as an individual* observer outside of court. The former [judicial knowledge] is in truth "known" to him merely in the fictional sense that it is known and notorious to all men, and the dilemma is only the result of using the term "knowledge" in two senses. Where to draw the line between knowledge by notoriety and knowledge by personal observation may sometimes be difficult, but the principle is plain.

J. Wigmore, Evidence, §2569, at 539-40 (3d ed. 1940). It is apparent that the trial judge's knowledge about Matron Foye falls into this latter category of personal knowledge and, therefore, does not qualify for judicial notice. It follows that the trial judge erred in rejecting Cappin's testimony on the ground stated. . . .

As an antidote to these errors in the fact-finding process, our inquiry into the validity of the verdict will assume . . . that Cappin's testimony was accurate. . . .

In the present case, Cappin did not indicate whether she considered herself influenced by the matron's statement. However, the trial judge found that she had voted guilty from the first ballot to the last. Since Cappin did not mention the incident to any of the other jurors, no juror could have been moved by the remarks to change his vote.

It thus appearing that no prejudice accrued to the defendants from the only occurrence which was both legally cognizable and sufficient to impeach the jury verdict, we find no abuse of discretion in the trial judge's refusal to order a new trial. The judgment of the district court will be affirmed.

NOTES ON JUDICIAL NOTICE OF ADJUDICATIVE FACTS

1. Was the court in *Gereau* right to conclude that the trial judge had taken judicial notice of an adjudicative fact? Regardless how the fact should be classified, is the decision sound?

2. The *Gereau* rule that judges may not base judicial notice on personal knowledge is well established but occasionally violated. See SEC v. Musella, 578 F. Supp. 425, 439 (S.D.N.Y. 1984), where the court took judicial notice of the following:

> [A]ll law firms, especially those such as Sullivan & Cromwell that routinely handle sensitive matters, impress upon their incoming employees the firm's expectation that they will not publicly discuss matters pertaining to their clients. . . . I have not been so long removed from the world inhabited by firms like Sullivan to have forgotten what life is like there.

See also In re National Airlines, 434 F. Supp. 269 (D. Fla. 1977).

3. The scope of judicial notice of adjudicative facts under FRE 201(b) is narrow. See Hardy v. Johns-Manville Sales Corp., 681 F.2d 334, 347 (5th Cir. 1982) (judicial notice "applies to self-evident truths that no reasonable person could question, truisms that approach platitudes or banalities"). Is the phrase of limitation in FRE 201 ("not subject to reasonable dispute") too stringent? Professors Thayer and Wigmore thought so, and Professor Davis agrees. They have urged that judicial notice should have a broader focus and should encompass not only indisputable facts but also facts that are unlikely to be challenged. Under the Thayer-Wigmore-Davis view, judicial notice would be like a presumption. The fact judicially noticed would not be binding upon the jury, and the opposing party could introduce evidence to the contrary. See J. Thayer, A Preliminary Treatise on Evidence at the Common Law 308 (1898); 9 J. Wigmore, Evidence §2567 (J. Chadbourn rev. 1981); Davis, Judicial Notice, 1969 Law & Social Order 513. Professors Morgan and McNaughton took the opposing position, ultimately adopted by FRE 201(b), that judicial notice should be limited to matters that are not subject to reasonable dispute. Under their view, because the matter must be indisputable, controverting proof is inappropriate. Hence taking notice is conclusive and conflicting evidence should not be admitted. E. Morgan, Basic Problems of Evidence 9 (1962); McNaughton, Judicial Notice—Excerpts Relating to the Morgan-Wigmore Controversy, 14 Vand. L. Rev. 779 (1961).

4. Does FRE 201 require a party to notify an opposing party that judicial notice is requested of a particular matter at trial? Does the Rule require a court to notify parties prior to taking judicial notice on its own motion? Compare Model Code, Rule 804(1) (1942): "The judge shall inform the parties of the tenor of any matter to be judicially noticed by him and afford each of them reasonable opportunity to present to him information relevant to the propriety of taking such judicial notice or to the tenor of the matter to be noticed."

5. Does the Constitution guarantee parties a right to be heard regarding the propriety of a court taking judicial notice? See Ohio Bell Telephone v. Public Utilities Commission, 301 U.S. 292, 302-303 (1937) (judicial notice without

providing opportunity for parties to be heard violates due process) (review of administrative determination).

6. Judicial notice is mandatory under FRE 201(d) on request by a party if the court is "supplied with the necessary information." A purpose of mandatory judicial notice is to assure attorneys that it will be possible to establish certain facts by judicial notice, thereby relieving them of the obligation to produce evidence on the point. Does the Rule accomplish this purpose? What uncertainties continue to exist? Is judicial notice mandatory on appeal when no request for judicial notice was made in the trial court?

7. For additional examples of judicial notice of facts viewed by the court as adjudicative, see Barnes v. Bosley, 568 F. Supp. 1406, 1410 n.4 (E.D. Mo. 1983) (judicial notice "that currently the Democratic Party is firmly in control of political offices within the city of St. Louis"), modified in part, rev'd in part on other grounds, 745 F.2d 501 (8th Cir. 1984), cert. denied, 471 U.S. 1017 (1985); Sinatra v. Heckler, 566 F. Supp. 1354 (E.D.N.Y. 1983) (substantial number of federal employees take vacations during year-end holiday period when the mails are heavily burdened, resulting in slowdown of office operations and retarded delivery); Allen v. Allen, 518 F. Supp. 1234, 1235 n.2 (E.D. Pa. 1981) (Father's Day occurred on June 17 in 1979); Caufield v. Board of Education, 486 F. Supp. 862, 885 (E.D.N.Y. 1979) (judicial notice that "historically in New York City, a large percentage of the teaching force, particularly at the lower school levels, has been composed of women"), aff'd, 632 F.2d 999 (2d Cir. 1980), cert. denied, 450 U.S. 1020 (1981); United Klans of America v. McGovern, 453 F. Supp. 836 (N.D. Ala. 1978) (judicial notice that United Klans "has been and continues to be a 'white supremacy' organization whose purposes and policies are implemented by acts of terror and intimidation"), aff'd, 621 F.2d 152 (5th Cir. 1980); State ex rel. Chalka v. Johnson, 292 N.W.2d 835, 840 (Wis. 1980) (judicial notice that Southern Comfort is "an intoxicating liquor and that excessive consumption of an intoxicating liquor can cause death").

8. In light of these examples, do you agree with Professor Davis' description that adjudicative facts are "facts concerning the immediate parties—who did what, where, when, how, and with what motive or intent"? 2 K. Davis, Administrative Law Treatise §15.03, at 353 (1984). Are not many adjudicative facts of a general nature and unrelated to the immediate parties?

C. JUDICIAL NOTICE IN CRIMINAL CASES

UNITED STATES v. JONES
United States Court of Appeals for the Sixth Circuit
580 F.2d 219 (1978)

[Defendant was convicted of illegally intercepting telephone conversations of his estranged wife. After the jury convicted defendant on three of five counts, the district judge granted defendant's motion for a judgment of acquittal on the ground that the government failed to prove that South Central Bell Telephone Company was "a common carrier . . . providing or operating . . . facilities

for the transmission of interstate or foreign communications," a requirement
of the federal eavesdropping statute under which defendant was prosecuted.
The government appealed the ruling of the trial court and urged that judicial
notice be taken by the appellate court of South Central Bell's status as a common
carrier.]

The government did not at any time during the jury trial specifically request
the district court to take judicial notice of the status of South Central Bell.
Nevertheless, it relies upon the provisions of Rule 201(f) which state that
"[j]udicial notice may be taken at any stage of the proceeding." It is true
that the Advisory Committee Note to 201(f) indicates that judicial notice is
appropriate "in the trial court *or on appeal.*" It is also true that the language
of 201(f) does not distinguish between judicial notice in civil or criminal cases.
There is, however, a critical difference in the manner in which the judicially
noticed fact is to be submitted to the jury in civil and criminal proceedings:

> *Instructing jury.* In a civil action or proceeding, the court shall instruct the jury
> to accept as conclusive any fact judicially noticed. In a criminal case, the court
> shall instruct the jury that it may, but is not required to, accept as conclusive any
> fact judicially noticed.

FRE 201(g). Thus under subsection (g) judicial notice of a fact in a civil case
is conclusive while in a criminal trial the jury is not bound to accept the judicially
noticed fact and may disregard it if it so chooses.

It is apparent from the legislative history that the congressional choice of
language in Rule 201 was deliberate. In adopting the present language, Congress
rejected a draft of subsection (g) proposed by the Supreme Court, which read:

> The judge shall instruct the jury to accept as established any facts judicially noticed.

The House Report explained its reason for the change:

> Rule 201(g) as received from the Supreme Court provided that when judicial
> notice of a fact is taken, the court shall instruct the jury to accept that fact as
> established. Being of the view that mandatory instruction to a jury in a criminal
> case to accept as conclusive any fact judicially noticed is inappropriate because
> contrary to the spirit of the Sixth Amendment right to a jury trial, the Committee
> adopted the 1969 Advisory Committee draft of this subsection, allowing a manda-
> tory instruction in civil actions and proceedings and a discretionary instruction
> in criminal cases.

H. Rep. No. 93-650, 93d Cong., 1st Sess. 6-7 (1973), U.S. Code Cong. & Admin.
News 7075, 7080 (1974). Congress intended to preserve the jury's traditional
prerogative to ignore even uncontroverted facts in reaching a verdict. The
legislature was concerned that the Supreme Court's rule violated the spirit, if
not the letter, of the constitutional right to a jury trial by effectively permitting
a partial directed verdict as to facts in a criminal case.[8]

___

8. The Supreme Court of Utah expressed a similar concern in State v. Lawrence, 234 P.2d
600 (Utah 1951): "If a court can take one important element of an offense from the jury and
determine the facts for them because such fact seems plain enough to him, then which element
cannot be similarly taken away, and where would the process stop?"

As enacted by Congress, Rule 201(g) plainly contemplates that the jury in a criminal case shall pass upon facts which are judicially noticed. This it could not do if this notice were taken for the first time after it had been discharged and the case was on appeal. We, therefore, hold that Rule 201(f), authorizing judicial notice at the appellate level, must yield in the face of the express congressional intent manifested in 201(g) for criminal jury trials. To the extent that the earlier practice may have been otherwise, we conceive that it has been altered by the enactment of Rule 201.

Accordingly, the judgment of the district court is affirmed.

NOTES ON JUDICIAL NOTICE IN CRIMINAL CASES

1. Was *Jones* correctly decided? Does the decision succeed in protecting the doctrine of jury nullification? Consider the following criticism:

> It is extremely difficult to see the working of the process of jury nullification under such circumstances. If they wished to exercise their power of nullification, they certainly did not need to do so by finding that South Central Bell was not engaged in interstate commerce. Moreover the jury already convicted the defendant. Whenever the fact judicially noticeable against the defendant is needed to support a conviction actually rendered by a jury, it makes no practical sense to discuss the possibility of jury nullification.

M. Graham, Handbook of Federal Evidence 84 n.15 (3d ed. 1991).

2. The Advisory Committee had trouble making up its mind on judicial notice in criminal cases. Originally it favored the nonbinding notice that FRE 201(g) now endorses, on the ground that "a verdict cannot be directed against the accused in a criminal case." 46 F.R.D. 161, 205 (1969). Later it concluded that mandatory notice was proper because "the right of jury trial does not extend to matters which are beyond reasonable dispute." 51 F.R.D. 315, 335 (1971). But Congress agreed with the Committee's first thought, and adopted the original proposal. The House Committee Report cites "the spirit of the Sixth Amendment right to a jury trial." Who is right here? Consider the following critique of FRE 201(g) as enacted:

> With deference, [FRE 201(g) as it emerged from Congress] is irrational. Actual application of the Congressional version makes fools of the judge, the law and the jury. If for example, the facts warrant a finding that a woman was taken by the defendant for immoral purposes from Newark, New Jersey, to New York City, New York, the judge under the Court's [proposed] Rule would by a proper instruction leave that issue to the jury, while further instructing them that such a journey would constitute a crossing of state lines. The Congressional rule, intended to preserve the power of the jury, requires him to instruct the jury that it "may, but is not required to accept" the proposition that to go from Newark to New York is to cross state lines. Under the Court's [proposed] rule the jury would still have the power to acquit the defendant though the evidence warranted a judgment of conviction—but on the ground of mercy and not under an instruction

permitting it to find that Newark is not really in New Jersey but is a New York suburb of "fun city," and that, after all, state lines were not crossed.

Under the Congressional rule, in the morning when the judge tries a civil case the world is round. That afternoon when he tries a criminal case the world is flat.

10 Moore's Federal Practice §201.70 (2d ed. 1985).

3. Consider the *Lawrence* case, which *Jones* cites in footnote 8. *Lawrence* involved a prosecution for grand larceny, arising out of the alleged theft in 1950 of a 1947 Ford two-door sedan. The trial judge instructed the jury to "take the value of this property as being in excess of $50.00," and the jury convicted. Not coincidentally, that sum represented the dividing line between grand and petty larceny. The Utah Supreme Court reversed, on the ground that judicial notice improperly took away the jury's power to "make findings which are not based on logic, nor even common sense." State v. Lawrence, 234 P.2d 600, 603 (Utah 1951). Do you agree with *Lawrence* that a mandatory instruction is out of line? A court applying FRE 201(g) could not give such an instruction. If the jury wanted to convict for petty larceny, would that be equivalent to finding that "the world is flat"?

4. On the facts in *Lawrence*, what exactly should a trial judge applying FRE 201(g) tell the jury? Consider the following proposal, advanced by the Federal Judicial Center Committee:

> Even though no evidence has been introduced about it, I have decided to accept as proved that [e.g.: the city of San Francisco is north of the city of Los Angeles]. I believe that this fact is of such common knowledge [or alternative justification per rule 201(b)(2) of the Federal Rules of Evidence] that it would be a waste of our time to hear evidence about it. Thus, you may treat it as proved, even though no evidence was brought out on the point. Of course, with this fact, as with any fact, you will have to make the final decision and you are not required to agree with me.

Federal Judicial Center, Committee to Study Jury Instructions 12 (1982). Would similar language work on the facts of *Lawrence*?

5. Does the Moore argument (Note 2, supra) overstate the degree to which FRE 201(g) protects the freedom of the jury? The ABA Section on Litigation thinks so: "Federal courts recognize a sound distinction between adjudicative facts and the legal significance of those facts. Thus, an instruction to a jury that, if it finds that a defendant traveled from Newark to New York, then the defendant traveled in interstate commerce is consistent with Rule 201." ABA Section of Litigation, Emerging Problems Under the Federal Rules of Evidence 36-37 (1983).

6. Uniform Rule of Evidence 201(g) (1974) provides for mandatory instructions in criminal cases, and a few states have agreed. See Maine Rule 201(g) and its Advisory Committee Comment: "It would be as absurd in a criminal case as in a civil action to allow jurors to question the accuracy of the court's instruction as to what day of the week December 4, 1972, actually was." Granting the force of this point, does it follow that a permissive instruction in *Lawrence* would be "absurd"?

7. The trend of judicial decisions has been to follow the lead of *Jones*.

See United States v. Dior, 671 F.2d 351 (9th Cir. 1982) (refusing to take judicial notice after trial that $13,690 in Canadian currency had a value of $5000 or more in United States currency); United States v. Bliss, 642 F.2d 390 (10th Cir. 1981); United States v. Thomas, 610 F.2d 1166 (3d Cir. 1979). But see Government of the Canal Zone v. Burjan, 596 F.2d 690 (5th Cir. 1979), and United States v. Lavender, 602 F.2d 639 (4th Cir. 1979) (judicial notice taken on appeal that place of crime was within federal jurisdiction).

8. Is there a drafting error in the second sentence of FRE 201(g)? Shouldn't judicial notice be binding when taken in favor of a criminal defendant?

PROBLEM 11-G. *Deadly Weapon*

Stimson, a karate expert, is charged with "assault with a deadly weapon, to wit, his hands" arising out of an attack on Boyer. Under the law of the jurisdiction, whether a weapon is deadly under the statute is an adjudicative fact for the jury. But on request by the prosecutor, the court instructs the jury under FRE 201(g) that "you may, but are not required to find, that the hands of karate expert qualify as a deadly weapon under the statute." In his case-in-chief, Stimson calls Osaga, a fellow karate expert, who will testify that karate is not a dangerous sport and that the hands of a karate expert are not a deadly weapon. The prosecutor objects, arguing that rebutting evidence cannot be presented with respect to a fact that has already been judicially noticed. What ruling?

D. EVALUATIVE FACTS

Thayer described evaluative facts as a part of judicial reasoning:

> In conducting a process of judicial reasoning, as of other reasoning, not a step can be taken without assuming something which has not been proved; and the capacity to do this, with competent judgment and efficiency, is imputed to judges and juries as part of their necessary mental outfit.

J. Thayer, Preliminary Treatise on Evidence at the Common Law 279-280 (1898).

PROBLEM 11-H. *"Okay, Maurie"*

Defendant is prosecuted for extortion in violation of federal law. At trial, the prosecution offers into evidence a note from the defendant to the alleged victim containing the following statements: "Okay, Maurie, this is it, get it and get it straight because you only have one chance. . . . Please Maurie, make it easy on yourself by cooperating fully." The prosecutor requests an instruction under FRE 201 telling the jury that it may, but is not required to find, that in the language of the criminal underworld such statements constitute an implicit death threat. What ruling?

NOTES ON NOTICE OF EVALUATIVE FACTS

1. Do you think jurors really need to be told that the language in the note to Maurie might convey a veiled death threat? If underworld code or jargon carries sinister meaning not common in ordinary discourse, shouldn't the prosecutor call an expert to testify on such points?

2. Courts have long understood that jurors bring certain "mental baggage" to the cases they decide. Indeed, this baggage seems part and parcel of the common sense that we seek from juries. Consider the following description of what jurors bring to their task:

> But any juror must consider the testimony in light of that knowledge and experience which is common to all men. For instance, it is a matter of common knowledge that a bullet piercing the brain of a human being will in all likelihood prove fatal. It is common knowledge also that a forest tree cut nearly in two at the butt will fall, if a high wind blows against it. If a witness should testify to the contrary of these ordinary phenomena the common knowledge of the juror derived from his experience in such matters would naturally compel him to discredit that witness. Many illustrations might be given where men are normally and legitimately influenced in considering testimony by their general knowledge and experience.

Rostad v. Portland Ry., Light & Power Co., 201 P. 184, 187 (Or. 1921). See also Head v. Hargrave, 105 U.S. 45, 49-50 (1882).

3. Is the doctrine described in *Rostad,* supra, subject to abuse? How can attorneys regulate the amount of relevant, extrarecord information possessed by jurors sitting on a case?

4. Isn't a jury's knowledge of evaluative facts one of the factors appropriately considered in determining questions of venue? See Pereza v. Mark, 423 F.2d 149, 151 (2d Cir. 1970) (Vermont jurors "are very likely better acquainted with rifles than we are"); Chance v. Du Pont De Nemours & Co., 371 F. Supp. 439, 449 (E.D.N.Y. 1974) (a federal court in West Virginia, with a West Virginia jury, "is best equipped to decide whether blasting caps are familiar articles around coal mines, and community standards comprise "a vital element in assessing the actions of the parties").

5. Isn't an attorney's most direct involvement with evaluative facts likely to be in closing argument? To what extent can an attorney in closing argument refer to matters outside the record, such as historical facts, scientific facts, and current events? See Levin and Levy, Persuading the Jury with Facts Not in Evidence: The Fiction-Science Spectrum, 105 U. Pa. L. Rev. 139 (1956) (references to current and historical events should be permitted).

6. What limits are imposed on a jury's use of information outside the record in deciding a case? Consider the following incident in a civil case, which the reviewing court considered jury misconduct calling for reversal:

After the jury was discharged on the afternoon of November 13, juror Noll borrowed a book on electricity from a friend, took it home with him, and thereafter read from it extensively until the early hours of the next morning, paying particular attention to the arcing and jumping characteristics of electricity while being transmitted through electric transmission lines. The next morning, after the jury returned to the jury room to resume its deliberations, he proceeded, in the presence of all the jurors, to discuss with most, if not all, of them matters and things he had learned from the book about the subject in question.

Thomas v. Kansas Power & Light Co., 340 P.2d 379 (Kan. 1959).

7. What if a juror does "original research"? Recall the movie classic *Twelve Angry Men*, in which a juror played by Henry Fonda went to a local pawnshop during a break in deliberations and purchased a switchblade knife identical to the alleged murder weapon. In part because the second knife suggested that its design and style were commonplace, he persuaded fellow jurors that defendants' ownership of such a weapon was not overwhelming proof of guilt, and the jury acquitted. To what extent would FRE 606(b) impede a determination of whether jurors have improperly relied on information outside the record of the case?

8. Two scholars who conducted extensive surveys regarding the jury system conclude:

Interviews with jurors and access to experimental jury deliberations abundantly show that jurors bring to their deliberations much extra knowledge—some of which certainly would not be known to the judge. The jury's extra information tends to be some item of personal experience not part of the trial, or some generalization about human nature. . . .

Bringing knowledge such as this to bear on its deliberations is, of course, one of the jury's most engaging and flavorsome characteristics. It raises the interesting problem of how the legal system expects the jurors to confine their deliberations to the trial record on the one hand, and yet on the other to bring into their deliberations their common experience with life. In any case, to the extent that the jury utilizes in its deliberations things it knows about life in general or about human nature, it is using a kind of knowledge which the judge, as a human being, must also have, although twelve jurors coming from many strata of the society may well produce more knowledge than one judge.

H. Kalven and H. Zeisel, The American Jury 131-132 (1966).

E. JUDICIAL NOTICE OF LEGISLATIVE FACTS

MULLER v. OREGON
United States Supreme Court
208 U.S. 412 (1907)

[In this case, the Court finds a rational basis for an Oregon statute limiting the hours women can work in laundries and factories to a maximum of ten hours per day, and therefore upholds its constitutionality.]

It may not be amiss, in the present case, before examining the constitutional question, to notice the course of legislation as well as expressions of opinion from other than judicial sources. In the brief filed by Mr. Louis D. Brandeis, for the defendant in error, is a very copious collection of all these matters, an epitome of which is found in the margin.[1]

The legislation and opinions referred to in the margin may not be, technically speaking, authorities, and in them is little or no discussion of the constitutional question presented to us for determination, yet they are significant of a widespread belief that woman's physical structure, and the functions she performs in consequence thereof, justify special legislation restricting or qualifying the conditions under which she should be permitted to toil. Constitutional questions, it is true, are not settled by even a consensus of present public opinion, for it is the peculiar value of a written constitution that it places in unchanging form limitations upon legislative action, and thus gives a permanence and stability to popular government which otherwise would be lacking. At the same time, when a question of fact is debated and debatable, and the extent to which a special constitutional limitation goes is affected by the truth in respect to that fact, a widespread and long continued belief concerning it is worthy of consideration. We take judicial cognizance of all matters of general knowledge.

HOUSER v. STATE
Washington Supreme Court
540 P.2d 412 (Wash. 1975)

UTTER, J.

Charles Houser, III, brought this action on his own behalf and that of the class of all 18- to 20-year-olds in this state, challenging the constitutionality of the legislation that established a minimum age of 21 for the consumption of alcoholic beverages. The trial court rendered summary judgment in favor of

---

1.   The following legislation of the States impose restrictions in some form or another upon the hours of labor that may be required of women.

In foreign legislation Mr. Brandeis calls attention to these statutes: Great Britain: Factories Act of 1844, chap. 15, pp. 161, 171; Factory and Workshop Act of 1901, chap. 22, pp. 60, 71; and see 1 Edw. VII, chap. 22. France, 1848; Act Nov. 2, 1892, and March 30, 1900. Switzerland, Canton of Glarus, 1848; Federal Law 1877, art. 2, §1. Austria, 1855; Acts 1897, art. 96a, §§1-3. Holland, 1889; art. 5, §1. Italy, June 19, 1902, art. 7. Germany, Laws 1891.

Then follow extracts from over ninety reports of committees, bureaus of statistics, commissioners of hygiene, inspectors of factories, both in this country and in Europe, to the effect that long hours of labor are dangerous for women, primarily because of their special physical organization. The matter is discussed in these reports in different aspects, but all agree as to the danger. It would of course take too much space to give these reports in detail. Following them are extracts from similar reports discussing the general benefits of short hours from an economic aspect of the question. In many of these reports individual instances are given tending to support the general conclusion. Perhaps the general scope and character of all these reports may be summed up in what an inspector for Hanover says: "The reasons for the reduction of the working day to ten hours—(a) the physical organization of women, (b) her maternal functions, (c) the rearing and education of the children, (d) the maintenance of the home—are all so important and so far reaching that the need for such reduction need hardly be discussed."

the defendant state agencies, and Houser appeals. We affirm the ruling of the trial court.

Appellant sought from the court below a declaratory judgment that the 21-year-old drinking age deprived persons between the ages of 18 and 20 of the equal protection of the laws in violation of the Fourteenth Amendment and Const. art. 1, §12. He contended that no rational basis exists for the present statutory scheme under which Washington citizens are considered to be adults at the age of 18 for all purposes except the possession and consumption of alcohol. He supported this contention with evidence in the form of an expert's affidavit that indicated that several traditional arguments for maintaining the drinking age at 21 were without scientific support. The State countered this claim by submitting to the court's notice two technical studies which contained data supporting the statutory age discrimination, and by citing the single federal case in point, Republican College Council v. Winner, 357 F. Supp. 739 (E.D. Pa. 1973), which upheld Pennsylvania's drinking age limitation against equal protection attack. The trial court found the State's studies and the reasoning of the *Republican College* case adequate to uphold the drinking-age statutes, regardless of the truth of the statements in appellant's expert's affidavit. It therefore granted the State's motion for summary judgment. Appellant's appeal challenges both the trial court's judicial notice of the State's studies and its refusal to grant him a trial on the merits of the contradictory factual claims. . . .

To ascertain whether a rational relationship existed between the 21-year-old drinking age and a legitimate state purpose, the trial court took judicial notice of the studies submitted to it by the State. Appellant contends these studies were not judicially noticeable because the facts they contain were not "well established and authoritatively settled." This argument misconceives the function the court was performing in ruling on the constitutional issue before it. The State's summary judgment motion required the court to inquire not into the facts of the particular case at bar but into the general relationship between the attainment of the age of 21 and the effect of alcohol consumption. The question it presented was essentially one of law, not fact: whether there was a "rational relationship" between the statutory distinction and the state purposes it was alleged to serve. The finding that it was rational to believe that the discrimination did correspond to a permissible state objective was a step in the court's legal reasoning, not a conclusion regarding the factual background of the particular dispute before it.

A court "may ascertain as it sees fit any fact that is merely a ground for laying down a rule of law.. . .." Chastleton Corp. v. Sinclair, 264 U.S. 543, 548 (1924). The restrictive rules governing judicial notice are not applicable to factual findings that simply supply premises in the process of legal reasoning. In interpreting and developing the constitution and laws, courts cannot operate in a vacuum. In order to determine whether there is a "rational relationship" between a statutory classification and an objective said to justify it, a court must look beyond the case reports and statute books into a world that is rich with probability and conjecture and almost devoid of settled certainty. It must make the best assessment it can from the best information it can obtain. Reputable scientific studies are one source of such information, increasingly utilized by courts in constitutional decision making. The trial court thus did not err in noticing the studies submitted to it in this case.

NOTES ON JUDICIAL NOTICE OF LEGISLATIVE FACTS

1.   Why don't the Federal Rules of Evidence regulate judicial notice of legislative facts? What policy arguments can be made against such regulation? What constitutional arguments?

2.   If a court intends to take judicial notice of legislative facts in making a ruling of law, should not the court advise the parties and provide them an opportunity to be heard on the propriety of relying upon such extrarecord facts?

3.   Why is judicial notice of legislative facts usually an invisible process? Do judges invite criticism when they reveal their extrarecord sources? Consider the following passage in a dissenting opinion by Judge Frank in *Triangle* in an appeal from an injunction prohibiting defendants, who made and sold girdles, from using the trade name Miss Seventeen Foundations Co. because of the likelihood of confusion with Seventeen magazine, which was published by the plaintiff:

> Like the trial judge's, our surmise [as to confusion between the names] must here rest on "judicial notice." As neither the trial judge nor any member of this court is (or resembles) a teen-age girl or the mother or sister of such a girl, our judicial notice apparatus will not work well unless we feed it with information directly obtained from "teen-agers" or from their female relatives accustomed to shop for them. Competently to inform ourselves, we should have a staff of investigators like those supplied to administrative agencies. As we have no such staff, I have questioned some adolescent girls and their mothers and sisters, persons I have chosen at random. I have been told uniformly by my questionees that no one could reasonably believe that any relation existed between plaintiff's magazine and defendant's girdles.

Triangle Publications v. Rohrlich, 167 F.2d 969, 976 (2d Cir. 1948).

4.   For other examples of judicial notice of legislative facts, see Population Services International v. Wilson, 398 F. Supp. 321, 332-333 (S.D.N.Y. 1975) (challenging the constitutionality of a New York statute prohibiting distribution of contraceptives to anyone under the age of 16; the court stated that "it is not beyond the power of this Court to note that some young persons under the age of sixteen do engage in sexual intercourse and the consequence of such activity is often venereal disease, unwanted pregnancy, or both."), aff'd, Carey v. Population Services International, 431 U.S. 678 (1977). See also Record Museum v. Lawrence Township, 481 F. Supp. 768, 771 (D.N.J. 1979) (challenge to drug paraphernalia ordinance; court takes "judicial notice of the phenomenon known as the Counterculture of the Seventies wherein untraditional attire such as spoons and hand-crafted pipes adorn both home and person").

F. JUDICIAL NOTICE OF LAW

As noted earlier, the term "judicial notice of law" is sometimes used to describe the process by which the court determines the applicable law, thereby relieving the parties of formally proving that law. At an earlier period, if judicial notice of law was not taken, the law had to be pleaded and, at least in the case of foreign law, proved to the jury as though it were a question of fact. Often an expert would be called and testimony would be given on the nature of the law or its proper interpretation. With respect to issues of foreign law, this testimony would then be weighed by the jury along with the other evidence in the case. Under the modern view, even if judicial notice of the law is not taken, the proof is presented to the court, and the determination of controlling law is made by the judge, not the jury. Once this determination is made, whether by judicial notice or formal proof to the court, the jury is instructed at the end of the trial to apply that law in deciding the case.

Judicial notice of law is not addressed by FRE 201. The ACN to Rule 201 says that "the manner in which law is fed into the judicial process is never a proper concern of the rules of evidence, but rather of the rules of procedure." Federal procedural rules, however, regulate this process only when it comes to proving the law of foreign nations. See FRCP 44.1 and FRCrimP 26.1.

Common law tradition requires federal judges to take judicial notice of all domestic statutory and case law, state as well as federal:

> The states of the Union are not foreign to the United States or to its courts. Such courts are required to take judicial notice of the statute and case law of each of the states. "The law of any State of the Union, whether depending upon statutes or *upon judicial opinions,* is a matter of which the courts of the United States are bound to take judicial notice, *without plea or proof.*"

Schultz v. Tecumseh Products, 310 F.2d 426, 433 (6th Cir. 1962) (emphasis in original). A few federal statutes also regulate judicial notice of law. See 44 U.S.C. §§1507, 1510 (authorizing judicial notice of the Code of Federal Regulations and content of Federal Register).

NOTES ON JUDICIAL NOTICE OF LAW

1. Many states have provisions in their evidence codes regulating judicial notice of law. See, e.g., Hawaii Rule of Evidence 202:
    (a) *Scope of rule.* This rule governs only judicial notice of law.
    (b) *Mandatory judicial notice of law.* The court shall take judicial notice of (1) the common law, (2) the constitutions and statutes of the United States and of every state, territory, and other jurisdiction of the United States, (3) all rules adopted by the U.S. Supreme Court or by the Hawaii Supreme Court, and (4) all duly enacted ordinances of cities or counties of this State.
    (c) *Optional judicial notice of law.* Upon reasonable notice to adverse parties, a party may request that the court take, and the court may take, judicial notice of (1) all duly adopted federal and state rules of court, (2) all duly published regulations of federal and state agencies, (3) all duly enacted ordinances of municipalities or other governmental subdivisions of other states, (4) any matter

of law which would fall within the scope of this subsection . . . but for the fact that it has been replaced, superseded, or otherwise rendered no longer in force, and (5) the laws of foreign countries, international law, and maritime law.

(d) *Determination by court.* All determinations of law made pursuant to this rule shall be made by the court and not by the jury, and the court may consider any relevant material or source, including testimony, whether or not submitted by a party or admissible under these rules.

Haw. Rev. Stat. §626 (1993).

2. Other states regulate judicial notice of law by statute outside their evidence code. Many of these statutes are based on the Uniform Judicial Notice of Foreign Law Act, which was drafted by the Conference of Commissioners on Uniform Laws in 1936 and adopted by approximately half the states. The Uniform Act provided that courts in an adopting state "shall take judicial notice of the common law and statutes of every state, territory and other jurisdiction of the United States." The Act required reasonable notice to the adverse party of the intention to request judicial notice and made clear that the determination of law was a question for the court, not the jury. However, the Act did not authorize judicial notice of the law of a foreign nation. In 1962, the Act was superseded by the Uniform Interstate and International Procedure Act, which extended judicial notice to the law of any foreign jurisdiction. The latter Act also has served as a model for legislation in several states. It provides:

§4.01 [Notice] A party who intends to raise an issue concerning the law of any jurisdiction or governmental unit thereof outside this state shall give notice in his pleadings or other reasonable written notice.

§4.02 [Materials to Be Considered] In determining the law of any jurisdiction, or governmental unit thereof outside this state, the court may consider any relevant material or source, including testimony whether or not submitted by a party or admissible under the rules of evidence.

§4.03 [Court Decision and Review] The court, not jury, shall determine the law of any governmental unit outside this state. Its determination is subject to review on appeal as a ruling on a question of law.

§4.04 [Other Provisions of Law Unaffected] This Article does not repeal or modify any other law of this state permitting another procedure for the determination of foreign law.

13 U.L.A. 459 (1980).

3. Courts seem reluctant to extend judicial notice of law to municipal ordinances. See Howard v. United States, 306 F.2d 392, 394 (10th Cir. 1962) (refusing to take judicial notice of Albuquerque vagrancy ordinance); Bryant v. Liberty Mutual Insurance Co., 407 F.2d 576, 579 n.2 (4th Cir. 1969) (collecting cases). Why this reluctance?

4. The limitations on the scope of judicial notice of law resulted from the historical unavailability or scarcity of legal materials and uncertainties regarding their accuracy. In this era of electronic publishing and computerized legal

research, are these concerns any longer valid? Consider the following observation:

> As all law has become increasingly accessible and judges have tended to assume the duty to rule on the tenor of all law, the notion that this process is part of judicial notice has become increasingly an anachronism. Evidence, after all, involves the proof of facts. How the law is fed into the judicial machine is more appropriately an aspect of the law pertaining to procedure.

McCormick on Evidence §335, at 507 (J. Strong 5th ed. 1999).

G. THE PROBLEM OF CLASSIFICATION

UNITED STATES v. GOULD
United States Court of Appeals for the Eighth Circuit
536 F.2d 216 (1976)

Defendants, Charles Gould and Joseph Carey, were convicted of conspiring to import (Count I) and actually importing (Count II) cocaine from Colombia, South America, into the United States in violation of the Controlled Substances Import and Export Act. . . .

The evidence persuasively showed that defendants and David Miller enlisted the cooperation of Miller's sister, Barbara Kenworthy, who agreed to travel to Colombia with defendants and smuggle the cocaine into the United States by placing it inside two pairs of hollowed-out platform shoes. In May of 1975, defendants and Ms. Kenworthy traveled to Colombia where the cocaine was purchased and packed in Ms. Kenworthy's shoes. The success of the importation scheme was foiled when, upon Ms. Kenworthy's arrival to the Miami airport from Colombia, a customs agent insisted upon x-raying the cocaine-laden shoes. Approximately two pounds of cocaine were discovered and seized by customs officials. . . .

At trial, two expert witnesses for the Government testified as to the composition of the powdered substance removed from Ms. Kenworthy's platform shoes at the Miami airport. One expert testified that the substance was comprised of approximately 60 percent cocaine hydrochloride. The other witness stated that the white powder consisted of 53 percent cocaine. There was no direct evidence to indicate that cocaine hydrochloride is a derivative of coca leaves. In its instructions to the jury, the District Court stated:

> If you find the substance was cocaine hydrochloride, you are instructed that cocaine hydrochloride is a schedule II controlled substance under the laws of the United States.

[Defendants claim the prosecutor should have been required to prove that the substance seized was on the schedule of controlled substances. The schedule listed "coca leaves" and any "derivative thereof" but did not specifically mention cocaine hydrochloride.]

Our inquiry on this first assignment of error is twofold. We must first determine whether it was error for the District Court to take judicial notice of the fact that cocaine hydrochloride is a schedule II controlled substance. Secondly, if we conclude that it was permissible to judicially notice this fact, we must then determine whether the District Court erred in instructing the jury that it must accept this fact as conclusive.

The first aspect of this inquiry merits little discussion. . . . The fact that cocaine hydrochloride is derived from coca leaves is, if not common knowledge, at least a matter which is capable of certain, easily accessible and indisputably accurate verification. See Webster's Third New International Dictionary 434 (1961). Therefore, it was proper for the District Court to judicially notice this fact. Our conclusion on this matter is amply supported by the weight of judicial authority. . . .

Our second inquiry involves the propriety of the District Court's instruction to the jurors that this judicially noticed fact must be accepted as conclusive by them. Defendants, relying upon FRE 201(g), urge that the jury should have been instructed that it could discretionarily accept or reject this fact. Rule 201(g) provides:

> In a civil action or proceeding, the court shall instruct the jury to accept as conclusive any fact judicially noticed. In a criminal case, the court shall instruct the jury that it may, but is not required to, accept as conclusive any fact judicially noticed.

It is clear that the reach of rule 201 extends only to adjudicative, not legislative, facts. FRE 201(a). Consequently, the viability of defendants' argument is dependent upon our characterization of the fact judicially noticed by the District Court as adjudicative, thus invoking the provisions of rule 201(g). In undertaking this analysis, we note at the outset that rule 201 is not all-encompassing. "Rule 201 . . . was deliberately drafted to cover only a small fraction of material usually subsumed under the concept of 'judicial notice.'" 1 J. Weinstein, Evidence ¶201[01] (1975).

The precise line of demarcation between adjudicative facts and legislative facts is not always easily identified. Adjudicative facts have been described as follows:

> When a court . . . finds facts concerning the immediate parties—who did what, where, when, how, and with what motive or intent—the court . . . is performing an adjudicative function, and the facts are conveniently called adjudicative facts. . . .
> Stated in other terms, the adjudicative facts are those to which the law is applied in the process of adjudication. They are the facts that normally go to the jury in a jury case. They relate to the parties, their activities, their properties, their businesses.

2 K. Davis, Administrative Law Treatise §15.03, at 353 (1958).

Legislative facts, on the other hand, do not relate specifically to the activities or characteristics of the litigants. A court generally relies upon legislative facts when it purports to develop a particular law or policy and thus considers material wholly unrelated to the activities of the parties.

Legislative facts are ordinarily general and do not concern the immediate parties. In the great mass of cases decided by courts . . . the legislative element is either absent or unimportant or interstitial, because in most cases the applicable law and policy have been previously established. But whenever a tribunal engages in the creation of law or of policy, it may need to resort to legislative facts, whether or not those facts have been developed on the record.

2 K. Davis, Administrative Law Treatise, supra, at §15.03. Legislative facts are established truths, facts or pronouncements that do not change from case to case but apply universally, while adjudicative facts are those developed in a particular case.

Applying these general definitions, we think it is clear that the District Court in the present case was judicially noticing a legislative fact rather than an adjudicative fact. Whether cocaine hydrochloride is or is not a derivative of the coca leaf is a question of scientific fact applicable to the administration of the Comprehensive Drug Abuse Prevention and Control Act of 1970. The District Court reviewed the schedule II classifications contained in 21 U.S.C. §812, construed the language in a manner which comports with common knowledge and understanding, and instructed the jury as to the proper law so interpreted. It is undisputed that the trial judge is required to fully and accurately instruct the jury as to the law to be applied in a case. When a court attempts to ascertain the governing law in a case for the purpose of instructing the jury, it must necessarily rely upon facts which are unrelated to the activities of the immediate parties. These extraneous, yet necessary, facts fit within the definition of legislative facts and are an indispensable tool used by judges when discerning the applicable law through interpretation. . . .

It is clear to us that the District Court took judicial notice of a legislative, rather than an adjudicative, fact in the present case and rule 201(g) is inapplicable. The District Court was not obligated to inform the jury that it could disregard the judicially noted fact. In fact, to do so would be preposterous, thus permitting juries to make conflicting findings on what constitutes controlled substances under federal law.

PROBLEM 11-I.   *Obscene Books*

Roost, an adult bookstore owner, is charged with possession of obscene material. At trial, the books in question are admitted. The court concludes as a matter of law that they are obscene within the meaning of the statute and so instructs the jury. The jury is left with only the question of whether the defendant possessed the books. Has the court erred? Is this case distinguishable from *Gould*?

NOTES ON THE PROBLEM OF CLASSIFICATION

1. Would *Gould* be a harder case if the noticed fact had been subject to reasonable dispute? Once a fact has been classified as legislative rather than

adjudicative, there is no requirement of indisputability. Should the *Gould* approach concern us for this reason?

2. Professor Davis has stated that it is important

> to recognize that many facts are not readily classifiable as either adjudicative or legislative. Just as some questions have to be regarded as mixed questions of law and fact and can be so regarded without destroying the necessary and useful distinction between law and fact, so some facts have to be regarded as mixed adjudicative and legislative facts and can be so regarded without destroying the necessary and useful distinction between adjudicative facts and legislative facts.

2 K. Davis, Administrative Law Treatise §15.03, at 528 (1970 Supp.). Nonetheless, under FRE 201 the classification has to be made, does it not, in order to determine whether the requirements of the rule are applicable?

3. Do you think FRE 201 regulates judicial notice in a useful way? Consider this observation:

> Since the adoption of the Federal Rules of Evidence there have been thousands of cases in which courts have taken judicial notice of some fact, but in only a few dozen of those cases did the court indicate that the fact it was noticing could be classified as either legislative or adjudicative. This phenomenon would suggest that the heart of F.R.E. 201 has not been well-received by the judges who actually have to work with it.

Turner, Judicial Notice and Federal Rule of Evidence 201—A Rule Ready for Change, 45 U. Pitt. L. Rev. 181, 185 (1983).

4. The problem of classification is of great practical importance to attorneys attempting to deal with precedents in the field of judicial notice. The case reports are laden with decisions taking "judicial notice" of multifarious facts. However, a previous decision taking judicial notice of a matter as a legislative fact is generally not authority for notice of the same matter as an adjudicative fact. Consider this comment by the Oregon Supreme Court:

> In determining the appropriateness of a court's action in taking judicial notice, it must constantly be borne in mind that judicial notice may be employed for a wide variety of purposes. A failure to distinguish between the purposes for which courts take judicial notice of fact creates the danger that someone will assume that once an appellate court has at one time or another taken judicial notice of a fact for one purpose it is a proper subject for notice for a completely different purpose.

Chartrand v. Coos Bay Tavern, 696 P.2d 513, 517 (Or. 1985).

PROBLEM 11-J.   *"Drunk as a Skunk"*

Prizi, a pedestrian, is seriously injured after being struck by a pickup truck driven by Davenport. The accident occurred one block from the Red Dog Saloon, where Davenport had spent the afternoon drinking. Davenport is described by one patron as "drunk as a skunk" at the time of his departure. Prizi sues the Red Dog Saloon for negligence in serving liquor to an intoxicated person whom the saloon should have foreseen was likely to drive off in a car. Prizi's action rests on a recent decision of the state supreme court recognizing a tort cause of action against tavern owners on behalf of third parties injured by patrons driving away in cars while intoxicated ("dramshop liability"). In deciding to create the new cause of action, the supreme court took "judicial notice that traveling by motor vehicle to and from a tavern is commonplace." Relying on this language, Prizi asks the trial judge to remove the issue of foreseeability from the jury. Prizi requests judicial notice that the employees of the Red Dog Saloon should have foreseen that Davenport would drive a motor vehicle upon leaving the tavern. What ruling?

PROBLEM 11-K. *Lighter Fluid Explosion*

Goodman sues Inland Chemical ("Inland") for injuries suffered when a can of charcoal lighter fluid manufactured by defendant exploded. Goodman had attempted to light the charcoal in his outdoor grill, but when he checked 15 minutes later he did not see any flames or feel much heat. He did notice that some of the briquettes were grayish-white at the corners. He poured more fluid on the charcoal. Immediately, a flame shot up the stream of fluid and the can blew up in his hand. Inland asserts the defense of contributory negligence, which under the applicable law constitutes a complete defense if proven. Inland moves for a summary judgment, on the ground that Goodman was contributorily negligent as a matter of law. Inland asks the court to take judicial notice that once combustion occurs in a bed of charcoal, the addition of flammable fluid is certain to result in instantaneous flare-up of the volatile liquid coming into contact with the charcoal. Should judicial notice be taken? Is this matter adjudicative, evaluative, or legislative?

PROBLEM 11-L. *Speed Trap*

Danielson is clocked by police radar driving 53 miles per hour in a 35 mile per hour speed zone. The jurisdiction requires that before scientific evidence may be received the court must find that there is general acceptance of the technique within the relevant scientific community. The prosecutor asks the court to take judicial notice that radar has achieved general scientific acceptance as a reliable speed-measuring technique. What ruling?

Twelve | PRIVILEGES

A. INTRODUCTION

Almost all the rules of evidence other than rules of privilege are designed to enhance the accuracy and efficiency of the factfinding process. Privileges have a different purpose. They are intended to protect certain societal relationships and values, even though such protection may impose significant costs upon the litigation process. Their effect in any given trial may be to impede the search for truth.

A primary goal of most privileges is to encourage the free flow of communication in various relationships. Some privileges are intended to prevent governmental interference with certain favored relationships, such as marriage. Others are designed to further the effective functioning of government by limiting the access of litigants to state secrets or confidential communications by public officials. The scope of privilege law is of concern to all citizens because it determines the balance struck between the interest of society in maintaining zones of privacy in human relationships and the right of litigants to obtain evidence needed to prosecute claims or defend themselves in court.

There is often confusion between evidentiary privileges and the related but distinct subject of a profession's ethical obligation of confidentiality. A profession may adopt a code of ethics imposing a duty on its members to protect the confidentiality of disclosures by the client or patient, regardless whether an evidentiary privilege is recognized for such disclosures. Violating this duty of confidentiality may lead to professional censure and (in the case of licensed professions) possible suspension or loss of license. Anyone may adopt an ethic of confidentiality as a matter of personal conscience, regardless whether it is imposed by professional standards or applicable licensing laws.

As a practical matter, this ethical obligation of confidentiality imposed by a profession may provide more protection for privacy than an evidentiary privilege, because a privilege can generally be asserted only in a judicial, legislative, or administrative proceeding. The duty of confidentiality imposes a more general proscription against disclosure by the professional person in any setting. Moreover, the ethical obligation of nondisclosure frequently extends to matters outside the scope of an evidentiary privilege, such as communications by the client or patient that do not meet the evidentiary requirement of confidentiality. For example, a client's communication to an attorney in the presence of an outsider is generally beyond reach of the attorney-client privilege, but it does not follow that the attorney is ethically free to discuss the communication publicly.

Nonetheless, evidentiary privileges are of fundamental importance. In the absence of a privilege, a professional person who is called as a witness may be judicially compelled to disclose confidential communications from a client or patient, regardless of the ethical standards of confidentiality adopted by that profession and regardless of what assurance of confidentiality was given to the client or patient. Therefore, well-advised practitioners are careful not to make a commitment to confidentiality in court proceedings beyond that allowed by privilege law, and the ethical codes of most professions specifically allow disclosure required by law or compelled by court order. See, e.g., ABA Model Code of Professional Responsibility, DR 4-101(C)(2); AMA Principles of Medical Ethics IV (2001). A practitioner who seeks to preserve a higher standard of confidentiality in a judicial proceeding than is recognized by evidence law may do so only at the risk of being held in contempt of court.

Privileges remain the most significant area of evidence law not codified by the Federal Rules of Evidence. The Advisory Committee drafted and the Supreme Court prescribed 13 rules governing privileges. But controversy arose in Congress regarding their scope and the propriety of any privileges being promulgated under the Rules Enabling Act, given their arguably substantive effect. There was particular concern about the omission of both the physician-patient privilege and the marital communications privilege and the inclusion of what some saw as an overly broad privilege for state secrets. There was also concern about the fact that the rules as promulgated would have applied to all actions in federal courts, overriding state privilege law, even where state law supplied the rule of decision.

The response of Congress was to delete the privilege provisions from the Rules as enacted and to substitute FRE 501 in their place. Congress went even further, and took rulemaking power away from the Supreme Court with respect to evidentiary privileges. The new Enabling Act provides that "[a]ny . . . rule creating, abolishing, or modifying an evidentiary privilege shall have no force or effect unless approved by Act of Congress." 28 U.S.C. §2074(b).

Under Rule 501, then, federal privilege law continues to be governed by "the principles of the common law as they may be interpreted by the courts of the United States in the light of reason and experience," except as otherwise provided by the Federal Constitution, a federal statute, or a rule "prescribed by the Supreme Court pursuant to statutory authority." Yet most states with evidence codes modeled after the Federal Rules have codified their rules of privilege. There is considerable variation from state to state regarding what privileges are recognized and the scope of those privileges.

NOTES ON FRE 501

1. Is deference to state privilege law in diversity cases required by the doctrine of Erie Railroad v. Tompkins, 304 U.S. 64 (1938)? Most rules of

evidence are regarded as "procedural" and thus can be applied in a federal court even when state law supplies the rule of decision. In what sense is privilege law more "substantive"?

2.   Does FRE 501 undermine state policy choices with respect to questions of privilege, given that it defers to state law only in diversity cases and other cases where state law supplies the rule of decision? What success will a state-created privilege have in facilitating and protecting communications within a particular relationship if that privilege is not also recognized in federal criminal proceedings and civil cases based on federal law? See, e.g., United States v. Schenheinz, 548 F.2d 1389 (9th Cir. 1977) (upholding an IRS summons to a stenographer to testify and produce records concerning the tax affairs of her employer despite the fact that this information was privileged under an employer-stenographer privilege recognized by state law).

3.   In light of the congressional insistence that any "amendment" to the Rules respecting privileges be approved by statute, should federal courts hesitate to change privilege law by judicial decision? Does it matter how sweeping the change is? Keep this question in mind as you read the decisions in *Trammel* and *Upjohn,* infra.

B. ATTORNEY-CLIENT PRIVILEGE

1. *Reasons for the Privilege*

5 J. BENTHAM, RATIONALE OF JUDICIAL EVIDENCE 301 (J.S. Mill ed. 1827)

When in consulting with a law adviser, attorney or advocate, a man has confessed his delinquency, or disclosed some fact which, if stated in court, might tend to operate in proof of it, such law adviser is not to be suffered to be examined as to any such point. The law adviser is neither to be compelled, nor so much as suffered, to betray the trust thus reposed in him. Not suffered? Why not? Oh, because to betray a trust is treachery; and an act of treachery is an immoral act. . . .

But if such confidence, when reposed, is permitted to be violated, and if this be known (which, if such be the law, it will be), the consequence will be, that no such confidence will be reposed. Not reposed?—Well: and if it be not, wherein will consist the mischief? The man by the supposition is guilty; if not, by the supposition there is nothing to betray: let the law adviser say every thing he has heard, every thing he can have heard from his client, the client cannot have any thing to fear from it. That it will often happen that in the case supposed no such confidence will be reposed, is natural enough: the first thing the advocate or attorney will say to his client, will be—Remember that, whatever you say to me, I shall be obliged to tell, if asked about it. What, then, will be the consequence? That a guilty person will not in general be able to derive quite so much assistance from his law adviser, in the way of concerting a false defence, as he may do at present.

Except the prevention of such pernicious confidence, of what other possible effect can the rule for the requisition of such evidence be productive? Either of none at all, or of the conviction of delinquents, in some instances in which, but for the lights thus obtained, they would not have been convicted. But in this effect, what imaginable circumstances is there that can render it in any degree pernicious and undesirable? None whatever. The conviction of delinquents is the very end of penal justice.

NOTES ON JUSTIFICATIONS FOR THE PRIVILEGE

1. Is Bentham correct that the attorney-client privilege protects only the guilty? The justifications for the attorney-client privilege are sometimes categorized as instrumental or humanistic, depending on whether they relate to the effective performance of the attorney's functions or to the preservation of other values. What instrumental justifications for the privilege can be offered in response to Bentham's arguments? What humanistic justifications?

2. Although Bentham takes the most extreme position, he does not stand alone as a critic of the privilege. See McCormick on Evidence §87, at 205 (E. Cleary 3d ed. 1984): "If one were legislating for a new commonwealth, without history or customs, it might be hard to maintain that a privilege for lawyer-client communications would facilitate more than it would obstruct the administration of justice." Even Wigmore, who was a supporter of the privilege, stated

> Its benefits are all indirect and speculative; its obstruction is plain and concrete. . . . It is worth preserving for the sake of a general policy, but it is nonetheless an obstacle to the investigation of the truth. It ought to be strictly confined within the narrowest possible limits consistent with the logic of its principle.

8 Wigmore on Evidence §2291, at 554 (J. McNaughton rev. 1961).

3. Do you agree that if we could just shed the habits of history, we would be better off without an attorney-client privilege? If we are stuck with it, do you agree that it should be narrowly construed? Consider Wigmore's own explanation and Professor Louisell's expansion:

> [I]t must be repugnant to any honorable man to feel that the confidences which his relation naturally invites are liable at the opponent's behest to be laid open through his own testimony. He cannot but feel the disagree able inconsistency of being at the same time solicitor and the revealer of the secrets of the cause. This double-minded attitude would create an unhealthy moral state in the practitioner.

8 Wigmore on Evidence §2291, at 553 (J. McNaughton rev. 1961).

> Why would compellability to reveal his clients' secrets "create an unhealthy moral state in the practitioner?" Because, it is submitted, he would know that he was perverting the function of counselling. Perhaps the notion is as well put by Francis

Bacon as anyone: "The great Truste, between Man and Man, is the Truste of *Giving Counsell*. For in other Confidences, Men commit the parts of their life; Their lands, their Goods, their Children, their Credit, some particular affaire; But to such, as they make their *Counsellors*, they commit the whole: By how much the more, they are obliged to all Faith and integrity."

Louisell, Confidentiality, Conformity and Confusion: Privileges in Federal Court Today, 31 Tulane L. Rev. 101, 112-113 (1956) (quoting Bacon's Essays, XX, Of Counsel).

4. How much does the attorney-client privilege actually obstruct truth? Recall that civil litigants enjoy the benefits of numerous discovery devices, including depositions (FRCP 30) and interrogatories (FRCP 31), and recall too that discovery under FRCP 26 may probe "any matter, not privileged, that is relevant to the claim or defense of any party" in the suit. Suppose that a civil plaintiff asks defendant in his deposition, "Isn't it a fact that you ran the red light?" If defendant previously told his lawyer that indeed the light was red for him, could she instruct him not to answer the question in the deposition because of the attorney-client privilege? What if plaintiff asked the same question in an interrogatory? (Recall that interrogatories are typically served on counsel, not on the client, and that counsel normally prepares the answers, even though her responses become those of the client. Those points should not matter, should they?)

5. In civil cases, a plaintiff can call the defendant as a witness during the plaintiff's case-in-chief and attempt to establish his case based on the defendant's own testimony. Even if the defendant discussed the underlying facts with his attorney, which he presumably did, he may not invoke the attorney-client privilege with respect to questions about the underlying facts. What if the plaintiff asks him about conversations with his attorney? Or what if plaintiff calls defendant's attorney as a witness? How does the situation differ in criminal cases, where the prosecutor cannot call the defendant to the witness stand? Does it thus appear that the privilege is more costly in criminal than in civil cases?

6. In the wake of the September 11, 2001 terrorist attacks, the Justice Department's Bureau of Prisons amended regulations governing federal prison inmates. The amendments allow the Attorney General to order monitoring of communications between prisoners and attorneys, when there is "reasonable suspicion" to believe that an inmate may use the communications "to further or facilitate acts of terrorism." 28 C.F.R. §501.3(d) (2001). Certain safeguards apply. Unless the feared acts are "imminent," there must be approval from a federal judge; written notice must be provided to the inmate and attorneys involved; monitoring is conducted by a team of persons uninvolved with the underlying case against the inmate. These protections notwithstanding, the regulations have spawned comment and criticism. See Lance Cole, Revoking Our Privileges: Federal Law Enforcement's Multi-Front Assault on the Attorney-Client Privilege (and Why It Is Misguided), 48 Vill. L. Rev 469 (2003); Paul R. Rice & Benjamin Parlin Saul, Is the War on Terrorism a War on Attorney-Client Privilege? 17 Crim. Just. 22 (2002); Avidan Y. Cover, A Rule Unfit for All Seasons: Monitoring Attorney-Client Communications Violates Privilege and the Sixth Amendment, 87 Cornell L. Rev. 1233 (2002).

PROBLEM 12-A.   "A Bum Rap"

After a lengthy and highly publicized trial, Dr. McNary is convicted of the brutal slaying of his wife and two children, who were found stabbed to death in the family home on October 20. Dr. McNary claimed innocence, and the case against him was based on circumstantial evidence. His attorney Ashbrooke made an eloquent argument for clemency, but McNary was given the death sentence. The night after the sentence is announced, Ashbrooke receives a call from Barton, an acquaintance who is also a criminal defense lawyer. On the phone, Barton tells Ashbrooke:

> I hesitate to call you, but I'm doing it because your client's facing a bum rap. You should know I'm the court-appointed lawyer for a man named Frank Gallo, who is charged with robbing a liquor store on October 20. Just between us, Gallo may be a little crazy. He's been in trouble before, but we don't need to talk about that. He tells me he didn't rob the liquor store, and I believe him because his alibi is too amazing to be false. He told me that at the very moment when the liquor store was being robbed, he—Gallo—was in fact in the McNary house committing what amounts to burglary and murder. Apparently the husband wasn't home, but the wife and kids were, and Gallo told me he killed them with a knife. Now he could have read the story in the paper and made up the part about him doing it, but I've listened to him and frankly I believe him. He even told me where he buried the knife, but I haven't looked for it. I'm not quite sure what to do with this information myself, but I felt I had to tell you about it.

The next day Ashbrooke files a motion for a new trial on the ground of newly discovered evidence. At the hearing on the motion, he calls Gallo and Barton to the stand. Gallo refuses to testify, claiming the privilege against self-incrimination. When Barton is called to testify, Gallo asserts the attorney-client privilege. Should the privilege claim be sustained? What constitutional arguments can be made on McNary's behalf for overriding the claim of privilege? What constitutional arguments can be made on Gallo's behalf for upholding it?

2.   Professional Services

The privilege applies only to confidential communications made for the purpose of rendering professional legal services to the client. Yet often attorneys are consulted for more than legal advice. They may also be asked questions soliciting business, financial, or personal advice. And often they are asked or expected to perform services on behalf of their clients that do not require formal legal training. How much of what attorneys do on behalf of their clients is protected by the attorney-client privilege?

PROBLEM 12-B.   The Bail Jumper

Woodburn is out on bail pending trial on an indictment charging him with bank robbery. One of the conditions is that he stay in touch with his attorney Nash and appear at the time set for trial. Woodburn fails to appear, and the government seeks to obtain an additional indictment against Woodburn for bail jumping. The government subpoenas Nash before the grand jury and asks him whether he advised his client of the time and place of the trial. Nash declines to answer, asserting the attorney-client privilege on behalf of Woodburn. The government obtains a court order requiring Nash to answer, but he continues in his refusal and is held in contempt. What ruling in an appeal by Nash from his contempt citation?

NOTES ON PROVIDING PROFESSIONAL SERVICES

1. Does the statement by Nash telling Woodburn the time and place of trial really constitute legal advice? Isn't he just serving as a conduit for information from the court? Is such a communication properly viewed as confidential? Most federal courts would hold that no privilege applies. See, e.g., United States v. Posin, 996 F.2d 1229, 1229 (9th Cir. 1993); United States v. Woodruff, 383 F. Supp. 696, 698 (E.D. Pa. 1974) (communications between counsel and defendant about trial date "do not involve the subject matter of defendant's legal problem"; they are "nonlegal in nature" and counsel "is simply performing a notice function").

In states adopting proposed FRE 503 (which extends the privilege to the provision of legal services rather than merely legal advice), courts have sometimes found the issue harder. See State v. Ogle, 297 Or. 84, 682 P.2d 267 (1984) (4-3 decision denying privilege on grounds of policy and precedent over dissent arguing that such notification of a client fits statutory language extending privilege to communications made in the "rendition of professional legal services").

2. For examples of activities by lawyers that courts have held not to constitute professional legal services, see United States v. Lawless, 709 F.2d 485 (7th Cir. 1983) (accounting); United States v. Palmer, 536 F.2d 1278 (9th Cir. 1976) (shipping agent); Canaday v. United States, 354 F.2d 849, 857 (8th Cir. 1966) (scrivener); Diamond v. City of Mobile, 86 F.R.D. 324 (S.D. Ala. 1978) (investigator); J.P. Foley & Co. v. Vanderbilt, 65 F.R.D. 523 (S.D.N.Y. 1974) (business agent; negotiator); Federal Savings & Loan Insurance Corp. v. Fielding, 343 F. Supp. 537, 546 (D. Nev. 1972) (business partner); Jones v. Smith, 56 S.E.2d 462, 465 (Ga. 1949) (attesting witness).

3. Is preparation of tax returns "professional legal services"? Compare United States v. Davis, 636 F.2d 1028, 1043 (5th Cir.) (since accountants do not have a privilege in preparing income tax returns, "[i]t would make little sense to permit a taxpayer to invoke a privilege merely because he hired an attorney to perform the same task"), cert. denied, 454 U.S. 862 (1981) with Colton v. United States, 306 F.2d 633, 637 (2d Cir. 1962) ("no question" that giving tax advice and preparing tax returns "are basically matters sufficiently within the professional competence of an attorney to make them prima facie subject to the attorney-client privilege"), cert. denied, 371 U.S. 951 (1963). Most courts hold that the privilege does not apply to matters intended for inclusion in the return, on the theory that such information was not intended to be kept

confidential. Most courts also hold that tax planning advice, as distinguished from the mechanical preparation of income tax returns, is privileged. See, e.g., United States v. Willis, 565 F. Supp. 1186, 1190 (S.D. Iowa 1983). Are you persuaded that there is a difference between enlisting the help of a lawyer in "filling out a tax return" and "seeking legal advice with respect to tax matters"? See, e.g., In re Grand Jury Investigation, 842 F.2d 1223, 1225 (11th Cir. 1987) ("Admittedly, the preparation of a tax return requires some knowledge of the law, and the manner in which a tax return is prepared can be viewed as an implicit interpretation of that law. . . . A taxpayer should not be able to invoke a privilege simply because he hires an attorney to prepare his tax returns.").

4.   How should we distinguish between business and legal advice? Should the privilege apply if the client seeks a mixture of business and legal advice? Most courts require that the lawyer's work be "primarily legal" before the privilege will attach. See, e.g., Sedco International, S.A. v. Cory, 683 F.2d 1201 (8th Cir.), cert. denied, 459 U.S. 1017 (1982). See also Bruce Kayle, The Tax Adviser's Privilege in Transactional Matters: A Synopsis and a Suggestion, 54 Tax L. 509 (2001) (suggesting "[e]limination of the attorney-client privilege in all but criminal tax matters").

3. *Communications*

The attorney-client privilege is described as a doctrine protecting "communications" from the client. Assume that a person charged with murder tells his lawyer, while seeking legal representation to defend the charges, that he was "really angry" at the victim on the day of the crime. If the two are speaking in private, there is no doubt that the statement is within the privilege, and the result would be the same if the client wrote such a message in a note or letter to the lawyer while seeking legal assistance.

It is hard to say how much further the privilege might reach. Assume, for example, that the client rolls up his sleeve and displays a scab-covered wound on his forearm that "came from the fight" with the victim or that he pulls out a knife and says "that's what I used" during the fray. Obviously both of these gestures have a communicative aspect, and yet neither is *solely* communicative. Does the privilege apply somehow to the viewing of the wound, or to the knife? And consider whether the privilege should apply to a page in the client's diary, written hours after the event, which the client might show to the lawyer later on, while seeking legal help. Finally, think about whether the privilege should apply if the lawyer tells the client, "Yes, you better take care of that wound, it looks like someone slashed you with a knife." Is the *lawyer's* statement covered by the privilege?

PROBLEM 12-C.   *The Tipsy Client*

Murphy arrives 35 minutes late for his afternoon appointment with Finch, his attorney, about a probate matter. Finch sees that Murphy has been drinking heavily, for he staggers as he is ushered into Finch's office and his breath smells of alcohol. In a slurred voice, he apologizes for being late, and explains that he had a "few drinks" with some friends and "lost track" of time. During the interview, Murphy is rambling and incoherent, and Finch finally suggests that the appointment be rescheduled.

As Murphy leaves the office, Finch offers to call a taxicab, but Murphy insists on driving. Finch watches with trepidation as Murphy drives away. Two blocks down the street Murphy collides with a parked car. He is not injured and flees the scene on foot. In his later trial for hit-and-run and drunken driving, Murphy is represented by another lawyer. The state calls Finch as a prosecution witness. To what may Finch be required to testify over Murphy's objection claiming the attorney-client privilege?

NOTES ON OBSERVATIONS AND ADVICE BY COUNSEL

1. If a lawyer in the position of Finch may be compelled to testify to matters he observes when his client comes in, does it follow that defense counsel in a criminal case may be compelled to testify on the matter of his client's mental capacity? Compare Clanton v. United States, 488 F.2d 1069, 1071 (5th Cir.) (lawyer was properly permitted to testify that his client was competent to stand trial, where the testimony "did not relate to private, confidential, communications with his client"), cert. denied, 419 U.S. 877 (1974) with Gunther v. United States, 230 F.2d 222, 223-224 (D.C. Cir. 1956) (lawyer should not have been allowed to testify that his client was competent to stand trial, for necessarily a lawyer who so testifies may "also be asked for the factual data upon which he premised his opinion," which would open up "the entire relationship," violating both the privilege and defendant's right of counsel). See generally Pizzi, Competency to Stand Trial in Federal Courts: Conceptual and Constitutional Problems, 45 U. Chi. L. Rev. 21, 57-64 (1977).

2. May a lawyer be compelled to testify to his client's physical appearance? See United States v. Kendrick, 331 F.2d 110, 113-114 (4th Cir. 1964) (dictum indicating that "physical characteristics of the client, such as his complexion, his demeanor, his bearing, his sobriety and his address," are not privileged, for such matters "are observable by anyone who talked with the client; there is nothing, in the usual case, to suggest that the client intends his attorney's observations of such matters to be confidential"). What about compelled testimony about a client's lifestyle? See In re Grand Jury Proceedings (Chesnoff), 13 F.2d 1293, 1296 (9th Cir. 1994) (no privilege for attorney's observations about his client's "expenditures during a European cruise, his income-producing activities, and his lifestyle").

3. Should statements by lawyer to client be within the privilege? If so, should the privilege cover only legal advice or all communications by the lawyer? Compare Wells v. Rushing, 755 F.2d 376, 379 n.2 (5th Cir. 1985) (communications from lawyer to client are privileged only to extent necessary to avoid revealing "confidential information provided by the client" or "advice or opinions of the attorney") with United States v. Ramirez, 608 F.2d 1261, 1268 n.12 (9th Cir. 1979) (lawyer-client communications "in both directions" are generally covered by privilege). See also Upjohn Co. v. United States, 449 U.S. 383, 389 (1981) (purpose of privilege is "to encourage full and frank

communication *between* attorneys and their clients") (emphasis added). And compare United States v. Silverman, 430 F.2d 106, 122 (2d Cir.), modified, 439 F.2d 1198 (communication from an attorney is not privileged "unless it has the effect of revealing a confidential communication from the client to the attorney"), cert. denied, 402 U.S. 953 (1970) with United States v. Amerada Hess Corp., 619 F.2d 980, 985-986 (3d Cir. 1980) (lawyer's advice to client is within the privilege because (a) it is necessary to prevent use of attorney's advice "to support inferences as to the content of confidential communications by the client" and (b) "independent of the content of any client communication, legal advice given to the client should remain confidential"). And consider this description:

> In practice, . . . advice does not spring from lawyers' heads as Athena did from the brow of Zeus. Inevitably, attorneys' opinions reflect an accumulation of education and experience in the law and the larger society law serves. In a given case, advice prompted by the client's disclosures may be further and inseparably informed by other knowledge and encounters. We have therefore stated that the privilege cloaks a communication from attorney to client " 'based, *in part at least,* upon a confidential communication [to the lawyer] from [the client].'"

In re Sealed Case, 737 F.2d 94, 99 (D.C. Cir. 1984).

PROBLEM 12-D.   The Transferred Tax Records

Kasmir learns that she is being investigated by a federal grand jury for possible tax evasion in the conduct of her business, the buying and selling of rare coins. She immediately contacts Hovet, a criminal defense attorney specializing in tax matters, who agrees to represent her. Kasmir delivers to Hovet all of her records pertaining to the conduct of her coin business. After the United States Attorney learns of the whereabouts of Kasmir's records, a grand jury subpoena is served on Hovet, demanding production of the records. Hovet moves to quash the subpoena, asserting the attorney-client privilege on behalf of Kasmir. What ruling? Would your answer differ if the Fifth Amendment privilege against self-incrimination would shield Kasmir from having to produce the records when they were in her own possession?

| **PEOPLE v. MEREDITH**
| **California Supreme Court**
| **631 P.2d 46 (Cal. 1981)**

TOBRINER, J.

Defendants Frank Earl Scott and Michael Meredith appeal from convictions for the first degree murder and first degree robbery of David Wade. Meredith's conviction rests on eyewitness testimony that he shot and killed Wade. Scott's conviction, however, depends on the theory that Scott conspired with Meredith and a third defendant, Jacqueline Otis, to bring about the killing and robbery.

To support the theory of conspiracy the prosecution sought to show the place where the victim's wallet was found, and, in the course of the case this piece of evidence became crucial. The admissibility of that evidence comprises the principal issue on this appeal. . . .

On the night of April 3, 1976, Wade (the victim) and Jacqueline Otis, a friend of the defendants, entered a club known as Rich Jimmy's. Defendant Scott remained outside by a shoeshine stand. A few minutes later codefendant Meredith arrived outside the club. He told Scott he planned to rob Wade, and asked Scott to go into the club, find Jacqueline Otis, and ask her to get Wade to go out to Wade's car parked outside the club.

In the meantime, Wade and Otis had left the club and walked to a liquor store to get some beer. Returning from the store, they left the beer in a bag by Wade's car and reentered the club. Scott then entered the club also and, according to the testimony of Laurie Ann Sam (a friend of Scott's who was already in the club), Scott asked Otis to get Wade to go back out to his car so Meredith could "knock him in the head."

When Wade and Otis did go out to the car, Meredith attacked Wade from behind. After a brief struggle, two shots were fired; Wade fell, and Meredith, witnessed by Scott and Sam, ran from the scene.

Scott went over to the body and, assuming Wade was dead, picked up the bag containing the beer and hid it behind a fence. Scott later returned, retrieved the bag, and took it home where Otis and Meredith joined him.

We now recount the evidence relating to Wade's wallet, basing our account primarily on the testimony of James Schenk, Scott's first appointed attorney. Schenk visited Scott in jail more than a month after the crime occurred and solicited information about the murder, stressing that he had to be fully acquainted with the facts to avoid being "sandbagged" by the prosecution during the trial. In response, Scott gave Schenk the same information that he had related earlier to the police. In addition, however, Scott told Schenk something Scott had not revealed to the police: that he had seen a wallet, as well as the paper bag, on the ground near Wade. Scott said that he picked up the wallet, put it in the paper bag, and placed both behind a parking lot fence. He also said that he later retrieved the bag, took it home, found $100 in the wallet and divided it with Meredith, and then tried to burn the wallet in his kitchen sink. He took the partially burned wallet, Scott told Schenk, placed it in a plastic bag, and threw it in a burn barrel behind his house.

Schenk, without further consulting Scott, retained Investigator Stephen Frick and sent Frick to find the wallet. Frick found it in the location described by Scott and brought it to Schenk. After examining the wallet and determining that it contained credit cards with Wade's name, Schenk turned the wallet and its contents over to Detective Payne, investigating officer in the case. Schenk told Payne only that, to the best of his knowledge, the wallet had belonged to Wade.

The prosecution subpoenaed Attorney Schenk and Investigator Frick to testify at the preliminary hearing. When questioned at that hearing, Schenk said that he received the wallet from Frick but refused to answer further questions on the ground that he learned about the wallet through a privileged communication. Eventually, however, the magistrate threatened Schenk with contempt if he did not respond "yes" or "no" when asked whether his contact with his client led to disclosure of the wallet's location. Schenk then replied "yes," and revealed on further questioning that this contact was the sole source of his information as to the wallet's location.

At the preliminary hearing Frick, the investigator who found the wallet, was then questioned by the district attorney. Over objections by counsel, Frick testified that he found the wallet in a garbage can behind Scott's residence.

Prior to trial, a third attorney, Hamilton Hintz, was appointed for Scott. Hintz unsuccessfully sought an in limine ruling that the wallet of the murder victim was inadmissible and that the attorney-client privilege precluded the admission of testimony concerning the wallet by Schenk or Frick.

At trial Frick, called by the prosecution, identified the wallet and testified that he found it in a garbage can behind Scott's residence. . . .

The jury found both Scott and Meredith guilty of first degree murder and first degree robbery. . . .

Defendant Scott concedes, and we agree, that the wallet itself was admissible in evidence. Scott maintains, however, that Evidence Code section 954 bars the testimony of the investigator concerning the location of the wallet. . . .

Section 954 provides, "[T]he client . . . has a privilege to refuse to disclose, and to prevent another from disclosing, a confidential communication between client and lawyer. . . ."

Scott's statements to Schenk regarding the location of the wallet clearly fulfilled the statutory requirements. Moreover, the privilege did not dissolve when Schenk disclosed the substance of that communication to his investigator, Frick. Under Evidence Code section 912, subdivision (d), a disclosure which is "reasonably necessary" to accomplish the purpose for which the attorney has been consulted does not constitute a waiver of the privilege. If Frick was to perform the investigative services for which Schenk had retained him, it was "reasonably necessary," that Schenk transmit to Frick the information regarding the wallet. Thus, Schenk's disclosure to Frick did not waive the statutory privilege.

The statutes codifying the attorney-client privilege do not, however, indicate whether that privilege protects facts viewed and observed as a direct result of confidential communication. . . .

Judicial decisions have recognized that the implementation of . . . [the policies underlying the attorney-client privilege] may require that the privilege extend not only to the initial communication between client and attorney but also to any information which the attorney or his investigator may subsequently acquire as a direct result of that communication. In a venerable decision involving facts analogous to those in the instant case, the Supreme Court of West Virginia held that the trial court erred in admitting an attorney's testimony as to the location of a pistol which he had discovered as the result of a privileged communication from his client. That the attorney had observed the pistol, the court pointed out, did not nullify the privilege: "All that the said attorney knew about this pistol, or where it was to be found, he knew only from the communications which had been made to him by his client confidentially and professionally, as counsel in this case. And it ought therefore, to have been entirely excluded from the jury. . . ." State of West Virginia v. Douglass (1882) 20 W. Va. 770, 783.

More recent decisions reach similar conclusions. In State v. Olwell, 394

P.2d 681 (Wash. 1964), the court reviewed contempt charges against an attorney who refused to produce a knife he obtained from his client. The court first observed that "[t]o be protected as a privileged communication . . . the securing of the knife . . . must have been *the direct result of information* given to Mr. Olwell by his client." (Emphasis added.) The court concluded that defense counsel, after examining the physical evidence, should deliver it to the prosecution, but should not reveal the source of the evidence; "[b]y thus allowing the prosecution to recover such evidence, the public interest is served, and by refusing the prosecution an opportunity to disclose the source of the evidence, the client's privilege is preserved and a balance reached between these conflicting interests."

Finally, we note the decisions of the New York courts in People v. Belge, 372 N.Y.S.2d 798 (Sup. Ct. 1975), affirmed in People v. Belge, 376 N.Y.S.2d 771 (App. Div. 1975). Defendant, charged with one murder, revealed to counsel that he had committed three others. Counsel, following defendant's directions, located one of the bodies. Counsel did not reveal the location of the body until trial, 10 months later, when he exposed the other murders to support an insanity defense.

Counsel was then indicted for violating two sections of the New York Public Health Law for failing to report the existence of the body to proper authorities in order that they could give it a decent burial. The trial court dismissed the indictment; the appellate division affirmed, holding that the attorney-client privilege shielded counsel from prosecution for actions which would otherwise violate the Public Health Law.

The foregoing decisions demonstrate that the attorney-client privilege is not strictly limited to communications, but extends to protect observations made as a consequence of protected communications. We turn therefore to the question whether that privilege encompasses a case in which the defense, by removing or altering evidence, interferes with the prosecution's opportunity to discover that evidence.[7] . . .

When defense counsel alters or removes physical evidence, he necessarily deprives the prosecution of the opportunity to observe that evidence in its original condition or location. As the Amicus Appellate Committee of the California District Attorneys Association points out, to bar admission of testimony concerning the original condition and location of the evidence in such a case permits the defense in effect to "destroy" critical information; it is as if, he explains, the wallet in this case bore a tag bearing the words "located in the trash can by Scott's residence," and the defense, by taking the wallet, destroyed this tag. To extend the attorney-client privilege to a case in which

---

7. We agree with the parties' suggestion that an attorney in Schenk's position often may best fulfill conflicting obligations to preserve the confidentiality of client confidences, investigate his case, and act as an officer of the court if he does not remove evidence located as the result of a privileged communication. We must recognize, however, that in some cases an examination of evidence may reveal information critical to the defense of a client accused of crime. If the usefulness of the evidence cannot be gauged without taking possession of it, as, for example, when a ballistics or fingerprint test is required, the attorney may properly take it for a reasonable time before turning it over to the prosecution. Similarly, in the present case the defense counsel could not be certain the burnt wallet belonged in fact to the victim: in taking the wallet to examine it for identification, he violated no ethical duty to his client or to the prosecution.

the defense removed evidence might encourage defense counsel to race the police to seize critical evidence.

We therefore conclude that courts must craft an exception to the protection extended by the attorney-client privilege in cases in which counsel has removed or altered evidence. Indeed, at oral argument defense counsel acknowledged that such an exception might be necessary in a case in which the police would have inevitably discovered the evidence in its original location if counsel had not removed it. Counsel argued, however, that the attorney-client privilege should protect observations of evidence, despite subsequent defense removal, unless the prosecution could prove that the police probably would have eventually discovered the evidence in the original site.

We have seriously considered counsel's proposal, but have concluded that a test based upon the probability of eventual discovery is unworkably speculative. Evidence turns up not only because the police deliberately search for it, but also because it comes to the attention of policemen or bystanders engaged in other business. In the present case, for example, the wallet might have been found by the trash collector. Moreover, one [sic] physical evidence (the wallet) is turned over to the police, they will obviously stop looking for it; to ask where, how long, and how carefully they would have looked is obviously to compel speculation as to theoretical future conduct of the police.

We therefore conclude that whenever defense counsel removes or alters evidence, the statutory privilege does not bar revelation of the original location or condition of the evidence in question.[8] We thus view the defense decision to remove evidence as a tactical choice. If defense counsel leaves the evidence where he discovers it, his observations derived from privileged communications are insulated from revelation. If, however, counsel chooses to remove evidence to examine or test it, the original location and condition of that evidence loses the protection of the privilege. Applying this analysis to the present case, we hold that the trial court did not err in admitting the investigator's testimony concerning the location of the wallet. . . .

NOTES ON APPLYING THE PRIVILEGE TO OBJECTS

1.   In *Meredith,* defendant concedes (and the court agrees) that the wallet itself is admissible, even if it was found only because of a confidential communication. Should defendant have conceded this point?

---

8.   In offering the evidence, the prosecution should present the information in a manner which avoids revealing the content of attorney-client communications or the original source of the information. In the present case, for example, the prosecutor simply asked Frick where he found the wallet; he did not identify Frick as a defense investigator or trace the discovery of the wallet to an attorney-client communication.

In other circumstances, when it is not possible to elicit such testimony without identifying the witness as the defendant's attorney or investigator, the defendant may be willing to enter a stipulation which will simply inform the jury as to the relevant location or condition of the evidence in question. When such a stipulation is proffered, the prosecution should not be permitted to reject the stipulation in the hope that by requiring defense counsel personally to testify to such facts, the jury might infer that counsel learned those facts from defendant.

2.   Didn't Scott reveal the information about the wallet to his lawyer Schenk only because he reasonably believed it would be protected by the attorney-client privilege? Yet because of this disclosure, his attorney arranged to have the wallet retrieved from his yard, delivered to the police, and the prosecutor is allowed to inform the jury that the wallet came from Scott's yard. Is the Court's decision fair to Scott?

3.   In light of this decision, what action *should* a criminal defense lawyer take when informed by his client of the existence and location of critical physical evidence?

4.   *Meredith* holds that an attorney who removes or alters physical evidence may be required to disclose its original location or condition. Is this rule consistent with State v. Olwell (discussed in the principal case), which held that a defense lawyer who receives physical evidence from a client must deliver it to the prosecutor, but need not reveal the source of the evidence? Does the *Olwell* doctrine mean that if Scott had brought the wallet to Schenk, instead of Schenk sending an investigator to retrieve it, that the jury would never have learned of Scott's connection with the wallet? Does the *Olwell* doctrine give too much protection to the client by enabling him to sever his connection with incriminating evidence by turning it over to his lawyer?

5.   Consider the compromise suggested by the defense in *Meredith*—that where counsel observes evidence and turns it over to the prosecution, the connecting information given by the accused should remain privileged unless the prosecutor demonstrates that police would have "inevitably" discovered the evidence. A similar doctrine has appeared in the context of the Fifth Amendment. If police obtain a confession that cannot itself be admitted because of the *Miranda* or *Massiah* doctrines (the one requiring warnings before custodial interrogation, the other barring ex parte questioning by police after proceedings have commenced, unless the accused clearly initiates discussions), evidence discovered as a result is nevertheless admissible if the prosecutor can show that police would "inevitably" have discovered it or that police found it because of an "independent source." See Nix v. Williams, 467 U.S. 431 (1984). Why shouldn't courts take the same approach in situations like *Meredith*?

6.   What if an attorney destroys or conceals evidence? See United States v. Kellington, 139 F.3d 909 (9th Cir. 1998) (affirming felony conviction of lawyer for burning envelope at request of client who was facing an extradition hearing; "[A]n honest and unwitting attorney would have wanted to know what he was causing to be destroyed for his fugitive client before putting the torch to it. Burning envelopes with contents unknown is not taught in American law schools."); In re Ryder, 263 F. Supp. 360 (E.D. Va. 1967) (attorney suspended from practice for 18 months for taking possession from a client and concealing in his own safe deposit box stolen money and a sawed-off shotgun, knowing that the money had been stolen and that the gun had been used in an armed robbery). See also ABA Model Rules of Professional Conduct, Rule 3.4:

A lawyer shall not:
     (a) unlawfully obstruct another party's access to evidence or unlawfully alter, destroy or conceal a document or other material having potential evidential value.
A lawyer shall not counsel or assist another person to do any such act. . . .

4. Required Confidentiality

It has long been understood that the privilege protects only communications intended by the client to be confidential. This limit confines the privilege within reasonable bounds and expresses the seemingly obvious point that a privilege for public statements to others would serve no purpose. However, it is also clear that disclosure may be made to selected persons other than the attorney without losing the cloak of confidentiality.

What obligation should be imposed on client and attorney to ensure the confidentiality of their communications? Certainly the privilege should be denied with respect to a conversation between lawyer and client in a room full of outsiders, conducted so as to be heard by all. But what should be the result where an eavesdropper or wiretapper hears what lawyer and client have said behind closed doors, or their confidential correspondence is stolen or otherwise obtained by outsiders?

a. Involving or Disclosing to Communicative Intermediaries

UNITED STATES v. KOVEL
United States Court of Appeals for the Second Circuit
296 F.2d 918 (1961)

FRIENDLY, J.

This appeal from a sentence for criminal contempt for refusing to answer a question asked in the course of an inquiry by a grand jury raises an important issue as to the application of the attorney-client privilege to a non-lawyer employed by a law firm. . . .

Kovel is a former Internal Revenue agent having accounting skills. Since 1943 he has been employed by Kamerman & Kamerman, a law firm specializing in tax law. A grand jury in the Southern District of New York was investigating alleged Federal income tax violations by Hopps, a client of the law firm; Kovel was subpoenaed to appear on September 6, 1961, a few days before the date, September 8, when the Government feared the statute of limitations might run. The law firm advised the Assistant United States Attorney that since Kovel was an employee under the direct supervision of the partners, Kovel could not disclose any communications by the client or the result of any work done for the client, unless the latter consented; the Assistant answered that the attorney-client privilege did not apply to one who was not an attorney. . . .

Nothing in the policy of the privilege suggests that attorneys, simply by placing accountants, scientists or investigators on their payrolls and maintaining them in their offices, should be able to invest all communications by clients to such persons with a privilege the law has not seen fit to extend when the latter are operating under their own steam. On the other hand, in contrast to the Tudor times when the privilege was first recognized, the complexities of modern existence prevent attorneys from effectively handling clients' affairs without the help of others; few lawyers could now practice without the assistance of secretaries, file clerks, telephone operators, messengers, clerks not yet admitted to the bar, and aides of other sorts. "The assistance of these agents being indispensable to his work and the communications of the client being often necessarily committed to them by the attorney or by the client himself, the privilege must include all the persons who act as the attorney's agents." 8 Wigmore, Evidence, §2301.

Indeed, the Government does not here dispute that the privilege covers communications to non-lawyer employees with "a menial or ministerial responsibility that involves relating communications *to an attorney.*" We cannot regard the privilege as confined to "menial or ministerial" employees. Thus, we can see no significant difference between a case where the attorney sends a client speaking a foreign language to an interpreter to make a literal translation of the client's story; a second where the attorney, himself having some little knowledge of the foreign tongue, has a more knowledgeable non-lawyer employee in the room to help out; a third where someone to perform that same function has been brought along by the client; and a fourth where the attorney, ignorant of the foreign language, sends the client to a non-lawyer proficient in it, with instructions to interview the client on the attorney's behalf and then render his own summary of the situation, perhaps drawing on his own knowledge in the process, so that the attorney can give the client proper legal advice. . . .

This analogy of the client speaking a foreign language is by no means irrelevant to the appeal at hand. Accounting concepts are a foreign language to some lawyers in almost all cases, and to almost all lawyers in some cases. Hence the presence of an accountant, whether hired by the lawyer or by the client, while the client is relating a complicated tax story to the lawyer, ought not destroy the privilege, any more than would that of the linguist in the second or third variations of the foreign language theme discussed above; the presence of the accountant is necessary, or at least highly useful, for the effective consultation between the client and the lawyer which the privilege is designed to permit. By the same token, if the lawyer has directed the client, either in the specific case or generally, to tell his story in the first instance to an accountant engaged by the lawyer, who is then to interpret it so that the lawyer may better give legal advice, communications by the client reasonably related to that purpose ought fall within the privilege; there can be no more virtue in requiring the lawyer to sit by while the client pursues these possibly tedious preliminary conversations with the accountant than in insisting on the lawyer's physical presence while the client dictates a statement to the lawyer's secretary or is interviewed by a clerk not yet admitted to practice. What is vital to the privilege is that the communication be made *in confidence* for the purpose of obtaining *legal* advice *from the lawyer.* If what is sought is not legal advice but only accounting service . . . or if the advice sought is the accountant's rather than the lawyer's, no privilege exists. We recognize this draws what may seem to some a rather arbitrary line between a case where the client communicates first to his own accountant (no privilege as to such communications, even though he later consults his lawyer on the same matter) and others, where the client in the first instance consults a lawyer who retains an accountant as a listening post, or consults the lawyer with his own accountant present. But that is the inevitable consequence of having to reconcile the absence of a privilege for accountants and the effective operation of the privilege of client and lawyer under conditions

where the lawyer needs outside help. We realize also that the line we have
drawn will not be so easy to apply as the simpler positions urged on us by the
parties—the district judges will scarcely be able to leave the decision of such
cases to computers; but the distinction has to be made if the privilege is neither
to be unduly expanded nor to become a trap. . . .

The judgment is vacated and the cause remanded for further proceedings
consistent with this opinion.

NOTES ON COMMUNICATIVE INTERMEDIARIES
AND OTHER AIDES

1. Is the *Kovel* doctrine incorporated in proposed FRE 503? See proposed
FRE 503(a)(3), (4), and (b). See also United States v. Schwimmer, 892 F.2d 237,
244 (2d Cir. 1989) (communications privileged between client and accountant
assisting lawyers conducting joint defense on behalf of client). But see United
States v. Brown, 478 F.2d 1038, 1040 (7th Cir. 1973) (privilege inapplicable
where the accountant was present at the invitation of the client and not at the
request of the lawyer).

2. If the attorney-client privilege is to survive in the modern world, the
doctrine endorsed in *Kovel* is necessary, isn't it? "Aides of other sorts" would
likely embrace paralegals who serve many modern law offices, wouldn't it? How
about a physician retained by a personal injury lawyer to diagnose the client
in preparation for litigation? See City & County of San Francisco v. Superior
Court, 231 P.2d 26 (Cal. 1951) (attorney-client privilege applies).

3. *Kovel* recognized that there is no federal accountant-client privilege, a
point that the Supreme Court confirmed more than 20 years later in United
States v. Arthur Young & Co., 465 U.S. 805 (1984). However, in the Internal
Revenue Service Restructuring and Reform Act of 1998 (105 Pub. L. No. 206;
112 Stat. 685), Congress created a privilege for taxpayer communications to
federally authorized tax practitioners (many of whom will be accountants),
although the privilege applies only in noncriminal federal proceedings.

4. Note that the primary concern of the court in *Kovel* was that the
privilege apply in cases where an expert is acting as an interpreter or intermedi-
ary between the client and the lawyer. Should the privilege apply in cases where
the communication from the expert to the attorney does not transmit or even
rely on communications from the client? For example, should the report of
an appraiser in a condemnation case or an engineer in a products liability case
be within the privilege if the report is not based upon communications from
the client? Would such a report be privileged under proposed FRE 503?
Wouldn't such a report be protected from discovery under the work product
doctrine? See FRCP 26(b)(3):

[A] party may obtain discovery of documents and tangible things . . . prepared
in anticipation of litigation or for trial by or for another party or by or for
that other party's representative (including the other party's attorney, consultant,
surety, indemnitor, insurer, or agent) only upon a showing that the party seeking
discovery has substantial need of the materials in the preparation of the party's

case and that the party is unable without undue hardship to obtain the substantial equivalent of the materials by other means.

Is it necessary also to make the report subject to the attorney-client privilege?

b. Joint Clients and Pooled Defenses

If two or more clients retain or consult the same attorney with respect to matters of common interest, the communications made between the joint clients and the attorney are privileged with respect to outsiders. Thus a joint client can communicate with an attorney in the presence of another joint client without destroying confidentiality.

What if the clients retain separate attorneys but still have a common interest in the matter being litigated, as happens when they are both on trial for the same crime? Can they pool information or otherwise collaborate (perhaps even mount a joint defense) without destroying confidentiality? Most courts say yes. Allowing such pooling of information among clients with overlapping interests is thought to encourage better case preparation and to conserve time and expense. Presumably little information is lost by recognizing the privilege in this situation because the collaborative communications are unlikely to be made in absence of the privilege.

PROBLEM 12-E.   A Failed Venture

Samuel and Thomas consult with lawyer Ullman on forming a partnership to import computer chips from Asia. The three discuss the venture, to be called Accu-Chip, Limited. Samuel indicates that he has "lots of contacts in Tokyo and Taipei who will supply quality chips," but he acknowledges that "many cheap chips available in those markets don't meet American specifications." Thomas provides most of the start-up money and some expertise on customs law and import fees.

The two sign a partnership and go into business. But Accu-Chip falls on hard times. It has difficulty with the chip quality; the market for chips declines because of technological changes and falling prices. The government brings criminal charges against Samuel and Thomas for alleged conspiracy to violate customs and import tariffs.

1. In a suit against Accu-Chip and the partners (Samuel and Thomas), dissatisfied customer Vanden alleges breach of implied warranty and misrepresentation of the quality of Accu-Chip products. Vanden takes the deposition of Ullman (who represents the defendants) and asks, "What did your clients tell you about the quality of the chips they intended to import?" On behalf of defendants, Ullman invokes the attorney-client privilege and refuses to answer. Vanden moves to compel answers. What result and why?

2. Samuel retains Wilson as counsel and files suit against Thomas for alleged breach of the partnership contract and an accounting for partnership profits. At trial, Samuel takes the witness stand and proposes to testify to what Thomas

said in Ullman's office when the partnership was formed. For Thomas, Ullman invokes the attorney-client privilege. What result, and why?

3. In the criminal trial of Samuel and Thomas for alleged conspiracy to evade customs inspections and import fees, Wilson represents Samuel and Ullman represents Thomas. The four meet together to coordinate strategy. During the meeting, Samuel angrily reminds Thomas that "you were supposed to be the expert on customs and taxes." Thomas replies, "I carried out that end and handled it as well as anybody could." At trial, Samuel proposes to testify to what Thomas said, but Ullman objects, raising the attorney-client privilege. What result, and why?

NOTES ON INTENTIONAL DISCLOSURE

1.   Courts considering the first situation described in Problem 12-E speak in terms of "joint clients." The assumption is that the clients have essentially the same interest. Here the privilege claim is usually sustained against outsiders suing the two clients. Why does that outcome seem right? Courts considering the third situation speak of "pooled strategy" or "defense," where the assumption is that the clients have overlapping but disparate interests. Here proposed Rule 503(b)(3) would uphold the privilege, and most courts agree. Why does that outcome seem right? The second situation stands between the first and the third. Once the clients had the same interest, but now they have conflicting interests. Here proposed Rule 503(d)(5) would deny the privilege, and most courts agree. Why?

2.   If joint clients have no privilege for their earlier attorney-client communications after they have a falling out, does the lawyer have an ethical obligation to advise them of this point before going forward with joint representation? See ABA Model Rules of Professional Conduct, Rule 1.7(b)(2) (in representing multiple clients on a single matter, lawyer shall provide "explanations of the implications of the common representation and the advantages and risks").

3.   Usually the privilege does not apply to attorney-client communications uttered in the known presence of an outsider. See United States v. Landof, 591 F.2d 36, 39 (9th Cir. 1978) (no privilege for statements uttered in presence of third person, who was a lawyer but was not acting as counsel). The same result obtains if the lawyer later discloses the communication to a third party at her client's direction. See United States v. El Paso Co., 682 F.2d 530, 538-541 (5th Cir. 1982) (tax pool analysis disclosed to outside auditors), cert. denied, 466 U.S. 944 (1984).

4.   Suppose a client communicates facts to his lawyer with the expectation that in due course they will be disclosed to a third party. Should the privilege apply in this situation? What if no disclosure is actually made? See United States v. (Under Seal), 748 F.2d 871, 875-876 (4th Cir. 1984) (where client communicates information to attorney with understanding that it will be revealed to others, privilege does not apply, even if "a fortuity" prevents actual publication, but information intended for disclosure may regain protection if client later "decides not to publish his communications and tells his attorney before the release").

5. Suppose the client conveys information to an attorney to be passed on to a government agency in an effort to comply with reporting requirements. Should protection of the privilege be denied even if the agency itself is obligated by statute to keep such reports confidential? Compare In re Subpoenas Duces Tecum (Fulbright & Jaworski; Vinson & Elkins), 738 F.2d 1367, 1369-1370 (D.C. Cir. 1984) (voluntary disclosure to SEC waived attorney-client privilege) with Diversified Industries v. Meredith, 572 F.2d 596, 611 (8th Cir. 1977) (surrender of documents to SEC under agency subpoena in connection with "separate and nonpublic SEC investigation" resulted in "only a limited waiver").

c. Leaks and Eavesdroppers

SUBURBAN SEW 'N SWEEP v. SWISS-BERNIA
United States District Court, Northern District of Illinois
91 F.R.D. 254 (N.D. Ill. 1981)

[Sewing machine retailers sue manufacturer Swiss-Bernia and others alleging antitrust violations (price discrimination and conspiracy). In building their case, plaintiffs search a dumpster in the parking lot of an office building occupied by Swiss-Bernia. Over a two-year period, they find hundreds of relevant documents, including handwritten drafts of confidential letters from the President of Swiss-Bernia to a lawyer for the corporation. These had been put in wastebaskets, which were emptied by a company employee into a large trash container, which was in turn emptied into the dumpster. Only Swiss-Bernia used the dumpster. Ultimately it was emptied by a scavenging company hired by Swiss-Bernia.

All agree that the drafts of letters were intended to remain confidential and would be privileged but for the fact that they were retrieved from the dumpster. The privilege issue arose in the setting of a motion to compel answers during discovery, when plaintiffs filed interrogatories seeking transcriptions and other information relating the letters. The Magistrate refused to compel, apparently because he considered the tactics pursued by the plaintiffs to be improper.

In reviewing what the Magistrate did, the District Court notes that property put in the garbage is "no longer protected by the Fourth Amendment." Even if it was, what plaintiffs did would not be a violation because the Fourth Amendment covers only government agents, and the exclusionary doctrine does not apply in civil cases anyway. The Court also notes a "diversity" in approaches to the question whether failure to maintain secrecy should be viewed in terms of waiver or voluntary disclosure, both of which result in loss of the attorney-client privilege.]

LEIGHTON, J. . . .

The traditional rule . . . placed near absolute responsibility for maintaining confidentiality on the parties to the communication. The underlying principle is well summarized by Wigmore:

The law provides subjective freedom for the client by assuring him of exemption from its processes of disclosure against himself or the attorney or their agents of communication. This much, but no more, is necessary for the maintenance of the privilege. Since the means of preserving secrecy of communication are largely in the client's hands and since the privilege is a derogation from the general testimonial duty and should be strictly construed, it would be improper to extend its prohibition to third persons who obtain knowledge of the communications.

8 Wigmore on Evidence §2326 (McNaughton Rev. 1961); see Id. §2325.

Under this rule, the privilege does not extend to prevent third parties who are not agents of the parties to the communication from testifying, with the result that a purloined letter, a stolen document, or a surreptitiously overheard conversation are not privileged. McCormick, Evidence §75 (2nd Ed. 1972). However, as McCormick points out:

Perhaps these incidental hazards may have been thought so remote as not to be likely to discourage disclosure; simple eavesdropping could be guarded against by taking simple precautions. With the advent of more sophisticated techniques for invading privacy in general and intercepting confidential communications in particular, the picture changed and a very different concept of the eavesdropper emerged. As a consequence . . . statutes and rules defining privileges began to include provisions entitling the holder to prevent anyone from disclosing a privileged confidential communication.

Id. One such provision is Rule 503 of the Proposed Federal Rules of Evidence which were prescribed and approved by the Supreme Court. . . .

The advisory committee notes specifically reject the former rule, adhered to by Wigmore. Commentators, noting that "(w)hile it may perhaps have been tolerable in Wigmore's day to penalize a client for failing to achieve secrecy, such a position is outmoded in an era of sophisticated eavesdropping devices against which no easily available protection exists," have endorsed the Supreme Court view, and rejected the older rule. 2 Weinstein's Evidence ¶503(b)[2] (1980). . . .

Nevertheless, "allowing the client to invoke the privilege to prevent testimony by eavesdroppers does not . . . in any way reduce the client's need to take all possible precautions to insure confidentiality." 2 Weinstein's Evidence ¶503(b)[2]. Nor does the new rule alter the well established principle that the privilege is to be strictly confined. The case before the court must be distinguished from the involuntary disclosure cases because the documents were not taken from some place where defendants had put them for safekeeping, diligently trying to safeguard their confidentiality, but rather were taken from defendants' garbage. This case lies between the inadvertent disclosure cases, where the information is transmitted in public or otherwise clearly not adequately safeguarded, and the involuntary disclosure cases, where the information is acquired by third parties in spite of all possible precautions.

Thus . . . the relevant consideration is the intent of the defendants to maintain the confidentiality of the documents as manifested in the precautions they took. In determining whether the precautions taken were adequate, two considerations are paramount: (1) the effect on uninhibited consultation between attorney and client of not allowing the privilege in these circumstances;

and (2) the ability of the parties to the communication to protect against the disclosures.

Though this case presents a very close question, the court concludes that consideration of these factors requires that the privilege not be applied to these documents. The likelihood that third parties will have the interest, ingenuity, perseverance and stamina, as well as risk possible criminal and civil sanctions, to search through mounds of garbage in hopes of finding privileged communications, and that they will then be successful, is not sufficiently great to deter open attorney-client communication. Furthermore, if the client or attorney fear such disclosure, it may be prevented by destroying the documents or rendering them unintelligible before placing them in a trash dumpster.[6] While requiring this degree of precaution may seem extreme, if the parties feel that the likelihood of disclosure is sufficiently great, the precautions may be justified, and it is within their power to decide what precautions to take, and so to protect against disclosure. Accordingly, that part of the Magistrate's order pertaining to the documents allegedly protected by the attorney-client privilege must also be reversed.

NOTES ON SCAVENGERS AND EAVESDROPPERS

1. Do you agree that the client in *Suburban Sew 'N Sweep* failed to take adequate precautions? Assuming that police can search trashcans for evidence without a warrant, does it follow that the attorney-client privilege should be lost if private parties recover discarded documents from the trash? Had you better buy a shredder when you enter law practice?

2. The confidentiality requirement generally imposes an obligation on parties who wish to claim the privilege both to ensure privacy at the time the communication is made and to preserve the continuing privacy of the communication. Is the obligation that of the client alone, or is it imposed equally upon the attorney? Should the nature of the obligation to safeguard confidentiality be more precisely defined, or is it sufficient to allow courts to gauge the intention of parties by the precautions they took? See proposed FRE 503(a)(4) (generally defining "confidential" to mean "not intended to be disclosed to third persons.") As you will see in Section B7b, infra, voluntary disclosure of a privileged communication to outsiders normally constitutes a waiver of the privilege.

3. Assume that a client, desperate for advice, telephones his lawyer at home after hours and tells her over the phone that he "just killed somebody." Unbeknownst to either, the lawyer's teen-aged child listens to the conversation on an extension phone. At the murder trial of the client, should the child be permitted to testify to the substance of the conversation over an objection raising the attorney-client privilege? What if the "eavesdropper" was a person standing in line behind the defendant at a pay phone where the call was placed?

4. Note how the issue of testimony by eavesdroppers is addressed by proposed FRE 503(b): "A client has a privilege to refuse to disclose *and to*

---

6. It was revealed at oral argument that defendants now have a paper shredder.

prevent any other person from disclosing confidential communications . . . " (emphasis added).

5. Should confidentiality (hence the privilege) be lost in the following situations:

    a. A letter from a client is stolen from her lawyer's office. Should it matter whether the door is locked? What if the thief is the night janitor?

    b. A letter from a client is left on her lawyer's desk, where it is seen and read by another client during an interview.

    c. A letter from the attorney is mistakenly addressed to and read by the wrong client, or is sent to the client at the wrong address, and read by the occupant.

    d. A fax from attorney to client is mistakenly sent to opposing counsel. The fax cover sheet contains instructions for recipients that material is privileged and should not be read by unintended recipients.

    e. An email from client to attorney is mistakenly forwarded by attorney to another client. The email did not contain a banner warning the recipient that the contents might be privileged.

The ABA Committee on Ethics and Professional Responsibility has taken the position that a recipient of a missent fax or email should refrain from examining the document once the inadvertence is discovered, notify the sending lawyer, and adhere to the sending lawyer's instructions for the unintended recipient. ABA Comm. on Ethics and Professional Responsibility, Formal Op. 92-368 (1992) and Formal Op. 99-413 (1999); see also Sampson Fire Sales, Inc. v. Oaks, 201 F.R.D. 351, 361-362 (M.D. Pa. 2001) (privilege not waived upon inadvertently sent fax; recipient lawyer ordered to return fax based on ABA Formal Op. 92-368). For commentary on privilege issues related to electronic communications, see Mitchel L. Winick et al., Playing "I Spy" with Client Confidences: Confidentiality, Privilege and Electronic Communications, 31 Tex. Tech. L. Re. 1225 (2000); David Hricik, Confidentiality and Privilege in High-Tech Communications, 60 Tex. Bar. J. 104 (1997); Anne G. Bruckner-Harvey, Inadvertent Disclosure in the Age of Fax Machines: Is the Cat Really Out of the Bag? 46 Baylor L. Rev. 385 (1994).

5. The Corporate Client

Before enactment of the Rules, it could be said with certainty that the attorney-client privilege extended to corporations, but it was not clear how many people in the corporate organization were within the charmed circle—that is, how many such people could communicate with corporate counsel in ways that would be protected by a corporate claim of the attorney-client privilege. In the development of federal case law on this issue, four approaches could be discerned, and some state cases took yet other approaches.

Two occupy extremes on the spectrum. One, which arose in an early opinion by a distinguished federal trial judge, suggested that a confidential statement to counsel by *any* "officer or employee" of the corporation might be privileged. See United States v. United Shoe Machinery, 89 F. Supp. 357,

359 (D.C. Mass. 1950) (opinion by Judge Wyzanski). Another said the privilege was "historically and fundamentally personal in nature," that the idea of confidentiality did not apply in the corporate setting, hence that corporate clients held no attorney-client privilege at all. See Radiant Burners v. American Gas Assn., 207 F. Supp. 771 (D.C. Ill.), rev'd, 320 F.2d 314 (7th Cir.), cert. denied, 375 U.S. 929 (1962).

Radiant Burners was reversed on appeal, but it sent shock waves through the corporate bar. In the interim, another District Court suggested a third approach, in the nature of a compromise: The privilege applied to corporate clients but covered only communications to counsel by persons in what has come to be called the "control group." See Philadelphia v. Westinghouse Electric Corp., 210 F. Supp. 483, 485 (E.D. Pa. 1962) (defining charmed circle to include people "of whatever rank" who are "in a position to control or even to take a substantial part in a decision about any action which the corporation may take upon the advice of the attorney").

In the drafting process, the Advisory Committee seized on the control group test and sought to write it into the Rules. It proposed a privilege that would cover communications to counsel by a "representative of the client," defined as

> one having authority to obtain professional legal services and to act on advice rendered pursuant thereto, on behalf of the client.

See Revised Draft of March, 1971, Rule 503, 51 F.R.D. 315, 361 (1971).

But before the Rules were enacted a fourth approach appeared, also something of a compromise. An opinion by the Seventh Circuit suggested what has come to be the "subject matter" test, described thus:

> [A]n employee of a corporation, though not a member of its control group, is sufficiently identified with the corporation so that his communication to the corporation's attorney is privileged where the employee makes the communication at the direction of his superiors in the corporation and where the subject matter upon which the attorney's advice is sought by the corporation and dealt with in the communication is the performance by the employee of the duties of his employment.

Harper & Row Publishers v. Decker, 423 F.2d 487 (7th Cir.), aff'd, 400 U.S. 348 (1970).

The Supreme Court affirmed the Seventh Circuit decision in *Harper & Row*, but the high court was divided 4-4, leaving the question of the appropriate test very much up in the air. In this environment, the Advisory Committee concluded that the matter was just "too hot to handle." See Hearings on Proposed Rules of Evidence Before the Special Subcommittee on Reform of Federal Criminal Laws of the House Committee on the Judiciary, 93d Cong., 1st Sess., Ser. 2, at 524 (1973) (testimony by Professor Cleary). The Committee withdrew its endorsement of the control group test, and Congress opted to reject all the privilege rules, leaving this question (and indeed all privilege issues) to the courts to resolve. The matter reached the Supreme Court in *Upjohn*.

UPJOHN CO. v. UNITED STATES
United States Supreme Court
449 U.S. 383 (1981)

JUSTICE REHNQUIST delivered the opinion of the Court.

We granted certiorari in this case to address important questions concerning the scope of the attorney-client privilege in the corporate context and the applicability of the work-product doctrine in proceedings to enforce tax summonses. With respect to the privilege question the parties and various *amici* have described our task as one of choosing between two "tests" which have gained adherents in the courts of appeals. We are acutely aware, however, that we sit to decide concrete cases and not abstract propositions of law. We decline to lay down a broad rule or series of rules to govern all conceivable future questions in this area, even were we able to do so. We can and do, however, conclude that the attorney-client privilege protects the communications involved in this case from compelled disclosure and that the work-product doctrine does apply in tax summons enforcement proceedings.

I

Petitioner Upjohn Co. manufactures and sells pharmaceuticals here and abroad. In January 1976 independent accountants conducting an audit of one of Upjohn's foreign subsidiaries discovered that the subsidiary made payments to or for the benefit of foreign government officials in order to secure government business. The accountants so informed Mr. Gerard Thomas, Upjohn's Vice-President, Secretary, and General Counsel. Thomas is a member of the Michigan and New York bars, and has been petitioner's General Counsel for 20 years. He consulted with outside counsel and R.T. Parfet, Jr., Upjohn's Chairman of the Board. It was decided that the company would conduct an internal investigation of what were termed "questionable payments." As part of this investigation the attorneys prepared a letter containing a questionnaire which was sent to "All Foreign General and Area Managers" over the Chairman's signature. The letter began by noting recent disclosures that several American companies made "possibly illegal" payments to foreign government officials and emphasized that the management needed full information concerning any such payments made by Upjohn. The letter indicated that the Chairman had asked Thomas, identified as "the company's General Counsel," "to conduct an investigation for the purpose of determining the nature and magnitude of any payments made by the Upjohn Company or any of its subsidiaries to any employee or official of a foreign government." The questionnaire sought detailed information concerning such payments. Managers were instructed to treat the investigation as "highly confidential" and not to discuss it with anyone other than Upjohn employees who might be helpful in providing the requested information. Responses were to be sent directly to Thomas. Thomas and outside counsel also interviewed the recipients of the questionnaire and some 33 other Upjohn officers or employees as part of the investigation.

On March 26, 1976, the company voluntarily submitted a preliminary report to the Securities and Exchange Commission on Form 8-K disclosing certain questionable payments. A copy of the report was simultaneously submitted to the Internal Revenue Service, which immediately began an investigation to determine the tax consequences of the payments. Special agents conducting the investigation were given lists by Upjohn of all those interviewed and all who had responded to the questionnaire. On November 23, 1976, the Service issued a summons pursuant to 26 U.S.C. §7602 demanding production of:

> All files relative to the investigation conducted under the supervision of Gerard Thomas to identify payments to employees of foreign governments and any political contributions made by the Upjohn Company or any of its affiliates since January 1, 1971 and to determine whether any funds of the Upjohn Company had been improperly accounted for on the corporate books during the same period.
>
> The records should include but not be limited to written questionnaires sent to managers of the Upjohn Company's foreign affiliates, and memoranda or notes of the interviews conducted in the United States and abroad with officers and employees of the Upjohn Company and its subsidiaries.

The company declined to produce the documents specified in the second paragraph on the grounds that they were protected from disclosure by the attorney-client privilege and constituted the work product of attorneys prepared in anticipation of litigation. On August 31, 1977, the United States filed a petition seeking enforcement of the summons. . . . That court adopted the recommendation of a Magistrate who concluded that the summons should be enforced. Petitioner appealed to the Court of Appeals for the Sixth Circuit which rejected the Magistrate's finding of a waiver of the attorney-client privilege, but agreed that the privilege did not apply "[t]o the extent that the communications were made by officers and agents not responsible for directing Upjohn's actions in response to legal advice . . . for the simple reason that the communications were not the 'client's.'" The court reasoned that accepting petitioner's claim for a broader application of the privilege would encourage upper-echelon management to ignore unpleasant facts and create too broad a "zone of silence." Noting that Upjohn's counsel had interviewed officials such as the Chairman and President, the Court of Appeals remanded to the District Court so that a determination of who was within the "control group" could be made. In a concluding footnote the court stated that the work-product doctrine "is not applicable to administrative summonses issued under 26 U.S.C. §7602."

II

FRE 501 provides that "the privilege of a witness . . . shall be governed by the principles of the common law as they may be interpreted by the courts of the United States in light of reason and experience." The attorney-client privilege is the oldest of the privileges for confidential communications known to the common law. Its purpose is to encourage full and frank communication between attorneys and their clients and thereby promote broader public interests in the observance of law and administration of justice. The privilege recognizes that sound legal advice or advocacy serves public ends and that such advice or advocacy depends upon the lawyer being fully informed by the client. . . . This rationale for the privilege has long been recognized by the Court. . . . Admittedly complications in the application of the privilege arise when the client is a corporation, which in theory is an artificial creature of the law, and not an individual; but this Court has assumed that the privilege applies when the client is a corporation, and the Government does not contest the general proposition.

The Court of Appeals, however, considered the application of the privilege in the corporate context to present a "different problem," since the client was an inanimate entity and "only the senior management, guiding and integrating the several operations, . . . can be said to possess an identity analogous to the corporation as a whole." The first case to articulate the so-called "control group test" adopted by the court below, Philadelphia v. Westinghouse Electric Corp., 210 F. Supp. 483, 485 (E.D. Pa.), reflected a similar conceptual approach:

> Keeping in mind that the question is, Is it the corporation which is seeking the lawyer's advice when the asserted privilege communication is made?, the most satisfactory solution, I think, is that if the employee making the communication, of whatever the rank he may be, is in a position to control or even to take a substantial part in a decision about any action which the corporation may take upon the advice of the attorney, . . . then, in effect, *he is (or personifies) the corporation* when he makes his disclosure to the lawyer and the privilege would apply. (Emphasis supplied.)

Such a view, we think, overlooks the fact that the privilege exists to protect not only the giving of professional advice to those who can act on it but also the giving of information to the lawyer to enable him to give sound and informed advice. The first step in the resolution of any legal problem is ascertaining the factual background and sifting through the facts with an eye to the legally relevant. [The Court quotes the Code of Professional Responsibility to the effect that a lawyer should be "fully informed of all the facts."]

In the case of the individual client the provider of information and the person who acts on the lawyer's advice are one and the same. In the corporate context, however, it will frequently be employees beyond the control group as defined by the court below—"officers and agents . . . responsible for directing [the company's] actions in response to legal advice"—who will possess the information needed by the corporation's lawyers. Middle-level—and indeed lower-level—employees can, by actions within the scope of their employment, embroil the corporation in serious legal difficulties, and it is only natural that these employees would have the relevant information needed by corporate counsel if he is adequately to advise the client with respect to such actual or potential difficulties. . . .

The control group test adopted by the court below thus frustrates the very purpose of the privilege by discouraging the communication of relevant information by employees of the client to attorneys seeking to render legal advice to the client corporation. The attorney's advice will also frequently be more significant to noncontrol group members than to those who officially sanction the advice, and the control group test makes it more difficult to convey full and frank legal advice to the employees who will put into effect the client corporation's policy.

The narrow scope given the attorney-client privilege by the court below not only makes it difficult for corporate attorneys to formulate sound advice when their client is faced with a specific legal problem but also threatens to limit the valuable efforts of corporate counsel to ensure their client's compliance with the law. In light of the vast and complicated array of regulatory legislation confronting the modern corporation, corporations, unlike most individuals, "constantly go to lawyers to find out how to obey the law," Burnham, The Attorney-Client Privilege in the Corporate Arena, 24 Bus. Law 901, 913 (1969), particularly since compliance with the law in this area is hardly an instinctive matter.[2] The test adopted by the court below is difficult to apply in practice, though no abstractly formulated and unvarying "test" will necessarily enable courts to decide questions such as this with mathematical precision. But if the purpose of the attorney-client privilege is to be served, the attorney and client must be able to predict with some degree of certainty whether particular discussions will be protected. An uncertain privilege, or one which purports to be certain but results in widely varying applications by the courts, is little better than no privilege at all. The very terms of the test adopted by the court below suggest the unpredictability of its application. The test restricts the availability of the privilege to those officers who play a "substantial role" in deciding and directing a corporation's legal response. Disparate decisions in cases applying this test illustrate its unpredictability. Compare, e.g., Hogan v. Zletz, 43 F.R.D. 308, 315-316 (N.D. Okla. 1967), aff'd in part sub nom. Natta v. Hogan, 392 F.2d 686 (CA10 1968) (control group includes managers and assistant managers of patent division and research and development department) with Congoleum Industries, Inc. v. GAF Corp., 49 F.R.D. 82, 83-85 (E.D. Pa. 1969), aff'd, 478 F.2d 1398 (CA3 1973) (control group includes only division and corporate vice presidents, and not two directors of research and vice president for production and research).

The communications at issue were made by Upjohn employees to counsel for Upjohn acting as such, at the direction of corporate superiors in order to secure legal advice from counsel. . . . Information, not available from upper-echelon management, was needed to supply a basis for legal advice concerning compliance with securities and tax laws, foreign laws, currency regulations, duties to shareholders, and potential litigation in each of these areas. The communications concerned matters within the scope of the employees' corporate duties, and the employees themselves were sufficiently aware that they were being questioned in order that the corporation could obtain legal advice. The questionnaire identified Thomas as "the company's General Counsel" and

2. The Government argues that the risk of civil or criminal liability suffices to ensure that corporations will seek legal advice in the absence of the protection of the privilege. This response ignores the fact that the depth and quality of any investigations to ensure compliance with the law would suffer, even were they undertaken. The response also proves too much, since it applies to all communications covered by the privilege: an individual trying to comply with the law or faced with a legal problem also has strong incentive to disclose information to his lawyer, yet the common law has recognized the value of the privilege in further facilitating communications.

referred in its opening sentence to the possible illegality of payments such as the ones on which information was sought. A statement of policy accompanying the questionnaire clearly indicated the legal implications of the investigation. . . . This statement was issued to Upjohn employees worldwide, so that even those interviewees not receiving a questionnaire were aware of the legal implications of the interviews. Pursuant to explicit instructions from the Chairman of the Board, the communications were considered "highly confidential" when made, and have been kept confidential by the company. Consistent with the underlying purposes of the attorney-client privilege, these communications must be protected against compelled disclosure.

The Court of Appeals declined to extend the attorney-client privilege beyond the limits of the control group test for fear that doing so would entail severe burdens on discovery and create a broad "zone of silence" over corporate affairs. Application of the attorney-client privilege to communications such as those involved here, however, puts the adversary in no worse position than if the communications had never taken place. The privilege only protects disclosure of communications; it does not protect disclosure of the underlying facts by those who communicated with the attorney. . . . Here the Government was free to question the employees who communicated with Thomas and outside counsel. Upjohn has provided the IRS with a list of such employees, and the IRS has already interviewed some 25 of them. While it would probably be more convenient for the Government to secure the results of petitioner's internal investigation by simply subpoenaing the questionnaires and notes taken by petitioner's attorneys, such considerations of convenience do not overcome the policies served by the attorney-client privilege. As Justice Jackson noted in his concurring opinion in Hickman v. Taylor, 329 U.S. at 516: "Discovery was hardly intended to enable a learned profession to perform its functions . . . on wits borrowed from the adversary."

Needless to say, we decide only the case before us, and do not undertake to draft a set of rules which should govern challenges to investigatory subpoenas. Any such approach would violate the spirit of FRE 501. . . . While such a "case-by-case" basis may to some slight extent undermine desirable certainty in the boundaries of the attorney-client privilege, it obeys the spirit of the Rules. At the same time we conclude that the narrow "control group test" sanctioned by the Court of Appeals in this case cannot, consistent with "the principles of the common law as . . . interpreted . . . in light of reason and experience," FRE 501, govern the development of the law in this area.

III

Our decision that the communications by Upjohn employees to counsel are covered by the attorney-client privilege disposes of the case so far as the responses to the questionnaires and any notes reflecting responses to interview questions are concerned. The summons reaches further, however, and Thomas has testified that his notes and memoranda of interviews go beyond recording responses to his questions. To the extent that the material subject to the summons is not protected by the attorney-client privilege as disclosing communications between an employee and counsel, we must reach the ruling by the Court of Appeals that the work-product doctrine does not apply to summonses issued under 26 U.S.C. §7602.

The Government concedes, wisely, that the Court of Appeals erred and that the work-product doctrine does apply to IRS summonses. This doctrine was announced by the Court over 30 years ago in Hickman v. Taylor, 329 U.S. 495 (1947). In the case the Court rejected "an attempt, without purported necessity or justification, to secure written statements, private memoranda and personal recollections prepared or formed by an adverse party's counsel in the course of his legal duties." The Court noted that "it is essential that a lawyer work with a certain degree of privacy" and reasoned that if discovery of the material sought were permitted

> much of what is now put down in writing would remain unwritten. An attorney's thoughts, heretofore inviolate, would not be his own. Inefficiency, unfairness and sharp practices would inevitably develop in the giving of legal advice and in the preparation of cases for trial. The effect on the legal profession would be demoralizing. And the interests of the clients and the cause of justice would be poorly served.

The "strong public policy" underlying the work-product doctrine was reaffirmed recently in United States v. Nobles, 422 U.S. 225, 236-240 (1975), and has been substantially incorporated in Federal Rule of Civil Procedure 26(b)(3).[7] . . . Rule 26(b)(3) codifies the work-product doctrine, and the Federal Rules of Civil Procedure are made applicable to summons enforcement proceedings by Rule 81(a)(3). While conceding the applicability of the work-product doctrine, the Government asserts that it has made a sufficient showing of necessity to overcome its protections. The Magistrate apparently so found. The Government relies on the following language in *Hickman*:

> We do not mean to say that all written materials obtained or prepared by an adversary's counsel with an eye toward litigation are necessarily free from discovery in all cases. Where relevant and nonprivileged facts remain hidden in an attorney's file and where production of those facts is essential to the preparation of one's case, discovery may properly be had. . . . And production might be justified where the witnesses are no longer available or can be reached only with difficulty.

The Government stresses that interviewees are scattered across the globe and that Upjohn has forbidden its employees to answer questions it considers irrelevant. The above-quoted language from *Hickman*, however, did not apply to "oral statements made by witnesses . . . whether presently in the form of [the

---

7. This provides, in pertinent part:

[A] party may obtain discovery of documents and tangible things otherwise discoverable under subdivision (b)(1) of this rule and prepared in anticipation of litigation or for trial by or for another party or by or for that other party's representative (including his attorney, consultant, surety, indemnitor, insurer, or agent) only upon a showing that the party seeking discovery has substantial need of the materials in the preparation of his case and that he is unable without undue hardship to obtain the substantial equivalent of the materials by other means. In ordering discovery of such materials when the required showing has been made, the court shall protect against disclosure of the mental impressions, conclusions, opinions, or legal theories of an attorney or other representative of a party concerning the litigation.

attorney's] mental impressions or memoranda." As to such material the Court did "not believe that any showing of necessity can be made under the circumstances of this case so as to justify production. . . . If there should be a rare situation justifying production of these matters, petitioner's case is not of that type." Forcing an attorney to disclose notes and memoranda of witnesses' oral statements is particularly disfavored because it tends to reveal the attorney's mental processes ("what he saw fit to write down regarding witnesses' remarks") ("the statement would be his [the attorney's] language, permeated with his inferences") (Jackson, J., concurring). . . .

. . . [S]ome courts have concluded that *no* showing of necessity can overcome protection of work product which is based on oral statements from witnesses. See, e.g., In re Grand Jury Proceedings, 473 F.2d 840, 848 (8th Cir. 1973) (personal recollections, notes, and memoranda pertaining to conversation with witnesses); In re Grand Jury Investigation, 412 F. Supp. 943, 949 (E.D. Pa. 1976) (notes of conversation with witness "are so much a product of the lawyer's thinking and so little probative of the witness's actual words that they are absolutely protected from disclosure"). Those courts declining to adopt an absolute rule have nonetheless recognized that such material is entitled to special protection. See, e.g., In re Grand Jury Investigation, 599 F.2d 1224, 1231 (CA3 1979) ("special considerations . . . must shape any ruling on the discoverability of interview memoranda. . . ; such documents will be discoverable only in a 'rare situation'"); cf. In re Grand Jury Subpoena, 599 F.2d 504, 511-512 (CA2 1979).

We do not decide the issue at this time. It is clear that the Magistrate applied the wrong standard when he concluded that the Government had made a sufficient showing of necessity to overcome the protections of the work-product doctrine. The Magistrate applied the "substantial need" and "without undue hardship" standard articulated in the first part of Rule 26(b)(3). The notes and memoranda sought by the Government here, however, are work product based on oral statements. If they reveal communications, they are, in this case, protected by the attorney-client privilege. To the extent they do not reveal communications, they reveal the attorney's mental process in evaluating the communications. As rule 26 and *Hickman* make clear, such work product cannot be disclosed simply on a showing of substantial need and inability to obtain the equivalent without undue hardship.

While we are not prepared at this juncture to say that such material is always protected by the work-product rule, we think a far stronger showing of necessity and unavailability by other means than was made by the Government or applied by the Magistrate in this case would be necessary to compel disclosure. Since the Court of Appeals thought that the work-product protection was never applicable in an enforcement proceeding such as this, and since the Magistrate whose recommendations the District Court adopted applied too lenient a standard of protection, we think the best procedure with respect to this aspect of the case would be to reverse the judgment of the Court of Appeals for the Sixth Circuit and remand the case to it for such further proceedings in connection with the work-product claim as are consistent with this opinion.

Accordingly, the judgment of the Court of Appeals is reversed, and the case remanded for further proceedings.

NOTES ON CORPORATE ATTORNEY-CLIENT PRIVILEGE

1. *Upjohn* lists numerous factors supporting the conclusion that the attorney-client privilege applies. Should all these be essential? *Upjohn* criticizes the control group test for vagueness. Does the *Upjohn* approach avoid that criticism? Does *Upjohn* adopt the "subject matter" test that had produced a stalemate in the Court when it reviewed *Harper & Row*?

2. If there is a need for a corporate privilege, why limit it at all? Why not take Judge Wyzanski's approach, under which a confidential statement to a lawyer by *any* officer or employee of the venture would be within the privilege? Recall the seminal decision on work product, where the Court refused to extend "the protective cloak" of the attorney-client privilege to "information which an attorney secures from a witness while acting for his client in anticipation of litigation," thus apparently indicating that statements by crew members on a tugboat that sank were not privileged, even though spoken to an attorney for the tugboat owners. Hickman v. Taylor, 329 U.S. 495 (1947). If the attorney spoke to the pilot of the vessel, wouldn't his statements be within the attorney-client privilege under *Upjohn*? If the attorney spoke to the galley cook as well, why shouldn't his statements also be privileged?

3. Do lower-echelon corporate employees need the protection of the privilege that *Upjohn* endorses, or are they likely to be motivated to make disclosures to corporate counsel by other factors? See generally Saltzburg, Corporate and Related Attorney-Client Privilege Claims: A Suggested Approach, 12 Hofstra L. Rev. 279 (1984) (inasmuch as individual employees do not own and cannot invoke the corporate attorney-client privilege themselves, extending its protection to them is unnecessary). Does *Upjohn* nonetheless serve a useful function in encouraging corporations to undertake investigations of the sort conducted here because they are assured that responses by lower-echelon employees are protected by the privilege?

4. Note that *Upjohn* also considers a claim of work product protection for the materials collected in this case. Does *Upjohn* demonstrate that the concerns of the privilege and those of the work product doctrine cannot be kept entirely separate in practice?

5. If the interests of the corporation are potentially adverse to those of the employee, does the corporate attorney have an ethical obligation to warn the employee that she does not represent the employee, that the employee may obtain separate counsel, and that the corporation will be the holder of the privilege with respect to any communications that are made? Would such warnings undermine the corporate attorney's ability to obtain information from employees, an objective that *Upjohn* sought to further? But see Diversified Industries v. Meredith, 572 F.2d 596, 611 n.5 (8th Cir. 1977) ("an employee's confidential communications to the corporation's counsel may reveal potential liability of the employee," so the employee himself "may have a privilege" where he seeks "legal advice from the corporation's counsel for himself" or where counsel acts as "joint attorney").

6. When corporate management changes, who then has the power to decide whether to claim the corporate attorney-client privilege with respect to

statements made by displaced officers? New management, says the Supreme Court:

> [W]hen control of a corporation passes to new management, the authority to assert and waive the corporation's attorney-client privilege passes as well. New managers installed as a result of a takeover, merger, loss of confidence by shareholders, or simply normal succession, may waive the attorney-client privilege with respect to communications made by former officers and directors. Displaced managers may not assert the privilege over the wishes of current managers, even as to statements that the former might have made to counsel concerning matters within the scope of their corporate duties.

Commodity Futures Trading Commission v. Weintraub, 470 U.S. 1026 (1985). The above quoted language does not mean that new management has the power to waive whatever claim the prior manager might have to a personal attorney-client privilege, does it?

7. Consider a claim of attorney-client privilege in the context of a stockholders' derivative suit. Recall that in such suits typically minority stockholders sue corporate managers to recover damages *for the corporation*. Can managers claim the corporate attorney-client privilege to block discovery by plaintiffs? See Garner v. Wolfinbarger, 430 F.2d 1093 (5th Cir. 1970), cert. denied, 401 U.S. 974 (1971) (recognizing qualified privilege that may be overcome on a showing of good cause); Saltzburg, Corporate-Attorney-Client Privilege in Shareholder Litigation and Similar Cases: *Garner* Revisited, 12 Hofstra L. Rev. 817 (1984).

8. Should the scope of the attorney-client privilege for governmental entities be similar to that of corporations? See Deuterium Corp. v. United States, 19 Cl. Ct. 697, 699 (1990) (applying "same reasoning" as in *Upjohn* to "Government employees at all levels"). But an important qualification is sometimes recognized. See, e.g., In re Lindsey, 148 F.3d 1100 (D.C. Cir. 1998) (governmental attorney-client privilege may not be used to shield information about possible criminal misconduct by public officials from disclosure to a grand jury).

6. Exceptions to Coverage

By common consensus, the attorney-client privilege gives way in several circumstances. Suits between client and lawyer present an obvious example: If the client sues for malpractice, she cannot invoke the privilege to prevent her lawyer from proving whatever was said on either side that might be relevant to defending the suit; similarly, if the lawyer sues for his fee, the client cannot invoke the privilege to block relevant proof of what was said on each side during the period of service.

A second example involves the lawyer who acts as attesting witness on a document executed by his client. The privilege survives the death of the client, but a lawyer who attests his client's will is usually permitted to testify to the execution of the document in probate proceedings, the theory being that the client would want such disclosure.

Two other exceptions are much harder in practice. One holds that certain basic facts about the attorney-client relationship are not privileged, even though the attorney may know such facts only through his confidential association with the client: Thus, it is usually said that the identity of the client and the fee arrangement with the lawyer are not privileged, and sometimes the same is said of the address or whereabouts of the client. Finally, all courts seem to agree that the privilege does not apply to communications in furtherance of a crime or fraud. But as you are about to see, sometimes identity *is* privileged (courts speak of "an exception," which means that the exception excluding identity from protection has its own exception in which identity is protected after all). And the crime or fraud exception is sometimes particularly difficult to apply.

a. Client Identity

IN RE GRAND JURY INVESTIGATION 83-2-35 (DURANT)
United States Court of Appeals for the Sixth Circuit
723 F.2d 447 (1983)

KRUPANSKY, J.

Attorney Richard Durant (Durant) appeals a finding of contempt for failure to disclose to the grand jury upon order of court the identity of his client. On March 1, 1983, Special Agent Edwards (Edwards), of the Federal Bureau of Investigation (FBI), visited Durant's office and explained that the FBI was investigating the theft of numerous checks made payable to International Business Machines, Inc. (IBM). He advised that a number of the stolen checks had been traced and deposited into various banking accounts under names of non-existent organizations, at least one of which included the initials "IBM." Edwards produced a photostatic copy of a check drawn upon one of these fictitious accounts which check was made payable to Durant's law firm. Upon FBI inquiry, Durant conceded that this check for $15,000 had been received and endorsed by his firm for services rendered to a client in two cases, one of which was "finished" and the other of which was "open." Durant refused to disclose the identity of his client to whose credit the proceeds had been applied, asserting the attorney-client privilege.

Durant was subpoenaed to appear before the grand jury the following day, March 2, 1983, where he again refused to identify his client, asserting the attorney-client privilege. The government immediately moved the United States District Court for the Eastern District of Michigan for an Order requiring Durant to provide the requested information. At a hearing that same afternoon, Durant informed the court that disclosure of his client's identity could incriminate that client in criminal activity so as to justify invoking the attorney-client privilege. Durant additionally stated that "I do not know any of the facts about this theft or anything else," and suggested that the requested information should be obtained through other methods. The court adjudged that the privilege did not attach and ordered Durant to identify his client. Upon refusal to comply with this Order, Durant was held in contempt. Further proceedings (e.g., bond) were stayed until March 16, 1983, and subsequently stayed until March 22, 1983.

In an obvious attempt to ascertain the identity of Durant's client in an alternate manner, the United States issued a second subpoena to Durant on March 9, 1983, ordering him to appear before the grand jury on March 16, 1983, and produce the following documents:

> A listing of all clients of the law firm of Durant & Durant, P.C., and Richard Durant as of February 18, 1983 including all clients with active cases and clients who owe fees or have provided a retainer to the firm and all client ledger cards and other books, records and documents reflecting or recording payments to the law firm for the period February 1, 1983 to March 1, 1983.

Durant moved to quash this subpoena duces tecum, again asserting the attorney-client privilege. At the March 22, 1983 hearing on this motion, Durant re-asserted that production of the subpoenaed documents could implicate his client in criminal activity. He additionally observed that the FBI had admitted before Durant and the district court judge in-chambers that an arrest would be effected by the FBI immediately following disclosure. In effect, the identity of Durant's client was the last link of evidence necessary to effect an indictment. . . .

The federal forum is unanimously in accord with the general rule that the identity of a client is, with limited exceptions, not within the protective ambit of the attorney-client privilege.

The Circuits have embraced various "exceptions" to the general rule that the identity of a client is not within the protective ambit of the attorney-client privilege. All such exceptions appear to be firmly grounded in the Ninth Circuit's seminal decision in Baird v. Koerner, 279 F.2d 623 (9th Cir. 1960). In *Baird* the IRS received a letter from an attorney stating that an enclosed check in the amount of $12,706 was being tendered for additional amounts due from undisclosed taxpayers. When the IRS summoned the attorney to ascertain the identity of the delinquent taxpayers the attorney refused identification asserting the attorney-client privilege. The Ninth Circuit, applying California law, adjudged that the "exception" to the general rule as pronounced in Ex parte McDonough, 149 P. 566 (Cal. 1915) controlled:

> The name of the client will be considered privileged matter where the circumstances of the case are such that the name of the client is material only for the purpose of showing an acknowledgement of guilt on the part of such client of the very offenses on account of which the attorney was employed.

The identity of the *Baird* taxpayer was adjudged within this exception to the general rule. The Ninth Circuit has continued to acknowledge this exception:

> A significant exception to this principle of nonconfidentiality holds that such information may be privileged when the person invoking the privilege is able to show that a strong possibility exists that disclosure of the information would implicate the client in the very matter for which legal advice was sought in the first case.

In re Grand Jury Subpoenas Duces Tecum (Marger/Merenbach), 695 F.2d 363, 365 (9th Cir. 1982). This exception, which can perhaps be most succinctly characterized as the "legal advice" exception, has also been recognized by other circuits. Since the legal advice exception is firmly grounded in the policy of protecting confidential communications, this Court adopts and applies its principles herein. . . .

Another exception to the general rule that the identity of a client is not privileged arises where disclosure of the identity would be tantamount to disclosing an otherwise protected confidential communication. In *Baird*, supra, the Ninth Circuit observed:

> If the identification of the client conveys information which ordinarily would be conceded to be part of the usual privileged communication between attorney and client, then the privilege should extend to such identification in the absence of other factors.

Citing *Baird*, the Fourth Circuit promulgated the following exception:

> To the general rule is an exception, firmly bedded as the rule itself. The privilege may be recognized where so much of the actual communication has already been disclosed that identification of the client amounts to disclosure of a confidential communication.

NLRB v. Harvey, 349 F.2d 900, 905 (4th Cir. 1965). The Seventh Circuit has added to the *Harvey* exception the following emphasized caveat:

> The privilege may be recognized where so much of the actual communication has already been disclosed [*not necessarily by the attorney, but by independent sources as well*] that identification of the client [*or of fees paid*] amounts to disclosure of a confidential communication.

United States v. Jeffers, 532 F.2d 1101, 1115 (7th Cir. 1976) (emphasis added). The Third Circuit, applying this exception, has emphasized that it is the link between the client and the *communication*, rather than the link between the client and the possibility of potential criminal *prosecution*, which serves to bring the client's identity within the protective ambit of the attorney-client privilege. See: In re Grand Jury Empanelled February 14, 1978 (Markowitz), 603 F.2d 469, 473 n.4 (3d Cir. 1979). Like the "legal advice" exception, this exception is also firmly rooted in principles of confidentiality.

Another exception, articulated in the Fifth Circuit's *en banc* decision of In re Grand Jury Proceedings (Pavlick), 680 F.2d 1026 (5th Cir. 1982) (en banc), is recognized when disclosure of the identity of the client would provide the "last link" of evidence:

> We have long recognized the general rule that matters involving the payment of fees and the identity of clients are not generally privileged. In re Grand Jury Proceedings, (United States v. Jones), 517 F.2d 666 (5th Cir. 1975); see cases collected id. at 670 n.2. There we also recognized, however, a limited and narrow exception to the general rule, one that obtains when the disclosure of the client's identity by his attorney would have supplied the last link in an existing chain of incriminating evidence likely to lead to the client's indictment.

Upon careful consideration this Court concludes that, although language exists in *Baird* to support viability of *Pavlick*'s "last link" exception, the exception is simply not grounded upon the preservation of confidential *communications* and hence not justifiable to support the attorney-client privilege. Although the last link exception may promote concepts of fundamental fairness against self-incrimination, these concepts are not proper considerations to invoke the attorney-client privilege. Rather, the focus of the inquiry is whether disclosure of the identity would adversely implicate the confidentiality of communications. Accordingly, this Court rejects the last link exception as articulated in *Pavlick*.

Turning to the facts at bar, it is observed that Durant asserted three justifications for invocation of the attorney-client privilege. First, at the March 2 hearing, he stated that disclosure might possibly implicate the client in criminal activity. As this justification has no roots in concepts of confidentiality or communication, it cannot be advanced to support an abdication of the general rule that identity of a client is not privileged. Second, at the March 22 hearing, Durant informed the Court that the FBI had informed him that an arrest would be effected upon disclosure of the identity of Durant's client. This is simply an assertion that disclosure would provide the last link of evidence to support an indictment as articulated in *Pavlick*—a precedent which is herein rejected.

Third, at the March 22 hearing, Durant submitted that disclosure was justified under the "legal advice" exception embraced by the Ninth Circuit. Seeking to invoke this exception, it was incumbent upon Durant to "show that a *strong possibility* exist[ed] that disclosure of the information would implicate the client in the very matter for which legal advice [had been] sought in the first case." A well recognized means for an attorney to *demonstrate* the existence of an exception to the general rule, while simultaneously preserving confidentiality of the identity of his client, is to move the court for an in camera ex parte hearing. . . .

Since the burden of establishing the existence of the privilege rests with the party asserting the privilege, it is incumbent upon the attorney to move for an in camera ex parte hearing if one is desired. In the action sub judice, Durant failed to so move. Rather, he rested on his blanket assertion that his client had initially sought legal advice relating to matters involving the theft of IBM checks. Such unsupported assertions of privilege are strongly disfavored. Further, it is pertinent to observe that at the first hearing on March 2 Durant had expressly disavowed knowledge of the existence of stolen IBM checks. This statement significantly diminishes the credibility of Durant's subsequent March 22 representation that his client had indeed engaged Durant's services for past activity relating to stolen IBM checks. Accordingly, Durant clearly failed to satisfy his burden of demonstrating a "strong possibility" that disclosure of the identity of his client would implicate that client in the very matter for which legal advice had been initially sought.

Last, it is observed that Durant did not represent to the district court that disclosure of the identity of his client would amount to a disclosure of a confidential communication. Not having advanced this exception to the general rule, it follows axiomatically that Durant failed to satisfy the burden of establishing its existence. Nor does the record suggest the viability of this exception so as to justify a remand.

In sum, Durant has failed to establish the existence of any exception to the general rule that disclosure of the identity of a client is not within the protective ambit of the attorney-client privilege. Therefore the contempt Order of the district court issued against Durant is hereby affirmed.

NOTES ON PRIVILEGE FOR CLIENT'S IDENTITY

1. Why should the identity of the client be excepted from coverage? If your answer is that normally the client does not expect to keep the fact of consultation confidential, what would you say in the case where the client *does* intend to keep this fact under wraps?

2. *Durant* cites the Ninth Circuit case of *Baird* as establishing three exceptions to the rule that the identity of the client is not privileged—the "legal advice" exception, the "last link" in a chain of incriminating evidence exception, and the disclosure of "confidential communications" exception. *Durant* rejects the "last link" exception. Why is evidence incriminating to the client not necessarily privileged? The Ninth Circuit has now reformulated its position to hold that the "confidential communications" exception is the only exception properly derived from *Baird*. See Tornay v. United States, 840 F.2d 1424, 1428 (9th Cir. 1988) ("careful reading" and "close examination of subsequent decisions" shows that *Baird* applies only where, because of exceptional circumstances, disclosure of client's identity "would reveal information that is tantamount to a confidential professional communication"). Other courts have similarly narrowed this exception to apply only to disclosures of identity that would reveal a confidential communication. See, e.g., In re Grand Jury Subpoena Served Upon Doe, 781 F.2d 238, 247-248 (2d Cir. 1985) (en banc); United States v. Liebman, 742 F.2d 807, 810 (3d Cir. 1984); In re Grand Jury Investigation No. 83-2-35, 723 F.2d 447, 453 (6th Cir. 1983), cert. denied, 467 U.S. 1246, 104 S. Ct. 3524, 82 L.Ed.2d 831 (1984); In re Witnesses Before the Special March 1980 Grand Jury, 729 F.2d 489, 494-495 (7th Cir. 1984); In re Grand Jury Proceedings (85 Misc. 140), 791 F.2d 663, 665 (8th Cir. 1986).

3. Consider three situations where an attorney claims the privilege when asked to identify her client:

   a. The attorney returns stolen property on behalf of an unnamed client. See Hughes v. Meade, 453 S.W.2d 538, 542 (Ky. Ct. App. 1970) (attorney-client privilege inapplicable to identity of client who hired attorney to return a stolen typewriter).

   b. The attorney reports illegal misdeeds or misconduct by some third person on behalf of an anonymous client. See In re Kozlov, 398 A.2d 882 (N.J. 1979) (privilege applies); In re Kaplan, 168 N.E.2d 660 (N.Y. 1960) (privilege applies).

   c. The attorney represents one person charged with a crime on the basis of fees paid by an anonymous third party. Compare In re Grand Jury Subpoena for Attorney Representing Criminal Defendant Reyes-Requena, 913 F.2d 1118, 1123 (5th Cir. 1990) (privilege denied where no contention made that fee payer was a current or former client) with Ralls v. United States, 52 F.3d 223, 226 (9th Cir. 1995) (fee payer was a previous client in same matter and his identity and fee arrangements were "intertwined" with confidential communications made for purposes of obtaining legal advice for fee payer himself).

Are there good reasons to permit nondisclosure in these cases? Is the attorney-client privilege the appropriate device? Is the attorney providing "professional legal services" to the client in these situations?

4.   While driving his car home late at night, Dale runs over Baltes, a pedestrian, killing him. Dale panics and speeds away from the scene of the accident. Media reports of the hit-and-run accident indicate that police are seeking the driver. They have a general description of Dale's car but not the license number or enough detail to identify him. Dale feels remorseful and retains Arnold as his attorney. He asks Arnold to contact the prosecutor and negotiate a plea bargain but not to reveal his identity if negotiations fail. The prosecutor refuses to negotiate without knowing who Arnold represents. The Baltes family learns from the district attorney that Arnold represents the hit-and-run driver. The family files a wrongful death action naming "John Doe" as the defendant and seeks a court order compelling Arnold to reveal the identity of his client. Arnold claims that the identity of the client is protected by the attorney-client privilege. How should the court rule? See Note, Public Assault on the Attorney-Client Privilege: Ramifications of Baltes v. Does, 3 Geo. J. Legal Ethics 351 (1989) (approving Florida trial court ruling that attorney-client privilege applies in situation described here); D'Alessio v. Gilbert, 617 N.Y.S.2d 484 (1994) (upholding privilege on similar facts).

5.   Sometimes courts have held other basic facts concerning the relationship to be unprivileged. See Matter of Walsh, 623 F.2d 489 (7th Cir.), cert. denied, 449 U.S. 994 (1980) (times and places when attorney met with client, along with bills sent and fees paid); In re Grand Jury Witness (Waxman), 695 F.2d 359, 361-362 (9th Cir. 1982) (amounts and form of attorney fees received); Condon v. Petacque, 90 F.R.D. 53 (N.D. Ill. 1981) (dates when attorney consulted); United States v. Blackman, 72 F.3d 1418, 1424-1426 (9th Cir. 1995) (identity of client who paid in cash fees exceeding $10,000, under government reporting requirement).

6.   Should the address or location of the client be disclosable where it relates directly to the legal advice that he sought? Consider Matter of Grand Jury Subpoenas Served upon Field, 408 F. Supp. 1169 (S.D.N.Y. 1976) (address privileged, where client sought advice concerning his relocation); In re Stolar, 397 F. Supp. 520 (S.D.N.Y. 1975) (address and telephone number privileged, where client sought legal advice regarding his right to refuse to be interviewed by FBI).

b. Future Crime or Fraud

STATE v. PHELPS
Oregon Court of Appeals
545 P.2d 901 (Or. App. 1976)

SCHWAB, C.J.
    A grand jury indicted defendant for one count of perjury . . . and three counts of tampering with a witness . . . in connection with his prior defense

of a charge of driving under the influence of intoxicating liquor. Defendant's original attorney in the DUIL case had been subpoenaed by the grand jury. Relying on a preliminary opinion by the Oregon State Bar Committee on Professional Responsibility, he had testified as to communications between defendant and him concerning the contemplated perjury. Defendant moved the court for an omnibus hearing . . . to determine the admissibility of the attorney's testimony. For the purposes of the hearing, the parties agreed to the following historical facts:

When defendant was charged with DUIL, he advised his attorney that he could produce several witnesses who would testify that he was not driving at the time of the alleged offense. After investigation, the attorney felt that defendant had not told him the truth. When the attorney confronted defendant and a witness with this possibility, they admitted that defendant had lied to the attorney with regard to who was driving the car. Upon receiving assurances that perjured testimony would not be used in the case, the attorney withdrew. Defendant then retained another lawyer and successfully defended the case by using perjured testimony.

Following the omnibus hearing, the circuit court ordered "that [the attorney] may not be compelled to testify as to any of the privileged communications between himself and the defendant as it relates to the subject case unless the defendant waives the privilege." The state appeals from the order. . . .

The question is whether the evidence which the circuit court suppressed before trial is protected by the attorney-client privilege or whether it falls within the future crime exception to the rule of privilege.

Disciplinary Rule DR 4-101(B) . . . states: "Except when permitted under DR 4-101(C), a lawyer shall not knowingly: (1) Reveal a confidence or secret of his client."

There are certain exceptions to this standard which are based on public policy considerations. For instance, Disciplinary Rule DR 4-101(C) states: "A lawyer may reveal: . . . (3) The intention of his client to commit a crime and the information necessary to prevent the crime. . . ."

As in this case, a conflict can arise between these competing duties imposed on attorneys.

If a client consults an attorney about prior wrongdoing, there is no doubt that the privilege protects their confidential communications. Defendant contends that this case falls within the privilege since the communication related to a past crime, i.e., the DUIL offense.

Defendant's position is illogical. The testimony which the state seeks to introduce into evidence concerns the crime of perjury for which defendant was indicted in this case. At the time of the attorney-client discussion, the crime of perjury had not been committed.

The privilege is not meant to protect discussion of future crime or fraud designed to conceal past wrongdoing. . . .

Defendant also suggests that the future crime or fraud exception to the attorney-client privilege does not apply where the crime could not be prevented by disclosure because it had already been committed at the time of trial even if it had not been committed when the attorney-client communications occurred. An examination of reasons other than crime prevention which justify the future crime exception reveals the weakness of defendant's argument. As stated in a leading English case:

. . . In order that the rule [of privilege] may apply there must be both professional confidence and professional employment, but if the client has a criminal object in view in his communications with his solicitor one of these elements must necessarily be absent. The client must either conspire with his solicitor or deceive him. If his criminal object is avowed, the client does not consult his advisor professionally, because it cannot be the solicitor's business to further any criminal object. If the client does not avow his object, he reposes no confidence, for the state of facts, which is the foundation of the supposed confidence, does not exist. The solicitor's advice is obtained by a fraud. . . .

Queen v. Cox (1884), 14 QBD 153, 168.

McCormick also explains why the future crime or fraud exception is well established:

> Since the policy of the privilege is that of promoting the administration of justice, it would be a perversion of the privilege to extend it to the client who seeks advice to aid him in carrying out an illegal or fraudulent scheme. Advice given for those purposes would not be a professional service but participation in a conspiracy. Accordingly, it is settled under modern authority that the privilege does not extend to communications between attorney and client where the client's purpose is the furtherance of a future intended crime or fraud. . . .

McCormick, Evidence 199, §95 (2d ed. Cleary 1972). . . . We find no reason why the exception to the attorney-client privilege should be applied differently if a client commits a contemplated crime before his attorney discloses his intention to do so.

What quantum of proof is necessary before the trial court should compel disclosure of the attorney-client communications is not considered by us at this time since the trial court's order was based on its memorandum opinion finding that the communications in question are privileged. We hold that they are not.

Reversed and remanded.

NOTES ON THE CRIME-FRAUD EXCEPTION

1.   The opinion discusses both the future crime exception to the lawyer's ethical duty of confidentiality and the future crime exception to the lawyer-client privilege without clearly distinguishing between them. Is there a distinction? Note that the cited exception to the ethical duty of confidentiality applies only to "[t]he intention of his client to commit a crime and the information necessary to prevent the crime," whereas the exception to the lawyer-client privilege applies to a "future crime or fraud."

2.   Should this exception to the privilege extend beyond future crimes and frauds to all future "torts"? This broader formulation of the exception was adopted by the Model Code of Evidence, Rule 212 (1942) and by Uniform Rule of Evidence 26(2)(a) (1974).

3.   What if the client does not know that the course of conduct about which she is seeking legal advice would be a crime? Is the communication to the lawyer outside of the privilege? See proposed FRE 503(d)(1) (no privilege

if the lawyer's services were obtained to enable client to commit "what the client knew or reasonably should have known to be a crime or fraud").

4.   In ruling on a claim that the crime-fraud exception applies to otherwise privileged communications, may the trial court order that the communications be produced for in camera inspection? Or would such disclosure, even though limited to the court, improperly invade the client's privilege? See United States v. Zolin, 491 U.S. 554 (1989) (proper for trial court to undertake in camera examination in determining whether the future crime-fraud exception applies; however, inspection is discretionary and can be ordered only upon a showing of "a factual basis adequate to support a good faith belief by a reasonable person" that such examination may reveal evidence of crime or fraud).

5.   Does an attorney have an ethical responsibility to report contemplated future crimes by a client? Compare ABA Model Code of Professional Responsibility, DR 4-101(C) (lawyer may reveal "intention of his client to commit a crime and the information necessary to prevent the crime") with ABA Model Rules of Professional Conduct, Rule 1.6(b), which was amended in 2003 in the wake of the Enron scandal (a lawyer may disclose client confidences to the extent necessary "to prevent reasonably certain death or substantial bodily harm; to prevent the client from committing crime or fraud that is reasonably certain to result in substantial injury to the financial interests or property of another and in furtherance of which the client has used or is using the lawyer's services" and "to prevent, mitigate or rectify substantial injury to the financial interests or property of another" resulting from such fraud). See also Restatement (Third) of the Law Governing Lawyers §117A. Could an attorney face civil liability for *not* reporting contemplated future crimes by a client?

7.   Assertion and Waiver

The client holds the privilege and must claim it at the appropriate moment or risk losing its protection. While the attorney cannot claim the privilege if her client wants disclosure (for the lawyer has no recognized stake in the protection provided), she is presumptively authorized to assert the privilege on behalf of the client. Although you have seen that disclosure to necessary intermediaries (and some disclosure to others, as in the pooled defense and joint client cases) does not cause loss of protection, disclosure to other parties during the discovery process often does. Problems of claim and waiver can become complicated.

a.   Asserting the Privilege

The client, as the holder of the attorney-client privilege, determines whether it should be asserted or waived. The client may claim the privilege independently or through the attorney. The attorney is ethically required to assert the privilege on the client's behalf, unless a waiver has been made or authorized by the client. The possible existence of the attorney-client privilege may be called to the attention of the court by third parties, and the court may seek assurance that the privilege is inapplicable or has been waived before permitting disclosure of the allegedly privileged matter.

The privilege claimant bears the burden of establishing his entitlement. The question whether the privilege claim should be sustained is for the court to resolve under FRE 104(a), and typically it can make a sensible ruling only if supplied with basic information, such as a description of the general nature of the communication, and the nature of the services rendered by counsel. Generally courts resolve the claim without requiring disclosure of the underlying communication itself, but they sometimes require at least partial disclosure, particularly in the case of documents. See Schwimmer v. United States, 232 F.2d 855, 864 (8th Cir.) (court may require production of documents for inspection to determine propriety of privilege claim), cert. denied, 352 U.S. 833 (1956).

When the information seeker contends that an exception applies, he bears the burden of proving that point. In the case of the crime or fraud exception, it is usually said that the information seeker can prevail by making a "prima facie case" that the exception applies. See Clark v. United States, 289 U.S. 1, 15 (1933). Requiring more certainty on a point so difficult to prove would seemingly risk the very evil that the exception seeks to discourage—abuse of the privilege to further ongoing criminal or fraudulent acts. How should the client respond? See Note, 51 Brooklyn L. Rev. 913, 918-919 (1985) ("[i]n the context of the fraud exception [the prima facie] standard is used to dispel the privilege altogether without affording the client an opportunity to rebut").

Review of privilege rulings. As noted in Chapter 1, ordinarily rulings on evidential issues are viewed as interlocutory and may not be reviewed until final judgment has been entered. Sometimes, however, immediate review is possible where a court overrules a claim of attorney-client privilege.

On this point, the cases are in disarray, even within the federal system. Under one approach, the threshold question is whether the person from whom information was sought has been held in contempt. If not, no review may be had. If so, some authority would permit the reviewing court to consider the privilege ruling on the merits only if the person has been held in criminal contempt. If the witness has been held in civil contempt, review is limited to the authority of the trial judge to impose the contempt sanction.

Under another approach, the threshold question is whether the nondisclosing person is a party to the action. If he is a party, he may be permitted to obtain review of the privilege ruling only by suffering an adverse judgment on the merits of the case, then raising the privilege issue (and all other points of error) on appeal from the judgment. See IBM Corp. v. United States, 493 F.2d 112, 117 (2d Cir. 1973) (IBM held in civil contempt and fined $150,000 per day, for refusing to produce documents under claims of attorney-client privilege and work product immunity; no interlocutory appeal possible), cert. denied, 416 U.S. 995 (1974). If he is not a party, he may obtain review of the privilege issue without suffering a judgment of contempt, simply because the final judgment in the proceedings will never afford him a chance to obtain such review.

Many modern cases present the issue of review in the context of orders of production directed to criminal defense lawyers during the course of grand jury proceedings. Of course, the lawyer is not herself a party, and technically the potential defendant is not a party either (since he has not yet been indicted). In this circumstance, some modern federal authority has applied the doctrine of Perlman v. United States, 247 U.S. 7 (1918) (party permitted to appeal, on ground of Fourth Amendment violation, from disclosure order directed to court clerk), and has permitted the client to intervene to appeal immediately from an order overruling her claim of privilege, and requiring her attorney to testify. One court explained the outcome thus:

> We suspect that the willingness of a lawyer to protect a client's privilege in the face of a contempt citation will vary greatly, and have a direct relationship to the value of the client's business and the power of the client in relation to the attorney. We are reluctant to pin the appealability of a district court order upon such precarious considerations. Moreover, there is a paradoxical element in even looking for indications of the lawyer's intent. If the attorney will submit to a contempt citation rather than testify, the efficient administration of justice is best served by hearing the client-intervenor's appeal immediately, rather than waiting for an appeal of the contempt judgment against the attorney. If the attorney will testify rather than risk contempt, the client-intervenor's appeal is most certainly proper because there will be no later opportunity to appeal and the order is definitely "final" as to the client.

In re Grand Jury Proceedings (Fine), 641 F.2d 199, 201-203 (5th Cir. 1981).

PROBLEM 12-F.   The Reluctant Lawyer

A federal grand jury is deciding whether to indict Kastin for fraud based on his alleged use of the mail to send false and misleading brochures soliciting investments in a real estate partnership. Walters, a real estate attorney who had represented Kastin, is called before the grand jury to describe discussions with Kastin relating to the brochure prior to mailing. The government is trying to show that Kastin knew there were false statements in the brochure, but Walters claims the attorney-client privilege on behalf of Kastin and refuses to testify. The court orders Walters to answer, finding that the discussions fit the future crime or fraud exception to the privilege.

Assume that Walters has a reasonable basis for believing that the court has erred. Does he have an ethical obligation to protect Kastin by defying the order, at the cost of being held in contempt, so the merits of the privilege claim can be reviewed? What if Walters is unwilling to be held in contempt? Should Kastin be allowed to intervene and to appeal the order requiring Walters to disclose?

NOTES ON APPELLATE REVIEW OF PRIVILEGE ISSUES

1. If the court *sustains* the privilege claim and bars the testimony by Walters, can the government take an interlocutory appeal? See 18 U.S.C. §3731 (allowing interlocutory appeals by the government under certain conditions when evidence has been suppressed in advance of trial). Why should the government be allowed an interlocutory appeal challenging the suppression of evidence? Could it be because Double Jeopardy would block an appeal by the government if the jury acquits Kastin after a trial on the merits?

2. If a party to a civil case refuses to testify after a privilege claim is

overruled, she can be cited for contempt of court. If she is cited only for civil contempt (which can be discharged by giving the ordered testimony), normally no interlocutory review on the merits is allowed. Why? Should an interlocutory appeal be allowed if the citation is for criminal contempt? Why? See Powers v. Chicago Transit Authority, 846 F.2d 1139, 1140 (7th Cir. 1988) (upholding $150 per day fine for failure to turn over material petitioner contended was privileged; refusing review on merits because an adjudication of civil contempt is not a "final judgment"; but criminal contempt is appealable "on the theory that it is the terminating order of a separate proceeding, the criminal prosecution").

3. If the privilege holder ultimately discloses privileged matter at trial pursuant to a court order after his privilege claim has been denied, can the privilege ruling be challenged on appeal from a final judgment or is the privilege waived? See proposed FRE 512 (disclosure of privileged matter is not a waiver if the disclosure "was compelled erroneously").

b. Waiver

There is a generally accepted rule of waiver (see proposed FRE 511). Under this rule, a privilege is waived if its holder "voluntarily discloses or consents to disclosure of any significant part of the matter or communication," except that the privilege is *not* lost "if the disclosure is itself a privileged communication." Thus the privilege is waived if a client discloses to his barber a conversation he had with his attorney, but not if he discloses the conversation to his wife in a confidential conversation with her. The privilege is also waived by disclosure of the privileged communication in court, as would happen if the client testified that "My attorney advised me that this deduction would be legal."

Under this general rule, the privilege is *not* waived if the lawyer discloses the privileged communication *without the client's consent*. Even though the communication has been revealed, the privilege remains available to prevent admission of the privileged communication at trial.

Ironically, however, while intentional-but-unauthorized disclosure by an attorney does not waive the privilege, still *negligent* disclosure by the attorney sometimes *does*. Such waiver-by-inadvertence occurs when a privileged document is mistakenly released to the opposing party during pretrial discovery, because an attorney is usually viewed as having authority to respond to discovery requests. Many courts find that such inadvertent disclosure waives the privilege, at least where reasonable precautions were not taken to maintain secrecy. See, e.g., Weil v. Investment/Indicators, Researchers & Management, 647 F.2d 18, 23-25 (9th Cir. 1981).

The doctrine of inadvertent waiver is viewed with great concern by trial lawyers, particularly if disclosure of *any part* of privileged matter is viewed as a waiver reaching *all related* matter on the same subject. Since such a broad rule of waiver would inhibit discovery and encourage broad claims of privilege, some courts hold that the inadvertent waiver reaches only those documents actually disclosed, and some courts even decline to find waiver where the attorney takes prompt steps to recover documents released by accident prior to reliance by the opposing side. See Hundley, "Inadvertent Waiver" of Evidentiary Privileges: Can Reformulating the Issue Lead to More Sensible Decisions? 19 S. Ill. U. L.J.

263 (1995); Davidson and Voth, Waiver of the Attorney-Client Privilege, 64 Or. L. Rev. 637 (1986).

NOTES ON WAIVER OF ATTORNEY-CLIENT PRIVILEGE

1.   Does it make sense to apply notions of waiver to apparently inadvertent disclosure? In one case Transamerica claimed that IBM waived its claim of attorney-client privilege for certain material by disclosing it in another suit. In that other suit, the judge had ordered IBM to produce 17 million pages in 90 days, leading to "herculean effort" to cull out privileged items. (IBM hired help and developed a complex review system in an effort to follow the schedule, which required some 34,000 work hours, moving at a pace of 500 pages per hour.) In the Transamerica litigation, the Ninth Circuit concluded that IBM's disclosure under such circumstances did not waive its privilege claim. Transamerica Computer Co. v. International Business Machines Corp., 573 F.2d 646, 648 (9th Cir. 1978). But see F.D.I.C. v. Singh, 140 F.R.D. 252 (D. Me 1992) (holding that inadvertent disclosure completely waives privilege, commenting that one "cannot unring a bell" and that courts grant "no greater protection to those who assert the privilege than their own precautions warrant") (internal quotation marks omitted).

2.   Does disclosure under a valid but erroneous court order waive the privilege? (The order is "valid" in the sense that the court has jurisdiction to resolve the issue, but the court might nevertheless err in ordering disclosure.) The authorities disagree, but arguably the sounder view is that no waiver occurs, and that was the result preferred by the Advisory Committee in proposed Rule 512 (privilege protection is not lost if disclosure is "compelled erroneously").

3. If a client waives the privilege by challenging the competency of his legal representation in a prior proceeding, does he waive the privilege for all purposes? See Bittaker v. Woodford, 331 F.3d 715 (9th Cir. 2003) (no; defendant's habeas corpus petition alleging inadequate assistance of counsel waived privilege only for purposes of litigating that claim; privileged communications not available for government to use in later reprosecution).

4.   If lawyer and client decide to disclose privileged material to other litigants in the same or connected suits, should such disclosure waive the privilege? Doesn't the logic of the pooled defense situation apply equally to such sharing of information?[1]

5.   Do strict notions of waiver reflect hostility to the privilege? Consider whether such hostility is justifiable, even under a strictly utilitarian view of the privilege. If it is easily lost in litigation, won't the result be increasing costs as parties take greater care to protect privileged matter? One astute modern commentator argues for a shift in emphasis in waiver analysis:

---

1.   Recall that work product protection is sometimes lost by disclosure, as happened in the *James Julian* case (Chapter 7B, supra). Recall too that the *AT&T* case (after *James Julian*, in Note 7 of Notes on Notes on Applying Rule 612) concludes that sharing among litigants with similar interests does not waive work product protection, although attorney-client privilege is more easily lost.

[W]aivers should be based on fairness, which is the emerging trend in the courts. The proper emphasis of the fairness analysis, in turn, is unfairness resulting from the act upon which the waiver argument is premised. The prime concern is that a privilege-holder may affirmatively use privileged material to garble the truth, while invoking the privilege to deny his opponent access to related privileged material that would put the proffered evidence in perspective.

Applying this fairness analysis to recurrent civil litigation situations suggests clear resolutions for some enduring problems. Thus, the "putting in issue" waiver should be limited to situations in which the privilege-holder makes affirmative use of privileged material as evidence; it should not be imposed as a tax on the decision to raise certain issues. Similarly, inadvertent revelation of damaging material to an opponent should not work a waiver. Beyond these situations, the fairness analysis requires a sometimes difficult assessment of the circumstances of the case in order to decide whether to find a waiver. Where privileged information has been shared, for example, a key question is whether the sharing has given it such currency that denying it to the opponent would threaten to make a mockery of justice. Similarly, where material has been used in witness preparation, the question is whether the opponent will be unfairly hampered in cross-examining the witness without the material.

Marcus, The Perils of Privilege: Waiver and the Litigator, 84 Mich. L. Rev. 1605, 1654-1655 (1986).

C. THE PSYCHOTHERAPIST-PATIENT PRIVILEGE

JAFFEE v. REDMOND
Supreme Court of the United States
518 U.S. 1 (1996)

JUSTICE STEVENS delivered the opinion of the Court.

After a traumatic incident in which she shot and killed a man, a police officer received extensive counseling from a licensed clinical social worker. The question we address is whether statements the officer made to her therapist during the counseling sessions are protected from compelled disclosure in a federal civil action brought by the family of the deceased. Stated otherwise, the question is whether it is appropriate for federal courts to recognize a "psychotherapist privilege" under FRE 501.

I

On June 27, 1991, Redmond was the first officer to respond to a "fight in progress" call at an apartment complex. As she arrived at the scene, two of Allen's sisters ran toward her squad car, waving their arms and shouting that there had been a stabbing in one of the apartments. Redmond testified at trial that she relayed this information to her dispatcher and requested an ambulance.

She then exited her car and walked toward the apartment building. Before Redmond reached the building, several men ran out, one waving a pipe. When the men ignored her order to get on the ground, Redmond drew her service revolver. Two other men then burst out of the building, one, Ricky Allen, chasing the other. According to Redmond, Allen was brandishing a butcher knife and disregarded her repeated commands to drop the weapon. Redmond shot Allen when she believed he was about to stab the man he was chasing. Allen died at the scene. Redmond testified that before other officers arrived to provide support, "people came pouring out of the buildings," and a threatening confrontation between her and the crowd ensued.

Petitioner filed suit in Federal District Court alleging that Redmond had violated Allen's constitutional rights by using excessive force during the encounter at the apartment complex. The complaint sought damages under 42 U.S.C. §1983 and the Illinois wrongful death statute. At trial, petitioner presented testimony from members of Allen's family that conflicted with Redmond's version of the incident in several important respects. They testified, for example, that Redmond drew her gun before exiting her squad car and that Allen was unarmed when he emerged from the apartment building.

During pretrial discovery petitioner learned that after the shooting Redmond had participated in about 50 counseling sessions with Karen Beyer, a clinical social worker licensed by the State of Illinois and employed at that time by the Village of Hoffman Estates. Petitioner sought access to Beyer's notes concerning the sessions for use in cross-examining Redmond. Respondents vigorously resisted the discovery. They asserted that the contents of the conversations between Beyer and Redmond were protected against involuntary disclosure by a psychotherapist-patient privilege. The district judge rejected this argument. Neither Beyer nor Redmond, however, complied with his order to disclose the contents of Beyer's notes. At depositions and on the witness stand both either refused to answer certain questions or professed an inability to recall details of their conversations.

In his instructions at the end of the trial, the judge advised the jury that the refusal to turn over Beyer's notes had no "legal justification" and that the jury could therefore presume that the contents of the notes would have been unfavorable to respondents. The jury awarded petitioner $45,000 on the federal claim and $500,000 on her state law claim.

II

FRE 501 authorizes federal courts to define new privileges by interpreting "common law principles . . . in the light of reason and experience." The authors of the Rule borrowed this phrase from our opinion in Wolfle v. United States, 291 U.S. 7, 12 (1934), which in turn referred to the oft-repeated observation that "the common law is not immutable but flexible, and by its own principles adapts itself to varying conditions." Funk v. United States, 290 U.S. 371, 383 (1933). See also Hawkins v. United States, 358 U.S. 74, 79 (1958) (changes in privileges may be "dictated by 'reason and experience'"). The Senate Report accompanying the 1975 adoption of the Rules indicates that FRE 501 "should be understood as reflecting the view that the recognition of a privilege based on a confidential relationship . . . should be determined on a case-by-case basis."[7] The Rule thus did not freeze the law governing the privileges of witnesses in federal trials at a particular point in our history, but rather directed federal courts to "continue the evolutionary development of testimonial privileges." Trammel v. United States, 445 U.S. 40, 47 (1980).

The common-law principles underlying the recognition of testimonial privileges can be stated simply. " 'For more than three centuries it has now been recognized as a fundamental maxim that the public . . . has a right to every man's evidence. When we come to examine the various claims of exemption, we start with the primary assumption that there is a general duty to give what testimony one is capable of giving, and that any exemptions which may exist are distinctly exceptional, being so many derogations from a positive general rule.' " United States v. Bryan, 339 U.S. 323, 331 (1950) (quoting 8 J. Wigmore, Evidence §2192, p. 64 (3d ed. 1940)). Exceptions from the general rule disfavoring testimonial privileges may be justified, however, by a " 'public good transcending the normally predominant principle of utilizing all rational means for ascertaining the truth.' " Trammel, quoting Alkanes v. United States, 364 U.S. 206, 234 (1960) (Frankfurter, J., dissenting).

Guided by these principles, the question we address today is whether a privilege protecting confidential communications between a psychotherapist and her patient "promotes sufficiently important interests to outweigh the need for probative evidence . . ." [quoting Trammel case]. Both "reason and experience" persuade us that it does.

III

Like the spousal and attorney-client privileges, the psychotherapist-patient privilege is "rooted in the imperative need for confidence and trust." Trammel. Treatment by a physician for physical ailments can often proceed successfully on the basis of a physical examination, objective information supplied by the patient, and the results of diagnostic tests. Effective psychotherapy, by contrast, depends upon an atmosphere of confidence and trust in which the patient is willing to make a frank and complete disclosure of facts, emotions, memories, and fears. Because of the sensitive nature of the problems for which individuals consult psychotherapists, disclosure of confidential communications made during counseling sessions may cause embarrassment or disgrace. For this reason, the mere possibility of disclosure may impede development of the confidential relationship necessary for successful treatment. As the Judicial Conference Advisory Committee observed in 1972 when it recommended that Congress

---

7. In 1972 the Chief Justice transmitted to Congress proposed Rules of Evidence for United States Courts and Magistrates. 56 F.R.D. 183 (hereinafter Proposed Rules). The rules had been formulated by the Judicial Conference Advisory Committee on Rules of Evidence and approved by the Judicial Conference of the United States and by this Court. Trammel v. United States, 445 U.S. 40, 47 (1980). The proposed rules defined nine specific testimonial privileges, including a psychotherapist-patient privilege, and indicated that these were to be the exclusive privileges absent constitutional mandate, Act of Congress, or revision of the Rules. Congress rejected this recommendation in favor of FRE 501's general mandate.

recognize a psychotherapist privilege as part of the Proposed Federal Rules of Evidence, a psychiatrist's ability to help her patients

> is completely dependent upon [the patients'] willingness and ability to talk freely. This makes it difficult if not impossible for [a psychiatrist] to function without being able to assure patients of confidentiality and, indeed, privileged communication. Where there may be exceptions to this general rule. . . , there is wide agreement that confidentiality is a sine qua non for successful psychiatric treatment.

ACN to Proposed Rules, 56 F.R.D. 183, 242 (1972).

By protecting confidential communications between a psychotherapist and her patient from involuntary disclosure, the proposed privilege thus serves important private interests.

Our cases make clear that an asserted privilege must also "serv[e] public ends." Upjohn Co. v. United States, 449 U.S. 383, 389 (1981). . . . The psychotherapist privilege serves the public interest by facilitating the provision of appropriate treatment for individuals suffering the effects of a mental or emotional problem. The mental health of our citizenry, no less than its physical health, is a public good of transcendent importance.[10]

In contrast to the significant public and private interests supporting recognition of the privilege, the likely evidentiary benefit that would result from the denial of the privilege is modest. If the privilege were rejected, confidential conversations between psychotherapists and their patients would surely be chilled, particularly when it is obvious that the circumstances that give rise to the need for treatment will probably result in litigation. Without a privilege, much of the desirable evidence to which litigants such as petitioner seek access—for example, admissions against interest by a party—is unlikely to come into being. This unspoken "evidence" will therefore serve no greater truth-seeking function than if it had been spoken and privileged.

That it is appropriate for the federal courts to recognize a psychotherapist privilege under FRE 501 is confirmed by the fact that all 50 States and the District of Columbia have enacted into law some form of psychotherapist privilege. [Court's footnote catalogues the state provisions.] We have previously observed that the policy decisions of the States bear on the question whether federal courts should recognize a new privilege or amend the coverage of an existing one. Because state legislatures are fully aware of the need to protect the integrity of the factfinding functions of their courts, the existence of a consensus among the States indicates that "reason and experience" support recognition of the privilege. In addition, given the importance of the patient's understanding that her communications with her therapist will not be publicly disclosed, any State's promise of confidentiality would have little value if the

10. This case amply demonstrates the importance of allowing individuals to receive confidential counseling. Police officers engaged in the dangerous and difficult tasks associated with protecting the safety of our communities not only confront the risk of physical harm but also face stressful circumstances that may give rise to anxiety, depression, fear, or anger. The entire community may suffer if police officers are not able to receive effective counseling and treatment after traumatic incidents, either because trained officers leave the profession prematurely or because those in need of treatment remain on the job.

patient were aware that the privilege would not be honored in a federal court.[12] Denial of the federal privilege therefore would frustrate the purposes of the state legislation that was enacted to foster these confidential communications.

The uniform judgment of the States is reinforced by the fact that a psychotherapist privilege was among the nine specific privileges recommended by the Advisory Committee in its proposed privilege rules. In United States v. Gillock, 445 U.S. 360, 367-368 (1980), our holding that FRE 501 did not include a state legislative privilege relied, in part, on the fact that no such privilege was included in the Advisory Committee's draft. The reasoning in Gillock thus supports the opposite conclusion in this case. In rejecting the proposed draft that had specifically identified each privilege rule and substituting the present more open-ended FRE 501, the Senate Judiciary Committee explicitly stated that its action "should not be understood as disapproving any recognition of a psychiatrist-patient . . . privileg[e] contained in the [proposed] rules."

Because we agree with the judgment of the state legislatures and the Advisory Committee that a psychotherapist-patient privilege will serve a "public good transcending the normally predominant principle of utilizing all rational means for ascertaining truth," Trammel, we hold that confidential communications between a licensed psychotherapist and her patients in the course of diagnosis or treatment are protected from compelled disclosure under FRE 501.

IV

All agree that a psychotherapist privilege covers confidential communications made to licensed psychiatrists and psychologists. We have no hesitation in concluding in this case that the federal privilege should also extend to confidential communications made to licensed social workers in the course of psychotherapy. The reasons for recognizing a privilege for treatment by psychiatrists and psychologists apply with equal force to treatment by a clinical social worker such as Karen Beyer.[15] Today, social workers provide a significant amount of

---

12. At the outset of their relationship, the ethical therapist must disclose to the patient "the relevant limits on confidentiality." See American Psychological Association, Ethical Principles of Psychologists and Code of Conduct, Standard 5.01 (Dec. 1992). See also National Federation of Societies for Clinical Social Work, Code of Ethics V(a) (May 1988); American Counseling Association, Code of Ethics and Standards of Practice A.3.a (effective July 1995).

15. If petitioner had filed her complaint in an Illinois state court, respondents' claim of privilege would surely have been upheld, at least with respect to the state wrongful death action. An Illinois statute provides that conversations between a therapist and her patients are privileged from compelled disclosure in any civil or criminal proceeding. Ill. Comp. Stat., ch. 740, §110/10 (1994). The term "therapist" is broadly defined to encompass a number of licensed professionals including social workers. Karen Beyer, having satisfied the strict standards for licensure, qualifies as a clinical social worker in Illinois.

Indeed, if only a state law claim had been asserted in federal court, the second sentence in FRE 501 would have extended the privilege to that proceeding. We note that there is disagreement concerning the proper rule in cases such as this in which both federal and state claims are asserted in federal court and relevant evidence would be privileged under state law but not under federal law. Because the parties do not raise this question and our resolution of the case does not depend on it, we express no opinion on the matter.

mental health treatment. Their clients often include the poor and those of modest means who could not afford the assistance of a psychiatrist or psychologist, but whose counseling sessions serve the same public goals.[16] Perhaps in recognition of these circumstances, the vast majority of States explicitly extend a testimonial privilege to licensed social workers.[17] We therefore agree with the Court of Appeals that "[d]rawing a distinction between the counseling provided by costly psychotherapists and the counseling provided by more readily accessible social workers serves no discernible public purpose."

We part company with the Court of Appeals on a separate point. We reject the balancing component of the privilege implemented by that court and a small number of States.[18] Making the promise of confidentiality contingent upon a trial judge's later evaluation of the relative importance of the patient's interest in privacy and the evidentiary need for disclosure would eviscerate the effectiveness of the privilege. As we explained in *Upjohn*, if the purpose of the privilege is to be served, the participants in the confidential conversation "must be able to predict with some degree of certainty whether particular discussions will be protected. An uncertain privilege, or one which purports to be certain but results in widely varying applications by the courts, is little better than no privilege at all."

These considerations are all that is necessary for decision of this case. A rule that authorizes the recognition of new privileges on a case-by-case basis makes it appropriate to define the details of new privileges in a like manner. Because this is the first case in which we have recognized a psychotherapist privilege, it is neither necessary nor feasible to delineate its full contours in a way that would "govern all conceivable future questions in this area."[19]

V

The conversations between Officer Redmond and Karen Beyer and the notes taken during their counseling sessions are protected from compelled disclosure under FRE 501. The judgment of the Court of Appeals is affirmed.

---

16. The Judicial Conference Advisory Committee's proposed psychotherapist privilege defined psychotherapists as psychologists and medical doctors who provide mental health services. This limitation in the 1972 recommendation does not counsel against recognition of a privilege for social workers practicing psychotherapy. In the quarter-century since the Committee adopted its recommendations, much has changed in the domains of social work and psychotherapy. While only 12 States regulated social workers in 1972, all 50 do today. Over the same period, the relative portion of therapeutic services provided by social workers has increased substantially.

17. [Court cites statutes of Arizona, Arkansas, California, Colorado, Connecticut, Delaware, Florida, Georgia, Idaho, Illinois, Indiana, Iowa, Kansas, Kentucky, Louisiana, Maine, Massachusetts, Minnesota, Mississippi, Missouri, Montana, Nebraska, Nevada, New Hampshire, New Jersey, New Mexico, New York, North Carolina, Ohio, Oklahoma, Oregon, Rhode Island, South Carolina, South Dakota, Tennessee, Texas, Utah, Vermont, Virginia, Washington, Wisconsin, and Wyoming.]

18. [Court cites statutes in Maine, New Hampshire, North Carolina, and Virginia.]

19. Although it would be premature to speculate about most future developments in the federal psychotherapist privilege, we do not doubt that there are situations in which the privilege must give way, for example, if a serious threat of harm to the patient or to others can be averted only by means of a disclosure by the therapist.

It is so ordered.

JUSTICE SCALIA, with whom THE CHIEF JUSTICE joins as to Part III, dissenting.

I

The case before us involves confidential communications made by a police officer to a state-licensed clinical social worker in the course of psychotherapeutic counseling. Before proceeding to a legal analysis of the case, I must observe that the Court makes its task deceptively simple by the manner in which it proceeds. It begins by characterizing the issue as "whether it is appropriate for federal courts to recognize a 'psychotherapist privilege,' " and devotes almost all of its opinion to that question. Having answered that question (to its satisfaction) in the affirmative, it then devotes less than a page of text to answering in the affirmative the small remaining question whether "the federal privilege should also extend to confidential communications made to licensed social workers in the course of psychotherapy."

Relegating the question actually posed by this case to an afterthought makes the impossible possible in a number of wonderful ways. For example, it enables the Court to treat the Proposed Federal Rules of Evidence developed in 1972 by the Judicial Conference Advisory Committee as strong support for its holding, whereas they in fact counsel clearly and directly against it. The Committee did indeed recommend a "psychotherapist privilege" of sorts; but more precisely, and more relevantly, it recommended a privilege for psychotherapy conducted by "a person authorized to practice medicine" or "a person licensed or certified as a psychologist," Proposed Rule of Evidence 504, 56 F.R.D. 183, 240 (1972), which is to say that it recommended against the privilege at issue here. That condemnation is obscured, and even converted into an endorsement, by pushing a "psychotherapist privilege" into the center ring. The Proposed Rule figures prominently in the Court's explanation of why that privilege deserves recognition, and is ignored in the single page devoted to the sideshow which happens to be the issue presented for decision.

II

To say that the Court devotes the bulk of its opinion to the much easier question of psychotherapist-patient privilege is not to say that its answer to that question is convincing. At bottom, the Court's decision to recognize such a privilege is based on its view that "successful [psychotherapeutic] treatment" serves "important private interests" (namely those of patients undergoing psychotherapy) as well as the "public good" of "[t]he mental health of our citizenry." I have no quarrel with these premises. Effective psychotherapy undoubtedly is beneficial to individuals with mental problems, and surely serves some larger social interest in maintaining a mentally stable society. But merely mentioning these values does not answer the critical question: are they of such importance, and is the contribution of psychotherapy to them so distinctive, and is the application of normal evidentiary rules so destructive to psychotherapy, as to justify making our federal courts occasional instruments of injustice? On that central question I find the Court's analysis insufficiently convincing to satisfy the high standard we have set for rules that "are in derogation of the search for truth."

When is it, one must wonder, that the psychotherapist came to play such an indispensable role in the maintenance of the citizenry's mental health? For most of history, men and women have worked out their difficulties by talking to, inter alios, parents, siblings, best friends and bartenders—none of whom was awarded a privilege against testifying in court. Ask the average citizen: Would your mental health be more significantly impaired by preventing you from seeing a psychotherapist, or by preventing you from getting advice from your mom? I have little doubt what the answer would be. Yet there is no mother-child privilege.

How likely is it that a person will be deterred from seeking psychological counseling, or from being completely truthful in the course of such counseling, because of fear of later disclosure in litigation? And even more pertinent to today's decision, to what extent will the evidentiary privilege reduce that deterrent? The Court does not try to answer the first of these questions; and it cannot possibly have any notion of what the answer is to the second, since that depends entirely upon the scope of the privilege, which the Court amazingly finds it "neither necessary nor feasible to delineate."

The Court confidently asserts that not much truth-finding capacity would be destroyed by the privilege anyway, since "[w]ithout a privilege, much of the desirable evidence to which litigants such as petitioner seek access . . . is unlikely to come into being." If that is so, how come psychotherapy got to be a thriving practice before the "psychotherapist privilege" was invented? Were the patients paying money to lie to their analysts all those years? Of course the evidence-generating effect of the privilege (if any) depends entirely upon its scope, which the Court steadfastly declines to consider. And even if one assumes that scope to be the broadest possible, is it really true that most, or even many, of those who seek psychological counseling have the worry of litigation in the back of their minds? I doubt that, and the Court provides no evidence to support it.

III

Turning from the general question that was not involved in this case to the specific one that is: The Court's conclusion that a social-worker psychotherapeutic privilege deserves recognition is even less persuasive. . . .

[The Court's] brief analysis like the earlier, more extensive, discussion of the general psychotherapist privilege contains no explanation of why the psychotherapy provided by social workers is a public good of such transcendent importance as to be purchased at the price of occasional injustice. Moreover, it considers only the respects in which social workers providing therapeutic services are similar to licensed psychiatrists and psychologists; not a word about the respects in which they are different. A licensed psychiatrist or psychologist is an expert in psychotherapy—and that may suffice (though I think it not so clear that this Court should make the judgment) to justify the use of extraordinary means to encourage counseling with him, as opposed to counseling with one's rabbi, minister, family or friends. One must presume that a social worker does not bring this greatly heightened degree of skill to bear, which is alone a reason for not encouraging that consultation as generously. Does a social worker bring to bear at least a significantly heightened degree of skill—more than a minister or rabbi, for example? I have no idea, and neither does the Court. The social worker in the present case, Karen Beyer, was a "licensed clinical social worker," a job title whose training requirements consist of "master's degree in social work from an approved program," and "3,000 hours of satisfactory, supervised clinical professional experience." It is not clear that the degree in social work requires any training in psychotherapy. . . .

Another critical distinction between psychiatrists and psychologists, on the one hand, and social workers, on the other, is that the former professionals, in their consultations with patients, do nothing but psychotherapy. Social workers, on the other hand, interview people for a multitude of reasons. The Illinois definition of "[l]icensed social worker," for example, is as follows:

> "Licensed social worker" means a person who holds a license authorizing the practice of social work, which includes social services to individuals, groups or communities in any one or more of the fields of social casework, social group work, community organization for social welfare, social work research, social welfare administration or social work education.

Thus, in applying the "social worker" variant of the "psychotherapist" privilege, it will be necessary to determine whether the information provided to the social worker was provided to him in his capacity as a psychotherapist, or in his capacity as an administrator of social welfare, a community organizer, etc. Worse still, if the privilege is to have its desired effect (and is not to mislead the client), it will presumably be necessary for the social caseworker to advise, as the conversation with his welfare client proceeds, which portions are privileged and which are not.

[A]lthough the Court is technically correct that "the vast majority of States explicitly extend a testimonial privilege to licensed social workers," that uniformity exists only at the most superficial level. No State has adopted the privilege without restriction; the nature of the restrictions varies enormously from jurisdiction to jurisdiction; and 10 States, I reiterate, effectively reject the privilege entirely. It is fair to say that there is scant national consensus even as to the propriety of a social-worker psychotherapist privilege, and none whatever as to its appropriate scope. In other words, the state laws to which the Court appeals for support demonstrate most convincingly that adoption of a social-worker psychotherapist privilege is a job for Congress. . . .

In its consideration of this case, the Court was the beneficiary of no fewer than 14 amicus briefs supporting respondents, most of which came from such organizations as the American Psychiatric Association, the American Psychoanalytic Association, the American Association of State Social Work Boards, the Employee Assistance Professionals Association, Inc., the American Counseling Association, and the National Association of Social Workers. Not a single amicus brief was filed in support of petitioner. That is no surprise. There is no self-interested organization out there devoted to pursuit of the truth in the federal courts. The expectation is, however, that this Court will have that interest prominently indeed, primarily in mind. Today we have failed that expectation, and that responsibility. It is no small matter to say that, in some cases, our federal courts will be the tools of injustice rather than unearth the truth where it is available to be found. The common law has identified a few instances where that is tolerable. Perhaps Congress may conclude that it is also tolerable for the purpose of encouraging psychotherapy by social workers. But that conclusion assuredly does not burst upon the mind with such clarity that a judgment in favor of suppressing the truth ought to be pronounced by this honorable Court. I respectfully dissent.

NOTES ON *JAFFEE* AND THE FEDERAL PSYCHOTHERAPIST-PATIENT PRIVILEGE

1. In ringing terms, *Jaffee* confirms the existence of a federal psychotherapist-patient privilege, derived as a matter of common law evolution under FRE 501. The Court of Appeals below stressed that the privilege rests on both instrumental and humanistic bases. See Jaffee v. Redmond, 51 F.3d 1346, 1355 (7th Cir. 1994) (citing need for confidentiality as a means of encouraging people to obtain counseling and the "right of privacy" as a "fundamental tenet of the American legal system"). The Supreme Court stresses mostly the instrumental rationale, doesn't it? To be sure, the majority opinion nods in the direction of privacy in recognizing that "the sensitive nature" of problems giving rise to the need for therapy means that disclosure "may cause embarrassment or disgrace," and the same paragraph concludes that the privilege "serves important private interests." But these observations are in a paragraph stressing the need to encourage therapy. Does *Jaffee* adequately deal with the privacy point?

2. Has the instrumental justification been adequately made? What do you think of the dissent's point that psychotherapy was a "thriving practice" before the privilege was "invented," and that we have no idea whether one is deterred from seeking therapy by the absence of a privilege (hence the risk that confidences will come out later)? Others have argued in a similar vein. See Daniel W. Shuman, Myron F. Weiner and Gilbert Pinard, The Privilege Study (Part III): Psychotherapist-Patient Communications in Canada, 9 Intl. J.L. & Psychiatry 393, at 416-417 (1986) (treatment occurs without regard to privilege); Myron F. Weiner and Daniel W. Shuman, The Privilege Study: An Empirical Examination of the Psychotherapist-Patient Privilege, 60 N.C. L. Rev. 893 (1982) (survey of lay persons, patients, therapists, and judges shows privilege may affect therapy for only a "small percentage" of people). And see Edward Imwinkelried, The Rivalry Between Truth and Privilege: The Weakness of the Supreme Court's Instrumental Reasoning in Jaffee v. Redmond, 49 Hastings L.J. 969 (1998) (arguing that the instrumentalist justification has not been made and that the Court should have rested its decision on the right of privacy). But consider these facts: Everyone believes trusting the therapist is essential, that therapy depends on frank disclosure of past acts, fears, and thoughts that are likely to be personal and embarrassing, and that therapists are ethically required to warn patients of the limits of confidentiality. In light of these points, should

we really hesitate to ground the privilege in an instrumentalist rationale merely because we cannot find empirical verification that the privilege is needed?

3. Sometimes critics argue that neither privacy nor the instrumental rationale justifies the privilege because so much of what we say is unprotected. Thus the dissent in Jaffee makes the point that there is no privilege for conversations with "parents, siblings, best friends and bartenders." And the dissent asks "the average citizen" whether "your mental health" would be more impaired by discouraging psychiatric treatment or "preventing you from getting advice from your mom?" On the law of privilege between parents and children, see Catherine J. Ross, Implementing Constitutional Rights for Children: The Parent-Child Privilege in Context, 14 Stanford L. & Policy Rev. 85 (2003) (proposing that privilege covering communications from minor child to parent, based on liberty interest of parent in freedom from governmental intrusion into parent-child relationship). Some might think Justice Scalia shot himself in the foot by putting the last question, but his more serious point is that many conversations that are doubtless crucial to psychological well-being are not privileged. So why a privilege here? One of us tried to answer this argument in these terms:

> [O]ther aspects of privacy are protected. The privilege for spousal confidences covers the most critical realm of private communications (the area that seems most important to the greatest number) and a privilege covers religious consultations (including the confessional). A broader familial privilege reaching conversations between parent and child and among siblings is not out of the question and may be warranted. It is true that other private conversations are not privileged, even if private, intimate and "therapeutic." People sometimes have such talks in the belief that what they say "cannot come back to haunt" them, like conversations with trusted friends, bartenders or running partners. And people sometimes "bear their souls" or "unload" on passing acquaintances in the belief that the conversation is "safe" because neither expects to see the other again, or to have overlapping contacts. But lack of privilege here does not mean the psychotherapist-patient privilege is fatally narrow, nor undercut the theory that it provides important protection for privacy as a value in itself. The area covered by the privileges mentioned above is, after all, very substantial. And what is not covered is often undiscoverable and unusable anyhow, meaning privacy is preserved even without a privilege: Familial communications are hard to get at if the witness is reluctant to cooperate, and conversations with bartenders and passing acquaintances are beyond reach in all but high-profile criminal prosecutions or civil litigation (O.J. Simpson, JonBenet Ramsey, the cigarette litigation).

Mueller, The Federal Psychotherapist-Patient Privilege After *Jaffee*: Truth and Other Values in a Therapeutic Age, 49 Hastings L.J. 947, 955-957 (1998) (also arguing that one can be "too embarrassed about crafting an imperfect rule" because we must choose between "a failsafe rule that is too general and uncertain for ready application and a clear rule that is too broad or narrow," and suggesting that *Jaffee* merits respect as "a compromise between functionality and precision").

4. Without apparent hesitation, *Jaffee* extends privilege protection to sessions with licensed clinical social workers. But in 1975, when the Court promulgated the Proposed Federal Rules, the relevant provision extended only to psychiatrists and psychologists, and not social workers. See Proposed Rule

504(a)(2). Should the privilege extend to clinical social workers? What about the arguments that social workers may have less training and often engage in activity other than psychotherapy?

5. Should the privilege extend to receptionists, secretaries, and other aides who work for psychotherapists? See State v. Miller, 709 P.2d 225 (Or. 1985) (defendant called state mental hospital and asked to speak to a psychiatrist; when the receptionist asked his problem he said "Murder. I just killed a man."; communications to aides of psychotherapist who are "reasonably necessary for the transmission of the communication" held to be privileged; even though no psychotherapist-patient privilege had yet been formally established privilege protects communications that defendant believed to be necessary to obtain diagnosis or treatment).

6. Although refusing to delineate the scope of the newly recognized psychotherapist-patient privilege, the Court in a footnote expresses "no doubt" that there are situations in which the privilege must "give way," including where "a serious threat of harm to the patient or to others can be averted only by means of a disclosure by the therapist." Should there be a "future crimes" exception to the psychotherapist-patient privilege? Proposed FRE 504 does not contain a "future crimes" exception. According to one commentator, this omission was based on the assumption "that less harm will [occur] if patients feel free to ventilate their intentions." 2 J. Weinstein and M. Berger, Weinstein's Evidence 504-524 (1981). Is a policy of allowing patients to "ventilate their intentions" undermined by developments in tort law allowing claims against psychotherapists who fail to warn potential victims of threats made by their clients? A famous California decision held that a therapist must disclose threats by the patient if he suspects that the patient may act on the treats, and this decision has a wide following. See Tarasoff v. Regents of University of California, 551 P.2d 334 (Cal. 1976). Should such state law doctrines apply in federal courts? See United States v. Hayes, 227 F.3d 578 (6th Cir. 2000) (discussing tension between privilege and *Tarasoff* doctrine, and recognizing obligation to warn and testify in proceedings to hospitalize patient, but refusing to find broad waiver of privilege). In addition, the Ninth Circuit has declined to recognize a "dangerous patient" exception to the psychotherapist privilege under federal law, because it would "significantly injure the interests justifying the existence of the privilege; would have little practical advantage; would encroach significantly on the policy prerogatives of the states; and would go against the experience of all but one of the states in the [Ninth] Circuit, as well as the persuasive Proposed Rules." United States v. Chase, 340 F.3d 978, 992 (9th Cir. 2003).

7. *Jaffee* stresses state law, and state statutory law at that, as important to the federal privilege that the Court crafts for use in the civil rights suit brought on behalf of Ricky Allen against Officer Redmond. From one perspective, this reference seems fitting, since state law (including state statutes) constitute legitimate expressions of social concerns and normative principles. From other perspectives, however, the stress on state law is more troublesome. For one thing, how is a federal court to fashion federal law in a manner that is consistent both with the methods of common law development mandated by FRE 501 and with the directive of *Jaffee* to look to state statutory law? In some states, for example, the statutory psychotherapist-patient privilege covers counseling obtained by a person charged with child abuse, but other states carve out an

exception in this situation, on the theory that getting at whatever the defendant told his psychotherapist is more important in this setting than encouraging therapy or protecting privacy. How should a federal court faced with the issue in this setting (as might happen if a Native American or a person working on a military base were prosecuted for child abuse) fashion the appropriate federal rule? Deciding which statute embodies the better policy is surely a difficult undertaking, and the process of choice here does not look much like common law evolution. See generally Mueller, supra Note 3, at 959-961 (1998) (arguing that it would be better to recognize that this privilege is substantive, and to direct federal courts to apply the law of the state where they sit).

8.   The psychotherapist-patient privilege is an outgrowth of the physician-patient privilege. The physician-patient privilege was not recognized at common law but has been adopted by statute in most states. The drafters of the Federal Rules of Evidence included only a psychotherapist-patient privilege and not a physician-client privilege in proposed FRE 504. The ACN to proposed FRE 504 concluded that "the exceptions which have been found necessary in order to obtain information required by the public interest or to avoid fraud are so numerous as to leave little if any basis for the [physician-patient] privilege." Commonly recognized exceptions make the physician-patient privilege inapplicable in criminal cases, in civil cases where the patient puts his medical condition in issue, or when reporting of certain illnesses or medical treatment is required by statute. See generally Shuman, The Origins of the Physician-Patient Privilege and Professional Secret, 39 Sw. L.J. 661 (1985).

D. SPOUSAL PRIVILEGES

1. Introduction

At early common law, one spouse was incompetent to testify for or against the other. This incompetency grew out of the rule making parties themselves incompetent as witnesses, combined with the legal fiction that husband and wife were but one person. When this ground of incompetency disappeared, the spouse of a party was still prevented from testifying adversely, but the issue came to be viewed in terms of privilege, based on considerations of marital harmony and privacy.

Common law and most modern statutes recognize two related but distinct spousal privileges. One bars adverse spousal testimony; the other protects spousal confidences. The two doctrines often overlap, but there are significant differences as well.

In one sense, the testimonial privilege is the broader of the two, for it goes beyond protecting communications and blocks all testimony by one spouse against another, including accounts of premarital events or acts. The spousal confidences privilege excludes only testimony concerning private communications between spouses (and perhaps some behavior in private settings) while they were married. In another sense, the testimonial privilege is the narrower of the two, for it applies only if the spouses are married when the testimony is sought. But the spousal confidences privilege is usually said to protect the interval of the marriage forever, hence blocking postdissolution testimony describing private communications occurring during marriage.

2. Testimonial Privilege

The testimonial privilege serves two purposes. The first is to preserve ongoing marriages:

> The basic reason the law has refused to pit wife against husband or husband against wife in a trial where life or liberty is at stake was a belief that such a policy was necessary to foster family peace, not only for the benefit of the husband, wife and children, but for the benefit of the public as well.

Hawkins v. United States, 358 U.S. 74, 77 (1958) (opinion by Justice Black). The other is somewhat harder to state, but it relates to the unseemliness of casting one spouse as the accuser of the other. Pitting spouse against spouse seems to invade and deny human dignity—an enterprise in which the government should not engage. Testifying against a spouse would likely amount to what Justice Black called an "unforgivable act" sealing the fate of any marriage.

The underlying logic suggests that the privilege should apply in civil and criminal cases alike. But it is only rarely claimed in civil litigation, and in federal courts it is doubtful that the privilege applies in civil suits. See Ryan v. Commissioner of Internal Revenue, 568 F.2d 531, 542-544 (7th Cir. 1977) (in civil suit, court leaves the question open but denies the privilege), cert. denied, 439 U.S. 820 (1978).

Jurisdictions disagree as to whether the testimonial privilege is held by both spouses or one, and if by one spouse, whether the holder should be the witness-spouse or the defendant-spouse. When held by both, the privilege allows one spouse to testify against the other only in the unlikely event that both agree, for the witness-spouse can refuse to testify, and (regardless what the witness-spouse might want) the defendant-spouse can block such testimony. If the witness-spouse is the holder, testimony can be given even over the objection of the defendant-spouse. If the defendant-spouse is the holder, testimony by the witness-spouse can be blocked, even if the latter is willing to testify.

| TRAMMEL v. UNITED STATES
United States Supreme Court
445 U.S. 40 (1980)

MR. CHIEF JUSTICE BURGER delivered the opinion of the Court.

We granted certiorari to consider whether an accused may invoke the privilege against adverse spousal testimony so as to exclude the voluntary testimony of his wife. This calls for a re-examination of Hawkins v. United States, 358 U.S. 74 (1958).

I

On March 10, 1976, petitioner Otis Trammel was indicted with two others, Edwin Lee Roberts and Joseph Freeman, for importing heroin into the United States from Thailand and the Philippine Islands and for conspiracy to import heroin. . . . The indictment also named six unindicted co-conspirators, including petitioner's wife Elizabeth Ann Trammel.

According to the indictment, petitioner and his wife flew from the Philippines to California in August 1975, carrying with them a quantity of heroin. Freeman and Roberts assisted them in its distribution. Elizabeth Trammel then traveled to Thailand where she purchased another supply of the drug. On November 3, 1975, with four ounces of heroin on her person, she boarded a plane for the United States. During a routine customs search in Hawaii, she was searched, the heroin was discovered, and she was arrested. After discussions with Drug Enforcement Administration agents, she agreed to cooperate with the Government.

Prior to trial on this indictment, petitioner moved to sever his case from that of Roberts and Freeman. He advised the court that the Government intended to call his wife as an adverse witness and asserted his claim to a privilege to prevent her from testifying against him. At a hearing on the motion, Mrs. Trammel was called as a Government witness under a grant of use immunity. She testified that she and petitioner were married in May 1975 and that they remained married.[1] She explained that her cooperation with the Government was based on assurances that she would be given lenient treatment.[2] She then described, in considerable detail, her role and that of her husband in the heroin distribution conspiracy.

After hearing this testimony, the District Court ruled that Mrs. Trammel could testify in support of the Government's case to any act she observed during the marriage and to any communication "made in the presence of a third person"; however, confidential communications between petitioner and his wife were held to be privileged and inadmissible. The motion to sever was denied.

At trial, Elizabeth Trammel testified within the limits of the court's pretrial ruling; her testimony, as the Government concedes, constituted virtually its entire case against petitioner. He was found guilty on both the substantive and conspiracy charges and sentenced to an indeterminate term of years pursuant to the Federal Youth Corrections Act.

In the Court of Appeals petitioner's only claim of error was that the admission of the adverse testimony of his wife, over his objection, contravened this Court's teaching in Hawkins v. United States, supra, and therefore constituted reversible error. The Court of Appeals rejected this contention. It concluded that *Hawkins* did not prohibit "the voluntary testimony of a spouse who appears as an unindicted co-conspirator under grant of immunity from the Government in return for her testimony."

---

1. In response to the question whether divorce was contemplated, Mrs. Trammel testified that her husband had said that "I would go my way and he would go his."

2. The Government represents to the Court that Elizabeth Trammel has not been prosecuted for her role in the conspiracy.

II

The privilege claimed by petitioner has ancient roots. Writing in 1628, Lord Coke observed that "it hath beene resolved by the Justices that a wife cannot be produced either against or for her husband." 1 E. Coke, A Commentarie upon Littleton 6b (1628). This spousal disqualification sprang from two canons of medieval jurisprudence: first, the rule that an accused was not permitted to testify in his own behalf because of his interest in the proceeding; second, the concept that husband and wife were one, and that since the woman had no recognized separate legal existence, the husband was that one. From those two now long-abandoned doctrines, it followed that what was inadmissible from the lips of the defendant-husband was also inadmissible from his wife.

Despite its medieval origins, this rule of spousal disqualification remained intact in most common-law jurisdictions well into the 19th century. It was applied by this Court in Stein v. Bowman, 13 Pet. 209, 220-223, 10 L. Ed. 129 (1839) . . . and again in Jin Fuey Moy v. United States, 254 U.S. 189 (1920), where it was deemed so well established a proposition as to "hardly requir[e] mention." Indeed, it was not until 1933, in Funk v. United States, 290 U.S. 371, that this Court abolished the testimonial disqualification in the federal courts, so as to permit the spouse of a defendant to testify in the defendant's behalf. *Funk,* however, left undisturbed the rule that either spouse could prevent the other from giving adverse testimony. The rule thus evolved into one of privilege rather than one of absolute disqualification.

The modern justification for this privilege against adverse spousal testimony is its perceived role in fostering the harmony and sanctity of the marriage relationship. Notwithstanding this benign purpose, the rule was sharply criticized. Professor Wigmore termed it "the merest anachronism in legal theory and an indefensible obstruction to truth in practice." 8 Wigmore, §2228, at 221. . . . In its place, Wigmore and others suggested a privilege protecting only private marital communications, modeled on the privilege between priest and penitent, attorney and client, and physician and patient.[5]

These criticisms influenced the American Law Institute, which, in its 1942 Model Code of Evidence, advocated a privilege for marital confidences, but expressly rejected a rule vesting in the defendant the right to exclude all adverse testimony of his spouse. [See Rule 215 (1942).] In 1953 the Uniform Rules of Evidence, drafted by the National Conference of Commissioners on Uniform State Laws, followed a similar course; it limited the privilege to confidential communications and "abolishe[d] the rule, still existing in some states, and largely a sentimental relic, of not requiring one spouse to testify against the other in a criminal action." See Rule 23(2) and comments. Several state legislatures enacted similarly patterned provisions into law.

In Hawkins v. United States, 358 U.S. 74 (1958), this Court considered the

---

5. This Court recognized just such a confidential marital communications privilege in Wolfle v. United States, 291 U.S. 7 (1934), and in Blau v. United States, 340 U.S. 332 (1951). In neither case, however, did the Court adopt the Wigmore view that the communications privilege be substituted *in place* of the privilege against adverse spousal testimony. The privilege as to confidential marital communications is not at issue in the instant case; accordingly, our holding today does not disturb *Wolfle* and *Blau.*

continued vitality of the privilege against adverse spousal testimony in the federal courts. There the District Court had permitted petitioner's wife, over his objection, to testify against him. With one questioning concurring opinion, the Court held the wife's testimony inadmissible; it took note of the critical comments that the common-law rule had engendered, but chose not to abandon it. Also rejected was the Government's suggestion that the Court modify the privilege by vesting it in the witness-spouse, with freedom to testify or not independent of the defendant's control. The Court viewed this proposed modification as antithetical to the widespread belief, evidenced in the rules then in effect in a majority of the States and in England, "that the law should not force or encourage testimony which might alienate husband and wife, or further inflame existing domestic differences."

Hawkins, then, left the federal privilege for adverse spousal testimony where it found it, continuing "a rule which bars the testimony of one spouse against the other unless both consent." Accord, Wyatt v. United States, 362 U.S. 525 (1960).[7] However, in so doing, the Court made clear that its decision was not meant to "foreclose whatever changes in the rule may eventually be dictated by 'reason and experience.' "

III

A

The Federal Rules of Evidence acknowledge the authority of the federal courts to continue the evolutionary development of testimonial privileges in federal criminal trials "governed by the principles of the common law as they may be interpreted . . . in the light of reason and experience." FRE 501. The general mandate of Rule 501 was substituted by the Congress for a set of privilege rules drafted by the Judicial Conference Advisory Committee on Rules of Evidence and approved by the Judicial Conference of the United States and by this Court. That proposal defined nine specific privileges, including a husband-wife privilege which would have codified the *Hawkins* rule and eliminated the privilege for confidential marital communications. See proposed FRE 505. In rejecting the proposed Rules and enacting Rule 501, Congress manifested an affirmative intention not to freeze the law of privilege. Its purpose rather was to "provide the courts with the flexibility to develop rules of privilege on a case-by-case basis," 120 Cong. Rec. 40891 (1974) (statement of Rep. Hungate), and to leave the door open to change.[8]

---

7. The decision in *Wyatt* recognized an exception to *Hawkins* for cases in which one spouse commits a crime against the other. This exception, placed on the ground of necessity, was a longstanding one at common law. It has been expanded since then to include crimes against the spouse's property, and in recent years crimes against children of either spouse. Similar exceptions have been found to the confidential marital communications privilege.

8. Petitioner's reliance on 28 U.S.C. §2076 for the proposition that this Court is without power to reconsider *Hawkins* is ill-founded. That provision limits this Court's *statutory* rulemaking authority by providing that rules "creating, abolishing, or modifying a privilege shall have no force or effect unless . . . approved by act of Congress." It was enacted principally to insure that state rules of privilege would apply in diversity jurisdiction cases unless Congress authorized otherwise. In Rule 501 Congress makes clear that §2076 was not intended to prevent the federal

Although Rule 501 confirms the authority of the federal courts to reconsider the continued validity of the *Hawkins* rule, the long history of the privilege suggests that it ought not to be casually cast aside. That the privilege is one affecting marriage, home, and family relationships—already subject to much erosion in our day—also counsels caution. At the same time, we cannot escape the reality that the law on occasion adheres to doctrinal concepts long after the reasons which gave them birth have disappeared and after experience suggests the need for change. . . . Mr. Justice Black admonished in another setting, "[w]hen precedent and precedent alone is all the argument that can be made to support a court-fashioned rule, it is time for the rule's creator to destroy it." Francis v. Southern Pacific Co., 333 U.S. 445, 471 (1948) (dissenting opinion).

B

Since 1958, when *Hawkins* was decided, support for the privilege against adverse spousal testimony has been eroded further. Thirty-one jurisdictions, including Alaska and Hawaii, then allowed an accused a privilege to prevent adverse spousal testimony. The number has now declined to 24.[9] In 1974, the National Conference on Uniform State Laws revised its Uniform Rules of Evidence, but again rejected the *Hawkins* rule in favor of a limited privilege for confidential communications. See Uniform Rules of Evidence, Rule 504. That proposed rule has been enacted in Arkansas, North Dakota, and Oklahoma—each of which in 1958 permitted an accused to exclude adverse spousal testimony.[10] The trend in state law toward divesting the accused of the privilege to bar adverse spousal testimony has special relevance because the laws of marriage and domestic relations are concerns traditionally reserved to the states. Scholarly criticism of the *Hawkins* rule has also continued unabated.

---

courts from developing testimonial privilege law in federal criminal cases on a case-by-case basis "in light of reason and experience"; indeed, Congress encouraged such development.

9. [Court collects state statutes and suggests that they show that (a) eight states "provide that one spouse is incompetent to testify against the other in a criminal proceeding," (b) sixteen states "provide a privilege against adverse spousal testimony and vest the privilege in both spouses or in the defendant-spouse alone," (c) nine states "entitle the witness-spouse alone to assert a privilege against adverse spousal testimony," and (d) seventeen states "have abolished the privilege in criminal cases." The District of Columbia has a statute "which vests the privilege against adverse spousal testimony in the witness spouse."]

10. In 1965, California took the privilege from the defendant-spouse and vested it in the witness-spouse, accepting a study commission recommendation that the "latter [was] more likely than the former to determine whether or not to claim the privilege on the basis of the probable effect on the marital relationship." See Cal. Evid. Code Ann. §§970-973 (West 1966 and Supp. 1979) and 1 California Law Revision Commission, Recommendation and Study Relating to the Marital "For and Against" Testimonial Privilege, at F-5 (1956). See also 6 California Law Revision Commission, Tentative Privileges Recommendation—Rule 27.5, pp. 243-244 (1964).

Support for the common-law rule has also diminished in England. In 1972, a study group there proposed giving the privilege to the witness-spouse, on the ground that "if [the wife] is willing to give evidence . . . the law would be showing excessive concern for the preservation of marital harmony if it were to say that she must not do so." Criminal Law Revision Committee, Eleventh Report, Evidence (General) 93.

C

Testimonial exclusionary rules and privileges contravene the fundamental principle that " 'the public . . . has a right to every man's evidence.'" United States v. Bryan, 339 U.S. 323, 331 (1950). As such, they must be strictly construed and accepted "only to the very limited extent that permitting a refusal to testify or excluding relevant evidence has a public good transcending the normally predominant principle of utilizing all rational means for ascertaining truth." Elkins v. United States, 364 U.S. 206, 234 (1960) (Frankfurter, J., dissenting). Here we must decide whether the privilege against adverse spousal testimony promotes sufficiently important interests to outweigh the need for probative evidence in the administration of criminal justice.

It is essential to remember that the *Hawkins* privilege is not needed to protect information privately disclosed between husband and wife in the confidence of the marital relationship—once described by this Court as "the best solace of human existence." Stein v. Bowman, 13 Pet., at 223, 10 L. Ed. 129 [1839]. Those confidences are privileged under the independent rule protecting confidential marital communications. The *Hawkins* privilege is invoked, not to exclude private marital communications, but rather to exclude evidence of criminal acts and of communications made in the presence of third persons.

No other testimonial privilege sweeps so broadly. The privileges between priest and penitent, attorney and client, and physician and patient limit protection to private communications. These privileges are rooted in the imperative need for confidence and trust. The priest-penitent privilege recognizes the human need to disclose to a spiritual counselor, in total and absolute confidence, what are believed to be flawed acts or thoughts and to receive priestly consolation and guidance in return. The lawyer-client privilege rests on the need for the advocate and counselor to know all that relates to the client's reasons for seeking representation if the professional mission is to be carried out. Similarly, the physician must know all that a patient can articulate in order to identify and to treat disease; barriers to full disclosure would impair diagnosis and treatment.

The *Hawkins* rule stands in marked contrast to these three privileges. Its protection is not limited to confidential communications; rather it permits an accused to exclude all adverse spousal testimony. As Jeremy Bentham observed more than a century and a half ago, such a privilege goes far beyond making "every man's house his castle," and permits a person to convert his house into "a den of thieves." 5 Rationale of Judicial Evidence 340 (1827). It "secures, to every man, one safe and unquestionable and ever ready accomplice for every imaginable crime."

The ancient foundations for so sweeping a privilege have long since disappeared. Nowhere in the common-law world—indeed in any modern society—is a woman regarded as chattel or demeaned by denial of a separate legal identity and the dignity associated with recognition as a whole human being. Chip by chip, over the years those archaic notions have been cast aside so that "[n]o longer is the female destined solely for the home and the rearing of the family, and only the male for the marketplace and the world of ideas."

The contemporary justification for affording an accused such a privilege is also unpersuasive. When one spouse is willing to testify against the other in a criminal proceeding—whatever the motivation—their relationship is almost certainly in disrepair; there is probably little in the way of marital harmony for the privilege to preserve. In these circumstances, a rule of evidence that permits an accused to prevent adverse spousal testimony seems far more likely to frustrate justice than to foster family peace. Indeed, there is reason to believe that vesting the privilege in the accused could actually undermine the marital relationship. For example, in a case such as this, the Government is unlikely to offer a wife immunity and lenient treatment if it knows that her husband can prevent her from giving adverse testimony. If the Government is dissuaded from making such an offer, the privilege can have the untoward effect of permitting one spouse to escape justice at the expense of the other. It hardly seems conducive to the preservation of the marital relation to place a wife in jeopardy solely by virtue of her husband's control over her testimony.

IV

Our consideration of the foundations for the privilege and its history satisfy us that "reason and experience" no longer justify so sweeping a rule as that found acceptable by the Court in *Hawkins*. Accordingly, we conclude that the existing rule should be modified so that the witness-spouse alone has a privilege to refuse to testify adversely; the witness may be neither compelled to testify nor foreclosed from testifying. This modification—vesting the privilege in the witness-spouse—furthers the important public interest in marital harmony without unduly burdening legitimate law enforcement needs.

Here, petitioner's spouse chose to testify against him. That she did so after a grant of immunity and assurances of lenient treatment does not render her testimony involuntary. Accordingly, the District Court and the Court of Appeals were correct in rejecting petitioner's claim of privilege, and the judgment of the Court of Appeals is Affirmed.

NOTES ON SPOUSAL TESTIMONIAL PRIVILEGE

1. *Trammel* endorses a testimonial privilege held only by the witness-spouse. Are you convinced by the Court's argument that when one spouse is willing to testify against the other, "their relationship is almost certainly in disrepair," and that enabling the defendant to bar the testimony could "undermine the marital relationship"? What new tool does *Trammel* provide to prosecutors when both spouses are implicated in criminal activity?

2. The Tenth Circuit in *Trammel* had denied the privilege by invoking a supposed "joint participants" exception. See United States v. Trammel, 583 F.2d 1166, 1168-1169 (10th Cir. 1980). Under such an exception, the testimonial privilege does not apply, regardless who is the holder, when the spouses were joint participants in the crime. Nowhere does the Supreme Court's opinion mention this point. Does that mean that there is, or that there is not, a joint participants exception after *Trammel*? Consider the case in which an unindicted wife is unwilling to testify against her husband in a criminal prosecution. If the two are coparticipants in the underlying venture, then the existence of a joint participants exception would enable the government to force her to testify,

even if it could not otherwise do so under *Trammel*. Should her testimony be compellable in such a case? Compare In re Grand Jury Subpoena (Koecher), 755 F.2d 1022, 1026-1027 (2d Cir. 1985) ("somewhat peculiar" that *Trammel* overlooked this point while engaging in a "much broader assault" on the privilege; *Trammel* has "negative implications" for the joint participants exception, and the reviewing court is "unable to accept the proposition that a marriage cannot be a devoted one simply because at some time the partners have decided to engage in a criminal activity"), vacated and dismissed as moot, 475 U.S. 133 (1986) with United States v. Clark, 712 F.2d 299, 300-301 (7th Cir. 1983) (joint participants exception survives, for "rehabilitative effect of a marriage, which in part justifies the privilege, is diminished when both spouses are participants in the crime").

3. Of course a marriage must be valid when the privilege is invoked, see People v. Catlin, 26 P.3d 357, 389 (2001) (denying privilege because murder defendant's second marriage was bigamous). Given *Trammel*'s comments about a relationship "in disrepair," should courts inquire broadly into the health of the marriage when the privilege is invoked, denying protection where the marriage seems "on the rocks"? Compare United States v. Brown, 605 F.2d 389, 396 (8th Cir.) (in overruling claim of privilege, court notes that wife had been with defendant husband for only two weeks and had not seen him for eight months after he left her, hence that it was "difficult to visualize" how the underlying values could be served by applying the privilege), cert. denied, 444 U.S. 972 (1979) with United States v. Lilley, 581 F.2d 182, 189 (8th Cir. 1978) (declining invitation to condition claim of spousal testimony privilege on "judicial determination that the marriage is a happy or successful one"). See Note, "Honey, the Judge Says We're History": Abrogating the Marital Privileges via Modern Doctrines of Marital Worthiness, 77 Cornell L. Rev. 843 (1992).

4. What if the spouses are recently married, and the primary purpose of the marriage seems to be blocking the testimony of one against the other? See Lutwak v. United States, 344 U.S. 604, 614-615 (1953) (war brides case in which defendants and aliens had apparently married abroad without intending to live together as spouses; such "sham, phony, empty ceremony" rendered testimonial privilege unavailable); United States v. Saniti, 604 F.2d 603, 604 (9th Cir.) (where marriage was a sham, wife of defendant was properly allowed to testify against him), cert. denied, 444 U.S. 969 (1979). Is a marriage entered into after the crime and just prior to trial *necessarily* a sham, for purposes of the privilege? See San Fratello v. United States, 340 F.2d 560, 566 (5th Cir. 1965) (fact that defendant marries witness after crime and shortly before trial did not entitle prosecutor to call spouse to testify).

5. Does the privilege apply to gay couples? See generally Peter Nicolas, "They Say He's Gay": The Admissibility of Evidence of Sexual Orientation, 37 Ga. L. Rev. 793, 871 (reporting "little consensus among the states as to the applicability of the spousal privileges to same-sex couples," noting that only Vermont recognizes such a privilege by statute, and that only one reported decision has "expressly considered and rejected" such a privilege, citing a New York case).

6. Consider the exceptions recognized by *Trammel* in footnote 7, which include prosecutions of one spouse for a crime against the other, or the children of either. Should that exception embrace situations in which a spouse is an

apparently willing victim in a consensual criminal act? See Wyatt v. United States, 362 U.S. 525 (1960) (spousal testimonial privilege inapplicable in Mann Act prosecution where defendant was charged with prostituting his own wife, even though both defendant-husband and witness-wife sought to invoke the privilege, for the statute assumes that husbands induce their wives against their will to engage in such acts).

7.   Five years before *Trammel* the Court had accepted the Advisory Committee's proposal of a privilege held only by the party spouse (see proposed Rule 505). And 20 years before that the Court in *Hawkins* had endorsed a privilege that either witness-spouse or party-spouse could invoke. Does *Trammel* represent the kind of common law evolution that Congress had in mind in adopting FRE 501 in preference to specific provisions? Is *Trammel* consistent with the spirit of the Enabling Act that bars rulemaking by the Court in the privilege area, unless Congress approves?

PROBLEM 12-G.   Hit-and-Run

Charley and his wife Edith were returning home late one night from a party where they both had too much to drink. Charley, who was driving, failed to see Max, an elderly pedestrian who was crossing the street at a properly marked crosswalk. He struck and killed him. Charley panicked and, over Edith's screams, fled the scene without stopping and returned to their home.

After they entered their house, Pam, the babysitter, asked Edith why she was so upset. She tearfully replied, "Because Charley ran over someone on the way home." After a police investigation, criminal charges are brought against Charley for vehicular manslaughter.

At trial, Edith refuses to testify for the prosecution, claiming the testimonial privilege. The prosecutor then calls Pam as a witness at trial to relate what Edith had said to her. The court finds that Edith's statement to Pam qualifies under the excited utterance exception to the hearsay rule, but both Charley and Edith object to Pam's testimony, again asserting the testimonial privilege. What ruling?

3.   Spousal Confidences Privilege

The privilege for spousal confidences has long been recognized as a necessary protection for the marital relationship. Long ago the Supreme Court praised the privilege as one based on "the deepest and soundest principles of our nature," suggesting that any inroad on the privilege would "destroy the best solace of human existence." Stein v. Bowman, 38 U.S. 209, 222-223 (1839). And recall that the modern Court, even as it sliced the testimonial privilege in half in *Trammel,* was at pains to say that the spousal confidences privilege was "not at issue" there, and that it did not "disturb" prior holdings on that privilege.

A doctrine under attack. Despite such statements of support, the privilege has come under siege. Modern courts, scholars, and reformers have attacked the doctrine.

Consider these arguments: Spousal confidences, covered at the time of their utterance, should be stripped of protection if the couple later obtains a divorce. McCormick on Evidence §85, at 131 (J. Strong 5th ed. 1999). The privilege should be abolished altogether (the position taken by the Advisory Committee that drafted the Rules) for these reasons:

> The traditional justifications for privileges not to testify against a spouse and not to be testified against by one's spouse have been the prevention of marital dissension and the repugnancy of requiring a person to condemn or be condemned by his spouse. These considerations bear no relevancy to marital communications. Nor can it be assumed that marital conduct will be affected by a privilege for confidential communications of whose existence the parties in all likelihood are unaware.

ACN to Proposed Rule 505, 56 F.R.D. 245-246 (1972).

The privilege defended. The Advisory Committee may have been surprised at the vigor of modern defenders of the privilege, whose reaction helped scuttle *all* of the specific privilege proposals in Congress. Consider this modern defense of the privilege, advanced by Professor Louisell in response to what he considered to be the overemphasis on the instrumentalist approach:

> A marriage without the right of complete privacy of communication would necessarily be an imperfect union. Utter freedom of marital communication from all government supervision, constraint, control or observation, save only when the communications are for an illegal purpose, is a psychological necessity for the perfect fulfillment of marriage. Recognition by the state that spouses possess such right of confidential communication by reason of the nature of their relationship, promotes the public policy of furthering and safeguarding the objectives of marriage just as other institutions in the area of domestic relations or family law promote it.

Louisell, Confidentiality, Conformity and Confusion: Privileges in Federal Court Today, 31 Tul. L. Rev. 101, 111-113 (1956). Recall too the constitutional right of privacy recognized in Griswold v. Connecticut, 381 U.S. 479 (1965) (state cannot bar use of contraceptives by married couples).

And consider this response by Professor Krattenmaker to the instrumentalist argument advanced by the Advisory Committee. Assuming that spousal conversations "take place without conscious, simultaneous awareness of the privilege," he replied:

> This proves little without the further assumption that subconscious, unarticulated knowledge never can influence human conduct. Surely, there is little reason to doubt that where they exist, interpersonal privileges such as that for confidential marital communications as well as confessions to clergymen provide at the very least a subconscious backdrop to the exercise of the right of privacy.

Krattenmaker, Testimonial Privileges in Federal Courts: An Alternative to the Proposed Federal Rules of Evidence, 62 Geo. L.J. 60, 92 (1973).

In protesting the Advisory Committee's decision to abolish the privilege for spousal confidences, Professor Black argued:

It ought to be enough to say of such a rule that it could easily—even often—force any decent person—anybody any of us would want to associate with—either to lie or to go to jail. No rule can be good that has that consequence—that compels the decent and honorable to evade or to disobey it.

Black, The Marital and Physician Privileges—A Reprint of a Letter to a Congressman, 1975 Duke L.J. 45, 48.

Consider this debate further in the context of the *Estes* case, where the court confronts a claim of the spousal confidences privilege in a particularly challenging factual setting.

UNITED STATES v. ESTES
United States Court of Appeals for the Second Circuit
793 F.2d 465 (2d Cir. 1986)

[Some of the ensuing facts are drawn from the trial court opinion in United States v. Estes, 609 F. Supp. 564 (D. Vt. 1985). Kenneth Estes was charged with bank robbery, arising out of the theft from a Purolator Armored Car of $55,000, and with committing perjury by lying to a grand jury investigating the theft. Estes worked for Purolator as a driver-guard. He arrived home one day with a motorcycle saddlebag full of cash. His wife Lydia noticed that he "had a strange look on his face." When she asked "what was wrong" he "showed her the money," which he "poured . . . onto the couple's bed." Defendant told Lydia that "he stole the money from Purolator." Initially she wanted to return it, but she changed her mind because the couple was so poor that "they could not adequately provide for their three children." Defendant removed and destroyed the top and bottom bills in each bundle, placed most of the loot in a plastic cooler, and buried it near a reservoir. Lydia hid the remaining $15,000 in a hollow place behind the stairs. She "laundered" some of the cash by exchanging numerous small-denomination stolen bills for larger bills, and the couple thereafter purchased "several items for their home, including a television, a stereo, mattresses and linens for their children's beds and kitchen supplies," as well as a used van. They returned several times to the reservoir to replenish their supply.

Before trial, Lydia and Kenneth were divorced. She had moved out and gone to live with a friend, but she purchased drugs for Kenneth for a time, apparently because he threatened "to file a claim for desertion." Lydia eventually contacted the FBI, obtaining a grant of immunity for herself and then taping conversations with Kenneth. Eventually she testified "willingly" before the grand jury and at the trial of Kenneth Estes, describing his arrival with the money, his confession, their activities in counting and hiding the money, and her acts in laundering the bills. Kenneth Estes was convicted of perjury, and he appealed.]

Van Graafeiland, J.

Appellant contends that all of Lydia's testimony should have been excluded on the ground that it involved the disclosure of confidential communications between them. The district court rejected this contention, citing cases from other circuits which hold that "confidential marital communications concerning ongoing criminal activity are not protected by the privilege" and opining that this is likely to be the rule followed by the Second Circuit. The district court's very statement of the rule shows, however, that it does not apply to the most damning testimony given by Lydia, viz., that appellant brought home a bag of money and told her that he had taken it from the Purolator truck.

At that time, the theft of the money had been completed and Lydia's involvement could be only as an accessory after the fact. Lydia could not become such an accessory until she knew that the theft had taken place. The communication to her of that knowledge was a necessary precursor to her involvement and therefore could not have been made as part of an ongoing joint criminal activity. Under the normal evidentiary rule applicable to confidential marital communications, this portion of Lydia's testimony should not have been admitted. . . .

Normally, the confidential communication privilege extends only to utterances and not to acts. Testimony concerning a spouse's conduct can be precluded upon the spouse's challenge only in the rare instances where the conduct was intended to convey a confidential message from the actor to the observer. The counting, hiding and laundering of the money conveyed no confidential message from appellant to Lydia. Acts do not become privileged communications simply because they are performed in the presence of the actor's spouse. "Nor does it appear that the essential qualities of communication and confidentiality flow automatically from the fact that the act seen by the other spouse is one that connotes criminal conduct." United States v. Lewis, 433 F.2d [1146] at 1151 [(D.C. Cir. 1970)]. Lydia's testimony concerning the handling and disposition of the money, much of which was done by Lydia herself, was properly heard by both the grand and petit juries.

Assuming for the argument that one or more of appellant's acts which followed the original disclosure of his theft might be construed as additional confidential communications of wrongdoing, we agree with so much of the opinion in United States v. Neal, 743 F.2d [1441] at 1446-47 [(10th Cir. 1984), cert. denied 470 U.S. 1086 (1985)], as would support the district court's holding that Lydia's testimony concerning those acts was admissible as evidence of joint criminal activity. . . . Although an accused does have the right to object to spousal testimony which violates confidential communications privilege, a number of circuits, in addition to the Tenth Circuit which decided United States v. Neal, supra, refuse to recognize that right where the testimony is not given under compulsion and the communications in question were made in furtherance of unlawful joint criminal activity. . . .

The above-cited courts which recognize the "partnership in crime" exception to the confidential communication privilege believe that greater public good will result from permitting the spouse of an accused to testify willingly concerning their joint criminal activities than would come from permitting the accused to erect a roadblock against the search for truth. We agree.

For all the reasons above stated, we hold that Lydia's testimony concerning appellant's initial disclosure of his theft should not have been admitted but that it was not error to admit the balance of Lydia's testimony dealing with the handling and disposition of the stolen money.

[The conviction is reversed and the case remanded for a new trial.]

NOTES ON SPOUSAL CONFIDENCES

1. Federal courts have generally limited the privilege to confidential communications. See Garcia-Jaramillo v. Immigration and Naturalization Service, 604 F.2d 1236, 1238 (9th Cir. 1979) (no privilege bars postdivorce testimony by spouse as to "sexual relations between former spouses"); United States v. Smith, 533 F.2d 1077, 1079 (8th Cir. 1976) (spousal confidences privilege could not block testimony by wife that husband hid heroin in her underclothing during airplane flight). State courts have different views regarding the extent to which the spousal confidences privilege reaches private acts by one spouse in the presence of the other. See Stewart v. Wilson, 88 S.E.2d 752 (Ga. App. 1955) (spousal confidences privilege bars wife's testimony concerning husband's drinking habits); People v. Daghita, 86 N.E.2d 172 (N.Y. 1949) (on facts similar to *Estes,* wife should not have been permitted to describe husband's display of proceeds of theft; privilege reaches "knowledge derived from the observance of disclosive acts done in the presence or view of one spouse by the other because of the confidence existing between them by reason of the marital relation and which would not have been performed except for the confidence so existing"). *Should* the spousal confidences privilege reach private acts done by one spouse in the presence of the other?

2. If Kenneth and Lydia Estes had still been married when Kenneth was tried, *Trammel* would have prevented him from resorting to the testimonial privilege to block her testimony (assuming her willingness to take the stand). But before *Trammel,* a still-married Kenneth Estes could have invoked the testimonial privilege to block *all* testimony by Lydia. Does *Trammel* mean that defendants married to spouses who collaborate with the prosecutor will push to expand the marital confidences privilege to cover acts?

3. Should there be an exception to the privilege in cases where one spouse is prosecuted for a crime against the other or against the child of either? See United States v. White, 974 F.2d 1135, 1138 (9th Cir. 1992) (privilege does not apply to "statements relating to a crime where a spouse or a spouse's children are the victims").

4. Courts generally recognize that the privilege does not apply in the case of spousal suits, such as divorce or child custody litigation. Cf. Chamberlain v. Chamberlain, 230 S.W.2d 184 (Mo. App. 1950) (wife's testimony describing the "unnatural sexual demands" of her husband held outside the communications privilege—because demands not shown to have been made verbally!).

5. Generally the confidences privilege does not apply to spousal communications in the presence of outsiders. How should courts handle conversations in the presence of children of the marriage? See Wolfle v. United States, 291 U.S. 7, 17 (1934) (citing with approval the principle that "communications between husband and wife, voluntarily made in the presence of their children,

old enough to comprehend them, or other members of the family within the
intimacy of the family circle, are not privileged").

PROBLEM 12-H.   The Child Molester

Rodney lives with Trish and her seven-year-old daughter Stacy in a trailer
that Trish obtained in her divorce settlement with her former husband (father
of Stacy). On August 30 Rodney and Trish marry, and in October Rodney is
charged with sexual abuse of Stacy and Rhonda (a friend of Stacy's who lives
next door).

The charges include allegations that Rodney abused both Stacy and Rhonda
while the two were having an overnight on July 14 in the trailer in Rodney's
care. The girls will testify that Rodney handcuffed them together and touched
them in inappropriate ways.

Trish recalls that Rodney was alone with the girls on the night of July 14
and that Stacy and Rhonda seemed subdued and secretive when she returned
late in the evening. Trish also recalls that during the following week she saw
Rodney experimenting on himself with a pair of handcuffs while the two were
watching TV in the living space of the trailer, and that he commented that he
had "used these cuffs on the girls last week when they wouldn't be quiet and
go to sleep."

After charges are filed in October (two months after Rodney and Trish
are married), Rodney admits to Trish that he sexually molested Stacy and
Rhonda on the night they were in his care. Rodney also tells Trish that he plans
"to deny everything because nobody can prove it anyway since the girls did
misbehave and it's just their word against mine."

Suppose Trish is called as a witness, but is reluctant to testify. (a) Can she
invoke either the spousal confidences privilege or the testimonial privilege to
avoid testifying about the handcuffs she saw in Rodney's possession or about
his being alone with the girls on July 14th? (b) Can she invoke the spousal
confidences privilege to avoid describing his confession of sexually molesting
the girls? (c) Can Rodney claim either the testimonial privilege or the spousal
confidences privilege? (d) Would your answers to these questions differ if
Rodney were charged only with molesting Rhonda?

E.   THE PRIVILEGE AGAINST SELF-INCRIMINATION

1. An Overview

The only privilege expressly recognized by the United States Constitution is
the privilege against self-incrimination, guaranteed by the Fifth Amendment.
Such a privilege is also recognized, in varying language, by most state constitutions. In Malloy v. Hogan, 378 U.S. 1 (1964), the Supreme Court held that the
federal privilege applies to the states as a component of Due Process under
the Fourteenth Amendment. Although the state provisions are important to
the extent that they may be interpreted to provide broader protection than the

federal privilege, the Fifth Amendment establishes a constitutional minimum in both state and federal proceedings.

The Fifth Amendment provides that "No person shall be . . . compelled in any criminal case to be a witness against himself." This language could be interpreted as guaranteeing the privilege only in criminal trials, and then only when asserted by the defendant. This narrow reading has been rejected by the Court. It is now settled that the privilege applies in civil cases as well as criminal, during pretrial as well as trial, and may be asserted not only by a criminal defendant but by any party or witness. The privilege is recognized in administrative and legislative proceedings as well as judicial proceedings. It applies whenever governmental power (most commonly the contempt power) may be used to compel testimony. The justification for this broader reading is that the privilege against self-incrimination would have little meaning if the government were free to compel an incriminating statement from a person in a noncriminal context and then offer the statement against the individual in a criminal proceeding.

The rationale for the privilege has been summarized by the Court as follows:

> It reflects many of our fundamental values and most noble aspirations; our unwillingness to subject those suspected of crime to the cruel trilemma of self-accusation, perjury or contempt; our preference for an accusatorial rather than an inquisitorial system of criminal justice; our fear that self-incriminating statements will be elicited by inhumane treatment and abuses; our sense of fair play which dictates "a fair state-individual balance by requiring the government to leave the individual alone until good cause is shown for disturbing him and by requiring the government in its contest with the individual to shoulder the entire load,". . . ; our respect for the inviolability of the human personality and of the right of each individual "to a private enclave where he may lead a private life,". . . ; our distrust of self-deprecatory statements; and our realization that the privilege, while sometimes "a shelter to the guilty," is often "a protection to the innocent."

Murphy v. Waterfront Commission, 378 U.S. 52, 55 (1964). See generally Dolinko, Is There a Rationale for the Privilege Against Self-Incrimination?, 33 UCLA L. Rev. 1063 (1986); Levy, Origins of the Fifth Amendment (1968); Gerstein, The Demise of *Boyd:* Self-Incrimination and Private Papers in the Burger Court, 27 UCLA L. Rev. 343 (1979); Friendly, The Fifth Amendment Tomorrow: The Case for Constitutional Change, 37 U. Cin. L. Rev. 671 (1968); Griswold, The Right to Be Let Alone, 55 Nw. U. L. Rev. 216 (1960).

2. Persons Protected

The privilege against self-incrimination belongs only to an individual. It cannot be asserted by corporations, labor unions, or, in most cases, other unincorporated associations or partnerships. According to the Court, the test is

> whether one can fairly say under all the circumstances that a particular type of organization has a character so impersonal in the scope of its membership and activities that it cannot be said to embody or represent the purely private or personal interest of its constituents, but rather to embody their common or group

interests only. If so, the privilege cannot be invoked on behalf of the organization or its representatives in their official capacity.

United States v. White, 322 U.S. 694, 701 (1944).

Because the privilege is personal, one of several codefendants cannot raise the privilege belonging to another. Nor can an attorney or agent rely on the Fifth Amendment as justification for refusing to testify or produce evidence that would be incriminating to the client or principal. A corporate employee is obligated to produce corporate records held in an official capacity even if they would incriminate him personally.

3. Scope of Privilege

The prohibition against compelling a person to "be a witness" against himself could be interpreted so broadly as to bar any action against a defendant that might produce incriminating evidence, even compelling him to come to court for trial, if it would facilitate eyewitness identification. Here the Court has adopted a narrower reading, holding that the privilege applies only to evidence that is "testimonial." The Fifth Amendment does not protect against compelled production of evidence, even though incriminating, that is not communicative in nature. In the leading case of Schmerber v. California, 384 U.S. 757 (1966), the Court held that the involuntary taking of a blood sample from the defendant did not violate his privilege against self-incrimination. Other cases have held that the privilege is not offended by requiring the defendant to be fingerprinted or photographed, to participate in a lineup, to submit a handwriting sample, to wear or remove certain clothing or a toupee for identification purposes, to speak for purposes of voice identification, or to submit a hair sample.

PROBLEM 12-I.   The Noncooperative Driver

While driving home from a tavern late one night, Darrell sideswipes a parked car. He does not stop, but a passerby notes his license number and phones the police. Darrell is stopped by a police officer ten minutes later. After failing a field sobriety test, he is placed under arrest for driving under the influence of intoxicants and failing to leave his name at the scene of an accident. At the police station, he is asked whether he would be willing to take a breathalyzer test. He is informed that under the state's implied consent law, refusal to take the test will result in automatic suspension of his driver's license for 90 days. Darrell nonetheless declines.

At trial, the prosecutor offers evidence of Darrell's refusal to take the breathalyzer test as evidence against him. Darrell objects, claiming the privilege against self-incrimination. In addition, he challenges the constitutionality of the statute requiring him to leave his name at the scene of an accident, claiming that this requirement also violates his privilege against self-incrimination. What result?

4. Incrimination

The privilege protects only against compelled disclosure that could lead to criminal liability, not disclosure that provides the basis for a civil damage claim or results in social embarrassment or public condemnation. In one case, the Supreme Court held that a claim of privilege should be upheld whenever it is "evident from the implications of the question, in the setting in which it was asked, that a responsive answer or an explanation of why it cannot be answered might be dangerous because injurious disclosure could result." But the Court added that a privilege claim may be overruled only when it is "perfectly clear, from a careful consideration of all the circumstances in the case, that the witness is mistaken, and the answer[s] cannot possibly have such tendency to incriminate." Hoffman v. United States, 341 U.S. 479, 486-488 (1951).

The privilege applies only where a danger of criminal liability still exists. Therefore, if the statute of limitations has run, the witness has received a pardon, or prosecution would be barred by the Double Jeopardy Clause, the privilege no longer applies. The fact that a privilege claimant has already been convicted does not necessarily end his protection, at least where an appeal is still available, because there is always the possibility of a reversal and a new trial. But where the only remaining challenge to the conviction is by collateral attack, courts are inclined to overrule a privilege claim in absence of a showing that the collateral attack is likely to be successful.

An important mechanism for eliminating the danger of incrimination, thereby obviating the privilege and making it possible to compel the witness to testify, is a grant of immunity. There are two types of immunity: "transactional immunity," which protects the witness against any future prosecution relating to the matter about which his testimony is being compelled, and "use immunity," which precludes future use of the testimony in any prosecution that might be brought, but which does not block future prosecution based on other evidence not derived from the testimony. Use immunity is obviously less protective of a witness, and for many years it was assumed that transactional immunity would have to be granted in order to vitiate the privilege. However, in Kastigar v. United States, 406 U.S. 441 (1972), the Supreme Court held that a grant of use immunity is sufficient to override the privilege and compel incriminating testimony. But if a later prosecution is brought, the government bears the burden of proving that the evidence it offers was derived from a source wholly independent of the compelled testimony.

The privilege is applicable even where the threat of criminal liability comes from another sovereign—one *other than* the jurisdiction seeking to compel the testimony. However, the fact that the testimony would be incriminating under the law of another jurisdiction does not necessarily provide a basis for refusal to testify, but rather a ground under the federal Constitution for preventing use of that testimony in the other jurisdiction.

In Murphy v. Waterfront Commission, 378 U.S. 52 (1964), the Court held that the privilege protects a witness whose testimony was compelled in a state proceeding from having that testimony used against him in a federal prosecution. The Court announced that it would exercise its supervisory powers over the federal courts to require exclusion of such testimony. In dictum, the Court indicated that testimony must also be excluded in the reverse situation, where it is compelled from a witness in a federal proceeding and later offered in a state proceeding. It also seems clear that testimony compelled from a witness in one state cannot be used against that witness in a prosecution in another state.

The most problematic case, where courts are divided, arises where the potential criminal liability exists under the laws of a foreign sovereign. Because it is not possible for courts in this country to prevent future use of that testimony in a foreign prosecution, recognition of such potential incrimination as a basis for the privilege could result in complete loss of the testimony. Such a result is more extreme than the outcome in domestic cases, where the testimony can be obtained if future use is restricted. Compare Mishima v. United States, 507 F. Supp. 131 (D. Alaska 1981) (privilege applies) with In re Campbell, 628 F.2d 1260 (9th Cir. 1980) ("the possibility of the use of grand jury testimony by a foreign jurisdiction does not violate a witness' privilege against self-incrimination").

5. Drawing of Adverse Inferences

The most common form of governmental compulsion against which the privilege is directed is a contempt citation for refusal to answer questions. However, compulsion can come in other forms, including physical force and psychological coercion. In Miranda v. Arizona, 384 U.S. 436 (1966), the Supreme Court held that even custodial police interrogation is sufficiently coercive to justify extension of the protections of the privilege to this context.

Sometimes a later penalty or adverse consequence is imposed on a witness because he has asserted the privilege. If the witness knows that such a consequence will be imposed, does the threat of such penalty or consequence amount to compulsion within the meaning of the Fifth Amendment? Consider the following case.

> ### GRIFFIN v. CALIFORNIA
> **United States Supreme Court**
> **380 U.S. 609 (1965)**

MR. JUSTICE DOUGLAS delivered the opinion of the Court.

Petitioner was convicted of murder in the first degree after a jury trial in a California court. He did not testify at the trial on the issue of guilt, though he did testify at the separate trial on the issue of penalty. The trial court instructed the jury on the issue of guilt, stating that a defendant has a constitutional right not to testify. But it told the jury:

> As to any evidence or facts against him which the defendant can reasonably be expected to deny or explain because of facts within his knowledge, if he does not testify or if, though he does testify, he fails to deny or explain such evidence, the jury may take that failure into consideration as tending to indicate the truth of

such evidence and as indicating that among the inferences that may be reasonably drawn therefrom those unfavorable to the defendant are the more probable . . .

Petitioner had been seen with the deceased the evening of her death, the evidence placing him with her in the alley where her body was found. The prosecutor made much of the failure of petitioner to testify:

> . . . He would know how she got down the alley. He would know how the blood got on the bottom of the concrete steps. He would know how long he was with her in that box. He would know how her wig got off. He would know whether he beat her or mistreated her. . . .
>
> These things he has not seen fit to take the stand and deny or explain.
>
> And in the whole world, if anybody would know, this defendant would know.
>
> Essie Mae is dead, she can't tell you her side of the story. The defendant won't.

The death penalty was imposed and the California Supreme Court affirmed. The case is here on a writ of certiorari. . . .

If this were a federal trial, reversible error would have been committed. Wilson v. United States, 149 U.S. 60, so holds. It is said, however, that the *Wilson* decision rested not on the Fifth Amendment, but on an Act of Congress, now 18 U.S.C. §3481. That indeed is the fact, as the opinion of the Court in the *Wilson* case states. But that is the beginning, not the end, of our inquiry. The question remains whether, statute or not, the comment rule, approved by California, violates the Fifth Amendment.

We think it does. It is in substance a rule of evidence that allows the State the privilege of tendering to the jury for its consideration the failure of the accused to testify. No formal offer of proof is made as in other situations; but the prosecutor's comment and the court's acquiescence are the equivalent of an offer of evidence and its acceptance. The Court in the *Wilson* case stated:

> . . . It is not every one who can safely venture on the witness stand though entirely innocent of the charge against him. Excessive timidity, nervousness when facing others and attempting to explain transactions of a suspicious character, and offences charged against him, will often confuse and embarrass him to such a degree as to increase rather than remove prejudices against him. It is not every one, however honest, who would, therefore, willingly be placed on the witness stand. The statute, in tenderness to the weakness of those who from the causes mentioned might refuse to ask to be a witness, particularly when they may have been in some degree compromised by their association with others, declares that the failure of the defendant in a criminal action to request to be a witness shall not create any presumption against him.

If the words "Fifth Amendment" are substituted for . . . "statute," the spirit of the Self-Incrimination Clause is reflected. For comment on the refusal to testify is a remnant of the "inquisitorial system of criminal justice," which the Fifth Amendment outlaws. It is a penalty imposed by courts for exercising a constitutional privilege. It cuts down on the privilege by making its assertion costly. It is said, however, that the inference of guilt for failure to testify as to facts peculiarly within the accused's knowledge is in any event natural and irresistible, and that comment on the failure does not magnify that inference into a penalty for asserting a constitutional privilege. People v. Modesto, 62 Cal. 2d 436, 452-453, 398 P.2d 753, 762-763. What the jury may infer, given no help from the court is one thing. What it may infer when the court solemnizes the silence of the accused into evidence against him is quite another. That the inference of guilt is not always so natural or irresistible is brought out in the *Modesto* opinion itself:

> Defendant contends that the reason a defendant refuses to testify is that his prior convictions will be introduced in evidence to impeach him and not that he is unable to deny the accusations. It is true that the defendant might fear that his prior convictions will prejudice the jury, and therefore another possible inference can be drawn from his refusal to take the stand.

We said in Malloy v. Hogan that "the same standards must determine whether an accused's silence in either a federal or state proceeding is justified." We take that in its literal sense and hold that the Fifth Amendment, in its direct application to the Federal Government, and in its bearing on the States by reason of the Fourteenth Amendment, forbids either comment by the prosecution on the accused's silence or instructions by the court that such silence is evidence of guilt.

Reversed.

MR. JUSTICE STEWART, with whom MR. JUSTICE WHITE joins, dissenting. . . .

We must determine whether the petitioner has been "compelled . . . to be a witness against himself." Compulsion is the focus of the inquiry. Certainly, if any compulsion be detected in the California procedure, it is of a dramatically different and less palpable nature than that involved in the procedures which historically gave rise to the Fifth Amendment guarantee. When a suspect was brought before the Court of High Commission or the Star Chamber, he was commanded to answer whatever was asked of him, and subjected to a far-reaching and deeply probing inquiry in an effort to ferret out some unknown and frequently unsuspected crime. He declined to answer on pain of incarceration, banishment, or mutilation. And if he spoke falsely, he was subject to further punishment. Faced with this formidable array of alternatives, his decision to speak was unquestionably coerced.

Those were the lurid realities which lay behind enactment of the Fifth Amendment, a far cry from the subject matter of the case before us. I think that the Court in this case stretches the concept of compulsion beyond all reasonable bounds, and that whatever compulsion may exist derives from the defendant's choice not to testify, not from any comment by court or counsel. In support of its conclusion that the California procedure does compel the accused to testify, the Court has only this to say: "It is a penalty imposed by courts for exercising a constitutional privilege. It cuts down on the privilege by making its assertion costly." Exactly what the penalty imposed consists of is not clear. . . .

It is not at all apparent to me, on any realistic view of the trial process, that a defendant will be at more of a disadvantage under the California practice than he would be in a court which permitted no comment at all on his failure to take the witness stand. How can it be said that the inferences drawn by a jury will be more detrimental to a defendant under the limiting and carefully controlling language of the instruction here involved than would result if the jury were left to roam at large with only its untutored instincts to guide it, to draw from the defendant's silence broad inferences of guilt? . . .

Moreover, no one can say where the balance of advantage might lie as a result of the attorneys' discussion of the matter. No doubt the prosecution's argument will seek to encourage the drawing of inferences unfavorable to the defendant. However, the defendant's counsel equally has an opportunity to explain the various other reasons why a defendant may not wish to take the stand, and thus rebut the natural if uneducated assumption that it is because the defendant cannot truthfully deny the accusations made.

I think the California comment rule is not a coercive device which impairs the right against self-incrimination but rather a means of articulating and bringing into the light of rational discussion a fact inescapably impressed on the jury's consciousness. . . .

. . . No constitution can prevent the operation of the human mind. Without limiting instructions, the danger exists that the inferences drawn by the jury may be unfairly broad. Some States have permitted this danger to go unchecked, by forbidding any comment at all upon the defendant's failure to take the witness stand. Other States have dealt with this danger in a variety of ways, as the Court's opinion indicates. Some might differ, as a matter of policy, with the way California has chosen to deal with the problem, or even disapprove of the judge's specific instructions in this case. But, so long as the constitutional command is obeyed, such matters of state policy are not for this Court to decide.

I would affirm the judgment.

NOTES ON GRIFFIN v. CALIFORNIA

1.   The outer limits of *Griffin* are unclear. Which of the following examples of prosecutorial questions and comments is proper under the *Griffin* standard?

   a.   Who else could have testified in this case? See Eberhardt v. Bordenkircher, 605 F.2d 275, 278 (6th Cir. 1979) (improper).
   b.   How many witnesses did the defense put on for your consideration? See Adams v. State, 566 S.W.2d 387 (Ark. 1978) (improper).
   c.   That question (the whereabouts of the defendant on the night of the crime) was the question that was never answered by the defendant. See State v. Cannon, 576 P.2d 132 (Ariz. 1978) (improper).
   d.   The defense has failed to produce any evidence in this case. See United States v. Bright, 630 F.2d 804, 825 (5th Cir. 1980) (proper, so long as prosecutor says *defense*, not *defendant*, failed to produce evidence).
   e.   "The government's evidence is uncontradicted," People v. Garcia, 420 N.E.2d 482 (Ill. App. 1981) (proper). With respect to the last comment, many courts find such argument to be error when the defendant's personal testimony would be required to supply the contradiction on the point to which the prosecutor refers. See Todd v. State, 598 S.W.2d 286 (Tex. App. 1980).

   f. Prosecutor told jury, during closing argument in capital murder trial: "Get [defendant] to explain 14 blows to you[,]." See State v. Barden, 572 S.E.2d 108 (N.C. 2002) (not improper; statement responded to argument that defendant lacked intent to kill and asked defense to explain why inflicting 14 blows to victim's head did not amount to premeditated and deliberate murder).

   2. Does a defendant have a constitutional right to have the trial judge instruct the jury on request that no inference may be drawn from the defendant's refusal to testify? See Carter v. Kentucky, 450 U.S. 288 (1981) (yes).

   3. What if the defendant does not want a "no inference" instruction given, out of concern that it will call the jury's attention to the defendant's refusal to testify? See Lakeside v. Oregon, 435 U.S. 333 (1978) (no Fifth Amendment violation to give "no inference" instruction over defendant's objection).

   4. Recall the Court's decision in Doyle v. Ohio, 426 U.S. 610 (1976) (Chapter 4B2, supra), which held that the prosecutor may not ask an accused who has been given *Miranda* warnings why he did not tell his story to police at the time of his arrest. Does *Griffin* require the decision in *Doyle*, or does *Doyle* represent an expansion of *Griffin*? Recall, if it be relevant, that the Court refused to extend the *Doyle* doctrine to cover postarrest prewarning silence. See Fletcher v. Weir, 455 U.S. 603 (1982), which is described in Notes on Use of Silence to Impeach (Chapter 8B1).

PROBLEM 12-J. *"He Claimed the Fifth"*

The City of St. Louis entered a contract with Bink's Armored Cars to collect and transport coins from the city parking meters. The City sues Bink's for alleged negligence in supervising its employees, claiming that substantial sums were lost because of pilferage by Carlton, the supervisor of the crew of Bink's employees assigned to collect the money from the meters. Carlton is also named as a defendant.

As proof that money was unlawfully taken by Carlton, the city, over the objection of both defendants, offers evidence that Carlton had asserted the privilege against self-incrimination when called before a grand jury investigating the incident. In addition, over defendants' objections, the city calls Carlton as a witness at trial, where he once more asserts the privilege against self-incrimination.

In her summation, the attorney for the City argues that the Fifth Amendment assertion by Carlton should be considered as circumstantial evidence in support of its claim against both Bink's and Carlton. In addition, the trial judge instructs the jury that "a witness has a constitutional right to decline to answer on the ground that it may tend to incriminate him. However, you may, but need not, infer by such refusal that the answers would have been adverse to the witness' interest."

A substantial judgment is entered against both defendants. On appeal, Bink's and Carlton argue error by the trial judge in (1) receiving evidence of Carlton's assertion of the privilege before the grand jury, (2) allowing the City to call Carlton as a witness at trial when the City knew he would claim the privilege, (3) allowing the City's attorney to comment on Carlton's assertion of the Fifth Amendment, and (4) instructing the jury that it could draw an adverse inference from Carlton's claim of privilege. What result?

6. Writings

It is clear that the Fifth Amendment protects against compelled writing as much as compelled testimony. Forcing a person to give an incriminating statement in writing is not different from compelling him to give it orally. But what if the statement sought is a preexisting, incriminating writing, so that the government only forces its production, not its making? Or what if such a writing is seized from the defendant during a lawful search and used against him at trial? Is the writer being compelled to "be a witness against himself" within the meaning of the Fifth Amendment?

PROBLEM 12-K.   The Inculpatory Diary

Acting pursuant to information supplied by a reliable informant, the Secret Service obtains a federal warrant to search a warehouse on the outskirts of Midville for "counterfeit currency and records pertaining to the printing and distribution of counterfeit currency." During the search, Secret Service agents locate and seize approximately $500,000 in counterfeit $20 bills along with personal papers, including a personal diary, kept by George Belknap, owner of the warehouse. The diary contains incriminating statements indicating that Belknap is the ringleader of a large counterfeit currency operation.

On further investigation, agents learn that he is the sole proprietor of his own printing company, "Andrew Jackson Offset Printing." They also discover that he is secretary-treasurer of an unincorporated association known as the "Society for a Return to the Gold Standard," which the Secret Service suspects is the distribution network for the counterfeit currency. The evidence is presented to a grand jury, which indicts Belknap for possession of counterfeit currency.

In connection with its continuing investigation into possible further charges against Belknap and others for the manufacture and distribution of counterfeit currency, the grand jury issues a subpoena to Belknap for production of the records of "Andrew Jackson Offset Printing" and the "Society for a Return to the Gold Standard." Belknap resists the subpoena, asserting the privilege against self-incrimination. In addition, he moves to suppress the personal diary that was seized during the initial search of the warehouse, asserting that its use against him would violate his privilege against self-incrimination.

What rulings? In formulating your answer, consider the following case.

UNITED STATES v. DOE
United States Supreme Court
465 U.S. 605 (1984)

JUSTICE POWELL delivered the opinion of the Court.

This case presents the issue whether, and to what extent, the Fifth Amendment privilege against compelled self-incrimination applies to the business records of a sole proprietorship.

Respondent is the owner of several sole proprietorships. In late 1980, a grand jury, during the course of an investigation of corruption in the awarding of county and municipal contracts, served five subpoenas on respondent. The first two demanded the production of the telephone records of several of respondent's companies and all records pertaining to four bank accounts of respondent and his companies. . . . The third subpoena demanded the production of a list of virtually all the business records of one of respondent's companies for the period between January 1, 1976, and the date of the subpoena. The fourth subpoena sought production of a similar list of business records belonging to another company. The final subpoena demanded production of all bank statements and cancelled checks of two of respondent's companies that had accounts at a bank in the Grand Cayman Islands.

Respondent filed a motion in federal district court seeking to quash the subpoenas. The District Court for the District of New Jersey granted his motion except with respect to those documents and records required by law to be kept or disclosed to a public agency. In reaching its decision, the District Court noted that the Government had conceded that the materials sought in the subpoena were or might be incriminating. The court stated that, therefore, "the relevant inquiry is . . . whether the *act* of producing the documents has communicative aspects which warrant Fifth Amendment protection." The court found that the act of production would compel respondent to "admit that the records exist, that they are in his possession, and that they are authentic." While not ruling out the possibility that the Government could devise a way to ensure that the act of turning over the documents would not incriminate respondent, the court held that the Government had not made such a showing.

The Court of Appeals for the Third Circuit affirmed. . . .

The Court of Appeals next considered whether the documents at issue in this case are privileged. The court noted that this Court held in Fisher v. United States, 425 U.S. 391 (1976), that the contents of business records ordinarily are not privileged because they are created voluntarily and without compulsion. The Court of Appeals nevertheless found that respondent's business records were privileged under either of two analyses. First, the court reasoned that, notwithstanding the holdings in *Bellis* and *Fisher,* the business records of a sole proprietorship are no different from the individual owner's personal records. Noting that Third Circuit cases had held that private papers, although created voluntarily, are protected by the Fifth Amendment, the court accorded the same protection to respondent's business papers. Second, it held that respondent's act of producing the subpoenaed records would have "communicative aspects of its own." 680 F.2d at 335. The turning over of the subpoenaed documents to the grand jury would admit their existence and authenticity. Accordingly, respondent was entitled to assert his Fifth Amendment privilege rather than produce the subpoenaed documents.

The Government contended that the court should enforce the subpoenas because of the Government's offer not to use respondent's act of production against respondent in any way. The Court of Appeals noted that no formal request for use immunity under 18 U.S.C. §§6002 and 6003 had been made. In light of this failure, the court held that the District Court did not err in rejecting the Government's attempt to compel delivery of the subpoenaed records.

We granted certiorari to resolve the apparent conflict between the Court of Appeals holding and the reasoning underlying this Court's holding in *Fisher*. We now affirm in part, reverse in part, and remand for further proceedings.

The Court in *Fisher* expressly declined to reach the question whether the Fifth Amendment privilege protects the contents of an individual's tax records in his possession.[7] The rationale underlying our holding in that case is, however, persuasive here. As we noted in *Fisher*, the Fifth Amendment protects the person asserting the privilege only from *compelled* self-incrimination. Where the preparation of business records is voluntary, no compulsion is present.[8] A subpoena that demands production of documents "does not compel oral testimony; nor would it ordinarily compel the taxpayer to restate, repeat, or affirm the truth of the contents of the documents sought." Applying this reasoning in *Fisher*, we stated:

> [T]he Fifth Amendment would not be violated by the fact alone that the papers on their face might incriminate the taxpayer, for the privilege protects a person only against being incriminated by his own compelled testimonial communications. Schmerber v. California [384 U.S. 757 (1966)]; United States v. Wade [388 U.S. 218 (1967)]; and Gilbert v. California [388 U.S. 263 (1967)]. The accountant's workpapers are not the taxpayer's. They were not prepared by the taxpayer, and they contain no testimonial declarations by him. Furthermore, as far as this record demonstrates, the preparation of all of the papers sought in these cases was wholly voluntary, and they cannot be said to contain compelled testimonial evidence, either of the taxpayers or of anyone else. The taxpayer cannot avoid compliance with the subpoena merely by asserting that the item of evidence which he is required to produce contains incriminating writing, whether his own or that of someone else.

Id., at 409-410.

---

7.   In *Fisher*, the Court stated: "Whether the Fifth Amendment would shield the taxpayer from producing his own tax records in his possession is a question not involved here; for the papers demanded here are not his 'private papers.' . . ." 425 U.S. at 414. We note that in some respects the documents sought in *Fisher* were more "personal" than those at issue here. The *Fisher* documents were accountant's workpapers in the possession of the taxpayers' lawyers. The workpapers related to the taxpayers' individual personal returns. To that extent, the documents were personal, even though in the possession of a third party. In contrast, each of the documents sought here pertained to respondent's businesses.

8.   Respondent's principal argument is that the Fifth Amendment should be read as creating a "zone of privacy which protects an individual and his personal records from compelled production." This argument derives from language in Boyd v. United States, 116 U.S. 616 (1886). This Court addressed substantially the same argument in *Fisher*:

> Within the limits imposed by the language of the Fifth Amendment, which we necessarily observe, the privilege truly serves privacy interests; but the Court has never on any ground, personal privacy included, applied the Fifth Amendment to prevent the otherwise proper acquisition or use of evidence which, in the Court's view, did not involve compelled testimonial self-incrimination of some sort.

425 U.S. at 399. In Andresen v. Maryland, 427 U.S. 463 (1976), the petitioner also relied on *Boyd*. In rejecting his argument, we observed that "the continued validity of the broad statements contained in some of the Court's earlier cases [has] been discredited by later opinions." Id. at 472. See also United States v. Nobles, 422 U.S. 225, 233, n.7 (1975).

This reasoning applies with equal force here. Respondent does not contend that he prepared the documents involuntarily or that the subpoena would force him to restate, repeat, or affirm the truth of their contents. The fact that the records are in respondent's possession is irrelevant to the determination of whether the creation of the records was compelled. We therefore hold that the contents of those records are not privileged.[10]

Although the contents of a document may not be privileged, the act of producing the document may be. A government subpoena compels the holder of the document to perform an act that may have testimonial aspects and an incriminating effect. As we noted in *Fisher:*

> Compliance with the subpoena tacitly concedes the existence of the papers demanded and their possession or control by the taxpayer. It also would indicate the taxpayer's belief that the papers are those described in the subpoena. Curcio v. United States, 354 U.S. 118, 125 (1957). The elements of compulsion are clearly present, but the more difficult issues are whether the tacit averments of the taxpayer are both "testimonial" and "incriminating" for purposes of applying the Fifth Amendment. These questions perhaps do not lend themselves to categorical answers; their resolution may instead depend on the facts and circumstances of particular cases or classes thereof.

In *Fisher,* the Court explored the effect that the act of production would have on the taxpayer and determined that the act of production would have only minimal testimonial value and would not operate to incriminate the taxpayer. Unlike the Court in *Fisher,* we have the explicit finding of the District Court that the act of producing the documents would involve testimonial self-incrimination.[11] The Court of Appeals agreed.[12] The District Court's finding

---

10. *Accord* In re Grand Jury Proceedings, 626 F.2d 1051, 1055 (C.A.1 1980) ("The line of cases culminating in *Fisher* have stripped the content of business records of any Fifth Amendment protection"). While not directly on point, Andresen v. Maryland, 427 U.S. 463 (1976), is consistent with our holding. In *Andresen,* investigators from a bicounty fraud unit obtained warrants to search the petitioner's office. During the search, the investigators seized several incriminating business records relating to the petitioner's practice as a sole practitioner of real estate law. The petitioner sought suppression of the documents on Fourth and Fifth Amendment grounds. The petitioner based his Fifth Amendment argument on "dicta in a number of cases which imply, or state, that the search for and seizure of a person's private papers violate the privilege against self-incrimination." The Court dismissed this argument and found the documents not to be privileged because the petitioner "had voluntarily committed to writing" any incriminating statements contained therein. Although *Andresen* involved a search warrant rather than a subpoena, the underlying principle is the same in this context. If the party asserting the Fifth Amendment privilege has voluntarily compiled the document, no compulsion is present and the contents of the document are not privileged.

11. The District Court stated:

> With few exceptions, enforcement of the subpoenas would compel [respondent] to admit that the records exist, that they are in his possession, and that they are authentic. These communications, if made under compulsion of a court decree, would violate [respondent's] Fifth Amendment rights. . . . The government argues that the existence, possession and authenticity of the documents can be proved without [respondent's] testimonial communication, but it cannot satisfy this court as to how that representation can be implemented to protect the witness in subsequent proceedings.

541 F. Supp., at 3.

12. The Court of Appeals stated:

> In the matter *sub judice,* however, we find nothing in the record that would indicate that

essentially rests on its determination of factual issues. Therefore, we will not overturn that finding unless it has no support in the record. Traditionally, we also have been reluctant to disturb findings of fact in which two courts below have concurred. We therefore decline to overturn the finding of the District Court in this regard, where, as here, it has been affirmed by the Court of Appeals.[13]

The Government, as it concedes, could have compelled respondent to produce the documents listed in the subpoena. [Sections 6002 and 6003 of Title 18] provide for the granting of use immunity with respect to the potentially incriminating evidence. The Court upheld the constitutionality of the use immunity statute in Kastigar v. United States, 406 U.S. 441 (1972).

The Government did state several times before the District Court that it would not use respondent's act of production against him in any way. But counsel for the Government never made a statutory request to the District Court to grant respondent use immunity.[15] We are urged to adopt a doctrine of constructive use immunity. Under this doctrine, the courts would impose a requirement on the Government not to use the incriminatory aspects of the act of production against the person claiming the privilege even though the statutory procedures have not been followed.

We decline to extend the jurisdiction of courts to include prospective grants of use immunity in the absence of the formal request that the statute requires. As we stated in Pillsbury Co. v. Conboy, 459 U.S. 248 (1983), in passing the use immunity statute, "Congress gave certain officials in the Department of Justice exclusive authority to grant immunities." "Congress foresaw the courts as playing only a minor role in the immunizing process. . . ." The decision to seek use immunity necessarily involves a balancing of the Government's interest in obtaining information against the risk that immunity will frustrate the

---

the United States knows, as a certainty, that each of the myriad documents demanded by the five subpoenas in fact is in the appellee's possession or subject to his control. The most plausible inference to be drawn from the broadsweeping subpoenas is that the Government, unable to prove that the subpoenaed documents exist—or that the appellee even is somehow connected to the business entities under investigation—is attempting to compensate for its lack of knowledge by requiring the appellee to become, in effect, the primary informant against himself.

680 F.2d at 335.

13. The Government concedes that the act of producing the subpoenaed documents might have had some testimonial aspects, but, it argues that any incrimination would be so trivial that the Fifth Amendment is not implicated. . . . On the basis of the findings made in this case we think it clear that the risk of incrimination was "substantial and real" and not "trifling or imaginary." Respondent did not concede in the District Court that the records listed in the subpoena actually existed or were in his possession. Respondent argued that by producing the records, he would tacitly admit their existence and his possession. Respondent also pointed out that if the Government obtained the documents from another source, it would have to authenticate them before they would be admissible at trial. See FRE 901. By producing the documents, respondent would relieve the Government of the need for authentication. These allegations were sufficient to establish a valid claim of the privilege against self-incrimination. This is not to say that the Government was foreclosed from rebutting respondent's claim by producing evidence that possession, existence, and authentication were a "foregone conclusion." *Fisher.* In this case, however, the Government failed to make such a showing.

15. Despite repeated questioning at oral argument, counsel for the Government gave no plausible explanation for the failure to request official use immunity rather than promising that the act of producing the documents would not be used against respondent.

Government's attempts to prosecute the subject of the investigation. Congress expressly left this decision exclusively to the Justice Department. If, on remand, the appropriate official concludes that it is desirable to compel respondent to produce his business records, the statutory procedure for requesting use immunity will be available.[17]

We conclude that the Court of Appeals erred in holding that the contents of the subpoenaed documents were privileged under the Fifth Amendment. The act of producing the documents at issue in this case is privileged and cannot be compelled without a statutory grant of use immunity pursuant to 18 U.S.C. §§6002 and 6003. The judgment of the Court of Appeals is, therefore, affirmed in part, reversed in part, and the case is remanded to the District Court for further proceedings in accordance with this decision.

JUSTICE O'CONNOR, concurring.

I concur in both the result and reasoning of Justice Powell's opinion for the Court. I write separately, however, just to make explicit what is implicit in the analysis of that opinion: that the Fifth Amendment provides absolutely no protection for the contents of private papers of any kind. The notion that the Fifth Amendment protects the privacy of papers originated in Boyd v. United States, 116 U.S. 616, 630 (1886), but our decision in Fisher v. United States, 425 U.S. 391 (1976), sounded the death-knell for *Boyd*. "Several of *Boyd*'s express or implicit declarations [had] not stood the test of time[,]" and its privacy of papers concept "had long been a rule searching for a rationale. . . ." Today's decision puts a long-overdue end to that fruitless search.

JUSTICE MARSHALL, with whom JUSTICE BRENNAN joins, concurring in part and dissenting in part.

I concur in the Court's affirmance of the Court of Appeals' ruling that the act of producing the documents could not be compelled without an explicit grant of use immunity pursuant to 18 U.S.C. §§6002 and 6003. I dissent, however, with respect to that part of the Court's opinion reversing the Court of Appeals. The basis for the reversal is the majority's disagreement with the Court of Appeals' discussion of whether the Fifth Amendment protected the contents of the documents respondent sought to withhold from disclosure. Inasmuch as the Court of Appeals' judgment did not rest upon the disposition of this issue, this Court errs by reaching out to decide it. As Justice Stevens rightly insists, "[t]his Court . . . reviews judgments, not statements in opinions."

Contrary to what Justice O'Connor contends, I do not view the Court's opinion in this case as having reconsidered whether the Fifth Amendment provides protection for the contents of "private papers of any kind." This case presented nothing remotely close to the question that Justice O'Connor eagerly poses and answers. First, as noted above, the issue whether the Fifth Amendment protects the contents of the documents was obviated by the Court of Appeals'

17. Respondent argues that any grant of use immunity must cover the contents of the documents as well as the act of production. We find this contention unfounded. To satisfy the requirements of the Fifth Amendment, a grant of immunity need be only as broad as the privilege against self-incrimination. Murphy v. Waterfront Commission, 378 U.S. 52, 107 (1964) (White, J., concurring); see *Pillsbury Co.*; United States v. Calandra, 414 U.S. 338 at 346 (1974). As discussed above, the privilege in this case extends only to the act of production. Therefore, any grant of use immunity need only protect respondent from the self-incrimination that might accompany the act of producing his business records.

rulings relating to the act of production and statutory use immunity. Second, the documents at stake here are business records which implicate a lesser degree of concern for privacy interests than, for example, personal diaries.

Were it true that the Court's opinion stands for the proposition that "the Fifth Amendment provides absolutely no protection for the contents of private papers of any kind," I would assuredly dissent. I continue to believe that under the Fifth Amendment "there are certain documents no person ought to be compelled to produce at the Government's request." Fisher v. United States, 425 U.S. 391 (Justice Marshall, concurring).

JUSTICE STEVENS, concurring in part and dissenting in part.

"This Court . . . reviews judgments, not statements in opinions." Black v. Cutter Laboratories, 351 U.S. 292 (1956). When both the District Court and the Court of Appeals correctly apply the law, and correctly dispose of the issue before them, I think it is poor appellate practice for this Court to reverse.

The question in this case is whether, without tendering statutory immunity, the Government can compel the sole proprietor of a business to produce incriminating records pursuant to a grand jury subpoena. Except for the records that are required by law to be kept or to be disclosed to public agencies, the District Court held that production could not be required. The basis for that decision turned, not on any suggestion that the contents of the documents were privileged, but rather on the significance of the act of producing them. . . .

This Court's opinion is entirely consistent with both the reasoning of the Court of Appeals and its disposition of the case. This Court agrees that the subpoena directed to respondent should have been quashed—which is all that the judgment we review today contains. Accordingly, the Court of Appeals' judgment should be affirmed.

To the extent that the Court purports to reverse the judgment of the Court of Appeals, I respectfully dissent.

NOTES ON REQUIRED DISCLOSURE AND THE FIFTH AMENDMENT

1. In 2002, the Supreme Court considered a claim of the Fifth Amendment privilege in connection with the private documents of Webster Hubbell, an Associate Attorney General during the Clinton administration. The question was whether the act of producing documents is a "testimonial communication" shielded by the Fifth Amendment. Unlike the defendant in *Doe*, Hubbell invoked his Fifth Amendment privilege against self-incrimination, declining to produce tax papers and other documents relating to the Whitewater investigation, in response to a subpoena issued by Independent Counsel Kenneth Starr. Already under indictment for one set of offenses, Hubbell produced this material only after the court granted him immunity with Starr's consent, but the information thus obtained led to a new indictment for tax-related crimes. The Supreme Court held that the immunity Hubbell obtained in the first case precluded later prosecution for tax evasion to the extent that the "testimonial aspect" of producing the subpoenaed documents was a necessary precursor to the second prosecution. See United States v. Hubbell, 530 U.S. 27 (2002).

2. As was true in *Doe,* so too in *Hubbell* the defendant could not "avoid compliance with the subpoena served on him merely because the demanded documents contained incriminating evidence." Yet the subpoena compelled communications (a clear testimonial aspect): Hubbell incriminated himself by identifying documents relevant to the subpoena in the Whitewater investigation. Consider whether *Hubbell,* fairly read, stands for the following: If a witness has a private document, and the government either does not know the document exists or does not know whether the witness has it, the document may be protected by the Fifth Amendment. If the witness produces the document under a grant of immunity, he performs a "testimonial act." The contents of the document, and of course its connection with the witness, may not be used as evidence against him. *Hubbell,* then, provides an important corrective to Justice O'Connor's statement in *Doe* that "the Fifth Amendment provides absolutely no protection for the contents of private papers of any kind."

3. Consider the following attempt to predict the consequences of the decision in the *Hubbell* case:

> [I]n *Hubbell,* the Supreme Court appeared to conclude that unless the government knows—really knows—of a particular document's existence, a subpoena's target is free to refuse to turn the document over, because the act of producing the document would testify to the fact that it does indeed exist. Of course, if the government really does know that the document exists, and hence knows what is in it . . . the government can probably get a warrant to search for and seize the document. Thus, after *Hubbell,* the working rule will be something like the following: When faced with subpoenas for documents, suspects can comply or not as they wish. For its part, the government can search for the evidence as it wants, so long as it satisfies the probable cause and warrant requirements.

William J. Stuntz, Commentary: O.J. Simpson, Bill Clinton, and the Transsubstantive Fourth Amendment, 114 Harv. L. Rev. 842, 865 (2001).

7. Required Records and Reports

If compelling the making or production of a writing can raise Fifth Amendment concerns, what is the constitutional status of records or reports required by law? Many governmental regulatory schemes mandate the keeping of various records or the submission of certain reports, often enforcing compliance by criminal sanctions.

The leading case upholding the government's right to require such records against a Fifth Amendment challenge is Shapiro v. United States, 335 U.S. 1 (1948). Shapiro was convicted under the Emergency Price Control Act of 1942, based on records that he was required by the Act to keep and that he had produced in response to a government subpoena duces tecum. The Court rejected his argument that he should have immunity from prosecution because the records were produced under compulsion. Although acknowledging limits on the extent to which the government could require the keeping and production of records for use in later criminal prosecutions, the Court held that such records could be required "when there is a sufficient relationship between the activity sought to be regulated and the public concern."

However, subsequent cases have been more sympathetic to the privilege claim. In Albertson v. Subversive Activities Control Board, 382 U.S. 70 (1965), the Court declared unconstitutional a provision of the Subversive Activities Control Act of 1950 requiring that officers of the Communist Party file a registration statement. In a trilogy of cases decided in 1968, the Court held that persons engaged in wagering activities could not be required to register or to pay an occupational tax, Marchetti v. United States, 390 U.S. 39 (1968); Grosso v. United States, 390 U.S. 62 (1968), nor could individuals be required to register a regulated firearm as required by a federal statute. Haynes v. United States, 390 U.S. 85 (1968). The Court delineated the limits of the doctrine allowing required records as follows:

> The premises of the doctrine, as it is described in *Shapiro*, are evidently three: first, the purposes of the United States' inquiry must be essentially regulatory; second, information is to be obtained by requiring the preservation of records of a kind which the regulating party has customarily kept; and third, the records themselves must have assumed "public aspects" which render them at least analogous to public documents.

Grosso v. United States, 390 U.S. 62, 67-68 (1968).

With respect to the federal wagering tax and firearm registration statutes, the Court found that these criteria were not satisfied. The Court concluded that these registration requirements were not "essentially regulatory," but instead were directed at "a highly selective group inherently suspect of criminal activities." Moreover, they were not related to the types of records customarily kept and lacked sufficient "public aspects."

Subsequent decisions have upheld amended versions of both the federal wagering tax and the firearm registration statutes, and these cases help illuminate further the boundaries of the required records doctrine. The federal wagering tax provisions were amended to allow information obtained from the required records to be used only in prosecutions under the tax statute, not in prosecutions for other gambling offenses. The act has been upheld in this more narrow form, apparently because the amended act is perceived as more "regulatory" in nature. See United States v. Haydel, 649 F.2d 1152 (5th Cir. 1981), cert. denied, 455 U.S. 1022 (1982).

The National Firearms Act was amended to apply to all possessors of regulated firearms, not just those suspected of unlawful activity. In addition, the registration filing is required only of the manufacturer or importer, not the transferee. The registration must include the transferee's photograph and fingerprints, and the Act prohibits receipt or possession of a firearm by anyone other than the person to whom the firearm is registered. In United States v. Freed, 401 U.S. 601 (1971), the defendant challenged the amended Act, arguing that requiring cooperation by the transferee in providing a photograph and fingerprints for the registration form was compelled self-incrimination. The Court upheld the amended Act, in part because it specifically prohibits use, in any prosecution for a violation occurring prior to or concurrently with the submission of the information or the compiling of the required records, of any evidence provided in complying with the statute. Justice Douglas commented:

> Appellee's argument assumes the existence of a periphery of the Self-Incrimination Clause which protects a person against incrimination not only against past or present transgressions but which supplies insulation for a career of crime about to be launched. We cannot give the Self-Incrimination Clause such an expansive interpretation.

Id. at 606-607.

NOTES ON THE REQUIRED RECORDS DOCTRINE

1.   Are you satisfied that the rationale and the boundaries of the required records doctrine have been adequately articulated by the Court? Is there a defensible rationale? See Saltzburg, The Required Records Doctrine: Its Lessons for the Privilege Against Self-Incrimination, 53 U. Chi. L. Rev. 6 (1986). And consider the following observation:

> The best approach seems simply in recognizing the doctrine as a limitation on the privilege based upon the public need for information in limited circumstances to make effective public regulation of certain activities. Thus in a specific case the question becomes whether there is a sufficient public interest to outweigh the strong policy in favor of maintaining the protection of the privilege.

McCormick on Evidence §142, at 352 (E. Cleary 3d ed. 1984).

2.   If a person furnishes incriminating information to the government in compliance with a reporting requirement rather than claiming the privilege, does he lose the right to assert the Fifth Amendment if the information is used against him in a subsequent prosecution? See Garner v. United States, 424 U.S. 648 (1976) (tax return reporting income from gambling properly admitted against taxpayer in later gambling prosecution; because he complied with the reporting requirement rather than asserting the privilege, the disclosure was not "compelled").

3.   If a court-appointed guardian of a child is suspected of abusing the child, can the guardian assert the Fifth Amendment privilege and refuse to comply with a court order to produce the child on the ground that production would be self-incriminating? See Baltimore City Department of Social Services v. Bouknight, 493 U.S. 549 (1990) (upholding order requiring parent who was a court-appointed custodian to produce the child despite claim that production would be incriminatory, relying upon the line of cases approving compelled production as part of "a regulatory scheme constructed to effect the State's public purposes unrelated to enforcement of its criminal laws"; Court leaves open the question of the "State's ability to use the testimonial aspects of Bouknight's act of production" in a subsequent criminal proceeding).

Thirteen
FOUNDATIONAL EVIDENCE, AUTHENTICATION

A. INTRODUCTION

A basic requirement before exhibits and other forms of nontestimonial evidence may be received is that they be properly authenticated. Under FRE 901(a), the authentication requirement is satisfied by the offering of "evidence sufficient to support a finding that the matter in question is what its proponent claims." Before a gun offered as the murder weapon may be received, a preliminary showing must be made that it really is the murder weapon. Before a contract purportedly signed by the defendant may be received, evidence must be offered that the signature really is that of the defendant. Before a photograph of an intersection may be admitted, it must be shown that the photograph accurately depicts the intersection. Failure to satisfy the authentication requirement can lead to the exclusion of evidence that may be essential for a party to prevail.

Common law courts were often strict with respect to the quantum of evidence demanded to satisfy the authentication requirement. See, e.g., Keegan v. Green Giant Co., 110 A.2d 599 (Me. 1954) (suit for personal injuries resulting from eating peas from can with defendant's label; court affirms trial judge's ruling excluding label as evidence of defendant's connection with the peas; directed verdict for defendant); Mancari v. Frank P. Smith, Inc., 114 F.2d 834 (D.C. Cir. 1940) (fact that allegedly tortious advertisement contained defendant's name and advertised defendant's product held to be insufficient evidence that defendant caused the advertisement to be written or published). While FRE 901 and 902 liberalize and expand the permissible methods of authentication,[1] the authentication requirement remains a significant evidentiary hurdle that must be surmounted before exhibits and other nontestimonial evidence will be received.

Authentication gives rise to issues of conditional relevancy under FRE 104(b). Here is a place where the literal language of this provision has some meaning: Something offered in evidence becomes relevant in the case only if

---

1. For example, FRE 902(7) rejects the holding of the *Green Giant* case and would accept a regularly affixed label as evidence of authenticity. See also FRE 901(b)(4).

the proponent proves that the thing is what he claims it to be. And here is a place where the division of functions contemplated by FRE 104 makes good sense. Authenticity speaks to common understanding, which means that we should be able to trust a jury to decide whether an object is the real thing and to ignore an item proffered for its consideration if it believes that the item has not been shown to be authentic.

FRE 104(b) clearly contemplates that the trial judge will play only a screening function, passing the ultimate decision on authenticity to the jury. Thus, the proponent must offer enough proof of authenticity to enable a jury to find an exhibit authentic. If he offers no proof (or not enough to support the necessary finding by a reasonable jury), the exhibit must be excluded. If he does offer enough proof, the exhibit will be received and the jury makes the ultimate decision regarding its authenticity. Of course the opponent remains free to challenge authenticity by offering evidence in rebuttal, in an attempt to persuade the jury to reject the exhibit as not authentic. The jury's usual function may be preempted in a case where the evidence for or against authenticity is so compelling as to permit only one conclusion by a reasonable jury. In such a case, the court itself may resolve the issue, by excluding the exhibit or by instructing the jury to accept it as authentic.

The required preliminary showing is often called "laying the foundation," and the kind of evidence needed depends on the nature of the thing in question. Often a single item may be authenticated in many different ways, and Rule 901(b) sets out an illustrative list of ten methods of authentication that satisfy the basic standard of Rule 901(a).

The traditional steps to authenticate and introduce an exhibit are the following: (1) having the exhibit marked for identification by the court reporter or other designated court officer; (2) authenticating the exhibit by the testimony of a witness unless the exhibit is self-authenticating; (3) offering the exhibit into evidence; (4) permitting adverse counsel to examine it; (5) allowing adverse counsel an opportunity to object; (6) submitting the exhibit to the court for examination if the court so desires; (7) obtaining the ruling of the court; (8) requesting permission to have the exhibit, if admitted, presented to the jury by reading it to them if it is a writing or having it passed among them. The sequence of these steps may vary somewhat, depending upon the jurisdiction.

Until any exhibit has been ruled admissible, an attorney should not display it to the jury, read its contents or ask the authenticating witness to do so, or even describe the nature of the exhibit in too great detail when handing it to the authenticating witness.

NOTES ON THE AUTHENTICATION REQUIREMENT

1.   FRE 901 assumes the existence of an authentication requirement and sets out a list of ways to satisfy it. But where do the Rules actually require parties to authenticate evidence?

2.   The Advisory Committee's Note to FRE 901 observes that the authentication requirement represents an "attitude of agnosticism" towards documents and other exhibits that "departs sharply from men's customs in ordinary affairs." Why should the trial judge screen exhibits before they are seen by the jury? If the jury

can be trusted to determine authenticity, why can't it be trusted to ignore exhibits for which no authenticating evidence has been offered? See generally Broun, Authentication and Contents of Writings, 1969 Law & Soc. Ord. 611.

3. What exactly must be authenticated? Only writings and physical exhibits? Or does the requirement of authentication also apply to other evidence, such as tape recordings and testimonial accounts of out-of-court statements, including telephone conversations?

4. To what extent does FRE 901(b)(4) permit the trier of fact to take exhibits at "face value," despite the general requirement of FRE 901 that authenticating evidence be offered? Consider United States v. Blackwell, 694 F.2d 1325, 1329-1333 (D.C. Cir. 1982) (approving receipt of photograph apparently showing defendant in hotel room holding gun like the one he was charged with possessing, despite the government's failure to establish where the photograph was taken or what gun he was holding).

5. In civil cases there are a number of discovery devices that allow parties to resolve questions of authentication in advance of trial. FRCP 26(a)(1)(b) requires parties, without awaiting a discovery request, to provide other parties with "a copy of, or a description by category and location of, all documents, data compilations, and tangible things that are in the possession, custody, or control of the party and that the disclosing party may use to support its claims or defenses." Production pursuant to this Rule authenticates the evidence as being what the producing party claims it to be. In addition, at least 30 days prior to trial each party must provide the others with "an appropriate identification of each document or other exhibit." FRCP 26(a)(3)(C). Any objections not made within 14 days after such disclosure (unless another time is provided by the court) are deemed waived (unless excused by the court for good cause) except for objections under FRE 402 or 403. These provisions go far toward removing issues of authentication from civil trials.

6. Authentication can also be accomplished by stipulation of the parties or, in civil cases, by use of FRCP 36, which allows a party to file a written request for admission of facts including the genuineness of documents. Under FRCP 37(c), if the opposing party refuses to admit the genuineness of the documents without good reason (and the requesting party subsequently proves their genuineness), the latter may seek an order requiring the former to pay reasonable expenses incurred in making that proof, including attorney's fees.

7. Authentication continues to be a much more significant evidentiary hurdle in criminal prosecutions and fewer authentication issues are resolved by stipulation. Why do you suppose that is so?

B. TANGIBLE OBJECTS

UNITED STATES v. JOHNSON
United States Court of Appeals for the Ninth Circuit
637 F.2d 1224 (1980)

[Johnson was convicted under 18 U.S.C. §1153 of assault resulting in serious bodily injury for an attack with an ax on a victim named Papse.]

Spencer Williams, J.

At Johnson's trial, the United States called Papse as a witness. A long-handled ax was offered into evidence during his testimony. Pursuant to a search warrant, this ax had been seized at Johnson's residence five days after the assault. Papse identified the ax, apparently with some hesitancy, as the weapon used to commit the assault on him. Over Johnson's objection that there had been insufficient foundation or authentication, the ax was admitted into evidence. . . .

Johnson argues the ax allegedly used in the assault was admitted into evidence without first being authenticated properly. He contends Papse's testimony was inadequate as authentication because the witness failed to state specifically that he could distinguish this ax from any other, because he did not identify specific characteristics of this ax which could tie it to the incident, and because he appeared to base his identification largely on an assumption, derived from his belief that this ax was the only ax on the premises, that this ax *must* have been the weapon in question. In addition, Johnson contends the ax introduced into evidence was in a changed condition from the ax noted at the scene of the incident, and for this reason the court should have been especially cautious about its admission.[34]

FRE 901(a) provides that "[t]he requirement of authentication or identification as a condition precedent to admissibility is satisfied by evidence sufficient to support a finding that the matter in question is what its proponent claims." The terms of the Rule are thus satisfied, and the proffered evidence should ordinarily be admitted, once a prima facie case has been made on the issue. At that point the matter is committed to the trier of fact to determine the evidence's credibility and probative force.

Here, although the trial record reveals the identification of the ax made by Papse may not have been entirely free from doubt, the witness did state that he was "pretty sure" this was the weapon Johnson had used against him, that he saw the ax in Johnson's hand, and that he was personally familiar with this particular ax because he had used it in the past. Based on Papse's testimony, a reasonable juror could have found that this ax was the weapon allegedly used in the assault. Papse's ability or inability to specify particular identifying features of the ax, as well as the evidence of the ax's alleged changed condition, should then go to the question of the weight to be accorded this evidence, which is precisely what the trial court ruled. In other words, although the jury remained free to reject the government's assertion that this ax had been used in the assault, the requirements for admissibility specified in Rule 901(a) had been met.

Finally, the trial court did not abuse its discretion in failing to exclude the ax for being more prejudicial than probative under Evidence Rule 403. "District judges have wide latitude in passing on the admissibility of evidence, and

---

34. Johnson inaccurately states in his brief that testimony revealed the ax observed at the crime scene had "blood and hair upon the blade end of it." In fact, the testimony was that Rose Edmo, a witness, had been told by Barney Dixie, another witness, only that "there was hair on the axe." The ax admitted as an exhibit did not have hair on it. Assuming the testimony about the hair is believed, the absence of hair represents the only change in the ax's condition which was noted between the time of the alleged assault and its seizure five days later.

admission will not be overturned on appeal absent an abuse of discretion."
United States v. Kearney, 560 F.2d 1358, 1369 (9th Cir.), cert. denied, 434 U.S.
971 (1977). The ax, as the suspected assault weapon, was very relevant to the
government's case and the jury was entitled to see it. . . .

NOTES ON AUTHENTICATING TANGIBLE OBJECTS

1. Does the nature of the required authentication depend on the purpose
for which the exhibit is offered? For what purpose was the prosecutor offering
the ax in the *Johnson* case? Would the required foundation be different if the
prosecutor were offering the ax for some other purpose—for example, to
impeach testimony by Johnson that he did not own an ax?

2. Could the prosecutor offer an ax into evidence for the limited purpose
of showing the jury the type of ax used in the assault? What type of foundation
would be necessary for such "illustrative" evidence? Could the prosecutor use
an ax seized from the defendant for this purpose if the prosecutor did not
show or claim any connection between the ax and the crime? See United States
v. Warledo, 557 F.2d 721, 725 (10th Cir. 1977) ("The courts have quite uniformly
condemned the introduction in evidence of testimony concerning dangerous
weapons, even though found in the possession of a defendant, which have
nothing to do with the crime charged").

3. When a tangible object such as a weapon is seized by the police to be
used as evidence, what should be done to facilitate identification of the exhibit
at trial?

PROBLEM 13-A. *A White Granular Substance*

Pursuant to a warrant, Swenson is arrested and three baggies containing
a white granular substance are seized from his person. The arresting officer
personally delivers the baggies to the state crime lab for analysis by a chemist,
who determines that they contain cocaine. The arresting officer picks up the
baggies from the chemist on the day of trial and brings them to court. You are
the prosecutor. What foundation is necessary to introduce the baggies into
evidence? What witnesses must be called?

UNITED STATES v. HOWARD-ARIAS
United States Court of Appeals for the Fourth Circuit
679 F.2d 363 (1982)

. . . Appellant was one of several crew members of the fishing trawler "Don
Frank" rescued when their ship became disabled sixty miles off the Virginia
coast on December 29, 1980. They were taken aboard an Italian ship, and
shortly thereafter units of the United States Coast Guard arrived on the scene.

An officer from one of the Coast Guard cutters boarded the wreckage of the "Don Frank" and discovered a large quantity of what was later determined to be marijuana. The Coast Guard cutter "Cherokee" attempted to tow the wreckage to shore, but thirty miles from Norfolk, Virginia, the "Don Frank" foundered and sank. All was not lost however, as approximately 240 bales of the marijuana from the "Don Frank" were salvaged. Upon return to port, the seized material was turned over to Coast Guard and Drug Enforcement Administration (DEA) investigators for testing and storage.

The appellant was indicted on three counts: possession of marijuana with the intent to distribute it while on a vessel subject to the jurisdiction of the United States, conspiracy to distribute marijuana, and possession of marijuana with intent to import it into the United States. . . .

The appellant's claims regarding the admission of certain evidence need not long detain us. His first argument is that the government failed to establish a continuous "chain of custody" for the marijuana from the time of its seizure on the seas off the Virginia coast until introduction at trial. It is conceded that one of the DEA agents involved in the transfer and testing of the bales and samples drawn from them did not testify at trial. The Coast Guard officer who seized and tested the marijuana, the officer to whom he surrendered it, the DEA custodian at Norfolk, and the DEA chemist all appeared as witnesses. The special agent who received the marijuana from the Coast Guard for transit to the DEA in Norfolk did not.

The "chain of custody" rule is but a variation of the principle that real evidence must be authenticated prior to its admission into evidence. The purpose of this threshold requirement is to establish that the item to be introduced, i.e., marijuana, is what it purports to be, i.e., marijuana seized from the "Don Frank." Therefore, the ultimate question is whether the authentication testimony was sufficiently complete so as to convince the court that it is improbable that the original item had been exchanged with another or otherwise tampered with. Contrary to the appellant's assertion, precision in developing the "chain of custody" is not an iron-clad requirement, and the fact of a "missing link does not prevent the admission of real evidence, so long as there is sufficient proof that the evidence is what it purports to be and has not been altered in any material aspect." United States v. Jackson, 649 F.2d 967 (3d Cir.), cert. denied, 454 U.S. 871, 1034 (1981). Resolution of this question rests with the sound discretion of the trial judge, and we cannot say that he abused that discretion in this case. . . .

NOTES ON CHAIN OF CUSTODY

1. How much of a break in the chain of custody can be tolerated before the attempt at authentication will be found insufficient? What if the Coast Guard officer who originally seized and tested the marijuana in this case were the missing link?

2. The chain of custody requirement tends to be enforced more stringently in criminal than civil cases. Why?

3. What procedures by law enforcement officers would help maintain a tight and complete chain of custody for trial exhibits? See generally Gianelli, *Chain of Custody and the Handling of Real Evidence*, 20 Am. Crim. L. Rev. 527 (1983). Should law enforcement agencies be required to maintain a round-the-clock watch on items offered in evidence? Should courts reject items kept in a property room on the basis of proof that unauthorized people sometimes gain entrance? See *United States v. Santiago*, 534 F.2d 768, 770 (7th Cir. 1976) (rejecting defense contention that evidence of narcotics should have been excluded because "many people had access to the safes," where the envelopes storing the material were sealed and there was no evidence of tampering).

C. WRITINGS

UNITED STATES v. BAGARIC
United States Court of Appeals for the Second Circuit
706 F.2d 42 (1983)

[Defendants Milan Bagaric, Mile Markich, Ante Ljubas, Vinko Logarusic, Ranko Primorac, and Drago Sudar were convicted of violations of the Racketeer Influenced and Corrupt Organizations Act (RICO). Miro Baresic was an unindicted co-racketeer, who participated in the enterprise's affairs during 1977 and 1978.]

KAUFMAN, J.

Logarusic challenges the admission of additional evidence linking him to Baresic. We refer to a letter discovered during a consent search of Logarusic's home on April 3, 1981, after his arrest. Appellant claims the letter was not properly authenticated. Fed. R. Evid. 901(a). We disagree. The requirement of authentication "is satisfied by evidence sufficient to support a finding that the matter is what its proponent claims," id. This finding may be based entirely on circumstantial evidence, including "[a]ppearance, contents, substance . . . and other distinctive characteristics" of the writing, id. 901(b)(4). Here, the letter was addressed to Logarusic and postmarked Asuncion, Paraguay, where Baresic resided. It began with the salutation "Dear Vinko" and ended "your Miro Baresic . . . your Miro Toni." "Toni Saric" was the alias Baresic had used in gaining entry into the United States. The letter referred to "our people in Chicago," where four of the defendants lived, and it asked Logarusic to contact "Crni," which the proof showed was Ljubas's sobriquet among his confederates. It also contained references to "Mercedes," a friend of Logarusic who testified on his behalf and admitted knowing Baresic, and to "the Razov family," Logarusic's landlord. Finally, the letter stated that "[t]he Swedes, Americans, and Yugoslavs are requesting expulsion because I am a terrorist and dangerous," a fact confirmed by testimony that Baresic was a fugitive from Sweden where he was sought for the murder of the Yugoslavian ambassador. In sum, as Chief Judge Motley found, there was ample demonstration "that the letter was in fact what the Government claimed, i.e., a letter from Miro Baresic to Vinko Logarusic."

NOTES ON AUTHENTICATING WRITINGS

1.   Can stylistic patterns, such as spelling errors, be used to authenticate writings? See United States v. Larson, 596 F.2d 759, 765 n.5 (8th Cir. 1979) (evidence received that defendant "misspelled approach as 'approuch' three times in one ransom note" and "previously did the same in a letter to the Pardon Board"); United States v. Clifford, 704 F.2d 86 (3d Cir. 1983) (letters allegedly from defendant authenticated in part by unusual misspellings).

2.   Can similar internal patterns of diction be useful when questions arise concerning the authenticity of evidence of the recorded voice? See United States v. Hearst, 563 F.2d 1331, 1349-1350 (9th Cir. 1977) (trial court excluded testimony by expert in psycholinguistics, offered by defense in trial of kidnapped heiress Patty Hearst as evidence that she "did not author" certain statements that she admittedly recorded, the latter having been offered by the prosecutor as proof that she "acted voluntarily in robbing the bank"; reviewing court approves the ruling, but only on narrow ground of avoiding "delay and needless cumulation"), cert. denied, 435 U.S. 1000 (1978). See generally Comment, Stylistics Evidence in the Trial of Patricia Hearst, 1977 Ariz. St. L.J. 387.

3.   Can a letter be authenticated as from the defendant by virtue of the fact that it is written on letterhead stationery of the defendant and appears to be signed by the defendant? See Strong, Liberalizing the Authentication of Private Writings, 52 Cornell L.Q. 284 (1967) (suggesting that the unlikelihood of fraud in this situation might support recognition of a "letterhead doctrine"). Is letterhead stationery so accessible to unauthorized persons, or so easily made up on private order, that such a doctrine is dangerous? Consider United States v. Gordon, 634 F.2d 639, 643-644 (1st Cir. 1980) (approving receipt of certain documents on basis of evidence that "on their face" all of them "purported to come from J. John Gordon, the President and Senior Counsel of the International Bank of Commerce, with a residential address at 8 Creswell Road, Worcester, and a telephone numbered 617-754-5000," where address and phone number matched those of the defendant).

PROBLEM 13-B.   The Land-Sale Contract

In a suit filed in 2002 to quiet title to Ridgeview Estates, plaintiff seeks to offer as an exhibit a land-sale contract between Greta Higgins, a previous owner, and plaintiff for the sale of the property to the plaintiff. The land-sale contract was executed in 1980, and the original was obtained from the property records office of the county courthouse. Identify all the ways this exhibit could be authenticated under FRE 901(b).

R. KEETON, BASIC EXPRESSIONS FOR TRIAL LAWYERS §2.25 (1979)

§2.25 OFFERING DOCUMENTARY EVIDENCE

Q: Have you ever before seen Plaintiff's Exhibit 7 for Identification?

A: Yes, I have.

Q: When did you first see it?

A: In the early part of February of this year.

Q: Where were you when you first saw it?

A: In my office.

Q: How did it come to your attention?

A: It came to me in the regular mail at my office.

Q: Please answer my next question just *yes* or *no:* Do you know who sent it to you?

A: Yes.

Q: How do you know?

A: I recognize the signature.

Q: Without saying whose signature you recognized it to be, please tell us how you were able to recognize that signature.

A: Well, I've been doing business with this person for more than ten years.

Q: Have you ever seen him sign his name during that period?

A: Yes, many times.

Q: Have you received letters from him during those ten years you have been doing business with him?

A: Yes, dozens of them.

Q: Have you completed transactions based on those letters?

A: Yes, often.

Q: Whose signature is it that appears on Plaintiff's Exhibit 7 for Identification?

A: John J. Jones.

Q: Is that the John J. Jones against whom you have brought this lawsuit?

A: Yes, it is.

Plaintiff's Counsel: Your Honor, . . . I offer in evidence what has been marked as Plaintiff's Exhibit 7 for Identification.

Defense Counsel: Objection, Your Honor.

Court: Objection overruled. The document is in evidence as Plaintiff's Exhibit 7.

Plaintiff's Counsel: Your honor, may I hand Plaintiff's Exhibit 7 to the jury for their examination?

Court: You _____ may.

[Wait until all jurors have read the document before proceeding.]

PROBLEM 13-C. *"The Wizard" and the Incriminating Email*

On Friday July 18, 2003, 14-year-old Tiffany is reported missing from her home in Phoenix, Arizona. Her anguished parents invite police to examine her computer files, where they discover a series of email messages from someone using the moniker "The Wizard." Apparently the two "met" in an online chatroom. Police recover the following messages from Tiffany's computer:

W: Think of it as the first of many road trips. Let's take a camera, so the pictures will show everyone just how grown up you are. Tickets are in my hand. Everyone knows the first visit to Vegas is the luckiest. Don't empty out your mom's purse until just before you leave. The more you play, the more they pay!

T: You promised it is only for the concert, and then we have to come back that night. I don't want to wind up on a milk carton. Anyway, after the concert I know my mom will lock me up for awhile, so don't be surprised if I can't take any more trips anytime soon. This concert better be worth it!

W: Not to worry. You can trust me. You'll love the band. Can't wait to see you on Friday.

On Sunday July 20, 2003, police find Tiffany at the Lucky Lady Hotel in Las Vegas, in a room with 28-year-old Morris Tate. Tate is arrested, and Tiffany is returned to her home in Phoenix.

Federal investigators learn that Tate is the internet account holder who calls himself "The Wizard." Tate is charged with inducing a minor to cross state lines for immoral purposes and with sexual assault against a minor.

As proof that Tate induced Tiffany to go with him from Arizona to Nevada, and to show how Tate persuaded Tiffany to meet him, the prosecutor offers the emails found on Tiffany's computer. Tiffany is willing to testify about her participation in the email exchange.

What foundation is needed to authenticate these emails? Is a different foundation required for The Wizard's emails than for those sent by Tiffany?

NOTES ON AUTHENTICATION OF EMAILS

1.   Which illustration in FRE 901(b) is most helpful in authenticating emails? Consider 901(b)(4) (allowing authentication of writings based on "appearance, contents, substance, internal patterns, or other distinctive characteristics."). How does an attorney authenticate emails based on content?

2.   Can authentication rest on the header and footer of an email message, which includes the IP address, date, and email addresses of the parties? How are these features similar to or different from markers on letters, such as return addresses, letterhead, or postmarks? Assuming Tate is shown to have an internet account in the name of The Wizard, is it sufficient that the email purports to have been sent by an internet account holder with the name of The Wizard?

3.   One method of authentication mentioned in the ACN to FRE 901(b)(4) is the "reply doctrine," under which a letter may be authenticated as coming from a person by showing that it replies to an earlier communication to that person, provided the earlier communication has itself been authenticated. Would the "reply doctrine" help here?

4.   Can emails be forged or fabricated or disguised as coming from a different person? See Munshani v. Signal Lake Venture Fund II, 2001 WL 1526954 (Mass. Super. Ct. 2001) (finding on basis of report by court-appointed computer forensics expert that plaintiff falsified email by fabricating the text

and altering the banner; dismissing lawsuit and imposing monetary sanctions on plaintiff).

5.   How is forgery of an email different from forgery of a document? Do the differences warrant separate criteria for authentication that are peculiar to email? What about claims that an email account may have been compromised or available to more than one person, so the email did not come personally from the holder of the account?

6.   On authentication of emails, see generally Jablon, *"God Mail": Authentication and Admissibility of Electronic Mail in Federal Courts*, 34 Am. Crim. L.R. 1387 (1997).

D.   TAPE RECORDINGS

PROBLEM 13-D.   The Hidden Microphone

Defendant is charged with the sale of heroin to Kirsch, an undercover agent. The transaction took place in a motel room where a hidden microphone was planted by narcotics officers. The entire conversation between defendant and Kirsch was recorded on a tape recorder in another room by Officer Enyart. Enyart could not hear the conversation as it was being recorded but can testify regarding the set up, operation, and reliability of the recording equipment. Enyart is also the person who has had custody of the tape for the entire period prior to trial. What foundation is necessary to authenticate this tape recording? Will the required foundation differ depending on whether Kirsch or Enyart is called as the authenticating witness, or must both be called? In formulating your answer, consider the following case.

UNITED STATES v. BIGGINS
United States Court of Appeals for the Fifth Circuit
551 F.2d 64 (1977)

GOLDBERG, J.
   Ulysses Biggins appeals from his conviction for possessing and distributing heroin in violation of 21 U.S.C. §841(a)(1). After a brief jury trial, Biggins was given concurrent three year sentences. . . .

1.   FACTS

Clarence Lydes was a confidential informant for the Drug Enforcement Administration. Lydes met Biggins at a bar and discussed with him the possibility of obtaining narcotics. Appellant told Lydes to contact him through Bertha Coudgo. On May 19, 1975, Lydes went to Coudgo's apartment to purchase narcotics from the appellant. The appellant told Lydes to return on the following day, when appellant would deliver the heroin. Appellant did not appear the next day. On May 30, 1975, Lydes and DEA agent Audis Wells returned to Coudgo's apartment. The appellant there agreed to sell one ounce of heroin for $1,600 at Lydes's apartment later that day.

Lydes's apartment was monitored by means of electronic surveillance. From his vantage point in an apartment across the street, Agent John Anderson of the Palm Beach County Sheriff's Department monitored and recorded the conversation that ensued within Lydes's apartment. During the course of that conversation, the appellant sold Wells one ounce of heroin for $1,500. Shortly thereafter, Wells obtained laboratory confirmation that the substance he had purchased was heroin.

At the appellant's trial, the government introduced the original tape recording of the conversation in Lydes's apartment and a re-recording of the original tape, ostensibly filtered for noise.

II. ESTABLISHING A FOUNDATION FOR THE ADMISSION OF SOUND RECORDINGS

Admitting sound recordings into evidence at a criminal trial presents discrete dangers to which courts have been justly sensitive. In the oft-cited case of United States v. McKeever, 169 F. Supp. 426 (S.D.N.Y. 1958), rev'd on other grounds, 271 F.2d 669 (2d Cir. 1959), the court established seven criteria as conditions precedent to admitting sound recordings. The Eighth Circuit has recently adopted that test in the context of electronic monitoring. United States v. McMillan, 508 F.2d 101, 104 (8th Cir. 1974), cert. denied, 421 U.S. 916 (1975).[1]

Although we neither adopt nor reject that test as a whole, we think that certain of its requirements may justifiably be imposed on the party seeking to introduce sound recording evidence. The court properly admits a sound recording into evidence only when the party introducing it carries its burden of going forward with foundation evidence demonstrating that the recording as played is an accurate reproduction of relevant sounds previously audited by a witness. As a general rule, at least in the context of a criminal trial, this requires the prosecution to go forward with respect to the competency of the operator, the fidelity of the recording equipment, the absence of material deletions, additions, or alterations in the relevant portions of the recording, and the identification of the relevant speakers.

---

1. *McKeever* and *McMillan* establish a test whereby the party introducing sound recordings must establish the following facts:

(1) That the recording device was capable of taking the conversation now offered in evidence.
(2) That the operator of the device was competent to operate the device.
(3) That the recording is authentic and correct.
(4) That changes, additions or deletions have not been made in the recording.
(5) That the recording has been preserved in a manner that is shown to the court.
(6) That the speakers are identified.
(7) That the conversation elicited was made voluntarily and in good faith, without any kind of inducement.

This burden properly falls to the government because it has access to such information in a way the criminal defendant does not. A defendant will often hear the tape recording for the first time in court. More so than photographs or other demonstrative evidence, sound recordings are susceptible to alterations that may be impossible to detect. It is therefore important that the defendant be alerted regarding any possible uncertainties or distortions in the recording before it is introduced as evidence against him.

Nevertheless, the trial judge has broad discretion in determining whether to allow a recording to be played before the jury. The standards for foundation evidence we adopt serve the paramount purpose of ensuring the accuracy of the recording. Strict compliance with the government's particularized burden is the preferred method of proceeding. If the trial judge independently determines that the recording accurately reproduces the auditory evidence, however, his discretion to admit the evidence is not to be sacrificed to a formalistic adherence to the standard we establish. If there is independent evidence of the accuracy of the tape recordings admitted at trial, we shall be extremely reluctant to disturb the trial court's decision even though at the time that decision was made the government had not carried its particularized burden of going forward.

In the case at bar the appellant objects that the government's foundation for the tape recordings was deficient because it failed to satisfy the *McMillan* test in several ways. First, appellant argues that the government failed to prove the competency of the operator. Second, the appellant contends that the government failed to establish the accuracy of the recording. Third, the appellant claims that the government's witness failed to identify a voice on the tape as that of the appellant.

The only foundation for the admission into evidence of the original or the filtered recording is found in the testimony of John Anderson, who monitored the conversation in Lydes's apartment. Anderson was not explicitly shown to be a competent operator of electronic monitoring equipment. We know neither that he was trained in the use of this equipment nor even whether he had ever used it before. Anderson averred only that he was "on electronic surveillance" for DEA. On the other hand, Anderson evinced some familiarity with the techniques of electronic surveillance, and it would be a reasonable inference that he was competent to use the monitor and tape recorder. But a greater uncertainty exists. Some person whom Anderson did not know and about whose competence there is no evidence both re-recorded and filtered the original tape of the conversation. These are not sophisticated operations, to be sure, but an incompetent operator could alter the conversation, perhaps without being aware that he had done so. Nevertheless, these defects in the government's foundation evidence are inconsequential under the circumstances of the case at bar. Because there was testimony that the re-recording was an accurate transcription of the original, the competency of the second operator is less important.

With respect to the most critical issue, the recording's accuracy, the government's foundation evidence is deficient in ways that, under other circumstances, might be fatal. Anderson testified that the re-recording was a "duplicate" of the original, but he did nothing to verify that the original was a faithful recording of the conversation that took place in Lydes's apartment. This stands in sharp contrast to the care with which the authenticity of the sound recording was established in *McMillan*. In that case, the agent testified that he replayed the tape of a conversation between defendant and informant in the informant's presence to verify the accuracy of the recording. . . .

Nevertheless, in the circumstances of this case there was sufficient evidence that the tape recording was authentic outside the foundation testimony established by Anderson. Lydes and Wells testified regarding the conversation in Lydes's apartment. The tape recording portrayed that conversation precisely as they described it. The record thus reveals a correspondence between the agents' accounts of the conversation and the version evidenced by the sound recording sufficiently close to lessen the importance of explicit testimony that the recording itself was accurate.

Similarly, neither Anderson nor anyone else testified that the tape has not been altered. Although no one affirmatively suggested that the tape had been altered, the party seeking to introduce such evidence has the burden of going forward. Here again, however, the government's proffer is saved by the close correspondence between Lydes's and Wells's testimony regarding the conversation in Lydes's apartment and the sound recording of that conversation.

Finally the appellant asserts that the government failed to identify Biggins's voice on the tape. This contention is meritless. Lydes, who participated in the conversation with defendant Biggins and thus was familiar with Biggins's voice, clearly identified the defendant's voice on the tape. FRE 901(b)(5) makes clear that the witness's familiarity with the voice sought to be identified, whether the familiarity developed before or after the time of the recording, is sufficient to ensure reliable voice identification. In this circuit, we have agreed that such familiarity is sufficient. . . .

In sum, the district judge acted correctly in admitting the sound recordings into evidence in the case at bar. . . .

NOTES ON AUTHENTICATING RECORDED CONVERSATIONS

1. Could the proponents in *Biggins* and Problem 13-D rely on "voiceprint" analysis to authenticate the recordings? The authorities conflict. Compare United States v. Williams, 583 F.2d 1194 (2d Cir. 1978) (yes; voiceprints are reliable and not misleading) with Cornett v. State, 450 N.E.2d 498 (Ind. 1983) (no; voiceprints do not satisfy standard for admissibility of scientific evidence). See the cases collected in Annot., Admissibility and Weight of Voiceprint Evidence, 97 A.L.R.3d 294 (1980).

2. Transcripts of tape recordings are sometimes provided to assist the jury, particularly when portions of the tape recording are difficult to hear. One court has articulated the following guidelines for the use of transcripts:

> The best evidence of the conversation is the tape itself; the transcript should normally be used only after the defendant has had an opportunity to verify its

accuracy and then only to assist the jury as it listens to the tape. . . . Transcripts should not ordinarily be read to the jury or given independent weight. The trial judge should carefully instruct the jury that differences in meaning may be caused by such factors as the inflection in a speaker's voice or inaccuracies in the transcript and that they should, therefore, rely on what they hear rather than on what they read when there is a difference. Transcripts should not ordinarily be admitted into evidence unless both sides stipulate to their accuracy. . . .

United States v. McMillan, 508 F.2d 101, 105-106 (8th Cir. 1974), cert. denied, 421 U.S. 916 (1975).

3.   What if the parties cannot agree to the accuracy of a transcript? Compare United States v. Onori, 535 F.2d 938, 948-949 (5th Cir. 1976) (endorsing receipt of divergent transcripts offered by government and defense) with United States v. Chiarizio, 525 F.2d 289, 293 (2d Cir. 1975) (trial judge should hold in camera hearing, personally listening to tapes and reading transcripts and hearing the objections of each side, before submitting the transcripts to jury).

E.   OTHER EXHIBITS

PROBLEM 13-E.   *The Photograph*

In an automobile accident case, Harris, the plaintiff, seeks to offer a photograph of the intersection where the accident occurred, taken one month afterwards. State the foundation necessary to authenticate the photograph. Must the photographer be the authenticating witness? What if the photograph shows a new traffic sign or billboard that was not there at the time of the accident? Is the photograph still admissible?

PROBLEM 13-F.   *X-Ray*

Mason, a pedestrian, is struck by a car while crossing a street. He sues to recover damages for a fractured leg. If Mason seeks to offer an X-ray of his leg, what foundation is necessary? What subparagraph of FRE 901(b) is most applicable? Why is the required foundation different than for a photograph?

PROBLEM 13-G.   *Computer Printout*

Georgia Pacific sues Allied Construction Company to recover on an unpaid account for the sale of lumber and other construction materials. To prove the amount of the account, Georgia Pacific offers a computer printout. What foundation is necessary to authenticate this exhibit?

F. TELEPHONE CONVERSATIONS

UNITED STATES v. POOL
United States Court of Appeals for the Fifth Circuit
660 F.2d 547 (1981)

[Eight defendants were convicted of several charges arising from participation in a scheme to import approximately 225,000 pounds of marijuana worth $60 million into the United States. Defendant Loye appealed his conviction under Count 9 of the indictment (for violation of 21 U.S.C. §843(b) for using a telephone to facilitate the illegal importation) on the ground that the phone call alleged to be from him was insufficiently authenticated.]

HILL, J.

. . . On August 5, 1978, at 10:40 a.m. DEA Agent Starratt received a call from a person who identified himself as "Chip," a nickname used by appellant Loye throughout the investigation. The caller told the agent that Petrulla wanted DEA Agent Story to obtain another boat. Based on this conversation Agent Starratt identified Loye as the telephone participant charged with the §843(b) violation in Count 9. The conversation was not recorded. Starratt never met Chip and he never made any voice comparison with Loye. The only way Starratt could identify the caller was through the caller's self-identification. Under these circumstances, Loye argues that Starratt's testimony identifying him is inadmissible because it was not authenticated, Fed. R. Evid. 901. Loye also argues that the identification was hearsay. Loye's contention that the identity of the caller was not properly authenticated finds support in our case law. . . .

We have previously remarked that "a telephone call out of the blue from one who identifies himself as X may not be, in itself, sufficient authentication of the call as in fact coming from X." United States v. Register, 496 F.2d 1072, 1077 (5th Cir. 1974). We agree with the government that the standard of admissibility of voice identification testimony is prima facie. We also agree that circumstantial evidence may be used in meeting this standard. However, there is not sufficient evidence to support the conclusion that Agent Starratt actually heard Loye's voice. As noted, Starratt had never met Loye and no voice comparisons were made. Under these circumstances, Loye's use of the nickname "Chip" does not make out a prima facie case that he was the caller. The possibility that someone else was using his nickname in this clandestine operation is too great to properly admit Agent Starratt's identification. This identification was essential to Loye's §843(b) conviction. Accordingly, we reverse Loye's conviction for Count 9. . . .

NOTES ON AUTHENTICATING TELEPHONE CALLS

1. The decision would be different, would it not, if Starratt had been able to recognize Loye's voice? How familiar does a witness have to be with a caller's voice before being allowed to testify to the identity of the caller? See

United States v. Axselle, 604 F.2d 1330, 1338 (10th Cir. 1979) (hearing voice one other time sufficient familiarity); United States v. Vitale, 549 F.2d 71 (8th Cir.) (two other occasions sufficient), cert. denied, 431 U.S. 907 (1977).

2. By what other methods might the telephone call have been authenticated as being from Loye?

3. In *Pool* the witness *received* an incoming call. How can a witness authenticate a call that he places himself? See FRE 901(b)(6).

PROBLEM 13-H.   *"This Is O'Rourke"*

Paul Michaud, a third-year law student, was a finalist for an associate position with O'Rourke & Kelly, the largest law firm in the state. He had recently returned from what he considered to be a successful interview with the firm and had been promised a decision within ten days. Although he did not have a chance to meet the senior partner, Jeremy O'Rourke, he learned that O'Rourke would make the final hiring decision. The firm was aware that he had two offers with deadlines, one from a prestigious firm in another city and the other from a federal judge.

On returning to his apartment on the fourth day after his interview, he found a phone message on his answering machine. The caller identified herself as the secretary to Jeremy O'Rourke of O'Rourke & Kelly. She stated that Mr. O'Rourke would like to speak with Paul and that "he will be leaving soon, but can be reached by phone at the Metropolitan Country Club, at 407-8965 after 5 p.m. this evening." Because it was after 5 p.m., Paul dialed the number indicated on the phone message. He asked to speak to Mr. O'Rourke. A voice came on the line and said "This is O'Rourke." Paul asked whether a decision had been made on the associate position. To his delight, the response was unhesitating, cordial, and positive—"When can you start?" After the negotiation of a starting date, the conversation was concluded.

The next day Paul wrote letters declining his other two offers. Paul heard nothing more for two months. Then he received the following letter:

Dear Mr. Michaud:

We are writing to inform you and our other job applicants that, because of recent internal restructuring within our law firm, we have decided not to hire any new associates for next year. We appreciate your interest in our firm.

Sincerely,
Jeremy O'Rourke

O'Rourke & Kelly

Paul was devastated. Against the recommendation of friends and ignoring possible legal impediments, he hired an attorney and filed suit against O'Rourke & Kelly for breach of contract. At trial, Paul takes the stand as the first witness. When Paul is asked to recount his telephone conversation with O'Rourke, the attorney for O'Rourke & Kelly objects on grounds of lack of authentication. What ruling?

G. SELF-AUTHENTICATING EXHIBITS

FRE 902 provides for the admissibility of "self-authenticating" exhibits, i.e., exhibits that do not require "[e]xtrinsic evidence of authenticity as a condition precedent to admissibility." The Advisory Committee's Note makes clear that the fact of self-authentication does not bar counterproof by the opponent.

What if no counterproof is offered? Does self-authentication merely create an inference of authenticity that satisfies a party's burden of production on the issue but does not bind the jury to find authenticity? Or does it shift the burden of production so that the trier of fact must find authenticity in the absence of counterproof by the opponent? Does self-authentication also shift the burden of persuasion, so the opponent is required not only to produce counterproof, but counterproof that persuades the trier of fact that the exhibit is not authentic? Consider the following problem.

PROBLEM 13-I.   *The Rejected Easement*

Byron sues Casey, alleging trespass on Greenacre. Casey claims to be entitled to drive on a dirt road over the parcel. At trial, Casey offers a document that purports to be an acknowledged grant of easement covering the road in question given to her by Arthur, who had later given a quitclaim deed for Greenacre to Byron. There is evidence that Arthur mentioned "some easement on the property" to Byron, and all agree that Casey has a good defense if indeed she holds the easement.

Casey offers the document without any foundation testimony, and Byron offers no evidence at all on the subject. At the end of trial, Casey seeks a directed verdict in her favor, arguing that the jury "cannot reject this easement, for the document is acknowledged and self-authenticating under FRE 902(8)." She seeks as well an instruction "telling the jury that they must accept this document for what it is, proof of the easement."

The court rejects Casey's motion and refuses the requested instruction. In his close, Byron argues that the purported easement is "obviously faked" and asks the jury to "pay no attention to that trumped up document."

The jury returns a verdict for Byron.

Should Casey have gotten her directed verdict or an instruction of the sort requested? Can the verdict for Byron be permitted to stand?

PROBLEM 13-J.   *The Death Certificate*

Walter Bellamy Jr. died in a single-car accident when his car went off the road while he was driving home. His life insurance company refused to pay death benefits to his widow, the designated beneficiary, claiming that his death was a suicide, hence outside the coverage of the policy. His widow files an action against the life insurance company. To prove the cause of his death at trial, she offers the certified copy of his death certificate shown here. Is it admissible as a self-authenticating document under FRE 902? Why or why not?

Certified Copy of a Death Record

REGISTRATION DISTRICT NO.	2.28	STATE OF ILLINOIS	STATE FILE NUMBER
REGISTERED NUMBER	48736	MEDICAL CERTIFICATE OF DEATH	

DECEASED – NAME	FIRST	MIDDLE	LAST	SEX	DATE OF DEATH (MONTH DAY YEAR)
1.	Walter	Herbert	Bellamy	2 M	3 Jan. 11, 1988

RACE – (WHITE, BLACK, AMERICAN INDIAN ETC.) (SPECIFY)	ORIGIN OR DESCENT	AGE – LAST BIRTHDAY (YRS)	UNDER 1 YEAR MOS DAYS	UNDER 1 DAY HOURS MIN	DATE OF BIRTH (MO DAY YEAR)	COUNTY OF DEATH
4a. White	4b. --	5a. 47	5b.	5c.	6 Oct. 27,1940	7a. Cook

CITY, TOWN, TWP OR ROAD DISTRICT NUMBER	HOSPITAL OR OTHER INSTITUTION – NAME (IF NOT IN EITHER GIVE STREET AND NUMBER)	IF HOSP OR INST INDICATE DOA OR DOA
7b. Chicago	7c. Metro General	7d. DOA

STATE OF BIRTH (IF NOT IN U.S.A. NAME COUNTRY)	CITIZEN OF WHAT COUNTRY	MARRIED NEVER MARRIED WIDOWED DIVORCED (SPECIFY)	NAME OF SURVIVING SPOUSE (IF WIFE GIVE MAIDEN NAME)
8. Mass.	9 USA	10. Married	11 Elaine Schwartz

SOCIAL SECURITY NUMBER	USUAL OCCUPATION	KIND OF BUSINESS OR INDUSTRY	U.S. WAR VETERAN (YES-NO)	WAR OR DATES OF SERVICE
12. 317-42-6307	13a Salesman	13b Electronics	13c No	13d N/A

RESIDENCE STREET AND NUMBER	CITY, TOWN, TWP OR ROAD DISTRICT NO	INSIDE CITY (YES-NO)	COUNTY	STATE
14a 1022 N. 141st	14b. Chicago	14c Yes	14d Cook	14e Ill.

FATHER – NAME	FIRST	MIDDLE	LAST	MOTHER – MAIDEN NAME	FIRST	MIDDLE	LAST
15.	George	Walter	Bellamy	16.	Karen	Kay	Dietz

INFORMANT'S SIGNATURE	RELATIONSHIP	MAILING ADDRESS (STREET AND OR R F D CITY OR TOWN STATE)
17a ▶ *Elaine Bellamy*	17b Wife	17c 1022 N. 141st, Chicago, IL 60627

18	DEATH WAS CAUSED BY	[ENTER ONLY ONE CAUSE PER LINE FOR (a) (b) and (c)]	APPROXIMATE INTERVAL BETWEEN ONSET AND DEATH
PART I.	IMMEDIATE CAUSE	(a) Head injury	Instantaneous
CONDITIONS IF ANY, WHICH GIVE RISE TO IMMEDIATE CAUSE (a) STATING THE UNDERLYING CAUSE LAST	DUE TO OR AS A CONSEQUENCE OF	(b) Automobile accident - Lake St. & Route 43	
	DUE TO OR AS A CONSEQUENCE OF	(c)	

PART II. OTHER SIGNIFICANT CONDITIONS	CONDITIONS CONTRIBUTING TO DEATH BUT NOT RELATED TO CAUSE GIVEN IN PART I (a)	AUTOPSY (YES-NO)	
		19a No	19b

DATE OF OPERATION IF ANY	MAJOR FINDINGS OF OPERATION
20a	20b

I ATTENDED THE DECEASED FROM (MONTH, DAY, YEAR)	TO (MONTH, DAY, YEAR)	AND LAST SAW HIM/HER ALIVE ON (MONTH DAY YEAR)	HOUR OF DEATH (MONTH DAY YEAR)
21a Jan. 11, 1988	21b Jan. 11, 1988	21c DOA	21d approximately 3:00 pm

TO THE BEST OF MY KNOWLEDGE DEATH OCCURRED AT THE TIME, DATE AND PLACE AND DUE TO THE CAUSE(S) STATED	DATE SIGNED
22a SIGNATURE ▶ *Randall Lewis*	22b Jan. 11, 1988

NAME AND ADDRESS OF CERTIFIER	(TYPE OR PRINT)	ILLINOIS LICENSE NUMBER
22c Randall Lewis, Metro General Hosp., Chicago, IL	22d 2837

NAME OF ATTENDING PHYSICIAN IF OTHER THAN CERTIFIER (TYPE OR PRINT)	NOTE IF AN INJURY WAS INVOLVED IN THIS DEATH THE CORONER MUST BE NOTIFIED
23	

BURIAL CREMATION REMOVAL (SPECIFY)	CEMETERY OR CREMATORY – NAME	LOCATION	CITY OR TOWN	STATE	DATE (MONTH DAY YEAR)
24a Burial	24b Forrest Park	24c	Glenview	IL	24d Jan. 14, 1988

FUNERAL HOME	NAME	STREET AND NUMBER	CITY OR TOWN	STATE	
25a Resthaven Mortuary 819 Main St.			Chicago	IL	60627

FUNERAL DIRECTOR'S SIGNATURE		FUNERAL DIRECTOR'S ILLINOIS LICENSE NUMBER
25b ▶ *Robert Babcox*		25c 4222

LOCAL REGISTRAR'S SIGNATURE	DATE REC'D BY LOCAL REGISTRAR (MONTH DAY YEAR)
26a ▶ *William Hutchinson*	26b Jan. 22, 1988

I HEREBY CERTIFY THAT the foregoing is a true and correct copy of the death record for the decedent named at Item 1, and that this record was established and filed in my office in accordance with the provisions of the Illinois Vital Records Act.

DATE March 21, 1988   SIGNED *Emily F. Bundy*

AT Chicago   Illinois OFFICIAL TITLE Deputy Clerk

The original record of this death is permanently filed with the ILLINOIS DEPARTMENT OF PUBLIC HEALTH at Springfield. County clerks and local registrars are authorized to make certifications from copies of the original record. The Illinois statutes provide that the certification of a death record by the Department of Public Health, local registrar or county clerk shall be prima facie evidence in all courts and places of the facts therein stated.

VR-201C (1978)   OFFICE OF VITAL RECORDS · ILLINOIS DEPARTMENT OF PUBLIC HEALTH · SPRINGFIELD 62761

Suppose that a second certificate were stapled to the death certificate, apparently signed by "Charles Burkett" above the title "Clerk of Cook County," bearing the apparent seal of the Office of County Clerk and containing the following statement:

> I certify that I am the Clerk of Cook County, and that Emily F. Bundy is personally known to me as the Deputy Clerk of Cook County, having legal custody of the records of the county pertaining to births, deaths, and motor vehicle registration.

Does *this* certificate authenticate the Death Certificate?

In addressing this problem, be sure to consult FRE 902(1), (2), and (4). Also consider FRCrimP 27 and FRCP 44(a)(1), both of which provide that an official record "may be evidenced by . . . a copy attested by the officer having the legal custody of the record, or by his deputy, and accompanied by a certificate that such officer has the custody," and that the requisite certificate "may be made by any public officer having a seal of office and having official duties in the district or political subdivision in which the record is kept, authenticated by the seal of his office." Are the requirements set out in the Civil and Criminal Rules perfectly consistent with FRE 902(2)? In case of conflict, which controls?

PROBLEM 13-K.   *The House of the Rising Sun*

Under the headline "Mayor Linked to Prostitution," the Daily Post ran a story stating that Mayor Cook was found to have a one-half ownership in the House of the Rising Sun, a local prostitution establishment. The story appeared under the by-line of Ron Bellamy, who was identified as "staff reporter." A week later, a letter to the editor was published in the Post, signed by George Ramsey, congratulating the Post on its expose of the mayor and stating that "Cook has been the prostitution kingpin in this town for years, and it is time the public knew about it." Mayor Cook files a libel action against the Post, Bellamy, and Ramsey. Bellamy defends on the ground that the published version of the story was not the same as the version he submitted to the city editor. Ramsey defends on the ground that he never wrote the letter in question. The Post settles prior to trial. At trial Mayor Cook offers as exhibits the two issues of the Post where the story and letter appeared. Bellamy and Ramsey object on grounds of lack of authentication. What ruling?

NOTES ON SELF-AUTHENTICATING EXHIBITS

1.   Which of the following qualify as self-authenticating exhibits: A copy of the New York Times? Webster's Dictionary? A volume of West Publishing Company's Supreme Court Reporter? A Sears catalog? Newsweek magazine? A candy bar in a wrapper labeled "Baby Ruth"? A map published by the government? The apparently signed and sealed minutes of the City Council of Fairbanks, Alaska? A census report by the government of France?

2.   Under FRE 902(9), commercial paper and related documents are self-authenticating "to the extent provided by general commercial law." General commercial law is now largely governed by the Uniform Commercial Code, and FRE 902(9) in effect incorporates certain provisions of the Code as rules of evidence. UCC §1-201(3) defines presumption to mean that the trier "must find the existence of the fact presumed unless and until evidence is introduced which would support a finding of its non-existence," and in other provisions the Code appears to use the term "prima facie" to mean essentially enough evidence to support (but not to require) a particular finding. There are at least five other pertinent provisions: UCC §1-202 provides that bills of lading and

certain other documents are "prima facie" authentic; UCC §3-114(3) provides that a date on an instrument is "presumed to be correct"; UCC §3-307(1)(b) provides that a signature on an instrument is "presumed to be genuine or authorized," except in certain cases; UCC §3-510 provides for the admissibility of certain documents that "create a presumption of dishonor and of any notice of dishonor therein shown"; and UCC §8-105(3)(b) provides that the signature on a security "is presumed to be genuine or authorized." Thus, in cases where the Uniform Commercial Code is applicable, a check or a security can generally be received as evidence that it was signed by the person whose signature appears thereon without calling a witness to identify the signature or to provide other evidence of authenticity.

3. FRE 902(10) incorporates by reference the multiplicity of federal statutes making certain documents "presumptively or prima facie genuine or authentic." Among the more important of such statutes is 28 U.S.C. §753(b), which provides:

> The transcript in any case certified by the reporter or other individual designated to produce the record shall be deemed prima facie a correct statement of the testimony taken and proceedings had. No transcripts of the proceedings of the court shall be considered as official except those made from the records certified by the reporter or other individual designated to produce the record.

H. DEMONSTRATIVE EVIDENCE

BELLI, DEMONSTRATIVE EVIDENCE: SEEING IS BELIEVING
16 Trial 70 (July 1980)

Everyone is familiar with the saying that a picture is worth a thousand words. To the trial lawyer, a picture can be worth much, much more. It could spell the difference between victory and defeat, or between a nominal award and an "adequate" one. Yet photographs comprise merely one fact of that vast expanse referred to as "demonstrative evidence." This article will examine the purposes and uses of demonstrative evidence, as well as some of its forms and variations. . . .

WHAT IS DEMONSTRATIVE EVIDENCE?

Broadly speaking, demonstrative evidence is anything which appeals to the jurors' senses. It can be something for them to look at, to touch, to smell, to taste, or listen to. Demonstrative evidence is premised upon the theory that it is easier and much more effective simply to show the jurors what is being described, rather than to waste time and to risk possible confusion by relying solely upon oral testimony.

Demonstrative evidence clearly and concisely communicates to the jury that precise image which no amount of verbal description by itself could convey. In addition, by giving jurors something they can see, feel, smell, taste, or hear, their attention spans and interests in the case are revived and renewed. More importantly, they now have something they can take back into the jury room with them as they begin their deliberations.

From this, one sees that another advantage to using demonstrative evidence is the *continual communication* with the jury that it provides. Unlike a witness' spoken testimony which disappears as soon as it is stated, tangible demonstrative evidence remains in the jury's presence throughout the trial, a constant reminder of the point it is intended to make. To illustrate this concept of continuous communications, I would like briefly to relate a burn case I recently tried with Vincent Igoe of East St. Louis, Illinois.

The case involved a plaintiff who had suffered thermal burns over 80 percent of his body. Among a myriad of other demonstrative evidence, we introduced and had accepted into evidence a six-foot high, full-color photograph of the plaintiff, who was clad only in a diaper-like cloth. The picture had been taken shortly after the incident occurred, and graphically illustrated the severity of the plaintiff's condition. Having the picture in the sight of the jury throughout the trial played a large factor in the defendant's decision to settle the case for $1 million.

One note on the continuous use of a single piece of demonstrative evidence throughout a trial such as this: Every once in a while, cases come about involving such "shocking" evidence. Sometimes it is more useful to bring in this evidence during the latter stage of the trial, so that the jurors do not become immune or indifferent to it, thereby losing some of its initial potency. This is a factor which must be taken into consideration and weighed on its own merits in every case involving such evidence, the trial lawyer then proceeding the way he deems best.

THE USES OF DEMONSTRATIVE EVIDENCE

Demonstrative evidence is utilized for three major purposes: (1) to establish the liability of the defendant; (2) to illustrate the full extent and severity of the plaintiff's injuries; and (3) to complement the written transcript for use on appeal.

1) As every trial lawyer is fully aware, without liability there is no case; there can be no recompense to an injured party. . . .

The use of models, tests, and experiments for reconstructing the accident in front of the jury to establish liability can prove invaluable. Simply telling a jury how one came to be injured involves not only general questions of the witness' credibility, but also the query of whether such an accident could have occurred even assuming all facts to be true as stated. To re-create the incident in the courtroom instantly removes this latter inquiry. Now the jury knows that such an accident can in fact occur, and is not quite so incredible as it may at one time have thought.

2) Demonstrative evidence, especially in the form of photographs and motion pictures—and particularly "day-in-the-life" films, which show the plain-

tiff's condition immediately after the accident and during the recovery period—is instrumental in communicating the plaintiff's injuries, pain, and suffering to the jury. . . .

. . . What often occurs is that, in the three to four years that it takes before the case goes to trial (and even considerably longer if one takes into consideration the possibility of various appeals followed by a second, or even third, trial), the plaintiff will have substantially recovered from the once horrendous scars, bruises, lacerations and other telltale markings of the distressful event. The jury, without such photos and movies, sees only the plaintiff as he now stands before them, in a fairly healthy, rehabilitated state. Once-hideous scars will have since faded away, leaving only faint traces of their one-time gruesome existence. . . .

3) Demonstrative evidence is also important as it aids in the creation of the record for review in the event the case is appealed. Many verdicts in favor of the plaintiff are appealed on the basis that there were insufficient facts upon which the jury or court could have found that the defendant was negligent, or frequently that the damages awarded the plaintiff were "excessive." By placing before the appellate justices a comprehensive record, replete with demonstrative evidence which clearly shows the defendant's liability and accurately reflects the *full* extent of the plaintiff's injuries, pain, and suffering, the plaintiff's lawyer stands a much better chance of not having the verdict overturned, or the damages awarded reduced.

TYPES OF DEMONSTRATIVE EVIDENCE

Of all types of demonstrative evidence, photographs have historically been the most frequently employed, and even today the trend continues. Although many restrictions were originally placed on the use of photographs, most of these have since disappeared. Color photographs and enlargements are routinely permitted. The fact that the scene captured on film is gory or gruesome does not make it any less admissible, unless it is being offered for the sole purpose of inflaming the jury. . . .

Motion pictures likewise may be utilized, but judges tend to exercise their discretion more frequently in refusing to admit this type of evidence, due to their susceptibility to editing and staging. One of the more common uses of motion pictures that has blossomed in the past few years is the use of a "day-in-the-life" film. The object of such a film is to record the injured plaintiff's daily routine since the injury was incurred. The camera begins rolling the moment the plaintiff wakes, and continues until he falls asleep.

The impact of these films is very powerful. The jury must watch as the plaintiff lives through one full day. These films are especially potent when the plaintiff has lost a limb, suffered severe internal injuries, has become a paraplegic, has sustained considerable brain damage, or someone, especially in the case of children, who for the rest of their lives will be confined to an iron lung.

Each juror sees how the plaintiff can no longer care for even his simplest needs. They learn how his condition demands constant care and attention. The jurors watch as the plaintiff's face writhes with pain as he tries to walk or make even the most elementary of movements. In short, the jurors watch as the plaintiff suffers through a typical day, which will be repeated over and over again until death.

Often, rather than show a picture of the injury, it is more effective to show the wound itself. Courts commonly allow scars, bruises, burnt tissue, and even the stump of an amputated limb to be bared and shown. In some cases, the court will allow the jurors to *touch* the injury. This is particularly true where the injury is hidden, such as a dent in the scalp. Often, jurors are given the chance to touch burned skin, so they may feel how hardened it has become.

Where the plaintiff has lost a limb due to the malfeasance of the defendant, the prosthesis he must wear for the remainder of his days may be admitted into evidence. The artificial limb may be put on and its workings demonstrated for the jury. Once in a while, in an amputation case, the courts are presented with the question of whether the amputated limb itself may be entered into evidence.

In one celebrated case, the plaintiff's hand was severed as he was operating a stamping press. One issue in the case involved exactly where the hand had been when it was caught. The Supreme Court of California held that the trial court had properly admitted into evidence a jar containing the plaintiff's amputated hand, which had been preserved in fluid. A streak of ink along the hand supported the plaintiff's contentions as to the whereabouts of the hand at the time of the injury. Other courts have admitted a severed kneecap, a bottle containing four ounces of brain matter and eight pieces of splintered bone, and a few toes.

Models, charts and diagrams are most effective tools for communicating with the jury. A skeleton, an electric train set, or a magnetized map upon which magnetic cars, trains, pedestrians and the like may be mounted play important roles in the successful handling of many cases. More often than not, the costs in having a model or chart prepared are not nearly as exorbitant as the trial lawyer may think. . . .

CONCLUSION

Many other forms of demonstrative evidence are widely employed. Tests, experiments, sound recordings, "real" evidence and untold others help the trial lawyer every day in making known to the jurors *exactly* what it is they should know. The varieties of demonstrative evidence available to the trial attorney are enormous. They are limited only by the creativity and originality of the trial lawyer's mind and the trial court's discretion. New forms of demonstrative evidence are being invented daily by innovative lawyers seeking to show the jurors precisely what they should consider.

The last 25 years have seen great advances in the field of demonstrative evidence and its uses. The next 25 years shall be at the very least equally exciting. Right now some trial lawyer may be formulating a new concept which will once again revolutionize this area. It is with eager anticipation that all trial lawyers await such new discoveries in further strengthening their skills and competence in the greatest of all professions.

NOTES ON DEMONSTRATIVE EVIDENCE

1.   Belli refers to demonstrative evidence as "anything which appeals to the jurors' senses." This is a broader definition than is often used because it could even encompass testimony. Most commentators and cases draw a distinction between "real evidence" and demonstrative evidence. Real evidence refers to tangible objects or matters that had a direct part in the events giving rise to the litigation. Demonstrative evidence is often viewed as having no independent probative value and serves merely as a visual aid to the jury in understanding the testimony of witnesses. Demonstrative evidence is also sometimes referred to as illustrative evidence.

2.   If evidence is received merely for illustrative purposes, in what ways, if any, should it be treated differently from other evidence?

3.   Is demonstrative evidence ever hearsay? See Grimes v. Employers Mutual Liability Insurance Co., 73 F.R.D. 607 (D. Alaska 1977) ("day in life" film of plaintiff is hearsay but admissible under the residual exception, FRE 803(24)). On what basis could a hearsay objection be made to a film of a reenactment of a crime offered by the prosecutor? Would it make a difference if the defendant voluntarily participated in the reenactment?

4.   The generally accepted standards for the admissibility of experiments or tests were stated as follows in Ramseyer v. General Motors Corp., 417 F.2d 859, 864 (8th Cir. 1969):

> Admissibility of evidence depends upon a foundational showing of substantial similarity between the tests conducted and actual conditions. Perfect identity between experimental and actual conditions is neither attainable nor required. Dissimilarities effect [sic] the weight of the evidence, not admissibility. . . . Finally, the decision whether to admit or exclude evidence of experiments in a particular case rests largely in the discretion of the trial judge and his decision will not be overturned on appeal absent a clear showing of an abuse of discretion.

When a litigant seeks to conduct an experiment in court, it is a form of demonstrative evidence. Trial courts have great discretion in deciding whether to allow in-court experiments, and are strongly influenced by considerations such as the amount of time the experiment will consume and the danger of unfair prejudice or of confusing or misleading the jury. If what the litigant seeks to offer is testimony regarding an experiment conducted out-of-court, prior to trial, the rules governing expert witnesses and scientific evidence must also be considered.

PROBLEM 13-L.   *"The Animation Will Help the Jury"*

Brandon Sayles is charged with involuntary manslaughter in connection with the death of Melissa, the seven-month-old daughter of his live-in girlfriend Naomi Lyell. Sayles and Lyell rushed Melissa to the emergency room, but Melissa died from severe neck injuries within an hour. As Melissa's treating physician, Dr. Gerdes concluded that her injuries resulted from "Shaken Baby Syndrome" and contacted police.

Interviewed by a detective, Sayles says Melissa fell down the stairs and was unconscious when he found her. Sayles tells the detective that he "panicked" and then shook Melissa "in the hope of reviving her." But he contends that her injuries were the result of the fall.

At trial the prosecutor offers a computer animation prepared by the National Center on Shaken Baby Syndrome. "The animation will help the jury understand the testimony by Dr. Gerdes," the prosecutor announces, "so it can comprehend how Melissa suffered her fatal injuries." The animation depicts a representational figure of a typical infant about six months in age being shaken so that the head is whipped forward and backward with such force that the chin touches the chest during the forward motion and the head almost touches the child's back at the other extreme. Later the animation depicts physical damage that occurs in blood vessels and nerves located in the brain and eyes of a child shaken in this manner.

As foundation, and on the basis of his medical training and experience, Dr. Gerdes testifies that (1) the computer animation accurately represents Shaken Baby Syndrome and the injuries it causes, and (2) his examination of Melissa persuades him that she suffered brain and eye damage similar to the injuries demonstrated on the animation. Sayles objects to the animation, claiming lack of adequate authentication and unfair prejudice.

How should the judge rule? Would it make a difference if the judge were willing to give the following instruction:

> Ladies and Gentlemen, we are going to watch a computer animation, and I want you to understand that it is not meant to be a recreation of events in this case. What happened in this case is for you to decide on the basis of the evidence presented, and not on the basis of the animation. The purpose of the animation is merely to help you understand the testimony by Dr. Gerdes and the concepts he is presenting here.

NOTES ON COMPUTER-CREATED ANIMATIONS

1. Is it important to your ruling that the defendant admitted shaking Melissa, even though he denied using enough force to inflict fatal injuries? He didn't concede that his conduct was the same as that depicted in the prosecution's video presentation, did he? Does that matter?

2. Is an expert required to authenticate such computer animations? What type of expert? Should the court also require testimony by the person who prepared the animation to explain the data or parameters on which the animation rests? Should such an exhibit be formally admitted as substantive evidence, or only as illustrative evidence? Should the jury be allowed to run the animation on a computer in the jury room during deliberations, or to see the animation run again in the courtroom if it requests?

3. What if a criminal defendant such as Sayles, or a civil litigant for that matter, cannot afford an expert to prepare computer-generated video imagery

to present his version of the facts, or even to challenge the preparation or accuracy of the opponent's imagery? Should an imbalance in available litigation resources bear on the judge's decision whether to allow such evidence?

4.   What role does FRE 403 play in this context? Consider the following suggestion:

> Computer-generated video imagery can have a powerful impact on the jury, perhaps overwhelming its fair consideration of other conflicting evidence. Moreover, unlike experimental evidence, computer-generated imagery is not restricted by the laws of gravity or other scientific principles. For these reasons, courts retain broad discretion under FRE 403 to exclude computer animations, particularly where they are based on questionable assumptions or project such a slanted or distorted view of the evidence as to be unfairly prejudicial or misleading.

C. Mueller and L. Kirkpatrick, Evidence §9.34 (3d ed. 2003). And see generally, Fred Galves, Where the Not-So-Wild Things Are: Computers in the Courtroom, The Federal Rules of Evidence, and the Need for Institutional Reform and More Judicial Acceptance, 13 Harv. J. L. & Tech. 161 (2000).

Fourteen

THE "BEST EVIDENCE" DOCTRINE

A. INTRODUCTION

Parties to litigation have a natural incentive to offer the most direct, reliable, and persuasive evidence available to them in order to satisfy their allocated proof burdens. Largely for this reason, it has been viewed as unnecessary for the law of evidence to compel parties to produce the "best" evidence. Litigants are generally allowed freedom of choice among admissible forms of evidence, and they may choose to offer "lesser" forms of proof for reasons of practicality, economy, or tactics. Testimony describing an accident scene may be given instead of taking the jury to the location for a view. A photograph or a testimonial description of a wrecked vehicle is almost always offered in lieu of the vehicle itself. A hearsay statement may be received in many circumstances (see FRE 803), even though the declarant could be called as a witness.

The primary exception where a rule of preference is imposed arises when a litigant seeks to prove the contents of a writing. At common law, it has long been required that when the contents of a writing are being proven, the original writing must be offered or its absence satisfactorily explained. The effect of this rule is to preclude proof of the terms of a writing not only by testimony but also by a copy, even a carbon copy, unless the original is shown to be unavailable through no serious fault of the party seeking to prove its contents. This rule is commonly called the "Best Evidence" doctrine, even though that name misleadingly suggests that it applies to all types of evidence. It is also known as the original writing or original document rule.

This special rule regulating proof of the contents of writings is based on several considerations. First, the written word has traditionally been regarded in law as having special sanctity, justifying more stringent proof requirements. Second, when the contents of a writing are in issue, any evidence other than the writing itself is distinctly inferior. Language is complex, and the slightest variation in wording can have enormous significance in determining the outcome of a legal dispute. Unless a writing is very short, it is beyond the power of most human memory to summarize the writing with the precision that is often needed in the courtroom. The burden on litigants of requiring them to produce an original writing when available is viewed as substantially outweighed by the increased accuracy of the factfinding process. Third, modern photocopy methods have not always been available, and historically copies of writings have been viewed with suspicion. A requirement of producing the original writing has been viewed as a convenient safeguard against either forgeries or inadvertent errors in the copying process. Such a safeguard was particularly important in earlier times when discovery was more limited and the adverse party was unlikely to be able to gain access to the original writing through discovery procedures. Fourth, production of the original writing assures completeness and prevents any segment from being presented out of context. Finally, examination of the original sometimes helps to resolve disputes regarding authenticity and claimed alteration.

NOTES ON THE "BEST EVIDENCE" DOCTRINE

1. FRE 1002 not only codifies the common law Best Evidence rule but extends it to recordings and photographs. What justification can be given for such an extension? On the other hand, does FRE 1003 have the effect of significantly modifying the Best Evidence doctrine?

2. In view of the general admissibility of duplicates in lieu of originals under FRE 1003, what type of secondary evidence proving the contents of a "writing, recording, or photograph" is now most likely to be excluded by FRE 1002?

3. Examine FRE 1005 carefully. It prevents disruption of public recordkeeping systems by making it unnecessary for litigants to produce the original of a public record. What qualifications does the Rule place on FRE 1003? Could FRE 1005 be more artfully drafted?

4. To what extent is an "escape clause" to FRE 1002 provided by FRE 1004(4), which dispenses with the requirement of producing the original when the writing, recording, or photograph is "not closely related to a controlling issue"? For examples of "collateral" writings, see the Advisory Committee's Note to FRE 1004(4). See also United States v. Johnson, 413 F.2d 1396, 1400 (5th Cir. 1969), on reh'g, 431 F.2d 441 (5th Cir. 1970) (alleged receipt and concealment of stolen motor vehicle; no error to allow FBI agent to testify that vehicle registration papers at courthouse did not match vehicle with that license number observed in front of defendant's house, resulting in further investigation and discovery that vehicle was stolen: "This item was not proof of identity but simply served to explain the reason for the agent's subsequent inspection, which did furnish conclusive [proof of] identity."); McCormick on Evidence §234, at 364 (J. Strong 5th ed. 1999) (reference by witness to newspaper in explaining why he knows the date a designated event occurred because the next day he saw the event described in the newspaper and made a mental note of the date); 5 C. Mueller and L. Kirkpatrick, Federal Evidence §580 (2d ed. 1994):

> It seems impossible to define "collateralness" or matters "not closely related to a controlling issue" with any precision, and perhaps for this reason the exception

is often invoked with little or no discussion of its intended meaning. But despite its vagueness, the exception is useful in preserving flexibility in administering the best evidence doctrine, enabling the trial judge to protect continuity and flow in the presentation of testimony and to avoid unnecessary distraction and delay—the exception is "a necessary concession to expedition of trials and clearness of narration."

5.   Are you persuaded that the Best Evidence rule is needed? To the extent that the parties want to present the most complete and accurate evidence of the content of a writing, recording, or photograph, they will certainly offer the thing itself, won't they? Does the Best Evidence rule serve to block parties from presenting inferior proof in precisely those circumstances in which they might be tempted to do so? See Cleary and Strong, The Best Evidence Rule: An Evaluation in Context, 51 Iowa L. Rev. 825 (1966) (concluding that Best Evidence rule does offer some minimal protection against inaccurate or fraudulent presentations and against attempts to present evidence out of context).

PROBLEM 14-A.   *The Defamatory Letter*

Paula brings a defamation action against Daniel based on statements made by Daniel in a letter to Paula's employer. At trial, the letter is neither produced nor shown to be unavailable. Over a Best Evidence objection, the employer is allowed to testify regarding the contents of the letter. Paula is awarded a substantial verdict. On appeal, Daniel contends that it was a clear violation of the Best Evidence rule to allow the employer to testify to the contents of the letter without being required to produce it. Assuming the appellate court agrees with this contention, should the judgment be reversed? At oral argument, what question is Daniel likely to be asked?

B.   DEFINING A "WRITING, RECORDING, OR PHOTOGRAPH"

UNITED STATES v. DUFFY
United States Court of Appeals for the Fifth Circuit
454 F.2d 809 (1972)

WISDOM, J.

The defendant-appellant James H. Duffy was convicted by a jury of transporting a motor vehicle in interstate commerce from Florida to California knowing it to have been stolen in violation of 18 U.S.C.A. §2312. He was sentenced to imprisonment for a term of two years and six months. On this appeal, Duffy complains of error in the admission of certain evidence and of prejudice resulting from members of the jury having been present during a sentencing in an unrelated case. We affirm.

At the trial, the Government established that Duffy was employed in the body shop of an automobile dealership in Homestead, Florida; that the stolen vehicle was taken by the dealership as a trade-in on the purchase of a new car; that the vehicle was sent to the body shop for repair; and that the vehicle and the defendant disappeared over the same weekend. The Government also presented testimony as to the discovery of the car in California including the testimony of (1) a witness who was found in possession of the vehicle and arrested and who testified he had received the vehicle from the defendant, (2) a San Fernando, California police officer who made the arrest and recovered the automobile, and (3) an F.B.I. agent who examined the vehicle, its contents, and the vehicle identification number. The defense stipulated to the authenticity of fingerprints, identified as Duffy's found on the rear-view mirror of the vehicle. The defense sought, through the testimony of three witnesses including the defendant, to establish that Duffy had hitchhiked to California and that, although he had worked on the stolen vehicle in the automobile dealership in Florida, he had not stolen it and had not transported it to California.

Both the local police officer and the F.B.I. agent testified that the trunk of the stolen car contained two suitcases. Found inside one of the suitcases, according to the witnesses, was a white shirt imprinted with a laundry mark reading "D-U-F." The defendant objected to the admission of testimony about the shirt and asked that the government be required to produce the shirt.[35] The trial judge overruled the objection and admitted the testimony. This ruling is assigned as error.

The appellant argues that the admission of the testimony violated the "Best Evidence Rule." According to his conception of the "Rule," the Government should have been required to produce the shirt itself rather than testimony about the shirt. This contention misses the import of the "Best Evidence Rule." The "Rule," as it exists today, may be stated as follows:

> [I]n proving the terms of *a writing*, where such terms are material, the original writing must be produced, unless it is shown to be unavailable for some reason other than the serious fault of the proponent.

(Emphasis supplied.) McCormick, Evidence §230, at 361 (J. Strong ed. 1999). Although the phrase "Best Evidence Rule" is frequently used in general terms, the "Rule" itself is applicable only to the proof of the contents of a writing. McCormick summarizes the policy-justifications for the rule preferring the original writing:

> (1). . . precision in presenting to the court the exact words of the writing is of more than average importance, particularly as respects operative or dispositive instruments, such as deeds, wills and contracts, since a slight variation in words may mean a great difference in rights, (2) . . . there is a substantial hazard of inaccuracy in the human process of making a copy by handwriting or typewriting, and (3) as respects oral testimony purporting to give from memory the terms of a writing, there is a special risk of error, greater than in the case of attempts at describing other situations generally. In the light of these dangers of mistransmis-

---

35. It is undisputed that the shirt was available to be produced and that there was no reason for failure to produce the shirt.

sion, accompanying the use of written copies or of recollection, largely avoided through proving the terms by presenting the writing itself, the preference for the original writing is justified.

McCormick, Evidence 410 (1954).

The "Rule" is not, by its terms or because of the policies underlying it, applicable to the instant case. The shirt with a laundry mark would not, under ordinary understanding, be considered a writing and would not, therefore, be covered by the "Best Evidence Rule." When the disputed evidence, such as the shirt in this case, is an object bearing a mark or inscription, and is, therefore, a chattel *and* a writing, the trial judge has discretion to treat the evidence as a chattel or as a writing. In reaching his decision, the trial judge should consider the policy-consideration behind the "Rule." In the instant case, the trial judge was correct in allowing testimony about the shirt without requiring the production of the shirt. Because the writing involved in this case was simple, the inscription "D-U-F," there was little danger that the witness would inaccurately remember the terms of the "writing." Also, the terms of the "writing" were by no means central or critical to the case against Duffy. The crime charged was not possession of a certain article, where the failure to produce the article might prejudice the defense. The shirt was collateral evidence of the crime. Furthermore, it was only one piece of evidence in a substantial case against Duffy.

The appellant relies on Watson v. United States, 5 Cir. 1955, 224 F.2d 910 for his contention that the testimony was inadmissible without production of the shirt. *Watson* involved a prosecution for possession of liquor without internal revenue stamps affixed to the containers in violation of what was then 26 U.S.C. §2803(a). This Court held that admission of testimony that there were no revenue stamps on seized containers without requiring production of the containers was erroneous. This case, however, does not provide support for appellant's assertion. First, the only case cited in *Watson* in support of application of the "Best Evidence Rule" to an object was a 1917 Ninth Circuit case involving a writing and not an object. See Simpson v. United States, 9 Cir. 1917, 245 F. 278. Second, the containers in *Watson* were critical to the proof of the crime. Possession of the containers was an element of the crime. As mentioned above, the shirt in the instant case, was not critical and possession of the shirt was not an element of the crime. Finally, *Watson,* although it has never been specifically overruled, has been distinguished into oblivion by this and other courts. Where *Watson* has been followed, a writing has been involved. In *Burney,* [5 Cir. 1965, 339 F.2d 91,] we held that oral testimony describing the contents of two containers as distilled spirits was admissible without producing the containers or their contents.

> The *Watson* decision is a minority decision on this point. As far as we are able to ascertain, the *Watson* case is the only case in all of the Circuits which does not confine the scope of the best evidence rule to the production of original documents or writings whenever feasible.

339 F.2d at 93.

In sum, the admission of the testimony in the instant case did not violate the "Best Evidence Rule.". . .

Affirmed.

NOTES ON DEFINING A "WRITING, RECORDING, OR PHOTOGRAPH"

1.   *Duffy* presents the question of the applicability of the Best Evidence rule to inscribed chattels. The question whether an inscription constitutes a "writing" may also arise when testimony is offered regarding the number on a police officer's badge or a license plate, the words on a tombstone or traffic sign, the odometer reading on an automobile service sticker, the words on a certificate or sales receipt, or the serial number on a manufactured product.

2.   Even if the Best Evidence doctrine is found to apply, courts can excuse nonproduction under the collateral writing exception of FRE 1004(4) if the inscription is sufficiently tangential to the dispute. Could the court have properly taken such an "end run" around the Best Evidence doctrine in the *Duffy* case?

3.   Is a painting or sculpture subject to the Best Evidence rule? See Seiler v. Lucasfilm 808 F.2d 1316 (9th Cir. 1986) (Best Evidence rule applies to drawings). Is a musical score? Is a live performance of a musical score? A recorded performance?

4.   Wide discretion is vested in trial judges to determine on the facts of each case whether the Best Evidence doctrine should apply to inscribed chattels. Consider the following suggested guidelines:

> The keys are (1) the relative importance of the communicative content of the inscribed object in the case, (2) the simplicity or complexity of that content and consequent risk of error in admitting other evidence, (3) the strength of the proffered evidence, taking into account corroborative witnesses or evidence and the presence or absence of bias or self-interest on the part of the witnesses, (4) the breadth of the margin for error within which mistake in any testimonial account or other proof would not undermine the point to be proved, (5) the presence or absence of an actual dispute as to content, (6) the ease or difficulty of producing the object itself, and (7) the reasons why the proponent of other evidence of content does not have or offer the object itself. . . .

5 C. Mueller and L. Kirkpatrick, Federal Evidence §552, at 234-235 (2d ed. 1994).

C.   DEFINING AN "ORIGINAL"

PROBLEM 14-B.   *The Unprivate Physician*

Denise allows Dr. Murphy to arrange for a private adoption of her newborn daughter with an express understanding that her identity as the mother would never be disclosed to either the adoptive parents or the child. Eighteen years later the daughter seeks to discover her biological parents and is put in touch with Dr. Murphy. At her request, Dr. Murphy furnishes her with a photocopy of his office adoption records, which clearly identify Denise as the mother. The daughter subsequently contacts Denise, and the reunion results in psychological anguish for Denise. She sues Dr. Murphy for outrageous conduct and for breach of the promise of confidentiality. At trial, Denise offers as evidence the photocopy of the adoption records that had been furnished to her daughter by Dr. Murphy. The attorney for Dr. Murphy objects, stating that the Best Evidence rule requires production of the original records, not a photocopy. Assume FRE 1003 has not been adopted in this jurisdiction. What ruling?

NOTES ON DEFINING AN "ORIGINAL"

1. The definition of an "original" writing, recording, or photograph is set forth in FRE 1001(3). When can a photocopy or carbon copy qualify as an original?

2. In determining which writing is the original, consideration must be given to the elements of the charge or claim, the intention of the parties, the surrounding circumstances, and the purposes of the party offering the writing. Consider United States v. Rangel, 585 F.2d 344, 346 (8th Cir. 1978) (photocopies of customer's carbon copies of Master Charge receipts were the "originals" when they were the documents submitted in support of a false claim for government travel expenses); Cartier v. Jackson, 59 F.3d 1046, 1048 (10th Cir. 1995) (copyright infringement action alleging that Michael Jackson appropriated to his own use a song from a demo tape sent to him by plaintiff; demo tape and not first-recorded "master" tape was "original" for purposes of this litigation because it was only tape heard by defendant).

3. Why is it generally not difficult to satisfy the best evidence requirement with respect to photographs and computer printouts?

D. USE OF DUPLICATES

In the days of Bob Cratchit, making copies involved enormous labor and great risk of inaccuracy or illegibility.[1] Little wonder, then, that common law tradition frowned as much on "copies" as on testimony describing what the original contained. Even the advent of more advanced copies (produced by carbon paper and the Thermofax machine) did not immediately open the door to receipt of copies.

This traditional skepticism, however, could not long survive the coming of the modern office copier. The genius of these machines is that they make full and accurate copies as readable as the original. (The technology involves an electrostatic process, but reproduction of black-and-white printed pages is so good that the product is sometimes called a "photocopy.") In recognition of

---

1. The scrivener often copied the original by hand, or used the "letterpress" or "blotterpress" method. These involved pressing the inked original on porous paper to produce a reverse (mirror image) of the original and then either pressing this reverse copy on a second porous sheet to make a second reversal (producing a faint forward-reading document) or, when times were slow in the bookkeeping department, simply using the first reversal as the basis for producing a new inked forward-reading handmade copy.

this technology, Rule 1003 permits the use in evidence of "duplicate[s]" *without* need to make excuses for nonproduction of the original under FRE 1004.

Note that a duplicate is admissible under FRE 1003 only if it meets the definition of a "duplicate" set forth in FRE 1001(4). Consider what types of copies are included in or excluded from this definition.

Rule 1003 does not quite open the door all the way to duplicates. A duplicate is *nearly* as usable in evidence as an original, but not quite, for Rule 1003 contains two escape clauses, permitting exclusion of duplicates when concerns arise over "authenticity of the original" or under the circumstances it would be "unfair to admit the duplicate."

In the following problems, consider whether duplicates should be admissible or required. Consider too the roles that Rule 1008 allocates to judge and jury when duplicates are offered.

PROBLEM 14-C.   *"There Never Was Such an Original"*

Dan sues Eva in contract and offers in evidence what he claims to be a "photocopy of the original agreement." On inspecting the proffered photocopy and consulting with his client, counsel for Eva raises a Best Evidence objection. In proceedings in aid of the objection, Eva takes the stand, and testifies thus:

Q *(defense counsel):*   Have you examined this so-called photocopy?
A *(Eva):* Yes, I have.
Q: Is that a copy of a written agreement between you and Dan?
A: I have no idea what that's a copy of. I never saw such a document in my life. We did have an agreement, and we did type it out, in a way that looks sort of like this, but *this* says that I promised not to go to work for any of Dan's competitors, and what we signed never contained anything like that. Our agreement, the original which we signed, never said that.

Counsel for Eva then states, "Your honor, there never was such an original as this. Therefore this purported copy—whatever it is—cannot be admitted. We've raised a genuine question about authenticity, and you cannot properly admit this purported copy—this forgery, if you want to call it what it really is."

You are counsel for Dan. How can you reply to Eva's objection? If Dan can testify that "I made this photocopy from the very agreement Eva and I signed, and it accurately reproduces our contract," should the judge resolve the issue produced by the conflict between Dan and Eva, or should the jury decide it? If the jury should decide it, does that mean that the copy should be admitted? Hasn't Eva raised a "genuine issue" about the authenticity of the original?

PROBLEM 14-D.   *Nine Hours or One?*

Gretchen sues St. Anne's Hospital and Dr. Mazo for negligence in an operation that caused her permanent brain damage. At the time, Gretchen was pregnant and had been admitted for emergency surgery. While under a general anesthetic, she vomited in her oxygen mask, which blocked the flow of oxygen to her brain. After the operation she was permanently comatose, living on life support, and her baby died unborn.

In his testimony, Dr. Mazo admits that it would be negligent to place Gretchen under anesthesia if she had eaten only one hour earlier. But St. Anne's introduces her admitting record, which shows that nine hours had passed since she last ate.

In a dramatic development during rebuttal, Gretchen's attorney calls Sally Abrams, the nurse who admitted Gretchen to St. Anne's. Abrams testifies that Gretchen told her she had eaten a meal just one hour prior to coming to the hospital. Abrams wrote the number "1" on the admitting form, and she testifies that after the failed surgery Dr. Mazo forced her (on threat of dismissal) to change the "1" to a "9." Before altering the form, however, she made a photocopy showing her prior entry.

Gretchen offers the photocopy. The defense raises a Best Evidence objection, both to the copy and to Abrams' testimony, arguing that the copy is a forgery that does not accurately reflect the contents of the original. How should the court rule, and why? What if the judge is personally persuaded that the photocopy is a forgery?

E.   BEST EVIDENCE DOCTRINE IN OPERATION

By its terms, the Best Evidence Doctrine always applied only when a party seeks to prove "the content" of a writing. On this point Rule 1002 made no change, though to be sure it did broaden the coverage of the doctrine to embrace recordings and photographs.

When the doctrine applies. Obviously it is critical to understand just when "the content" is what a party seeks to prove. Speaking broadly and focusing mostly on writings, there are two situations in which necessarily content is indeed the point to be proved. First is the circumstance in which the substantive law forces the content of a writing into prominence, and in effect simply requires one party or another to prove that content. Second is the circumstance in which a party chooses to prove content, even though she might theoretically present an adequate claim or defense without such proof—the situation, in other words, in which party strategy forces the writing into prominence.

Recall, as one instance in which substantive law forces the content of a writing into prominence, what you learned in the contracts course about the parol evidence doctrine and the statute of frauds. Here is not the place to exhaust those subjects, but we can agree that the former holds essentially that when the parties have integrated their agreement into a writing, they may not later alter or vary the terms of that agreement by "parol evidence" (meaning, for the most part, evidence of oral statements uttered during negotiation or signing), and that the latter holds essentially that when a contract is "within the statute of frauds" (such as an agreement for the sale of goods at a price exceeding $500, to name a common example), there must be an adequate writing memorializing the agreement.

Imagine now that a party sues on a contract covered by either of these substantive doctrines. What is the effect of the doctrine? Its effect is to force any party who would rely on the agreement to prove "the content" of the writing. And what is the effect of the Best Evidence doctrine? Its effect (oversimplifying for a moment) is to force the party to offer the writing itself. Note well that the substantive law, standing alone, does not require production of the document, for its focus is on the rights of the parties, not the mechanics of proof at trial. Nevertheless the effect of these substantive principles is to force the parties to prove content, and then the Best Evidence doctrine steps in to require production of the document itself, as the proper means of proving content.

Now consider a case in which party strategy forces a writing into prominence. Recall Baker v. Elcona Homes, 588 F.2d 551 (6th Cir. 1978), cert. denied, 441 U.S. 933 (1979) (Chapter 4C6, supra), where defendant sought to prove that the Valiant ran a red light and offered as proof the accident report prepared by Officer Hendrickson. As long as defendant chose to rely on the report as proof that the light was red for the Valiant, the Best Evidence doctrine required it to offer the report itself. No principle of substantive law required proof in that form, for testimony by an eyewitness who saw the accident would serve as well—and possibly better. Nor did the Best Evidence doctrine require defendant to offer the report in preference to eyewitness testimony. But the Best Evidence doctrine says, in effect, that if defendant wants to prove, by means of the police report, that the Valiant ran a red light, then defendant must offer the report itself.

Probably there was no bystander, or at least none known to the defendant in *Elcona Homes,* who may have had no real options in deciding to prove the point by using the report. Necessity may have been the mother of this strategy, but it was strategy plus the Best Evidence doctrine that led defendant to proceed this way, rather than substantive law or the Best Evidence doctrine alone.

When the doctrine does not apply. As you are soon to discover, there are many cases in which it might appear at first glance that the Best Evidence doctrine applies, though in fact it does not. Speaking broadly once again, most of these cases are commonly described as situations in which the matter to be proved has been "incidentally recorded," but in which neither substantive law nor party strategy actually forces the writing into prominence.

Think once again about the *Elcona Homes* case. If Officer Hendrickson had remained on the witness stand (in fact he had left), and if defendant had succeeded in qualifying him as an expert in accident investigation and had asked him which vehicle probably had the light, could plaintiffs raise a Best Evidence objection? Again clearly not, at least if Officer Hendrickson could testify from present memory as to the conclusions he had earlier reached and memorialized in his written report. Can you see why?

With that much as prologue, consider now some problems and cases that illustrate the application of the Best Evidence doctrine.

PROBLEM 14-E. *The XXX-Rated Movies*

In a prosecution for alleged interstate transportation of obscene films, the prosecutor attempts to establish the obscene content of the films seized from the defendant by the testimony of a police officer who viewed them. The films themselves are not offered into evidence or shown to the jury. The attorney for the defendant makes a Best Evidence objection to the police officer's testimony. What ruling?

PROBLEM 14-F.   The Surveillance Photograph

During a bank robbery, a photograph of the robber is taken by a hidden surveillance camera. At trial the bank security officer, who was not present at the time of the robbery, testifies that he removed the film from the camera after the robbery, supervised its development, and examined the photograph that was produced. He offers to testify that the person shown by the photograph to be robbing the bank is the defendant. The photograph is not offered into evidence. The defendant makes a Best Evidence objection to this testimony. What ruling?

MEYERS v. UNITED STATES
United States Court of Appeals,District of Columbia Circuit
171 F.2d 800 (1948)

[In the trial of Bleriot Lamarre for perjury, and of Bennett Meyers for suborning perjury, the government sought to prove that Lamarre lied in his testimony before a Senate Committee. To prove what Lamarre had said, the government called William P. Rogers, then Chief Counsel to the Committee. Rogers had examined Lamarre before the Committee and consequently heard all his testimony. Later in the trial the government also introduced in evidence a stenographic transcript of Lamarre's testimony.

According to the indictment, Lamarre falsely testified to the Committee that (a) he was "not financially interested" in Aviation Electric Corporation in the years 1940-1947, (b) a Cadillac purchased by Meyers was for company use; and (c) the payment of $10,000 to decorate and furnish Meyers' Washington apartment was made by Lamarre when actually the money was paid by means of an Aviation Electric check.

On appeal, Meyers claimed that using Rogers to prove what Lamarre had said represented a "bizarre procedure."]

WILBUR K. MILLER, J.

The dissenting opinion. . . asserts it was reversible error to allow Rogers to testify at all as to what Lamarre had said to the subcommittee, on the theory that the transcript itself was the best evidence of Lamarre's testimony before the subcommittee.

That theory is, in our view, based upon a misconception of the best evidence rule. As applied generally in federal courts, the rule is limited to cases where the contents of a writing are to be proved. Here there was no attempt to prove the contents of a writing; the issue was what Lamarre had said, not what the transcript contained. The transcript made from shorthand notes of his testimony was, to be sure, evidence of what he had said, but it was not the only admissible evidence concerning it. Rogers' testimony was equally competent, and was admissible whether given before or after the transcript was received in evidence. Statements alleged to be perjurious may be proved by any person who heard them, as well as by a reporter who recorded them in shorthand. . . .

As we have pointed out, there was no issue as to the contents of the transcript, and the government was not attempting to prove what it contained; the issue was what Lamarre actually had said. Rogers was not asked what the transcript contained but what Lamarre's testimony had been.

After remarking, ". . . there is a line of cases which holds that a stenographic transcript is not the best evidence of what was said. There is also a legal cliche that the best evidence rule applies only to documentary evidence," the dissenting opinion asserts that the rule is outmoded and that "the courts ought to establish a new and correct rule." We regard the principle set forth in the cases which we have cited as being, not a legal cliche, but an established and sound doctrine which we are not prepared to renounce.

With the best evidence rule shown to be inapplicable, it is clearly seen that it was neither "preposterously unfair," as the appellant asserts, nor unfair at all, to permit the transcript of Lamarre's evidence to be introduced after Rogers had testified. Since both methods of proving the perjury were permissible, the prosecution could present its proof in any order it chose.

There is no substance in the criticism, voiced by the appellant and in the dissent, of the fact that Rogers testified early in the unduly protracted trial and the transcript was introduced near its close. Appellant's counsel had a copy of the transcript from the second day of the trial, and had full opportunity to study it and to cross-examine Rogers in the light of that study. The mistaken notion that, had the transcript been first put in evidence, Rogers' testimony would have been incompetent is, of course, based on the erroneous idea that the best evidence rule had application.

It is quite clear that Meyers was in no way prejudiced by the order in which the evidence against him was introduced, nor does it appear that his position before the jury would have been more favorable had the transcript been offered on an earlier day of the trial. . . .

Since we perceive no prejudicial error in appellant's trial, the judgment entered pursuant to the jury's verdict will not be disturbed.

Affirmed.

PRETTYMAN, J. (dissenting).

I am of strong opinion that the judgment in this case should be reversed.

The testimony given by Lamarre before the Senate Committee was presented to the jury upon the trial in so unfair and prejudicial a fashion as to constitute reversible error.

Lamarre testified before the Committee in executive session, only Senators, Mr. William P. Rogers, who was counsel to the Committee, the clerk, the reporter, and the witness being present. An official stenographic record was made of the proceedings. The testimony continued for two days, and the transcript is 315 typewritten pages. When Meyers was indicted, he moved for a copy of the transcript. The United States Attorney opposed, on the ground that the executive proceedings of a Senate Committee are confidential. The court denied Meyers' motion.

When the trial began, the principal witness called by the Government was Mr. Rogers. He was asked by the United States Attorney, "Now, will you tell the

Court and the jury in substance what the testimony was that the defendant Lamarre gave before the Committee concerning the Cadillac automobile?" Two counts of the indictment related to this automobile.

The court at once called counsel to the bench and said to the prosecutor:

> Of course, technically, you have the right to proceed the way you are doing. . . . I do not think that is hearsay under the hearsay rule, but it seems to me. . . that, after all, when you have a prosecution based on perjury, and you have a transcript of particular testimony on which the indictment is based, that you ought to lay a foundation for it or ought to put the transcript in evidence, instead of proving what the testimony was by someone who happens to be present, who has to depend on his memory as to what was said.

Counsel for the defense, objecting, insisted that the procedure was "preposterously unfair." The trial judge said that it seemed to him that the transcript ought to be made available to defense counsel. That was then done, but the prosecutor insisted upon proceeding as he had planned with the witness.

Mr. Rogers then testified: "I will try to give the substance of the testimony. . . . I am sure your Honor appreciates that I do not remember exactly the substance of the testimony. The substance of testimony was this,. . . ." And then he gave "in substance" the testimony in respect to the Cadillac car. The same process was followed in respect to the matters covered by the other counts of the indictment, i.e., the redecoration of Meyers' apartment and Meyers' interest in the Aviation Electric Corporation. Defense counsel reserved part of his cross-examination until he could read the transcript.

The notable characteristics of this testimony of Rogers are important. In each instance, the "substance" was a short summation, about half a printed page in length. The witness did not purport to be absolute in his reproduction but merely recited his unrefreshed recollection, and his recollection on each of the three matters bears a striking resemblance to the succinct summations of the indictment. . . .

From the theoretical viewpoint, I realize that there is a line of authority that (absent or incompetent the original witness) a bystander who hears testimony or other conversation may testify as to what was said, even though there be a stenographic report. And there is a line of cases which holds that a stenographic transcript is not the best evidence of what was said. There is also a legal cliche that the best evidence rule applies only to documentary evidence. The trial judge in this case was confronted with that authority, and a trial court is probably not the place to inaugurate a new line of authority. But I do not know why an appellate court should perpetuate a rule clearly outmoded by scientific development. I know that courts are reluctant to do so. I recognize the view that such matters should be left to Congress. But rules of evidence were originally judge-made and are an essential part of the judicial function. I know of no reason why the judicial branch of Government should abdicate to the legislative branch so important a part of its responsibility.

I am of opinion, and quite ready to hold, that the rules of evidence. . . are outmoded and at variance with known fact, and that the courts ought to establish a new and correct rule. The rationale of the so-called "best evidence rule" requires that a party having available evidence which is relatively certain may not submit evidence which is far less certain. The law is concerned with the true fact, and with that alone; its procedures are directed to that objective, and to that alone. It should permit no procedure the sole use of which is to obscure and confuse that which is otherwise plain and certain. . . .

The doctrine that stenographic notes are not the best evidence of testimony was established when stenography was not an accurate science. The basis for the decisions is succinctly stated in the 1892 case quoted as leading by Professor Wigmore:

> Stenographers are no more infallible than any other human beings, and while as a rule they may be accurate, intelligent, and honest, they are not always so; and therefore it will not do to lay down as a rule that the stenographer's notes when translated by him are the best evidence of what a witness has said, in such a sense as to exclude the testimony of an intelligent bystander who has heard and paid particular attention to the testimony of the witness.

[4 Wigmore, Evidence, §1330 (3d ed. 1940), quoting McIver, C.J., in Brice v. Miller, 1892, 35 S.C. 537, 549, 15 S.E. 272.]

But we have before us no such situation. Stenographic reporting has become highly developed, and official stenographic reports are relied upon in many of the most important affairs of life. . . . In the present instance, at least, no one has disputed the correctness of the transcript.

From the theoretical point of view, the case poses this question: Given both (1) an accurate stenographic transcription of a witness' testimony during a two-day hearing and (2) the recollection of one of the complainants as to the substance of that testimony, is the latter admissible as evidence in a trial of the witness for perjury? I think not. To say that it is, is to apply a meaningless formula and ignore crystal-clear actualities. The transcript is, as a matter of simple, indisputable fact, the best evidence. The principle and not the rote of the law ought to be applied. . . .

NOTES ON *MEYERS* AND THE LIMITS OF THE BEST EVIDENCE DOCTRINE

1.   This case would be decided the same way, would it not, if the prosecutor had never offered the transcript and had relied solely on Rogers' testimony? If the same case arose today, would it be decided the same way under the Federal Rules? Is the case made harder or easier by the fact that the transcript was also offered? What consideration should be given to the fact that the transcript was not made available to the defendant until after Rogers had testified?

2.   Would this case be decided differently if Rogers had not been present at the subcommittee hearing and had learned of Lamarre's testimony only by reading the transcript? When a witness testifies regarding a matter that has been recorded, does application of the Best Evidence doctrine turn on whether the witness has independent knowledge of the matter apart from the recording?

3.   Judge Prettyman's dissent is premised on the assumption that a transcript is the best evidence of former testimony. What if the only available transcript had been prepared by an unofficial court reporter? By a secretary to the defendant's attorney? Can a court always judge what is the "best evidence"?

Should not the government be allowed to try its own case and choose its own form of proof? On the other hand, should the government be allowed to use two forms of proof, both the testimony of Rogers and the transcript, to establish Lamarre's former testimony?

4.   If the transcript of Lamarre's testimony had been introduced first, and Rogers had been asked to summarize or interpret the transcript, Meyers would have an objection available. But would it be a Best Evidence objection?

PROBLEM 14-G.   *The Recorded Conversation*

In a drug surveillance operation, DEA agent Nolan monitors a conversation between Peter and Quinn that takes place in a room in the Quality Court Motel. Using a planted bug and recording equipment in an adjacent room, Nolan both hears and records what Peter and Quinn are saying. The conversations relate to drug transactions, past and ongoing.

After arresting Peter and Quinn, Nolan interrogates them separately at DEA headquarters. First Nolan questions Peter, who admits his involvement in a drug scheme and implicates Quinn. After getting Peter's story, Nolan summons a stenographer and has Peter repeat his statement. The stenographer prints out a hardcopy, and Peter signs it. Then Nolan questions Quinn and tape records the interview.

Consider the following evidence issues:

(1) At the trial of Peter and Quinn, should Nolan be allowed to testify to the conversation he overheard at the Quality Court Motel or does the Best Evidence Doctrine require the government to produce the recording?

(2) Can Nolan testify to Peter's admissions about his own conduct, or does a Best Evidence objection by Peter force the government to offer the signed written statement instead? What if Nolan thinks the signed statement omits important points that Peter uttered in his original recitation, before the retelling that the stenographer used in making the written version?

(3) Can Nolan testify to what Quinn said at DEA headquarters, or does a Best Evidence objection force the government to offer the recording?

PROBLEM 14-H.   *The Sick Chickens*

Best Chix, a company that specializes in breeding chickens and selling them to poultry farmers, sues one such farmer, Curt Duval, to recover the balance owed on the purchase price for a flock of chickens. Duval, who claims he is entitled to a price adjustment because many of the chickens were infected with leukosis, seeks to prove this point by testifying to the substance of a veterinarian's report he received, but does not offer the report itself. Best Chix makes a Best Evidence objection. What ruling, and why?

PROBLEM 14-I.   *Cash Payment*

Teresa Feiler, who rents apartments to students in College Station, seeks to evict Ashley Gibson for nonpayment of rent for the month of October.

Gibson testifies that she paid the October rent in cash. Under questioning in aid of an objection, counsel for Feiler gets Gibson to admit that Feiler always gave her a written receipt for her rent payments. Then Feiler's lawyer objects to Gibson's testimony, arguing that "the receipt constitutes the Best Evidence of payment, your Honor, and she cannot testify that she made the October payment unless she has a good reason for not producing the receipt." What result, and why?

PROBLEM 14-J. The Unreported Burglary

In a suit by homeowner Eric Hoskins against Frontier Casualty Company to recover losses suffered when a burglar allegedly stole a valuable Jackson Pollock painting from his home in St. Louis on December 14th, Frontier denies liability and asserts that any coverage that might have existed was lost when Hoskins failed to report the theft to the police. As proof, Frontier offers testimony by its claims examiner Jensen, who would testify that she "looked through the records of reported burglaries in every police station in greater St. Louis for the time period December 14th through December 20th, and found no record of a report by Hoskins and no record of any complaint regarding stolen artwork." Hoskins makes a Best Evidence objection, arguing that "Frontier must produce the logs and records themselves, not just testimony by someone who looked through the written materials." What result, and why? Notice, if helpful, the comments in the ACN to FRE 1002.

PROBLEM 14-K. The Unproduced X-Ray

In a personal injury suit brought by Sid Landon against Leigh Mills following a two-car collision, Dr. Sherry Nash (Landon's treating physician) testifies on behalf of Landon that the X-ray of his leg showed a fractured femur. Landon does not offer the X-ray itself. Mills objects to this testimony, citing the Best Evidence rule. What ruling? Does it make any difference whether the doctor is relying on the X-ray as part of the basis of a medical opinion rather than merely describing what the X-ray depicts? See FRE 703 and the Advisory Committee's Note to FRE 1002.

F. PRODUCTION OF ORIGINAL EXCUSED

SYLVANIA ELECTRIC PRODUCTS v. FLANAGAN
United States Court of Appeals for the First Circuit
352 F.2d 1005 (1965)

McENTEE, J.
    Plaintiff, Paul L. Flanagan, d/b/a Paul L. Flanagan and Sons, is a trucker and hauler of sand, gravel, stone and other similar materials. In the spring of

1963, defendant, Sylvania Electric Products, Inc., engaged a general contractor to construct a parking lot for it at its plant in Needham, Massachusetts. There was a hill or ledge on this site which had to be removed at the beginning of the job. Although the general contractor was obliged to level off the hill, he was not required under his contract to truck the ledge material away. Plaintiff alleges that on May 27, 1963, which is the date the parking lot job was commenced, the defendant made an oral agreement with him whereby he agreed to supply the trucks and haul this ledge material away and the defendant agreed to pay him for this work at the rate of $13 per hour per truck. Plaintiff proceeded immediately with the hauling operation which extended over two periods: May 27 to June 10, 1963 and June 17 to July 1, 1963. In the performance of this work he used his own trucks and trucks rented from others, as was his practice on jobs of this size. Plaintiff claimed that the entire job took a total of 1932 1/2 truck hours work for which he billed defendant at the rate of $13 an hour. This amount, plus an item of $145 for bulldozer hire, which was not disputed, came to $25,267.50. Defendant refused to pay this bill. Whereupon plaintiff brought suit in the Massachusetts Superior Court for breach of contract. The case was removed to the United States District Court for the District of Massachusetts on the ground of diversity. The jury found for the plaintiff in the full amount of his claim. This is an appeal by the defendant from the judgment entered by the district court based on the jury verdict. Defendant's principal ground of appeal is that the district court erred in admitting certain evidence in violation of the best evidence rule; that this evidence should have been excluded and a verdict should have been directed for the defendant.

Plaintiff offered the following evidence in support of his claim, all of which he alleged is based on daily truck hour slips on tally sheets made at the site of the job which recorded the number of trucks on the job and the number of hours worked by each truck: (1) Exhibit A in the declaration filed in this case, which he says is a summary of the data contained in the invoices and the tally sheets. (2) A number of photostatic copies of bills and invoices sent to plaintiff by other truckers for the rental of their trucks on this job. (3) Copies of two bills sent by plaintiff to defendant, one in the amount of $12,521 for work done during the first period and the other reflecting the total amount of $25,267.50 due for both periods. The contents of these two bills is identical with the claim set forth in Schedule A of the plaintiff's declaration (supra).

Plaintiff testified that the data contained in the above exhibits is the same as that contained in the tally sheets. In the course of the trial when plaintiff was asked whether the information contained in these exhibits was the same as that contained in the tally sheets, defendant objected on the ground that this was secondary evidence and thus was barred by the best evidence rule. At this point, the trial court inquired as to whether the plaintiff had those tally sheets, to which he replied that he knew he had some at home but was not sure whether he had them all. The court then suggested that he bring in those that he had. Later in the course of the trial this line of inquiry was resumed by plaintiff's counsel and again defendant objected. The court allowed plaintiff's testimony that the information contained in the invoices "checked out" with that contained in the tally sheets. The defendant adequately objected. None of the tally sheets were ever produced at the trial.

It is well settled that the best evidence that is obtainable in the circumstances of the case must be adduced to prove any disputed fact. Here, the plaintiff's claim is based on performance of the work. The best evidence of his performance is the truck hour records (tally sheets). Those records were made for the very purpose of recording this performance. Instead of producing these records plaintiff offered the secondary evidence of their content enumerated above. In proving the terms of a writing, which terms are material to the issues in the case, the original writing must be produced unless it is shown to be unavailable for some reason other than the serious fault of the proponent. McCormick, Evidence §196 (1954). Upon a proper showing of the unavailability of the original writing, secondary evidence of its contents may be received. However, secondary evidence of the content of the original is not admissible unless the proponent of the testimony shows that a reasonable and diligent search has been made for the original without success.

From a careful examination of the evidence in this case we feel there is not sufficient proof that the original tally sheets in question were in fact unavailable or that a reasonable search had been made to find them. Although plaintiff stated that it was not his practice to keep these tally sheets after checking them with the truckers' invoices, he did testify on several occasions that he knew he had some of them at home and that he would bring into court what he had. This he did not do. It is also apparent from the evidence that plaintiff had tally sheets in his possession when he conferred with officials of the defendant in June 1963, at which time he knew there was a dispute concerning the work and payment for it. Although plaintiff stated in open court that he would make a search for the tally sheets there is little if any evidence that he in fact made such a search and there is no evidence at all as to the extent of any such search. There is no universal or fixed rule that determines the sufficiency of the proof required to show that a reasonable or diligent search has been made. Each case is governed in large measure by its own particular facts and circumstances. He who seeks to introduce secondary evidence must show that he has used all reasonable means to obtain the original, i.e., such search as the nature of the case would suggest. The best evidence rule should not be applied as a mere technicality. But where the missing original writings in dispute are the very foundation of the claim, which is the situation in this case, more strictness in proof is required than where the writings are only involved collaterally. Plaintiff failed to satisfy this requirement.

Moreover, under the best evidence rule, in order to permit proof by secondary evidence of the allegedly lost or otherwise unavailable original writing, the trial judge must make preliminary findings that the original had become unavailable, otherwise than through the fault of the proponent of the testimony and that reasonable search had been made for it. The record in this case does not reveal that the trial court made these necessary preliminary findings.

In a similar case decided by this court it was held that an itemized bill sent to defendant was inadmissible in evidence where the bill was made from work sheets which were not produced at the trial and where there was no evidence that these original work sheets were lost or unavailable.

Ordinarily prejudicial error with respect to damages should require that the new trial be on damages only. However, in this case the whole case depended largely upon plaintiff's credibility. The record was left in such condition that he was never called upon to explain the absence of his records, his search, if any, therefor, or why, when he knew from the beginning that there was a dispute, he had not preserved them, if, in fact, he had not. Actually, plaintiff has never denied that the records no longer exist. In view of the fact that examination of the records might well corroborate the defendant's account, rather than plaintiff's, as to other issues between the parties, we believe that justice would be best served by ordering an entirely new trial.

We find it unnecessary to decide any other questions raised in the case.

The judgment of the district court will be vacated, the verdict set aside and the case remanded for a new trial consistent with this opinion.

NOTES ON ADMISSIBILITY OF "OTHER EVIDENCE OF CONTENTS"

1. Is there any doubt that the "bills and invoices" for the work that Paul Flanagan claimed that he had performed were business records? Recall the hearsay exception for business records, now contained in FRE 803(6). Don't the "bills and invoices" amount to the Best Evidence of the content of those records, and doesn't the business records exception permit their use to prove exactly what Paul Flanagan sought to prove? Then why did the court say he had to produce the "tally sheets"? Is it that the tally sheets were in some sense more reliable proof?

2. If Paul Flanagan testified, in a hearing before the judge, that he had asked his bookkeeper where the tally sheets were and that the bookkeeper had replied, "Paul, I'm afraid those were lost when we moved the office from the first floor to the second, and the only records we still have are the copies of the bills and invoices," would Paul's testimony restating what his bookkeeper had told him be admissible to prove loss of the records? (Note that FRE 1004(1), which also restates a common law tradition, would permit resort to secondary evidence of what the tally sheets contained if their loss without bad faith were satisfactorily explained.) Does the question of loss of records raise an issue of "admissibility" under FRE 104(a) or one of "conditional relevancy" under FRE 104(b)?

3. As the principal case suggests, the extent of search required for the original is a matter to be determined by the trial judge. The appellate cases provide relatively few guidelines. A cursory search should not suffice:

Ordinarily it is not sufficient that the paper is not found in its usual place of deposit, but all papers in the office or place should be examined. . . . It is true the party need not search every possible place where it might be found, for then the search might be interminable, but he must search every place where there is a reasonable possibility that it might be found.

Stipe v. First National Bank, 301 P.2d 175, 181 (Or. 1956).

4. Whether a writing, recording, or photograph is beyond the reach of judicial process under FRE 1004(2) depends on the applicable process statutes or rules. Process provisions usually extend farther in criminal cases than civil.

If the writing, recording, or photograph is in the hands of a third party, the process typically used to compel production is a subpoena duces tecum. The party seeking discovery is usually able to obtain only a duplicate, not the original. Does inability to obtain the original through discovery mean that at trial the party will be allowed to offer any form of secondary evidence? Or if a duplicate was available through discovery is the party required to offer that duplicate? The literal language of FRE 1004(2) appears to excuse a party from compliance with the Best Evidence doctrine on a showing that the *original* is unobtainable. But see 5 C. Mueller and L. Kirkpatrick, Federal Evidence §578 (2d ed. 1994) (suggesting that FRE 1004(2) should be read as requiring a party who can obtain a duplicate through discovery to prove contents by offering that duplicate).

5.   FRE 1004 recognizes two categories of unavailability that justify proof by secondary evidence. Would a showing of extreme difficulty or impracticality of producing a certain writing, such as a billboard or tombstone, qualify as a sufficient justification for nonproduction of the original? See People v. Mastin, 171 Cal. Rptr. 780, 783 (Cal. App. 1981) ("We can visualize situations in which the best evidence rule should not be applicable, such as an inscription on a 30 ton piece of heavy equipment or an item of personal property which should be promptly returned to the owner.").

6.   FRE 1004(3) establishes a procedure that permits the use of secondary evidence of contents when the writing, recording, or photograph is under the control of the opponent and the opponent has been put on notice, by pleadings or otherwise, of the party's intent to prove contents at the hearing. This procedure is not the same as a request for production, and the rule does not require showing of an inability to obtain the original through discovery or other means.

PROBLEM 14-L.   *Testimony versus Photocopy*

In a breach of contract action, Corrigan, the plaintiff, establishes that the original written contract was destroyed in a fire through no fault of his own. Even though Corrigan has an accurate and legible photocopy of the original contract, he chooses at trial to prove the terms of the contract by his testimony rather than by offering the photocopy. Defendant Gregor makes a Best Evidence objection to the testimony, arguing that the photocopy must be introduced. What ruling? See FRE 1004 and the Advisory Committee's Note to FRE 1004.

PROBLEM 14-M.   *The Tax Evader*

Brad Trimble is prosecuted for alleged tax evasion, and the government calls Charles Urban, an IRS accountant, to testify. Urban has examined Trimble's bank records, which reflect more than 90 deposits and 300 withdrawals over the year, and the prosecutor offers (1) Urban's testimonial summary of deposits and disbursements from the account and (2) a chart prepared by Urban from the bank records summarizing entries deemed significant from the prosecutor's perspective.

Trimble raises a Best Evidence objection, but the prosecutor invokes FRE 1006. What result, and why?

PROBLEM 14-N. "No Pets"

Owner Ann Brindon seeks to evict tenant Clay Dobbs from the apartment he rents from her because he has broken his lease by keeping a dog on the premises. At the hearing, Brindon seeks to testify that the lease contains a "no pets" provision, but Dobbs' Best Evidence objection is sustained.

Counsel for Brindon does not have the lease at hand, but she discovers in the file a signed letter from Dobbs acknowledging that "the lease says I cannot have any pets" and requesting special permission to keep the dog. She offers the letter, but Dobbs renews his Best Evidence objection. Brindon invokes FRE 1007. How should the court rule, and why? If Dobbs had written no letter but had orally sought exemption from the "no pets" provision from Brindon, could she prove the clause by testifying to what he said?

NOTES ON OTHER ESCAPES FROM PRODUCING THE ORIGINAL

1. When a summary is offered under FRE 1006, should the jury be told that it is not "evidence" because only the documents themselves have that status? Does it matter whether the underlying documents themselves are admitted? See United States v. Bray, 139 F.3d 1104, 1111 (6th Cir. 1998) (FRE 1006 summary, whether or not underlying documents are introduced, is "evidence to be considered by the factfinder").

2. Sometimes a summary of exhibits or other trial evidence is introduced for "pedagogical" purposes to assist the jury in understanding the evidence rather than to prove its content. Such use of summaries is governed by FRE 611(a) rather than FRE 1006. See Gomez v. Great Lakes Steel Division National Steel Corp., 803 F.2d 250, 257-258 (6th Cir. 1986) (charts used only as visual aid or "pedagogical device" should generally be "accompanied by a limiting instruction which informs the jury of the summary's purpose and that it does not itself constitute evidence").

3. When a summary is offered, does it matter whether the underlying documents are *admissible?* See Hackett v. Housing Authority of San Antonio, 750 F.2d 1308, 1312 (5th Cir.) (summary inadmissible when based on inadmissible hearsay), cert. denied, 474 U.S. 50 (1985). Given the result in *Hackett,* what foundation must the government lay when offering Urban's testimony in Problem 14-M?

4. Does the proponent of summary evidence have to offer the underlying documents as well? Must he give advance notice of intent to offer a summary? See FRCP 26(a)(3)(C) (requiring pretrial disclosure "of each document or other exhibit, including summaries of other evidence").

TABLE OF CASES

TABLE OF RULES

TABLE OF AUTHORITIES

Books and Treatises

AMA Principles of Medical Ethics IV (2001), 758
Appleman, J., Insurance Law and Practice (rev. ed. 1981), 670 n.2
Barker, S., The Elements of Logic (3d ed. 1980), 61
Bentham, J., Rationale of Judicial Evidence (J.S. Mill ed., 1827), 759
Brennan, J., Handbook of Logic (1957), 68, 70
Cohen, L., The Probable and the Provable (1977), 104
Couch on Insurance (1982), 670 n.2
Cound, J., J. Friedenthal, A. Miller, & J. Sexton, Civil Procedure Cases and Materials (8th ed. 2001), 670 n.1
Davis, K., Administrative Law Treatise (1984), 739, 754
Devitt, E., & C. Blackmar, Federal Jury Practice and Instructions (4th ed. 1992), 66
Dombroff, M., Direct and Cross-Examination (1985), 21
Faigman, D., D. Kaye, M. Saks, & J. Sanders, Modern Scientific Evidence (1997), 644 n.9
Gianelli, P., & E. Imwinkelried, Scientific Evidence (2d ed. 1993), 644 n.9
Goodman, N., Fact, Fiction, and Forecast (4th ed. 1983), 70
Graham, M., Handbook of Federal Evidence (3d ed. 1991), 741
Greenleaf, S., Evidence (1892), 450
_____, Evidence (1883), 449
Huber, P., Galileo's Revenge: Junk Science in the Courtroom (1991), 640
Hume, D., An Enquiry Concerning Human Understanding (1777 ed., reprinted 1975), 68, 69
Imwinkelried, E., Uncharged Misconduct (1994), 426, 427
Kalven, H., & H. Zeisel, The American Jury (1966), 745
Kamisar, Police Interrogation and Confessions: Essays in Law and Policy (1980), 201
Keeton, R., Basic Expressions for Trial Lawyers (1979), 857
LaFave, Israel, & King, Criminal Procedure (1999), 179
Levy, Origins of the Fifth Amendment (1968), 831
Lilly, G., Introduction to the Law of Evidence (3d ed. 1996), 525, 589, 590
Longfellow, H.W., Tales of a Wayside Inn (1864-1873), 111 n.3
McCormick, Evidence (J. Strong 5th ed. 1999), 23, 670 n.1, 751, 825, 878
_____, Evidence (J. Strong 4th ed. 1992), 428
_____, Evidence (E. Cleary 3d ed. 1984), 64, 133, 760, 848
Moenssens, A., F. Inbau, & J. Starrs, Scientific Evidence in Criminal Cases (3d ed. 1986), 644 n.9
Moore's Federal Practice (2d ed. 1985), 742
Morgan, E., Basic Problems of Evidence (1962), 738
Moriarty, J., Psychological and Scientific Evidence in Criminal Trials (2002), 644 n.9
Mueller, C., & L. Kirkpatrick, Evidence (3d ed. 2003), 58, 66, 198, 211, 212, 223, 339, 354, 385, 412, 542, 621, 681, 875
_____, Evidence (2d ed. 1999), 242, 271, 422, 587
_____, Federal Evidence (2d ed. 1994), 20, 86, 178, 179, 428, 440, 878, 882, 896
O'Malley, K., J. Grenig, & W. Lee, Federal Jury Practice and Instructions (5th ed. 2000), 103, 730

Park, R., D. Leonard, & S. Goldberg, Evidence Law: A Student's Guide to the Law of Evidence as Applied in American Trials (1998), 32

Reference Manual on Scientific Evidence (1994), 644 n.9

Restatement (Third) of the Law Governing Lawyers, 799

Russell, B., The Art of Philosophizing and Other Essays (1968), 69

Saltzburg, S., & M. Martin, Federal Rules of Evidence Manual (5th ed. 1990), 149

Sandburg, C., The People, Yes (1936), 53

Skyrms, New Readings in Philosophical Analysis (H. Feigl, W. Sellars, & Lehrer eds., 1972), 70

Starkie, T., Evidence (1824), 451

Thayer, J., A Preliminary Treatise on Evidence at the Common Law (1898), 51, 52, 738, 743

Traynor, R., The Riddle of Harmless Error (1970), 43 n.7

Weinstein, J., & M. Berger, Weinstein's Evidence (1981), 815

Wigmore, J., Code of Evidence (1909), 3, 52

————, Evidence (1943), 61, 64

————, Evidence (1923), 133

————, Evidence (3d ed. 1940), 398

————, Evidence (J. Chadbourn rev. 1981), 738

————, Evidence (J. Chadbourn ed. 1979), 450

————, Evidence (J. Chadbourn rev. 1978), 595

————, Evidence (J. Chadbourn rev. 1974), 21, 362

————, Evidence (J. McNaughton rev. 1961), 760

Articles

ABA Section of Litigation, Emerging Problems Under the Federal Rules of Evidence (1983), 742

Allen, Presumptions, Inferences and Burden of Proof in Federal Civil Actions—An Anatomy of Unnnecessary Ambiguity and a Proposal for Reform, 76 Nw. L. Rev. 892 (1982), 692

————, Rationality, Mythology, and the "Acceptability of Verdicts" Thesis, 66 B.U. L. Rev. 541 (1986), 105, 643

Ashford & Risinger, Presumptions, Assumptions, and Due Process in Criminal Cases: A Theoretical Overview, 79 Yale L.J. 165 (1969), 713

Ball, The Myth of Conditional Relevancy, 14 Ga. L. Rev. 435 (1980), 89

Beaver, Memory Restored or Confabulated by Hypnosis—Is It Competent?, 6 U. Puget Sound L. Rev. 155 (1983), 464

Belli, Demonstrative Evidence: Seeing Is Believing, 16 Trial 70 (July 1980), 869

Berger, Upsetting the Balance Between Adverse Interests: The Impact of the Supreme Court's Trilogy on Expert Testimony in Toxic Tort Litigation, 64 Law & Contemp. Probs. 289 (2001), 645

Black, The Marital and Physician Privileges—A Reprint of a Letter to a Congressman, 1975 Duke L.J. 45, 826

Bohlen, The Effect of Rebuttable Resumptions of Law upon the Burden of Proof, 68 U. Pa. L. Rev. 307 (1920), 677 n.6

Broun, Authentication and Contents of Writings, 1969 Law & Soc. Ord. 611, 851

Bruckner-Harvey, Inadvertent Disclosure in the Age of Fax Machines: Is the Cat Really Out of the Bag?, 46 Baylor L. Rev. 385 (1994), 780

Bryden & Park, "Other Crimes" Evidence in Sex Offense Cases, 78 Minn. L. Rev. 529 (1994), 427

Bulkley, Background and Overview of Child Sexual Abuse: Law Reforms in the Mid-1980's, 40 U. Miami L. Rev. 5 (1985), 457

Callen, Hearsay and Informal Reasoning, 47 Vand. L. Rev. 43 (1994), 141

Carlson, Collision Course in Expert Testimony: Limitations on Affirmative Introduction of Underlying Data, 36 U. Fla. L. Rev. 234 (1984), 610

————, Cross-Examination of the Accused, 52 Cornell L.Q. 705 (1967), 24

————, Policing the Bases of Modern Expert Testimony, 59 Vand. L. Rev. 577 (1986), 610

————, Scope of Cross-Examination and the Proposed Federal Rules, 32 Fed. B.J. 244 (1973), 24

Cassell, Balancing the Scales of Justice: The Case for and the Effects of Utah's Victim's Rights Amendment, 1994 Utah L. Rev. 1373, 498

Cassell & Strassberg, Evidence of Repeated Acts of Rape and Child Molestation: Reforming Utah Law to Permit the Propensity Inference, 1998 Utah L. Rev. 145, 423

Chafee, The Progress of the Law—Evidence, 1919-1922, 35 Harv. L. Rev. 428 (1922), 241

Cleary, Preliminary Notes on Reading the Rules of Evidence, 57 Neb. L. Rev. 908 (1978), 526

————, Presuming and Pleading: An Essay on Juristic Immaturity, 12 Stan. L. Rev. 5 (1959), 668, 669, 677 n.6

Cleary & Strong, The Best Evidence Rule: An Evaluation in Context, 51 Iowa L. Rev. 825 (1966), 879

Cohen, The Costs of Acceptability: Blue Buses, Agent Orange, and Aversion to Statistical Evidence, 66 B.U. L. Rev. 563 (1986), 105

INDEX